LECTIONARY
II

WEEKDAYS IN ORDINARY TIME
PROPER OF SAINTS
COMMONS

THE ROMAN MISSAL

REVISED BY DECREE OF THE SECOND VATICAN COUNCIL
AND PUBLISHED BY AUTHORITY OF POPE PAUL VI

LECTIONARY
II

WEEKDAYS IN ORDINARY TIME
PROPER OF SAINTS
COMMONS

Revised Edition approved for use in the dioceses of Australia and New Zealand

COLLINS GEOFFREY CHAPMAN

Altar Edition first published 1981 in three volumes
I Proper of Seasons. Sundays in Ordinary Time
II Weekdays in Ordinary Time. Proper of Saints, Commons
III Ritual Celebrations. Masses for Various Needs and Occasions. Votive Masses.
Masses for the Dead

This Study Edition first published 1983

Collins Liturgical Publications
187 Piccadilly, London W1V 9DA

Collins Liturgical Australia
PO Box 3023 (55 Clarence Street)
Sydney 2001

Geoffrey Chapman, a division of Cassell Ltd
1 Vincent Square, London SW1P 2PN

This edition of the Lectionary is based on *Ordo Lectionum Missae* Editio Typica Altera, Typis
Polyglottis Vaticanis 1981.
Confirmed by Decree of the Sacred Congregation for Divine Worship, 12 June 1981.
Prot number for Australia: CD 2188/80

Concordat cum originali: Denis J. Hart
Imprimatur: Edward B. Clancy
Archbishop of Sydney
10 May 1983

	ISBN Collins		Cassell
Volume I	0 00 599764-X	Volume I	0 225 66374 0
Volume II	0 00 599765-8	Volume II	0 225 66375 9
Volume III	0 00 599766-6	Volume III	0 225 66376 7
complete set	0 00 599709 7	complete set	0 225 66377 5

Typographical design by Colin Reed in Century Schoolbook
Data capture and manipulation by Morton Word Processing Ltd, Scarborough
Typeset by Filmtype Services Ltd, Scarborough
Printed in Japan

iv

CONTENTS

ACKNOWLEDGEMENTS

The Scripture quotations in this publication are from the Jerusalem Bible version of the Scriptures, copyrighted © in 1966, 1967 and 1968 by Darton, Longman and Todd Ltd and Doubleday and Company, Inc., and used by permission.

The version of the Psalms used for the Responsorial Psalms is that translated from the Hebrew by the Grail, © The Grail (England) 1963, and published by Collins in Fontana Books, London, 1963. It is used by permission.

The version of the Canticles from the Old Testament (Exodus, Deuteronomy, 1 Samuel, 1 Chronicles, Ecclesiasticus, Judith, Tobit, Isaiah, Jeremiah, Habakkuk, Daniel), and the version of the Magnificat, the Song of Zechariah, and the Song of Simeon printed here are translated from Hebrew and Greek by the Grail, © The Grail (England) 1963.

The Sequences for Whit Sunday and Corpus Christi are copyrighted © 1967, by the National Liturgical Commission of England and Wales. The Sequence for Easter Sunday is © 1966, the Hierarchy of England and Wales.

The Sequence for the feast of the blessed Virgin Mary of Sorrows is taken from the *Saint Andrew Bible Missal*, © 1962, Abbaye de St André, A.S.B.L., Bruges, Belgium, © 1960 Darton, Longman & Todd Ltd.

English translation of the Lectionary: Introduction, headings to the readings, responsories (responses to the psalms), and Gospel Acclamations, copyright © 1969, 1980 and 1981, International Committee on English in the Liturgy, Inc. All rights reserved.

INTRODUCTION TO THIS EDITION

The introduction to the second edition of the *Ordo Lectionum Missae* envisages that vernacular editions will necessarily consist of several volumes, although no specific division is prescribed.

This second volume of this edition contains all the readings for the Weekdays in Ordinary Time in the two separate sections of the two-year cycle; all the readings for the Proper of Saints and all the readings for the Commons.

The readings for the Weekdays in Ordinary Time appear in this volume, separated from the Sundays in Ordinary Time, because they follow a different cycle, unrelated to the Sundays. For convenience, the Gospel passages, which are common to both years of the cycle, appear in each section of the two-year cycle.

For each Weekday in Ordinary Time a Gospel Acclamation is provided, as in the second edition of the *Ordo Lectionum Missae*. These are suggestions only and on any Weekday any acclamation may be chosen from the appropriate collection provided at the end of the Weekdays section.

One of the features of the second edition of the *Ordo Lectionum Missae* is that it suggests appropriate sets of readings from the Commons for each of the days in the Proper of Saints on which, in the first edition of the *Ordo Lectionum Missae*, no sets of readings were provided or where there was only an incomplete set. However, these are suggestions only; for pastoral reasons other readings from the Commons may be chosen on celebrations in honour of the saints.

In regard to the Commons this edition of the Lectionary follows the arrangement of readings adopted in the Latin *Lectionarium*: in each section of the Commons the responsorial psalms are paired with the first readings and the Gospel acclamations are paired with the Gospel passages.

<h1>Extracts from</h1>
<h1>GENERAL INTRODUCTION</h1>

69. The weekday readings have been arranged in the following way:

1. Each Mass has two readings: the first is from the Old Testament or from an apostle (from a letter or Apocalypse) and during the Easter season from Acts; the second, from the gospels.

2. For the thirty-four weeks of Ordinary Time, the gospel readings are arranged in a single cycle, repeated each year. But the first reading is arranged in a two-year cycle and is thus read every other year. Year I is used during odd-numbered years; Year II, during even-numbered years.

Like the Order for Sundays and the solemnities of the Lord, then, the weekday Order of Readings is governed by similar application of the principles of harmony and of semicontinuous reading, especially in the case of seasons with their own distinctive character.

82. The arrangement of weekday readings provides texts for every day of the week throughout the year. In most cases, therefore, these readings are to be used on their assigned days, unless a solemnity, feast, or memorial with proper readings occurs.[107]

The one using the Order of Readings for weekdays must check to see whether one reading or another from the same biblical book will have to be omitted because of some celebration occuring during the week. With the plan of readings for the entire week in mind, the priest in that case arranges to omit the less significant selections or suitably combines them with other readings, if they contribute to an integral view of a particular theme.

109. 1) The *gospels* are so arranged that Mark is read first (First to Ninth Week), then Matthew (Tenth to Twenty-first Week), then Luke (Twenty-second to Thirty-fourth Week). Mark 1-12 are read in their entirety, with the exception only of the two passages of Mark 6 that are read on weekdays in other seasons. From Matthew and Luke the readings comprise all the matters not contained in Mark. From all three Synoptics or from two of them, as the case may be, all those passages are read that either are distinctively presented in each Gospel or are needed for a proper understanding of its progression. Jesus' eschatological discourse as contained in its entirety in Luke is read at the end of the liturgical year.

110. 2) The *first reading* is taken in periods of weeks from the Old then from the New Testament; the number of weeks depends on the length of the biblical books read.

Rather large sections are read from the New Testament books in order to give the substance, as it were, of each of the letters of the apostles.

From the Old Testament there is room only for select passages that, as far as possible, bring out the character of the individual books. The historical texts have been chosen in such a way as to provide an overall view of the history of salvation before the Lord's incarnation. But lengthy narratives could hardly be presented; sometimes verses have been selected that make for a reading of moderate length. In

107   See General Instruction of the Roman Missal, no. 319.

addition, the religious significance of the historical events is sometimes brought out by means of certain texts from the wisdom books that are placed as prologues or conclusions to a series of historical readings.

[. . .]

Tables are given to list the way the books of the Old and the New Testament are distributed over the weekdays in Ordinary Time in the course of two years.

At the end of the liturgical year the readings are from Daniel and Apocalypse, the books that correspond to the eschatological character of this period.

CELEBRATIONS OF THE SAINTS

70. Two groups of readings are provided for celebrations of the saints:

1. The proper of Saints provides the first group, for solemnities, feasts, or memorials and particularly when there are proper texts for such celebrations. Sometimes in the Proper, however, there is a reference to the most appropriate among the texts in the Commons as the one to be given preference.

2. The Common of Saints provide the second, more extensive group of readings. There are, first, appropriate texts for the different classes of saints (martyrs, pastors, virgins, etc.), then a great many texts that deal with holiness in general. These are for alternative use wherever the Commons are indicated as the source for the choice of readings.

83. When they exist, proper readings are given for celebrations of the saints, that is, biblical passages about the saint or the event in the saint's life that the Mass is celebrating. Even in the case of a memorial these readings must take the place of the weekday readings for the same day. This Order of Readings makes explicit note of every case of proper readings on a memorial.

In some cases there are accommodated readings, those, namely, that bring out some particular aspect of a saint's spiritual life or apostolate. Use of such readings does not seem binding, except for compelling pastoral reasons. For the most part references are given to readings in the Commons in order to facilitate choice. But these are merely suggestions: in place of an accommodated reading or the particular reading proposed from a Common, any other reading from the Commons referred to may be selected.

The first concern of a priest celebrating with a congregation is the spiritual benefit of the faithful and he will be careful not to impose his personal preference on them. Above all he will make sure not to omit too often or needlessly the readings assigned for each day in the weekday Lectionary: the Church's desire is to provide the faithful with a richer share at the table of God's word.[108]

There are also general readings, that is, those placed in the Commons either for some determined class of saints (martyrs, virgins, pastors, etc.) or for the saints in general. Because in these cases several texts are listed for the same reading, it will be up to the priest to choose the one best suited to the congregation.

In all celebrations of saints the readings may be taken not only from the Commons to which the references are given in each case, but also from the Common of Holy Men and Women, whenever there is special reason for doing so.

84. For celebrations of the saints:

a. On solemnities and feasts the readings must be those that are given in the Proper of the Commons. For solemnities and feasts of the General Roman

---

108   See ibid., no. 316c. Vatican Council II, Constitution on the Liturgy, no. 51.

Calendar proper readings are always assigned.

b. On solemnities belonging to particular calendars, three readings are to be assigned, unless the conference of bishops has decreed that there are to be only two readings.[109] The first reading is from the Old Testament (but during the Easter season, from Acts or Revelation); the second, from an apostle; the third, from the gospels.

c. On feasts and memorials, which have only two readings, the first can be chosen from either the Old Testament or from an apostle; the second is from the gospels. Following the Church's traditional practice, however, the first reading in the Easter season is to be taken from an apostle, the second, as far as possible, from the Gospel of John.

Table I
ORDER FOR THE READINGS FOR THE
WEEKDAYS IN ORDINARY TIME: YEAR I

Week	First Reading	Gospel Reading
1	Hebrews	Mark 1:14–2:17
2	"	2:18–3:19
3	"	3:22–4:34
4	"	5:1–6:30
5	Genesis 1–11	6:53–8:10
6	"	8:11–9:13
7	Ecclesiasticus	9:14–10:16
8	"	10:17–11:33
9	Tobit	12:1–12:44
10	2 Corinthians	Matthew 5:1-37
11	"	5:38–6:34
12	Genesis 12–50	7:1–8:17
13	"	8:18–9:17
14	"	9:18–10:33
15	Exodus	10:34–12:21
16	"	12:38–13:30
17	Exodus; Leviticus	13:31–14:12
18	Numbers; Deuteronomy	14:13–17:20
19	Deuteronomy; Joshua	17:22–19:15
20	Judges; Ruth	19:16–23:12
21	1 Thessalonians	23:13–25:30
22	1 Thessalonians; Colossians	Luke 4:16–6:5
23	Colossians; 1 Timothy	6:6-49
24	1 Timothy	7:1–8:15
25	Ezra; Haggai; Zechariah	8:16–9:45
26	Zecheriah; Nehemiah; Baruch	9:46–10:24
27	Jonah; Malachi; Joel	10:25–11:28
28	Romans	11:29–12:12
29	"	12:13–13:9
30	"	13:10–14:11
31	"	14:12–16:15
32	Wisdom	17:1–18:8
33	1 and 2 Maccabees	18:35–20:40
34	Daniel	21:1-36

Table II
ORDER FOR THE READINGS FOR THE
WEEKDAYS IN ORDINARY TIME: YEAR II

Week	First Reading	Gospel Reading
1	1 Samuel	Mark 1:14–2:17
2	"	2:18–3:19
3	2 Samuel	3:22–4:34
4	2 Samuel; 1 Kings 1–16	5:1–6:30
5	1 Kings 1–16	6:53–8:10
6	James	8:11–9:13
7	"	9:14–10:16
8	1 Peter; Jude	10:17–11:33
0	2 Peter; 2 Timothy	12:1–12:44
10	1 Kings 17–22	Matthew 5:1-37
11	1 Kings 17–22; 2 Kings	5:38–6:34
12	2 Kings; Lamentations	7:1–8:17
13	Amos	8:18–9:17
14	Hosea; Isaiah	9:18–10:33
15	Isaiah; Micah	10:34–12:21
16	Micah; Jeremiah	12:38–13:30
17	Jeremiah	13:31–14:12
18	Numbers; Deuteronomy	14:13–17:20
19	Ezekiel	17:22–19:15
20	"	19:16–23:12
21	2 Thessalonians; 1 Corinthians	23:13–25:30
22	1 Corinthians	Luke 4:16–6:5
23	"	6:6-49
24	"	7:1–8:15
25	Proverbs; Ecclesiastes	8:16–9:45
26	Job	9:46–10:24
27	Galatians	10:25–11:28
28	Galatians; Ephesians	11:29–12:12
29	Ephesians	12:13–13:9
30	"	13:10–14:11
31	Ephesians; Philippians	14:12–16:15
32	Titus; Philemon; 2 and 3 John	17:1–18:8
33	Apocalypse	18:35–20:40
34	"	21:1-36

GENERAL ROMAN CALENDAR

JANUARY

1	Octave of Christmas	
	SOLEMNITY OF MARY, MOTHER OF GOD	Solemnity
2	Ss Basil the Great and Gregory Nazianzen,	Memorial
	bishops and doctors of the Church	
3		
4		
5		
6	THE EPIPHANY	Solemnity
7	*St Raymond of Penyafort, priest**	
8		
9		
10		
11		
12		
13	*St Hilary, bishop and doctor of the Church*	
14		
15		
16		
17	St Anthony, abbot	Memorial
18		
19		
20	*St Fabian, pope and martyr*	
	St Sebastian, martyr	
21	St Agnes, virgin and martyr	Memorial
22	*St Vincent, deacon and martyr*	
23		
24	*St Francis de Sales, bishop and doctor of the Church*	Memorial
25	THE CONVERSION OF ST PAUL, APOSTLE	Feast
26	Ss Timothy and Titus, bishops	Memorial
27	*St Angela Merici, virgin*	
28	St Thomas Aquinas, priest and doctor of the Church	Memorial
29		
30		
31	St John Bosco, priest	Memorial
Sunday after 6 January:	BAPTISM OF THE LORD	Feast

*When no rank is given, it is an optional memorial.

FEBRUARY

1		
2	THE PRESENTATION OF THE LORD	Feast
3	*St Blaise, bishop and martyr*	
	St Ansgar, bishop	
4		
5	St Agatha, virgin and martyr	Memorial
6	Ss Paul Miki and companions, martyrs	Memorial
7		
8	*St Jerome Emiliani*	
9		
10	St Scholastica, virgin	Memorial
11	*Our Lady of Lourdes*	
12		
13		
14	Ss Cyril, monk, and Methodius, bishop	Memorial
15		
16		
17	*The Seven Founders of the Order of Servites*	
18		
19		
20		
21	*St Peter Damian, bishop and doctor of the Church*	
22	THE CHAIR OF ST PETER, APOSTLE	Feast
23	St Polycarp, bishop and martyr	Memorial
24		
25		
26		
27		
28		

MARCH

1		
2		
3		
4	*St Casimir*	
5		
6		
7	Ss Perpetua and Felicity, martyrs	Memorial
8	*St John of God, religious*	
9	*St Frances of Rome, religious*	
10		
11		
12		
13		
14		
15		
16		
17	*St Patrick, bishop*	
18	*St Cyril of Jerusalem, bishop and doctor of the Church*	
19	ST JOSEPH, HUSBAND OF THE BLESSED VIRGIN MARY	Solemnity
20		
21		
22		
23	*St Turibius de Mongrovejo, bishop*	
24		
25	THE ANNUNCIATION OF THE LORD	Solemnity
26		
27		
28		
29		
30		
31		

APRIL

1		
2	*St Francis of Paola, hermit*	
3		
4	*St Isidore, bishop and doctor of the Church*	
5	*St Vincent Ferrer, priest*	
6		
7	St John Baptist de la Salle, priest	Memorial
8		
9		
10		
11	St Stanislaus, bishop and martyr	Memorial
12		
13	*St Martin I, pope and martyr*	
14		
15		
16		
17		
18		
19		
20		
21	*St Anselm, bishop and doctor of the Church*	
22		
23	*St George, martyr*	
24	*St Fidelis of Sigmaringen, priest and martyr*	
25	ST MARK, EVANGELIST	Feast
26		
27		
28	*St Peter Chanel, priest and martyr*	
29	St Catherine of Siena, virgin and doctor of the Church	Memorial
30	*St Pius V, pope*	

MAY

1	*St Joseph the Worker*	
2	St Athanasius, bishop and doctor of the Church	Memorial
3	SS PHILIP AND JAMES, APOSTLES	Feast
4		
5		
6		
7		
8		
9		
10		
11		
12	*Ss Nereus and Achilleus, martyrs. St Pancras, martyr*	
13		
14	ST MATTHIAS, APOSTLE	Feast
15		
16		
17		
18	*St John I, pope and martyr*	
19		
20	*St Bernardine of Siena, priest*	
21		
22		
23		
24		
25	*St Bede the Venerable, priest and doctor of the Church*	
	St Gregory VII, pope. St Mary Magdalene de Pazzi, virgin	
26	St Philip Neri, priest	Memorial
27	*St Augustine of Canterbury, bishop*	
28		
29		
30		
31	THE VISITATION OF THE BLESSED VIRGIN MARY	Feast
	First Sunday after Pentecost: HOLY TRINITY	Solemnity
	Thursday after Holy Trinity: THE BODY AND BLOOD OF CHRIST (CORPUS CHRISTI)	Solemnity
	Friday following Second Sunday after Pentecost: THE SACRED HEART OF JESUS	Solemnity
	Saturday following Second Sunday after Pentecost: *The Immaculate Heart of Mary*	

JUNE

1	St Justin, martyr	Memorial
2	*Ss Marcellinus and Peter, martyrs*	
3	Ss Charles Lwanga and companions, martyrs	Memorial
4		
5	St Boniface, bishop and martyr	Memorial
6	*St Norbert, bishop*	
7		
8		
9	*St Ephrem, deacon and doctor of the Church*	
10		
11	St Barnabas, apostle	Memorial
12		
13	St Anthony of Padua, priest and doctor of the Church	Memorial
14		
15		
16		
17		
18		
19	*St Romuald, abbot*	
20		
21	St Aloysius Gonzaga, religious	Memorial
22	*St Paulinus of Nola, bishop*	
	Ss John Fisher, bishop, and Thomas More, martyrs	
23		
24	THE BIRTH OF ST JOHN THE BAPTIST	Solemnity
25		
26		
27	*St Cyril of Alexandria, bishop and doctor of the Church*	
28	St Irenaeus, bishop and martyr	Memorial
29	SS PETER AND PAUL, APOSTLES	Solemnity
30	*The First Martyrs of the Church of Rome*	

JULY

1		
2		
3	ST THOMAS, APOSTLE	Feast
4	*St Elizabeth of Portugal*	
5	*St Anthony Zaccaria, priest*	
6	*St Maria Goretti, virgin and martyr*	
7		
8		
9		
10		
11	St Benedict, abbot	Memorial
12		
13	*St Henry*	
14	*St Camillus de Lellis, priest*	
15	St Bonaventure, bishop and doctor of the Church	Memorial
16	*Our Lady of Mount Carmel*	
17		
18		
19		
20		
21	*St Lawrence of Brindisi, priest and doctor of the Church*	
22	St Mary Magdalene	Memorial
23	*St Bridget, religious*	
24		
25	ST JAMES, APOSTLE	Feast
26	SS Joachim and Anne, parents of Mary	Memorial
27		
28		
29	St Martha	Memorial
30	*St Peter Chrysologus, bishop and doctor of the Church*	
31	St Ignatius of Loyola, priest	Memorial

AUGUST

1	St Alphonsus Liguori, bishop and doctor of the Church	Memorial
2	*St Eusebius of Vercelli, bishop*	
3		
4	St John Vianney, priest	Memorial
5	*The Dedication of the Basilica of St Mary Major*	
6	THE TRANSFIGURATION OF THE LORD	Feast
7	*Ss Sixtus II, pope and martyr, and companions, martyrs*	
	St Cajetan, priest	
8	St Dominic, priest	Memorial
9		
10	ST LAWRENCE, DEACON AND MARTYR	Feast
11	St Clare, virgin	Memorial
12		
13	*Ss Pontian, pope, and Hippolytus, priest, martyrs*	
14		
15	THE ASSUMPTION OF THE BLESSED VIRGIN MARY	Solemnity
16	*St Stephen of Hungary*	
17		
18		
19	*St John Eudes, priest*	
20	St Bernard, abbot and doctor of the Church	Memorial
21	St Pius X, pope	Memorial
22	The Queenship of Mary	Memorial
23	*St Rose of Lima, virgin*	
24	ST BARTHOLOMEW, APOSTLE	Feast
25	*St Louis*	
	St Joseph Calasanz, priest	
26		
27	St Monica	Memorial
28	St Augustine, bishop and doctor of the Church	Memorial
29	The Beheading of St John the Baptist, martyr	Memorial
30		
31		

SEPTEMBER

1		
2		
3	St Gregory the Great, pope and doctor of the Church	Memorial
4		
5		
6		
7		
8	THE BIRTHDAY OF THE BLESSED VIRGIN MARY	Feast
9		
10		
11		
12		
13	St John Chrysostom, bishop and doctor of the Church	Memorial
14	THE TRIUMPH OF THE CROSS	Feast
15	Our Lady of Sorrows	Memorial
16	Ss Cornelius, pope, and Cyprian, bishop, martyrs	Memorial
17	*St Robert Bellarmine, bishop and doctor of the Church*	
18		
19	*St Januarius, bishop and martyr*	
20		
21	ST MATTHEW, APOSTLE AND EVANGELIST	Feast
22		
23		
24		
25		
26	*Ss Cosmas and Damian, martyrs*	
27	St Vincent de Paul, priest	Memorial
28	*St Wenceslaus, martyr*	
29	SS MICHAEL, GABRIEL, AND RAPHAEL, ARCHANGELS	Feast
30	St Jerome, priest and doctor of the Church	Memorial

OCTOBER

1	St Teresa of the child Jesus, virgin	Memorial
2	The Guardian Angels	Memorial
3		
4	St Francis of Assisi	Memorial
5		
6	*St Bruno, priest*	
7	Our Lady of the Rosary	Memorial
8		
9	*Ss Denis, bishop and martyr, and companions, martyrs*	
	St John Leonardi, priest	
10		
11		
12		
13		
14	*St Callistus I, pope and martyr*	
15	St Teresa of Avila, virgin and doctor of the Church	Memorial
16	*St Hedwig, religious*	
	St Margaret Mary Alacoque, virgin	
17	St Ignatius of Antioch, bishop and martyr	Memorial
18	ST LUKE, EVANGELIST	Feast
19	*Ss John de Brébeuf and Isaac Jogues, priest, and companions, martyrs*	
	St Paul of the Cross, priest	
20		
21		
22		
23	*St John of Capistrano, priest*	
24	*St Anthony Claret, bishop*	
25		
26		
27		
28	SS SIMON AND JUDE, APOSTLES	Feast
29		
30		
31		

NOVEMBER

1	ALL SAINTS	Solemnity
2	THE COMMEMORATION OF ALL THE FAITHFUL DEPARTED (ALL SOULS)	
3	*St Martin de Porres, Religious*	
4	St Charles Borromeo, bishop	Memorial
5		
6		
7		
8		
9	THE DEDICATION OF THE LATERAN BASILICA	Feast
10	St Leo the Great, pope and doctor of the Church	Memorial
11	St Martin of Tours, bishop	Memorial
12	St Josaphat, bishop and martyr	Memorial
13		
14		
15	*St Albert the Great, bishop and doctor of the Church*	
16	*St Margaret of Scotland*	
	St Gertrude, virgin	
17	St Elizabeth of Hungary, religious	Memorial
18	*The Dedication of the Basilicas of Ss Peter and Paul, apostles*	
19		
20		
21	The Presentation of the blessed Virgin Mary	Memorial
22	St Cecilia, virgin and martyr	Memorial
23	*St Clement I, pope and martyr*	
	St Columban, abbot	
24		
25		
26		
27		
28		
29		
30	ST ANDREW, APOSTLE	Feast
	Last Sunday in Ordinary Time: CHRIST THE KING	Solemnity

DECEMBER

1		
2		
3	St Francis Xavier, priest	Memorial
4	*St John Damascene, priest and doctor of the Church*	
5		
6	*St Nicholas, bishop*	
7	St Ambrose, bishop and doctor of the Church	Memorial
8	THE IMMACULATE CONCEPTION OF THE BLESSED VIRGIN MARY	Solemnity
9		
10		
11	*St Damasus I, pope*	
12	*St Jane Frances de Chantal, religious*	
13	St Lucy, virgin and martyr	Memorial
14	St John of the Cross, priest and doctor of the Church	Memorial
15		
16		
17		
18		
19		
20		
21	*St Peter Canisius, priest and doctor of the Church*	
22		
23	*St John of Kanty, priest*	
24		
25	THE NATIVITY OF OUR LORD	Solemnity
26	ST STEPHEN, FIRST MARTYR	Feast
27	ST JOHN, APOSTLE AND EVANGELIST	Feast
28	THE HOLY INNOCENTS, MARTYRS	Feast
29	*St Thomas à Becket, bishop and martyr*	
30		
31	*St Sylvester I, pope*	

Sunday within the octave of Chrismas
or if there is no Sunday within the octave, 30 December:
THE HOLY FAMILY OF JESUS, MARY AND JOSEPH — Feast

Weekdays in Ordinary Time

Year I

FIRST WEEK IN ORDINARY TIME

Year I

Monday

FIRST READING

A reading from the letter to the Hebrews   1:1-6

God has spoken to us through his Son.

At various times in the past and in various different ways, God spoke to our ancestors through the prophets; but in our own time, the last days, he has spoken to us through his Son, the Son that he has appointed to inherit everything and through whom he made everything there is. He is the radiant light of God's glory and the perfect copy of his nature, sustaining the universe by his powerful command; and now that he has destroyed the defilement of sin, he has gone to take his place in heaven at the right hand of divine Majesty. So he is now as far above the angels as the title he has inherited is higher than their own name.

God has never said to any angel: You are my Son, today I have become your father; or: I will be a father to him and he a son to me. Again, when he brings the First-born into the world, he says: Let all the angels of God worship him.

This is the word of the Lord.

Responsorial Psalm   Ps 96:1-2. 6-7. 9. ℟ cf. v.7

℟   Let all his angels worship him.

1 The Lord is king, let earth rejoice,
   the many coastlands be glad.
   Cloud and darkness are his raiment;
   his throne, justice and right.   ℟

2 The skies proclaim his justice;
   all peoples see his glory.
   All you spirits, worship him.   ℟

3 For you indeed are the Lord
   most high above all the earth
   exalted far above all spirits.   ℟

Gospel Acclamation   Mk 1:15

Alleluia, alleluia!
The kingdom of God is near:
repent and believe the Good News!
Alleluia!

Alternative Acclamations pp.838ff.

GOSPEL

A reading from the holy Gospel according to Mark   1:14-20

Repent and believe the Good News.

After John had been arrested, Jesus went into Galilee. There he
proclaimed the Good News from God. 'The time has come' he said 'and
the kingdom of God is close at hand. Repent, and believe the Good
News.'

As he was walking along by the Sea of Galilee he saw Simon and
his brother Andrew casting a net in the lake – for they were
fishermen. And Jesus said to them, 'Follow me and I will make you
into fishers of men.' And at once they left their nets and followed him.

Going on a little further, he saw James son of Zebedee and his
brother John; they too were in their boat, mending their nets. He
called them at once and, leaving their father Zebedee in the boat with
the men he employed, they went after him.

This is the Gospel of the Lord.

In years when the feast of the Baptism of the Lord occurs on Monday of the first
week in Ordinary Time, the readings given for Monday may be added to those given
for Tuesday, so that the beginning of each book is read.

Tuesday

FIRST READING

A reading from the letter to the Hebrews   2:5-12

He perfected the author of our salvation through suffering.

God did not appoint angels to be rulers of the world to come, and that world is what we are talking about. Somewhere there is a passage that shows us this. It runs: What is man that you should spare a thought for him, the son of man that you should care for him? For a short while you made him lower than the angels; you crowned him with glory and splendour. You have put him in command of everything. Well then, if he has put him in command of everything, he has left nothing which is not under his command. At present, it is true, we are not able to see that everything has been put under his command, but we do see in Jesus one who was for a short while made lower than the angels and is now crowned with glory and splendour because he submitted to death; by God's grace he had to experience death for all mankind.

As it was his purpose to bring a great many of his sons into glory, it was appropriate that God, for whom everything exists and through whom everything exists, should make perfect, through suffering, the leader who would take them to their salvation. For the one who sanctifies, and the ones who are sanctified, are of the same stock; that is why he openly calls them brothers in the text: I shall announce your name to my brothers, praise you in full assembly.

This is the word of the Lord.

Responsorial Psalm   Ps 8:2. 5-9. ℟ v.7

℟   You gave your Son authority
    over all your creation.

1 How great is your name, O Lord our God,
   through all the earth!
   What is man that you should keep him in mind,
   mortal man that you care for him?   ℟

2 Yet you have made him little less than a god;
   with glory and honour you crowned him,
   gave him power over the works of your hand,
   put all things under his feet.   ℟

(continued)

3   All of them, sheep and cattle,
    yes, even the savage beasts,
    birds of the air, and fish
    that make their way through the waters.

℟   You gave your Son authority
    over all your creation.

Gospel Acclamation   cf. 1 Thess 2:13

Alleluia, alleluia!
Receive this messsage not as human words,
but as truly the word of God.
Alleluia!

GOSPEL

A reading from the holy Gospel according to Mark   1:21-28

Here was a teaching with authority behind it.

Jesus and his disciples went as far as Capernaum, and as soon as the
sabbath came he went to the synagogue and began to teach. And his
teaching made a deep impression on them because, unlike the scribes,
he taught them with authority.

In their synagogue just then there was a man possessed by an
unclean spirit, and it shouted, 'What do you want with us, Jesus of
Nazareth? Have you come to destroy us? I know who you are: the Holy
One of God.' But Jesus said sharply, 'Be quiet! Come out of him!' And
the unclean spirit threw the man into convulsions and with a loud cry
went out of him. The people were so astonished that they started
asking each other what it all meant. 'Here is a teaching that is new'
they said 'and with authority behind it: he gives orders even to
unclean spirits and they obey him.' And his reputation rapidly spread
everywhere, through all the surrounding Galilean countryside.

This is the Gospel of the Lord.

Wednesday

FIRST READING

A reading from the letter to the Hebrews   2:14-18

He became like all the brothers and sisters that he might share
their suffering.

Since all the children share the same blood and flesh, Jesus too shared equally in it, so that by his death he could take away all the power of the devil, who had power over death, and set free all those who had been held in slavery all their lives by the fear of death. For it was not the angels that he took to himself; he took to himself descent from Abraham. It was essential that he should in this way become completely like his brothers so that he could be a compassionate and trustworthy high priest of God's religion, able to atone for human sins. That is, because he has himself been through temptation he is able to help others who are tempted.

This is the word of the Lord.

Responsorial Psalm   Ps 104:1-4. 6-9. ℟ v.8

℟   The Lord remembers his covenant for ever.

or

℟   Alleluia!

1   Give thanks to the Lord, tell his name,
      make known his deeds among the peoples.
      O sing to him, sing his praise;
      tell all his wonderful works! ℟

2   Be proud of his holy name,
      let the hearts that seek the Lord rejoice.
      Consider the Lord and his strength;
      constantly seek his face. ℟

3   O children of Abraham, his servant,
      O sons of the Jacob he chose.
      He, the Lord, is our God:
      his judgements prevail in all the earth. ℟

4   He remembers his covenant for ever,
      his promise for a thousand generations,
      the covenant he made with Abraham,
      the oath he swore to Isaac. ℟

7

Gospel Acclamation   Jn 10:27

Alleluia, alleluia!
My sheep listen to my voice, says the Lord;
I know them, and they follow me.
Alleluia!

GOSPEL

A reading from the holy Gospel according to Mark   1:29-39

He healed many who were suffering from diseases.

On leaving the synagogue, Jesus went with James and John straight
to the house of Simon and Andrew. Now Simon's mother-in-law had
gone to bed with fever, and they told him about her straightaway. He
went to her, took her by the hand and helped her up. And the fever left
her and she began to wait on them.

That evening, after sunset, they brought to him all who were sick
and those who were possessed by devils. The whole town came
crowding round the door, and he cured many who were suffering from
diseases of one kind or another; he also cast out many devils, but he
would not allow them to speak, because they knew who he was.

In the morning, long before dawn, he got up and left the house, and
went off to a lonely place and prayed there. Simon and his companions
set out in search of him, and when they found him they said,
'Everybody is looking for you.' He answered, 'Let us go elsewhere, to
the neighbouring country towns, so that I can preach there too,
because that is why I came.' And he went all through Galilee,
preaching in their synagogues and casting out devils.

This is the Gospel of the Lord.

Thursday

FIRST READING

A reading from the letter to the Hebrews   3:7-14

Encourage one another daily while it is still today.

The Holy Spirit says: If only you would listen to him today; do not
harden your hearts, as happened in the Rebellion, on the Day of
Temptation in the wilderness, when your ancestors challenged me
and tested me, though they had seen what I could do for forty years.
That was why I was angry with that generation and said: How
unreliable these people who refuse to grasp my ways! And so, in
anger, I swore that not one would reach the place of rest I had for
them. Take care, brothers, that there is not in any one of your
community a wicked mind, so unbelieving as to turn away from the
living God. Every day, as long as this 'today' lasts, keep encouraging
one another so that none of you is hardened by the lure of sin, because
we shall remain co-heirs with Christ only if we keep a grasp on our
first confidence right to the end.

This is the word of the Lord.

Responsorial Psalm   Ps 94:6-11. ℟ v.8

℟   If today you hear his voice,
    harden not your hearts.

1   Come in; let us bow and bend low;
    let us kneel before the God who made us
    for he is our God and we
    the people who belong to his pasture,
    the flock that is led by his hand.   ℟

2   O that today you would listen to his voice!
    'Harden not your hearts as at Meribah,
    as on that day at Massah in the desert
    when your fathers put me to the test;
    when they tried me, though they saw my work.   ℟

3   For forty years I was wearied of these people
    and I said: "Their hearts are astray,
    these people do not know my ways."
    Then I took an oath in my anger:
    "Never shall they enter my rest." '   ℟

Gospel Acclamation   cf. Mt 4:23

Alleluia, alleluia!
Jesus preached the Good News of the kingdom
and healed all who were sick.
Alleluia!

GOSPEL

A reading from the holy Gospel according to Mark   1:40-45

The leper went away from him, cleansed.

A leper came to Jesus and pleaded on his knees: 'If you want to' he
said 'you can cure me.' Feeling sorry for him, Jesus stretched out his
hand and touched him. 'Of course I want to!' he said. 'Be cured!' And
the leprosy left him at once and he was cured. Jesus immediately sent
him away and sternly ordered him, 'Mind you say nothing to anyone,
but go and show yourself to the priest, and make the offering for your
healing prescribed by Moses as evidence of your recovery.' The man
went away, but then started talking about it freely and telling the
story everywhere, so that Jesus could no longer go openly into any
town, but had to stay outside in places where nobody lived. Even so,
people from all around would come to him.

This is the Gospel of the Lord.

Friday

FIRST READING

A reading from the letter to the Hebrews   4:1-5. 11

We must be eager to reach the place of rest.

Be careful: the promise of reaching the place of rest God had for the
Israelites still holds good, and none of you must think that he has
come too late for it. We received the Good News exactly as they did;
but hearing the message did them no good because they did not share
the faith of those who listened. We, however, who have faith, shall
reach a place of rest, as in the text: And so, in anger, I swore

that not one would reach the place of rest I had for them. God's work was undoubtedly all finished at the beginning of the world; as one text says, referring to the seventh day: After all his work God rested on the seventh day. The text we are considering says: they shall not reach the place of rest I had for them.

We must therefore do everything we can to reach this place of rest, or some of you might copy this example of disobedience and be lost.

This is the word of the Lord.

Responsorial Psalm   Ps 77:3-4. 6-8. ℟ cf. v.7

℟   Do not forget the works of the Lord!

1   The things we have heard and understood,
    the things our fathers have told us
    we will not hide from their children
    but will tell them to the next generation:
    the glories of the Lord and his might
    and the marvellous deeds he has done.   ℟

2   They too should arise and tell their sons
    that they too should set their hope in God
    and never forget God's deeds
    but keep every one of his commands.   ℟

3   So that they might not be like their fathers,
    a defiant and rebellious race,
    a race whose heart was fickle,
    whose spirit was unfaithful to God.   ℟

Gospel Acclamation   Lk 7:16

    Alleluia, alleluia!
    A great prophet has appeared among us;
    God has visited his people.
    Alleluia!

GOSPEL

A reading from the holy Gospel according to Mark   2:1-12

The Son of Man has authority on earth to forgive sins.

When Jesus returned to Capernaum, word went round that he was back; and so many people collected there that there was no room left, even in front of the door. He was preaching the word to them when some people came bringing him a paralytic carried by four men, but as the crowd made it impossible to get the man to him, they stripped the roof over the place where Jesus was; and when they had made an opening, they lowered the stretcher on which the paralytic lay. Seeing their faith, Jesus said to the paralytic, 'My child, your sins are forgiven.' Now some scribes were sitting there, and they thought to themselves, 'How can this man talk like that? He is blaspheming. Who can forgive sins but God?' Jesus, inwardly aware that this was what they were thinking, said to them, 'Why do you have these thoughts in your hearts? Which of these is easier: to say to the paralytic, "Your sins are forgiven" or to say, "Get up, pick up your stretcher and walk"? But to prove to you that the Son of Man has authority on earth to forgive sins,' – he said to the paralytic – 'I order you: get up, pick up your stretcher, and go off home.' And the man got up, picked up his stretcher at once and walked out in front of everyone, so that they were all astounded and praised God saying, 'We have never seen anything like this.'

This is the Gospel of the Lord.

Saturday

FIRST READING

A reading from the letter to the Hebrews   4:12-16

Let us approach the throne of grace with confidence.

The word of God is something alive and active: it cuts like any double-edged sword but more finely: it can slip through the place where the soul is divided from the spirit, or joints from the marrow; it can judge the secret emotions and thoughts. No created thing can hide from him; everything is uncovered and open to the eyes of the one to whom we must give account of ourselves.

Since in Jesus, the Son of God, we have the supreme high priest who has gone through to the highest heaven, we must never let go of the faith that we have professed. For it is not as if we had a high priest who was incapable of feeling our weaknesses with us; but we have one who has been tempted in every way that we are, though he is without sin. Let us be confident, then, in approaching the throne of grace, that we shall have mercy from him and find grace when we are in need of help.

This is the word of the Lord.

Responsorial Psalm   Ps 18:8-10. 15. ℟ cf. Jn 6:63

℟   Your words, Lord,
       are spirit and life.

1   The law of the Lord is perfect,
       it revives the soul.
       The rule of the Lord is to be trusted,
       it gives wisdom to the simple.   ℟

2   The precepts of the Lord are right,
       they gladden the heart.
       The command of the Lord is clear,
       it gives light to the eyes.   ℟

3   The fear of the Lord is holy,
       abiding for ever.
       The decrees of the Lord are truth
       and all of them just.   ℟

4   May the spoken words of my mouth,
       the thoughts of my heart,
       win favour in your sight, O Lord,
       my rescuer, my rock!   ℟

Gospel Acclamation   Lk 4:18

Alleluia, alleluia!
The Lord sent me to bring Good News to the poor
and freedom to prisoners.
Alleluia!

GOSPEL

A reading from the holy Gospel according to Mark   2:13-17

I have not come to call the just, but sinners.

Jesus went out to the shore of the lake; and all the people came to him, and he taught them. As he was walking on he saw Levi the son of Alphaeus, sitting by the customs house, and he said to him, 'Follow me.' And he got up and followed him.

When Jesus was at dinner in his house, a number of tax collectors and sinners were also sitting at the table with Jesus and his disciples; for there were many of them among his followers. When the scribes of the Pharisee party saw him eating with sinners and tax collectors, they said to his disciples, 'Why does he eat with tax collectors and sinners?' When Jesus heard this he said to them, 'It is not the healthy who need the doctor, but the sick. I did not come to call the virtuous, but sinners.'

This is the Gospel of the Lord.

SECOND WEEK IN ORDINARY TIME
Year I

Monday

FIRST READING

A reading from the letter to the Hebrews   5:1-10

Although he was the Son of God, he learned obedience from what he suffered.

Every high priest has been taken out of mankind and is appointed to act for men in their relations with God, to offer gifts and sacrifices for sins; and so he can sympathise with those who are ignorant or uncertain because he too lives in the limitations of weakness. That is why he has to make sin offerings for himself as well as for the people. No one takes this honour on himself, but each one is called by God, as Aaron was. Nor did Christ give himself the glory of becoming high priest, but he had it from the one who said to him: You are my son, today I have become your father, and in another text: You are a priest of the order of Melchizedek, and for ever. During his life on earth, he offered up prayer and entreaty, aloud and in silent tears, to the one who had the power to save him out of death, and he submitted so humbly that his prayer was heard. Although he was Son, he learnt to obey through suffering; but having been made perfect, he became for all who obey him the source of eternal salvation and was acclaimed by God with the title of high priest of the order of Melchizedek.

This is the word of the Lord.

Responsorial Psalm   Ps 109:1-4. ℟ v.4

℟   You are a priest for ever,
     in the line of Melchizedek.

1   The Lord's revelation to my Master:
    'Sit on my right:
    I will put your foes beneath your feet.'   ℟

2   The Lord will send from Zion
    your sceptre of power:
    rule in the midst of all your foes.   ℟

3   A prince from the day of your birth
    on the holy mountains;
    from the womb before the daybreak I begot you.   ℟

4   The Lord has sworn an oath he will not change.
    'You are a priest for ever,
    a priest like Melchizedek of old.'   ℟

Gospel Acclamation   Heb 4:12

Alleluia, alleluia!
The word of God is living and active;
it probes the thoughts and motives of our heart.
Alleluia!

GOSPEL

A reading from the holy Gospel according to Mark   2:18-22

The bridegroom is still with them.

One day when John's disciples and the Pharisees were fasting, some people came and said to Jesus, 'Why is it that John's disciples and the disciples of the Pharisees fast, but your disciples do not?'

Jesus replied, 'Surely the bridegroom's attendants would never think of fasting while the bridegroom is still with them? As long as they have the bridegroom with them, they could not think of fasting. But the time will come for the bridegroom to be taken away from them, and then, on that day, they will fast. No one sews a piece of unshrunken cloth on an old cloak; if he does, the patch pulls away from it, the new from the old, and the tear gets worse. And nobody puts new wine into old wineskins; if he does, the wine will burst the skins, and the wine is lost and the skins too. No! New wine, fresh skins!'

This is the Gospel of the Lord.

Tuesday

FIRST READING

A reading from the letter to the Hebrews   6:10-20

We have a source of strength to take firm grip of the hope that is
held out to us.

God would not be so unjust as to forget all you have done, the love that you have for his name or the services you have done, and are still doing, for the saints. Our one desire is that every one of you should go on showing the same earnestness to the end, to the perfect fulfilment of our hopes, never growing careless, but imitating those who have the faith and the perseverance to inherit the promises.

When God made the promise to Abraham, he swore by his own self, since it was impossible for him to swear by anyone greater: I will shower blessings on you and give you many descendants. Because of that, Abraham persevered and saw the promise fulfilled. Men, of course, swear an oath by something greater than themselves, and between men, confirmation by an oath puts an end to all dispute. In the same way, when God wanted to make the heirs to the promise thoroughly realise that his purpose was unalterable, he conveyed this by an oath; so that there would be two unalterable things in which it was impossible for God to be lying, and so that we, now we have found safety, should have a strong encouragement to take a firm grip on the hope that is held out to us. Here we have an anchor for our soul, as sure as it is firm, and reaching right through beyond the veil where Jesus has entered before us and on our behalf, to become a high priest of the order of Melchizedek, and for ever.

This is the word of the Lord.

Responsorial Psalm   Ps 110:1-2. 4-5. 9. 10. ℟ v.5

℟   The Lord will remember his covenant for ever.

or

℟   Alleluia!

1   I will thank the Lord with all my heart
     in the meeting of the just and their assembly.
     Great are the works of the Lord;
     to be pondered by all who love them. ℟

2   He makes us remember his wonders.
     The Lord is compassion and love.
     He gives food to those who fear him;
     keeps his covenant ever in mind. ℟

3   He has sent deliverance to his people
     and established his covenant for ever.
     Holy his name, to be feared.
     His praise shall last for ever! ℟

Gospel Acclamation   cf. Eph 1:17-18

Alleluia, alleluia!
May the Father of our Lord Jesus Christ
enlighten the eyes of our heart
that we might see how great is the hope
to which we are called.
Alleluia!

GOSPEL

A reading from the holy Gospel according to Mark   2:23-28

The sabbath was made for people, not people for the sabbath.

One sabbath day Jesus happened to be taking a walk through the cornfields, and his disciples began to pick ears of corn as they went along. And the Pharisees said to him, 'Look, why are they doing

17

something on the sabbath day that is forbidden?' And he replied, 'Did you never read what David did in his time of need when he and his followers were hungry – how he went into the house of God when Abiathar was high priest, and ate the loaves of offering which only the priests are allowed to eat, and how he also gave some to the men with him?'

And he said to them, 'The sabbath was made for man, not man for the sabbath; so the Son of Man is master even of the sabbath.'

This is the Gospel of the Lord.

Wednesday

FIRST READING

A reading from the letter to the Hebrews   7:1-3. 15-17

You are a priest for ever, in the line of Melchizedek.

You remember that Melchizedek, king of Salem, a priest of God most High, went to meet Abraham who was on his way back after defeating the kings, and blessed him; and also that it was to him that Abraham gave a tenth of all that he had. By the interpretation of his name, he is, first, 'king of righteousness' and also king of Salem, that is, 'king of peace'; he has no father, mother or ancestry, and his life has no beginning or ending; he is like the Son of God. He remains a priest for ever.

This becomes even more clearly evident when there appears a second Melchizedek, who is a priest not by virtue of a law about physical descent, but by the power of an indestructible life. For it was about him that the prophecy was made: You are a priest of the order of Melchizedek, and for ever.

This is the word of the Lord.

Responsorial Psalm   Ps 109:1-4. ℞ v.4

℞   You are a priest for ever,
     in the line of Melchizedek.

1   The Lord's revelation to my Master:
    'Sit on my right:
    I will put your foes beneath your feet.'   ℞

2   The Lord will send from Zion
    your sceptre of power;
    rule in the midst of all your foes.   ℟

3   A prince from the day of your birth
    on the holy mountains;
    from the womb before the daybreak I begot you.   ℟

4   The Lord has sworn an oath he will not change.
    'You are a priest for ever,
    a priest like Melchizedek of old.'   ℟

Gospel Acclamation   cf. Mt 4:23

    Alleluia, alleluia!
    Jesus preached the Good News of the kingdom
    and healed all who were sick.
    Alleluia!

GOSPEL

A reading from the holy Gospel according to Mark   3:1-6

    Is it against the law on the sabbath day to do good – to save life or to kill?

Jesus went into a synagogue, and there was a man there who had a
withered hand. And they were watching him to see if he would cure
him on the sabbath day, hoping for something to use against him. He
said to the man with the withered hand, 'Stand up out in the middle!'
Then he said to them, 'Is it against the law on the sabbath day to do
good, or to do evil; to save life, or to kill?' But they said nothing. Then,
grieved to find them so obstinate, he looked angrily round at them,
and said to the man, 'Stretch out your hand.' He stretched it out and
his hand was better. The Pharisees went out and at once began to plot
with the Herodians against him, discussing how to destroy him.

    This is the Gospel of the Lord.

Thursday

FIRST READING

A reading from the letter to the Hebrews 7:25–8:6

He offered his sacrifice once and for all when he offered himself.

The power of Jesus to save is utterly certain, since he is living for ever to intercede for all who come to God through him.

To suit us, the ideal high priest would have to be holy, innocent and uncontaminated, beyond the influence of sinners, and raised up above the heavens; one who would not need to offer sacrifices every day, as the other high priests do for their own sins and then for those of the people, because he has done this once and for all by offering himself. The Law appoints high priests who are men subject to weakness; but the promise on oath, which came after the Law, appointed the Son who is made perfect for ever.

The great point of all that we have said is that we have a high priest of exactly this kind. He has his place at the right of the throne of divine Majesty in the heavens, and he is the minister of the sanctuary and of the true Tent of Meeting which the Lord, and not any man, set up. It is the duty of every high priest to offer gifts and sacrifices, and so this one too must have something to offer. In fact, if he were on earth, he would not be a priest at all, since there are others who make the offerings laid down by the Law and these only maintain the service of a model or a reflection of the heavenly realities. For Moses, when he had the Tent to build, was warned by God who said: See that you make everything according to the pattern shown you on the mountain.

We have seen that he has been given a ministry of a far higher order, and to the same degree it is a better covenant of which he is the mediator, founded on better promises.

This is the word of the Lord.

Responsorial Psalm Ps 39:7-10. 17. ℟ cf. vv.8. 9

℟ Here am I, Lord;
I come to do your will.

1 You do not ask for sacrifice and offerings,
but an open ear.

You do not ask for holocaust and victim.
Instead, here am I. ℟

2 In the scroll of the book it stands written
that I should do your will.
My God, I delight in your law
in the depth of my heart. ℟

3 Your justice I have proclaimed
in the great assembly.
My lips I have not sealed;
you know it, O Lord. ℟

4 O let there be rejoicing and gladness
for all who seek you
Let them ever say: 'The Lord is great',
who love your saving help. ℟

Gospel Acclamation   cf. 2 Tim 1:10

Alleluia, alleluia!
Our Saviour Jesus Christ has done away with death
and brought us life through his gospel.
Alleluia!

GOSPEL

A reading from the holy Gospel according to Mark   3:7-12

The unclean spirits shouted, you are the Son of God, but he
warned them not to make him known.

Jesus withdrew with his disciples to the lakeside, and great crowds
from Galilee followed him. From Judaea, Jerusalem, Idumaea, Transjordania and the region of Tyre and Sidon, great numbers who had
heard of all he was doing came to him. And he asked his disciples to
have a boat ready for him because of the crowd, to keep him from
being crushed. For he had cured so many that all who were afflicted in
any way were crowding forward to touch him. And the unclean spirits,
whenever they saw him, would fall down before him and shout, 'You
are the Son of God!' But he warned them strongly not to make him
known.

This is the Gospel of the Lord.

Friday

FIRST READING

A reading from the letter to the Hebrews   8:6-13

He is mediator of a better covenant.

We have seen that Jesus has been given a ministry of a far higher order, and to the same degree it is a better covenant of which he is the mediator, founded on better promises. If that first covenant had been without a fault, there would have been no need for a second one to replace it. And in fact God does find fault with them; he says:

See, the days are coming – it is the Lord who speaks –
when I will establish a new covenant
with the House of Israel and the House of Judah,
but not a covenant like the one I made with their ancestors
on the day I took them by the hand
to bring them out of the land of Egypt.
They abandoned that covenant of mine,
and so I on my side deserted them. It is the Lord who speaks.
No, this is the covenant I will make
with the House of Israel
when those days arrive – it is the Lord who speaks.
I will put my laws into their minds
and write them on their hearts.
Then I will be their God
and they shall be my people.
There will be no further need for neighbour to try to teach
    neighbour,
or brother to say to brother,
'Learn to know the Lord.'
No, they will all know me,
the least no less than the greatest,
since I will forgive their iniquities
and never call their sins to mind.

By speaking of a new covenant, he implies that the first one is already old. Now anything old only gets more antiquated until in the end it disappears.

This is the word of the Lord.

Responsorial Psalm   Ps 84:8. 10-14. ℟ v.11

℟ Kindness and truth shall meet.

1 Let us see, O Lord, your mercy
   and give us your saving help.
   His help is near for those who fear him
   and his glory will dwell in our land. ℟

2 Mercy and faithfulness have met;
   justice and peace have embraced.
   Faithfulness shall spring from the earth
   and justice look down from heaven. ℟

3 The Lord will make us prosper
   and our earth shall yield its fruit.
   Justice shall march before him
   and peace shall follow his steps. ℟

Gospel Acclamation   2 Cor 5:19

Alleluia, alleluia!
God was in Christ, to reconcile the world to himself;
and the Good News of reconciliation he has entrusted to us.
Alleluia!

GOSPEL

A reading from the holy Gospel according to Mark   3:13-19

He called those he wanted and they went with him.

Jesus went up into the hills and summoned those he wanted. So they
came to him and he appointed twelve; they were to be his companions
and to be sent out to preach, with power to cast out devils. And so he
appointed the Twelve: Simon to whom he gave the name Peter, James
the son of Zebedee and John the brother of James, to whom he gave
the name Boanerges or 'Sons of Thunder'; then Andrew, Philip,
Bartholomew, Matthew, Thomas, James the son of Alphaeus, Thaddaeus, Simon the Zealot and Judas Iscariot, the man who was to
betray him.

This is the Gospel of the Lord.

Saturday

FIRST READING

A reading from the letter to the Hebrews   9:2-3. 11-14

He offered his sacrifice once and for all when he offered himself.

There was a tent which comprised two compartments: the first, in which the lamp-stand, the table and the presentation loaves were kept, was called the Holy Place; then beyond the second veil, an innermost part which was called the Holy of Holies.

But now Christ has come, as the high priest of all the blessings which were to come. He has passed through the greater, the more perfect tent, which is better than the one made by men's hands because it is not of this created order; and he has entered the sanctuary once and for all, taking with him not the blood of goats and bull calves, but his own blood, having won an eternal redemption for us. The blood of goats and bulls and the ashes of a heifer are sprinkled on those who have incurred defilement and they restore the holiness of their outward lives; how much more effectively the blood of Christ, who offered himself as the perfect sacrifice to God through the eternal Spirit, can purify our inner self from dead actions so that we do our service to the living God.

This is the word of the Lord.

Responsorial Psalm   Ps 46:2-3. 6-9. ℟ v.6

℟   God mounts his throne to shouts of joy;
a blare of trumpets for the Lord.

1   All peoples, clap your hands,
cry to God with shouts of joy!
For the Lord, the Most High, we must fear,
great king over all the earth.   ℟

2   God goes up with shouts of joy;
the Lord goes up with trumpet blast.
Sing praise for God, sing praise,
sing praise to our king, sing praise.   ℟

3   God is king of all the earth.
Sing praise with all your skill.
God is king over the nations;
God reigns on his holy throne.   ℟

Gospel Acclamation   cf. Acts 16:14

Alleluia, alleluia!
Open our hearts, O Lord,
to listen to the words of your Son.
Alleluia!

GOSPEL

A reading from the holy Gospel according to Mark   3:20-21

The people said that he was out of his mind.

Jesus went home, and such a crowd collected that they could not even
have a meal. When his relatives heard of this, they set out to take
charge of him, convinced he was out of his mind.

This is the Gospel of the Lord.

THIRD WEEK IN ORDINARY TIME

Year I

Monday

FIRST READING

A reading from the letter to the Hebrews   9:15. 24-28

*He offered himself to take the faults of many away; he will appear
a second time to those who are awaiting him.*

Christ brings a new covenant, as the mediator, only so that the
people who were called to an eternal inheritance may actually
receive what was promised: his death took place to cancel the sins
that infringed the earlier covenant. It is not as though Christ had
entered a man-made sanctuary which was only modelled on the
real one; but it was heaven itself, so that he could appear in the
actual presence of God on our behalf. And he does not have to offer
himself again and again, like the high priest going into the sanctuary year after year with the blood that is not his own, or else he
would have had to suffer over and over again since the world
began. Instead of that, he has made his appearance once and for all,
now at the end of the last age, to do away with sin by sacrificing
himself. Since men only die once, and after that comes judgement,
so Christ, too, offers himself only once to take the faults of many on

himself, and when he appears a second time, it will not be to deal with sin but to reward with salvation those who are waiting for him.

This is the word of the Lord.

Responsorial Psalm   Ps 97:1-6. ℟ v.1

℟   Sing to the Lord a new song,
      for he has done marvellous deeds.

1   Sing a new song to the Lord
     for he has worked wonders.
     His right hand and his holy arm
     have brought salvation. ℟

2   The Lord has made known his salvation;
     has shown his justice to the nations.
     He has remembered his truth and love
     for the house of Israel. ℟

3   All the ends of the earth have seen
     the salvation of our God.
     Shout to the Lord all the earth,
     ring out your joy. ℟

4   Sing psalms to the Lord with the harp
     with the sound of music.
     With trumpets and the sound of the horn
     acclaim the King, the Lord. ℟

Gospel Acclamation   cf. 2 Tim 1:10

     Alleluia, alleluia!
     Our Saviour Jesus Christ has done away with death
     and brought us life through his gospel.
     Alleluia!

GOSPEL

A reading from the holy Gospel according to Mark   3:22-30

It is the end of Satan.

The scribes who had come down from Jerusalem were saying: 'Beelzebul is in him' and, 'It is through the prince of devils that he casts devils out.' So Jesus called them to him and spoke to them in parables, 'How can Satan cast out Satan? If a kingdom is divided against itself, that kingdom cannot last. And if a household is divided against itself, that household can never stand. Now if Satan has rebelled against himself and is divided, he cannot stand either – it is the end of him. But no one can make his way into a strong man's house and burgle his property unless he has tied up the strong man first. Only then can he burgle his house.

'I tell you solemnly, all men's sins will be forgiven, and all their blasphemies: but let anyone blaspheme against the Holy Spirit and he will never have forgiveness: he is guilty of an eternal sin.' This was because they were saying, 'An unclean spirit is in him.'

This is the Gospel of the Lord.

Tuesday

FIRST READING

A reading from the letter to the Hebrews   10:1-10

God, I am coming to do your will.

Since the Law has no more than a reflection of these realities, and no finished picture of them, it is quite incapable of bringing the worshippers to perfection, with the same sacrifices repeatedly offered year after year. Otherwise, the offering of them would have stopped, because the worshippers, when they had been purified once, would have no awareness of sins. Instead of that, the sins are recalled year after year in the sacrifices. Bulls' blood and goats' blood are useless for taking away sins, and this is what he said, on coming into the world:

You who wanted no sacrifice or oblation,
prepared a body for me.
You took no pleasure in holocausts or sacrifices for sin;
then I said,
just as I was commanded in the scroll of the book,
'God, here I am! I am coming to obey your will.'

Notice that he says first: You did not want what the Law lays down as the things to be offered, that is: the sacrifices, the oblations, the holocausts and the sacrifices for sin, and you took no pleasure in them; and then he says: Here I am! I am coming to obey your will.

He is abolishing the first sort to replace it with the second. And this will was for us to be made holy by the offering of his body made once and for all by Jesus Christ.

This is the word of the Lord.

Responsorial Psalm   Ps 39:2. 4. 7-8. 10.11. ℟ cf. vv.8. 9

℟ Here am I, Lord;
    I come to do your will.

1 I waited, I waited for the Lord
    and he stooped down to me;
    he heard my cry.
    He put a new song into my mouth,
    praise of our God. ℟

2 You do not ask for sacrifice and offerings,
    but an open ear.
    You do not ask for holocaust and victim.
    Instead, here am I. ℟

3 Your justice I have proclaimed
    in the great assembly.
    My lips I have not sealed;
    you know it, O Lord. ℟

4 I have not hidden your justice in my heart
    but declared your faithful help.
    I have not hidden your love and your truth
    from the great assembly. ℟

Gospel Acclamation   cf. Mt 11:25

Alleluia, alleluia!
Blessed are you, Father, Lord of heaven and earth;
you have revealed to little ones the mysteries of the kingdom.
Alleluia!

GOSPEL

A reading from the holy Gospel according to Mark   3:31-35

Here are my mother and my brother: anyone who does the will of God.

The mother and brothers of Jesus arrived and, standing outside, sent in a message asking for him. A crowd was sitting round him at the time the message was passed to him, 'Your mother and brothers and sisters are outside asking for you.' He replied, 'Who are my mother and my brothers?' And looking round at those sitting in a circle about him, he said, 'Here are my mother and my brothers. Anyone who does the will of God, that person is my brother and sister and mother.'

This is the Gospel of the Lord.

Wednesday

FIRST READING

A reading from the letter to the Hebrews   10:11-18

He has achieved the eternal perfection of all whom he is sanctifying.

All the priests stand at their duties every day, offering over and over again the same sacrifices which are quite incapable of taking sins away. Jesus, on the other hand, has offered one single sacrifice for sins, and then taken his place for ever, at the right hand of God, where he is now waiting until his enemies are made into a footstool for him. By virtue of that one single offering, he has achieved the eternal perfection of all whom he is sanctifying. The Holy Spirit assures us of this; for he says, first:

This is the covenant I will make with them
when those days arrive;

and the Lord then goes on to say:

I will put my laws into their hearts
and write them on their minds.
I will never call their sins to mind,
or their offences.

When all sins have been forgiven, there can be no more sin offerings.

This is the word of the Lord.

Responsorial Psalm   Ps 109:1-4. ℟ v.4

℟ You are a priest for ever,
    in the line of Melchizedek.

1 The Lord's revelation to my Master:
   'Sit on my right:
   I will put your foes beneath your feet.' ℟

2 The Lord will send from Zion
   your sceptre of power:
   rule in the midst of all your foes. ℟

3 A prince from the day of your birth
   on the holy mountains;
   from the womb before the daybreak I begot you. ℟

4 The Lord has sworn an oath he will not change.
   'You are a priest for ever,
   a priest like Melchizedek of old.' ℟

Gospel Acclamation

Alleluia, alleluia!
The seed is the word of God, Christ is the sower;
all who come to him will live for ever.
Alleluia!

GOSPEL

A reading from the holy Gospel according to Mark   4:1-20

The sower goes out to sow.

Jesus began to teach by the lakeside, but such a huge crowd gathered round him that he got into a boat on the lake and sat there. The people were all along the shore, at the water's edge. He taught them many things in parables, and in the course of his teaching he said to them, 'Listen! Imagine a sower going out to sow. Now it happened that, as he sowed, some of the seed fell on the edge of the path, and the birds came and ate it up. Some seed fell on rocky ground where it found little soil and sprang up straightaway, because there was no depth of earth; and when the sun came up it was scorched and, not having any roots, it withered away. Some seed fell into thorns, and the thorns grew up and choked it, and it produced no crop. And some seed fell into rich soil and, growing tall and strong, produced crop; and yielded thirty, sixty, even a hundredfold.' And he said, 'Listen, anyone who has ears to hear!'

When he was alone, the Twelve, together with the others who formed his company, asked what the parables meant. He told them, 'The secret of the kingdom of God is given to you, but to those who are outside everything comes in parables, so that they may see and see again, but not perceive; may hear and hear again, but not understand; otherwise they might be converted and be forgiven.'

He said to them, 'Do you not understand this parable? Then how will you understand any of the parables? What the sower is sowing is the word. Those on the edge of the path where the word is sown are people who have no sooner heard it than Satan comes and carries away the word that was sown in them. Similarly, those who receive the seed on patches of rock are people who, when first they hear the word, welcome it at once with joy. But they have no root in them, they do not last; should some trial come, or some persecution on account of the word, they fall away at once. Then there are others who receive the seed in thorns. These have heard the word, but the worries of this world, the lure of riches and all the other passions come in to choke the word, and so it produces nothing. And there are those who have received the seed in rich soil: they hear the word and accept it and yield a harvest, thirty and sixty and a hundredfold.'

This is the Gospel of the Lord.

Thursday

FIRST READING

A reading from the letter to the Hebrews   10:19-25

Let us be filled with faith, firm in the hope we profess and encourage each other in love.

Through the blood of Jesus we have the right to enter the sanctuary, by a new way which he has opened for us, a living opening through the curtain, that is to say, his body. And we have the supreme high priest over all the house of God. So as we go in, let us be sincere in heart and filled with faith, our minds sprinkled and free from any trace of bad conscience and our bodies washed with pure water. Let us keep firm in the hope we profess, because the one who made the promise is faithful. Let us be concerned for each other, to stir a

31

response in love and good works. Do not stay away from the meetings of the community, as some do, but encourage each other to go; the more so as you see the Day drawing near.

This is the word of the Lord.

Responsorial Psalm   Ps 23:1-6. ℟ cf. v.6

℟ Lord, this is the people that longs to see your face.

1   The Lord's is the earth and its fullness,
    the world and all its peoples.
    It is he who set it on the seas;
    on the waters he made it firm.   ℟

2   Who shall climb the mountain of the Lord?
    Who shall stand in his holy place?
    The man with clean hands and pure heart,
    who desires not worthless things.   ℟

3   He shall receive blessings from the Lord
    and reward from the God who saves him.
    Such are the men who seek him,
    seek the face of the God of Jacob.   ℟

Gospel Acclamation   Ps 118:105

Alleluia, alleluia!
Your word is a lamp for my feet
and a light on my path.
Alleluia!

GOSPEL

A reading from the holy Gospel according to Mark   4:21-25

*Come and place your lamp on a stand. In the measure you give you
shall receive.*

Jesus said to the crowd: 'Would you bring in a lamp to put it under a tub or under the bed? Surely you will put it on the lampstand? For there is nothing hidden but it must be disclosed, nothing kept secret except to be brought to light. If anyone has ears to hear, let him listen to this.'

He also said to them, 'Take notice of what you are hearing. The amount you measure out is the amount you will be given – and more besides; for the man who has will be given more; from the man who has not, even what he has will be taken away.'

This is the Gospel of the Lord.

Friday

FIRST READING

A reading from the letter to the Hebrews   10:32-39

Do not throw your confidence away. It will have a great reward.

Remember all the sufferings that you had to meet after you received the light, in earlier days: sometimes by being yourselves publicly exposed to insults and violence, and sometimes as associates of others who were treated in the same way. For you not only shared in the sufferings of those who were in prison, but you happily accepted being stripped of your belongings, knowing that you owned something that was better and lasting. Be as confident now, then, since the reward is so great. You will need endurance to do God's will and gain what he has promised.

Only a little while now, a very little while,
and the one that is coming will have come; he will not delay.
The righteous man will live by faith,
but if he draws back, my soul will take no pleasure in him.

You and I are not the sort of people who draw back, and are lost by it; we are the sort who keep faithful until our souls are saved.

This is the word of the Lord.

Responsorial Psalm   Ps 36:3-6. 23-24. 39-40. ℟ v.39

℟   The salvation of the just comes from the Lord.

1   If you trust in the Lord and do good,
then you will live in the land and be secure.
If you find your delight in the Lord,
he will grant your heart's desire.   ℟

2   Commit your life to the Lord,
     trust in him and he will act,
     so that your justice breaks forth like the light,
     your cause like the noon-day sun.

     ℟   The salvation of the just comes from the Lord.

3   The Lord guides the steps of a man
     and makes safe the path of one he loves.
     Though he stumble he shall never fall
     for the Lord holds him by the hand.   ℟

4   The salvation of the just comes from the Lord,
     their stronghold in time of distress.
     The Lord helps them and delivers them
     and saves them: for their refuge is in him.   ℟

Gospel Acclamation   cf. Mt 11:25

Alleluia, alleluia!
Blessed are you, Father, Lord of heaven and earth;
     you have revealed to little ones the mysteries of the kingdom.
Alleluia!

GOSPEL

A reading from the holy Gospel according to Mark   4:26-34

A man scatters seed and while he sleeps it grows even though he
does not know how.

Jesus said to the crowd: 'This is what the kingdom of God is like. A
man throws seed on the land. Night and day, while he sleeps, when he
is awake, the seed is sprouting and growing; how, he does not know.
Of its own accord the land produces first the shoot, then the ear, then
the full grain in the ear. And when the crop is ready, he loses no time:
he starts to reap because the harvest has come.'

He also said, 'What can we say the kingdom of God is like? What
parable can we find for it? It is like a mustard seed which at the time
of its sowing in the soil is the smallest of all the seeds on earth; yet
once it is sown it grows into the biggest shrub of them all and puts out
big branches so that the birds of the air can shelter in its shade.'

Using many parables like these, he spoke the word to them, so far
as they were capable of understanding it. He would not speak to them

except in parables, but he explained everything to his disciples when they were alone.

This is the Gospel of the Lord.

Saturday

FIRST READING

A reading from the letter to the Hebrews   11:1-2. 8-19

They look forward to a city founded, designed, and built by God.

Only faith can guarantee the blessings that we hope for, or prove the existence of the realities that at present remain unseen. It was for faith that our ancestors were commended.

It was by faith that Abraham obeyed the call to set out for a country that was the inheritance given to him and his descendants, and that he set out without knowing where he was going. By faith he arrived, as a foreigner, in the Promised Land, and lived there as if in a strange country, with Isaac and Jacob, who were heirs with him of the same promise. They lived there in tents while he looked forward to a city founded, designed and built by God.

It was equally by faith that Sarah, in spite of being past the age, was made able to conceive, because she believed that he who had made the promise would be faithful to it. Because of this, there came from one man, and one who was already as good as dead himself, more descendants than could be counted, as many as the stars of heaven or the grains of sand on the seashore.

All these died in faith, before receiving any of the things that had been promised, but they saw them in the far distance and welcomed them, recognising that they were only strangers and nomads on earth. People who use such terms about themselves make it quite plain that they are in search of their real homeland. They can hardly have meant the country they came from, since they had the opportunity to go back to it; but in fact they were longing for a better homeland, their heavenly homeland. That is why God is not ashamed to be called their God, since he has founded the city for them.

It was by faith that Abraham, when put to the test, offered up Isaac. He offered to sacrifice his only son even though the promises had been made to him and he had been told: It is through Isaac that your name will be carried on. He was confident that God had the power even to raise the dead; and so, figuratively speaking he was given back Isaac from the dead.

This is the word of the Lord.

Responsorial Psalm   Lk 1:69-75. ℟ cf. v.68

℟ Blessed be the Lord, the God of Israel;
    he has come to his people.

1 He has raised up for us a mighty saviour
   in the house of David his servant,
   as he promised by the lips of holy men,
   those who were his prophets from of old.   ℟

2 A Saviour who would free us from our foes,
   from the hands of all who hate us.
   So his love for our fathers is fulfilled
   and his holy covenant remembered.   ℟

3 He swore to Abraham our father
   to grant us, that free from fear,
   and saved from the hands of our foes,
   we might serve him in holiness and justice
   all the days of our life in his presence.   ℟

Gospel Acclamation   Jn 3:16

Alleluia, alleluia!
God loved the world so much, he gave us his only Son,
that all who believe in him might have eternal life.
Alleluia!

GOSPEL

A reading from the holy Gospel according to Mark   4:35-41

Who can this be? Even the wind and the sea obey him.

With the coming of evening, Jesus said to his disciples, 'Let us cross over to the other side.' And leaving the crowd behind they took him, just as he was, in the boat; and there were other boats with him. Then it began to blow a gale and the waves were breaking into the boat so that it was almost swamped. But he was in the stern, his head on the cushion, asleep. They woke him and said to him, 'Master, do you not care? We are going down!' And he woke up and rebuked the wind and said to the sea, 'Quiet now! Be calm!' And the wind dropped, and all was calm again. Then he said to them, 'Why are you so frightened? How is it that you have no faith?' They were filled with awe and said to one another, 'Who can this be? Even the wind and the sea obey him.'

This is the Gospel of the Lord.

FOURTH WEEK IN ORDINARY TIME
Year I

Monday

FIRST READING

A reading from the letter to the Hebrews   11:32-40

Through faith they conquered kingdoms. God will provide for us
something better.

Gideon, Barak, Samson, Jephthah, David, Samuel and the prophets – these were men who through faith conquered kingdoms, did what is right and earned the promises. They could keep a lion's mouth shut, put out blazing fires and emerge unscathed from battle. They were weak people who were given strength, to be brave in war and drive back foreign invaders. Some came back to their wives from the dead, by resurrection; and others submitted to torture, refusing release so that they would rise again to a better life. Some had to bear being pilloried and flogged, or even chained up in prison. They were stoned, or sawn in half, or beheaded; they were homeless, and dressed in the skins of sheep and goats; they were penniless and were given nothing but ill-treatment. They were too good for the world and they went out to live in deserts and mountains and in caves and ravines. These are all heroes of faith, but they did not receive what was promised, since God had made provision for us to have something better, and they were not to reach perfection except with us.

This is the word of the Lord.

Responsorial Psalm   Ps 30:20-24. ℟ v.25

℟ Let your hearts take comfort,
   all who hope in the Lord.

1 How great is the goodness, Lord,
   that you keep for those who fear you,
   that you show to those who trust you
   in the sight of men. ℟

2 You hide them in the shelter of your presence
   from the plotting of men:
   you keep them safe within your tent
   from disputing tongues. ℟

3 Blessed be the Lord who has shown me
   the wonders of his love
   in a fortified city. ℟

4 'I am far removed from your sight'
   I said in my alarm.
   Yet you heard the voice of my plea
   when I cried for help. ℟

5 Love the Lord, all you saints.
   He guards the faithful
   but the Lord will repay to the full
   those who act with pride. ℟

Gospel Acclamation   Lk 7:16

Alleluia, alleluia!
A great prophet has appeared among us;
God has visited his people.
Alleluia!

GOSPEL

A reading from the holy Gospel according to Mark   5:1-20

Unclean spirit, come out of the man!

Jesus and his disciples reached the country of the Gerasenes on the other side of the lake, and no sooner had he left the boat than a man with an unclean spirit came out from the tombs towards him. The man lived in the tombs and no one could secure him any more, even with a chain, because he had often been secured with fetters and chains but had snapped the chains and broken the fetters, and no one had the strength to control him. All night and all day, among the tombs and in the mountains, he would howl and gash himself with stones. Catching sight of Jesus from a distance, he ran up and fell at his feet and shouted at the top of his voice, 'What do you want with me, Jesus, son of the Most High God? Swear by God you will not torture me!' – For Jesus had been saying to him, 'Come out of the man, unclean spirit.' 'What is your name?' Jesus asked. 'My name is legion,' he answered 'for there are many of us.' And he begged him earnestly not to send them out of the district. Now there was there on the mountainside a great herd of pigs feeding and the unclean spirits begged him, 'Send us to the pigs, let us go into them.' So he gave them leave. With that, the unclean spirits came out and went into the pigs, and the herd of about two thousand pigs charged down the cliff into the lake, and there they were drowned. The swineherds ran off and told their story in the town and in the country round about; and the people came to see what had really happened. They came to Jesus and saw the demoniac sitting there, clothed and in his full senses – the very man who had had the legion in him before – and they were afraid. And those who had witnessed it reported what had happened to the demoniac and what had become of the pigs. Then they began to implore Jesus to leave the neighbourhood. As he was getting into the boat, the man who had been possessed begged to be allowed to stay with him. Jesus would not let him but said to him, 'Go home to your people and tell them all that the Lord in his mercy has done for you.' So the man went off and proceeded to spread throughout the Decapolis all that Jesus had done for him. And everyone was amazed.

This is the Gospel of the Lord.

Tuesday

FIRST READING

A reading from the letter to the Hebrews   12:1-4

Let us persevere in running the race that lies ahead.

With so many witnesses in a great cloud on every side of us, we too, then, should throw off everything that hinders us, especially the sin that clings so easily, and keep running steadily in the race we have started. Let us not lose sight of Jesus, who leads us in our faith and brings it to perfection: for the sake of the joy which was still in the future, he endured the cross, disregarding the shamefulness of it, and from now on has taken his place at the right of God's throne. Think of the way he stood such opposition from sinners and then you will not give up for want of courage. In the fight against sin, you have not yet had to keep fighting to the point of death.

This is the word of the Lord.

Responsorial Psalm   Ps 21:26-28. 30-32. ℟ cf. v.27

℟   They will praise you, Lord, who long for you.

1   My vows I will pay before those who fear him.
     The poor shall eat and shall have their fill.
     They shall praise the Lord, those who seek him.
     May their hearts live for ever and ever! ℟

2   All the earth shall remember and return to the Lord,
     all families of the nations worship before him.
     They shall worship him, all the mighty of the earth;
     before him shall bow all who go down to the dust. ℟

3   And my soul shall live for him, my children serve him.
     They shall tell of the Lord to generations yet to come,
     declare his faithfulness to peoples yet unborn:
     'These things the Lord has done.' ℟

Gospel Acclamation   Mt 8:17

     Alleluia, alleluia!
     He bore our sickness,
     and endured our suffering.
     Alleluia!

GOSPEL

A reading from the holy Gospel according to Mark   5:21-43

Young woman, I say to you, arise.

When Jesus had crossed in the boat to the other side a large crowd gathered round him and he stayed by the lakeside. Then one of the synagogue officials came up, Jairus by name, and seeing him, fell at his feet and pleaded with him earnestly, saying, 'My little daughter is desperately sick. Do come and lay your hands on her to make her better and save her life.' Jesus went with him and a large crowd followed him; they were pressing all round him.

Now there was a woman who had suffered from a haemorrhage for twelve years; after long and painful treatment under various doctors, she had spent all she had without being any the better for it, in fact, she was getting worse. She had heard about Jesus, and she came up behind him through the crowd and touched his cloak. 'If I can touch even his clothes,' she had told herself 'I shall be well again.' And the source of the bleeding dried up instantly, and she felt in herself that she was cured of her complaint. Immediately aware that power had gone out from him, Jesus turned round in the crowd and said, 'Who touched my clothes?' His disciples said to him, 'You see how the crowd is pressing round you and yet you say, "Who touched me?" But he continued to look all round to see who had done it. Then the woman came forward, frightened and trembling because she knew what had happened to her, and she fell at his feet and told him the whole truth. 'My daughter,' he said 'your faith has restored you to health; go in peace and be free from your complaint.'

While he was still speaking some people arrived from the house of the synagogue official to say, 'Your daughter is dead: why put the Master to any further trouble?' But Jesus had overheard this remark of theirs and he said to the official, 'Do not be afraid; only have faith.' And he allowed no one to go with him except Peter and James and John the brother of James. So they came to the official's house and Jesus noticed all the commotion, with people weeping and wailing unrestrainedly. He went in and said to them, 'Why all this commotion and crying? The child is not dead, but asleep.' But they laughed at him. So he turned them all out and, taking with him the child's father and mother and his own companions, he went into the place where the child lay. And taking the child by the hand he said to her, 'Talitha, kum!' which means, 'Little girl, I tell you to get up.' The little girl got up at once and began to walk about, for she was twelve years old. At this they were overcome with astonishment, and he ordered them strictly not to let anyone know about it, and told them to give her something to eat.

This is the Gospel of the Lord.

Wednesday

FIRST READING

A reading from the letter to the Hebrews   12:4-7. 11-15

The Lord disciplines those he loves.

In the fight against sin, you have not yet had to keep fighting to the point of death.

Have you forgotten that encouraging text in which you are addressed as sons? My son, when the Lord corrects you, do not treat it lightly; but do not get discouraged when he reprimands you. For the Lord trains the ones that he loves and he punishes all those that he acknowledges as his son. Suffering is part of your training; God is treating you as his sons. Has there ever been any son whose father did not train him?

Of course, any punishment is most painful at the time, and far from pleasant; but later, in those on whom it has been used, it bears fruit in peace and goodness. So hold up your limp arms and steady your trembling knees and smooth out the path you tread; then the injured limb will not be wrenched, it will grow strong again.

Always be wanting peace with all people, and the holiness without which no one can ever see the Lord. Be careful that no one is deprived of the grace of God and that no root of bitterness should begin to grow and make trouble; this can poison a whole community.

This is the word of the Lord.

Responsorial Psalm   Ps 102:1-2. 13-14. 17-18. ℟ cf. 17

℟ The Lord's kindness is everlasting to those who fear him.

1 My soul, give thanks to the Lord,
   all my being, bless his holy name.
   My soul, give thanks to the Lord
   and never forget all his blessings. ℟

2 As a father has compassion on his sons,
   the Lord has pity on those who fear him;
   for he knows of what we are made,
   he remembers that we are dust. ℟

3 But the love of the Lord is everlasting
   upon those who hold him in fear;
   his justice reaches out to children's children
   when they keep his covenant in truth. ℟

Gospel Acclamation   Jn 10:27

Alleluia, alleluia!
My sheep listen to my voice, says the Lord;
I know them, and they follow me.
Alleluia!

GOSPEL

A reading from the holy Gospel according to Mark   6:1-6

A prophet is without honour in his own country.

Jesus went to his home town and his disciples accompanied him. With
the coming of the sabbath he began teaching in the synagogue and
most of them were astonished when they heard him. They said,
'Where did the man get all this? What is this wisdom that has been
granted him, and these miracles that are worked through him? This is
the carpenter, surely, the son of Mary, the brother of James and Joset
and Jude and Simon? His sisters, too, are they not here with us?' And
they would not accept him. And Jesus said to them, 'A prophet is only
despised in his own country, among his own relations and in his own
house'; and he could work no miracle there, though he cured a few sick
people by laying his hands on them. He was amazed at their lack of
faith.

   This is the Gospel of the Lord.

Thursday

FIRST READING

A reading from the letter to the Hebrews 12:18-19. 21-24

You have come to Mount Zion and the city of the living God.

What you have come to is nothing known to the senses: not a blazing fire, or a gloom turning to total darkness, or a storm; or trumpeting thunder or the great voice speaking which made everyone that heard it beg that no more should be said to them. The whole scene was so terrible that Moses said: I am afraid, and was trembling with fright. But what you have come to is Mount Zion and the city of the living God, the heavenly Jerusalem where the millions of angels have gathered for the festival, with the whole Church in which everyone is a 'first-born son' and a citizen of heaven. You have come to God himself, the supreme Judge, and been placed with spirits of the saints who have been made perfect; and to Jesus, the mediator who brings a new covenant and a blood for purification which pleads more insistently than Abel's.

This is the word of the Lord.

Responsorial Psalm Ps 47:2-4. 9-11. ℟ cf. v.10

℟ God, in your temple, we ponder your love.

1 The Lord is great and worthy to be praised
in the city of our God.
His holy mountain rises in beauty,
the joy of all the earth. ℟

2 Mount Zion, true pole of the earth,
the Great King's city!
God, in the midst of its citadels,
has shown himself its stronghold. ℟

3 As we have heard, so we have seen
in the city of our God,
in the city of the Lord of hosts
which God upholds for ever. ℟

44

4　O God, we ponder your love
　　within your temple.
　　Your praise, O God, like your name
　　reaches to the ends of the earth.
　　With justice your right hand is filled. ℟

Gospel Acclamation   Mk 1:15

　　Alleluia, alleluia!
　　The kingdom of God is near:
　　believe the Good News!
　　Alleluia!

GOSPEL

A reading from the holy Gospel according to Mark   6:7-13

He summoned the Twelve and sent them out in pairs.

Jesus made a tour round the villages, teaching. Then he summoned the Twelve and began to send them out in pairs giving them authority over the unclean spirits. And he instructed them to take nothing for the journey except a staff – no bread, no haversack, no coppers for their purses. They were to wear sandals but, he added, 'Do not take a spare tunic.' And he said to them, 'If you enter a house anywhere, stay there until you leave the district. And if any place does not welcome you and people refuse to listen to you, as you walk away shake off the dust from under your feet as a sign to them.' So they set off to preach repentance; and they cast out many devils, and anointed many sick people with oil and cured them.

　　This is the Gospel of the Lord.

Friday

FIRST READING

A reading from the letter to the Hebrews   13:1-8

Jesus Christ is the same yesterday, and today, and for ever.

Continue to love each other like brothers, and remember always to welcome strangers, for by doing this, some people have entertained angels without knowing it. Keep in mind those who are in prison, as though you were in prison with them; and those who are being badly treated, since you too are in the one body. Marriage is to be honoured by all, and marriages are to be kept undefiled, because fornicators and adulterers will come under God's judgement. Put greed out of your lives and be content with whatever you have; God himself has said: I will not fail you or desert you, and so we can say with confidence: With the Lord to help me, I fear nothing: what can man do to me?

Remember your leaders, who preached the word of God to you, and as you reflect on the outcome of their lives, imitate their faith. Jesus Christ is the same today as he was yesterday and as he will be for ever.

This is the word of the Lord.

Responsorial Psalm   Ps 26:1. 3. 5. 8-9. ℟ v.1

℟   The Lord is my light and my salvation.

1   The Lord is my light and my help;
    whom shall I fear?
    The Lord is the stronghold of my life;
    before whom shall I shrink?   ℟

2   Though an army encamp against me
    my heart would not fear.
    Though war break out against me
    even then would I trust.   ℟

3   For there he keeps me safe in his tent
    in the day of evil.
    He hides me in the shelter of his tent,
    on a rock he sets me safe.   ℟

4   It is your face, O Lord, that I seek;
    hide not your face.
    Dismiss not your servant in anger;
    you have been my help.   ℞

Gospel Acclamation   cf. Lk 8:15

    Alleluia, alleluia!
    Happy are they who have kept the word
    with a generous heart
    and yield a harvest through perseverance.
    Alleluia!

GOSPEL

A reading from the holy Gospel according to Mark   6:14-29

It is John whose head I have cut off. He has risen from the dead.

King Herod had heard about Jesus, since by now his name was
well-known. Some were saying, 'John the Baptist has risen from the
dead, and that is why miraculous powers are at work in him.' Others
said, 'He is Elijah'; others again, 'He is a prophet, like the prophets we
used to have.' But when Herod heard this he said, 'It is John whose
head I cut off; he has risen from the dead.'

Now it was this same Herod who had sent to have John arrested,
and had him chained up in prison because of Herodias, his brother
Philip's wife whom he had married. For John had told Herod, 'It is
against the law for you to have your brother's wife.' As for Herodias,
she was furious with him and wanted to kill him; but she was not able
to, because Herod was afraid of John, knowing him to be a good and
holy man, and gave him his protection. When he had heard him speak
he was greatly perplexed, and yet he liked to listen to him.

An opportunity came on Herod's birthday when he gave a banquet
for the nobles of his court, for his army officers and for the leading
figures in Galilee. When the daughter of this same Herodias came in
and danced, she delighted Herod and his guests; so the king said to the
girl, 'Ask me anything you like and I will give it you.' And he swore
her an oath, 'I will give you anything you ask, even half my kingdom.'
She went out and said to her mother, 'What shall I ask for?' She
replied, 'The head of John the Baptist.' The girl hurried straight back

47

to the king and made her request, 'I want you to give me John the Baptist's head, here and now, on a dish.' The king was deeply distressed but, thinking of the oaths he had sworn and of his guests, he was reluctant to break his word to her. So the king at once sent one of the bodyguard with orders to bring John's head. The man went off and beheaded him in prison; then he brought the head on a dish and gave it to the girl, and the girl gave it to her mother. When John's disciples heard about this, they came and took his body and laid it in a tomb.

This is the Gospel of the Lord.

Saturday

FIRST READING

A reading from the letter to the Hebrews   13:15-17. 20-21

May the God of peace who brought back from the dead, the great shepherd, lead you in all good things.

Through Jesus, let us offer God an unending sacrifice of praise, a verbal sacrifice that is offered every time we acknowledge his name. Keep doing good works and sharing your resources, for these are sacrifices that please God.

Obey your leaders and do as they tell you, because they must give an account of the way they look after your souls; make this a joy for them to do, and not a grief – you yourselves would be the losers.

I pray that the God of peace, who brought our Lord Jesus back from the dead to become the great Shepherd of the sheep by the blood that sealed an eternal covenant, may make you ready to do his will in any kind of good action; and turn us all into whatever is acceptable to himself through Jesus Christ, to whom be glory for ever and ever, Amen.

This is the word of the Lord.

Responsorial Psalm   Ps 22. ℟ v.1

℟ The Lord is my shepherd;
    there is nothing I shall want.

1 The Lord is my shepherd;
    there is nothing I shall want.

Fresh and green are the pastures
where he gives me repose.
Near restful waters he leads me,
to revive my drooping spirit. ℟

2 He guides me along the right path;
he is true to his name.
If I should walk in the valley of darkness
no evil would I fear.
You are there with your crook and your staff;
with these you give me comfort. ℟

3 You have prepared a banquet for me
in the sight of my foes.
My head you have anointed with oil;
my cup is overflowing. ℟

4 Surely goodness and kindness shall follow me
all the days of my life.
In the Lord's own house shall I dwell
for ever and ever. ℟

Gospel Acclamation   Jn 10:27

Alleluia, alleluia!
My sheep listen to my voice, says the Lord;
I know them, and they follow me.
Alleluia!

GOSPEL

A reading from the holy Gospel according to Mark   6:30-34

They were sheep without a shepherd.

The apostles rejoined Jesus and told him all they had done and
taught. Then he said to them, 'You must come away to some lonely
place all by yourselves and rest for a while'; for there were so many
coming and going that the apostles had no time even to eat. So they
went off in a boat to a lonely place where they could be by themselves.
But people saw them going, and many could guess where; and from
every town they all hurried to the place on foot and reached it

before them. So as he stepped ashore he saw a large crowd; and he took pity on them because they were like sheep without a shepherd, and he set himself to teach them at some length.

This is the Gospel of the Lord.

FIFTH WEEK IN ORDINARY TIME
Year I

Monday

FIRST READING

A reading from the book of Genesis   1:1-19

God spoke, and it was done.

In the beginning God created the heavens and the earth. Now the earth was a formless void, there was darkness over the deep, and God's spirit hovered over the water.

God said, 'Let there be light,' and there was light. God saw that light was good, and God divided light from darkness. God called light 'day,' and darkness he called 'night'. Evening came and morning came: the first day.

God said, 'Let there be a vault in the waters to divide the waters in two.' And so it was. God made the vault, and it divided the waters above the vault from the waters under the vault. God called the vault 'heaven'. Evening came and morning came: the second day.

God said, 'Let the waters under heaven come together into a single mass, and let dry land appear.' And so it was. God called the dry land 'earth' and the mass of waters 'seas', and God saw that it was good.

God said, 'Let the earth produce vegetation: seed-bearing plants, and trees bearing fruit with their seed inside, on the earth.' And so it was. The earth produced vegetation: plants bearing seed in their several kinds, and trees bearing fruit with their seed inside in their several kinds. God saw that it was good. Evening came and morning came: the third day.

God said, 'Let there be lights in the vault of heaven to divide day from night, and let them indicate festivals, days and years. Let

50

them be lights in the vault of heaven to shine on the earth.' And so it was God made the two great lights: the greater light to govern the day, the smaller light to govern the night, and the stars. God set them in the vault of heaven to shine on the earth, to govern the day and the night and to divide light from darkness. God saw that it was good. Evening came and morning came: the fourth day.

This is the word of the Lord.

Responsorial Psalm   Ps 103:1-2. 5-6. 10. 12. 24. 35. ℞ v.31

℞ May the Lord be glad in his works.

1 Bless the Lord, my soul!
   Lord God, how great you are,
   clothed in majesty and glory,
   wrapped in light as in a robe! ℞

2 You founded the earth on its base,
   to stand firm from age to age.
   You wrapped it with the ocean like a cloak:
   the waters stood higher than the mountains. ℞

3 You make springs gush forth in the valleys:
   they flow in between the hills.
   On their banks dwell the birds of heaven;
   from the branches they sing their song. ℞

4 How many are your works, O Lord!
   In wisdom you have made them all.
   The earth is full of your riches.
   Bless the Lord, my soul! ℞

Gospel Acclamation   cf. Mt 4:23

   Alleluia, alleluia!
   Jesus preached the Good News of the kingdom
   and healed all who were sick.
   Alleluia!

GOSPEL

A reading from the holy Gospel according to Mark   6:53-56

All those who touched him were cured.

Having made the crossing, Jesus and his disciples came to land at Genessaret and tied up. No sooner had they stepped out of the boat than people recognised him, and started hurrying all through the countryside and brought the sick on stretchers to wherever they heard he was. And wherever he went, to village, or town, or farm, they laid down the sick in the open spaces, begging him to let them touch even the fringe of his cloak. And all those who touched him were cured.

This is the Gospel of the Lord.

Tuesday

FIRST READING

A reading from the book of Genesis   1:20–2:4

Let us make man in our own image and likeness.

God said, 'Let the waters teem with living creatures, and let birds fly above the earth within the vault of heaven.' And so it was. God created great sea-serpents and every kind of living creature with which the waters teem, and every kind of winged creature.

God saw that it was good. God blessed them, saying, 'Be fruitful, multiply, and fill the waters of the seas; and let the birds multiply upon the earth.' Evening came and morning came: the fifth day.

God said, 'Let the earth produce every kind of living creature: cattle, reptiles, and every kind of wild beast.' And so it was. God made every kind of wild beast, every kind of cattle, and every kind of land reptile. God saw that it was good.

God said, 'Let us make man in our own image, in the likeness of ourselves, and let them be masters of the fish of the sea, the birds of heaven, the cattle, all the wild beasts and all the reptiles that crawl upon the earth.'

God created man in the image of himself,
in the image of God he created him,
male and female he created them.

God blessed them, saying to them, 'Be fruitful, multiply, fill the earth and conquer it. Be masters of the fish of the sea, the birds of heaven and all living animals on the earth.' God said, 'See, I give you all the seed-bearing plants that are upon the whole earth, and all the trees with seed-bearing fruit; this shall be your food. To all wild beasts, all birds of heaven and all living reptiles on the earth I give all the foliage of plants for food.' And so it was. God saw all he had made, and indeed it was very good. Evening came and morning came: the sixth day.

Thus heaven and earth were completed with all their array. On the seventh day God completed the work he had been doing. He rested on the seventh day after all the work he had been doing. God blessed the seventh day and made it holy, because on that day he had rested after all his work of creating.

Such were the origins of heaven and earth when they were created.

This is the word of the Lord.

Responsorial Psalm   Ps 8:4-9. ℟ v.2

℟   O Lord our God,
      how wonderful your name in all the earth!

1   When I see the heavens, the work of your hands,
    the moon and the stars which you arranged,
    what is man that you should keep him in mind,
    mortal man that you care for him?   ℟

2   Yet you have made him little less than a god;
    with glory and honour you crowned him,
    gave him power over the works of your hand,
    put all things under his feet.   ℟

3   All of them, sheep and cattle,
    yes, even the savage beasts,
    birds of the air, and fish
    that make their way through the waters.   ℟

Gospel Acclamation   Ps 118:36. 29

> Alleluia, alleluia!
> Turn my heart to do your will;
> teach me your law, O God.
> Alleluia!

GOSPEL

A reading from the holy Gospel according to Mark   7:1-13

You put aside the commandments of God to hold on to human traditions.

The Pharisees and some of the scribes who had come from Jerusalem gathered round Jesus, and they noticed that some of his disciples were eating with unclean hands, that is, without washing them. For the Pharisees, and the Jews in general, follow the tradition of the elders and never eat without washing their arms as far as the elbow; and on returning from the market place they never eat without first sprinkling themselves. There are also many other observances which have been handed down to them concerning the washing of cups and pots and bronze dishes. So these Pharisees and scribes asked him, 'Why do your disciples not respect the tradition of the elders but eat their food with unclean hands?' He answered, 'It was of you hypocrites that Isaiah so rightly prophesied in this passage of scripture:

> This people honours me only with lip-service,
> while their hearts are far from me.
> The worship they offer me is worthless,
> the doctrines they teach are only human regulations.

You put aside the commandment of God to cling to human traditions.' And he said to them, 'How ingeniously you get round the commandment of God in order to preserve your own tradition! For Moses said: Do your duty to your father and your mother, and, Anyone who curses father or mother must be put to death. But you say, "If a man says to his father or mother: Anything I have that I might have used to help you is Corban (that is, dedicated to God), then he is forbidden from that moment to do anything for his father or mother." In this way you make God's word null and void for the sake of your tradition which you have handed down. And you do many other things like this.'

This is the Gospel of the Lord.

Wednesday

FIRST READING

A reading from the book of Genesis   2:4-9. 15-17

The Lord God planted a garden in Eden, and there he put the man he had formed.

At the time when the Lord God made earth and heaven there was as yet no wild bush on the earth nor had any wild plant yet sprung up, for the Lord God had not sent rain on the earth, nor was there any man to till the soil. However, a flood was rising from the earth and watering all the surface of the soil. The Lord God fashioned man of dust from the soil. Then he breathed into his nostrils a breath of life, and thus man became a living being.

The Lord God planted a garden in Eden which is in the east, and there he put the man he had fashioned. The Lord God caused to spring up from the soil every kind of tree, enticing to look at and good to eat, with the tree of life and the tree of the knowledge of good and evil in the middle of the garden. The Lord God took the man and settled him in the garden of Eden to cultivate and take care of it. Then the Lord God gave the man this admonition, 'You may eat indeed of all the trees in the garden. Nevertheless of the tree of the knowledge of good and evil you are not to eat, for on the day you eat of it you shall most surely die.'

This is the word of the Lord.

Responsorial Psalm   Ps 103:1-2. 27-30. ℟ v.1

℟ Bless the Lord, my soul!

1 Bless the Lord my soul!
   Lord God, how great you are,
   clothed in majesty and glory,
   wrapped in light as in a robe.   ℟

2 All of these look to you
   to give them their food in due season.
   You give it, they gather it up:
   you open your hand, they have their fill.   ℟

3 You take back your spirit, they die,
   returning from the dust from which they came.
   You send forth your spirit, they are created;
   and you renew the face of the earth.   ℟

Gospel Acclamation   cf. Jn 17:17

Alleluia, alleluia!
Your word, O Lord, is truth:
make us holy in the truth.
Alleluia!

GOSPEL

A reading from the holy Gospel according to Mark   7:14-23

It is the things that come out of a person that make one unclean.

Jesus called the people to him and said, 'Listen to me, all of you, and understand. Nothing that goes into a man from outside can make him unclean; it is the things that come out of a man that make him unclean. If anyone has ears to hear, let him listen to this.'

When he had gone back into the house, away from the crowd, his disciples questioned him about the parable. He said to them, 'Do you not understand either? Can you not see that whatever goes into a man from outside cannot make him unclean, because it does not go into his heart but through his stomach and passes out in the sewer?' (Thus he pronounced all foods clean.) And he went on, 'It is what comes out of a man that makes him unclean. For it is from within, from men's hearts, that evil intentions emerge: fornication, theft, murder, adultery, avarice, malice, deceit, indecency, envy, slander, pride, folly. All these evil things come from within and make a man unclean.'

This is the Gospel of the Lord.

Thursday

FIRST READING

A reading from the book of Genesis   2:18-25

The Lord God led her to Adam, and they became two in one body.

The Lord God said, 'It is not good that the man should be alone. I will make him a helpmate.' So from the soil the Lord God fashioned all the wild beasts and all the birds of heaven. These he brought to the man to see what he would call them; each one was to bear the name the man would give it. The man gave names to all the cattle, all the birds of heaven, and all the wild beasts. But no helpmate suitable for man was found for him. So the Lord God made the man fall into a deep sleep. And while he slept, he took one of his ribs and enclosed it in flesh. The Lord God built the rib he had taken from the man into a woman, and brought her to the man. The man exclaimed:

'This at last is bone from my bones,
and flesh from my flesh!
This is to be called woman,
for this was taken from man.'

This is why a man leaves his father and mother and joins himself to his wife, and they become one body.

Now both of them were naked, the man and his wife, but they felt no shame in front of each other.

This is the word of the Lord.

Responsorial Psalm   Ps 127:1-5. ℟ cf. v.1

℟   Happy are those who fear the Lord.

1   O blessed are those who fear the Lord
    and walk in his ways!
    By the labour of your hands you shall eat.
    You will be happy and prosper. ℟

2   Your wife like a fruitful vine
    in the heart of your house;
    your children like shoots of the olive
    around your table. ℟

3   Indeed thus shall be blessed
    the man who fears the Lord.
    May the Lord bless you from Zion
    all the days of your life! ℟

Gospel Acclamation   James 1:21

Alleluia, alleluia!
Receive and submit to the word planted in you;
it can save your souls.
Alleluia!

GOSPEL

A reading from the holy Gospel according to Mark   7:24-30

The dogs under the table can eat the children's scraps.

Jesus left Gennesaret and set out for the territory of Tyre. There he went into a house and did not want anyone to know he was there, but he could not pass unrecognised. A woman whose little daughter had an unclean spirit heard about him straightaway and came and fell at his feet. Now the woman was a pagan, by birth a Syrophoenician, and she begged him to cast the devil out of her daughter. And he said to her, 'The children should be fed first, because it is not fair to take the children's food and throw it to the house-dogs.' But she spoke up: 'Ah yes, sir,' she replied, 'but the house-dogs under the table can eat the children's scraps.' And he said to her, 'For saying this, you may go home happy: the devil has gone out of your daughter.' So she went off to her home and found the child lying on the bed and the devil gone.

This is the Gospel of the Lord.

Friday

FIRST READING

A reading from the book of Genesis   3:1-8

You will be like God, knowing good and evil.

The serpent was the most subtle of all the wild beasts that the Lord God had made. It asked the woman, 'Did God really say you were not to eat from any of the trees in the garden?' The woman answered the serpent, 'We may eat the fruit of the trees in the garden. But of the fruit of the tree in the middle of the garden God said, "You must not eat it, nor touch it, under pain of death."' Then the serpent said to the woman, 'No! You will not die! God knows in fact that on the day you eat it your eyes will be opened and you will be like gods, knowing good and evil.' The woman saw that the tree was good to eat and pleasing to the eye, and that it was desirable for the knowledge that it could give. So she took some of its fruit and ate it. She gave some also to her husband who was with her, and he ate it. Then the eyes of both of them were opened and they realised that they were naked. So they sewed fig-leaves together to make themselves loin-cloths.

The man and his wife heard the sound of the Lord God walking in the garden in the cool of the day, and they hid from the Lord God among the trees of the garden.

This is the word of the Lord.

Responsorial Psalm   Ps 31:1-2. 5-7. ℞ v.1

℞ Happy are those whose sins are forgiven.

1 Happy the man whose offence is forgiven,
   whose sin is remitted.
   O happy the man to whom the Lord
   imputes no guilt,
   in whose spirit is no guile. ℞

2 But now I have acknowledged my sins;
   my guilt I did not hide.
   I said: 'I will confess
   my offence to the Lord.'
   And you, Lord, have forgiven
   the guilt of my sin. ℞

3 So let every good man pray to you
   in the time of need.
   The floods of water may reach high
   but him they shall not reach. ℞

4 You are my hiding place, O Lord;
   you save me from distress.
   You surround me with cries of deliverance. ℞

Gospel Acclamation   cf. Acts 16:14

Alleluia, alleluia!
Open our hearts, O Lord,
to listen to the words of your Son.
Alleluia!

GOSPEL

A reading from the holy Gospel according to Mark   7:31-37

He makes the deaf hear and the dumb speak.

Returning from the district of Tyre, Jesus went by way of Sidon towards the Sea of Galilee, right through the Decapolis region. And they brought him a deaf man who had an impediment in his speech; and they asked him to lay his hand on him. He took him aside in private, away from the crowd, put his fingers into the man's ears and touched his tongue with spittle. Then looking up to heaven he sighed; and he said to him, 'Ephphatha,' that is, 'Be opened.' And his ears were opened, and the ligament of his tongue was loosened and he spoke clearly. And Jesus ordered them to tell no one about it, but the more he insisted, the more widely they published it. Their admiration was unbounded. 'He has done all things well,' they said 'he makes the deaf hear and the dumb speak.'

This is the Gospel of the Lord.

Saturday

FIRST READING

A reading from the book of Genesis   3:9-24

The Lord God expelled him from the garden of Eden, to till the soil.

The Lord God called to the man. 'Where are you?' he asked. 'I heard the sound of you in the garden,' he replied 'I was afraid because I was naked, so I hid.' 'Who told you that you were naked?' he asked. 'Have you been eating of the tree I forbade you to eat?' The man replied, 'It was the woman you put with me; she gave me the fruit, and I ate it.' Then the Lord God asked the woman, 'What is this you have done?' The woman replied, 'The serpent tempted me and I ate.'

Then the Lord God said to the serpent, 'Because you have done this,

'Be accursed beyond all cattle,
all wild beasts.
You shall crawl on your belly and eat dust
every day of your life.
I will make you enemies of each other:

you and the woman,
your offspring and her offspring.
It will crush your head
and you will strike its heel.'

To the woman he said:

'I will multiply your pains in childbearing,
you shall give birth to your children in pain.
Your yearning shall be for your husband,
yet he will lord it over you.'

To the man he said, 'Because you listened to the voice of your wife
and ate from the tree of which I had forbidden you to eat,

'Accursed be the soil because of you.
With suffering shall you get your food from it
every day of your life.
It shall yield you brambles and thistles,
and you shall eat wild plants.
With sweat on your brow
shall you eat your bread,
until you return to the soil,
as you were taken from it.
For dust you are
and to dust you shall return.'

The man named his wife 'Eve' because she was the mother of all those who live. The Lord God made clothes out of skins for the man and his wife, and they put them on. Then the Lord God said, 'See, the man has become like one of us, with his knowlege of good and evil. He must not be allowed to stretch his hand out next and pick from the tree of life also, and eat some and live for ever.' So the Lord God expelled him from the garden of Eden, to till the soil from which he had been taken. He banished the man, and in front of the garden of Eden he posted cherubs, and the flame of a flashing sword, to guard the way to the tree of life.

This is the word of the Lord.

Responsorial Psalm   Ps 89:2-6. 12-13. ℟ v.1

℟   In every age, O Lord, you have been our refuge.

1   Before the mountains were born
     or the earth or the world brought forth,
     you are God, without beginning or end. ℟

2   You turn men back into dust
     and say: 'Go back, sons of men.'
     To your eyes a thousand years
     are like yesterday, come and gone,
     no more than a watch in the night. ℟

3   You sweep men away like a dream,
     like grass which springs up in the morning.
     In the morning it springs up and flowers:
     by evening it withers and fades. ℟

4   Make us know the shortness of our life
     that we may gain wisdom of heart.
     Lord, relent! Is your anger for ever?
     Show pity on your servants. ℟

Gospel Acclamation   Mt 4:4

     Alleluia, alleluia!
     No one lives on bread alone,
     but on every word that comes from the mouth of God.
     Alleluia!

GOSPEL

A reading from the holy Gospel according to Mark   8:1-10

They ate and were filled.

A great crowd had gathered, and they had nothing to eat. So Jesus
called his disciples to him and said to them, 'I feel sorry for all these
people; they have been with me for three days now and have nothing
to eat. If I send them off home hungry they will collapse on the way;
some have come a great distance.' His disciples replied, 'Where could
anyone get bread to feed these people in a deserted place like this?' He
asked them, 'How many loaves have you?' 'Seven' they said. Then he

instructed the crowd to sit down on the ground, and he took the seven loaves, and after giving thanks he broke them and handed them to his disciples to distribute; and they distributed them among the crowd. They had a few small fish as well, and over these he said a blessing and ordered them to be distributed also. They ate as much as they wanted, and they collected seven basketfuls of the scraps left over. Now there had been about four thousand people. He sent them away and immediately, getting into the boat with his disciples, went to the region of Dalmanutha.

This is the Gospel of the Lord.

SIXTH WEEK IN ORDINARY TIME

Year I

Monday

FIRST READING

A reading from the book of Genesis

4:1-15. 25

Cain set on his brother and killed him.

The man had intercourse with his wife Eve, and she conceived and gave birth to Cain. 'I have acquired a man with the help of the Lord' she said. She gave birth to a second child, Abel, the brother of Cain. Now Abel became a shepherd and kept flocks, while Cain tilled the soil. Time passed and Cain brought some of the produce of the soil as an offering for the Lord, while Abel for his part brought the first-born of his flock and some of their fat as well. The Lord looked with favour on Abel and his offering. But he did not look with favour on Cain and his offering, and Cain was very angry and downcast. The Lord asked Cain, 'Why are you angry and downcast? If you are well disposed, ought you not to lift up your head? But if you are ill disposed, is not sin at the door like a crouching beast hungering for you, which you must master?' Cain said to his brother Abel, 'Let us go out'; and while they were in the open country, Cain set on his brother Abel and killed him.

The Lord asked Cain, 'Where is your brother Abel?' 'I do not know' he replied. 'Am I my brother's guardian?' 'What have you done?' the Lord asked. 'Listen to the sound of your brother's blood, crying out to me from the ground. Now be accursed and driven from the ground that has opened its mouth to receive your brother's blood at your hands. When you till the ground it shall no longer yield you any of its produce. You shall be a fugitive and a wanderer over the earth.' Then Cain said to the Lord, 'My punishment is greater than I can bear. See! Today you drive me from this ground. I must hide from you, and be a fugitive and a wanderer over the earth. Why, whoever comes across me will kill me!' 'Very well, then,' the Lord replied 'if anyone kills Cain, sevenfold vengeance shall be taken from him.' So the Lord put a mark on Cain, to prevent whoever might come across him from striking him down.

Adam had intercourse with his wife, and she gave birth to a son whom she named Seth, 'because God has granted me other offspring' she said 'in place of Abel, since Cain has killed him.'

This is the word of the Lord.

Responsorial Psalm   Ps 49:1. 8. 16-17. 20-21. ℟ v.14

℟   Offer to God a sacrifice of praise.

1   The God of gods, the Lord,
     has spoken and summoned the earth,
     from the rising of the sun to its setting.
     'I find no fault with your sacrifices,
     your offerings are always before me.   ℟

2   'But how can you recite my commandments
     and take my covenant on your lips,
     you who despise my law
     and throw my words to the winds.   ℟

3   'You who sit and malign your brother
     and slander your own mother's son.
     You do this, and should I keep silence?
     Do you think that I am like you?'   ℟

Gospel Acclamation   Jn 14:16

Alleluia, alleluia!
I am the way, the truth, and the life, says the Lord;
no one comes to the Father, except through me.
Alleluia!

GOSPEL

A reading from the holy Gospel according to Mark   8:11-13

Why does this generation demand a sign?

The Pharisees came up and started a discussion with Jesus; they demanded of him a sign from heaven, to test him. And with a sigh that came straight from the heart he said, 'Why does this generation demand a sign? I tell you solemnly, no sign shall be given to this generation.' And leaving them again and re-embarking he went away to the opposite shore.

This is the Gospel of the Lord.

Tuesday

FIRST READING

A reading from the book of Genesis   6:5-8; 7:1-5. 10

I will rid all people, my own creation, from the face of the earth.

The Lord saw that the wickedness of man was great on the earth, and that the thoughts in his heart fashioned nothing but wickedness all day long. The Lord regretted having made man on the earth, and his heart grieved. 'I will rid the earth's face of man, my own creation,' the Lord said 'and of animals also, reptiles too, and the birds of heaven; for I regret having made them.' But Noah had found favour with the Lord.

The Lord said to Noah, 'Go aboard the ark, you and all your household, for you alone among this generation do I see as a good man in my judgement. Of all the clean animals you must take seven of each kind, both male and female; of the unclean animals you must take two, a male and its female (and of the birds of heaven also, seven of each kind, both male and female), to propagate their kind over the whole earth. For in seven days' time I mean to make it rain on the earth for forty days and nights, and I will rid the earth of every living thing that I made.' Noah did all that the Lord ordered.

Seven days later the waters of the flood appeared on the earth.

This is the word of the Lord.

Responsorial Psalm   Ps 28:1-4. 9-10. ℟ v.11

℟ The Lord will bless his people with peace.

1 O give the Lord you sons of God,
   give the Lord glory and power;
   give the Lord the glory of his name.
   Adore the Lord in his holy court. ℟

2 The Lord's voice resounding on the waters,
   the Lord on the immensity of waters;
   the voice of the Lord, full of power,
   the voice of the Lord, full of splendour. ℟

3 The God of glory thunders.
   In his temple they all cry: 'Glory!'
   The Lord sat enthroned over the flood;
   the Lord sits as king for ever. ℟

Gospel Acclamation   Jn 14:23

Alleluia, alleluia!
All who love me will keep my words,
and my Father will love them and we will come to them.
Alleluia!

GOSPEL

A reading from the holy Gospel according to Mark   8:14-21

Be on your guard against the yeast of the Pharisees and the yeast of Herod.

The disciples had forgotten to take any food and they had only one loaf
with them in the boat. Then Jesus gave them this warning, 'Keep
your eyes open; be on your guard against the yeast of the Pharisees
and the yeast of Herod.' And they said to one another, 'It is because we
have no bread.' And Jesus knew it, and he said to them, 'Why are you
talking about having no bread? Do you not yet understand? Have you
no perception? Are your minds closed? Have you eyes that do not see,
ears that do not hear? Or do you not remember? When I broke the five
loaves among the five thousand, how many baskets full of scraps did
you collect?' They answered, 'Twelve.' 'And when I broke the seven
loaves for the four thousand, how many baskets full of scraps did you

collect?' And they answered, 'Seven.' Then he said to them, 'Are you still without perception?'

This is the Gospel of the Lord.

Wednesday

FIRST READING

A reading from the book of Genesis   8:6-13. 20-22

He saw that the surface of the earth was dry.

At the end of forty days Noah opened the porthole he had made in the ark and he sent out the raven. This went off, and flew back and forth until the waters dried up from the earth. Then he sent out the dove, to see whether the waters were receding from the surface of the earth. The dove, finding nowhere to perch, returned to him in the ark, for there was water over the whole surface of the earth; putting out his hand he took hold of it and brought it back into the ark with him. After waiting seven more days, again he sent out the dove from the ark. In the evening, the dove came back to him and there it was with a new olive-branch in its beak. So Noah realised that the waters were receding from the earth. After waiting seven more days he sent out the dove, and now it returned to him no more.

It was in the six hundred and first year of Noah's life, in the first month and on the first of the month, that the water dried up from the earth. Noah lifted back the hatch of the ark and looked out. The surface of the ground was dry!

Noah built an altar for the Lord, and choosing from all the clean animals and all the clean birds he offered burnt offerings on the altar. The Lord smelt the appeasing fragrance and said to himself, 'Never again will I curse the earth because of man, because his heart contrives evil from his infancy. Never again will I strike down every living thing as I have done.

'As long as earth lasts,
sowing and reaping,
cold and heat,
summer and winter,
day and night
shall cease no more.'

This is the word of the Lord.

Responsorial Psalm   Ps 115:12-15. 18-19. ℟ v.17

℟   To you, Lord, I will offer a sacrifice of praise.

or

℟   Alleluia!

1   How can I repay the Lord
    for his goodness to me?
    The cup of salvation I will raise;
    I will call on the Lord's name.   ℟

2   My vows to the Lord I will fulfil
    before all his people.
    O precious in the eyes of the Lord
    is the death of his faithful.   ℟

3   My vows to the Lord I will fulfil
    before all his people,
    in the courts of the house of the Lord,
    in your midst, O Jerusalem.   ℟

Gospel Acclamation   cf. Eph 1:17-18

Alleluia, alleluia!
May the Father of our Lord Jesus Christ
enlighten the eyes of our heart
that we might see how great is the hope
to which we are called.
Alleluia!

GOSPEL

A reading from the holy Gospel according to Mark   8:22-26

He restored sight to the blind man and he could see everything clearly.

Jesus and his disciples came to Bethsaida, and some people brought to him a blind man whom they begged him to touch. He took the blind man by the hand and led him outside the village. Then putting spittle on his eyes and laying his hands on him, he asked, 'Can you see anything?' The man, who was beginning to see, replied, 'I can see people; they look like trees to me, but they are walking about.' Then he laid his hands on the man's eyes again and he saw clearly; he was cured, and he could see everything plainly and distinctly. And Jesus sent him home, saying, 'Do not even go into the village.'

This is the Gospel of the Lord.

Thursday

FIRST READING

A reading from the book of Genesis   9:1-13

I set my bow in the clouds and it shall be a sign of the covenant between me and the earth.

God blessed Noah and his sons, saying to them, 'Be fruitful, multiply and fill the earth. Be the terror and the dread of all the wild beasts and all the birds of heaven, of everything that crawls on the ground and all the fish of the sea; they are handed over to you. Every living and crawling thing shall provide food for you, no less than the foliage of plants. I give you everything, with this exception: you must not eat flesh with life, that is to say blood, in it. I will demand an account of your life-blood. I will demand an account from every beast and from man. I will demand an account of every man's life from his fellow men.

'He who sheds man's blood,
shall have his blood shed by man,
for in the image of God
man was made.

'As for you, be fruitful, multiply, teem over the earth and be lord of it.'

God spoke to Noah and his sons, 'See, I establish my Covenant with you, and with your descendants after you; also with every living creature to be found with you, birds, cattle and every wild beast with you: everthing that came out of the ark, everything that lives on the earth. I establish my Covenant with you: no thing of flesh shall be swept away again by the waters of the flood. There shall be no flood to destroy the earth again.'

God said, 'Here is the sign of the Covenant I make between myself and you and every living creature with you for all generations: I set my bow in the clouds and it shall be a sign of the Covenant between me and the earth.'

This is the word of the Lord.

Responsorial Psalm   Ps 101:16-21. 29. 22-23. ℟ v.20

℟   From heaven the Lord looks down on the earth.

1   The nations shall fear the name of the Lord
    and all the earth's kings your glory,
    when the Lord shall build up Zion again
    and appear in all his glory.
    Then he will turn to the prayers of the helpless;
    he will not despise their prayers. ℟

2   Let this be written for ages to come
    that a people yet unborn may praise the Lord;
    for the Lord leaned down from his sanctuary on high.
    He looked down from heaven to the earth
    that he might hear the groans of the prisoners
    and free those condemned to die. ℟

3   The sons of your servants shall dwell untroubled
    and their race shall endure before you
    that the name of the Lord may be proclaimed in Zion
    and his praise in the heart of Jerusalem,
    when peoples and kingdoms are gathered together
    to pay their homage to the Lord. ℟

Gospel Acclamation   cf. Jn 6:63. 68

    Alleluia, alleluia!
    Your words, Lord, are spirit and life;
    you have the words of everlasting life.
    Alleluia!

GOSPEL

A reading from the holy Gospel according to Mark   8:27-33

You are the Christ. The Son of Man must suffer many things.

Jesus and his disciples left for the villages round Caesarea Philippi.
On the way he put this question to his disciples, 'Who do people say I
am?' And they told him, 'John the Baptist,' they said, 'others Elijah;
others again, one of the prophets.' 'But you,' he asked, 'who do you say
I am?' Peter spoke up and said to him, 'You are the Christ.' And he

gave them strict orders not to tell anyone about him. And he began to teach them that the Son of Man was destined to suffer grievously, to be rejected by the elders and the chief priests and the scribes, and to be put to death, and after three days to rise again; and he said all this quite openly. Then, taking him aside, Peter started to remonstrate with him. But, turning and seeing his disciples, he rebuked Peter and said to him, 'Get behind me, Satan! Because the way you think is not God's way but man's.'

This is the Gospel of the Lord.

Friday

FIRST READING

A reading from the book of Genesis   11:1-9

Let us go down and confuse their language.

Throughout the earth men spoke the same language, with the same vocabulary. Now as they moved eastwards they found a plain in the land of Shinar where they settled. They said to one another, 'Come, let us make bricks and bake them in the fire.' – For stone they used bricks, and for mortar they used bitumen. – 'Come,' they said, 'let us build ourselves a town and a tower with its top reaching heaven. Let us make a name for ourselves, so that we may not be scattered about the whole earth.'

Now the Lord came down to see the town and the tower that the sons of man had built. 'So they are all a single people with a single language!' said the Lord. 'This is but the start of their undertakings! There will be nothing too hard for them to do. Come, let us go down and confuse their language on the spot so that they can no longer understand one another.' The Lord scattered them hence over the whole face of the earth, and they stopped building the town. It was named Babel therefore, because there the Lord confused the language of the whole earth. It was from there that the Lord scattered them over the whole face of the earth.

This is the word of the Lord.

Responsorial Psalm   Ps 32:10-15. ℟ v.12

℟ Happy the people the Lord has chosen to be his own.

1 He frustrates the designs of the nations,
   he defeats the plans of the peoples.
   His own designs shall stand for ever,
   the plans of his heart from age to age. ℟

2 They are happy, whose God is the Lord,
   the people he has chosen as his own.
   From the heavens the Lord looks forth,
   he sees all the children of men. ℟

3 From the place where he dwells he gazes
   on all the dwellers on the earth,
   he who shapes the hearts of them all
   and considers all their deeds. ℟

Gospel Acclamation   Jn 15:15

Alleluia, alleluia!
I call you my friends, says the Lord,
for I have made known to you all that the Father has told me.
Alleluia!

GOSPEL

A reading from the holy Gospel according to Mark   8:34–9:1

Whoever loses his life for my sake and the sake of the gospel, will save it.

Jesus called the people and his disciples to him and said, 'If anyone
wants to be a follower of mine, let him renounce himself and take up
his cross and follow me. For anyone who wants to save his life will lose
it; but anyone who loses his life for my sake, and for the sake of the
gospel, will save it. What gain, then, is it for a man to win the whole
world and ruin his life? And indeed what can man offer in exchange
for his life? For if anyone in this adulterous and sinful generation is
ashamed of me and of my words, the Son of Man will also be ashamed
of him when he comes in the glory of his Father with the holy angels.'

   And he said to them, 'I tell you solemnly, there are some standing
here who will not taste death before they see the kingdom of God come
with power.'

   This is the Gospel of the Lord.

Saturday

FIRST READING

A reading from the letter to the Hebrews   11:1-7

By faith we understand that the world was created by God.

Only faith can guarantee the blessings that we hope for, or prove the existence of the realities that at present remain unseen. It was for faith that our ancestors were commended.

It is by faith that we understand that the world was created by one word from God, so that no apparent cause can account for the things we can see.

It was because of his faith that Abel offered God a better sacrifice than Cain, and for that he was declared to be righteous when God made acknowledgement of his offerings. Though he is dead, he still speaks by faith.

It was because of his faith that Enoch was taken up and did not have to experience death: he was not to be found because God had taken him. This was because before his assumption it is attested that he had pleased God. Now it is impossible to please God without faith, since anyone who comes to him must believe that he exists and rewards those who try to find him.

It was through his faith that Noah, when he had been warned by God of something that had never been seen before, felt a holy fear and built an ark to save his family. By his faith the world was convicted, and he was able to claim the righteousness which is the reward of faith.

This is the word of the Lord.

Responsorial Psalm   Ps 144:2-5. 10-11. ℟ cf. v.1

℟ I will praise your name for ever, Lord.

1 I will bless you day after day
   and praise your name for ever.
   The Lord is great, highly to be praised,
   his greatness cannot be measured.   ℟

2 Age to age shall proclaim your works,
   shall declare your mighty deeds,
   shall speak of your splendour and glory,
   tell the tale of your wonderful works.   ℟

(continued)

3   All your creatures shall thank you, O Lord,
and your friends shall repeat their blessing.
They shall speak of the glory of your reign
and declare your might, O God.

℟   I will praise your name for ever, Lord.

Gospel Acclamation

cf. Mk 9:6

Alleluia, alleluia!
The heavens were opened and the Father's voice was heard:
this is my beloved Son, hear him.
Alleluia.

GOSPEL

A reading from the holy Gospel according to Mark   9:2-13

He was transfigured in their presence.

Jesus took with him Peter and James and John and led them up a high mountain where they could be alone by themselves. There in their presence he was transfigured: his clothes became dazzlingly white, whiter than any earthly bleacher could make them. Elijah appeared to them with Moses; and they were talking with Jesus. Then Peter spoke to Jesus: 'Rabbi,' he said, 'it is wonderful for us to be here; so let us make three tents, one for you, one for Moses and one for Elijah.' He did not know what to say; they were so frightened. And a cloud came, covering them in shadow; and there came a voice from the cloud, 'This is my Son, the Beloved. Listen to him.' Then suddenly, when they looked round, they saw no one with them any more but only Jesus.

As they came down from the mountain he warned them to tell no one what they had seen, until after the Son of Man had risen from the dead. They observed the warning faithfully, though among themselves they discussed what 'rising from the dead' could mean. And they put this question to him, 'Why do the scribes say that Elijah has to come first?' 'True,' he said, 'Elijah is to come first and to see that everything is as it should be; yet how is it that the scriptures say about the Son of Man that he is to suffer grievously and be treated with contempt? However, I tell you that Elijah has come and they have treated him as they pleased, just as the scriptures say about him.'

This is the Gospel of the Lord.

SEVENTH WEEK IN ORDINARY TIME

Year I

Monday

FIRST READING

A reading from the book of Ecclesiasticus   1:1-10

Before all other things, wisdom was created.

All wisdom is from the Lord,
and it is his own for ever.
The sand of the sea and the raindrops,
and the days of eternity, who can assess them?
The height of the sky and the breadth of the earth,
and the depth of the abyss, who can probe them?
Before all other things wisdom was created,
shrewd understanding is everlasting.
For whom has the root of wisdom ever been uncovered?
Her resourceful ways, who knows them?
One only is wise, terrible indeed,
seated on his throne, the Lord.
He himself has created her, looked on her and assessed her,
and poured her out on all his works
to be with all mankind as his gift,
and he conveyed her to those who love him.

This is the word of the Lord.

Responsorial Psalm   Ps 92:1-2. 5. ℟ v.1

℟   The Lord is king;
     he is robed in majesty.

1   The Lord is king, with majesty enrobed;
     the Lord has robed himself with might,
     he has girded himself with power.   ℟

2   The world you made firm, not to be moved;
     your throne has stood firm from of old.
     From all eternity, O Lord, you are.   ℟

3   Truly your decrees are to be trusted.
     Holiness is fitting to your house,
     O Lord, until the end of time.   ℟

Gospel Acclamation   cf. 2 Tim 1:10

Alleluia, alleluia!
Our Saviour Jesus Christ has done away with death
and brought us life through his gospel.
Alleluia!

GOSPEL

A reading from the holy Gospel according to Mark   9:14-29

I believe, Lord, help my unbelief.

When Jesus, with Peter, James and John came down from the
mountain and rejoined the disciples they saw a large crowd round
them and some scribes arguing with them. The moment they saw him
the whole crowd were struck with amazement and ran to greet him.
'What are you arguing about with them?' he asked. A man answered
him from the crowd, 'Master, I have brought my son to you; there is a
spirit of dumbness in him, and when it takes hold of him it throws him
to the ground, and he foams at the mouth and grinds his teeth and
goes rigid. And I asked your disciples to cast it out and they were
unable to.' 'You faithless generation,' he said to them in reply. 'How
much longer must I be with you? How much longer must I put up with
you? Bring him to me.' They brought the boy to him, and as soon as
the spirit saw Jesus it threw the boy into convulsions, and he fell to
the ground and lay writhing there, foaming at the mouth. Jesus asked
the father, 'How long has this been happening to him?' 'From
childhood,' he replied, 'and it has often thrown him into the fire and
into the water, in order to destroy him. But if you can do anything,
have pity on us and help us.' 'If you can?' retorted Jesus. 'Everything
is possible for anyone who has faith.' Immediately the father of the
boy cried out, 'I do have faith. Help the little faith I have!' And when
Jesus saw how many people were pressing round him, he rebuked the
unclean spirit. 'Deaf and dumb spirit,' he said, 'I command you: come
out of him and never enter him again.' Then throwing the boy into
violent convulsions it came out shouting, and the boy lay there so like
a corpse that most of them said, 'He is dead.' But Jesus took him by
the hand and helped him up, and he was able to stand. When he had
gone indoors his disciples asked him privately, 'Why were we unable
to cast it out?' 'This is the kind,' he answered 'that can only be driven
out by prayer.'

This is the Gospel of the Lord.

Tuesday

FIRST READING

A reading from the book of Ecclesiasticus   2:1-11

Prepare yourself for the trials.

My son, if you aspire to serve the Lord,
prepare yourself for an ordeal.
Be sincere of heart, be steadfast,
and do not be alarmed when disaster comes.
Cling to him and do not leave him,
so that you may be honoured at the end of your days.
Whatever happens to you, accept it,
and in the uncertainties of your humble state, be patient,
since gold is tested in the fire,
and chosen men in the furnace of humiliation.
Trust him and he will uphold you,
follow a straight path and hope in him.
You who fear the Lord, wait for his mercy;
do not turn aside in case you fall.
You who fear the Lord, trust him,
you who will not be baulked of your reward.
You who fear the Lord hope for good things,
for everlasting happiness and mercy.
Look at the generations of old and see:
who ever trusted in the Lord and was put to shame?
Or who ever feared him steadfastly and was left forsaken?
Or who ever called out to him, and was ignored?
For the Lord is compassionate and merciful,
he forgives sins, and saves in days of distress.

This is the word of the Lord.

Responsorial Psalm   Ps 36:3-4. 18-19. 27-28. 39-40. ℟ v.5

℟   Commit your life to the Lord,
        and he will help you.

1   If you trust in the Lord and do good,
        then you will live in the land and be secure.
        If you find your delight in the Lord,
        he will grant your heart's desire. ℟

2   He protects the lives of the upright,
    their heritage will last for ever.
    They shall not be put to shame in evil days,
    in time of famine their food shall not fail.

    ℟ Commit your life to the Lord,
       and he will help you.

3   Then turn away from evil and do good
    and you shall have a home for ever;
    for the Lord loves justice
    and will never forsake his friends. ℟

4   The salvation of the just comes from the Lord,
    their stronghold in time of distress.
    The Lord helps them and delivers them
    and saves them: for their refuge is in him. ℟

Gospel Acclamation   Gal 6:14

    Alleluia, alleluia!
    My only glory is the cross of our Lord Jesus Christ,
    which crucifies the world to me and me to the world.
    Alleluia!

GOSPEL

A reading from the holy Gospel according to Mark   9:30-37

The Son of Man will be betrayed. Whoever wishes to be first must be last.

Jesus and his disciples made their way through Galilee; and he did not want anyone to know, because he was instructing his disciples; he was telling them, 'The Son of Man will be delivered into the hands of men; they will put him to death; and three days after he has been put to death he will rise again.' But they did not understand what he said and were afraid to ask him.

They came to Capernaum, and when he was in the house he asked them, 'What were you arguing about on the road?' They said nothing because they had been arguing which of them was the greatest. So he sat down, called the Twelve to him and said, 'If anyone wants to be first, he must make himself last of all and servant of all.' He then took a little child, set him in front of them, put his arms round him, and said to them, 'Anyone who welcomes one of these little children in my name, welcomes me; and anyone who welcomes me welcomes not me but the one who sent me.'

This is the Gospel of the Lord.

Wednesday

FIRST READING

A reading from the book of Ecclesiasticus 4:11-19

God loves those who love wisdom.

Wisdom brings up her own sons,
and cares for those who seek her.
Whoever loves her loves life,
those who wait on her early will be filled with happiness.
Whoever holds her close will inherit honour,
and wherever he walks the Lord will bless him.
Those who serve her minister to the Holy One,
and the Lord loves those who love her.
Whoever obeys her judges aright,
and whoever pays attention to her dwells secure.
If he trusts himself to her he will inherit her,
and his descendants will remain in possession of her;
for though she takes him at first through winding ways,
bringing fear and faintness on him,
plaguing him with her discipline until she can trust him,
and testing him with her ordeals,
in the end she will lead him back to the straight road,
and reveal her secrets to him.
If he wanders away she will abandon him,
and hand him over to his fate.

This is the word of the Lord.

Responsorial Psalm Ps 118:165. 168. 171-2. 174-5. ℟ v.165

℟ O Lord, great peace have they who love your law.

1 The lovers of your law have great peace;
they never stumble.
I obey your precepts and your will;
all that I do is before you. ℟

79

2 Let my lips proclaim your praise
   because you teach me your statutes.
   Let my tongue sing your promise
   for your commands are just.

   ℟ O Lord, great peace have they who love your law.

3 Give life to my soul that I may praise you.
   Let your decrees give me help.
   Lord, I long for your saving help
   and your law is my delight. ℟

Gospel Acclamation   Jn 14:16

   Alleluia, alleluia!
   I am the way, the truth, and the life, says the Lord;
   no one comes to the Father, except through me.
   Alleluia!

                          GOSPEL

A reading from the holy Gospel according to Mark   9:38-40

                          Anyone who is not against us is for us.

John said to Jesus, 'Master, we saw a man who is not one of us casting
out devils in your name; and because he was not one of us we tried to
stop him.' But Jesus said, 'You must not stop him: no one who works a
miracle in my name is likely to speak evil of me. Anyone who is not
against us is for us.'

   This is the Gospel of the Lord.

Thursday

FIRST READING

A reading from the book of Ecclesiasticus   5:1-8

Do not delay your return to the Lord.

Do not give your heart to your money,
or say, 'With this I am self-sufficient.'
Do not be led by your appetites and energy
to follow the passions of your heart.
And do not say, 'Who has authority over me?'
for the Lord will certainly be avenged on you.
Do not say, 'I sinned, and what happened to me?'
for the Lord's forbearance is long.
Do not be so sure of forgiveness
that you add sin to sin.
And do not say, 'His compassion is great,
he will forgive me my many sins';
for with him are both mercy and wrath,
and his rage bears heavy on sinners.
Do not delay your return to the Lord,
do not put it off day after day;
for suddenly the Lord's wrath will blaze out,
and at the time of vengeance you will be utterly destroyed.
Do not set your heart on ill-gotten gains,
they will be of no use to you on the day of disaster.

This is the word of the Lord.

Responsorial Psalm   Ps 1:1-4. 6. ℟ Ps 39:5

℟   Happy are they who hope in the Lord.

1   Happy indeed is the man
    who follows not the counsel of the wicked;
    nor lingers in the way of sinners
    nor sits in the company of scorners,
    but whose delight is the law of the Lord
    and who ponders his law day and night.   ℟

2   He is like a tree that is planted
    beside the flowing waters,

that yields its fruit in due season
and whose leaves shall never fade;
and all that he does shall prosper.

℟ Happy are they who hope in the Lord.

3   Not so are the wicked, not so!
For they like winnowed chaff
shall be driven away by the wind.
For the Lord guards the way of the just
but the way of the wicked leads to doom.   ℟

Gospel Acclamation   cf. 1 Thess 2:13

Alleluia, alleluia!
Receive this message not as human words,
but as truly the word of God.
Alleluia!

GOSPEL

A reading from the holy Gospel according to Mark   9:41-50

It is better to enter into life crippled, than to have two hands and go to hell.

Jesus said to his disciples: 'If anyone gives you a cup of water to drink just because you belong to Christ, then I tell you solemnly, he will most certainly not lose his reward.

'But anyone who is an obstacle to bring down one of these little ones who have faith, would be better thrown into the sea with a great millstone round his neck. And if your hand should cause you to sin, cut it off; it is better for you to enter into life crippled, than to have two hands and go to hell, into the fire that cannot be put out. And if your foot should cause you to sin, cut it off; it is better for you to enter into life lame, than to have two feet and be thrown into hell. And if your eye should cause you to sin, tear it out; it is better for you to enter into the kingdom of God with one eye, than to have two eyes and be thrown into hell where their worm does not die nor their fire go out. For everyone will be salted with fire. Salt is a good thing, but if salt has become insipid, how can you season it again? Have salt in yourselves and be at peace with one another.'

This is the Gospel of the Lord.

Friday

FIRST READING

A reading from the book of Ecclesiasticus   6:5-17

A faithful friend is beyond comparison.

A kindly turn of speech multiplies a man's friends,
and a courteous way of speaking invites many a friendly reply.
Let your acquaintances be many,
but your advisers one in a thousand.
If you want to make a friend, take him on trial,
and be in no hurry to trust him;
for one kind of friend is only so when it suits him
but will not stand by you in your day of trouble.
Another kind of friend will fall out with you
and to your dismay make your quarrel public,
and a third kind of friend will share your table,
but not stand by you in your day of trouble:
when you are doing well he will be your second self,
ordering your servants about;
but if ever you are brought low he will turn against you
and will hide himself from you.
Keep well clear of your enemies,
and be wary of your friends.
A faithful friend is a sure shelter,
whoever finds one has found a rare treasure.
A faithful friend is something beyond price,
there is no measuring his worth.
A faithful friend is the elixir of life,
and those who fear the Lord will find one.
Whoever fears the Lord makes true friends,
for as a man is, so is his friend.

This is the word of the Lord.

Responsorial Psalm   Ps 118:12. 16. 18. 27. 34-35. ℟ v.35

℟   Guide me, Lord, in the way of your commands.

1   Blessed are you, O Lord;
teach me your statutes.
I take delight in your statutes;
I will not forget your word. ℟

2　Open my eyes that I may consider
the wonders of your law.
Make me grasp the way of your precepts
and I will muse on your wonders.

℟　Guide me, Lord, in the way of your commands.

3　Train me to observe your law,
to keep it with my heart.
Guide me in the path of your commands;
for there is my delight.　℟

Gospel Acclamation　　　　　　　　　　　　　　　　　　cf. Jn 17:17

Alleluia, alleluia!
Your word, O Lord, is truth:
make us holy in the truth.
Alleluia!

GOSPEL

A reading from the holy Gospel according to Mark　　　　10:1-12

What God has joined together, no one must divide.

Jesus came to the district of Judaea and the far side of the Jordan.
And again crowds gathered round him, and again he taught them, as
his custom was. Some Pharisees approached him and asked, 'Is it
against the law for a man to divorce his wife?' They were testing him.
He answered them, 'What did Moses command you?' 'Moses allowed
us' they said 'to draw up a writ of dismissal and so to divorce.' Then
Jesus said to them, 'It was because you were so unteachable that he
wrote this commandment for you. But from the beginning of creation
God made them male and female. This is why a man must leave father
and mother, and the two become one body. They are no longer two,
therefore, but one body. So then, what God has united, man must not
divide.' Back in the house the disciples questioned him again about
this, and he said to them, 'The man who divorces his wife and marries
another is guilty of adultery against her. And if a woman divorces her
husband and marries another she is guilty of adultery too.'

This is the Gospel of the Lord.

Saturday

FIRST READING

A reading from the book of Ecclesiasticus 17:1-15

The Lord made us in his own image.

The Lord fashioned man from the earth,
to consign him back to it.
He gave them so many days' determined time,
he gave them authority over everything on earth.
He clothed them with strength like his own,
and made them in his own image.
He filled all living things with dread of man,
making him master over beasts and birds.
He shaped for them a mouth and tongue, eyes and ears,
and gave them a heart to think with.
He filled them with knowledge and understanding,
and revealed to them good and evil.
He put his own light in their hearts
to show them the magnificence of his works.
They will praise his holy name,
as they tell of his magnificent works.
He set knowledge before them,
he endowed them with the law of life.
He established an eternal covenant with them,
and revealed his judgements to them.
Their eyes saw his glorious majesty,
and their ears heard the glory of his voice.
He said to them, 'Beware of all wrong-doing';
he gave each a commandment concerning his neighbour.
Their ways are always under his eye,
they cannot be hidden from his sight.

This is the word of the Lord.

Responsorial Psalm   Ps 102:13-18. ℟ cf. v.17

℟ The Lord's kindness is everlasting to those who fear him.

1 As a father has compassion on his sons,
   the Lord has pity on those who fear him;
   for he knows of what we are made,
   he remembers that we are dust. ℟

2 As for man, his days are like grass;
   he flowers like the flower of the field
   the wind blows and he is gone
   and his place never sees him again. ℟

3 But the love of the Lord is everlasting
   upon those who hold him in fear;
   his justice reaches out to children's children
   when they keep his covenant in truth. ℟

Gospel Acclamation   cf. Mt 11:25

Alleluia, alleluia!
Blessed are you, Father, Lord of heaven and earth;
you have revealed to little ones the mysteries of the kingdom.
Alleluia!

GOSPEL

A reading from the holy Gospel according to Mark   10:13-16

*Whoever does not accept the kingdom of God like a child will
never enter it.*

People were bringing little children to Jesus, for him to touch them.
The disciples turned them away, but when Jesus saw this he was
indignant and said to them, 'Let the little children come to me; do not
stop them; for it is to such as these that the kingdom of God belongs. I
tell you solemnly, anyone who does not welcome the kingdom of God
like a little child will never enter it.' Then he put his arms round
them, laid his hands on them and gave them his blessing.

This is the Gospel of the Lord.

EIGHTH WEEK IN ORDINARY TIME

Year I

Monday

FIRST READING

A reading from the book of Ecclesiasticus   17:24-29

Turn to the Lord, plead before his face and lessen your offence.

To those who repent God permits return,
and he encourages those who were losing hope.
Return to the Lord and leave sin behind,
plead before his face and lessen your offence.
Come back to the Most High and turn away from iniquity,
and hold in abhorrence all that is foul.
Who will praise the Most High in Sheol,
if the living do not do so by giving glory to him?
To the dead, as to those who do not exist, praise is unknown,
only those with life and health can praise the Lord.
How great is the mercy of the Lord,
his pardon on all those who turn towards him!

This is the word of the Lord.

Responsorial Psalm   Ps 31:1-2. 5-7. ℞ v.11

℞   Let the just exult and rejoice in the Lord.

1   Happy the man whose offence is forgiven,
     whose sin is remitted.
     O happy the man to whom the Lord
     imputes no guilt,
     in whose spirit is no guile.   ℞

2   But now I have acknowledged my sins;
     my guilt I did not hide.
     I said: 'I will confess
     my offence to the Lord.'
     And you, Lord, have forgiven
     the guilt of my sin.   ℞

3   So let every good man pray to you
    in the time of need.
    The floods of water may reach high
    but him they shall not reach.

    ℟   Let the just exult and rejoice in the Lord.

4   You are my hiding place, O Lord;
    you save me from distress.
    You surround me with cries of deliverance.   ℟

Gospel Acclamation   2 Cor 8:9

    Alleluia, alleluia!
    Jesus Christ was rich but he became poor
    to make you rich out of his poverty.
    Alleluia!

GOSPEL

A reading from the holy Gospel according to Mark   10:17-27

Go, sell everything you have and follow me.

Jesus was setting out on a journey when a man ran up, knelt before
him and put this question to him, 'Good master, what must I do to
inherit eternal life?' Jesus said to him, 'Why do you call me good? No
one is good but God alone. You know the commandments: You must
not kill; You must not commit adultery; You must not steal; You must
not bring false witness; You must not defraud; Honour your father
and mother.' And he said to him, 'Master, I have kept all these from
my earliest days.' Jesus looked steadily at him and loved him, and he
said, 'There is one thing you lack. Go and sell everything you own and
give the money to the poor, and you will have treasure in heaven; then
come, follow me.' But his face fell at these words and he went away
sad, for he was a man of great wealth.

    Jesus looked round and said to his disciples, 'How hard it is for
those who have riches to enter the kingdom of God!' The disciples were
astounded by these words, but Jesus insisted, 'My children,' he said to
them 'how hard it is to enter the kingdom of God! It is easier for a
camel to pass through the eye of a needle than for a rich man to enter
the kingdom of God.' They were more astonished than ever. 'In that
case' they said to one another 'who can be saved?' Jesus gazed at them.

'For men' he said 'it is impossible, but not for God: because everything is possible for God.'

This is the Gospel of the Lord.

Tuesday

FIRST READING

A reading from the book of Ecclesiasticus 35:1-12

A person offers sacrifice by following the law.

A man multiplies offerings by keeping the Law;
he offers communion sacrifices by following the commandments.
By showing gratitude he makes an offering of fine flour,
by giving alms he offers a sacrifice of praise.
Withdraw from wickedness and the Lord will be pleased,
withdraw from injustice and you make atonement.
Do not appear empty-handed in the Lord's presence;
for all these things are due under the commandment.
A virtuous man's offering graces the altar,
and its savour rises before the Most High.
A virtuous man's sacrifice is acceptable,
its memorial will not be forgotten.
Honour the Lord with generosity,
do not stint the first fruits you bring.
Add a smiling face to all your gifts,
and be cheerful as you dedicate your tithes.
Give to the Most High as he has given to you,
generously as your means can afford;
for the Lord is a good rewarder,
he will reward you seven times over.
Offer him no bribe, he will not accept it,
do not put your faith in an unvirtuous sacrifice;
since the Lord is a judge
who is no respecter of personages.

This is the word of the Lord.

Responsorial Psalm   Ps 49:5-8. 14. 23. ℟ v.23

℟   To the upright I will show the saving power of God.

1   'Summon before me my people
     who made covenant with me by sacrifice.'
     The heavens proclaim his justice,
     for he, God, is the judge.   ℟

2   'Listen, my people, I will speak;
     Israel, I will testify against you,
     for I am God your God.
     I find no fault with your sacrifices,
     your offerings are always before me.   ℟

3   'Pay your sacrifice of thanksgiving to God
     and render him your votive offerings.
     A sacrifice of thanksgiving honours me
     and I will show God's salvation to the upright.'   ℟

Gospel Acclamation   cf. Mt 11:25

     Alleluia, alleluia!
     Blessed are you, Father, Lord of heaven and earth;
     you have revealed to little ones the mysteries of the kingdom.
     Alleluia!

GOSPEL

A reading from the holy Gospel according to Mark   10:28-31

You will receive a hundred times as much persecution in this present
time, and in the world to come, eternal life.

'What about us?' Peter asked Jesus. 'We have left everything and
followed you.' Jesus said, 'I tell you solemnly, there is no one who has
left house, brothers, sisters, father, children or land for my sake and
for the sake of the gospel who will not be repaid a hundred times over,
houses, brothers, sisters, mothers, children and land – not without
persecutions – now in this present time and, in the world to come,
eternal life.

    'Many who are first will be last, and the last first.'

    This is the Gospel of the Lord.

Wednesday

FIRST READING

A reading from the book of Ecclesiasticus   36:1. 4-5. 10-17

The nations have acknowledged that there is no God but you.

Have mercy on us, Master, Lord of all, and look on us,
cast the fear of yourself over every nation.
Let them acknowledge you, just as we have acknowledged
that there is no God but you, Lord.
Send new portents, do fresh wonders,
win glory for your hand and your right arm.
Gather together all the tribes of Jacob,
restore them their inheritance as in the beginning.
Have mercy, Lord, on the people who have invoked your name,
on Israel whom you have treated as a first-born.
Show compassion on your holy city,
on Jerusalem the place of your rest.
Fill Zion with songs of your praise,
and your sanctuary with your glory.
Bear witness to those you created in the beginning,
and bring about what has been prophesied in your name.
Give those who wait for you their reward,
and let your prophets be proved worthy of belief.
Grant, Lord, the prayer of your servants,
in accordance with Aaron's blessing on your people,
so that all the earth's inhabitants may acknowledge
that you are the Lord, the everlasting God.

This is the word of the Lord.

Responsorial Psalm   Ps 78:8-9. 11. 13. ℟ Ecclus 36:1

℟   Show us, O Lord,
     the light of your kindness.

1   Do not hold the guilt of our fathers against us.
     Let your compassion hasten to meet us
     for we are in the depths of distress.   ℟

2   O God our saviour, come to our help,
     come for the sake of the glory of your name.
     O Lord our God, forgive us our sins
     rescue us for the sake of your name.   ℟

91

3   Let the groans of the prisoners come before you;
    let your strong arm reprieve those condemned to die.
    But we, your people, the flock of your pasture,
    will give you thanks for ever and ever.
    We will tell your praise from age to age.

  ℟   Show us, O Lord,
      the light of your kindness.

Gospel Acclamation   Mk 10:45

    Alleluia, alleluia!
    The Son of Man came to serve
    and to give his life as a ransom for all.
    Alleluia!

GOSPEL

A reading from the holy Gospel according to Mark   10:32-45

*Now we are going up to Jerusalem, and the Son of Man will be
handed over.*

The disciples were on the road, going up to Jerusalem; Jesus was
walking on ahead of them; they were in a daze, and those who
followed were apprehensive. Once more taking the Twelve aside he
began to tell them what was going to happen to him: 'Now we are
going up to Jerusalem, and the Son of Man is about to be handed over
to the chief priests and the scribes. They will condemn him to death
and will hand him over to the pagans, who will mock him and spit at
him and scourge him and put him to death; and after three days he
will rise again.'

James and John, the sons of Zebedee, approached him. 'Master,'
they said to him 'we want you to do us a favour.' He said to them,
'What is it you want me to do for you?' They said to him, 'Allow us to
sit one at your right hand and the other at your left in your glory.'
'You do not know what you are asking' Jesus said to them. 'Can you
drink the cup that I must drink, or be baptised with the baptism with
which I must be baptised?' They replied, 'We can.' Jesus said to them,
'The cup that I must drink you shall drink, and with the baptism with
which I must be baptised you shall be baptised, but as for seats at my
right hand or my left, these are not mine to grant; they belong to those
to whom they have been allotted.'

When the other ten heard this they began to feel indignant with
James and John, so Jesus called them to him and said to them, 'You
know that among the pagans their so-called rulers lord it over them,
and their great men make their authority felt. This is not to happen
among you. No; anyone who wants to become great among you must
be your servant, and anyone who wants to be first among you must be
slave to all. For the Son of Man himself did not come to be served but
to serve, and to give his life as a ransom for many.'

This is the Gospel of the Lord.

Thursday

FIRST READING

A reading from the book of Ecclesiasticus   42:15-25

The work of the Lord is filled with his glory.

I will remind you of the works of the Lord,
and tell of what I have seen.
By the words of the Lord his works come into being
and all creation obeys his will.
As the sun in shining looks on all things,
so the work of the Lord is full of his glory.
The Lord has not granted to the holy ones
to tell of all his marvels
which the Almighty Lord has solidly constructed
for the universe to stand firm in his glory.
He has fathomed the deep and the heart,
and seen into their devious ways;
for the Most High knows all the knowledge there is,
and has observed the signs of the times.
He declares what is past and what will be,
and uncovers the traces of hidden things.
Not a thought escapes him,
not a single word is hidden from him.
He has imposed an order on the magnificent works of his wisdom,
he is from everlasting to everlasting,
nothing can be added to him, nothing taken away.
He needs no one's advice.
How desirable are all his works,
how dazzling to the eye!

They all live and last for ever,
whatever the circumstances all obey him.
All things go in pairs, by opposites,
and he has made nothing defective;
the one consolidates the excellence of the other,
who could ever be sated with gazing at his glory?

This is the word of the Lord.

Responsorial Psalm   Ps 32:2-9. ℟ v.6

℟ By the word of the Lord the heavens were made.

1 Give thanks to the Lord upon the harp,
   with a ten-stringed lute sing him songs.
   O sing him a song that is new,
   play loudly, with all your skill. ℟

2 For the word of the Lord is faithful
   and all his works to be trusted.
   The Lord loves justice and right
   and fills the earth with his love. ℟

3 By his word the heavens were made,
   by the breath of his mouth all the stars.
   He collects the waves of the ocean;
   he stores up the depths of the sea. ℟

4 Let all the earth fear the Lord,
   all who live in the world revere him.
   He spoke; and it came to be.
   He commanded; it sprang into being. ℟

Gospel Acclamation   Jn 8:12

Alleluia, alleluia!
I am the light of the world, says the Lord;
whoever follows me will have the light of life.
Alleluia!

GOSPEL

A reading from the holy Gospel according to Mark   10:46-52

Master, let me see again.

As Jesus was leaving Jericho with his disciples and a large crowd, Bartimaeus (that is, the son of Timaeus), a blind beggar, was sitting at the side of the road. When he heard that it was Jesus of Nazareth, he began to shout and to say, 'Son of David, Jesus, have pity on me.' And many of them scolded him and told him to keep quiet, but he only shouted all the louder, 'Son of David, have pity on me.' Jesus stopped and said, 'Call him here.' So they called the blind man. 'Courage,' they said 'get up; he is calling you.' So throwing off his cloak, he jumped up and went to Jesus. Then Jesus spoke, 'What do you want me to do for you?' 'Rabbuni,' the blind man said to him 'Master, let me see again.' Jesus said to him, 'Go; your faith has saved you.' And immediately his sight returned and he followed him along the road.

This is the Gospel of the Lord.

Friday

FIRST READING

A reading from the book of Ecclesiasticus   44:1. 9-13

Our ancestors were merciful, and their name will live for generations.

Let us praise illustrious men,
our ancestors in their successive generations.
While others have left no memory,
and disappeared as though they had not existed,
they are now as though they had never been,
and so too, their children after them.

But here is a list of generous men
whose good works have not been forgotten.
In their descendants there remains
a rich inheritance born of them.
Their descendants stand by the covenants
and, thanks to them, so do their children's children.
Their offspring will last for ever,
their glory will not fade.

This is the word of the Lord.

Responsorial Psalm   Ps 149:1-6. 9. ℟ v.4

> ℟   The Lord takes delight in his people.

or

> ℟   Alleluia!

1   Sing a new song to the Lord,
    his praise in the assembly of the faithful.
    Let Israel rejoice in its Maker,
    let Zion's sons exult in their king.   ℟

2   Let them praise his name with dancing
    and make music with timbrel and harp.
    For the Lord takes delight in his people.
    He crowns the poor with salvation.   ℟

3   Let the faithful rejoice in their glory,
    shout for joy and take their rest.
    Let the praise of God be on their lips;
    this honour is for all his faithful.   ℟

Gospel Acclamation   cf. Jn 15:16

Alleluia, alleluia!
I have chosen you from the world, says the Lord,
to go and bear fruit that will last.
Alleluia!

GOSPEL

A reading from the holy Gospel according to Mark   11:11-26

My house will be called a house of prayer for all people. Have faith in God.

After he had been acclaimed by the crowds, Jesus entered Jerusalem
and went into the Temple. He looked all round him, but as it was now
late, he went out to Bethany with the Twelve.
    Next day as they were leaving Bethany, he felt hungry. Seeing a
fig tree in leaf some distance away, he went to see if he could find any
fruit on it, but when he came up to it he found nothing but leaves; for
it was not the season for figs. And he addressed the fig tree. 'May no
one ever eat fruit from you again' he said. And his disciples heard him
say this.

So they reached Jerusalem and he went into the Temple and began driving out those who were selling and buying there; he upset the tables of the money changers and the chairs of those who were selling pigeons. Nor would he allow anyone to carry anything through the Temple. And he taught them and said, 'Does not scripture say: My house will be called a house of prayer for all the peoples? But you have turned it into a robber's den.' This came to the ears of the chief priests and the scribes, and they tried to find some way of doing away with him; they were afraid of him because the people were carried away by his teaching. And when evening came he went out of the city.

Next morning, as they passed by, they saw the fig tree withered to the roots. Peter remembered. 'Look, Rabbi,' he said to Jesus 'the fig tree you cursed has withered away.' Jesus answered, 'Have faith in God. I tell you solemnly, if anyone says to this mountain, "Get up and throw yourself into the sea," with no hesitation in his heart but believing that what he says will happen, it will be done for him. I tell you therefore: everything you ask and pray for, believe that you have it already, and it will be yours. And when you stand in prayer, forgive whatever you have against anybody, so that your Father in heaven may forgive your failings too. But if you do not forgive, your Father in heaven will not forgive your failings either.'

This is the Gospel of the Lord.

Saturday

FIRST READING

A reading from the book of Ecclesiasticus   51:12-20

Give me wisdom and I will give you glory.

I will thank you and praise you,
and bless the name of the Lord.
When I was still a youth, before I went travelling,
in my prayers I asked outright for wisdom.
Outside the sanctuary I would pray for her,
and to the last I will continue to seek her.
From her blossoming to the ripening of her grape
my heart has taken its delight in her.
My foot has pursued a straight path,
I have been following her steps ever since my youth.
By bowing my ear a little I have received her,

and have found much instruction.
Thanks to her I have advanced;
the glory be to him who has given me wisdom!
For I am determined to put her into practice,
I have earnestly pursued what is good, I will not be put to shame.
My soul has fought to possess her,
I have been scrupulous in keeping the law;
I have stretched out my hands to heaven
and bewailed my ignorance of her;
I have directed my soul towards her,
and in purity have found her.

This is the word of the Lord.

Responsorial Psalm

Ps 18:8-11. ℟ v.9

℟   The precepts of the Lord give joy to the heart.

1   The law of the Lord is perfect,
     it revives the soul.
     The rule of the Lord is to be trusted,
     it gives wisdom to the simple. ℟

2   The precepts of the Lord are right,
     they gladden the heart.
     The command of the Lord is clear,
     it gives light to the eyes. ℟

3   The fear of the Lord is holy,
     abiding for ever.
     The decrees of the Lord are truth
     and all of them just. ℟

4   They are more to be desired than gold,
     than the purest of gold,
     and sweeter are they than honey,
     than honey from the comb. ℟

Gospel Acclamation

cf. Col 3:16.17

Alleluia, alleluia!
Give thanks to God our Father through Jesus Christ our Lord,
and may the fullness of his message live within you.
Alleluia!

GOSPEL

A reading from the holy Gospel according to Mark   11:27-33

By what authority have you done this?

Jesus and his disciples came to Jerusalem, and as Jesus was walking in the Temple, the chief priests and the scribes and the elders came to him, and they said to him, 'What authority have you for acting like this? Or who gave you authority to do these things?' Jesus said to them, 'I will ask you a question, only one; answer me and I will tell you my authority for acting like this. John's baptism: did it come from heaven, or from man? Answer me that.' And they argued it out this way among themselves: 'If we say from heaven, he will say, "Then why did you refuse to believe him?" But dare we say from man?' – they had the people to fear, for everyone held that John was a real prophet. So their reply to Jesus was, 'We do not know.' And Jesus said to them, 'Nor will I tell you my authority for acting like this.'

This is the Gospel of the Lord.

NINTH WEEK IN ORDINARY TIME

Year I

Monday

FIRST READING

A reading from the book of Tobit   1:3; 2:1-8

Tobias feared the Lord more than the king.

I, Tobit, have walked in paths of truth and in good works all the days of my life. I have given much in alms to my brothers and fellow countrymen exiled like me to Nineveh in the country of Assyria.

At our feast of Pentecost (the feast of Weeks) there was a good dinner. I took my place for the meal; the table was brought to me and various dishes were brought. Then I said to my son Tobias, 'Go, my child, and seek out some poor, loyal-hearted man among our brothers exiled in Nineveh, and bring him to share my meal. I will wait until you come back, my child.' So Tobias went out to look for some poor man among our brothers, but he came back again and said, 'Father!' I answered, 'What is it, my child?' He went on, 'Father, one of our nation has just been murdered; he has been

strangled and then thrown down in the market place; he is there still.'
I sprang up at once, left my meal untouched, took the man from the
market place and laid him in one of my rooms, waiting until sunset to
bury him. I came in again and washed myself and ate my bread in
sorrow, remembering the words of the prophet Amos concerning
Bethel:

Your feasts will be turned to mourning,
and all your songs to lamentation.

And I wept. When the sun was down, I went and dug a grave and
buried him. My neighbours laughed and said, 'See! He is not afraid
any more.' (You must remember that a price had been set on my head
earlier for this very thing.) 'The time before this he had to flee, yet
here he is, beginning to bury the dead again.'

This the word of the Lord.

Responsorial Psalm   Ps 111:1-6. ℟ v.1

    ℟   Happy are those who fear the Lord.

or

    ℟   Alleluia!

1   Happy the man who fears the Lord,
    who takes delight in his commands.
    His sons will be powerful on earth;
    the children of the upright are blessed   ℟

2   Riches and wealth are in his house;
    his justice stands firm for ever.
    He is a light in the darkness for the upright:
    he is generous, merciful and just.   ℟

3   The good man takes pity and lends,
    he conducts his affairs with honour.
    The just man will never waver:
    he will be remembered for ever.   ℟

Gospel Acclamation   cf. Apoc 1:5

Alleluia, alleluia!
Jesus Christ, you are the faithful witness, firstborn from the dead;
you have loved us and washed away our sins in your blood.
Alleluia!

GOSPEL

A reading from the holy Gospel according to Mark 12:1-12

They seized the beloved son, killed him, and threw him out of the vineyard.

Jesus began to speak to the chief priests, the scribes and the elders in parables, 'A man planted a vineyard; he fenced it round, dug out a trough for the winepress and built a tower; then he leased it to tenants and went abroad. When the time came, he sent a servant to the tenants to collect from them his share of the produce from the vineyard. But they seized the man, thrashed him and sent him away empty-handed. Next he sent another servant to them; him they beat about the head and treated shamefully. And he sent another and him they killed; then a number of others, and they thrashed some and killed the rest. He had still someone left: his beloved son. He sent him to them last of all. 'They will respect my son' he said. But those tenants said to each other, 'This is the heir. Come on, let us kill him, and the inheritance will be ours.' So they seized him and killed him and threw him out of the vineyard. Now what will the owner of the vineyard do? He will come and make an end to the tenants and give the vineyard to others. Have you not read this text of scripture:

It was the stone rejected by the builders
that became the keystone.
This was the Lord's doing
and it is wonderful to see'?

And they would have liked to arrest him, because they realised that the parable was aimed at them, but they were afraid of the crowds. So they left him alone and went away.

This is the Gospel of the Lord.

Tuesday

FIRST READING

A reading from the book of Tobit 2:9-14

Even though he was blind he did not turn against God.

I, Tobit, took a bath; then I went into the courtyard and lay down by the courtyard wall. Since it was hot I left my face uncovered. I did not know that there were sparrows in the wall above my head; their hot droppings fell into my eyes. White spots then formed which I was obliged to have treated by the doctors. But the more ointments they tried me with, the more the spots blinded me, and in the end I became blind altogether. I remained without sight four years; all my brothers were distressed; and Ahikar provided for my upkeep for two years, till he left for Elymais.

My wife Anna then undertook woman's work; she would spin wool and take cloth to weave; she used to deliver whatever had been ordered from her and then receive payment. Now on March the seventh she finished a piece of work and delivered it to her customers. They paid her all that was due, and into the bargain presented her with a kid for a meal. When the kid came into my house, it began to bleat. I called to my wife and said, 'Where does this creature come from? Suppose it has been stolen! Quick, let the owners have it back; we have no right to eat stolen goods.' She said, 'No, it was a present given me over and above my wages.' I did not believe her, and told her to give it back to the owners (I blushed at this in her presence). Then she answered, 'What about your own alms? What about your own good works? Everyone knows what return you have had for them.'

This is the word of the Lord.

Responsorial Psalm   Ps 111:1-2. 7-9. ℟ cf. v.7

℟   The hearts of the just are secure, trusting in the Lord.

or

℟   Alleluia!

1   Happy the man who fears the Lord,
    who takes delight in his commands.
    His sons will be powerful on earth;
    the children of the upright are blessed.   ℟

2   He has no fear of evil news:
    with a firm heart he trusts in the Lord.
    With a steadfast heart he will not fear;
    he will see the downfall of his foes.   ℟

3   Open-handed, he gives to the poor;
    his justice stands firm for ever.
    His head will be raised in glory.   ℟

Gospel Acclamation cf. Eph 1:17-18

> Alleluia, alleluia!
> May the Father of our Lord Jesus Christ
> enlighten the eyes of our heart
> that we might see how great is the hope
> to which we are called.
> Alleluia!

GOSPEL

A reading from the holy Gospel according to Mark 12:13-17

Give to Caesar what belongs to Caesar and to God what belongs to God.

The chief priests and the scribes and the elders sent to Jesus some Pharisees and some Herodians to catch him out in what he said. These came and said to him, 'Master, we know you are an honest man, that you are not afraid of anyone, because a man's rank means nothing to you, and that you teach the way of God in all honesty. Is it permissible to pay taxes to Caesar or not? Should we pay, yes or no?' Seeing through their hypocrisy he said to them, 'Why do you set this trap for me? Hand me a denarius and let me see it.' They handed him one and he said, 'Whose head is this? Whose name?' 'Caesar's' they told him. Jesus said to them, 'Give back to Caesar what belongs to Caesar – and to God what belongs to God.' This reply took them completely by surprise.

This is the Gospel of the Lord.

Wednesday

FIRST READING

A reading from the book of Tobit 3:1-11. 16-17

Their prayers were heard by the Lord and found favour in his sight.

Sad at heart, I, Tobit, sighed and wept, and began this prayer of lamentation:

> 'You are just, O Lord,
> and just are all your works.
> All your ways are grace and truth,
> and you are the Judge of the world.

'Therefore, Lord,
remember me, look on me.
Do not punish me for my sins
or for my heedless faults
or for those of my fathers.

'For we have sinned against you
and broken your commandments;
and you have given us over to be plundered,
to captivity and death,
to be the talk, the laughing-stock and scorn
of all the nations among whom you have dispersed us.

'Whereas all your decrees are true
when you deal with me as my faults deserve,
and those of my fathers,
since we have neither kept your commandments
nor walked in truth before you;
so now, do with me as you will;
be pleased to take my life from me;
I desire to be delivered from earth
and to become earth again.
For death is better for me than life.
I have been reviled without a cause
and I am distressed beyond measure.

'Lord, I wait for the sentence you will give
to deliver me from this affliction.
Let me go away to my everlasting home;
do not turn your face from me, O Lord.
For it is better to die than still to live
in the face of trouble that knows no pity;
I am weary of hearing myself traduced.'

It chanced on the same day that Sarah the daughter of Raguel, who lived in Media at Ecbatana, also heard insults from one of her father's maids. You must know that she had been given in marriage seven times, and that Asmodeus, that worst of demons, had killed her bridegrooms one after another before ever they had slept with her as man with wife. The servant-girl said, 'Yes, you kill your bridegrooms yourself. That makes seven already to whom you have been given, and you have not once been in luck yet. Just because your bridegrooms have died, that is no reason for punishing us. Go and join them, and may we be spared the sight of any child of yours!' That day she grieved, she sobbed, and went up to her father's room intending to hang herself. But then she thought, 'Suppose they blamed my father! They will say, "You had an only daughter whom you loved, and now she has hanged herself for grief." I cannot cause my father a sorrow which would bring down his old age to the dwelling of the dead. I should do better not to hang myself, but to beg the Lord to let me die and not live to hear any more insults.'

This time the prayer of each of them found favour before the glory of God, and Raphael was sent to bring remedy to them both.

This is the word of the Lord.

Responsorial Psalm   Ps 24:2-9. ℟ v.1

℟ To you, O Lord, I lift my soul.

1 I trust you, let me not be disappointed;
   do not let my enemies triumph.
   Those who hope in you shall not be disappointed,
   but only those who wantonly break faith. ℟

2 Lord, make me know your ways.
   Lord, teach me your paths.
   Make me walk in your truth, and teach me:
   for you are God my saviour. ℟

3 In you I hope all the day long
   because of your goodness, O Lord.
   Remember your mercy, Lord,
   and the love you have shown from of old.
   Do not remember the sins of my youth.
   In your love remember me. ℟

4 The Lord is good and upright.
   He shows the path to those who stray,
   He guides the humble in the right path;
   he teaches his way to the poor. ℟

Gospel Acclamation   Jn 11:25.26

Alleluia, alleluia!
I am the resurrection and the life, says the Lord;
whoever believes in me will not die for ever.
Alleluia!

GOSPEL

A reading from the holy Gospel according to Mark   12:18-27

He is God, not of the dead, but of the living.

Some Sadducees – who deny that there is a resurrection – came to Jesus and they put this question to him, 'Master, we have it from Moses in writing, if a man's brother dies leaving a wife but no child, the man must marry the widow to raise up children for his brother. Now there were seven brothers. The first married a wife and then died leaving no children. The second married the widow, and he too died leaving no children; with the third it was the same, and none of the seven left any children. Last of all the woman herself died. Now at the resurrection, when they rise again, whose wife will she be, since she had been married to all seven?'

Jesus said to them, 'Is not the reason why you go wrong, that you understand neither the scriptures nor the power of God? For when they rise from the dead, men and women do not marry; no, they are like the angels in heaven. Now about the dead rising again, have you never read in the Book of Moses, in the passage about the Bush, how God spoke to him and said: I am the God of Abraham, the God of Isaac and the God of Jacob? He is God, not of the dead, but of the living. You are very much mistaken.'

This is the Gospel of the Lord.

Thursday

FIRST READING

A reading from the book of Tobit   6:10-11; 7:1. 9-14; 8:4-9

The Lord made you come to me that we might be joined together.

Raphael and Tobit entered Media and had nearly reached Ecbatana when Raphael said to the boy, 'Brother Tobias.' 'Yes?' he answered. The angel went on, 'Tonight we shall be staying with Raguel, who is a kinsman of yours. He has a daughter called Sarah.' As they entered Ecbatana, Tobias said, 'Brother Azarias, take me at once to our brother Raguel's.' And he showed him the way to the house of Raguel, whom they found sitting beside his courtyard door. They greeted him first, and he replied, 'Welcome and greetings, brothers.' And he took them into his house. Raguel killed a sheep from the flock, and he and his wife Edna gave them a warmhearted welcome.

They washed and bathed and sat down to table. Then Tobias said to Raphael, 'Brother Azarias, will you ask Raguel to give me my sister Sarah?' Raguel overheard the words, and said to the young man, 'Eat and drink, and make the most of your evening; no one else has the right to take my daughter Sarah – no one but you, my brother. In any case I, for my own part, am not at liberty to give her to anyone else, since you are her next of kin. However, my boy, I must be frank with you: I have tried to find a husband for her seven times among our kinsmen, and all of them have died the first evening, on going to her room. But for the present, my boy, eat and drink; the Lord will grant you his grace and peace.' Tobias spoke out, 'I will not hear of eating and drinking till you have come to a decision about me.' Raguel answered, 'Very well. Since, as prescribed by the Book of Moses, she is given to you, heaven itself decrees she shall be yours. I therefore entrust your sister to you. From now you are her brother and she is your sister. She is given to you from today for ever. The Lord of heaven favour you tonight, my child, and grant you his grace and peace.' Raguel called for his daughter Sarah, took her by the hand and gave her to Tobias with these words, 'I entrust her to you; the law and the ruling recorded in the Book of Moses assign her to you as your wife. Take her; take her home to your father's house with a good conscience. The God of heaven grant you a good journey in peace.' Then he turned to her mother and asked her to fetch him writing paper. He drew up the marriage contract, how he gave his daughter as bride to Tobias according to the ordinance in the Law of Moses.

After this they began to eat and drink. The parents meanwhile had gone out and shut the door behind them. Tobias said to Sarah, 'Get up, my sister! You and I must pray and petition our Lord to win his grace and his protection.' She stood up, and they began praying for protection, and this was how he began:

'You are blessed, O God of our fathers;
blessed, too, is your name
for ever and ever.
Let the heavens bless you
and all things you have made
for evermore.

It was you who created Adam,
you who created Eve his wife

to be his help and support;
and from these two the human race was born.
It was you who said,
"It is not good that the man should be alone;
let us make him a helpmate like himself."
And so I do not take my sister
for any lustful motive;
I do it in singleness of heart.
Be kind enough to have pity on her and on me
and bring us to old age together.'

And together they said 'Amen, Amen', and lay down for the night.

This is the word of the Lord.

Responsorial Psalm   Ps 127:1-5. ℟ cf. v.1

℟   Happy are those who fear the Lord.

1   O blessed are those who fear the Lord
      and walk in his ways!
      By the labour of your hands you shall eat.
      You will be happy and prosper.   ℟

2   Your wife like a fruitful vine
      in the heart of your house;
      your children like shoots of the olive,
      around your table.   ℟

3   Indeed thus shall be blessed
      the man who fears the Lord.
      May the Lord bless you from Zion
      all the days of your life!   ℟

Gospel Acclamation   cf. 2 Tim 1:10

Alleluia, alleluia!
Our Saviour Jesus Christ has done away with death,
and brought us life through his gospel.
Alleluia!

GOSPEL

A reading from the holy Gospel according to Mark 12:28-34

This is the first commandment. The second is similar to it.

One of the scribes came up to Jesus and put a question to him, 'Which is the first of all the commandments?' Jesus replied, 'This is the first: Listen, Israel, the Lord our God is the one Lord, and you must love the Lord your God with all your heart, with all your soul, with all your mind and with all your strength. The second is this: you must love your neighbour as yourself. There is no commandment greater than these.' The scribe said to him, 'Well spoken, Master; what you have said is true: that he is one and there is no other. To love him with all your heart, with all your understanding and strength, and to love your neighbour as yourself, this is far more important than any holocaust or sacrifice.' Jesus, seeing how wisely he had spoken, said, 'You are not far from the kingdom of God.' And after that no one dared to question him any more.

This is the Gospel of the Lord.

Friday

FIRST READING

A reading from the book of Tobit 11:5-17

You have scourged me and now you have saved me, Lord; I can see my son.

Anna was sitting, watching the road by which her son would come. She was sure at once it must be he and said to the father, 'Here comes your son, with his companion.'

Raphael said to Tobias before he reached his father, 'I give you my word that your father's eyes will open. You must put the fish's gall to his eyes; the medicine will smart and will draw a filmy white skin off his eyes. And your father will be able to see and look on the light.'

The mother ran forward and threw her arms round her son's neck. 'Now I can die,' she said 'I have seen you again.' And she wept. Tobit rose to his feet and stumbled across the courtyard through the door. Tobias came on towards him (he had the fish's gall in his hand). He blew into his eyes and said, steadying him, 'Take courage, father!' With this he applied the medicine, left it there a while, then with both hands peeled away a filmy skin from the corners of his eyes. Then his father fell on his neck and wept. He exclaimed, 'I can see, my son, the light of my eyes!' And he said:

'Blessed be God!
Blessed be his great name!
Blessed be all his holy angels!
Blessed be his great name
for evermore!
For he had scourged me
and now has had pity on me
and I see my son Tobias.'

Tobias went into the house, and with a loud voice joyfully blessed God. Then he told his father everything: how his journey had been successful and he had brought the silver back; how he had married Sarah, the daughter of Raguel; how she was following him now, close behind, and could not be far from the gates of Nineveh.

Tobit set off to the gates of Nineveh to meet his daughter-in-law, giving joyful praise to God as he went. When the people of Nineveh saw him walking without a guide and stepping forward as briskly as of old, they were astonished. Tobit described to them how God had taken pity on him and had opened his eyes. Then Tobit met Sarah, the bride of his son Tobias, and blessed her in these words, 'Welcome, daughter! Blessed be your God for sending you to us, my daughter. Blessings on your father, blessings on my son Tobias, blessings on yourself, my daughter. Welcome now to your own house in joyfulness and in blessedness. Come in, my daughter.' He held a feast that day for all the Jews of Nineveh.

This is the word of the Lord.

Responsorial Psalm   Ps 145:2. 7-10. ℟ v.2

℟   Praise the Lord, my soul!

or

℟   Alleluia!

1   My soul, give praise to the Lord;
    I will praise the Lord all my days,
      make music to my God while I live. ℟

2 It is the Lord who keeps faith for ever,
who is just to those who are oppressed.
It is he who gives bread to the hungry,
the Lord, who sets prisoners free. ℟

3 It is the Lord who gives sight to the blind,
who raises up those who are bowed down,
the Lord, who protects the stranger
and upholds the widow and orphan. ℟

4 It is the Lord who loves the just
but thwarts the path of the wicked.
The Lord will reign for ever,
Zion's God, from age to age. ℟

Gospel Acclamation

Jn 14:23

Alleluia, alleluia!
All who love me will keep my words,
and my Father will love them, and we will come to them.
Alleluia!

GOSPEL

A reading from the holy Gospel according to Mark

12:35-37

How can the scribes maintain that Christ is the son of David?

While teaching in the Temple, Jesus said, 'How can the scribes maintain that the Christ is the son of David? David himself, moved by the Holy Spirit, said:

The Lord said to my Lord:
Sit at my right hand
and I will put your enemies
under your feet.

David himself calls him Lord, in what way then can he be his son?' And the great majority of the people heard this with delight.

This is the Gospel of the Lord.

Saturday

FIRST READING

A reading from the book of Tobit   12:1. 5-15. 20

I will return to him who sent me; bless the Lord.

When the feasting was over, Tobit called his son Tobias and said, 'My son, you ought to think about paying the amount due to your fellow traveller; give him more than the figure agreed on.' So Tobias called his companion and said, 'Take half of what you brought back, in payment for all you have done, and go in peace.'

Then Raphael took them both aside and said, 'Bless God, utter his praise before all the living for all the favours he has given you. Bless and extol his name. Proclaim before all men the deeds of God as they deserve, and never tire of giving him thanks. It is right to keep the secret of a king, yet right to reveal and publish the works of God. Thank him worthily. Do what is good, and no evil can befall you.

'Prayer with fasting and alms with right conduct are better than riches with iniquity. Better to practise almsgiving than to hoard up gold. Almsgiving saves from death and purges every kind of sin. Those who give alms have their fill of days; those who commit sin and do evil, bring harm on themselves.

'I am going to tell you the whole truth, hiding nothing from you. I have already told you that it is right to keep the secret of a king, yet right too to reveal in worthy fashion the works of God. So you must know that when you and Sarah were at prayer, it was I who offered your supplications before the glory of the Lord and who read them; so too when you were burying the dead. When you did not hesitate to get up and leave the table to go and bury a dead man, I was sent to test your faith, and at the same time God sent me to heal you and your daughter-in-law Sarah. I am Raphael, one of the seven angels who stand ever ready to enter the presence of the glory of the Lord.

'Now bless the Lord on earth and give thanks to God. I am about to return to him above who sent me.'

This is the word of the Lord.

Responsorial Psalm   Tob 13:2. 6-8. ℟ v.1

℟   Blessed be God, who lives for ever.

1   By turns he punishes and pardons;
    he sends men down to the depths of the underworld
    and draws them up from supreme Destruction;
    no one can escape his hand.   ℟

2   If you return to him
    with all your heart and all your soul,
    behaving honestly towards him,
    then he will return to you
    and hide his face from you no longer.   ℟

3   Consider how well he has treated you;
    loudly give him thanks.
    Bless the Lord of justice
    and extol the King of the ages.   ℟

4   I for my part sing his praise
    in the country of my exile;
    I make his power and greatness known
    to a nation that has sinned.   ℟

5   Sinners, return to him;
    let your conduct be upright before him;
    perhaps he will be gracious to you
    and take pity on you.   ℟

Gospel Acclamation   Mt 5:3

    Alleluia, alleluia!
    Happy the poor in spirit;
    the kingdom of heaven is theirs!
    Alleluia!

GOSPEL

A reading from the holy Gospel according to Mark   12:38-44

This poor widow has given more than all others.

In his teaching Jesus said, 'Beware of the scribes who like to walk
about in long robes, to be greeted obsequiously in the market squares,

to take the front seats in the synagogues and the places of honour at banquets; these are the men who swallow the property of widows, while making a show of lengthy prayers. The more severe will be the sentence they receive.'

He sat down opposite the treasury and watched the people putting money into the treasury, and many of the rich put in a great deal. A poor widow came and put in two small coins, the equivalent of a penny. Then he called his disciples and said to them, 'I tell you solemnly, this poor widow has put more in than all who have contributed to the treasury; for they have all put in money they had over, but she from the little she had has put in everything she possessed, all she had to live on.'

This is the Gospel of the Lord.

TENTH WEEK IN ORDINARY TIME
Year I

Monday

FIRST READING

A reading from the second letter of St Paul   1:1-7
to the Corinthians

God comforts us that we might comfort others in their sorrows.

From Paul, appointed by God to be an apostle of Christ Jesus, and from Timothy, one of the brothers, to the church of God at Corinth and to all the saints in the whole of Achaia. Grace and peace to you from God our Father and the Lord Jesus Christ.

Blessed be the God and Father of our Lord Jesus Christ, a gentle Father and the God of all consolation, who comforts us in all our sorrows, so that we can offer others, in their sorrows, the consolation that we have received from God ourselves. Indeed, as the sufferings of Christ overflow to us, so, through Christ, does our consolation overflow. When we are made to suffer, it is for your consolation and salvation. When, instead, we are comforted, this should be a consolation to you, supporting you in patiently bearing the same sufferings as we bear. And our hope for you is confident, since we know that, sharing our sufferings, you will also share our consolations.

This is the word of the Lord.

Responsorial Psalm   Ps 33:2-9. ℟ v.9

℟   Taste and see the goodness of the Lord.

1   I will bless the Lord at all times,
    his praise always on my lips;
    in the Lord my soul shall make its boast.
    The humble shall hear and be glad.   ℟

2   Glorify the Lord with me.
    Together let us praise his name.
    I sought the Lord and he answered me;
    from all my terrors he set me free.   ℟

3   Look towards him and be radiant;
    let your faces not be abashed.
    This poor man called; the Lord heard him
    and rescued him from all his distress.   ℟

4   The angel of the Lord is encamped
    around those who revere him, to rescue them.
    Taste and see that the Lord is good.
    He is happy who seeks refuge in him.   ℟

Gospel Acclamation   Mt 5:12

    Alleluia, alleluia!
    Rejoice and be glad;
    your reward will be great in heaven.
    Alleluia!

GOSPEL

A reading from the holy Gospel according to Matthew   5:1-12

Happy are the poor in spirit.

Seeing the crowds, Jesus went up the hill. There he sat down and was
joined by his disciples. Then he began to speak. This is what he taught
them:

    'How happy are the poor in spirit;
    theirs is the kingdom of heaven.
    Happy the gentle:

they shall have the earth for their heritage.
Happy those who mourn:
they shall be comforted.
Happy those who hunger and thirst for what is right:
they shall be satisfied.
Happy the merciful:
they shall have mercy shown them.
Happy the pure in heart:
they shall see God.
Happy the peacemakers:
they shall be called sons of God.
Happy those who are persecuted in the cause of right:
theirs is the kingdom of heaven.

'Happy are you when people abuse you and persecute you and speak all kinds of calumny against you on my account. Rejoice and be glad, for your reward will be great in heaven; this is how they persecuted the prophets before you.'

This is the Gospel of the Lord.

Tuesday

FIRST READING

A reading from the second letter of St Paul   1:18-22
to the Corinthians

The Son of God, Jesus Christ, was not yes and no, in him it is always yes.

I swear by God's truth, there is no Yes and No about what we say to you. The Son of God, the Christ Jesus that we proclaimed among you – I mean Silvanus and Timothy and I – was never Yes and No: with him it was always Yes, and however many the promises God made, the Yes to them all is in him. That is why it is 'through him' that we answer Amen to the praise of God. Remember it is God himself who assures us all, and you, of our standing in Christ, and has anointed us, marking us with his seal and giving us the pledge, the Spirit, that we carry in our hearts.

This is the word of the Lord.

Responsorial Psalm   Ps 118:129-133. 135. ℟ v.135

℟   Lord, let your face shine on me.

1   Your will is wonderful indeed;
    therefore I obey it.
    The unfolding of your word gives light
    and teaches the simple.   ℟

2   I open my mouth and I sigh
    as I yearn for your commands.
    Turn and show me your mercy;
    show justice to your friends.   ℟

3   Let my steps be guided by your promise;
    let no evil rule me.
    Let your face shine on your servant
    and teach me your decrees.   ℟

Gospel Acclamation   Mt 5:16

    Alleluia, alleluia!
    Let your light shine before all,
    that they may see your good works and glorify your Father.
    Alleluia!

GOSPEL

A reading from the holy Gospel according to Matthew   5:13-16

You are the light of the world.

Jesus said to his disciples: 'You are the salt of the earth. But if salt
becomes tasteless, what can make it salty again? It is good for
nothing, and can only be thrown out to be trampled underfoot by men.

'You are the light of the world. A city built on a hill-top cannot be
hidden. No one lights a lamp to put it under a tub; they put it on the
lamp-stand where it shines for everyone in the house. In the same way
your light must shine in the sight of men, so that, seeing your good
works, they may give the praise to your Father in heaven.'

This is the Gospel of the Lord.

Wednesday

FIRST READING

A reading from the second letter of St Paul
to the Corinthians   3:4-11

*He made us ministers of the new covenant, a covenant of spirit not
of letters.*

Before God, we are confident of this through Christ: not that we are
qualified in ourselves to claim anything as our own work: all our
qualifications come from God. He is the one who has given us the
qualifications to be the administrators of this new covenant, which is
not a covenant of written letters but of the Spirit: the written letters
bring death, but the Spirit gives life. Now if the administering of
death, in the written letters engraved on stones, was accompanied by
such a brightness that the Israelites could not bear looking at the face
of Moses, though it was a brightness that faded, then how much
greater will be the brightness that surrounds the administering of the
Spirit! For if there was any splendour in administering condemnation,
there must be very much greater splendour in administering justification. In fact, compared with this greater splendour, the thing that
used to have such splendour now seems to have none; and if what was
so temporary had any splendour, there must be much more in what is
going to last for ever.

This is the word of the Lord.

Responsorial Psalm   Ps 98:5-9. ℟ v.9

℟   Holy is the Lord our God.

1   Exalt the Lord our God;
    bow down before Zion, his footstool.
    He the Lord is holy. ℟

2   Among his priests were Aaron and Moses,
    among those who invoked his name was Samuel.
    They invoked the Lord and he answered. ℟

3   To them he spoke in the pillar of cloud.
    They did his will; they kept the law,
    which he, the Lord, had given. ℟

4   O Lord our God, you answered them.
    For them you were a God who forgives;
    yet you punished all their offences. ℟

5   Exalt the Lord our God;
    bow down before his holy mountain
    for the Lord our God is holy. ℟

Gospel Acclamation   Ps 24:4. 5

    Alleluia, alleluia!
    Teach me your paths, my God,
    and lead me in your truth.
    Alleluia!

GOSPEL

A reading from the holy Gospel according to Matthew   5:17-19

I have come not to abolish the law, but to complete it.

Jesus said to his disciples: 'Do not imagine that I have come to abolish the Law or the Prophets. I have come not to abolish but to complete them. I tell you solemnly, till heaven and earth disappear, not one dot, not one little stroke, shall disappear from the Law until its purpose is achieved. Therefore, the man who infringes even one of the least of these commandments and teaches others to do the same will be considered the least in the kingdom of heaven; but the man who keeps them and teaches them will be considered great in the kingdom of heaven.'

    This is the Gospel of the Lord.

Thursday

FIRST READING

A reading from the second letter of St Paul   3:15–4:1. 3-6
to the Corinthians

God has shone in our minds to radiate the light of God's glory.

Even today, whenever Moses is read, the veil is over the minds of the
Israelites. It will not be removed until they turn to the Lord. Now this
Lord is the Spirit, and where the Spirit of the Lord is, there is freedom.
And we, with our unveiled faces reflecting like mirrors the brightness
of the Lord, all grow brighter and brighter as we are turned into the
image that we reflect; this is the work of the Lord who is Spirit.

Since we have by an act of mercy been entrusted with this work of
administration, there is no weakening on our part. If our gospel does
not penetrate the veil, then the veil is on those who are not on the way
to salvation; the unbelievers whose minds the god of this world has
blinded, to stop them seeing the light shed by the Good News of the
glory of Christ, who is the image of God. For it is not ourselves that we
are preaching, but Christ Jesus as the Lord, and ourselves as your
servants for Jesus' sake. It is the same God that said, 'Let there be
light shining out of darkness,' who has shone in our minds to radiate
the light of the knowledge of God's glory, the glory on the face of
Christ.

This is the word of the Lord.

Responsorial Psalm   Ps 84:9-14. ℟ cf. v.10

℟ The glory of the Lord will dwell in our land.

1 I will hear what the Lord God has to say,
   a voice that speaks of peace.
   His help is near for those who fear him
   and his glory will dwell in our land.   ℟

2 Mercy and faithfulness have met,
   justice and peace have embraced.
   Faithfulness shall spring from the earth
   and justice look down from heaven.   ℟

3   The Lord will make us prosper
    and our earth shall yield its fruit.
    Justice shall march before him
    and peace shall follow his steps.   ℟

Gospel Acclamation   Jn 13:34

Alleluia, alleluia!
I give you a new commandment:
love one another as I have loved you.
Alleluia!

GOSPEL

A reading from the holy Gospel according to Matthew   5:20-26

Whoever is angry with his brother or sister will be judged for it.

Jesus said to his disciples: 'If your virtue goes no deeper than that of
the scribes and Pharisees, you will never get into the kingdom of
heaven.

'You have learnt how it was said to our ancestors: You must not
kill; and if anyone does kill he must answer for it before the court. But
I say this to you: anyone who is angry with his brother will answer for
it before the court; if a man calls his brother "Fool" he will answer for
it before the Sanhedrin; and if a man calls him "Renegade" he will
answer for it in hell fire. So then, if you are bringing your offering to
the altar and there remember that your brother has something
against you, leave your offering there before the altar, go and be
reconciled with your brother first, and then come back and present
your offering. Come to terms with your opponent in good time while
you are still on the way to the court with him, or he may hand you
over to the judge and the judge to the officer, and you will be thrown
into prison. I tell you solemnly, you will not get out till you have paid
the last penny.'

This is the Gospel of the Lord.

Friday

FIRST READING

A reading from the second letter of St Paul
to the Corinthians   4:7-15

He who raised the Lord Jesus to life will raise us with him in our turn.

We are only the earthenware jars that hold this treasure, to make it
clear that such an overwhelming power comes from God and not from
us. We are in difficulties on all sides, but never cornered; we see no
answer to our problems, but never despair; we have been persecuted,
but never deserted; knocked down, but never killed; always, wherever
we may be, we carry with us in our body the death of Jesus, so that the
life of Jesus, too, may always be seen in our body. Indeed, while we are
still alive, we are consigned to our death every day, for the sake of
Jesus, so that in our mortal flesh the life of Jesus, too, may be openly
shown. So death is at work in us, but life in you.

But as we have the same spirit of faith that is mentioned in
scripture – I believed, and therefore I spoke – we too believe and
therefore we too speak, knowing that he who raised the Lord Jesus to
life will raise us with Jesus in our turn, and put us by his side and you
with us. You see, all this is for your benefit, so that the more grace is
multiplied among people, the more thanksgiving there will be to the
glory of God.

This is the word of the Lord.

Responsorial Psalm   Ps 115:10-11. 15-18. ℟ v.17

℟   To you, Lord, I will offer a sacrifice of praise.

or

℟   Alleluia!

1   I trusted, even when I said:
    'I am sorely afflicted,'
    and when I said in my alarm:
    'No man can be trusted.'   ℟

2   O precious in the eyes of the Lord
    is the death of his faithful.
    Your servant, Lord, your servant am I;
    you have loosened my bonds.   ℟

3   A thanksgiving sacrifice I make:
     I will call on the Lord's name.
     My vows to the Lord I will fulfil
     before all his people. ℞

Gospel Acclamation   Phil 2:15.16

    Alleluia, alleluia!
    Shine on the world like bright stars;
    you are offering it the word of life.
    Alleluia!

GOSPEL

A reading from the holy Gospel according to Matthew   5:27-32

If a man looks at a woman lustfully, he has already sinned.

Jesus said to his disciples: 'You have learnt how it was said: You must not commit adultery. But I say this to you: if a man looks at a woman lustfully, he has already committed adultery with her in his heart. If your right eye should cause you to sin, tear it out and throw it away; for it will do you less harm to lose one part of you than to have your whole body thrown into hell. And if your right hand should cause you to sin, cut it off and throw it away; for it will do you less harm to lose one part of you than to have your whole body go to hell.

'It has also been said: Anyone who divorces his wife must give her a writ of dismissal. But I say this to you: everyone who divorces his wife, except for the case of fornication, makes her an adulteress; and anyone who marries a divorced woman commits adultery.'

    This is the Gospel of the Lord.

Saturday

FIRST READING

A reading from the second letter of St Paul
to the Corinthians

For our sake God made the sinless one into sin.

The love of Christ overwhelms us when we reflect that if one man has died for all, then all men should be dead; and the reason he died for all was so that living men should live no longer for themselves but for him who died and was raised to life for them.

From now onwards, therefore, we do not judge anyone by the standards of the flesh. Even if we did once know Christ in the flesh, that is not how we know him now. And for anyone who is in Christ, there is a new creation; the old creation has gone, and now the new one is here. It is all God's work. It was God who reconciled us to himself through Christ and gave us the work of handing on this reconciliation. In other words, God in Christ was reconciling the world to himself, not holding men's faults against them, and he has entrusted to us the news that they are reconciled. So we are ambassadors for Christ; it is as though God were appealing through us, and the appeal that we make in Christ's name is: be reconciled to God. For our sake God made the sinless one into sin, so that in him we might become the goodness of God.

This is the word of the Lord.

Responsorial Psalm   Ps 102:1-4. 8-9. 11-12. ℟ v.8

℟   The Lord is kind and merciful

1   My soul, give thanks to the Lord,
     all my being, bless his holy name.
     My soul, give thanks to the Lord
     and never forget all his blessings.   ℟

2   It is he who forgives all your guilt,
     who heals every one of your ills,
     who redeems your life from the grave,
     who crowns you with love and compassion.   ℟

3   The Lord is compassion and love,
     slow to anger and rich in mercy.

His wrath will come to an end;
he will not be angry for ever.   ℞

4   For as the heavens are high above the earth
so strong is his love for those who fear him.
As far as the east is from the west
so far does he remove our sins.   ℞

Gospel Acclamation   Ps 118:36. 29

Alleluia, alleluia!
Turn my heart to do your will;
teach me your law, O God.
Alleluia!

GOSPEL

A reading from the holy Gospel according to Matthew   5:33-37

I say to you: do not swear at all.

Jesus said to his disciples: 'You have learnt how it was said to our ancestors: You must not break your oath, but must fulfil your oaths to the Lord. But I say this to you: do not swear at all, either by heaven, since that is God's throne; or by the earth, since that is his footstool; or by Jerusalem, since that is the city of the great king. Do not swear by your own head either, since you cannot turn a single hair white or black. All you need say is "Yes" if you mean yes, "No" if you mean no; anything more than this comes from the evil one.'

This is the Gospel of the Lord.

ELEVENTH WEEK IN ORDINARY TIME

Year I

Monday

FIRST READING

A reading from the second letter of St Paul
to the Corinthians   6:1-10

Let us show that we are the servants of God.

As God's fellow workers, we beg you once again not to neglect the
grace of God that you have received. For he says: At the favourable
time, I have listened to you; on the day of salvation I came to your
help. Well, now is the favourable time; this is the day of salvation.

We do nothing that people might object to, so as not to bring
discredit on our function as God's servants. Instead, we prove we are
servants of God by great fortitude in times of suffering: in times of
hardship and distress; when we are flogged, or sent to prison, or
mobbed; labouring, sleepless, starving. We prove we are God's servants by our purity, knowledge, patience and kindness; by a spirit of
holiness, by a love free from affectation; by the word of truth and by
the power of God; by being armed with the weapons of righteousness
in the right hand and in the left, prepared for honour or disgrace, for
blame or praise; taken for impostors while we are genuine; obscure
yet famous; said to be dying and here are we alive; rumoured to be
executed before we are sentenced; thought most miserable and yet we
are always rejoicing; taken for paupers though we make others rich,
for people having nothing though we have everything.

This is the word of the Lord.

Responsorial Psalm   Ps 97:1-4. ℟ v.2

℟   The Lord has made known his salvation.

1   Sing a new song to the Lord
     for he has worked wonders.
     His right hand and his holy arm
     have brought salvation.   ℟

2   The Lord has made known his salvation;
has shown his justice to the nations.
He has remembered his truth and love
for the house of Israel. ℟

3   All the ends of the earth have seen
the salvation of our God.
Shout to the Lord all the earth,
ring out your joy. ℟

Gospel Acclamation   Ps 118:105

Alleluia, alleluia!
Your word is a lamp for my feet
and a light on my path.
Alleluia!

GOSPEL

A reading from the holy Gospel according to Matthew   5:38-42

I say to you, offer the wicked no resistance.

Jesus said to his disciples: 'You have learnt how it was said: Eye for eye and tooth for tooth. But I say this to you: offer the wicked man no resistance. On the contrary, if anyone hits you on the right cheek, offer him the other as well; if a man takes you to law and would have your tunic, let him have your cloak as well. And if anyone orders you to go one mile, go two miles with him. Give to anyone who asks, and if anyone wants to borrow, do not turn away.'

This is the Gospel of the Lord.

Tuesday

FIRST READING

A reading from the second letter of St Paul
to the Corinthians

8:1-9

Christ became poor for our sake.

Here, brothers, is the news of the grace of God which was given in the
churches in Macedonia; and of how, throughout great trials by
suffering, their constant cheerfulness and their intense poverty have
overflowed in a wealth of generosity. I can swear that they gave not
only as much as they could afford, but far more, and quite spon-
taneously, begging and begging us for the favour of sharing in this
service to the saints and, what was quite unexpected, they offered
their own selves first to God and, under God, to us.

Because of this, we have asked Titus, since he has already made a
beginning, to bring this work of mercy to the same point of success
among you. You always have the most of everything – of faith, of
eloquence, of understanding, of keenness for any cause, and the
biggest share of our affection – so we expect you to put the most into
this work of mercy too. It is not an order that I am giving you ; I am
just testing the genuineness of your love against the keenness of
others. Remember how generous the Lord Jesus was: he was rich, but
he became poor for your sake, to make you rich out of his poverty.

This is the word of the Lord.

Responsorial Psalm

Ps 145:2. 5-9. ℟ v.2

℟   Praise the Lord, my soul!

or

℟   Alleluia!

1   I will praise the Lord all my days,
     make music to my God while I live.   ℟

2   He is happy who is helped by Jacob's God,
     whose hope is in the Lord his God,
     who alone made heaven and earth,
     the seas and all they contain.   ℟

3 It is he who keeps faith for ever,
  who is just to those who are oppressed.
  It is he who gives bread to the hungry,
  the Lord, who sets prisoners free. ℟

4 It is the Lord who gives sight to the blind,
  who raises up those who are bowed down,
  the Lord, who protects the stranger
  and upholds the widow and orphan. ℟

Gospel Acclamation   Jn 13:34

Alleluia, alleluia!
I give you a new commandment:
love one another as I have loved you.
Alleluia!

GOSPEL

A reading from the holy Gospel according to Matthew   5:43-48

Love your enemies.

Jesus said to his disciples: 'You have learnt how it was said: You must love your neighbour and hate your enemy. But I say to you: love your enemies and pray for those who persecute you; in this way you will be sons of your Father in heaven, for he causes his sun to rise on bad men as well as good, and his rain to fall on honest and dishonest men alike. For if you love those who love you, what right have you to claim any credit? Even the tax collectors do as much, do they not? And if you save your greetings for your brothers, are you doing anything exceptional? Even the pagans do as much, do they not? You must therefore be perfect just as your heavenly Father is perfect.'

This is the Gospel of the Lord.

Wednesday

FIRST READING

A reading from the second letter of St Paul 9:6-11
to the Corinthians

God loves a cheerful giver.

Do not forget: thin sowing means thin reaping; the more you sow, the more you reap. Each one should give what he has decided in his own mind, not grudgingly or because he is made to, for God loves a cheerful giver. And there is no limit to the blessings which God can send you – he will make sure that you will always have all you need for yourselves in every possible circumstance, and still have something to spare for all sorts of good works. As scripture says: He was free in almsgiving, and gave to the poor: his good deeds will never be forgotten.

The one who provides seed for the sower and bread for food will provide you with all the seed you want and make the harvest of your good deeds a larger one, and, made richer in every way, you will be able to do all the generous things which, through us, are the cause of thanksgiving to God.

This is the word of the Lord.

Responsorial Psalm   Ps 111:1-4. 9. ℟ v.1

℟   Happy are those who fear the Lord.

or

℟   Alleluia!

1   Happy the man who fears the Lord,
    who takes delight in his commands.
    His sons will be powerful on earth;
    the children of the upright are blessed.   ℟

2   Riches and wealth are in his house;
    his justice stands firm for ever.
    He is a light in the darkness for the upright:
    he is generous, merciful and just.   ℟

3   Open-handed, he gives to the poor;
    his justice stands firm for ever.
    His head will be raised in glory.   ℟

Gospel Acclamation   Jn 14:23

> Alleluia, alleluia!
> All who love me will keep my words,
> and my Father will love them, and we will come to them.
> Alleluia!

GOSPEL

A reading from the holy Gospel according   6:1-6. 16-18
to Matthew

Your Father who sees all that is done in secret will reward you.

Jesus said to his disciples: 'Be careful not to parade your good deeds before men to attract their notice; by doing this you will lose all reward from your Father in heaven. So when you give alms, do not have it trumpeted before you ; that is what the hypocrites do in the synagogues and in the streets to win men's admiration. I tell you solemnly, they have had their reward. But when you give alms, your left hand must not know what your right is doing; your almsgiving must be secret, and your Father who sees all that is done in secret will reward you.

'And when you pray, do not imitate the hypocrites: they love to say their prayers standing up in the synagogues and at the street corners for people to see them. I tell you solemnly, they have had their reward. But when you pray, go to your private room and, when you have shut your door, pray to your Father who is in that secret place, and your Father who sees all that is done in secret will reward you.

'When you fast do not put on a gloomy look as the hypocrites do: they pull long faces to let men know they are fasting. I tell you solemnly, they have had their reward. But when you fast, put oil on your head and wash your face, so that no one will know you are fasting except your Father who sees all that is done in secret; and your Father who sees all that is done in secret will reward you.'

This is the Gospel of the Lord.

Thursday

FIRST READING

A reading from the second letter of St Paul
to the Corinthians

11:1-11

I preached the gospel of God to you freely.

I only wish you were able to tolerate a little foolishness from me. But of course: you are tolerant towards me. You see, the jealousy that I feel for you is God's own jealousy: I arranged for you to marry Christ so that I might give you away as a chaste virgin to this one husband. But the serpent, with his cunning, seduced Eve, and I am afraid that in the same way your ideas may get corrupted and turned away from simple devotion to Christ. Because any newcomer has only to proclaim a new Jesus, different from the one that we preached, or you have only to receive a new spirit, different from the one you have already received, or a new gospel, different from the one you have already accepted – and you welcome it with open arms. As far as I can tell, these arch-apostles have nothing more than I have. I may not be a polished speechmaker, but as for knowledge, that is a different matter; surely we have made this plain, speaking on every subject in front of all of you.

Or was I wrong, lowering myself so as to lift you high, by preaching the gospel of God to you and taking no fee for it? I was robbing other churches, living on them so that I could serve you. When I was with you and ran out of money, I was no burden to anyone; the brothers who came from Macedonia provided me with everything I wanted. I was very careful, and I always shall be, not to be a burden to you in any way, and by Christ's truth in me, this cause of boasting will never be taken from me in the regions of Achaia. Would I do that if I did not love you? God knows I do.

This is the word of the Lord.

Responsorial Psalm

Ps 110:1-4. 7-8. ℟ v.7

℟   Your works, O Lord, are justice and truth.

or

℟   Alleluia!

1   I will thank the Lord with all my heart
    in the meeting of the just and their assembly.

Great are the works of the Lord;
to be pondered by all who love them. ℟

2 Majestic and glorious his work,
his justice stands firm for ever.
He makes us remember his wonders.
The Lord is compassion and love. ℟

3 His works are justice and truth:
his precepts are all of them sure,
standing firm for ever and ever:
they are made in uprightness and truth. ℟

Gospel Acclamation   Rom 8:15

Alleluia, alleluia!
You have received the Spirit which makes us God's children,
and in that Spirit we call God our Father.
Alleluia!

GOSPEL

A reading from the holy Gospel according to Matthew   6:7-15

You should pray like this: Our Father . . .

Jesus said to his disciples: 'In your prayers do not babble as the
pagans do, for they think that by using many words they will make
themselves heard. Do not be like them; your Father knows what you
need before you ask him. So you should pray like this:

Our Father in heaven,
may your name be held holy,
your kingdom come,
your will be done,
on earth as in heaven.
Give us today our daily bread.
as we have forgiven those who are in debt to us.
And do not put us to the test,
but save us from the evil one.

'Yes, if you forgive others their failings, your heavenly Father will
forgive you yours; but if you do not forgive others, your Father will not
forgive your failings either.'

This is the Gospel of the Lord.

Friday

FIRST READING

A reading from the second letter of St Paul to the Corinthians 11:18. 21-30

Besides all the other important things, there is my daily preoccupation, my anxiety for all the churches.

So many others have been boasting of their worldly achievements, that I will boast myself. But if anyone wants some brazen speaking – I am still talking as a fool – then I can be as brazen as any of them, and about the same things. Hebrews, are they? So am I. Israelites? So am I. Descendants of Abraham? So am I. The servants of Christ? I must be mad to say this, but so am I, and more than they: more, because I have worked harder, I have been sent to prison more often, and whipped so many times more, often almost to death. Five times I had the thirty-nine lashes from the Jews; three times I have been beaten with sticks; once I was stoned; three times I have been shipwrecked and once adrift in the open sea for a night and a day. Constantly travelling, I have been in danger from rivers and in danger from brigands, in danger from my own people and in danger from pagans; in danger in the towns, in danger in the open country, danger at sea and danger from so-called brothers. I have worked and laboured, often without sleep; I have been hungry and thirsty and often starving; I have been in the cold without clothes. And, to leave out much more, there is my daily preoccupation: my anxiety for all the churches. When any man has had scruples, I have had scruples with him; when any man is made to fall, I am tortured.

If I am to boast, then let me boast of my own feebleness.

This is the word of the Lord.

Responsorial Psalm   Ps 33:2-7. ℟ cf. v.18

℟   From all their afflictions God will deliver the just.

1   I will bless the Lord at all times,
      his praise always on my lips;
      in the Lord my soul shall make its boast.
      The humble shall hear and be glad.   ℟

2 Glorify the Lord with me.
  Together let us praise his name.
  I sought the Lord and he answered me;
  from all my terrors he set me free. ℟

3 Look towards him and be radiant;
  let your faces not be abashed.
  This poor man called; the Lord heard him
  and rescued him from all his distress. ℟

Gospel Acclamation   Mt 5:3

Alleluia, alleluia!
Happy the poor in spirit;
the kingdom of heaven is theirs!
Alleluia!

GOSPEL

A reading from the holy Gospel according to Matthew   6:19-23

Where your treasure is, there will your heart be also.

Jesus said to his disciples: 'Do not store up treasures for yourselves on earth, where moths and woodworms destroy them and thieves can break in and steal. But store up treasures for yourselves in heaven, where neither moth or woodworms destroy them and thieves cannot break in and steal. For where your treasure is, there will your heart be also.

'The lamp of the body is the eye. It follows that if your eye is sound, your whole body will be filled with light. But if your eye is diseased, your whole body will be all darkness. If then, the light inside you is darkness, what darkness that will be!'

This is the Gospel of the Lord.

Saturday

FIRST READING

A reading from the second letter of St Paul to the Corinthians   12:1-10

Gladly will I boast of my weaknesses.

Must I go on boasting, though there is nothing to be gained by it? But I will move on to the visions and revelations I have had from the Lord. I know a man in Christ who, fourteen years ago, was caught up – whether still in the body or out of the body, I do not know; God knows – right into the third heaven. I do know, however, that this same person – whether in the body or out of the body, I do not know; God knows – was caught up into paradise and heard things which must not and cannot be put into human language. I will boast about a man like that, but not about anything of my own except my weaknesses. If I should decide to boast, I should not be made to look foolish, because I should only be speaking the truth; but I am not going to, in case anyone should begin to think I am better than he can actually see and hear me to be.

In view of the extraordinary nature of these revelations, to stop me from getting too proud I was given a thorn in the flesh, an angel of Satan to beat me and stop me from getting too proud! About this thing, I have pleaded with the Lord three times for it to leave me, but he has said, 'My grace is enough for you: my power is at its best in weakness.' So I shall be very happy to make my weaknesses my special boast so that the power of Christ may stay over me, and that is why I am quite content with my weaknesses, and with insults, hardships, persecutions, and the agonies I go through for Christ's sake. For it is when I am weak that I am strong.

This is the word of the Lord.

Responsorial Psalm   Ps 33:8-13. ℟ v.9

℟   Taste and see the goodness of the Lord.

1   The angel of the Lord is encamped
     around those who revere him, to rescue them.
     Taste and see that the Lord is good.
     He is happy who seeks refuge in him.   ℟

2   Revere the Lord, you his saints.
     They lack nothing, those who revere him.

Strong lions suffer want and go hungry
but those who seek the Lord lack no blessing. ℟

3 Come, children, and hear me
that I may teach you the fear of the Lord.
Who is he who longs for life
and many days, to enjoy his prosperity? ℟

Gospel Acclamation   2 Cor 8:9

Alleluia, alleluia!
Jesus Christ was rich but he became poor,
to make you rich out of his poverty.
Alleluia!

GOSPEL

A reading from the holy Gospel according to Matthew   6:24-34

Do not worry about tomorrow.

Jesus said to his disciples: 'No one can be the slave of two masters: he
will either hate the first and love the second, or treat the first with
respect and the second with scorn. You cannot be the slave both of God
and money.

'That is why I am telling you not to worry about your life and what
you are to eat, nor about your body and how you are to clothe it.
Surely life means more than food, and the body more than clothing!
Look at the birds in the sky. They do not sow or reap or gather into
barns; yet your heavenly Father feeds them. Are you not worth much
more than they are? Can any of you, for all his worrying, add one
single cubit to his span of life? And why worry about clothing? Think
of the flowers growing in the fields; they never have to work or spin;
yet I assure you that not even Solomon in all his regalia was robed
like one of these. Now if that is how God clothes the grass in the field
which is there today and thrown into the furnace tomorrow, will he
not much more look after you, you men of little faith? So do not worry;
do not say, 'What are we to eat? What are we to drink? How are we to
be clothed?' It is the pagans who set their hearts on all these things.
Your heavenly Father knows you need them all. Set your hearts on
his kingdom first, and on his righteousness, and all these other things
will be given you as well. So do not worry about tomorrow: tomorrow
will take care of itself. Each day has enough trouble of its own.'

This is the Gospel of the Lord.

TWELFTH WEEK IN ORDINARY TIME

Year I

Monday

FIRST READING

A reading from the book of Genesis   12:1-9

Abraham went out as God had told him.

The Lord said to Abram, 'Leave your country, your family and your
father's house, for the land I will show you. I will make you a great
nation; I will bless you and make your name so famous that it will be
used as a blessing.

'I will bless those who bless you:
I will curse those who slight you.
All the tribes of the earth
shall bless themselves by you.'

So Abram went as the Lord told him, and Lot went with him. Abram
was seventy-five years old when he left Haran. Abram took his wife
Sarai, his nephew Lot, all the possessions they had amassed and the
people they had acquired in Haran. They set off for the land of
Canaan, and arrived there.

Abram passed through the land as far as Shechem's holy place, the
Oak of Moreh. At that time the Canaanites were in the land. The Lord
appeared to Abram and said, 'It is to your descendants that I will give
this land.' So Abram built there an altar for the Lord who had
appeared to him. From there he moved on to the mountainous district
east of Bethel, where he pitched his tent, with Bethel to the west and
Ai to the east. There he built an altar to the Lord and invoked the
name of the Lord. Then Abram made his way stage by stage to the
Negeb.

This is the word of the Lord.

Responsorial Psalm   Ps 32:12-13. 18-20. 22. ℟ v.12

℟ Happy the people the Lord has chosen to be his own.

1 They are happy, whose God is the Lord,
   the people he has chosen as his own.
   From the heavens the Lord looks forth,
   he sees all the children of men.   ℟

2 The Lord looks on those who revere him,
   on those who hope in his love,
   to rescue their souls from death,
   to keep them alive in famine.   ℟

3 Our soul is waiting for the Lord.
   The Lord is our help and our shield.
   May your love be upon us, O Lord,
   as we place all our hope in you.   ℟

Gospel Acclamation   Heb 4:12

Alleluia, alleluia!
The word of God is living and active;
it probes the thoughts and motives of our heart.
Alleluia!

GOSPEL

A reading from the holy Gospel according to Matthew   7:1-5

Take the beam out of your own eye first.

Jesus said to his disciples: 'Do not judge, and you will not be judged;
because the judgements you give are the judgements you will get, and
the amount you measure out is the amount you will be given. Why do
you observe the splinter in your brother's eye and never notice the
plank in your own? How dare you say to your brother, "Let me take
the splinter out of your eye", when all the time there is a plank in your
own? Hypocrite! Take the plank out of your own eye first, and then
you will see clearly enough to take the splinter out of your brother's
eye.'

This is the Gospel of the Lord.

Tuesday

FIRST READING

A reading from the book of Genesis 13:2. 5-18

Let there be no dispute between me and you, for we are brothers.

Abram was a very rich man, with livestock, silver and gold. Lot, who was travelling with Abram, had flocks and cattle of his own, and tents too. The land was not sufficient to accommodate them both at once, for they had too many possessions to be able to live together. Dispute broke out between the herdsmen of Abram's livestock and those of Lot's. (The Canaanites and the Perizzites were then living in the land.) Accordingly Abram said to Lot, 'Let there be no dispute between me and you, nor between my herdsmen and yours, for we are brothers. Is not the whole land open before you? Part company with me: if you take the left, I will go right; if you take the right, I will go left.'

Looking round, Lot saw all the Jordan plain, irrigated everywhere – this was before the Lord destroyed Sodom and Gomorrah – like the garden of the Lord or the land of Egypt, as far as Zoar. So Lot chose all the Jordan plain for himself and moved off eastwards. Thus they parted company: Abram settled in the land of Canaan; Lot settled among the towns of the plain, pitching his tents on the outskirts of Sodom. Now the people of Sodom were vicious men, great sinners against the Lord.

The Lord said to Abram after Lot had parted company with him, 'Look all round from where you are towards the north and the south, towards the east and the west. All the land within sight I will give to you and your descendants for ever. I will make your descendants like the dust on the ground: when men succeed in counting the specks of dust on the ground, then they will be able to count your descendants! Come, travel through the length and breadth of the land, for I mean to give it to you.'

So Abram went with his tents to settle at the Oak of Mamre, at Hebron, and there he built an altar to the Lord.

This is the word of the Lord.

Responsial Psalm

Ps 14:2-5. ℟ v.1

℟ The just will live in the presence of the Lord.

1 Lord, who shall dwell on your holy mountain?
   He who walks without fault;
   he who acts with justice
   and speaks the truth from his heart;
   he who does not slander with his tongue. ℟

2 He who does no wrong to his brother,
   who casts no slur on his neighbour,
   who holds the godless in disdain,
   but honours those who fear the Lord. ℟

3 He who keeps his pledge, come what may;
   who takes no interest on a loan
   and accepts no bribes against the innocent.
   Such a man will stand firm for ever. ℟

Gospel Acclamation

Jn 8:12

Alleluia, alleluia!
I am the light of the world, says the Lord;
whoever follows me will have the light of life.
Alleluia!

GOSPEL

A reading from the holy Gospel according to Matthew   7: 6. 12-14

Always treat others as you would like them to treat you.

Jesus said to his disciples: 'Do not give dogs what is holy; and do not throw your pearls in front of pigs, or they may trample them and then turn on you and tear you to pieces.

'So always treat others as you would like them to treat you; that is the meaning of the Law and the Prophets.

'Enter by the narrow gate, since the road that leads to perdition is wide and spacious, and many take it; but it is a narrow gate and a hard road that leads to life, and only a few find it.'

This is the Gospel of the Lord.

Wednesday

FIRST READING

A reading from the book of Genesis   15:1-12. 17-18

*Abraham put his faith in the Lord God, who counted this as
making him justified, and the Lord made a covenant with him.*

It happened that the word of the Lord was spoken to Abram in a
vision, 'Have no fear, Abram, I am your shield; your reward will be
very great.'

'My Lord,' Abram replied 'what do you intend to give me? I go
childless ... ' Then Abram said, 'See, you have given me no descendants; some man of my household will be my heir.' And then this word
of the Lord was spoken to him, 'He shall not be your heir; your heir
shall be of your own flesh and blood.' Then taking him outside he said,
'Look up to heaven and count the stars if you can. Such will be your
descendants' he told him. Abram put his faith in the Lord, who
counted this as making him justified.

'I am the Lord' he said to him 'who brought you out of Ur of the
Chaldaeans to make you heir to this land.' 'My Lord,' Abram replied
'how am I to know that I shall inherit it?' He said to him, 'Get me a
three-year-old heifer, a three-year-old goat, a three-year-old ram, a
turtledove and a young pigeon.' He brought him all these, cut them in
half and put half on one side and half facing it on the other; but the
birds he did not cut in half. Birds of prey came down on the carcasses
but Abram drove them off.

Now as the sun was setting Abram fell into a deep sleep, and terror
seized him. When the sun had set and darkness had fallen, there
appeared a smoking furnace and a firebrand that went between the
halves. That day the Lord made a Covenant with Abram in these
terms:

'To your descendants I give this land,
from the wadi of Egypt to the Great River,
the river Euphrates.'

This is the word of the Lord.

Responsorial Psalm   Ps 104:1-4. 6-9. ℟ v.8

℟   The Lord remembers his covenant for ever.

or

℟   Alleluia!

1   Give thanks to the Lord, tell his name,
     make known his deeds among the peoples.
     O sing to him, sing his praise;
     tell all his wonderful works! ℟

2   Be proud of his holy name,
     let the hearts that seek the Lord rejoice.
     Consider the Lord and his strength;
     constantly seek his face. ℟

3   O children of Abraham, his servant,
     O sons of the Jacob he chose.
     He, the Lord, is our God:
     his judgements prevail in all the earth. ℟

4   He remembers his covenant for ever,
     his promise for a thousand generations,
     the covenant he made with Abraham,
     the oath he swore to Isaac. ℟

Gospel Acclamation   Jn 15:4. 5

     Alleluia, alleluia!
     Live in me and let me live in you, says the Lord;
     my branches bear much fruit.
     Alleluia!

GOSPEL

A reading from the holy Gospel according to Matthew   7:15-20

By their fruits you will know them.

Jesus said to his disciples: 'Beware of false prophets who come to you
disguised as sheep but underneath are ravenous wolves. You will be
able to tell them by their fruits. Can people pick grapes from thorns,
or figs from thistles? In the same way, a sound tree produces good fruit
but a rotten tree bad fruit. A sound tree cannot bear bad fruit, nor a

rotten tree bear good fruit. Any tree that does not produce good fruit is cut down and thrown on the fire. I repeat, you will be able to tell them by their fruits.'

This is the Gospel of the Lord.

Thursday

FIRST READING

A reading from the book of Genesis 16:1-12. 15-16

Hagar bore Abraham a son and he called him Ishmael.

Abram's wife Sarai had borne him no child, but she had an Egyptian maidservant named Hagar. So Sarai said to Abram, 'Listen, now! Since the Lord has kept me from having children, go to my slave-girl. Perhaps I shall get children through her.' Abram agreed to what Sarai had said.

Thus after Abram had lived in the land of Canaan for ten years Sarai took Hagar her Egyptian slave-girl and gave her to Abram as his wife. He went to Hagar and she conceived. And once she knew she had conceived, her mistress counted for nothing in her eyes. Then Sarai said to Abram, 'May this insult to me come home to you! It was I who put my slave-girl into your arms but now she knows that she has conceived, I count for nothing in her eyes. Let the Lord judge between me and you.' 'Very well,' Abram said to Sarai, 'your slave-girl is at your disposal. Treat her as you think fit.' Sarai accordingly treated her so badly that she ran away from her.

The angel of the Lord met Hagar near a spring in the wilderness, the spring that is on the road to Shur. He said, 'Hagar, slave-girl of Sarai, where have you come from, and where are you going?' 'I am running away from my mistress Sarai' she replied. The angel of the Lord said to her, 'Go back to your mistress and submit to her.' The angel of the Lord said to her, 'I will make your descendants too numerous to be counted.' Then the angel of the Lord said to her:

'Now you have conceived, and you will bear a son,
and you shall name him Ishmael,
for the Lord has heard your cries of distress.
A wild-ass of a man he will be,
against every man, and every man against him,
setting himself to defy all his brothers.'

Hagar bore Abram a son, and Abram gave to the son that Hagar bore the name Ishmael. Abram was eighty-six years old when Hagar bore him Ishmael.

This is the word of the Lord.

Shorter form
A reading from the book of Genesis   16:6-12. 15-16

Hagar bore Abraham a son and he called him Ishmael.

Sarai treated Hagar so badly that she ran away from her. The angel of the Lord met her near a spring in the wilderness, the spring that is on the road to Shur. He said, 'Hagar, slave-girl of Sarai, where have you come from, and where are you going?' 'I am running away from my mistress Sarai' she replied. The angel of the Lord said to her, 'Go back to your mistress and submit to her.' The angel of the Lord said to her, 'I will make your descendants too numerous to be counted.' Then the angel of the Lord said to her:

'Now you have conceived, and you will bear a son,
and you shall name him Ishmael,
for the Lord has heard your cries of distress.
A wild-ass of a man he will be,
against every man, and every man against him,
setting himself to defy all his brothers.'

Hagar bore Abram a son, and Abram gave to the son that Hagar bore the name Ishmael. Abram was eighty-six years old when Hagar bore him Ishmael.

This is the word of the Lord.

Responsorial Psalm   Ps 105:1-5. ℟ v.1

℟   Give thanks to the Lord for he is good.

or

℟   Alleluia!

1   O give thanks to the Lord for he is good;
    for his great love is without end.
    Who can tell the Lord's mighty deeds?
    Who can recount all his praise?   ℟

2   They are happy who do what is right,
who at all times do what is just.
O Lord, remember me
out of the love you have for your people.

℟   Give thanks to the Lord for he is good.

3   Come to me, Lord, with your help
that I may see the joy of your chosen ones
and may rejoice in the gladness of your nation
and share the glory of your people.   ℟

Gospel Acclamation   Jn 14:23

Alleluia, alleluia!
All who love me will keep my words,
and my Father will love them and we will come to them.
Alleluia!

GOSPEL

A reading from the holy Gospel according to Matthew   7:21-29

The house built on rock is compared to the house built on sand.

Jesus said to his disciples: 'It is not those who say to me, "Lord, Lord,"
who will enter the kingdom of heaven, but the person who does the
will of my Father in heaven. When the day comes many will say to
me, "Lord, Lord, did we not prophesy in your name, cast out demons in
your name, work miracles in your name?" Then I shall tell them to
their faces: I have never known you; away from me, you evil men!

'Therefore, everyone who listens to these words of mine and acts on
them will be like a sensible man who built his house on rock. Rain
came down, floods rose, gales blew and hurled themselves against the
house, and it did not fall: it was founded on rock. But everyone who
listens to these words of mine and does not act on them will be like a
stupid man who built his house on sand. Rain came down, floods rose,
gales blew and struck that house, and it fell; and what a fall it had!'

Jesus had now finished what he wanted to say, and his teaching
made a deep impression on the people because he taught them with
authority, and not like their own scribes.

This is the Gospel of the Lord.

Friday

FIRST READING

A reading from the book of Genesis   17:1. 9-10. 15-22

All your males must be circumcised as a sign of my covenant. I will
give you a son by Sarah.

When Abram was ninety-nine years old the Lord appeared to him and said, 'I am El Shaddai. Bear yourself blameless in my presence.

'You shall maintain my Covenant, yourself and your descendants after you, generation after generation. Now this is my Covenant which you are to maintain between myself and you, and your descendants after you: all your males must be circumcised.

'As for Sarai your wife, you shall not call her Sarai, but Sarah. I will bless her and moreover give you a son by her. I will bless her and nations shall come out of her; kings of peoples shall descend from her.' Abraham bowed to the ground, and he laughed, thinking to himself, 'Is a child to be born to a man one hundred years old, and will Sarah have a child at the age of ninety?' Abraham said to God, 'Oh, let Ishmael live in your presence!' But God replied, 'No, but your wife Sarah shall bear you a son whom you are to name Isaac. With him I will establish my Covenant, a Covenant in perpetuity, to be his God and the God of his descendants after him. For Ishmael too I grant you your request: I bless him and I will make him fruitful and greatly increased in numbers. He shall be the father of twelve princes, and I will make him into a great nation. But my Covenant I will establish with Isaac, whom Sarah will bear you at this time next year.' When he had finished speaking to Abraham God went up from him.

This is the word of the Lord.

Responsorial Psalm   Ps 127:1-5. ℞ v.4

℞ See how the Lord blesses those who fear him.

1   O blessed are those who fear the Lord
     and walk in his ways!
     By the labour of your hands you shall eat.
     You will be happy and prosper.   ℞

2   Your wife like a fruitful vine
    in the heart of your house;
    your children like shoots of the olive,
    around your table.

℟   See how the Lord blesses those who fear him.

3   Indeed thus shall be blessed
    the man who fears the Lord.
    May the Lord bless you from Zion
    all the days of your life!   ℟

Gospel Acclamation   Mt 8:17

    Alleluia, alleluia!
    He bore our sicknesses,
    and endured our suffering.
    Alleluia!

GOSPEL

A reading from the holy Gospel according to Matthew   8:1-4

If you will, you can cure me.

After Jesus had come down from the mountain large crowds followed
him. A leper now came up and bowed low in front of him. 'Sir,' he said,
'if you want to, you can cure me.' Jesus stretched out his hand,
touched him and said, 'Of course I want to! Be cured!' And his leprosy
was cured at once. Then Jesus said to him, 'Mind you do not tell
anyone, but go and show yourself to the priest and make the offering
prescribed by Moses, as evidence for them.'

    This is the Gospel of the Lord.

Saturday

FIRST READING

A reading from the book of Genesis   18:1-15

Is anything too difficult for the Lord God? I will visit you again and
Sarah will have a son.

The Lord appeared to Abraham at the Oak of Mamre while he was sitting by the entrance of the tent during the hottest part of the day. He looked up, and there he saw three men standing near him. As soon as he saw them he ran from the entrance of the tent to meet them, and bowed to the ground. 'My lord,' he said 'I beg you, if I find favour with you, kindly do not pass your servant by. A little water shall be brought; you shall wash your feet and lie down under the tree. Let me fetch a little bread and you shall refresh yourselves before going further. That is why you have come in your servant's direction.' They replied, 'Do as you say.'

Abraham hastened to the tent to find Sarah. 'Hurry,' he said 'knead three bushels of flour and make loaves.' Then running to the cattle Abraham took a fine and tender calf and gave it to the servant, who hurried to prepare it. Then taking cream, milk and the calf he had prepared, he laid all before them, and they ate while he remained standing near them under the tree.

'Where is your wife Sarah?' they asked him. 'She is in the tent' he replied. Then his guest said, 'I shall visit you again next year without fail, and your wife will then have a son.' Sarah was listening at the entrance of the tent behind him. Now Abraham and Sarah were old, well on in years, and Sarah had ceased to have her monthly periods. So Sarah laughed to herself, thinking, 'Now that I am past the age of child-bearing, and my husband is an old man, is pleasure to come my way again!' But the Lord asked Abraham, 'Why did Sarah laugh and say, "Am I really going to have a child now that I am old?" Is anything too wonderful for the Lord? At the same time next year I shall visit you again and Sarah will have a son.' 'I did not laugh' Sarah said, lying because she was afraid. But he replied, 'Oh yes, you did laugh.'

This is the word of the Lord.

Responsorial Psalm   Lk 1:46-50. 53-55. ℟ cf. v.54

℟   The Lord has remembered his mercy.

1   My soul glorifies the Lord,
    my spirit rejoices in God my saviour.   ℟

2   He looks on his servant in her nothingness;
    henceforth all ages will call me blessed.
    The Almighty works marvels for me.
    Holy his name!   ℟

3   His mercy is from age to age,
    on those who fear him.
    He fills the starving with good things,
    sends the rich away empty.   ℟

4   He protects Israel, his servant,
    remembering his mercy,
    the mercy promised to our fathers,
    for Abraham and his sons for ever.   ℟

Gospel Acclamation   Mt 8:17

    Alleluia, alleluia!
    He bore our sicknesses,
    and endured our suffering.
    Alleluia!

GOSPEL

A reading from the holy Gospel according to Matthew   8:5-17

*Many will come from East and West and take their places
with Abraham, Isaac, and Jacob at the feast.*

When Jesus went into Capernaum a centurion came up and pleaded
with him. 'Sir,' he said 'my servant is lying at home paralysed, and in
great pain.' 'I will come myself and cure him' said Jesus. The
centurion replied, 'Sir, I am not worthy to have you under my roof;
just give the word and my servant will be cured. For I am under
authority myself, and have soldiers under me; and I say to one man:
Go, and he goes; to another: Come here, and he comes; to my servant:
Do this, and he does it.' When Jesus heard this he was astonished and
said to those following him, 'I tell you solemnly, nowhere in Israel

have I found faith like this. And I tell you that many will come from east and west to take their places with Abraham and Isaac and Jacob at the feast in the kingdom of heaven; but the subjects of the kingdom will be turned out into the dark, where there will be weeping and grinding of teeth.' And to the centurion Jesus said, 'Go back, then; you have believed, so let this be done for you.' And the servant was cured at that moment.

And going into Peter's house Jesus found Peter's mother-in-law in bed with fever. He touched her hand and the fever left her, and she got up and began to wait on him.

That evening they brought him many who were possessed by devils. He cast out the spirits with a word and cured all who were sick. This was to fulfil the prophecy of Isaiah:

He took our sicknesses away and carried our diseases for us.

This is the Gospel of the Lord.

THIRTEENTH WEEK IN ORDINARY TIME

Year I

Monday

FIRST READING

A reading from the book of Genesis   18:16-33

Are you going to destroy the just person with the sinner?

From Mamre the men set out and arrived within sight of Sodom, with Abraham accompanying them to show them the way. Now the Lord had wondered, 'Shall I conceal from Abraham what I am going to do, seeing that Abraham will become a great nation with all the nations of the earth blessing themselves by him? For I have singled him out to command his sons and his household after him to maintain the way of the Lord by just and upright living. In this way the Lord will carry out for Abraham what he has promised him.' Then the Lord said, 'How great an outcry there is against Sodom and Gomorrah! How grievous is their sin! I propose to go down and see whether or not they have done all that is alleged in the outcry against them that has come up to me. I am determined to know.'

The men left there and went to Sodom while Abraham remained standing before the Lord. Approaching him he said, 'Are you really going to destroy the just man with the sinner? Perhaps there are fifty just men in the town. Will you really overwhelm them, will you not spare the place for the fifty just men in it? Do not think of doing such a thing: to kill the just man with the sinner, treating just and sinner alike! Do not think of it! Will the judge of the whole earth not administer justice?' The Lord replied, 'If at Sodom I find fifty just men in the town, I will spare the whole place because of them.'

Abraham replied, 'I am bold indeed to speak like this to my Lord, I who am dust and ashes. But perhaps the fifty just men lack five: will you destroy the whole city for five?' 'No,' he replied, 'I will not destroy it if I find forty-five just men there.' Again Abraham said to him, 'Perhaps there will only be forty there.' 'I will not do it,' he replied 'for the sake of the forty.'

Abraham said, 'I trust my Lord will not be angry, but give me leave to speak: perhaps there will only be thirty there.' 'I will not do it' he replied 'if I find thirty there.' He said, 'I am bold indeed to speak like this, but perhaps there will only be twenty there.' 'I will not destroy it' he replied 'for the sake of the twenty.' He said, 'I trust my Lord will not be angry if I speak once more: perhaps there will only be ten.' 'I will not destroy it' he replied 'for the sake of the ten.'

When he had finished talking to Abraham the Lord went away, and Abraham returned home.

This is the word of the Lord.

Responsorial Psalm   Ps 102:1-4. 8-11. ℟ v.8

℟   The Lord is kind and merciful.

1   My soul, give thanks to the Lord,
     all my being, bless his holy name.
     My soul, give thanks to the Lord
     and never forget all his blessings.   ℟

2 It is he who forgives all your guilt,
who heals every one of your ills,
who redeems your life from the grave,
who crowns you with love and compassion. ℟

3 The Lord is compassion and love,
slow to anger and rich in mercy.
His wrath will come to an end;
he will not be angry for ever. ℟

4 He does not treat us according to our sins
nor repay us according to our faults.
For as the heavens are high above the earth
so strong is his love for those who fear him. ℟

Gospel Acclamation   cf. Ps 94:8

Alleluia, alleluia!
If today you hear his voice,
harden not your hearts.
Alleluia!

GOSPEL

A reading from the holy Gospel according to Matthew   8:18-22

Follow me.

When Jesus saw the great crowds all about him he gave orders to leave for the other side. One of the scribes then came up and said to him, 'Master, I will follow you wherever you go.' Jesus replied, 'Foxes have holes and the birds of the air have nests, but the Son of Man has nowhere to lay his head.'

Another man, one of his disciples, said to him, 'Sir, let me go and bury my father first.' But Jesus replied, 'Follow me, and leave the dead to bury their dead.'

This is the Gospel of the Lord.

Tuesday

FIRST READING

A reading from the book of Genesis   19:15-29

The Lord God rained brimstone and fire on Sodom and Gomorrah.

The angels urged Lot, 'Come, take your wife and these two daughters of yours, or you will be overwhelmed in the punishment of the town.' And as he hesitated, the men took him by the hand, and his wife and his two daughters, because of the pity the Lord felt for him. They led him out and left him outside the town.

As they were leading him out he said, 'Run for your life. Neither look behind you nor stop anywhere on the plain. Make for the hills if you would not be overwhelmed.' 'No, I beg you, my lord,' Lot said to them 'your servant has won your favour and you have shown great kindness to me in saving my life. But I could not reach the hills before this calamity overtook me, and death with it. The town over there is near enough to flee to, and is a little one. Let me make for that – is it not little? – and my life will be saved.' He answered, 'I grant you this favour too, and will not destroy the town you speak of. Hurry, escape to it, for I can do nothing until you reach it.' That is why the town is named Zoar.

As the sun rose over the land and Lot entered Zoar, the Lord rained on Sodom and Gomorrah brimstone and fire from the Lord. He overthrew these towns and the whole plain, with all the inhabitants of the towns, and everything that grew there. But the wife of Lot looked back, and was turned into a pillar of salt.

Rising early in the morning Abraham went to the place where he had stood before the Lord, and looking towards Sodom and Gomorrah, and across all the plain, he saw the smoke rising from the land, like smoke from a furnace.

Thus it was that when God destroyed the towns of the plain, he kept Abraham in mind and rescued Lot out of disaster when he overwhelmed the towns where Lot lived.

This is the word of the Lord.

Responsorial Psalm   Ps 25:2-3. 9-12. ℟ v.3

℟   O Lord, your kindness is before my eyes.

1   Examine me, Lord, and try me;
    O test my heart and my mind,
    for your love is before my eyes
    and I walk according to your truth. ℟

2   Do not sweep me away with sinners,
    nor my life with bloodthirsty men
    in whose hands are evil plots,
    whose right hands are filled with gold. ℟

3   As for me, I walk the path of perfection.
    Redeem me and show me your mercy.
    My foot stands on level ground:
    I will bless the Lord in the assembly. ℟

Gospel Acclamation   Ps 129:5

Alleluia, alleluia!
I hope in the Lord,
I trust in his word.
Alleluia!

GOSPEL

A reading from the holy Gospel according to Matthew   8:23-27

He commanded the wind and the sea, and all was calm again.

Jesus got into the boat followed by his disciples. Without warning a
storm broke over the lake, so violent that the waves were breaking
right over the boat. But he was asleep. So they went to him and woke
him saying, 'Save us, Lord, we are going down!' And he said to them,
'Why are you so frightened, you men of little faith?' And with that he
stood up and rebuked the winds and the seas; and all was calm again.
The men were astounded and said, 'Whatever kind of man is this?
Even the winds and the sea obey him.'

This is the Gospel of the Lord.

Wednesday

FIRST READING

A reading from the book of Genesis 21:5. 8-20

The slave girl's son will not share the inheritance with my son Isaac.

Abraham was a hundred years old when his son Isaac was born to him. The child grew and was weaned, and Abraham gave a great banquet on the day Isaac was weaned. Now Sarah watched the son that Hagar the Egyptian had borne to Abraham, playing with her son Isaac. 'Drive away that slave-girl and her son,' she said to Abraham; 'this slave-girl's son is not to share the inheritance with my son Isaac.' This greatly distressed Abraham because of his son, but God said to him, 'Do not distress yourself on account of the boy and your slave-girl. Grant Sarah all she asks of you, for it is through Isaac that your name will be carried on. But the slave-girl's son I will also make into a nation, for he is your child too.' Rising early next morning Abraham took some bread and a skin of water and, giving them to Hagar, he put the child on her shoulder and sent her away.

She wandered off into the wilderness of Beersheba. When the skin of water was finished she abandoned the child under a bush. Then she went and sat down at a distance, about a bowshot away, saying to herself, 'I cannot see the child die.' So she sat at a distance; and the child wailed and wept.

But God heard the boy wailing, and the angel of God called to Hagar from heaven. 'What is wrong, Hagar?' he asked, 'Do not be afraid, for God has heard the boy's cry where he lies. Come, pick up the boy and hold him safe, for I will make him into a great nation.' Then God opened Hagar's eyes and she saw a well, so she went and filled the skin with water and gave the boy a drink.

God was with the boy. He grew up and made his home in the wilderness, and he became a bowman.

This is the word of the Lord.

Responsorial Psalm Ps 33:7-8. 10-13. ℟ v.7

℟ The Lord hears the cry of the poor.

1 This poor man called; the Lord heard him
   and rescued him from all his distress.

The angel of the Lord is encamped
around those who revere him, to rescue them.   ℟

2   Revere the Lord, you his saints.
    They lack nothing, those who revere him.
    Strong lions suffer want and go hungry
    but those who seek the Lord lack no blessing.   ℟

3   Come, children, and hear me
    that I may teach you the fear of the Lord.
    Who is he who longs for life
    and many days, to enjoy his prosperity?   ℟

Gospel Acclamation   James 1:18

Alleluia, alleluia!
The Father gave us birth by his message of truth,
that we might be as the first fruits of his creation.
Alleluia!

GOSPEL

A reading from the holy Gospel according to Matthew   8:28-34

He came at this time to torture the demons.

When Jesus reached the country of the Gadarenes on the other side of
the lake, two demoniacs came towards him out of the tombs –
creatures so fierce that no one could pass that way. They stood there
shouting, 'What do you want with us, Son of God? Have you come here
to torture us before the time?' Now some distance away there was a
large herd of pigs feeding, and the devils pleaded with Jesus, 'If you
cast us out, send us into the herd of pigs.' And he said to them, 'Go
then,' and they came out and made for the pigs; and at that the whole
herd charged down the cliff into the lake and perished in the water.
The swineherds ran off and made for the town, where they told the
whole story, including what had happened to the demoniacs. At this
the whole town set out to meet Jesus; and as soon as they saw him
they implored him to leave the neighbourhood.

This is the Gospel of the Lord.

Thursday

FIRST READING

A reading from the book of Genesis   22:1-19

The sacrifice of Abraham, our father in faith.

It happened that God put Abraham to the test. 'Abraham, Abraham,' he called. 'Here I am' he replied. 'Take your son,' God said 'your only child Isaac, whom you love, and go to the land of Moriah. There you shall offer him as a burnt offering on a mountain I will point out to you.'

Rising early next morning Abraham saddled his ass and took with him two of his servants and his son Isaac. He chopped wood for the burnt offering and started on his journey to the place God had pointed out to him. On the third day Abraham looked up and saw the place in the distance. Then Abraham said to his servants, 'Stay here with the donkey. The boy and I will go over there; we will worship and come back to you.'

Abraham took the wood for the burnt offering, loaded it on Isaac, and carried in his own hands the fire and the knife. Then the two of them set out together. Isaac spoke to his father Abraham. 'Father' he said. 'Yes, my son' he replied. 'Look,' he said 'here are the fire and the wood, but where is the lamb for the burnt offering?' Abraham answered, 'My son, God himself will provide the lamb for the burnt offering.' Then the two of them went on together.

When they arrived at the place God had pointed out to him, Abraham built an altar there, and arranged the wood. Then he bound his son Isaac and put him on the altar on top of the wood. Abraham stretched out his hands and seized the knife to kill his son.

But the angel of the Lord called to him from heaven. 'Abraham, Abraham' he said. 'I am here' he replied. 'Do not raise your hand against the boy' the angel said. 'Do not harm him, for now I know you fear God. You have not refused me your son, your only son.' Then looking up, Abraham saw a ram caught by its horns in a bush. Abraham took the ram and offered it as a burnt-offering in place of his son. Abraham called this place 'The Lord provides', and hence the saying today: On the mountain the Lord provides.

The angel of the Lord called Abraham a second time from heaven. 'I swear by my own self – it is the Lord who speaks – because you have done this, because you have not refused me your son, your only son, I will shower blessings on you, I will make your descendants as many as the stars of heaven and the grains of sand on the seashore. Your descendants shall gain possession of the gates of their enemies. All the nations of the earth shall bless themselves by your descendants, as a reward for your obedience.'

Abraham went back to his servants, and together they set out for Beersheba, and he settled in Beersheba.

This is the word of the Lord

Responsorial Psalm   Ps 114:1-6. 8-9. ℟ v.9

℟   I will walk in the presence of the Lord
      in the land of the living.

or

℟   Alleluia!

1   I love the Lord for he has heard
      the cry of my appeal;
      for he turned his ear to me
      in the day when I called him.   ℟

2   They surrounded me, the snares of death,
      with the anguish of the tomb;
      they caught me, sorrow and distress.
      I called on the Lord's name.
      O Lord my God, deliver me!   ℟

3   How gracious is the Lord, and just;
      our God has compassion.
      The Lord protects the simple hearts;
      I was helpless so he saved me.   ℟

4   He has kept my soul from death,
      (my eyes from tears)
      and my feet from stumbling.
      I will walk in the presence of the Lord
      in the land of the living.   ℟

Gospel Acclamation   2 Cor 5:19

Alleluia, alleluia!
God was in Christ, to reconcile the world to himself;
and the Good News of reconciliation he has entrusted to us.
Alleluia!

GOSPEL

A reading from the holy Gospel according to Matthew   9:1-8

They praised God for giving such power to men.

Jesus got in the boat, crossed the water and came to his own town. Then some people appeared, bringing him a paralytic stretched out on a bed. Seeing their faith, Jesus said to the paralytic, 'Courage, my child, your sins are forgiven.' And at this some scribes said to themselves, 'This man is blaspheming.' Knowing what was in their minds Jesus said, 'Why do you have such wicked thoughts in your hearts? Now, which of these is easier: to say, "Your sins are forgiven", or to say, "Get up and walk"? But to prove to you that the Son of Man has authority on earth to forgive sins,' – he said to the paralytic – 'get up, and pick up your bed and go off home.' And the man got up and went home. A feeling of awe came over the crowd when they saw this, and they praised God for giving such power to men.

This is the Gospel of the Lord.

Friday

FIRST READING

A reading from the book of Genesis   23:1-4. 19; 24:1-8. 62-67

Isaac loved Rebecca – he made her his wife, and was consoled for the loss of his mother.

The length of Sarah's life was a hundred and twenty-seven years. She died at Kiriath-arba, or Hebron, in the land of Canaan, and Abraham went to mourn and grieve for her.

Then leaving his dead, Abraham spoke to the sons of Heth: 'I am a stranger and a settler among you' he said. 'Let me own a burial-plot among you, so that I may take my dead wife and bury her.'

After this Abraham buried his wife Sarah in the cave of the field of Machpelah opposite Mamre, in the country of Canaan.

By now Abraham was an old man well on in years, and the Lord had blessed him in every way. Abraham said to the eldest servant of his household, the steward of all his property, 'Place your hand under my thigh, I would have you swear by the Lord God of heaven and God of earth, that you will not choose a wife for my son from the daughters of the Canaanites among whom I live. Instead, go to my own land and my own kinsfolk to choose a wife for my son Isaac.' The servant asked him, 'What if the woman does not want to come with me to this country? Must I take your son back to the country from which you came?' Abraham answered, 'On no account take my son back there. The Lord, God of heaven and God of earth, took me from my father's home, and from the land of my father's home, and from the land of my kinsfolk, and he swore to me that he would give this country to my descendants. He will now send his angel ahead of you, so that you may choose a wife for my son there. And if the woman does not want to come with you, you will be free from this oath of mine. Only do not take my son back there.'

Isaac, who lived in the Negeb, had meanwhile come into the wilderness of the well of Lahai Roi. Now Isaac went walking in the fields as evening fell, and looking up saw camels approaching. And Rebekah looked up and saw Isaac. She jumped down from her camel, and asked the servant, 'Who is that man walking through the fields to meet us?' The servant replied, 'That is my master'; then she took her veil and hid her face. The servant told Isaac the whole story, and Isaac led Rebekah into his tent and made her his wife; and he loved her. And so Isaac was consoled for the loss of his mother.

This is the word of the Lord.

Responsorial Psalm   Ps 105:1-5. ℟ v.1

℟   Give thanks to the Lord for he is good.

or

℟   Alleluia!

1   O give thanks to the Lord for he is good;
     for his great love is without end.
     Who can tell the Lord's mighty deeds?
     Who can recount all his praise?   ℟

2   They are happy who do what is right,
     who at all times do what is just.
     O Lord, remember me
     out of the love you have for your people.   ℟

3   Come to me, Lord, with your help
     that I may see the joy of your chosen ones
     and may rejoice in the gladness of your nation
     and share the glory of your people.   ℟

Gospel Acclamation   Mt 11:28

Alleluia, alleluia!
Come to me, all you that labour and are burdened,
and I will give you rest, says the Lord.
Alleluia!

GOSPEL

A reading from the holy Gospel according to Matthew   9:9-13

It is not the healthy who need the doctor; what I want is mercy, not sacrifice.

As Jesus was walking he saw a man named Matthew sitting by the customs house, and he said to him, 'Follow me.' And he got up and followed him.

While he was at dinner in the house it happened that a number of tax collectors and sinners came to sit at the table with Jesus and his disciples. When the Pharisees saw this, they said to his disciples, 'Why does your master eat with tax collectors and sinners?' When he heard this he replied, 'It is not the healthy who need the doctor, but the sick. Go and learn the meaning of the words: What I want is mercy, not sacrifice. And indeed I did not come to call the virtuous, but sinners.'

This is the Gospel of the Lord.

Saturday

FIRST READING

A reading from the book of Genesis   27:1-5. 15-29

Jacob took his brother's place and by fraud received the blessing.

Isaac had grown old, and his eyes were so weak that he could no longer see. He summoned his elder son Esau. 'My son!' he said to him, and the latter answered, 'I am here.' Then he said, 'See, I am old and do not know when I may die. Now take your weapons, your quiver and bow; go out into the country and hunt me some game. Make me the kind of savoury I like and bring it to me, so that I may eat, and give you my blessing before I die.'

Rebekah happened to be listening while Isaac was talking to his son Esau. So when Esau went into the country to hunt game for his father, Rebekah took her elder son Esau's best clothes, which she had in the house, and dressed her younger son Jacob in them, covering his arms and the smooth part of his neck with the skins of the kids. Then she handed the savoury and the bread she had made to her son Jacob.

He presented himself before his father and said, 'Father.' 'I am here' was the reply, 'who are you, my son?' Jacob said to his father, 'I am Esau your firstborn; I have done as you told me. Please get up and take your place and eat the game I have brought and then give me your blessing.' Isaac said to his son, 'How quickly you found it, my son!' 'It was the Lord your God' he answered 'who put it in my path.' Isaac said to Jacob, 'Come here, then, and let me touch you, my son, to know if you are my son Esau or not.' Jacob came close to his father Isaac, who touched him and said, 'The voice is Jacob's voice but the arms are the arms of Esau!' He did not recognise him, for his arms were hairy like his brother Esau's, and so he blessed him. He said, 'Are you really my son Esau?' And he replied, 'I am.' Isaac said, 'Bring it here that I may eat the game my son has brought, and so may give you my blessing.' He brought it to him and he ate; he offered him wine, and he drank. His father Isaac said to him, 'Come closer, and kiss me, my son.' He went closer and kissed his father, who smelled the smell of his clothes.

He blessed him saying:

'Yes, the smell of my son
is like the smell of a fertile field blessed by the Lord.
May God give you
dew from heaven,
and the richness of the earth,
abundance of grain and wine!
May nations serve you
and peoples bow down before you!
Be master of your brothers;
may the sons of your mother bow down before you!
Cursed be he who curses you;
blessed be he who blesses you!'

This is the word of the Lord.

Responsorial Psalm   Ps 134:1-6. ℟ v.3

℟   Praise the Lord for he is good!

or

℟   Alleluia!

1   Praise the name of the Lord,
    praise him, servants of the Lord,
    who stand in the house of the Lord
    in the courts of the house of our God. ℟

2   Praise the Lord for the Lord is good.
    Sing a psalm to his name for he is loving.
    For the Lord has chosen Jacob for himself
    and Israel for his own possession. ℟

3   For I know the Lord is great,
    that our Lord is high above all gods.
    The Lord does whatever he wills,
    in heaven, on earth, in the seas. ℟

Gospel Acclamation   Jn 10:27

Alleluia, alleluia!
My sheep listen to my voice, says the Lord;
I know them, and they follow me.
Alleluia!

GOSPEL

A reading from the holy Gospel according to Matthew   9:14-17

The wedding guests would never mourn while the bridegroom is still with them.

John's disciples came to Jesus and said, 'Why is it that we and the Pharisees fast, but your disciples do not?' Jesus replied, 'Surely the bridegroom's attendants would never think of mourning as long as the bridegroom is still with them? But the time will come for the bridegroom to be taken away from them, and then they will fast. No one puts a piece of unshrunken cloth on to an old cloak, because the patch pulls away from the cloak and the tear gets worse. Nor do people put new wine into old wineskins; if they do, the skins burst, the wine runs out, and the skins are lost. No; they put new wine into fresh skins and both are preserved.'

This is the Gospel of the Lord.

FOURTEENTH WEEK IN ORDINARY TIME

Year I

Monday

FIRST READING

A reading from the book of Genesis   28:10-22

He saw a ladder standing there, angels of God going up and coming down, and God speaking.

Jacob left Beersheba and set out for Haran. When he had reached a certain place he passed the night there, since the sun had set. Taking one of the stones to be found at that place, he made it his pillow and lay down where he was. He had a dream: a ladder was there, standing on the ground with its top reaching to heaven; and there were angels of God going up it and coming down. And the Lord was there, standing over him, saying, 'I am the Lord, the God of Abraham your father, and the God of Isaac. I will give to you and your descendants the land on which you are lying. Your descendants shall be like the specks of dust on the ground; you shall spread to the west and the east, to the north and the south, and all the tribes of the earth shall bless themselves by you and your descendants. Be sure that I am with you; I will keep you safe wherever you go, and bring you back to this land, for I will not desert you before I have done all that I have promised you.' Then Jacob awoke from his sleep and said, 'Truly, the Lord is in this place and I never knew it!' He was afraid and said, 'How awe-inspiring this place is! This is nothing less than a house of God; this is the gate of heaven!' Rising early in the morning, Jacob took the stone he had used for his pillow, and set it up as a monument, pouring oil over the top of it. He named the place Bethel, but before that the town was called Luz.

Jacob made this vow, 'If God goes with me and keeps me safe on this journey I am making, if he gives me bread to eat and clothes to wear, and if I return home safely to my father, then the Lord shall be my God. This stone I have set up as a monument shall be a house of God.'

This is the word of the Lord.

Responsorial Psalm   Ps 90:1-4. 14-15. ℟ cf. v.2

℟   In you, my God, I place my trust.

1   He who dwells in the shelter of the Most High
    and abides in the shade of the Almighty
    says to the Lord: 'My refuge,
    my stronghold, my God in whom I trust!'   ℟

2   It is he who will free you from the snare
    of the fowler who seeks to destroy you;
    he will conceal you with his pinions
    and under his wings you will find refuge.   ℟

3   His love he set on me, so I will rescue him;
    protect him for he knows my name.
    When he calls I shall answer: 'I am with you.'
    I will save him in distress.   ℟

Gospel Acclamation   cf. 2 Tim 1:10

    Alleluia, alleluia!
    Our Saviour Jesus Christ has done away with death
    and brought us life through his gospel.
    Alleluia!

GOSPEL

A reading from the holy Gospel according to Matthew   9:18-26

My daughter has just died, but come to her and she will live.

While Jesus was speaking, up came one of the officials, who bowed low
in front of him and said, 'My daughter has just died, but come and lay
your hand on her and her life will be saved.' Jesus rose and, with his
disciples, followed him.

Then from behind him came a woman, who had suffered from a
haemorrhage for twelve years, and she touched the fringe of his cloak,
for she said to herself, 'If I can only touch his cloak I shall be well
again.' Jesus turned round and saw her; and he said to her, 'Courage,
my daughter, your faith has restored you to health.' And from that
moment the woman was well again.

When Jesus reached the official's house and saw the fluteplayers, with the crowd making a commotion he said, 'Get out of here; the little girl is not dead, she is asleep.' And they laughed at him. But when the people had been turned out he went inside and took the little girl by the hand; and she stood up. And the news spread all round the countryside.

This is the Gospel of the Lord.

Tuesday

FIRST READING

A reading from the book of Genesis   32:23-33

Your name shall be called Israel, because you have been strong against God.

Jacob rose, and taking his two wives and his two slave-girls and his eleven children he crossed the ford of the Jabbok. He took them and sent them across the stream and sent all his possessions over too. And Jacob was left alone.

And there was one that wrestled with him until daybreak who, seeing that he could not master him, struck him in the socket of his hip, and Jacob's hip was dislocated as he wrestled with him. He said, 'Let me go, for day is breaking.' But Jacob answered, 'I will not let you go unless you bless me.' He then asked, 'What is your name?' 'Jacob,' he replied. He said, 'Your name shall no longer be Jacob, but Israel; because you have been strong against God, you shall prevail against men.' Jacob then made this request, 'I beg you, tell me your name,' but he replied, 'Why do you ask my name?' And he blessed him there.

Jacob named the place Peniel, 'Because I have seen God face to face,' he said 'and I have survived.' The sun rose as he left Peniel, limping because of his hip. That is the reason why to this day the Israelites do not eat the sciatic nerve which is in the socket of the hip, because he had struck Jacob in the socket of the hip on the sciatic nerve.

This is the word of the Lord.

Responsorial Psalm   Ps 16:1-3. 6-8. 15. ℟ v.15

℟   In my justice, I shall see your face, O Lord.

1 Lord, hear a cause that is just,
   pay heed to my cry.
   Turn your ear to my prayer:
   no deceit is on my lips. ℟

2 From you may my judgement come forth.
   Your eyes discern the truth.
   You search my heart, you visit me by night.
   You test me and you find in me no wrong. ℟

3 I am here and I call, you will hear me, O God.
   Turn your ear to me; hear my words.
   Display your great love, you whose right hand saves
   your friends from those who rebel against them. ℟

4 Guard me as the apple of your eye.
   Hide me in the shadow of your wings.
   In my justice I shall see your face
   and be filled, when I awake, with the sight of your glory. ℟

Gospel Acclamation   Jn 10:14

   Alleluia, alleluia!
   I am the good shepherd, says the Lord;
   I know my sheep, and mine know me.
   Alleluia!

GOSPEL

A reading from the holy Gospel according to Matthew   9:32-38

The harvest is rich but the labourers are few.

A man was brought to Jesus, a dumb demoniac. And when the devil
was cast out, the dumb man spoke and the people were amazed.
'Nothing like this has ever been seen in Israel' they said. But the
Pharisees said, 'It is through the prince of devils that he casts out
devils.'

Jesus made a tour through all the towns and villages, teaching
in their synagogues, proclaiming the Good News of the kingdom

and curing all kinds of diseases and sickness.

And when he saw the crowds he felt sorry for them because they were harassed and dejected, like sheep without a shepherd. Then he said to his disciples, 'The harvest is rich but the labourers are few, so ask the Lord of the harvest to send labourers to his harvest.'

This is the Gospel of the Lord.

Wednesday

FIRST READING

A reading from the book of Genesis   41:55-57; 42:5-7. 17-24

We have merited this misery because we have sinned against our brother.

When the country of Egypt began to feel the famine, the people cried out to Pharaoh for bread. But Pharaoh told all the Egyptians, 'Go to Joseph and do what he tells you.' – There was famine all over the world. – Then Joseph opened all the granaries and sold grain to the Egyptians. The famine grew worse in the land of Egypt. People came to Egypt from all over the world to buy grain from Joseph, for the famine had grown severe throughout the world.

Israel's sons with others making the same journey went to buy grain, for there was famine in the land of Canaan. It was Joseph, as the man in authority over the country, who sold the grain to all comers. So Joseph's brothers went and bowed down before him, their faces touching the ground. When Joseph saw his brothers he recognised them. Then he kept them all in custody for three days.

On the third day Joseph said to them, 'Do this and you shall keep your lives, for I am a man who fears God. If you are honest men let one of your brothers be kept in the place of your detention; as for you, go and take grain to relieve the famine of your families. You shall bring me your youngest brother; this way your words will be proved true, and you will not have to die!' This they did. They said to one another, 'Truly we are being called to account for our brother. We saw his misery of soul when he begged our mercy, but we did not listen to him and now this misery has come home to us.' Reuben answered them, 'Did I not tell you not to wrong the boy? But you did not listen, and now we are brought to account for his blood.' They did not know that Joseph understood, because there was an interpreter between them. He left them and wept.

This is the word of the Lord.

Responsorial Psalm   Ps 32:2-3. 10-11. 18-19. ℟ v.22

℟   Lord, let your mercy be on us,
     as we place our trust in you.

1   Give thanks to the Lord upon the harp,
     with a ten-stringed lute sing him songs.
     O sing him a song that is new,
     play loudly, with all your skill. ℟

2   He frustrates the designs of the nations,
     he defeats the plans of the peoples.
     His own designs shall stand for ever,
     the plans of his heart from age to age. ℟

3   The Lord looks on those who revere him,
     on those who hope in his love,
     to rescue their souls from death,
     to keep them alive in famine. ℟

Gospel Acclamation   Mk 1:15

     Alleluia, alleluia!
     The kingdom of God is near:
     repent and believe the Good News!
     Alleluia!

GOSPEL

A reading from the holy Gospel according to Matthew   10:1-7

Go to the lost sheep of the house of Israel.

Jesus summoned his twelve disciples, and gave them authority over
unclean spirits with power to cast them out and to cure all kinds of
diseases and sickness.

These are the names of the twelve apostles: first, Simon who is
called Peter, and his brother Andrew; James the son of Zebedee, and
his brother John; Philip and Bartholomew; Thomas, and Matthew the
tax collector; James the son of Alphaeus, and Thaddaeus; Simon the
Zealot and Judas Iscariot, the one who was to betray him. These
twelve Jesus sent out, instructing them as follows:

'Do not turn your steps to pagan territory, and do not enter any Samaritan town; go rather to the lost sheep of the House of Israel. And as you go, proclaim that the kingdom of heaven is close at hand.'

This is the Gospel of the Lord.

Thursday

FIRST READING

A reading from the book of Genesis   44:18-21. 23-29; 45:1-5

God sent me before you into Egypt to preserve your lives.

Judah went up to Joseph and said, 'May it please my lord, let your servant have a word privately with my lord. Do not be angry with your servant, for you are like Pharaoh himself. My lord questioned his servants, "Have you father or brother?" And we said to my lord, "We have an old father, and a younger brother born of his old age. His brother is dead, so he is the only one left of his mother, and his father loves him." Then you said to your servants, "Bring him down to me that my eyes may look on him. If your youngest brother does not come down with you, you will not be admitted to my presence again." When we went back to your servant my father, we repeated to him what my lord had said. So when our father said, "Go back and buy us a little food," we said, "We cannot go down. If our youngest brother is with us, we will go down, for we cannot be admitted to the man's presence unless our youngest brother is with us." So your servant our father said to us, "You know that my wife bore me two children. When one left me, I said that he must have been torn to pieces. And I have not seen him to this day. If you take this one from me too and any harm comes to him, you will send me down to Sheol with my white head bowed in misery."'

Then Joseph could not control his feelings in front of all his retainers, and he exclaimed, 'Let everyone leave me.' No one therefore was present with him while Joseph made himself known to his brothers, but he wept so loudly that all the Egyptians heard, and the news reached Pharaoh's palace.

Joseph said to his brothers, 'I am Joseph. Is my father really still alive?' His brothers could not answer him, they were so dismayed at the sight of him. Then Joseph said to his brothers, 'Come closer to me.' When they had come closer to him he said, 'I am your brother

Joseph whom you sold into Egypt. But now, do not grieve, do not reproach yourselves for having sold me here, since God sent me before you to preserve your lives.'

This is the word of the Lord.

Responsorial Psalm   Ps 104:16-21. ℟ v.5

℟   Remember the marvels the Lord has done.

or

℟   Alleluia!

1   The Lord called down a famine on the land;
    he broke the staff that supported them.
    He had sent a man before them,
    Joseph, sold as a slave.   ℟

2   His feet were put in chains,
    his neck was bound with iron,
    until what he said came to pass
    and the Lord's word proved him true.   ℟

3   Then the king sent and released him;
    the ruler of the peoples set him free,
    making him master of his house
    and ruler of all he possessed.   ℟

Gospel Acclamation   Mk 1:15

Alleluia, alleluia!
The kingdom of God is near:
repent and believe the Good News!
Alleluia!

GOSPEL

A reading from the holy Gospel according to Matthew   10:7-15

You received without charge, give without charge.

Jesus instructed the Twelve as follows: 'As you go, proclaim that the kingdom of heaven is close at hand. Cure the sick, raise the dead, cleanse the lepers, cast out devils. You received without charge, give without charge. Provide yourselves with no gold or silver, not even with a few coppers for your purses, with no haversack for the journey or spare tunic or footwear or a staff, for the workman deserves his keep.

'Whatever town or village you go into, ask for someone trustworthy and stay with him until you leave. As you enter his house, salute it, and if the house deserves it, let your peace descend upon it; if it does not, let your peace come back to you. And if anyone does not welcome you or listen to what you have to say, as you walk out of the house or town shake the dust from your feet. I tell you solemnly, on the day of Judgement it will not go as hard with the land of Sodom and Gomorrah as with that town.'

This is the Gospel of the Lord.

Friday

FIRST READING

A reading from the book of Genesis   46:1-7. 28-30

Now I can die, because I have seen you again.

Israel left Canaan with his possessions, and reached Beersheba. There he offered sacrifices to the God of his father Isaac. God spoke to Israel in a vision at night, 'Jacob, Jacob,' he said. 'I am here,' he replied. 'I am God, the God of your father,' he continued. 'Do not be afraid of going down to Egypt, for I will make you a great nation there. I myself will go down to Egypt with you. I myself will bring you back again, and Joseph's hand shall close your eyes.' Then Jacob left Beersheba. Israel's sons conveyed their father Jacob, their little children and their wives in the waggons Pharaoh had sent to fetch him.

Taking their livestock and all that they had acquired in the land of Canaan, they went to Egypt, Jacob and all his family with him: his sons and his grandsons, his daughters and his grand-daughters, in a word, all his children he took with him to Egypt.

Israel sent Judah ahead to Joseph, so that the latter might present himself to him in Goshen. When they arrived in the land of Goshen, Joseph had his chariot made ready and went up to meet his father Israel in Goshen. As soon as he appeared he threw his arms round his neck and for a long time wept on his shoulder. Israel said to Joseph, 'Now I can die, now that I have seen you again, and seen you still alive.'

This is the word of the Lord.

Responsorial Psalm   Ps 36:3-4. 18-19. 27-28. 39-40. ℟ v.39

℟ The salvation of the just comes from the Lord.

1   If you trust in the Lord and do good,
    then you will live in the land and be secure.
    If you find your delight in the Lord,
    he will grant your heart's desire.   ℟

2   He protects the lives of the upright,
    their heritage will last for ever.
    They shall not be put to shame in evil days,
    in time of famine their food shall not fail.   ℟

3   Then turn away from evil and do good
    and you shall have a home for ever;
    for the Lord loves justice
    and will never forsake his friends.   ℟

4   The salvation of the just comes from the Lord,
    their stronghold in time of distress.
    The Lord helps them and delivers them
    and saves them: for their refuge is in him.   ℟

Gospel Acclamation   Jn 16:13; 14:26

    Alleluia, alleluia!
    When the Spirit of truth comes, he will teach you all truth
    and bring to your mind all I have told you.
    Alleluia!

GOSPEL

A reading from the holy Gospel according to Matthew   10:16-23

It is not you who speak, but the Spirit of your Father speaking in you.

Jesus instructed the Twelve as follows: 'Remember, I am sending you
out like sheep among wolves; so be cunning as serpents and yet as
harmless as doves.

   'Beware of men: they will hand you over to sanhedrins and scourge
you in their synagogues. You will be dragged before governors and
kings for my sake, to bear witness before them and the pagans. But
when they hand you over, do not worry about how to speak or what to

say; what you are to say will be given to you when the time comes; because it is not you who will be speaking; the Spirit of your Father will be speaking in you.

'Brother will betray brother to death, and the father his child; children will rise against their parents and have them put to death. You will be hated by all men on account of my name; but the man who stands firm to the end will be saved. If they persecute you in one town, take refuge in the next; and if they persecute you in that, take refuge in another. I tell you solemnly, you will not have gone the round of the towns of Israel before the Son of Man comes.'

This is the Gospel of the Lord.

Saturday

FIRST READING

A reading from the book of Genesis   49:29-33; 50:15-26

God will visit you and bring about the deliverance of many people.

Jacob gave his sons these instructions, 'I am about to be gathered to my people. Bury me near my fathers, in the cave that is in the field of Ephron the Hittite, in the cave in the field at Machpelah, opposite Mamre, in the land of Canaan, which Abraham bought from Ephron the Hittite as a burial-plot. There Abraham was buried and his wife Sarah. There Isaac was buried and his wife Rebekah. There I buried Leah. I mean the field and the cave in it that were bought from the sons of Heth.'

When Jacob had finished giving his instructions to his sons, he drew his feet up into the bed, and breathing his last was gathered to his people.

Seeing that their father was dead, Joseph's brothers said, 'What if Joseph intends to treat us as enemies and repay us in full for all the wrong we did him?' So they sent this message to Joseph: 'Before your father died he gave us this order: "You must say to Joseph: Oh forgive your brothers their crime and their sin and all the wrong they did you." Now therefore, we beg you, forgive the crime of the servants of your father's God.' Joseph wept at the message they sent to him.

His brothers came themselves and fell down before him. 'We present ourselves before you' they said 'as your slaves.' But Joseph answered them, 'Do not be afraid; is it for me to put myself in God's place? The evil you planned to do me has by God's design been turned to good, that he might bring about, as indeed he has, the deliverance of a numerous people. So you need not be afraid; I myself will provide for you and your dependants.' In this way he reassured them with words that touched their hearts.

So Joseph stayed in Egypt with his father's family; and Joseph lived a hundred and ten years. Joseph saw the third generation of Ephraim's children, as also the children of Machir, Manasseh's son, who were born on Joseph's lap. At length Joseph said to his brothers, 'I am about to die; but God will be sure to remember you kindly and take you back from this country to the land that he promised on oath to Abraham, Isaac and Jacob.' And Joseph made Israel's sons swear an oath, 'When God remembers you with kindness be sure to take my bones from here.'

Joseph died at the age of a hundred and ten; they embalmed him and laid him in his coffin in Egypt.

This is the word of the Lord.

Responsorial Psalm   Ps 104:1-4. 6-7. ℟ cf. Ps 68:33

℟   Turn to the Lord in your need and you will live.

1   Give thanks to the Lord, tell his name,
     make known his deeds among the peoples.
     O sing to him, sing his praise;
     tell all his wonderful works!   ℟

2   Be proud of his holy name,
     let the hearts that seek the Lord rejoice.
     Consider the Lord and his strength;
     constantly seek his face.   ℟

3   O children of Abraham, his servant,
     O sons of the Jacob he chose.
     He, the Lord, is our God:
     his judgements prevail in all the earth.   ℟

Gospel Acclamation   1 Peter 4:14

Alleluia, alleluia!
If you are insulted for the name of Christ, blessed are you,
for the Spirit of God rests upon you.
Alleluia!

GOSPEL

A reading from the holy Gospel according to Matthew   10:24-33

Do not be afraid of those who can kill the body.

Jesus instructed the Twelve as follows: 'The disciple is not superior to
his teacher, nor the slave to his master. It is enough for the disciple
that he should grow to be like his teacher, and the slave like his
master. If they have called the master of the house Beelzebul, what
will they not say of his household?

'Do not be afraid of them therefore. For everything that is now
covered will be uncovered, and everything now hidden will be made
clear. What I say to you in the dark, tell in the daylight; what you
hear in whispers, proclaim from the housetops.

'Do not be afraid of those who kill the body but cannot kill the soul;
fear him rather who can destroy both body and soul in hell. Can you
not buy two sparrows for a penny? And yet not one falls to the ground
without your Father knowing. Why, every hair on your head has been
counted. So there is no need to be afraid; you are worth more than
hundreds of sparrows.

'So if anyone declares himself for me in the presence of men, I will
declare myself for him in the presence of my Father in heaven. But
the one who disowns me in the presence of men, I will disown in the
presence of my Father in heaven.'

This is the Gospel of the Lord.

FIFTEENTH WEEK IN ORDINARY TIME

Year I

Monday

FIRST READING

A reading from the book of Exodus   1:8-14. 22

We must move against Israel lest they become greater in number.

There came to power in Egypt a new king who knew nothing of Joseph. 'Look,' he said to his subjects 'these people, the sons of Israel, have become so numerous and strong that they are a threat to us. We must be prudent and take steps against their increasing any further, or if war should break out, they might add to the number of our enemies. They might take arms against us and so escape out of the country.' Accordingly they put slave-drivers over the Israelites to wear them down under heavy loads. In this way they built the store-cities of Pithom and Rameses for Pharaoh. But the more they were crushed, the more they increased and spread, and men came to dread the sons of Israel. The Egyptians forced the sons of Israel into slavery, and made their lives unbearable with hard labour, work with clay and with brick, all kinds of work in the fields; they forced on them every kind of labour.

Pharaoh then gave his subjects this command: 'Throw all the boys born to the Hebrews into the river, but let all the girls live.'

This is the word of the Lord.

Responsorial Psalm   Ps 123. ℟ v.8

℟   Our help is in the name of the Lord.

1   'If the Lord had not been on our side,'
    this is Israel's song,
    'If the Lord had not been on our side
    when men rose against us,
    then would they have swallowed us alive
    when their anger was kindled.   ℟

2   Then would the waters have engulfed us,
    the torrent gone over us;
    over our head would have swept
    the raging waters.'

Blessed be the Lord who did not give us
a prey to their teeth! ℟

3   Our life, like a bird, has escaped
from the snare of the fowler.
Indeed the snare has been broken
and we have escaped.
Our help is in the name of the Lord,
who made heaven and earth. ℟

Gospel Acclamation   Mt 5:10

Alleluia, alleluia!
Happy are they who suffer persecution for justice' sake;
the kingdom of heaven is theirs.
Alleluia!

GOSPEL

A reading from the holy Gospel according to Matthew   10:34–11:1

I have not come to bring peace, but the sword.

Jesus instructed the Twelve as follows: 'Do not suppose that I have
come to bring peace to the earth: it is not peace I have come to bring,
but a sword. For I have come to set a man against his father, a
daughter against her mother, a daughter-in-law against her mother-
in-law. A man's enemies will be those of his own household.

'Anyone who prefers father or mother to me is not worthy of me.
Anyone who prefers son or daughter to me is not worthy of me.
Anyone who does not take his cross and follow in my footsteps is not
worthy of me. Anyone who finds his life will lose it; anyone who loses
his life for my sake will find it.

'Anyone who welcomes you welcomes me; and those who welcome
me welcome the one who sent me.

'Anyone who welcomes a prophet because he is a prophet will have
a prophet's reward; and anyone who welcomes a holy man because he
is a holy man will have a holy man's reward.

'If anyone gives so much as a cup of cold water to one of these little
ones because he is a disciple, then I tell you solemnly, he will most
certainly not lose his reward.'

When Jesus had finished instructing his twelve disciples he moved
on from there to teach and preach in their towns.

This is the Gospel of the Lord.

Tuesday

FIRST READING

A reading from the book of Exodus 2:1-15

He was called by the name Moses because he was taken from the water.
Afterwards he grew up to lead his people.

There was a man of the tribe of Levi who had taken a woman of Levi as his wife. She conceived and gave birth to a son and, seeing what a fine child he was, she kept him hidden for three months. When she could hide him no longer, she got a papyrus basket for him; coating it with bitumen and pitch, she put the child inside and laid it among the reeds at the river's edge. His sister stood some distance away to see what would happen to him.

Now Pharaoh's daughter went down to bathe in the river, and the girls attending her were walking along by the riverside. Among the reeds she noticed the basket, and she sent her maid to fetch it. She opened it and looked, and saw a baby boy, crying; and she was sorry for him. 'This is a child of one of the Hebrews' she said. Then the child's sister said to Pharaoh's daughter, 'Shall I go and find you a nurse among the Hebrew women to suckle the child for you?' 'Yes, go' Pharaoh's daughter said to her; and the girl went off to find the baby's own mother. To her the daughter of Pharaoh said, 'Take this child away and suckle it for me. I will see you are paid.' So the woman took the child and suckled it. When the child grew up, she brought him to Pharaoh's daughter who treated him like a son; she named him Moses because, she said, 'I drew him out of the water.'

Moses, a man by now, set out at this time to visit his countrymen, and he saw what a hard life they were having; and he saw an Egyptian strike a Hebrew, one of his countrymen. Looking round he could see no one in sight, so he killed the Egyptian and hid him in the sand. On the following day he came back, and there were two Hebrews, fighting. He said to the man who was in the wrong, 'What do you mean by hitting your fellow countryman?' 'And who appointed you' the man retorted 'to be prince over us, and judge? Do you intend to kill me as you killed the Egyptian?' Moses was frightened. 'Clearly that business has come to light' he thought. When Pharaoh heard of the matter he would have killed Moses, but Moses fled from Pharaoh and made for the land of Midian.

This is the word of the Lord.

Responsorial Psalm   Ps 68:3. 14. 30-31. 33-34. ℟ cf. v.33

℟ Turn to the Lord in your need,
and you will live.

1   I have sunk into the mud of the deep
and there is no foothold.
I have entered the waters of the deep
and the waves overwhelm me.   ℟

2   This is my prayer to you,
my prayer for your favour.
In your great love, answer me, O God,
with your help that never fails.   ℟

3   As for me in my poverty and pain
let your help, O God, lift me up.
I will praise God's name with a song;
I will glorify him with thanksgiving.   ℟

4   The poor when they see it will be glad
and God-seeking hearts will revive;
for the Lord listens to the needy
and does not spurn his servants in their chains.   ℟

Gospel Acclamation   cf. Ps 94:8

Alleluia, alleluia!
If today you hear his voice,
harden not your hearts.
Alleluia!

GOSPEL

A reading from the holy Gospel according to Matthew   11:20-24

It will not go as hard with Tyre and Sidon and the land of Sodom
on Judgement Day as with you.

Jesus began to reproach the towns in which most of his miracles had
been worked, because they refused to repent.

'Alas for you, Chorazin! Alas for you, Bethsaida! For if the
miracles done in you had been done in Tyre and Sidon, they would
have repented long ago in sackcloth and ashes. And still, I tell you

that it will not go as hard on Judgement day with Tyre and Sidon as with you. And as for you, Capernaum, did you want to be exalted as high as heaven? You shall be thrown down to hell. For if the miracles done in you had been done in Sodom, it would have been standing yet. And still, I tell you that it will not go as hard with the land of Sodom on Judgement day as with you.'

This is the Gospel of the Lord.

Wednesday

FIRST READING

A reading from the book of Exodus   3:1-6. 9-12

The Lord appeared to Moses in the form of a fire in the midst of a bush.

Moses was looking after the flock of Jethro, his father-in-law, priest of Midian. He led his flock to the far side of the wilderness and came to Horeb, the mountain of God. There the angel of the Lord appeared to him in the shape of a flame of fire, coming from the middle of a bush. Moses looked; there was the bush blazing but it was not being burnt up. 'I must go and look at this strange sight,' Moses said 'and see why the bush is not burnt.' Now the Lord saw him go forward to look, and God called to him from the middle of the bush. 'Moses, Moses!' he said. 'Here I am' he answered. 'Come no nearer' he said. 'Take off your shoes, for the place on which you stand is holy ground. I am the God of your father,' he said 'the God of Abraham, the God of Isaac and the God of Jacob.' At this Moses covered his face, afraid to look at God.

And the Lord said, 'And now the cry of the sons of Israel has come to me, and I have witnessed the way in which the Egyptians oppress them, so come, I send you to Pharaoh to bring the sons of Israel, my people, out of Egypt.'

Moses said to God, 'Who am I to go to Pharaoh and bring the sons of Israel out of Egypt?' 'I shall be with you,' was the answer 'and this is the sign by which you shall know that it is I who have sent you ... After you have led the people out of Egypt, you are to offer worship to God on this mountain.'

This is the word of the Lord.

Responsorial Psalm   Ps 102:1-4. 6-7. ℟ v.8

   ℟   The Lord is kind and merciful.

1   My soul, give thanks to the Lord,
    all my being, bless his holy name.
    My soul, give thanks to the Lord
    and never forget all his blessings.   ℟

2   It is he who forgives all your guilt,
    who heals every one of your ills,
    who redeems your life from the grave,
    who crowns you with love and compassion.   ℟

3   The Lord does deeds of justice,
    gives judgement for all who are oppressed.
    He made known his ways to Moses
    and his deeds to Israel's sons.   ℟

Gospel Acclamation   cf. Mt 11:25

   Alleluia, alleluia!
   Blessed are you, Father, Lord of heaven and earth;
   you have revealed to little ones the mysteries of the kingdom.
   Alleluia!

GOSPEL

A reading from the holy Gospel according to Matthew   11:25-27

*The Lord hides these things from the wise and reveals them to
children.*

Jesus exclaimed, 'I bless you, Father, Lord of heaven and of earth, for
hiding these things from the learned and the clever and revealing
them to mere children. Yes, Father, for that is what it pleased you to
do. Everything has been entrusted to me by my Father; and no one
knows the Son except the Father, just as no one knows the Father
except the Son and those to whom the Son chooses to reveal him.'

   This is the Gospel of the Lord.

Thursday

FIRST READING

A reading from the book of Exodus   3:13-20

I am who am. I am has sent me to you.

Moses, hearing the voice of God coming from the middle of the bush, said to him 'I am to go, then, to the sons of Israel and say to them, "The God of your fathers has sent me to you." But if they ask me what his name is, what am I to tell them?' And God said to Moses, 'I Am who I Am. This' he added 'is what you must say to the sons of Israel: "I Am has sent me to you." ' And God also said to Moses, 'You are to say to the sons of Israel: "The Lord, the God of your fathers, the God of Abraham, the God of Isaac, and the God of Jacob, has sent me to you." This is my name for all time; by this name I shall be invoked for all generations to come.

'Go and gather the elders of Israel together and tell them, "The Lord, the God of your fathers, has appeared to me, – the God of Abraham, of Isaac, and of Jacob; and he has said to me: I have visited you and seen all that the Egyptians are doing to you. And so I have resolved to bring you up out of Egypt where you are oppressed, into the land of the Canaanites, the Hittites, the Amorites, the Perizzites. the Hivites and the Jebusites, to a land where milk and honey flow." They will listen to your words, and with the elders of Israel you are to go to the king of Egypt and say to him, "The Lord, the God of the Hebrews, has come to meet us. Give us leave, then, to make a three days' journey into the wilderness to offer sacrifice to the Lord our God." For myself , knowing that the king of Egypt will not let you go unless he is forced by a mighty hand, I shall show my power and strike Egypt with all the wonders I am going to work there. After this he will let you go.'

This is the word of the Lord.

Responsorial Psalm   Ps 104:1. 5. 8-9. 24-27. ℟ v.8

℟   The Lord remembers his covenant for ever.

or

℟   Alleluia!

1   Give thanks to the Lord, tell his name,
    make known his deeds among the peoples.
    Remember the wonders he has done,
    his miracles, the judgements he spoke.   ℟

2   He remembers his covenant for ever,
    his promise for a thousand generations,
    the covenant he made with Abraham,
    the oath he swore to Isaac.   ℟

3   He gave his people increase;
    he made them stronger than their foes,
    whose hearts he turned to hate his people
    and to deal deceitfully with his servants.   ℟

4   Then he sent Moses his servant
    and Aaron the man he had chosen.
    Through them he showed his marvels
    and his wonders in the country of Ham.   ℟

Gospel Acclamation   Mt 11:28

Alleluia, alleluia!
Come to me, all you that labour and are burdened,
and I will give you rest, says the Lord.
Alleluia!

GOSPEL

A reading from the holy Gospel according to Matthew   11:28-30

I am gentle and humble in heart.

Jesus exclaimed: 'Come to me, all you who labour and are overburdened, and I will give you rest. Shoulder my yoke and learn from me,
for I am gentle and humble in heart, and you will find rest for your
souls. Yes, my yoke is easy and my burden light.'

This is the Gospel of the Lord.

Friday

FIRST READING

A reading from the book of Exodus   11:10–12:14

The lamb must be slain in the evening; when I see the blood I will passover you.

Moses and Aaron worked many wonders in the presence of Pharaoh. But the Lord made Pharaoh's heart stubborn, and he did not let the sons of Israel leave his country.

The Lord said to Moses and Aaron in the land of Egypt, 'This month is to be the first of all the others for you, the first month of your year. Speak to the whole community of Israel and say, 'On the tenth day of this month each man must take an animal from the flock, one for each family: one animal for each household. If the household is too small to eat the animal, a man must join with his neighbour, the nearest to his house, as the number of persons requires. You must take into account what each can eat in deciding the number for the animal. It must be an animal without blemish, a male one year old; you may take it from either sheep or goats. You must keep it till the fourteenth day of the month when the whole assembly of the community of Israel shall slaughter it between the two evenings. Some of the blood must then be taken and put on the two doorposts and the lintel of the houses where it is eaten. That night, the flesh is to be eaten, roasted over the fire; it must be eaten with unleavened bread and bitter herbs. Do not eat any of it raw or boiled, but roasted over the fire, head, feet and entrails. You must not leave any over till the morning: whatever is left till morning you are to burn. You shall eat it like this: with a girdle round your waist, sandals on your feet, a staff in your hand. You shall eat it hastily: it is a passover in honour of the Lord. That night, I will go through the land of Egypt and strike down all the first-born in the land of Egypt, man and beast alike, and I shall deal out punishment to all the gods of Egypt. I am the Lord! The blood shall serve to mark the houses that you live in. When I see the blood I will pass over you and you shall escape the destroying plague when I strike the land of Egypt. This day is to be a day of remembrance for you, and you must celebrate it as a feast in the Lord's honour. For all generations you are to declare it a day of festival, for ever.'

This is the word of the Lord.

Responsorial Psalm   Ps 115:12-13. 15-18. ℟ v.13

> ℟ I will take the cup of salvation,
>   and call on the name of the Lord.

or

> ℟ Alleluia!

1   How can I repay the Lord
    for his goodness to me?
    The cup of salvation I will raise;
    I will call on the Lord's name.   ℟

2   O precious in the eyes of the Lord
    is the death of his faithful.
    Your servant, Lord, your servant am I;
    you have loosened my bonds.   ℟

3   A thanksgiving sacrifice I make:
    I will call on the Lord's name.
    My vows to the Lord I will fulfil
    before all his people.   ℟

Gospel Acclamation   Jn 10:27

> Alleluia, alleluia!
> My sheep listen to my voice, says the Lord;
> I know them, and they follow me.
> Alleluia!

GOSPEL

A reading from the holy Gospel according to Matthew   12:1-8

The Son of Man is master of the sabbath.

Jesus took a walk one sabbath day through the cornfields. His disciples were hungry and began to pick ears of corn and eat them. The Pharisees noticed it and said to him, 'Look, your disciples are doing something that is forbidden on the sabbath.' But he said to them, 'Have you not read what David did when he and his followers were hungry – how he went into the house of God and how they ate the loaves of offering which neither he nor his followers were allowed to eat, but which were for the priests alone? Or again, have you not read in the Law that on the sabbath day the Temple priests break the sabbath without being blamed for it? Now here, I tell you, is something greater than the Temple. And if you had understood the meaning of the words: What I want is mercy, not sacrifice, you would not have condemned the blameless. For the Son of Man is master of the sabbath.'

This is the Gospel of the Lord.

Saturday

FIRST READING

A reading from the book of Exodus 12:37-42

The night is here when the Lord will lead Israel out of the land of Egypt.

The sons of Israel left Rameses for Succoth, about six hundred thousand on the march – all men – not counting their families. People of various sorts joined them in great numbers; there were flocks, too, and herds in immense droves. They baked cakes with the dough which they had brought from Egypt, unleavened because the dough was not leavened; they had been driven out of Egypt, with no time for dallying, and had not provided themselves with food for the journey. The time that the sons of Israel had spent in Egypt was four hundred and thirty years. And on the very day the four hundred and thirty years ended, all the array of the Lord left the land of Egypt. The night, when the Lord kept vigil to bring them out of the land of Egypt, must be kept as a vigil in honour of the Lord for all their generations.

This is the word of the Lord.

Responsorial Psalm Ps 135:1. 10-15. 23-24

1 O give thanks to the Lord for he is good,
℟ His love is everlasting.
He remembered us in our distress,
℟ His love is everlasting.
And he snatched us away from our foes,
℟ His love is everlasting.

2   The first-born of the Egyptians he smote,
    ℟   His love is everlasting.
    He brought Israel out from their midst,
    ℟   His love is everlasting.
    arm outstretched, with power in his hand,
    ℟   His love is everlasting.

3   He divided the Red Sea in two,
    ℟   His love is everlasting.
    he made Israel pass through the midst,
    ℟   His love is everlasting.
    he flung Pharaoh and his force in the sea,
    ℟   His love is everlasting.

or

    ℟   Alleluia!

Gospel Acclamation   2 Cor 5:19

    Alleluia, alleluia!
    God was in Christ, to reconcile the world to himself;
    and the Good News of reconciliation he has entrusted to us.
    Alleluia!

GOSPEL

A reading from the holy Gospel according to Matthew   12:14-21

   He did not show himself to them that what had been said would be fulfilled.

The Pharisees went out and began to plot against Jesus, discussing
how to destroy him.

   Jesus knew this and withdrew from the district. Many followed
him and he cured them all, but warned them not to make him known.
This was to fulfil the prophecy of Isaiah:

    Here is my servant whom I have chosen,
    my beloved, the favourite of my soul.
    I will endow him with my spirit,
    and he will proclaim the true faith to the nations.
    He will not brawl or shout,
    nor will anyone hear his voice in the streets.
    He will not break the crushed reed,

nor put out the smouldering wick
till he has led the truth to victory:
in his name the nations will put their hope.

This is the Gospel of the Lord.

SIXTEENTH WEEK IN ORDINARY TIME

Year I

Monday

FIRST READING

A reading from the book of Exodus   14:5-18

*They will know that I am the Lord God when I glorify myself at
the expense of pharaoh.*

When Pharaoh, king of Egypt, was told that the Israelites had made
their escape, he and his courtiers changed their minds about the
people. 'What have we done,' they said 'allowing Israel to leave our
service?' So Pharaoh had his chariot harnessed and gathered his
troops about him, taking six hundred of the best chariots and all the
other chariots in Egypt, each manned by a picked team. The Lord
made Pharaoh, king of Egypt, stubborn, and he gave chase to the sons
of Israel as they made their triumphant escape. So the Egyptians gave
chase and came up with them where they lay encamped beside the sea
– all the horses, the chariots of Pharaoh, his horsemen, his army –
near Pi-hahiroth, facing Baal-zephon. And as Pharaoh approached,
the sons of Israel looked round – and there were the Egyptians in
pursuit of them! The sons of Israel were terrified and cried out to the
Lord. To Moses they said, 'Were there no graves in Egypt that you
must lead us out to die in the wilderness? What good have you done
us, bringing us out of Egypt? We spoke of this in Egypt, did we not?
Leave us alone, we said, we would rather work for the Egyptians!
Better to work for the Egyptians than die in the wilderness!' Moses
answered the people, 'Have no fear! Stand firm, and you will see what
the Lord will do to save you today: the Egyptians you see today, you
will never see again. The Lord will do the fighting for you: you have
only to keep still.'

The Lord said to Moses, 'Why do you cry to me so? Tell the sons of
Israel to march on. For yourself, raise your staff and stretch out

your hand over the sea and part it for the sons of Israel to walk through the sea on dry ground. I for my part will make the heart of the Egyptians so stubborn that they will follow them. So shall I win myself glory at the expense of Pharaoh, of all his army, his chariots, his horsemen. And when I have won glory for myself, at the expense of Pharaoh and his chariots and his army, the Egyptians will learn that I am the Lord.'

This is the word of the Lord.

Responsorial Psalm   Ex 15:1-6. ℟ v.1

℟   Let us sing to the Lord;
     he has covered himself in glory.

1   I will sing to the Lord, glorious his triumph!
     Horse and rider he has thrown into the sea!
     The Lord is my strength, my song, my salvation.
     This is my God and I extol him,
     my father's God and I give him praise. ℟

2   The Lord is a warrior! The Lord is his name.
     The chariots of Pharaoh he hurled into the sea,
     the flower of his army is drowned in the sea. ℟

3   The deeps hide them; they sank like a stone.
     Your right hand, Lord, glorious in its power,
     your right hand, Lord, has shattered the enemy. ℟

Gospel Acclamation   cf. Ps 94:8

     Alleluia, alleluia!
     If today you hear his voice,
     harden not your hearts.
     Alleluia!

GOSPEL

A reading from the holy Gospel according to Matthew   12:38-42

*On Judgement Day the Queen of the South will rise up with this
generation and condemn it.*

Some of the scribes and Pharisees spoke up. 'Master,' they said 'we should like to see a sign from you.' Jesus replied, 'It is an evil and unfaithful generation that asks for a sign! The only sign it will be given is the sign of the prophet Jonah. For as Jonah was in the belly of the sea-monster for three days and three nights, so will the Son of Man be in the heart of the earth for three days and three nights. On Judgement day the men of Nineveh will stand up with this generation and condemn it, because when Jonah preached they repented; and there is something greater than Jonah here. On Judgement day the Queen of the South will rise up with this generation and condemn it, because she came from the ends of the earth to hear the wisdom of Solomon; and there is something greater than Solomon here.'

This is the Gospel of the Lord.

Tuesday

FIRST READING

A reading from the book of Exodus   14:21–15:1

The children of Israel went on dry ground right into the sea.

Moses stretched out his hand over the sea. The Lord drove back the sea with a strong easterly wind all night, and he made dry land of the sea. The waters parted and the sons of Israel went on dry ground right into the sea, walls of water to right and to left of them. The Egyptians gave chase: after them they went, right into the sea, all Pharaoh's horses, his chariots, and his horsemen. In the morning watch, the Lord looked down on the army of the Egyptians from the pillar of fire and of cloud, and threw the army into confusion. He so clogged their chariot wheels that they could scarcely make headway. 'Let us flee from the Israelites,' the Egyptians cried 'the Lord is fighting for them against the Egyptians!' 'Stretch out your hand over the sea,' the Lord said to Moses 'that the waters may flow back on the Egyptians and their chariots and their horsemen.' Moses stretched out his hand over the sea and, as day broke, the sea returned to its bed. The fleeing Egyptians marched right into it, and the Lord overthrew the Egyptians in the very middle of the sea. The returning waters overwhelmed the chariots and the horsemen of Pharaoh's whole army, which had followed the Israelites into the sea; not a single one of them was left. But the sons of Israel had marched through the sea on dry ground, walls of water to right and to left of them. That day, the Lord rescued Israel from the Egyptians, and Israel saw the Egyptians lying dead on the shore. Israel witnessed the great act that the Lord had performed against the Egyptians, and the people venerated the Lord; they put their faith in the Lord and in Moses, his servant.

It was then that Moses and the sons of Israel sang this song in honour of the Lord:*

*The Responsorial Psalm may follow immediately, as at the Easter Vigil.

Responsorial Psalm   Ex 15:8-10. 12. 17. ℟ v.1

℟   Let us sing to the Lord;
     he has covered himself in glory.

1   At the breath of your anger the waters piled high;
     the moving waters stood up like a dam.
     The deeps turned solid in the midst of the sea.
     The enemy said: 'I will pursue and overtake them,
     I will divide the plunder, I shall have my will.
     I will draw my sword, my hand shall destroy them.'   ℟

2   You blew with your breath, the sea closed over them.
     They went down like lead into the mighty waters.
     You stretched forth your hand, the earth engulfed them.   ℟

3   You will lead your people and plant them on your mountain,
     the place, O Lord, where you have made your home,
     the sanctuary, Lord, which your hands have made.   ℟

Gospel Acclamation   Jn 14:23

Alleluia, alleluia!
All who love me will keep my words,
and my Father will love them, and we will come to them.
Alleluia!

GOSPEL

A reading from the holy Gospel according to Matthew   12:46-50

*Extending his hands toward the disciples, he said: Here are my
mother and my brothers.*

Jesus was speaking to the crowds when his mother and his brothers appeared; they were standing outside and were anxious to have a word with him. But to the man who told him this Jesus replied, 'Who is my mother? Who are my brothers?' And stretching out his hand towards his disciples he said, 'Here are my mother and my brothers. Anyone who does the will of my Father in heaven, he is my brother and sister and mother.'

This is the Gospel of the Lord.

Wednesday

FIRST READING

A reading from the book of Exodus   16:1-5. 9-15

I will rain down bread from heaven for you.

From Elim they set out, and the whole community of the sons of Israel reached the wilderness of Sin – between Elim and Sinai – on the fifteenth day of the second month after they had left Egypt. And the whole community of the sons of Israel began to complain against Moses and Aaron in the wilderness and said to them, 'Why did we not die at the Lord's hand in the land of Egypt, when we were able to sit down to pans of meat and could eat bread to our heart's content! As it is, you have brought us to this wilderness to starve this whole company to death!'

Then the Lord said to Moses, 'Now I will rain down bread for you from the heavens. Each day the people are to go out and gather the day's portion; I propose to test them in this way to see whether they will follow my law or not. On the sixth day, when they prepare what they have brought in, this will be twice as much as the daily gathering.'

Moses said to Aaron, 'To the whole community of the sons of Israel say this, "Present yourselves before the Lord, for he has heard your complaints." ' As Aaron was speaking to the whole community of the sons of Israel, they turned towards the wilderness, and there was the glory of the Lord appearing in the form of a cloud. Then the Lord spoke to Moses and said, 'I have heard the complaints of the sons of Israel. Say this to them, "Between the two evenings you shall eat meat, and in the morning you shall have bread to your heart's content. Then you will learn that I, the Lord, am your God." ' And so it came about: quails flew up in the evening, and they covered the camp; in the morning there was a coating of dew all round the camp. When the coating of dew lifted, there on the surface of the desert was a thing delicate, powdery, as fine as hoarfrost on the ground. When they saw this, the sons of Israel said to one another, 'What is that?' not knowing what it was. 'That' said Moses to them 'is the bread the Lord gives you to eat.'

This is the word of the Lord.

Responsorial Psalm   Ps 77:18-19. 23-28. ℟ v.24

℟   The Lord gave them bread from heaven.

1   In their heart they put God to the test
    by demanding the food they craved.
    They even spoke against God.
    They said: 'Is it possible for God
    to prepare a table in the desert?'   ℟

2   Yet he commanded the clouds above
    and opened the gates of heaven.
    He rained down manna for their food,
    and gave them bread from heaven.   ℟

3   Mere men ate the bread of angels.
    He sent them abundance of food;
    he made the east wind blow from heaven
    and roused the south wind by his might.   ℟

4   He rained food on them like dust,
    winged fowl like the sands of the sea.
    He let it fall in the midst of their camp
    and all around their tents.   ℟

Gospel Acclamation

    Alleluia, alleluia!
    The seed is the word of God, Christ is the sower;
    all who come to him will live for ever.
    Alleluia!

GOSPEL

A reading from the holy Gospel according to Matthew   13:1-9

He increased the harvest a hundredfold.

Jesus left the house and sat by the lakeside, but such crowds gathered round him that he got into a boat and sat there. The people all stood on the beach, and he told them many things in parables.

He said, 'Imagine a sower going out to sow. As he sowed, some seeds fell on the edge of the path, and the birds came and ate them up. Others fell on patches of rock where they found little soil and sprang up straight away, because there was no depth of earth; but as soon as the sun came up they were scorched and, not having any roots, they withered away. Others fell among thorns, and the thorns grew up and choked them. Others fell on rich soil and produced their crop, some a hundredfold, some sixty, some thirty. Listen, anyone who has ears!'

This is the Gospel of the Lord.

Thursday

FIRST READING

A reading from the book of Exodus   19:1-2. 9-11. 16-20

The Lord descended on Mount Sinai before all the people.

Three months after they came out of the land of Egypt, on that day the sons of Israel came to the wilderness of Sinai. From Rephidim they set out again; and when they reached the wilderness of Sinai, there in the wilderness they pitched their camp; there facing the mountain Israel pitched camp.

The Lord said to Moses, 'I am coming to you in a dense cloud so that the people may hear when I speak to you and may trust you always.' And Moses took the people's reply back to the Lord.

The Lord said Moses, 'Go to the people and tell them to prepare themselves today and tomorrow. Let them wash their clothing and hold themselves in readiness for the third day, because on the third day the Lord will descend on the mountain of Sinai in the sight of all the people.'

Now at daybreak on the third day there were peals of thunder on the mountain and lightning flashes, a dense cloud, and a loud trumpet blast, and inside the camp all the people trembled. Then Moses led the people out of the camp to meet God; and they stood at the bottom of the mountain. The mountain of Sinai was entirely wrapped in smoke, because the Lord had descended on it in the form of fire. Like smoke from a furnace the smoke went up, and the whole mountain shook violently. Louder and louder grew the sound of the trumpet. Moses spoke, and God answered him with peals of thunder. The Lord came down on the mountain of Sinai, on the mountain top, and the Lord called Moses to the top of the mountain.

This is the word of the Lord.

Responsorial Psalm   Dan 3:52-56. ℟ v.52

1   You are blest, Lord God of our fathers.
     ℟   Glory and praise for ever!
     Blest your glorious holy name.
     ℟   Glory and praise for ever!

2   You are blest in the temple of your glory.
     ℟   Glory and praise for ever!
     You are blest on the throne of your kingdom.
     ℟   Glory and praise for ever!

3   You are blest who gaze into the depths.
     ℟   Glory and praise for ever!
     You are blest in the firmament of heaven.
     ℟   Glory and praise for ever!

Gospel Acclamation   cf. Mt 11:25

    Alleluia, alleluia!
    Blessed are you, Father, Lord of heaven and earth;
    you have revealed to little ones the mysteries of the kingdom.
    Alleluia!

GOSPEL

A reading from the holy Gospel according to Matthew   13:10-17

*To you it is given to know the mysteries of the kingdom of heaven, but
to them it has not been given.*

The disciples went up to Jesus and asked, 'Why do you talk to the crowds in parables?' 'Because' he replied, 'the mysteries of the kingdom of heaven are revealed to you, but they are not revealed to them. For anyone who has will be given more, and he will have more than enough; but from anyone who has not, even what he has will be taken away. The reason I talk to them in parables is that they look without seeing and listen without hearing or understanding. So in their case the prophecy of Isaiah is being fulfilled:

You will listen and listen again, but not understand,
see and see again, but not perceive.
For the heart of this nation has grown coarse,
their ears are dull of hearing, and they have shut their eyes
for fear they should see with their eyes,
hear with their ears,
understand with their heart,
and be converted
and be healed by me.

But happy are your eyes because they see, your ears because they hear! I tell you solemnly, many prophets and holy men longed to see what you see, and never saw it; to hear what you hear, and never heard it.'

This is the Gospel of the Lord.

Friday

FIRST READING

A reading from the book of Exodus   20:1-17

The law was given through Moses.

The Lord spoke all these words. He said, 'I am the Lord your God who brought you out of the land of Egypt, out of the house of slavery.

'You shall have no gods except me.

'You shall not make yourself a carved image or any likeness of anything in heaven or earth beneath or in the waters under the earth; you shall not bow down to them or serve them. For I, the Lord your God, am a jealous God and I punish the father's fault in the sons, the grandsons, and the great-grandsons of those who hate me; but I show kindness to thousands of those who love me and keep my commandments.

'You shall not utter the name of the Lord your God to misuse it, for the Lord will not leave unpunished the man who utters his name to misuse it.

'Remember the sabbath day and keep it holy. For six days you shall labour and do all your work, but the seventh day is a sabbath for the Lord your God. You shall do no work that day, neither you nor your son nor your daughter nor your servants, men or women, nor your animals nor the stranger who lives with you. For in six days the Lord made the heavens and the earth and the sea and all that these hold, but on the seventh day he rested; that is why the Lord has blessed the sabbath day and made it sacred.

'Honour your father and your mother so that you may have a long life in the land that the Lord your God has given you.

'You shall not kill.

'You shall not commit adultery.

'You shall not steal.

'You shall not bear false witness against your neighbour.

'You shall not covet your neighbour's house. You shall not covet your neighbour's wife, or his servant, man or woman, or his ox, or his donkey, or anything that is his.'

This is the word of the Lord.

Responsorial Psalm   Ps 18:8-11. ℟ Jn 6:68

℟ Lord, you have the words of everlasting life.

1   The law of the Lord is perfect,
     it revives the soul.
     The rule of the Lord is to be trusted,
     it gives wisdom to the simple.   ℟

2   The precepts of the Lord are right,
     they gladden the heart.
     The command of the Lord is clear,
     it gives light to the eyes.   ℟

3   The fear of the Lord is holy,
     abiding for ever.
     The decrees of the Lord are truth
     and all of them just.

   ℟   Lord, you have the words of everlasting life.

4   They are more to be desired than gold,
     than the purest of gold
     and sweeter are they than honey,
     than honey from the comb. ℟

Gospel Acclamation   cf. Lk 8:15

    Alleluia, alleluia!
    Happy are they who have kept the word with a generous heart
    and yield a harvest through perseverance.
    Alleluia!

GOSPEL

A reading from the holy Gospel according to Matthew   13:18-23

All who hear the word of God and understand it, yield much fruit.

Jesus said to his disciples: 'You are to hear the parable of the sower. When anyone hears the word of the kingdom without understanding, the evil one comes and carries off what was sown in his heart; this is the man who received the seed on the edge of the path. The one who received it on patches of rock is the man who hears the word and welcomes it at once with joy. But he has no root in him, he does not last; let some trial come, or some persecution on account of the word, and he falls away at once. The one who received the seed in thorns is the man who hears the word, but the worries of this world and the lure of riches choke the word and so he produces nothing. And the one who received the seed in rich soil is the man who hears the word and understands it; he is the one who yields a harvest and produces now a hundredfold, now sixty, now thirty.'

    This is the Gospel of the Lord.

Saturday

FIRST READING

A reading from the book of Exodus   24:3-8

This is the blood of the covenant which the Lord God has made with you.

Moses went and told the people all the commands of the Lord and all the ordinances. In answer, all the people said with one voice, 'We will observe all the commands that the Lord has decreed.' Moses put all the commands of the Lord into writing, and early next morning he built an altar at the foot of the mountain, with twelve standing-stones for the twelve tribes of Israel. Then he directed certain young Israelites to offer holocausts and to immolate bullocks to the Lord as communion sacrifices. Half of the blood Moses took up and put into basins, the other half he cast on the altar. And taking the Book of the Covenant he read it to the listening people, and they said, 'We will observe all that the Lord has decreed; we will obey.' Then Moses took the blood and cast it towards the people. 'This' he said 'is the blood of the Covenant that the Lord has made with you, containing all these rules.'

This is the word of the Lord.

Responsorial Psalm   Ps 49:1-2. 5-6. 14-15. ℟ v.14

℟   Offer to God a sacrifice of praise.

1   The God of gods, the Lord,
     has spoken and summoned the earth,
     from the rising of the sun to its setting.
     Out of Zion's perfect beauty he shines.   ℟

2   'Summon before me my people
     who made covenant with me by sacrifice.'
     The heavens proclaim his justice,
     for he, God, is the judge.   ℟

3   Pay your sacrifice of thanksgiving to God
     and render him your votive offerings.
     'Call on me in the day of distress.
     I will free you and you shall honour me.'   ℟

Gospel Acclamation   James 1:21

> Alleluia, alleluia!
> Receive and submit to the word planted in you;
> it can save your souls.
> Alleluia!

GOSPEL

A reading from the holy Gospel according to Matthew   13:24-30

Let them both grow until the harvest time.

Jesus put a parable before the crowds, 'The kingdom of heaven may be compared to a man who sowed good seed in his field. While everybody was asleep his enemy came, sowed darnel all among the wheat, and made off. When the new wheat sprouted and ripened, the darnel appeared as well. The owner's servants went to him and said, "Sir, was it not good seed that you sowed in your field? If so, where does the darnel come from?" "Some enemy has done this" he answered. And the servants said, "Do you want us to go and weed it out?" But he said, "No, because when you weed out the darnel you might pull up the wheat with it. Let them both grow till the harvest; and at harvest time I shall say to the reapers: First collect the darnel and tie it in bundles to be burnt, then gather the wheat into my barn." '

This is the Gospel of the Lord.

SEVENTEENTH WEEK IN ORDINARY TIME

Year I

Monday

FIRST READING

A reading from the book of Exodus   32:15-24. 30-34

This people has committed a grave sin, making themselves gods of gold.

Moses made his way back down the mountain with the two tablets of the Testimony in his hands, tablets inscribed on both sides, inscribed on the front and on the back. These tablets were the work of God, and the writing on them was God's writing engraved on the tablets.

Joshua heard the noise of the people shouting. 'There is the sound of battle in the camp,' he told Moses. Moses answered him:

'No song of victory is this sound,
no wailing for defeat this sound;
it is the sound of chanting that I hear.'

As he approached the camp and saw the calf and the groups dancing, Moses' anger blazed. He threw down the tablets he was holding and broke them at the foot of the mountain. He seized the calf they had made and burned it, grinding it into powder which he scattered on the water; and he made the sons of Israel drink it. To Aaron Moses said, 'What has this people done to you, for you to bring such a great sin on them?' 'Let not my lord's anger blaze like this' Aaron answered. 'You know yourself how prone this people is to evil. They said to me, "Make us a god to go at our head; this Moses, the man who brought us up from Egypt, we do not know what has become of him." So I said to them, "Who has gold?" and they took it off and brought it to me. I threw it into the fire and out came this calf.'

On the following day Moses said to the people, 'You have committed a grave sin. But now I shall go up to the Lord: perhaps I can make atonement for your sin.' And Moses returned to the Lord. 'I am grieved,' he cried 'this people has committed a grave sin making themselves a god of gold. And yet, if it pleased you to forgive this sin of theirs ... ! But if not, then blot me out from the book that you have written.' The Lord answered Moses, 'It is the man who has sinned against me that I shall blot out from my book. Go now, lead the people to the place of which I told you. My angel shall go before you but, on the day of my visitation, I shall punish them for their sin.'

This is the word of the Lord.

Responsorial Psalm   Ps 105:19-23. ℟ v.1

℟   Give thanks to the Lord for he is good.

or

℟   Alleluia!

1   They fashioned a calf at Horeb
     and worshipped an image of metal,
     exchanging the God who was their glory
     for the image of a bull that eats grass.   ℟

2   They forgot the God who was their saviour,
     who had done such great things in Egypt,
     such portents in the land of Ham,
     such marvels at the Red Sea.   ℟

3   For this he said he would destroy them,
     but Moses, the man he had chosen,
     stood in the breach before him,
     to turn back his anger from destruction.   ℟

Gospel Acclamation   James 1:18

     Alleluia, alleluia!
     The Father gave us birth by his message of truth,
     that we might be as the first fruits of his creation.
     Alleluia!

GOSPEL

A reading from the holy Gospel according to Matthew   13:31-35

When the seeds grows it is the biggest shrub of all and the birds of
the air come and nest in its branches.

Jesus put a parable before the crowds, 'The kingdom of heaven is like
a mustard seed which a man took and sowed in his field. It is the
smallest of all the seeds, but when it has grown it is the biggest shrub
of all and becomes a tree so that the birds of the air come and shelter
in its branches.'

He told them another parable, 'The kingdom of heaven is like the
yeast a woman took and mixed in with three measures of flour till it
was leavened all through.'

In all this Jesus spoke to the crowds in parables; indeed, he would
never speak to them except in parables. This was to fulfill the
prophecy:

I will speak to you in parables
and expound things hidden since the foundation of the world.

This is the Gospel of the Lord.

Tuesday

FIRST READING

A reading from the book of Exodus   33:7-11; 34:5-9. 28

The Lord God spoke to Moses face to face.

Moses used to take the Tent and pitch it outside the camp, at some
distance from the camp. He called it the Tent of Meeting. Anyone
who had to consult the Lord would go out to the Tent of Meeting,
outside the camp. Whenever Moses went out to the Tent, all the
people would rise. Every man would stand at the door of his tent
and watch Moses until he reached the Tent; the pillar of cloud
would come down and station itself at the entrance to the Tent, and
the Lord would speak with Moses. When they saw the pillar of
cloud stationed at the entrance to the Tent, all the people
would rise and bow low, each at the door of his tent. The Lord would
speak with Moses face to face, as a man speaks with his friend.
Then Moses would turn back to the camp, but the young man who

was his servant, Joshua son of Nun, would not leave the Tent.

Moses stood with the Lord on the mountain. He called on the name of the Lord. The Lord passed before him and proclaimed, 'The Lord, the Lord, a God of tenderness and compassion, slow to anger, rich in kindness and faithfulness; for thousands he maintains his kindness, forgives faults, transgression, sin; yet he lets nothing go unchecked, punishing the father's fault in the sons and in the grandsons to the third and fourth generation.' And Moses bowed down to the ground at once and worshipped. 'If I have indeed won your favour, Lord,' he said 'let my Lord come with us, I beg. True, they are a headstrong people, but forgive us our faults and our sins, and adopt us as your heritage.'

He stayed there with the Lord for forty days and forty nights, eating and drinking nothing. He inscribed on the tablets the words of the Covenant – the Ten Words.

This is the word of the Lord.

Responsorial Psalm   Ps 102:6-13. ℟ v.8

℟   The Lord is kind and merciful.

1   The Lord does deeds of justice,
       gives judgement for all who are oppressed.
       He made known his ways to Moses
       and his deeds to Israel's sons. ℟

2   The Lord is compassion and love,
       slow to anger and rich in mercy.
       His wrath will come to an end:
       he will not be angry for ever. ℟

3   He does not treat us according to our sins
       nor repay us according to our faults.
       For as the heavens are high above the earth
       so strong is his love for those who fear him. ℟

4   As far as the east is from the west
       so far does he remove our sins.
       As a father has compassion on his sons,
       the Lord has pity on those who fear him. ℟

Gospel Acclamation

Alleluia, alleluia!
The seed is the word of the God, Christ is the sower;
all who come to him will live for ever.
Alleluia!

GOSPEL

A reading from the holy Gospel according to Matthew   13:36-43

Just as the weeds are gathered up and burnt in the fire, so it will
be at the end of time.

Leaving the crowds, Jesus went to the house; and his disciples came to
him and said, 'Explain the parable about the darnel in the field to us.'
He said in reply, 'The sower of the good seed is the Son of Man. The
field is the world; the good seed is the subjects of the kingdom; the
darnel, the subjects of the evil one; the enemy who sowed them, the
devil; the harvest is the end of the world; the reapers are the angels.
Well then, just as the darnel is gathered up and burnt in the fire, so it
will be at the end of time. The Son of Man will send his angels and
they will gather out of his kingdom all things that provoke offences
and all who do evil, and throw them into the blazing furnace, where
there will be weeping and grinding of teeth. Then the virtuous will
shine like the sun in the kingdom of their Father. Listen, anyone who
has ears!'

This is the Gospel of the Lord.

Wednesday

FIRST READING

A reading from the book of Exodus   34:29-35

Seeing Moses' face, they would not approach him.

When Moses came down from the mountain of Sinai – as he came
down from the mountain, Moses had the two tablets of the Testimony
in his hands – he did not know that the skin on his face was radiant
after speaking with the Lord. And when Aaron and all the sons of
Israel saw Moses, the skin on his face shone so much that

they would not venture near him. But Moses called to them, and Aaron with all the leaders of the community came back to him; and he spoke to them. Then all the sons of Israel came closer, and he passed on to them all the orders that the Lord had given him on the mountain of Sinai. And when Moses had finished speaking to them, he put a veil over his face. Whenever he went into the Lord's presence to speak with him, Moses would remove the veil until he came out again. And when he came out, he would tell the sons of Israel what he had been ordered to pass on to them, and the sons of Israel would see the face of Moses radiant. Then Moses would put the veil back over his face until he returned to speak with the Lord.

This is the word of the Lord.

Responsorial Psalm   Ps 98:5-7. 9. ℟ cf. v.9

℟   Holy is the Lord our God.

1   Exalt the Lord our God;
    bow down before Zion, his footstool.
    He the Lord is holy.   ℟

2   Among his priests were Aaron and Moses,
    among those who invoked his name were Samuel.
    They invoked the Lord and he answered.   ℟

3   To them he spoke in the pillar of cloud.
    They did his will; they kept the law,
    which he, the Lord, had given.   ℟

4   Exalt the Lord our God;
    bow down before his holy mountain
    for the Lord our God is holy.   ℟

Gospel Acclamation   Jn 15:15

Alleluia, alleluia!
I call you my friends, says the Lord,
for I have made known to you all that the Father has told me.
Alleluia!

GOSPEL

A reading from the holy Gospel according to Matthew   13:44-46

He sold everything he had and went and bought the field.

Jesus said to the crowds: 'The kingdom of heaven is like treasure hidden in a field which someone has found; he hides it again, goes off happy, sells everything he owns and buys the field.

'Again, the kingdom of heaven is like a merchant looking for fine pearls; when he finds one of great value he goes and sells everything he owns and buys it.'

This is the Gospel of the Lord.

Thursday

FIRST READING

A reading from the book of Exodus   40:16-21. 34-38

The cloud covered the Tent of Meeting and the glory of the Lord
God filled the tabernacle.

Moses did exactly as the Lord had directed him. The tabernacle was set up on the first day of the first month in the second year. Moses erected the tabernacle. He fixed the sockets for it, put up its frames, put its cross-bars in position, set up its posts. He spread the tent over the tabernacle and on top of this the covering for the tent, as the Lord had directed Moses. He took the Testimony and placed it inside the ark. He set the shafts to the ark and placed the throne of mercy on it. He brought the ark into the tabernacle and put the screening veil in place; thus he screened the ark of the Lord, as the Lord had directed Moses.

The cloud covered the Tent of Meeting and the glory of the Lord filled the tabernacle. Moses could not enter the Tent of Meeting because of the cloud that rested on it and because of the glory of the Lord that filled the tabernacle.

At every stage of their journey, whenever the cloud rose from the tabernacle the sons of Israel would resume their march. If the cloud did not rise, they waited and would not march until it did. For the cloud of the Lord rested on the tabernacle by day, and a fire shone within the cloud by night, for all the House of Israel to see. And so it was for every stage of their journey.

This is the word of the Lord.

209

Responsorial Psalm   Ps 83:3-6. 8. 11. ℟ v.2

℟ How lovely is your dwelling-place,
    Lord, mighty God!

1 My soul is longing and yearning,
   is yearning for the courts of the Lord.
   My heart and my soul ring out their joy
   to God, the living God. ℟

2 The sparrow herself finds a home
   and the swallow a nest for her brood;
   she lays her young by your altars,
   Lord of hosts, my king and my God. ℟

3 They are happy, who dwell in your house,
   for ever singing your praise.
   They are happy, whose strength is in you,
   they walk with ever growing strength. ℟

4 One day within your courts
   is better than a thousand elsewhere.
   The threshold of the house of God
   I prefer to the dwellings of the wicked. ℟

Gospel Acclamation   cf. Acts 16:14

Alleluia, alleluia!
Open our hearts, O Lord,
to listen to the words of your Son.
Alleluia!

GOSPEL

A reading from the holy Gospel according to Matthew   13:47. 53

They gather the good ones in a basket, and the bad are thrown away.

Jesus said to the crowds: 'The kingdom of heaven is like a dragnet cast
into the sea that brings in a haul of all kinds. When it is full, the
fishermen haul it ashore; then, sitting down, they collect the good
ones in a basket and throw away those that are no use. This is how it
will be at the end of time; the angels will appear and separate the

wicked from the just to throw them into the blazing furnace where there will be weeping and grinding of teeth.

'Have you understood all this?' They said, 'Yes.' And he said to them, 'Well then, every scribe who becomes a disciple of the kingdom of heaven is like a householder who brings out from his storeroom things both new and old.'

When Jesus had finished these parables he left the district.

This is the Gospel of the Lord.

Friday

FIRST READING

A reading from the book of Leviticus   23:1. 4-11. 15-16. 27. 34-37

The solemn feasts of the Lord God are sacred assemblies.

The Lord spoke to Moses; he said:

'These are the Lord's solemn festivals, the sacred assemblies to which you are to summon the sons of Israel on the appointed day.

'The fourteenth day of the first month, between the two evenings, is the Passover of the Lord; and the fifteenth day of the same month is the feast of Unleavened Bread for the Lord. For seven days you shall eat bread without leaven. On the first day you are to hold a sacred assembly; you must do no heavy work. For seven days you shall offer a burnt offering to the Lord. The seventh day is to be a day of sacred assembly; you must do no work.'

The Lord spoke to Moses; he said:

'Speak to the sons of Israel and say to them:

'When you enter the land that I give you, and gather in the harvest there, you must bring the first sheaf of your harvest to the priest, and he is to present it to the Lord with the gesture of offering, so that you may be acceptable. The priest shall make this offering on the day after the sabbath.

'From the day after the sabbath, the day on which you bring the sheaf of offering, you are to count seven full weeks. You are to count fifty days, to the day after the seventh sabbath, and then you are to offer the Lord a new oblation.

'But the tenth day of this seventh month shall be the Day of Atonement. You are to hold a sacred assembly. You must fast, and you must offer a burnt offering to the Lord.

'The fifteenth day of this seventh month shall be the feast of Tabernacles for the Lord, lasting seven days. The first day is a day of sacred assembly; you must do no heavy work. For seven days you must offer a burnt offering to the Lord. On the eighth day you are to hold a sacred assembly, you must offer a burnt offering to the Lord. It is a day of solemn meeting; you must do no heavy work.

'These are the solemn festivals of the Lord to which you are to summon the children of Israel, sacred assemblies for the purpose of offering burnt offerings, holocausts, oblations, sacrifices and libations to the Lord, according to the ritual of each day.'

This is the word of the Lord.

Responsial Psalm   Ps 80:3-6. 10-11. ℟ v.2

℟   Sing with joy to God our help.

1   Raise a song and sound the timbrel,
     the sweet-sounding harp and the lute,
     blow the trumpet at the new moon,
     when the moon is full, on our feast.   ℟

2   For this is Israel's law,
     a command of the God of Jacob.
     He imposed it as a rule on Joseph,
     when he went out against the land of Egypt.   ℟

2   Let there be no foreign god among you,
     no worship of an alien god.
     I am the Lord your God,
     who brought you from the land of Egypt.   ℟

Gospel Acclamation   1 Peter 1:25

     Alleluia, alleluia!
     The word of the Lord stands for ever;
     it is the word given to you, the Good News.
     Alleluia!

GOSPEL

A reading from the holy Gospel according to Matthew   13:54-58

Is this not the son of the carpenter? Where did he get all his wisdom?

Coming to his home town, Jesus taught the people in their synagogue in such a way that they were astonished and said, 'Where did the man get this wisdom and these miraculous powers? This is the carpenter's son, surely? Is not his mother the woman called Mary, and his brothers James and Joseph and Simon and Jude? His sisters, too, are they not all here with us? So where did the man get it all?' And they would not accept him. But Jesus said to them, 'A prophet is only despised in his own country and in his own house,' and he did not work many miracles there because of their lack of faith.

This is the Gospel of the Lord.

Saturday

FIRST READING

A reading from the book of Leviticus   25:1. 8-17

In the jubilee year you will reap all you possess.

The Lord spoke to Moses on Mount Sinai; he said: 'You are to count seven weeks of years – seven times seven years, that is to say a period of seven weeks of years, forty-nine years. And on the tenth day of the seventh month you shall sound the trumpet; on the Day of Atonement you shall sound the trumpet throughout the land. You will declare this fiftieth year sacred and proclaim the liberation of all the inhabitants of the land. This is to be a jubilee for you; each of you will return to his ancestral home, each to his own clan. This fiftieth year is to be a jubilee year for you: you will not sow, you will not harvest the ungathered corn, you will not gather from the untrimmed vine. The jubilee is to be a holy thing to you, you will eat what comes from the fields.

'In this year of jubilee each of you is to return to his ancestral home. If you buy or sell with your neighbour, let no one wrong his brother. If you buy from your neighbour, this must take into account the number of years since the jubilee: according to the number of productive years he will fix the price. The greater the number of years, the higher shall be the price demanded; the less the number of years, the greater the reduction; for what he is selling you is a certain number of harvests. Let none of you wrong his neighbour, but fear your God; I am the Lord your God.'

This is the word of the Lord.

Responsorial Psalm   Ps 66:2-3. 5. 7-8. ℟ v.4

℟   O God, let all the nations praise you!

1   O God, be gracious and bless us
    and let your face shed its light upon us.
    So will your ways be known upon earth
    and all nations learn your saving help.   ℟

2   Let the nations be glad and exult
    for you rule the world with justice.
    With fairness you rule the peoples,
    you guide the nations on earth.   ℟

3   The earth has yielded its fruit
    for God, our God, has blessed us.
    May God still give us his blessing
    till the ends of the earth revere him.   ℟

Gospel Acclamation   Mt 5:10

    Alleluia, alleluia!
    Happy are they who suffer persecution for justice' sake;
    the kingdom of heaven is theirs.
    Alleluia!

GOSPEL

A reading from the holy Gospel according to Matthew   14:1-12

Herod had John beheaded; the disciples went and told Jesus.

Herod the tetrarch heard about the reputation of Jesus, and said to his court, 'This is John the Baptist himself; he has risen from the dead, and that is why miraculous powers are at work in him.'

Now it was Herod who had arrested John, chained him up and put him in prison because of Herodias, his brother Philip's wife. For John had told him, 'It is against the Law for you to have her.' He had wanted to kill him but was afraid of the people, who regarded John as a prophet. Then, during the celebrations for Herod's birthday, the daughter of Herodias danced before the company, and so delighted Herod that he promised on oath to give her anything she asked. Prompted by her mother she said, 'Give me John the Baptist's head, here, on a dish.' The king was distressed but, thinking of the oaths he had sworn and of his guests, he ordered it to be given her, and sent and had John beheaded in the prison. The head was brought in on a dish and given to the girl who took it to her mother. John's disciples came and took the body and buried it; then they went off to tell Jesus.

This is the Gospel of the Lord.

EIGHTEENTH WEEK IN ORDINARY TIME
Year I

Monday

FIRST READING

A reading from the book of Numbers   11:4-15

I am not able to carry this nation by myself alone.

The sons of Israel began to wail, 'Who will give us meat to eat?' they said. 'Think of the fish we used to eat free in Egypt, the cucumbers, melons, leeks, onions and garlic! Here we are wasting away, stripped of everything; there is nothing but manna for us to look at!'

The manna was like coriander seed, and had the appearance of bdellium. The people went round gathering it, and ground it in a mill or crushed it with a pestle; it was then cooked in a pot and made into pancakes. It tasted like cake made with oil. When the dew fell on the camp at night-time, the manna fell with it.

Moses heard the people wailing, every family at the door of its tent. The anger of the Lord flared out, and Moses greatly worried over this. And he spoke to the Lord:

'Why do you treat your servant so badly? Why have I not found favour with you, so that you load on me the weight of all this nation? Was it I who conceived all this people, was it I who gave them birth, that you should say to me, "Carry them in your bosom, like a nurse with a baby at the breast, to the land that I swore to give their fathers?" Where am I to find meat to give to all this people, when they come worrying me so tearfully and say, "Give us meat to eat"? I am not able to carry this nation by myself alone; the weight is too much for me. If this is how you want to deal with me, I would rather you killed me! If only I had found favour in your eyes, and not lived to see such misery as this!'

This is the word of the Lord.

Responsial Psalm   Ps 80:12-17. ℟ v.2

℟   Sing with joy to God our help.

1   My people did not heed my voice
     and Israel would not obey,
     so I left them in their stubbornness of heart
     to follow their own designs.   ℟

2   O that my people would heed me,
     that Israel would walk in my ways!
     At once I would subdue their foes,
     turn my hand against their enemies.   ℟

3   The Lord's enemies would cringe at their feet
     and their subjection would last for ever.
     But Israel I would feed with finest wheat
     and fill them with honey from the rock.   ℟

Gospel Acclamation   Mt 4:4

     Alleluia, alleluia!
     No one lives on bread alone,
     but on every word that comes from the mouth of God.
     Alleluia!

GOSPEL

A reading from the holy Gospel according to Matthew   14:13-21

*Raising his eyes to heaven he said the blessing and gave the bread
to his disciples who in turn gave it to the crowds.*

When Jesus received the news of John the Baptist's death he
withdrew by boat to a lonely place where they could be by themselves.
But the people heard of this and, leaving the towns, went after him on
foot. So as he stepped ashore he saw a large crowd; and he took pity on
them and healed their sick.

When evening came, the disciples went to him and said, 'This is a
lonely place, and the time has slipped by; so send the people away, and
they can go to the villages to buy themselves some food.' Jesus replied,
'There is no need for them to go: give them something to eat
yourselves.' But they answered, 'All we have with us is five loaves and
two fish.' 'Bring them here to me,' he said. He gave orders that the
people were to sit down on the grass; then he took the five loaves and
the two fish, raised his eyes to heaven and said the blessing. And
breaking the loaves he handed them to his disciples who gave them to
the crowds. They all ate as much as they wanted, and they collected
the scraps remaining, twelve baskets full. Those who ate numbered
about five thousand men, to say nothing of women and children.

This is the Gospel of the Lord.

Alternative Gospel

This is to be used in Year A, when the Gospel given above is read on the preceding
Sunday.

A reading from the holy Gospel according to Matthew   14:22-36

Order me to come to you across the water.

When Jesus heard of the death of John the Baptist, he made the
disciples get into the boat, and go on ahead to the other side while he
would send the crowds away. After sending the crowds away he went
up into the hills by himself to pray. When evening came, he was there
alone, while the boat, by now far out on the lake, was battling with a
heavy sea, for there was a head-wind. In the fourth watch of the night
he went towards them, walking on the lake, and when the disciples
saw him on the lake they were terrified. 'It is a ghost' they said,

and cried out in fear. But at once Jesus called out to them, saying, 'Courage! It is I! Do not be afraid.' It was Peter who answered. 'Lord', he said 'if it is you, tell me to come to you across the water.' 'Come' said Jesus. Then Peter got out of the boat and started walking towards Jesus across the water, but as soon as he felt the force of the wind, he took fright and began to sink. 'Lord! Save me!' he cried. Jesus put out his hand at once and held him. 'Man of little faith,' he said 'why did you doubt?' And as they got into the boat the wind dropped. The men in the boat bowed down before him and said, 'Truly, you are the Son of God.'

Having made the crossing, they came to land at Gennesaret. When the local people recognised him they spread the news through the whole neighbourhood and took all that were sick to him, begging him just to let them touch the fringe of his cloak. And all those who touched it were completely cured.

This is the Gospel of the Lord.

Tuesday

FIRST READING

A reading from the book of Numbers   12:1-13

Moses is not like other prophets. How have you dared to speak against him?

Miriam, and Aaron too, spoke against Moses in connexion with the Cushite woman he had taken. (For he had married a Cushite woman.) They said, 'Has the Lord spoken to Moses only? Has he not spoken to us too?' The Lord heard this. Now Moses was the most humble of men, the humblest man on earth.

Suddenly, the Lord said to Moses and Aaron and Miriam, 'Come, all three of you, to the Tent of Meeting.' They went, all three of them, and the Lord came down in a pillar of cloud and stood at the entrance of the Tent. He called Aaron and Miriam and they both came forward. The Lord said, 'Listen now to my words:

If any man among you is a prophet
I make myself known to him in a vision,
I speak to him in a dream.
Not so with my servant Moses:

he is at home in my house;
I speak with him face to face,
plainly and not in riddles,
and he sees the form of the Lord.

How then have you dared to speak against my servant Moses?'

The anger of the Lord blazed out against them. He departed, and as soon as the cloud withdrew from the Tent, there was Miriam a leper, white as snow! Aaron turned to look at her; she had become a leper.

Aaron said to Moses:

'Help me, my lord! Do not punish us for a sin committed in folly of which we are guilty. I entreat you, do not let her be like a monster, coming from its mother's womb with flesh half corrupted.'

Moses cried to the Lord, 'O God,' he said 'please heal her, I beg you!'

This is the word of the Lord.

Responsial Psalm   Ps 50:3-7. 12-13. ℟ cf. v.3

℟ Be merciful, O Lord, for we have sinned.

1 Have mercy on me, God, in your kindness.
   In your compassion blot out my offence.
   O wash me more and more from my guilt
   and cleanse me from my sin. ℟

2 My offences truly I know them;
   my sin is always before me.
   Against you, you alone, have I sinned;
   what is evil in your sight I have done. ℟

3 That you may be justified when you give sentence
   and be without reproach when you judge,
   O see, in guilt I was born,
   a sinner was I conceived. ℟

4 A pure heart create for me, O God,
   put a steadfast spirit within me.
   Do not cast me away from your presence,
   nor deprive me of your holy spirit. ℟

Gospel Acclamation   Jn 1:49

> Alleluia, alleluia!
> Master, you are the Son of God,
> you are the king of Israel.
> Alleluia!

GOSPEL

A reading from the holy Gospel according to Matthew   14:22-36

Order me to come to you across the water.

Jesus made the disciples get into the boat and go on ahead to the other side while he would send the crowds away. After sending the crowds away he went up into the hills by himself to pray. When evening came, he was there alone, while the boat, by now far out on the lake, was battling with a heavy sea, for there was a head-wind. In the fourth watch of the night he went towards them, walking on the lake, and when the disciples saw him walking on the lake they were terrified. 'It is a ghost' they said, and cried out in fear. But at once Jesus called out to them, saying, 'Courage! It is I! Do not be afraid.' It was Peter who answered. 'Lord,' he said 'if it is you, tell me to come to you across the water.' 'Come' said Jesus. Then Peter got out of the boat and started walking towards Jesus across the water, but as soon as he felt the force of the wind he took fright and began to sink. 'Lord! Save me!' he cried. Jesus put out his hand at once and held him. 'Man of little faith,' he said 'why did you doubt?' And as they got into the boat the wind dropped. The men in the boat bowed down before him and said, 'Truly, you are the Son of God.'

Having made the crossing, they came to land at Gennesaret. When the local people recognised him they spread the news through the whole neighbourhood and took all that were sick to him, begging him just to let them touch the fringe of his cloak. And all those who touched it were completely cured.

This is the Gospel of the Lord.

Alternative Gospel

This is to be used in Year A, when the Gospel given above is read on the preceding Monday.

A reading from the holy Gospel according to Matthew   15:1-2. 10-14

Any plant my heavenly Father has not planted will be pulled up by the roots.

Pharisees and scribes from Jerusalem came to Jesus and said, 'Why do your disciples break away from the tradition of the elders? They do not wash their hands when they eat food.'

He called the people to him and said, 'Listen, and understand. What goes into the mouth does not make a man unclean; it is what comes out of the mouth that makes him unclean.'

Then the disciples came to him and said, 'Do you know that the Pharisees were shocked when they heard what you said?' He replied, 'Any plant my heavenly Father has not planted will be pulled up by the roots. Leave them alone. They are blind men leading blind men; and if one blind man leads another, both will fall into a pit.'

This is the Gospel of the Lord.

Wednesday

FIRST READING

A reading from the book of Numbers   13:1-2. 25–14:1. 26-29. 34-35

They will have nothing of the land they desired.

The Lord spoke to Moses in the wilderness of Paran and said, 'Send out men, one from each tribe, to make a reconnaissance of this land of Canaan which I am giving to the sons of Israel. Send the leader of each tribe.' At the end of forty days, they came back from their reconnaissance of the land. They sought out Moses, Aaron and the whole community of Israel, in the wilderness of Paran, at Kadesh. They made their report to them, and to the whole community, and showed them the produce of the country.

They told them this story, 'We went into the land to which you sent us. It does indeed flow with milk and honey; this is its produce. At the same time, its inhabitants are a powerful people; the towns are fortified and very big; yes, and we saw the descendants of Anak there.

The Amalekite holds the Negeb area, the Hittite, Amorite and Jebusite the highlands, and the Canaanite the sea coast and the banks of the Jordan.'

Caleb harangued the people gathered about Moses: 'We must march in,' he said 'and conquer this land: we are well able to do it.' But the men who had gone up with him answered, 'We are not able to march against this people; they are stronger than we are.' And they began to disparage the country they had reconnoitred to the sons of Israel, 'The country we went to reconnoitre is a country that devours its inhabitants. Every man we saw there was of enormous size. Yes, and we saw giants there (the sons of Anak, descendants of the Giants). We felt like grasshoppers, and so we seemed to them.'

At this, the whole community raised their voices and cried aloud, and the people wailed all that night. The Lord spoke to Moses and Aaron. He said:

'How long does this perverse community complain against me? I have heard the complaints which the sons of Israel make against me. Say to them, "As I live – it is the Lord who speaks – I will deal with you according to the very words you have used in my hearing. In this wilderness your dead bodies will fall, all you men of the census, all you who were numbered from the age of twenty years and over, you who have complained against me. For forty days you reconnoitred the land. Each day shall count for a year: for forty years you shall bear the burden of your sins, and you shall learn what it means to reject me." I, the Lord, have spoken: this is how I will deal with this perverse community that has conspired against me. Here in this wilderness, to the last man, they shall die.'

This is the word of the Lord.

Responsorial Psalm   Ps 105:6-7. 13-14. 21-23. ℟ v.4

℟ Lord, remember us,
      for the love you bear your people.

or

℟ Alleluia!

1 Our sin is the sin of our fathers;
      we have done wrong, our deeds have been evil.
      Our fathers when they were in Egypt
      paid no heed to your wonderful deeds.   ℟

2 But they soon forgot his deeds
and would not wait upon his will.
They yielded to their cravings in the desert
and put God to the test in the wilderness. ℞

3 They forgot the God who was their saviour,
who had done such great things in Egypt,
such portents in the land of Ham,
such marvels at the Red Sea. ℞

4 For this he said he would destroy them,
but Moses, the man he had chosen,
stood in the breach before him,
to turn back his anger from destruction. ℞

Gospel Acclamation   Lk 7:16

Alleluia, alleluia!
A great prophet has appeared among us;
God has visited his people.
Alleluia!

GOSPEL

A reading from the holy Gospel according to Matthew   15:21-28

Woman, you have great faith.

Jesus left Gennesaret and withdrew to the region of Tyre and Sidon. Then out came a Canaanite woman from that district and started shouting, 'Sir, Son of David, take pity on me. My daughter is tormented by a devil.' But he answered her not a word. And his disciples went and pleaded with him. 'Give her what she wants,' they said 'because she is shouting after us.' He said in reply, 'I was sent only to the lost sheep of the House of Israel.' But the woman had come up and was kneeling at his feet. 'Lord,' she said 'help me.' He replied, 'It is not fair to take the children's food and throw it to the house-dogs.' She retorted, 'Ah yes, sir, but even house-dogs can eat the scraps that fall from their master's table.' Then Jesus answered her, 'Woman, you have great faith. Let your wish be granted.' And from that moment her daughter was well again.

This is the Gospel of the Lord.

Thursday

FIRST READING

A reading from the book of Numbers   20:1-13

He showed them his treasure, the font of living water.

The sons of Israel, the whole community, arrived in the first month at the desert of Zin. The people settled at Kadesh. It was there that Miriam died and was buried.

There was no water for the community, and they were all united against Moses and Aaron. The people challenged Moses: 'We would rather have died,' they said 'as our brothers died before the Lord! Why did you bring the assembly of the Lord into this wilderness, only to let us die here, ourselves and our cattle? Why did you lead us out of Egypt, only to bring us to this wretched place? It is a place unfit for sowing, it has no figs, no vines, no pomegranates, and there is not even water to drink!'

Leaving the assembly, Moses and Aaron went to the door of the Tent of Meeting. They threw themselves face downward on the ground, and the glory of the Lord appeared to them. The Lord spoke to Moses and said, 'Take the branch and call the community together, you and your brother Aaron. Then, in full view of them, order this rock to give water. You will make water flow for them out of the rock, and provide drink for the community and their cattle.'

Moses took up the branch from before the Lord, as he had directed him. Then Moses and Aaron called the assembly together in front of the rock and addressed them, 'Listen now, you rebels. Shall we make water gush from this rock for you?' And Moses raised his hand and struck the rock twice with the branch; water gushed in abundance, and the community drank and their cattle too.

Then the Lord said to Moses and Aaron, 'Because you did not believe that I could proclaim my holiness in the eyes of the sons of Israel, you shall not lead this assembly into the land I am giving them.'

These are the waters of Meribah, where the sons of Israel challenged the Lord and he proclaimed his holiness.

This is the word of the Lord.

Responsorial Psalm   Ps 94:1-2. 6-9. ℟ v.8

℟   If today you hear his voice,
      harden not your hearts.

1   Come, ring out our joy to the Lord:
    hail the rock who saves us.
    Let us come before him, giving thanks,
    with songs let us hail the Lord.   ℟

2   Come in; let us bow and bend low;
    let us kneel before the God who made us
    for he is our God and we
    the people who belong to his pasture,
    the flock that is led by his hand.   ℟

3   O that today you would listen to his voice!
    'Harden not your hearts as at Meribah,
    as on that day at Massah in the desert
    when your fathers put me to the test;
    when they tried me, though they saw my work.'   ℟

Gospel Acclamation   Mt 16:18

    Alleluia, alleluia!
    You are Peter, the rock on which I will build my Church;
    the gates of hell will not hold out against it.
    Alleluia!

GOSPEL

A reading from the holy Gospel according to Matthew   16:13-23

You are Peter, to you I will give the keys of the kingdom of heaven.

When Jesus came to the region of Casesarea Philippi he put this
question to his disciples, 'Who do people say the Son of Man is?' And
they said, 'Some say he is John the Baptist, some Elijah, and others
Jeremiah or one of the prophets.' 'But you,' he said, 'who do you say I
am?' Then Simon Peter spoke up, 'You are the Christ,' he said 'the Son
of the living God.' Jesus replied, 'Simon son of Jonah, you are a happy
man! Because it was not flesh and blood that revealed this to you but
my Father in heaven. So I now say to you: You are Peter and on this
rock I will build my Church. And the gates of the underworld can

never hold out against it. I will give you the keys of the kingdom of heaven; whatever you bind on earth shall be considered bound in heaven; whatever you loose on earth shall be considered loosed in heaven.' Then he gave the disciples strict orders not to tell anyone that he was the Christ.

From that time Jesus began to make it clear to his disciples that he was destined to go to Jerusalem and suffer grievously at the hands of the elders and chief priests and scribes, to be put to death and to be raised up on the third day. Then, taking him aside, Peter started to remonstrate with him. 'Heaven preserve you, Lord,' he said 'this must not happen to you.' But he turned and said to Peter, 'Get behind me, Satan! You are an obstacle in my path, because the way you think is not God's way but man's.'

This is the Gospel of the Lord.

Friday

FIRST READING

A reading from the book of Deuteronomy   4:32-40

The Lord God loved your ancestors and chose their descendants after them.

Moses said to the people: 'Put this question to the ages that are past, that went before you, from the time God created man on earth: Was there ever a word so majestic, from one end of heaven to the other? Was anything ever heard? Did ever a people hear the voice of the living God speaking from the heart of the fire, as you heard it, and remain alive? Has any god ventured to take to himself one nation from the midst of another by ordeals, signs, wonders, war with mighty hand and outstretched arm, by fearsome terrors – all this that the Lord your God did for you before your eyes in Egypt?

'This he showed you so that you might know that the Lord is God indeed and that there is no other. He let you hear his voice out of heaven for your instruction; on earth he let you see his great fire, and from the heart of the fire you heard his word. Because he loved your fathers and chose their descendants after them, he brought you out from Egypt, openly showing his presence and his great power, driving out in front of you nations greater and more powerful than yourself, and brought you into their land to give it you for your heritage, as it is still today.

'Understand this today, therefore, and take it to heart: the Lord is God indeed, in heaven above as on earth beneath, he and no other. Keep his laws and commandments as I give them to you today, so that you and your children may prosper and live long in the land that the Lord your God gives you for ever.'

This is the word of the Lord.

Responsorial Psalm   Ps 76:12-16. 21. ℟ v.12

℟   I remember the deeds of the Lord.

1   I remember the deeds of the Lord,
      I remember your wonders of old,
      I muse on all your works
      and ponder your mighty deeds. ℟

2   Your ways, O God, are holy.
      What god is great as our God?
      You are the God who works wonders
      You showed your power among the peoples. ℟

3   Your strong arm redeemed your people,
      the sons of Jacob and Joseph.
      You guided your people like a flock
      by the hand of Moses and Aaron. ℟

Gospel Acclamation   Mt 16:18

      Alleluia, alleluia!
      Happy are they who suffer persecution for justice' sake;
      the kingdom of heaven is theirs.
      Alleluia!

GOSPEL

A reading from the holy Gospel according to Matthew   16:24-28

What can anyone give in exchange for his life?

Jesus said to his disciples, 'If anyone wants to be a follower of mine, let him renounce himself and take up his cross and follow me. For anyone who wants to save his life will lose it; but anyone who loses his life for my sake will find it. What, then, will a man gain if he wins the whole world and ruins his life? Or what has a man to offer in exchange for his life?

'For the Son of Man is going to come in the glory of his Father with his angels, and, when he does, he will reward each one according to his behaviour. I tell you solemnly, there are some of these standing here who will not taste death before they see the Son of Man coming with his kingdom.'

This is the Gospel of the Lord.

Saturday

FIRST READING

A reading from the book of Deuteronomy   6:4-13

You shall love the Lord your God with your whole heart.

Moses said to the people: 'Listen, Israel: the Lord our God is the one Lord. You shall love the Lord your God with all your heart, with all your soul, with all your strength. Let these words I urge on you today be written on you heart. You shall repeat them to your children and say them over to them whether at rest in your house or walking abroad, at your lying down or at your rising; you shall fasten them on your hands as a sign and on your forehead as a circlet; you shall write them on the doorposts of your house and on your gates.

'When the Lord has brought you into the land which he swore to your fathers Abraham, Isaac and Jacob that he would give you, with great and prosperous cities not of your building, houses full of good things not furnished by you, wells you did not dig, vineyards and olives you did not plant, when you have eaten these and had your fill, then take care you do not forget the Lord who brought you out of the land of Egypt, out of the house of slavery. You must fear the Lord your God, you must serve him, by his name you must swear.'

This is the word of the Lord.

Responsorial Psalm   Ps 17:2-4. 47. 51. ℟ v.2

℟   I love you, Lord, my strength.

1   I love you, Lord, my strength,
     my rock, my fortress, my saviour.   ℟

2 My God is the rock where I take refuge;
   my shield, my mighty help, my stronghold.
   The Lord is worthy of all praise:
   when I call I am saved from my foes.   ℟

3 Long life to the Lord, my rock!
   Praised be the God who saves me.
   He has given great victories to his king
   and shown his love for his anointed.   ℟

Gospel Acclamation   cf. 2 Tim 1:10

   Alleluia, alleluia!
   Our Saviour Jesus Christ has done away with death
   and brought us life through his gospel.
   Alleluia!

GOSPEL

A reading from the holy Gospel according to Matthew   17:14-20

If you have faith, nothing is impossible for you.

A man came up to Jesus and went down on his knees before him.
'Lord,' he said 'take pity on my son: he is a lunatic and in a wretched
state; he is always falling into the fire or into the water. I took him to
your disciples and they were unable to cure him.' 'Faithless and
perverse generation!' Jesus said in reply 'How much longer must I be
with you? How much longer must I put up with you? Bring him here
to me.' And when Jesus rebuked it the devil came out of the boy who
was cured from that moment.

   Then the disciples came privately to Jesus. 'Why were we unable
to cast it out?' they asked. He answered, 'Because you have little faith.
I tell you solemnly, if your faith were the size of a mustard seed you
could say to this mountain, "Move from here to there", and it would
move; nothing would be impossible for you.'

   This is the Gospel of the Lord.

NINETEENTH WEEK IN ORDINARY TIME

Year I

Monday

FIRST READING

A reading from the book of Deuteronomy   10:12-22

Circumcise your hearts. Love the strangers, for you yourselves were
strangers in the land of Egypt.

Moses said to the people: 'What does the Lord your God ask of you?
Only this: to fear the Lord our God, to follow all his ways, to love him,
to serve the Lord your God with all your heart and all your soul, to
keep the commandments and laws of the Lord that for your good I lay
down for you today.

'To the Lord your God belong indeed heaven and the heaven of
heavens, and the earth and all it contains; yet it was on your fathers
that the Lord set his heart for love of them, and after them of all the
nations chose their descendants, you yourselves up to the present day.
Circumcise your heart then and be obstinate no longer; for the Lord
your God is God of gods and Lord of lords, the great God, triumphant
and terrible, never partial, never to be bribed. It is he who sees justice
done for the orphan and the widow, who loves the stranger and gives
him food and clothing. Love the stranger then, for you were strangers
in the land of Egypt. It is the Lord your God you must fear and serve;
you must cling to him; in his name take your oaths. He it is you must
praise, he is your God: for you he has done these great and terrible
things you have seen with your own eyes; and though your fathers
numbered only seventy when they went down to Egypt, the Lord your
God has made you as many as the stars of heaven.'

This is the word of the Lord.

Responsorial Psalm   Ps 147:12-15. 19-20. ℟ v.12

℟   Praise the Lord, Jerusalem.

or

℟   Alleluia!

1   O praise the Lord, Jerusalem!
    Zion, praise your God!

He has strengthened the bars of your gates,
he has blessed the children within you.   ℟

2   He established peace on your borders,
he feeds you with finest wheat.
He sends out his word to the earth
and swiftly runs his command.   ℟

3   He makes his word known to Jacob,
to Israel his laws and decrees.
He has not dealt thus with other nations;
he has not taught them his decrees.   ℟

Gospel Acclamation   cf. 2 Thess 2:14

Alleluia, alleluia!
God has called us with the gospel
to share in the glory of our Lord Jesus Christ.
Alleluia!

GOSPEL

A reading from the holy Gospel according to Matthew   17:22-27

They put him to death and he rose. We are freed from tribute.

One day when they were together in Galilee, Jesus said to his
disciples 'The Son of Man is going to be handed over into the power of
men; they will put him to death, and on the third day he will be raised
to life again.' And a great sadness came over them.

When they reached Capernaum, the collectors of the half-shekel
came to Peter and said, 'Does your master not pay the half-shekel?'
'Oh yes' he replied, and went into the house. But before he could
speak, Jesus said, 'Simon, what is your opinion? From whom do the
kings of the earth take toll or tribute? From their sons or from
foreigners?' And when he replied, 'From foreigners,' Jesus said, 'Well
then, the sons are exempt. However, so as not to offend these people,
go to the lake and cast a hook; take the first fish that bites, open its
mouth and there you will find a shekel; take it and give it to them for
me and for you.'

This is the Gospel of the Lord.

Tuesday

FIRST READING

A reading from the book of Deuteronomy 31:1-8

Be strong, Joshua, stand firm, you will lead this people into the land of promise.

Moses proceeded to address these words to the whole of Israel, 'I am one hundred and twenty years old now, and can no longer come and go as I will. The Lord has said to me, "You shall not cross this Jordan." It is the Lord your God who will cross it at your head to destroy these nations facing you and dispossess them; and Joshua too shall cross at your head, as the Lord has said. The Lord will treat them as he treated Sihon and Og the Amorite kings and their land, destroying them. The Lord will hand them over to you, and you will deal with them in exact accordance with the commandments I have enjoined on you. Be strong, stand firm, have no fear of them, no terror, for the Lord your God is going with you; he will not fail you or desert you.'

Then Moses summoned Joshua and in the presence of all Israel said to him, 'Be strong, stand firm; you are going with this people into the land the Lord swore to their fathers he would give them; you are to give it into their possession. The Lord himself will lead you; he will be with you; he will not fail you or desert you. Have no fear, do not be disheartened by anything.'

This is the word of the Lord.

Responsorial Psalm   Deut 32:3-4. 7-9. ℟ v.9

℟   The portion of the Lord is his people.

1   I proclaim the name of the Lord.
    Oh, tell the greatness of our God!
    He is the Rock, his work is perfect,
    for all his ways are Equity.   ℟

2   Think back on the days of old,
    think over the years, down the ages.
    Ask of your father, let him teach you;
    of your elders, let them enlighten you.   ℟

3 When the Most High gave the nations their inheritance,
  when he divided the sons of men,
  he fixed their bounds according to the number of the sons of
   God;
  but the Lord's portion was his people,
  Jacob his share of inheritance. ℟

4 The Lord alone is his guide,
  with him is no alien god. ℟

Gospel Acclamation   Mt 11:29

  Alleluia, alleluia!
  Take my yoke upon you;
  learn from me, for I am gentle and lowly in heart.
  Alleluia!

GOSPEL

A reading from the holy Gospel according   18:1-5. 10. 12-14
to Matthew

Be careful never to despise one of these little ones.

The disciples came to Jesus and said, 'Who is the greatest in the kingdom of heaven?' So he called a little child to him and set the child in front of them. Then he said, 'I tell you solemnly, unless you change and become like little children you will never enter the kingdom of heaven. And so, the one who makes himself as little as this little child is the greatest in the kingdom of heaven.

'Anyone who welcomes a little child like this in my name welcomes me.

'See that you never despise any of these little ones, for I tell you that their angels in heaven are continually in the presence of my Father in heaven.

'Tell me. Suppose a man has a hundred sheep and one of them strays; will he not leave the ninety-nine on the hillside and go in search of the stray? I tell you solemnly, if he finds it, it gives him more joy than do the ninety-nine that did not stray at all. Similarly, it is never the will of your Father in heaven that one of these little ones should be lost.'

This is the Gospel of the Lord.

Wednesday

FIRST READING

A reading from the book of Deuteronomy   34:1-12

Moses died here praising the Lord; since then there has not been
raised such a prophet in Israel.

Leaving the plains of Moab, Moses went up Mount Nebo, the peak of Pisgah opposite Jericho, and the Lord showed him the whole land; Gilead as far as Dan, all Naphtali, the land of Ephraim and Manasseh, all the land of Judah as far as the Western Sea, the Negeb, and the stretch of the Valley of Jericho, city of palm trees, as far as Zoar. The Lord said to him, 'This is the land I swore to give to Abraham, Isaac and Jacob, saying: I will give it to your descendants. I have let you see it with your own eyes, but you shall not cross into it.' There in the land of Moab, Moses the servant of the Lord died as the Lord decreed; he buried him in the valley, in the land of Moab, opposite Beth-peor; but to this day no one has ever found his grave. Moses was a hundred and twenty years old when he died, his eye undimmed, his vigour unimpaired. The sons of Israel wept for Moses in the plains of Moab for thirty days. The days of weeping for the mourning rites of Moses came to an end. Joshua son of Nun was filled with the spirit of wisdom, for Moses had laid his hands on him. It was he that the sons of Israel obeyed, carrying out the order that the Lord had given to Moses.

Since then, never has there been such a prophet in Israel as Moses, the man the Lord knew face to face. What signs and wonders the Lord caused him to perform in the land of Egypt against Pharaoh and all his servants and his whole land! How mighty the hand and great the fear that Moses wielded in the sight of all Israel!

This is the word of the Lord.

Responsorial Psalm   Ps 65:1-3. 5. 16-17. ℟ cf. vv.20. 9

℟ Blessed be God who filled my soul with life!

1 Cry out with joy to God all the earth,
    O sing to the glory of his name.
    O render him glorious praise.
    Say to God: 'How tremendous your deeds!'   ℟

2 Come and see the works of God,
   tremendous his deeds among men.
   Come and hear, all who fear God.
   I will tell what he did for my soul:
   to him I cried aloud,
   with high praise ready on my tongue. ℟

Gospel Acclamation   2 Cor 5:19

   Alleluia, alleluia!
   God was in Christ, to reconcile the world to himself;
   and the Good News of reconciliation he has entrusted to us.
   Alleluia!

GOSPEL

A reading from the holy Gospel according to Matthew   18:15-20

If your brother or sister listens to you, you will have won that person back.

Jesus said to his disciples: 'If your brother does something wrong, go and have it out with him alone, between your two selves. If he listens to you, you have won back your brother. If he does not listen, take one or two others along with you: the evidence of two or three witnesses is required to sustain any charge. But if he refuses to listen to these, report it to the community; and if he refuses to listen to the community, treat him like a pagan or a tax collector.

'I tell you solemnly, whatever you bind on earth shall be considered bound in heaven; whatever you loose on earth shall be considered loosed in heaven.

'I tell you solemnly once again, if two of you on earth agree to ask anything at all, it will be granted to you by my Father in heaven. For where two or three meet in my name, I shall be there with them.'

   This is the Gospel of the Lord.

Thursday

FIRST READING

A reading from the book of Joshua   3:7-11. 13-17

The ark of the Lord God will precede you across the Jordan.

The Lord said to Joshua, 'This very day I will begin to make you a great man in the eyes of all Israel, to let them be sure that I am going to be with you even as I was with Moses. As for you, give this order to the priests carrying the ark of the covenant: "When you have reached the brink of the waters of the Jordan, you are to stand still in the Jordan itself." ' Then Joshua said to the Israelites, 'Come closer and hear the words of the Lord your God.' Joshua said, 'By this you shall know that a living God is with you and without a doubt will expel the Canaanite. Look, the ark of the Lord, the Lord of the whole earth, is about to cross the Jordan at your head. As soon as the priests with the ark of the Lord, the Lord of the whole earth, have set their feet in the waters of the Jordan, the upper waters of the Jordan flowing down will be stopped in their course and stand still in one mass.'

Accordingly, when the people struck camp to cross the Jordan, the priests carried the ark of the covenant in front of the people. As soon as the bearers of the ark reached the Jordan and the feet of the priests who carried it touched the waters (the Jordan overflows the whole length of its banks throughout the harvest season) the upper waters stood still and made one heap over a wide space – from Adam to the fortress of Zarethan – while those flowing down to the Sea of the Arabah, that is, the Salt Sea, stopped running altogether. The people crossed opposite Jericho. The priests who carried the ark of the covenant of the Lord stood still on dry ground in mid-Jordan, and all Israel continued to cross dry-shod till the whole nation had finished its crossing of the river.

This is the word of the Lord.

Responsorial Psalm   Ps 113A:1-6

℟   Alleluia!

1   When Israel came forth from Egypt,
    Jacob's sons from an alien people,
    Judah became the Lord's temple,
    Israel became his kingdom.   ℟

2   The sea fled at the sight:
    the Jordan turned back on its course,
    the mountains leapt like rams
    and the hills like yearling sheep. ℟

3   Why was it, sea, that you fled,
    that you turned back, Jordan, on your course?
    Mountains, that you leapt like rams,
    hills, like yearling sheep? ℟

Gospel Acclamation   Ps 118:135

    Alleluia, alleluia!
    Let your face shine on your servant,
    and teach me your laws.
    Alleluia!

GOSPEL

A reading from the holy Gospel according to Matthew   18:21–19:1

I did not say to you to forgive seven times, but seventy times seven.

Peter went up to Jesus and said, 'Lord, how often must I forgive my brother if he wrongs me? As often as seven times?' Jesus answered, 'Not seven, I tell you, but seventy-seven times.

   'And so the kingdom of heaven may be compared to a king who decided to settle his accounts with his servants. When the reckoning began, they brought him a man who owed ten thousand talents; but he had no means of paying, so his master gave orders that he should be sold, together with his wife and children and all his possessions, to meet the debt. At this, the servant threw himself down at his master's feet. "Give me time" he said "and I will pay the whole sum." And the servant's master felt so sorry for him that he let him go and cancelled the debt. Now as this servant went out, he happened to meet a fellow servant who owed him one hundred denarii; and he seized him by the throat and began to throttle him. "Pay what you owe me" he said. His fellow servant fell at his feet and implored him, saying, "Give me time and I will pay you." But the other would not agree; on the contrary, he had him thrown into prison till he should pay the debt. His fellow servants were deeply distressed when they saw what had happened, and they went to their master and reported the whole affair to him. Then the master sent for him. "You wicked servant," he said, "I cancelled all that debt of yours when you appealed to me. Were you not bound, then, to have pity on your fellow servant just as I had pity on you?" And in his anger the master handed him over to the torturers till he should pay all his debt. And that is how my heavenly Father will deal with you unless you each forgive your brother from your heart.'

Jesus had now finished what he wanted to say, and he left Galilee and came into the part of the Judaea which is on the far side of the Jordan.

This is the Gospel of the Lord.

Friday

FIRST READING

A reading from the book of Joshua   24:1-13

I brought your father from Mesopotamia, out of the land of Egypt and took you to your own land.

Joshua gathered all the tribes of Israel together at Shechem; then he called the elders, leaders, judges and scribes of Israel, and they presented themselves before God. Then Joshua said to all the people: 'The Lord the God of Israel says this, "In ancient days your ancestors lived beyond the River – such was Terah the father of Abraham and of Nahor – and they served other gods. Then I brought your father Abraham from beyond the River and led him through all the land of Canaan. I increased his descendants and gave him Isaac. To Isaac I gave Jacob and Esau. To Esau I gave the mountain country of Seir as his possession. Jacob and his sons went down into Egypt. Then I sent Moses and Aaron and plagued Egypt with the wonders that I worked there. So I brought you out of it. I brought your ancestors out of Egypt, and you came to the Sea; the Egyptians pursued your ancestors with chariots and horsemen as far as the Sea of Reeds. There they called to the Lord, and he spread a thick fog between you and the Egyptians, and made the sea go back on them and cover them. You saw with your own eyes the things I did in Egypt. Then for a long time you lived in the wilderness, until I brought you into the land of the Amorites who lived beyond the Jordan; they made war on you and I gave them into your hands; you took possession of their country because I destroyed them before you. Next, Balak son of Zippor the king of Moab arose to make war on Israel, and sent for

Balaam son of Beor to come and curse you. But I would not listen to Balaam; instead, he had to bless you, and I saved you from his hand.

"When you crossed the Jordan and came to Jericho, those who held Jericho fought against you, as did the Amorites and Perizzites, the Canaanites, Hittites, Girgashites, Hivites and Jebusites, but I put them all into your power. I sent out hornets in front of you, which drove the two Amorite kings before you; this was not the work of your sword or your bow. I gave you a land where you never toiled, you live in towns you never built; you eat now from vineyards and olive groves you never planted."'

This is the word of the Lord.

Responsorial Psalm   Ps 135:1-3. 16-18. 21-22. 24

1 O give thanks to the Lord for he is good.
   ℟ His love is everlasting.
   Give thanks to the God of gods.
   ℟ His love is everlasting.
   Give thanks to the Lord of lords.
   ℟ His love is everlasting.

2 Through the desert his people he led.
   ℟ His love is everlasting.
   Nations in their greatness he struck.
   ℟ His love is everlasting.
   Kings in their splendour he slew.
   ℟ His love is everlasting.

3 He let Israel inherit their land.
   ℟ His love is everlasting.
   On his servant their land he bestowed.
   ℟ His love is everlasting.
   And he snatched us away from our foes.
   ℟ His love is everlasting.

or

   ℟ Alleluia!

Gospel Acclamation   cf. 1 Thess 2:13

Alleluia, alleluia!
Receive this message not as human words,
but as truly the word of God.
Alleluia!

GOSPEL

A reading from the holy Gospel according to Matthew   19:3-12

Because of the hardness of your hearts Moses permitted you to divorce
your wives, but it was not like this from the beginning.

Some Pharisees approached Jesus, and to test him they said, 'Is it
against the Law for a man to divorce his wife on any pretext
whatever?' He answered, 'Have you not read that the creator from the
beginning made them male and female and that he said: This is why a
man must leave father and mother, and cling to his wife, and the two
become one body? They are no longer two, therefore, but one body. So
then, what God has united, man must not divide.'

They said to him, 'Then why did Moses command that a writ of
dismissal should be given in cases of divorce?' 'It was because you
were so unteachable' he said 'that Moses allowed you to divorce your
wives, but it was not like this from the beginning. Now I say this to
you: the man who divorces his wife – I am not speaking of fornication
– and marries another, is guilty of adultery.'

The disciples said to him, 'If that is how things are between
husband and wife, it is not advisable to marry.' But he replied, 'It is
not everyone who can accept what I have said, but only those to whom
it is granted. There are eunuchs born that way from their mother's
womb, there are eunuchs made so by men and there are eunuchs who
have made themselves that way for the sake of the kingdom of
heaven. Let anyone accept this who can.'

This is the Gospel of the Lord.

Saturday

FIRST READING

A reading from the book of Joshua   24:14-29

Choose today whom you wish to serve.

Joshua said to all the people: 'Fear the Lord and serve him perfectly and sincerely; put away the gods that your ancestors served beyond the River and in Egypt, and serve the Lord. But if you will not serve the Lord, choose today whom you wish to serve, whether the gods that your ancestors served beyond the River, or the gods of the Amorites in whose land you are now living. As for me in my House, we will serve the Lord.'

The people answered, 'We have no intention of deserting the Lord and serving other gods! Was it not the Lord our God who brought us and our ancestors out of the land of Egypt, the house of slavery, who worked those great wonders before our eyes and preserved us all along the way we travelled and among all the peoples through whom we journeyed? What is more, the Lord drove all those people out before us, as well as the Amorites who used to live in this country. We too will serve the Lord, for he is our God.'

Then Joshua said to the people, 'You cannot serve the Lord, because he is a holy God, he is a jealous God who will not forgive your transgressions or your sins. If you desert the Lord to follow alien gods he in turn will afflict and destroy you after the goodness he has shown you.' The people answered Joshua, 'No; it is the Lord we wish to serve.' Then Joshua said to the people, 'You are witnesses against yourselves that you have chosen the Lord, to serve him.' They answered, 'We are witnesses.' 'Then cast away the alien gods among you and give your hearts to the Lord the God of Israel!' The people answered Joshua, 'It is the Lord our God we choose to serve; it is his voice that we will obey.'

That day, Joshua made a covenant for the people; he laid down a statute and ordinance for them at Shechem. Joshua wrote these words in the Book of the Law of God. Then he took a great stone and set it up there, under the oak in the sanctuary of the Lord, and Joshua said to all the people, 'See! This stone shall be a witness against us because it has heard all the words that the Lord has spoken to us: it shall be a witness against you in case you deny your God.' Then Joshua sent the people away, and each returned to his own inheritance.

After these things Joshua son of Nun, the servant of the Lord, died; he was a hundred and ten years old.

This is the word of the Lord.

Responsorial Psalm   Ps 15:1-2. 5. 7-8. 11. ℟ cf. v.5

℟   You are my inheritance, O Lord.

1   Preserve me, God, I take refuge in you.
    I say to the Lord: 'You are my God.'
    O Lord, it is you who are my portion and cup;
    it is you yourself who are my prize.   ℟

2   I will bless the Lord who gives me counsel,
    who even at night directs my heart.
    I keep the Lord ever in my sight:
    since he is at my right hand, I shall stand firm.   ℟

3   You will show me the path of life,
    the fullness of joy in your presence,
    at your right hand happiness for ever.   ℟

Gospel Acclamation   cf. Mt 11:25

Alleluia, alleluia!
Blessed are you, Father, Lord of heaven and earth;
you have revealed to little ones the mysteries of the kingdom.
Alleluia!

GOSPEL

A reading from the holy Gospel according to Matthew   19:13-15

*Do not prevent the little children from coming to me: to them belongs
the kingdom of heaven.*

People brought little children to Jesus, for him to lay his hands on them and say a prayer. The disciples turned them away, but Jesus said, 'Let the little children alone, and do not stop them coming to me; for it is to such as these that the kingdom of heaven belongs.' Then he laid his hands on them and went on his way.

This is the Gospel of the Lord.

TWENTIETH WEEK IN ORDINARY TIME

Year I

Monday

FIRST READING

A reading from the book of Judges   2:11-19

The Lord God appointed judges for them, but they would not listen to them.

The sons of Israel did what displeases the Lord and served the Baals. They deserted the Lord, the God of their ancestors, who had brought them out of the land of Egypt, and followed other gods from the gods of the peoples round them. They bowed down to these; they provoked the Lord; they deserted the Lord to serve Baal and Astarte. Then the Lord's anger flamed out against Israel. He handed them over to pillagers who plundered them; he delivered them to the enemies surrounding them, and they were not able to resist them. In every warlike venture, the hand of the Lord was there to foil them, as the Lord had warned, as the Lord had sworn to them. Thus he reduced them to dire distress.

Then the Lord appointed judges for them, and rescued the men of Israel from the hands of their plunderers. But they would not listen to their judges. They prostituted themselves to other gods, and bowed down before these. Very quickly they left the path their ancestors had trodden in obedience to the orders of the Lord; they did not follow their example. When the Lord appointed judges for them, the Lord was with the judge and rescued them from the hands of their enemies as long as the judge lived, for the Lord felt pity for them as they groaned under the iron grip of their oppressors. But once the judge was dead, they relapsed and behaved even worse than their ancestors. They followed other gods; they served them and bowed before them, and would not give up the practices and stubborn ways of their ancestors at all.

This is the word of the Lord.

Responsorial Psalm   Ps 105:34-37. 39-40. 43-44. ℟ v.4

℟   Lord, remember us,
        for the love you bear your people.

1   They failed to destroy the peoples
      as the Lord had given command,
      but instead they mingled with the nations
      and learned to act like them.   ℟

2   They worshipped the idols of the nations
      and these became a snare to entrap them.
      They even offered their own sons
      and their daughters in sacrifice to demons.   ℟

3   So they defiled themselves by their deeds
      and broke their marriage bond with the Lord
      till his anger blazed against his people:
      he was filled with horror at his chosen ones.   ℟

4   Time after time he rescued them,
      but in their malice they dared to defy him.
      In spite of this he paid heed to their distress,
      so often as he heard their cry.   ℟

Gospel Acclamation   Mt 5:3

      Alleluia, alleluia!
      Happy the poor in spirit;
      the kingdom of heaven is theirs!
      Alleluia!

GOSPEL

A reading from the holy Gospel according to Matthew   19:16-22

If you wish to be perfect, sell what you own, and your treasure will
be in heaven.

There was a man who came to Jesus and asked, 'Master, what good
deed must I do to possess eternal life?' Jesus said to him, 'Why do you
ask me about what is good? There is one alone who is good. But if you
wish to enter into life, keep the commandments.' He said, 'Which?'
'These,' Jesus replied, 'You must not kill. You must not commit

adultery. You must not bring false witness. Honour your father and mother, and: You must love your neighbour as yourself.' The young man said to him 'I have kept all these. What more do I need to do?' Jesus said, 'If you wish to be perfect, go and sell what you own and give the money to the poor, and you will have treasure in heaven; then come, follow me.' But when the young man heard these words he went away sad, for he was a man of great wealth.

This is the Gospel of the Lord.

Tuesday

FIRST READING

A reading from the book of Judges   6:11-24

Gideon, you will free Israel. Do I not send you?

The angel of the Lord came and sat under the terebinth at Ophrah which belonged to Joash of Abiezer. Gideon his son was threshing wheat inside the winepress to keep it hidden from Midian, when the angel of the Lord appeared to him and said, 'The Lord is with you, valiant warrior!' Gideon answered him, 'Forgive me, my lord, but if the Lord is with us, then why is it that all this is happening to us now? And where are all the wonders our ancestors tell us of when they say, "Did not the Lord bring us out of Egypt?" But now the Lord has deserted us; he has abandoned us to Midian.'

At this the Lord turned to him and said, 'Go in the strength now upholding you, and you will rescue Israel from the power of Midian. Do I not send you myself?' Gideon answered him, 'Forgive me, my lord, but how can I deliver Israel? My clan, you must know, is the weakest in Manasseh and I am the least important in my family.' The Lord answered him, 'I will be with you and you shall crush Midian as though it were a single man.' Gideon said to him, 'If I have found favour in your sight, give me a sign that it is you who speak to me. I beg you, do not go away until I come back, I will bring you my offering and set it down before you.' And he answered, 'I will stay until you return.'

Gideon went away and prepared a young goat and made un-leavened cakes with an ephah of flour. He put the meat into a basket and the broth into a pot, then brought it all to him under the terebinth. As he came near, the angel of the Lord said to him,

'Take the meat and unleavened cakes, put them on this rock and pour the broth over them.' Gideon did so. Then the angel of the Lord reached out the tip of the staff in his hand and touched the meat and unleavened cakes. Fire sprang from the rock and consumed the meat and unleavened cakes, and the angel of the Lord vanished before his eyes. Then Gideon knew this was the angel of the Lord, and he said, 'Alas, my Lord! I have seen the angel of the Lord face to face!' The Lord answered him, 'Peace be with you; have no fear; you will not die.' Gideon built an altar there to the Lord and called it The-Lord-is-Peace.

This is the word of the Lord.

Responsorial Psalm   Ps 84:9. 11-14. ℟ v.9

℟   The Lord speaks of peace to his people.

1   I will hear what the Lord God has to say,
    a voice that speaks of peace,
       peace for his people and his friends
       and those who turn to him in their hearts.   ℟

2   Mercy and faithfulness have met;
       justice and peace have embraced.
    Faithfulness shall spring from the earth
       and justice look down from heaven.   ℟

3   The Lord will make us prosper
       and our earth shall yield its fruit.
    Justice shall march before him
       and peace shall follow his steps.   ℟

Gospel Acclamation   2 Cor 8:9

    Alleluia, alleluia!
    Jesus Christ was rich but he became poor,
    to make you rich out of his poverty.
    Alleluia!

GOSPEL

A reading from the holy Gospel according to Matthew   19:23-30

It is easier for a camel to pass through the eye of a needle than for
a rich person to enter the kingdom of heaven.

Jesus said to his disciples, 'I tell you solemnly, it will be hard for a rich man to enter the kingdom of heaven. Yes, I tell you again, it is easier for a camel to pass through the eye of a needle than for a rich man to enter the kingdom of heaven.' When the disciples heard this they were astonished. 'Who can be saved, then?' they said. Jesus gazed at them. 'For men' he told them 'this is impossible; for God everything is possible.'

Then Peter spoke. 'What about us?' he said to him. 'We have left everything and followed you. What are we to have, then?' Jesus said to him, 'I tell you solemnly, when all is made new and the Son of Man sits on his throne of glory, you will yourselves sit on twelve thrones to judge the twelve tribes of Israel. And everyone who has left houses, brothers, sisters, father, mother, children or land for the sake of my name will be repaid a hundred times over, and also inherit eternal life.

'Many who are first will be last, and the last, first.'

This is the Gospel of the Lord.

Wednesday

FIRST READING

A reading from the book of Judges   9:6-15

It is said, the king will reign over us, when the Lord God reigns
among you.

All the leading men of Shechem and all Bethmillo gathered, and proclaimed Abimelech king by the terebinth of the pillar at Shechem.

News of this was brought to Jotham. He came and stood on the top of Mount Gerizim and shouted aloud for them to hear:

'Hear me, leaders of Shechem,
that God may also hear you!

'One day the trees went out
to anoint a king to rule over them.
They said to the olive tree, "Be our king!"

'The olive tree answered them,
"Must I forego my oil
which gives honour to gods and men,
to stand swaying above the trees?"

'Then the trees said to the fig tree,
"Come now, you be our king!"

'The fig tree answered them,
"Must I forego my sweetness,
forego my excellent fruit,
to stand swaying above the trees?"

'Then the trees said to the vine,
"Come now, you be our king!"

'The vine answered them,
"Must I forego my wine
which cheers the heart of gods and men,
to stand swaying above the trees?"

'Then all the trees said to the thorn bush,
"Come now, you be our king!"

'And the thorn bush answered the trees,
"If in all good faith you anoint me king to reign over you,
then come and shelter in my shade.
If not, fire will come from the thorn bush
and devour the cedars of Lebanon." '

This is the word of the Lord.

Responsorial Psalm   Ps 20:2-7. ℟ v.2

℟   Lord, your strength gives joy to the king.

1   O Lord, your strength gives joy to the king;
    how your saving help makes him glad!
    You have granted him his heart's desire;
    you have not refused the prayer of his lips.   ℟

2   You came to meet him with the blessings of success,
    you have set on his head a crown of pure gold.

He asked you for life and this you have given,
days that will last from age to age.   ℟

3   Your saving help has given him glory.
You have laid upon him majesty and splendour,
you have granted your blessings to him for ever.
You have made him rejoice with the joy of your presence.   ℟

Gospel Acclamation   Heb 4:12

Alleluia! alleluia!
The word of God is living and active;
it probes the thoughts and motives of our heart.
Alleluia!

GOSPEL

A reading from the holy Gospel according to Matthew   20:1-16

Are you jealous because I am generous?

Jesus said to his disciples: 'The kingdom of heaven is like a landowner
going out at daybreak to hire workers for his vineyard. He made an
agreement with the workers for one denarius a day, and sent them to
his vineyard. Going out at about the third hour he saw others
standing idle in the market place and said to them, "You go to my
vineyard too and I will give you a fair wage." So they went. At about
the sixth hour and again at about the ninth hour, he went out and did
the same. Then at about the eleventh hour he went out and found
more men standing round, and he said to them, "Why have you been
standing here idle all day?" "Because no one has hired us" they
answered. He said to them, "You go into my vineyard too." In the
evening, the owner of the vineyard said to his bailiff, "Call the
workers and pay them their wages, starting with the last arrivals and
ending with the first." So those who were hired at about the eleventh
hour came forward and received one denarius each. When the first
came, they expected to get more, but they too received one denarius
each. They took it, but grumbled at the landowner. "The men who
came last" they said "have done only one hour, and you have treated
them the same as us, though we have done a heavy day's work in all
the heat." He answered one of them and said, "My friend, I am not
being unjust to you; did we not agree on one denarius? Take

your earnings and go. I choose to pay the last-comer as much as I pay you. Have I no right to do what I like with my own? Why be envious because I am generous?" Thus the last will be first, and the first, last.'

This is the Gospel of the Lord.

Thursday

FIRST READING

A reading from the book of Judges   11:29-39

Whoever first comes from the door of my house I will offer up as a holocaust.

The spirit of the Lord came on Jephthah, who crossed Gilead and Manasseh, passed through to Mizpah in Gilead and from Mizpah in Gilead made his way to the rear of the Ammonites. And Jephthah made a vow to the Lord, 'If you deliver the Ammonites into my hands, then the first person to meet me from the door of my house when I return in triumph from fighting the Ammonites shall belong to the Lord, and I will offer him up as a holocaust.' Jephthah marched against the Ammonites to attack them, and the Lord delivered them into his power. He harassed them from Aroer almost to Minnith (twenty towns) and to Abel-keramim. It was a very severe defeat, and the Ammonites were humbled before the Israelites.

As Jephthah returned to his house at Mizpah, his daughter came out from it to meet him; she was dancing to the sound of timbrels. This was his only child; apart from her he had neither son nor daughter. When he saw her, he tore his clothes and exclaimed, 'Oh my daughter, what sorrow you are bringing me! Must it be you, the cause of my ill-fortune! I have given a promise to the Lord, and I cannot unsay what I have said.' She answered him, 'My father, you have given a promise to the Lord; treat me as the vow you took binds you to, since the Lord has given you vengeance on your enemies the Ammonites.' Then she said to her father, 'Grant me one request. Let me be free for two months. I shall go and wander in the mountains, and with my companions bewail my virginity.' He answered, 'Go,' and let her depart for two months. So she went away with her companions and bewailed her virginity in the mountains. When the two months were over, she returned to her father, and he treated her as the vow he had uttered bound him.

This is the word of the Lord.

Responsorial Psalm   Ps 39:5. 7-10. ℟ vv.8-9

> ℟ Here am I, Lord;
>   I come to do your will.

1   Happy the man who has placed
    his trust in the Lord
    and has not gone over to the rebels
    who follow false gods. ℟

2   You do not ask for sacrifice and offerings,
    but an open ear.
    You do not ask for holocaust and victim.
    Instead, here am I. ℟

3   In the scroll of the book it stands written
    that I should do your will.
    My God, I delight in your law
    in the depth of my heart. ℟

4   Your justice I have proclaimed
    in the great assembly.
    My lips I have not sealed;
    you know it, O Lord. ℟

Gospel Acclamation   cf. Ps 94:8

> Alleluia, alleluia!
> If today you hear his voice,
> harden not your hearts.
> Alleluia!

GOSPEL

A reading from the holy Gospel according to Matthew   22:1-14

Go out and find whomever you can, and invite them to the wedding.

Jesus began to speak to the chief priests and the elders of the people in
parables, 'The kingdom of heaven may be compared to a king who
gave a feast for his son's wedding. He sent his servants to call those
who had been invited, but they would not come. Next he sent some
more servants. "Tell those who have been invited" he said "that I have
my banquet all prepared, my oxen and fattened cattle have been

slaughtered, everything is ready. Come to the wedding." But they were not interested: one went off to his farm, another to his business, and the rest seized his servants, maltreated them and killed them. The king was furious. He despatched his troops, destroyed those murderers and burnt their town. Then he said to his servants, "The wedding is ready; but as those who were invited proved to be unworthy, go to the crossroads in the town and invite everyone you can find to the wedding." So these servants went out on to the roads and collected together everyone they could find, bad and good alike; and the wedding hall was filled with guests. When the king came in to look at the guests he noticed one man who was not wearing a wedding garment, and said to him, "How did you get in here, my friend, without a wedding garment?" And the man was silent. Then the king said to the attendants, "Bind him hand and foot and throw him out into the dark, where there will be weeping and grinding of teeth." For many are called, but few are chosen.'

This is the Gospel of the Lord.

Friday

FIRST READING

A reading from the book of Ruth   1:1. 3-6. 14-16. 22

Naomi came with Ruth the Moabitess and returned to Bethlehem.

In the days of the Judges famine came to the land and a certain man from Bethlehem of Judah went – he, his wife and his two sons – to live in the country of Moab. Elimelech, Naomi's husband, died, and she and her two sons were left. These married Moabite women: one was named Orpah and the other Ruth. They lived there about ten years. Then both Mahlon and Chilion also died and the woman was bereft of her two sons and her husband. So she and her daughters-in-law prepared to return from the country of Moab, for she had heard that the Lord had visited his people and given them food. Then Orpah kissed her mother-in-law and went back to her people. But Ruth clung to her.

Naomi said to her, 'Look, your sister-in-law has gone back to her people and to her god. You must return too; follow your sister-in-law.'

But Ruth said, 'Do not press me to leave you and to turn back from your company, for

'wherever you go, I will go,
wherever you live, I will live.
Your people shall be my people,
and your God, my God.'

This was how Naomi, she who returned from the country of Moab, came back with Ruth the Moabitess her daughter-in-law. And they came to Bethlehem at the beginning of the barley harvest.

This is the word of the Lord.

Responsial Psalm   Ps 145:5-10. ℞ v.2

℞   Praise the Lord, my soul!

or

℞   Alleluia!

1   He is happy who is helped by Jacob's God,
     whose hope is in the Lord his God,
     who alone made heaven and earth,
     the seas and all they contain.   ℞

2   It is he who keeps faith for ever,
     who is just to those who are oppressed.
     It is he who gives bread to the hungry,
     the Lord, who sets prisoners free.   ℞

3   It is the Lord who gives sight to the blind,
     who raises up those who are bowed down,
     the Lord, who protects the stranger
     and upholds the widow and orphan.   ℞

4   It is the Lord who loves the just
     but thwarts the path of the wicked.
     The Lord will reign for ever,
     Zion's God, from age to age.   ℞

Gospel Acclamation   Ps 24:4. 5

Alleluia, alleluia!
Teach me your paths, my God,
and lead me in your truth.
Alleluia!

GOSPEL

A reading from the holy Gospel according to Matthew   22:34-40

Love the Lord your God, and your neighbour as yourself.

When the Pharisees heard that Jesus had silenced the Sadducees they got together and, to disconcert him, one of them put a question, 'Master, which is the greatest commandment of the Law?' Jesus said, 'You must love the Lord your God with all your heart, with all your soul, and with all your mind. This is the greatest and the first commandment. The second resembles it: You must love your neighbour as yourself. On these two commandments hang the whole Law, and the Prophets also.'

This is the Gospel of the Lord.

Saturday

FIRST READING

A reading from the book of Ruth   2:1-3. 8-11; 4:13-17

The Lord has not left your family without a successor.
This was the father of David's father.

Naomi had a kinsman on her husband's side, well-to-do and of Elimelech's clan. His name was Boaz.

Ruth the Moabitess said to Naomi, 'Let me go into the fields and glean among the ears of corn in the footsteps of some man who will look on me with favour.' And she said to her, 'Go, my daughter.' So she set out and went to glean in the fields after the reapers. And it chanced that she came to that part of the fields which belonged to Boaz of Elimelech's clan.

Boaz said to Ruth, 'Listen, my daughter, and understand this. You are not to glean in any other field, do not leave here but stay with my servants. Keep your eyes on whatever part of the field they are reaping and follow behind. I have ordered my servants not to molest you. And if you are thirsty, go to the pitchers and drink what the servants have drawn.' Then she fell on her face, bowing to the ground. And she said to him, 'How have I so earned your favour that you take notice of me, even though I am a foreigner?' And Boaz answered her, 'I have been told all you have done for your mother-in-law since your husband's death, and how you left your own father and mother and the land where you were born to come among a people whom you knew nothing about before you came here.'

So Boaz took Ruth and she became his wife. And when they came together, the Lord made her conceive and she bore a son. And the women said to Naomi, 'Blessed be the Lord who has not left the dead man without next of kin this day to perpetuate his name in Israel. The child will be a comfort to you and the prop of your old age, for your daughter-in-law who loves you and is more to you than seven sons has given him birth.' And Naomi took the child to her own bosom and she became his nurse.

And the women of the neighbourhood gave him a name. 'A son has been born for Naomi' they said; and they named him Obed. This was the father of David's father, Jesse.

This is the word of the Lord.

Responsorial Psalm   Ps 127:1-5. ℟ v.4

℟   See how the Lord blesses those who fear him.

1   O blessed are those who fear the Lord
    and walk in his ways!
    By the labour of your hands you shall eat.
    You will be happy and prosper.   ℟

2   Your wife like a fruitful vine
    in the heart of your house;
    your children like shoots of the olive,
    around your table.   ℟

3   Indeed thus shall be blessed
    the man who fears the Lord.
    May the Lord bless you from Zion
    all the days of your life!   ℟

Gospel Acclamation   Mt 23:9. 10

    Alleluia, alleluia!
    You have one Father, your Father in heaven;
    you have one teacher: the Lord Jesus Christ!
    Alleluia!

GOSPEL

A reading from the holy Gospel according to Matthew   23:1-12

They speak, but do not practise what they preach.

Addressing the people and his disciples Jesus said, 'The scribes and the Pharisees occupy the chair of Moses. You must therefore do what they tell you and listen to what they say; but do not be guided by what they do: since they do not practise what they preach. They tie up heavy burdens and lay them on men's shoulders, but will they lift a finger to move them? Not they! Everything they do is done to attract attention, like wearing broader phylacteries and longer tassels, like wanting to take the place of honour at banquets and the front seats in the synagogues, being greeted obsequiously in the market squares and having people call them Rabbi.

'You, however, must not allow yourselves to be called Rabbi, since you have only one Master, and you are all brothers. You must call no one on earth your father, since you have only one Father, and he is in heaven. Nor must you allow yourselves to be called teachers, for you have only one Teacher, the Christ. The greatest among you must be your servant. Anyone who exalts himself will be humbled, and anyone who humbles himself will be exalted.'

This is the Gospel of the Lord.

TWENTY-FIRST WEEK IN ORDINARY TIME

Year I

Monday

FIRST READING

A reading from the first letter of St Paul   1:1-5. 8-10
to the Thessalonians

You converted to God from idolatry, expecting his Son whom he raised from the dead.

From Paul, Silvanus and Timothy, to the Church in Thessalonika which is in God our Father and the Lord Jesus Christ; wishing you grace and peace from God the Father and the Lord Jesus Christ.

We always mention you in our prayers and thank God for you all, and constantly remember before God our Father how you have shown your faith in action, worked for love and persevered through hope, in our Lord Jesus Christ.

We know, brothers, that God loves you and that you have been chosen, because when we brought the Good News to you, it came to you not only as words, but as power and as the Holy Spirit and as utter conviction. And you observed the sort of life we lived when we were with you, which was for your instruction. We do not need to tell other people about it: other people tell us how we started the work among you, how you broke with idolatry when you were converted to God and became servants of the real, living God; and how you are now waiting for Jesus, his Son, whom he raised from the dead, to come from heaven to save us from the retribution which is coming.

This is the word of the Lord.

Responsorial Psalm   Ps 149:1-6. 9. ℟ v.4

℟   The Lord takes delight in his people.

or

℟   Alleluia!

1   Sing a new song to the Lord,
    his praise in the assembly of the faithful.
    Let Israel rejoice in its Maker,
    let Zion's sons exult in their king.   ℟

2   Let them praise his name with dancing
    and make music with timbrel and harp.
    For the Lord takes delight in his people.
    He crowns the poor with salvation.   ℟

3   Let the faithful rejoice in their glory,
    shout for joy and take their rest.
    Let the praise of God be on their lips:
    this honour is for all his faithful.   ℟

Gospel Acclamation   Jn 10:27

    Alleluia, alleluia!
    My sheep listen to my voice, says the Lord;
    I know them, and they follow me.
    Alleluia!

GOSPEL

A reading from the holy Gospel according to Matthew   23:13-22

Woe to you, blind leaders.

Jesus said: 'Alas for you, scribes and Pharisees, you hypocrites! You who shut up the kingdom of heaven in men's faces, neither going in yourselves nor allowing others to go in who want to.

'Alas for you, scribes and Pharisees, you hypocrites! You who travel over sea and land to make a single proselyte, and when you have him you make him twice as fit for hell as you are.

'Alas for you, blind guides! You who say, "If a man swears by the Temple, it has no force; but if a man swears by the gold of the Temple, he is bound." Fools and blind! For which is of greater worth, the gold or the Temple that makes the gold sacred? Or else, "If a man swears by the altar it has no force; but if a man swears by the offering that is on the altar, he is bound." You blind men! For which is of greater worth, the offering or the altar that makes the offering sacred? Therefore, when a man swears by the altar he is swearing by that and by everything on it. And when a man swears by the Temple he is swearing by that and by the One who dwells in it. And when a man swears by heaven he is swearing by the throne of God and by the One who is seated there.'

This is the Gospel of the Lord.

Tuesday

FIRST READING

A reading from the first letter of St Paul   2:1-8
to the Thessalonians

We wish to hand over to you not only the Good News, but our lives as well.

You know yourselves, my brothers, that our visit to you has not proved ineffectual.

We had, as you know, been given rough treatment and been grossly insulted at Philippi, and it was our God who gave us the courage to proclaim his Good News to you in the face of great opposition. We have not taken to preaching because we are deluded, or immoral, or trying to deceive anyone; it was God who decided that we were fit to be entrusted with the Good News, and when we are speaking, we are not trying to please men but God, who can read our inmost thoughts. You know very well, and we can swear it before God, that never at any time have our speeches been simply flattery, or a cover for trying to get money; nor have we ever looked for any special honour from men, either from you or anybody else, when we could have imposed ourselves on you with full weight, as apostles of Christ.

Instead, we were unassuming. Like a mother feeding and looking after her own children, we felt so devoted and protective towards you, and had come to love you so much, that we were eager to hand over to you not only the Good News but our whole lives as well.

This is the word of the Lord.

Responsorial Psalm   Ps 138:1-3. 4-6. ℟ v.1

℟   You have searched me and you know me, Lord.

1   O Lord, you search me and you know me,
      you know my resting and my rising,
      you discern my purpose from afar.   ℟

2   You mark when I walk or lie down,
      all my ways lie open to you.
      Before ever a word is on my tongue
      you know it, O Lord, through and through.   ℟

3   Behind and before you besiege me,
      your hand ever laid upon me.
      Too wonderful for me, this knowledge,
      too high, beyond my reach.   ℟

Gospel Acclamation   Heb 4:12

Alleluia, alleluia!
The word of God is living and active;
it probes the thoughts and motives of our heart.
Alleluia!

GOSPEL

A reading from the holy Gospel according to Matthew 23:23-26

You should have practised these without neglecting other things.

Jesus said, 'Alas for you, scribes and Pharisees, you hypocrites! You who pay your tithe of mint and dill and cummin and have neglected the weightier matters of the Law – justice, mercy, good faith! These you should have practised, without neglecting the others. You blind guides! Straining out gnats and swallowing camels!

'Alas for you, scribes and Pharisees, you hypocrites! You who clean the outside of cup and dish and leave the inside full of extortion and intemperance. Blind Pharisee! Clean the inside of cup and dish first so that the outside may become clean as well.'

This is the Gospel of the Lord.

Wednesday

FIRST READING

A reading from the first letter of St Paul to the Thessalonians 2:9-13

Night and day we have worked among you preaching the Good News.

Let me remind you, brothers, how hard we used to work, slaving night and day so as not to be a burden on any one of you while we were proclaiming God's Good News to you. You are witnesses, and so is God, that our treatment of you, since you became believers, has been impeccably right and fair. You can remember how we treated every one of you as a father treats his children, teaching you what was right, encouraging you and appealing to you to live a life worthy of God, who is calling you to share the glory of his kingdom.

Another reason why we constantly thank God for you is that as soon as you heard the message that we brought you as God's message, you accepted it for what it really is, God's message and not some human thinking; and it is still a living power among you who believe it.

This is the word of the Lord.

Responsorial Psalm   Ps 138:7-12. ℟ v.1

℟   You have searched me and you know me, Lord.

1   O where can I go from your spirit,
     or where can I flee from your face?
     If I climb the heavens, you are there.
     If I lie in the grave, you are there. ℟

2   If I take the wings of the dawn
     and dwell at the sea's furthest end,
     even there your hand would lead me,
     your right hand would hold me fast. ℟

3   If I say: 'Let the darkness hide me
     and the light around me be night,'
     even darkness is not dark for you
     and the night is as clear as the day. ℟

Gospel Acclamation   1 Jn 2:5

     Alleluia, alleluia!
     Whoever keeps the word of Christ,
     grows perfect in the love of God.
     Alleluia!

GOSPEL

A reading from the holy Gospel according to Matthew   23:27-32

You are the children of those who murdered the prophets.

Jesus said, 'Alas for you, scribes and Pharisees, you hypocrites! You who are like whitewashed tombs that look handsome on the outside, but inside are full of dead men's bones and every kind of corruption. In the same way you appear to people from the outside like good honest men, but inside you are full of hypocrisy and lawlessness.

'Alas for you, scribes and Pharisees, you hypocrites! You who build the sepulchres of the prophets and decorate the tombs of holy men, saying, "We would never have joined in shedding the blood of the prophets, had we lived in our fathers' day." So! Your own evidence tells against you! You are the sons of those who murdered the prophets! Very well then, finish off the work that your fathers began.'

This is the Gospel of the Lord.

Thursday

FIRST READING

A reading from the first letter of St Paul
to the Thessalonians

3:7-13

*May the Lord be generous in increasing your love for one another and
for the whole human race.*

Brothers, your faith has been a great comfort to us in the middle of our
own troubles and sorrows; now we can breathe again, as you are still
holding firm in the Lord. How can we thank God enough for you, for
all the joy we feel before our God on your account? We are earnestly
praying night and day to be able to see you face to face again and
make up any shortcomings in your faith.

May God our Father himself, and our Lord Jesus Christ, make it
easy for us to come to you. May the Lord be generous in increasing
your love and make you love one another and the whole human race
as much as we love you. And may he so confirm your hearts in
holiness that you may be blameless in the sight of our God and Father
when our Lord Jesus Christ comes with all his saints.

This is the word of the Lord.

Responsorial Psalm

Ps 89:3-4. 12-14. 17. ℟ v.14

℟   Fill us with your love, O Lord,
and we will sing for joy!

1   You turn men back into dust
and say: 'Go back, sons of men.'
To your eyes a thousand years
are like yesterday, come and gone,
no more than a watch in the night.   ℟

2   Make us know the shortness of our life
that we may gain wisdom of heart.
Lord, relent! Is your anger for ever?
Show pity to your servants.   ℟

3   In the morning, fill us with your love;
we shall exult and rejoice all our days.
Let the favour of the Lord be upon us:
give success to the work of our hands.   ℟

Gospel Acclamation   Mt 24:42. 44

Alleluia, alleluia!
Be watchful and ready:
you know not when the Son of Man is coming.
Alleluia!

GOSPEL

A reading from the holy Gospel according to Matthew   24:42-51

Stay awake and be ready.

Jesus said to his disciples: 'Stay awake, because you do not know the day when your master is coming. You may be quite sure of this, that if the householder had known at what time of the night the burglar would come, he would have stayed awake and would not have allowed anyone to break the wall of his house. Therefore, you too must stand ready because the Son of Man is coming at an hour you do not expect.

'What sort of servant, then, is faithful and wise enough for the master to place him over his household to give them their food at the proper time? Happy that servant if his master's arrival finds him at this employment. I tell you solemnly, he will place him over everything he owns. But as for the dishonest servant who says to himself, "My master is taking his time," and sets about beating his fellow servants and eating and drinking with drunkards, his master will come on a day he does not expect and at an hour he does not know. The master will cut him off and send him to the same fate as the hypocrites, where there will be weeping and grinding of teeth.'

This is the Gospel of the Lord.

Friday

FIRST READING

A reading from the first letter of St Paul
to the Thessalonians .

4:1-8

This is the will of God, your holiness of life.

Brothers, we urge you and appeal to you in the Lord Jesus to make
more and more progress in the kind of life that you are meant to live:
the life that God wants, as you learnt from us, and as you are already
living it. You have not forgotten the instructions we gave you on the
authority of the Lord Jesus.

What God wants is for you all to be holy. He wants you to keep
away from fornication, and each one of you to know how to use the
body that belongs to him in a way that is holy and honourable, not
giving way to selfish lust like the pagans who do not know God. He
wants nobody at all ever to sin by taking advantage of a brother in
these matters; the Lord always punishes sins of that sort, as we told
you before and assured you. We have been called by God to be holy,
not to be immoral; in other words, anyone who objects is not objecting
to a human authority, but to God, who gives you his Holy Spirit.

This is the word of the Lord.

Responsorial Psalm

Ps 96:1-2. 5-6. 10-12. ℟ v.12

℟   Let the just rejoice in the Lord.

1   The Lord is king, let earth rejoice,
     the many coastlands be glad.
     Cloud and darkness are his raiment;
     his throne, justice and right. ℟

2   The mountains melt like wax
     before the Lord of all the earth.
     The skies proclaim his justice;
     all peoples see his glory. ℟

3   The Lord loves those who hate evil:
     he guards the souls of his saints;
     he sets them free from the wicked. ℟

4   Light shines forth for the just
    and joy for the upright of heart.
    Rejoice, you just, in the Lord;
    give glory to his holy name.   ℟

Gospel Acclamation   Lk 21:36

Alleluia, alleluia!
Be watchful, pray constantly,
that you may be worthy to stand before the Son of Man.
Alleluia!

GOSPEL

A reading from the holy Gospel according to Matthew   25:1-13

The bridegroom is here, go out and meet him.

Jesus said to his disciples: 'The kingdom of heaven will be like this:
Ten bridesmaids took their lamps and went to meet the bridegroom.
Five of them were foolish and five were sensible: the foolish ones did
take their lamps, but they brought no oil, whereas the sensible ones
took flasks of oil as well as their lamps. The bridegroom was late, and
they all grew drowsy and fell asleep. But at midnight there was a cry,
"The bridegroom is here! Go out and meet him." At this, all those
bridesmaids woke up and trimmed their lamps, and the foolish ones
said to the sensible ones, "Give us some of your oil: our lamps are
going out." But they replied, "There may not be enough for us and for
you; you had better go to those who sell it and buy some for
yourselves." They had gone off to buy it when the bridegroom arrived.
Those who were ready went in with him to the wedding hall and the
door was closed. The other bridesmaids arrived later. "Lord, Lord,"
they said, "open the door for us." But he replied, "I tell you solemnly, I
do not know you." So stay awake, because you do not know either the
day or the hour.'

This is the Gospel of the Lord.

Saturday

FIRST READING

A reading from the first letter of St Paul
to the Thessalonians

4:9-11

You have learned from God himself to love one another.

As for loving our brothers, there is no need for anyone to write to you
about that, since you have learnt from God yourselves to love one
another, and in fact this is what you are doing with all the brothers
throughout the whole of Macedonia. However, we do urge you,
brothers, to go on making even greater progress and to make a point
of living quietly, attending to your own business and earning your
living, just as we told you to.

This is the word of the Lord.

Responsorial Psalm

Ps 97:1. 7-9. ℟ v.9

℟   The Lord comes to rule the earth with justice.

1   Sing a new song to the Lord
    for he has worked wonders.
    His right hand and his holy arm
    have brought salvation.   ℟

2   Let the sea and all within it, thunder;
    the world, and all its peoples.
    Let the rivers clap their hands
    and the hills ring out their joy
    at the presence of the Lord.   ℟

3   For the Lord comes,
    he comes to rule the earth.
    He will rule the world with justice
    and the peoples with fairness.   ℟

Gospel Acclamation

Jn 13:34

Alleluia, alleluia!
I give you a new commandment:
love one another as I have loved you.
Alleluia!

GOSPEL

A reading from the holy Gospel according to Matthew   25:14-30

You have been faithful in small things, enter into the joy of your Master.

Jesus told his disciples this parable: 'A man on his way abroad summoned his servants and entrusted his property to them. To one he gave five talents, to another two, to a third one; each in proportion to his ability. Then he set out. The man who had received the five talents promptly went and traded with them and made five more. The man who had received two made two more in the same way. But the man who had received one went off and dug a hole in the ground and hid his master's money. Now a long time after, the master of those servants came back and went through his accounts with them. The man who had received the five talents came forward bringing five more. "Sir," he said, "you entrusted me with five talents; here are five more that I have made." His master said to him, "Well done, good and faithful servant; you have shown you can be faithful in small things, I will trust you with greater; come and join in your master's happiness." Next the man with the two talents came forward. "Sir," he said, "you entrusted me with two talents; here are two more that I have made." His master said to him, "Well done, good and faithful servant; you have shown you can be faithful in small things, I will trust you with greater; come and join in your master's happiness." Last came forward the man who had the one talent. "Sir," said he, "I heard you were a hard man, reaping where you have not sown and gathering where you have not scattered; so I was afraid, and I went off and hid your talent in the ground. Here it is; it was yours, you have it back." But his master answered him, "You wicked and lazy servant! So you knew that I reap where I have not sown and gather where I have not scattered? Well then, you should have deposited my money with the bankers, and on my return I would have recovered my capital with interest. So now, take the talent from him and give it to the man who has the five talents. For to everyone who has will be given more, and he will have more than enough; but from the man who has not, even what he has will be taken away. As for this good-for-nothing servant, throw him out into the dark, where there will be weeping and grinding of teeth." '

This is the Gospel of the Lord.

TWENTY-SECOND WEEK IN ORDINARY TIME

Year I

Monday

FIRST READING

A reading from the first letter of St Paul
to the Thessalonians

4:13-18

The Lord himself will lead all who are asleep in Jesus with him.

We want you to be quite certain, brothers, about those who have died, to make sure that you do not grieve about them, like the other people who have no hope. We believe that Jesus died and rose again, and that it will be the same for those who have died in Jesus: God will bring them with him. We can tell you this from the Lord's own teaching, that any of us who are left alive until the Lord's coming will not have any advantage over those who have died. At the trumpet of God, the voice of the archangel will call out the command and the Lord himself will come down from heaven; those who have died in Christ will be the first to rise, and then those of us who are still alive will be taken up in the clouds, together with them, to meet the Lord in the air. So we shall stay with the Lord for ever. With such thoughts as these you should comfort one another.

This is the word of the Lord.

Responsorial Psalm

Ps 95:1. 3-5. 11-13. ℟ v.13

℟   The Lord comes to judge the earth.

1   O sing a new song to the Lord,
    sing to the Lord all the earth.
    Tell among the nations his glory
    and his wonders among all the peoples.   ℟

2   The Lord is great and worthy of praise,
    to be feared above all gods;
    the gods of the heathens are naught.
    It was the Lord who made the heavens.   ℟

268

3   Let the heavens rejoice and earth be glad,
    let the sea and all within it thunder praise,
    let the land and all it bears rejoice,
    all the trees of the wood shout for joy
    at the presence of the Lord for he comes,
    he comes to rule the earth.   ℟

4   With justice he will rule the world,
    he will judge the peoples with his truth.   ℟

Gospel Acclamation   cf. Lk 4:18

    Alleluia, alleluia!
    The Spirit of the Lord is upon me;
    he sent me to bring Good News to the poor.
    Alleluia!

GOSPEL

A reading from the holy Gospel according to Luke   4:16-30

> *He has sent me to bring the Good News to the poor. No prophet is*
> *ever accepted in his own country.*

Jesus came to Nazara, where he had been brought up, and went into
the synagogue on the sabbath day as he usually did. He stood up to
read, and they handed him the scroll of the prophet Isaiah. Unrolling
the scroll he found the place where it is written:

    The spirit of the Lord has been given to me,
    for he has anointed me.
    He has sent me to bring the good news to the poor,
    to proclaim liberty to captives
    and to the blind new sight,
    to set the downtrodden free,
    to proclaim the Lord's year of favour.

He then rolled up the scroll, gave it back to the assistant and sat
down. And all eyes in the synagogue were fixed on him. Then he
began to speak to them, 'This text is being fulfilled today even as you
listen.' And he won the approval of all, and they were astonished by
the gracious words that came from his lips.

    They said, 'This is Joseph's son, surely?' But he replied, 'No doubt you will quote me the saying, "Physician, heal yourself" and tell me, "We have heard all that happened in Capernaum, do the same here in your own countryside." ' And he went on, 'I tell you solemnly, no prophet is ever accepted in his own country.

'There were many widows in Israel, I can assure you, in Elijah's day, when heaven remained shut for three years and six months and a great famine raged throughout the land, but Elijah was not sent to any one of these: he was sent to a widow at Zarephath, a Sidonian town. And in the prophet Elisha's time there were many lepers in Israel, but none of these was cured, except the Syrian, Naaman.'

When they heard this everyone in the synagogue was enraged. They sprang to their feet and hustled him out of the town; and they took him up to the brow of the hill their town was built on, intending to throw him down the cliff, but he slipped through the crowd and walked away.

This is the Gospel of the Lord.

Tuesday

FIRST READING

A reading from the first letter of St Paul   5:1-6. 9-11
to the Thessalonians

Christ has died for us, that we might live.

You will not be expecting us to write anything to you, brothers, about 'times and seasons', since you know very well that the Day of the Lord is going to come like a thief in the night. It is when people are saying, 'How quiet and peaceful it is' that the worst suddenly happens, as suddenly as labour pains come on a pregnant woman; and there will be no way for anybody to evade it.

But it is not as if you live in the dark, my brothers, for that Day to overtake you like a thief. No, you are all sons of light and sons of the day: we do not belong to the night or to darkness, so we should not go on sleeping, as everyone else does, but stay wide awake and sober. God never meant us to experience the Retribution, but to win salvation through our Lord Jesus Christ, who died for us so that, alive or dead, we should still live united to him. So give encouragement to each other, and keep strengthening one another, as you do already.

This is the word of the Lord.

Responsorial Psalm   Ps 26:1. 4. 13-14. ℟ v.13

> ℟ I believe that I shall see the good things of the Lord
>   in the land of the living.

1 The Lord is my light and my help;
   whom shall I fear?
   The Lord is the stronghold of my life;
   before whom shall I shrink? ℟

2 There is one thing I ask of the Lord,
   for this I long,
   to live in the house of the Lord,
   all the days of my life,
   to savour the sweetness of the Lord,
   to behold his temple. ℟

3 I am sure I shall see the Lord's goodness
   in the land of the living.
   Hope in him, hold firm and take heart.
   Hope in the Lord! ℟

Gospel Acclamation   Lk 7:16

> Alleluia, alleluia!
> A great prophet has appeared among us;
> God has visited his people.
> Alleluia!

GOSPEL

A reading from the holy Gospel according to Luke   4:31-37

I know who you are, the Holy One of God.

Jesus went down to Capernaum, a town in Galilee, and taught them
on the sabbath. And his teaching made a deep impression on them
because he spoke with authority.

In the synagogue there was a man who was possessed by the spirit
of an unclean devil, and it shouted at the top of its voice, 'Ha! What do
you want with us, Jesus of Nazareth? Have you come to destroy us? I
know who you are: the Holy One of God.' But Jesus said sharply, 'Be
quiet! Come out of him!' And the devil, throwing the man down in
front of everyone, went out of him without hurting him at all.

271

Astonishment seized them and they were all saying to one another, 'What teaching! He gives orders to unclean spirits with authority and power and they come out.' And reports of him went all through the surrounding countryside.

This is the Gospel of the Lord.

Wednesday

FIRST READING

A reading from the letter of St Paul to the Colossians   1:1-8

The Good News which has reached you is spreading all over the world.

From Paul, appointed by God to be an apostle of Christ Jesus, and from our brother Timothy to the saints in Colossae, our faithful brothers in Christ: Grace and peace to you from God our Father.

We have never failed to remember you in our prayers and to give thanks for you to God, the Father of our Lord Jesus Christ, ever since we heard about your faith in Christ and the love that you show towards all the saints because of the hope which is stored up for you in heaven. It is only recently that you heard of this, when it was announced in the message of the truth. The Good News which has reached you is spreading all over the world and producing the same results as it has among you ever since the day when you heard about God's grace and understood what this really is. Epaphras, who taught you, is one of our closest fellow workers and a faithful deputy for us as Christ's servant, and it was he who told us all about your love in the Spirit.

This is the word of the Lord.

Responsorial Psalm   Ps 51:10-11. ℟ v.10

℟   I trust in the kindness of God for ever.

1   I am like a growing olive tree
     in the house of God.
     I trust in the goodness of God
     for ever and ever. ℟

2 I will thank you for evermore;
for this is your doing.
I will proclaim that your name is good,
in the presence of your friends. ℟

Gospel Acclamation   Lk 4:18

Alleluia, alleluia!
The Lord sent me to bring Good News to the poor
and freedom to prisoners.
Alleluia!

GOSPEL

A reading from the holy Gospel according to Luke   4:38-44

I must preach the Good News to other towns as well, because that is what I was sent to do.

Leaving the synagogue Jesus went to Simon's house. Now Simon's mother-in-law was suffering from a high fever and they asked him to do something for her. Leaning over her he rebuked the fever and it left her. And she immediately got up and began to wait on them.

At sunset all those who had friends suffering from diseases of one kind or another brought them to him, and laying his hands on each he cured them. Devils too came out of many people, howling, 'You are the Son of God.' But he rebuked them and would not allow them to speak because they knew that he was the Christ.

When daylight came he left the house and made his way to a lonely place. The crowds went to look for him, and when they had caught up with him they wanted to prevent him leaving them, but he answered, 'I must proclaim the Good News of the kingdom of God to the other towns too, because that is what I was sent to do.' And he continued his preaching in the synagogues of Judaea.

This is the Gospel of the Lord.

Thursday

FIRST READING

A reading from the letter of St Paul to the Colossians   1:9-14

He has taken us out of the power of darkness and created a place for us in the kingdom of his Son.

Ever since the day we heard about you, we have never failed to pray for you, and what we ask God is that through perfect wisdom and spiritual understanding you should reach the fullest knowledge of his will. So you will be able to lead the kind of life which the Lord expects of you, a life acceptable to him in all its aspects; showing the results in all the good actions you do and increasing your knowledge of God. You will have in you the strength, based on his own glorious power, never to give in, but to bear anything joyfully, thanking the Father who has made it possible for you to join the saints and with them to inherit the light.

Because that is what he has done: he has taken us out of the power of darkness and created a place for us in the kingdom of the Son that he loves, and in him, we gain our freedom, the forgiveness of our sins.

This is the word of the Lord.

Responsorial Psalm   Ps 97:2-6. ℟ v.2

℟   The Lord has made known his salvation.

1   The Lord has made known his salvation;
    has shown his justice to the nations.
    He has remembered his truth and love
    for the house of Israel.   ℟

2   All the ends of the earth have seen
    the salvation of our God.
    Shout to the Lord all the earth,
    ring out your joy.   ℟

3   Sing psalms to the Lord with the harp
    with the sound of music.
    With trumpets and the sound of the horn
    acclaim the King, the Lord.   ℟

Gospel Acclamation   Mt 4:19

Alleluia, alleluia!
Come follow me, says the Lord,
and I will make you fishers of my people.
Alleluia!

GOSPEL

A reading from the holy Gospel according to Luke   5:1-11

They left everything and followed him.

Jesus was standing one day by the Lake of Gennesaret, with the crowd pressing round him listening to the word of God, when he caught sight of two boats close to the bank. The fishermen had gone out of them and were washing their nets. He got into one of the boats – it was Simon's – and asked him to put out a little from the shore. Then he sat down and taught the crowds from the boat.

When he had finished speaking he said to Simon, 'Put out into deep water and pay out your nets for a catch.' 'Master,' Simon replied 'we worked hard all night long and caught nothing, but if you say so, I will pay out the nets.' And when they had done this they netted such a huge number of fish that their nets began to tear, so they signalled to their companions in the other boat to come and help them; when these came, they filled the two boats to sinking point.

When Simon Peter saw this he fell at the knees of Jesus saying, 'Leave me, Lord; I am a sinful man.' For he and all his companions were completely overcome by the catch they had made; so also were James and John, sons of Zebedee, who were Simon's partners. But Jesus said to Simon, 'Do not be afraid; from now on it is men you will catch.' Then, bringing their boats back to land, they left everything and followed him.

This is the Gospel of the Lord.

Friday

FIRST READING

A reading from the letter of St Paul to the Colossians   1:15-20

All things were created through him and for him.

Christ Jesus is the image of the unseen God
and the first-born of all creation,
for in him were created
all things in heaven and on earth:
everything visible and everything invisible,
Thrones, Dominations, Sovereignties, Powers –
all things were created through him and for him.
Before anything was created, he existed,
and he holds all things in unity.
Now the Church is his body,
he is its head.
As he is the Beginning,
he was first to be born from the dead,
so that he should be first in every way;
because God wanted all perfection
to be found in him
and all things to be reconciled through him and for him,
everything in heaven and everything on earth,
when he made peace
by his death on the cross.

This is the word of the Lord.

Responsorial Psalm   Ps 99:2-5. ℟ v.2

℟ Come with joy into the presence of the Lord.

1 Cry out with joy to the Lord, all the earth.
   Serve the Lord with gladness.
   Come before him, singing for joy.   ℟

2 Know that he, the Lord, is God.
   He made us, we belong to him,
   we are his people, the sheep of his flock.   ℟

3 Go within his gates, giving thanks.
   Enter his courts with songs of praise.
   Give thanks to him and bless his name.   ℟

4   Indeed, how good is the Lord,
    eternal his merciful love.
    He is faithful from age to age.   ℟

Gospel Acclamation   Jn 8:12

    Alleluia, alleluia!
    I am the light of the world, says the Lord;
    whoever follows me will have the light of life.
    Alleluia!

GOSPEL

A reading from the holy Gospel according to Luke   5:33-39

When the bridegroom is taken from them, then they will fast.

The Pharisees and the scribes said to Jesus, 'John's disciples are always fasting and saying prayers, and the disciples of the Pharisees too, but yours go on eating and drinking.' Jesus replied, 'Surely you cannot make the bridegroom's attendants fast while the bridegroom is still with them? But the time will come, the time for the bridegroom to be taken away from them; that will be the time when they will fast.'

He also told them this parable. 'No one tears a piece from a new cloak to put it on an old cloak; if he does, not only will he have torn the new one, but the piece taken from the new will not match the old.

'And nobody puts new wine into old skins; if he does, the new wine will burst the skins and then run out, and the skins will be lost. No; new wine must be put into fresh skins. And nobody who has been drinking old wine wants new. "The old is good" he says.'

This is the Gospel of the Lord.

Saturday

FIRST READING

A reading from the letter of St Paul to the Colossians   1:21-23

He has reconciled you that you can appear holy and pure.

Not long ago, you were foreigners and enemies, in the way that you used to think and the evil things that you did; but now God has reconciled you, by Christ's death in his mortal body. Now you are able to appear before him holy, pure and blameless – as long as you persevere and stand firm on the solid base of the faith, never letting yourselves drift away from the hope promised by the Good News, which you have heard, which has been preached to the whole human race, and of which I, Paul, have become the servant.

This is the word of the Lord.

Responsorial Psalm
Ps 53:3-4. 6. 8. ℟ v.6

℟   God himself is my help.

1   O God, save me by your name;
     by your power, uphold my cause.
     O God, hear my prayer;
     listen to the words of my mouth.   ℟

2   But I have God for my help.
     The Lord upholds my life.
     I will sacrifice to you with willing heart
     and praise your name for it is good.   ℟

Gospel Acclamation
Jn 14:6

Alleluia, alleluia!
I am the way, the truth, and the life, says the Lord;
no one comes to the Father, except through me.
Alleluia!

GOSPEL

A reading from the holy Gospel according to Luke   6:1-5

Why are you doing something that is forbidden on the sabbath?

One sabbath Jesus happened to be taking a walk through the cornfields, and his disciples were picking ears of corn, rubbing them in their hands and eating them. Some of the Pharisees said, 'Why are you doing something that is forbidden on the sabbath day?' Jesus answered them, 'So you have not read what David did when he and his followers were hungry – how he went into the House of God, took the loaves of offering and ate them and gave them to his followers, loaves which only the priests are allowed to eat?' And he said to them, 'The Son of Man is master of the sabbath.'

This is the Gospel of the Lord.

TWENTY-THIRD WEEK IN ORDINARY TIME

Year I

Monday

FIRST READING

A reading from the letter of St Paul to the Colossians   1:24–2:3

I am the servant of the Church to make known the word of God, a
mystery hidden for generations.

It makes me happy to suffer for you, as I am suffering now, and in my own body to do what I can to make up all that has still to be undergone by Christ for the sake of his body, the Church. I became the servant of the Church when God made me responsible for delivering God's message to you, the message which was a mystery hidden for generations and centuries and has now been revealed to his saints. It was God's purpose to reveal it to them and to show all the rich glory of this mystery to pagans. The mystery is Christ among you, your hope of glory: this is the Christ we proclaim, this is the wisdom in which we thoroughly train everyone and instruct everyone, to make them all perfect in Christ. It is for this I struggle wearily on, helped only by his power driving me irresistibly.

Yes, I want you to know that I do have to struggle hard for you, and for those in Laodicea, and for so many others who have never seen me face to face. It is all to bind you together in love and to stir your minds, so that your understanding may come to full development, until you really know God's secret in which all the jewels of wisdom and knowledge are hidden.

This is the word of the Lord.

Responsorial Psalm   Ps 61:6-7.9. ℟ v.8

℟   In God is my safety and my glory.

1   In God alone be at rest, my soul;
    for my hope comes from him.
    He alone is my rock, my stronghold,
    my fortress; I stand firm.   ℟

2   Take refuge in God all you people.
    Trust him at all times.
    Pour out your hearts before him
    for God is our refuge.   ℟

Gospel Acclamation   Jn 10:27

Alleluia, alleluia!
My sheep listen to my voice, says the Lord;
I know them, and they follow me.
Alleluia!

GOSPEL

A reading from the holy Gospel according to Luke   6:6-11

They watched him to see if he would cure a man on the sabbath.

On the sabbath Jesus went into the synagogue and began to teach, and a man was there whose right hand was withered. The scribes and the Pharisees were watching him to see if he would cure a man on the sabbath, hoping to find something to use against him. But he knew their thoughts; and he said to the man with the withered hand, 'Stand up! Come out into the middle.' And he came out and stood there. Then Jesus said to them, 'I put it to you: is it against the law on the sabbath to do good, or to do evil; to save life, or to destroy it?' Then he looked around at them all and said to the man, 'Stretch out your hand.' He did so, and his hand was better. But they were furious, and began to discuss the best way of dealing with Jesus.

This is the Gospel of the Lord.

Tuesday

FIRST READING

A reading from the letter of St Paul to the Colossians   2:6-15

You must live your life in Christ, who has given you all forgiveness.

You must live your whole life according to the Christ you have received – Jesus the Lord; you must be rooted in him and built on him and held firm by the faith you have been taught, and full of thanksgiving.

Make sure that no one traps you and deprives you of your freedom by some secondhand, empty, rational philosophy based on the principles of this world instead of on Christ.

In his body lives the fullness of divinity, and in him you too find your own fulfilment, in the one who is the head of every Sovereignty and Power.

In him you have been circumcised, with circumcision not performed by human hand, but by the complete stripping of your body of flesh. This is circumcision according to Christ. You have been buried with him, when you were baptised; and by baptism, too, you have been raised up with him through your belief in the power of God who raised him from the dead. You were dead, because you were sinners and had not been circumcised: he has brought you to life with him, he has forgiven us all our sins.

He has overridden the Law, and cancelled every record of the debt that we had to pay; he has done away with it by nailing it to the cross; and so he got rid of the Sovereignties and the Powers, and paraded them in public, behind him in his triumphal procession.

This is the word of the Lord.

Responsorial Psalm   Ps 144:1-2. 8-11. ℟ v.9

℟   The Lord is compassionate to all his creatures.

1   I will give you glory, O God my King,
    I will bless your name for ever.
    I will bless you day after day
    and praise your name for ever. ℟

2   The Lord is kind and full of compassion,
    slow to anger, abounding in love.
    How good is the Lord to all,
    compassionate to all his creatures. ℟

3   All your creatures shall thank you, O Lord,
    and your friends shall repeat their blessing.
    They shall speak of the glory of your reign
    and declare your might, O God. ℟

Gospel Acclamation   cf. Jn 15:16

Alleluia, alleluia!
I have chosen you from the world, says the Lord,
to go and bear fruit that will last.
Alleluia!

GOSPEL

A reading from the holy Gospel according to Luke   6:12-19

He spent the night in prayer. He chose twelve from his disciples and called them Apostles.

Jesus went out into the hills to pray; and he spent the whole night in prayer to God. When day came he summoned his disciples and picked out twelve of them; he called them 'apostles': Simon whom he called Peter, and his brother Andrew; James, John, Philip, Bartholomew, Matthew, Thomas, James son of Alphaeus, Simon called the Zealot, Judas son of James, and Judas Iscariot who became a traitor.

He then came down with them and stopped at a piece of level ground where there was a large gathering of his disciples with a great crowd of people from all parts of Judaea and from Jerusalem and from the coastal region of Tyre and Sidon who had come to hear him and to be cured of their diseases. People tormented by unclean spirits were also cured, and everyone in the crowd was trying to touch him because power came out of him that cured them all.

This is the Gospel of the Lord.

Wednesday

FIRST READING

A reading from the letter of St Paul to the Colossians   3:1-11

You must die with Christ; put to death everything in you that belongs to earthly life.

Since you have been brought back to true life with Christ, you must look for the things that are in heaven, where Christ is, sitting at God's right hand. Let your thoughts be on heavenly things, not on the things that are on the earth, because you have died, and now the life you have is hidden with Christ in God. But when Christ is revealed – and he is your life – you too will be revealed in all your glory with him.

That is why you must kill everything in you that belongs only to earthly life: fornication, impurity, guilty passion, evil desires and especially greed, which is the same thing as worshipping a false god; all this is the sort of behaviour that makes God angry. And it is the way in which you used to live when you were surrounded by people doing the same thing, but now you, of all people, must give all these things up: getting angry, being bad-tempered, spitefulness, abusive language and dirty talk; and never tell each other lies. You have stripped off your old behaviour with your old self, and you have put on a new self which will progress towards true knowledge the more it is renewed in the image of its creator; and in that image there is no room for distinction between Greek and Jew, between the circumcised or the uncircumcised, or between barbarian and Scythian, slave and free man. There is only Christ: he is everything and he is in everything.

This is the word of the Lord.

Responsorial Psalm   Ps 144:2-3. 10-13. ℟ v.9

℟   The Lord is compassionate to all his creatures.

1   I will bless you day after day
    and praise your name for ever.
    The Lord is great, highly to be praised,
    his greatness cannot be measured.   ℟

2   All your creatures shall thank you, O Lord,
    and your friends shall repeat their blessing.
    They shall speak of the glory of your reign
    and declare your might, O God.   ℟

3   To make known to men your mighty deeds
    and the glorious splendour of your reign.
    Yours is an everlasting kingdom;
    your rule lasts from age to age.   ℟

Gospel Acclamation   Lk 6:23

Alleluia, alleluia!
Rejoice and be glad;
your reward will be great in heaven.
Alleluia!

283

GOSPEL

A reading from the holy Gospel according to Luke 6:20-26

Happy are the poor. Woe to you who are rich.

Fixing his eyes on his disciples Jesus said:

'How happy are you who are poor: yours is the kingdom of God.
Happy you who are hungry now: you shall be satisfied.
Happy you who weep now: you shall laugh.

'Happy are you when people hate you, drive you out, abuse you, denounce your name as criminal, on account of the Son of Man. Rejoice when that day comes and dance for joy, for then your reward will be great in heaven. This was the way their ancestors treated the prophets.

'But alas for you who are rich: you are having your consolation now.
Alas for you who have your fill now: you shall go hungry.
Alas for you who laugh now: you shall mourn and weep.

'Alas for you when the world speaks well of you! This was the way their ancestors treated the false prophets.'

This is the Gospel of the Lord.

Thursday

FIRST READING

A reading from the letter of St Paul to the Colossians 3:12-17

Have charity, which is the bond of perfection.

You are God's chosen race, his saints; he loves you, and you should be clothed in sincere compassion, in kindness and humility, gentleness and patience. Bear with one another; forgive each other as soon as a quarrel begins. The Lord has forgiven you; now you must do the same. Over all these clothes, to keep them together and complete them, put on love. And may the peace of Christ reign in your hearts, because it is for this that you were called together as parts of one body. Always be thankful.

Let the message of Christ, in all its richness, find a home with you. Teach each other, and advise each other, in all wisdom. With gratitude in your hearts sing psalms and hymns and inspired songs to

God; and never say or do anything except in the name of the Lord
Jesus, giving thanks to God the Father through him.

This is the word of the Lord.

Responsorial Psalm   Ps 150:1-6. ℟ v.6

℟   Let everything that breathes praise the Lord!

or

℟   Alleluia!

1   Praise God in his holy place,
    praise him in his mighty heavens.
    Praise him for his powerful deeds,
    praise his surpassing greatness.   ℟

2   O praise him with sound of trumpet,
    praise him with lute and harp.
    Praise him with timbrel and dance,
    praise him with strings and pipes.   ℟

3   O praise him with resounding cymbals,
    praise him with clashing of cymbals.
    Let everything that lives and that breathes
    give praise to the Lord.   ℟

Gospel Acclamation   1 Jn 4:12

    Alleluia, alleluia!
    If we love one another,
    God will live in us in perfect love.
    Alleluia!

GOSPEL

A reading from the holy Gospel according to Luke   6:27-38

Be merciful, as your Father is merciful.

Jesus said to his disciples: 'I say this to you who are listening: Love
your enemies, do good to those who hate you, bless those who curse
you, pray for those who treat you badly. To the man who slaps you on
one cheek, present the other cheek too; to the man who takes your

cloak from you, do not refuse your tunic. Give to everyone who asks you, and do not ask for your property back from the man who robs you. Treat others as you would like them to treat you. If you love those who love you, what thanks can you expect? Even sinners love those who love them. And if you do good to those who do good to you, what thanks can you expect? For even sinners do that much. And if you lend to those from whom you hope to receive, what thanks can you expect? Even sinners lend to get back the same amount. Instead, love your enemies and do good, and lend without any hope of return. You will have a great reward, and you will be sons of the Most High, for he himself is kind to the ungrateful and the wicked.

'Be compassionate as your Father is compassionate. Do not judge, and you will not be judged yourselves; do not condemn, and you will not be condemned yourselves; grant pardon, and you will be pardoned. Give, and there will be gifts for you: a full measure, pressed down, shaken together, and running over, will be poured into your lap; because the amount you measure out is the amount you will be given back.'

This is the Gospel of the Lord.

Friday

FIRST READING

A reading from the first letter of St Paul to Timothy   1:1-2. 12-14

I used to be a blasphemer, but the mercy of God was shown me.

From Paul, apostle of Christ Jesus appointed by the command of God our saviour and of Christ Jesus our hope, to Timothy, true child of mine in the faith; wishing you grace, mercy and peace from God the Father and from Christ Jesus our Lord.

I thank Christ Jesus our Lord, who has given me strength, and who judged me faithful enough to call me into his service even though I used to be a blasphemer and did all I could to injure and discredit the faith. Mercy, however, was shown me, because until I became a believer I had been acting in ignorance; and the grace of our Lord filled me with faith and with the love that is in Christ Jesus.

This is the word of the Lord.

Responsorial Psalm   Ps 15:1-2. 5. 7-8. 11. ℞ cf. v.5

℞   You are my inheritance, O Lord.

1   Preserve me, God, I take refuge in you.
     I say to the Lord: 'You are my God.
     My happiness lies in you alone.'
     O Lord, it is you who are my portion and cup;
     it is you yourself who are my prize. ℞

2   I will bless the Lord who gives me counsel,
     who even at night directs my heart.
     I keep the Lord ever in my sight:
     since he is at my right hand, I shall stand firm. ℞

3   You will show me the path of life,
     the fullness of joy in your presence,
     at your right hand happiness for ever. ℞

Gospel Acclamation   cf. Jn 17:17

     Alleluia, alleluia!
     Your word, O Lord, is truth:
     make us holy in the truth.
     Alleluia!

GOSPEL

A reading from the holy Gospel according to Luke   6:39-42

Can the blind lead the blind?

Jesus told a parable to the disciples, 'Can one blind man guide another? Surely both will fall into a pit? The disciple is not superior to his teacher; the fully trained disciple will always be like his teacher. Why do you observe the splinter in your brother's eye and never notice the plank in your own? How can you say to your brother, "Brother, let me take out the splinter that is in your eye", when you cannot see the plank in your own? Hypocrite! Take the plank out of your own eye first, and then you will see clearly enough to take out the splinter that is in your brother's eye.'

     This is the Gospel of the Lord.

Saturday

FIRST READING

A reading from the first letter of St Paul
to Timothy

1:15-17

He came into the world to save sinners.

Here is a saying that you can rely on and nobody should doubt: that
Christ Jesus came into the world to save sinners. I myself am the
greatest of them; and if mercy has been shown to me, it is because
Jesus Christ meant to make me the greatest evidence of his inexhaustible patience for all the other people who would later have to trust in
him to come to eternal life. To the eternal King, the undying, invisible
and only God, be honour and glory for ever and ever. Amen.

This is the word of the Lord.

Responsorial Psalm

Ps 112:1-7. ℟ v.2

℟   Blessed be the name of the Lord for ever.

or

℟   Alleluia!

1   Praise, O servants of the Lord,
    praise the name of the Lord!
    May the name of the Lord be blessed
    both now and for evermore!   ℟

2   From the rising of the sun to its setting
    praised be the name of the Lord!
    High above all nations is the Lord,
    above the heavens his glory.   ℟

3   Who is like the Lord, our God,
    who has risen on high to his throne
    yet stoops from the heights to look down,
    to look down upon heaven and earth?
    From the dust he lifts up the lowly,
    from the dungheap he raises the poor.   ℟

Gospel Acclamation   Jn 14:23

Alleluia, alleluia!
All who love me will keep my words,
and my Father will love them, and we will come to them.
Alleluia!

GOSPEL

A reading from the holy Gospel according to Luke   6:43-49

Why do you call me, 'Lord, Lord' and not do what I say?

Jesus said to his disciples: 'There is no sound tree that produces rotten fruit, nor again a rotten tree that produces sound fruit. For every tree can be told by its own fruit: people do not pick figs from thorns, nor gather grapes from brambles. A good man draws what is good from the store of goodness in his heart; a bad man draws what is bad from the store of badness. For a man's words flow out of what fills his heart.

'Why do you call me, "Lord, Lord" and not do what I say?'

'Everyone who comes to me and listens to my words and acts on them – I will show you what he is like. He is like the man who when he built his house dug, and dug deep, and laid the foundations on rock; when the river was in flood it bore down on that house but could not shake it, it was so well built. But the one who listens and does nothing is like the man who built his house on soil, with no foundations: as soon as the river bore down on it, it collapsed; and what a ruin that house became!'

This is the Gospel of the Lord.

TWENTY-FOURTH WEEK IN ORDINARY TIME

Year I

Monday

FIRST READING

A reading from the first letter of St Paul to Timothy   2:1-8

Let prayers be offered to God for everyone; he wants all people to be saved.

My advice is that, first of all, there should be prayers offered for everyone – petitions, intercessions and thanksgiving – and especially for kings and others in authority, so that we may be able to live religious and reverent lives in peace and quiet. To do this is right, and will please God our saviour: he wants everyone to be saved and reach full knowledge of the truth. For there is only one God, and there is only one mediator between God and mankind, himself a man, Christ Jesus, who sacrificed himself as a ransom for them all. He is the evidence of this, sent at the appointed time, and I have been named a herald and apostle of it and – I am telling the truth and no lie – a teacher of the faith and the truth to the pagans.

In every place, then, I want the men to lift their hands up reverently in prayer, with no anger or argument.

This is the word of the Lord.

Responsorial Psalm   Ps 27:2. 7-9. ℞ v.6

℞ Blest be the Lord for he has heard my prayer.

1 Hear the voice of my pleading
     as I call for help,
     as I lift up my hands in prayer
     to your holy place. ℞

2 The Lord is my strength and my shield;
     in him my heart trusts.
     I was helped, my heart rejoices
     and I praise him with my song. ℞

3 The Lord is the strength of his people,
     the stronghold where his anointed find salvation.
     Save your people; bless Israel your heritage.
     Be their shepherd and carry them for ever. ℞

Gospel Acclamation   Jn 3:16

Alleluia, alleluia!
God loved the world so much, he gave us his only Son,
that all who believe in him might have eternal life.
Alleluia!

GOSPEL

A reading from the holy Gospel according to Luke   7:1-10

Not even in Israel have I found such faith.

When Jesus had come to the end of all he wanted the people to hear,
he went into Capernaum. A centurion there had a servant, a favourite
of his, who was sick and near death. Having heard about Jesus he sent
some Jewish elders to him to ask him to come and heal his servant.
When they came to Jesus they pleaded earnestly with him. 'He
deserves this of you' they said 'because he is friendly towards our
people; in fact, he is the one who built the synagogue.' So Jesus went
with them, and was not very far from the house when the centurion
sent word to him by some friends: 'Sir,' he said 'do not put yourself to
trouble; because I am not worthy to have you under my roof; and for
this same reason I did not presume to come to you myself; but give the
word and let my servant be cured. For I am under authority myself,
and have soldiers under me; and I say to one man: Go, and he goes; to
another: Come here, and he comes; to my servant: Do this, and he does
it.' When Jesus heard these words he was astonished at him and,
turning round, said to the crowd following him, 'I tell you, not even in
Israel have I found faith like this.' And when the messengers got back
to the house they found the servant in perfect health.

This is the Gospel of the Lord.

Tuesday

FIRST READING

A reading from the first letter of St Paul to Timothy   3:1-13

The bishop must be blameless; deacons also must be conscientious
believers in the mystery of the faith.

Here is a saying that you can rely on: To want to be a presiding elder is to want to do a noble work. That is why the president must have an impeccable character. He must not have been married more than once, and he must be temperate, discreet and courteous, hospitable and a good teacher; not a heavy drinker, not hot-tempered, but kind and peaceable. He must not be a lover of money. He must be a man who manages his own family well and brings his children up to obey him and be well-behaved: how can any man who does not understand how to manage his own family have responsibility for the church of God? He should not be a new convert, in case pride might turn his head and then he might be condemned as the devil was condemned. It is also necessary that people outside the Church should speak well of him, so that he never gets a bad reputation and falls into the devil's trap.

In the same way, deacons must be respectable men whose word can be trusted, moderate in the amount of wine they drink and with no squalid greed for money. They must be conscientious believers in the mystery of the faith. They are to be examined first, and only admitted to serve as deacons if there is nothing against them. In the same way, the women must be respectable, not gossips but sober and quite reliable. Deacons must not have been married more than once, and must be men who manage their children and families well. Those of them who carry out their duties well as deacons will earn a high standing for themselves and be rewarded with great assurance in their work for the faith in Christ Jesus.

This is the word of the Lord.

Responsorial Psalm   Ps 100:1-3. 5. 6. ℟ v.2

℟   I will walk with blameless heart.

1   My song is of mercy and justice;
    I sing to you, O Lord.
    I will walk in the way of perfection.
    O when, Lord, will you come? ℟

2   I will walk with blameless heart
within my house;
I will not set before my eyes
whatever is base. ℟

3   The man who slanders his neighbour in secret
I will bring to silence.
The man of proud looks and haughty heart
I will never endure. ℟

4   I look to the faithful in the land
that they may dwell with me.
He who walks in the way of perfection
shall be my friend. ℟

Gospel Acclamation   Lk 7:16

    Alleluia, alleluia!
    A great prophet has appeared among us;
    God has visited his people.
    Alleluia!

GOSPEL

A reading from the holy Gospel according to Luke   7:11-17

Young man, I tell you, arise.

Jesus went to a town called Nain, accompanied by his disciples and a great number of people. When he was near the gate of the town it happened that a dead man was being carried out for burial, the only son of his mother, and she was a widow. And a considerable number of the townspeople were with her. When the Lord saw her he felt sorry for her. 'Do not cry' he said. Then he went up and put his hand on the bier and the bearers stood still, and he said, 'Young man, I tell you to get up.' And the dead man sat up and began to talk, and Jesus gave him to his mother. Everyone was filled with awe and praised God saying, 'A great prophet has appeared among us; God has visited his people.' And this opinion of him spread throughout Judaea and all over the countryside.

    This is the Gospel of the Lord.

Wednesday

FIRST READING

A reading from the first letter of St Paul to Timothy   3:14-16

The mystery of our religion is very deep.

At the moment of writing to you, I am hoping that I may be with you soon; but in case I should be delayed, I wanted you to know how people ought to behave in God's family – that is, in the Church of the living God, which upholds the truth and keeps it safe. Without any doubt, the mystery of our religion is very deep indeed:

He was made visible in the flesh,
attested by the Spirit,
seen by angels,
proclaimed to the pagans,
believed in by the world,
taken up in glory.

This is the word of the Lord.

Responsorial Psalm   Ps 110:1-6. ℟ v.2

℟   How great are the works of the Lord!

or

℟   Alleluia!

1   I will thank the Lord with all my heart
   in the meeting of the just and their assembly.
   Great are the works of the Lord;
   to be pondered by all who love them.   ℟

2   Majestic and glorious his work,
   his justice stands firm for ever.
   He makes us remember his wonders.
   The Lord is compassion and love.   ℟

3   He gives food to those who fear him;
   keeps his covenant ever in mind.
   He has shown his might to his people
   by giving them the lands of the nations.   ℟

Gospel Acclamation   cf. Jn 6:63. 68

Alleluia, alleluia!
Your words, Lord, are spirit and life;
you have the words of everlasting life.
Alleluia!

GOSPEL

A reading from the holy Gospel according to Luke   7:31-35

We played the pipes for you, and you wouldn't dance; we sang
dirges, and you wouldn't cry.

Jesus said to the people: 'What description can I find for the men of
this generation? What are they like? They are like children shouting
to one another while they sit in the market place:

"We played the pipes for you,
  and you wouldn't dance;
we sang dirges,
  and you wouldn't cry."

'For John the Baptist comes, not eating bread, not drinking wine,
and you say, "He is possessed." The Son of Man comes, eating and
drinking, and you say, "Look, a glutton and a drunkard, a friend of tax
collectors and sinners." Yet Wisdom has been proved right by all her
children.'

This is the Gospel of the Lord.

Thursday

FIRST READING

A reading from the first letter of St Paul to Timothy   4:12-16

Take care about what you do and teach; in this way you will save
both yourself and those who listen to you.

Do not let people disregard you because you are young, but be an
example to all the believers in the way you speak and behave, and in
your love, your faith and your purity. Make use of the time until I
arrive by reading to the people, preaching and teaching. You have in
you a spiritual gift which was given to you when the prophets spoke
and the body of elders laid their hands on you; do not let it lie unused.
Think hard about all this, and put it into practice, and everyone will
be able to see how you are advancing. Take great care about what you
do and what you teach; always do this, and in this way you will save
both yourself and those who listen to you.

This is the word of the Lord.

Responsorial Psalm   Ps 110:7-10. ℟ v.2

℟   How great are the works of the Lord!

or

℟   Alleluia!

1   His works are justice and truth:
    his precepts are all of them sure,
    standing firm for ever and ever:
    they are made in uprightness and truth.   ℟

2   He has sent deliverance to his people
    and established his covenant for ever.
    Holy his name, to be feared.   ℟

3   To fear the Lord is the beginning of wisdom;
    all who do so prove themselves wise.
    His praise shall last for ever!   ℟

Gospel Acclamation   Mt 11:28

Alleluia, alleluia!
Come to me, all you that labour and are burdened,
and I will give you rest, says the Lord.
Alleluia!

GOSPEL

A reading from the holy Gospel according to Luke   7:36-50

Her many sins must have been forgiven her, because she loved much.

One of the Pharisees invited Jesus to a meal. When he arrived at the
Pharisee's house and took his place at table, a woman came in, who
had a bad name in the town. She had heard he was dining with the
Pharisee and had brought with her an alabaster jar of ointment. She
waited behind him at his feet, weeping, and her tears fell on his feet,
and she wiped them away with her hair; then she covered his feet with
kisses and anointed them with the ointment.

When the Pharisee who had invited him saw this, he said to
himself, 'If this man were a prophet, he would know who this woman
is that is touching him and what a bad name she has.' Then Jesus took
him up and said, 'Simon, I have something to say to you.' 'Speak,
Master' was the reply. 'There was once a creditor who had two men in
his debt; one owed him five hundred denarii, the other fifty. They
were unable to pay, so he pardoned them both. Which of them will
love him more?' 'The one who was pardoned more, I suppose' answered
Simon. Jesus said, 'You are right.'

Then he turned to the woman. 'Simon,' he said 'you see this
woman? I came into your house, and you poured no water over my
feet, but she has poured out her tears over my feet and wiped them
away with her hair. You gave me no kiss, but she has been covering
my feet with kisses ever since I came in. You did not anoint my head
with oil, but she has anointed my feet with ointment. For this reason I
tell you that her sins, her many sins, must have been forgiven her, or
she would not have shown such great love. It is the man who is
forgiven little who shows little love.' Then he said to her, 'Your sins
are forgiven.' Those who were with him at table began to say to
themselves, 'Who is this man, that he even forgives sins?' But he said
to the woman, 'Your faith has saved you; go in peace.'

This is the Gospel of the Lord.

Friday

FIRST READING

A reading from the first letter of St Paul to Timothy   6:2-12

As a person dedicated to God, you must be just.

This is what you are to teach the brothers to believe and persuade them to do. Anyone who teaches anything different, and does not keep to the sound teaching which is that of our Lord Jesus Christ, the doctrine which is in accordance with true religion, is simply ignorant and must be full of self-conceit – with a craze for questioning everything and arguing about words. All that can come of this is jealousy, contention, abuse and wicked mistrust of one another; and unending disputes by people who are neither rational nor informed and imagine that religion is a way of making a profit. Religion, of course, does bring large profits, but only to those who are content with what they have. We brought nothing into the world, and we can take nothing out of it; but as long as we have food and clothing, let us be content with that. People who long to be rich are a prey to temptation; they get trapped into all sorts of foolish and dangerous ambitions which eventually plunge them into ruin and destruction. 'The love of money is the root of all evils' and there are some who, pursuing it, have wandered away from the faith, and so given their souls any number of fatal wounds.

But, as a man dedicated to God, you must avoid all that. You must aim to be saintly and religious, filled with faith and love, patient and gentle. Fight the good fight of the faith and win for yourself the eternal life to which you were called when you made your profession and spoke up for the truth in front of many witnesses.

This is the word of the Lord.

Responsorial Psalm   Ps 48:6-10. 17-20. ℟ Mt 5:3

℟ Happy the poor in spirit;
     the kingdom of heaven is theirs!

1 Why should I fear in evil days
    the malice of the foes who surround me,
    men who trust in their wealth,
    and boast of the vastness of their riches? ℟

2   For no man can buy his own ransom,
    or pay a price to God for his life.
    The ransom of his soul is beyond him.
    He cannot buy life without end,
    nor avoid coming to the grave. ℟

3   Then do not fear when a man grows rich,
    when the glory of his house increases.
    He takes nothing with him when he dies,
    his glory does not follow him below. ℟

4   Though he flattered himself while he lived:
    'Men will praise me for doing well for myself,'
    yet he will go to join his fathers,
    who will never see the light any more. ℟

Gospel Acclamation   cf. Mt 11:25

    Alleluia, alleluia!
    Blessed are you, Father, Lord of heaven and earth;
    you have revealed to little ones the mysteries of the kingdom.
    Alleluia!

GOSPEL

A reading from the holy Gospel according to Luke   8:1-3

> *There were women with them who provided for them out of their*
> *own resources.*

Jesus made his way through towns and villages preaching, and proclaiming the Good News of the kingdom of God. With him went the Twelve, as well as certain women who had been cured of evil spirits and ailments: Mary surnamed the Magdalene, from whom seven demons had gone out, Joanna the wife of Herod's steward Chuza, Susanna, and several others who provided for them out of their own resources.

    This is the Gospel of the Lord.

Saturday

FIRST READING

A reading from the first letter of St Paul to Timothy   6:13-16

Do all that you have been told until the appearance of our Lord Jesus Christ.

Before God the source of all life and before Jesus Christ, who spoke up as a witness for the truth in front of Pontius Pilate, I put to you the duty of doing all that you have been told, with no faults or failures, until the Appearing of our Lord Jesus Christ,

who at the due time will be revealed
by God, the blessed and only Ruler of all,
the King of kings and the Lord of lords,
who alone is immortal,
whose home is in inaccessible light,
whom no man has seen and no man is able to see:
to him be honour and everlasting power. Amen.

This is the word of the Lord.

Responsorial Psalm   Ps 99. ℟ v.2

℟   Come with joy into the presence of the Lord.

1   Cry out with joy to the Lord, all the earth.
    Serve the Lord with gladness.
    Come before him, singing for joy.   ℟

2   Know that he, the Lord, is God.
    He made us, we belong to him,
    we are his people, the sheep of his flock.   ℟

3   Go within his gates, giving thanks.
    Enter his courts with songs of praise.
    Give thanks to him and bless his name.   ℟

4   Indeed, how good is the Lord,
    eternal his merciful love.
    He is faithful from age to age.   ℟

Gospel Acclamation   cf. Lk 8:15

Alleluia, alleluia!
Happy are they who have kept the word with a generous heart
and yield a harvest through perseverance.
Alleluia!

GOSPEL

A reading from the holy Gospel according to Luke   8:4-15

*As for the seed in good ground, this is the people who have heard the word
and take it to themselves and yield a harvest through their perseverance.*

With a large crowd gathering and people from every town finding
their way to him, Jesus used this parable:
'A sower went out to sow his seed. As he sowed, some fell on the
edge of the path and was trampled on; and the birds of the air ate it
up. Some seed fell on rock, and when it came up it withered away,
having no moisture. Some seed fell amongst thorns and the thorns
grew with it and choked it. And some seed fell into rich soil and grew
and produced its crop a hundredfold.' Saying this he cried, 'Listen,
anyone who has ears to hear!'
His disciples asked him what this parable might mean, and he
said, 'The mysteries of the kingdom of God are revealed to you; for the
rest there are only parables, so that

they may see but not perceive,
listen but not understand.

'This, then, is what the parable means: the seed is the word of God.
Those on the edge of the path are people who have heard it, and then
the devil comes and carries away the word from their hearts in case
they should believe and be saved. Those on the rock are people who,
when they first hear it, welcome the word with joy. But these have no
root; they believe for a while, and in time of trial they give up. As for
the part that fell into thorns, this is people who have heard, but as
they go on their way they are choked by the worries and riches and
pleasures of life and do not reach maturity. As for the part in the rich
soil, this is people with a noble and generous heart who have heard
the word and take it to themselves and yield a harvest through their
perseverance.'

This is the Gospel of the Lord.

TWENTY-FIFTH WEEK IN ORDINARY TIME

Year I

Monday

FIRST READING

A reading from the book of Ezra   1:1-6

*These are the people of the Lord who went to Jerusalem to build
the temple of the Lord God.*

In the first year of Cyrus king of Persia, to fulfil the word of the Lord
that was spoken through Jeremiah, the Lord roused the spirit of
Cyrus king of Persia to issue a proclamation and to have it publicly
displayed throughout his kingdom: 'Thus speaks Cyrus king of Persia,
"The Lord, the God of heaven, has given me all the kingdoms of the
earth; he has ordered me to build him a Temple in Jerusalem, in
Judah. Whoever there is among you of all his people, may his God be
with him! Let him go up to Jerusalem in Judah to build the Temple of
the Lord, the God of Israel – he is the God who is in Jerusalem. And let
each survivor, wherever he lives, be helped by the people of that place
with silver and gold, with goods and cattle, as well as voluntary
offerings for the Temple of God which is in Jerusalem." '

Then the heads of families of Judah and of Benjamin, the priests
and the Levites, in fact all whose spirit had been roused by God,
prepared to go and rebuild the Temple of the Lord in Jerusalem; and
all their neighbours gave them every assistance with silver, gold,
goods, cattle, quantities of costly gifts and with voluntary offerings of
every kind.

This is the word of the Lord.

Responsorial Psalm   Ps 125. ℟ v.3

℟   The Lord has done marvels for us.

1   When the Lord delivered Zion from bondage,
     it seemed like a dream.
     Then was our mouth filled with laughter,
     on our lips there were songs.   ℟

302

2   The heathens themselves said: 'What marvels
    the Lord worked for them!'
    What marvels the Lord worked for us!
    Indeed we were glad.   ℟

3   Deliver us, O Lord, from our bondage
    as streams in dry land.
    Those who are sowing in tears
    will sing when they reap.   ℟

4   They go out, they go out, full of tears,
    carrying seed for the sowing:
    they come back, they come back, full of song,
    carrying their sheaves.   ℟

Gospel Acclamation   Mt 5:16

Alleluia, alleluia!
Let your light shine before all,
that they may see your good works and glorify your Father.
Alleluia!

GOSPEL

A reading from the holy Gospel according to Luke   8:16-18

Place your light on a stand so that people may see it when they enter.

Jesus said to his disciples: 'No one lights a lamp to cover it with a bowl
or to put it under a bed. No, he puts it on a lamp-stand so that people
may see the light when they come in. For nothing is hidden but it will
be made clear, nothing secret but it will be known and brought to
light. So take care how you hear; for anyone who has will be given
more; from anyone who has not, even what he thinks he has will be
taken away.'

    This is the Gospel of the Lord.

Tuesday

FIRST READING

A reading from the book of Ezra   6:7-8. 12. 14-20

They completed the temple of God, and ate the passover.

King Darius wrote to the satrap of Transeuphrates and his colleagues: 'Leave the high commissioner of Judah and the elders of the Jews to work on this Temple of God; they are to rebuild this Temple of God on its ancient site. This, I decree, is how you must assist the elders of the Jews in the reconstruction of this Temple of God: the expenses of these people are to be paid, promptly and without fail, from the royal revenue – that is, from the tribute of Transeuphrates. I, Darius, have issued this decree. Let it be obeyed to the letter!'

The elders of the Jews, for their part, prospered with their building, inspired by Haggai the prophet and Zechariah son of Iddo. They finished the building in accordance with the order of the God of Israel and the order of Cyrus and of Darius. This temple was finished on the twenty-third day of the month of Adar; it was the sixth year of the reign of King Darius. The Israelites – the priests, the Levites and the remainder of the exiles – joyfully dedicated this Temple of God; for the dedication of this Temple of God they offered one hundred bulls, two hundred rams, four hundred lambs and, as a sacrifice for sin for the whole of Israel, twelve he-goats, corresponding to the number of the tribes of Israel. Then they installed the priests according to their orders in the service of the Temple of God in Jerusalem, as is written in the Book of Moses.

The exiles celebrated the Passover on the fourteenth day of the first month. The Levites, as one man, had purified themselves; all were pure, so they sacrificed the passover for all the exiles, for their brothers the priests and for themselves.

This is the word of the Lord.

Responsorial Psalm   Ps 121:1-5. ℟ v.1

℟   Let us go rejoicing to the house of the Lord.

1   I rejoiced when I heard them say:
     'Let us go to God's house.'
     And now our feet are standing
     within your gates, O Jerusalem. ℟

2   Jerusalem is built as a city
    strongly compact.
    It is there that the tribes go up,
    the tribes of the Lord. ℟

3   For Israel's law it is,
    there to praise the Lord's name.
    There were set the thrones of judgement
    of the house of David. ℟

Gospel Acclamation   Lk 11:28

    Alleluia, alleluia!
    Blessed are they who hear the word of God
    and keep it.
    Alleluia!

GOSPEL

A reading from the holy Gospel according to Luke   8:19-21

*My mother and my brothers are those who hear the word of God
and put it into practice.*

The mother and the brothers of Jesus came looking for him, but they could not get to him because of the crowd. He was told, 'Your mother and brothers are standing outside and want to see you.' But he said in answer, 'My mother and my brothers are those who hear the word of God and put it into practice.

    This is the Gospel of the Lord.

Wednesday

FIRST READING

A reading from the book of Ezra   9:5-9

Our God has not forgotten us in our slavery.

At the evening sacrifice I, Ezra, came out of my stupor and falling on my knees, with my garment and cloak torn, I stretched out my hands to the Lord my God, and said:
    'My God, I am ashamed, I blush to lift my face to you, my God. For

our crimes have increased, until they are higher than our heads, and our sin has piled up to heaven. From the days of our ancestors until now our guilt has been great; on account of our crimes we, our kings and our priests, were given into the power of the kings of other countries, given to the sword, to captivity, to pillage and to shame, as is the case today. But now, suddenly, the Lord our God by his favour has left us a remnant and granted us a refuge in his holy place; this is how our God has cheered our eyes and given us a little respite in our slavery. For we are slaves: but God has not forgotten us in our slavery; he has shown us kindness in the eyes of the kings of Persia, obtaining permission for us to rebuild the Temple of our God and restore its ruins, and he has found us safety and shelter in Judah and in Jerusalem.'

This is the word of the Lord.

Responsorial Psalm   Tob 13:2. 4. 6-8. ℟ v.1

℟   Blessed be God who lives for ever.

1   God punishes, he also has mercy,
    he leads men to the depths of the grave,
    he restores them from the great destruction.
    No man can escape his hand.   ℟

2   It is he who scattered us among the nations.
    Among them must we show forth his greatness
    and exalt him in the presence of all living;
    for he is our Lord and our God,
    our Father and our God for ever.   ℟

3   Now think what he has done for you,
    give thanks to him with all your voice.
    Give praise to the Lord for his justice
    and exalt the kings of all ages.   ℟

4   In this land of exile I will thank him,
    and show forth his greatness and might
    to the race of sinful men.   ℟

5   Sinners, come back to him,
    do what is right before him.
    Who knows but he will receive you with pity?   ℟

Gospel Acclamation   Mk 1:15

> Alleluia, alleluia!
> The kingdom of God is near:
> repent and believe the Good News!
> Alleluia!

GOSPEL

A reading from the holy Gospel according to Luke   9:1-6

He sent them to proclaim the kingdom of God and to heal the sick.

Jesus called the Twelve together and gave them power and authority over all devils and to cure diseases, and he sent them out to proclaim the kingdom of God and to heal. He said to them, 'Take nothing for the journey: neither staff, nor haversack, nor bread, nor money; and let none of you take a spare tunic. Whatever house you enter, stay there; and when you leave, let it be from there. As for those who do not welcome you, when you leave their town shake the dust from your feet as a sign to them.' So they set out and went from village to village proclaiming the Good News and healing everywhere.

This is the Gospel of the Lord.

Thursday

FIRST READING

A reading from the prophet Haggai   1:1-8

Build the temple and you will be acceptable to me.

In the second year of King Darius, on the first day of the sixth month, the word of the Lord was addressed through the prophet Haggai to Zerubbabel son of Shealtiel, high commissioner of Judah, and to Joshua son of Jehozadak, the high priest, as follows, 'The Lord of hosts says this, "This people says: The time has not yet come to rebuild the Temple of the Lord. (And the word of the Lord was addressed through the prophet Haggai, as follows:) Is this a time for you to live in your panelled houses, when this House lies in ruins? So now, the Lord of hosts says this: Reflect carefully how things have gone for you.

You have sown much and harvested little; you eat but never have enough, drink but never have your fill, put on clothes but do not feel warm. The wage earner gets his wages only to put them in a purse riddled with holes. Reflect carefully how things have gone for you. So go to the hill country, fetch wood, and rebuild the House: I shall then take pleasure in it, and be glorified there, says the Lord." '

This is the word of the Lord.

Responsial Psalm   Ps 149:1-6. 9. ℟ v.4

℟   The Lord takes delight in his people.

or

℟   Alleluia!

1   Sing a new song to the Lord,
    his praise in the assembly of the faithful.
    Let Israel rejoice in its Maker,
    let Zion's sons exult in their king. ℟

2   Let them praise his name with dancing
    and make music with timbrel and harp.
    For the Lord takes delight in his people.
    He crowns the poor with salvation. ℟

3   Let the faithful rejoice in their glory,
    shout for joy and take their rest.
    Let the praise of God be on their lips,
    this honour is for all his faithful. ℟

Gospel Acclamation   Jn 14:6

Alleluia, alleluia!
I am the way, the truth, and the life, says the Lord;
no one comes to the Father, except through me.
Alleluia!

GOSPEL

A reading from the holy Gospel according to Luke 9:7-9

I beheaded John, so who is this I hear so much about?

Herod the tetrarch had heard about all that was being done by Jesus; and he was puzzled, because some people were saying that John had risen from the dead, others that Elijah had reappeared, still others that one of the ancient prophets had come back to life. But Herod said, 'John? I beheaded him. So who is this I hear such reports about?' And he was anxious to see Jesus.

This is the Gospel of the Lord.

Friday

FIRST READING

A reading from the prophet Haggai 1:15–2:9

A little while and I shall fill the temple with glory.

In the second year of King Darius, on the twenty-first day of the seventh month, the word of the Lord was addressed through the prophet Haggai, as follows, 'You are to speak to Zerubbabel son of Shealtiel, the high commissioner of Judah, to Joshua son of Jehozadak, the high priest, and to all the remnant of the people. Say this, "Who is there left among you that saw this Temple in its former glory? And how does it look to you now? Does it seem nothing to you? But take courage now, Zerubbabel – it is the Lord who speaks. Courage, High Priest Joshua son of Jehozadak! Courage, all you people of the country! – it is the Lord who speaks. To work! I am with you – it is the Lord of hosts who speaks – and my spirit remains among you. Do not be afraid! For the Lord of hosts says this: A little while now, and I am going to shake the heavens and the earth, the sea and the dry land. I will shake all the nations and the treasures of all the nations shall flow in, and I will fill this Temple with glory, says the Lord of hosts. Mine is the silver, mine the gold! – it is the Lord of hosts who speaks. The new glory of this Temple is going to surpass the old, says the Lord of hosts, and in this place I will give peace – it is the Lord of hosts who speaks." '

This is the word of the Lord.

Responsorial Psalm   Ps 42:1-4. ℟ cf. v.5

℟   Hope in God, I will praise him,
      my saviour and my God.

1   Defend me, O God, and plead my cause
     against a godless nation.
     From deceitful and cunning men
     rescue me, O God.   ℟

2   Since you, O God, are my stronghold,
     why have you rejected me?
     Why do I go mourning
     oppressed by the foe?   ℟

3   O send forth your light and your truth;
     let these be my guide.
     Let them bring me to your holy mountain
     to the place where you dwell.   ℟

4   And I will come to the altar of God,
     the God of my joy.
     My redeemer, I will thank you on the harp,
     O God, my God.   ℟

Gospel Acclamation   Mk 10:45

    Alleluia, alleluia!
    The Son of Man came to serve
    and to give his life as a ransom for all.
    Alleluia!

GOSPEL

A reading from the holy Gospel according to Luke   9:18-22

You are the Christ of God. The Son of Man must suffer much.

One day when Jesus was praying alone in the presence of his disciples
he put this question to them, 'Who do the crowds say I am?' And they
answered, 'John the Baptist; others Elijah; and others say one of the
ancient prophets come back to life.' 'But you,' he said 'who do you say I
am?' It was Peter who spoke up. 'The Christ of God' he said. But he
gave them strict orders not to tell anyone anything about this.

'The Son of Man' he said 'is destined to suffer grievously, to be rejected by the elders and chief priests and scribes and to be put to death, and to be raised up on the third day.'

This is the Gospel of the Lord.

Saturday

FIRST READING

A reading from the prophet Zechariah   2:5-9. 14-15

I am coming, and I will live in your midst.

Raising my eyes, I saw a vision. It was this: there was a man with a measuring line in his hand. I asked him, 'Where are you going?' He said, 'To measure Jerusalem, to find out her breadth and her length.' And then, while the angel who was talking to me stood still, another angel came forward to meet him. He said to him, 'Run, and tell that young man this, "Jerusalem is to remain unwalled, because of the great number of men and cattle there will be in her. But I – it is the Lord who speaks – I will be a wall of fire for her all round her, and I will be her glory in the midst of her." '

Sing, rejoice,
daughter of Zion;
for I am coming
to dwell in the middle of you
– it is the Lord who speaks.
Many nations will join the Lord,
on that day;
they will become his people.

This is the word of the Lord.

Responsorial Psalm ⟨Jer 31:10-13. ℟ v.10⟩

℟ The Lord will guard us,
   like a shepherd guarding his flock.

1 O nations, hear the word of the Lord,
   proclaim it to the far-off coasts.
   Say: 'He who scattered Israel will gather him,
   and guard him as a shepherd guards his flock.' ℟

2 For the Lord has ransomed Jacob,
   has saved him from an overpowering hand.
   They will come and shout for joy on Mount Zion,
   they will stream to the blessings of the Lord. ℟

3 Then the young girls will rejoice and will dance,
   the men, young and old, will be glad.
   I will turn their mourning into joy,
   I will console them, give gladness for grief. ℟

Gospel Acclamation ⟨cf. 2 Tim 1:10⟩

Alleluia, alleluia!
Our Saviour Jesus Christ has done away with death
and brought us life through his gospel.
Alleluia!

GOSPEL

A reading from the holy Gospel according to Luke ⟨9:43-45⟩

The Son of Man will be delivered into the hands of humanity . . .
All who wish to be first must make themselves servants of all.

At a time when everyone was full of admiration for all he did, Jesus
said to his disciples, 'For your part, you must have these words
constantly in your mind: The Son of Man is going to be handed over
into the power of men.' But they did not understand him when he said
this; it was hidden from them so that they should not see the meaning
of it, and they were afraid to ask him about what he had just said.

   This is the Gospel of the Lord.

TWENTY-SIXTH WEEK IN ORDINARY TIME
Year I

Monday

FIRST READING

A reading from the prophet Zechariah   8:1-8

I will save my people from the East and the West.

The word of the Lord of hosts was addressed to me as follows:

'The Lord of hosts says this.
I am burning with jealousy for Zion,
with great anger for her sake.

'The Lord of hosts says this.
I am coming back to Zion
and shall dwell in the middle of Jerusalem.
Jerusalem will be called Faithful City
and the mountain of the Lord of hosts, the Holy Mountain.

'The Lord of hosts says this.
Old men and old women will again sit down
in the squares of Jerusalem;
every one of them staff in hand
because of their great age.
And the squares of the city will be full
of boys and girls
playing in the squares.

'The Lord of hosts says this.
If this seems a miracle
to the remnant of this people (in those days),
will it seem one to me?
It is the Lord of hosts who speaks.
The Lord of hosts says this.
Now I am going to save my people
from the countries of the East
and from the countries of the West.
I will bring them back
to live inside Jerusalem.
They shall be my people

and I will be their God
in faithfulness and integrity.'

This is the word of the Lord.

Responsorial Psalm   Ps 101:16-21. 29. 22-23. ℞ v.17

℞   The Lord will build up Zion again,
       and appear in all his glory.

1   The nations shall fear the name of the Lord
     and all the earth's kings your glory,
     when the Lord shall build up Zion again
     and appear in all his glory.
     Then he will turn to the prayers of the helpless;
     he will not despise their prayers.   ℞

2   Let this be written for ages to come
     that a people yet unborn may praise the Lord;
     for the Lord leaned down from his sanctuary on high.
     He looked down from heaven to the earth
     that he might hear the groans of the prisoners
     and free those condemned to die.   ℞

3   The sons of your servants shall dwell untroubled
     and their race shall endure before you
     that the name of the Lord may be proclaimed in Zion
     and his praise in the heart of Jerusalem,
     when peoples and kingdoms are gathered together
     to pay their homage to the Lord.   ℞

Gospel Acclamation   Mk 10:45

     Alleluia, alleluia!
     The Son of Man came to serve
     and to give his life as a ransom for all.
     Alleluia!

GOSPEL

A reading from the holy Gospel according to Luke   9:46-50

The least among you all is the one who is great.

An argument started between the disciples about which of them was the greatest. Jesus knew what thoughts were going through their minds, and he took a little child and set him by his side and then said to them, 'Anyone who welcomes this little child in my name welcomes me; and anyone who welcomes me welcomes the one who sent me. For the least among you all, that is the one who is great.'

John spoke up. 'Master,' he said 'we saw a man casting out devils in your name, and because he is not with us we tried to stop him.' But Jesus said to him, 'You must not stop him: anyone who is not against you is for you.'

This is the Gospel of the Lord.

Tuesday

FIRST READING

A reading from the prophet Zechariah   8:20-23

Many peoples will come to seek the Lord God in Jerusalem.

The Lord of hosts says this. 'There will be other peoples yet, and citizens of great cities. And the inhabitants of one city will go to the next and say, "Come, let us go and entreat the favour of the Lord, and seek the Lord of hosts; I am going myself." And many peoples and great nations will come to seek the Lord of hosts in Jerusalem and to entreat the favour of the Lord.'

The Lord of hosts says this. 'In those days, ten men of nations of every language will take a Jew by the sleeve and say, "We want to go with you, since we have learnt that God is with you." '

This is the word of the Lord.

Responsorial Psalm   Ps 86. ℟ Zech 8:23

℟   God is with us.

1   On the holy mountain is his city
    cherished by the Lord.
    The Lord prefers the gates of Zion
    to all Jacob's dwellings.
    Of you are told glorious things,
    O city of God!   ℟

2   Babylon and Egypt I will count
    among those who know me;
    Philistia, Tyre, Ethiopia,
    these will be her children
    and Zion shall be called 'Mother'
    for all shall be her children.   ℟

3   It is he, the Lord Most High,
    who gives each his place.
    In his register of peoples he writes:
    'These are her children'
    and while they dance they will sing;
    'In you all find their home.'   ℟

Gospel Acclamation   Mk 10:45

    Alleluia, alleluia!
    The Son of Man came to serve
    and to give his life as a ransom for all.
    Alleluia!

GOSPEL

A reading from the holy Gospel according to Luke   9:51-56

He resolutely took the road to Jerusalem.

As the time drew near for him to be taken up to heaven, Jesus
resolutely took the road for Jerusalem and sent messengers ahead of
him. These set out, and they went into a Samaritan village to make
preparations for him, but the people would not receive him because he
was making for Jerusalem. Seeing this, the disciples James and John
said, 'Lord, do you want us to call down fire from heaven to burn them
up?' But he turned and rebuked them, and they went off to another
village.

    This is the Gospel of the Lord.

Wednesday

FIRST READING

A reading from the book of Nehemiah   2:1-8

If it pleases the king, send me to the city of my ancestors and I will rebuild it.

In the month of Nisan, in the twentieth year of King Artaxerxes, the wine being my concern, I took up the wine and offered it to the king. Now I had never been downcast before. So the king said, 'Why is your face so sad? You are not sick, surely? This must be a sadness of your heart.' A great fear came over me and I said to the king, 'May the king live for ever! How could my face be other than sad when the city where the tombs of my ancestors are lies in ruins, and its gates have been burnt down?' 'What' the king asked 'is your request?' I called on the God of heaven and made this reply to the king, 'If it pleases the king, and if you are satisfied with your servant, give me leave to go to Judah, to the city of my ancestors' tombs, and rebuild it.' The king, with the queen sitting there beside him, said, 'How long will your journey take, and when will you return?' So I named a date that seemed acceptable to the king and he gave me leave to go. I spoke to the king once more, 'If it pleases the king, could letters be given me for the governors of Transeuphrates to allow me to pass through to Judah? And also a letter for Asaph, keeper of the king's park, to supply me with timber for the gates of the citadel of the Temple, for the city walls and for the house I am to occupy?' This the king granted me, for the kindly favour of my God was with me.

This is the word of the Lord.

Responsorial Psalm   Ps 136:1-6. ℟ v.6

℟   Let my tongue be silenced
     if I ever forget you!

1   By the rivers of Babylon
     there we sat and wept,
     remembering Zion;
     on the poplars that grew there
     we hung up our harps.   ℟

2 For it was there that they asked us,
    our captors, for songs,
    our oppressors, for joy.
    'Sing to us,' they said,
    'one of Zion's songs.'

    ℟ Let my tongue be silenced,
        if I ever forget you!

3 O how could we sing
    the song of the Lord
    on alien soil?
    If I forget you, Jerusalem,
    let my right hand wither! ℟

4 O let my tongue
    cleave to my mouth
    if I remember you not,
    if I prize not Jerusalem
    above all my joys! ℟

Gospel Acclamation   Phil 3:8-9

    Alleluia, alleluia!
    I count all things worthless but this:
    to gain Jesus Christ and to be found in him.
    Alleluia!

GOSPEL

A reading from the holy Gospel according to Luke   9:57-62

                                    I will follow you wherever you go.

As Jesus and his disciples travelled along they met a man on the road
who said to him, 'I will follow you wherever you go.' Jesus answered,
'Foxes have holes and the birds of the air have nests, but the Son of
Man has nowhere to lay his head.'

Another to whom he said, 'Follow me', replied, 'Let me go and bury
my father first.' But he answered, 'Leave the dead to bury the dead;
your duty is to go and spread the news of the kingdom of God.'

Another said, 'I will follow you, sir, but first let me go and say
good-bye to my people at home.' Jesus said to him, 'Once the hand is
laid on the plough, no one who looks back is fit for the kingdom of
God.'

This is the Gospel of the Lord.

Thursday

FIRST READING

A reading from the book of Nehemiah   8:1-12

*Ezra opened the Book of the Law, blessed the Lord, and all the
people responded, 'Amen! Amen!'*

When the seventh month came, all the people gathered as one man on
the square before the Water Gate. They asked Ezra the scribe to bring
the Book of the Law of Moses which the Lord had prescribed for Israel.
Accordingly Ezra the priest brought the Law before the assembly,
consisting of men, women, and children old enough to understand.
This was the first day of the seventh month. On the square before the
Water Gate, in the presence of the men and women, and children old
enough to understand, he read from the book from early morning till
noon; all the people listened attentively to the Book of the Law.

Ezra the scribe stood on a wooden dais erected for the purpose. In
full view of all the people – since he stood higher than all the people –
Ezra opened the book; and when he opened it all the people stood up.
Then Ezra blessed the Lord, the great God, and all the people raised
their hands and answered, 'Amen! Amen!'; then they bowed down and,
face to the ground, prostrated themselves before the Lord.

The Levites explained the Law to the people while the people
remained standing. And Ezra read from the Law of God, translating
and giving the sense, so that the people understood what was read.

Then Nehemiah – His Excellency – and Ezra, priest and scribe
(and the Levites who were instructing the people) said to all the
people, 'This day is sacred to the Lord your God. Do not be mournful,
do not weep.' For the people were all in tears as they listened to the
words of the Law.

He then said, 'Go, eat the fat, drink the sweet wine, and send a
portion to the man who has nothing prepared ready. For this day is
sacred to our Lord. Do not be sad: the joy of the Lord is your
stronghold.' And the Levites calmed all the people, saying, 'Be at ease;
this is a sacred day. Do not be sad.' And all the people went off to eat
and drink and give shares away and begin to enjoy themselves since
they had understood the meaning of what had been proclaimed to
them.

This is the word of the Lord.

Responsorial Psalm   Ps 18:8-11. ℟ v.9

℟   The precepts of the Lord give joy to the heart.

1   The law of the Lord is perfect,
    it revives the soul.
    The rule of the Lord is to be trusted,
    it gives wisdom to the simple.   ℟

2   The precepts of the Lord are right,
    they gladden the heart.
    The command of the Lord is clear,
    it gives light to the eyes.   ℟

3   The fear of the Lord is holy,
    abiding for ever.
    The decrees of the Lord are truth
    and all of them just.   ℟

4   They are more to be desired than gold,
    than the purest of gold
    and sweeter are they than honey,
    than honey from the comb.   ℟

Gospel Acclamation   Mk 1:15

    Alleluia, alleluia!
    The kingdom of God is near:
    repent and believe the Good News!
    Alleluia!

GOSPEL

A reading from the holy Gospel according to Luke   10:1-12

Your peace will rest on them.

The Lord appointed seventy-two others and sent them out ahead of
him, in pairs, to all the towns and places he himself was to visit. He
said to them, 'The harvest is rich but the labourers are few, so ask the
Lord of the harvest to send labourers to his harvest. Start off now, but
remember, I am sending you out like lambs among wolves. Carry no
purse, no haversack, no sandals. Salute no one on the road. Whatever
house you go into, let your first words be, "Peace to this house!"

And if a man of peace lives there, your peace will go and rest on him; if not, it will come back to you. Stay in the same house, taking what food and drink they have to offer, for the labourer deserves his wages; do not move from house to house. Whenever you go into a town where they make you welcome, eat what is set before you. Cure those in it who are sick, and say, "The kingdom of God is very near to you." But whenever you enter a town and they do not make you welcome, go into its street and say, "We wipe off the very dust of your town that clings to our feet, and leave it with you. Yet be sure of this: the kingdom of God is very near." I tell you, on that day it will not go as hard with Sodom as with that town.'

This is the Gospel of the Lord.

Friday

FIRST READING

A reading from the book of Baruch   1:15-22

We have sinned in the sight of the Lord and have not believed.

Integrity belongs to the Lord our God; to us the look of shame we wear today, to us, the people of Judah and the citizens of Jerusalem, to our kings and princes, our priests, our prophets, as to our ancestors, because we have sinned in the sight of the Lord, have disobeyed him, and have not listened to the voice of the Lord our God telling us to follow the commandments which the Lord had ordained for us. From the day when the Lord brought our ancestors out of the land of Egypt until today we have been disobedient to the Lord our God, we have been disloyal, refusing to listen to his voice. And so the disasters, and the curse which the Lord pronounced through his servant Moses the day he brought our fathers out of Egypt to give us a land where milk and honey flow, have seized on us, disasters we experience today. Despite all the words of those prophets whom he sent us, we have not listened to the voice of the Lord our God, but, each following the dictates of his evil heart, we have taken to serving alien gods, and doing what is displeasing to the Lord our God.

This is the word of the Lord.

Responsorial Psalm   Ps 78:1-5. 8-9. ℟ v.9

℟ For the glory of your name,
    O Lord, deliver us.

1 O God, the nations have invaded your land,
   they have profaned your holy temple.
   They have made Jerusalem a heap of ruins.
   They have handed over the bodies of your servants as food
   to feed the birds of heaven
   and the flesh of your faithful to the beasts of the earth. ℟

2 They have poured out blood like water in Jerusalem,
   leaving no one to bury the dead.
   We have become the taunt of our neighbours,
   the mockery and scorn of those who surround us.
   How long, O Lord? Will you be angry for ever,
   how long will your anger burn like fire? ℟

3 Do not hold the guilt of our fathers against us.
   Let your compassion hasten to meet us
   for we are in the depths of distress. ℟

4 O God our saviour, come to our help,
   come for the sake of the glory of your name.
   O Lord our God, forgive us our sins;
   rescue us for the sake of your name. ℟

Gospel Acclamation   cf. Ps 94:8

Alleluia, alleluia!
If today you hear his voice,
harden not your hearts.
Alleluia!

GOSPEL

A reading from the holy Gospel according to Luke   10:13-16

Whoever rejects me, rejects him who sent me.

Jesus said to his disciples: 'Alas for you, Chorazin! Alas for you,
Bethsaida! For if the miracles done in you had been done in Tyre and
Sidon, they would have repented long ago, sitting in sackcloth and
ashes. And still, it will not go as hard with Tyre and Sidon at

the Judgement as with you. And as for you, Capernaum, did you want to be exalted high as heaven? You shall be thrown down to hell.

'Anyone who listens to you listens to me; anyone who rejects you rejects me, and those who reject me reject the one who sent me.'

This is the Gospel of the Lord.

Saturday

FIRST READING

A reading from the book of Baruch   4:5-12. 27-29

He who delivered you to your enemies, will rescue you and give you
eternal joy.

Take courage, my people,
constant reminder of Israel.
You were sold to the nations,
but not for extermination.
You provoked God;
and so were delivered to your enemies,
since you had angered your creator
by offering sacrifices to demons, not to God.
You had forgotten the eternal God who reared you.
You had also grieved Jerusalem who nursed you,
for when she saw the anger fall on you
from God, she said:

Listen, you neighbours of Zion:
God has sent me great sorrow.
I have seen my sons and daughters taken into captivity,
to which they have been sentenced by the Eternal.
I had reared them joyfully;
in tears, in sorrow, I watched them go away.
Do not, any of you, exult over me,
a widow, deserted by so many;
I suffer loneliness because of the sins of my own children,
who turned away from the Law of God.

Take courage, my children, call on God:
he who brought disaster on you will remember you.
As by your will you first strayed away from God,

so now turn back and search for him ten times as hard;
for as he brought down those disasters on you,
so will he rescue you and give you eternal joy.

This is the word of the Lord.

Responsorial Psalm   Ps 68:33-37. ℟ v.34

℟   The Lord listens to the poor.

1   The poor when they see it will be glad
and God-seeking hearts will revive;
for the Lord listens to the needy
and does not spurn his servants in their chains.
Let the heavens and the earth give him praise,
the sea and all its living creatures.   ℟

2   For God will bring help to Zion
and rebuild the cities of Judah
and men shall dwell there in possession.
The sons of his servants shall inherit it;
those who love his name shall dwell there.   ℟

Gospel Acclamation   cf. Mt 11:25

Alleluia, alleluia!
Blessed are you, Father, Lord of heaven and earth;
you have revealed to little ones the mysteries of the kingdom.
Alleluia!

GOSPEL

A reading from the holy Gospel according to Luke   10:17-24

Rejoice because your names are written in heaven.

The seventy-two came back rejoicing. 'Lord,' they said 'even the devils submit to us when we use your name.' Jesus said to them, 'I watched Satan fall like lightning from heaven. Yes, I have given you power to tread underfoot serpents and scorpions and the whole strength of the enemy; nothing shall ever hurt you. Yet do not rejoice that the spirits submit to you; rejoice rather that your names are written in heaven.'

It was then that, filled with joy by the Holy Spirit, he said, 'I bless you, Father, Lord of heaven and of earth, for hiding these things from the learned and the clever and revealing them to mere children. Yes, Father, for that is what it pleased you to do. Everything has been entrusted to me by my Father; and no one knows who the Son is except the Father, and who the Father is except the Son and those to whom the Son chooses to reveal him.'

Then turning to his disciples he spoke to them in private, 'Happy the eyes that see what you see, for I tell you that many prophets and kings wanted to see what you see, and never saw it; to hear what you hear, and never heard it.'

This is the Gospel of the Lord.

TWENTY-SEVENTH WEEK IN ORDINARY TIME
Year I

Monday

FIRST READING

A reading from the prophet Jonah   1:1 – 2:1.11

Jonah rose up and fled from the face of the Lord.

The word of the Lord was addressed to Jonah son of Amittai:

'Up!' he said 'Go to Nineveh, the great city, and inform them that their wickedness has become known to me.' Jonah decided to run away from the Lord, and to go to Tarshish. He went down to Joppa and found a ship bound for Tarshish; he paid his fare and went aboard, to go with them to Tarshish, to get away from the Lord. But the Lord unleashed a violent wind on the sea, and there was such a great storm at sea that the ship threatened to break up. The sailors took fright, and each of them called on his own god, and to lighten the ship they threw the cargo overboard. Jonah, however, had gone below and lain down in the hold and fallen fast alseep. The boatswain came upon him and said 'What do you mean by sleeping? Get up! Call on your God! Perhaps he will spare us a thought, and not leave us to die.' Then they said to each other, 'Come on, let us draw lots to find out who is responsible for bringing this evil on us.' So they cast lots, and the lot fell to Jonah. Then they said to him, 'Tell us, what is your business? Where do you come from? What is your country? What is your nationality?' He replied, 'I am a Hebrew, and I worship the Lord, the God of heaven, who made the sea and the land.' The sailors were seized with terror at this and said, 'What have you done?' They knew that he was trying to escape from the Lord, because he had told them so. They then said, 'What are we to do with you, to make the sea grow calm for us?' For the sea was growing rougher and rougher. He replied, 'Take me and throw me into the sea, and then it will grow calm for you. For I can see it is my fault this violent storm has happened to you.' The sailors rowed hard in an effort to reach the shore, but in vain, since the sea grew still rougher for them. They then called on the Lord and said, 'O Lord, do not let us perish for taking this man's life; do not hold us guilty of innocent blood; for you, Lord, have acted as you thought right.' And taking hold of Jonah they threw him into the sea; and the sea grew calm again. At this the men were seized with dread of the Lord; they offered a sacrifice to the Lord and made vows. The Lord had arranged that a great fish should be there to swallow Jonah; and Jonah remained in the belly of the fish for three days and three nights. The Lord spoke to the fish, which then vomited Jonah on to the shore.

This is the word of the Lord.

Responsorial Psalm   Jonah 2:3-5. 8. ℟ v.7

℟   You will rescue my life from the pit, O Lord.

1   Out of my distress I cried to the Lord
     and he answered me;
     from the belly of Sheol I cried,
     and you have heard my voice. ℟

2   You cast me into the abyss, into the heart of the sea,
     and the flood surrounded me.
     All your waves, your billows,
     washed over me. ℟

3   And I said: I am cast out
     from your sight.
     How shall I ever look again
     on your Holy Temple? ℟

4　While my soul was fainting within me,
　　I remembered the Lord,
　　and my prayer came before you
　　into your holy Temple.　℟

Gospel Acclamation　　　　　　　　　　　　　　　　Jn 13:34

　　Alleluia, alleluia!
　　I give you a new commandment:
　　love one another as I have loved you.
　　Alleluia!

GOSPEL

A reading from the holy Gospel according to Luke　　10:25-37

Who is my neighbour?

There was a lawyer who, to disconcert Jesus, stood up and said to him, 'Master, what must I do to inherit eternal life?' He said to him, 'What is written in the Law? What do you read there?' He replied, 'You must love the Lord your God with all your heart, with all your soul, with all your strength, and with all your mind, and your neighbour as yourself.' 'You have answered right,' said Jesus 'do this and life is yours.'

　　But the man was anxious to justify himself and said to Jesus, 'And who is my neighbour?' Jesus replied, 'A man was once on his way down from Jerusalem to Jericho and fell into the hands of brigands; they took all he had, beat him and then made off, leaving him half dead. Now a priest happened to be travelling down the same road, but when he saw the man, he passed by on the other side. In the same way a Levite who came to the place saw him, and passed by on the other side. But a Samaritan traveller who came upon him was moved with compassion when he saw him. He went up and bandaged his wounds, pouring oil and wine on them. He then lifted him on to his own mount, carried him to the inn and looked after him. Next day, he took out two denarii and handed them to the innkeeper. "Look after him," he said "and on my way back I will make good any extra expense you have." Which of these three, do you think, proved himself a neighbour to the man who fell into the brigands' hands?' 'The one who took pity on him' he replied. Jesus said to him, 'Go, and do the same yourself.'

　　This is the Gospel of the Lord.

Tuesday

FIRST READING

A reading from the prophet Jonah   3:1-10

Nineveh was converted from its evil ways and was spared by the Lord.

The word of the Lord was addressed to Jonah: 'Up!' he said. 'Go to
Nineveh, the great city, and preach to them as I told you to.' Jonah set
out and went to Nineveh in obedience to the word of the Lord. Now
Nineveh was a city great beyond compare: it took three days to cross
it. Jonah went on into the city, making a day's journey. He preached
in these words, 'Only forty days more and Nineveh is going to be
destroyed.' And the people of Nineveh believed in God; they proclaimed a fast and put on sackcloth from the greatest to the least. The
news reached the king of Nineveh, who rose from his throne, took off
his robe, put on sackcloth and sat down in ashes. A proclamation was
then promulgated throughout Nineveh, by decree of the king and his
ministers, as follows: 'Men and beasts, herds and flocks, are to taste
nothing; they must not eat, they must not drink water. All are to put
on sackcloth and call on God with all their might; and let everyone
renounce his evil behaviour and the wicked things he has done. Who
knows if God will not change his mind and relent, if he will not
renounce his burning wrath, so that we do not perish?' God saw their
efforts to renounce their evil behaviour. And God relented: he did not
inflict on them the disaster which he had threatened.

This is the word of the Lord.

Responsorial Psalm   Ps 129:1-4. 7-8. ℟ v.3

℟   If you, O Lord, laid bare our guilt,
    who could endure it?

1   Out of the depths I cry to you, O Lord,
    Lord, hear my voice!
    O let your ears be attentive
    to the voice of my pleading.   ℟

2   If you, O Lord, should mark our guilt,
    Lord, who would survive?
    But with you is found forgiveness:
    for this we revere you.   ℟

3   Because with the Lord there is mercy
    and fullness of redemption,
    Israel indeed he will redeem
    from all its iniquity.   ℟

Gospel Acclamation   Lk 11:28

    Alleluia, alleluia!
    Blessed are they who hear the word of God
    and keep it.
    Alleluia!

GOSPEL

A reading from the holy Gospel according to Luke   10:38-42

Martha took up the duties in the house. Mary chose the better part.

Jesus came to a village, and a woman named Martha welcomed him
into her house. She had a sister called Mary, who sat down at the
Lord's feet and listened to him speaking. Now Martha who was
distracted with all the serving said, 'Lord, do you not care that my
sister is leaving me to do the serving all by myself? Please tell her to
help me.' But the Lord answered: 'Martha, Martha,' he said 'you worry
and fret about so many things, and yet few are needed, indeed only
one. It is Mary who has chosen the better part; it is not to be taken
from her.'

    This is the Gospel of the Lord.

Wednesday

FIRST READING

A reading from the prophet Jonah   4:1-11

*Jonah, you worry over a plant. Am I not to feel sorry for the
great city Nineveh?*

Jonah was very indignant; he fell into a rage. He prayed to the Lord
and said, 'Ah! Lord, is not this just as I said would happen when I was
still at home? That was why I went and fled to Tarshish: I knew that
you were a God of tenderness and compassion, slow to anger, rich in
graciousness, relenting from evil. So now Lord, please take away my
life, for I might as well be dead as go on living.' The Lord replied, 'Are
you right to be angry?' Jonah then went out of the city and sat down
to the east of the city. There he made himself a shelter and sat under
it in the shade, to see what would happen to the city. Then the Lord
God arranged that a castor-oil plant should grow up over Jonah to
give shade for his head and soothe his ill-humour; Jonah was
delighted with the castor-oil plant. But at dawn the next day, God
arranged that a worm should attack the castor-oil plant – and it
withered. Next, when the sun rose, God arranged that there should be
a scorching east wind; the sun beat down so hard on Jonah's head that
he was overcome and begged for death, saying, 'I might as well be
dead as go on living.' God said to Jonah, 'Are you right to be angry
about the castor-oil plant?' He replied, 'I have every right to be angry,
to the point of death.' The Lord replied, 'You are only upset about a
castor-oil plant which cost you no labour, which you did not make
grow, which sprouted in a night and has perished in a night. And am I
not to feel sorry for Nineveh, the great city, in which there are more
than a hundred and twenty thousand people who cannot tell their
right hand from their left, to say nothing of all the animals?'

This is the word of the Lord.

Responsorial Psalm   Ps 85:3-6. 9-10. ℟ v.15

℟   Lord, you are tender and full of love.

1   You are my God, have mercy on me, Lord,
    for I cry to you all the day long.
    Give joy to your servant, O Lord,
    for to you I lift up my soul.   ℟

2   O Lord, you are good and forgiving,
    full of love to all who call.
    Give heed, O Lord, to my prayer
    and attend to the sound of my voice.   ℟

3   All the nations shall come to adore you
    and glorify your name, O Lord:
    for you are great and do marvellous deeds,
    you who alone are God.   ℟

Gospel Acclamation   Rom 8:15

    Alleluia, alleluia!
    You have received the Spirit which makes us God's children,
    and in that Spirit we call God our Father.
    Alleluia!

GOSPEL

A reading from the holy Gospel according to Luke   11:1-4

Lord, teach us to pray.

Once Jesus was in a certain place praying, and when he had finished,
one of his disciples said, 'Lord, teach us to pray, just as John taught
his disciples.' He said to them, 'Say this when you pray:

    "Father, may your name be held holy,
    your kingdom come;
    give us each day our daily bread,
    and forgive us our sins,
    for we ourselves forgive each one who is in debt to us.
    And do not put us to the test." '

This is the Gospel of the Lord.

Thursday

FIRST READING

A reading from the prophet Malachi   3:13-20

The day is coming now like a burning furnace.

You say harsh things about me, says the Lord. You ask, 'What have we said against you?' You say, 'It is useless to serve God; what is the good of keeping his commands or of walking mournfully before the Lord of hosts? Now we have reached the point when we call the arrogant blessed; yes, they prosper, these evildoers; they try God's patience and yet go free.' This is what those who fear the Lord used to say to one another. But the Lord took note and heard them: a book of remembrance was written in his presence recording those who fear him and take refuge in his name. On the day which I am preparing, says the Lord of hosts, they are going to be my own special possession. I will make allowances for them as a man makes allowances for the son who obeys him. Then once again you will see the difference between an upright man and a wicked one, between the one who serves God and the one who does not serve him. For the day is coming now, burning like a furnace; and all the arrogant and the evil-doers will be like stubble. The day that is coming is going to burn them up, says the Lord of hosts, leaving them neither root nor stalk. But for you who fear my name, the sun of righteousness will shine out with healing in its rays.

This is the word of the Lord.

Responsorial Psalm   Ps 1. ℟ Ps 39:5

℟   Happy are they who hope in the Lord.

1   Happy indeed is the man
     who follows not the counsel of the wicked;
     nor lingers in the way of sinners
     nor sits in the company of scorners,
     but whose delight is the law of the Lord
     and who ponders his law day and night.   ℟

2   He is like a tree that is planted
     beside the flowing waters,
     that yields its fruit in due season

and whose leaves shall never fade;
and all that he does shall prosper.   ℟

3   Not so are the wicked, not so!
For they like winnowed chaff
shall be driven away by the wind.
For the Lord guards the way of the just
but the way of the wicked leads to doom.   ℟

Gospel Acclamation   cf. Acts 16:14

Alleluia, alleluia!
Open our hearts, O Lord,
to listen to the words of your Son.
Alleluia!

GOSPEL

A reading from the holy Gospel according to Luke   11:5-13

Seek and it will be given to you.

Jesus said to his disciples: 'Suppose one of you has a friend and goes to him in the middle of the night to say, "My friend, lend me three loaves, because a friend of mine on his travels has just arrived at my house and I have nothing to offer him;" and the man answers from inside the house, "Do not bother me. The door is bolted now, and my children and I are in bed; I cannot get up to give it you." I tell you, if the man does not get up and give it him for friendship's sake, persistence will be enough to make him get up and give his friend all he wants.

'So I say to you: Ask, and it will be given to you; search, and you will find; knock, and the door will be opened to you. For the one who asks always receives; the one who searches always finds; the one who knocks will always have the door opened to him. What father among you would hand his son a stone when he asked for bread? Or hand him a snake instead of a fish? Or hand him a scorpion if he asked for an egg? If you then, who are evil, know how to give your children what is good, how much more will the heavenly Father give the Holy Spirit to those who ask him!'

This is the Gospel of the Lord.

Friday

FIRST READING

A reading from the prophet Joel   1:13-15; 2:1-2

The day of the Lord God is coming, a day of darkness and gloom.

Priests, put on sackcloth and lament.
Ministers of the altar, wail.
Come, pass the night in sackcloth,
you ministers of my God.
For the house of our God has been deprived
of oblation and libation.
Order a fast,
proclaim a solemn assembly;
elders, call together
all the inhabitants of the country
to the house of the Lord your God.
Cry out to the Lord,
'Oh, what a day!
For the day of the Lord is near,
it comes as a devastation from Shaddai.'
Sound the trumpet in Zion,
give the alarm on my holy mountain!
Let all the inhabitants of the country tremble,
for the day of the Lord is coming,
yes, it is near.

Day of darkness and gloom,
day of cloud and blackness.
Like the dawn there spreads across the mountains
a vast and mighty host,
such as has never been before,
such as will never be again
to the remotest ages.

    This is the word of the Lord.

Responsorial Psalm   Ps 9:2-3. 6. 16. 8-9. ℟ v.9

> ℟   The Lord will judge the world with justice.

1   I will praise you, Lord, with all my heart;
    I will recount all your wonders.
    I will rejoice in you and be glad,
    and sing psalms to your name O Most High.   ℟

2   You have checked the nations, destroyed the wicked;
    you have wiped out their name for ever and ever.
    The nations have fallen in the pit which they made,
    their feet caught in the snare they laid.   ℟

3   But the Lord sits enthroned for ever.
    He has set up his throne for judgement;
    he will judge the world with justice,
    he will judge the peoples with his truth.   ℟

Gospel Acclamation   Jn 12:31-32

> Alleluia, alleluia!
> The prince of this world will now be cast out,
> and when I am lifted up from the earth
> I will draw all to myself, says the Lord.
> Alleluia!

GOSPEL

A reading from the holy Gospel according to Luke   11:15-26

> *If by the finger of God I cast out devils, the kingdom of God has*
> *overtaken you.*

When Jesus had cast out a devil, some of the people said, 'It is through
Beelzebul, the prince of devils, that he casts out devils.' Others asked
Jesus, as a test, for a sign from heaven; but, knowing what they were
thinking, he said to them, 'Every kingdom divided against itself is
heading for ruin, and a household divided against itself collapses. So
too with Satan: if he is divided against himself, how can his kingdom
stand? – since you assert that it is through Beelzebul that I cast out
devils. Now if it is through Beelzebul that I cast out devils, through
whom do your own experts cast them out? Let them be your judges,
then. But if it is through the finger of God that I cast out

devils, then know that the kingdom of God has overtaken you. So long as a strong man fully armed guards his own palace, his goods are undisturbed; but when someone stronger than he is attacks and defeats him, the stronger man takes away all the weapons he relied on and shares out his spoil.

'He who is not with me is against me; and he who does not gather with me scatters.

'When an unclean spirit goes out of a man it wanders through waterless country looking for a place to rest, and not finding one it says, "I will go back to the home I came from." But on arrival, finding it swept and tidied, it then goes off and brings seven other spirits more wicked than itself, and they go in and set up house there, so that the man ends up by being worse than he was before.'

This is the Gospel of the Lord.

Saturday

FIRST READING

A reading from the prophet Joel   4:12-21

Put the sickle in because the harvest is ripe.

The Lord says this:

'Let the nations rouse themselves, let them march
to the Valley of Jehoshaphat,
for I am going to sit in judgement there
on all the nations round.
Put the sickle in:
the harvest is ripe;
come and tread:
the winepress is full,
the vats are overflowing,
so great is their wickedness!'

Host on host
in the Valley of Decision!
For the day of the Lord is near
in the Valley of Decision!
Sun and moon grow dark,
the stars lose their brilliance.
The Lord roars from Zion,

makes his voice heard from Jerusalem;
heaven and earth tremble.
But the Lord will be a shelter for his people,
a stronghold for the sons of Israel.

'You will learn then that I am the Lord your God,
dwelling in Zion, my holy mountain.
Jerusalem will be a holy place,
no alien will ever pass through it again.'

When that day comes,
the mountains will run with new wine
and the hills flow with milk,
and all the river beds of Judah
will run with water.
A fountain will spring from the house of the Lord
to water the wadi of Acacias.
Egypt will become a desolation,
Edom a desert waste
on account of the violence done to the sons of Judah
whose innocent blood they shed in their country.
But Judah will be inhabited for ever,
Jerusalem from age to age.
'I will avenge their blood and let none go unpunished,'
and the Lord shall make his home in Zion.

This is the word of the Lord.

Responsorial Psalm   Ps 96:1-2. 5-6. 11-12. ℟ v.12

℟   Let the just rejoice in the Lord.

1   The Lord is king, let earth rejoice,
    the many coastlands be glad.
    Cloud and darkness are his raiment;
    his throne, justice and right. ℟

2   The mountains melt like wax
    before the Lord of all the earth.
    The skies proclaim his justice;
    all peoples see his glory. ℟

3   Light shines forth for the just
    and joy for the upright of heart,
    Rejoice, you just, in the Lord;
    give glory to his holy name. ℟

Gospel Acclamation   Lk 11:28

Alleluia, alleluia!
Blessed are they who hear the word of God
and keep it.
Alleluia!

GOSPEL

A reading from the holy Gospel according to Luke   11:27-28

*Happy the womb that bore you! Happier still are those who hear
the word of God.*

As Jesus was speaking, a woman in the crowd raised her voice and
said, 'Happy the womb that bore you and the breasts you sucked!' But
he replied, 'Still happier those who hear the word of God and keep it!'

This is the Gospel of the Lord.

TWENTY-EIGHTH WEEK IN ORDINARY TIME

Year I

Monday

FIRST READING

A reading from the letter of St Paul to the Romans   1:1-7

*Through Christ we received grace and our apostolic mission to
preach the obedience of faith to the gentiles.*

From Paul, a servant of Christ Jesus who has been called to be an
apostle, and specially chosen to preach the Good News that God
promised long ago through his prophets in the scriptures.

This news is about the Son of God who, according to the human
nature he took, was a descendant of David: it is about Jesus Christ our
Lord who, in the order of the spirit, the spirit of holiness that was in
him, was proclaimed Son of God in all his power through his
resurrection from the dead. Through him we received grace and our
apostolic mission to preach the obedience of faith to all pagan

nations in honour of his name. You are one of these nations, and by his call belong to Jesus Christ. To you all, then, who are God's beloved in Rome, called to be saints, may God our Father and the Lord Jesus Christ send grace and peace.

This is the word of the Lord.

Responsorial Psalm   Ps 97: 1-4. ℟ v.2

℟ The Lord has made known his salvation.

1 Sing a new song to the Lord
   for he has worked wonders.
   His right hand and his holy arm
   have brought salvation. ℟

2 The Lord has made known his salvation;
   has shown his justice to the nations.
   He has remembered his truth and love
   for the house of Israel. ℟

3 All the ends of the earth have seen
   the salvation of our God.
   Shout to the Lord all the earth,
   ring out your joy. ℟

Gospel Acclamation   cf. Ps 94:8

   Alleluia, alleluia!
   If today you hear his voice,
   harden not your hearts.
   Alleluia!

GOSPEL

A reading from the holy Gospel according to Luke   11:29-32

No sign will be given to this generation except the sign of Jonah the prophet.

The crowds got even bigger and Jesus addressed them, 'This is a wicked generation; it is asking for a sign. The only sign it will be given is the sign of Jonah. For just as Jonah became a sign to the Ninevites, so will the Son of Man be to this generation. On Judgement day the Queen of the South will rise up with the men of this generation and condemn them, because she came from the ends of the earth to hear the wisdom of Solomon; and there is something greater than Solomon here. On Judgement day the men of Nineveh will stand up with this generation and condemn it, because when Jonah preached they repented; and there is something greater than Jonah here.'

This is the Gospel of the Lord.

Tuesday

FIRST READING

A reading from the letter of St Paul to the Romans   1:16-25

People have known God, yet they refused to honour him.

I am not ashamed of the Good News: it is the power of God saving all who have faith – Jews first, but Greeks as well – since this is what reveals the justice of God to us: it shows how faith leads to faith, or as scripture says: The upright man finds life through faith.

The anger of God is being revealed from heaven against all the impiety and depravity of men who keep truth imprisoned in their wickedness. For what can be known about God is perfectly plain to them since God himself has made it plain. Ever since God created the world his everlasting power and deity – however invisible – have been there for the mind to see in the things he has made. That is why such people are without excuse: they knew God and yet refused to honour him as God or to thank him; instead, they made nonsense out of logic and their empty minds were darkened. The more they called themselves philosophers, the more stupid they grew, until they exchanged the glory of the immortal God for a worthless imitation, for the image of mortal man, of birds, of quadrupeds and reptiles. That is why God left them to their filthy enjoyments and the practices with which they dishonour their own bodies, since they have given up divine truth for a lie and have worshipped and served creatures instead of the creator, who is blessed for ever. Amen!

This is the word of the Lord.

Responsorial Psalm   Ps 18:2-5. ℟ v.2

℟   The heavens proclaim the glory of God.

1   The heavens proclaim the glory of God
    and the firmament shows forth the work of his hands.
    Day unto day takes up the story
    and night unto night makes known the message.   ℟

2   No speech, no word, no voice is heard
    yet their span goes forth through all the earth,
    their words to the utmost bounds of the world.   ℟

Gospel Acclamation   Heb 4:12

    Alleluia, alleluia!
    The word of God is living and active;
    it probes the thoughts and motives of our heart.
    Alleluia!

                          GOSPEL

A reading from the holy Gospel according to Luke   11:37-41

                Give alms and everything will be made clean for you.

Jesus had just finished speaking when a Pharisee invited him to dine
at his house. He went in and sat down at the table. The Pharisee saw
this and was surprised that he had not first washed before the meal.
But the Lord said to him, 'Oh, you Pharisees! You clean the outside of
cup and plate, while inside yourselves you are filled with extortion
and wickedness. Fools! Did not he who made the outside make the
inside too? Instead, give alms from what you have and then indeed
everything will be clean for you.'

    This is the Gospel of the Lord.

Wednesday

FIRST READING

A reading from the letter of St Paul to the Romans   2:1-11

He will repay each one according to his works, Jews first, but
Greeks as well.

No matter who you are, if you pass judgement you have no excuse. In
judging others you condemn yourself, since you behave no differently
from those you judge. We know that God condemns that sort of
behaviour impartially: and when you judge those who behave like this
while you are doing exactly the same, do you think you will escape
God's judgement? Or are you abusing his abundant goodness, patience
and toleration, not realising that this goodness of God is meant to lead
you to repentance? Your stubborn refusal to repent is only adding to
the anger God will have towards you on that day of anger when his
just judgements will be made known. He will repay each one as his
works deserve. For those who sought renown and honour and immortality by always doing good there will be eternal life; for the
unsubmissive who refused to take truth for their guide and took
depravity instead, there will be anger and fury. Pain and suffering
will come to every human being who employs himself in evil – Jews
first, but Greeks as well; renown, honour and peace will come to
everyone who does good – Jews first, but Greeks as well. God has no
favourites.

This is the word of the Lord.

Responsorial Psalm   Ps 61:2-3. 6-7. 9. ℞ v.13

℞   Lord, you give back to all
     according to their works.

1   In God alone is my soul at rest;
     my help comes from him.
     He alone is my rock, my stronghold,
     my fortress: I stand firm.   ℞

2   In God alone be at rest, my soul;
     for my hope comes from him.
     He alone is my rock, my stronghold,
     my fortress: I stand firm.   ℞

3   Take refuge in God all you people.
Trust him at all times,
Pour out your hearts before him
for God is our refuge.   ℟

Gospel Acclamation   Jn 10:27

Alleluia, alleluia!
My sheep listen to my voice, says the Lord;
I know them, and they follow me.
Alleluia!

GOSPEL

A reading from the holy Gospel according to Luke   11:42-46

Alas for you pharisees – and you lawyers, woe to you!

The Lord said to the Pharisees: 'Alas for you Pharisees! You who pay
your tithe of mint and rue and all sorts of garden herbs and overlook
justice and the love of God! These you should have practised, without
leaving the others undone. Alas for you Pharisees who like taking the
seats of honour in the synagogues and being greeted obsequiously in
the market squares! Alas for you, because you are like the unmarked
tombs that men walk on without knowing it!'

A lawyer then spoke up. 'Master,' he said 'when you speak like this
you insult us too.' 'Alas for you lawyers also,' he replied, 'because you
load on men burdens that are unendurable, burdens that you
yourselves do not move a finger to lift.'

This is the Gospel of the Lord.

Thursday

FIRST READING

A reading from the letter of St Paul to the Romans   3:21-30

A person is justified by faith apart from the law.

God's justice that was made known through the Law and the Prophets
has now been revealed outside the Law, since it is the same justice
of God that comes through faith to everyone, Jew and pagan

alike, who believes in Jesus Christ. Both Jew and pagan sinned and forfeited God's glory, and both are justified through the free gift of his grace by being redeemed in Christ Jesus who was appointed by God to sacrifice his life so as to win reconciliation through faith. In this way God makes his justice known; first, for the past, when sins went unpunished because he held his hand, then, for the present age, by showing positively that he is just, and that he justifies everyone who believes in Jesus.

So what becomes of our boasts? There is no room for them. What sort of law excludes them? The sort of law that tells us what to do? On the contrary, it is the law of faith, since, as we see it, a man is justified by faith and not by doing something the Law tells him to do. Is God the God of Jews alone and not of the pagans too? Of the pagans too, most certainly, since there is only one God.

This is the word of the Lord.

Responsorial Psalm   Ps 129:1-6. ℟ v.7

℟ With the Lord there is mercy,
   and fullness of redemption.

1 Out of the depths I cry to you, O Lord,
   Lord, hear my voice!
   O let your ears be attentive
   to the voice of my pleading. ℟

2 If you, O Lord, should mark our guilt,
   Lord, who would survive?
   But with you is found forgiveness:
   for this we revere you. ℟

3 My soul is waiting for the Lord,
   I count on his word.
   My soul is longing for the Lord
   more than watchman for daybreak. ℟

Gospel Acclamation   Jn 14:6

Alleluia, alleluia!
I am the way, the truth, and the life, says the Lord;
no one comes to the Father, except through me.
Alleluia!

GOSPEL

A reading from the holy Gospel according to Luke   11:47-54

The blood of the prophets is required, from the blood of Abel to the blood of Zechariah.

Jesus said: 'Alas for you who build the tombs of the prophets, the men your ancestors killed! In this way you both witness what your ancestors did and approve it; they did the killing, you do the building.

'And that is why the Wisdom of God said, "I will send them prophets and apostles; some they will slaughter and persecute, so that this generation will have to answer for every prophet's blood that has been shed since the foundation of the world, from the blood of Abel to the blood of Zechariah, who was murdered between the altar and the sanctuary." Yes, I tell you, this generation will have to answer for it all.

'Alas for you lawyers who have taken away the key of knowledge! You have not gone in yourselves, and have prevented others going in who wanted to.'

When he left the house, the scribes and the Pharisees began a furious attack on him and tried to force answers from him on innumerable questions, setting traps to catch him out in something he might say.

This is the Gospel of the Lord.

Friday

FIRST READING

A reading from the letter of St Paul to the Romans   4:1-8

Abraham believed in God, and his faith justified him.

What shall we say about Abraham, the ancestor from whom we are all descended? If Abraham was justified as a reward for doing something, he would really have had something to boast about, though not in God's sight because scripture says: Abraham put his faith in God, and this faith was considered as justifying him. If a man has work to show, his wages are not considered as a favour but as his due; but when a man has nothing to show except faith in the one who justifies sinners, then his faith is considered as justifying him. And David says the same: a man is happy if God considers him righteous, irrespective of good deeds:

> Happy those whose crimes are forgiven,
> whose sins are blotted out;
> happy the man whom the Lord considers sinless.

This is the word of the Lord.

Responsorial Psalm
Ps 31:1-2. 5. 11. ℟ cf. v.7

> ℟ I turn to you Lord in time of trouble,
> and you fill me with the joy of salvation.

1 Happy the man whose offence is forgiven,
whose sin is remitted.
O happy the man to whom the Lord
imputes no guilt,
in whose spirit is no guile. ℟

2 But now I have acknowledged my sins;
my guilt I did not hide.
I said: 'I will confess
my offence to the Lord.'
And you, Lord, have forgiven
the guilt of my sin. ℟

3 Rejoice, rejoice in the Lord,
exult, you just!
O come, ring out your joy,
all you upright of heart. ℟

Gospel Acclamation
Ps 32:22

> Alleluia, alleluia!
> Lord, let your mercy be on us,
> as we place our trust in you.
> Alleluia!

GOSPEL

A reading from the holy Gospel according to Luke 12:1-7

Every hair on your head has been numbered.

The people had gathered in their thousands so that they were treading on one another. And Jesus began to speak, first of all to his disciples. 'Be on your guard against the yeast of the Pharisees – that is, their hypocrisy. Everything that is now covered will be uncovered, and everything now hidden will be made clear. For this reason, whatever you have said in the dark will be heard in the daylight, and what you have whispered in hidden places will be proclaimed on the housetops.

'To you my friends I say: Do not be afraid of those who kill the body and after that can do no more. I will tell you whom to fear: fear him who, after he has killed, has the power to cast into hell. Yes, I tell you, fear him. Can you not buy five sparrows for two pennies? And yet not one is forgotten in God's sight. Why, every hair on your head has been counted. There is no need to be afraid: you are worth more than hundreds of sparrows.'

This is the Gospel of the Lord.

Saturday

FIRST READING

A reading from the letter of St Paul to the Romans 4:13. 16-18

In hope he believed against hope.

The promise of inheriting the world was not made to Abraham and his descendants on account of any law but on account of the righteousness which consists in faith. That is why what fulfils the promise depends on faith, so that it may be a free gift and be available to all of Abraham's descendants, not only those who belong to the Law but also those who belong to the faith of Abraham who is the father of all of us. As scripture says: I have made you the ancestor of many nations – Abraham is our father in the eyes of God, in whom he put his faith, and who brings the dead to life and calls into being what does not exist.

Though it seemed Abraham's hope could not be fulfilled, he hoped and he believed, and through doing so he did become the father of many nations exactly as he had been promised: Your descendants will be as many as the stars.

This is the word of the Lord.

Responsorial Psalm   Ps 104:6-9. 42-43. ℟ v.8

℟   The Lord remembers his covenant for ever.

or

℟   Alleluia!

1   O children of Abraham, his servant,
    O sons of the Jacob he chose.
    He, the Lord, is our God:
    his judgements prevail in all the earth.   ℟

2   He remembers his covenant for ever,
    his promise for a thousand generations,
    the covenant he made with Abraham,
    the oath he swore to Isaac.   ℟

3   For he remembered his holy word,
    which he gave to Abraham his servant.
    So he brought out his people with joy,
    his chosen ones with shouts of rejoicing.   ℟

Gospel Acclamation   Jn 15:26. 27

    Alleluia, alleluia!
    The Spirit of Truth will bear witness to me, says the Lord,
    and you also will be my witnesses.
    Alleluia!

GOSPEL

A reading from the holy Gospel according to Luke   12:9-12

When the time comes, the Holy Spirit will teach you what you must say.

Jesus said to his disciples, 'I tell you, if anyone openly declares himself for me in the presence of men, the Son of Man will declare himself for him in the presence of God's angels. But the man who disowns me in the presence of men will be disowned in the presence of God's angels.

'Everyone who says a word against the Son of Man will be forgiven, but he who blasphemes against the Holy Spirit will not be forgiven.

'When they take you before synagogues and magistrates and authorities, do not worry about how to defend yourselves or what to say, because when the time comes, the Holy Spirit will teach you what you must say.'

This is the Gospel of the Lord.

TWENTY-NINTH WEEK IN ORDINARY TIME
Year I

Monday

FIRST READING

A reading from the letter of St Paul to the Romans   4:20-25

It was written for us when it says that our faith in him will be counted.

Since God had made him a promise, Abraham refused either to deny it or even to doubt it, but drew strength from faith and gave glory to God, convinced that God had power to do what he had promised. This is the faith that was 'considered as justifying him'. Scripture however does not refer only to him but to us as well when it says that his faith was thus 'considered'; our faith too will be 'considered' if we believe in him who raised Jesus our Lord from the dead, Jesus who was put to death for our sins and raised to life to justify us.

This is the word of the Lord.

Responsorial Psalm   Lk 1:69-75. ℟ cf. v.68

℟   Blessed be the Lord God of Israel;
     he has come to his people.

1   He has raised up for us a mighty saviour
     in the house of David his servant,
     as he promised by the lips of holy men,
     those who were his prophets from of old.   ℟

2 A saviour who would free us from our foes,
   from the hands of all who hate us.
   So his love for our fathers is fulfilled
   and his holy covenant remembered.

   ℟ Blessed be the Lord God of Israel;
        he has come to his people.

3 He swore to Abraham our father
   to grant us, that free from fear,
   and saved from the hands of our foes,
   we might serve him in holiness and justice
   all the days of our life in his presence. ℟

Gospel Acclamation   Mt 5:3

   Alleluia, alleluia!
   Happy the poor in spirit;
   the kingdom of heaven is theirs!
   Alleluia!

GOSPEL

A reading from the holy Gospel according to Luke   12:13-21

To whom will all this wealth of yours go?

A man in the crowd said to Jesus, 'Master, tell my brother to give me a share of our inheritance.' 'My friend,' he replied 'who appointed me your judge, or the arbitrator of your claims?' Then he said to them, 'Watch, and be on your guard against avarice of any kind, for a man's life is not made secure by what he owns, even when he has more than he needs.'

Then he told them a parable: 'There was once a rich man who, having had a good harvest from his land, thought to himself, "What am I to do? I have not enough room to store my crops." Then he said, "This is what I will do: I will pull down my barns and build bigger ones, and store all my grain and my goods in them, and I will say to my soul: My soul, you have plenty of good things laid by for many years to come; take things easy, eat, drink, have a good time." But God said to him, "Fool! This very night the demand will be made for your soul; and this hoard of yours, whose will it be then?" So it is when a man stores up treasure for himself in place of making himself rich in the sight of God.'

This is the Gospel of the Lord.

Tuesday

FIRST READING

A reading from the letter of St Paul to the Romans   5:12. 15. 17-21

If death reigns from one man's sin, how much more will those who receive the gift of grace reign.

Sin entered the world through one man, and through sin death, and thus death has spread through the whole human race because everyone has sinned.

If it is certain that through one man's fall so many died, it is even more certain that divine grace, coming through the one man, Jesus Christ, came to so many as an abundant free gift. If it is certain that death reigned over everyone as the consequence of one man's fall, it is even more certain that one man, Jesus Christ, will cause everyone to reign in life who receives the free gift that he does not deserve, of being made righteous. Again, as one man's fall brought condemnation on everyone, so the good act of one man brings everyone life and makes them justified. As by one man's disobedience many were made sinners, so by one man's obedience many will be made righteous. But however great the number of sins committed, grace was even greater; and so, just as sin reigned wherever there was death, so grace will reign to bring eternal life, thanks to the righteousness that comes through Jesus Christ our Lord.

This is the word of the Lord.

Responsorial Psalm   Ps 39:7-10. 17. ℟ cf. vv.8. 9

℟   Here am I, Lord;
      I come to do your will.

1   You do not ask for sacrifice and offerings,
      but an open ear.
      You do not ask for holocaust and victim.
      Instead, here am I.   ℟

2 In the scroll of the book it stands written
   that I should do your will.
   My God, I delight in your law
   in the depth of my heart.

   ℟   Here am I, Lord;
       I come to do your will.

3 Your justice I have proclaimed
   in the great assembly.
   My lips I have not sealed;
   you know it, O Lord. ℟

4 O let there be rejoicing and gladness
   for all who seek you.
   Let them ever say: 'The Lord is great',
   who love your saving help. ℟

Gospel Acclamation   Lk 21:36

   Alleluia, alleluia!
   Be watchful, pray constantly,
   that you may be worthy to stand before the Son of Man.
   Alleluia!

GOSPEL

A reading from the holy Gospel according to Luke   12:35-38

Happy those servants whom the master finds awake when he comes.

Jesus said to his disciples: 'See that you are dressed for action and
have your lamps lit. Be like men waiting for their master to return
from the wedding feast, ready to open the door as soon as he comes and
knocks. Happy those servants whom the master finds awake when he
comes. I tell you solemnly, he will put on an apron, sit them down at
table and wait on them. It may be in the second watch he comes, or in
the third, but happy those servants if he finds them ready.'

   This is the Gospel of the Lord.

Wednesday

FIRST READING

A reading from the letter of St Paul to the Romans   6:12-18

Offer yourselves to God as people brought back from death to life.

You must not let sin reign in your mortal bodies or command your obedience to bodily passions, you must not let any part of your body turn into an unholy weapon fighting on the side of sin; you should, instead, offer yourselves to God, and consider yourselves dead men brought back to life; you should make every part of your body into a weapon fighting on the side of God; and then sin will no longer dominate your life, since you are living by grace and not by law.

Does the fact that we are living by grace and not by law mean that we are free to sin? Of course not. You know that if you agree to serve and obey a master you become his slaves. You cannot be slaves of sin that leads to death and at the same time slaves of obedience that leads to righteousness. You were once slaves of sin, but thank God you submitted without reservation to the creed you were taught. You may have been freed from the slavery of sin, but only to become 'slaves' of righteousness.

This is the word of the Lord.

Responsorial Psalm   Ps 123. ℟ v.8

℟   Our help is in the name of the Lord.

1   'If the Lord had not been on our side,'
     this is Israel's song.
     'If the Lord had not been on our side
     when men rose against us,
     then would they have swallowed us alive
     when their anger was kindled. ℟

2   'Then would the waters have engulfed us,
     the torrent gone over us;
     over our head would have swept
     the raging waters.'
     Blessed be the Lord who did not give us
     a prey to their teeth! ℟

(continued)

3   Our life, like a bird, has escaped
    from the snare of the fowler.
    Indeed the snare has been broken
    and we have escaped.
    Our help is in the name of the Lord,
    who made heaven and earth.

℟   Our help is in the name of the Lord.

Gospel Acclamation   Mt 24:42. 44

    Alleluia, alleluia!
    Be watchful and ready:
    you know not when the Son of Man is coming.
    Alleluia!

GOSPEL

A reading from the holy Gospel according to Luke   12:39-48

From the person who has received much, much will be demanded.

Jesus said to his disciples: 'You may be quite sure of this, that if the householder had known at what hour the burglar would come, he would not have let anyone break through the wall of his house. You too must stand ready, because the Son of Man is coming at an hour you do not expect.'

Peter said, 'Lord, do you mean this parable for us, or for everyone?' The Lord replied, 'What sort of steward, then, is faithful and wise enough for the master to place him over his household to give them their allowance of food at the proper time? Happy that servant if his master's arrival finds him at this employment. I tell you truly, he will place him over everything he owns. But as for the servant who says to himself, "My master is taking his time coming", and sets about beating the menservants and the maids, and eating and drinking and getting drunk, his master will come on a day he does not expect and at an hour he does not know. The master will cut him off and send him to the same fate as the unfaithful.

'The servant who knows what his master wants, but has not even started to carry out those wishes, will receive very many strokes of the lash. The one who did not know, but deserves to be beaten for what he has done, will receive fewer strokes. When a man has had a great deal given him, a great deal will be demanded of him; when a man has had a great deal given him on trust, even more will be expected of him.'

This is the Gospel of the Lord.

Thursday

FIRST READING

A reading from the letter of St Paul to the Romans   6:19-23

Now that you have been freed from sin, you have been made slaves of God.

If I may use human terms to help your natural weakness: as once you put your bodies at the service of vice and immorality, so now you must put them at the service of righteousness for your sanctification.

When you were slaves of sin, you felt no obligation to righteousness, and what did you get from this? Nothing but experiences that now make you blush, since that sort of behaviour ends in death. Now, however, you have been set free from sin, you have been made slaves of God, and you get a reward leading to your sanctification and ending in eternal life. For the wage paid by sin is death; the present given by God is eternal life in Christ Jesus our Lord.

This is the word of the Lord.

Responsorial Psalm   Ps 1:1-4. 6. ℟ Ps 39:5

℟ Happy are they who hope in the Lord.

1   Happy indeed is the man
    who follows not the counsel of the wicked;
    nor lingers in the way of sinners
    nor sits in the company of scorners,
    but whose delight is the law of the Lord
    and who ponders his law day and night.   ℟

2   He is like a tree that is planted
    beside the flowing waters,
    that yields its fruit in due season
    and whose leaves shall never fade;
    and all that he does shall prosper.   ℟   (continued)

3 Not so are the wicked, not so!
    For they like winnowed chaff
    shall be driven away by the wind.
    For the Lord guards the way of the just
    but the way of the wicked leads to doom.

  ℟   Happy are they who hope in the Lord.

Gospel Acclamation   Phil 3:8-9

    Alleluia, alleluia!
    I count all things worthless but this:
    to gain Jesus Christ and to be found in him.
    Alleluia!

GOSPEL

A reading from the holy Gospel according to Luke   12:49-53

I have not come to bring peace, but separation.

Jesus said to his disciples: 'I have come to bring fire to the earth, and how I wish it were blazing already! There is a baptism I must still receive, and how great is my distress till it is over!

'Do you suppose that I am here to bring peace on earth? No, I tell you, but rather division. For from now on a household of five will be divided: three against two and two against three; the father divided against the son, son against father, mother against daughter, daughter against mother, mother-in-law against daughter-in-law, daughter-in-law against mother-in-law.'

This is the Gospel of the Lord.

Friday

FIRST READING

A reading from the letter of St Paul to the Romans 7:18-25

Who will rescue me from this body of death?

I know of nothing good living in me – living, that is, in my unspiritual self – for though the will to do what is good is in me, the performance is not, with the result that instead of doing the good things I want to do, I carry out the sinful things I do not want. When I act against my will, then, it is not my true self doing it, but sin which lives in me.

In fact, this seems to be the rule, that every single time I want to do good it is something evil that comes to hand. In my inmost self I dearly love God's Law, but I can see that my body follows a different law that battles against the law which my reason dictates. This is what makes me a prisoner of that law of sin which lives inside my body.

What a wretched man I am! Who will rescue me from this body doomed to death? Thanks be to God through Jesus Christ our Lord!

This is the word of the Lord.

Responsorial Psalm Ps 118:66. 68. 76-77. 93-94. ℟ v.68

℟ Teach me your laws, O Lord.

1 Teach me discernment and knowledge
  for I trust in your commands.
  You are good and your deeds are good;
  teach me your statutes. ℟

2 Let your love be ready to console me
  by your promise to your servant.
  Let your love come to me and I shall live
  for your law is my delight. ℟

3 I will never forget your precepts
  for with them you give me life.
  Save me, for I am yours
  since I seek your precepts. ℟

Gospel Acclamation   cf. Mt 11:25

Alleluia, alleluia!
Blessed are you, Father, Lord of heaven and earth;
you have revealed to little ones the mysteries of the kingdom.
Alleluia!

GOSPEL

A reading from the holy Gospel according to Luke   12:54-59

You know how to interpret the face of the earth and the sky. How is it
you do not know how to interpret these times?

Jesus said to the crowds, 'When you see a cloud looming up in the west
you say at once that rain is coming, and so it does. And when the wind
is from the south you say it will be hot, and it is. Hypocrites! You
know how to interpret the face of the earth and the sky. How is it you
do not know how to interpret these times?

'Why not judge for yourselves what is right? For example: when
you go to court with your opponent, try to settle with him on the way,
or he may drag you before the judge and the judge hand you over to
the bailiff and the bailiff have you thrown into prison. I tell you, you
will not get out till you have paid the very last penny.'

This is the Gospel of the Lord.

Saturday

FIRST READING

A reading from the letter of St Paul to the Romans   8:1-11

The Spirit of him who raised Jesus from the dead lives in you.

The reason why those who are in Christ Jesus are not condemned, is
that the law of the spirit of life in Christ Jesus has set you free from
the law of sin and death. God has done what the Law, because of our
unspiritual nature, was unable to do. God dealt with sin by sending
his own Son in a body as physical as any sinful body, and in that body
God condemned sin. He did this in order that the Law's just demands
might be satisfied in us, who behave not as our unspiritual nature but
as the spirit dictates.

The unspiritual are interested only in what is unspiritual, but the spiritual are interested in spiritual things. It is death to limit oneself to what is unspiritual; life and peace can only come with concern for the spiritual. That is because to limit oneself to what is unspiritual is to be at enmity with God: such a limitation never could and never does submit to God's law. People who are interested only in unspiritual things can never be pleasing to God. Your interests, however, are not in the unspiritual, but in the spiritual, since the Spirit of God has made his home in you. In fact, unless you possessed the Spirit of Christ you would not belong to him. Though your body may be dead it is because of sin, but if Christ is in you then your spirit is life itself because you have been justified; and if the Spirit of him who raised Jesus from the dead is living in you, then he who raised Jesus from the dead will give life to your own mortal bodies through his Spirit living in you.

This is the word of the Lord.

Responsorial Psalm   Ps 23:1-6. ℟ v.6

℟   Lord, this is the people that longs to see your face.

1   The Lord's is the earth and its fullness,
     the world and all its peoples.
     It is he who set it on the seas;
     on the waters he made it firm.   ℟

2   Who shall climb the mountain of the Lord?
     Who shall stand in his holy place?
     The man with clean hands and pure heart,
     who desires not worthless things.   ℟

3   He shall receive blessings from the Lord
     and reward from the God who saves him.
     Such are the men who seek him,
     seek the face of the God of Jacob.   ℟

Gospel Acclamation   Ez 33:11

     Alleluia, alleluia!
     I do not wish the sinner to die, says the Lord,
     but to turn to me and live.
     Alleluia!

GOSPEL

A reading from the holy Gospel according to Luke   13:1-9

Unless you repent, you will all perish as they did.

Some people arrived and told Jesus about the Galileans whose blood
Pilate had mingled with that of their sacrifices. At this he said to
them, 'Do you suppose these Galileans who suffered like that were
greater sinners than any other Galileans? They were not, I tell you.
No; but unless you repent you will all perish as they did. Or those
eighteen on whom the tower at Siloam fell and killed them? Do you
suppose that they were more guilty than all the other people living in
Jerusalem? They were not, I tell you. No; but unless you repent you
will all perish as they did.'

He told this parable: 'A man had a fig tree planted in his vineyard,
and he came looking for fruit on it but found none. He said to the man
who looked after the vineyard, "Look here, for three years now I have
been coming to look for fruit on this fig tree and finding none. Cut it
down: why should it be taking up the ground?" "Sir," the man replied
"leave it one more year and give me time to dig round it and manure
it: it may bear fruit next year; if not, then you can cut it down." '

This is the Gospel of the Lord.

THIRTIETH WEEK IN ORDINARY TIME

Year I

Monday

FIRST READING

A reading from the letter of St Paul to the Romans   8:12-17

You have received the Spirit which makes us God's children, and
with that Spirit we cry out: Abba, Father.

My brothers, there is no necessity for us to obey our unspiritual selves
or to live unspiritual lives. If you do live in that way, you are doomed
to die; but if by the Spirit you put an end to the misdeeds of the body
you will live.

Everyone moved by the Spirit is a son of God. The spirit you
received is not the spirit of slaves bringing fear into your lives
again; it is the spirit of sons, and it makes us cry out, 'Abba, Father!'
The Spirit himself and our spirit bear united witness that

we are children of God. And if we are children we are heirs as well: heirs of God and coheirs with Christ, sharing his sufferings so as to share his glory.

This is the word of the Lord.

Responsorial Psalm   Ps 67:2. 4. 6-7. 20-21. ℟ v.21

℟   Our God is the God of salvation.

1   Let God arise, let his foes be scattered.
    Let those who hate him flee before him.
    But the just shall rejoice at the presence of God,
    they shall exult and dance for joy.   ℟

2   Father of the orphan, defender of the widow,
    such is God in his holy place.
    God gives the lonely a home to live in;
    he leads the prisoners forth into freedom.   ℟

3   May the Lord be blessed day after day.
    He bears our burdens, God our saviour.
    This God of ours is a God who saves.
    The Lord our God holds the keys of death.   ℟

Gospel Acclamation   cf. Jn 17:17

Alleluia, alleluia!
Your word, O Lord, is truth:
make us holy in the truth.
Alleluia!

GOSPEL

A reading from the holy Gospel according to Luke   13:10-17

*This daughter of Abraham, was it not right to free her from
the bondage on the sabbath day?*

One sabbath day Jesus was teaching in one of the synagogues, and a woman was there who for eighteen years had been possessed by a spirit that left her enfeebled: she was bent double and quite unable to stand upright. When Jesus saw her he called her over and said, 'Woman, you are rid of your infirmity' and he laid his hands on her.

361

And at once she straightened up, and she glorified God.

But the synagogue official was indignant because Jesus had healed on the sabbath, and he addressed the people present. 'There are six days' he said 'when work is to be done. Come and be healed on one of those days and not on the sabbath.' But the Lord answered him. 'Hypocrites!' he said 'Is there one of you who does not untie his ox or his donkey from the manger on the sabbath and take it out for watering? And this woman, a daughter of Abraham whom Satan has held bound these eighteen years – was it not right to untie her bonds on the sabbath day?' When he said this, all his adversaries were covered with confusion, and all the people were overjoyed at all the wonders he worked.

This is the Gospel of the Lord.

Tuesday

FIRST READING

A reading from the letter of St Paul to the Romans   8:18-25

The whole creation is eagerly waiting for God to reveal his children.

I think that what we suffer in this life can never be compared to the glory, as yet unrevealed, which is waiting for us. The whole creation is eagerly waiting for God to reveal his sons. It was not for any fault on the part of creation that it was made unable to attain its purpose, it was made so by God; but creation still retains the hope of being freed, like us, from its slavery to decadence, to enjoy the same freedom and glory as the children of God. From the beginning till now the entire creation, as we know, has been groaning in one great act of giving birth; and not only creation, but all of us who possess the first-fruits of the Spirit, we too groan inwardly as we wait for our bodies to be set free. For we must be content to hope that we shall be saved – our salvation is not in sight, we should not have to be hoping for it if it were – but, as I say, we must hope to be saved since we are not saved yet – it is something we must wait for with patience.

This is the word of the Lord.

Responsorial Psalm   Ps 125. ℟ v.3

℟   The Lord has done marvels for us.

1   When the Lord delivered Zion from bondage,
    it seemed like a dream.
    Then was our mouth filled with laughter,
    on our lips there were songs.   ℟

2   The heathens themselves said: 'What marvels
    the Lord worked for them!'
    What marvels the Lord worked for us!
    Indeed we were glad.   ℟

3   Deliver us, O Lord, from our bondage
    as streams in dry land.
    Those who are sowing in tears.
    will sing when they reap.   ℟

4   They go out, they go out, full of tears,
    carrying seed for the sowing:
    they come back, they come back, full of song,
    carrying their sheaves.   ℟

Gospel Acclamation   cf. Mt. 11:25

    Alleluia, alleluia!
    Blessed are you, Father, Lord of heaven and earth;
    you have revealed to little ones the mysteries of the kingdom.
    Alleluia!

GOSPEL

A reading from the holy Gospel according to Luke   13:18-21

The seed grew and became a mighty tree.

Jesus said, 'What is the kingdom of God like? What shall I compare it
with? It is like a mustard seed which a man took and threw into his
garden: it grew and became a tree, and the birds of the air sheltered in
its branches.'

    Another thing he said, 'What shall I compare the kingdom of God
with? It is like the yeast a woman took and mixed in with three
measures of flour till it was leavened all through.'

    This is the Gospel of the Lord.

Wednesday

FIRST READING

A reading from the letter of St Paul to the Romans   8:26-30

All things work to the good for those who love God.

The Spirit comes to help us in our weakness. For when we cannot choose words in order to pray properly, the Spirit himself expresses our plea in a way that could never be put into words, and God who knows everything in our hearts knows perfectly well what he means, and that the pleas of the saints expressed by the Spirit are according to the mind of God.

We know that by turning everything to their good God co-operates with all those who love him, with all those that he has called according to his purpose. They are the ones he chose specially long ago and intended to become true images of his Son, so that his Son might be the eldest of many brothers. He called those he intended for this; those he called he justified, and with those he justified he shared his glory.

This is the word of the Lord.

Responsorial Psalm   Ps 12:4-6. ℟ v.6

℟   All my hope, O Lord,
     is in your loving kindness.

1   Look at me, answer me, Lord my God!
     Give light to my eyes lest I fall asleep in death,
     lest my enemy say: 'I have overcome him';
     lest my foes rejoice to see my fall.   ℟

2   As for me, I trust in your merciful love.
     Let my heart rejoice in your saving help:
     Let me sing to the Lord for his goodness to me,
     singing psalms to the name of the Lord, the Most High.   ℟

Gospel Acclamation   cf. 2 Thess 2:14

     Alleluia, alleluia!
     God has called us with the gospel,
     to share in the glory of our Lord Jesus Christ.
     Alleluia!

GOSPEL

A reading from the holy Gospel according to Luke　　　13:22-30

They will come from East and West to take their places at the feast in the kingdom of God.

Through towns and villages Jesus went teaching, making his way to Jerusalem. Someone said to him, 'Sir, will there be only a few saved?' He said to them, 'Try your best to enter by the narrow door, because, I tell you, many will try to enter and will not succeed.

'Once the master of the house has got up and locked the door, you may find yourself knocking on the door, saying, "Lord, open to us" but he will answer, "I do not know where you come from." Then you will find yourself saying, "We once ate and drank in your company; you taught in our streets" but he will reply, "I do not know where you come from. Away from me, all you wicked men!"

'Then there will be weeping and grinding of teeth, when you see Abraham and Isaac and Jacob and all the prophets in the kingdom of God, and yourselves turned outside. And men from east and west, from north and south, will come to take their places at the feast in the kingdom of God.

'Yes, there are those now last who will be first, and those now first who will be last.'

This is the Gospel of the Lord.

Thursday

FIRST READING

A reading from the letter of St Paul to the Romans　　　8:31-39

Nothing can come between us and the love of God made visible in Christ Jesus our Lord.

With God on our side who can be against us? Since God did not spare his own Son, but gave him up to benefit us all, we may be certain, after such a gift, that he will not refuse anything he can give. Could anyone accuse those that God has chosen? When God acquits, could anyone condemn? Could Christ Jesus? No! He not only died for us – he rose from the dead, and there at God's right hand he stands and pleads for us.

Nothing therefore can come between us and the love of Christ, even if we are troubled or worried, or being persecuted, or lacking food or clothes, or being threatened or even attacked. As scripture promised: For your sake we are being massacred daily, and reckoned as sheep for the slaughter. These are the trials through which we triumph, by the power of him who loved us.

For I am certain of this: neither death nor life, no angel, no prince, nothing that exists, nothing still to come, not any power, or height or depth, nor any created thing, can ever come between us and the love of God made visible in Christ Jesus our Lord.

This is the word of the Lord.

Responsorial Psalm   Ps 108:21-22. 26-27. 30-31. ℟ v.26

℟   Save me, O Lord, in your kindness.

1   For your name's sake act in my defence;
    in the goodness of your love be my rescuer.
    For I am poor and needy
    and my heart is pierced within me.   ℟

2   Help me, Lord my God;
    save me because of your love.
    Let them know that this is your work,
    that this is your doing, O Lord.   ℟

3   Loud thanks to the Lord are on my lips.
    I will praise him in the midst of the throng,
    for he stands at the poor man's side
    to save him from those who condemn him.   ℟

Gospel Acclamation   cf. Lk 19:38; 2:14

Alleluia, alleluia!
Blessed is the king who comes in the name of the Lord:
glory to God in the highest and peace to his people on earth.
Alleluia!

GOSPEL

A reading from the holy Gospel according to Luke   13:31-35

It is not right for the prophet to die outside Jerusalem.

Some Pharisees came up to Jesus. 'Go away' they said. 'Leave this place, because Herod means to kill you.' He replied, 'You may go and give that fox this message: Learn that today and tomorrow I cast out devils and on the third day attain my end. But for today and tomorrow and the next day I must go on, since it would not be right for a prophet to die outside Jerusalem.

'Jerusalem, Jerusalem, you that kill the prophets and stone those who are sent to you! How often have I longed to gather your children, as a hen gathers her brood under her wings, and you refused! So be it! Your house will be left to you. Yes, I promise you, you shall not see me till the time comes when you say:

Blessings on him who comes in the name of the Lord!'

This is the Gospel of the Lord.

Friday

FIRST READING

A reading from the letter of St Paul to the Romans   9:1-5

I would willingly be condemned for the sake of my people.

What I want to say now is no pretence; I say it in union with Christ – it is the truth – my conscience in union with the Holy Spirit assures me of it too. What I want to say is this: my sorrow is so great, my mental anguish so endless, I would willingly be condemned and be cut off from Christ if it could help my brothers of Israel, my own flesh and blood. They were adopted as sons, they were given the glory and the covenants; the Law and the ritual were drawn up for them, and the promises were made to them. They are descended from the patriarchs and from their flesh and blood came Christ who is above all, God for ever blessed! Amen.

This is the word of the Lord.

Responsorial Psalm   Ps 147:12-15. 19-20. ℟ v.12

℟   Praise the Lord, Jerusalem.

1   O praise the Lord, Jerusalem!
Zion, praise your God!
He has strengthened the bars of your gates,
he has blessed the children within you.   ℟

2 He established peace on your borders,
   he feeds you with finest wheat.
   He sends out his word to the earth
   and swiftly runs his command.

   ℟ Praise the Lord, Jerusalem.

3 He makes his word known to Jacob,
   to Israel his laws and decrees.
   He has not dealt thus with other nations;
   he has not taught them his decrees.   ℟

Gospel Acclamation   Jn 10:27

   Alleluia, alleluia!
   My sheep listen to my voice, says the Lord;
   I know them, and they follow me.
   Alleluia!

GOSPEL

A reading from the holy Gospel according to Luke   14:1-6

*Which of you here, if his ass or ox falls into a well, will not pull him
out on the sabbath day?*

Now on a sabbath day Jesus had gone for a meal to the house of one of
the leading Pharisees; and they watched him closely. There in front of
him was a man with dropsy, and Jesus addressed the lawyers and
Pharisees. 'Is it against the law' he asked 'to cure a man on the
sabbath, or not?' But they remained silent, so he took the man and
cured him and sent him away. Then he said to them, 'Which of you
here, if his son falls into a well, or his ox, will not pull him out on a
sabbath day without hesitation?' And to this they could find no
answer.

   This is the Gospel of the Lord.

Saturday

FIRST READING

A reading from the letter of St Paul to the Romans   11:1-2. 11-12. 25-29

*If the loss of the Jews brings reconciliation to the world, what can we
assume but that life comes from death?*

Let me put a question: is it possible that God has rejected his people?
Of course not. I, an Israelite, descended from Abraham through the
tribe of Benjamin, could never agree that God had rejected his people,
the people he chose specially long ago.

Let me put another question then: have the Jews fallen for ever, or
have they just stumbled? Obviously they have not fallen for ever:
their fall, though, has saved the pagans in a way the Jews may now
well emulate. Think of the extent to which the world, the pagan
world, has benefited from their fall and defection – then think how
much more it will benefit from the conversion of them all.

There is a hidden reason for all this, brothers, of which I do not
want you to be ignorant, in case you think you know more than you
do. One section of Israel has become blind, but this will last only until
the whole pagan world has entered, and then after this the rest of
Israel will be saved as well. As scripture says: The liberator will come
from Zion, he will banish godlessness from Jacob. And this is the
covenant I will make with them when I take their sins away.

The Jews are enemies of God only with regard to the Good News,
and enemies only for your sake; but as the chosen people, they are still
loved by God, loved for the sake of their ancestors. God never takes
back his gifts or revokes his choice.

This is the word of the Lord.

Responsorial Psalm   Ps 93:12-15. 17-18. ℟ v.14

℟   The Lord will not abandon his people.

1   Happy the man whom you teach, O Lord,
    whom you train by means of your law:
    to him you give peace in evil days.   ℟

2   The Lord will not abandon his people
    nor forsake those who are his own:
    for judgement shall again be just
    and all true hearts shall uphold it.

    ℟   The Lord will not abandon his people.

3   If the Lord were not to help me,
    I would soon go down into the silence.
    When I think: 'I have lost my foothold;'
    your mercy, Lord, holds me up. ℟

Gospel Acclamation

Mt 11:29

Alleluia, alleluia!
Take my yoke upon you;
learn from me, for I am gentle and lowly in heart.
Alleluia!

GOSPEL

A reading from the holy Gospel according to Luke

14:1. 7-11

All who exalt themselves shall be humbled, and all who humble themselves shall be exalted.

Now on a sabbath day Jesus had gone for a meal to the house of one of the leading Pharisees; and they watched him closely.

He then told the guests a parable, because he had noticed how they picked the places of honour. He said this, 'When someone invites you to a wedding feast, do not take your seat in the place of honour. A more distinguished person than you may have been invited, and the person who invited you both may come and say, "Give up your place to this man." And then, to your embarrassment, you would have to go and take the lowest place. No; when you are a guest, make your way to the lowest place and sit there, so that, when your host comes, he may say, "My friend, move up higher." In that way, everyone with you at the table will see you honoured. For everyone who exalts himself will be humbled, and the man who humbles himself will be exalted.'

This is the Gospel of the Lord.

THIRTY-FIRST WEEK IN ORDINARY TIME

Year I

Monday

FIRST READING

A reading from the letter of St Paul to the Romans   11:29-36

God has consigned all people to disobedience only to show mercy to them.

God never takes back his gifts or revokes his choice.

Just as you changed from being disobedient to God, and now enjoy mercy because of their disobedience, so those who are disobedient now – and only because of the mercy shown to you – will also enjoy mercy eventually. God has imprisoned all men in their own disobedience only to show mercy to all mankind.

How rich are the depths of God – how deep his wisdom and knowledge – and how impossible to penetrate his motives or understand his methods! Who could ever know the mind of the Lord? Who could ever be his counsellor? Who could ever give him anything or lend him anything? All that exists comes from him; all is by him and for him. To him be glory for ever! Amen.

This is the word of the Lord.

Responsorial Psalm   Ps 68:30-31. 33-34. 36-37. ℟ v.14

℟   Lord, in your great love, answer me.

1   As for me in my poverty and pain
    let your help, O God, lift me up.
    I will praise God's name with a song;
    I will glorify him with thanksgiving.   ℟

2   The poor when they see it will be glad
    and God-seeking hearts will revive;
    for the Lord listens to the needy
    and does not spurn his servants in their chains.   ℟   (continued)

3   For God will bring help to Zion
    and rebuild the cities of Judah
    and men shall dwell there in possession.
    The sons of his servants shall inherit it;
    those who love his name shall dwell there.   ℟

   ℟ Lord, in your great love, answer me.

Gospel Acclamation   Jn 8:31-32

   Alleluia, alleluia!
   If you stay in my word, you will indeed be my disciples,
   and you will know the truth, says the Lord.
   Alleluia!

GOSPEL

A reading from the holy Gospel according to Luke   14:12-14

Do not invite just your friends, but the poor and the crippled.

Jesus said to his host, one of the leading Pharisees, 'When you give a lunch or a dinner, do not ask your friends, brothers, relations or rich neighbours, for fear they repay your courtesy by inviting you in return. No; when you have a party, invite the poor, the crippled, the lame, the blind; that they cannot pay you back means that you are fortunate, because repayment will be made to you when the virtuous rise again.'

   This is the Gospel of the Lord.

Tuesday

FIRST READING

A reading from the letter of St Paul to the Romans   12:5-16

We form one body and as parts of it we belong to each other.

All of us, in union with Christ, form one body, and as parts of it we belong to each other. Our gifts differ according to the grace given us. If your gift is prophecy, then use it as your faith suggests; if administration, then use it for administration; if teaching, then use it for teaching. Let the preachers deliver sermons, the almsgivers give freely, the officials be diligent, and those who do works of mercy do them cheerfully.

Do not let your love be a pretence, but sincerely prefer good to evil. Love each other as much as brothers should, and have a profound respect for each other. Work for the Lord with untiring effort and with great earnestness of spirit. If you have hope, this will make you cheerful. Do not give up if trials come; and keep on praying. If any of the saints are in need you must share with them; and you should make hospitality your special care.

Bless those who persecute you: never curse them, bless them. Rejoice with those who rejoice and be sad with those in sorrow. Treat everyone with equal kindness; never be condescending but make real friends with the poor.

This is the word of the Lord.

Responsorial Psalm   Ps 130

℟   In you, Lord, I have found my peace.

1   O Lord, my heart is not proud
    nor haughty my eyes.
    I have not gone after things too great
    nor marvels beyond me.   ℟

2   Truly I have set my soul
    in silence and peace.
    A weaned child on its mother's breast,
    even so is my soul.   ℟

3   O Israel, hope in the Lord
    both now and for ever.   ℟

Gospel Acclamation   Mt 11:28

    Alleluia, alleluia!
    Come to me, all you that labour and are burdened,
    and I will give you rest, says the Lord.
    Alleluia!

GOSPEL

A reading from the holy Gospel according to Luke   14:15-24

Go to the highway and force people to come that my house will be filled.

One of those gathered round the table said to Jesus, 'Happy the man who will be at the feast in the kingdom of God!' But he said to him, 'There was a man who gave a great banquet, and he invited a large number of people. When the time for the banquet came, he sent his servant to say to those who had been invited, "Come along: everything is ready now." But all alike started to make excuses. The first said, "I have bought a piece of land and must go and see it. Please accept my apologies." Another said, "I have bought five yoke of oxen and am on my way to try them out. Please accept my apologies." Yet another said, "I have just got married and so am unable to come."

'The servant returned and reported this to his master. Then the householder, in a rage, said to his servant, "Go out quickly into the streets and alleys of the town and bring in here the poor, the crippled, the blind and the lame." "Sir," said the servant "your orders have been carried out and there is still room." Then the master said to his servant, "Go to the open roads and the hedgerows and force people to come in to make sure my house is full; because, I tell you, not one of those who were invited shall have a taste of my banquet." '

This is the Gospel of the Lord.

Wednesday

FIRST READING

A reading from the letter of St Paul to the Romans   13:8-10

You fulfil the law if you love your neighbour.

Avoid getting into debt, except the debt of mutual love. If you love your fellow men you have carried out your obligations. All the commandments: You shall not commit adultery, you shall not kill, you shall not steal, you shall not covet, and so on, are summed up in this single command: You must love your neighbour as yourself. Love is the one thing that cannot hurt your neighbour; that is why it is the answer to every one of the commandments.

This is the word of the Lord.

Responsorial Psalm   Ps 111:1-2. 4-5. 9. ℟ v.5

℟ Happy the merciful who give to those in need.

or

℟ Alleluia!

1 Happy the man who fears the Lord,
   who takes delight in his commands.
   His sons will be powerful on earth;
   the children of the upright are blessed. ℟

2 He is a light in the darkness for the upright:
   he is generous, merciful and just.
   The good man takes pity and lends,
   he conducts his affairs with honour. ℟

3 Open-handed, he gives to the poor;
   his justice stands firm for ever.
   His head will be raised in glory. ℟

Gospel Acclamation   1 Peter 4:14

Alleluia, alleluia!
If you are insulted for the name of Christ, blessed are you,
for the Spirit of God rests upon you.
Alleluia!

GOSPEL

A reading from the holy Gospel according to Luke   14:25-33

All who do not give up all their possessions cannot be my disciples.

Great crowds accompanied Jesus on his way and he turned and spoke
to them. 'If any man comes to me without hating his father, mother,
wife, children, brothers, sisters, yes and his own life too, he cannot be
my disciple. Anyone who does not carry his cross and come after me
cannot be my disciple.

   'And indeed, which of you here, intending to build a tower, would
not first sit down and work out the cost to see if he had enough to
complete it? Otherwise, if he laid the foundation and then found
himself unable to finish the work, the onlookers would all start
making fun of him and saying, "Here is a man who started to build
and was unable to finish." Or again, what king marching to war

against another king would not first sit down and consider whether with ten thousand men he could stand up to the other who advanced against him with twenty thousand? If not, then while the other king was still a long way off, he would send envoys to sue for peace. So in the same way, none of you can be my disciples unless he gives up all his possessions.'

This is the Gospel of the Lord.

Thursday

FIRST READING

A reading from the letter of St Paul to the Romans   14:7-12

If we live, we live for the Lord; if we die, we die for the Lord.

The life and death of each of us has its influence on others; if we live, we live for the Lord; and if we die, we die for the Lord, so that alive or dead we belong to the Lord. This explains why Christ both died and came to life, it was so that he might be Lord both of the dead and of the living. This is also why you should never pass judgement on a brother or treat him with contempt, as some of you have done. We shall all have to stand before the judgement seat of God; as scripture says: By my life – it is the Lord who speaks – every knee shall bend before me, and every tongue shall praise God. It is to God, therefore, that each of us must give an account of himself.

This is the word of the Lord.

Responsorial Psalm   Ps 26:1. 4. 13-14. ℟ v.13

℟   I believe that I shall see the good things of the Lord
      in the land of the living.

1   The Lord is my light and my help;
    whom shall I fear?
    The Lord is the stronghold of my life;
    before whom shall I shrink?   ℟

2   There is one thing I ask of the Lord,
    for this I long,
    to live in the house of the Lord,

all the days of my life,
to savour the sweetness of the Lord,
to behold his temple.   ℟

3   I am sure I shall see the Lord's goodness
in the land of the living.
Hope in him, hold firm and take heart.
Hope in the Lord!   ℟

Gospel Acclamation

Mt 11:28

Alleluia, alleluia!
Come to me, all you that labour and are burdened,
and I will give you rest, says the Lord.
Alleluia!

GOSPEL

A reading from the holy Gospel according to Luke   15:1-10

There will be great rejoicing in heaven over one repentant sinner.

The tax collectors and the sinners were all seeking the company of Jesus to hear what he had to say, and the Pharisees and the scribes complained. 'This man' they said 'welcomes sinners and eats with them.' So he spoke this parable to them:

'What man among you with a hundred sheep, losing one, would not leave the ninety-nine in the wilderness and go after the missing one till he found it? And when he found it, would he not joyfully take it on his shoulders and then, when he got home, call together his friends and neighbours? "Rejoice with me," he would say "I have found my sheep that was lost." In the same way, I tell you, there will be more rejoicing in heaven over one repentant sinner than over ninety-nine virtuous men who have no need of repentance.

'Or again, what woman with ten drachmas would not, if she lost one, light a lamp and sweep out the house and search thoroughly till she found it? And then, when she had found it, call together her friends and neighbours? "Rejoice with me," she would say "I have found the drachma I lost." In the same way, I tell you, there is rejoicing among the angels of God over one repentant sinner.'

This is the Gospel of the Lord.

Friday

FIRST READING

A reading from the letter of St Paul to the Romans   15:14-21

He has appointed me as a minister of Jesus Christ to make the gentiles
acceptable as an offering.

My brothers, I am quite certain that you are full of good intentions, perfectly well instructed and able to advise each other. The reason why I have written to you, and put some things rather strongly, is to refresh your memories, since God has given me this special position. He has appointed me as a priest of Jesus Christ, and I am to carry out my priestly duty by bringing the Good News from God to the pagans, and so make them acceptable as an offering, made holy by the Holy Spirit.

I think I have some reason to be proud of what I, in union with Christ Jesus, have been able to do for God. What I am presuming to speak of, of course, is only what Christ himself has done to win the allegiance of the pagans, using what I have said and done by the power of signs and wonders, by the power of the Holy Spirit. Thus, all the way along, from Jerusalem to Illyricum, I have preached Christ's Good News to the utmost of my capacity. I have always, however, made it an unbroken rule never to preach where Christ's name has already been heard. The reason for that was that I had no wish to build on other men's foundations; on the contrary, my chief concern has been to fulfil the text: Those who have never been told about him will see him, and those who have never heard about him will understand.

This is the word of the Lord.

Responsorial Psalm   Ps 97:1-4. ℟ cf. v.2

℟   The Lord has revealed to the nations his saving power.

1   Sing a new song to the Lord
    for he has worked wonders.
    His right hand and his holy arm
    have brought salvation.   ℟

2   The Lord has made known his salvation;
    has shown his justice to the nations.

He has remembered his truth and love
for the house of Israel. ℟

3 All the ends of the earth have seen
the salvation of our God.
Shout to the Lord all the earth,
ring out your joy. ℟

Gospel Acclamation   1 Jn 2:5

Alleluia, alleluia!
Whoever keeps the word of Christ
grows perfect in the love of God.
Alleluia!

GOSPEL

A reading from the holy Gospel according to Luke   16:1-8

The children of this world are wiser in dealing with their own kind
than are the children of light.

Jesus said to his disciples, 'There was a rich man and he had a steward
who was denounced to him for being wasteful with his property. He
called for the man and said, "What is this I hear about you? Draw me
up an account of your stewardship because you are not to be my
steward any longer." Then the steward said to himself, "Now that my
master is taking the stewardship from me, what am I to do? Dig? I am
not strong enough. Go begging? I should be too ashamed. Ah, I know
what I will do to make sure that when I am dismissed from office there
will be some to welcome me into their homes."

'Then he called his master's debtors one by one. To the first he
said, "How much do you owe my master?" "One hundred measures of
oil" was the reply. The steward said, "Here, take your bond; sit down
straight away and write fifty." To another he said, "And you, sir, how
much do you owe?" "One hundred measures of wheat" was the reply.
The steward said, "Here, take your bond and write eighty."

'The master praised the dishonest steward for his astuteness. For
the children of this world are more astute in dealing with their own
kind than are the children of light.'

This is the Gospel of the Lord.

Saturday

FIRST READING

A reading from the letter of St Paul to the Romans   16:3-9. 16. 22-27

Greet each other with a holy kiss.

My greetings to Prisca and Aquila, my fellow workers in Christ Jesus, who risked death to save my life: I am not the only one to owe them a debt of gratitude, all the churches among the pagans do as well. My greetings also to the church that meets at their house.

Greetings to my friend Epaenetus, the first of Asia's gifts to Christ; greetings to Mary who worked so hard for you; to those outstanding apostles Andronicus and Junias, my compatriots and fellow prisoners who became Christians before me; to Ampliatus, my friend in the Lord; to Urban, my fellow worker in Christ; to my friend Stachys. Greet each other with a holy kiss. All the churches of Christ send greetings.

I, Tertius, who wrote out this letter, greet you in the Lord. Greetings from Gaius, who is entertaining me and from the whole church that meets in his house. Erastus, the city treasurer, sends his greetings; so does our brother Quartus.

Glory to him who is able to give you the strength to live according to the Good News I preach, and in which I proclaim Jesus Christ, the revelation of a mystery kept secret for endless ages, but now so clear that it must be broadcast to pagans everywhere to bring them to the obedience of faith. This is only what scripture has predicted, and it is all part of the way the eternal God wants things to be. He alone is wisdom; give glory therefore to him through Jesus Christ for ever and ever. Amen.

This is the word of the Lord.

Responsorial Psalm   Ps 144:2-5. 10-11. ℟ v.1

℟   I will praise your name for ever, Lord.

1   I will bless you day after day
     and praise your name for ever.
     The Lord is great, highly to be praised,
     his greatness cannot be measured.   ℟

2   Age to age shall proclaim your works,
    shall declare your mighty deeds,
    shall speak of your splendour and glory,
    tell the tale of your wonderful works.   ℞

3   All your creatures shall thank you, O Lord,
    and your friends shall repeat their blessing.
    They shall speak of the glory of your reign
    and declare your might, O God.   ℞

Gospel Acclamation   2 Cor 8:9

    Alleluia, alleluia!
    Jesus Christ was rich but he became poor,
    to make you rich out of his poverty.
    Alleluia!

GOSPEL

A reading from the holy Gospel according to Luke   16:9-15

If you cannot be trusted with money, who will trust you with the true riches.

Jesus said to his disciples, 'I tell you this: use money, tainted as it is, to win you friends, and thus make sure that when it fails you, they will welcome you into the tents of eternity. The man who can be trusted in little things can be trusted in great; the man who is dishonest in little things will be dishonest in great. If then you cannot be trusted with money, that tainted thing, who will trust you with genuine riches? And if you cannot be trusted with what is not yours, who will give you what is your very own?

'No servant can be the slave of two masters: he will either hate the first and love the second, or treat the first with respect and the second with scorn. You cannot be the slave both of God and of money.'

The Pharisees, who loved money, heard all this and laughed at him. He said to them, 'You are the very ones who pass yourselves off as virtuous in people's sight, but God knows your hearts. For what is thought highly of by men is loathsome in the sight of God.'

This is the Gospel of the Lord.

THIRTY-SECOND WEEK IN ORDINARY TIME
Year I

Monday

FIRST READING

A reading from the book of Wisdom   1:1-7

Wisdom is a kindly spirit; the Spirit of the Lord fills the whole world.

Love virtue, you who are judges on earth,
let honesty prompt your thinking about the Lord,
seek him in simplicity of heart;
since he is to be found by those who do not put him to the test,
he shows himself to those who do not distrust him.
But selfish intentions divorce from God;
and Omnipotence, put to the test, confounds the foolish.
No, Wisdom will never make its way into a crafty soul
nor stay in a body that is in debt to sin;
the holy spirit of instruction shuns deceit,
it stands aloof from reckless purposes,
is taken aback when iniquity appears.

Wisdom is a spirit, a friend to man,
though she will not pardon the words of a blasphemer,
since God sees into the innermost parts of him,
truly observes his heart,
and listens to his tongue.
The Spirit of the Lord, indeed, fills the whole world,
and that which holds all things together knows every word that is
      said.

This is the word of the Lord.

Responsorial Psalm   Ps 138:1-10. ℟ v.24

℟   Guide me, Lord, along the everlasting way.

1   O Lord, you search me and you know me,
    you know my resting and my rising,
    you discern my purpose from afar.
    You mark when I walk or lie down,
    all my ways lie open to you.   ℟

2　Before ever a word is on my tongue
　　you know it, O Lord, through and through.
　　Behind and before you besiege me,
　　your hand ever laid upon me.
　　Too wonderful for me, this knowledge,
　　too high, beyond my reach.　℟

3　O where can I go from your spirit,
　　or where can I flee from your face?
　　If I climb the heavens, you are there.
　　If I lie in the grave, you are there.　℟

4　If I take the wings of the dawn
　　and dwell at the sea's furthest end,
　　even there your hand would lead me,
　　your right hand would hold me fast.　℟

Gospel Acclamation　　　　　　　　　　　　　　　　Phil 2:15-16

　　Alleluia, alleluia!
　　Shine on the world like bright stars;
　　you are offering it the word of life.
　　Alleluia!

GOSPEL

A reading from the holy Gospel according to Luke　　　17:1-6

*If your neighbour returns to you seven times a day and says I am
sorry, you must forgive that person.*

Jesus said to his disciples, 'Obstacles are sure to come, but alas for the
one who provides them! It would be better for him to be thrown into
the sea with a millstone put round his neck than that he should lead
astray a single one of these little ones. Watch yourselves!

　'If your brother does something wrong, reprove him and, if he is
sorry, forgive him. And if he wrongs you seven times a day and seven
times comes back to you and says, "I am sorry," you must forgive him.'

　The apostles said to the Lord, 'Increase our faith.' The Lord
replied, 'Were your faith the size of a mustard seed you could say to
this mulberry tree, "Be uprooted and planted in the sea," and it would
obey you.'

　This is the Gospel of the Lord.

Tuesday

FIRST READING

A reading from the book of Wisdom   2:23 – 3:9

In the eyes of fools they were dead, but they are at peace.

God made man imperishable,
he made him in the image of his own nature;
it was the devil's envy that brought death into the world,
as those who are his partners will discover.

But the souls of the virtuous are in the hands of God,
no torment shall ever touch them.
In the eyes of the unwise, they did appear to die,
their going looked like a disaster;
their leaving us, like annihilation;
but they are in peace.
If they experienced punishment as men see it,
their hope was rich with immortality;
slight was their affliction, great will their blessing be.
God has put them to the test
and proved them worthy to be with him;
he has tested them like gold in a furnace,
and accepted them as a holocaust.
When the time comes for his visitation they will shine out;
as sparks run through the stubble, so will they.
They shall judge nations, rule over peoples,
and the Lord will be their king for ever.
They who trust in him will understand the truth,
those who are faithful will live with him in love;
for grace and mercy await those he has chosen.

This is the word of the Lord.

Responsorial Psalm   Ps 33:2-3. 16-19. ℟ v.2

℟   I will bless the Lord at all times.

1   I will bless the Lord at all times,
     his praise always on my lips;
     in the Lord my soul shall make its boast.
     The humble shall hear and be glad.   ℟

2   The Lord turns his face against the wicked
    to destroy their remembrance from the earth.
    The Lord turns his eyes to the just
    and his ears to their appeal.   ℟

3   They call and the Lord hears
    and rescues them in all their distress.
    The Lord is close to the broken-hearted;
    those whose spirit is crushed he will save.   ℟

Gospel Acclamation   Jn 14:23

    Alleluia, alleluia!
    All who love me will keep my words,
    and my Father will love them, and we will come to them.
    Alleluia!

GOSPEL

A reading from the holy Gospel according to Luke   17:7-10

We are only servants: we have done our duty.

Jesus said to his disciples: 'Which of you, with a servant ploughing or
minding sheep, would say to him when he returned from the fields,
"Come and have your meal immediately?" Would he not be more
likely to say, "Get my supper laid; make yourself tidy and wait on me
while I eat and drink. You can eat and drink yourself afterwards"?
Must he be grateful to the servant for doing what he was told? So with
you: when you have done all you have been told to do, say, "We are
merely servants: we have done no more than our duty." '

    This is the Gospel of the Lord.

Wednesday

FIRST READING

A reading from the book of Wisdom   6:1-11

Listen, kings, that you may learn wisdom.

Listen, kings, and understand;
rulers of remotest lands, take warning;
hear this, you who have thousands under your rule,
who boast of your hordes of subjects.
For power is a gift to you from the Lord,
sovereignty is from the Most High;
he himself will probe your acts and scrutinise your intentions.

If, as administrators of his kingdom, you have not governed justly
nor observed the law,
nor behaved as God would have you behave,
he will fall on you swiftly and terribly.
Ruthless judgement is reserved for the high and mighty;
the lowly will be compassionately pardoned,
the mighty will be mightily punished.
For the Lord of All does not cower before a personage,
he does not stand in awe of greatness,
since he himself has made small and great
and provides for all alike;
but strict scrutiny awaits those in power.

Yes, despots, my words are for you,
that you may learn what wisdom is and not transgress;
for they who observe holy things holily will be adjudged holy,
and, accepting instruction from them, will find their defence in them.
Look forward, therefore, to my words;
yearn for them, and they will instruct you.

This is the word of the Lord.

Responsorial Psalm   Ps 81:3-4. 6-7. ℟ v.8

℟   Rise up, O God, bring judgment to the earth.

1   Do justice for the weak and the orphan,
    defend the afflicted and the needy.
    Rescue the weak and the poor;
    set them free from the hand of the wicked.   ℟

2   I have said to you: 'You are gods
    and all of you, sons of the Most High.'
    And yet, you shall die like men,
    you shall fall like any of the princes.   ℟

Gospel Acclamation   1 Thess 5:18

Alleluia, alleluia!
For all things give thanks to God,
because this is what he expects of you in Christ Jesus.
Alleluia!

GOSPEL

A reading from the holy Gospel according to Luke   17:11-19

It seems that no one has returned to give thanks to God except this foreigner.

On the way to Jerusalem Jesus travelled along the border between
Samaria and Galilee. As he entered one of the villages, ten lepers
came to meet him. They stood some way off and called to him, 'Jesus!
Master! Take pity on us.' When he saw them he said, 'Go and show
yourselves to the priests.' Now as they were going away they were
cleansed. Finding himself cured, one of them turned back praising
God at the top of his voice and threw himself at the feet of Jesus and
thanked him. The man was a Samaritan. This made Jesus say, 'Were
not all ten made clean? The other nine, where are they? It seems that
no one has come back to give praise to God, except this foreigner.' And
he said to the man, 'Stand up and go on your way. Your faith has
saved you.'

This is the Gospel of the Lord.

Thursday

FIRST READING

A reading from the book of Wisdom   7:22 – 8:1

Wisdom is reflection of eternal light, a spotless mirror of the majesty of God.

Within Wisdom is a spirit intelligent, holy,
unique, manifold, subtle,
active, incisive, unsullied,
lucid, invulnerable, benevolent, sharp,
irresistible, beneficent, loving to man,
steadfast, dependable, unperturbed,
almighty, all-surveying,
penetrating all intelligent, pure
and most subtle spirits;
for Wisdom is quicker to move than any motion;
she is so pure, she pervades and permeates all things.

She is a breath of the power of God,
pure emanation of the glory of the Almighty;
hence nothing impure can find a way into her.
She is a reflection of the eternal light,
untarnished mirror of God's active power,
image of his goodness.

Although alone, she can do all;
herself unchanging, she makes all things new.
In each generation she passes into holy souls,
she makes them friends of God and prophets;
for God loves only the man who lives with Wisdom.
She is indeed more splendid than the sun,
she outshines all the constellations;
compared with light, she takes first place,
for light must yield to night,
but over Wisdom evil can never triumph.
She deploys her strength from one end of the earth to the other,
ordering all things for good.

This is the word of the Lord.

Responsorial Psalm   Ps 118:89-91. 130. 135. 175. ℟ v.89

℟   Your word is for ever, O Lord.

1   Your word, O Lord, for ever
    stands firm in the heavens:
    your truth lasts from age to age,
    like the earth you created.   ℟

2   By your decree it endures to this day;
    for all things serve you.
    The unfolding of your word gives light
    and teaches the simple.   ℟

3   Let your face shine on your servant
    and teach me your decrees.
    Give life to my soul that I may praise you.
    Let your decrees give me help.   ℟

Gospel Acclamation   Jn 15:5

    Alleluia, alleluia!
    I am the vine and you are the branches, says the Lord;
    those who live in me, and I in them, will bear much fruit.
    Alleluia!

GOSPEL

A reading from the holy Gospel according to Luke   17:20-25

The kingdom of God is among you.

Asked by the Pharisees when the kingdom of God was to come, Jesus
gave them this answer, 'The coming of the kingdom of God does not
admit of observation and there will be no one to say, "Look here! Look
there!" For, you must know, the kingdom of God is among you.'

    He said to the disciples, 'A time will come when you will long to see
one of the days of the Son of Man and will not see it. They will say to
you, "Look there!" or, "Look here!" Make no move; do not set off in
pursuit; for as the lightning flashing from one part of heaven lights up
the other, so will be the Son of Man when his day comes. But first he
must suffer grievously and be rejected by this generation.'

    This is the Gospel of the Lord.

Friday

FIRST READING

A reading from the book of Wisdom   13:1-9

*If they are able to investigate the world, how have they been so slow to
find its master?*

Naturally stupid are all men who have not known God
and who, from the good things that are seen, have not been able to
    discover Him-who-is,
or, by studying the works, have failed to recognise the Artificer.
Fire however, or wind, or the swift air,
the sphere of the stars, impetuous water, heaven's lamps,
are what they have held to be the gods who govern the world.

If, charmed by their beauty, they have taken things for gods,
let them know how much the Lord of these excels them,
since the very Author of beauty has created them.
And if they have been impressed by their power and energy,
let them deduce from these how much mightier is he that has formed
    them,
since through the grandeur and beauty of the creatures
we may, by analogy, contemplate their Author.

Small blame, however, attaches to these men,
for perhaps they only go astray
in their search for God and their eagerness to find him;
living among his works, they strive to comprehend them
and fall victim to appearances, seeing so much beauty.

Even so, they are not to be excused:
if they are capable of acquiring enough knowledge
to be able to investigate the world,
how have they been so slow to find its Master?

This is the word of the Lord.

Responsorial Psalm   Ps 18:2-5. ℟ v.2

℟   The heavens proclaim the glory of God.

1   The heavens proclaim the glory of God
    and the firmament shows forth the work of his hands.
    Day unto day takes up the story
    and night unto night makes known the message. ℟

2   No speech, no word, no voice is heard
    yet their span extends through all the earth,
    their words to the utmost bounds of the world. ℟

Gospel Acclamation   Lk 21:28

    Alleluia, alleluia!
    Lift up your heads and see;
    your redemption is near at hand.
    Alleluia!

GOSPEL

A reading from the holy Gospel according to Luke   17:26-37

It will be the same when the day comes the Son of Man is revealed.

Jesus said to the disciples: 'As it was in Noah's day, so will it also be in the days of the Son of Man. People were eating and drinking, marrying wives and husbands, right up to the day Noah went into the ark, and the Flood came and destroyed them all. It will be the same as it was in Lot's day: people were eating and drinking, buying and selling, planting and building, but the day Lot left Sodom, God rained fire and brimstone from heaven and it destroyed them all. It will be the same when the day comes for the Son of Man to be revealed.

'When that day comes, anyone on the housetop, with his possessions in the house, must not come down to collect them, nor must anyone in the fields turn back either. Remember Lot's wife. Anyone who tries to preserve his life will lose it; and anyone who loses it will keep it safe. I tell you, on that night two will be in one bed: one will be taken, the other left; two women will be grinding corn together: one will be taken, the other left.' The disciples interrupted. 'Where Lord?' they asked. He said, 'Where the body is, there too will the vultures gather.'

    This is the Gospel of the Lord

Saturday

FIRST READING

A reading from the book of Wisdom   18:14-16; 19:6-9

*It appeared over the Red Sea, the way was opened and they rejoiced
like lambs.*

When peaceful silence lay over all,
and night had run the half of her swift course,
down from the heavens, from the royal throne, leapt your all-powerful
    Word;
into the heart of a doomed land the stern warrior leapt.
Carrying your unambiguous command like a sharp sword,
he stood, and filled the universe with death;
he touched the sky, yet trod the earth.
For, to keep your children from all harm,
the whole creation, obedient to your commands,
was once more, and newly, fashioned in its nature.
Overshadowing the camp there was the cloud,
where water had been, dry land was seen to rise,
the Red Sea became an unimpeded way,
the tempestuous flood a green plain;
sheltered by your hand, the whole nation passd across,
gazing at these amazing miracles.
They were like horses at pasture,
they skipped like lambs,
singing your praises, Lord, their deliverer.

This is the word of the Lord.

Responsorial Psalm   Ps 104: 2-3. 36-37. 42-43. ℞ v.5

℞   Remember the marvels the Lord has done.

or

℞   Alleluia!

1   O sing to the Lord, sing his praise;
     tell all his wonderful works!
     Be proud of his holy name,
     let the hearts that seek the Lord rejoice.   ℞

2   He struck all the first-born in their land,
    the finest flower of their sons.
    He led out Israel with silver and gold.
    In his tribes were none who fell behind.   ℟

3   For he remembered his holy word,
    which he gave to Abraham his servant.
    So he brought out his people with joy,
    his chosen ones with shouts of rejoicing.   ℟

Gospel Acclamation   cf. 2 Thess 2:14

   Alleluia, alleluia!
   God has called us with the gospel
   to share in the glory of our Lord Jesus Christ.
   Alleluia!

GOSPEL

A reading from the holy Gospel according to Luke   18:1-8

God will see justice done to his chosen who cry to him.

Jesus told his disciples a parable about the need to pray continually
and never lose heart. 'There was a judge in a certain town' he said
'who had neither fear of God nor respect for men. In the same town
there was a widow who kept on coming to him and saying, "I want
justice from you against my enemy!" For a long time he refused, but at
last he said to himself, "Maybe I have neither fear of God nor respect
for man, but since she keeps pestering me I must give the widow her
just rights, or she will persist in coming and worry me to death." '
    And the Lord said, 'You notice what the unjust judge has to say?
Now will not God see justice done to his chosen who cry to him day and
night even when he delays to help them? I promise you, he will see
justice done to them, and done speedily. But when the Son of Man
comes, will he find any faith on earth?'

    This is the Gospel of the Lord.

Monday

FIRST READING

A reading from the first book   1:10-15. 41-43. 54-57. 62-64
of Maccabees

A dreadful wrath visited Israel.

There grew a sinful offshoot, Antiochus Epiphanes, son of King Antiochus; once a hostage in Rome, he became king in the one hundred and thirty-seventh year of the kingdom of the Greeks. It was then that there emerged from Israel a set of renegades who led many people astray. 'Come,' they said 'let us reach an understanding with the pagans surrounding us. For since we separated ourselves from them many misfortunes have overtaken us.' This proposal proved acceptable, and a number of the people eagerly approached the king, who authorised them to practise the pagan observances. So they built a gymnasium in Jerusalem, such as the pagans have, disguised their circumcision, and abandoned the holy covenant, submitting to the heathen rule as willing slaves of impiety.

Then the king issued a proclamation to his whole kingdom that all were to become a single people, each renouncing his particular customs. All the pagans conformed to the king's decree, and many Israelites chose to accept his religion, sacrificing to idols and profaning the sabbath. On the fifteenth day of Chislev in the year one hundred and forty-five the king erected the abomination of desolation above the altar; and altars were built in the surrounding towns of Judah and incense offered at the doors of houses and in the streets. Any books of the Law that came to light were torn up and burned. Whenever anyone was discovered possessing a copy of the covenant or practising the Law, the king's decree sentenced him to death.

Yet there were many in Israel who stood firm and found the courage to refuse unclean food. They chose death rather than contamination by such fare or profanation of the holy covenant, and they were executed. It was a dreadful wrath that visited Israel.

This is the word of the Lord.

Responsorial Psalm   Ps 118:53. 61. 134. 150. 155. 158. ℟ cf. v.88

℟   Give me life, O lord,
       and I will do your commands.

1   I am seized with indignation at the wicked
     who forsake your law.
     Though the nets of the wicked ensnared me
     I remembered your law.   ℟

2   Redeem me from man's oppression
     and I will keep your precepts.
     Those who harm me unjustly draw near:
     they are far from your law.   ℟

3   Salvation is far from the wicked
     who are heedless of your statutes.
     I look at the faithless with disgust;
     they ignore your promise.   ℟

Gospel Acclamation   Jn 8:12

Alleluia, alleluia!
I am the light of the world, says the Lord:
whoever follows me will have the light of life.
Alleluia!

GOSPEL

A reading from the holy Gospel according to Luke   18:35-43

What do you want me to do? Lord, that I may see.

As Jesus drew near to Jericho there was a blind man sitting at the
side of the road begging. When he heard the crowd going past he
asked what it was all about, and they told him that Jesus the
Nazarene was passing by. So he called out, 'Jesus, Son of David, have
pity on me.' The people in front scolded him and told him to keep
quiet, but he shouted all the louder, 'Son of David, have pity on me.'
Jesus stopped and ordered them to bring the man to him, and when he
came up, asked him, 'What do you want me to do for you?' 'Sir,' he
replied 'let me see again.' Jesus said to him, 'Receive your sight. Your
faith has saved you.' And instantly his sight returned and he followed
him praising God, and all the people who saw it gave praise to God for
what had happened.

   This is the Gospel of the Lord.

Tuesday

FIRST READING

A reading from the second book of Maccabees 6:18-31

I have left the young an example of how to die a good death for the venerable and holy laws.

Eleazar, one of the foremost teachers of the Law, a man already advanced in years and of most noble appearance, was being forced to open his mouth wide to swallow pig's flesh. But he, resolving to die with honour rather than to live disgraced, went to the block of his own accord, spitting the stuff out, the plain duty of anyone with the courage to reject what it is not lawful to taste, even from a natural tenderness for his own life. Those in charge of the impious banquet, because of their long-standing friendship with him, took him aside and privately urged him to have meat brought of a kind he could properly use, prepared by himself, and only pretend to eat the portions of sacrificial meat as prescribed by the king; this action would enable him to escape death, by availing himself of an act of kindness prompted by their long friendship. But having taken a noble decision worthy of his years and the dignity of his great age and the well earned distinction of his grey hairs, worthy too of his impeccable conduct from boyhood, and above all of the holy legislation established by God himself, he publicly stated his convictions, telling them to send him at once to Hades. 'Such pretence' he said 'does not square with our time of life; many young people would suppose that Eleazar at the age of ninety had conformed to the foreigners' way of life, and because I had played this part for the sake of a paltry brief spell of life might themselves be led astray on my account; I should only bring defilement and disgrace on my old age. Even though for the moment I avoid execution by man, I can never, living or dead, elude the grasp of the Almighty. Therefore if I am man enough to quit this life here and now I shall prove myself worthy of my old age, and I shall have left the young a noble example of how to make a good death, eagerly and generously, for the venerable and holy laws.'

With these words he went straight to the block. His escorts, so recently well disposed towards him, turned against him after this declaration, which they regarded as sheer madness. Just before he died under the blows, he groaned aloud and said, 'The Lord whose knowledge is holy sees clearly that, though I might have escaped death, whatever agonies of body I now endure under this bludgeoning, in my soul I am glad to suffer, because of the awe which he inspires in me.'

This was how he died, leaving his death as an example of nobility and a record of virtue not only for the young but for the great majority of the nation.

This is the word of the Lord.

Responsial Psalm   Ps 3:2-7. ℟ v.6

℟ The Lord upholds me.

1 How many are my foes, O Lord!
   How many are rising up against me!
   How many are saying about me:
   'There is no help for him in God.'   ℟

2 But you, Lord, are a shield about me,
   my glory, who lift up my head.
   I cry aloud to the Lord.
   He answers from his holy mountain.   ℟

3 I lie down to rest and I sleep.
   I wake, for the Lord upholds me.
   I will not fear even thousands of people
   who are ranged on every side against me.   ℟

Gospel Acclamation   1 Jn 4:10

Alleluia, alleluia!
God first loved us
and sent his Son to take away our sins.
Alleluia!

GOSPEL

A reading from the holy Gospel according to Luke   19:1-10

The Son of Man has come to seek out and save what was lost.

Jesus entered Jericho and was going through the town when a man whose name was Zacchaeus made his appearance; he was one of the senior tax collectors and a wealthy man. He was anxious to see what kind of man Jesus was, but he was too short and could not see him for the crowd; so he ran ahead and climbed a sycamore tree to catch a glimpse of Jesus who was to pass that way. When Jesus reached the spot he looked up and spoke to him: 'Zacchaeus, come down. Hurry, because I must stay at your house today.' And he hurried down and welcomed him joyfully. They all complained when they saw what was happening. 'He has gone to stay at a sinner's house' they said. But Zacchaeus stood his ground and said to the Lord, 'Look, sir, I am going to give half my property to the poor, and if I have cheated anybody I will pay him back four times the amount.' And Jesus said to him, 'Today salvation has come to this house, because this man too is a son of Abraham; for the Son of Man has come to seek out and save what was lost.'

This is the Gospel of the Lord.

Wednesday

FIRST READING

A reading from the second book of Maccabees   7:1. 20-31

The creator of the world will give you breath and life.

There were seven brothers who were arrested with their mother. The king tried to force them to taste pig's flesh, which the Law forbids, by torturing them with whips and scourges.

The mother was especially admirable and worthy of honourable remembrance, for she watched the death of seven sons in the course of a single day, and endured it resolutely because of her hopes in the Lord. Indeed she encouraged each of them in the language of their ancestors; filled with noble conviction, she reinforced her womanly argument with manly courage, saying to them, 'I do not know how you appeared in my womb; it was not I who endowed you with breath and life, I had not the shaping of your every part. It is the creator of the world, ordaining the process of man's birth and presiding over the origin of all things, who in his mercy will most surely give you back both breath and life, seeing that you now despise your own existence for the sake of his laws.'

Antiochus thought he was being ridiculed, suspecting insult in the tone of her voice; and as the youngest was still alive he appealed to him not with mere words but with promises on oath to make him both rich and happy if he would abandon the traditions of his ancestors; he would make him his Friend and entrust him with public office. The young man took no notice at all, and so the king then appealed to the mother, urging her to advise the youth to save his life. After a great deal of urging on his part she agreed to try persuasion on her son. Bending over him, she fooled the cruel tyrant with these words, uttered in the language of their ancestors, 'My son, have pity on me; I carried you nine months in my womb and suckled you three years, fed you and reared you to the age you are now and cherished you. I implore you, my child, observe heaven and earth, consider all that is in them, and acknowledge that God made them out of what did not exist, and that mankind comes into being in the same way. Do not fear this executioner, but prove yourself worthy of your brothers, and make death welcome, so that in the day of mercy I may receive you back in your brothers' company.'

She had scarcely ended when the young man said, 'What are you all waiting for? I will not comply with the king's ordinance; I obey the ordinance of the Law given to our ancestors through Moses. As for you, sir, who have contrived every kind of evil against the Hebrews, you will certainly not escape the hands of God.'

This is the word of the Lord.

Responsorial Psalm   Ps 16:1. 5-6. 8. 15. ℟ v.15

℟ Lord, when your glory appears,
   my joy will be full.

1 Lord, hear a cause that is just,
   pay heed to my cry.
   Turn your ear to my prayer:
   no deceit is on my lips. ℟

2 I kept my feet firmly in your paths;
   there was no faltering in my steps.
   I am here and I call, you will hear me, O God.
   Turn your ear to me; hear my words. ℟

3 Guard me as the apple of your eye.
   Hide me in the shadow of your wings.
   As for me, in my justice I shall see your face
   and be filled, when I awake, with the sight of your glory. ℟

Gospel Acclamation

cf. Jn 15:16

Alleluia, alleluia!
I have chosen you from the world, says the Lord,
to go and bear fruit that will last.
Alleluia!

GOSPEL

A reading from the holy Gospel according to Luke   19:11-28

Why did you not lend my money out?

While the people were listening, Jesus went on to tell a parable, because he was near Jerusalem and they imagined that the kingdom of God was going to show itself then and there. Accordingly he said, 'A man of noble birth went to a distant country to be appointed king and afterwards return. He summoned ten of his servants and gave them ten pounds. "Do business with these" he told them "until I get back." But his compatriots detested him and sent a delegation to follow him with this message, "We do not want this man to be our king."

'Now on his return, having received his appointment as king, he sent for those servants to whom he had given the money, to find out what profit each had made. The first came in and said, "Sir, your one pound has brought in ten." "Well done, my good servant!" he replied. "Since you have proved yourself faithful in a very small thing, you shall have the government of ten cities." Then came the second and said, "Sir, your one pound has made five." To this one also he said, "And you shall be in charge of five cities." Next came the other and said, "Sir, here is your pound. I put it away safely in a piece of linen because I was afraid of you; for you are an exacting man: you pick up what you have not put down and reap what you have not sown." "You wicked servant!" he said "Out of your own mouth I condemn you. So you knew I was an exacting man, picking up what I have not put down and reaping what I have not sown? Then why did you not put my money in the bank? On my return I could have drawn it out with interest." And he said to those standing by, "Take the pound from him and give it to the man who has ten pounds." And they said to him, "But, sir, he has ten pounds ..." "I tell you, to everyone who has will be given more; but from the man who has not, even what he has will be taken away.

' "But as for my enemies who did not want me for their king, bring them here and execute them in my presence." '

When he had said this he went on ahead, going up to Jerusalem.

This is the Gospel of the Lord.

Thursday

FIRST READING

A reading from the first book of Maccabees   2:15-29

We will still follow the law of our ancestors.

The commissioners of King Antiochus who were enforcing the apostasy came to the town of Modein to make the Israelites sacrifice. Many Israelites gathered round them, but Mattathias and his sons drew apart. The king's commissioners then addressed Mattathias as follows, 'You are a respected leader, a great man in this town; you have sons and brothers to support you. Be the first to step forward and conform to the king's decree, as all the nations have done, and the leaders of Judah and the survivors in Jerusalem; you and your sons shall be reckoned among the Friends of the King, you and your sons shall be honoured with gold and silver and many presents.' Raising his voice, Mattathias retorted, 'Even if every nation living in the king's dominions obeys him, each forsaking its ancestral religion to conform to his decrees, I, my sons and my brothers will still follow the covenant of our ancestors. Heaven preserve us from forsaking the Law and its observances. As for the king's orders, we will not follow them; we will not swerve from our own religion either to right or to left.' As he finished speaking, a Jew came forward in the sight of all to offer sacrifice on the altar in Modein as the royal edict required. When Mattathias saw this, he was fired with zeal; stirred to the depth of his being, he gave vent to his legitimate anger, threw himself on the man and slaughtered him on the altar. At the same time he killed the king's commissioner who was there to enforce the sacrifice, and tore down the altar. In his zeal for the Law he acted as Phinehas did against Zimri son of Salu. Then Mattathias went through the town, shouting at the top of his voice, 'Let everyone who has a fervour for the Law and takes his stand on the covenant come out and follow me.' Then he fled with his sons into the hills, leaving all their possessions behind in the town.

At this many who were concerned for virtue and justice went down to the desert and stayed there.

This is the word of the Lord.

Responsorial Psalm   Ps 49:1-2. 5-6. 14-15. ℟ v.23

℟   To the upright I will show the saving power of God.

1   The God of gods, the Lord,
    has spoken and summoned the earth,
    from the rising of the sun to its setting.
    Out of Zion's perfect beauty he shines.   ℟

2   'Summon before me my people
    who made covenant with me by sacrifice.'
    The heavens proclaim his justice,
    for he, God, is the judge.   ℟

3   'Pay your sacrifice of thanksgiving to God
    and render him your votive offerings.
    Call on me in the day of distress.
    I will free you and you shall honour me.'   ℟

Gospel Acclamation   cf. Ps 94:8

Alleluia, alleluia!
If today you hear his voice,
harden not your hearts.
Alleluia!

GOSPEL

A reading from the holy Gospel according to Luke   19:41-44

If only you knew on what your peace depends.

As Jesus drew near Jerusalem and came in sight of the city he shed tears over it and said, 'If you in your turn had only understood on this day the message of peace! But, alas, it is hidden from your eyes! Yes, a time is coming when your enemies will raise fortifications all round you, when they will encircle you and hem you in on every side; they will dash you and the children inside your walls to the ground; they will leave not one stone standing on another within you – and all because you did not recognise your opportunity when God offered it!'

This is the Gospel of the Lord.

Friday

FIRST READING

A reading from the first book of Maccabees   4:36-37. 52-59

They offered with joy a sacrifice on the new altar which they had dedicated.

Judas and his brothers said, 'Now that our enemies have been defeated, let us go up to purify the sanctuary and dedicate it.' So they marshalled the whole army, and went up to Mount Zion.

On the twenty-fifth of the ninth month, Chislev, in the year one hundred and forty-eight, they rose at dawn and offered a lawful sacrifice on the new altar of holocausts which they had made. The altar was dedicated, to the sound of zithers, harps and cymbals, at the same time of year and on the same day on which the pagans had originally profaned it. The whole people fell prostrate in adoration, praising to the skies him who had made them so successful. For eight days they celebrated the dedication of the altar, joyfully offering holocausts, communion sacrifices and thanksgivings. They ornamented the front of the Temple with crowns and bosses of gold, repaired the gates and the storerooms and fitted them with doors. There was no end to the rejoicing among the people, and the reproach of the pagans was lifted from them. Judas, with his brothers and the whole assembly of Israel, made it a law that the days of the dedication of the altar should be celebrated yearly at the proper season, for eight days beginning on the twenty-fifth of the month Chislev, with rejoicing and gladness.

This is the word of the Lord.

Responsorial Psalm   1 Chron 29:10-12. ℟ v.13

℟ We praise your glorious name, O mighty God.

1 Blessed are you, O Lord,
   the God of Israel our father,
   for ever, for ages unending.   ℟

2 Yours, Lord, are greatness and power,
   and splendour, triumph and glory.
   All is yours, in heaven and on earth.   ℟

3 Yours, O Lord, is the kingdom,
   you are supreme over all.
   Both honour and riches come from you.   ℟

4 You are the ruler of all,
   from your hand come strength and power,
   from your hand come greatness and might.   ℟

Gospel Acclamation   Jn 10:27

   Alleluia, alleluia!
   My sheep listen to my voice, says the Lord;
   I know them, and they follow me.
   Alleluia!

GOSPEL

A reading from the holy Gospel according to Luke   19:45-48

You have turned the house of the Lord into a robber's den.

Jesus went into the Temple and began driving out those who were
selling. 'According to scripture,' he said 'my house will be a house of
prayer. But you have turned it into a robbers' den.'

He taught in the Temple every day. The chief priests and the
scribes, with the support of the leading citizens, tried to do away with
him, but they did not see how they could carry this out because the
people as a whole hung on his words.

This is the Gospel of the Lord.

Saturday

FIRST READING

A reading from the first book of Maccabees   6:1-13

On account of the evil I did in Jerusalem, I have suffered great misfortunes.

King Antiochus was making his way across the upper provinces; he had heard that in Persia there was a city called Elymais, renowned for its riches, its silver and gold, and its very wealthy temple containing golden armour, breastplates and weapons, left there by Alexander son of Philip, the king of Macedon, the first to reign over the Greeks. He therefore went and attempted to take the city and pillage it, but without success, since the citizens learnt of his intention, and offered him a stiff resistance, whereupon he turned about and retreated, disconsolate, in the direction of Babylon. But while he was still in Persia news reached him that the armies that had invaded the land of Judah had been defeated, and that Lysias in particular had advanced in massive strength, only to be forced to turn and flee before the Jews; these had been strengthened by the acquisition of arms, supplies and abundant spoils from the armies they had cut to pieces; they had overthrown the abomination he had erected over the altar in Jerusalem, and had encircled the sanctuary with high walls as in the past, and had fortified Bethzur, one of his cities. When the king heard this news he was amazed and profoundly shaken; he threw himself on his bed and fell into a lethargy from acute disappointment, because things had not turned out for him as he had planned. And there he remained for many days, subject to deep and recurrent fits of melancholy, until he understood that he was dying. Then summoning all his Friends, he said to them, 'Sleep evades my eyes, and my heart is cowed by anxiety. I have been asking myself how I could have come to such a pitch of distress, so great a flood as that which now engulfs me – I who was so generous and well-loved in my heyday. But now I remember the wrong I did in Jerusalem when I seized all the vessels of silver and gold there, and ordered the extermination of the inhabitants of Judah for no reason at all. This, I am convinced, is why these misfortunes have overtaken me, and why I am dying of melancholy in a foreign land.'

This is the word of the Lord.

Responsorial Psalm   Ps 9:2-4. 6. 16. 19. ℟ cf. v.16

℟   I will rejoice in your salvation, O Lord.

1   I will praise you, Lord, with all my heart;
    I will recount all your wonders.
    I will rejoice in you and be glad,
    and sing psalms to your name, O Most High.   ℟

2   See how my enemies turn back,
    how they stumble and perish before you.
    You have checked the nations, destroyed the wicked;
    you have wiped out their name for ever and ever.   ℟

3   The nations' feet have been caught
    in the snare they laid;
    for the needy shall not always be forgotten
    nor the hopes of the poor be in vain.   ℟

Gospel Acclamation   cf. 2 Tim 1:10

Alleluia, alleluia!
Our Saviour Jesus Christ has done away with death
and brought us life through his gospel.
Alleluia!

GOSPEL

A reading from the holy Gospel according to Luke   20:27-40

He is God not of the dead, but of the living.

Some Sadducees – those who say that there is no resurrection –
approached Jesus and they put this question to him, 'Master, we have
it from Moses in writing, that if a man's married brother dies
childless, the man must marry the widow to raise up children for his
brother. Well then, there were seven brothers. The first, having
married a wife, died childless. The second and then the third married
the widow. And the same with all seven, they died leaving no
children. Finally the woman herself died. Now, at the resurrection, to
which of them will she be wife since she had been married to all
seven?'

Jesus replied, 'The children of this world take wives and husbands,
but those who are judged worthy of a place in the other world and in
the resurrection from the dead do not marry because they can no

longer die, for they are the same as the angels, and being children of the resurrection they are sons of God. And Moses himself implies that the dead rise again, in the passage about the bush where he calls the Lord the God of Abraham, the God of Isaac and the God of Jacob. Now he is God, not of the dead, but of the living; for to him all men are in fact alive.'

Some scribes then spoke up. 'Well put, Master' they said – because they would not dare to ask him any more questions.

This is the Gospel of the Lord.

LAST WEEK IN ORDINARY TIME

Year I

Monday

FIRST READING

A reading from the prophet Daniel   1:1-6. 8-20

They have not found the equal of Daniel, Hananiah, Mishael, and Azariah.

In the third year of the reign of Jehoiakim king of Judah, Nebuchadnezzar king of Babylon marched on Jerusalem and besieged it. The Lord delivered Jehoiakim king of Judah into his hands, with some of the furnishings of the Temple of God. He took them away to the land of Shinar, and stored the sacred vessels in the treasury of his own gods.

The king ordered Ashpenaz, his chief eunuch, to select from the Israelites a certain number of boys of either royal or noble descent; they had to be without any physical defect, of good appearance, trained in every kind of wisdom, well-informed, quick at learning, suitable for service in the palace of the king. Ashpenaz himself was to teach them the language and literature of the Chaldaeans. The king assigned them a daily allowance of food and wine from his own royal table. They were to receive an education lasting for three years, after which they were expected to be fit for the king's society. Among them were Daniel, Hananiah, Mishael and Azariah, who were Judaeans. Daniel, who was most anxious not to defile himself with the food and wine from the royal table, begged the chief eunuch to spare him this defilement; and by the grace of

God Daniel met goodwill and sympathy on the part of the chief eunuch. But he warned Daniel, 'I am afraid of my lord the king: he has assigned you food and drink, and if he sees you looking thinner in the face than the other boys of your age, my head will be in danger with the king because of you.' At this Daniel turned to the guard whom the chief eunuch had assigned to Daniel, Hananiah, Mishael and Azariah. He said, 'Please allow your servants a ten days' trial, during which we are given only vegetables to eat and water to drink. You can then compare our looks with those of the boys who eat the king's food; go by what you see, and treat your servants accordingly.' The man agreed to do what they asked and put them on ten days' trial. When the ten days were over they looked and were in better health than any of the boys who had eaten their allowance from the royal table; so the guard withdrew their allowance of food and the wine they were to drink, and gave them vegetables. And God favoured these four boys with knowledge and intelligence in everything connected with literature, and in wisdom; while Daniel had the gift of interpreting every kind of vision and dream. When the period stipulated by the king for the boys' training was over, the chief eunuch presented them to Nebuchadnezzar. The king conversed with them, and among all the boys found none to equal Daniel, Hananiah, Mishael and Azariah. So they became members of the king's court, and on whatever point of wisdom or information he might question them, he found them ten times better than all the magicians and enchanters in his entire kingdom.

This is the word of the Lord.

Responsorial Psalm   Dan 3: 52-56. ℟ v.52

1   You are blest, Lord God of our fathers.
    ℟   Glory and praise for ever.
    Blest your glorious holy name.
    ℟   Glory and praise for ever.

2   You are blest in the temple of your glory.
    ℟   Glory and praise for ever.
    You are blest on the throne of your kingdom.
    ℟   Glory and praise for ever.

3   You are blest who gaze into the depths.
    ℟ Glory and praise for ever.
    You are blest in the firmament of heaven.
    ℟ Glory and praise for ever.

Gospel Acclamation   Mt 24:42. 44

    Alleluia, alleluia!
    Be watchful and ready:
    you know not when the Son of Man is coming.
    Alleluia!

GOSPEL

A reading from the holy Gospel according to Luke   21:1-4

He saw the poor widow give two small coins.

As Jesus looked up he saw rich people putting their offerings into the treasury; then he happened to notice a poverty-stricken widow putting in two small coins, and he said, 'I tell you truly, this poor widow has put in more than any of them; for these have all contributed money they had over, but she from the little she had has put in all she had to live on.'

    This is the Gospel of the Lord.

Tuesday

FIRST READING

A reading from the prophet Daniel   2:31-45

The God of heaven will set up a kingdom which will never be destroyed, and it will absorb all the kingdoms of the world.

Daniel said to Nebuchadnezzar, 'You have had a vision, O king; this is what you saw: a statue, a great statue of extreme brightness, stood before you, terrible to see. The head of this statue was of fine gold, its chest and arms were of silver, its belly and thighs of bronze, its legs of iron, its feet part iron, part earthenware. While you were gazing, a stone broke away, untouched by any hand, and struck the statue, struck its feet of iron and earthenware and shattered them. And then, iron and earthenware, bronze, silver, gold all broke into small pieces as fine as chaff on the threshing-floor in summer. The wind blew them away, leaving not a trace behind. And the stone that had struck the statue grew into a great mountain, filling the whole earth. This was the dream; now we will explain to the king what it means. You, O king, king of kings, to whom the God of heaven has given sovereignty, power, strength and glory – the sons of men, the beasts of the field, the birds of heaven, wherever they live, he has entrusted to your rule, making you king of them all – you are the golden head. And after you another kingdom will rise, not so great as you, and then a third, of bronze, which will rule the whole world. There will be a fourth kingdom, hard as iron, as iron that shatters and crushes all. Like iron that breaks everything to pieces, it will crush and break all the earlier kingdoms. The feet you saw, part earthenware, part iron, are a kingdom which will be split in two, but which will retain something of the strength of iron, just as you saw the iron and the clay of the earthenware mixed together. The feet were part iron, part earthenware; the kingdom will be partly strong and partly weak. And just as you saw the iron and the clay of the earthenware mixed together, so the two will be mixed together in the seed of man; but they will not hold together any more than iron will blend with earthenware. In the time of these kings the God of heaven will set up a kingdom which shall never be destroyed, and this kingdom will not pass into the hands of another race: it will shatter and absorb all the previous kingdoms, and itself last for ever – just as you saw the stone untouched by hand break from the mountain and shatter iron, bronze, earthenware, silver and gold. The great God has shown the king what is to take place. The dream is true, the interpretation exact.'

This is the word of the Lord.

Responsorial Psalm   Dan 3:57-61. ℟ v.59

1 All things the Lord has made, bless the Lord.
   ℟ Give glory and eternal praise to him!

2 Angels of the Lord! all bless the Lord.
   ℟ Give glory and eternal praise to him!

3 Heavens! bless the Lord.
   ℟ Give glory and eternal praise to him!

4   Waters above the heavens! bless the Lord.
    ℟   Give glory and eternal praise to him!

5   Powers of the Lord! all bless the Lord.
    ℟   Give glory and eternal praise to him.

Gospel Acclamation   Apoc 2:10

   Alleluia, alleluia!
   Be faithful until death, says the Lord,
   and I will give you the crown of the life.
   Alleluia!

GOSPEL

A reading from the holy Gospel according to Luke   21:5-11

Not a single stone will be left on the other.

When some were talking about the Temple, remarking how it was
adorned with fine stonework and votive offerings, Jesus said, 'All
these things you are staring at now – the time will come when not a
single stone will be left on another: everything will be destroyed.' And
they put to him this question: 'Master,' they said 'when will this
happen, then, and what sign will there be that this is about to take
place?'

   'Take care not to be deceived,' he said 'because many will come
using my name and saying, "I am he" and, "The time is near at hand."
Refuse to join them. And when you hear of wars and revolutions, do
not be frightened, for this is something that must happen but the end
is not so soon.' Then he said to them, 'Nation will fight against nation,
and kingdom against kingdom. There will be great earthquakes, and
plagues and famines here and there; there will be fearful sights and
great signs from heaven.'

   This is the Gospel of the Lord.

Wednesday

FIRST READING

A reading from the prophet Daniel   5:1-6. 13-14. 16-17. 23-28

The fingers of a human hand appeared and began to write on the wall.

King Belshazzar gave a great banquet for his noblemen; a thousand of them attended, and he drank wine in company with this thousand. As he sipped his wine, Belshazzar gave orders for the gold and silver vessels to be brought which his father Nebuchadnezzar had looted from the sanctuary in Jerusalem, so that the king, his noblemen, his wives and his singing women could drink out of them. The gold and silver vessels looted from the sanctuary of the Temple of God in Jerusalem were brought in, and the king, his noblemen, his wives and his singing women drank out of them. They drank their wine and praised their gods of gold and silver, of bronze and iron, of wood and stone. Suddenly the fingers of a human hand appeared, and began to write on the plaster of the palace wall, directly behind the lamp-stand; and the king could see the hand as it wrote. The king turned pale with alarm; his thigh-joints went slack and his knees began to knock. Daniel was brought into the king's presence; the king said to Daniel, 'Are you the Daniel who was one of the Judean exiles brought by my father the king from Judah? I am told that the spirit of God Most Holy lives in you, and that you are known for your perception, intelligence and marvellous wisdom. As I am told that you are able to give interpretations and to unravel difficult problems, if you can read the writing and tell me what it means, you shall be dressed in purple, and have a chain of gold put round your neck, and be third in rank in the kingdom.'

Then Daniel spoke up in the presence of the king. 'Keep your gifts for yourself,' he said 'and give your rewards to others. I will read the writing to the king without them, and tell him what it means. You have defied the Lord of heaven, you have had the vessels from his Temple brought to you, and you, your noblemen, your wives and your singing women have drunk your wine out of them. You have praised gods of gold and silver, of bronze and iron, of wood and stone, which cannot either see, hear or understand; but you have given no glory to the God who holds your breath and all your fortunes in his hands. That is why he has sent the hand which, by itself, has written these words. The writing reads: Mene, Mene, Tekel and Parsin. The meaning of the words is this: Mene: God has measured your sovereignty and put an end to it; Tekel: you have been weighed in the balance and found wanting; Parsin: your kingdom has been divided and given to the Medes and the Persians.'

This is the word of the Lord.

Responsorial Psalm   Dan 3:62-67. ℟ v.59

1   Sun and moon! bless the Lord.
    ℟   Give glory and eternal praise to him.
    Stars of heaven! bless the Lord.
    ℟   Give glory and eternal praise to him.

2   Showers and dews! all bless the Lord.
    ℟   Give glory and eternal praise to him.
    Winds! all bless the Lord.
    ℟   Give glory and eternal praise to him.

3   Fire and heat! bless the Lord.
    ℟   Give glory and eternal praise to him.
    Cold and heat! bless the Lord.
    ℟   Give glory and eternal praise to him.

Gospel Acclamation   Apoc 2:10

    Alleluia, alleluia!
    Be faithful until death, says the Lord,
    and I will give you the crown of life.
    Alleluia!

GOSPEL

A reading from the holy Gospel according to Luke   21:12-19

You will be hated by all because of my name, but not a hair of your
head will be lost.

Jesus said to his disciples: 'Men will seize you and persecute you; they will hand you over to the synagogues and to imprisonment, and bring you before kings and governors because of my name – and that will be your opportunity to bear witness. Keep this carefully in mind: you are not to prepare your defence, because I myself shall give you an eloquence and a wisdom that none of your opponents will be able to

413

resist or contradict. You will be betrayed even by parents and brothers, relations and friends; and some of you will be put to death. You will be hated by all men on account of my name, but not a hair of your head will be lost. Your endurance will win you your lives.'

This is the Gospel of the Lord.

Thursday

FIRST READING

A reading from the prophet Daniel   6:12-28

God sent his angels to seal the lions' jaws.

The presidents and satraps came along in a body and found Daniel praying and pleading with God. They then came to the king and said, 'Have you not just signed an edict forbidding any man for the next thirty days to pray to anyone, god or man, other than to yourself, O king, on pain of being thrown into the lions' den?' 'The decision stands,' the king replied 'as befits the law of the Medes and the Persians, which cannot be revoked.' Then they said to the king, 'O king, this man Daniel, one of the exiles from Judah, disregards both you and the edict which you have signed: he is at his prayers three times each day.' When the king heard these words he was deeply distressed, and determined to save Daniel; he racked his brains until sunset to find some way out. But the men came back in a body to the king and said, 'O king, remember that in conformity with the law of the Medes and the Persians, no edict or decree can be altered when once issued by the king.'

The king then ordered Daniel to be fetched and thrown into the lion pit. The king said to Daniel, 'Your God himself, whom you have served so faithfully, will have to save you.' A stone was then brought and laid over the mouth of the pit; and the king sealed it with his own signet and with that of his noblemen, so that there could be no going back on the original decision about Daniel. The king returned to his palace, spent the night in fasting and refused to receive any of his concubines. Sleep eluded him, and at the first sign of dawn he was up, and hurried off to the lion pit. As he approached the pit he shouted in anguished tones, 'Daniel, servant of the living God! Has your God, whom you serve so faithfully, been able to save you from the lions?' Daniel replied, 'O king, live for ever! My God sent his angel who sealed the lions' jaws, they did me no harm, since in his sight I am blameless, and I have never done you any wrong either, O king.' The king was overjoyed, and ordered Daniel to be released from the pit. Daniel was released from the pit, and found to be quite unhurt, because he had trusted in his God. The king sent for the men who had accused Daniel and had them thrown into the lion pit, they, their wives and their children: and they had not reached the floor of the pit before the lions had seized them and crushed their bones to pieces.

King Darius then wrote to men of all nations, peoples and languages throughout the world. 'May peace be always with you! I decree: in every kingdom of my empire let all tremble with fear before the God of Daniel:

'He is the living God, he endures for ever,
his sovereignty will never be destroyed
and his kingship never end.
He saves, sets free, and works signs and wonders
in the heavens and on earth;
he has saved Daniel from the power of the lions.'

This is the word of the Lord.

Responsorial Psalm   Dan 3:68-74. ℟ v.59

1 Dews and sleets! bless the Lord.
   ℟ Give glory and eternal praise to him.

2 Frost and cold! bless the Lord.
   ℟ Give glory and eternal praise to him.

3 Ice and snow! bless the Lord.
   ℟ Give glory and eternal praise to him.

4 Nights and days! bless the Lord.
   ℟ Give glory and eternal praise to him.

5 Light and darkness! bless the Lord.
   ℟ Give glory and eternal praise to him.

6 Lightning and clouds! bless the Lord.
   ℟ Give glory and eternal praise to him.

7 Let the earth bless the Lord.
   ℟ Give glory and eternal praise to him.

Gospel Acclamation   Lk 21:28

Alleluia, alleluia!
Lift up your heads and see;
your redemption is near at hand.
Alleluia!

GOSPEL

A reading from the holy Gospel according to Luke   21:20-28

Jerusalem will be trampled by the Gentiles until the time of the Gentiles is
fulfilled.

Jesus said to his disciples: 'When you see Jerusalem surrounded by
armies, you must realise that she will soon be laid desolate. Then
those in Judaea must escape to the mountains, those inside the city
must leave it, and those in country districts must not take refuge in it.
For this is the time of vengeance when all that scripture says must be
fulfilled. Alas for those with child, or with babies at the breast, when
those days come!

'For great misery will descend on the land and wrath on this
people. They will fall by the edge of the sword and be led captive to
every pagan country; and Jerusalem will be trampled down by the
pagans until the age of the pagans is completely over.

'There will be signs in the sun and moon and stars; on earth
nations in agony, bewildered by the clamour of the ocean and its
waves; men dying of fear as they await what menaces the world, for
the powers of heaven will be shaken. And then they will see the Son of
Man coming in a cloud with power and great glory. When these things
begin to take place, stand erect, hold your heads high, because your
liberation is near at hand.'

This is the Gospel of the Lord.

Friday

FIRST READING

A reading from the prophet Daniel   7:2-14

I saw, coming out of the clouds, one like a son of man.

I, Daniel, have been seeing visions in the night. I saw that the four winds of heaven were stirring up the great sea; four great beasts emerged from the sea, each different from the other. The first was like a lion with eagle's wings; and as I looked its wings were torn off, and it was lifted from the ground and set standing on its feet like a man; and it was given a human heart. The second beast I saw was different, like a bear, raised up on one of its sides, with three ribs in its mouth, between its teeth. 'Up!' came the command 'Eat quantities of flesh!' After this I looked, and saw another beast, like a leopard, and with four bird's wings on its flanks; it had four heads, and power was given to it. Next I saw another vision in the visions of the night: I saw a fourth beast, fearful, terrifying, very strong; it had great iron teeth, and it ate, crushed and trampled underfoot what remained. It was different from the previous beasts and had ten horns.

While I was looking at these horns, I saw another horn sprouting among them, a little one; three of the original horns were pulled out by the roots to make way for it; and in this horn I saw eyes like human eyes, and a mouth that was full of boasts. As I watched:

Thrones were set in place
and one of great age took his seat.
His robe was white as snow,
the hair of his head as pure as wool.
His throne was a blaze of flames,
its wheels were a burning fire.
A stream of fire poured out,
issuing from his presence.
A thousand thousand waited on him,
ten thousand times ten thousand stood before him.
A court was held
and the books were opened.

The great things the horn was saying were still ringing in my ears, and as I watched, the beast was killed, and its body destroyed and committed to the flames. The other beasts were deprived of their power, but received a lease of life for a season and a time.

I gazed into the visions of the night.
And I saw, coming on the clouds of heaven,
one like a son of man.
He came to the one of great age
and was led into his presence.
On him was conferred sovereignty,
glory and kingship,
and men of all peoples, nations and languages became his
　　servants.
His sovereignty is an eternal sovereignty
which shall never pass away,
nor will his empire ever be destroyed.

This is the word of the Lord.

Responsorial Psalm
Dan 3:75-81. ℟ v.59

1　Mountains and hills! bless the Lord.
　℟　Give glory and eternal praise to him.

2　Everything that grows on the earth! bless the Lord.
　℟　Give glory and eternal praise to him.

3　Springs of water! bless the Lord.
　℟　Give glory and eternal praise to him.

4　Seas and rivers! bless the Lord.
　℟　Give glory and eternal praise to him.

5　Sea beasts and everything that lives in water! bless the Lord.
　℟　Give glory and eternal praise to him.

6　Birds of heaven! bless the Lord.
　℟　Give glory and eternal praise to him.

7　Animals, wild and tame! bless the Lord.
　℟　Give glory and eternal praise to him.

Gospel Acclamation
Lk 21:28

Alleluia, alleluia!
Lift up your heads and see;
your redemption is near at hand.
Alleluia!

GOSPEL

A reading from the holy Gospel according to Luke   21:29-33

When you see these things happening, know that the kingdom of God is near.

Jesus told his disciples a parable. 'Think of the fig tree and indeed every tree. As soon as you see them bud, you know that summer is now near. So with you when you see these things happening: know that the kingdom of God is near. I tell you solemnly, before this generation has passed away all will have taken place. Heaven and earth will pass away, but my words will never pass away.'

This is the Gospel of the Lord.

Saturday

FIRST READING

A reading from the prophet Daniel   7:15-27

Kingdoms and power will be given to the people of the Most High.

I, Daniel, was deeply disturbed and the visions that passed through my head alarmed me. So I approached one of those who were standing by and asked him to tell me the truth about all this. And in reply he revealed to me what these things meant. 'These four great beasts are four kings who will rise from the earth. Those who are granted sovereignty are the saints of the Most High, and the kingdom will be theirs for ever, for ever and ever.' Then I asked to know the truth about the fourth beast, different from all the rest, very terrifying, with iron teeth, and bronze claws, eating, crushing and trampling underfoot what remained; and the truth about the ten horns on its head – and why the other horn sprouted and the three original horns fell, and why this horn had eyes and a mouth that was full of boasts, and why it made a greater show than the other horns. This was the horn I had watched making war on the saints and proving the stronger, until the coming of the one of great age who gave judgement in favour of the saints of the Most High, when the time came for the saints to take over the kingdom. This is what he said:

'The fourth beast
is to be a fourth kingdom on earth,
different from all other kingdoms.

It will devour the whole earth,
trample it underfoot and crush it.
As for the ten horns: from this kingdom
will rise ten kings, and another after them;
this one will be different from the previous ones
and will bring down three kings;
he is going to speak words against the Most High,
and harass the saints of the Most High.
He will consider changing seasons and the Law,
and the saints will be put into his power
for a time, two times, and half a time.
But a court will be held and his power will be stripped from him,
consumed, and utterly destroyed.
And sovereignty and kingship,
and the splendours of all the kingdoms under heaven
will be given to the people of the saints of the Most High.
His sovereignty is an eternal sovereignty
and every empire will serve and obey him.

This is the word of the Lord.

Responsial Psalm   Dan 3:82-87. ℟ v.59

1 Sons of men! bless the Lord.
   ℟ Give glory and eternal praise to him.
   Israel! bless the Lord.
   ℟ Give glory and eternal praise to him.

2 Priests! bless the Lord.
   ℟ Give glory and eternal praise to him.
   Servants of the Lord! bless the Lord.
   ℟ Give glory and eternal praise to him.

3 Spirits and souls of the virtuous! bless the Lord.
   ℟ Give glory and eternal praise to him.
   Devout and humble-hearted men! bless the Lord.
   ℟ Give glory and eternal praise to him.

Gospel Acclamation   Lk 21:36

> Alleluia, alleluia!
> Be watchful, pray constantly,
> that you may be worthy to stand before the son of Man.
> Alleluia!

GOSPEL

A reading from the holy Gospel according to Luke   21:34-36

Stay awake, that you might have the strength to survive all that is
going to happen.

Jesus said to his disciples: 'Watch yourselves, or your hearts will be coarsened with debauchery and drunkenness and the cares of life, and that day will be sprung on you suddenly, like a trap. For it will come down on every living man on the face of the earth. Stay awake, praying at all times for the strength to survive all that is going to happen, and to stand with confidence before the Son of Man.'

This is the Gospel of the Lord.

Weekdays in Ordinary Time

Year II

FIRST WEEK IN ORDINARY TIME
Year II

Monday

FIRST READING

A reading from the first book of Samuel   1:1-8

Hannah was tormented by her rival because God had made her barren.

There was a man of Ramathaim, a Zuphite from the highlands of
Ephraim whose name was Elkanah son of Jeroham, son of Elihu, son
of Tohu, son of Zuph, an Ephraimite. He had two wives, one called
Hannah, the other Peninnah; Peninnah had children but Hannah had
none. Every year this man used to go up from his town to worship and
to sacrifice to the Lord of hosts in Shiloh. The two sons of Eli, Hophni
and Phinehas, were there as priests of the Lord.

One day Elkanah offered sacrifice. He used to give portions to
Peninnah and to all her sons and daughters; to Hannah, however, he
would give only one portion, although he loved her more, since the
Lord had made her barren. Her rival would taunt her to annoy her,
because the Lord had made her barren. And this went on year after
year: every time they went up to the temple of the Lord she used to
taunt her. And so Hannah wept and would not eat. Then Elkanah her
husband said to her, 'Hannah, why are you crying and why are you
not eating? Why so sad? Am I not more to you than ten sons?'

This is the word of the Lord.

Responsorial Psalm   Ps 115:12-19. ℟ v.17

℟   To you, Lord, I will offer a sacrifice of praise.

or

℟   Alleluia!

1   How can I repay the Lord
     for his goodness to me?
     The cup of salvation I will raise;
     I will call on the Lord's name.   ℟

2　My vows to the Lord I will fulfil
before all his people.
O precious in the eyes of the Lord
is the death of his faithful.

℟　To you, Lord, I will offer a sacrifice of parise.

or

℟　Alleluia!

3　Your servant, Lord, your servant am I;
you have loosened my bonds.
A thanksgiving sacrifice I make;
I will call on the Lord's name.　℟

4　My vows to the Lord I will fulfil
before all his people,
in the courts of the house of the Lord,
in your midst, O Jerusalem.　℟

Gospel Acclamation

Mk 1:15

Alleluia, alleluia!
The kingdom of God is near:
repent and believe the Good News!
Alleluia!

Alternative Acclamations pp.838ff.

GOSPEL

A reading from the holy Gospel according to Mark

1:14-20

Repent and believe the Good News.

After John had been arrested, Jesus went into Galilee. There he proclaimed the Good News from God. 'The time has come' he said 'and the kingdom of God is close to hand. Repent, and believe the Good News.'

As he was walking along by the Sea of Galilee he saw Simon and his brother Andrew casting a net in the lake – for they were fishermen. And Jesus said to them, 'Follow me and I will make you into fishers of men.' And at once they left their nets and followed him.

Going on a little further, he saw James son of Zebedee and his brother John: they too were in their boat, mending their nets. He called them at once and, leaving their father Zebedee in the boat with the men he employed, they went after him.

This is the Gospel of the Lord.

In years when the feast of the Baptism of the Lord is celebrated on Monday of the first week in Ordinary Time, the readings given for the Monday may be added to those given for Tuesday, so that the beginning of each book may be read.

Tuesday

FIRST READING

A reading from the first book of Samuel   1:9-20

The Lord God remembered Hannah and she gave birth to Samuel.

After they had eaten in the hall, Hannah rose and took her stand before the Lord, while Eli the priest was sitting on his seat by the doorpost of the temple of the Lord. In the bitterness of her soul she prayed to the Lord with many tears and made a vow, saying, 'Lord of hosts! If you will take notice of the distress of your servant, and bear me in mind and not forget your servant and give her a man-child, I will give him to the Lord for the whole of his life and no razor shall ever touch his head.'

While she prayed before the Lord which she did for some time, Eli was watching her mouth, for she was speaking under her breath; her lips were moving but her voice could not be heard. He therefore supposed that she was drunk and said to her, 'How long are you going to be in this drunken state? Rid yourself of your wine.' 'No, my lord,' Hannah replied 'I am a woman in great trouble; I have taken neither wine nor strong drink – I was pouring out my soul before the Lord. Do not take your maidservant for a worthless woman; all this time I have been speaking from the depth of my grief and my resentment.' Then Eli answered her: 'Go in peace,' he said 'and may the God of Israel grant what you have asked of him.' And she said, 'May your maidservant find favour in your sight'; and with that the woman went away; she returned to the hall and ate and was dejected no longer.

They rose early in the morning and worshipped before the Lord and then set out and returned to their home in Ramah. Elkanah had intercourse with Hannah his wife and the Lord was mindful of her. She conceived and gave birth to a son, and called him Samuel 'since' she said 'I asked the Lord for him.'

This is the word of the Lord.

Responsorial Psalm · 1 Sam 2:1. 4-8. ℟ cf. v.1

℟ My heart rejoices in the Lord, my Saviour.

1 My heart exults in the Lord.
  I find my strength in my God;
  my mouth laughs at my enemies
  as I rejoice in your saving help. ℟

2 The bows of the mighty are broken,
  but the weak are clothed with strength.
  Those with plenty must labour for bread,
  but the hungry need work no more.
  The childless wife has children now
  but the fruitful wife bears no more. ℟

3 It is the Lord who gives life and death,
  he brings men to the grave and back;
  it is the Lord who gives poverty and riches.
  He brings men low and raises them on high. ℟

4 He lifts up the lowly from the dust,
  from the dungheap he raises the poor
  to set him in the company of princes,
  to give him a glorious throne. ℟

Gospel Acclamation · cf. 1 Thess 2:13

Alleluia, alleluia!
Receive this message not as human words,
but as truly the word of God.
Alleluia!

GOSPEL

A reading from the holy Gospel acording to Mark · 1:21-28

Here was a teaching with authority behind it.

Jesus and his disciples went as far as Capernaum, and as soon as the sabbath came he went to the synagogue and began to teach. And his teaching made a deep impression on them because, unlike the scribes, he taught them with authority.

In their synagogue just then there was a man possessed by an unclean spirit, and it shouted, 'What do you want with us, Jesus of

Nazareth? Have you come to destroy us? I know who you are: the Holy One of God.' But Jesus said sharply, 'Be quiet! Come out of him!' And the unclean spirit threw the man into convulsions and with a loud cry went out of him. The people were so astonished that they started asking each other what it all meant. 'Here is a teaching that is new' they said 'and with authority behind it: he gives orders even to unclean spirits and they obey him.' And his reputation rapidly spread everywhere, through all the surrounding Galilean countryside.

This is the Gospel of the Lord.

Wednesday

FIRST READING

A reading from the first book of Samuel   3:1-10. 19-20

Speak, O Lord, your servant is listening.

The boy Samuel was ministering to the Lord in the presence of Eli; it was rare for the Lord to speak in those days; visions were uncommon. One day, it happened that Eli was lying down in his room. His eyes were beginning to grow dim; he could no longer see. The lamp of God had not yet gone out, and Samuel was lying in the sanctuary of the Lord where the ark of God was, when the Lord called, 'Samuel! Samuel!' He answered, 'Here I am.' Then he ran to Eli and said, 'Here I am, since you called me.' Eli said, 'I did not call. Go back and lie down.' So he went and lay down. Once again the Lord called, 'Samuel! Samuel!' Samuel got up and went to Eli and said, 'Here I am, since you called me.' He replied, 'I did not call you, my son; go back and lie down.' Samuel had as yet no knowledge of the Lord and the word of the Lord had not yet been revealed to him. Once again the Lord called, the third time. He got up and went to Eli and said, 'Here I am, since you called me.' Eli then understood that it was the Lord who was calling the boy, and he said to Samuel, 'Go and lie down, and if someone calls say, "Speak, Lord, your servant is listening." ' So Samuel went and lay down in his place.

The Lord then came and stood by, calling as he had done before, 'Samuel! Samuel!' Samuel answered, 'Speak, Lord, your servant is listening.'

Samuel grew up and the Lord was with him and let no word of his fall to the ground. All Israel from Dan to Beersheba came to know that Samuel was accredited as a prophet of the Lord.

This is the word of the Lord.

Responsorial Psalm
Ps 39:2. 5. 7-10. ℟ vv.8. 9

℟ Here am I, Lord;
I come to do your will.

1 I waited, I waited for the Lord
and he stooped down to me;
he heard my cry.
Happy the man who has placed
his trust in the Lord
and has not gone over to the rebels
who follow false gods. ℟

2 You do not ask for sacrifice and offerings,
but an open ear.
You do not ask for holocaust and victim.
Instead, here am I. ℟

3 In the scroll of the book it stands written
that I should do your will.
My God, I delight in your law
in the depth of my heart. ℟

4 Your justice I have proclaimed
in the great assembly.
My lips I have not sealed;
you know it, O Lord. ℟

Gospel Acclamation
Jn 10:27

Alleluia, alleluia!
My sheep listen to my voice, says the Lord;
I know them, and they follow me.
Alleluia!

GOSPEL

A reading from the holy Gospel according to Mark
1:29-39

He healed many who were suffering from diseases.

On leaving the synagogue, Jesus went with James and John straight
to the house of Simon and Andrew. Now Simon's mother-in-law had
gone to bed with fever, and they told him about her straightaway. He

430

went to her, took her by the hand and helped her up. And the fever left her and she began to wait on them.

That evening, after sunset, they brought to him all who were sick and those who were possessed by devils. The whole town came crowding round the door, and he cured many who were suffering from diseases of one kind or another; he also cast out many devils, but he would not allow them to speak, because they knew who he was.

In the morning, long before dawn, he got up and left the house, and went off to a lonely place and prayed there. Simon and his companions set out in search of him, and when they found him they said, 'Everybody is looking for you.' He answered, 'Let us go elsewhere, to the neighbouring country towns, so that I can preach there too, because that is why I came.' And he went all through Galilee, preaching in their synagogues and casting out devils.

This is the Gospel of the Lord.

Thursday

FIRST READING

A reading from the first book of Samuel   4:1-11

Israel was defeated and the ark of God was captured.

It happened that the Philistines mustered to fight Israel and Israel went out to meet them in battle, encamping near Ebenezer while the Philistines were encamped at Aphek. The Philistines drew up their battle line against Israel, the battle was hotly engaged, and Israel was defeated by the Philistines and about four thousand of their army were killed on the field. The troops returned to the camp and the elders of Israel said, 'Why has the Lord allowed us to be defeated today by the Philistines? Let us fetch the ark of our God from Shiloh so that it may come among us and rescue us from the power of our enemies.' So the troops sent to Shiloh and brought away the ark of the Lord of hosts, he who is seated on the cherubs; the two sons of Eli, Hophni and Phinehas, came with the ark. When the ark of the Lord arrived in the camp, all Israel gave a great shout so that the earth resounded. When the Philistines heard the noise of the shouting, they said, 'What can this great shouting in the Hebrew camp mean?' And they realised that the ark of the Lord had come into the camp. At this the Philistines were afraid; and they said, 'God has come to the camp.'

'Alas!' they cried 'This has never happened before. Alas! Who will save us from the power of this mighty God? It was he who struck down Egypt with every kind of plague! But take courage and be men, Philistines, or you will become slaves to the Hebrews as they have been slaves to you. Be men and fight.' So the Philistines joined battle and Israel was defeated, each man fleeing to his tent. The slaughter was great indeed, and there fell of the Israelites thirty thousand foot soldiers. The ark of God was captured too, and the two sons of Eli died, Hophni and Phinehas.

This is the word of the Lord.

Responsorial Psalm
Ps 43:10-11. 14-15. 24-25. ℟ v.27

℟ Save us, Lord, in your mercy.

1 Yet now you have rejected us, disgraced us:
   you no longer go forth with our armies.
   You make us retreat from the foe
   and our enemies plunder us at will. ℟

2 You make us the taunt of our neighbours,
   the mockery and scorn of all who are near.
   Among the nations, you make us a byword,
   among the peoples a thing of derision. ℟

3 Awake, O Lord, why do you sleep?
   Arise, do not reject us for ever!
   Why do you hide your face
   and forget our oppression and misery. ℟

Gospel Acclamation
cf. Mt 4.23

Alleluia, alleluia!
Jesus preached the Good News of the kingdom
and healed all who were sick.
Alleluia!

GOSPEL

A reading from the holy Gospel according to Mark   1:40-45

The leper went away from him cleansed.

A leper came to Jesus and pleaded on his knees: 'If you want to' he said 'you can cure me.' Feeling sorry for him, Jesus stretched out his hand and touched him. 'Of course I want to!' he said. 'Be cured!'And the leprosy left him at once and he was cured. Jesus immediately sent him away and sternly ordered him, 'Mind you say nothing to anyone, but go and show yourself to the priest, and make the offering for your healing prescribed by Moses as evidence of your recovery.' The man went away, but then started talking about it freely and telling the story everywhere, so that Jesus could no longer go openly into any town, but had to stay outside in places where nobody lived. Even so, people from all around would come to him.

This is the Gospel of the Lord.

Friday

FIRST READING

A reading from the first book of Samuel   8:4-7. 10-22

You will cry out because of your king, but the Lord will not answer you because you have chosen him yourselves.

All the elders of Israel gathered together and came to Samuel at Ramah. 'Look,' they said to him 'you are old, and your sons do not follow your ways. So give us a king to rule over us, like the other nations.' It displeased Samuel that they should say, 'Let us have a king to rule us,' so he prayed to the Lord. But the Lord said to Samuel, 'Obey the voice of the people in all that they say to you, for it is not you they have rejected; they have rejected me from ruling over them.'

All that the Lord had said Samuel repeated to the people who were asking him for a king. He said, 'These will be the rights of the king who is to reign over you. He will take your sons and assign them to his chariotry and cavalry, and they will run in front of his chariot. He will use them as leaders of a thousand and leaders of fifty; he will make them plough his ploughland and harvest his harvest and make his weapons of war and the gear for his chariots. He will also take your daughters as perfumers, cooks and bakers. He will take the best of your fields, of your vineyards and olive groves and give them to his officials. He will tithe your crops and vineyards to provide for his eunuchs and his officials. He will take the best of your manservants and maidservants, of your cattle and your donkeys, and make them work for him. He will tithe your flocks, and you yourselves will become his slaves. When that day comes, you will cry out on account of the king you have chosen for yourselves, but on that day God will not answer you.'

The people refused to listen to the words of Samuel. They said, 'No! We want a king, so that we in our turn can be like the other nations; our king shall rule us and be our leader and fight our battles.' Samuel listened to all that the people had to say and repeated it in the ears of the Lord. The Lord then said to Samuel, 'Obey their voice and give them a king.'

This is the word of the Lord.

Responsorial Psalm   Ps 88:16-19. ℟ cf. v.2

℟   For ever I will sing the goodness of the Lord.

1   Happy the people who acclaim such a king,
    who walk, O Lord, in the light of your face,
    who find their joy every day in your name,
    who make your justice the source of their bliss.   ℟

2   For it is you, O Lord, who are the glory of their strength;
    it is by your favour that our might is exalted:
    for our ruler is in the keeping of the Lord;
    our king in the keeping of the Holy One of Israel.   ℟

Gospel Acclamation   Lk 7:16

    Alleluia, alleluia!
    A great prophet has appeared among us;
    God has visited his people.
    Alleluia!

GOSPEL

A reading from the holy Gospel according to Mark 2:1-12

The Son of Man has authority on earth to forgive sins.

When Jesus returned to Capernaum, word went round that he was back; and so many people collected there that there was no room left, even in front of the door. He was preaching the word to them when some people came bringing him a paralytic carried by four men, but as the crowd made it impossible to get the man to him, they stripped the roof over the place where Jesus was; and when they had made an opening, they lowered the stretcher on which the paralytic lay. Seeing their faith, Jesus said to the paralytic, 'My child, your sins are forgiven.' Now some scribes were sitting there, and they thought to themselves, 'How can this man talk like that? He is blaspheming. Who can forgive sins but God?' Jesus, inwardly aware that this was what they were thinking, said to them, 'Why do you have these thoughts in your hearts? Which of these is easier: to say to the paralytic, "Your sins are forgiven" or to say, "Get up, pick up your stretcher and walk"? But to prove to you that the Son of Man has authority on earth to forgive sins,' – he said to the paralytic – 'I order you: get up, pick up your stretcher, and go off home.' And the man got up, picked up his stretcher at once and walked out in front of everyone, so that they were all astounded and praised God saying, 'We have never seen anything like this.'

This is the Gospel of the Lord.

Saturday

FIRST READING

A reading from the first book of Samuel 9:1-4. 17-19; 10:1

This is the man of whom the Lord God spoke, Saul who will rule his people.

Among the men of Benjamin there was a man named Kish son of Abiel, son of Zeror, son of Becorath, son of Aphiah; a Benjaminite and a man of rank. He had a son named Saul, a handsome man in the prime of life. Of all the Israelites there was no one more handsome than he; he stood head and shoulders taller than the rest of the people. Now some of the she-donkeys of Saul's father Kish had strayed, so

Kish said to Saul, 'My son, take one of the servants with you and be off; go and look for the she-donkeys.' They passed through the highlands of Ephraim and passed through the land of Shalishah, but did not find them; they passed through the land of Shaalim, they were not there; they passed through the land of Benjamin, but did not find them.

When Samuel saw Saul, the Lord told him, 'That is the man of whom I told you; he shall rule my people.' Saul accosted Samuel in the gateway and said, 'Tell me, please, where the seer's house is?' Samuel replied to Saul, 'I am the seer. Go up ahead of me to the high place. You are to eat with me today. In the morning I shall take leave of you and tell you all that is in your heart.'

Samuel took a phial of oil and poured it on Saul's head; then he kissed him, saying, 'Has not the Lord anointed you prince over his people Israel? You are the man who must rule the Lord's people, and who must save them from the power of the enemies surrounding them.'

This is the word of the Lord.

Responsorial Psalm   Ps 20:2-7. ℟ v.2

℟   Lord, your strength gives joy to the king.

1   O Lord, your strength gives joy to the king;
    how your saving help makes him glad!
    You have granted him his heart's desire;
    you have not refused the prayer of his lips.   ℟

2   You came to meet him with the blessings of success,
    you have set on his head a crown of pure gold.
    He asked you for life and this you have given,
    days that will last from age to age.   ℟

3   Your saving help has given him glory.
    You have laid upon him majesty and splendour,
    you have granted your blessings to him for ever.
    You have made him rejoice with the joy of your presence.   ℟

Gospel Acclamation   Lk 4:18

Alleluia, alleluia!
The Lord sent me to bring Good News to the poor
and freedom to prisoners.
Alleluia!

GOSPEL

A reading from the holy Gospel according to Mark   2:13-17

I have not come to call the just, but sinners.

Jesus went out to the shore of the lake; and all the people came to him,
and he taught them. As he was walking on he saw Levi the son of
Alphaeus, sitting by the customs house, and he said to him, 'Follow
me.' And he got up and followed him.

When Jesus was at dinner in his house, a number of tax collectors
and sinners were also sitting at the table with Jesus and his disciples;
for there were many of them among his followers. When the scribes of
the Pharisee party saw him eating with sinners and tax collectors,
they said to his disciples, 'Why does he eat with tax collectors and
sinners?' When Jesus heard this he said to them, 'It is not the healthy
who need the doctor, but the sick. I did not come to call the virtuous,
but sinners.'

This is the Gospel of the Lord.

SECOND WEEK IN ORDINARY TIME

Year II

Monday

FIRST READING

A reading from the first book of Samuel   15:16-23

Obedience is better than sacrifice. Since you have rejected the voice of the Lord God, he has rejected you as king.

Samuel said to Saul, 'Stop! Let me tell you what the Lord said to me last night.' Saul said, 'Tell me.' Samuel continued, 'Small as you may be in your own eyes, are you not head of the tribes of Israel? The Lord has anointed you king over Israel. The Lord sent you on a mission and said to you, "Go, put these sinners, the Amalekites, under the ban and make war on them until they are exterminated." Why then did you not obey the voice of the Lord? Why did you fall on the booty and do what is displeasing to the Lord?' Saul replied to Samuel, 'But I did obey the voice of the Lord. I went on the mission which the Lord gave me; I brought back Agag king of the Amalekites; I put the Amalekites under the ban. From the booty the people took the best sheep and oxen of what was under the ban to sacrifice them to the Lord your God in Gilgal.' But Samuel replied:

'Is the pleasure of the Lord in holocausts and sacrifices
or in obedience to the voice of the Lord?
Yes, obedience is better than sacrifice,
submissiveness better than the fat of rams.
Rebellion is a sin of sorcery,
presumption a crime of teraphim.

'Since you have rejected the word of the Lord, he has rejected you as king.'

This is the word of the Lord.

Responsorial Psalm   Ps 49:8-9. 16-17. 21. 23. ℟ v.23

    ℟ To the upright I will show the saving power of God.

1 'I find no fault with your sacrifices,
     your offerings are always before me.
     I do not ask more bullocks from your farms,
     nor goats from among your herds. ℟

2 'But how can you recite my commandments
     and take my covenant on your lips,
     you who despise my law
     and throw my words to the winds. ℟

3 'You do this, and should I keep silence?
     Do you think that I am like you?
     a sacrifice of thanksgiving honours me
     and I will show God's salvation to the upright.' ℟

Gospel Acclamation   Heb 4:12

    Alleluia, alleluia!
    The word of the God is living and active;
    it probes the thoughts and motives of our heart.
    Alleluia!

GOSPEL

A reading from the holy Gospel according to Mark   2:18-22

The bridegroom is still with them.

One day when John's disciples and the Pharisees were fasting, some people came and said to Jesus, 'Why is it that John's disciples and the disciples of the Pharisees fast, but your disciples do not?' Jesus replied, 'Surely the bridegroom's attendants would never think of fasting while the bridegroom is still with them? As long as they have the bridegroom with them, they could not think of fasting. But the time will come for the bridegroom to be taken away from them, and then, on that day, they will fast. No one sews a piece of unshrunken cloth on an old cloak; if he does, the patch pulls away from it, the new from the old, and the tear gets worse. And nobody puts new wine into old wineskins; if he does, the wine will burst the skins, and the wine is lost and the skins too. No! New wine, fresh skins!'

    This is the Gospel of the Lord.

Tuesday

FIRST READING

A reading from the first book of Samuel   16:1-13

Samuel anointed David where he stood with his brothers, and the
Spirit of the Lord God was with him.

The Lord said to Samuel, 'How long will you go on mourning over Saul
when I have rejected him as king of Israel? Fill your horn with oil and
go. I am sending you to Jesse of Bethlehem, for I have chosen myself a
king among his sons.' Samuel replied, 'How can I go? When Saul hears
of it he will kill me.' Then the Lord said, 'Take a heifer with you and
say, "I have come to sacrifice to the Lord." Invite Jesse to the sacrifice,
and then I myself will tell you what you must do; you must anoint to
me the one I point out to you.'

Samuel did what the Lord ordered and went to Bethlehem. The
elders of the town came trembling to meet him and asked, 'Seer, have
you come with good intentions towards us?' 'Yes,' he replied 'I have
come to sacrifice to the Lord. Purify yourselves and come with me to
the sacrifice.' He purified Jesse and his sons and invited them to the
sacrifice.

When they arrived, he caught sight of Eliab and thought, 'Surely
the Lord's anointed one stands there before him,' but the Lord said to
Samuel, 'Take no notice of his appearance or his height for I have
rejected him; God does not see as man sees; man looks at appearances
but the Lord looks at the heart.' Jesse then called Abinadab and
presented him to Samuel, who said, 'The Lord has not chosen this one
either.' Jesse then presented Shammah, but Samuel said, 'The Lord
has not chosen this one either.' Jesse presented his seven sons to
Samuel, but Samuel said to Jesse, 'The Lord has not chosen these.' He
then asked Jesse, 'Are these all the sons you have?' He answered,
'There is still one left, the youngest; he is out looking after the sheep.'
Then Samuel said to Jesse, 'Send for him; we will not sit down to eat
until he comes.' Jesse had him sent for, a boy of fresh complexion, with
fine eyes and pleasant bearing. The Lord said, 'Come, anoint him, for
this is the one.' At this, Samuel took the horn of oil and anointed him
where he stood with his brothers; and the spirit of the Lord seized on
David and stayed with him from that day on. As for Samuel, he rose
and went to Ramah.

This is the word of the Lord.

Responsorial Psalm   Ps 88:20-22. 27-28. ℟ v.21

℟   I have found David, my servant.

1   Of old you spoke in a vision.
    To your friends the prophets you said:
    'I have set the crown on a warrior,
    I have exalted one chosen from the people.   ℟

2   'I have found David my servant
    and with my holy oil anointed him.
    My hand shall always be with him
    and my arm shall make him strong.   ℟

3   'He will say to me: "You are my father,
    my God, the rock who saves me."
    And I will make him my first-born,
    the highest of the kings of the earth.'   ℟

Gospel Acclamation   cf. Eph 1:17.18

    Alleluia, alleluia!
    May the Father of our Lord Jesus Christ
    enlighten the eyes of our heart
    that we might see how great is the hope
    to which we are called.
    Alleluia!

GOSPEL

A reading from the holy Gospel according to Mark   2:23-28

The sabbath was made for people, not people for the sabbath.

One sabbath day Jesus happened to be taking a walk through the cornfields, and his disciples began to pick ears of corn as they went along. And the Pharisees said to him. 'Look, why are they doing something on the sabbath day that is forbidden?' And he replied, 'Did you never read what David did in his time of need when he and his followers were hungry – how he went into the house of God when Abiathar was high priest, and ate the loaves of offering which only the priests are allowed to eat, and how he also gave some to the men with him?'

    And he said to them, 'The sabbath was made for man, not man for the sabbath; so the Son of Man is master even of the sabbath.'

    This is the Gospel of the Lord.

Wednesday

FIRST READING

A reading from the first book of Samuel   17:32-33. 37. 40-51

David triumphed over the Philistine with a sling and a stone.

David said to Saul, 'Let no one lose heart on his account; your servant will go and fight this Philistine.' But Saul answered David, 'You cannot go and fight the Philistine; you are only a boy and he has been a warrior from his youth.' 'The Lord who rescued me from the claws of lion and bear,' David said, 'will rescue me from the power of this Philistine.' Then Saul said to David, 'Go, and the Lord be with you!'

He took his staff in his hand, picked five smooth stones from the river bed, put them in his shepherd's bag, in his pouch, and with his sling in his hand he went to meet the Philistine. The Philistine, his shield-bearer in front of him, came nearer and nearer to David; and the Philistine looked at David, and what he saw filled him with scorn, because David was only a youth, a boy of fresh complexion and pleasant bearing. The Philistine said to him, 'Am I a dog for you to come against me with sticks?' And the Philistine cursed David by his gods. The Philistine said to David, 'Come over here and I will give your flesh to the birds of the air and the beasts of the field.' But David answered the Philistine, 'You come against me with sword and spear and javelin, but I come against you in the name of the Lord of hosts, the God of the armies of Israel that you have dared to insult. Today the Lord will deliver you into my hand and I shall kill you; I will cut off your head, and this very day I will give your dead body and the bodies of the Philistine army to the birds of the air and the wild beasts of the earth, so that all the earth may know that there is a God in Israel, and that all this assembly may know that it is not by sword or by spear that the Lord gives the victory, for he is lord of the battle and he will deliver you into our power.'

No sooner had the Philistine started forward to confront David than David left the line of battle and ran to meet the Philistine. Putting his hand in his bag, he took out a stone and slung it and struck the Philistine on the forehead; the stone penetrated his forehead and he fell on his face to the ground. Thus David triumphed over the Philistine with a sling and a stone and struck the Philistine down and killed him. David had no sword in his hand. Then David ran and, standing over the Philistine, seized his sword and drew it from the scabbard, and with this he killed him, cutting off his head. The Philistines saw that their champion was dead and took to flight.

This is the word of the Lord.

Responsorial Psalm   Ps 143:1-2. 9-10. ℟ v.1

℟   Blessed be the Lord, my Rock!

1   Blessed be the Lord, my rock
     who trains my arms for battle,
     who prepares my hands for war.   ℟

2   He is my love, my fortress;
     he is my stronghold, my saviour,
     my shield, my place of refuge.
     He brings peoples under my rule.   ℟

3   To you, O God, will I sing a new song;
     I will play on the ten-stringed lute
     to you who give kings their victory,
     who set David your servant free.   ℟

Gospel Acclamation   cf. Mt 4:23

     Alleluia, alleluia!
     Jesus preached the Good News of the kingdom
     and healed all who were sick.
     Alleluia!

GOSPEL

A reading from the holy Gospel according to Mark   3:1-6

Is it against the law on the sabbath day to do good – to save life or to kill?

Jesus went into a synagogue, and there was a man there who had a withered hand. And they were watching him to see if he would cure him on the sabbath day, hoping for something to use against him. He said to the man with the withered hand, 'Stand up out in the middle!' Then he said to them, 'Is it against the law on the sabbath day to do good or to do evil; to save life, or to kill?' But they said nothing. Then, grieved to find them so obstinate, he looked angrily round at them, and said to the man, 'Stretch out your hand.' He stretched it out and his hand was better. The Pharisees went out and at once began to plot with the Herodians against him, discussing how to destroy him.

This is the Gospel of the Lord.

Thursday

FIRST READING

A reading from the first book of Samuel   18:6-9; 19:1-7

My father Saul is looking for a way to kill you.

On their way back, as David was returning after killing the Philistine, the women came out to meet King Saul from all the towns of Israel, singing and dancing to the sound of tambourine and lyre and cries of joy; and as they danced the women sang:

'Saul has killed his thousands,
and David his tens of thousands.'

Saul was very angry; the incident was not to his liking. 'They have given David the tens of thousands,' he said, 'but me only the thousands; he has all but the kingship now.' And Saul turned a jealous eye on David from that day forward.

Saul told Jonathan his son and all his servants of his intention to kill David. Now Jonathan, Saul's son, held David in great affection; and so Jonathan warned David; 'My father Saul is looking for a way to kill you,' he said, 'so be on your guard tomorrow morning; hide away in some secret place. Then I will go and keep my father company in the fields where you are hiding, and will talk to my father about you; I will find out what the situation is and let you know.'

So Jonathan spoke well of David to Saul his father; he said, 'Let not the king sin against his servant David, for he has not sinned against you, and what he has done has been greatly to your advantage. He took his life in his hands when he killed the Philistine, and the Lord brought about a great victory for all Israel. You saw it yourself and rejoiced; why then sin against innocent blood in killing David without cause?' Saul was impressed by Jonathan's words and took an oath, 'As the Lord lives, I will not kill him.' Jonathan called David and told him all these things. Then Jonathan brought him to Saul, and David attended on him as before.

This is the word of the Lord.

Responsorial Psalm   Ps 55:2-3. 9-14. ℟ v.5

℟   In God I trust;
    I shall not fear.

1   Have mercy on me, God, men crush me;
    they fight me all day long and oppress me.
    My foes crush me all the day long,
    for many fight proudly against me.   ℟

2   You have kept an account of my wanderings;
    you have kept a record of my tears;
    (are they not written in your book?)
    Then my foes will be put to flight
    on the day I call to you.   ℟

3   This I know, that God is on my side.
    In God, whose word I praise,
    in the Lord, whose word I praise,
    in God I trust; I shall not fear;
    what can mortal man do to me?   ℟

4   I am bound by the vows I have made you.
    O God, I will offer you praise
    for you rescued my soul from death,
    you kept my feet from stumbling
    that I may walk in the presence of God
    in the light of the living.   ℟

Gospel Acclamation   cf. 2 Tim 1:10

    Alleluia, alleluia!
    Our Saviour Jesus Christ has done away with death
    and brought us life through his gospel.
    Alleluia!

GOSPEL

A reading from the holy Gospel according to Mark   3:7-12

The unclean spirits shouted, you are the Son of God, but he warned them not to make him known.

Jesus withdrew with his disciples to the lakeside, and great crowds from Galilee followed him. From Judaea, Jerusalem, Idumaea,

Transjordania and the region of Tyre and Sidon, great numbers who had heard of all he was doing came to him. And he asked his disciples to have a boat ready for him because of the crowd, to keep him from being crushed. For he had cured so many that all who were afflicted in any way were crowding forward to touch him. And the unclean spirits, whenever they saw him, would fall down before him and shout, 'You are the Son of God!' But he warned them strongly not to make him known.

This is the Gospel of the Lord.

Friday

FIRST READING

A reading from the first book of Samuel   24:3-21

I shall not raise my hand against him, for he is the anointed of the Lord God.

Saul took three thousand men chosen from the whole of Israel and went in search of David and his men east of the Rocks of the Wild Goats. He came to the sheep-folds along the route where there was a cave, and went in to cover his feet. Now David and his men were sitting in the recesses of the cave; David's men said to him, 'Today is the day of which the Lord said to you, "I will deliver your enemy into your power, do what you like with him."' David stood up and, unobserved, cut off the border of Saul's cloak. Afterwards David reproached himself for having cut off the border of Saul's cloak. He said to his men, 'The Lord preserve me from doing such a thing to my lord and raising my hand against him, for he is the anointed of the Lord.' David gave his men strict instructions, forbidding them to attack Saul.

Saul then left the cave and went on his way. After this, David too left the cave and called after Saul, 'My lord king!' Saul looked behind him and David bowed to the ground and did homage. Then David said to Saul, 'Why do you listen to the men who say to you, "David means to harm you"? Why, your own eyes have seen today how the Lord put you in my power in the cave and how I refused to kill you, but spared you. "I will not raise my hand against my lord," I said, "for he is the anointed of the Lord." O my father, see, look at the border of your cloak in my hand. Since I cut off the border of your cloak, yet did not kill you, you must acknowledge frankly that there is neither malice nor treason in my mind. I have not offended against you, yet you hunt me down to take my life. May the Lord be judge between me and you, and may the Lord avenge me on you; but my hand shall not be laid on you. (As the old proverb says: Wickedness goes out from the wicked, and my hand will not be laid on you.) On whose trail has the king of Israel set out? On whose trail are you in hot pursuit? On the trail of a dead dog! On the trail of a single flea! May the Lord be the judge and decide between me and you ; may he take up my cause and defend it and give judgement for me, freeing me from your power.'

When David had finished saying these words to Saul, Saul said, 'Is that your voice, my son David?' And Saul wept aloud. 'You are a more upright man than I,' he said to David, 'for you have repaid me with good while I have repaid you with evil. Today you have crowned your goodness towards me since the Lord had put me in your power yet you did not kill me. When a man comes on his enemy, does he let him go unmolested? May the Lord reward you for the goodness you have shown me today. Now I know you will indeed reign and that the sovereignty in Israel will be secure in your hands.'

This is the word of the Lord.

Responsorial Psalm   Ps 56:2-4. 6. 11. ℟ v.2

 ℟ Have mercy on me, God, have mercy.

1 Have mercy on me, God, have mercy
 for in you my soul has taken refuge.
 In the shadow of your wings I take refuge
 till the storms of destruction pass by. ℟

2 I call to God the Most High,
 to God who has always been my help.
 May he send from heaven and save me
 and shame those who assail me.
 May God send his truth and his love. ℟

3 O God, arise above the heavens;
 may your glory shine on earth,
 for your love reaches to the heavens
 and your truth to the skies. ℟

Gospel Acclamation   2 Cor 5:19

> Alleluia, alleluia!
> God was in Christ, to reconcile the world to himself;
> and the Good News of reconciliation he has entrusted to us.
> Alleluia!

GOSPEL

A reading from the holy Gospel according to Mark   3:13-19

He called those he wanted and they went with him.

Jesus went up into the hills and summ⌐ned those he wanted. So they came to him and he appointed twelve; they were to be his companions and to be sent out to preach, with power to cast out devils. And so he appointed the Twelve: Simon to whom he gave the name Peter, James the son of Zebedee and John the brother of James, to whom he gave the name Boanerges or 'Sons of Thunder'; then Andrew, Philip, Bartholomew, Matthew, Thomas, James the son of Alphaeus, Thaddaeus, Simon the Zealot and Judas Iscariot, the man who was to betray him.

This is the Gospel of the Lord.

Saturday

FIRST READING

A reading from the second book   1:1-4. 11-12. 17. 19. 23-27
of Samuel

How were the heroes killed in the battle?

David returned from his rout of the Amalekites and spent two days in Ziklag. On the third day a man came from the camp where Saul had been, his garments torn and earth on his head. When he came to David, he fell to the ground and did homage. 'Where do you come from?' David asked him. 'I have escaped from the Israelite camp,' he said. David said to him, 'What happened? Tell me.' He replied, 'The people have fled from the battlefield and many of them have fallen. Saul and his son Jonathan are dead too.'

Then David took hold of his garments and tore them, and all the men did the same. They mourned and wept and fasted until the evening for Saul and his son Jonathan, for the people of the Lord and for the House of Israel, because they had fallen by the sword.

Then David made this lament over Saul and his son Jonathan:

Alas, the glory of Israel has been slain on your heights!
How did the heroes fall?
Saul and Jonathan, loved and lovely,
neither in life, nor in death, were divided.
Swifter than eagles were they,
stronger were they than lions.
O daughters of Israel, weep for Saul
who clothed you in scarlet and fine linen,
who set brooches of gold
on your garments.
How did the heroes fall
in the thick of the battle?
O Jonathan, in your death I am stricken,
I am desolate for you, Jonathan my brother.
Very dear to me you were,
your love to me more wonderful
than the love of a woman.
How did the heroes fall
and the battle armour fail?

This is the word of the Lord.

Responsorial Psalm   Ps 79:2-3. 5-7. ℟ v.4

℟   Let us see your face, Lord,
      and we shall be saved.

1   O shepherd of Israel, hear us,
      you who lead Joseph's flock,
      shine forth from your cherubim throne
      upon Ephraim, Benjamin, Manasseh.
      O Lord, rouse up your might,
      O Lord, come to our help.   ℟

2   Lord God of hosts, how long
      will you frown on your people's plea?
      You have fed them with tears for their bread,
      an abundance of tears for their drink.
      You have made us the taunt of our neighbours,
      our enemies laugh us to scorn.   ℟

449

Gospel Acclamation   cf. Acts 16:14

Alleluia, alleluia!
Open our hearts, O Lord,
to listen to the words of your Son.
Alleluia!

GOSPEL

A reading from the holy Gospel according to Mark   3:20-21

The people said that he was out of his mind.

Jesus went home, and such a crowd collected that they could not even have a meal. When his relatives heard of this, they set out to take charge of him, convinced he was out of his mind.

This is the Gospel of the Lord.

THIRD WEEK IN ORDINARY TIME
Year II

Monday

FIRST READING

A reading from the second book of Samuel   5:1-7. 10

You shall be the leader of my people Israel.

All the tribes of Israel came to David at Hebron. 'Look' they said 'we are your own flesh and blood. In days past when Saul was our king, it was you who led Israel in all their exploits; and the Lord said to you, "You are the man who shall be shepherd of my people Israel, you shall be the leader of Israel." ' So all the elders of Israel came to the king at Hebron, and King David made a pact with them at Hebron in the presence of the Lord, and they anointed David king of Israel.

David was thirty years old when he became king, and he reigned for forty years. He reigned in Hebron over Judah for seven years and six months; then he reigned in Jerusalem over all Israel and Judah for thirty-three years.

David and his men marched on Jerusalem against the Jebusites living there. These said to David, 'You will not get in here. The blind and the lame will hold you off.' (That is to say: David will never get in here.) But David captured the fortress of Zion, that is, the Citadel of David.

He grew greater and greater, and the Lord, the God of hosts, was with him.

This is the word of the Lord.

Responsorial Psalm   Ps 88:20-22. 25-26. ℟ v.25

℟   My faithfulness and love shall be with him.

1   Of old you spoke in a vision.
    To your friends the prophets you said:
    'I have set the crown on a warrior,
    I have exalted one chosen from the people.   ℟

2   'I have found David my servant
    and with my holy oil anointed him.
    My hand shall always be with him
    and my arm shall make him strong.   ℟

3   'My truth and my love shall be with him;
    by my name his might shall be exalted.
    I will stretch out his hand to the Sea
    and his right hand as far as the River.'   ℟

Gospel Acclamation   cf. 2 Tim 1:10

Alleluia, alleluia!
Our Saviour Jesus Christ has done away with death
and brought us life through his gospel.
Alleluia!

GOSPEL

A reading from the holy Gospel according to Mark   3:22-30

It is the end of Satan.

The scribes who had come down from Jerusalem were saying: 'Beelzebul is in him' and, 'It is through the prince of devils that he casts devils out.' So Jesus called them to him and spoke to them in parables, 'How can Satan cast out Satan? If a kingdom is divided against itself, that kingdom cannot last. And if a household is divided against itself, that household can never stand. Now if Satan has rebelled against himself and is divided, he cannot stand either – it is the end of him. But no one can make his way into a strong man's house and burgle his property unless he has tied up the strong man first. Only then can he burgle his house.

'I tell you solemnly, all men's sins will be forgiven, and all their blasphemies; but let anyone blaspheme against the Holy Spirit and he will never have forgiveness: he is guilty of an eternal sin.' This was because they were saying, 'An unclean spirit is in him.'

This is the Gospel of the Lord.

Tuesday

FIRST READING

A reading from the second book of Samuel   6:12-15. 17-19

David and all the house of Israel led the ark of the Lord God in jubilation.

David went and brought the ark of God up from Obed-edom's house to the Citadel of David with great rejoicing. When the bearers of the ark of the Lord had gone six paces, he sacrificed an ox and a fat sheep. And David danced whirling round before the Lord with all his might, wearing a linen loincloth round him. Thus David and all the House of Israel brought up the ark of the Lord with acclaim and the sound of the horn. They brought the ark of the Lord and put it in position inside the tent that David had pitched for it; and David offered holocausts before the Lord, and communion sacrifices. And when David had finished offering holocausts and communion sacrifices, he blessed the people in the name of the Lord of hosts. He then distributed among all the people, among the whole multitude of Israelites, men and women, a roll of bread to each, a portion of dates, and a raisin cake. Then they all went away, each to his own house.

This is the word of the Lord.

Responsorial Psalm   Ps 23:7-10. ℞ v.8

   ℞   Who is this king of glory?
       It is the Lord!

1   O gates, lift high your heads;
     grow higher, ancient doors.
     Let him enter, the king of glory! ℞

2   Who is the king of glory?
     The Lord, the mighty, the valiant,
     the Lord, the valiant in war. ℞

3   O gates, lift high your heads;
     grow higher, ancient doors.
     Let him enter, the king of glory! ℞

4   Who is he, the king of glory?
     He, the Lord of armies,
     he is the king of glory. ℞

Gospel Acclamation   cf. Mt 11:25

   Alleluia, alleluia!
   Blessed are you, Father, Lord of heaven and earth;
   you have revealed to little ones the mysteries of the kingdom.
   Alleluia!

GOSPEL

A reading from the holy Gospel according to Mark   3:31-35

Here are my mother and my brother: anyone who does the will of God.

The mother and brothers of Jesus arrived and, standing outside, sent in a message asking for him. A crowd was sitting round him at the time the message was passed to him, 'Your mother and brothers and sisters are outside asking for you.' He replied, 'Who are my mother and my brothers?' And looking round at those sitting in a circle about him, he said, 'Here are my mother and my brothers. Anyone who does the will of God, that person is my brother and sister and mother.'

This is the Gospel of the Lord.

Wednesday

FIRST READING

A reading from the second book of Samuel   7:4-17

*I will preserve the offspring of your body after you and make his
sovereignty secure.*

The word of the Lord came to Nathan:

'Go and tell my servant David, "Thus the Lord speaks: Are you the
man to build me a house to dwell in? I have never stayed in a house
from the day I brought the Israelites out of Egypt until today, but
have always led a wanderer's life in a tent. In all my journeying with
the whole people of Israel, did I say to any one of the judges of Israel,
whom I had appointed as shepherds of Israel my people: Why have you
not built me a house of cedar?" This is what you must say to my
servant David, "The Lord of hosts says this: I took you from the
pasture, from following the sheep, to be leader of my people Israel; I
have been with you on all your expeditions; I have cut off all your
enemies before you. I will give you fame as great as the fame of the
greatest on earth. I will provide a place for my people Israel; I will
plant them there and they shall dwell in that place and never be
disturbed again; nor shall the wicked continue to oppress them as
they did, in the days when I appointed judges over my people Israel; I
will give them rest from all their enemies. The Lord will make you
great; the Lord will make you a House. And when your days are ended
and you are laid to rest with your ancestors, I will preserve the
offspring of your body after you and make his sovereignty secure. (It is
he who shall build a house for my name, and I will make his royal
throne secure for ever.) I will be a father to him and he a son to me; if
he does evil, I will punish him with the rod such as men use, with
strokes such as mankind gives. Yet I will not withdraw my favour
from him, as I withdrew it from your predecessor. Your House and
your sovereignty will always stand secure before me and your throne
be established for ever." '

Nathan related all these words to David and this whole revelation.

This is the word of the Lord.

Responsorial Psalm   Ps 88:4-5. 27-30. ℞ v.29

℞ For ever I will keep my love for him.

1 I have made a covenant with my chosen one;
   I have sworn to David my servant:
   I will establish your dynasty for ever
   and set up your throne through all ages. ℞

2 He will say to me: 'You are my father,
   my God, the rock who saves me.'
   And I will make him my first-born,
   the highest of the kings of the earth. ℞

3 I will keep my love for him always;
   for him my covenant shall endure.
   I will establish his dynasty for ever,
   make his throne as lasting as the heavens. ℞

Gospel Acclamation

    Alleluia, alleluia!
    The seed is the word of God, Christ is the sower;
    all who come to him will live for ever.
    Alleluia!

GOSPEL

A reading from the holy Gospel according to Mark   4:1-20

The sower goes out to sow.

Jesus began to teach by the lakeside, but such a huge crowd gathered round him that he got into a boat on the lake and sat there. The people were all along the shore, at the water's edge. He taught them many things in parables, and in the course of his teaching he said to them, 'Listen! Imagine a sower going out to sow. Now it happened that, as he sowed, some of the seed fell on the edge of the path, and the birds came and ate it up. Some seed fell on rocky ground where it found little soil and sprang up straightaway, because there was no depth of earth; and when the sun came up it was scorched and, not having any roots, it withered away. Some seed fell into thorns, and the thorns grew up and choked it, and it produced no crop. And some seed fell into rich soil and, growing tall and strong, produced crop; and yielded thirty, sixty, even a hundredfold.' And he said, 'Listen, anyone who has ears to hear.'

When he was alone, the Twelve, together with the others who formed his company, asked what the parables meant. He told them, 'The secret of the kingdom of God is given to you, but to those who are outside everything comes in parables, so that they may see and see again, but not perceive; may hear and hear again, but not understand; otherwise they might be converted and be forgiven.'

He said to them, 'Do you not understand this parable? Then how will you understand any of the parables? What the sower is sowing is the word. Those on the edge of the path where the word is sown are people who have no sooner heard it than Satan comes and carries away the word that was sown in them. Similarly, those who receive the seed on patches of rock are people who, when first they hear the word, welcome it at once with joy. But they have no root in them, they do not last; should some trial come, or some persecution on account of the word, they fall away at once. Then there are others who receive the seed in thorns. These have heard the word, but the worries of this world, the lure of riches and all the other passions come in to choke the word, and so it produces nothing. And there are those who have received the seed in rich soil: they hear the word and accept it and yield a harvest, thirty and sixty and a hundredfold.'

This is the Gospel of the Lord.

Thursday

FIRST READING

A reading from the second book of Samuel   7:18-19. 24-29

Who am I, the Lord God, and what is my house?

After Nathan had spoken to David, the King went in and, seated before the Lord, said:

'Who am I, Lord, and what is my House, that you have led me as far as this? Yet in your sight, Lord, this is still not far enough, and you make your promises extend to the House of your servant for a far-distant future. You have constituted your people Israel to be your own people for ever; and you, Lord, have become their God. Now, Lord, always keep the promise you have made your servant and his House, and do as you have said. Your name will be exalted for ever and men will say, "The Lord of hosts is God over Israel." The House of your servant David will be made secure in your presence, since you yourself, Lord of hosts, God of Israel, have made this revelation to your servant, "I will build you a House;" hence your servant has ventured to offer this prayer to you. Yes, Lord, you are God indeed, your words are true and you have made this fair promise to your servant. Be pleased, then, to bless the House of your servant, that it may continue for ever in your presence; for you, Lord, have spoken; and with your blessing the House of your servant will be for ever blessed.'

This is the word of the Lord.

Responsorial Psalm   Ps 131:1-5. 11-14. ℟ Lk 1:32

℟   God will give him the throne of David, his father.

1   O Lord, remember David
    and all the hardships he endured,
    the oath he swore to the Lord,
    his vow to the Strong One of Jacob.   ℟

2   'I will not enter the house where I live
    nor go to the bed where I rest.
    I will give no sleep to my eyes
    to my eyelids will give no slumber
    till I find a place for the Lord,
    a dwelling for the Strong One of Jacob.'   ℟

3   The Lord swore an oath to David;
    he will not go back on his word:
    'A son, the fruit of your body,
    will I set upon your throne.   ℟

4   'If they keep my covenant in truth
    and my laws that I have taught them,
    their sons also shall rule
    on your throne from age to age.'   ℟

5   For the Lord has chosen Zion;
    he has desired it for his dwelling:
    'This is my resting-place for ever,
    here have I chosen to live.'   ℟

Gospel Acclamation   Ps 118:105

> Alleluia, alleluia!
> Your word is a lamp for my feet
> and a light on my path.
> Alleluia!

GOSPEL

A reading from the holy Gospel according to Mark   4:21-25

Come and place your lamp on a stand. In the measure you give you
shall receive.

Jesus said to the crowd: 'Would you bring in a lamp to put it under a tub or under the bed? Surely you will put it on the lamp-stand? For there is nothing hidden but it must be disclosed, nothing kept secret except to be brought to light. If anyone has ears to hear, let him listen to this.'

He also said to them, 'Take notice of what you are hearing. The amount you measure out is the amount you will be given – and more besides; for the man who has will be given more; from the man who has not, even what he has will be taken away.'

This is the Gospel of the Lord.

Friday

FIRST READING

A reading from the second book of Samuel   11:1-10. 13-17

You have defied me and taken the wife of Uriah for your own wife.

At the turn of the year, the time when kings go campaigning, David sent Joab and with him his own guards and the whole of Israel. They massacred the Ammonites and laid siege to Rabbah. David however remained in Jerusalem.

It happened towards evening when David had risen from his couch and was strolling on the palace roof, that he saw from the roof a woman bathing; the woman was very beautiful. David made inquiries about this woman and was told, 'Why, that is Bathsheba, Eliam's daughter, the wife of Uriah the Hittite.' Then David sent messengers and had her brought. She came to him, and he slept with her. She then went home again. The woman conceived and sent word to David, 'I am with child.'

Then David sent Joab a message, 'Send me Uriah the Hittite,' whereupon Joab sent Uriah to David. When Uriah came into his presence, David asked after Joab and the army and how the war was going. David then said to Uriah, 'Go down to your house and enjoy yourself.' Uriah left the palace, and was followed by a present from the king's table. Uriah however slept by the palace door with his master's bodyguard and did not go down to his house.

This was reported to David; 'Uriah' they said 'did not go down to his house.' The next day David invited him to eat and drink in his presence and made him drunk. In the evening Uriah went out and lay on his couch with his master's bodyguard, but he did not go down to his house.

Next morning David wrote a letter to Joab and sent it by Uriah. In the letter he wrote, 'Station Uriah in the thick of the fight and then fall back behind him so that he may be struck down and die.' Joab, then besieging the town, posted Uriah in a place where he knew there were fierce fighters. The men of the town sallied out and engaged Joab; the army suffered casualties, including some of David's body-guard; and Uriah the Hittite was killed too.

This is the word of the Lord.

Responsorial Psalm   Ps 50:3-7. 10-11. ℟ cf. v.3

℟ Be merciful, O Lord, for we have sinned.

1 Have mercy on me, God, in your kindness.
   In your compassion blot out my offence.
   O wash me more and more from my guilt
   and cleanse me from my sin. ℟

2 My offences truly I know them;
   my sin is always before me.
   Against you, you alone, have I sinned;
   what is evil in your sight I have done. ℟

3 That you may be justified when you give sentence
   and be without reproach when you judge,
   O see, in guilt I was born,
   a sinner was I conceived. ℟   (continued)

459

4   Make me hear rejoicing and gladness,
that the bones you have crushed may thrill.
From my sins turn away your face
and blot out all my guilt.

℟   Be merciful, O Lord, for we have sinned.

Gospel Acclamation

cf. Mt 11:25

Alleluia, alleluia!
Blessed are you, Father, Lord of heaven and earth;
you have revealed to little ones the mysteries of the kingdom.
Alleluia!

GOSPEL

A reading from the holy Gospel according to Mark   4:26-34

*A man scatters seed and while he sleeps it grows even though he does
not know how.*

Jesus said to the crowd: 'This is what the kingdom of God is like. A
man throws seed on the land. Night and day, while he sleeps, when he
is awake, the seed is sprouting and growing; how, he does not know.
Of its own accord the land produces first the shoot, then the ear, then
the full grain in the ear. And when the crop is ready, he loses no time:
he starts to reap because the harvest has come.'

He also said, 'What can we say the kingdom of God is like? What
parable can we find for it? It is like a mustard seed which at the time
of its sowing in the soil is the smallest of all the seeds on earth; yet
once it is sown it grows into the biggest shrub of them all and puts out
big branches so that the birds of the air can shelter in its shade.'

Using many parables like these, he spoke the word to them, so far
as they were capable of understanding it. He would not speak to them
except in parables, but he explained everything to his disciples when
they were alone.

This is the Gospel of the Lord.

Saturday

FIRST READING

A reading from the second book of Samuel   12:1-7. 10-17

I have sinned against the Lord God.

The Lord sent Nathan the prophet to David. He came to him and said:

'In the same town were two men,
one rich, the other poor.
The rich man had flocks and herds
in great abundance;
the poor man had nothing but a ewe lamb,
one only, a small one he had bought.
This he fed, and it grew up with him and his children,
eating his bread, drinking from his cup,
sleeping on his breast; it was like a daughter to him.
When there came a traveller to stay the rich man
refused to take one of his own flock or herd
to provide for the wayfarer who had come to him.
Instead he took the poor man's lamb
and prepared it for his guest.'

David's anger flared up against the man. 'As the Lord lives,' he said to Nathan 'the man who did this deserves to die! He must make fourfold restitution for the lamb, for doing such a thing and showing no compassion.'

Then Nathan said to David, 'You are the man. So now the sword will never be far from your House, since you have shown contempt for me and taken the wife of Uriah the Hittite to be your wife.

'Thus the Lord speaks, "I will stir up evil for you out of your own House. Before your very eyes I will take your wives and give them to your neighbour, and he shall lie with your wives in the sight of this sun. You worked in secret, I will work this in the face of all Israel and in the face of the sun." '

David said to Nathan, 'I have sinned against the Lord.' Then Nathan said to David, 'The Lord, for his part, forgives your sin; you are not to die. Yet because you have outraged the Lord by doing this, the child that is born to you is to die.' Then Nathan went home.

The Lord struck the child that Uriah's wife had borne to David and it fell gravely ill. David pleaded with the Lord for the child; he kept a strict fast and went home and spent the night on the bare ground,

461

covered with sacking. The officials of his household came and stood round him to get him to rise from the ground, but he refused, nor would he take food with them.

This is the word of the Lord.

Responsorial Psalm Ps 50:12-17. ℟ v.12

℟ Create a clean heart in me, O God.

1 A pure heart create for me, O God,
   put a steadfast spirit within me.
   Do not cast me away from your presence,
   nor deprive me of your holy spirit. ℟

2 Give me again the joy of your help;
   with a spirit of fervour sustain me,
   that I may teach transgressors your ways
   and sinners may return to you. ℟

3 O rescue me, God, my helper,
   and my tongue shall ring out your goodness.
   O Lord, open my lips
   and my mouth shall declare your praise. ℟

Gospel Acclamation Jn 3:16

Alleluia, alleluia!
God loved the world so much, he gave us his only Son,
that all who believe in him might have eternal life.
Alleluia!

GOSPEL

A reading from the holy Gospel according to Mark 4:35-41

Who can this be? Even the wind and the sea obey him.

With the coming of evening, Jesus said to his disciples, 'Let us cross over to the other side.' And leaving the crowd behind they took him, just as he was, in the boat; and there were other boats with him. Then it began to blow a gale and the waves were breaking into the boat so that it was almost swamped. But he was in the stern, his head on the cushion, asleep. They woke him and said to him, 'Master, do you not care? We are going down!' And he woke up and rebuked the wind and said to the sea, 'Quiet now! Be calm!' And the wind dropped, and all was calm again. Then he said to them, 'Why are you so frightened? How is it that you have no faith?' They were filled with awe and said to one another, 'Who can this be? Even the wind and the sea obey him.'

This is the Gospel of the Lord.

FOURTH WEEK IN ORDINARY TIME
Year II

Monday

FIRST READING

A reading from the second book of Samuel   15:13-14. 30; 16:5-13

Let us fly from the face of Absalom. Shimei was sent to bring the curse by precept of the Lord God.

A messenger came to tell David, 'The hearts of the men of Israel are now with Absalom.' So David said to all his officers who were with him in Jerusalem, 'Let us be off, let us fly, or we shall never escape from Absalom. Leave as quickly as you can in case he mounts a surprise attack and worsts us and puts the city to the sword.'

David then made his way up the Mount of Olives, weeping as he went, his head covered and his feet bare. And all the people with him had their heads covered and made their way up, weeping as they went.

As David was reaching Bahurim, out came a man of the same clan as Saul's family. His name was Shimei son of Gera, and as he came he uttered curse after curse and threw stones at David and at all King David's officers, though the whole army and all the champions flanked the king right and left. The words of his curse were these, 'Be off, be off, man of blood, scoundrel! The Lord has brought on you all the blood of the House of Saul whose sovereignty you have usurped; and the Lord has transferred that same sovereignty to Absalom your son. Now your doom has overtaken you, man of blood that you are.' Abishai son of Zeruiah said to the king, 'Is this dead dog to curse my lord the king? Let me go over and cut his

463

head off.' But the king replied, 'What business is it of mine and yours, son of Zeruiah? Let him curse. If the Lord said to him, "Curse David," what right has anyone to say, "Why have you done this?" ' David said to Abishai and all his officers, 'Why, my own son, sprung from my body, is now seeking my life; so now how much the more this Benjaminite? Let him curse on if the Lord has told him to. Perhaps the Lord will look on my misery and repay me with good for his curse today.' So David and his men went on their way.

This is the word of the Lord.

Responsorial Psalm   Ps 3:2-8. ℟ v.8

℟   Lord, rise up and save me.

1   How many are my foes, O Lord!
    How many are rising up against me!
    How many are saying about me:
    'There is no help for him in God.'   ℟

2   But you, Lord, are a shield about me,
    my glory, who lift up my head.
    I cry aloud to the Lord.
    He answers from his holy mountain.   ℟

3   I lie down to rest and I sleep.
    I wake, for the Lord upholds me.
    I will not fear even thousands of people
    who are ranged on every side against me.
    Arise, Lord; save me, my God.   ℟

Gospel Acclamation   Lk 7:16

    Alleluia, alleluia!
    A great prophet has appeared among us;
    God has visited his people.
    Alleluia!

GOSPEL

A reading from the holy Gospel according to Mark 5:1-20

Unclean spirit, come out of the man!

Jesus and his disciples reached the country of the Gerasenes on the other side of the lake, and no sooner had he left the boat than a man with an unclean spirit came out from the tombs towards him. The man lived in the tombs and no one could secure him any more, even with a chain, because he had often been secured with fetters and chains but had snapped the chains and broken the fetters, and no one had the strength to control him. All night and all day, among the tombs and in the mountains, he would howl and gash himself with stones. Catching sight of Jesus from a distance, he ran up and fell at his feet and shouted at the top of his voice, 'What do you want with me, Jesus, son of the Most High God? Swear by God you will not torture me!' – For Jesus had been saying to him, 'Come out of the man, unclean spirit.' 'What is your name?' Jesus asked. 'My name is legion,' he answered 'for there are many of us.' And he begged him earnestly not to send them out of the district. Now there was there on the mountainside a great herd of pigs feeding, and the unclean spirits begged him, 'Send us to the pigs, let us go into them.' So he gave them leave. With that, the unclean spirits came out and went into the pigs, and the herd of about two thousand pigs charged down the cliff into the lake, and there they were drowned. The swineherds ran off and told their story in the town and in the country round about; and the people came to see what had really happened. They came to Jesus and saw the demoniac sitting there, clothed and in his full senses – the very man who had had the legion in him before – and they were afraid. And those who had witnessed it reported what had happened to the demoniac and what had become of the pigs. Then they began to implore Jesus to leave the neighbourhood. As he was getting into the boat, the man who had been possessed begged to be allowed to stay with him. Jesus would not let him but said to him, 'Go home to your people and tell them all that the Lord in his mercy has done for you.' So the man went off and proceeded to spread throughout the Decapolis all that Jesus had done for him. And everyone was amazed.

This is the Gospel of the Lord.

Tuesday

FIRST READING

A reading from the second book of Samuel   18:9-10. 14. 24-25. 30–19:3

My son Absalom, would that I had died in your place.

Absalom happened to run into some of David's followers. Absalom was riding a mule and the mule passed under the thick branches of a great oak. Absalom's head caught fast in the oak and he was left hanging between heaven and earth, while the mule he was riding went on. Someone saw this and told Joab. 'I have just seen Absalom,' he said, 'hanging from an oak.' And Joab took three lances in his hand and thrust them into Absalom's heart while he was still alive there in the oak tree.

David was sitting between the two gates. The look-out had gone up to the roof of the gate, on the ramparts; he looked up and saw a man running all by himself. The watch called out to the king and told him. The king said, 'Move aside and stand there.' He moved aside and stood waiting.

Then the Cushite arrived. 'Good news for my lord the king!' cried the Cushite. 'The Lord has vindicated your cause today by ridding you of all who rebelled against you.' 'Is all well with young Absalom?' the king asked the Cushite. 'May the enemies of my lord the king,' the Cushite answered, 'and all who rebelled against you to your hurt, share the lot of that young man.'

The king shuddered. He went up to the room over the gate and burst into tears, and weeping said, 'My son Absalom! My son! My son Absalom! Would I had died in your place! Absalom, my son, my son!' Word was brought to Joab, 'The king is now weeping and mourning for Absalom.' And the day's victory was turned to mourning for all the troops, because they learned that the king was grieving for his son. And the troops returned stealthily that day to the town, as troops creep back ashamed when routed in battle.

This is the word of the Lord.

Responsorial Psalm   Ps 85:1-6. ℟ v.1

℟   Listen Lord, and answer me.

1   Turn your ear, O Lord, and give answer
     for I am poor and needy.

Preserve my life, for I am faithful:
save the servant who trusts in you. ℟

2 You are my God, have mercy on me, Lord,
   for I cry to you all the day long.
   Give joy to your servant, O Lord,
   for to you I lift up my soul. ℟

3 O Lord, you are good and forgiving,
   full of love to all who call.
   Give heed, O Lord, to my prayer
   and attend to the sound of my voice. ℟

Gospel Acclamation   Mt 8:17

Alleluia, alleluia!
He bore our sickness,
and endured our suffering.
Alleluia!

GOSPEL

A reading from the holy Gospel according to Mark   5:21-43

Young woman, I say to you, arise.

When Jesus had crossed in the boat to the other side, a large crowd gathered round him and he stayed by the lakeside. Then one of the synagogue officials came up, Jairus by name, and seeing him, fell at his feet and pleaded with him earnestly, saying, 'My little daughter is desperately sick. Do come and lay your hands on her to make her better and save her life.' Jesus went with him and a large crowd followed him; they were pressing all round him.

Now there was a woman who had suffered from a haemorrhage for twelve years; after long and painful treatment under various doctors, she had spent all she had without being any the better for it, in fact, she was getting worse. She had heard about Jesus, and she came up behind him through the crowd and touched his cloak. 'If I can touch even his clothes,' she had told herself 'I shall be well again.' And the source of the bleeding dried up instantly, and she felt in herself that she was cured of her complaint. Immediately aware that power had gone out from him, Jesus turned round in the crowd and said, 'Who touched my clothes?' His disciples said to him, 'You see how the crowd is pressing round you and yet you say, "Who touched me?" ' But he continued to look all round to see who had done it. Then the woman came forward, frightened and trembling because she knew what had happened to her, and she fell at his feet and told him the whole truth. 'My daughter,' he said 'your faith has restored you to health; go in peace and be free from your complaint.'

While he was still speaking some people arrived from the house of the synagogue official to say, 'Your daughter is dead: why put the Master to any further trouble?' But Jesus had overheard this remark of theirs and he said to the official, 'Do not be afraid; only have faith.' And he allowed no one to go with him except Peter and James and John the brother of James. So they came to the official's house and Jesus noticed all the commotion, with people weeping and wailing unrestrainedly. He went in and said to them, 'Why all this commotion and crying? The child is not dead, but asleep.' But they laughed at him. So he turned them all out and, taking with him the child's father and mother and his own companions, he went into the place where the child lay. And taking the child by the hand he said to her, 'Talitha, kum!' which means, 'Little girl, I tell you to get up.' The little girl got up at once and began to walk about, for she was twelve years old. At this they were overcome with astonishment, and he ordered them strictly not to let anyone know about it, and told them to give her something to eat.

This is the Gospel of the Lord.

Wednesday

FIRST READING

A reading from the second book of Samuel   24:2. 9-17

I have sinned, but these people, this flock, what have they done?

King David said to Joab and to the senior army officers who were with him, 'Now go throughout the tribes of Israel from Dan to Beersheba and take a census of the people; I wish to know the size of the population.'

Joab gave the king the figures for the census of the people; Israel numbered eight hundred thousand armed men capable of drawing sword, and Judah five hundred thousand men.

But afterwards David's heart misgave him for having taken a census of the people. 'I have committed a grave sin,' David said to the

Lord. 'But now, Lord, I beg you to forgive your servant for this fault. I have been very foolish.' But when David got up the next morning, the following message had come from the Lord to the prophet Gad, David's seer, 'Go and say to David, "The Lord says this: I offer you three things; choose one of them for me to do to you." '

So Gad went to David and told him. 'Are three years of famine to come on you in your country,' he said, 'or will you flee for three months before your pursuing enemy, or would you rather have three days' pestilence in your country? Now think, and decide how I am to answer him who sends me.' David said to Gad, 'This is a hard choice. But let us rather fall into the power of the Lord, since his mercy is great, and not into the power of men.' So David chose pestilence.

It was the time of the wheat harvest. The Lord sent a pestilence on Israel from the morning till the time appointed and plague ravaged the people, and from Dan to Beersheba seventy thousand men of them died. The angel stretched out his hand towards Jerusalem to destroy it, but the Lord thought better of this evil, and he said to the angel who was destroying the people, 'Enough! now withdraw your hand.' The angel of the Lord was beside the threshing-floor of Araunah the Jebusite. When David saw the angel who was ravaging the people, he spoke to the Lord. 'It was I who sinned;' he said, 'I who did this wicked thing. But these, this flock, what have they done? Let your hand lie heavy on me then, and on my family.'

This is the word of the Lord.

Responsorial Psalm   Ps 31:1-2. 5-7. ℟ cf. v.5

℟   Lord, forgive the wrong I have done.

1   Happy the man whose offence is forgiven,
    whose sin is remitted.
    O happy the man to whom the Lord
    imputes no guilt,
    in whose spirit is no guile.   ℟

2   But now I have acknowledged my sins,
    my guilt I did not hide.
    I said: 'I will confess
    my offence to the Lord.'
    And you, Lord, have forgiven
    the guilt of my sin.   ℟

(continued)

3   So let every good man pray to you
     in the time of need.
     The floods of water may reach high
     but him they shall not reach.

     ℟   Lord, forgive the wrong I have done.

4   You are my hiding place, O Lord;
     you save me from distress.
     You surround me with cries of deliverance. ℟

Gospel Acclamation   Jn 10:27

     Alleluia, alleluia!
     My sheep listen to my voice, says the Lord;
     I know them, and they follow me.
     Alleluia!

GOSPEL

A reading from the holy Gospel according to Mark   6:1-6

A prophet is without honour in his own country.

Jesus went to his home town and his disciples accompanied him. With the coming of the sabbath he began teaching in the synagogue and most of them were astonished when they heard him. They said, 'Where did the man get all this? What is this wisdom that has been granted him, and these miracles that are worked through him? This is the carpenter, surely, the son of Mary, the brother of James and Joset and Jude and Simon? His sisters, too, are they not here with us?' And they would not accept him. And Jesus said to them, 'A prophet is only despised in his own country, among his own relations and in his own house'; and he could work no miracle there, though he cured a few sick people by laying his hands on them. He was amazed at their lack of faith.

     This is the Gospel of the Lord.

470

Thursday

FIRST READING

A reading from the first book of the Kings   2:1-4. 10-12

I am going the way of all the earth; be strong, Solomon, and show yourself a man.

As David's life drew to its close he laid this charge on his son Solomon, 'I am going the way of all the earth. Be strong and show yourself a man. Observe the injunctions of the Lord your God, following his ways and keeping his laws, his commandments, his customs and his decrees, as it stands written in the Law of Moses, that so you may be successful in all you do and undertake, so that the Lord may fulfil the promise he made me, "If your sons are careful how they behave, and walk loyally before me with all their heart and soul, you shall never lack for a man on the throne of Israel." '

So David slept with his ancestors and was buried in the Citadel of David. David's reign over Israel lasted forty years: he reigned in Hebron for seven years, and in Jerusalem for thirty-three.

Solomon was seated upon the throne of David, and his sovereignty was securely established.

This is the word of the Lord.

Responsorial Psalm   1 Chron 29:10-12. ℟ v.12

> ℟   Lord, you are exalted over all.

1   Blessed are you, O Lord,
    the God of Israel, our father,
    for ever, for ages unending.   ℟

2   Yours, Lord, are greatness and power,
    and splendour, triumph and glory.
    All is yours, in heaven and on earth.   ℟

3   Yours, O Lord, is the kingdom,
    you are supreme over all.
    Both honour and riches come from you.   ℟

4   You are the ruler of all,
    from your hand come strength and power,
    from your hand come greatness and might.   ℟

Gospel Acclamation   Mk 1:15

> Alleluia, alleluia!
> The kingdom of God is near:
> believe the Good News!
> Alleluia!

GOSPEL

A reading from the holy Gospel according to Mark   6:7-13

He summoned the Twelve and sent them out in pairs.

Jesus made a tour round the villages, teaching. Then he summoned the Twelve and began to send them out in pairs giving them authority over the unclean spirits. And he instructed them to take nothing for the journey except a staff – no bread, no haversack, no coppers for their purses. They were to wear sandals but, he added, 'Do not take a spare tunic.' And he said to them, 'If you enter a house anywhere, stay there until you leave the district. And if any place does not welcome you and people refuse to listen to you, as you walk away shake off the dust from under your feet as a sign to them.' So they set off to preach repentance; and they cast out many devils, and anointed many sick people with oil and cured them.

> This is the Gospel of the Lord.

Friday

FIRST READING

A reading from the book of Ecclesiasticus   47:2-11

David praised the Lord God with all his heart and loved him.

As the fat is set apart from the communion sacrifice,
so David was chosen out of all the sons of Israel.
He played with lions as though with kids,
and with bears as though with lambs of the flock.
While still a boy, did he not slay the giant,
and relieve the people of their shame,
by putting out a hand to sling a stone
which brought down the arrogance of Goliath?
For he called on the Lord Most High,

who gave strength to his right arm
to put a mighty warrior to death,
and lift up the horn of his people.
Hence they gave him credit for ten thousand,
and praised him while they blessed the Lord,
by offering him a crown of glory;
for he massacred enemies on every side,
he annihilated his foes the Philistines,
and crushed their horn to this very day.
In all his activities he gave thanks
to the Holy One, the Most High, in words of glory;
he put all his heart into his songs
out of love for his Maker.
He placed harps before the altar
to make the singing sweeter with their music;
he gave the feasts their splendour,
the festivals their solemn pomp,
causing the Lord's holy name to be praised
and the sanctuary to resound from dawn.
The Lord took away his sins,
and exalted his horn for ever;
he gave him a royal covenant,
and a glorious throne in Israel.

This is the word of the Lord.

Responsorial Psalm   Ps 17:31. 47. 50-51. ℟ cf. v.47

℟   Blessed be God my salvation!

1   The ways of God are perfect;
    the word of the Lord, purest gold.
    He indeed is the shield
    of all who make him their refuge.   ℟

2   Long life to the Lord, my rock!
    Praised be the God who saves me.
    I will praise you, Lord, among the nations:
    I will sing a psalm to your name.   ℟

3   He has given great victories to his king
    and shown his love for his anointed,
    for David and his sons for ever.   ℟

Gospel Acclamation
cf. Lk 8:15

Alleluia, alleluia!
Happy are they who have kept the word
with a generous heart
and yield a harvest through perseverance.
Alleluia!

GOSPEL

A reading from the holy Gospel according to Mark
6:14-29

It is John whose head I cut off. He has risen from the dead.

King Herod had heard about Jesus, since by now his name was well-known. Some were saying, 'John the Baptist has risen from the dead, and that is why miraculous powers are at work in him.' Others said, 'He is Elijah'; others again, 'He is a prophet, like the prophets we used to have.' But when Herod heard this he said, 'It is John whose head I cut off; he has risen from the dead.'

Now it was this same Herod who had sent to have John arrested, and had him chained up in prison because of Herodias, his brother Philip's wife whom he had married. For John had told Herod, 'It is against the law for you to have your brother's wife.' As for Herodias, she was furious with him and wanted to kill him; but she was not able to, because Herod was afraid of John, knowing him to be a good and holy man, and gave him his protection. When he had heard him speak he was greatly perplexed, and yet he liked to listen to him.

An opportunity came on Herod's birthday when he gave a banquet for the nobles of his court, for his army officers and for the leading figures in Galilee. When the daughter of this same Herodias came in and danced, she delighted Herod and his guests; so the king said to the girl, 'Ask me anything you like and I will give it you.' And he swore her an oath, 'I will give you anything you ask, even half my kingdom.' She went out and said to her mother, 'What shall I ask for?' She replied, 'The head of John the Baptist.' The girl hurried straight back to the king and made her request. 'I want you to give me John the Baptist's head, here and now, on a dish.' The king was deeply distressed but, thinking of the oaths he had sworn and of his guests, he was reluctant to break his word to her. So the king at once sent one of the bodyguard with orders to bring John's head. The man went off and beheaded him in prison; then he brought the head on a dish and gave it to the girl, and the girl gave it to her mother. When John's disciples heard about this, they came and took his body and laid it in a tomb.

This is the Gospel of the Lord.

Saturday

FIRST READING

A reading from the first book of the Kings   3:4-13

Give your servant an understanding heart to govern your people.

King Solomon went to Gibeon to sacrifice there, since that was the greatest of the high places – he offered a thousand holocausts on that altar. At Gibeon the Lord appeared in a dream to Solomon during the night. God said, 'Ask what you would like me to give you.' Solomon replied, 'You showed great kindness to your servant David, my father, when he lived his life before you in faithfulness and justice and integrity of heart; you have continued this great kindness to him by allowing a son of his to sit on his throne today. Now, Lord my God, you have made your servant king in succession to David my father. But I am a very young man, unskilled in leadership. Your servant finds himself in the midst of this people of yours that you have chosen, a people so many its number cannot be counted or reckoned. Give your servant a heart to understand how to discern between good and evil, for who could govern this people of yours that is so great?' It pleased the Lord that Solomon should have asked for this. 'Since you have asked for this' the Lord said 'and not asked for long life for yourself or riches or the lives of your enemies, but have asked for a discerning judgement for yourself, here and now I do what you ask. I give you a heart wise and shrewd as none before you has had and none will have after you. What you have not asked I shall give you too: such riches and glory as no other king ever had.'

This is the word of the Lord.

Responsorial Psalm   Ps 118:9-14. ℟ v. 12

℟ Lord, teach me your decrees.

1 How shall the young remain sinless?
   By obeying your word.
   I have sought you with all my heart:
   let me not stray from your commands. ℟

2 I treasure your promise in my heart
   lest I sin against you.
   Blessed are you, O Lord:
   teach me your statutes. ℟

3 With my tongue I have recounted
   the decrees of your lips.
   I rejoiced to do your will
   as though all riches were mine. ℟

Gospel Acclamation   Jn 10:27

Alleluia, alleluia!
My sheep listen to my voice, says the Lord;
I know them, and they follow me.
Alleluia!

GOSPEL

A reading from the holy Gospel according to Mark   6:30-34

They were sheep without a shepherd.

The apostles rejoined Jesus and told him all they had done and
taught. Then he said to them, 'You must come away to some lonely
place all by yourselves and rest for a while'; for there were so many
coming and going that the apostles had no time even to eat. So they
went off in a boat to a lonely place where they could be by themselves.
But people saw them going, and many could guess where; and from
every town they all hurried to the place on foot and reached it before
them. So as he stepped ashore he saw a large crowd; and he took pity
on them because they were like sheep without a shepherd, and he set
himself to teach them at some length.

This is the Gospel of the Lord.

FIFTH WEEK IN ORDINARY TIME

Year II

Monday

FIRST READING

A reading from the first book of the Kings   8:1-7. 9-13

They carried the ark of the covenant to the Holy of Holies and a
cloud filled the house of the Lord God.

Solomon called the elders of Israel together in Jerusalem to bring the
ark of the covenant of the Lord up from the Citadel of David, which is
Zion. All the men of Israel assembled round King Solomon in the
month of Ethanim, at the time of the feast (that is, the seventh
month), and the priests took up the ark and the Tent of Meeting with
all the sacred vessels that were in it. In the presence of the ark, King
Solomon and all Israel sacrificed sheep and oxen, countless, innumerable. The priests brought the ark of the covenant of the Lord to its
place, in the Debir of the Temple, that is, in the Holy of Holies, under
the cherubs' wings. For there where the ark was placed the cherubs
spread out their wings and sheltered the ark and its shafts. There was
nothing in the ark except the two stone tablets Moses had placed in it
at Horeb, the tablets of the covenant which the Lord had made with
the Israelites when they came out of the land of Egypt; they are still
there today.

Now when the priests came out of the sanctuary, the cloud filled
the Temple of the Lord, and because of the cloud the priests could no
longer perform their duties: the glory of the Lord filled the Lord's
Temple.

Then Solomon said:

'The Lord has chosen to dwell in the thick cloud.
Yes, I have built you a dwelling,
a place for you to live in for ever.'

This is the word of the Lord.

Responsorial Psalm   Ps 131:6-10. ℟ v.8

℟ Lord, go up to the place of your rest!

1 At Ephrata we heard of the ark;
   we found it in the plains of Yearim.
   'Let us go to the place of his dwelling;
   let us go to kneel at his footstool.' ℟

2 Go up, Lord, to the place of your rest,
   you and the ark of your strength.
   Your priests shall be clothed with holiness;
   your faithful shall ring out their joy.
   For the sake of David your servant
   do not reject your anointed. ℟

Gospel Acclamation   cf. Mt 4:23

Alleluia, alleluia!
Jesus preached the Good News of the kingdom
and healed all who were sick.
Alleluia!

GOSPEL

A reading from the holy Gospel according to Mark   6:53-56

All those who touched him were cured.

Having made the crossing, Jesus and his disciples came to land at
Genessaret and tied up. No sooner had they stepped out of the boat
than people recognised him, and started hurrying all through the
countryside and brought the sick on stretchers to wherever they heard
he was. And wherever he went, to village, or town, or farm, they laid
down the sick in the open spaces, begging him to let them touch even
the fringe of his cloak. And all those who touched him were cured.

This is the Gospel of the Lord.

Tuesday

FIRST READING

A reading from the first book of the Kings   8:22-23. 27-30

You have said, my name shall be there, to hear the prayers of your
people Israel.

In the presence of the whole assembly of Israel, Solomon stood before
the altar of the Lord and, stretching out his hands towards heaven,
said, 'Lord God of Israel, not in heaven above nor on earth beneath is
there such a God as you, true to your covenant and your kindness
towards your servants when they walk wholeheartedly in your way.
Yet will God really live with men on the earth? Why, the heavens and
their own heavens cannot contain you. How much less this house that
I have built! Listen to the prayer and entreaty of your servant, Lord
my God; listen to the cry and to the prayer your servant makes to you
today. Day and night let your eyes watch over this house, over this
place of which you have said, 'My name shall be there.' Listen to the
prayer that your servant will offer in this place.

'Hear the entreaty of your servant and of Israel your people as they
pray in this place. From heaven where your dwelling is, hear; and as
you hear, forgive.'

This is the word of the Lord.

Responsorial Psalm   Ps 83:3-5. 10-11. ℟ v.2

℟   How lovely is your dwelling-place,
    Lord, mighty God!

1   My soul is longing and yearning,
    is yearning for the courts of the Lord.
    My heart and my soul ring out their joy
    to God, the living God.   ℟

2   The sparrow herself finds a home
    and the swallow a nest for her brood;
    she lays her young by your altars,
    Lord of hosts, my king and my God.   ℟

3   They are happy, who dwell in your house,
    for ever singing your praise.
    Turn your eyes, O God, our shield,
    look on the face of your anointed.   ℟

(continued)

4   One day within your courts
    is better than a thousand elsewhere.
    The threshold of the house of God
    I prefer to the dwellings of the wicked.

    ℟   How lovely is your dwelling-place,
        Lord, mighty God.

Gospel Acclamation   Ps 118:36. 29

    Alleluia, alleluia!
    Turn my heart to do your will;
    teach me your law, O God.
    Alleluia!

GOSPEL

A reading from the holy Gospel according to Mark   7:1-13

You put aside the commandments of God to hold on to human traditions.

The Pharisees and some of the scribes who had come from Jerusalem
gathered round Jesus, and they noticed that some of his disciples were
eating with unclean hands, that is without washing them. For the
Pharisees, and the Jews in general, follow the tradition of the elders
and never eat without washing their arms as far as the elbow; and on
returning from the market place they never eat without first sprinkling themselves. There are also many other observances which have
been handed down to them concerning the washing of cups and pots
and bronze dishes. So these Pharisees and scribes asked him, 'Why do
your disciples not respect the tradition of the elders but eat their food
with unclean hands?' He answered, 'It was of you hypocrites that
Isaiah so rightly prophesised in this passage of scripture:

    This people honours me only with lip-service,
    while their hearts are far from me.
    The worship they offer me is worthless,
    the doctrines they teach are only human regulations.

You put aside the commandment of God to cling to human traditions.'
And he said to them, 'How ingeniously you get round the commandment of God in order to preserve your own tradition! For Moses said:

Do your duty to your father and your mother, and, Anyone who curses father or mother must be put to death. But you say, "If a man says to his father or mother: Anything I have that I might have used to help you is Corban (that is, dedicated to God), then he is forbidden from that moment to do anything for his father or mother." In this way you make God's word null and void for the sake of your tradition which you have handed down. And you do many other things like this.'

This is the Gospel of the Lord.

Wednesday

FIRST READING

A reading from the first book of the Kings   10:1-10

The queen of Sheba saw all the wisdom of Solomon.

The fame of Solomon having reached the queen of Sheba, she came to test him with difficult questions. She brought immense riches to Jerusalem with her, camels laden with spices, great quantities of gold, and precious stones. On coming to Solomon, she opened her mind freely to him; and Solomon had an answer for all her questions, not one of them was too obscure for the king to expound. When the queen of Sheba saw all the wisdom of Solomon, the palace he had built, the food at his table, the accommodation for his officials, the organisation of his staff and the way they were dressed, his cup-bearers, and the holocausts he offered in the Temple of the Lord, it left her breathless, and she said to the king, 'What I heard in my own country about you and your wisdom was true, then! Until I came and saw it with my own eyes I could not believe what they told me, but clearly they told me less than half: for wisdom and prosperity you surpass the report I heard. How happy your wives are! How happy are these servants of yours who wait on you always and hear your wisdom! Blessed be the Lord your God who has granted you his favour, setting you on the throne of Israel! Because of the Lord's everlasting love for Israel, he has made you king to deal out law and justice.' And she presented the king with a hundred and twenty talents of gold and great quantities of spices and precious stones; no such wealth of spices ever came again as those given to King Solomon by the queen of Sheba.

This is the word of the Lord.

Responsorial Psalm   Ps 36:5-6. 30-31. 39-40. ℟ v.30

℟   The mouths of the just murmur wisdom.

1   Commit your life to the Lord,
    trust in him and he will act,
    so that your justice breaks forth like the light,
    your cause like the noon-day sun.   ℟

2   The just man's mouth utters wisdom
    and his lips speak what is right;
    the law of his God is in his heart,
    his steps shall be saved from stumbling.   ℟

3   The salvation of the just comes from the Lord,
    their stronghold in time of distress.
    The Lord helps them and delivers them
    and saves them: for their refuge is in him.   ℟

Gospel Acclamation   cf. Jn 17:17

Alleluia, alleluia!
Your word, O Lord, is truth:
make us holy in the truth.
Alleluia!

GOSPEL

A reading from the holy Gospel according to Mark   7:14-23

It is the things that come out of a person that make one unclean.

Jesus called the people to him and said, 'Listen to me, all of you, and
understand. Nothing that goes into a man from outside can make him
unclean; it is the things that come out of a man that make him
unclean. If anyone has ears to hear, let him listen to this.'

When he had gone back into the house, away from the crowd, his
disciples questioned him about the parable. He said to them, 'Do you
not understand either? Can you not see that whatever goes into a man
from outside cannot make him unclean, because it does not go into his
heart but through his stomach and passes out into the sewer?' (Thus
he pronounced all foods clean.) And he went on, 'It is what comes out
of a man that makes him unclean. For it is from within, from men's
hearts, that evil intentions emerge; fornication, theft, murder,

adultery, avarice, malice, deceit, indecency, envy, slander, pride, folly. All these evil things come from within and make a man unclean.'

This is the Gospel of the Lord.

Thursday

FIRST READING

A reading from the first book of the Kings   11:4-13

Since you did not keep my covenant, I will tear the kingdom away from you and I will leave your son one tribe for the sake of my servant, David.

When Solomon grew old his wives swayed his heart to other gods; and his heart was not wholly with the Lord his God as his father David's had been. Solomon became a follower of Astarte, the goddess of the Sidonians, and of Milcom, the Ammonite abomination. He did what was displeasing to the Lord, and was not a wholehearted follower of the Lord, as his father David had been. Then it was that Solomon built a high place for Chemosh the god of Moab on the mountain to the east of Jerusalem, and to Milcom the god of the Ammonites. He did the same for all his foreign wives, who offered incense and sacrifice to their gods.

The Lord was angry with Solomon because his heart had turned from the Lord the God of Israel who had twice appeared to him and who had then forbidden him to follow other gods; but he did not carry out the Lord's order. The Lord therefore said to Solomon, 'Since you behave like this and do not keep my covenant or the laws I laid down for you, I will most surely tear the kingdom away from you and give it to one of your servants. For your father David's sake, however, I will not do this during your lifetime, but will tear it out of your son's hands. Even so, I will not tear the whole kingdom from him. For the sake of my servant David, and for the sake of Jerusalem which I have chosen, I will leave your son one tribe.'

This is the word of the Lord.

Responsorial Psalm ⬩ Ps 105:3-4. 35-37. 40. ℞ v.4

℞ Lord, remember us,
for the love you bear your people.

1 They are happy who do what is right,
who at all times do what is just.
O Lord, remember me
out of the love you have for your people. ℞

2 But instead they mingled with the nations
and learned to act like them.
They worshipped the idols of the nations
and these became a snare to entrap them. ℞

3 They even offered their own sons
and their daughters in sacrifice to demons,
till his anger blazed against his people:
he was filled with horror at his chosen ones. ℞

Gospel Acclamation ⬩ James 1:21

Alleluia, alleluia!
Receive and submit to the word planted in you;
it can save your souls.
Alleluia!

GOSPEL

A reading from the holy Gospel according to Mark ⬩ 7:24-30

The dogs under the table can eat the children's scraps.

Jesus left Gennesaret and set out for the territory of Tyre. There he went into a house and did not want anyone to know he was there, but he could not pass unrecognised. A woman whose little daughter had an unclean spirit heard about him straightaway and came and fell at his feet. Now the woman was a pagan, by birth a Syrophoenician, and she begged him to cast the devil out of her daughter. And he said to her, 'The children should be fed first, because it is not fair to take the children's food and throw it to the house-dogs.' But she spoke up: 'Ah yes, sir,' she replied 'but the house-dogs under the table can eat the children's scraps.' And he said to her, 'For saying this, you may go home happy: the devil has gone out of your daughter.' So she went off to her home and found the child lying on the bed and the devil gone.

This is the Gospel of the Lord.

Friday

FIRST READING

A reading from the first book of the Kings 11:29-32; 12:19

All Israel has been separated from the house of David.

One day when Jeroboam had gone out of Jerusalem, the prophet Ahijah of Shiloh accosted him on the road. Ahijah was wearing a new cloak; the two of them were in the open country by themselves. Ahijah took the new cloak he was wearing and tore it into twelve strips, saying to Jeroboam, 'Take ten strips for yourself, for thus the Lord God speaks, the God of Israel, "I am going to tear the kingdom from Solomon's hand and give ten tribes to you. He shall keep one tribe for the sake of my servant David and for the sake of Jerusalem, the city I have chosen out of all the tribes of Israel." ' And Israel has been separated from the House of David until the present day.

This is the word of the Lord.

Responsorial Psalm Ps 80:10-15. ℟ vv.11. 9

℟ I am the Lord, your God:
hear my voice.

1 Let there be no foreign god among you,
no worship of an alien god.
I am the Lord your God,
who brought you from the land of Egypt. ℟

2 But my people did not heed my voice
and Israel would not obey,
so I left them in their stubbornness of heart
to follow their own designs. ℟

3 O that my people would heed me,
that Israel would walk in my ways!
At once I would subdue their foes,
turn my hand against their enemies. ℟

485

Gospel Acclamation   cf. Acts 16:14

Alleluia, alleluia!
Open our hearts, O Lord,
to listen to the words of your Son.
Alleluia!

GOSPEL

A reading from the holy Gospel according to Mark   7:31-37

He makes the deaf hear and the dumb speak.

Returning from the district of Tyre, Jesus went by way of Sidon
towards the Sea of Galilee, right through the Decapolis region. And
they brought him a deaf man who had an impediment in his speech;
and they asked him to lay his hand on him. He took him aside in
private, away from the crowd, put his fingers into the man's ears and
touched his tongue with spittle. Then looking up to heaven he sighed;
and he said to him, 'Ephphatha,' that is, 'Be opened.' And his ears
were opened, and the ligament of his tongue was loosened and he
spoke clearly. And Jesus ordered them to tell no one about it, but the
more he insisted, the more widely they published it. Their admiration
was unbounded. 'He has done all things well,' they said 'he makes the
deaf hear and the dumb speak.'

This is the Gospel of the Lord.

Saturday

FIRST READING

A reading from the first book of the Kings   12:26-32; 13:33-34

Jeroboam made two golden calves.

Jeroboam thought to himself, 'As things are, the kingdom will revert
to the House of David. If this people continues to go up to the Temple
of the Lord in Jerusalem to offer sacrifices, the people's heart will turn
back again to their lord, Rehoboam king of Judah, and they will put
me to death.' So the king thought this over and then made two golden
calves; he said to the people. 'You have been going up to Jerusalem
long enough. Here are your gods, Israel; these brought you up out of

the land of Egypt!' He set up one in Bethel and the people went in procession all the way to Dan in front of the other. He set up the temple of the high places and appointed priests from ordinary families, who were not of the sons of Levi. Jeroboam also instituted a feast in the eighth month, on the fifteenth of the month, like the feast that was kept in Judah, and he went up to the altar. That was how he behaved in Bethel, sacrificing to the calves he had made; and at Bethel he put the priests of the high places he had established.

Jeroboam did not give up his wicked ways after this incident, but went on appointing priests for the high places from the common people. He consecrated as priests of the high places any who wished to be. Such conduct made the House of Jeroboam a sinful House, and caused its ruin and extinction from the face of the earth.

This the word of the Lord.

Responsorial Psalm   Ps 105:6-7. 19-22. ℟ v.4

℟   Lord, remember us,
     for the love you bear your people.

1   Our sin is the sin of our fathers;
    we have done wrong, our deeds have been evil.
    Our fathers when they were in Egypt
    paid no heed to your wonderful deeds.   ℟

2   They fashioned a calf at Horeb
    and worshipped an image of metal,
    exchanging the God who was their glory
    for the image of a bull that eats grass.   ℟

3   They forgot the God who was their saviour,
    who had done such great things in Egypt,
    such portents in the land of Ham,
    such marvels at the Red Sea.   ℟

Gospel Acclamation   Mt 4:4

     Alleluia, alleluia!
     No one lives on bread alone,
     but on every word that comes from the mouth of God.
     Alleluia!

GOSPEL

A reading from the holy Gospel according to Mark   8:1-10

They ate and were filled.

A great crowd had gathered, and they had nothing to eat. So Jesus called his disciples to him and said to them, 'I feel sorry for all these people; they have been with me for three days now and have nothing to eat. If I send them off home hungry they will collapse on the way; some have come a great distance.' His disciples replied, 'Where could anyone get bread to feed these people in a deserted place like this?' He asked them, 'How many loaves have you?' 'Seven,' they said. Then he instructed the crowd to sit down on the ground, and he took the seven loaves, and after giving thanks he broke them and handed them to his disciples to distribute; and they distributed them among the crowd. They had a few small fish as well, and over these he said a blessing and ordered them to be distributed also. They ate as much as they wanted, and they collected seven basketfuls of the scraps left over. Now there had been about four thousand people. He sent them away and immediately, getting into the boat with his disciples, went to the region of Dalmanutha.

This is the Gospel of the Lord.

SIXTH WEEK IN ORDINARY TIME

Year II

Monday

FIRST READING

A reading from the letter of St James   1:1-11

Your faith is put to the test to make you patient, so that you will become perfect and complete.

From James, servant of God and of the Lord Jesus Christ. Greetings to the twelve tribes of the Dispersion.

My brothers, you will always have your trials but, when they come, try to treat them as a happy privilege; you understand that your faith is only put to the test to make you patient, but patience too is to have its practical results so that you will become fully-developed, complete, with nothing missing.

If there is any one of you who needs wisdom, he must ask God, who gives to all freely and ungrudgingly; it will be given to him. But he must ask with faith, and no trace of doubt, because a person who has doubts is like the waves thrown up in the sea when the wind drives. That sort of person, in two minds, wavering between going different ways, must not expect that the Lord will give him anything.

It is right for the poor brother to be proud of his high rank, and the rich one to be thankful that he has been humbled, because riches last no longer than the flowers in the grass; the scorching sun comes up, and the grass withers, the flower falls; what looked so beautiful now disappears. It is the same with the rich man: his business goes on; he himself perishes.

This is the word of the Lord.

Responsorial Psalm   Ps 118:67-68. 71-72. 75-76. ℟ v.77

℟   Be kind to me, Lord, and I shall live.

1   Before I was afflicted I went astray
    but now I keep your word.
    You are good and your deeds are good;
    teach me your statutes.   ℟

2   It was good for me to be afflicted,
    to learn your statutes.
    The law from your mouth means more to me
    than silver and gold.   ℟

3   Lord, I know that your decrees are right,
    that you afflicted me justly.
    Let your love be ready to console me
    by your promise to your servant.   ℟

Gospel Acclamation   Jn 14:6

    Alleluia, alleluia!
    I am the way, the truth, and the life, says the Lord;
    no one comes to the Father, except through me.
    Alleluia!

GOSPEL

A reading from the holy Gospel according to Mark   8:11-13

Why does this generation demand a sign?

The Pharisees came up and started a discussion with Jesus; they demanded of him a sign from heaven, to test him. And with a sigh that came straight from the heart he said, 'Why does this generation demand a sign? I tell you solemnly, no sign shall be given to this generation.' And leaving them again and re-embarking he went away to the opposite shore.

This is the Gospel of the Lord.

Tuesday

FIRST READING

A reading from the letter of St James   1:12-18

God tempts no one.

Happy the man who stands firm when trials come. He has proved himself, and will win the prize of life, the crown that the Lord has promised to those who love him.

Never, when you have been tempted, say, 'God sent the temptation'; God cannot be tempted to do anything wrong, and he does not tempt anybody. Everyone who is tempted is attracted and seduced by his own wrong desire. Then the desire conceives and gives birth to sin, and when sin is fully grown, it too has a child, and the child is death.

Make no mistake about this, my dear brothers; it is all that is good, everything that is perfect, which is given us from above; it comes down from the Father of all light; with him there is no such thing as alteration, no shadow of a change. By his own choice he made us his children by the message of the truth so that we should be a sort of first-fruits of all that he had created.

This is the word of the Lord.

Responsorial Psalm   Ps 93:12-15. 18-19. ℟ v.12

℟   Happy are those you teach, O Lord.

1   Happy the man whom you teach, O Lord,
    whom you train by means of your law:
    to him you give peace in evil days.   ℟

2   The Lord will not abandon his people
    nor forsake those who are his own;
    for judgement shall again be just
    and all true hearts shall uphold it.   ℟

3   When I think: 'I have lost my foothold',
    your mercy, Lord, holds me up.
    When cares increase in my heart
    your consolation calms my soul.   ℟

Gospel Acclamation   Jn 14:23

    Alleluia, alleluia!
    All who love me will keep my words,
    and my Father will love them and we will come to them.
    Alleluia!

GOSPEL

A reading from the holy Gospel according to Mark   8:14-21

  Be on your guard against the yeast of the Pharisees and the yeast of Herod.

The disciples had forgotten to take any food and they had only one loaf
with them in the boat. Then Jesus gave them this warning, 'Keep
your eyes open; be on your guard against the yeast of the Pharisees
and the yeast of Herod.' And they said to one another, 'It is because we
have no bread.' And Jesus knew it, and he said to them, 'Why are you
talking about having no bread? Do you not yet understand? Have you
no perception? Are your minds closed? Have you eyes that do not see,
ears that do not hear? Or do you not remember? When I broke the five
loaves among the five thousand, how many baskets full of scraps did
you collect?' They answered, 'Twelve.' 'And when I broke the seven
loaves for the four thousand, how many baskets full of scraps did you
collect?' And they answered, 'Seven'. Then he said to them, 'Are you
still without perception?'

    This is the Gospel of the Lord.

Wednesday

FIRST READING

A reading from the letter of St James   1:19-27

Be doers of the word and not just listeners.

Remember this, my dear brothers: be quick to listen but slow to speak and slow to rouse your temper; God's righteousness is never served by man's anger; so do away with all the impurities and bad habits that are still left in you – accept and submit to the word which has been planted in you and can save your souls. But you must do what the word tells you, and not just listen to it and deceive yourselves. To listen to the word and not obey is like looking at your own features in a mirror and then, after a quick look, going off and immediately forgetting what you looked like. But the man who looks steadily at the perfect law of freedom and makes that his habit – not listening and then forgetting, but actively putting it into practice – will be happy in all that he does.

Nobody must imagine that he is religious while he still goes on deceiving himself and not keeping control over his tongue; anyone who does this has the wrong idea of religion. Pure, unspoilt religion, in the eyes of God our Father is this: coming to the help of orphans and widows when they need it, and keeping oneself uncontaminated by the world.

This is the word of the Lord.

Responsorial Psalm   Ps 14:2-5. ℟ v.1

℟   The just shall live on your holy mountain, O Lord.

1   Lord, who shall dwell on your holy mountain?
     He who walks without fault;
     he who acts with justice
     and speaks the truth from his heart;
     he who does not slander with his tongue.   ℟

2   He who does no wrong to his brother,
     who casts no slur on his neighbour,
     who holds the godless in disdain.
     but honours those who fear the Lord.   ℟

3 He who keep his pledge, come what may;
   who takes no interest on a loan
   and accepts no bribes against the innocent.
   Such a man will stand firm for ever.   ℟

Gospel Acclamation   cf. Eph 1:17. 18

   Alleluia, alleluia!
   May the Father of our Lord Jesus Christ
   enlighten the eyes of our heart
   that we might see how great is the hope
   to which we are called.
   Alleluia!

GOSPEL

A reading from the holy Gospel according to Mark   8:22-26

He restored sight to the blind man and he could see everything clearly.

Jesus and his disciples came to Bethsaida, and some people brought to
him a blind man whom they begged him to touch. He took the blind
man by the hand and led him outside the village. Then putting spittle
on his eyes and laying his hands on him, he asked, 'Can you see
anything?' The man, who was beginning to see, replied, 'I can see
people; they look like trees to me, but they are walking about.' Then
he laid his hands on the man's eyes again and he saw clearly; he was
cured, and he could see everything plainly and distinctly. And Jesus
sent him home, saying, 'Do not even go into the village.'

   This is the Gospel of the Lord.

Thursday

FIRST READING

A reading from the letter of St James   2:1-9

Did not God choose the poor? You, however, do not respect them.

My brothers, do not try to combine faith in Jesus Christ, our glorified
Lord, with the making of distinctions between classes of people. Now
suppose a man comes into your synagogue, beautifully dressed and

with a gold ring on, and at the same time a poor man comes in, in shabby clothes, and you take notice of the well-dressed man, and say, 'Come this way to the best seats'; then you tell the poor man, 'Stand over there' or 'You can sit on the floor by my foot-rest.' Can't you see that you have used two different standards in your mind, and turned yourselves into judges, and corrupt judges at that?

Listen, my dear brothers: it was those who are poor according to the world that God chose, to be rich in faith and to be the heirs to the kingdom which he promised to those who love him. In spite of this, you have no respect for anybody who is poor. Isn't it always the rich who are against you? Isn't it always their doing when you are dragged before the court? Aren't they the ones who insult the honourable name to which you have been dedicated? Well, the right thing to do is to keep the supreme law of scripture: you must love your neighbour as yourself; but as soon as you make distinctions between classes of people, you are committing sin, and under condemnation for breaking the Law.

This is the word of the Lord.

Responsorial Psalm
Ps 33:2-7. ℟ v.7

℟ The Lord hears the cry of the poor.

1 I will bless the Lord at all times,
    his praise always on my lips;
    in the Lord my soul shall make its boast.
    The humble shall hear and be glad. ℟

2 Glorify the Lord with me.
    Together let us praise his name.
    I sought the Lord and he answered me;
    from all my terrors he set me free. ℟

3 Look towards him and be radiant;
    let your faces not be abashed.
    This poor man called; the Lord heard him
    and rescued him from all his distress. ℟

Gospel Acclamation   cf. Jn 6:63. 68

> Alleluia, alleluia!
> Your words, Lord, are spirit and life;
> you have the words of everlasting life.
> Alleluia!

GOSPEL

A reading from the holy Gospel according to Mark   8:27-33

You are the Christ. The Son of Man must suffer many things.

Jesus and his disciples left for the villages round Caesarea Philippi.
On the way he put this question to his disciples, 'Who do people say I
am?' And they told him, 'John the Baptist,' they said 'others Elijah;
others again, one of the prophets.' 'But you,' he asked 'who do you say I
am?' Peter spoke up and said to him, 'You are the Christ.' And he gave
them strict orders not to tell anyone about him.

And he began to teach them that the Son of Man was destined to
suffer grievously, to be rejected by the elders and the chief priests and
the scribes, and to be put to death, and after three days to rise again;
and he said all this quite openly. Then, taking him aside, Peter
started to remonstrate with him. But, turning and seeing his disciples, he rebuked Peter and said to him, 'Get behind me, Satan!
Because the way you think is not God's way but man's.'

This is the Gospel of the Lord.

Friday

FIRST READING

A reading from the letter of St James   2:14-24. 26

*A body dies when it is separated from the spirit, and in the same way
faith is dead if it is separated from good works.*

Take the case, my brothers, of someone who has never done a single
good act but claims that he has faith. Will that faith save him? If one
of the brothers or one of the sisters is in need of clothes and has not
enough food to live on, and one of you says to them, 'I wish you well;
keep yourself warm and eat plenty,' without giving them these bare
necessities of life, then what good is that? Faith is like that: if good

works do not go with it, it is quite dead.

This is the way to talk to people of that kind: 'You say you have faith and I have good deeds; I will prove to you that I have faith by showing you my good deeds – now you prove to me that you have faith without any good deeds to show. You believe in the one God – that is creditable enough, but the demons have the same belief, and they tremble with fear. Do realise, you senseless man, that faith without good deeds is useless. You surely know that Abraham our father was justified by his deed, because he offered his son Isaac on the altar? There you see it: faith and deeds were working together; his faith became perfect by what he did. This is what scripture really means when it says: Abraham put his faith in God, and this was counted as making him justified; and that is why he was called 'the friend of God.'

You see now that it is by doing something good, and not only by believing, that a man is justified. A body dies when it is separated from the spirit, and in the same way faith is dead if it is separated from good deeds.

This is the word of the Lord.

Responsorial Psalm   Ps 111:1-6. ℟ cf. v.1

> ℟   Happy are those who do what the Lord commands.

1   Happy the man who fears the Lord,
   who takes delight in his commands.
   His sons will be powerful on earth;
   the children of the upright are blessed.   ℟

2   Riches and wealth are in his house;
   his justice stands firm for ever.
   He is a light in the darkness for the upright:
   he is generous, merciful and just.   ℟

3   The good man takes pity and lends,
   he conducts his affairs with honour.
   The just man will never waver:
   he will be remembered for ever.   ℟

Gospel Acclamation   Jn 15:15

Alleluia, alleluia!
I call you my friends, says the Lord,
for I have made known to you all that the Father has told me.
Alleluia!

GOSPEL

A reading from the holy Gospel according to Mark   8:34–9:1

Whoever loses his life for my sake and the sake of the gospel, will save it.

Jesus called the people and his disciples to him and said, 'If anyone wants to be a follower of mine, let him renounce himself and take up his cross and follow me. For anyone who wants to save his life will lose it: but anyone who loses his life for my sake, and for the sake of the gospel, will save it. What gain, then, is it for a man to win the whole world and ruin his life? And indeed what can man offer in exchange for his life? For if anyone in this adulterous and sinful generation is ashamed of me and of my words, the Son of Man will also be ashamed of him when he comes in the glory of his Father with the holy angels.'

And he said to them, 'I tell you solemnly, there are some standing here who will not taste death before they see the kingdom of God come with power.'

This is the Gospel of the Lord.

Saturday

FIRST READING

A reading from the letter of St James   3:1-10

No human being can tame the tongue.

Only a few of you, my brothers, should be teachers, bearing in mind that those of us who teach can expect a stricter judgement.

After all, every one of us does something wrong, over and over again; the only man who could reach perfection would be someone who never said anything wrong – he would be able to control every part of himself. Once we put a bit into the horse's mouth, to make it do what we want, we have the whole animal under our control. Or think of ships: no matter how big they are, even if a gale is driving them, the man at the helm can steer them anywhere he likes by controlling a tiny rudder. So is the tongue only a tiny part of the body, but it can proudly claim that it does great things. Think how small a flame can set fire to a huge forest; the tongue is a flame like that. Among all the parts of the body, the tongue is a whole wicked world in itself: it infects the whole body; catching fire from hell, it sets fire to the whole wheel of creation. Wild animals and birds, reptiles and fish can all be tamed by man, and often are; but nobody can tame the tongue – it is a pest that will not keep still, full of deadly poison. We use it to bless the Lord and Father, but we also use it to curse men who are made in God's image: the blessing and the curse come out of the same mouth. My brothers, this must be wrong.

This is the word of the Lord.

Responsorial Psalm

Ps 11:2-5. 7-8. ℟ v.8

℟ You will protect us, Lord.

1 Help, O Lord, for good men have vanished:
truth has gone from the sons of men.
Falsehood they speak one to another,
with lying lips, with a false heart. ℟

2 May the Lord destroy all lying lips,
the tongue speaking high-sounding words,
those who say: 'Our tongue is our strength;
our lips are our own, who is our master?' ℟

3 The words of the Lord are words without alloy,
silver from the furnace, seven times refined.
It is you, O Lord, who will take us in your care
and protect us for ever from this generation. ℟

Gospel Acclamation

cf. Mk 9:6

Alleluia, alleluia!
The heavens were opened and the Father's voice was heard:
this is my beloved Son, hear him.
Alleluia!

GOSPEL

A reading from the holy Gospel according to Mark   9:2-13

He was transfigured in their presence.

Jesus took with him Peter and James and John and led them up a high mountain where they could be alone by themselves. There in their presence he was transfigured: his clothes became dazzlingly white, whiter than any earthly bleacher could make them. Elijah appeared to them with Moses; and they were talking with Jesus. Then Peter spoke to Jesus: 'Rabbi,' he said 'it is wonderful for us to be here; so let us make three tents, one for you, one for Moses and one for Elijah.' He did not know what to say; they were so frightened. And a cloud came, covering them in shadow; and there came a voice from the cloud, 'This is my Son, the Beloved. Listen to him.' Then suddenly, when they looked round, they saw no one with them any more but only Jesus.

As they came down from the mountain he warned them to tell no one what they had seen, until after the Son of Man had risen from the dead. They observed the warning faithfully, though among themselves they discussed what 'rising from the dead' could mean. And they put this question to him, 'Why do the scribes say that Elijah has to come first?' 'True,' he said 'Elijah is to come first and to see that everything is as it should be; yet how is it that the scriptures say about the Son of Man that he is to suffer grievously and be treated with contempt? However, I tell you that Elijah has come and they have treated him as they pleased, just as the scriptures say about him.'

This is the Gospel of the Lord.

SEVENTH WEEK IN ORDINARY TIME

Year II

Monday

FIRST READING

A reading from the letter of St James   3:13-18

If there is disharmony in your hearts, you cannot give glory.

If there are any wise or learned men among you, let them show it by their good lives, with humility and wisdom in their actions. But if at heart you have the bitterness of jealousy, or a self-seeking ambition, never make any claims for yourself or cover up the truth with lies – principles of this kind are not the wisdom that comes down from above: they are only earthly, animal and devilish. Wherever you find jealousy and ambition, you find disharmony, and wicked things of every kind being done; whereas the wisdom that comes down from above is essentially something pure; it also makes for peace, and is kindly and considerate; it is full of compassion and shows itself by doing good; nor is there any trace of partiality or hypocrisy in it. Peacemakers, when they work for peace, sow the seeds which will bear fruit in holiness.

This is the word of the Lord.

Responsorial Psalm   Ps 18:8-10. 15. ℟ v.9

℟   The precepts of the Lord give joy to the heart.

1   The law of the Lord is perfect,
      it revives the soul.
      The rule of the Lord is to be trusted,
      it gives wisdom to the simple.   ℟

2   The precepts of the Lord are right,
      they gladden the heart.
      The command of the Lord is clear,
      it gives light to the eyes.   ℟

3   The fear of the Lord is holy,
    abiding for ever,
    The decrees of the Lord are truth
    and all of them just.   ℟

4   May the spoken words of my mouth,
    the thoughts of my heart,
    win favour in your sight, O Lord,
    my rescuer, my rock.   ℟

Gospel Acclamation   cf. 2 Tim 1:10

    Alleluia, alleluia!
    Our Saviour Jesus Christ has done away with death
    and brought us life through his gospel.
    Alleluia!

GOSPEL

A reading from the holy Gospel according to Mark   9:14-29

I believe, Lord, help my unbelief.

When Jesus, with Peter, James and John came down from the
mountain and rejoined the disciples they saw a large crowd round
them and some scribes arguing with them. The moment they saw him
the whole crowd were struck with amazement and ran to greet him.
'What are you arguing about with them?' he asked. A man answered
him from the crowd, 'Master, I have brought my son to you; there is a
spirit of dumbness in him, and when it takes hold of him it throws him
to the ground, and he foams at the mouth and grinds his teeth and
goes rigid. And I asked your disciples to cast it out and they were
unable to.' 'You faithless generation' he said to them in reply. 'How
much longer must I be with you? How much longer must I put up with
you? Bring him to me.' They brought the boy to him, and as soon as
the spirit saw Jesus it threw the boy into convulsions, and he fell to
the ground and lay writhing there, foaming at the mouth. Jesus asked
the father, 'How long has this been happening to him?' 'From
childhood,' he replied 'and it has often thrown him into the fire and
into the water, in order to destroy him. But if you can do anything,
have pity on us and help us.' 'If you can?' retorted Jesus. 'Everything
is possible for anyone who has faith.' Immediately the father of the
boy cried out, 'I do have faith. Help the little faith I have!' And

when Jesus saw how many people were pressing round him, he rebuked the unclean spirit. 'Deaf and dumb spirit,' he said 'I command you: come out of him and never enter him again.' Then throwing the boy into violent convulsions it came out shouting, and the boy lay there so like a corpse that most of them said, 'He is dead.' But Jesus took him by the hand and helped him up, and he was able to stand. When he had gone indoors his disciples asked him privately, 'Why were we unable to cast it out?' 'This is the kind' he answered 'that can only be driven out by prayer.'

This is the Gospel of the Lord.

Tuesday

FIRST READING

A reading from the letter of St James   4:1-10

You ask and you do not receive because you ask wrongly.

Where do these wars and battles between yourselves first start? Isn't it precisely in the desires fighting inside your own selves? You want something and you haven't got it; so you are prepared to kill. You have an ambition that you cannot satisfy; so you fight to get your way by force. Why you don't have what you want is because you don't pray for it; when you do pray and don't get it, it is because you have not prayed properly, you have prayed for something to indulge your own desires.

You are as unfaithful as adulterous wives; don't you realise that making the world your friend is making God your enemy? Anyone who chooses the world for his friend turns himself into God's enemy. Surely you don't think scripture is wrong when it says: the spirit which he sent to live in us wants us for himself alone? But he has been even more generous to us, as scripture says: God opposes the proud but he gives generously to the humble. Give in to God, then; resist the devil, and he will run away from you. The nearer you go to God, the nearer he will come to you. Clean your hands, you sinners, and clear your minds, you waverers. Look at your wretched condition, and weep for it in misery; be miserable instead of laughing, gloomy instead of happy. Humble yourselves before the Lord and he will lift you up.

This is the word of the Lord.

Responsorial Psalm   Ps 54:7-11. 23. ℞ v.23

℞   Throw your cares on the Lord,
      and he will support you.

1   O that I had wings like a dove
      to fly away and be at rest.
      So I would escape far away
      and take refuge in the desert.   ℞

2   I would hasten to find a shelter
      from the raging wind,
      from the destructive storm, O Lord,
      and from their plotting tongues.   ℞

3   For I can see nothing but violence
      and strife in the city.
      Night and day they patrol
      high on the city walls.   ℞

4   Entrust your cares to the Lord
      and he will support you.
      He will never allow
      the just man to stumble.   ℞

Gospel Acclamation   Gal 6:14

      Alleluia, alleluia!
      My only glory is the cross of our Lord Jesus Christ,
      which crucifies the world to me and me to the world.
      Alleluia!

GOSPEL

A reading from the holy Gospel according to Mark   9:30-37

The Son of Man will be betrayed. Whoever wishes to be first must be last.

Jesus and his disciples made their way through Galilee; and he did
not want anyone to know, because he was instructing his disciples; he
was telling them, 'The Son of Man will be delivered into the hands of
men; they will put him to death; and three days after he has been put
to death he will rise again.' But they did not understand what he said
and were afraid to ask him.

They came to Capernaum, and when he was in the house he asked them, 'What were you arguing about on the road?' They said nothing because they had been arguing which of them was the greatest. So he sat down, called the Twelve to him and said, 'If anyone wants to be first, he must make himself last of all and servant of all.' He then took a little child, set him in front of them, put his arms round him, and said to them, 'Anyone who welcomes one of these little children in my name, welcomes me; and anyone who welcomes me welcomes not me but the one who sent me.'

This is the Gospel of the Lord.

Wednesday

FIRST READING

A reading from the letter of St James   4:13-17

What about your life? You should say: If it is the Lord's will.

Here is the answer for those of you who talk like this: 'Today or tomorrow, we are off to this or that town; we are going to spend a year there, trading, and make some money.' You never know what will happen tomorrow: you are no more than a mist that is here for a little while and then disappears. The most you should ever say is: 'If it is the Lord's will, we shall still be alive to do this or that.' But how proud and sure of yourselves you are now! Pride of this kind is always wicked. Everyone who knows what is the right thing to do and doesn't do it commits a sin.

This is the word of the Lord.

Responsorial Psalm   Ps 48:2-3. 6-11. ℟ Mt 5:3

℟ Happy the poor in spirit;
the kingdom of heaven is theirs!

1 Hear this, all you peoples,
give heed, all who dwell in the world,
men both low and high,
rich and poor alike! ℟

2 Why should I fear in evil days
the malice of the foes who surround me,

men who trust in their wealth,
and boast of the vastness of their riches?   ℟

3   For no man can buy his own ransom,
     or pay a price to God for his life.
     The ransom of his soul is beyond him.
     He cannot buy life without end,
     nor avoid coming to the grave.   ℟

4   He knows that wise men and fools must both perish
     and leave their wealth to others.   ℟

Gospel Acclamation   Jn 14:6

Alleluia, alleluia!
I am the way, the truth and the life, says the Lord;
no one comes to the Father, except through me.
Alleluia!

GOSPEL

A reading from the holy Gospel according to Mark   9:38-40

Anyone who is not against us is for us.

John said to Jesus, 'Master, we saw a man who is not one of us casting
out devils in your name; and because he was not one of us we tried to
stop him.' But Jesus said, 'You must not stop him: no one who works a
miracle in my name is likely to speak evil of me. Anyone who is not
against us is for us.'

This is the Gospel of the Lord.

Thursday

FIRST READING

A reading from the letter of St James   5:1-6

*The hired workers you cheated cry out, and their cries reach the ears
of the Lord.*

The answer for the rich: start crying, weep for the miseries that are
coming to you. Your wealth is all rotting, your clothes are all eaten up
by moths. All your gold and your silver are corroding away, and the

same corrosion will be your own sentence, and eat into your body. It was a burning fire that you stored up as your treasure for the last days. Labourers mowed your fields, and you cheated them – listen to the wages that you kept back, calling out; realise that the cries of the reapers have reached the ears of the Lord of hosts. On earth you have had a life of comfort and luxury; in the time of slaughter you went on eating to your heart's content. It was you who condemned the innocent and killed them; they offered you no resistance.

This is the word of the Lord.

Responsorial Psalm   Ps 48:14-20. ℟ Mt 5:3

℟   Happy the poor in spirit;
      the kingdom of heaven is theirs!

1   This is the lot of the self-confident,
      who have others at their beck and call.
      Like sheep they are driven to the grave,
      where death shall be their shepherd
      and the just shall become their rulers.   ℟

2   With the morning their outward show vanishes
      and the grave becomes their home.
      But God will ransom me from death
      and take my soul to himself.   ℟

3   Then do not fear when a man grows rich,
      when the glory of his house increases.
      He takes nothing with him when he dies,
      his glory does not follow him below.   ℟

4   Though he flattered himself while he lived:
      'Men will praise me for doing well for myself,'
      yet he will go to join his fathers,
      who will never see the light any more.   ℟

Gospel Acclamation   cf. 1 Thess 2:13

Alleluia, alleluia!
Receive this message not as human words,
but as truly the word of God.
Alleluia!

506

GOSPEL

A reading from the holy Gospel according to Mark   9:41-50

It is better for you to enter into life crippled, than to have two hands and go to hell.

Jesus said to his disciples: 'If anyone gives you a cup of water to drink just because you belong to Christ, then I tell you solemnly, he will most certainly not lose his reward.

'But anyone who is an obstacle to bring down one of these little ones who have faith, would be better thrown into the sea with a great millstone round his neck. And if your hand should cause you to sin, cut it off; it is better for you to enter into life crippled, than to have two hands and go to hell, into the fire that cannot be put out. And if your foot should cause you to sin, cut if off; it is better for you to enter into life lame, than to have two feet and be thrown into hell. And if your eye should cause you to sin, tear it out; it is better for you to enter into the kingdom of God with one eye, than to have two eyes and be thrown into hell where their worm does not die nor their fire go out. For everyone will be salted with fire. Salt is a good thing, but if salt has become insipid, how can you season it again? Have salt in yourselves and be at peace with one another.'

This is the Gospel of the Lord.

Friday

A reading from the letter of St James   5:9-12

The judge is waiting at the gates.

Do not make complaints against one another, brothers, so as not to be brought to judgement yourselves; the Judge is already to be seen waiting at the gates. For your example, brothers, in submitting with patience, take the prophets who spoke in the name of the Lord; remember it is those who had endurance that we say are the blessed ones. You have heard of the patience of Job, and understood the Lord's purpose, realising that the Lord is kind and compassionate.

Above all, my brothers, do not swear by heaven or by the earth, or use any oaths at all. If you mean 'yes', you must say 'yes'; if you mean 'no', say 'no'. Otherwise you make yourselves liable to judgement.

This is the word of the Lord.

507

Responsorial Psalm   Ps 102:1-4. 8-9. 11-12. ℟ v.8

℟   The Lord is kind and merciful.

1   My soul, give thanks to the Lord,
      all my being, bless his holy name.
      My soul, give thanks to the Lord
      and never forget all his blessings. ℟

2   It is he who forgives all your guilt,
      who heals every one of your ills,
      who redeems your life from the grave,
      who crowns you with love and compassion. ℟

3   The Lord is compassion and love,
      slow to anger and rich in mercy.
      His wrath will come to an end;
      he will not be angry for ever. ℟

4   For as the heavens are high above the earth
      so strong is his love for those who fear him.
      As far as the east is from the west
      so far does he remove our sins. ℟

Gospel Acclamation   cf. Jn 17:17

      Alleluia, alleluia!
      Your word, O Lord, is truth:
      make us holy in the truth.
      Alleluia!

GOSPEL

A reading from the holy Gospel according to Mark   10:1-12

What God has joined together, no one must divide.

Jesus came to the district of Judaea and the far side of the Jordan.
And again crowds gathered round him, and again he taught them, as
his custom was. Some Pharisees approached him and asked, 'Is it
against the law for a man to divorce his wife?' They were testing him.
He answered them, 'What did Moses command you?' 'Moses allowed
us' they said 'to draw up a writ of dismissal and so to divorce.' Then
Jesus said to them, 'It was because you were so unteachable that he
wrote this commandment for you. But from the beginning of creation
God made them male and female. This is why a man must leave father

508

and mother, and the two become one body. They are no longer two, therefore, but one body. So then, what God has united, man must not divide.' Back in the house the disciples questioned him again about this, and he said to them, 'The man who divorces his wife and marries another is guilty of adultery against her. And if a woman divorces her husband and marries another she is guilty of adultery too.'

This is the Gospel of the Lord.

Saturday

FIRST READING

A reading from the letter of St James   5:13-20

The prayer of the just has great power.

If any one of you is in trouble, he should pray; if anyone is feeling happy, he should sing a psalm. If one of you is ill, he should send for the elders of the church, and they must anoint him with oil in the name of the Lord and pray over him. The prayer of faith will save the sick man and the Lord will raise him up again; and if he has committed any sins, he will be forgiven. So confess your sins to one another, and pray for one another, and this will cure you; the heartfelt prayer of a good man works very powerfully. Elijah was a human being like ourselves – he prayed hard for it not to rain, and no rain fell for three-and-a-half years; then he prayed again and the sky gave rain and the earth gave crops.

My brothers, if one of you strays away from the truth, and another brings him back to it, he may be sure that anyone who can bring back a sinner from the wrong way that he has taken will be saving a soul from death and covering up a great number of sins.

This is the word of the Lord.

Responsorial Psalm   Ps 140:1-3. 8. ℟ v.2

℟   Let my prayer come like incense before you.

1   I have called to you, Lord; hasten to help me!
     Hear my voice when I cry to you.
     Let my prayer come before you like incense,
     the raising of my hands like an evening oblation.   ℟

2 Lord, set a guard over my mouth;
   keep watch at the door of my lips!
   To you, Lord God, my eyes are turned;
   in you I take refuge; spare my soul!

℟ Let my prayer come like incense before you.

Gospel Acclamation   cf. Mt 11:25

Alleluia, alleluia!
Blessed are you, Father, Lord of heaven and earth;
you have revealed to little ones the mysteries of the kingdom.
Alleluia!

GOSPEL

A reading from the holy Gospel according to Mark   10:13-16

*Whoever does not accept the kingdom of God like a child will never
enter it.*

People were bringing little children to Jesus, for him to touch them.
The disciples turned them away, but when Jesus saw this he was
indignant and said to them, 'Let the little children come to me; do not
stop them; for it is to such as these that the kingdom of God belongs. I
tell you solemnly, anyone who does not welcome the kingdom of God
like a little child will never enter it.' Then he put his arms round
them, laid his hands on them and gave them his blessing.

This is the Gospel of the Lord.

EIGHTH WEEK IN ORDINARY TIME
Year II

Monday

FIRST READING

A reading from the first letter of St Peter   1:3-9

*You did not see Christ, yet you love him, and because you believe
you are filled with a joy that cannot be described.*

Blessed be God the Father of our Lord Jesus Christ, who in his great
mercy has given us a new birth as his sons, by raising Jesus Christ
from the dead, so that we have a sure hope and the promise of an
inheritance that can never be spoilt or soiled and never fade away,
because it is being kept for you in the heavens. Through your faith,
God's power will guard you until the salvation which has been
prepared is revealed at the end of time. This is a cause of great joy for
you, even though you may for a short time have to bear being plagued
by all sorts of trials; so that, when Jesus Christ is revealed, your faith
will have been tested and proved like gold – only it is more precious
than gold, which is corruptible even though it bears testing by fire –
and then you will have praise and glory and honour. You did not see
him, yet you love him; and still without seeing him, you are already
filled with a joy so glorious that it cannot be described, because you
believe; and you are sure of the end to which your faith looks forward,
that is, the salvation of your souls.

This is the word of the Lord.

Responsorial Psalm   Ps 110:1-2. 5-6. 9-10. ℟ v.5

℟   The Lord will remember his covenant for ever.

or

℟   Alleluia!

1   I will thank the Lord with all my heart
     in the meeting of the just and their assembly.
     Great are the works of the Lord;
     to be pondered by all who love them. ℟

2   He gives food to those who fear him;
    keeps his covenant ever in mind.
    He has shown his might to his people
    by giving them the lands of the nations.   ℟

3   He has sent deliverance to his people
    and established his covenant for ever.
    Holy his name, to be feared.   ℟

4   To fear the Lord is the beginning of wisdom;
    all who do so prove themselves wise.
    His praise shall last for ever!   ℟

Gospel Acclamation   2 Cor 8:9

    Alleluia, alleluia!
    Jesus Christ was rich but he became poor
    to make you rich out of his poverty.
    Alleluia!

GOSPEL

A reading from the holy Gospel according to Mark   10:17-27

Go, sell everything you have and follow me.

Jesus was setting out on a journey when a man ran up, knelt before
him and put this question to him, 'Good master, what must I do to
inherit eternal life?' Jesus said to him, 'Why do you call me good? No
one is good but God alone. You know the commandments: You must
not kill; You must not commit adultery; You must not steal; You must
not bring false witness; You must not defraud; Honour your father
and mother.' And he said to him, 'Master, I have kept all these from
my earliest days.' Jesus looked steadily at him and loved him, and he
said, 'There is one thing you lack. Go and sell everything you own and
give the money to the poor, and you will have treasure in heaven; then
come, follow me.' But his face fell at these words and he went away
sad, for he was a man of great wealth.

    Jesus looked round and said to his disciples, 'How hard it is for
those who have riches to enter the kingdom of God!' The disciples were
astounded by these words, but Jesus insisted, 'My children,' he said to
them 'how hard it is to enter the kingdom of God! It is easier for a
camel to pass through the eye of a needle than for a rich man

to enter the kingdom of God.' They were more astonished than ever. 'In that case' they said to one another 'who can be saved?' Jesus gazed at them. 'For men' he said 'it is impossible, but not for God: because everything is possible for God.'

This is the Gospel of the Lord.

Tuesday

FIRST READING

A reading from the first letter of St Peter   1:10-16

They prophesied about the grace which was to come to you, so
be watchful and perfect in hope.

It was this salvation that the prophets were looking and searching so hard for; their prophecies were about the grace which was to come to you. The Spirit of Christ which was in them foretold the sufferings of Christ and the glories that would come after them, and they tried to find out at what time and in what circumstances all this was to be expected. It was revealed to them that the news they brought of all the things which have now been announced to you, by those who preached to you the Good News through the Holy Spirit sent from heaven, was for you and not for themselves. Even the angels long to catch a glimpse of these things.

Free your minds, then, of encumbrances; control them, and put your trust in nothing but the grace that will be given you when Jesus Christ is revealed. Do not behave in the way that you liked to before you learnt the truth; make a habit of obedience: be holy in all you do, since it is the Holy One who has called you, and scripture says: Be holy, for I am holy.

This is the word of the Lord.

Responsorial Psalm   Ps 97:1-4. ℟ v.2

℟   The Lord has made known his salvation.

1   Sing a new song to the Lord
    for he has worked wonders.
    His right hand and his holy arm
    have brought salvation.   ℟

2   The Lord has made known his salvation;
    has shown his justice to the nations.
    He has remembered his truth and love
    for the house of Israel.   ℟

3   All the ends of the earth have seen
    the salvation of our God.
    Shout to the Lord all the earth,
    ring out your joy.   ℟

Gospel Acclamation   cf. Mt 11:25

    Alleluia, alleluia!
    Blessed are you, Father, Lord of heaven and earth;
    you have revealed to little ones the mysteries of the kingdom.
    Alleluia!

GOSPEL

A reading from the holy Gospel according to Mark   10:28-31

You will receive a hundred times as much persecution in
this present time, and in the world to come, eternal life.

'What about us?' Peter asked Jesus. 'We have left everything and
followed you.' Jesus said, 'I tell you solemnly, there is no one who has
left house, brothers, sisters, father, children or land for my sake and
for the sake of the gospel who will not be repaid a hundred times over,
houses, brothers, sisters, mothers, children and land – not without
persecution – now in this present time and, in the world to come,
eternal life.

    'Many who are first will be last, and the last first.'

    This is the Gospel of the Lord.

Wednesday

FIRST READING

A reading from the first letter of St Peter   1:18-25

You have been ransomed in the precious blood of Christ, a spotless lamb.

Remember, the ransom that was paid to free you from the useless way of life your ancestors handed down was not paid in anything corruptible, neither in silver nor gold, but in the precious blood of a lamb without spot or stain, namely Christ; who, though known since before the world was made, has been revealed only in our time, the end of the ages, for your sake. Through him you now have faith in God, who raised him from the dead and gave him glory for that very reason – so that you would have faith and hope in God.

You have been obedient to the truth and purified your souls until you can love like brothers, in sincerity; let your love for each other be real and from the heart – your new birth was not from any mortal seed but from the everlasting word of the living and eternal God. All flesh is grass and its glory like the wild flower's. The grass withers, the flower falls, but the word of the Lord remains for ever. What is this word? It is the Good News that has been brought to you.

This is the word of the Lord.

Responsorial Psalm   Ps 147:12-15. 19-20. ℟ v.12

℟ Praise the Lord, Jerusalem.

or

℟ Alleluia!

1 O praise the Lord, Jerusalem!
   Zion, praise your God!
   He has strengthened the bars of your gates,
   he has blessed the children within you.   ℟

2 He established peace on your borders,
   he feeds you with finest wheat.
   He sends out his word to the earth
   and swiftly runs his command.   ℟   (continued)

3   He makes his word known to Jacob,
    to Israel his laws and decrees.
    He has not dealt thus with other nations,
    he has not taught them his decrees.

    ℟   Praise the Lord, Jerusalem.

or

    ℟   Alleluia!

Gospel Acclamation   Mk 10:45

    Alleluia, alleluia!
    The Son of Man came to serve
    and to give his life as a ransom for all.
    Alleluia!

GOSPEL

A reading from the holy Gospel according to Mark   10:32-45

*Now we are going up to Jerusalem, and the Son of Man will be
handed over.*

The disciples were on the road, going up to Jerusalem; Jesus was walking on ahead of them; they were in a daze, and those who followed were apprehensive. Once more taking the Twelve aside he began to tell them what was going to happen to him: 'Now we are going up to Jerusalem, and the Son of Man is about to be handed over to the chief priests and the scribes. They will condemn him to death and will hand him over to the pagans, who will mock him and spit at him and scourge him and put him to death; and after three days he will rise again.'

James and John, the sons of Zebedee, approached him. 'Master,' they said to him 'we want you to do us a favour.' He said to them, 'What is it you want me to do for you?' They said to him, 'Allow us to sit one at your right hand and the other at your left in your glory.' 'You do not know what you are asking' Jesus said to them. 'Can you drink the cup that I must drink, or be baptised with the baptism with which I must be baptised?' They replied, 'We can.' Jesus said to them. 'The cup that I must drink you shall drink, and with the baptism with which I must be baptised you shall be baptised, but as for seats at my right hand or my left, these are not mine to grant; they belong to those to whom they have been allotted.'

When the other ten heard this they began to feel indignant with James and John, so Jesus called them to him and said to them, 'You know that among the pagans their so-called rulers lord it over them, and their great men make their authority felt. This is not to happen among you. No; anyone who wants to become great among you must be your servant, and anyone who wants to be first among you must be slave to all. For the Son of Man himself did not come to be served but to serve, and to give his life as a ransom for many.'

This is the Gospel of the Lord.

Thursday

FIRST READING

A reading from the first letter of St Peter   2:2-5. 9-12

You are a chosen race, a royal priesthood, sing the praises of God who called you out of darkness.

You are new born, and, like babies, you should be hungry for nothing but milk – the spiritual honesty which will help you to grow up to salvation – now that you have tasted the goodness of the Lord.

He is the living stone, rejected by men but chosen by God and precious to him; set yourselves close to him so that you too, the holy priesthood that offers the spiritual sacrifices which Jesus Christ has made acceptable to God, may be living stones making a spiritual house.

But you are a chosen race, a royal priesthood, a consecrated nation, a people set apart to sing the praises of God who called you out of the darkness into his wonderful light. Once you were not a people at all and now you are the People of God; once you were outside the mercy and now you have been given mercy.

I urge you, my dear people, while you are visitors and pilgrims to keep yourselves free from the selfish passions that attack the soul. Always behave honourably among pagans so that they can see your good works for themselves and, when the day of reckoning comes, give thanks to God for the things which now make them denounce you as criminals.

This is the word of the Lord.

Responsorial Psalm   Ps 99:2-5.℟ v.2

℟   Come with joy into the presence of the Lord.

1   Cry out with joy to the Lord, all the earth.
    Serve the Lord with gladness.
    Come before him, singing for joy.   ℟

2   Know that he, the Lord, is God.
    He made us, we belong to him,
    we are his people, the sheep of his flock.   ℟

3   Go within his gates, giving thanks.
    Enter his courts with songs of praise.
    Give thanks to him and bless his name.   ℟

4   Indeed, how good is the Lord,
    eternal his merciful love.
    He is faithful from age to age.   ℟

Gospel Acclamation   Jn 8:12

    Alleluia, alleluia!
    I am the light of the world, says the Lord:
    whoever follows me will have the light of life.
    Alleluia!

GOSPEL

A reading from the holy Gospel according to Mark   10:46-52

Master, let me see again.

As Jesus was leaving Jericho with his disciples and a large crowd,
Bartimaeus (that is, the son of Timaeus), a blind beggar, was sitting
at the side of the road. When he heard that it was Jesus of Nazareth,
he began to shout and to say, 'Son of David, Jesus, have pity on me.'
And many of them scolded him and told him to keep quiet, but he only
shouted all the louder, 'Son of David, have pity on me.' Jesus stopped
and said, 'Call him here'. So they called the blind man. 'Courage,' they
said 'get up; he is calling you.' So throwing off his cloak, he jumped up
and went to Jesus. Then Jesus spoke, 'What do you want me to do for
you?' 'Rabbuni,' the blind man said to him 'Master, let me see again.'
Jesus said to him, 'Go; your faith has saved you.' And immediately his
sight returned and he followed him along the road.

    This is the Gospel of the Lord.

Friday

FIRST READING

A reading from the first letter of St Peter   4:7-13

Be good stewards of the many graces you have received.

Everything will soon come to an end, so, to pray better, keep a calm and sober mind. Above all, never let your love for each other grow insincere, since love covers over many a sin. Welcome each other into your houses without grumbling. Each one of you has received a special grace, so, like good stewards responsible for all these different graces of God, put yourselves at the service of others. If you are a speaker, speak in words which seem to come from God; if you are a helper, help as though every action was done at God's orders; so that in everything God may receive the glory, through Jesus Christ, since to him alone belong all glory and power for ever and ever. Amen.

My dear people, you must not think it unaccountable that you should be tested by fire. There is nothing extraordinary in what has happened to you. If you can have some share in the sufferings of Christ, be glad, because you will enjoy a much greater gladness when his glory is revealed.

This is the word of the Lord.

Responsorial Psalm   Ps 95:10-13. ℟ v.13

℟   The Lord comes to judge the earth.

1   Proclaim to the nations: 'God is king.'
    The world he made firm in its place;
    he will judge the peoples in fairness.   ℟

2   Let the heavens rejoice and earth be glad.
    Let the sea and all within it thunder praise,
    let the land and all it bears rejoice,
    all the trees of the wood shout for joy
    at the presence of the Lord for he comes,
    he comes to rule the earth.   ℟

3   With justice he will rule the world,
    he will judge the peoples with his truth.   ℟

Gospel Acclamation   cf. Jn 15:16

Alleluia, alleluia!
I have chosen you from the world, says the Lord,
to go and bear fruit that will last.
Alleluia!

GOSPEL

A reading from the holy Gospel according to Mark   11:11-26

My house will be called a house of prayer for all the people. Have faith in God.

After he had been acclaimed by the crowds, Jesus entered Jerusalem
and went into the Temple. He looked all round him, but as it was now
late, he went out to Bethany with the Twelve.

Next day as they were leaving Bethany, he felt hungry. Seeing a
fig tree in leaf some distance away, he went to see if he could find any
fruit on it, but when he came up to it he found nothing but leaves; for
it was not the season for figs. And he addressed the fig tree. 'May no
one ever eat fruit from you again' he said. And his disciples heard him
say this.

So they reached Jerusalem and he went into the Temple and began
driving out those who were selling and buying there; he upset the
tables of the money changers and the chairs of those who were selling
pigeons. Nor would he allow anyone to carry anything through the
Temple. And he taught them and said, 'Does not scripture say: My
house will be called a house of prayer for all the peoples? But you have
turned it into a robber's den.' This came to the ears of the chief priests
and the scribes, and they tried to find some way of doing away with
him; they were afraid of him because the people were carried away by
his teaching. And when evening came he went out of the city.

Next morning, as they passed by, they saw the fig tree withered to
the roots. Peter remembered. 'Look, Rabbi,' he said to Jesus 'the fig
tree you cursed has withered away.' Jesus answered, 'Have faith in
God. I tell you solemnly, if anyone says to this mountain, "Get up and
throw yourself into the sea," with no hesitation in his heart but
believing that what he says will happen, it will be done for him. I tell
you therefore: everything you ask and pray for, believe that you have
it already, and it will be yours. And when you stand in prayer, forgive
whatever you have against anybody, so that your Father in heaven
may forgive your failings too. But if you do not forgive, your Father in
heaven will not forgive your failings either.'

This is the Gospel of the Lord.

Saturday

FIRST READING

A reading from the letter of St Jude   17. 20-25

Glory be to him who can keep you from falling and bring you safe
to his presence.

Remember, my dear friends, what the apostles of our Lord Jesus
Christ told you to expect. You must use your holy faith as your
foundation and build on that, praying in the Holy Spirit; keep
yourselves within the love of God and wait for the mercy of our Lord
Jesus Christ to give you eternal life. When there are some who have
doubts, reassure them; when there are some to be saved from the fire,
pull them out; but there are others to whom you must be kind with
great caution, keeping your distance even from outside clothing which
is contaminated by vice.

Glory be to him who can keep you from falling and bring you safe
to his glorious presence, innocent and happy. To God, the only God,
who saves us through Jesus Christ our Lord, be the glory, majesty,
authority and power, which he had before time began, now and for
ever. Amen.

This is the word of the Lord.

Responsorial Psalm   Ps 62:2-6. ℟ v.2

℟   My soul is thirsting for you,
    O Lord my God.

1   O God, you are my God, for you I long;
    for you my soul is thirsting.
    My body pines for you
    like a dry weary land without water.   ℟

2   So I gaze on you in the sanctuary
    to see your strength and your glory.
    For your love is better than life,
    my lips will speak your praise.   ℟

3   So I will bless you all my life,
    in your name I will lift up my hands.
    My soul shall be filled as with a banquet,
    my mouth shall praise you with joy.   ℟

Gospel Acclamation   cf. Col 3:16. 17

> Alleluia, alleluia!
> Give thanks to God our Father through Jesus Christ our Lord,
> and may the fullness of his message live within you.
> Alleluia!

GOSPEL

A reading from the holy Gospel according to Mark   11:27-33

What authority have you for acting like this?

Jesus and his disciples came to Jerusalem, and as Jesus was walking in the Temple, the chief priests and the scribes and the elders came to him, and they said to him, 'What authority have you for acting like this? Or who gave you authority to do these things?' Jesus said to them, 'I will ask you a question, only one; answer me and I will tell you my authority for acting like this. John's baptism: did it come from heaven, or from man? Answer me that.' And they argued it out this way among themselves: 'If we say from heaven, he will say, "Then why did you refuse to believe him?" But dare we say from man?' – they had the people to fear, for everyone held that John was a real prophet. So their reply to Jesus was, 'We do not know.' And Jesus said to them, 'Nor will I tell you my authority for acting like this.'

This is the Gospel of the Lord.

NINTH WEEK IN ORDINARY TIME

Year II

Monday

FIRST READING

A reading from the second letter of St Peter   1:2-7

He has promised and bestowed on us precious gifts to enable us
to share divine nature.

May you have more and more grace and peace as you come to know
our Lord more and more.

By his divine power, he has given us all the things that we need for
life and for true devotion, bringing us to know God himself, who has
called us by his own glory and goodness. In making these gifts, he has
given us the guarantee of something very great and wonderful to
come: through them you will be able to share the divine nature and to
escape corruption in a world that is sunk in vice. But to attain this,
you will have to do your utmost yourselves, adding goodness to the
faith that you have, understanding to your goodness, self-control to
your understanding, patience to your self-control, true devotion to
your patience, kindness towards your fellow men to your devotion,
and, to this kindness, love.

This is the word of the Lord.

Responsorial Psalm   Ps 90:1-2. 14-16. ℟ v. cf. 2

℟   In you, my God, I place my trust.

1   He who dwells in the shelter of the Most High
    and abides in the shade of the Almighty
    says to the Lord: 'My refuge,
    my stronghold, my God in whom I trust!'   ℟

2   His love he set on me, so I will rescue him;
    protect him for he knows my name.
    When he calls I shall answer: 'I am with you.'   ℟

3   I will save him in distress and give him glory.
    With length of life I will content him;
    I shall let him see my saving power.   ℟

Gospel Acclamation   cf. Apoc 1:5

Alleluia, alleluia!
Jesus Christ, you are the faithful witness, firstborn from the dead;
you have loved us and washed away our sins in your blood.
Alleluia!

GOSPEL

A reading from the holy Gospel according to Mark   12:1-12

They seized the beloved son, killed him, and threw him out of the vineyard.

Jesus began to speak to the chief priests, the scribes and the elders in
parables, 'A man planted a vineyard; he fenced it round, dug out a
trough for the winepress and built a tower; then he leased it to tenants
and went abroad. When the time came, he sent a servant to the
tenants to collect from them his share of the produce from the
vineyard. But they seized the man, thrashed him and sent him away
empty-handed. Next he sent another servant to them; him they beat
about the head and treated shamefully. And he sent another and him
they killed; then a number of others, and they thrashed some and
killed the rest. He had still someone left: his beloved son. He sent him
to them last of all. 'They will respect my son' he said. But those
tenants said to each other, 'This is the heir. Come on, let us kill him,
and the inheritance will be ours.' So they seized him and killed him
and threw him out of the vineyard. Now what will the owner of the
vineyard do? He will come and make an end of the tenants and give
the vineyard to others. Have you not read this text of scripture:

It was the stone rejected by the builders
that became the keystone.
This was the Lord's doing
and it is wonderful to see?'

And they would have liked to arrest him, because they realised
that the parable was aimed at them, but they were afraid of the
crowds. So they left him alone and went away.

This is the Gospel of the Lord.

Tuesday

FIRST READING

A reading from the second letter of St Peter   3:11-15. 17-18

We are waiting for the new heavens and the new earth.

You should be living holy and saintly lives while you wait and long for
the Day of God to come, when the sky will dissolve in flames and the
elements melt in the heat. What we are waiting for is what he
promised: the new heavens and new earth, the place where righteousness will be at home. So then, my friends, while you are waiting, do
your best to live lives without spot or stain so that he will find you at
peace. Think of our Lord's patience as your opportunity to be saved.
You have been warned about this, my friends; be careful not to get
carried away by the errors of unprincipled people, from the firm
ground that you are standing on. Instead, go on growing in the grace
and in the knowledge of our Lord and saviour Jesus Christ. To him be
glory, in time and in eternity. Amen.

This is the word of the Lord.

Responsorial Psalm   Ps 89:2-4. 10. 14. 16. ℟ v.1

℟   In every age, O Lord, you have been our refuge.

1   Before the mountains were born
     or the earth or the world brought forth,
     you are God, without beginning or end.   ℟

2   You turn men back into dust
     and say: 'Go back, sons of men.'
     To your eyes a thousand years
     are like yesterday, come and gone,
     no more than a watch in the night.   ℟

3   Our span is seventy years
     or eighty for those who are strong.
     And most of these are emptiness and pain.
     They pass swiftly and we are gone.   ℟

4   In the morning, fill us with your love;
     we shall exult and rejoice all our days.
     Show forth your work to your servants;
     let your glory shine on their children.   ℟

Gospel Acclamation cf. Eph 1:17-18

Alleluia, alleluia!
May the Father of our Lord Jesus Christ
enlighten the eyes of our heart
that we might see how great is the hope
to which we are called
Alleluia!

GOSPEL

A reading from the holy Gospel according to Mark 12:13-17

Give to Caesar what belongs to Caesar and to God what belongs to God.

The chief priests and the scribes and the elders sent to Jesus some Pharisees and some Herodians to catch him out in what he said. These came and said to him, 'Master, we know you are an honest man, that you are not afraid of anyone, because a man's rank means nothing to you, and that you teach the way of God in all honesty. Is it permissible to pay taxes to Caesar or not? Should we pay, yes or no?' Seeing through their hyprocrisy he said to them, 'Why do you set this trap for me? Hand me a denarius and let me see it.' They handed him one and he said, 'Whose head is this? Whose name?' 'Caesar's' they told him. Jesus said to them, 'Give back to Caesar what belongs to Caesar – and to God what belongs to God.' This reply took them completely by surprise.

This is the Gospel of the Lord.

Wednesday

FIRST READING

A reading from the second letter of St Paul to Timothy 1:1-3. 6-12

Rekindle the gift God gave you when I laid my hands on you.

From Paul, appointed by God to be an apostle of Christ Jesus in his design to promise life in Christ Jesus; to Timothy, dear child of mine, wishing you grace, mercy and peace from God the Father and from Christ Jesus our Lord.

Night and day I thank God, keeping my conscience clear and

remembering my duty to him as my ancestors did, and always I remember you in my prayers

This is why I am reminding you now to fan into a flame the gift that God gave you when I laid my hands on you. God's gift was not a spirit of timidity, but the Spirit of power, and love, and self-control. So you are never to be ashamed of witnessing to the Lord, or ashamed of me for being his prisoner; but with me bear the hardships for the sake of the Good News, relying on the power of God who has saved us and called us to be holy – not because of anything we ourselves have done but for his own purpose and by his own grace. This grace had already been granted to us, in Christ Jesus, before the beginning of time, but it has only been revealed by the Appearing of our saviour Christ Jesus. He abolished death, and he has proclaimed life and immortality through the Good News; and I have been named its herald, its apostle and its teacher.

It is only on account of this that I am experiencing fresh hardships here now; but I have not lost confidence, because I know who it is that I have put my trust in, and I have no doubt at all that he is able to take care of all that I have entrusted to him until that Day.

This is the word of the Lord.

Responsorial Psalm   Ps 122:1-2. ℟ v.1

℟   To you, O Lord, I lift up my eyes.

1   To you have I lifted up my eyes,
    you who dwell in the heavens:
    my eyes, like the eyes of slaves
    on the hand of their lord.   ℟

2   Like the eyes of a servant
    on the hand of her mistress,
    so our eyes are on the Lord our God
    till he show us his mercy.   ℟

Gospel Acclamation   Jn 11:25. 26

Alleluia, alleluia!
I am the resurrection and the life, says the Lord;
whoever believes in me will not die for ever.
Alleluia!

GOSPEL

A reading from the holy Gospel according to Mark 12:18-27

He is God, not of the dead, but of the living.

Some Sadducees – who deny that there is a resurrection – came to Jesus and they put this question to him, 'Master, we have it from Moses in writing, if a man's brother dies leaving a wife but no child, the man must marry the widow to raise up children for his brother. Now there were seven brothers. The first married a wife and then died leaving no children. The second married the widow, and he too died leaving no children; with the third it was the same, and none of the seven left any children. Last of all the woman herself died. Now at the resurrection, when they rise again, whose wife will she be, since she had been married to all seven?'

Jesus said to them, 'Is not the reason why you go wrong, that you understand neither the scriptures nor the power of God? For when they rise from the dead, men and women do not marry; no, they are like the angels in heaven. Now about the dead rising again, have you never read in the Book of Moses, in the passage about the Bush, how God spoke to him and said: I am the God of Abraham, the God of Isaac and the God of Jacob? He is God, not of the dead, but of the living. You are very much mistaken.'

This is the Gospel of the Lord.

Thursday

FIRST READING

A reading from the second letter of St Paul to Timothy 2:8-15

The word of God is not chained. If we have died with him, we shall live with him.

Remember the Good News that I carry, 'Jesus Christ risen from the dead, sprung from the race of David'; it is on account of this that I have my own hardships to bear, even to being chained like a criminal – but they cannot chain up God's news. So I bear it all for the sake of those who are chosen, so that in the end they may have the salvation that is in Christ Jesus and the eternal glory that comes with it.

Here is a saying that you can rely on:

If we have died with him, then we shall live with him.
If we hold firm, then we shall reign with him.
If we disown him, then he will disown us.
We may be unfaithful, but he is always faithful,
for he cannot disown his own self.

Remind them of this; and tell them in the name of God that there is to be no wrangling about words: all that this ever achieves is the destruction of those who are listening. Do all you can to present yourself in front of God as a man who has come through his trials, and a man who has no cause to be ashamed of his life's work and has kept a straight course with the message of the truth.

This is the word of the Lord.

Responsorial Psalm   Ps 24:4-5. 8-10. 14. ℟ v.4

℟   Teach me your ways, O Lord.

1   Lord, make me know your ways.
    Lord, teach me your paths.
    Make me walk in your truth, and teach me:
    for you are God my saviour.   ℟

2   The Lord is good and upright.
    He shows the path to those who stray,
    he guides the humble in the right path;
    he teaches his way to the poor.   ℟

3   His ways are faithfulness and love
    for those who keep his covenant and will.
    The Lord's friendship is for those who revere him;
    to them he reveals his covenant.   ℟

Gospel Acclamation   cf. 2 Tim 1:10

Alleluia, alleluia!
Our Saviour Jesus Christ has done away with death
and brought us life through his gospel.
Alleluia!

GOSPEL

A reading from the holy Gospel according to Mark   12:28-34

This is the first commandment. The second is similar to it.

One of the scribes came up to Jesus and put a question to him, 'Which is the first of all the commandments?' Jesus replied, 'This is the first: Listen, Israel, the Lord our God is the one Lord, and you must love the Lord your God with all your heart, with all your soul, with all your mind and with all your strength. The second is this: You must love your neighbour as yourself. There is no commandment greater than these.' The scribe said to him, 'Well spoken, Master; what you have said is true: that he is one and there is no other. To love him with all your heart, with all your understanding and strength, and to love your neighbour as yourself, this is far more important than any holocaust or sacrifice.' Jesus, seeing how wisely he had spoken, said, 'You are not far from the kingdom of God.' And after that no one dared to question him any more.

This is the Gospel of the Lord.

Friday

FIRST READING

A reading from the second letter of St Paul to Timothy   3:10-17

Whoever tries to live for Christ will be persecuted.

You know what I have taught, how I have lived, what I have aimed at; you know my faith, my patience and my love; my constancy and the persecutions and hardships that came to me in places like Antioch, Iconium and Lystra – all the persecutions I have endured; and the Lord has rescued me from every one of them. You are well aware, then, that anybody who tries to live in devotion to Christ is certain to be attacked; while these wicked impostors will go from bad to worse, deceiving others and deceived themselves.

You must keep to what you have been taught and know to be true; remember who your teachers were, and how, ever since you were a child, you have known the holy scriptures – from these you can learn the wisdom that leads to salvation through faith in Christ Jesus. All scripture is inspired by God and can profitably be used for teaching, for refuting error, for guiding people's lives and teaching them to be holy. This is how the man who is dedicated to God becomes fully equipped and ready for any good work.

This is the word of the Lord.

Responsorial Psalm   Ps 118:157. 160-161. 165-166. 168. ℟ v.165

℟   O Lord, great peace have they who love your law.

1   Though my foes and oppressors are countless
    I have not swerved from your will.
    Your word is founded on truth:
    your decrees are eternal.   ℟

2   Though princes oppress me without cause
    I stand in awe of your word.
    The lovers of your law have great peace;
    they never stumble.   ℟

3   I await your saving help, O Lord,
    I fulfil your commands.
    I obey your precepts and your will;
    all that I do is before you.   ℟

Gospel Acclamation   Jn 14:23

Alleluia, alleluia!
All who love me will keep my words,
and my Father will love them, and we will come to them.
Alleluia!

GOSPEL

A reading from the holy Gospel according to Mark   12:35-37

How can the scribes maintain that Christ is the son of David?

While teaching in the Temple, Jesus said, 'How can the scribes maintain that the Christ is the son of David? David himself, moved by the Holy Spirit, said:

The Lord said to my Lord:
Sit at my right hand
and I will put your enemies

under your feet.

David himself calls him Lord, in what way then can he be his son?'
And the great majority of the people heard this with delight.

This is the Gospel of the Lord.

Saturday

FIRST READING

A reading from the second letter of St Paul to Timothy   4:1-8

*Proclaim the Good News. I am already being destroyed and the Lord
will give me the crown of righteousness.*

Before God and before Christ Jesus who is to be judge of the living and
the dead, I put this duty to you, in the name of his Appearing and of
his kingdom: proclaim the message and, welcome or unwelcome,
insist on it. Refute falsehood, correct error, call to obedience – but do
all with patience and with the intention of teaching. The time is sure
to come when, far from being content with sound teaching, people will
be avid for the latest novelty and collect themselves a whole series of
teachers according to their own tastes; and then, instead of listening
to the truth, they will turn to myths. Be careful always to choose the
right course; be brave under trials; make the preaching of the Good
News your life's work, in thoroughgoing service.

As for me, my life is already being poured away as a libation, and
the time has come for me to be gone. I have fought the good fight to the
end; I have run the race to the finish; I have kept the faith; all there is
to come now is the crown of righteousness reserved for me, which the
Lord, the righteous judge, will give me on that Day; and not only to
me but to all those who have longed for his Appearing.

This is the word of the Lord.

Responsorial Psalm   Ps 70:8-9. 14-17. 22. ℟ cf. v.15

℟   I will sing of your salvation.

1   My lips are filled with your praise,
     with your glory all the day long.
     Do not reject me now that I am old;
     when my strength fails do not forsake me.   ℟

2   But as for me, I will always hope
     and praise you more and more.
     My lips will tell of your justice
     and day by day of your help
     (though I can never tell it all). ℟

3   I will declare the Lord's mighty deeds
     proclaiming your justice, yours alone.
     O God, you have taught me from my youth
     and I proclaim your wonders still. ℟

4   So I will give thanks on the lyre
     for your faithful love, my God.
     To you will I sing with the harp
     to you, the Holy One of Israel. ℟

Gospel Acclamation   Mt 5:3

    Alleluia, alleluia!
    Happy the poor in spirit;
    the kingdom of heaven is theirs!
    Alleluia!

GOSPEL

A reading from the holy Gospel according to Mark   12:38-44

This poor widow has given more than all others.

In his teaching Jesus said, 'Beware of the scribes who like to walk about in long robes, to be greeted obsequiously in the market squares, to take the front seats in the synagogues and the places of honour at banquets; these are the men who swallow the property of widows, while making a show of lengthy prayers. The more severe will be the sentence they receive.'

He sat down opposite the treasury and watched the people putting money into the treasury, and many of the rich put in a great deal. A poor widow came and put in two small coins, the equivalent of a penny. Then he called his disciples and said to them, 'I tell you solemnly, this poor widow has put more in than all who have contributed to the treasury; for they have all put in money they had over, but she from the little she had has put in everything she possessed, all she had to live on.'

This is the Gospel of the Lord.

TENTH WEEK IN ORDINARY TIME
Year II

Monday

FIRST READING

A reading from the first book of the Kings   17:1-6

Elias stands before the Lord God of Israel.

Elijah the Tishbite, of Tishbe in Gilead said to Ahab, 'As the Lord
lives, the God of Israel whom I serve, there shall be neither dew nor
rain these years except at my order.'

The word of the Lord came to him, 'Go away from here, go
eastwards, and hide yourself in the wadi Cherith which lies east of
Jordan. You can drink from the stream, and I have ordered the ravens
to bring you food there.' He did as the Lord had said; he went and
stayed in the wadi Cherith which lies east of Jordan. The ravens
brought him bread in the morning and meat in the evening, and he
quenched his thirst at the stream.

This is the word of the Lord.

Responsorial Psalm   Ps 120:1-8. ℟ cf. v.2

℟   Our help is from the Lord
      who made heaven and earth.

1   I lift up my eyes to the mountains:
      from where shall come my help?
      My help shall come from the Lord
      who made heaven and earth.   ℟

2   May he never allow you to stumble!
      Let him sleep not, your guard.
      No, he sleeps not nor slumbers,
      Israel's guard. ℟

3   The Lord is your guard and your shade;
      at your right side he stands.
      By day the sun shall not smite you
      nor the moon in the night. ℟

4 The Lord will guard you from evil,
  he will guard your soul.
  The Lord will guard your going and coming
  both now and for ever. ℟

Gospel Acclamation   Mt 5:12

  Alleluia, alleluia!
  Rejoice and be glad;
  your reward will be great in heaven.
  Alleluia!

GOSPEL

A reading from the holy Gospel according to Matthew   5:1-12

Happy are the poor in spirit.

Seeing the crowds, Jesus went up the hill. There he sat down and was
joined by his disciples. Then he began to speak. This is what he taught
them:

  'How happy are the poor in spirit;
  theirs is the kingdom of heaven.
  Happy the gentle:
  they shall have the earth for their heritage.
  Happy those who mourn:
  they shall be comforted.
  Happy those who hunger and thirst for what is right:
  they shall be satisfied.
  Happy the merciful:
  they shall have mercy shown them.
  Happy the pure in heart:
  they shall see God.
  Happy the peacemakers:
  they shall be called sons of God.
  Happy those who are persecuted in the cause of right:
  theirs is the kingdom of heaven.

'Happy are you when people abuse you and persecute you and speak
all kinds of calumny against you on my account. Rejoice and be glad,
for your reward will be great in heaven; this is how they persecuted
the prophets before you.'

  This is the Gospel of the Lord.

Tuesday

FIRST READING

A reading from the first book of the Kings   17:7-16

The jar of meal shall not be spent according to the word of the
Lord spoken through Elias.

The stream in the place where Elijah lay hidden dried up, for the country had no rain. And then the word of the Lord came to Elijah, 'Up and go to Zarephath, a Sidonian town, and stay there. I have ordered a widow there to give you food.' So he went off to Sidon. And when he reached the city gate, there was a widow gathering sticks; addressing her he said, 'Please bring a little water in a vessel for me to drink.' She was setting off to bring it when he called after her. 'Please' he said 'bring me a scrap of bread in your hand.' 'As the Lord your God lives,' she replied 'I have no baked bread, but only a handful of meal in a jar and a little oil in a jug; I am just gathering a stick or two to go and prepare this for myself and my son to eat, and then we shall die.' But Elijah said to her, 'Do not be afraid, go and do as you have said; but first make a little scone of it for me and bring it to me, and then make some for yourself and for your son. For thus the Lord speaks, the God of Israel:

> "Jar of meal shall not be spent,
> jug of oil shall not be emptied,
> before the day when the Lord sends
> rain on the face of the earth" '

The woman went and did as Elijah told her and they ate the food, she, himself and her son. The jar of meal was not spent nor the jug of oil emptied, just as the Lord had foretold through Elijah.

This is the word of the Lord.

Responsorial Psalm   Ps 4:2-5. 7-8. ℟ v.7

℟   Lord, let your face shine on us.

1   When I call, answer me, O God of justice;
    from anguish you released me, have mercy and hear me!
    O men, how long will your hearts be closed,
    will you love what is futile and seek what is false?   ℟

2   It is the Lord who grants favours to those whom he loves;
    the Lord hears me whenever I call him.
    Fear him; do not sin: ponder on your bed and be still.   ℟

3   'What can bring us happiness?' many say.
    Lift up the light of your face on us, O Lord.
    You have put into my heart a greater joy
    than they have from abundance of corn and new wine.   ℟

Gospel Acclamation   Mt 5:16

    Alleluia, alleluia!
    Let your light shine before all,
    that they may see your good works and glorify your Father.
    Alleluia!

                         GOSPEL

A reading from the holy Gospel according to Matthew   5:13-16

                              You are the light of the world.

Jesus said to his disciples: 'You are the salt of the earth. But if salt
becomes tasteless, what can make it salty again? It is good for
nothing, and can only be thrown out to be trampled underfoot by men.
    'You are the light of the world. A city built on a hilltop cannot be
hidden. No one lights a lamp to put it under a tub; they put it on the
lamp-stand where it shines for everyone in the house. In the same way
your light must shine in the sight of men, so that, seeing your good
works, they may give the praise to your Father in heaven.'

    This is the Gospel of the Lord.

Wednesday

FIRST READING

A reading from the first book of the Kings   18:20-39

*Let his people know that you are the Lord God and are winning
back their hearts.*

King Ahab called all Israel together and assembled the prophets of
Baal on Mount Carmel. Elijah stepped out in front of all the people.
'How long' he said 'do you mean to hobble first on one leg then on the
other? If the Lord is God, follow him; if Baal, follow him.' But the
people never said a word. Elijah then said to them, 'I, I alone, am left
as a prophet of the Lord, while the prophets of Baal are four hundred
and fifty. Let two bulls be given us; let them choose one for themselves, dismember it and lay it on the wood, but not set fire to it. I in
my turn will prepare the other bull, but not set fire to it. You must call
on the name of your god, and I shall call on the name of mine; the god
who answers with fire, is God indeed.' The people all answered,
'Agreed!' Elijah then said to the prophets of Baal, 'Choose one bull and
begin, for there are more of you. Call on the name of your god but light
no fire.' They took the bull and prepared it, and from morning to
midday they called on the name of Baal. 'O Baal, answer us!' they
cried, but there was no voice, no answer, as they performed their
hobbling dance round the altar they had made. Midday came, and
Elijah mocked them. 'Call louder,' he said 'for he is a god: he is
preoccupied or he is busy, or he has gone on a journey; perhaps he is
asleep and will wake up.' So they shouted louder and gashed themselves, as their custom was, with swords and spears until the blood
flowed down them. Midday passed, and they ranted on until the time
the offering is presented; but there was no voice, no answer, no
attention given to them.

Then Elijah said to all the peoplg, 'Come closer to me,' and all the
people came closer to him. He repaired the altar of the Lord which had
been broken down. Elijah took twelve stones, corresponding to the
number of the tribes of the sons of Jacob, to whom the word of the Lord
had come, 'Israel shall be your name,' and built an altar in the name
of the Lord. Round the altar he dug a trench of a size to hold two
measures of seed. He then arranged the wood, dismembered the bull,
and laid it on the wood. Then he said, 'Fill four jars with water and
pour it on the holocaust and on the wood'; this they did. He said, 'Do it
a second time'; they did it a second time. He said, 'Do it a third

time'; they did it a third time. The water flowed round the altar and the trench itself was full of water. At the time when the offering is presented, Elijah the prophet stepped forward, 'Lord, God of Abraham, Isaac and Israel,' he said 'let them know today that you are God in Israel, and that I am your servant, that I have done all these things at your command. Answer me, Lord, answer me, so that this people may know that you, Lord, are God and are winning back their hearts.'

Then the fire of the Lord fell and consumed the holocaust and wood and licked up the water in the trench. When all the people saw this they fell on their faces. 'The Lord is God,' they cried 'the Lord is God.'

This is the word of the Lord.

Responsorial Psalm   Ps 15:1-2. 4-5. 8. 11. ℟ v.1

℟   Keep me safe, O God;
      you are my hope.

1   Preserve me, God, I take refuge in you.
    I say to the Lord: 'You are my God.'   ℟

2   Those who choose other gods increase their sorrows.
    Never will I offer their offerings of blood.
    Never will I take their name upon my lips.   ℟

3   O Lord, it is you who are my portion and cup;
    it is you yourself who are my prize.
    I keep the Lord ever in my sight:
    since he is at my right hand, I shall stand firm.   ℟

4   You will show me the path of life,
    the fullness of joy in your presence,
    at your right hand happiness for ever.   ℟

Gospel Acclamation   Ps 24:4. 5

    Alleluia, alleluia!
    Teach me your paths, my God,
    and lead me in your truth.
    Alleluia!

GOSPEL

A reading from the holy Gospel according to Matthew 5:17-19

I have come not to abolish the law, but to complete it.

Jesus said to his disciples: 'Do not imagine that I have come to abolish the Law or the Prophets. I have come not to abolish but to complete them. I tell you solemnly, till heaven and earth disappear, not one dot, not one little stroke, shall disappear from the Law until its purpose is achieved. Therefore, the man who infringes even one of the least of these commandments and teaches others to do the same will be considered the least in the kingdom of heaven; but the man who keeps them and teaches them will be considered great in the kingdom of heaven.'

This is the Gospel of the Lord.

Thursday

FIRST READING

A reading from the first book of the Kings 18:41-46

Elijah prayed and the rain fell in torrents.

Elijah said to Ahab, 'Go back, eat and drink; for I hear the sound of rain.' While Ahab went back to eat and drink, Elijah climbed to the top of Carmel and bowed down to the earth, putting his face between his knees. 'Now go up,' he told his servant 'and look out to the sea.' He went up and looked. 'There is nothing at all' he said. 'Go back seven times' Elijah said. The seventh time, the servant said, 'Now there is a cloud, small as a man's hand, rising from the sea.' Elijah said, 'Go and say to Ahab, "Harness the chariot and go down before the rain stops you." ' And with that the sky grew dark with cloud and storm, and rain fell in torrents. Ahab mounted his chariot and made for Jezreel. The hand of the Lord was on Elijah, and tucking up his cloak he ran in front of Ahab as far as the outskirts of Jezreel.

This is the word of the Lord.

Responsorial Psalm   Ps 64:10-13. ℞ v.2

℞ It is right to praise you in Zion, O God.

1   You care for the earth, give it water,
    you fill it with riches.
    Your river in heaven brims over
    to provide its grain.   ℞

2   And thus you provide for the earth;
    you drench its furrows,
    you level it, soften it with showers,
    you bless its growth.   ℞

3   You crown the year with your goodness.
    Abundance flows in your steps,
    in the pastures of the wilderness it flows.
    The hills are girded with joy.   ℞

Gospel Acclamation   Jn 13:34

    Alleluia, alleluia!
    I give you a new commandment:
    love one another as I have loved you.
    Alleluia!

GOSPEL

A reading from the holy Gospel according to Matthew   5:20-26

Whoever is angry with his brother or sister will be judged for it.

Jesus said to his disciples: 'If your virtue goes no deeper than that of
the scribes and Pharisees, you will never get into the kingdom of
heaven.

'You have learnt how it was said to our ancestors: You must not
kill; and if anyone does kill he must answer for it before the court. But
I say this to you: anyone who is angry with his brother will answer for
it before the court; if a man calls his brother, "Fool" he will answer for
it before the Sanhedrin; and if a man calls him "Renegade" he will
answer for it in hell fire. So then, if you are bringing your offering to
the altar and there remember that your brother has something
against you, leave your offering there before the altar, go and be
reconciled with your brother first, and then come back and present

your offering. Come to terms with your opponent in good time while you are still on the way to the court with him, or he may hand you over to the judge and the judge to the officer, and you will be thrown into prison. I tell you solemnly, you will not get out till you have paid the last penny.'

This is the Gospel of the Lord.

Friday

FIRST READING

A reading from the first book of the Kings   19:9. 11-16

Stand on the mountain before the Lord God.

When Elijah reached Horeb, the mountain of God, he went into the cave and spent the night in it. Then he was told, 'Go out and stand on the mountain before the Lord.' Then the Lord himself went by. There came a mighty wind, so strong it tore the mountains and shattered the rocks before the Lord. But the Lord was not in the wind. After the wind came an earthquake. But the Lord was not in the earthquake. After the earthquake came a fire. But the Lord was not in the fire. And after the fire there came the sound of a gentle breeze. And when Elijah heard this, he covered his face with his cloak and went out and stood at the entrance of the cave. Then a voice came to him, which said, 'What are you doing here, Elijah?' He replied, 'I am filled with jealous zeal for the Lord of hosts, because the sons of Israel have deserted you, broken down your altars and put your prophets to the sword. I am the only one left and they want to kill me.'

'Go,' the Lord said 'go back by the same way to the wilderness of Damascus. You are to go and anoint Hazael as king of Aram. You are to anoint Jehu son of Nimshi as king of Israel, and to anoint Elisha son of Shaphat, of Abel Meholah, as prophet to succeed you.'

This is the word of the Lord.

Responsorial Psalm   Ps 26:7-9. 13-14. ℟ v.8

℟   I long to see your face, O Lord.

1   O Lord, hear my voice when I call;
     have mercy and answer.
     Of you my heart has spoken:
     'Seek his face.'   ℟

2   It is your face, O Lord, that I seek;
     hide not your face.
     Dismiss not your servant in anger;
     you have been my help.   ℟

3   I am sure I shall see the Lord's goodness
     in the land of the living.
     Hope in him, hold firm and take heart.
     Hope in the Lord!   ℟

Gospel Acclamation   Phil 2:15. 16

     Alleluia, alleluia!
     Shine on the world like bright stars;
     you are offering it the word of life.
     Alleluia!

GOSPEL

A reading from the holy Gospel according to Matthew   5:27-32

If a man looks at a woman lustfully, he has already sinned.

Jesus said to his disciples: 'You have learnt how it was said: You must not commit adultery. But I say this to you: if a man looks at a woman lustfully, he has already committed adultery with her in his heart. If your right eye should cause you to sin, tear it out and throw it away; for it will do you less harm to lose one part of you than to have your whole body thrown into hell. And if your right hand should cause you to sin, cut it off and throw it away; for it will do you less harm to lose one part of you than to have your whole body go to hell.

It has also been said: Anyone who divorces his wife must give her a writ of dismissal. But I say this to you: everyone who divorces his wife, except for the case of fornication, makes her an adulteress; and anyone who marries a divorced woman commits adultery.'

This is the Gospel of the Lord.

Saturday

FIRST READING

A reading from the first book of the Kings   19:19-21

Elisha rose and followed Elijah and became his servant.

Leaving Mount Horeb, Elijah came on Elisha son of Shaphat as he
was ploughing behind twelve yoke of oxen, he himself being with the
twelfth. Elijah passed near to him and threw his cloak over him.
Elisha left his oxen and ran after Elijah. 'Let me kiss my father and
mother, then I will follow you' he said. Elijah answered, 'Go, go back;
for have I done anything to you?' Elisha turned away, took the pair of
oxen and slaughtered them. He used the plough for cooking the oxen,
then gave to his men, who ate. He then rose, and followed Elijah and
became his servant.

This is the word of the Lord.

Responsorial Psalm   Ps 15:1-2. 5. 7-10. ℟ cf. v.5

℟   You are my inheritance, O Lord.

1   Preserve me, God, I take refuge in you.
    I say to the Lord: 'You are my God.'
    O Lord, it is you who are my portion and cup;
    it is you yourself who are my prize.   ℟

2   I will bless the Lord who gives me counsel,
    who even at night directs my heart.
    I keep the Lord ever in my sight:
    since he is at my right hand, I shall stand firm.   ℟

3   And so my heart rejoices, my soul is glad;
    even my body shall rest in safety.
    For you will not leave my soul among the dead,
    nor let your beloved know decay.   ℟

Gospel Acclamation   Ps 118:36. 29

    Alleluia, alleluia!
    Turn my heart to do your will;
    teach me your law, O God.
    Alleluia!

GOSPEL

A reading from the holy Gospel according to Matthew   5:33-37

I say to you: do not swear at all.

Jesus said to his disciples: 'You have learnt how it was said to our ancestors: You must not break your oath, but must fulfil your oaths to the Lord. But I say this to you: do not swear at all, either by heaven, since that is God's throne; or by the earth, since that is his footstool; or by Jerusalem, since that is the city of the great king. Do not swear by your own head either, since you cannot turn a single hair white or black. All you need say is "Yes" if you mean yes, "No" if you mean no; anything more than this comes from the evil one.'

This is the Gospel of the Lord.

ELEVENTH WEEK IN ORDINARY TIME

Year II

Monday

FIRST READING

A reading from the first book of the Kings   21:1-16

Naboth has been stoned to death.

Naboth of Jezreel had a vineyard close by the palace of Ahab king of Samaria, and Ahab said to Naboth, 'Give me your vineyard to be my vegetable garden, since it adjoins my house; I will give you a better vineyard for it or, if you prefer, I will give you its worth in money.' But Naboth answered Ahab, 'The Lord forbid that I should give you the inheritance of my ancestors!'

Ahab went home gloomy and out of temper at the words of Naboth of Jezreel, 'I will not give you the inheritance of my fathers.' He lay down on his bed and turned his face away and refused to eat. His wife Jezebel came to him. 'Why are you so dispirited' she said 'that you will not eat?' He said, 'I have been speaking to Naboth of Jezreel; I said: Give me your vineyard either for money or, if you prefer, for another vineyard in exchange. But he said, "I will not give you my vineyard." ' Then his wife Jezebel said, 'You make a fine king of Israel, and no mistake! Get up and eat; cheer up, and you will feel better; I will get you the vineyard of Naboth of Jezreel myself.'

So she wrote letters in Ahab's name and sealed them with his seal, sending them to the elders and nobles who lived where Naboth lived. In the letters she wrote, 'Proclaim a fast, and put Naboth in the forefront of the people. Confront him with a couple of scoundrels who will accuse him like this, "You have cursed God and the king". Then take him outside and stone him to death.'

The men of Naboth's town, the elders and nobles who lived in his town, did what Jezebel ordered, what was written in the letters she had sent them. They proclaimed a fast and put Naboth in the forefront of the people. Then the two scoundrels came and stood in front of him and made their accusation, 'Naboth has cursed God and the king.' They led him outside the town and stoned him to death. They then sent word to Jezebel, 'Naboth has been stoned to death.' When Jezebel heard that Naboth had been stoned to death, she said to Ahab, 'Get up! Take possession of the vineyard which Naboth of Jezreel would not give you for money, for Naboth is no longer alive, he is dead.' When Ahab heard that Naboth was dead, he got up to go down to the vineyard of Naboth of Jezreel and take possession of it.

This is the word of the Lord.

Responsorial Psalm   Ps 5:2-3. 5-7. ℟ v.2

℟   Lord, listen to my groaning.

1   To my words give ear, O Lord,
    give heed to my groaning.
    Attend to the sound of my cries,
    my King and my God.   ℟

2   You are no God who loves evil;
    no sinner is your guest.
    The boastful shall not stand their ground
    before your face.   ℟

3   You hate all who do evil:
    you destroy all who lie.
    The deceitful and bloodthirsty man
    the Lord detests.   ℟

Gospel Acclamation   Ps 118:105

Alleluia, alleluia!
Your word is a lamp for my feet
and a light on my path.
Alleluia!

GOSPEL

A reading from the holy Gospel according to Matthew   5:38-42

I say to you, offer the wicked no resistance.

Jesus said to his disciples: 'You have learnt how it was said: Eye for eye and tooth for tooth. But I say this to you: offer the wicked man no resistance. On the contrary, if anyone hits you on the right cheek, offer him the other as well; if a man takes you to law and would have your tunic, let him have your cloak as well. And if anyone orders you to go one mile, go two miles with him. Give to anyone who asks, and if anyone wants to borrow, do not turn away.'

This is the Gospel of the Lord.

Tuesday

FIRST READING

A reading from the first book of the Kings   21:17-29

Israel was led into sin.

After the death of Naboth, the word of the Lord came to Elijah the Tishbite. 'Up! Go down to meet Ahab king of Israel, in Samaria. You will find him in Naboth's vineyard; he has gone down to take possession of it. You are to say this to him. "The Lord says this: You have committed murder; now you usurp as well. For this – and the Lord says this – in the place where the dogs licked the blood of Naboth, the dogs will lick your blood too." ' Ahab said to Elijah, 'So you have found me out, O my enemy!' Elijah answered, 'I have found you out. For your double dealing, and since you have done what is displeasing to the Lord, I will now bring disaster down on you; I will sweep away your descendants, and wipe out every male belonging to the family of Ahab, fettered or free in Israel. I will treat your House as I treated the House of Jeroboam son of Nebat and of Baasha son of

Ahijah, for provoking my anger and leading Israel into sin. (Against Jezebel too the Lord spoke these words: The dogs will eat Jezebel in the Field of Jezreel.) Those of Ahab's family who die in the city, the dogs will eat; and those who die in the open country, the birds of the air will eat.'

And indeed there never was anyone like Ahab for double dealing and for doing what is displeasing to the Lord, urged on by Jezebel his wife. He behaved in the most abominable way, adhering to idols, just as the Amorites used to do whom the Lord had dispossessed for the sons of Israel.

When Ahab heard these words, he tore his garments and put sackcloth next his skin and fasted; he slept in the sackcloth; he walked with slow steps. Then the word of the Lord came to Elijah the Tishbite, 'Have you seen how Ahab has humbled himself before me? Since he has humbled himself before me, I will not bring the disaster in his days; I will bring the disaster down on his House in the days of his son.'

This is the word of the Lord.

Responsorial Psalm   Ps 50:3-6. 11. 16. ℟ cf. v.3

℟   Be merciful, O Lord, for we have sinned.

1   Have mercy on me, God, in your kindness.
    In your compassion blot out my offence.
    O wash me more and more from my guilt
    and cleanse me from sin.   ℟

2   My offences truly I know them;
    my sin is always before me.
    Against you, you alone, have I sinned;
    what is evil in your sight I have done.   ℟

3   From my sins turn away your face
    and blot out all my guilt.
    O rescue me, God, my helper,
    and my tongue shall ring out your goodness.   ℟

Gospel Acclamation   Jn 13:34

Alleluia, alleluia!
I give you a new commandment:
love one another as I have loved you.
Alleluia!

GOSPEL

A reading from the holy Gospel according to Matthew   5:43-48

Love your enemies.

Jesus said to his disciples: 'You have learnt how it was said: You must love your neighbour and hate your enemy. But I say this to you: love your enemies and pray for those who persecute you; in this way you will be sons of your Father in heaven, for he causes his sun to rise on bad men as well as good, and his rain to fall on honest and dishonest men alike. For if you love those who love you, what right have you to claim any credit? Even the tax collectors do as much, do they not? And if you save your greetings for your brothers, are you doing anything exceptional? Even the pagans do as much, do they not? You must therefore be perfect just as your heavenly Father is perfect.'

This is the Gospel of the Lord.

Wednesday

FIRST READING

A reading from the second book of the Kings   2:1. 6-14

A chariot of fire appeared and Elijah went up to heaven.

This is what happened when the Lord took Elijah up to heaven in the whirlwind: Elijah and Elisha set out from Gilgal. Elijah said, 'Elisha, please stay here, the Lord is only sending me to the Jordan.' But he replied, 'As the Lord lives and as you yourself live, I will not leave you!' And they went on together.

Fifty of the brotherhood of prophets followed them, halting some distance away as the two of them stood beside the Jordan. Elijah took his cloak, rolled it up and struck the water; and the water divided to left and right, and the two of them crossed over dry-shod. When they had crossed, Elijah said to Elisha, 'Make your request. What can I do for you before I am taken from you?' Elisha answered, 'Let me inherit a double share of your spirit.' 'Your request is a difficult one' Elijah said. 'If you see me while I am being taken from you, it shall be as you ask; if not, it will not be so.' Now as they walked on, talking as they went, a chariot of fire appeared and horses of fire, coming between the two of them; and Elijah went up to heaven in the whirlwind. Elisha saw it, and shouted, 'My father! My father! Chariot of Israel and its chargers!' Then he lost sight of him, and taking hold of his clothes he tore them in half. He picked up the cloak of Elijah which had fallen, and went back and stood on the bank of the Jordan.

He took the cloak of Elijah and struck the water. 'Where is the Lord, the God of Elijah?' he cried. He struck the water, and it divided to right and left, and Elisha crossed over.

This is the word of the Lord.

Responsorial Psalm   Ps 30:20. 21. 24. ℟ v.25

℟ Let your hearts take comfort,
    all who hope in the Lord.

1 How great is the goodness, Lord,
    that you keep for those who fear you,
    that you show to those who trust you
    in the sight of men.   ℟

2 You hide them in the shelter of your presence
    from the plotting of men:
    you keep them safe within your tent
    from disputing tongues.   ℟

3 Love the Lord, all you saints.
    He guards his faithful
    but the Lord will repay to the full
    those who act with pride.   ℟

Gospel Acclamation   Jn 14:23

Alleluia, alleluia!
All who love me will keep my words,
and my Father will love them, and we will come to them.
Alleluia!

GOSPEL

A reading from the holy Gospel according to Matthew   6:1-6. 16-18

Your Father who sees all that is done in secret will reward you.

Jesus said to his disciples: 'Be careful not to parade your good deeds before men to attract their notice; by doing this you will lose all reward from your Father in heaven. So when you give alms, do not have it trumpeted before you ; this is what the hypocrites do in the synagogues and in the streets to win men's admiration. I tell you solemnly, they have had their reward. But when you give alms, your left hand must not know what your right is doing; your almsgiving must be secret, and your Father who sees all that is done in secret will reward you.

'And when you pray, do not imitate the hypocrites: they love to say their prayers standing up in the synagogues and at the street corners for people to see them. I tell you solemnly, they have had their reward. But when you pray, go to your private room and, when you have shut your door, pray to your Father who is in that secret place, and your Father who sees all that is done in secret will reward you.

'When you fast do not put on a gloomy look as the hypocrites do: they pull long faces to let men know they are fasting. I tell you solemnly, they have had their reward. But when you fast, put oil on your head and wash your face, so that no one will know you are fasting except your Father who sees all that is done in secret; and your Father who sees all that is done in secret will reward you.'

This is the Gospel of the Lord.

Thursday

FIRST READING

A reading from the book of Ecclesiasticus   48:1-14

Elijah was shrouded in the whirlwind, and Elisha was filled with his spirit.

The prophet Elijah arose like a fire,
his word flaring like a torch.
It was he who brought famine on them,
and who decimated them in his zeal.
By the word of the Lord, he shut up the heavens,
he also, three times, brought down fire.
How glorious you were in your miracles, Elijah!

Has anyone reason to boast as you have? –
rousing a corpse from death,
from Sheol by the word of the Most High;
dragging kings down to destruction,
and high dignitaries from their beds;
hearing reproof on Sinai,
and decrees of punishment on Horeb;
anointing kings as avengers,
and prophets to succeed you;
taken up in the whirlwind of fire,
in a chariot with fiery horses;
designated in the prophecies of doom
to allay God's wrath before the fury breaks,
to turn the hearts of fathers towards their children,
and to restore the tribes of Jacob.
Happy shall they be who see you,
and those who have fallen asleep in love;
for we too will have life.

Elijah was shrouded in the whirlwind,
and Elisha was filled with his spirit;
throughout his life no ruler could shake him,
and no one could subdue him.
No task was too hard for him,
and even in death his body prophesied.
In his lifetime he performed wonders,
and in death his works were marvellous.

This is the word of the Lord.

Responsorial Psalm   Ps 96:1-7. ℟ v.12

℟   Let the just rejoice in the Lord.

1   The Lord is king, let earth rejoice,
    the many coastlands be glad.
    Cloud and darkness are his raiment;
    his throne, justice and right.   ℟

2   A fire prepares his path;
    it burns up his foes on every side.
    His lightnings light up the world,
    the earth trembles at the sight.   ℟

3 The mountains melt like wax
   before the Lord of all the earth.
   The skies proclaim his justice;
   all peoples see his glory.   ℟

4 Let those who serve idols be ashamed,
   those who boast of their worthless gods.
   All you spirits, worship him.   ℟

Gospel Acclamation   Rom 8:15

   Alleluia, alleluia!
   You have received the Spirit which makes us God's children,
   and in that Spirit we call God our Father.
   Alleluia!

GOSPEL

A reading from the holy Gospel according to Matthew   6:7-15

You should pray like this: Our Father ...

Jesus said to his disciples: 'In your prayers do not babble as the
pagans do, for they think that by using many words they will make
themselves heard. Do not be like them; your Father knows what you
need before you ask him. So you should pray like this:

   Our Father in heaven,
   may your name be held holy,
   your kingdom come,
   your will be done,
   on earth as in heaven.
   Give us today our daily bread.
   And forgive us our debts,
   as we have forgiven those who are in debt to us.
   And do not put us to the test,
   but save us from the evil one.

'Yes, if you forgive others their failings, your heavenly Father will
forgive you yours; but if you do not forgive others, your Father will not
forgive your failings either.'

   This is the Gospel of the Lord.

Friday

FIRST READING

A reading from the second book of the Kings   11:1-4. 9-18. 20

Jehoash was anointed king and they shouted: Long live the king.

When Athaliah the mother of Ahaziah learned that her son was dead, she promptly did away with all those of royal stock. But Jehosheba, daughter of King Jehoram and sister of Ahaziah, secretly took away Jehoash, her brother's son, from among the sons of the king who were being murdered, and put him with his nurse in the sleeping quarters; in this way she hid him from Athaliah, and he was not put to death. He stayed with her for six years, hidden in the Temple of the Lord, while Athaliah governed the country.

In the seventh year, Jehoiada sent for the commanders of hundreds of the Carians and of the guards, and had them brought to him in the Temple of the Lord. He made a pact with them, and, putting them under oath, showed them the king's son.

The commanders of hundreds did everything as Jehoiada the priest had ordered. They brought their men, those coming off duty on the sabbath together with those mounting guard on the sabbath, and came to Jehoiada the priest. The priests equipped the commanders of hundreds with King David's spears and shields which were in the Temple of the Lord. The guards formed up, each man with his weapon in his hand, from the south corner to the north corner of the Temple, surrounding the altar and the Temple. Then Jehoiada brought out the king's son, put the crown and armlets on him, and he anointed him king. They clapped their hands and shouted, 'Long live the king!'

Athaliah, on hearing the shouts of the people, made for the Temple of the Lord where the people were. When she saw the king standing there beside the pillar, as the custom was, with the captains and trumpeters at the king's side, and all the country people rejoicing and sounding trumpets, Athaliah tore her garments and shouted, 'Treason, treason!' Then Jehoiada the priest gave the order to the army officers: 'Take her outside the precincts and put to death anyone who follows her.' 'For,' the priest had reasoned, 'she must not be put to death in the Temple of the Lord.' They seized her, and when she had reached the palace through the Entry of the Horses, she was put to death there.

Jehoiada made a covenant between the Lord and king and people, by which the latter undertook to be the people of the Lord; and also

between king and people. All the country people then went to the
temple of Baal and demolished it; they smashed his altars and his
images and killed Mattan, priest of Baal, in front of the altars.

The priest posted entries to guard the Temple of the Lord. All the
country people were delighted, and the city made no move. And they
put Athaliah to death in the royal palace.

This is the word of the Lord.

Responsorial Psalm   Ps 131:11-14. 17-18. ℟ v.13

℟   The Lord has chosen Zion for his dwelling.

1   The Lord swore an oath to David;
    he will not go back on his word:
    'A son, the fruit of your body,
    will I set upon your throne.   ℟

2   'If they keep my covenant in truth
    and my laws that I have taught them,
    their sons also shall rule
    on your throne from age to age.'   ℟

3   For the Lord has chosen Zion;
    he has desired it for his dwelling:
    'This is my resting-place for ever,
    here have I chosen to live.'   ℟

4   There the stock of David will flower:
    'I will prepare a lamp for my anointed.
    I will cover his enemies with shame
    but on him my crown shall shine.'   ℟

Gospel Acclamation   Mt 5:3

    Alleluia, alleluia!
    Happy the poor in spirit;
    the kingdom of heaven is theirs!
    Alleluia!

GOSPEL

A reading from the holy Gospel according to Matthew   6:19-23

Where your treasure is, there will your heart be also.

Jesus said to his disciples: 'Do not store up treasures for yourselves on earth, where moths and woodworms destroy them and thieves can break in and steal. But store up treasures for yourselves in heaven, where neither moth or woodworms destroy them and thieves cannot break in and steal. For where your treasure is, there will your heart be also.

'The lamp of the body is the eye. It follows that if your eye is sound, your whole body will be filled with light. But if your eye is diseased, your whole body will be all darkness. If then, the light inside you is darkness, what darkness that will be!'

This is the Gospel of the Lord.

Saturday

FIRST READING

A reading from the second book of Chronicles   24:17-25

They killed Zechariah in the court of the temple.

After the death of Jehoiada, the officials of Judah came to pay court to the king, and the king now turned to them for advice. The Judaeans abandoned the Temple of the Lord, the God of their ancestors, for the worship of sacred poles and idols. Because of their guilt, God's anger fell on Judah and Jerusalem. He sent them prophets to bring them back to the Lord, but when these gave their message, they would not listen. The spirit of God took possession of Zechariah son of Jehoiada the priest. He stood up before the people and said, 'God says this, "Why do you transgress the commandments of the Lord to no good purpose? You have deserted the Lord, now he deserts you."' They then plotted against him and by order of the king stoned him in the court of the Temple of the Lord. King Joash, forgetful of the kindness that Jehoiada, the father of Zechariah, had shown him, killed Jehoiada's son who cried out as he died, 'The Lord sees and he will avenge!'

When a year had gone by, the Aramaean army made war on Joash. They reached Judah and Jerusalem, and executed all the officials among the people, sending back to the king at Damascus all that they had plundered from them. Though the Aramaean army had by no means come in force, the Lord delivered into its power an army of great size for having deserted him, the God of their ancestors.

The Aramaeans treated Joash as he had deserved, and when they retired they left him a very sick man; and his officers, plotting against him to avenge the death of the son of Jehoiada the priest, murdered him in his bed. So he died, and they buried him in the Citadel of David, though not in the tombs of the kings.

This is the word of the Lord.

Responsorial Psalm   Ps 88:4-5. 29-34. ℟ v.29

 ℟ For ever I will keep my love for him.

1 'I have made a covenant with my chosen one;
  I have sworn to David my servant:
  I will establish your dynasty for ever
  and set up your throne through all ages. ℟

2 'I will keep my love for him always;
  for him my covenant shall endure.
  I will establish his dynasty for ever,
  make his throne as lasting as the heavens. ℟

3 'If his sons forsake my law
  and refuse to walk as I decree
  and if ever they violate my statutes,
  refusing to keep my commands;
  then I will punish their offences with the rod,
  then I will scourge them on account of their guilt. ℟

4 'But I will never take back my love:
  my truth will never fail.' ℟

Gospel Acclamation   2 Cor 8:9

 Alleluia, alleluia!
 Jesus Christ was rich but he became poor,
 to make you rich out of his poverty.
 Alleluia!

GOSPEL

A reading from the holy Gospel according to Matthew   6:24-34

Do not worry about tomorrow.

Jesus said to his disciples: 'No one can be the slave of two masters: he will either hate the first and love the second, or treat the first with respect and the second with scorn. You cannot be the slave both of God and money.

'That is why I am telling you not to worry about your life and what you are to eat, nor about your body and how you are to clothe it. Surely life means more than food, and the body more than clothing! Look at the birds in the sky. They do not sow or reap or gather into barns; yet your heavenly Father feeds them. Are you not worth much more than they are? Can any of you, for all his worrying, add one single cubit to his span of life? And why worry about clothing? Think of the flowers growing in the fields: they never have to work or spin; yet I assure you that not even Solomon in all his regalia was robed like one of these. Now if that is how God clothes the grass in the field which is there today and thrown into the furnace tomorrow, will he not much more look after you, you men of little faith? So do not worry; do not say, "What are we to eat? What are we to drink? How are we to be clothed?" It is the pagans who set their hearts on all these things. Your heavenly Father knows you need them all. Set your hearts on his kingdom first, and on his righteousness, and all these other things will be given you as well. So do not worry about tomorrow: tomorrow will take care of itself. Each day has enough trouble of its own.'

This is the Gospel of the Lord.

TWELFTH WEEK IN ORDINARY TIME

Year II

Monday

FIRST READING

A reading from the second book of the Kings   17:5-8. 13-15. 18

The Lord thrust Israel away from him and there was none left but the tribe of Judah.

The king of Assyria invaded the whole country and, coming to Samaria, laid seige to it for three years. In the ninth year of Hoshea, the king of Assyria captured Samaria and deported the Israelites to Assyria. He settled them in Halah on the Habor, a river of Gozan, and in the cities of the Medes.

This happened because the Israelites had sinned against the Lord their God who had brought them out of the land of Egypt, out of the grip of Pharaoh, king of Egypt. They worshipped other gods, they followed the practices of the nations that the Lord had dispossessed for them.

And yet through all the prophets and all the seers the Lord had given Israel and Judah this warning, 'Turn from your wicked ways and keep my commandments and my law in accordance with the entire Law I laid down for your fathers and delivered to them through my servants the prophets.' But they would not listen, they were more stubborn than their ancestors had been who had no faith in the Lord their God. They despised his laws and the covenant he had made with their ancestors, and the warnings he had given them. For this, the Lord was enraged with Israel and thrust them away from him. There was none left but the tribe of Judah only.

This is the word of the Lord.

Responsorial Psalm   Ps 59:3-5. 12-13. ℟ v.7

℟ Help us with your right hand, O Lord,
and answer us.

1 O God you have rejected us and broken us.
You have been angry; come back to us.   ℟

2 You have made the earth quake, torn it open.
   Repair what is shattered for it sways.
   You have inflicted hardships on your people
   and made us drink a wine that dazed us.

   ℟ Help us with your right hand, O Lord,
      and answer us.

3 Will you utterly reject us, O God,
   and no longer march with our armies?
   Give us help against the foe:
   for the help of man is vain. ℟

Gospel Acclamation   Heb 4:12

   Alleluia, alleluia!
   The word of God is living and active;
   it probes the thoughts and motives of our heart.
   Alleluia!

GOSPEL

A reading from the holy Gospel according to Matthew   7:1-5

                              Take the beam out of your own eye first.

Jesus said to his disciples: 'Do not judge, and you will not be judged;
because the judgements you give are the judgements you will get, and
the amount you measure out is the amount you will be given. Why do
you observe the splinter in your brother's eye and never notice the
plank in your own? How dare you say to your brother, "Let me take
the splinter out of your eye", when all the time there is a plank in your
own? Hypocrite! Take the plank out of your own eye first, and then
you will see clearly enough to take the splinter out of your brother's
eye.'

   This is the Gospel of the Lord.

Tuesday

FIRST READING

A reading from the second book of
the Kings

19:9-11. 14-21. 31-36

I will protect this city and save it for my own sake and for the sake of David.

Sennacherib, King of the Assyrians, sent messengers to Hezekiah saying, 'Tell this to Hezekiah king of Judah, "Do not let your God on whom you are relying deceive you, when he says: Jerusalem shall not fall into the power of the king of Assyria. You have learnt by now what the kings of Assyria have done to every country, putting them all under the ban. Are you likely to be spared?" '

Hezekiah took the letter from the hands of the messenger and read it; he then went up to the Temple of the Lord and spread it out before the Lord. Hezekiah said this prayer in the presence of the Lord, 'Lord of hosts, God of Israel, enthroned on the cherubs, you alone are God of all the kingdoms of the earth, you have made heaven and earth.

'Give ear, Lord, and listen.
Open your eyes, Lord, and see.
Hear the words of Sennacherib
who has sent to insult the living God.

'It is true, Lord, that the kings of Assyria have exterminated all the nations, they have thrown their gods on the fire, for these were not gods but the work of men's hands, wood and stone, and hence they have destroyed them. But now, Lord our God, save us from his hand, I pray you, and let all the kingdoms of the earth know that you alone are God, Lord.'

Then Isaiah son of Amoz sent to Hezekiah. 'The Lord, the God of Israel' he said 'says this, "I have heard the prayer you have addressed to me about Sennacherib king of Assyria." Here is the oracle that the Lord has pronounced against him:

' "She despises you, she scorns you,
the virgin daughter of Zion:
she tosses her head behind you,
the daughter of Jerusalem.
A remnant shall go out from Jerusalem,
and survivors from Mount Zion.
The jealous love of the Lord of Hosts shall accomplish this."

'This, then, is what the Lord says about the king of Assyria:

' "He will not enter this city,
he will let fly no arrow against it,
confront it with no shield,
throw up no earthwork against it.
By the road that he came on he will return;
he shall not enter this city. It is the Lord who speaks.
I will protect this city and save it
for my own sake and for the sake of my servant David." '

That same night the angel of the Lord went out and struck down a hundred and eighty-five thousand men in the Assyrian camp. Sennacherib struck camp and left; he returned home and stayed in Nineveh.

This is the word of the Lord.

Responsorial Psalm   Ps 47:2-4. 10-11. ℟ cf. v.9

℟ God upholds his city for ever.

1   The Lord is great and worthy to be praised
    in the city of our God.
    His holy mountain rises in beauty,
    the joy of all the earth.   ℟

2   Mount Zion, true pole of the earth,
    the Great King's city!
    God, in the midst of its citadels,
    has shown himself its stronghold.   ℟

3   O God, we ponder your love
    within your temple.
    Your praise, O God, like your name
    reaches to the ends of the earth.   ℟

Gospel Acclamation   Jn 8:12

Alleluia, alleluia!
I am the light of the world, says the Lord;
whoever follows me will have the light of life.
Alleluia!

GOSPEL

A reading from the holy Gospel according to Matthew   7:6. 12-14

Always treat others as you would like them to treat you.

Jesus said to his disciples: 'Do not give dogs what is holy; and do not throw your pearls in front of pigs, or they may trample them and then turn on you and tear you to pieces.

'So always treat others as you would like them to treat you; that is the meaning of the Law and the Prophets.

'Enter by the narrow gate, since the road that leads to perdition is wide and spacious, and many take it; but it is a narrow gate and a hard road that leads to life, and only a few find it.'

This is the Gospel of the Lord.

Wednesday

FIRST READING

A reading from the second book of the Kings   22:8-13; 23:1-3

The king read out everything that was in the covenant found in the temple of the Lord, and he made a covenant in the presence of the Lord.

The high priest Hilkiah said to Shaphan the secretary, 'I have found the Book of the Law in the Temple of the Lord.' And Hilkiah gave the book to Shaphan, who read it. Shaphan the secretary went to King Josiah and reported to him as follows, 'Your servants' he said 'have melted down the silver which was in the Temple and have handed it over to the masters of works attached to the Temple of the Lord.' Then Shaphan the secretary informed the king, 'Hilkiah the priest has given me a book'; and Shaphan read it aloud in the king's presence.

On hearing the contents of the Book of the Law, the king tore his garments, and gave the following order to Hilkiah the priest, Ahikam son of Shaphan, Achbor son of Micaiah, Shaphan the secretary and Asaiah the king's minister: 'Go and consult the Lord, on behalf of me and the people, about the contents of this book that has been found. Great indeed must be the anger of the Lord blazing out against us because our ancestors did not obey what this book says by practising everything written in it.'

The king then had all the elders of Judah and of Jerusalem summoned to him, and the king went up to the Temple of the Lord with all the men of Judah and all the inhabitants of Jerusalem, priests, prophets and all the people, of high or low degree. In their hearing he read out everything that was said in the book of the covenant found in the Temple of the Lord. The king stood beside the pillar, and in the presence of the Lord he made a covenant to follow the Lord and keep his commandments and decrees and laws with all his heart and soul, in order to enforce the terms of the covenant as written in that book. All the people gave their allegiance to the covenant.

This is the word of the Lord.

Responsorial Psalm   Ps 118:33-37. 40. ℟ v.33

℟   Teach me the way of your decrees, O Lord.

1   Teach me the demands of your statutes
    and I will keep them to the end.
    Train me to observe your law,
    to keep it with my heart.   ℟

2   Guide me in the path of your commands;
    for there is my delight.
    Bend my heart to your will
    and not to love of gain.   ℟

3   Keep my eyes from what is false:
    by your word, give me life.
    See, I long for your precepts:
    then in your justice, give me life.   ℟

Gospel Acclamation   Jn 15:4. 5

    Alleluia, alleluia!
    Live in me and let me live in you, says the Lord;
    my branches bear much fruit.
    Alleluia!

GOSPEL

A reading from the holy Gospel according to Matthew   7:15-20

By their fruits you will know them.

Jesus said to his disciples: 'Beware of false prophets who come to you disguised as sheep but underneath are ravenous wolves. You will be able to tell them by their fruits. Can people pick grapes from thorns, or figs from thistles? In the same way, a sound tree produces good fruit but a rotten tree bad fruit. A sound tree cannot bear bad fruit, nor a rotten tree bear good fruit. Any tree that does not produce good fruit is cut down and thrown on the fire. I repeat, you will be able to tell them by their fruits.'

This is the Gospel of the Lord.

Thursday

FIRST READING

A reading from the second book of the Kings   24:8-17

Joachim and all his leaders surrendered to the king of Babylon and were prisoners in Babylon.

Jehoiachin was eighteen years old when he came to the throne, and he reigned for three months in Jerusalem. His mother's name was Nehushta, daughter of Elnathan, from Jerusalem. He did what is displeasing to the Lord, just as his father had done.

At that time the troops of Nebuchadnezzar king of Babylon marched on Jerusalem, and the city was besieged. Nebuchadnezzar king of Babylon himself came to attack the city while his troops were besieging it. Then Jehoiachin king of Judah surrendered to the king of Babylon, he, his mother, his officers, his nobles and his eunuchs, and the king of Babylon took them prisoner. This was in the eighth year of King Nebuchadnezzar.

The latter carried off all the treasures of the Temple of the Lord and the treasures of the royal palace, and broke up all the golden furnishings that Solomon king of Israel had made for the sanctuary of the Lord, as the Lord had foretold. He carried off all Jerusalem into exile, all the nobles and all the notables, ten thousand of these were exiled, with all the blacksmiths and metalworkers; only the poorest people in the country were left behind. He deported Jehoiachin to Babylon, as also the king's mother, his eunuchs and the nobility of the country; he made them all leave Jerusalem for exile in Babylon. All the men of distinction, seven thousand of them, the blacksmiths and metalworkers, one thousand of them, all of them men capable of bearing arms, were led into exile in Babylon by the king of Babylon.

The king of Babylon made Mattaniah, Jehoiachin's uncle, king in succession to him, and changed his name to Zedekiah.

This is the word of the Lord.

Responsorial Psalm   Ps 78:1-5. 8-9. ℟ v.9

℟   For the glory of your name,
      O Lord, deliver us.

1   O God, the nations have invaded your land,
      they have profaned your holy temple.
      they have made Jerusalem a heap of ruins.
      They have handed over the bodies of your servants
      as food to feed the birds of heaven
      and the flesh of your faithful to the beasts of the earth.   ℟

2   They have poured out blood like water in Jerusalem,
      leaving no one to bury the dead.
      We have become the taunt of our neighbours,
      the mockery and scorn of those who surround us.
      How long, O Lord? Will you be angry for ever,
      how long will your anger burn like fire?   ℟

3   Do not hold the guilt of our fathers against us.
      Let your compassion hasten to meet us
      for we are in the depths of distress.   ℟

4   O God our saviour, come to our help,
      come for the sake of the glory of your name.
      O Lord our God, forgive us our sins;
      rescue us for the sake of your name.   ℟

Gospel Acclamation   Jn 14:23

      Alleluia, alleluia!
      All who love me will keep my words,
      and my Father will love them and we will come to them.
      Alleluia!

GOSPEL

A reading from the holy Gospel according to Matthew 7:21-29

The house built on rock is compared to the house built on sand.

Jesus said to his disciples: 'It is not those who say to me, "Lord, Lord," who will enter the kingdom of heaven, but the person who does the will of my Father in heaven. When the day comes many will say to me, "Lord, Lord, did we not prophesy in your name, cast out demons in your name, work many miracles in your name?" Then I shall tell them to their faces: I have never known you; away from me, you evil men!

'Therefore, everyone who listens to these words of mine and acts on them will be like a sensible man who built his house on rock. Rain came down, floods rose, gales blew and hurled themselves against that house, and it did not fall: it was founded on rock. But everyone who listens to these words of mine and does not act on them will be like a stupid man who built his house on sand. Rain came down, floods rose, gales blew and struck that house, and it fell; and what a fall it had!'

Jesus had now finished what he wanted to say, and his teaching made a deep impression on the people because he taught them with authority, and not like their own scribes.

This is the Gospel of the Lord.

Friday

FIRST READING

A reading from the second book of the Kings 25:1-12

The land of Juda was taken away.

In the ninth year of Zedekiah's reign, in the tenth month, on the tenth day of the month, Nebuchadnezzar king of Bablyon came with his whole army to attack Jerusalem; he pitched camp in front of the city and threw up earthworks round it. The city lay under siege till the eleventh year of King Zedekiah. In the fourth month, on the ninth day of the month, when famine was raging in the city and there was no food for the populace, a breach was made in the city wall. At once, the king made his escape under cover of dark, with all the fighting men, by way of the gate between the two walls, which is near the king's garden – the Chaldaeans had surrounded the city – and made his way towards the Arabah. The Chaldaean troops pursued the king and caught up with him in the plains of Jericho, where all his troops deserted. The Chaldaeans captured the king and took him to the king of Babylon at Riblah, who passed sentence on him. He had the sons of Zedekiah slaughtered before his eyes, then put out Zedekiah's eyes and, loading him with chains, carried him off to Babylon.

In the fifth month, on the seventh day of the month – it was in the nineteenth year of Nebuchadnezzar king of Babylon – Nebuzaradan, commander of the guard, an officer of the king of Babylon, entered Jerusalem. He burned down the Temple of the Lord, the royal palace and all the houses in Jerusalem. The Chaldaean troops who accompanied the commander of the guard demolished the walls surrounding Jerusalem. Nebuzaradan, commander of the guard, deported the remainder of the population left behind in the city, the deserters who had gone over to the king of Babylon, and the rest of the common people. The commander of the guard left some of the humbler country people as vineyard workers and ploughmen.

This is the word of the Lord.

Responsial Psalm   Ps 136:1-6. ℟ v.6

℟   Let my tongue be silenced,
     if I ever forget you!

1   By the rivers of Babylon
     there we sat and wept,
     remembering Zion;
     on the poplars that grew there
     we hung up our harps. ℟

2   For it was there that they asked us,
     our captors, for songs,
     our oppressors, for joy.
     'Sing to us,' they said,
     'one of Zion's songs.' ℟

3   O how could we sing
     the song of the Lord
     on alien soil?
     If I forget you, Jerusalem,
     let my right hand wither! ℟

4   O let my tongue
    cleave to my mouth
    if I remember you not,
    if I prize not Jerusalem
    above all my joys!   ℟

Gospel Acclamation   Mt 8:17

    Alleluia, alleluia!
    He bore our sicknesses,
    and endured our suffering.
    Alleluia!

GOSPEL

A reading from the holy Gospel according to Matthew   8:1-4

If you will, you can cure me.

After Jesus had come down from the mountain large crowds followed
him. A leper now came up and bowed low in front of him, 'Sir,' he said
'if you want to, you can cure me.' Jesus stretched out his hand,
touched him and said, 'Of course I want to! Be cured!' And his leprosy
was cured at once. Then Jesus said to him, 'Mind you do not tell
anyone, but go and show yourself to the priest and make the offering
prescribed by Moses, as evidence for them.'

    This is the Gospel of the Lord.

Saturday

FIRST READING

A reading from the book of Lamentations   2:2. 10-14. 18-19

Cry out to the Lord, O Daughter Zion.

The Lord has pitilessly destroyed
all the homes of Jacob;
in his displeasure he has shattered
the strongholds of the daughter of Judah;
he has thrown to the ground, he has left accursed
the kingdom and its rulers.

Mutely they sit on the ground,
the elders of the daughter of Zion;
they have put dust on their heads,
and wrapped themselves in sackcloth.
The virgins of Jerusalem hang their heads
down to the ground.

My eyes wasted away with weeping,
my entrails shuddered,
my liver spilled on the ground
at the ruin of the daughters of my people,
as children, mere infants, fainted
in the squares of the Citadel.

They kept saying to their mothers,
'Where is the bread?'
as they fainted like wounded men
in the squares of the City,
as they poured out their souls
on their mother's breasts.

How can I describe you, to what compare you,
daughter of Jerusalem?
Who can rescue and comfort you,
virgin daughter of Zion?
For huge as the sea is your affliction;
who can possibly cure you?

The visions your prophets had on your behalf
were delusive, tinsel things,
they never pointed out your sin,
to ward off your exile.
The visions they proffered you were false,
fallacious, misleading.

Cry aloud, then, to the Lord,
groan, daugher of Zion;
let your tears flow like a torrent,
day and night;
give yourself no relief,
grant your eyes no rest.

Up, cry out in the night-time,
in the early hours of darkness;

pour your heart out like water
before the Lord.
Stretch out your hands to him
for the lives of your children
who faint with hunger at the entrance to every street.

This is the word of the Lord.

Responsorial Psalm   Ps 73:1-7. 20-21. ℟ v.19

℟   Lord, forget not the life of your poor ones.

1   Why, O God, have you cast us off for ever?
     Why blaze with anger against the sheep of your pasture?
     Remember your people whom you chose long ago,
     the tribe you redeemed to be your own possession,
     the mountain of Zion where you made your dwelling.   ℟

2   Turn your steps to these places that are utterly ruined!
     The enemy has laid waste the whole of the sanctuary.
     Your foes have made uproar in your house of prayer:
     they have set up their emblems, their foreign emblems,
     high above the entrance to the sanctuary.   ℟

3   Their axes have battered the wood of its doors.
     They have struck together with hatchet and pickaxe.
     O God, they have set your sanctuary on fire:
     they have razed and profaned the place where you dwell.   ℟

4   Remember your covenant; every cave in the land
     is a place where violence makes its home.
     Do not let the oppressed return disappointed:
     let the poor and the needy bless your name.   ℟

Gospel Acclamation   Mt 8:17

     Alleluia, alleluia!
     He bore our sicknesses,
     and endured our suffering.
     Alleluia!

GOSPEL

A reading from the holy Gospel according to Matthew   8:5-17

Many will come from East and West and take their places with
Abraham, Isaac, and Jacob at the feast.

When Jesus went into Capernaum, a centurion came up and pleaded with him. 'Sir,' he said, 'my servant is lying at home paralysed, and in great pain.' 'I will come myself and cure him,' said Jesus. The centurion replied, 'Sir, I am not worthy to have you under my roof; just give the word and my servant will be cured. For I am under authority myself, and have soldiers under me; and I say to one man: Go, and he goes; to another: Come here, and he comes; to my servant: Do this, and he does it.' When Jesus heard this he was astonished and said to those following him, 'I tell you solemnly, nowhere in Israel have I found faith like this. And I tell you that many will come from east and west to take their places with Abraham and Isaac and Jacob at the feast in the kingdom of heaven; but the subjects of the kingdom will be turned out into the dark, where there will be weeping and grinding of teeth.' And to the centurion Jesus said, 'Go back, then; you have believed, so let this be done for you.' And the servant was cured at that moment.

And going into Peter's house Jesus found Peter's mother-in-law in bed with fever. He touched her hand and the fever left her, and she got up and began to wait on him.

That evening they brought him many who were possessed by devils. He cast out the spirits with a word and cured all who were sick. This was to fulfill the prophecy of Isaiah:

He took our sicknesses away and carried our diseases for us.

This is the Gospel of the Lord.

THIRTEENTH WEEK IN ORDINARY TIME
Year II

Monday

FIRST READING

A reading from the prophet Amos   2:6-10. 13-16

They trample the head of the poor into the dust.

The Lord says this:

For the three crimes, the four crimes, of Israel
I have made my decree and will not relent:
because they have sold the virtuous man for silver
and the poor man for a pair of sandals,
because they trample on the heads of ordinary people
and push the poor out of their path,
because father and son have both resorted to the same girl,
profaning my holy name,
because they stretch themselves out by the side of every altar
on clothes acquired as pledges,
and drink the wine of the people they have fined
in the house of their god ...
Yet it was I who overthrew the Amorites when they attacked,
men tall as cedars and strong as oaks,
I who destroyed them,
both fruit above ground
and root below.
It was I who brought you out of the land of Egypt
and for forty years led you through the wilderness
to take possession of the Amorite's country.
See then how I am going to crush you into the ground
as the threshing-sledge crushes when clogged by straw;
flight will not save even the swift,
the strong man will find his strength useless,
the mighty man will be powerless to save himself.
The bowman will not stand his ground,
the fast runner will not escape,
the horseman will not save himself,
the bravest warriors will run away naked that day.
It is the Lord who speaks.

This is the word of the Lord.

Responsorial Psalm   Ps 49:16-23. ℟ v.22

℟   Remember this, you who never think of God.

1   'How can you recite my commandments
    and take my covenant on your lips,
    you who despise my law
    and throw my words to the winds?   ℟

2   'You who see a thief and go with him;
    who throw in your lot with adulterers,
    who unbridle your mouth for evil
    and whose tongue is plotting crime.   ℟

3   'You who sit and malign your brother
    and slander your own mother's son.
    You do this, and should I keep silence?
    Do you think I am like you?   ℟

4   'Mark this, you who never think of God,
    lest I seize you and you cannot escape;
    a sacrifice of thanksgiving honours me
    and I will show God's salvation to the upright.'   ℟

Gospel Acclamation   cf. Ps 94:8

    Alleluia, alleluia!
    If today you hear his voice,
    harden not your hearts.
    Alleluia!

GOSPEL

A reading from the holy Gospel according to Matthew   8:18-22

Follow me.

When Jesus saw the great crowds all about him he gave orders to
leave for the other side. One of the scribes then came up and said to
him, 'Master, I will follow you wherever you go.' Jesus replied, 'Foxes
have holes and the birds of the air have nests, but the Son of Man has
nowhere to lay his head.'

Another man, one of his disciples, said to him, 'Sir, let me go and
bury my father first.' But Jesus replied, 'Follow me, and leave the
dead to bury their dead.'

This is the Gospel of the Lord.

Tuesday

FIRST READING

A reading from the prophet Amos　　　　　　　　　3:1-8; 4:11-12

The Lord God spoke: who will refuse to prophesy.

Listen, sons of Israel, to this oracle the Lord speaks against you, against the whole family I brought out of the land of Egypt:

> You alone, of all the families of earth, have I acknowledged,
> therefore it is for all your sins that I mean to punish you.
> Do two men take the road together
> if they have not planned to do so?
> Does the lion roar in the jungle
> if no prey has been found?
> Does the young lion growl in his lair
> if he has captured nothing?
> Does the bird fall to the ground
> if no trap has been set?
> Does the snare spring up from the ground
> if nothing has been caught?
> Does the trumpet sound in the city
> without the populace becoming alarmed?
> Does misfortune come to a city
> if the Lord has not sent it?
> No more does the Lord do anything
> without revealing his plans to his servants the prophets.
> The lion roars: who can help feeling afraid?
> The Lord speaks: who can refuse to prophesy?
>
> I overthrew you as God overthrew Sodom and Gomorrah,
> and you were like a brand snatched from the blaze;
> and yet you never came back to me.
> It is the Lord who speaks.
> This therefore, Israel, is what I plan to do to you,
> and because I am going to do this to you,
> Israel, prepare to meet your God!

This is the word of the Lord.

Responsorial Psalm   Ps 5:5-8. ℟ v.9

℟   Lead me in your justice, Lord.

1   You are no God who loves evil;
    no sinner is your guest.
    The boastful shall not stand their ground
    before your face.   ℟

2   You hate all who do evil:
    you destroy all who lie.
    The deceitful and bloodthirsty man
    the Lord detests.   ℟

3   But I through the greatness of your love
    have access to your house.
    I bow down before your holy temple,
    filled with awe.   ℟

Gospel Acclamation   Ps 129:5

    Alleluia, alleluia!
    I hope in the Lord,
    I trust in his word.
    Alleluia!

GOSPEL

A reading from the holy Gospel according to Matthew   8:23-27

He commanded the wind and the sea, and all was calm again.

Jesus got into the boat followed by his disciples. Without warning a
storm broke over the lake, so violent that the waves were breaking
right over the boat. But he was asleep. So they went to him and woke
him saying, 'Save us, Lord, we are going down!' And he said to them,
'Why are you so frightened, you men of little faith?' And with that he
stood up and rebuked the winds and the sea; and all was calm again.
The men were astounded and said, 'Whatever kind of man is this?
Even the winds and the sea obey him.'

    This is the Gospel of the Lord.

Wednesday

FIRST READING

A reading from the prophet Amos   5:14-15. 21-24

Take away your sacrifices, but let your justice flow like an unfailing stream.

Seek good and not evil
so that you may live,
and that the Lord, God of hosts, may really be with you
as you claim he is.
Hate evil, love good,
maintain justice at the city gate,
and it may be that the Lord, God of hosts, will take pity
on the remnant of Joseph.

The Lord says this:
I hate and despise your feasts,
I take no pleasure in your solemn festivals.
When you offer me holocausts,
I reject your oblations,
and refuse to look at your sacrifices of fattened cattle.
Let me have no more of the din of your chanting,
no more of your strumming on harps.
But let justice flow like water,
and integrity like an unfailing stream.

This is the word of the Lord.

Responsorial Psalm   Ps 49:7-13. 16-17. ℟ v.23

℟   To the upright I will show the saving power of God.

1   'Listen, my people, I will speak;
    Israel, I will testify against you,
    for I am God your God.   ℟

2   'I find no fault with your sacrifices,
    your offerings are always before me.
    I do not ask more bullocks from your farms,
    nor goats from among your herds.   ℟   (continued)

3 'I own all the beasts of the forest,
   beasts in their thousands on my hills.
   I know all the birds in the sky,
   all that moves in the field belongs to me.

℟ To the upright I will show the saving power of God.

4 'Were I hungry, I would not tell you,
   for I own the world and all it holds.
   Do you think I eat the flesh of bulls,
   or drink the blood of goats? ℟

5 'How can you recite my commandments
   and take my covenant on your lips,
   you who despise my law
   and throw my words to the winds?' ℟

Gospel Acclamation   James 1:18

Alleluia, alleluia!
The Father gave us birth by his message of truth,
that we might be as the first fruits of his creation.
Alleluia!

GOSPEL

A reading from the holy Gospel according to Matthew   8:28-34

He came at this time to torture the demons.

When Jesus reached the country of the Gadarenes on the other side of
the Lake, two demoniacs came towards him out of the tombs –
creatures so fierce that no one could pass that way. They stood there
shouting, 'What do you want with us, Son of God? Have you come here
to torture us before the time?' Now some distance away there was a
large herd of pigs feeding, and the devils pleaded with Jesus, 'If you
cast us out, send us into the herd of pigs.' And he said to them, 'Go
then,' and they came out and made for the pigs; and at that the whole
herd charged down the cliff into the lake and perished in the water.
The swineherds ran off and made for the town, where they told the
whole story, including what had happened to the demoniacs. At this
the whole town set out to meet Jesus; and as soon as they saw him
they implored him to leave the neighbourhood.

This is the Gospel of the Lord.

Thursday

FIRST READING

A reading from the prophet Amos 7:10-17

Go prophesy to my people.

Amaziah the priest of Bethel sent word to Jeroboam king of Israel as follows. 'Amos is plotting against you in the heart of the House of Israel; the country can no longer tolerate what he keeps saying. For this is what he says, "Jeroboam is going to die by the sword, and Israel go into exile far from its country." ' To Amos, Amaziah said, 'Go away, seer; get back to the land of Judah; earn your bread there, do your prophesying there. We want no more prophesying in Bethel; this is the royal sanctuary, the national temple.' 'I was no prophet, neither did I belong to any of the brotherhoods of prophets,' Amos replied to Amaziah. 'I was a shepherd, and looked after sycamores: but it was the Lord who took me from herding the flock, and the Lord who said, "Go, prophesy to my people Israel." So listen to the word of the Lord. You say:

"Do not prophesy against Israel,
utter no oracles against the House of Isaac."

Very well, this is what the Lord says,

"Your wife will be forced to go on the streets,
your sons and daughters will fall by the sword,
your land be parcelled out by measuring line,
and you yourself die on unclean soil
and Israel will go into exile far distant from its own land." '

This is the word of the Lord.

Responsorial Psalm Ps 18:8-11. ℟ v.10

℟ The judgements of the Lord are true
and all of them just.

1 The law of the Lord is perfect,
it revives the soul.
The rule of the Lord is to be trusted,
it gives wisdom to the simple.   ℟

2 The precepts of the Lord are right,
they gladden the heart.

The command of the Lord is clear,
it gives light to the eyes.

℟   The judgements of the Lord are true
and all of them just.

3   The fear of the Lord is holy,
abiding for ever.
The decrees of the Lord are truth
and all of them just.   ℟

4   They are more to be desired than gold,
than the purest of gold
and sweeter are they than honey,
than honey from the comb.   ℟

Gospel Acclamation   2 Cor 5:19

Alleluia, alleluia!
God was in Christ, to reconcile the world to himself;
and the Good News of reconciliation he has entrusted to us.
Alleluia!

GOSPEL

A reading from the holy Gospel according to Matthew   9:1-8

They praised God for giving power to men.

Jesus got back in the boat, crossed the water and came to his own
town. Then some people appeared, bringing him a paralytic stretched
out on a bed. Seeing their faith, Jesus said to the paralytic, 'Courage,
my child, your sins are forgiven.' And at this some scribes said to
themselves, 'This man is blaspheming.' Knowing what was in their
minds Jesus said, 'Why do you have such wicked thoughts in your
hearts? Now, which of these is easier: to say, 'Your sins are forgiven',
or to say, 'Get up and walk'? But to prove to you that the Son of Man
has authority on earth to forgive sins,' – he said to the paralytic – 'get
up, and pick up your bed and go off home.' And the man got up and
went home. A feeling of awe came over the crowd when they saw this,
and they praised God for giving such power to men.

This is the Gospel of the Lord.

Friday

FIRST READING

A reading from the prophet Amos   8:4-6. 9-12

I will send famine on the earth, not of bread but of hearing the word of God.

Listen to this, you who trample on the needy
and try to suppress the poor people of the country,
you who say, 'When will New Moon be over
so that we can sell our corn,
and sabbath, so that we can market our wheat?
Then by lowering the bushel, raising the shekel,
by swindling and tampering with the scales,
we can buy up the poor for money,
and the needy for a pair of sandals,
and get a price even for the sweepings of the wheat.'

'That day – it is the Lord who speaks –
I will make the sun go down at noon,
and darken the earth in broad daylight.
I am going to turn your feasts into funerals,
all your singing into lamentation;
I will have your loins all in sackcloth,
your heads all shaved.
I will make it a mourning like the mourning for an only son,
as long as it lasts it will be like a day of bitterness.
See what days are coming – it is the Lord who speaks –
days when I will bring famine on the country,
a famine not of bread, a drought not of water,
but of hearing the word of the Lord.
They will stagger from sea to sea,
wander from north to east,
seeking the word of the Lord
and failing to find it.'

This is the word of the Lord.

Responsorial Psalm   Ps 118:2. 10. 20. 30. 40. 131. ℟ Mt 4:4

℟   No one lives on bread alone,
    but on every word that comes from the mouth of God.

1   They are happy those who do his will,
    seeking him with all their hearts.
    I have sought you with all my heart:
    let me not stray from your commands.   ℟

2   My soul is ever consumed
    in longing for your decrees.
    I have chosen the way of truth
    with your decrees before me.   ℟

3   See, I long for your precepts:
    then in your justice, give me life.
    I open my mouth and I sigh
    as I yearn for your commands.   ℟

Gospel Acclamation   Mt 11:28

Alleluia, alleluia!
Come to me, all you that labour and are burdened,
and I will give you rest, says the Lord.
Alleluia!

GOSPEL

A reading from the holy Gospel according to Matthew   9:9-13

It is not the healthy who need the doctor. What I want is mercy, not sacrifice.

As Jesus was walking he saw a man named Matthew sitting by the
customs house, and he said to him, 'Follow me.' And he got up and
followed him.

While he was at dinner in the house it happened that a number of
tax collectors and sinners came to sit at the table with Jesus and his
disciples. When the Pharisees saw this, they said to his disciples,
'Why does your master eat with tax collectors and sinners?' When he
heard this he replied, 'It is not the healthy who need the doctor, but
the sick. Go and learn the meaning of the word: What I want is mercy,

not sacrifice. And indeed I did not come to call the virtuous, but sinners.'

This is the Gospel of the Lord.

Saturday

FIRST READING

A reading from the prophet Amos   9:11-15

I will restore my people Israel and plant them in their own country.

It is the Lord who speaks:

'That day I will re-erect the tottering hut of David,
make good the gaps in it, restore its ruins
and rebuild it as it was in the days of old,
so that they can conquer the remnant of Edom
and all the nations that belonged to me.'

It is the Lord who speaks, and he will carry this out.

'The days are coming now – it is the Lord who speaks –
when harvest will follow directly after ploughing,
the treading of grapes soon after sowing,
when the mountains will run with new wine
and the hills all flow with it.
I mean to restore the fortunes of my people Israel;
they will rebuild the ruined cities and live in them,
plant vineyards and drink their wine,
dig gardens and eat their produce.
I will plant them in their own country,
never to be rooted up again
out of the land I have given them,
says the Lord, your God.'

This is the word of the Lord.

Responsorial Psalm   Ps 84:9. 11-14.℟ v.9

℟   The Lord speaks of peace to his people.

1   I will hear what the Lord God has to say,
     a voice that speaks of peace,
     peace for his people and his friends
     and those who turn to him in their hearts.   ℟

2   Mercy and faithfulness have met;
     justice and peace have embraced.
     Faithfulness shall spring from the earth
     and justice look down from heaven.   ℟

3   The Lord will make us prosper
     and our earth shall yield its fruit.
     Justice shall march before him
     and peace shall follow his steps.   ℟

Gospel Acclamation   Jn 10:27

     Alleluia, alleluia!
     My sheep listen to my voice, says the Lord
     I know them, and they follow me.
     Alleluia!

GOSPEL

A reading from the holy Gospel according to Matthew   9:14-17

*The wedding guests would never mourn while the bridegroom is
still with them?*

John's disciples came to Jesus and said, 'Why is it that we and the
Pharisees fast, but your disciples do not?' Jesus replied, 'Surely the
bridegroom's attendants would never think of mourning as long as the
bridegroom is still with them? But the time will come for the
bridegroom to be taken away from them, and then they will fast. No
one puts a piece of unshrunken cloth on to an old cloak, because the
patch pulls away from the cloak and the tear gets worse. Nor do people
put new wine into old wineskins; if they do, the skins burst, the wine
runs out, and the skins are lost. No; they put new wine into fresh
skins and both are preserved.'

This is the Gospel of the Lord.

FOURTEENTH WEEK IN ORDINARY TIME
Year II

Monday

FIRST READING

A reading from the prophet Hosea   2:16-18. 21-22

I will betroth you to myself for ever.

It is the Lord who speaks:

I am going to lure her
and lead her out into the wilderness
and speak to her heart.
There she will respond to me as she did when she was young,
as she did when she came out of the land of Egypt.
When that day comes – it is the Lord who speaks –
she will call me, 'My husband',
no longer will she call me, 'My Baal.'
I will betroth you to myself for ever,
betroth you with integrity and justice,
with tenderness and love;
I will betroth you to myself with faithfulness,
and you will come to know the Lord.

This is the word of the Lord.

Responsorial Psalm   Ps 144:2-9. ℟ v.8

℟   The Lord is kind and merciful.

1   I will bless you day after day
     and praise your name for ever.
     The Lord is great, highly to be praised,
     his greatness cannot be measured.   ℟

2   Age to age shall proclaim your works,
     shall declare your mighty deeds,
     shall speak of your splendour and glory,
     tell the tale of your wonderful works.   ℟   (continued)

3   They will speak of your terrible deeds,
    recount your greatness and might.
    They will recall your abundant goodness;
    age to age shall ring out your justice.

    ℟   The Lord is kind and merciful.

4   The Lord is kind and full of compassion,
    slow to anger, abounding in love.
    How good is the Lord to all,
    compassionate to all his creatures.   ℟

Gospel Acclamation   cf. 2 Tim 1:10

    Alleluia, alleluia!
    Our Saviour Jesus Christ has done away with death
    and brought us life through his gospel.
    Alleluia!

GOSPEL

A reading from the holy Gospel according to Matthew   9:18-26

My daughter has just died, but come to her and she will live.

While Jesus was speaking, up came one of the officials,who bowed low
in front of him and said, 'My daughter has just died, but come and lay
your hand on her and her life will be saved.' Jesus rose and, with his
disciples, followed him.

Then from behind him came a woman, who had suffered from a
haemorrhage for twelve years, and she touched the fringe of his cloak,
for she said to herself, 'If I can only touch his cloak I shall be well
again.' Jesus turned round and saw her; and he said to her, 'Courage,
my daughter, your faith has restored you to health.' And from that
moment the woman was well again.

When Jesus reached the official's house, and saw the fluteplayers,
with the crowd making a commotion he said, 'Get out of here; the little
girl is not dead, she is asleep.' And they laughed at him. But when the
people had been turned out he went inside and took the little girl by
the hand; and she stood up. And the news spread all round the
countryside.

    This is the Gospel of the Lord.

Tuesday

FIRST READING

A reading from the prophet Hosea   8:4-7. 11-13

They sow the wind and reap the whirlwind.

Thus says the Lord:

They have set up kings, but not with my consent,
and appointed princes, but without my knowledge.
Out of their own silver and gold they have made idols,
which are doomed to destruction.
I spurn your calf, Samaria,
my anger blazes against it.
(How long will it be before they purge themselves of this,
the sons of Israel?)
A workman made the thing,
this cannot be God!
Yes, the calf of Samaria shall go up in flames.

They sow the wind, they will reap the whirlwind;
their wheat will yield no ear,
the ear will yield no flour,
or, if it does, foreigners will swallow it.
Ephraim has built altar after altar,
they have only served him as occasion for sin.
Were I to write out the thousand precepts of my Law for him,
they would be paid no more attention than those of a stranger.
They love sacrificing; right, let them sacrifice!
They love meat; right, let them eat it!
The Lord takes no pleasure in these.
He is now going to remember their iniquity
and punish their sins;
they will have to go back to Egypt.

This is the word of the Lord.

Responsorial Psalm   Ps 113B:3-10. ℟ v.9

℟   The house of Israel trusts in the Lord.

or

℟   Alleluia!

1   Our God, he is in the heavens;
    he does whatever he wills.
    The idols of the heathen are silver and gold,
    the work of human hands.   ℟

2   They have mouths but they cannot speak;
    they have eyes but they cannot see;
    they have ears but they cannot hear;
    they have nostrils but they cannot smell.   ℟

3   With their hands they cannot feel;
    with their feet they cannot walk.
    Their makers will become like them:
    so will all who trust in them.   ℟

4   Sons of Israel, trust in the Lord;
    he is their help and their shield.
    Sons of Aaron, trust in the Lord;
    he is their help and their shield.   ℟

Gospel Acclamation   Jn 10:14

Alleluia, alleluia!
I am the good shepherd, says the Lord;
I know my sheep, and mine know me.
Alleluia!

GOSPEL

A reading from the holy Gospel according to Matthew   9:32-38

The harvest is rich but the labourers are few.

A man was brought to Jesus, a dumb demoniac. And when the devil
was cast out, the dumb man spoke and the people were amazed.
'Nothing like this has ever been seen in Israel' they said. But the
Pharisees said, 'It is through the prince of devils that he casts out
devils.'

Jesus made a tour through all the towns and villages, teaching in their synagogues, proclaiming the Good News of the kingdom and curing all kinds of diseases and sickness.

And when he saw the crowds he felt sorry for them because they were harassed and dejected, like sheep without a shepherd. Then he said to his disciples, 'The harvest is rich but the labourers are few, so ask the Lord of the harvest to send labourers to his harvest.'

This is the Gospel of the Lord.

Wednesday

FIRST READING

A reading from the prophet Hosea   10:1-3. 7-8. 12

It is time to go seeking the Lord God.

Israel was a luxuriant vine
yielding plenty of fruit.
The more his fruit increased,
the more altars he built;
the richer his land became,
the richer he made the sacred stones.
Their heart is a divided heart;
very well, they must pay for it;
the Lord is going to break their altars down
and destroy their sacred stones.
Then they will say,
'We have no king
because we have not feared the Lord.'
But what can a king do for us?

Samaria has had her day.
Her king is like a straw drifting on the water.
The idolatrous high places shall be destroyed –
that sin of Israel;
thorn and thistle will grow on their altars.
Then they will say to the mountains, 'Cover us!'
and to the hills, 'Fall on us!'

Sow integrity for yourselves,
reap a harvest of kindness,

break up your fallow ground:
it is time to go seeking the Lord
until he comes to rain salvation on you.

This is the word of the Lord.

Responsorial Psalm

Ps 104:2-7. ℟ v.4

℟   Seek always the face of the Lord.

or

℟   Alleluia!

1   O sing to him, sing his praise;
tell all his wonderful works!
Be proud of his holy name,
let the hearts that seek the Lord rejoice.   ℟

2   Consider the Lord and his strength;
constantly seek his face.
Remember the wonders he has done,
his miracles, the judgements he spoke.   ℟

3   O children of Abraham, his servant,
O sons of the Jacob he chose.
He, the Lord, is our God:
his judgements prevail in all the earth.   ℟

Gospel Acclamation

Mk 1:15

Alleluia, alleluia!
The kingdom of God is near:
repent and believe the Good News!
Alleluia!

GOSPEL

A reading from the holy Gospel according to Matthew   10:1-7

Go to the lost sheep of the House of Israel.

Jesus summoned his twelve disciples, and gave them authority over
unclean spirits with power to cast them out and to cure all kinds of
diseases and sickness.

These are the names of the twelve apostles: first, Simon who is called Peter, and his brother Andrew; James the son of Zebedee, and his brother John; Philip and Bartholomew; Thomas, and Matthew the tax collector; James the son of Alphaeus, and Thaddaeus; Simon the Zealot and Judas Iscariot, the one who was to betray him. These twelve Jesus sent out, instructing them as follows:

'Do not turn your steps to pagan territory, and do not enter any Samaritan town; go rather to the lost sheep of the House of Israel. And as you go, proclaim that the kingdom of heaven is close at hand.'

This is the Gospel of the Lord.

Thursday

FIRST READING

A reading from the prophet Hosea   11:1-4. 8-9

Israel, how could I give you up? My heart turns against it.

Thus says the Lord:

When Israel was a child I loved him,
and I called my son out of Egypt.
But the more I called to them, the further they went from me;
they have offered sacrifice to the Baals
and set their offerings smoking before the idols.
I myself taught Ephraim to walk,
I took them in my arms;
yet they have not understood that I was the one looking after
    them.
I led them with reins of kindness,
with leading-strings of love.

I was like someone who lifts an infant close against his cheek;
stooping down to him I gave him his food.
My heart recoils from it,
my whole being trembles at the thought.
I will not give rein to my fierce anger,
I will not destroy Ephraim again,
for I am God, not man:
I am the Holy One in your midst
and have no wish to destroy.

This is the word of the Lord.

591

Responsial Psalm   Ps 79:2-3. 15-16. ℟ v.4

℟   Let us see your face, Lord,
      and we shall be saved.

1   O shepherd of Israel, hear us,
      shine forth from your cherubim throne.
      O Lord, rouse up your might,
      O Lord, come to our help.   ℟

2   God of hosts, turn again, we implore,
      look down from heaven and see.
      Visit this vine and protect it,
      the vine your right hand has planted.   ℟

Gospel Acclamation   Mk 1:15

      Alleluia, alleluia!
      The kingdom of God is near:
      repent and believe the Good News!
      Alleluia!

GOSPEL

A reading from the holy Gospel according to Matthew   10:7-15

You received without charge, give without charge.

Jesus instructed the Twelve as follows: 'As you go, proclaim that the
kingdom of heaven is close at hand. Cure the sick, raise the dead,
cleanse the lepers, cast out devils. You received without charge, give
without charge. Provide yourselves with no gold or silver, not even
with a few coppers for your purses, with no haversack for the journey
or spare tunic or footwear or a staff, for the workman deserves his
keep.

      'Whatever town or village you go into, ask for someone trust-
worthy and stay with him until you leave. As you enter his house,
salute it, and if the house deserves it, let your peace descend upon it; if
it does not, let your peace come back to you. And if anyone does not
welcome you or listen to what you have to say, as you walk out of the
house or town shake the dust from your feet. I tell you solemnly, on
the day of Judgement it will not go as hard with the land of Sodom and
Gomorrah as with that town.'

      This is the Gospel of the Lord.

Friday

FIRST READING

A reading from the prophet Hosea   14:2-10

We will say no more: Our God, to the work of our hands.

The Lord says this:

Israel, come back to the Lord your God;
your iniquity was the cause of your downfall.
Provide yourself with words
and come back to the Lord.
Say to him, 'Take all iniquity away
so that we may have happiness again
and offer you our words of praise.
Assyria cannot save us,
we will not ride horses any more,
or say, "Our God!" to what our own hands have made,
for you are the one in whom orphans find compassion.'
– I will heal their disloyalty,
I will love them with all my heart,
for my anger has turned from them.
I will fall like dew on Israel.
He shall bloom like the lily,
and thrust out roots like the poplar,
his shoots will spread far;
he will have the beauty of the olive
and the fragrance of Lebanon.
They will come back to live in my shade;
they will grow corn that flourishes,
they will cultivate vines
as renowned as the wine of Helbon.
What has Ephraim to do with idols any more
when it is I who hear his prayer and care for him?
I am like a cypress ever green,
all your fruitfulness comes from me.

Let the wise man understand these words.
Let the intelligent man grasp their meaning.
For the ways of the Lord are straight,
and virtuous men walk in them,
but sinners stumble.

This is the word of the Lord.

Responsorial Psalm   Ps 50:3-4. 8-9. 12-14. 17. ℟ v.17

℟   My mouth will declare your praise.

1   Have mercy on me, God, in your kindness.
    In your compassion blot out my offence.
    O wash me more and more from my guilt
    and cleanse me from my sin.   ℟

2   Indeed you love truth in the heart;
    then in the secret of my heart teach me wisdom.
    O purify me, then I shall be clean;
    O wash me, I shall be whiter than snow.   ℟

3   A pure heart create for me, O God,
    put a steadfast spirit within me.
    Do not cast me away from your presence,
    nor deprive me of your holy spirit.   ℟

4   Give me again the joy of your help;
    with a spirit of fervour sustain me.
    O Lord, open my lips
    and my mouth shall declare your praise.   ℟

Gospel Acclamation   Jn 16:13; 14:26

    Alleluia, alleluia!
    When the Spirit of truth comes, he will teach you all truth
    and bring to your mind all I have told you.
    Alleluia!

GOSPEL

A reading from the holy Gospel according to Matthew   10:16-23

It is not you who speak, but the Spirit of your Father speaking in you.

Jesus instructed the Twelve as follows: 'Remember, I am sending you out like sheep among wolves; so be cunning as serpents and yet as harmless as doves.

'Beware of men: they will hand you over to sanhedrins and scourge you in their synagogues. You will be dragged before governors and kings for my sake, to bear witness before them and the pagans. But when they hand you over, do not worry about how to speak or what to say; what you are to say will be given to you when the time comes; because it is not you who will be speaking; the Spirit of your Father will be speaking in you.

'Brother will betray brother to death, and the father his child; children will rise against their parents and have them put to death. You will be hated by all men on account of my name; but the man who stands firm to the end will be saved. If they persecute you in one town, take refuge in the next; and if they persecute you in that, take refuge in another. I tell you solemnly, you will not have gone the round of the towns of Israel before the Son of Man comes.'

This is the Gospel of the Lord.

Saturday

FIRST READING

A reading from the prophet Isaiah   6:1-8

What a wretched state I am in, my eyes have looked at the king, the Lord God.

In the year of King Uzziah's death I saw the Lord seated on a high throne; his train filled the sanctuary; above him stood seraphs, each one with six wings: two to cover its face, two to cover its feet and two for flying.

And they cried out to one another in this way,
'Holy, holy, holy is the Lord of hosts.
His glory fills the whole earth.'

The foundations of the threshold shook with the voice of the one who cried out, and the Temple was filled with smoke. I said:

'What a wretched state I am in! I am lost,
for I am a man of unclean lips
and I live among a people of unclean lips,
and my eyes have looked at the King, the Lord of hosts.'

Then one of the seraphs flew to me, holding in his hand a live coal which he had taken from the altar with a pair of tongs. With this he touched my mouth and said:

'See now, this has touched your lips,

your sin is taken away,
your iniquity is purged.'

Then I heard the voice of the Lord saying:

'Whom shall I send? Who will be our messenger?'

I answered, 'Here I am, send me.'

This is the word of the Lord.

Responsorial Psalm

Ps 92:1-2. 5. ℟ v.1

℟ The Lord is king;
    he is robed in majesty.

1 The Lord is king, with majesty enrobed;
   the Lord has robed himself with might,
   he has girded himself with power.   ℟

2 The world you made firm, not to be moved;
   your throne has stood firm from of old.
   From all eternity, O Lord, you are.   ℟

3 Truly your decrees are to be trusted.
   Holiness is fitting to your house,
   O Lord, until the end of time.   ℟

Gospel Acclamation

1 Peter 4:14

Alleluia, alleluia!
If you are insulted for the name of Christ, blessed are you,
for the Spirit of God rests upon you.
Alleluia!

GOSPEL

A reading from the holy Gospel according to Matthew   10:24-33

Do not be afraid of those who can kill the body.

Jesus instructed the Twelve as follows: 'The disciple is not superior to
his teacher, nor the slave to his master. It is enough for the disciple
that he should grow to be like his teacher, and the slave like his
master. If they have called the master of the house Beelzebul, what
will they not say of his household?

'Do not be afraid of them therefore. For everything that is now covered will be uncovered, and everything now hidden will be made clear. What I say to you in the dark, tell in the daylight; what you hear in whispers, proclaim from the housetops.

'Do not be afraid of those who kill the body but cannot kill the soul; fear him rather who can destroy both body and soul in hell. Can you not buy two sparrows for a penny? And yet not one falls to the ground without your Father knowing. Why, every hair on your head has been counted. So there is no need to be afraid; you are worth more than hundreds of sparrows.

'So if anyone declares himself for me in the presence of men, I will declare myself for him in the presence of my Father in heaven. But the one who disowns me in the presence of men, I will disown in the presence of my Father in heaven.'

This is the Gospel of the Lord.

FIFTEENTH WEEK IN ORDINARY TIME
Year II

Monday

FIRST READING

A reading from the prophet Isaiah   1:10-17

Make yourselves clean, take your evil out of my sight.

Hear the word of the Lord,
you rulers of Sodom:
listen to the command of our God,
you people of Gomorrah.

'What are your endless sacrifices to me?
says the Lord.
I am sick of holocausts of rams
and the fat of calves.
The blood of bulls and of goats revolts me.
When you come to present yourselves before me,
who asked you to trample over my courts?
Bring me your worthless offerings no more,
the smoke of them fills me with disgust.
New Moons, sabbaths, assemblies –
I cannot endure festival and solemnity.

Your New Moons and your pilgrimages
I hate with all my soul.
They lie heavy on me,
I am tired of bearing them.

'When you stretch out your hands
I turn my eyes away.
You may multiply your prayers,
I shall not listen.
Your hands are covered with blood,
wash, make yourselves clean.

'Take your wrong-doing out of my sight.
Cease to do evil.
Learn to do good,
search for justice,
help the oppressed,
be just to the orphan,
plead for the widow.'

This is the word of the Lord.

Responsorial Psalm   Ps 49:8-9. 16-17. 21. 23. ℟ v.23

℟   To the upright I will show the saving power of God.

1   'I find no fault with your sacrifices,
    your offerings are always before me.
    I do not ask more bullocks from your farms,
    nor goats from among your herds.   ℟

2   'How can you recite my commandments
    and take my covenant on your lips,
    you who despise my law
    and throw my words to the winds?   ℟

3   'You do this, and should I keep silence?
    Do you think that I am like you?
    A sacrifice of thanksgiving honours me
    and I will show God's salvation to the upright.'   ℟

Gospel Acclamation   Mt 5:10

> Alleluia, alleluia!
> Happy are they who suffer persecution for justice' sake;
> the kingdom of heaven is theirs.
> Alleluia!

GOSPEL

A reading from the holy Gospel according to Matthew   10:34 – 11:1

I have not come to bring peace, but the sword.

Jesus instructed the Twelve as follows: 'Do not suppose that I have come to bring peace to the earth: it is not peace I have come to bring, but a sword. For I have come to set a man against his father, a daughter against her mother, a daughter-in-law against her mother-in-law. A man's enemies will be those of his own household.

'Anyone who prefers father or mother to me is not worthy of me. Anyone who prefers son or daughter to me is not worthy of me. Anyone who does not take his cross and follow in my footsteps is not worthy of me. Anyone who finds his life will lose it; anyone who loses his life for my sake will find it.

'Anyone who welcomes you welcomes me; and those who welcome me welcome the one who sent me.

'Anyone who welcomes a prophet because he is a prophet will have a prophet's reward; and anyone who welcomes a holy man because he is a holy man will have a holy man's reward.

'If anyone gives so much as a cup of cold water to one of these little ones because he is a disciple, then I tell you solemnly, he will most certainly not lose his reward.'

When Jesus had finished instructing his twelve disciples he moved on from there to teach and preach in their towns.

This is the Gospel of the Lord.

Tuesday

FIRST READING

A reading from the prophet Isaiah   7:1-9

If you do not stand by me, you will perish.

In the reign of Ahaz son of Jotham, son of Uzziah, king of Judah, Razon the king of Afam went up against Jerusalem with Pekah son of Remaliah, king of Israel, to lay siege to it; but he was unable to capture it.

The news was brought to the House of David. 'Aram,' they said, 'has reached Ephraim.' Then the heart of the king and the hearts of the people shuddered as the trees of the forest shudder in front of the wind. The Lord said to Isaiah, 'Go with your son Shear-jashub, and meet Ahaz at the end of the conduit of the upper pool on the Fuller's Field road, and say to him:

"Pay attention, keep calm, have no fear,
do not let your heart sink
because of these two smouldering stumps of firebrands,
or because Aram, Ephraim and the son of Remaliah
have plotted to ruin you, and have said:
Let us invade Judah and terrorise it
and seize it for ourselves,
and set up a king there,
the son of Tabeel.
The Lord says this:
It shall not come true; it shall not be.
The capital of Aram is Damascus,
the head of Damascus, Razon;
the capital of Ephraim, Samaria,
the head of Samaria, the son of Remaliah.
Six or five years more
and shattered Ephraim shall no longer be a people.
But if you do not stand by me,
you will not stand at all." '

This is the word of the Lord.

Responsorial Psalm   Ps 47:2-8. ℟ v.9

℟   God upholds his city for ever.

1   The Lord is great and worthy to be praised
    in the city of our God.
    His holy mountain rises in beauty,
    the joy of all the earth.   ℟

2   Mount Zion, true pole of the earth,
    the Great King's city!
    God, in the midst of its citadels,
    has shown himself its stronghold.   ℟

3   For the kings assembled together,
    together they advanced.
    They saw; at once they were astounded;
    dismayed, they fled in fear.   ℟

4   A trembling seized them there,
    like the pangs of birth,
    or as the east wind destroys
    the ships of Tarshish.   ℟

Gospel Acclamation   cf. Ps 94:8

    Alleluia, alleluia!
    If today you hear his voice,
    harden not your hearts.
    Alleluia!

GOSPEL

A reading from the holy Gospel according to Matthew   11:20-24

*It will not go as hard with Tyre and Sidon and the land of Sodom
on Judgement Day as with you.*

Jesus began to reproach the towns in which most of his miracles had
been worked, because they refused to repent.

'Alas for you, Chorazin! Alas for you, Bethsaida! For if the
miracles done in you had been done in Tyre and Sidon, they would
have repented long ago in sackcloth and ashes. And still, I tell you
that it will not go as hard on Judgement day with Tyre and Sidon

as with you. And as for you, Capernaum, did you want to be exalted as high as heaven? You shall be thrown down to hell. For if the miracles done in you had been done in Sodom, it would have been standing yet. And still, I tell you it will not go as hard with the land of Sodom on Judgement day as with you.'

This is the Gospel of the Lord.

Wednesday

FIRST READING

A reading from the prophet Isaiah   10:5-7. 13-16

Does the axe claim more credit than the one who wields it?

The Lord of hosts says this:

'Woe to Assyria, the rod of my anger,
the club brandished by me in my fury!
I sent him against a godless nation;
I gave him commission against a people that provokes me,
to pillage and to plunder freely
and to stamp down like the mud in the streets.
But he did not intend this,
his heart did not plan it so.
No, in his heart was to destroy,
to go on cutting nations to pieces without limit.'

For he has said:

'By the strength of my own arm I have done this
and by my own intelligence, for understanding is mine;
I have pushed back the frontiers of peoples
and plundered their treasures.
I have brought their inhabitants down to the dust.
As if they were a bird's nest, my hand has seized
the riches of the peoples.
As people pick up deserted eggs
I have picked up the whole earth,
with not a wing fluttering,
not a beak opening, not a chirp.'

Does the axe claim more credit than the man who wields it,
or the saw more strength than the man who handles it?
It would be like the cudgel controlling the man who raises it,
or the club moving what is not made of wood!
And so the Lord of hosts is going to send
a wasting sickness on his stout warriors;
beneath his plenty, a burning will burn
like a consuming fire.

This is the word of the Lord.

Responsorial Psalm   Ps 93:5-10. 14-15. ℟ v.14

℟   The Lord will not abandon his people.

They crush your people, Lord,
they afflict the ones you have chosen.
They kill the widow and the stranger
and murder the fatherless child.   ℟

And they say: 'The Lord does not see;
the God of Jacob pays no heed.'
Mark this, most senseless of people;
fools, when will you understand?   ℟

Can he who made the ear not hear?
Can he who formed the eye not see?
Will he who trains nations not punish?
Will he who teaches men not have knowledge?   ℟

The Lord will not abandon his people
nor forsake those who are his own:
for judgement shall again be just
and all true hearts shall uphold it.   ℟

Gospel Acclamation   cf. Mt 11:25

Alleluia, alleluia!
Blessed are you, Father, Lord of heaven and earth;
you have revealed to little ones the mysteries of the kingdom.
Alleluia!

GOSPEL

A reading from the holy Gospel according to Matthew   11:25-27

The Lord hides these things from the wise and reveals them to children

Jesus exclaimed, 'I bless you, Father, Lord of heaven and of earth, for hiding these things from the learned and the clever and revealing them to mere children. Yes, Father, for that is what it pleased you to do. Everything has been entrusted to me by my Father; and no one knows the Son except the Father, just as no one knows the Father except the Son and those to whom the Son chooses to reveal him.'

This is the Gospel of the Lord.

Thursday

FIRST READING

A reading from the prophet Isaiah   26:7-9. 12. 16-19

Come to life and rejoice, all you who lie in the dust.

The path of the upright man is straight,
you smooth the way of the upright.
Following the path of your judgements,
we hoped in you, Lord,
your name, your memory are all my soul desires.

At night my soul longs for you
and my spirit in me seeks for you;
when your judgements appear on earth
the inhabitants of the world learn the meaning of integrity.

Lord, you are giving us peace,
since you treat us
as our deeds deserve.

Distressed, we search for you, Lord;
the misery of oppression was your punishment for us.
As a woman with child near her time
writhes and cries out in her pangs,

so are we, O Lord, in your presence:
we have conceived, we writhe
as if we were giving birth;

we have not given the spirit of salvation to the earth,
no more inhabitants of the world are born.

Your dead will come to life,
their corpses will rise;
awake, exult,
all you who lie in the dust,
for your dew is a radiant dew
and the land of ghosts will give birth.

This is the word of the Lord.

Responsorial Psalm   Ps 101:13-21. ℟ v.20

℟   From heaven the Lord looks down on the earth.

1   You, O Lord, will endure for ever
    and your name from age to age.
    You will arise and have mercy on Zion:
    for this is the time to have mercy,
    for your servants love her very stones,
    are moved with pity even for her dust.   ℟

2   The nations shall fear the name of the Lord
    and all the earth's kings your glory,
    when the Lord shall build up Zion again
    and appear in all his glory.
    Then he will turn to the prayers of the helpless;
    he will not despise their prayers.   ℟

3   Let this be written for ages to come
    that a people yet unborn may praise the Lord;
    for the Lord leaned down from his sanctuary on high.
    He looked down from heaven to the earth
    that he might hear the groans of the prisoners
    and free those condemned to die.   ℟

Gospel Acclamation   Mt 11:28

    Alleluia, alleluia!
    Come to me, all you that labour and are burdened,
    and I will give you rest, says the Lord.
    Alleluia!

GOSPEL

A reading from the holy Gospel according to Matthew   11:28-30

I am gentle and humble in heart.

Jesus exclaimed: 'Come to me, all you who labour and are overburdened, and I will give you rest. Shoulder my yoke and learn from me, for I am gentle and humble in heart, and you will find rest for your souls. Yes, my yoke is easy and my burden light.'

This is the Gospel of the Lord.

Friday

FIRST READING

A reading from the prophet Isaiah   38:1-6. 21-22. 7-8

I have heard your prayer and seen your tears.

Hezekiah fell ill and was at the point of death. The prophet Isaiah son of Amoz came and said to him, 'The Lord says this, "Put your affairs in order, for you are going to die, you will not live." ' Hezekiah turned his face to the wall and addressed this prayer to the Lord, 'Ah, Lord, remember, I beg you, how I have behaved faithfully and with sincerity of heart in your presence and done what is right in your eyes.' And Hezekiah shed many tears.

Then the word of the Lord came to Isaiah, 'Go and say to Hezekiah, "The Lord, the God of David your ancestor, says this: I have heard your prayer and seen your tears. I will cure you: in three days' time you shall go up to the Temple of the Lord. I will add fifteen years to your life. I will save you from the hands of the king of Assyria, I will protect this city." '

'Bring a fig poultice,' Isaiah said. 'Apply it to the ulcer and he will recover.' Hezekiah said, 'What is the sign to tell me that I shall be going up to the Temple of the Lord?' 'Here' Isaiah replied 'is the sign from the Lord that he will do what he has said. Look, I shall make the shadow cast by the declining sun go back ten steps on the steps of Ahaz.' And the sun went back the ten steps by which it had declined.

This is the word of the Lord.

Responsorial Psalm   Is 38:10-12. 16. ℟ cf. v.27

℟ You saved my life, O Lord,
    I shall not die.

I said, 'So I must go away,
my life half spent,
assigned to the world below
for the rest of my years.'   ℟

I said, 'No more shall I see the Lord
in the land of the living,
no more shall I look upon men
within this world.   ℟

'My home is pulled up and removed
like a shepherd's tent.
Like a weaver you have rolled up my life,
you cut it from the loom.   ℟

'For you, Lord, my heart will live,
you gave me back my spirit;
you cured me, kept me alive,
changed my sickness into health.'   ℟

Gospel Acclamation   Jn 10:27

Alleluia, alleluia!
My sheep listen to my voice, says the Lord;
I know them, and they follow me.
Alleluia!

GOSPEL

A reading from the holy Gospel according to Matthew   12:1-8

The Son of Man is master of the sabbath.

Jesus took a walk one sabbath day through the cornfields. His
disciples were hungry and began to pick ears of corn and eat them.
The Pharisees noticed it and said to him, 'Look, your disciples are
doing something that is forbidden on the sabbath.' But he said to
them, 'Have you not read what David did when he and his followers
were hungry – how he went into the house of God and how they ate
the loaves of offering which neither he nor his followers were allowed

607

to eat, but which were for the priests alone? Or again, have you no
read in the Law that on the sabbath day the Temple priests break the
sabbath without being blamed for it? Now here, I tell you, is
something greater than the Temple. And if you had understood the
meaning of the words: What I want is mercy, not sacrifice, you would
not have condemned the blameless. For the Son of Man is master of
the sabbath.'

This is the Gospel of the Lord.

Saturday

FIRST READING

A reading from the prophet Micah   2:1-

They seized the fields and houses that they coveted

Woe to those who plot evil,
who lie in bed planning mischief!
No sooner is it dawn than they do it
– their hands have the strength for it.
Seizing the fields that they covet,
they take over houses as well,
owner and house they confiscate together,
taking both man and inheritance.
So the Lord says this:
Now it is I who plot
such mischief against this breed
as your necks will not escape;
nor will you be able to walk proudly,
so evil will the time be.
On that day they will make a satire on you,
sing a dirge and say,
'We are stripped of everything;
my people's portion is measured out and shared,
no one will give it back to them,
our fields are awarded to our despoiler.'
Therefore you will have no one
to measure out a share
in the community of the Lord.

This is the word of the Lord.

Responsorial Psalm   Ps 9B:1-4. 7-8. 14. ℟ v.12

℟   Do not forget the poor, O Lord!

1   Lord, why do you stand afar off
     and hide yourself in times of distress?
     The poor man is devoured by the pride of the wicked:
     he is caught in the schemes that others have made. ℟

2   For the wicked man boasts of his heart's desires;
     the covetous blasphemes and spurns the Lord.
     In his pride the wicked says: 'He will not punish.
     There is no God.' Such are his thoughts. ℟

3   His mouth is full of cursing, guile, oppression,
     mischief and deceit under his tongue.
     He lies in wait among the reeds;
     the innocent he murders in secret. ℟

4   But you have seen the trouble and sorrow,
     you note it, you take it in hand.
     The helpless trusts himself to you;
     for you are the helper of the orphan. ℟

Gospel Acclamation   2 Cor 5:19

     Alleluia, alleluia!
     God was in Christ, to reconcile the world to himself;
     and the Good News of reconciliation he has entrusted to us.
     Alleluia!

GOSPEL

A reading from the holy Gospel according to Matthew   12:14-21

He did not show himself to them that what had been said would be fulfilled.

The Pharisees went out and began to plot against Jesus, discussing
how to destroy him.

    Jesus knew this and withdrew from the district. Many followed
him and he cured them all, but warned them not to make him known.
This was to fulfil the prophecy of Isaiah:

     Here is my servant whom I have chosen,
     my beloved, the favourite of my soul.
     I will endow him with my spirit,

and he will proclaim the true faith to the nations.
He will not brawl or shout,
nor will anyone hear his voice in the streets.
He will not break the crushed reed,
nor put out the smouldering wick
till he has led the truth to victory:
in his name the nations will put their hope.

This is the Gospel of the Lord.

SIXTEENTH WEEK IN ORDINARY TIME
Year II

Monday

FIRST READING

A reading from the prophet Micah   6:1-4. 6-8

I will explain to you, people, what it is the Lord God asks of you.

Listen to what the Lord is saying:

Stand up and let the case begin in the hearing of the mountains
and let the hills hear what you say.
Listen, you mountains, to the Lord's accusation,
give ear, you foundations of the earth,
for the Lord is accusing his people,
pleading against Israel:
My people, what have I done to you,
how have I been a burden to you? Answer me.
I brought you out of the land of Egypt,
I rescued you from the house of slavery;
I sent Moses to lead you,
with Aaron and Miriam.

– 'With what gift shall I come into the Lord's presence
and bow down before God on high?
Shall I come with holocausts,
with calves one year old?
Will he be pleased with rams by the thousand,
with libations of oil in torrents?
Must I give my first-born for what I have done wrong,

the fruit of my body for my own sin?'

– What is good has been explained to you, man;
this is what the Lord asks of you:
only this, to act justly,
to love tenderly
and to walk humbly with your God.

This is the word of the Lord.

Responsorial Psalm   Ps 49:5-6. 8-9. 16-17. 21. 23. ℟ v.23

℟   To the upright I will show the saving power of God.

1   'Summon before me my people
    who made covenant with me by sacrifice.'
    The heavens proclaim his justice,
    you forgave the guilt of your people
    and covered all their sins.
    You averted all your rage,
    you calmed the heat of your anger.   ℟

2   Revive us now, God, our helper!
    Put an end to your grievance against us.
    Will you be angry with us for ever,
    will your anger never cease?   ℟

3   Will you not restore again our life
    that your people may rejoice in you?
    Let us see, O Lord, your mercy
    and give us your saving help.   ℟

Gospel Acclamation   cf. Ps 94:8

    Alleluia, alleluia!
    If today you hear his voice,
    harden not your hearts.
    Alleluia!

GOSPEL

A reading from the holy Gospel according to Matthew   12:38-42

On Judgement Day the Queen of the South will rise up with this
generation and condemn it.

Some of the scribes and Pharisees spoke up. 'Master,' they said 'we
should like to see a sign from you.' Jesus replied, 'It is an evil and
unfaithful generation that asks for a sign! The only sign it will be
given is the sign of the prophet Jonah. For as Jonah was in the belly of
the sea-monster for three days and three nights, so will the Son of
Man be in the heart of the earth for three days and three nights. On
Judgement day the men of Nineveh will stand up with this generation
and condemn it, because when Jonah preached they repented; and
there is something greater than Jonah here. On Judgement day the
Queen of the South will rise up with this generation and condemn it,
because she came from the ends of the earth to hear the wisdom of
Solomon; and there is something greater than Solomon here.'

This is the Gospel of the Lord.

Tuesday

FIRST READING

A reading from the prophet Micah   7:14-15. 18-20

He will cast our faults to the bottom of the sea.

With shepherd's crook, O Lord, lead your people to pasture
the flock that is your heritage,
living confined in a forest
with meadow land all around.
Let them pasture in Bashan and Gilead
as in the days of old.
As in the days when you came out of Egypt
grant us to see wonders.
What god can compare with you: taking fault away,
pardoning crime,
not cherishing anger for ever
but delighting in showing mercy?
Once more have pity on us,
tread down our faults,

to the bottom of the sea
throw all our sins.
Grant Jacob your faithfulness,
and Abraham your mercy,
as you swore to our fathers
from the days of long ago.

This is the word of the Lord.

Responsorial Psalm   Ps 84:2-8. ℟ v.8

℟   Lord, show us your mercy and love.

1   O Lord, you once favoured your land
    and revived the fortunes of Jacob,
    you forgave the guilt of your people
    and covered all their sins.
    You averted all your rage,
    you calmed the heat of your anger.   ℟

2   Revive us now, God, our helper!
    Put an end to your grievance against us.
    Will you be angry with us for ever,
    will your anger never cease?   ℟

3   Will you not restore again our life
    that your people may rejoice in you?
    Let us see, O Lord, your mercy
    and give us your saving help.   ℟

Gospel Acclamation   Jn 14:23

Alleluia, alleluia!
All who love me will keep my words,
and my Father will love them, and we will come to them.
Alleluia!

GOSPEL

A reading from the holy Gospel according to Matthew 12:46-50

*Extending his hand toward the disciples, he said: Here are my
mother and my brothers.*

Jesus was speaking to the crowds when his mother and his brothers
appeared; they were standing outside and were anxious to have a
word with him. But to the man who told him this Jesus replied, 'Who
is my mother? Who are my brothers?' And stretching out his hand
towards his disciples he said, 'Here are my mother and my brothers.
Anyone who does the will of my Father in heaven, he is my brother
and sister and mother.'

This is the Gospel of the Lord.

Wednesday

FIRST READING

A reading from the prophet Jeremiah 1:1. 4-10

I have appointed you as prophet to the nations.

The words of Jeremiah son of Hilkiah, of a priestly family living at
Anathoth in the territory of Benjamin.

The word of the Lord was addressed to me, saying,

'Before I formed you in the womb I knew you;
before you came to birth I consecrated you;
I have appointed you as prophet to the nations.'

I said, 'Ah, Lord; look, I do not know how to speak: I am a child!'
But the Lord replied,

'Do not say, "I am a child."
Go now to those to whom I send you
and say whatever I command you.
Do not be afraid of them,
for I am with you to protect you –
it is the Lord who speaks!'

Then the Lord put out his hand and touched my mouth and said
to me:

'There! I am putting my words into your mouth.
Look, today I am setting you
over nations and over kingdoms,
to tear up and to knock down,
to destroy and to overthrow,
to build and to plant.'

This is the word of the Lord.

Responsorial Psalm   Ps 70:1-6. 15. 17. ℞ cf. v.15

℞   I will sing of your salvation.

1 In you, O Lord, I take refuge;
   let me never be put to shame.
   In your justice rescue me, free me:
   pay heed to me and save me.   ℞

2 Be a rock where I can take refuge,
   a mighty stronghold to save me;
   for you are my rock, my stronghold.
   Free me from the hand of the wicked.   ℞

3 It is you, O Lord, who are my hope,
   my trust, O Lord, since my youth.
   On you I have leaned from my birth,
   from my mother's womb you have been my help.   ℞

4 My lips will tell of your justice
   and day by day of your help.
   O God, you have taught me from my youth
   and I proclaim your wonders still.   ℞

Gospel Acclamation

   Alleluia alleluia!
   The seed is the word of God, Christ is the sower;
   all who come to him will live for ever.
   Alleluia!

615

GOSPEL

A reading from the holy Gospel according to Matthew   13:1-9

He increased the harvest a hundredfold.

Jesus left the house and sat by the lakeside, but such crowds gathered round him that he got into a boat and sat there. The people all stood on the beach, and he told them many things in parables.

He said, 'Imagine a sower going out to sow. As he sowed, some seeds fell on the edge of the path, and the birds came and ate them up. Others fell on patches of rock where they found little soil and sprang up straight away, because there was no depth of earth; but as soon as the sun came up they were scorched and, not having any roots, they withered away. Others fell among thorns, and the thorns grew up and choked them. Others fell on rich soil and produced their crop, some a hundredfold, some sixty, some thirty. Listen, anyone who has ears!'

This is the Gospel of the Lord.

Thursday

FIRST READING

A reading from the prophet Jeremiah   2:1-3. 7-8. 12-13

They have abandoned me, the fountain of living water, to dig broken cisterns for themselves.

The word of the Lord was addressed to me saying, 'Go and shout this in the hearing of Jerusalem:

' "The Lord says this:
I remember the affection of your youth,
the love of your bridal days:
you followed me through the wilderness,
through a land unsown.
Israel was sacred to the Lord,
the first-fruits of his harvest;
anyone who ate of this had to pay for it,
misfortune came to them –
it is the Lord who speaks."

'I brought you to a fertile country
to enjoy its produce and good things;
but no sooner had you entered than you defiled my land,

and made my heritage detestable.
The priests have never asked, "Where is the Lord?"
Those who administer the Law have no knowledge of me.
The shepherds have rebelled against me;
the prophets have prophesied in the name of Baal,
following things with no power in them.

'You heavens, stand aghast at this,
stand stupefied, stand utterly appalled
– it is the Lord who speaks –
since my people have committed a double crime:
they have abandoned me,
the fountain of living water,
only to dig cisterns for themselves,
leaky cisterns
that hold no water.'

This is the word of the Lord

Responsorial Psalm   Ps 35:6-11. ℟ v.10

℟   You are the source of life, O Lord.

1   Your love, Lord, reaches to heaven;
    your truth to the skies.
    Your justice is like God's mountain,
    your judgements like the deep.   ℟

2   O Lord, how precious is your love.
    My God, the sons of men
    find refuge in the shelter of your wings.
    They feast on the riches of your house;
    they drink from the stream of your delight.   ℟

3   In you is the source of life
    and in your light we see light.
    Keep on loving those who know you,
    doing justice for upright hearts.   ℟

Gospel Acclamation   cf. Mt 11:25

Alleluia, alleluia!
Blessed are you, Father, Lord of heaven and earth;
you have revealed to little ones the mysteries of the kingdom.
Alleluia!

GOSPEL

A reading from the holy Gospel according to Matthew   13:10-17

*To you it is given to know the mysteries of the kingdom of heaven, but
to them it has not been given.*

The disciples went up to Jesus and asked, 'Why do you talk to the
crowds in parables?' 'Because' he replied, 'the mysteries of the
kingdom of heaven are revealed to you, but they are not revealed to
them. For anyone who has will be given more, and he will have more
than enough; but from anyone who has not, even what he has will be
taken away. The reason I talk to them in parables is that they look
without seeing and listen without hearing or understanding. So in
their case this prophecy of Isaiah is being fulfilled:

You will listen and listen again, but not understand,
see and see again, but not perceive.
For the heart of this nation has grown coarse,
their ears are dull of hearing and they have shut their eyes
for fear they should see with their eyes,
hear with their ears,
understand with their heart,
and be converted
and be healed by me.

'But happy are your eyes because they see, your ears because they
hear! I tell you solemnly, many prophets and holy men longed to see
what you see, and never saw it; to hear what you hear, and never
heard it.'

This is the Gospel of the Lord.

Friday

FIRST READING

A reading from the prophet Jeremiah   3:14-17

I will give you shepherds after my own heart. When that time comes,
Jerusalem shall be called.

'Come back, disloyal children – it is the Lord who speaks – for I alone
am your Master. I will take one from a town, two from a clan, and
bring you to Zion. I will give you shepherds after my own heart, and
these shall feed you on knowledge and discretion. And when you have
increased and become many in the land, then – it is the Lord who
speaks – no one will ever say again: Where is the ark of the covenant
of the Lord? There will be no thought of it, no memory of it, no regret
for it, no making of another. When that time comes, Jerusalem shall
be called: The Throne of the Lord; all the nations will gather there in
the name of the Lord and will no longer follow the dictates of their
own stubborn hearts.'

This is the word of the Lord.

Responsorial Psalm   Jer 31:10-13. ℟ cf. v.10

℟ The Lord will guard us,
    like a shepherd guarding his flock.

1 O nations, hear the word of the Lord,
   proclaim it to the far-off coasts.
   Say: 'He who scattered Israel will gather him
   and guard him as a shepherd guards his flock.' ℟

2 For the Lord has ransomed Jacob,
   has saved him from an overpowering hand.
   They will come and shout for joy on Mount Zion,
   they will stream to the blessings of the Lord. ℟

3 Then the young girls will rejoice and dance,
   the men, young and old, will be glad.
   I will turn their mourning into joy,
   I will console them, give gladness for grief. ℟

Gospel Acclamation   cf. Lk 8:15

Alleluia, alleluia!
Happy are they who have kept the word with a generous heart
and yield a harvest through perseverance.
Alleluia!

GOSPEL

A reading from the holy Gospel according to Matthew   13:18-23

All who hear the word of God and understand it, yield much fruit.

Jesus said to his disciples: 'You are to hear the parable of the sower. When anyone hears the word of the kingdom without understanding, the evil one comes and carries off what was sown in his heart: this is the man who received the seed on the edge of the path. The one who received it on patches of rock is the man who hears the word and welcomes it at once with joy. But he has no root in him, he does not last; let some trial come, or some persecution on account of the word, and he falls away at once. The one who received the seed in thorns is the man who hears the word, but the worries of this world and the lure of riches choke the word and so he produces nothing. And the one who received the seed in rich soil is the man who hears the word and understands it; he is the one who yields a harvest and produces now a hundredfold, now sixty, now thirty.'

This is the Gospel of the Lord.

Saturday

FIRST READING

A reading from the prophet Jeremiah   7:1-11

Do you take this temple that bears my name for a robber's den?

The word that was addressed to Jeremiah by the Lord, 'Go and stand at the gate of the Temple of the Lord and there proclaim this message. Say, "Listen to the word of the Lord, all you men of Judah who come in by these gates to worship the Lord. The Lord of hosts, the God of Israel, says this: Amend your behaviour and your actions and I will stay with you here in this place. Put no trust in delusive words like these: This is the sanctuary of the Lord, the sanctuary of the Lord, the sanctuary of the Lord! But if you do amend your behaviour and your actions, if you treat each other fairly, if you do not exploit the stranger, the orphan and the widow (if you do not shed innocent blood in this place), and if you do not follow alien gods, to your own ruin, then here in this place I will stay with you, in the land that long ago I gave to your father for ever. Yet here you are, trusting in delusive words, to no purpose! Steal, would you, murder, commit adultery, perjure yourselves, burn incense to Baal, follow alien gods that you do not know? – and then come presenting yourselves in this Temple that bears my name, saying: Now we are safe – safe to go on committing all these abominations! Do you take this Temple that bears my name for a robbers' den? I, at any rate, am not blind – it is the Lord who speaks." '

This is the word of the Lord.

Responsorial Psalm

Ps 83:3-6. 8. 11. ℟ v.2

℟   How lovely is your dwelling-place,
       Lord, mighty God!

1   My soul is longing and yearning,
     is yearning for the courts of the Lord.
     My heart and my soul ring out their joy
     to God, the living God. ℟

2   The sparrow herself finds a home
     and the swallow a nest for her brood;
     she lays her young by your altars,
     Lord of hosts, my king and my God. ℟

3   They are happy, who dwell in your house,
     for ever singing your praise.
     They are happy, whose strength is in you;
     they walk with ever growing strength. ℟

4   One day within your courts
     is better than a thousand elsewhere.
     The threshold of the house of God
     I prefer to the dwellings of the wicked. ℟

Gospel Acclamation   James 1:21

Alleluia, alleluia!
Receive and submit to the word planted in you;
it can save your souls.
Alleluia!

GOSPEL

A reading from the holy Gospel according to Matthew   13:24-30

Let them both grow until the harvest time.

Jesus put a parable before the crowds, 'The kingdom of heaven may be
compared to a man who sowed good seed in his field. While everybody
was asleep his enemy came, sowed darnel all among the wheat, and
made off. When the new wheat sprouted and ripened, the darnel
appeared as well. The owner's servants went to him and said, "Sir,
was it not good seed that you sowed in your field? If so, where does the
darnel come from?" "Some enemy has done this," he answered. And
the servants said, "Do you want us to go and weed it out?" But he said,
"No, because when you weed out the darnel you might pull up the
wheat with it. Let them both grow till the harvest; and at harvest
time I shall say to the reapers: First collect the darnel and tie it in
bundles to be burnt, then gather the wheat into my barn." '

This is the Gospel of the Lord.

SEVENTEENTH WEEK IN ORDINARY TIME
Year II

Monday

FIRST READING

A reading from the prophet Jeremiah   13:1-11

This people shall be like this waist cloth, which is good for nothing.

The Lord said this to me, 'Go and buy a linen loincloth and put it round your waist. But do not dip it in water.' And so, as the Lord has ordered, I bought a loincloth and put it round my waist. A second time the word of the Lord was spoken to me, 'Take the loincloth that you have bought and are wearing round your waist; up! Go to the Euphrates and hide it in a hole in the rock.' So I went and hid it near the Euphrates as the Lord had ordered me. Many days afterwards the Lord said to me, 'Get up and go to the Euphrates and fetch the loincloth I ordered you to hide there.' So I went to the Euphrates, and I searched, and I took the loincloth from the place where I had hidden it. The loincloth was spoilt, good for nothing. Then the word of the Lord was addressed to me, 'Thus says the Lord: In the same way I will spoil the arrogance of Judah and Jerusalem. This evil people who refuse to listen to my words, who follow the dictates of their own hard hearts, who have followed alien gods, and served them and worshipped them, let them become like this loincloth, good for nothing. For just as a loincloth clings to a man's waist, so I had intended the whole House of Judah to cling to me – it is the Lord who speaks – to be my people, my glory, my honour and my boast. But they have not listened.'

This is the word of the Lord.

Responsorial Psalm   Deut 32:18-21. ℟ cf. v.18

℟   You have forgotten God who gave you birth.

1   You forget the Rock who begot you,
      unmindful now of the God who fathered you.
      The Lord had seen this, and in his anger
      cast off his sons and his daughters.   ℟

2 'I shall hide my face from them,' he says
   'and see what becomes of them.
   For they are a deceitful brood,
   children with no loyalty in them.

   ℟ You have forgotten God who gave you birth.

3 'They have roused me to jealousy with what is no god,
   they have angered me with their beings of nothing;
   I, then, will rouse them to jealousy with what is no people.
   I will anger them with an empty-headed nation.' ℟

Gospel Acclamation   James 1:18

   Alleluia, alleluia!
   The Father gave us birth, by his message of truth
   that we might be as the first fruits of his creation.
   Alleluia!

GOSPEL

A reading from the holy Gospel according to Matthew   13:31-35

   When the seed grows it is the biggest shrub of all and the birds of the air come
   and nest in its branches.

Jesus put a parable before the crowds, 'The kingdom of heaven is like
a mustard seed which a man took and sowed in his field. It is the
smallest of all the seeds, but when it has grown it is the biggest shrub
of all and becomes a tree so that the birds of the air come and shelter
in its branches.'

He told them another parable, 'The kingdom of heaven is like the
yeast a woman took and mixed in with three measures of flour till it
was leavened all through.'

In all this Jesus spoke to the crowds in parables; indeed, he would
never speak to them except in parables. This was to fulfil the
prophecy:

   I will speak to you in parables
   and expound things hidden since the foundation of the world.

This is the Gospel of the Lord.

Tuesday

FIRST READING

A reading from the prophet Jeremiah   14:17-22

Remember, Lord, do not break your covenant with us.

The Lord said to me:

> Say this word to the people:
> 'Tears flood my eyes
> night and day, unceasingly,
> since a crushing blow falls on the daughter of my people,
> a most grievous injury.
> If I go into the countryside,
> there lie men killed by the sword;
> if I go into the city,
> I see people sick with hunger;
> even prophets and priests
> plough the land: they are at their wit's end.'

> 'Have you rejected Judah altogether?
> Does your very soul revolt at Zion?
> Why have you struck us down without hope of cure?
> We were hoping for peace – no good came of it!
> For the moment of cure – nothing but terror!
> Lord, we do confess our wickedness
> and our father's guilt:
> we have indeed sinned against you.
> For your name's sake do not reject us,
> do not dishonour the throne of your glory.
> Remember us; do not break your covenant with us.
> Can any of the pagan Nothings make it rain?
> Can the heavens produce showers?
> No, it is you, Lord.
> O our God, you are our hope,
> since it is you who do all this.'

This is the word of the Lord.

Responsorial Psalm   Ps 78:8-9. 11. 13. ℟ v.9

℟   For the glory of your name,
    O Lord, deliver us.

1   Do not hold the guilt of our fathers against us.
    Let your compassion hasten to meet us.
    for we are in the depths of distress.   ℟

2   O God our saviour, come to our help,
    come for the sake of the glory of your name.
    O Lord our God, forgive us our sins;
    rescue us for the sake of your name.   ℟

3   Let the groans of the prisoners come before you;
    let your strong arm reprieve those condemned to die.
    But we, your people, the flock of your pasture,
    will give you thanks for ever and ever.
    We will tell your praise from age to age.   ℟

Gospel Acclamation

    Alleluia, alleluia!
    The seed is the word of God, Christ is the sower;
    all who come to him will live for ever.
    Alleluia!

GOSPEL

A reading from the holy Gospel according to Matthew   13:36-43

Just as the weeds are gathered up and burnt in the fire,
so it will be at the end of time.

Leaving the crowds, Jesus went to the house; and his disciples came to
him and said, 'Explain the parable about the darnel in the field to us.'
He said in reply, 'The sower of the good seed is the Son of Man. The
field is the world; the good seed is the subjects of the kingdom; the
darnel, the subjects of the evil one; the enemy who sowed them, the
devil; the harvest is the end of the world; the reapers are the angels.
Well then, just as the darnel is gathered up and burnt in the fire, so it
will be at the end of time. The Son of Man will send his angels and
they will gather out of his kingdom all things that provoke offences
and all who do evil, and throw them into the blazing furnace, where

there will be weeping and grinding of teeth. Then the virtuous will shine like the sun in the kingdom of their Father. Listen, anyone who has ears!'

This is the Gospel of the Lord.

Wednesday

FIRST READING

A reading from the prophet Jeremiah   15:10. 16-21

*Why is my suffering continued, Lord? If you come back, I will take you
into my service.*

Woe is me, my mother, for you have borne me
to be a man of strife and of dissension for all the land.
I neither lend nor borrow,
yet all of them curse me
and avenge me on my persecutors.
Your anger is very slow: do not let me be snatched away.
Realise that I suffer insult for your sake.
When your words came, I devoured them:
your word was my delight
and the joy of my heart;
for I was called by your name,
Lord, God of hosts.
I never took pleasure in sitting in scoffers' company;
with your hand on me I held myself aloof,
since you had filled me with indignation.
Why is my suffering continual,
my wound incurable, refusing to be healed?
Do you mean to be for me a deceptive stream
with inconstant waters?

To which the Lord replied,

'If you come back,
I will take you back into my service;
and if you utter noble, not despicable, thoughts,
you shall be as my own mouth.
They will come back to you,
but you must not go back to them.
I will make you
a bronze wall fortified against this people.

627

They will fight against you
but they will not overcome you,
because I am with you
to save you and to deliver you
– it is the Lord who speaks.
I mean to deliver you from the hands of the wicked
and redeem you from the clutches of the violent.'

This is the word of the Lord.

Responsial Psalm   Ps 58:2-5. 10-11. 17-18. ℟ v.17

℟ God is my refuge on the day of distress.

1 Rescue me, God, from my foes;
  protect me from those who attack me.
  O rescue me from those who do evil
  and save me from blood-thirsty men. ℟

2 See, they lie in wait for my life;
  powerful men band together against me.
  For no offence, no sin of mine, Lord,
  for no guilt of mine they rush to take their stand. ℟

3 O my Strength, it is you to whom I turn,
  for you, O God, are my stronghold,
  the God who shows me love. ℟

4 As for me, I will sing of your strength
  and each morning acclaim your love
  for you have been my stronghold,
  a refuge in the day of my distress. ℟

5 O my Strength, it is you to whom I turn,
  for you, O God, are my stronghold,
  the God who shows me love. ℟

Gospel Acclamation   Jn 15:15

Alleluia, alleluia!
I call you my friends, says the Lord,
for I have made known to you all that the Father has told me.
Alleluia!

GOSPEL

A reading from the holy Gospel according to Matthew   13:44-46

He sold everything he had and went and bought a field.

Jesus said to the crowds: 'The kingdom of heaven is like treasure hidden in a field which someone has found; he hides it again, goes off happy, sells everything he owns and buys the field.

'Again, the kingdom of heaven is like a merchant looking for fine pearls; when he finds one of great value he goes and sells everything he owns and buys it.'

This is the Gospel of the Lord.

Thursday

FIRST READING

A reading from the prophet Jeremiah   18:1-6

As the clay in the potter's hand, so you are in mine, house of Israel.

The word that was addressed to Jeremiah by the Lord, 'Get up and make your way down to the potter's house; there I shall let you hear what I have to say.' So I went down to the potter's house; and there he was, working at the wheel. And whenever the vessel he was making came out wrong, as happens with the clay handled by potters, he would start afresh and work it into another vessel, as potters do. Then this word of the Lord was addressed to me, 'House of Israel, can not I do to you what this potter does? – it is the Lord who speaks. Yes, as the clay is in the potter's hand, so you are in mine, House of Israel.'

This is the word of the Lord.

Responsorial Psalm   Ps 145:2-6. ℞ v.5

℞   Blest are they whose help is the God of Jacob.

or

℞   Alleluia!

1   My soul, give praise to the Lord;
    I will praise the Lord all my days,
    make music to my God while I live.   ℞

2   Put no trust in princes,
    in mortal men in whom there is no help.
    Take their breath, they return to clay
    and their plans that day come to nothing.

    ℟   Blest are they whose help is the God of Jacob.

or

    ℟   Alleluia!

3   He is happy who is helped by Jacob's God,
    whose hope is in the Lord his God,
    who alone made heaven and earth,
    the seas and all they contain.   ℟

Gospel Acclamation   cf. Acts 16:14

    Alleluia, alleluia!
    Open our hearts, O Lord,
    to listen to the words of your Son.
    Alleluia!

GOSPEL

A reading from the holy Gospel according to Matthew   13:47-53

They gather the good ones in a basket, and the bad are thrown away.

Jesus said to the crowds: 'The kingdom of heaven is like a dragnet cast into the sea that brings in a haul of all kinds. When it is full, the fishermen haul it ashore; then, sitting down, they collect the good ones in a basket and throw away those that are no use. This is how it will be at the end of time; the angels will appear and separate the wicked from the just to throw them into the blazing furnace where there will be weeping and grinding of teeth.

    'Have you understood all this?' They said, 'Yes.' And he said to them, 'Well then, every scribe who becomes a disciple of the kingdom of heaven is like a householder who brings out from his storeroom things both new and old.'

    When Jesus had finished these parables he left the district.

    This is the Gospel of the Lord.

Friday

FIRST READING

A reading from the prophet Jeremiah   26:1-9

All the people gathered to worship the Lord.

At the beginning of the reign of Jehoiakim son of Josiah, king of Judah, this word was addressed to Jeremiah by the Lord. The Lord says this: Stand in the court of the Temple of the Lord. To all the people of the towns of Judah who come to worship in the Temple of the Lord you must speak all the words I have commanded you to tell them; do not omit one syllable. Perhaps they will listen and each turn from his evil way: if so, I shall relent and not bring the disaster on them which I intended for their misdeeds. Say to them, "The Lord says this: If you will not listen to me by following my Law which I put before you, by paying attention to the words of my servants the prophets whom I send so persistently to you, without you ever listening to them, I will treat this Temple as I treated Shiloh, and make this city a curse for all the nations of the earth." '

The priests and prophets and all the people heard Jeremiah say these words in the Temple of the Lord. When Jeremiah had finished saying everything that the Lord had ordered him to say to all the people, the priests and prophets seized hold of him and said, 'You shall die! Why have you made this prophecy in the name of the Lord, "This Temple will be like Shiloh, and this city will be desolate, and uninhabited"?' And the people were all crowding round Jeremiah in the Temple of the Lord.

This is the word of the Lord.

Responsorial Psalm   Ps 68:5. 8-10. 14. ℟ v.14

℟   Lord, in your great love, answer me.

1   More numerous than the hairs on my head
    are those who hate me without cause.
    Those who attack me with lies
    are too much for my strength.
    How can I restore
    what I have never stolen?   ℟

2 It is for you that I suffer taunts,
   that shame covers my face,
   that I have become a stranger to my brothers,
   an alien to my own mother's sons.
   I burn with zeal for your house
   and taunts against you fall on me.

    ℟   Lord, in your great love, answer me.

3 This is my prayer to you,
   my prayer for your favour.
   In your great love, answer me, O God,
   with your help that never fails.   ℟

Gospel Acclamation   1 Peter 1:25

   Alleluia, alleluia!
   The word of the Lord stands for ever;
   it is the word given to you, the Good News.
   Alleluia!

GOSPEL

A reading from the holy Gospel according to Matthew   13:54-58

Is this not the son of the carpenter? Where did he get all his wisdom?

Coming to his home town, Jesus taught the people in their synagogue in such a way that they were astonished and said, 'Where did the man get this wisdom and these miraculous powers? This is the carpenter's son, surely? Is not his mother the woman called Mary, and his brothers James and Joseph and Simon and Jude? His sisters, too, are they not all here with us? So where did the man get it all?' And they would not accept him. But Jesus said to them, 'A prophet is only despised in his own country and in his own house,' and he did not work many miracles there because of their lack of faith.

   This is the Gospel of the Lord.

Saturday

FIRST READING

A reading from the prophet Jeremiah   26:11-16. 24

The Lord God himself sent me to say all the things you have heard.

The priests and prophets addressed the officials and all the people:
'This man deserves to die, since he has prophesied against this city, as
you have heard with your own ears.' Jeremiah, however, replied to the
people as follows, 'The Lord himself sent me to say all the things you
have heard against this Temple and this city. So now amend your
behaviour and actions, listen to the voice of the Lord your God: if you
do, he will relent and not bring down on you the disaster he has
pronounced against you. For myself, I am as you see in your hands. Do
whatever you please or think right with me. But be sure of this, that if
you put me to death, you will be bringing innocent blood on
yourselves, on this city and on its citizens, since the Lord has truly
sent me to you to say all these words in your hearing.'

The officials and all the people then said to the priests and
prophets, 'This man does not deserve to die: he has spoken to us in the
name of the Lord our God.' And Jeremiah had a protector in Ahikam
son of Shaphan, so he was not handed over to the people to be put to
death.

This is the word of the Lord.

Responsorial Psalm   Ps 68:15-16. 30-31. 33-34. ℞ cf. v.14

℞   Lord, in your great love, answer me.

1   Rescue me from sinking in the mud;
     save me from my foes.
     Save me from the waters of the deep
     lest the waves overwhelm me.
     Do not let the deep engulf me
     nor death close its mouth on me.   ℞

2   As for me in my poverty and pain
     let your help, O God, lift me up.
     I will praise God's name with a song;
     I will glorify him with thanksgiving.   ℞

3 The poor when they see it will be glad
   and God-seeking hearts will revive;
   For the Lord listens to the needy
   and does not spurn his servants in their chains.

   ℟ Lord, in your great love, answer me.

Gospel Acclamation

Mt 5:10

Alleluia, alleluia!
Happy are they who suffer persecution for justice' sake;
the kingdom of heaven is theirs.
Alleluia!

GOSPEL

A reading from the holy Gospel according to Matthew   14:1-12

Herod had John beheaded; the disciples went and told Jesus.

Herod the tetrarch heard about the reputation of Jesus, and said to his court, 'This is John the Baptist himself; he has risen from the dead, and that is why miraculous powers are at work in him.'

Now it was Herod who had arrested John, chained him up and put him in prison because of Herodias, his brother Philip's wife. For John had told him, 'It is against the Law for you to have her.' He had wanted to kill him but was afraid of the people, who regarded John as a prophet. Then, during the celebrations for Herod's birthday, the daughter of Herodias danced before the company, and so delighted Herod that he promised on oath to give her anything she asked. Prompted by her mother she said, 'Give me John the Baptist's head, here, on a dish.' The king was distressed but, thinking of the oaths he had sworn and of his guests, he ordered it to be given her, and sent and had John beheaded in the prison. The head was brought in on a dish and given to the girl who took it to her mother. John's disciples came and took the body and buried it; then they went off to tell Jesus.

   This is the Gospel of the Lord.

EIGHTEENTH WEEK IN ORDINARY TIME

Year II

Monday

FIRST READING

A reading from the prophet Jeremiah   28:1-17

*Hananiah, the Lord God has not sent you, you have confided to the
people what is false.*

At the beginning of the reign of Zedekiah king of Judah in the fifth
month of the fourth year, the prophet Hananiah son of Azzur, a
Gibeonite, spoke as follows to Jeremiah in the Temple of the Lord
in the presence of the priests and of all the people. 'The Lord, the
God of Israel, says this, "I have broken the yoke of the king of
Babylon. In two years' time I will bring back all the vessels of the
Temple of the Lord which Nebuchadnezzar king of Babylon carried
off from this place and took to Babylon. And I will also bring back
Jeconiah son of Jehoiakim, king of Judah, and all the exiles of
Judah who have gone to Babylon – it is the Lord who speaks. Yes, I
am going to break the yoke of the king of Babylon." '

The prophet Jeremiah then replied to the prophet Hananiah in
front of the priests and all the people there in the Temple of the
Lord. 'I hope so' the prophet Jeremiah said. 'May the Lord do so.
May he fulfil the words that you have prophesied and bring the
vessels of the Temple of the Lord and all the exiles back to this
place from Babylon. Listen carefully, however, to this word I am
now going to say for you and all the people to hear: From remote
times, the prophets who preceded you and me prophesied war,
famine and plague for many countries and for great kingdoms; but
the prophet who prophesies peace can only be recognised as one
truly sent by the Lord when his word comes true.'

The prophet Hananiah then took the yoke off the neck of the
prophet Jeremiah and broke it. In front of all the people Hananiah
then said, 'The Lord says this, "This is how, two years hence, I will
break the yoke of Nebuchadnezzar king of Babylon and take it off
the necks of all the nations." ' At this, the prophet Jeremiah went
away.

After the prophet Hananiah had broken the yoke which he had
taken off the neck of the prophet Jeremiah the word of the Lord was

addressed to Jeremiah, 'Go to Hananiah and tell him this, "The Lord says this: You can break wooden yokes? Right, I will make them iron yokes instead! For the Lord of hosts, the God of Israel, says this: An iron yoke is what I now lay on the necks of all these nations to subject them to Nebuchadnezzar king of Babylon. (They will be subject to him; I have even given him the wild animals.)"'

The prophet Jeremiah said to the prophet Hananiah, 'Listen carefully Hananiah: the Lord has not sent you; and thanks to you this people are now relying on what is false. Hence – the Lord says this, "I am going to throw you off the face of the earth: you are going to die this year (since you have preached apostasy from the Lord)."'

The prophet Hananiah died the same year, in the seventh month.

This is the word of the Lord.

Responsorial Psalm   Ps 118:29. 43. 79-80. 95. 102. ℟ v.68

℟   Teach me your laws, O Lord.

1   Keep me from the way of error
    and teach me your law.
    Do not take the word of truth from my mouth
    for I trust in your decrees.   ℟

2   Let your faithful turn to me,
    those who know your will.
    Let my heart be blameless in your statutes
    lest I be ashamed.   ℟

3   Though the wicked lie in wait to destroy me
    yet I ponder on your will.
    I have not turned away from your decrees;
    you yourself have taught me.   ℟

Gospel Acclamation   Mt 4:4

    Alleluia, alleluia!
    No one lives on bread alone,
    but on every word that comes from the mouth of God.
    Alleluia!

GOSPEL

A reading from the holy Gospel according to Matthew   14:13-21

*Raising his eyes to heaven he said the blessing and gave the bread
to his disciples who in turn gave it to the crowds.*

When Jesus received the news of John the Baptist's death he withdrew by boat to a lonely place where they could be by themselves. But the people heard of this and, leaving the towns, went after him on foot. So as he stepped ashore he saw a large crowd; and he took pity on them and healed their sick.

When evening came, the disciples went to him and said, 'This is a lonely place, and the time has slipped by; so send the people away, and they can go to the villages to buy themselves some food.' Jesus replied, 'There is no need for them to go: give them something to eat yourselves.' But they answered, 'All we have with us is five loaves and two fish.' 'Bring them here to me,' he said. He gave orders that the people were to sit down on the grass; then he took the five loaves and the two fish, raised his eyes to heaven and said the blessing. And breaking the loaves he handed them to his disciples who gave them to the crowds. They all ate as much as they wanted, and they collected the scraps remaining, twelve baskets full. Those who ate numbered about five thousand men, to say nothing of women and children.

This is the Gospel of the Lord.

Alternative Gospel

This is to be used in Year A, when the Gospel given above is read on the preceding Sunday.

A reading from the holy Gospel according to Matthew   14:22-36

Order me to come to you across the water.

When Jesus heard of the death of John the Baptist, he made the disciples get into the boat and go on ahead to the other side while he would send the crowds away. After sending the crowds away he went up into the hills by himself to pray. When evening came, he was there alone, while the boat, by now far out on the lake, was battling with a heavy sea, for there was a head-wind. In the fourth watch of the night he went towards them, walking on the lake, and when the disciples saw him on the lake they were terrified. 'It is a ghost' they said, and cried out in fear. But at once Jesus called out to them, saying,

'Courage! It is I! do not be afraid.' It was Peter who answered. 'Lord,' he said 'if it is you, tell me to come to you across the water.' 'Come' said Jesus. Then Peter got out of the boat and started walking towards Jesus across the water, but as soon as he felt the force of the wind, he took fright and began to sink. 'Lord! Save me!' he cried. Jesus put out his hand at once and held him. 'Man of little faith,' he said 'why did you doubt?' And as they got into the boat the wind dropped. The men in the boat bowed down before him and said, 'Truly, you are the Son of God.'

Having made the crossing, they came to land at Gennesaret. When the local people recognised him they spread the news through the whole neighbourhood and took all that were sick to him, begging him just to let them touch the fringe of his cloak. And all those who touched it were completely cured.

This is the Gospel of the Lord.

Tuesday

FIRST READING

A reading from the prophet Jeremiah
30:1-2. 12-15. 18-22

Your sins are so great that I have done all this to you. Now I will restore the tents of Jacob.

The word addressed to Jeremiah by the Lord: The Lord, the God of Israel says this: Write all the words I have spoken to you in a book.

Yes, the Lord says this:
Your wound is incurable,
your injury past healing.
There is no one to care for your sore,
no medicine to make you well again.
All your lovers have forgotten you,
they look for you no more.
Yes, I have struck you as an enemy strikes,
with harsh punishment
(so great is your guilt, so many your sins).
Why bother to complain about your wound?
Your pain is incurable.
So great is your guilt, so many your sins,

that I have done all this to you.

The Lord says this:
Now I will restore the tents of Jacob,
and take pity on his dwellings:
the city shall be rebuilt on its ruins,
the citadel restored on its site.
From them will come thanksgiving
and shouts of joy.
I will make them increase, and not diminish them,
make them honoured, and not disdained.
Their sons shall be as once they were,
their community fixed firm in my presence,
and I will punish all their oppressors.
Their prince will be one of their own,
their ruler come from their own people.
I will let him come freely into my presence and he can come close to
    me;
who else, indeed, would risk his life
by coming close to me? – it is the Lord who speaks.
And you shall be my people and I will be your God.

This is the word of the Lord.

Responsorial Psalm   Ps 101:16-21. 29. 22-3. ℟ v.17

℟ The Lord will build up Zion again,
    and appear in all his glory.

1   The nations shall fear the name of the Lord
    and all the earth's kings your glory,
    when the Lord shall build up Zion again
    and appear in all his glory.
    Then he will turn to the prayers of the helpless;
    he will not despise their prayers. ℟

2   Let this be written for ages to come
    that a people yet unborn may praise the Lord;
    for the Lord leaned down from his sanctuary on high.
    He looked down from heaven to the earth
    that he might hear the groans of the prisoners
    and free those condemned to die. ℟   (continued)

3 The sons of your servants shall dwell untroubled
   and their race shall endure before you
   that the name of the Lord may be proclaimed to Zion
   and his praise in the heart of Jerusalem,
   when peoples and kingdoms are gathered together
   to pay their homage to the Lord.

   ℟ The Lord will build up Zion again,
      and appear in all his glory.

Gospel Acclamation   Jn 1:49

   Alleluia, alleluia!
   Master, you are the Son of God,
   you are the king of Israel.
   Alleluia!

GOSPEL

A reading from the holy Gospel according to Matthew   14:22-36

Order me to come to you across the water.

When the crowds had eaten their fill Jesus made the disciples get into
the boat and go on ahead to the other side while he would send the
crowds away. After sending the crowds away he went up into the hills
by himself to pray. When evening came, he was there alone, while the
boat, by now far out on the lake, was battling with a heavy sea, for
there was a headwind. In the fourth watch of the night he went
towards them, walking on the lake, and when the disciples saw him
walking on the lake they were terrified. 'It is a ghost' they said, and
cried out in fear. But at once Jesus called out to them, saying,
'Courage! It is I! Do not be afraid.' It was Peter who answered. 'Lord,'
he said 'if it is you, tell me to come to you across the water.' 'Come'
said Jesus. Then Peter got out of the boat and started walking towards
Jesus across the water, but as soon as he felt the force of the wind, he
took fright and began to sink. 'Lord! Save me!' he cried. Jesus put out
his hand at once and held him. 'Man of little faith,' he said 'why did
you doubt?' And as they got into the boat the wind dropped. The men
in the boat bowed down before him and said, 'Truly, you are the Son of
God.'
    Having made the crossing, they came to land at Gennesaret. When
the local people recognised him they spread the news through

the whole neighbourhood and took all that were sick to him, begging him just to let them touch the fringe of his cloak. And all those who touched it were completely cured.

This is the Gospel of the Lord.

Alternative Gospel

This is to be used in Year A, when the Gospel given above is read on the preceding Monday.

A reading from the holy Gospel according to Matthew   15:1-2. 10-14

Any plant my heavenly Father has not planted will be pulled up by the roots.

Pharisees and scribes from Jerusalem came to Jesus and said, 'Why do your disciples break away from the tradition of the elders? They do not wash their hands when they eat food.'

He called the people to him and said, 'Listen, and understand. What goes into the mouth does not make a man unclean; it is what comes out of the mouth that makes him unclean.'

Then the disciples came to him and said, 'Do you know that the Pharisees were shocked when they heard what you said?' He replied, 'Any plant my heavenly Father has not planted will be pulled up by the roots. Leave them alone. They are blind men leading blind men; and if one blind man leads another, both will fall into a pit.'

This is the Gospel of the Lord.

Wednesday

FIRST READING

A reading from the prophet Jeremiah   31:1-7

I have loved you with an everlasting love.

I will be the God of all the clans of Israel – it is the Lord who speaks – they shall be my people.

The Lord says this:
They have found pardon in the wilderness,
those who have survived the sword.

Israel is marching to his rest.
The Lord has appeared to him from afar:
I have loved you with an everlasting love,
so I am constant in my affection for you.
I build you once more; you shall be rebuilt,
virgin of Israel.
Adorned once more, and with your tambourines,
you will go out dancing gaily.
You will plant vineyards once more
on the mountains of Samaria
(the planters have done their planting: they will gather the fruit).
Yes, a day will come when the watchmen shout
on the mountains of Ephraim,
'Up! Let us go up to Zion,
to the Lord our God!'

For the Lord says this:
Shout with joy for Jacob!
Hail the chief of nations!
Proclaim! Praise! Shout:
'The Lord has saved his people,
the remnant of Israel!'

This is the word of the Lord.

Responsorial Psalm   Jer 31:10-13. ℟ cf. v.10

℟   The Lord will guard us,
     like a shepherd guarding his flock.

1   O nations, hear the word of the Lord,
     proclaim it to the far-off coasts.
     Say: 'He who scattered Israel will gather him
     and guard him as a shepherd guards his flock.'   ℟

2   For the Lord has ransomed Jacob,
     has saved him from an overpowering hand.
     They will come and shout for joy on Mount Zion,
     they will stream to the blessings of the Lord.   ℟

3   Then the young girls will rejoice and dance,
     the men, young and old, will be glad.
     I will turn their mourning into joy,
     I will console them, give gladness for grief.   ℟

Gospel Acclamation   Lk 7:16

> Alleluia, alleluia!
> A great prophet has appeared among us;
> God has visited his people.
> Alleluia!

GOSPEL

A reading from the holy Gospel according to Matthew   15:21-28

Woman, you have great faith.

Jesus left Gennesaret and withdrew to the region of Tyre and Sidon. Then out came a Canaanite woman from that district and started shouting, 'Sir, Son of David, take pity on me. My daughter is tormented by a devil.' But he answered her not a word. And his disciples went and pleaded with him. 'Give her what she wants,' they said 'because she is shouting after us.' He said in reply, 'I was sent only to the lost sheep of the House of Israel.' But the woman had come up and was kneeling at his feet. 'Lord,' she said 'help me.' He replied. 'It is not fair to take the children's food and throw it to the house-dogs.' She retorted, 'Ah yes, sir; but even house-dogs can eat the scraps that fall from their master's table.' Then Jesus answered her, 'Woman, you have great faith. Let your wish be granted.' And from that moment her daughter was well again.

> This is the Gospel of the Lord.

Thursday

FIRST READING

A reading from the prophet Jeremiah   31:31-34

I will make a new covenant with the house of Israel
and never call their sin to mind.

See, the days are coming – it is the Lord who speaks – when I will make a new covenant with the House of Israel and the House of Judah, but not a covenant like the one I made with their ancestors on the day I took them by the hand to bring them out of the land of Egypt.

They broke that covenant of mine, so I had to show them who was master. It is the Lord who speaks. No, this is the covenant I will make with the House of Israel when those days arrive – it is the Lord who speaks. Deep within them I will plant my law, writing it on their hearts. Then I will be their God and they shall be my people. There will be no further need for neighbour to try to teach neighbour, or brother to say to brother, 'Learn to know the Lord!' No, they will all know me, the least no less than the greatest – it is the Lord who speaks – since I will forgive their iniquity and never call their sin to mind.

This is the word of the Lord.

Responsorial Psalm   Ps 50:12-15. 18-19. ℟ v.12

℟   Create a clean heart in me, O God.

1   A pure heart create for me, O God,
    put a steadfast spirit within me.
    Do not cast me away from your presence,
    nor deprive me of your holy spirit.   ℟

2   Give me again the joy of your help;
    with a spirit of fervour sustain me,
    that I may teach transgressors your ways
    and sinners may return to you.   ℟

3   For in sacrifice you take no delight,
    burnt offering from me you would refuse,
    my sacrifice, a contrite spirit.
    A humbled, contrite heart you will not spurn.   ℟

Gospel Acclamation   Mt 16:18

    Alleluia, alleluia!
    You are Peter, the rock on which I will build my Church;
    the gates of hell will not hold against it.
    Alleluia!

GOSPEL

A reading from the holy Gospel according to Matthew   16:13-23

You are Peter, to you I will give you the keys of the kingdom of heaven.

When Jesus came to the region of Caesarea Philippi he put this question to his disciples, 'Who do people say the Son of Man is?' And they said, 'Some say he is John the Baptist, some Elijah, and others Jeremiah or one of the prophets.' 'But you,' he said 'who do you say I am?' Then Simon Peter spoke up, 'You are the Christ,' he said 'the Son of the living God.' Jesus replied, 'Simon son of Jonah, you are a happy man! Because it was not flesh and blood that revealed this to you but my Father in heaven. So I now say to you: You are Peter and on this rock I will build my Church. And the gates of the underworld can never hold out against it. I will give you the keys of the kingdom of heaven; whatever you bind on earth shall be considered bound in heaven; whatever you loose on earth shall be considered loosed in heaven.' Then he gave the disciples strict orders not to tell anyone that he was the Christ.

From that time Jesus began to make it clear to his disciples that he was destined to go to Jerusalem and suffer grievously at the hands of the elders and chief priests and scribes, to be put to death and to be raised up on the third day. Then, taking him aside, Peter started to remonstrate with him. 'Heaven preserve you, Lord,' he said 'this must not happen to you.' But he turned and said to Peter, 'Get behind me, Satan! You are an obstacle in my path, because the way you think is not God's way but man's.'

This is the Gospel of the Lord.

Friday

FIRST READING

A reading from the prophet Nahum   2:1. 3; 3:1-3. 6-7

Woe to the city soaked in blood.

See, over the mountains the messenger hurries!
'Peace!' he proclaims.
Judah, celebrate your feasts,
carry out your vows,
for Belial will never pass through you again;

he is utterly annihilated.
Yes, the Lord is restoring the vineyard of Jacob
and the vineyard of Israel.
For the plunderers had plundered them,
they had broken off their branches.
Woe to the city soaked in blood,
full of lies,
stuffed with booty,
whose plunderings know no end!
The crack of the whip!
The rumble of wheels!
Galloping horse,
jolting chariot,
charging cavalry,
flash of swords,
gleam of spears ...
a mass of wounded,
hosts of dead,
countless corpses;
they stumble over the dead.
I am going to pelt you with filth,
shame you, make you a public show.
And all who look on you
will turn their backs on you and say,
'Nineveh is a ruin.'
Could anyone pity her?
Where can I find anyone to comfort her?

This is the word of the Lord.

Responsorial Psalm   Deut 32:35-36. 39. 41. ℟ v.39

℟   It is I who deal death and give life.

1   It is close, the day of their ruin;
    their doom comes at speed.
    For the Lord will see his people righted,
    he will take pity on his servants.   ℟

2   See now that I, I am He,
    and beside me there is no other god.
    It is I who deal death and life:
    when I have struck it is I who heal.   ℟

3 When I have whetted my flashing sword
  I will take up the cause of Right,
  I will give my foes as good again,
  I will repay those who hate me. ℟

Gospel Acclamation   Mt 5:10

   Alleluia, alleluia!
   Happy are they who suffer persecution for justice' sake;
   the kingdom of heaven is theirs.
   Alleluia!

GOSPEL

A reading from the holy Gospel according to Matthew   16:24-28

What can anyone give in exchange for his life?

Jesus said to his disciples, 'If anyone wants to be a follower of mine, let him renounce himself and take up his cross and follow me. For anyone who wants to save his life will lose it; but anyone who loses his life for my sake will find it. What, then, will a man gain if he wins the whole world and ruins his life? Or what has a man to offer in exchange for his life?

   'For the Son of Man is going to come in the glory of his Father with his angels, and, when he does, he will reward each one according to his behaviour. I tell you solemnly, there are some of these standing here who will not taste death before they see the Son of Man coming with his kingdom.'

   This is the Gospel of the Lord.

Saturday

FIRST READING

A reading from the prophet Habakkuk   1:12 – 2:4

The upright will live by faithfulness.

Are not you, from ancient times Lord,
my God, my Holy One, who never dies?
Lord, you have made this people an instrument of justice,
set it firm as a rock in order to punish.

Your eyes are too pure to rest on wickedness,
you cannot look on at tyranny.
Why do you look on while men are treacherous,
and stay silent while the evil man swallows a better man than he?

You treat mankind like fishes in the sea,
like creeping, masterless things.
A people, these, who catch all on their hook,
who draw them with their net,
in their dragnet gather them,
and so, triumphantly, rejoice.

At this, they offer a sacrifice to their net,
and burn incense to their dragnet,
for providing them with luxury
and lavish food.
Are they then to empty their net unceasingly,
slaughtering nations without pity?

I will stand on my watchtower,
and take up my post on my battlements,
watching to see what he will say to me,
what answer he will make to my complaints.

Then the Lord answered and said,

> 'Write the vision down,
> inscribe it on tablets
> to be easily read,
> since this vision is for its own time only:
> eager for its own fulfilment, it does not deceive;
> if it comes slowly, wait,
> for come it will, without fail.

> 'See, how he flags, he whose soul is not at rights,
> but the upright man will live by his faithfulness.'

This is the word of the Lord.

Responsorial Psalm   Ps 9:8-13. ℟ v.11

℟   You will never abandon those who seek you, Lord.

1   The Lord sits enthroned for ever.
    He has set up his throne for judgement;

he will judge the world with justice,
he will judge the peoples with his truth.   ℟

2   For the oppressed let the Lord be a stronghold,
a stronghold in times of distress.
Those who know your name will trust you:
you will never forsake those who seek you.   ℟

3   Sing psalms to the Lord who dwells in Zion.
Proclaim his mighty works among the peoples;
for the Avenger of blood has remembered them,
and has not forgotten the cry of the poor.   ℟

Gospel Acclamation   cf. 2 Tim 1:10

Alleluia, alleluia!
Our Saviour Jesus Christ has done away with death
and brought us life through his gospel.
Alleluia!

GOSPEL

A reading from the holy Gospel according to Matthew   17:14-20

If you have faith, nothing is impossible for you.

A man came up to Jesus and went down on his knees before him.
'Lord,' he said 'take pity on my son: he is a lunatic and in a wretched
state; he is always falling into the fire or into the water. I took him to
your disciples and they were unable to cure him.' 'Faithless and
perverse generation!' Jesus said in reply 'How much longer must I be
with you? How much longer must I put up with you? Bring him here
to me.' And when Jesus rebuked it the devil came out of the boy who
was cured from that moment.

Then the disciples came privately to Jesus. 'Why were we unable
to cast it out?' they asked. He answered, 'Because you have little faith.
I tell you solemnly, if your faith were the size of a mustard seed you
could say to this mountain, "Move from here to there", and it would
move; nothing would be impossible for you.'

This is the Gospel of the Lord.

NINETEENTH WEEK IN ORDINARY TIME
Year II

Monday

FIRST READING

A reading from the prophet Ezekiel   1:2-5. 24-28

Ezekiel's vision of the likeness of the glory of the Lord

On the fifth of the month – it was the fifth year of exile for King
Jehoiachin – the word of the Lord was addressed to the priest
Ezekiel son of Buzi, in the land of the Chaldaeans, on the bank of
the river Chebar.

There the hand of the Lord came on me. I looked; a stormy wind
blew from the north, a great cloud with light around it, a fire from
which flashes of lightning darted, and in the centre a sheen like
bronze at the heart of the fire. In the centre I saw what seemed
four animals. They looked like this. They were of human form.
heard the noise of their wings as they moved; it sounded like
rushing water, like the voice of Shaddai, a noise like a storm, like
the noise of a camp; when they halted, they folded their wings, and
there was a noise.

Above the vault over their heads was something that looked like
a sapphire; it was shaped like a throne and high up on this throne
was a being that looked like a man. I saw him shine like bronze
and close to and all around him from what seemed his loins upwards was what looked like fire; and from what seemed his loins
downwards I saw what looked like fire, and a light all round like a
bow in the clouds on rainy days; that is how the surrounding light
appeared. It was something that looked like the glory of the Lord.
looked, and prostrated myself.

This is the word of the Lord.

650

Responsorial Psalm   Ps 148:1-2. 11-14

℟   Heaven and earth are filled with your glory.

or

℟   Alleluia!

1   Praise the Lord from the heavens,
     praise him, in the heights.
     Praise him, all his angels,
     praise him, all his host.   ℟

2   All earth's kings and peoples, praise him,
     earth's princes and rulers;
     young men and maidens,
     old men together with children.   ℟

3   Let them praise the name of the Lord
     for he alone is exalted.
     The splendour of his name
     reaches beyond heaven and earth.   ℟

4   He exalts the strength of his people.
     He is the praise of all his saints,
     of the sons of Israel,
     of the people to whom he comes close.   ℟

Gospel Acclamation   cf. 2 Thess 2:14

     Alleluia, alleluia!
     God has called us with the gospel
     to share in the glory of our Lord Jesus Christ.
     Alleluia!

GOSPEL

A reading from the holy Gospel according to Matthew   17:22-27

They put him to death and he rose. We are freed from tribute.

One day when they were together in Galilee, Jesus said to his disciples 'The Son of Man is going to be handed over into the power of men; they will put him to death, and on the third day he will be raised to life again.' And a great sadness came over them.

     When they reached Capernaum, the collectors of the half-shekel came to Peter and said, 'Does your master not pay the half-shekel?' 'Oh yes' he replied, and went into the house. But before he could speak, Jesus said, 'Simon, what is your opinion? From whom do the kings of the earth take toll or tribute? From their sons or from foreigners?' And when he replied, 'From foreigners,' Jesus said, 'Well then, the sons are exempt. However, so as not offend these people, go to the lake and cast a hook; take the first fish that bites, open its mouth and there you will find a shekel; take it and give it to them for me and for you.'

This is the Gospel of the Lord.

Tuesday

FIRST READING

A reading from the prophet Ezekiel   2:8 – 3:4

He gave me the scroll to eat, and it tasted as sweet as honey.

I, Ezekiel, heard a voice speaking. It said, 'You, son of man, listen to the words I say; do not be a rebel like that rebellious set. Open your mouth and eat what I am about to give you.' I looked. A hand was there, stretching out to me and holding a scroll. He unrolled it in front of me; it was written on back and front; on it was written 'lamentations, wailings, moanings'. He said, 'Son of man, eat what is given to you; eat this scroll, then go and speak to the House of Israel.' I opened my mouth; he gave me the scroll to eat and said, 'Son of man, feed and be satisfied by the scroll I am giving you.' I ate it, and it tasted sweet as honey.

Then he said, 'Son of man, go to the House of Israel and tell them what I have said.'

This is the word of the Lord.

Responsorial Psalm   Ps 118:14. 24. 72. 103. 111. 131. ℟ v.103

℟ How sweet to my taste is your promise!

1 I rejoice to do your will
   as though all riches were mine.
   Your will is my delight;
   your statutes are my counsellors. ℟

2   The law from your mouth means more to me
    than silver and gold.
    Your promise is sweeter to my taste
    than honey in the mouth.   ℟

3   Your will is my heritage for ever,
    the joy of my heart.
    I open my mouth and I sigh
    as I yearn for your commands.   ℟

Gospel Acclamation   Mt 11:29

Alleluia, alleluia!
Take my yoke upon you;
learn from me, for I am gentle and lowly in heart.
Alleluia!

GOSPEL

A reading from the holy Gospel according   18:1-5. 10. 12-14
to Matthew

Be careful never to despise one of these little ones.

The disciples came to Jesus and said, 'Who is the greatest in the kingdom of heaven?' So he called a little child to him and set the child in front of them. Then he said, 'I tell you solemnly, unless you change and become like little children you will never enter the kingdom of heaven. And so, the one who makes himself as little as this little child is the greatest in the kingdom of heaven.

'Anyone who welcomes a little child like this in my name welcomes me.

'See that you never despise any of these little ones, for I tell you that their angels in heaven are continually in the presence of my Father in heaven.

'Tell me. Suppose a man has a hundred sheep and one of them strays; will he not leave the ninety-nine on the hillside and go in search of the stray? I tell you solemnly, if he finds it, it gives him more joy than do the ninety-nine that did not stray at all. Similarly, it is never the will of your Father in heaven that one of these little ones should be lost.'

This is the Gospel of the Lord.

Wednesday

FIRST READING

A reading from the prophet Ezekiel   9:1-7; 10:18-22

*Mark a cross on the foreheads of all who deplore the filth practised
in Jerusalem.*

As I, Ezekiel, listened God shouted, 'Come here, you scourges of the
city, and bring your weapons of destruction.' Immediately six men
advanced from the upper north gate, each holding a deadly weapon. In
the middle of them was a man in white, with a scribe's ink horn in his
belt. They came in and halted in front of the bronze altar. The glory of
the God of Israel rose off the cherubs where it had been and went up to
the threshold of the Temple. He called the man in white with a
scribe's ink horn in his belt and said, 'Go all through the city, all
through Jerusalem, and mark a cross on the foreheads of all who
deplore and disapprove of all the filth practised in it.' I heard him say
to the others, 'Follow him through the city, and strike. Show neither
pity nor mercy; old men, young men, virgins, children, women, kill
and exterminate them all. But do not touch anyone with a cross on his
forehead. Begin at my sanctuary.' So they began with the old men in
front of the Temple. He said to them, 'Defile the Temple; fill the courts
with corpses, and go.' They went out and hacked their way through
the city.

The glory of the Lord came out from the Temple threshold and
paused over the cherubs. The cherubs spread their wings and rose
from the ground to leave, and as I watched the wheels rose with them.
They paused at the entrance to the east gate of the Temple of the Lord,
and the glory of the God of Israel hovered over them. This was the
creature that I had seen supporting the God of Israel beside the river
Chebar, and I was now certain that these were cherubs. Each had four
faces and four wings and what seemed to be human hands under their
wings. Their faces were just as I had seen them beside the river
Chebar. Each moved straight forward.

This is the word of the Lord.

Responsorial Psalm   Ps 112:1-6. ℟ v.4

℟   The glory of the Lord is higher than the skies.

or

℟   Alleluia!

1   Praise, O servants of the Lord,
     praise the name of the Lord!
     May the name of the Lord be blessed
     both now and for evermore!   ℟

2   From the rising of the sun to its setting
     praised be the name of the Lord!
     High above all nations is the Lord,
     above the heavens his glory.   ℟

3   Who is like the Lord, our God,
     who has risen on high to his throne
     yet stoops from the heights to look down,
     to look down upon heaven and earth?   ℟

Gospel Acclamation   2 Cor 5:19

Alleluia, alleluia!
God was in Christ, to reconcile the world to himself;
and the Good News of reconciliation he has entrusted to us.
Alleluia!

GOSPEL

A reading from the holy Gospel according to Matthew   18:15-20

If your brother or sister listens to you, you will have won that
person back.

Jesus said to his disciples: If your brother does something wrong, go
and have it out with him alone, between your two selves. If he listens
to you, you have won back your brother. If he does not listen, take one
or two others along with you: the evidence of two or three witnesses is
required to sustain any charge. But if he refuses to listen to these,
report it to the community; and if he refuses to listen to the
community, treat him like a pagan or a tax collector.

   'I tell you solemnly, whatever you bind on earth shall be considered bound in heaven; whatever you loose on earth shall be considered loosed in heaven.

'I tell you solemnly once again, if two of you on earth agree to ask anything at all, it will be granted to you by my Father in heaven. For where two or three meet in my name, I shall be there with them.'

This is the Gospel of the Lord.

Thursday

FIRST READING

A reading from the prophet Ezekiel   12:1-12

You will leave in the daylight for them to see.

The word of the Lord was addressed to me as follows, 'Son of man, you are living with that set of rebels who have eyes and never see, ears and never hear, for they are a set of rebels. You, son of man, pack an exile's bundle and emigrate by daylight when they can see you, emigrate from where you are to somewhere else while they watch. Perhaps they will admit then that they are a set of rebels. You will pack your baggage like an exile's bundle, by daylight, for them to see, and leave like an exile in the evening, making sure that they are looking. As they watch, make a hole in the wall, and go out through it. As they watch, you will shoulder your pack and go out into the dark; you will cover your face so that you cannot see the country, since I have made you a symbol for the House of Israel.'

I did as I had been told. I packed my baggage like an exile's bundle, by daylight; and in the evening I made a hole through the wall with my hand. I went out into the dark and shouldered my pack as they watched.

The next morning the word of the Lord was addressed to me as follows, 'Son of man, did not the House of Israel, did not that set of rebels, ask you what you were doing? Say, "The Lord says this: This oracle is directed against Jerusalem and the whole House of Israel wherever they are living." Say, "I am a symbol of you; the thing I have done will be done to them; they will go into exile, into banishment." Their ruler will shoulder his pack in the dark and go out through the wall; a hole will be made to let him out; he will cover his face rather than see the country.'

This is the word of the Lord.

Responsorial Psalm   Ps 77:56-59. 61-62. ℟ cf. v.7

℟   Do not forget the works of the Lord!

1   They put God to the proof and defied him;
    they refused to obey the Most High.
    They strayed, as faithless as their fathers,
    like a bow on which the archer cannot count.   ℟

2   With their mountain shrines they angered him;
    made him jealous with the idols they served.
    God saw and was filled with fury:
    he utterly rejected Israel.   ℟

3   He gave his ark into captivity,
    his glorious ark into the hand of the foe.
    He gave up his people to the sword,
    in his anger against his chosen ones.   ℟

Gospel Acclamation   Ps 118:135

    Alleluia, alleluia!
    Let your face shine on your servant,
    and teach me your laws.
    Alleluia!

GOSPEL

A reading from the holy Gospel according to Matthew   18:21 – 19:1

I did not say to you to forgive seven times, but seventy times seven.

Peter went up to Jesus and said, 'Lord, how often must I forgive my brother if he wrongs me? As often as seven times?' Jesus answered, 'Not seven, I tell you, but seventy-seven times.

    'And so the kingdom of heaven may be compared to a king who decided to settle his accounts with his servants. When the reckoning began, they brought him a man who owed ten thousand talents; but he had no means of paying, so his master gave orders that he should be sold, together with his wife and children and all his possessions, to meet the debt. At this, the servant threw himself down at his master's feet. "Give me time" he said "and I will pay the whole sum." And the servant's master felt so sorry for him that he let him go and cancelled the debt. Now as this servant went out, he happened to meet a fellow servant who owed him one hundred denarii; and he seized him by the throat and began to throttle him. "Pay what you owe me" he said. His fellow servant fell at his feet and implored him, saying, "Give me time and I will pay you." But the other would not agree; on the contrary, he had him thrown into prison till he should pay the debt. His fellow servants were deeply distressed when they saw what had happened, and they went to their master and reported the whole affair to him. Then the master sent for him. "You wicked servant," he said. "I cancelled all that debt of yours when you appealed to me. Were you not bound, then, to have pity on your fellow servant just as I had pity on you?" And in his anger the master handed him over to the torturers till he should pay all his debt. And that is how my heavenly Father will deal with you unless you each forgive your brother from your heart.'

Jesus had now finished what he wanted to say, and he left Galilee and came into the part of Judaea which is on the far side of the Jordan.

This is the Gospel of the Lord.

Friday

FIRST READING

A reading from the prophet Ezekiel   16:1-15. 60. 63

I clothed you with my own splendour; you became a prostitute.

The word of the Lord was addressed to me as follows, 'Son of man, confront Jerusalem with her filthy crimes. Say, "The Lord says this: By origin and birth you belong to the land of Canaan. Your father was an Amorite and your mother a Hittite. At birth, the very day you were born, there was no one to cut your navel-string, or wash you in cleansing water, or rub you with salt, or wrap you in napkins. No one leaned kindly over you to do anything like that for you. You were exposed in the open fields; you were as unloved as that on the day you were born.

"I saw you struggling in your blood as I was passing, and I said to you as you lay in your blood: Live, and grow like the grass of the fields. You developed, you grew, you reached marriageable age. Your breasts and your hair both grew, but you were quite naked. Then I saw you as I was passing. Your time had come, the time for love. I spread part of my cloak over you and covered your nakedness; I bound myself by oath, I made a covenant with you – it is the Lord who speaks

– and you became mine. I bathed you in water, I washed the blood off you, I anointed you with oil. I gave you embroidered dresses, fine leather shoes, a linen headband and a cloak of silk. I loaded you with jewels, gave you bracelets for your wrists and a necklace for your throat. I gave you nose-ring and earrings; I put a beautiful diadem on your head. You were loaded with gold and silver, and dressed in fine linen and embroidered silks. Your food was the finest flour, honey and oil. You grew more and more beautiful; and you rose to be queen. The fame of your beauty spread through the nations, since it was perfect, because I had clothed you with my own splendour – it is the Lord who speaks.

"You have become infatuated with your own beauty; you have used your fame to make yourself a prostitute; you have offered your services to all comers. But I will remember the covenant that I made with you when you were a girl, and I will conclude a covenant with you that shall last for ever. So remember and be covered with shame, and in your confusion be reduced to silence, when I have pardoned you for all that you have done – it is the Lord who speaks." '

This is the word of the Lord.

Alternative First Reading

A reading from the prophet Ezekiel   16:59-63

> *I will keep my covenant with you and you will be ashamed.*

'The Lord says this: "Jerusalem, I will treat you as you deserve, you who have despised your oath even to the extent of breaking a covenant, but I will remember the covenant that I made with you when you were a girl, and I will conclude a covenant with you that shall last for ever. And you for your part will remember your past behaviour and be covered with shame when I take your elder and younger sisters and make them your daughters, although this was not included in this covenant. I am going to renew my covenant with you; and you will learn that I am the Lord, and so remember and be covered with shame, and in your confusion be reduced to silence, when I have pardoned you for all that you have done – it is the Lord who speaks." '

This is the word of the Lord.

Responsorial Psalm   Is 12:2-6. ℟ v.1

℟   You have turned from your anger to comfort me.

1   Truly, God is my salvation,
    I trust, I shall not fear.
    For the Lord is my strength, my song,
    he became my saviour.   ℟

2   With joy you will draw water
    from the wells of salvation.
    Give thanks to the Lord, give praise to his name,
    make his mighty deeds known to the peoples!   ℟

3   Declare the greatness of his name,
    sing a psalm to the Lord!
    For he has done glorious deeds,
    make them known to all the earth!
    People of Zion, sing and shout for joy
    for great in your midst is the Holy One of Israel.   ℟

Gospel Acclamation   cf. 1 Thess 2:13

Alleluia, alleluia!
Receive this message not as human words,
but as truly the word of God.
Alleluia!

GOSPEL

A reading from the holy Gospel according to Matthew   19:3-12

Because of the hardness of your hearts Moses permitted you to divorce
your wives, but it was not like this from the beginning.

Some Pharisees approached Jesus, and to test him they said, 'Is it
against the Law for a man to divorce his wife on any pretext
whatever?' He answered, 'Have you not read that the creator from the
beginning made them male and female and that he said: This is why a
man must leave father and mother, and cling to his wife, and the two
become one body? They are no longer two, therefore, but one body. So
then, what God has united, man must not divide.'

They said to him, 'Then why did Moses command that a writ of
dismissal should be given in cases of divorce?' 'It was because you
were so unteachable' he said 'that Moses allowed you to divorce your
wives, but it was not like this from the beginning. Now I say this to
you: the man who divorces his wife – I am not speaking of fornication

- and marries another, is guilty of adultery.'

The disciples said to him, 'If that is how things are between husband and wife, it is not advisable to marry.' But he replied, 'It is not everyone who can accept what I have said, but only those to whom it is granted. There are eunuchs born that way from their mother's womb, there are eunuchs made so by men and there are eunuchs who have made themselves that way for the sake of the kingdom of heaven. Let anyone accept this who can.'

This is the Gospel of the Lord.

Saturday

FIRST READING

A reading from the prophet Ezekiel   18:1-10. 13. 30-32

I will judge everyone according to his ways.

The word of the Lord was addressed to me as follows, 'Why do you keep repeating this proverb in the land of Israel:

The fathers have eaten unripe grapes;
and the children's teeth are set on edge?

'As I live – it is the Lord who speaks – there will no longer be any reason to repeat this proverb in Israel. See now: all life belongs to me; the father's life and the son's life, both alike belong to me. The man who has sinned, he is the one who shall die.

'The upright man is law-abiding and honest; he does not eat on the mountains or raise his eyes to the idols of the House of Israel, does not seduce his neighbour's wife or sleep with a woman during her periods. He oppresses no one, returns pledges, never steals, gives his own bread to the hungry, his clothes to the naked. He never charges usury on loans, takes no interest, abstains from evil, gives honest judgement between man and man, keeps my laws and sincerely respects my observances – such a man is truly upright. It is the Lord who speaks.

'But if anyone has a son prone to violence and bloodshed, who commits one of these misdeeds, then this son shall certainly not live; having committed all these appalling crimes he will have to die, and his blood be on his own head.

'House of Israel, in future I mean to judge each of you by what he does – it is the Lord who speaks. Repent, renounce all your sins, avoid all occasions of sin! Shake off all the sins you have committed against me, and make yourselves a new heart and a new spirit! Why are you so anxious to die, House of Israel? I take no pleasure in the death of anyone – it is the Lord who speaks. Repent and live!'

This is the word of the Lord.

Responsorial Psalm

Ps 50:12-15. 18-19. ℟ v.12

℟   Create a clean heart in me, O God.

1   A pure heart create for me, O God,
    put a steadfast spirit within me.
    Do not cast me away from your presence,
    nor deprive me of your holy spirit.   ℟

2   Give me again the joy of your help;
    with a spirit of fervour sustain me,
    that I may teach transgressors your ways
    and sinners may return to you.   ℟

3   For in sacrifice you take no delight,
    burnt offering from me you would refuse,
    my sacrifice, a contrite spirit.
    A humbled, contrite heart you will not spurn.   ℟

Gospel Acclamation

cf. Mt 11:25

Alleluia, alleluia!
Blessed are you, Father, Lord of heaven and earth;
you have revealed to little ones the mysteries of the kingdom.
Alleluia!

GOSPEL

A reading from the holy Gospel according to Matthew   19:13-15

Do not stop the little children coming to me: for it is to such as these that the kingdom of heaven belongs.

People brought little children to Jesus, for him to lay his hands on them and say a prayer. The disciples turned them away, but Jesus said, 'Let the little children alone, and do not stop them coming to me; for it is to such as these that the kingdom of heaven belongs.' Then he laid his hands on them and went on his way.

This is the Gospel of the Lord.

TWENTIETH WEEK IN ORDINARY TIME
Year II

Monday

FIRST READING

A reading from the prophet Ezekiel   24:15-24

Thus shall Ezekiel be to you a sign; all that he has done, you will do.

The word of the Lord was addressed to me as follows, 'Son of man, I am about to deprive you suddenly of the delight of your eyes. But you are not to lament, not to weep, not to let your tears run down. Groan in silence, do not go into mourning for the dead, knot your turban round your head, put your sandals on your feet, do not cover your beard, do not eat common bread.' I told this to the people in the morning, and my wife died in the evening, and the next morning I did as I had been ordered. The people then said to me, 'Are you not going to explain what meaning these actions have for us?' I replied, 'The word of the Lord has been addressed to me as follows, "Say to the House of Israel: The Lord says this. I am about to profane my sanctuary, the pride of your strength, the delight of your eyes, the passion of your souls. Those of your sons and daughters whom you have left behind will fall by the sword. And you are to do as I have done; you must not cover your beards or eat common bread; you must keep your turbans on your heads and your sandals on your feet; you must not lament or weep. You shall waste away owing to your sins and groan among yourselves. Ezekiel is to be a sign for you. You are to do just as he has done. And when this happens, you will learn that I am the Lord." '

This is the word of the Lord.

Responsorial Psalm   Deut 32:18-21. ℟ cf. v.18

℟   You have forgotten God who gave you birth.

1   You forget the Rock who begot you,
      unmindful now of the God who fathered you.
      The Lord has seen this, and in his anger
      cast off his sons and his daughters.   ℟

2 'I shall hide my face from them,' he says
   'and see what becomes of them.
   For they are a deceitful brood,
   children with no loyalty in them.

   ℟   You have forgotten God who gave you birth.

3 'They have roused me to jealousy with what is no god,
   they have angered me with their beings of nothing;
   I, then, will rouse them to jealousy with what is no people,
   I will anger them with an empty-headed nation.'   ℟

Gospel Acclamation   Mt 5:3

   Alleluia, alleluia!
   Happy the poor in spirit;
   the kingdom of heaven is theirs!
   Alleluia!

GOSPEL

A reading from the holy Gospel according to Matthew   19:16-22

*If you wish to be perfect, sell what you own, and your treasure will
be in heaven.*

There was a man who came to Jesus and asked, 'Master, what good
deed must I do to possess eternal life.' Jesus said to him, 'Why do you
ask me about what is good? There is one alone who is good. But if you
wish to enter into life, keep the commandments.' He said, 'Which?'
'These,' Jesus replied. 'You must not kill. You must not commit
adultery. You must not bring false witness. Honour your father and
mother, and: you must love your neighbour as yourself.' The young
man said to him, 'I have kept all these. What more do I need to do?'
Jesus said, 'If you wish to be perfect, go and sell what you own and
give the money to the poor, and you will have treasure in heaven; then
come, follow me.' But when the young man heard these words he went
away sad, for he was a man of great wealth.

   This is the Gospel of the Lord.

Tuesday

FIRST READING

A reading from the prophet Ezekiel   28:1-10

You are a man and not God, yet you consider yourself equal to God.

The word of the Lord was addressed to me as follows, 'Son of man, tell the ruler of Tyre, "The Lord says this:

Being swollen with pride,
you have said: I am a god;
I am sitting on the throne of God,
surrounded by the seas.
Though you are a man and not a god,
you consider yourself the equal of God.
You are wiser now than Daniel;
there is no sage as wise as you.
By your wisdom and your intelligence
you have amassed great wealth;
you have piles of gold and silver
inside your treasure-houses.
Such is your skill in trading,
your wealth has continued to increase,
and with this your heart has grown more arrogant.
And so, the Lord says this:
Since you consider yourself the equal of God,
very well, I am going to bring foreigners against you,
the most barbarous of the nations.
They will draw sword against your fine wisdom,
they will defile your glory;
they will throw you down into the pit
and you will die a violent death
surrounded by the seas.
Are you still going to say: I am a god,
when your murderers confront you?
No, you are a man and not a god
in the clutches of your murderers!
You will die like the uncircumcised
at the hand of foreigners.
For I have spoken – it is the Lord who speaks." '

This is the word of the Lord.

665

Responsorial Psalm
Deut 32:26-28. 30. 35-36. ℟ v.39

℟   It is I who deal death and give life.

1   I should crush them to dust, said the Lord.
    I should wipe out their memory among men,
    did I not fear the boasting of the enemy.
    But let not their foes be mistaken!   ℟

2   Let them not say: Our own power wins the victory,
    the Lord plays no part in this.
    What a nation of short sight it is;
    in them there is no understanding.   ℟

3   How else could one man rout a thousand,
    how could two put ten thousand to flight,
    were it not that their Rock has sold them,
    that the Lord has delivered them up?   ℟

4   For it is close, the day of their ruin;
    their doom comes at speed.
    For the Lord will see his people righted,
    he will take pity on his servants.   ℟

Gospel Acclamation
2 Cor 8:9

Alleluia, alleluia!
Jesus Christ was rich but he became poor,
to make you rich out of his poverty.
Alleluia!

GOSPEL

A reading from the holy Gospel according to Mattthew   19:23-30

It is easier for a camel to pass through the eye of a needle than for
a rich person to enter the kingdom of heaven.

Jesus said to his disciples, 'I tell you solemnly, it will be hard for a rich man to enter the kingdom of heaven. Yes, I tell you again, it is easier for a camel to pass through the eye of a needle than for a rich man to enter the kingdom of heaven.' When the disciples heard this they were astonished. 'Who can be saved, then?' they said. Jesus gazed at them. 'For men' he told them 'this is impossible; for God everything is possible.'

Then Peter spoke. 'What about us?' he said to him. 'We have left everything and followed you. What are we to have, then?' Jesus said to him, 'I tell you solemnly, when all is made new and the Son of Man sits on his throne of glory, you will yourselves sit on twelve thrones to judge the twelve tribes of Israel. And everyone who has left houses, brothers, sisters, father, mother, children or land for the sake of my name will be repaid a hundred times over, and also inherit eternal life.

'Many who are first will be last, and the last, first.'

This is the Gospel of the Lord.

Wednesday

FIRST READING

A reading from the prophet Ezekiel   34:1-11

I will free my sheep from their hands and they will not prey on them
any more.

The word of the Lord was addressed to me as follows: 'Son of man, prophesy against the shepherds of Israel; prophesy and say to them, "Shepherds, the Lord says this: Trouble for the shepherds of Israel who feed themselves! Shepherds ought to feed their flock, yet you have fed on milk, you have dressed yourselves in wool, you have sacrificed the fattest sheep, but failed to feed the flock. You have failed to make weak sheep strong, or to care for the sick ones, or bandage the wounded ones. You have failed to bring back strays or look for the lost. On the contrary, you have ruled them cruelly and violently. For lack of a shepherd they have scattered, to become the prey of any wild animal; they have scattered far. My flock is straying this way and that, on mountains and on high hills; my flock has been scattered all over the country; no one bothers about them and no one looks for them.

"Well then, shepherds, hear the word of the Lord. As I live, I swear it – it is the Lord who speaks – since my flock has been looted and for lack of a shepherd is now the prey of any wild animal, since my shepherds have stopped bothering about my flock, since my shepherds feed themselves rather than my flock, in view of all this, shepherds, hear the word of the Lord. The Lord says this: I am going to call the shepherds to account. I am going to take my flock back from them and I shall not allow them to feed my flock. In this way the shepherds will

667

stop feeding themselves. I shall rescue my sheep from their mouths; they will not prey on them any more." '

'For the Lord says this: "I am going to look after my flock myself and keep all of it in view." '

This is the word of the Lord.

Responsorial Psalm

Ps 22. ℟ v.1

℟ The Lord is my shepherd;
there is nothing I shall want.

1 The Lord is my shepherd;
there is nothing I shall want.
Fresh and green are the pastures
where he gives me repose.
Near restful waters he leads me,
to revive my drooping spirit. ℟

2 He guides me along the right path;
he is true to his name.
If I should walk in the valley of darkness
no evil would I fear.
You are there with your crook and your staff;
with these you give me comfort. ℟

3 You have prepared a banquet for me
in the sight of my foes.
My head you have anointed with oil;
my cup is overflowing. ℟

4 Surely goodness and kindness shall follow me
all the days of my life.
In the Lord's own house shall I dwell
for ever and ever. ℟

Gospel Acclamation

Heb 4:12

Alleluia! alleluia!
The word of God is living and active;
it probes the thoughts and motives of our heart.
Alleluia!

GOSPEL

A reading from the holy Gospel according to Matthew   20:1-16

Are you jealous because I am generous?

Jesus said to his disciples: 'The kingdom of heaven is like a landowner going out at daybreak to hire workers for his vineyard. He made an agreement with the workers for one denarius a day, and sent them to his vineyard. Going out at about the third hour he saw others standing idle in the market place and said to them, "You go to my vineyard too and I will give you a fair wage." So they went. At about the sixth hour and again at about the ninth hour, he went out and did the same. Then at about the eleventh hour he went out and found more men standing round, and he said to them, "Why have you been standing here idle all day?" "Because no one has hired us" they answered. He said to them, "You go into my vineyard too." In the evening, the owner of the vineyard said to his bailiff, "Call the workers and pay them their wages, starting with the last arrivals and ending with the first." So those who were hired at about the eleventh hour came forward and received one denarius each. When the first came, they expected to get more, but they too received one denarius each. They took it, but grumbled at the landowner. "The men who came last" they said "have done only one hour, and you have treated them the same as us, though we have done a heavy day's work in all the heat." He answered one of them and said, "My friend, I am not being unjust to you; did we not agree on one denarius? Take your earnings and go. I choose to pay the last-comer as much as I pay you. Have I no right to do what I like with my own? Why be envious because I am generous?" Thus the last will be first, and the first, last.'

This is the Gospel of the Lord.

Thursday

FIRST READING

A reading from the prophet Ezekiel   36:23-28

I will give you a new heart and put a new spirit in you.

The word of the Lord was addressed to me as follows: I mean to display the holiness of my great name, which has been profaned among the nations, which you have profaned among them. And the nations will learn that I am the Lord – it is the Lord who speaks – when I display my holiness for your sake before their eyes. Then I am going to take you from among the nations and gather you together from all the foreign countries, and bring you home to your own land. I shall pour clean water over you and you will be cleansed; I shall cleanse you of all your defilement and all your idols. I shall give you a new heart, and put a new spirit in you; I shall remove the heart of stone from your bodies and give you a heart of flesh instead. I shall put my spirit in you, and make you keep my laws and sincerely respect my observances. You will live in the land which I gave your ancestors. You shall be my people and I will be your God.

This is the word of the Lord.

Responsorial Psalm   Ps 50:12-15. 18-19. ℟ Ez 36:25

℟ I will pour clean water on you
     and wash away all your sins.

1 A pure heart create for me, O God,
    put a steadfast spirit within me.
    Do not cast me away from your presence,
    nor deprive me of your holy spirit.   ℟

2 Give me again the joy of your help;
    with a spirit of fervour sustain me,
    that I may teach transgressors your ways
    and sinners may return to you.   ℟

3 For in sacrifice you take no delight,
    burnt offering from me you would refuse,
    my sacrifice, a contrite spirit.
    A humbled, contrite heart you will not spurn.   ℟

Gospel Acclamation   cf. Ps 94:8

Alleluia, alleluia!
If today you hear his voice,
harden not your hearts.
Alleluia!

GOSPEL

A reading from the holy Gospel according to Matthew 22:1-14

Go out and find whoever you can, and invite them to the wedding.

Jesus began to speak to the chief priests and the elders of the people in parables, 'The kingdom of heaven may be compared to a king who gave a feast for his son's wedding. He sent his servants to call those who had been invited, but they would not come. Next he sent some more servants. "Tell those who have been invited" he said "that I have my banquet all prepared, my oxen and fattened cattle have been slaughtered, everything is ready. Come to the wedding." But they were not interested: one went off to his farm, another to his business and the rest seized his servants, maltreated them and killed them. The king was furious. He despatched his troops, destroyed those murderers and burnt their town. Then he said to his servants, "The wedding is ready; but as those who were invited proved to be unworthy, go to the crossroads in the town and invite everyone you can find to the wedding." So these servants went out on to the roads and collected together everyone they could find, bad and good alike; and the wedding hall was filled with guests. When the king came in to look at the guests he noticed one man who was not wearing a wedding garment, and said to him, "How did you get in here, my friend, without a wedding garment?" And the man was silent. Then the king said to the attendants, "Bind him hand and foot and throw him out into the dark, where there will be weeping and grinding of teeth." For many are called, but few are chosen.'

This is the Gospel of the Lord.

Friday

FIRST READING

A reading from the prophet Ezekiel 37:1-4

Dry bones, hear the word of the Lord. I will lead you back to the soil, O house of Israel.

The hand of the Lord was laid on me, and he carried me away by the spirit of the Lord and set me down in the middle of a valley, a valley full of bones. He made me walk up and down among them. There were vast quantities of these bones on the ground the whole length of the valley; and they were quite dried up. He said to me, 'Son of man, can these bones live?' I said, 'You know, Lord.' He said, 'Prophesy over these bones. Say, "Dry bones, hear the word of the Lord. The Lord says this to these bones: I am now going to make the breath enter you, and you will live. I shall put sinews on you, I shall make flesh grow on you. I shall cover you with skin and give you breath, and you will live; and you will learn that I am the Lord." ' I prophesied as I had been ordered. While I was prophesying, there was a noise, a sound of clattering; and the bones joined together. I looked, and saw that they were covered with sinews; flesh was growing on them and skin was covering them, but there was no breath in them. He said to me, 'Prophesy to the breath; prophesy, son of man. Say to the breath, "The Lord says this: Come from the four winds, breath; breathe on these dead; let them live!" ' I prophesied as he had ordered me, and the breath entered them; they came to life again and stood up on their feet, a great, an immense army.

Then he said, 'Son of man, these bones are the whole House of Israel. They keep saying, "Our bones are dried up, our hope has gone; we are as good as dead." So prophesy. Say to them, "The Lord says this: I am now going to open your graves; I mean to raise you from your graves, my people, and lead you back to the soil of Israel. And you will know that I am the Lord, when I open your graves and raise you from your graves, my people. And I shall put my spirit in you, and you will live, and I shall resettle you on your own soil; and you will know that I, the Lord, have said and done this – it is the Lord who speaks." '

This is the word of the Lord.

Responsorial Psalm   Ps 106:2-9. ℟ v.1

℟ Give thanks to the Lord,
    his love is everlasting.

or

℟ Alleluia!

1 Let them say this, the Lord's redeemed,
   whom he redeemed from the hand of the foe
   and gathered from far-off lands,
   from east and west, north and south.   ℟

2 Some wandered in the desert, in the wilderness,
finding no way to a city they could dwell in.
Hungry they were and thirsty;
their soul was fainting within them.   ℟

3 Then they cried to the Lord in their need
and he rescued them from their distress
and he led them along the right way,
to reach a city they could dwell in.   ℟

4 Let them thank the Lord for his love,
for the wonders he does for men.
For he satisfies the thirsty soul;
he fills the hungry with good things.   ℟

Gospel Acclamation   Ps 24:4. 5

Alleluia, alleluia!
Teach me your paths, my God,
and lead me in your truth.
Alleluia!

GOSPEL

A reading from the holy Gospel according to Matthew   22:34-40

Love the Lord your God, and your neighbour as yourself.

When the Pharisees heard that Jesus had silenced the Sadducees they got together and, to disconcert him, one of them put a question, 'Master, which is the greatest commandment of the Law?' Jesus said, 'You must love the Lord your God with all your heart, with all your soul, and with all your mind. This is the greatest and the first commandment. The second resembles it: You must love your neighbour as yourself. On these two commandments hang the whole Law, and the Prophets also.'

This is the Gospel of the Lord.

Saturday

FIRST READING

A reading from the prophet Ezekiel   43:1-7

The glory of God filled the temple

The angel took me to the gate, the one facing east. I saw the glory o
the God of Israel approaching from the east. A sound came with it
like the sound of the ocean, and the earth shone with his glory. Thi
vision was like the one I had seen when I had come for the destructior
of the city, and like the one I had seen on the bank of the river Chebar
Then I prostrated myself.

The glory of the Lord arrived at the Temple by the east gate. Th
spirit lifted me up and brought me into the inner court; I saw the glory
of the Lord fill the Temple. And I heard someone speaking to me from
the Temple while the man stood beside me. The voice said, 'Son o
man, this is the dais of my throne, the step on which I rest my feet. I
shall live here among the sons of Israel for ever.'

This is the word of the Lord.

Responsorial Psalm   Ps 84:9-14. ℟ cf. v.10

℟   The glory of the Lord will dwell in our land.

1   I will hear what the Lord God has to say,
     a voice that speaks of peace,
     peace for his people and his friends.
     His help is near for those who fear him
     and his glory will dwell in our land. ℟

2   Mercy and faithfulness have met;
     justice and peace have embraced.
     Faithfulness shall spring from the earth
     and justice look down from heaven. ℟

3   The Lord will make us prosper
     and our earth shall yield its fruit.
     Justice shall march before him
     and peace shall follow his steps. ℟

Gospel Acclamation   Mt 23:9. 10

Alleluia, alleluia!
You have one Father, your Father in heaven;
you have one teacher: the Lord Jesus Christ!
Alleluia!

GOSPEL

A reading from the holy Gospel according to Matthew   23:1-12

They speak, but do not practise what they preach.

Addressing the people and his disciples Jesus said, 'The scribes and
the Pharisees occupy the chair of Moses. You must therefore do what
they tell you and listen to what they say; but do not be guided by what
they do: since they do not practise what they preach. They tie up
heavy burdens and lay them on men's shoulders, but will they lift a
finger to move them? Not they! Everything they do is done to attract
attention, like wearing broader phylacteries and longer tassels, like
wanting to take the place of honour at banquets and the front seats in
the synagogues, being greeted obsequiously in the market squares
and having people call them Rabbi.

'You, however, must not allow yourselves to be called Rabbi, since
you have only one Master, and you are all brothers. You must call no
one on earth your father, since you have only one Father, and he is in
heaven. Nor must you allow yourselves to be called teachers, for you
have only one Teacher, the Christ. The greatest among you must be
your servant. Anyone who exalts himself will be humbled, and anyone
who humbles himself will be exalted.'

This is the Gospel of the Lord.

TWENTY-FIRST WEEK IN ORDINARY TIME
Year II

Monday

FIRST READING

A reading from the second letter of St Paul   1:1-5. 11-12
to the Thessalonians

> *The name of our Lord Jesus Christ will be glorified in you and*
> *you in him*

From Paul, Silvanus and Timothy, to the Church in Thessalonika
which is in God our Father and the Lord Jesus Christ; wishing you
grace and peace from God the Father and the Lord Jesus Christ.

We feel we must be continually thanking God for you, brothers,
quite rightly, because your faith is growing so wonderfully and the
love that you have for one another never stops increasing; and among
the churches of God we can take special pride in you for your
constancy and faith under all the persecutions and troubles you have
to bear. It all shows that God's judgement is just, and the purpose of it
is that you may be found worthy of the kingdom of God; it is for the
sake of this that you are suffering now. We pray continually that our
God will, by his power, fulfil all your desires for goodness and
complete all that you have been doing through faith; because in this
way the name of our Lord Jesus Christ will be glorified in you and you
in him, by the grace of our God and the Lord Jesus Christ.

This is the word of the Lord.

Responsorial Psalm   Ps 95:1-5. ℟ v.3

℟   Proclaim his marvellous deeds to all the nations.

1   O sing a new song to the Lord,
     sing to the Lord all the earth.
     O sing to the Lord, bless his name. ℟

2   Proclaim his help day by day,
     tell among the nations his glory
     and his wonders among all the peoples. ℟

3   The Lord is great and worthy of praise,
to be feared above all gods;
the gods of the heathens are naught.   ℞

Gospel Acclamation   Jn 10:27

Alleluia, alleluia!
My sheep listen to my voice, says the Lord;
I know them, and they follow me.
Alleluia!

GOSPEL

A reading from the holy Gospel according to Matthew   23:13-22

Woe to you, blind leaders.

Jesus said: 'Alas for you, scribes and Pharisees, you hypocrites! You who shut up the kingdom of heaven in men's faces, neither going in yourselves nor allowing others to go in who want to.

'Alas for you, scribes and Pharisees, you hypocrites! You who travel over sea and land to make a single proselyte, and when you have him you make him twice as fit for hell as you are.

'Alas for you, blind guides! You who say, "If a man swears by the Temple, it has no force; but if a man swears by the gold of the Temple, he is bound." Fools and blind! For which is of greater worth, the gold or the Temple that makes the gold sacred? Or else, "If a man swears by the altar it has no force; but if a man swears by the offering that is on the altar, he is bound." You blind men! For which is of greater worth, the offering or the altar that makes the offering sacred? Therefore, when a man swears by the altar he is swearing by that and by everything on it. And when a man swears by the Temple he is swearing by that and by the One who dwells in it. And when a man swears by heaven he is swearing by the throne of God and by the One who is seated there.'

This is the Gospel of the Lord.

Tuesday

FIRST READING

A reading from the second letter of St Paul
to the Thessalonians

2:1-3. 14-17

Keep the traditions that we taught you.

To turn, brothers, to the coming of our Lord Jesus Christ and how we
shall all be gathered round him: please do not get excited too soon or
alarmed by any prediction or rumour or any letter claiming to come
from us, implying that the Day of the Lord has already arrived. Never
let anyone deceive you in this way.

Through the Good News that we brought God called you so that
you should share the glory of our Lord Jesus Christ. Stand firm, then,
brothers, and keep the traditions that we taught you, whether by
word of mouth or by letter. May our Lord Jesus Christ himself, and
God our Father who has given us his love and, through his grace,
such inexhaustible comfort and such sure hope, comfort you and
strengthen you in everything good that you do or say.

This is the word of the Lord.

Responsorial Psalm   Ps 95:10-13. ℟ v.13

℟ The Lord comes to judge the earth.

1 Proclaim to the nations: 'God is king.'
   The world he made firm in its place;
   he will judge the peoples in fairness. ℟

2 Let the heavens rejoice and earth be glad,
   let the sea and all within it thunder praise,
   let the land and all it bears rejoice,
   all the trees of the wood shout for joy
   at the presence of the Lord for he comes,
   he comes to rule the earth. ℟

3 With justice he will rule the world,
   he will judge the peoples with his truth. ℟

Gospel Acclamation   Heb 4:12

Alleluia, alleluia!
The word of God is living and active;
  it probes the thoughts and motives of our heart.
Alleluia!

GOSPEL

A reading from the holy Gospel according to Matthew   23:23-26

You should have practised these without neglecting other things.

Jesus said, 'Alas for you, scribes and Pharisees, you hypocrites! you who pay your tithe of mint and dill and cummin and have neglected the weightier matters of the Law – justice, mercy, good faith! These you should have practised, without neglecting the others. You blind guides! Straining out gnats and swallowing camels!

'Alas for you, scribes and Pharisees, you hypocrites. You who clean the outside of cup and dish and leave the inside full of extortion and imtemperance. Blind Pharisee! Clean the inside of cup and dish first so that the outside may become clean as well.'

This is the Gospel of the Lord.

Wednesday

FIRST READING

A reading from the second letter of St Paul   3:6-10. 16-18
to the Thessalonians

Whoever does not wish to work cannot eat.

In the name of the Lord Jesus Christ, we urge you, brothers, to keep away from any of the brothers who refuses to work or to live according to the tradition we passed on to you.

You know how you are supposed to imitate us: now we were not idle when we were with you, nor did we ever have our meals at anyone's table without paying for them; no, we worked night and day, slaving and straining, so as not to be a burden on any of you. This was not because we had no right to be, but in order to make ourselves an example for you to follow.

We gave you a rule when we were with you: not to let anyone

have any food if he refused to do any work.

May the Lord of peace himself give you peace all the time and in every way. The Lord be with you all.

From me, PAUL, these greetings in my own handwriting, which is the mark of genuineness in every letter; this is my own writing. May the grace of our Lord Jesus Christ be with you all.

This is the word of the Lord.

Responsorial Psalm   Ps 127:1-2. 4-5. ℟ cf. v.1

℟   Happy are those who fear the Lord.

1   O blessed are those who fear the Lord
    and walk in his ways!
    By the labour of your hands you shall eat.
    You will be happy and prosper.   ℟

2   Indeed thus shall be blessed
    the man who fears the Lord.
    May the Lord bless you from Zion
    all the days of your life!   ℟

Gospel Acclamation   1 Jn 2:5

    Alleluia, alleluia!
    Whoever keeps the word of Christ,
    grows perfect in the love of God.
    Alleluia!

GOSPEL

A reading from the holy Gospel according to Matthew   23:27-32

You are the children of those who murdered the prophets.

Jesus said, 'Alas for you, scribes and Pharisees, you hypocrites! You who are like whitewashed tombs that look handsome on the outside, but inside are full of dead men's bones and every kind of corruption. In the same way you appear to people from the outside like good honest men, but inside you are full of hypocrisy and lawlessness.

'Alas for you, scribes and Pharisees, you hypocrites! You who build the sepulchres of the prophets and decorate the tombs of holy men, saying, "We would never have joined in shedding the blood of the prophets, had we lived in our fathers' day." So! Your own evidence tells against you! You are the sons of those who murdered the prophets! Very well then, finish off the work that your fathers began.'

This is the Gospel of the Lord.

Thursday

FIRST READING

A reading from the first letter from St Paul to the Corinthians   1:1-9

You have been enriched in so many ways by Christ.

I, Paul, appointed by God to be an apostle, together with brother Sosthenes, send greetings to the church of God in Corinth, to the holy people of Jesus Christ, who are called to take their place among all the saints everywhere who pray to our Lord Jesus Christ; for he is their Lord no less than ours. May God our Father and the Lord Jesus Christ send you grace and peace.

I never stop thanking God for all the graces you have received through Jesus Christ. I thank him that you have been enriched in so many ways, especially in your teachers and preachers; the witness to Christ has indeed been strong among you so that you will not be without any of the gifts of the Spirit while you are waiting for our Lord Jesus Christ to be revealed; and he will keep you steady and without blame until the last day, the day of our Lord Jesus Christ, because God by calling you has joined you to his Son, Jesus Christ; and God is faithful.

This is the word of the Lord.

Responsorial Psalm   Ps 144:2-7. ℟ cf. v.1

℟   I will praise your name for ever, Lord.

1   I will bless you day after day
    and praise your name for ever.
    The Lord is great, highly to be praised,
    his greatness cannot be measured.   ℟

2 Age to age shall proclaim your works,
　shall declare your mighty deeds,
　shall speak of your splendour and glory,
　tell the tale of your wonderful works.

　　℟　I will praise your name for ever, Lord.

3 They will speak of your terrible deeds,
　recount your greatness and might.
　They will recall your abundant goodness;
　age to age shall ring out your justice.　℟

Gospel Acclamation

Mt 24:42. 44

Alleluia, alleluia!
Be watchful and ready:
you know not when the Son of Man is coming.
Alleluia!

GOSPEL

A reading from the holy Gospel according to Matthew　24:42-51

Stay awake and be ready.

Jesus said to his disciples: 'Stay awake, because you do not know the day when your master is coming. You may be quite sure of this, that if the householder had known at what time of the night the burglar would come, he would have stayed awake and would not have allowed anyone to break the wall of his house. Therefore, you too must stand ready because the Son of Man is coming at an hour you do not expect.

'What sort of servant, then, is faithful and wise enough for the master to place him over his household to give them their food at the proper time? Happy that servant if his master's arrival finds him at this employment. I tell you solemnly, he will place him over everything he owns. But as for the dishonest servant who says to himself, "My master is taking his time," and sets about beating his fellow servants and eating and drinking with drunkards, his master will come on a day he does not expect and at an hour he does not know. The master will cut him off and send him to the same fate as the hypocrites, where there will be weeping and grinding of teeth.'

This is the Gospel of the Lord.

Friday

FIRST READING

A reading from the first letter of St Paul
to the Corinthians   1:17-25

*We are preaching a crucified Christ, to people a scandal but to those
who have been called, the wisdom of God.*

Christ did not send me to baptise, but to preach the Good News, and
not to preach that in the terms of philosophy in which the crucifixion of
Christ cannot be expressed. The language of the cross may be illogical
to those who are not on the way to salvation, but those of us who are
on the way see it as God's power to save. As scripture says: I shall
destroy the wisdom of the wise and bring to nothing all the learning of
the learned. Where are the philosophers now? Where are the scribes?
Where are any of our thinkers today? Do you see now how God has
shown up the foolishness of human wisdom? If it was God's wisdom
that human wisdom should not know God, it was because God wanted
to save those who have faith through the foolishness of the message
that we preach. And so, while the Jews demand miracles and the
Greeks look for wisdom, here are we preaching a crucified Christ; to
the Jews an obstacle that they cannot get over, to the pagans
madness, but to those who have been called, whether they are Jews or
Greeks, a Christ who is the power and the wisdom of God. For God's
foolishness is wiser than human wisdom, and God's weakness is
stronger than human strength.

This is the word of the Lord.

Responsorial Psalm   Ps 32:1-2. 4-5. 10-11. ℟ v.5

℟   The earth is full of the goodness of the Lord.

1   Ring out your joy to the Lord, O you just;
    for praise is fitting for loyal hearts.
    Give thanks to the Lord upon the harp,
    with a ten-stringed lute sing him songs. ℟

2   For the word of the Lord is faithful
    and all his works to be trusted.
    The Lord loves justice and right
    and fills the earth with his love. ℟   (continued)

683

3   He frustrates the designs of the nations,
he defeats the plans of the peoples.
His own designs shall stand for ever,
the plans of his heart from age to age.

℟   The earth is full of the goodness of the Lord.

Gospel Acclamation   Lk 21:36

Alleluia, alleluia!
Be watchful, pray constantly,
that we may be worthy to stand before the Son of Man.
Alleluia!

GOSPEL

A reading from the holy Gospel according to Matthew   25:1-13

The bridegroom is here! Go out and meet him.

Jesus said to his disciples: 'The kingdom of heaven will be like this: Ten bridesmaids took their lamps and went to meet the bridegroom. Five of them were foolish and five were sensible: the foolish ones did take their lamps, but they brought no oil, whereas the sensible ones took flasks of oil as well as their lamps. The bridegroom was late, and they all grew drowsy and fell asleep. But at midnight there was a cry, "The bridegroom is here! Go out and meet him." At this, all those bridesmaids woke up and trimmed their lamps, and the foolish ones said to the sensible ones, "Give us some of your oil: our lamps are going out." But they replied, "There may not be enough for us and for you; you had better go to those who sell it and buy some for yourselves." They had gone off to buy it when the bridegroom arrived. Those who were ready went in with him to the wedding hall and the door was closed. The other bridesmaids arrived later. "Lord, Lord," they said, "open the door for us." But he replied, "I tell you solemnly, I do not know you." So stay awake, because you do not know either the day or the hour.'

This is the Gospel of the Lord.

Saturday

FIRST READING

A reading from the first letter of St Paul   1:26-31
to the Corinthians

God has chosen what the world would consider weak.

Take yourselves, brothers, at the time when you were called: how
many of you were wise in the ordinary sense of the word, how many
were influential people, or came from noble families? No, it was to
shame the wise that God chose what is foolish by human reckoning,
and to shame what is strong that he chose what is weak by human
reckoning; those whom the world thinks common and contemptible
are the ones that God has chosen – those who are nothing at all to
show up those who are everything. The human race has nothing to
boast about to God, but you, God has made members of Christ Jesus
and by God's doing he has become our wisdom, and our virtue, and our
holiness, and our freedom. As scripture says: if anyone wants to boast,
let him boast about the Lord.

This is the word of the Lord.

Responsorial Psalm   Ps 32:12-13. 18-21. ℟ cf. v.12

℟ Happy the people the Lord has chosen to be his own.

1   They are happy, whose God is the Lord,
    the people he has chosen as his own.
    From the heavens the Lord looks forth,
    he sees all the children of men.   ℟

2   The Lord looks on those who revere him,
    on those who hope in his love,
    to rescue their souls from death,
    to keep them alive in famine.   ℟

3   Our soul is waiting for the Lord.
    The Lord is our help and our shield.
    In him do our hearts find joy.
    We trust in his holy name.   ℟

Gospel Acclamation   Jn 13:34

> Alleluia, alleluia!
> I give you a new commandment:
> love one another as I have loved you.
> Alleluia!

GOSPEL

A reading from the holy Gospel according to Matthew   25:14-30

You have been faithful in small things, enter into the joy of your Master.

Jesus told his disciples this parable: 'A man on his way abroad summoned his servants and entrusted his property to them. To one he gave five talents, to another two, to a third one; each in proportion to his ability. Then he set out. The man who had received the five talents promptly went and traded with them and made five more. The man who had received two made two more in the same way. But the man who had received one went off and dug a hole in the ground and hid his master's money. Now a long time after, the master of those servants came back and went through his accounts with them. The man who had received the five talents came forward bringing five more. "Sir," he said "you entrusted me with five talents; here are five more that I have made." His master said to him, "Well done, good and faithful servant; you have shown you can be faithful in small things, I will trust you with greater; come and join in your master's happiness." Next the man with the two talents came forward. "Sir," he said "you entrusted me with two talents; here are two more that I have made." His master said to him, "Well done, good and faithful servant; you have shown you can be faithful in small things, I will trust you with greater; come and join in your master's happiness." Last came forward the man who had the one talent. "Sir," said he "I have heard you were a hard man, reaping where you have not sown and gathering where you have not scattered; so I was afraid, and I went off and hid your talent in the ground. Here it is; it was yours, you have it back." But his master answered him, "You wicked and lazy servant! So you knew that I reap where I have not sown and gather where I have not scattered? Well then, you should have deposited my money with the bankers, and on my return I would have recovered my capital with interest. So now, take the talent from him and give it to the man who has the five talents. For to everyone who has will be given more, and he will have more than enough; but from the man who has not, even what he has will be taken away. As for this good-for-nothing servant, throw him out into the dark, where there will be weeping and grinding of teeth." '

This is the Gospel of the Lord.

TWENTY-SECOND WEEK IN ORDINARY TIME
Year II

Monday

FIRST READING

A reading from the first letter of St Paul   2:1-5
to the Corinthians

I have announced to you the knowledge of Christ crucified.

Brothers, when I came to you, it was not with any show of oratory or philosophy, but simply to tell you what God had guaranteed. During my stay with you, the only knowledge I claimed to have was about Jesus, and only about him as the crucified Christ. Far from relying on any power of my own, I came among you in great 'fear and trembling' and in my speeches and the sermons that I gave, there were none of the arguments that belong to philosophy; only a demonstration of the power of the Spirit. And I did this so that your faith should not depend on human philosophy but on the power of God.

This is the word of the Lord.

Responsorial Psalm   Ps 118:97-102. ℟ v.97

℟   Lord, I love your commands.

1 Lord, how I love your law!
   It is ever in my mind.
   Your command makes me wiser than my foes;
   for it is mine for ever.   ℟

2   I have more insight than all who teach me
for I ponder your will.
I have more understanding than the old
for I keep your precepts.

℞   Lord, I love your commands.

3   I turn my feet from evil paths
to obey your word.
I have not turned away from your decrees;
you yourself have taught me. ℞

Gospel Acclamation

cf. Lk 4:18

Alleluia, alleluia!
The Spirit of the Lord is upon me;
he sent me to bring Good News to the poor.
Alleluia!

GOSPEL

A reading from the holy Gospel according to Luke   4:16-30

*He has sent me to bring the Good News to the poor. No prophet is
ever accepted in his own country.*

Jesus came to Nazara, where he had been brought up, and went into
the synagogue on the sabbath day as he usually did. He stood up to
read, and they handed him the scroll of the prophet Isaiah. Unrolling
the scroll he found the place where it is written:

The spirit of the Lord has been given to me,
for he has anointed me.
He has sent me to bring the good news to the poor,
to proclaim liberty to captives
and to the blind new sight,
to set the downtrodden free,
to proclaim the Lord's year of favour.

He then rolled up the scroll, gave it back to the assistant and sat
down. And all eyes in the synagogue were fixed on him. Then he
began to speak to them, 'This text is being fulfilled today even as you
listen.' And he won the approval of all, and they were astonished by
the gracious words that came from his lips.

They said, 'This is Joseph's son, surely?' But he replied, 'No doubt you will quote me the saying, "Physician, heal yourself" and tell me, "We have heard all that happened in Capernaum, do the same here in your own countryside." ' And he went on, 'I tell you solemnly, no prophet is ever accepted in his own country.

'There were many widows in Israel, I can assure you, in Elijah's day, when heaven remained shut for three years and six months and a great famine raged throughout the land, but Elijah was not sent to any one of these: he was sent to a widow at Zarephath, a Sidonian town. And in the prophet Elisha's time there were many lepers in Israel, but none of these was cured, except the Syrian, Naaman.'

When they heard this everyone in the synagogue was enraged. They sprang to their feet and hustled him out of the town; and they took him up to the brow of the hill their town was built on, intending to throw him down the cliff, but he slipped through the crowd and walked away.

This is the Gospel of the Lord.

Tuesday

FIRST READING

A reading from the first letter of St Paul to the Corinthians   2:10-16

The unspiritual person does not receive the gifts of God; the spiritual person judges all things.

The Spirit reaches the depths of everything, even the depths of God. After all, the depths of a man can only be known by his own spirit, not by any other man, and in the same way the depths of God can only be known by the Spirit of God. Now instead of the spirit of the world, we have received the Spirit that comes from God, to teach us to understand the gifts that he has given us. Therefore we teach, not in the way in which philosophy is taught, but in the way that the Spirit teaches us: we teach spiritual things spiritually. An unspiritual person is one who does not accept anything of the Spirit of God: he sees it all as nonsense; it is beyond his understanding because it can only be understood by means of the Spirit. A spiritual man, on the other hand, is able to judge the value of everything, and his own value is not to be judged by other men. As scripture says: Who can know the mind of the Lord, so who can teach him? But we are those who have the mind of Christ.

This is the word of the Lord.

Responsorial Psalm

Ps 144:8-14. ℟ v.17

℟ The Lord is just in all his ways.

1 The Lord is kind and full of compassion,
   slow to anger, abounding in love.
   How good is the Lord to all,
   compassionate to all his creatures.   ℟

2 All your creaures shall thank you, O Lord,
   and your friends shall repeat their blessing.
   They shall speak of the glory of your reign
   and declare your might, O God,
   to make known to men your mighty deeds
   and the glorious splendour of your reign.   ℟

3 Yours is an everlasting kingdom;
   your rule lasts from age to age.
   The Lord is faithful in all his words
   and loving in all his deeds.
   The Lord supports all who fall
   and raises all who are bowed down.   ℟

Gospel Acclamation

Lk 7:16

Alleluia, alleluia!
A great prophet has appeared among us;
God has visited his people.
Alleluia!

GOSPEL

A reading from the holy Gospel according to Luke   4:31-37

I know who you are: the Holy One of God.

Jesus went down to Capernaum, a town in Galilee, and taught them on the sabbath. And his teaching made a deep impression on them because he spoke with authority.

In the synagogue there was a man who was possessed by the spirit of an unclean devil, and it shouted at the top of its voice, 'Ha! What do you want with us, Jesus of Nazareth? Have you come to destroy us? I know who you are: the Holy One of God.' But Jesus said sharply, 'Be quiet! Come out of him!' And the devil, throwing the man down in front of everyone, went out of him without hurting him at all. Astonishment seized them and they were all saying to one another, 'What teaching! He gives orders to unclean spirits with authority and power and they come out.' And reports of him went all through the surrounding countryside.

This is the Gospel of the Lord.

Wednesday

FIRST READING

A reading from the first letter of St Paul   3:1-9
to the Corinthians

We are fellow workers with God; you are God's farm, God's building.

Brothers, I myself was unable to speak to you as people of the Spirit: I treated you as sensual men, still infants in Christ. What I fed you with was milk, not solid food, for you were not ready for it; and indeed, you are still not ready for it since you are still un-spiritual. Isn't that obvious from all the jealousy and wrangling that there is among you, from the way that you go on behaving like ordinary people? What could be more unspiritual than your slogans, 'I am for Paul' and 'I am for Apollos'?

After all, what is Apollos and what is Paul? They are servants who brought the faith to you. Even the different ways in which they brought it were assigned to them by the Lord. I did the planting, Apollos did the watering, but God made things grow. Neither the planter nor the waterer matters: only God, who makes things grow. It is all one who does the planting and who does the watering, and each will duly be paid according to his share in the work. We are fellow workers with God; you are God's farm, God's building.

This is the word of the Lord.

Responsorial Psalm   Ps 32:12-15. 20-21. ℟ v.12

℟   Happy the people the Lord has chosen to be his own.

1   They are happy, whose God is the Lord,
     the people he has chosen as his own.
     From the heavens the Lord looks forth,
     he sees all the children of men. ℟

2   From the place where he dwells he gazes
     on all the dwellers on the earth,
     he who shapes the hearts of them all
     and considers all their deeds. ℟

3   Our soul is waiting for the Lord.
     The Lord is our help and our shield.
     In him do our hearts find joy.
     We trust in his holy name. ℟

Gospel Acclamation   Lk 4:18

     Alleluia, alleluia!
     The Lord sent me to bring Good News to the poor
     and freedom to prisoners.
     Alleluia!

GOSPEL

A reading from the holy Gospel according to Luke   4:38-44

*I must preach the Good News to other towns as well, because this
is what I was sent to do.*

Leaving the synagogue Jesus went to Simon's house. Now Simon's
mother-in-law was suffering from a high fever and they asked him to
do something for her. Leaning over her he rebuked the fever and it left
her. And she immediately got up and began to wait on them.

    At sunset all those who had friends suffering from diseases of one
kind or another brought them to him, and laying his hands on each he
cured them. Devils too came out of many people, howling, 'You are the
Son of God.' But he rebuked them and would not allow them to speak
because they knew that he was the Christ.

    When daylight came he left the house and made his way to a

lonely place. The crowds went to look for him, and when they had caught up with him they wanted to prevent him leaving them, but he answered, 'I must proclaim the Good News of the kingdom of God to the other towns too, because that is what I was sent to do.' And he continued his preaching in the synagogues of Judaea.

This is the Gospel of the Lord.

Thursday

FIRST READING

A reading from the first letter of St Paul to the Corinthians
3:18-23

All things are yours, but you belong to Christ and Christ belongs to God.

Make no mistake about it: if any one of you thinks of himself as wise, in the ordinary sense of the word, then he must learn to be a fool before he really can be wise. Why? Because the wisdom of this world is foolishness to God. As scripture says: The Lord knows wise men's thoughts: he knows how useless they are: or again: God is not convinced by the arguments of the wise. So there is nothing to boast about in anything human: Paul, Apollos, Cephas, the world, life and death, the present and the future, are all your servants; but you belong to Christ and Christ belongs to God.

This is the word of the Lord.

Responsorial Psalm
Ps 23:1-6. ℟ v.1

℟ To the Lord belongs the earth and all that fills it.

1 The Lord's is the earth and its fullness,
   the world and all its peoples.
   It is he who set it on the seas;
   on the waters he made it firm. ℟

2 Who shall climb the mountain of the Lord?
   Who shall stand in his holy place?
   The man with clean hands and pure heart,
   who desires not worthless things. ℟

(continued)

3   He shall receive blessings from the Lord
    and reward from the God who saves him.
    Such are the men who seek him,
    seek the face of the God of Jacob.

    ℟   To the Lord belongs the earth and all that fills it.

Gospel Acclamation   Mt 4:19

    Alleluia, alleluia!
    Come follow me, says the Lord,
    and I will make you fishers of my people.
    Alleluia!

GOSPEL

A reading from the holy Gospel according to Luke   5:1-11
They left everything and followed him.

Jesus was standing one day by the Lake of Gennesaret, with the
crowd pressing round him listening to the word of God, when he
caught sight of two boats close to the bank. The fishermen had gone
out of them and were washing their nets. He got into one of the boats –
it was Simon's – and asked him to put out a little from the shore. Then
he sat down and taught the crowds from the boat.

    When he had finished speaking he said to Simon, 'Put out into
deep water and pay out your nets for a catch.' 'Master,' Simon replied
'we worked hard all night long and caught nothing but if you say so, I
will pay out the nets.' And when they had done this they netted such a
huge number of fish that their nets began to tear, so they signalled to
their companions in the other boat to come and help them; when these
came, they filled the two boats to sinking point.

    When Simon Peter saw this he fell at the knees of Jesus saying,
'Leave me, Lord; I am a sinful man.' For he and all his companions
were completely overcome by the catch they had made; so also were
James and John, sons of Zebedee, who were Simon's partners. But
Jesus said to Simon, 'Do not be afraid; from now on it is men you will
catch.' Then, bringing their boats back to land, they left everything
and followed him.

    This is the Gospel of the Lord.

Friday

FIRST READING

A reading from the first letter of St Paul
to the Corinthians

4:1-5

The Lord will reveal the intentions of our hearts.

People must think of us as Christ's servants, stewards entrusted with the mysteries of God. What is expected of stewards is that each one should be found worthy of his trust. Not that it makes the slightest difference to me whether you, or indeed any human tribunal, find me worthy or not. I will not even pass judgement on myself. True, my conscience does not reproach me at all, but that does not prove that I am acquitted: the Lord alone is my judge. There must be no passing of premature judgement. Leave that until the Lord comes: he will light up all that is hidden in the dark and reveal the secret intentions of men's hearts. Then will be the time for each one to have whatever praise he deserves, from God.

This is the word of the Lord.

Responsorial Psalm   Ps 36:3-6. 27-28. 39-40. ℟ v.39

℟   The salvation of the just comes from the Lord.

1   If you trust in the Lord and do good,
    then you will live in the land and be secure.
    If you find your delight in the Lord,
    he will grant your heart's desire.   ℟

2   Commit your life to the Lord,
    trust in him and he will act,
    so that your justice breaks forth like the light,
    your cause like the noon-day sun.   ℟

3   Then turn away from evil and do good
    and you shall have a home for ever;
    for the Lord loves justice
    and will never forsake his friends.   ℟

4   The salvation of the just comes from the Lord,
    their stronghold in time of distress.
    The Lord helps them and delivers them
    and saves them: for their refuge is in him.   ℟

Gospel Acclamation   Jn 8:12

Alleluia, alleluia!
I am the light of the world, says the Lord;
whoever follows me will have the light of life.
Alleluia!

GOSPEL

A reading from the holy Gospel according to Luke   5:33-39

When the bridegroom is taken away from them, then they will fast.

The Pharisees and the scribes said to Jesus, 'John's disciples are always fasting and saying prayers, and the disciples of the Pharisees too, but yours go on eating and drinking.' Jesus replied, 'Surely you cannot make the bridegrooms' attendants fast while the bridegroom is still with them? But the time will come, the time for the bridegroom to be taken away from them; that will be the time when they will fast.'

He also told them this parable, 'No one tears a piece from a new cloak to put it on an old cloak; if he does, not only will he have torn the new one, but the piece taken from the new will not match the old.

'And nobody puts new wine into old skins; if he does, the new wine will burst the skins and then run out, and the skins will be lost. No; new wine must be put into fresh skins. And nobody who has been drinking old wine wants new. "The old is good" he says.'

This is the Gospel of the Lord.

Saturday

FIRST READING

A reading from the first letter of St Paul   4:6-15
to the Corinthians

We hunger and thirst and are naked.

Take Apollos and myself as an example and remember the maxim, 'Keep to what is written'; it is not for you, so full of your own importance, to go taking sides for one man against another. In any case, brother, has anybody given you some special right? What do you have that was not given to you? And if it was given, how can you boast as though it were not? Is it that you have everything that you want – that you are rich already, in possession of your kingdom, with us left outside? Indeed I wish you were really kings, and we could be kings with you! But instead, it seems to me, God has put us apostles at the end of his parade, with the men sentenced to death; it is true – we have been put on show in front of the whole universe, angels as well as men. Here we are, fools for the sake of Christ, while you are the learned men in Christ; we have no power, but you are influential; you are celebrities, we are nobodies. To this day, we go without food and drink and clothes; we are beaten and have no homes; we work for our living with our own hands. When we are cursed, we answer with a blessing; when we are hounded, we put up with it; we are insulted and we answer politely. We are treated as the offal of the world, still to this day, the scum of the earth.

I am saying all this not just to make you ashamed but to bring you, as my dearest children, to your senses. You might have thousands of guardians in Christ, but no more than one father and it was I who begot you in Christ Jesus by preaching the Good News.

This is the word of the Lord.

Responsorial Psalm   Ps 144:17-21. ℟ v.18

℟   The Lord is near to all who call him.

1   The Lord is just in all his ways
     and loving in all his deeds.
     He is close to all who call him,
     who call on him from their hearts.   ℟

2   He grants the desires of those who fear him,
     he hears their cry and he saves them.
     The Lord protects all who love him;
     but the wicked he will utterly destroy.   ℟

3   Let me speak the praise of the Lord,
     let all mankind bless his holy name
     for ever, for ages unending.   ℟

Gospel Acclamation

Jn 14:6

Alleluia, alleluia!
I am the way, the truth, and the life, says the Lord;
no one comes to the Father, except through me.
Alleluia!

GOSPEL

A reading from the holy Gospel according to Luke   6:1-5

Why are you doing something that is forbidden on the sabbath?

One sabbath Jesus happened to be taking a walk through the cornfields, and his disciples were picking ears of corn, rubbing them in their hands and eating them. Some of the Pharisees said, 'Why are you doing something that is forbidden on the sabbath day?' Jesus answered them, 'So you have not read what David did when he and his followers were hungry – how he went into the House of God, took the loaves of offering and ate them and gave them to his followers, loaves which only the priests are allowed to eat?' And he said to them, 'The Son of Man is master of the sabbath.'

This is the Gospel of the Lord.

TWENTY-THIRD WEEK IN ORDINARY TIME
Year II

Monday

FIRST READING

A reading from the first letter of St Paul
to the Corinthians   5:1-8

Get rid of the old yeast, Christ our passover has been sacrificed.

I have been told as an undoubted fact that one of you is living with his father's wife. This is a case of sexual immorality among you that must be unparalleled even among pagans. How can you be so proud of yourselves? You should be in mourning. A man who does a thing like that ought to have been expelled from the community. Though I am far away in body, I am with you in spirit, and have already condemned the man who did this thing as if I were actually present. When you are assembled together in the name of the Lord Jesus, and I am spiritually present with you, then with the power of our Lord Jesus he is to be handed over to Satan so that his sensual body may be destroyed and his spirit saved on the day of the Lord.

The pride that you take in yourselves is hardly to your credit. You must know how even a small amount of yeast is enough to leaven all the dough, so get rid of all the old yeast, and make yourselves into a completely new batch of bread, unleavened as you are meant to be. Christ, our passover, has been sacrificed; let us celebrate the feast, then, by getting rid of all the old yeast of evil and wickedness, having only the unleavened bread of sincerity and truth.

This is the word of the Lord.

Responsorial Psalm   Ps 5:5-7. 12. ℟ v.9

℟   Lead me in your justice, Lord.

1   You are no God who loves evil;
    no sinner is your guest.
    The boastful shall not stand their ground
    before your face.   ℟

2   You hate all who do evil:
    you destroy all who lie.
    The deceitful and bloodthirsty man
    the Lord detests.   ℟

3   All those you protect shall be glad
    and ring out their joy.
    You shelter them; in you they rejoice,
    those who love your name.   ℟

Gospel Acclamation   Jn 10:27

Alleluia, alleluia!
My sheep listen to my voice, says the Lord;
I know them, and they follow me.
Alleluia!

GOSPEL

A reading from the holy Gospel according to Luke   6:6-11

They watched him to see if he would cure a man on the sabbath.

On the sabbath Jesus went into the synagogue and began to teach, and a man was there whose right hand was withered. The scribes and the Pharisees were watching him to see if he would cure a man on the sabbath, hoping to find something to use against him. But he knew their thoughts; and he said to the man with the withered hand, 'Stand up! Come out into the middle.' And he came out and stood there. Then Jesus said to them, 'I put it to you: is it against the law on the sabbath to do good, or to do evil; to save life, or to destroy it?' Then he looked round at them all and said to the man, 'Stretch out your hand.' He did so, and his hand was better. But they were furious, and began to discuss the best way of dealing with Jesus.

This is the Gospel of the Lord.

Tuesday

FIRST READING

A reading from the first letter of St Paul   6:1-11
to the Corinthians

One believer contests another in front of unbelievers.

How dare one of your members take up a complaint against another in the lawcourts of the unjust instead of before the saints? As you know, it is the saints who are to 'judge the world'; and if the world is to be judged by you, how can you be unfit to judge trifling cases? Since we are also to judge angels, it follows that we can judge matters of everyday life; but when you have had cases of that kind, the people you appointed to try them were not even respected in the Church. You should be ashamed: is there really not one reliable man among you to settle differences between brothers and so one brother brings a court case against another in front of unbelievers? It is bad enough for you to have lawsuits at all against one another: oughtn't you to let yourselves be wronged, and let yourselves be cheated? But you are doing the wronging and the cheating, and to your own brothers.

You know perfectly well that people who do wrong will not inherit the kingdom of God: people of immoral lives, idolators, adulterers, catamites, sodomites, thieves, usurers, drunkards, slanderers and swindlers will never inherit the kingdom of God. These are the sort of people some of you were once, but now you have been washed clean, and sanctified, and justified through the name of the Lord Jesus Christ and through the Spirit of our God.

This is the word of the Lord.

Responsorial Psalm   Ps 149:1-6. 9. ℟ v.4

℟   The Lord takes delight in his people.

or

℟   Alleluia!

1   Sing a new song to the Lord,
    his praise in the assembly of the faithful.
    Let Israel rejoice in its Maker,
    let Zion's sons exult in their king.   ℟

2   Let them praise his name with dancing
    and make music with timbrel and harp.
    For the Lord takes delight in his people.
    He crowns the poor with salvation.   ℟

3   Let the faithful rejoice in their glory,
    shout for joy and take their rest.
    Let the praise of God be on their lips:
    this honour·is for all his faithful.   ℟

Gospel Acclamation   cf. Jn 15:16

Alleluia, alleluia!
I have chosen you from the world, says the Lord,
to go and bear fruit that will last.
Alleluia!

GOSPEL

A reading from the holy Gospel according to Luke   6:12-19

He spent the night in prayer. He chose twelve from his disciples
and called them Apostles.

Jesus went out into the hills to pray; and he spent the whole night in
prayer to God. When day came he summoned his disciples and picked
out twelve of them; he called them 'apostles': Simon whom he called
Peter, and his brother Andrew; James, John, Philip, Bartholomew,
Matthew, Thomas, James son of Alphaeus, Simon called the Zealot,
Judas son of James, and Judas Iscariot who became a traitor.

He then came down with them and stopped at a piece of level
ground where there was a large gathering of his disciples with a great
crowd of people from all parts of Judaea and from Jerusalem and from
the coastal region of Tyre and Sidon who had come to hear him and to
be cured of their diseases. People tormented by unclean spirits were
also cured, and everyone in the crowd was trying to touch him because
power came out of him that cured them all.

This is the Gospel of the Lord.

Wednesday

FIRST READING

A reading from the first letter of St Paul   7:25-31
to the Corinthians

Are you bound to a wife? Do not seek to be free. Are you free from
a wife? Do not seek marriage.

About remaining celibate, I have no directions from the Lord but give
my own opinion as one who, by the Lord's mercy, has stayed faithful.
Well then, I believe that in these present times of stress this is right:
that it is good for a man to stay as he is. If you are tied to a wife, do not
look for freedom; if you are free of a wife, then do not look for one. But
if you marry, it is no sin, and it is not a sin for a young girl to get
married. They will have their troubles, though, in their married life,
and I should like to spare you that.

Brothers, this is what I mean: our time is growing short. Those
who have wives should live as though they had none, and those who
mourn should live as though they had nothing to mourn for; those who

are enjoying life should live as though there were nothing to laugh about; those whose life is buying things should live as though they had nothing of their own; and those who have to deal with the world should not become engrossed in it. I say this because the world as we know it is passing away.

This is the word of the Lord.

Responsorial Psalm   Ps 44:11-12. 14-17. ℟ v.11

℟   Listen to me, daughter;
     see and bend your ear.

1   Listen, O daughter, give ear to my words:
     forget your own people and your father's house.
     So will the king desire your beauty:
     He is your lord, pay homage to him. ℟

2   The daughter of the king is clothed with splendour,
     her robes embroidered with pearls set in gold.
     She is led to the king with her maiden companions. ℟

3   They are escorted amid gladness and joy;
     they pass within the palace of the king.
     Sons shall be yours in place of your fathers;
     you will make them princes over all the earth. ℟

Gospel Acclamation   Lk 6:23

     Alleluia, alleluia!
     Rejoice and be glad;
     your reward will be great in heaven.
     Alleluia!

GOSPEL

A reading from the holy Gospel according to Luke   6:20-26

Happy are the poor. Woe to you who are rich.

Fixing his eyes on his disciples Jesus said:

'How happy are you who are poor: yours is the kingdom of God.
Happy you who are hungry now: you shall be satisfied.
Happy you who weep now: you shall laugh.

'Happy are you when people hate you, drive you out, abuse you, denounce your name as criminal, on account of the Son of Man. Rejoice when that day comes and dance for joy, for then your reward will be great in heaven. This was the way their ancestors treated the prophets.

'But alas for you who are rich: you are having your consolation now.
Alas for you who have your fill now: you shall go hungry.
Alas for you who laugh now: you shall mourn and weep.

'Alas for you when the world speaks well of you! This was the way their ancestors treated the false prophets.'

This is the Gospel of the Lord.

Thursday

FIRST READING

A reading from the first letter of St Paul   8:1-7. 11-13
to the Corinthians

By sinning against the weak, you have sinned against Christ.

'We all have knowledge'; yes, that is so, but knowledge gives self-importance – it is love that makes the building grow. A man may imagine he understands something, but still not understand anything in the way that he ought to. But any man who loves God is known by him. Well then, about eating food sacrificed to idols: we know that idols do not really exist in the world and that there is no god but the One. And even if there were things called gods, either in the sky or on earth – where there certainly seem to be 'gods' and 'lords' in plenty – still for us there is one God, the Father, from whom all things come and for whom we exist; and there is one Lord, Jesus Christ, through whom all things come and through whom we exist.

Some people, however, do not have this knowledge. There are some who have been so long used to idols that they eat this food as though it really had been sacrificed to the idol, and their conscience, being weak, is defiled by it. In this way your knowledge could become the ruin of someone weak, of a brother for whom Christ died. By sinning in this way against your brothers, and injuring their weak consciences, it would be Christ against whom you sinned. That is why, since food can be the occasion of my brother's downfall, I shall never eat meat again in case I am the cause of a brother's downfall.

This is the word of the Lord.

Responsorial Psalm   Ps 138:1-3. 13-14. 23-24. ℟ v.24

℟   Guide me, Lord, along the everlasting way.

1   O Lord, you search me and you know me,
      you know my resting and my rising,
      you discern my purpose from afar.
      You mark when I walk or lie down,
      all my ways lie open to you.   ℟

2   For it was you who created my being,
      knit me together in my mother's womb.
      I thank you for the wonder of my being,
      for the wonders of all your creation.   ℟

3   O search me, God, and know my heart.
      O test me and know my thoughts.
      See that I follow not the wrong path
      and lead me in the path of life eternal.   ℟

Gospel Acclamation   1 Jn 4:12

      Alleluia, alleluia!
      If we love one another,
      God will live in us in perfect love.
      Alleluia!

GOSPEL

A reading from the holy Gospel according to Luke   6:27-38

Be merciful, as your Father is merciful.

Jesus said to his disciples: 'I say this to you who are listening: Love your enemies, do good to those who hate you, bless those who curse you, pray for those who treat you badly. To the man who slaps you on one cheek, present the other cheek too; to the man who takes your cloak from you, do not refuse your tunic. Give to everyone who asks you, and do not ask for your property back from the man who robs you.

Treat others as you would like them to treat you. If you love those who love you, what thanks can you expect? Even sinners love those who love them. And if you do good to those who do good to you, what thanks can you expect? For even sinners do that much. And if you lend to those from whom you hope to receive, what thanks can you expect? Even sinners lend to sinners to get back the same amount. Instead, love your enemies and do good, and lend without any hope of return. You will have a great reward, and you will be sons of the Most High, for he himself is kind to the ungrateful and the wicked.

'Be compassionate as your Father is compassionate. Do not judge, and you will not be judged yourselves; do not condemn, and you will not be condemned yourselves; grant pardon, and you will be pardoned. Give, and there will be gifts for you: a full measure, pressed down, shaken together, and running over, will be poured into your lap; because the amount you measure out is the amount you will be given back.'

This is the Gospel of the Lord.

Friday

FIRST READING

A reading from the first letter of St Paul to the Corinthians
9:16-19. 22-27

I made myself all things to all people, to save some at any cost.

I do not boast of preaching the gospel, since it is a duty which has been laid on me; I should be punished if I did not preach it! If I had chosen this work myself, I might have been paid for it, but as I have not, it is a responsibility which has been put into my hands. Do you know what my reward is? It is this: in my preaching, to be able to offer the Good News free, and not insist on the rights which the gospel gives me.

So though I am not a slave of any man I have made myself the slave of everyone so as to win as many as I could. I made myself all things to all men in order to save some at any cost; and I still do this, for the sake of the gospel, to have a share in its blessing.

All the runners at the stadium are trying to win, but only one of them gets the prize. You must run in the same way, meaning to win. All the fighters at the games go into strict training; they do this just to win a wreath that will wither away, but we do it for a wreath that will never wither. That is how I run, intent on winning; that is how I fight, not beating the air. I treat my body hard and make it obey me, for, having been an announcer myself, I should not want to be disqualified.

This is the word of the Lord.

Responsorial Psalm Ps 83:3-6. 12. ℟ v.2

℟ How lovely is your dwelling-place,
   Lord, mighty God!

1 My soul is longing and yearning,
   is yearning for the courts of the Lord.
   My heart and my soul ring out their joy
   to God, the living God. ℟

2 The sparrow herself finds a home
   and the swallow a nest for her brood;
   she lays her young by your altars,
   Lord of hosts, my king and my God. ℟

3 They are happy, who dwell in your house,
   for ever singing your praise.
   They are happy, whose strength is in you,
   in whose hearts are the roads to Zion. ℟

4 For the Lord God is a rampart, a shield;
   he will give us his favour and glory.
   The Lord will not refuse any good
   to those who walk without blame. ℟

Gospel Acclamation cf. Jn 17:17

Alleluia, alleluia!
Your word, O Lord, is truth:
make us holy in the truth.
Alleluia!

GOSPEL

A reading from the holy Gospel according to Luke   6:39-42

Can the blind lead the blind?

Jesus told a parable to the disciples, 'Can one blind man guide another? Surely both will fall into a pit? The disciple is not superior to his teacher; the fully trained disciple will always be like his teacher. Why do you observe the splinter in your brother's eye and never notice the plank in your own? How can you say to your brother, "Brother, let me take out the splinter that is in your eye," when you cannot see the plank in your own? Hypocrite! Take the plank out of your own eye first, and then you will see clearly enough to take out the splinter that is in your brother's eye.'

This is the Gospel of the Lord.

Saturday

FIRST READING

A reading from the first letter of St Paul   10:14-22
to the Corinthians

Though there are many of us, we are one body, because we share in
this one bread.

My dear brothers, you must keep clear of idolatry. I say to you as sensible people: judge for yourselves what I am saying. The blessing-cup that we bless is a communion with the blood of Christ, and the bread that we break is a communion with the body of Christ. The fact that there is only one loaf means that, though there are many of us, we form a single body because we all have a share in this one loaf. Look at the other Israel, the race, where those who eat the sacrifices are in communion with the altar. Does this mean that the food sacrificed to idols has a real value, or that the idol itself is real? Not at all. It simply means that the sacrifices that they offer they sacrifice to demons who are not God. I have no desire to see you in communion with demons. You cannot drink the cup of the Lord and the cup of demons. You cannot take your share at the table of the Lord and at the table of demons. Do we want to make the Lord angry; are we stronger than he is?

This is the word of the Lord.

Responsorial Psalm   Ps 115:12-13. 17-18. ℞ v.17

℞   To you, Lord, I will offer a sacrifice of praise.

1   How can I repay the Lord
     for his goodness to me?
     The cup of salvation I will raise;
     I will call on the Lord's name.   ℞

2   A thanksgiving sacrifice I make:
     I will call on the Lord's name.
     My vows to the Lord I will fulfil
     before all his people.   ℞

Gospel Acclamation   Jn 14:23

     Alleluia, alleluia!
     All who love me will keep my words,
     and my Father will love them, and we will come to them.
     Alleluia!

GOSPEL

A reading from the holy Gospel according to Luke   6:43-49

Why do you call me, 'Lord, Lord' and not do what I say?

Jesus said to his disciples: 'There is no sound tree that produces rotten fruit, nor again a rotten tree that produces sound fruit. For every tree can be told by its own fruit: people do not pick figs from thorns, nor gather grapes from brambles. A good man draws what is good from the store of goodness in his heart; a bad man draws what is bad from the store of badness. For a man's words flow out of what fills his heart.

'Why do you call me, "Lord, Lord" and not do what I say?

'Everyone who comes to me and listens to my words and acts on them – I will show you what he is like. He is like the man who when he built his house dug, and dug deep, and laid the foundations on rock; when the river was in flood it bore down on that house but could not shake it, it was so well built. But the one who listens and does nothing is like the man who built his house on soil, with no foundations: as soon as the river bore down on it, it collapsed; and what a ruin that house became!'

     This is the Gospel of the Lord.

TWENTY-FOURTH WEEK IN ORDINARY TIME

Year II

Monday

FIRST READING

A reading from the first letter of St Paul
to the Corinthians

11:17-26. 33

If there are factions among you, it is not the Lord's supper that you eat.

On the subject of instructions, I cannot say that you have done well in holding meetings that do you more harm than good. In the first place, I hear that when you all come together as a community, there are separate factions among you, and I half believe it – since there must no doubt be separate groups among you, to distinguish those who are to be trusted. The point is, when you hold these meetings, it is not the Lord's Supper that you are eating, since when the time comes to eat, everyone is in such a hurry to start his own supper that one person goes hungry while another is getting drunk. Surely you have homes for eating and drinking in? Surely you have enough respect for the community of God not to make poor people embarrassed? What am I to say to you? Congratulate you? I cannot congratulate you on this.

For this is what I received from the Lord, and in turn passed on to you: that on the same night that he was betrayed, the Lord Jesus took some bread, and thanked God for it and broke it, and he said, 'This is my body, which is for you; do this as a memorial of me.' In the same way he took the cup after supper, and said, 'This cup is the new covenant in my blood. Whenever you drink it, do this as a memorial of me.' Until the Lord comes, therefore, every time you eat this bread and drink this cup, you are proclaiming his death.

So to sum up, my dear brothers, when you meet for the Meal, wait for one another.

This is the word of the Lord.

Responsorial Psalm   Ps 39:7-10. 17. ℟ 1 Cor 11:26

  ℟ Proclaim the death of the Lord
     until he comes again.

1 You do not ask for sacrifice and offerings,
   but an open ear.
   You do not ask for holocaust and victim.
   Instead, here am I.   ℟

2 In the scroll of the book it stands written
   that I should do your will.
   My God, I delight in your law
   in the depth of my heart.   ℟

3 Your justice I have proclaimed
   in the great assembly.
   My lips I have not sealed;
   you know it, O Lord.   ℟

4 O let there be rejoicing and gladness
   for all who seek you.
   Let them ever say: 'The Lord is great,'
   who love your saving help.   ℟

Gospel Acclamation   Jn 3:16

   Alleluia, alleluia!
   God loved the world so much, he gave us his only Son,
   that all who believe in him might have eternal life.
   Alleluia!

GOSPEL

A reading from the holy Gospel according to Luke   7:1-10

Not even in Israel have I found such faith.

When Jesus had come to the end of all he wanted the people to hear, he went into Capernaum. A centurion there had a servant, a favourite of his, who was sick and near death. Having heard about Jesus he sent some Jewish elders to him to ask him to come and heal his servant. When they came to Jesus they pleaded earnestly with him. 'He deserves this of you' they said 'because he is friendly towards our people; in fact, he is the one who built the synagogue.' So Jesus went with them, and was not very far from the house when the centurion sent word to him by some friends: 'Sir,' he said 'do not put yourself to trouble; because I am not worthy to have you under my roof; and for this same reason I did not presume to come to you myself; but give the word and let my servant be cured. For I am under authority myself, and have soldiers under me; and I say to one man: Go, and he goes; to another: Come here, and he comes; to my servant: Do this, and he does it.' When Jesus heard these words he was astonished at him and, turning round, said to the crowd following him, 'I tell you, not even in Israel have I found faith like this.' And when the messengers got back to the house they found the servant in perfect health.

This is the Gospel of the Lord.

Tuesday

FIRST READING

A reading from the first letter of St Paul   12:12-14. 27-31
to the Corinthians

Now you together are Christ's body, but each of you is a different part of it.

Just as a human body, though it is made up of many parts, is a single unit because all these parts, though many, make one body, so it is with Christ. In the one Spirit we were all baptised, Jews as well as Greeks, slaves as well as citizens, and one Spirit was given to us all to drink.

Nor is the body to be identified with any one of its many parts. Now you together are Christ's body; but each of you is a different part of it. In the Church, God has given the first place to apostles, the second to prophets, the third to teachers; after them, miracles, and after them the gift of healing; helpers, good leaders, those with many languages. Are all of them apostles, or all of them prophets, or all of them teachers? Do they all have the gift of miracles, or all have the gift of healing? Do all speak strange languages, and all interpret them? Be ambitious for the higher gifts.

This is the word of the Lord.

Responsorial Psalm   Ps 99. ℟ v.3

℟   We are his people:
    the sheep of his flock.

1   Cry out with joy to the Lord, all the earth.
    Serve the Lord with gladness.
    Come before him, singing for joy.   ℟

2   Know that he, the Lord, is God.
    He made us, we belong to him,
    we are his people, the sheep of his flock.   ℟

3   Go within his gates, giving thanks.
    Enter his courts with songs of praise.
    Give thanks to him and bless his name.   ℟

4   Indeed, how good is the Lord,
    eternal his merciful love.
    He is faithful from age to age.   ℟

Gospel Acclamation   Lk 7:16

Alleluia, alleluia!
A great prophet has appeared among us;
God has visited his people.
Alleluia!

GOSPEL

A reading from the holy Gospel according to Luke   7:11-17

Young man, I tell you, arise.

Jesus went to a town called Nain, accompanied by his disciples and a great number of people. When he was near the gate of the town it happened that a dead man was being carried out for burial, the only son of his mother, and she was a widow. And a considerable number of the townspeople were with her. When the Lord saw her he felt sorry for her. 'Do not cry' he said. Then he went up and put his hand on the bier and the bearers stood still, and he said, 'Young man, I tell you to get up.' And the dead man sat up and began to talk, and Jesus gave him to his mother. Everyone was filled with awe and praised God saying, 'A great prophet has appeared among us; God has visited his people.' And this opinion of him spread throughout Judaea and all over the countryside.

This is the Gospel of the Lord.

Wednesday

FIRST READING

A reading from the first letter of St Paul
to the Corinthians   12:31–13: 13

There are three things that last: faith, hope and love, and the greatest
of these is love

Be ambitious for the higher gifts. And I am going to show you a way
that is better than any of them.

If I have all the eloquence of men or of angels, but speak without
love, I am simply a gong booming or a cymbal clashing. If I have the
gift of prophecy, understanding all the mysteries there are, and
knowing everything, and if I have faith in all its fullness, to move
mountains, but without love, then I am nothing at all. If I give away
all that I possess, piece by piece, and if I even let them take my body to
burn it, but am without love, it will do me no good whatever.

Love is always patient and kind; it is never jealous; love is never
boastful or conceited; it is never rude or selfish; it does not take
offence, and is not resentful. Love takes no pleasure in other people's
sins but delights in the truth; it is always ready to excuse, to trust, to
hope, and to endure whatever comes.

Love does not come to an end. But if there are gifts of prophecy, the
time will come when they must fail; or the gift of languages, it will not
continue for ever; and knowledge – for this, too, the time will come
when it must fail. For our knowledge is imperfect and our prophesying is imperfect; but once perfection comes, all imperfect things will
disappear. When I was a child, I used to talk like a child, and think
like a child, and argue like a child, but now I am a man, all childish
ways are put behind me. Now we are seeing a dim reflection in a
mirror; but then we shall be seeing face to face. The knowledge that I
have now is imperfect; but then I shall know as fully as I am known.

In short, there are three things that last: faith, hope and love; and
the greatest of these is love.

This is the word of the Lord.

Responsorial Psalm   Ps 32:2-5. 12. 22. ℟ v.12

℟   Happy the people the Lord has chosen to be his own.

1   Give thanks to the Lord upon the harp,
      with a ten-stringed lute sing him songs.

O sing him a song that is new,
play loudly, with all your skill. ℟

2   For the word of the Lord is faithful
and all his works to be trusted.
The Lord loves justice and right
and fills the earth with his love. ℟

3   They are happy, whose God is the Lord,
the people he has chosen as his own.
May your love be upon us, O Lord,
as we place all our hope in you. ℟

Gospel Acclamation   cf. Jn 6:63. 68

Alleluia, alleluia!
Your words, Lord, are spirit and life;
you have the words of everlasting life.
Alleluia!

GOSPEL

A reading from the holy Gospel according to Luke   7:31-35

We played the pipes for you, and you wouldn't dance; we sang dirges,
and you wouldn't cry.

Jesus said to the people: 'What description can I find for the men of
this generation? What are they like? They are like children shouting
to one another while they sit in the market place:

"We played the pipes for you,
and you wouldn't dance;
we sang dirges,
and you wouldn't cry."

'For John the Baptist comes, not eating bread, not drinking wine,
and you say, "He is possessed." The Son of Man comes, eating and
drinking, and you say, "Look, a glutton and a drunkard, a friend of tax
collectors and sinners." Yet Wisdom has been proved right by all her
children.'

This is the Gospel of the Lord.

Thursday

FIRST READING

A reading from the first letter of St Paul   15:1-11
to the Corinthians

We preached and this is what you believed.

Brothers, I want to remind you of the gospel I preached to you, the gospel that you received and in which you are firmly established; because the gospel will save you only if you keep believing exactly what I preached to you – believing anything else will not lead to anything.

Well then, in the first place, I taught you what I had been taught myself, namely that Christ died for our sins, in accordance with the scriptures; that he was buried; and that he was raised to life on the third day, in accordance with the scriptures; that he appeared first to Cephas and secondly to the Twelve. Next he appeared to more than five hundred of the brothers at the same time, most of whom are still alive, though some have died; then he appeared to James, and then to all the apostles; and last of all he appeared to me too; it was as though I was born when no one expected it.

I am the least of the apostles; in fact, since I persecuted the Church of God, I hardly deserve the name apostle; but by God's grace that is what I am, and the grace that he gave me has not been fruitless. On the contrary, I, or rather the grace of God that is with me, have worked harder than any of the others; but what matters is that I preach what they preach, and this is what you all believed.

This is the word of the Lord.

Responsorial Psalm   Ps 117:1-2. 15-17. 28. ℟ v.1

℟   Give thanks to the Lord, for he is good.

or

℟   Alleluia!

1   Give thanks to the Lord for he is good,
    for his love has no end.
    Let the sons of Israel say:
    'His love has no end.'   ℟

2   The Lord's right hand has triumphed;
    his right hand raised me up.
    I shall not die, I shall live
    and recount his deeds.   ℟

3   You are my God, I thank you.
    My God, I praise you.
    I will thank you for you have given answer
    and you are my saviour.   ℟

Gospel Acclamation   Mt 11:28

    Alleluia, alleluia!
    Come to me, all you that labour and are burdened,
    and I will give you rest, says the Lord.
    Alleluia!

GOSPEL

A reading from the holy Gospel according to Luke   7:36-50

Her many sins must have been forgiven her, because she loved much.

One of the Pharisees invited Jesus to a meal. When he arrived at the
Pharisee's house and took his place at table, a woman came in, who
had a bad name in the town. She had heard he was dining with the
Pharisee and had brought with her an alabaster jar of ointment. She
waited behind him at his feet, weeping, and her tears fell on his feet,
and she wiped them away with her hair; then she covered his feet with
kisses and anointed them with the ointment.

    When the Pharisee who had invited him saw this, he said to
himself, 'If this man were a prophet, he would know who this woman
is that is touching him and what a bad name she has.' Then Jesus took
him up and said, 'Simon, I have something to say to you.' 'Speak,
Master' was the reply. 'There was once a creditor who had two men in
his debt; one owed him five hundred denarii, the other fifty. They
were unable to pay, so he pardoned them both. Which of them will
love him more?' 'The one who was pardoned more, I suppose' answered
Simon. Jesus said, 'You are right.'

    Then he turned to the woman. 'Simon,' he said 'you see this
woman? I came into your house, and you poured no water over my
feet, but she has poured out her tears over my feet and wiped them
away with her hair. You gave me no kiss, but she has been covering

my feet with kisses ever since I came in. You did not anoint my head with oil, but she has anointed my feet with ointment. For this reason I tell you that her sins, her many sins, must have been forgiven her, or she would not have shown such great love. It is the man who is forgiven little who shows little love.' Then he said to her, 'Your sins are forgiven.' Those who were with him at the table began to say to themselves, 'Who is this man, that he even forgives sins?' But he said to the woman, 'Your faith has saved you; go in peace.'

This is the Gospel of the Lord.

Friday

FIRST READING

A reading from the first letter of St Paul
to the Corinthians

15:12-20

If Christ has not risen, your faith is in vain.

If Christ raised from the dead is what has been preached, how can some of you be saying that there is no resurrection of the dead? If there is no resurrection of the dead, Christ himself cannot have been raised and if Christ has not been raised then our preaching is useless and your believing it is useless; indeed, we are shown up as witnesses who have committed perjury before God, because we swore in evidence before God that he had raised Christ to life. For if the dead are not raised, Christ has not been raised, and if Christ has not been raised, you are still in your sins. And what is more serious, all who have died in Christ have perished. If our hope in Christ has been for this life only, we are the most unfortunate of all people.

But Christ has in fact been raised from the dead, the first-fruits of all who have fallen asleep.

This is the word of the Lord.

Responsorial Psalm   Ps 16:1. 6-8. 15. ℟ v.15

℟ Lord, when your glory appears,
    my joy will be full.

1 Lord, hear a cause that is just,
   pay heed to my cry.
   Turn your ear to my prayer:
   no deceit is on my lips. ℟

2 I am here and I call, you will hear me, O God.
   Turn your ear to me; hear my words.
   Display your great love, you whose right hand saves
   your friends from those who rebel against them. ℟

3 Hide me in the shadow of your wings.
   As for me, in my justice I shall see your face
   and be filled, when I awake,
   with the sight of your glory. ℟

Gospel Acclamation   cf. Mt 11:25

Alleluia, alleluia!
Blessed are you, Father, Lord of heaven and earth;
   you have revealed to little ones the mysteries of the kingdom.
Alleluia!

GOSPEL

A reading from the holy Gospel according to Luke   8:1-3

There were women with them who provided for them out of their
own resources.

Jesus made his way through towns and villages preaching, and
proclaiming the Good News of the kingdom of God. With him went the
Twelve, as well as certain women, who had been cured of evil spirits
and ailments: Mary surnamed the Magdalene, from whom seven
demons had gone out, Joanna the wife of Herod's steward Chuza,
Susanna, and several others who provided for them out of their own
resources.

This is the Gospel of the Lord.

Saturday

FIRST READING

A reading from the first letter of St Paul
to the Corinthians   15:35-37. 42-49

What is sown is perishable, but what is raised is imperishable.

Someone may ask, 'How are dead people raised, and what sort of body
do they have when they come back?' They are stupid questions.
Whatever you sow in the ground has to die before it is given new life
and the thing that you sow is not what is going to come; you sow a
bare grain, say of wheat or something like that. It is the same with the
resurrection of the dead: the thing that is sown is perishable but what
is raised is imperishable; the thing that is sown is contemptible but
what is raised is glorious; the thing that is sown is weak but what is
raised is powerful; when it is sown it embodies the soul, when it is
raised it embodies the spirit.

If the soul has its own embodiment, so does the spirit have its own
embodiment. The first man, Adam, as scripture says, became a living
soul; but the last Adam has become a life-giving spirit. That is, first
the one with the soul, not the spirit, and after that, the one with the
spirit. The first man, being from the earth, is earthly by nature; the
second man is from heaven. As this earthly man was, so are we on
earth; and as the heavenly man is, so are we in heaven. And we, who
have been modelled on the earthly man, will be modelled on the
heavenly man.

This is the word of the Lord.

Responsorial Psalm   Ps 55:10-14. ℟ cf. v.14

℟   I will walk in the presence of God,
     with the light of the living.

1   My foes will be put to flight
    on the day that I call to you.
    This I know, that God is on my side.   ℟

2   In God, whose word I praise,
    in the Lord, whose word I praise,
    in God I trust; I shall not fear:
    what can mortal man do to me?   ℟

3   I am bound by the vows I have made you.
    O God, I will offer you praise
    for you rescued my soul from death,
    you kept my feet from stumbling
    that I may walk in the presence of God
    in the light of the living.   ℟

Gospel Acclamation   cf. Lk 8:15

Alleluia, alleluia!
Happy are they who have kept the word with a generous heart
and yield a harvest through perseverance.
Alleluia!

GOSPEL

A reading from the holy Gospel according to Luke   8:4-15

*As for the seed in good ground, this is the people who have heard the word
and take it to themselves and yield a harvest through their perseverance.*

With a large crowd gathering and people from every town finding
their way to him, Jesus used this parable:
    'A sower went out to sow his seed. As he sowed, some fell on the
edge of the path and was trampled on; and the birds of the air ate it
up. Some seed fell on rock, and when it came up it withered away,
having no moisture. Some seed fell amongst thorns and the thorns
grew with it and choked it. And some seed fell into rich soil and grew
and produced its crop a hundredfold.' Saying this he cried, 'Listen,
anyone who has ears to hear!'
    The disciples asked him what this parable might mean, and he
said, 'The mysteries of the kingdom of God are revealed to you; for the
rest there are only parables, so that

    they may see but not perceive,
    listen but not understand.

'This, then, is what the parable means: the seed is the word of God.
Those on the edge of the path are people who have heard it, and then
the devil comes and carries away the word from their hearts in case
they should believe and be saved. Those on the rock are people who,
when they first hear it, welcome the word with joy. But these have no
root; they believe for a while, and in time of trial they give up. As for
the part that fell into thorns, this is people who have heard, but as

they go on their way they are choked by the worries and riches and pleasures of life and do not reach maturity. As for the part in the rich soil, this is people with a noble and generous heart who have heard the word and take it to themselves and yield a harvest through their perseverance.'

This is the Gospel of the Lord.

TWENTY-FIFTH WEEK IN ORDINARY TIME
Year II

Monday

FIRST READING

A reading from the book of Proverbs   3:27-34

The Lord God's curse lies on the house of the wicked.

My son,
do not refuse a kindness to anyone who begs it,
if it is in your power to perform it.
Do not say to your neighbour, 'Go away! Come another time!
I will give it you tomorrow,' if you can do it now.
Do not plot harm against your neighbour
as he lives unsuspecting next door.
Do not pick a groundless quarrel with a man
who has done you no harm.
Do not emulate the man of violence,
never model your conduct on his;
for the wilful wrong-doer is abhorrent to the Lord,
who confides only in honest men.
The Lord's curse lies on the house of the wicked,
but he blesses the home of the virtuous.
He mocks those who mock,
but accords his favour to the humble.

This is the word of the Lord.

Responsorial Psalm   Ps 14:2-5. ℟ v.1

℟   Whoever does justice shall live on the Lord's holy mountain.

1   Lord, who shall dwell on your holy mountain?
    He who walks without fault;
    he who acts with justice
    and speaks the truth from his heart;
    he who does not slander with his tongue.   ℟

2   He who does no wrong to his brother,
    who casts no slur on his neighbour,
    who holds the godless in disdain,
    but honours those who fear the Lord.   ℟

3   He who keeps his pledge, come what may;
    who takes no interest on a loan
    and accepts no bribes against the innocent.
    Such a man will stand firm for ever.   ℟

Gospel Acclamation   Mt 5:16

    Alleluia, alleluia!
    Let your light shine before all,
    that they may see your good works and glorify your Father.
    Alleluia!

GOSPEL

A reading from the holy Gospel according to Luke   8:16-18

Place your light on a stand so that people may see it when they enter.

Jesus said to his disciples: 'No one lights a lamp to cover it with a bowl or to put it under a bed. No, he puts it on a lamp-stand so that people may see the light when they come in. For nothing is hidden but it will be made clear, nothing secret but it will be known and brought to light. So take care how you hear; for anyone who has will be given more; from anyone who has not, even what he thinks he has will be taken away.'

    This is the Gospel of the Lord.

Tuesday

FIRST READING

A reading from the book of Proverbs   21:1-6. 10-13

Various proverbs.

Like flowing water is the heart of the king in the hand of the Lord,
who turns it where he pleases.

A man's conduct may strike him as upright,
the Lord, however, weighs the heart.

To act virtuously and with justice
is more pleasing to the Lord than sacrifice.

Haughty eye, proud heart,
lamp of the wicked, nothing but sin.

The hardworking man is thoughtful, and all is gain;
too much haste, and all that comes of it is want.

To make a fortune with the help of a lying tongue,
such the idle fantasy of those who look for death.

The wicked man's soul is intent on evil,
he looks on his neighbour with dislike.

When a mocker is punished, the ignorant man grows wiser,
when a wise man is instructed he acquires more knowledge.

The Just One watches the house of the wicked:
he hurls the wicked to destruction.

He who shuts his ear to the poor man's cry
shall himself plead and not be heard.

This is the word of the Lord.

Responsorial Psalm   Ps 118:1. 27. 30. 34-35. 44. ℟ v.35

℟   Guide me, Lord, in the way of your commands.

1   They are happy whose life is blameless,
     who follow God's law!
     Make me grasp the way of your precepts
     and I will muse on your wonders.   ℟

2   I have chosen the way of truth
with your decrees before me.
Train me to observe your law,
to keep it with my heart. ℟

3   Guide me in the path of your commands;
for there is my delight.
I shall always keep your law
for ever and ever. ℟

Gospel Acclamation   Lk 11:28

Alleluia, alleluia!
Blessed are they who hear the word of God
and keep it.
Alleluia!

GOSPEL

A reading from the holy Gospel according to Luke   8:19-21

My mother and my brothers are those who hear the word of God and
put it into practice.

The mother and brothers of Jesus came looking for him, but they could not get to him because of the crowd. He was told, 'Your mother and brothers are standing outside and want to see you.' But he said in answer, 'My mother and my brothers are those who hear the word of God and put it into practice.'

This is the Gospel of the Lord.

Wednesday

FIRST READING

A reading from the book of Proverbs   30:5-9

Give me neither poverty nor riches, but only the food which is necessary.

Every word of God is unalloyed,
he is the shield of those who take refuge in him.
To his words make no addition,
lest he reprove you and know you for a fraud.

Two things I beg of you,
do not grudge me them before I die:
keep falsehood and lies far from me,
give me neither poverty nor riches,
grant me only my share of bread to eat,
for fear that surrounded by plenty, I should fall away
and say, 'The Lord – who is the Lord?'
or else, in destitution, take to stealing
and profane the name of my God.

This is the word of the Lord.

Responsorial Psalm   Ps 118:29. 72. 89. 101. 104. 163. ℟ v.105

℟   Your word, O Lord, is a lamp for my feet.

1   Keep me, Lord, from the way of error
    and teach me your law.
    The law from your mouth means more to me
    than silver and gold.   ℟

2   Your word, O Lord, for ever
    stands firm in the heavens.
    I turn my feet from evil paths
    to obey your word.   ℟

3   I gain understanding from your precepts
    and so I hate false ways.
    Lies I hate and detest
    but your law is my love.   ℟

Gospel Acclamation   Mk 1:15

> Alleluia, alleluia!
> The kingdom of God is near:
> repent and believe the Good News!
> Alleluia!

GOSPEL

A reading from the holy Gospel according to Luke   9:1-6

He sent them to proclaim the kingdom of God and to heal the sick.

Jesus called the Twelve together and gave them power and authority over all devils and to cure diseases, and he sent them out to proclaim the kingdom of God and to heal. He said to them, 'Take nothing for the journey: neither staff, nor haversack, nor bread, nor money, and let none of you take a spare tunic. Whatever house you enter, stay there; and when you leave, let it be from there. As for those who do not welcome you, when you leave their town shake the dust from your feet as a sign to them.' So they set out and went from village to village proclaiming the Good News and healing everywhere.

This is the Gospel of the Lord.

Thursday

FIRST READING

A reading from the book of Ecclesiastes   1:2-11

There is nothing new under the sun.

Vanity of vanities, the Preacher says. Vanity of vanities. All is vanity! For all his toil, his toil under the sun, what does man gain by it?

A generation goes, a generation comes, yet the earth stands firm for ever. The sun rises, the sun sets; then to its place it speeds and there it rises. Southward goes the wind, then turns to the north; it turns and turns again; back then to its circling goes the wind. Into the sea all the rivers go, and yet the sea is never filled, and still to their goal the rivers go. All things are wearisome. No man can say that eyes have not had enough of seeing, ears their fill of hearing. What was will be again; what has been done will be done again; and there is nothing new under the sun. Take anything of which it may be said,

'Look now, this is new.' Already, long before our time, it existed. Only no memory remains of earlier times, just as in times to come next year itself will not be remembered.

This is the word of the Lord.

Responsorial Psalm   Ps 89:3-6. 12-14.17. ℟ v.1

℟   In every age, O Lord, you have been our refuge.

1   You turn men back into dust
    and say: 'Go back, sons of men.'
    To your eyes a thousand years
    are like yesterday, come and gone,
    no more than a watch in the night.   ℟

2   You sweep men away like a dream,
    like grass which springs up in the morning.
    In the morning it springs up and flowers:
    by evening it withers and fades.   ℟

3   Make us know the shortness of our life
    that we may gain wisdom of heart.
    Lord, relent! Is your anger for ever?
    Show pity to your servants.   ℟

4   In the morning, fill us with your love;
    we shall exult and rejoice all our days.
    Let the favour of the Lord be upon us:
    give success to the work of our hands.   ℟

Gospel Acclamation   Jn 14:6

Alleluia, alleluia!
I am the way, the truth, and the life, says the Lord;
no one comes to the Father, except through me.
Alleluia!

GOSPEL

A reading from the holy Gospel according to Luke 9:7-9

I beheaded John, so who is this I hear so much about?

Herod the tetrarch had heard about all that was being done by Jesus; and he was puzzled, because some people were saying that John had risen from the dead, others that Elijah had reappeared, still others that one of the ancient prophets had come back to life. But Herod said, 'John? I beheaded him. So who is this I hear such reports about?' And he was anxious to see Jesus.

This is the Gospel of the Lord.

Friday

FIRST READING

A reading from the book of Ecclesiastes 3:1-11

There is a time for everything under heaven.

There is a season for everything, a time for every occupation under heaven:

A time for giving birth, a time for dying;
a time for planting, a time for uprooting what has been planted.
A time for killing, a time for healing;
a time for knocking down, a time for building.
A time for tears, a time for laughter;
a time for mourning, a time for dancing.
A time for throwing stones away, a time for gathering them up;
a time for embracing, a time to refrain from embracing.
A time for searching, a time for losing;
a time for keeping, a time for throwing away.
A time for tearing, a time for sewing;
a time for keeping silent, a time for speaking.
A time for loving, a time for hating;
a time for war, a time for peace.

What does a man gain for the efforts that he makes? I contemplate the task that God gives mankind to labour at. All that he does is apt for its time; but though he has permitted man to consider time in its wholeness, man cannot comprehend the work of God from beginning to end.

This is the word of the Lord.

Responsorial Psalm   Ps 143:1-4. ℟ v.1

℟ Blessed be the Lord, my Rock!

1 Blessed be the Lord, my rock.
  He is my love, my fortress;
  he is my stronghold, my saviour,
  my shield, my place of refuge. ℟

2 Lord, what is man that you care for him,
  mortal man, that you keep him in mind;
  man, who is merely a breath
  whose life fades like a passing shadow? ℟

Gospel Acclamation   Mk 10:45

Alleluia, alleluia!
The Son of Man came to serve
and to give his life as a ransom for all.
Alleluia!

GOSPEL

A reading from the holy Gospel according to Luke   9:18-22

You are the Christ of God. The Son of Man must suffer much.

One day when Jesus was praying alone in the presence of his disciples he put this question to them, 'Who do the crowds say I am?' And they answered, 'John the Baptist; others Elijah; and others say one of the ancient prophets come back to life.' 'But you,' he said 'who do you say I am?' It was Peter who spoke up. 'The Christ of God' he said. But he gave them strict orders not to tell anyone anything about this.

'The Son of Man' he said 'is destined to suffer grievously, to be rejected by the elders and chief priests and scribes and to be put to death, and to be raised up on the third day.'

This is the Gospel of the Lord.

Saturday

FIRST READING

A reading from the book of Ecclesiastes   11:9–12:8

Remember your creator in the days of your youth before the dust returns to the
earth and the spirit to God.

Rejoice in your youth, you who are young;
let your heart give you joy in your young days.
Follow the promptings of your heart
and the desires of your eyes.

But this you must know: for all these things God will bring you to
judgement.

Cast worry from your heart,
shield your flesh from pain.

Yet youth, the age of dark hair, is vanity. And remember your creator
in the days of your youth, before evil days come and the years
approach when you say, 'These give me no pleasure', before sun and
light and moon and stars grow dark, and the clouds return after the
rain;

the day when those who keep the house tremble
and strong men are bowed;
when the women grind no longer at the mill,
because day is darkening at the windows
and the street doors are shut;
when the sound of the mill is faint,
when the voice of the bird is silenced,
and song notes are stilled,
when to go uphill is an ordeal
and a walk is something to dread.

Yet the almond tree is in flower,
the grasshopper is heavy with food
and the caper bush bears its fruit,

while man goes to his everlasting home. And the mourners are
already walking to and fro in the street

before the silver cord has snapped,
or the golden lamp been broken,
or the pitcher shattered at the spring,
or the pulley cracked at the well,

or before the dust returns to the earth as it once came from it, and the breath of God who gave it.

Vanity of vanities, the Preacher says. All is vanity.

This is the word of the Lord.

Responsorial Psalm   Ps 89:3-6. 12-14. 17. ℟ v.1

℟   In every age, O Lord, you have been our refuge.

1   You turn men back into dust
    and say: 'Go back, sons of men.'
    To your eyes a thousand years
    are like yesterday, come and gone,
    no more than a watch in the night.   ℟

2   You sweep men away like a dream,
    like grass which springs up in the morning.
    In the morning it springs up and flowers:
    by evening it withers and fades.   ℟

3   Make us know the shortness of our life
    that we may gain wisdom of heart.
    Lord, relent! Is your anger for ever?
    Show pity to your servants.   ℟

4   In the morning, fill us with your love;
    we shall exult and rejoice all our days.
    Let the favour of the Lord be upon us:
    give success to the work of our hands.   ℟

Gospel Acclamation   cf. 2 Tim 1:10

Alleluia, alleluia!
Our Saviour Jesus Christ has done away with death
and brought us life through his gospel.
Alleluia!

GOSPEL

A reading from the holy Gospel according to Luke 9:43-45

The Son of Man will be delivered into the hands of humanity ... All
who wish to be first must make themselves the servants of all.

At a time when everyone was full of admiration for all he did, Jesus said to his disciples, 'For your part, you must have these words constantly in your mind: The Son of Man is going to be handed over into the power of men.' But they did not understand him when he said this; it was hidden from them so that they should not see the meaning of it, and they were afraid to ask him about what he had just said.

This is the Gospel of the Lord.

TWENTY-SIXTH WEEK IN ORDINARY TIME

Year II

Monday

FIRST READING

A reading from the book of Job 1:6-22

The Lord gave, the Lord has taken away, blessed be the name of the Lord.

One day the Sons of God came to attend on the Lord, and among them was Satan. So the Lord said to Satan, 'Where have you been?' 'Round the earth,' he answered 'roaming about.' So the Lord asked him, 'Did you notice my servant Job? There is no one like him on the earth: a sound and honest man who fears God and shuns evil.' 'Yes,' Satan said 'but Job is not God-fearing for nothing, is he? Have you not put a wall round him and his house and all his domain? You have blessed all he undertakes, and his flocks throng the countryside. But stretch out your hand and lay a finger on his possessions: I warrant you, he will curse you to your face.' 'Very well,' the Lord said to Satan 'all he has is in your power. But keep your hands off his person.' So Satan left the presence of the Lord.

On the day when Job's sons and daughters were at their meal and drinking wine at their eldest brother's house, a messenger came to Job. 'Your oxen' he said 'were at the plough, with the donkeys grazing at their side, when the Sabaeans swept down on them and carried them off. Your servants they put to the sword: I

733

alone escaped to tell you.' He had not finished speaking when another messenger arrived. 'The fire of God' he said 'has fallen from the heavens and burnt up all your sheep, and your shepherds too: I alone escaped to tell you.' He had not finished speaking when another messenger arrived. 'The Chaldaeans', he said 'three bands of them, have raided your camels and made off with them. Your servants they put to the sword: I alone escaped to tell you.' He had not finished speaking when another messenger arrived. 'Your sons and daughters' he said 'were at their meals and drinking wine at their eldest brother's house, when suddenly from the wilderness a gale sprang up, and it battered all four corners of the house which fell in on the young people. They are dead: I alone escaped to tell you.'

Job rose and tore his gown and shaved his head. Then falling to the ground he worshipped and said:

'Naked I came from my mother's womb,
naked I shall return.
The Lord gave, the Lord has taken back.
Blessed be the name of the Lord!'

In all this misfortune Job committed no sin nor offered any insult to God.

This is the word of the Lord.

Responsorial Psalm   Ps 16:1-3. 6-7. ℟ v.6

℟   Lord, bend your ear and hear my prayer.

1   Lord, hear a cause that is just,
    pay heed to my cry.
    Turn your ear to my prayer:
    no deceit is on my lips.   ℟

2   From you may my judgement come forth.
    Your eyes discern the truth.
    You search my heart, you visit me by night.
    You test me and you find in me no wrong.   ℟

3   I am here and I call, you will hear me, O God.
    Turn your ear to me; hear my words.
    Display your great love, you whose right hand saves
    your friends from those who rebel against them.   ℟

Gospel Acclamation   Mk 10:45

> Alleluia, alleluia!
> The Son of Man came to serve
> and to give his life as a ransom for all.
> Alleluia!

GOSPEL

A reading from the holy Gospel according to Luke   9:46-50

The least among you all is the one who is great.

An argument started between the disciples about which of them was the greatest. Jesus knew what thoughts were going through their minds, and he took a little child and set him by his side and then said to them, 'Anyone who welcomes this little child in my name welcomes me; and anyone who welcomes me welcomes the one who sent me. For the least among you all, that is the one who is great.'

John spoke up. 'Master,' he said 'we saw a man casting out devils in your name, and because he is not with us we tried to stop him.' But Jesus said to him, 'You must not stop him: anyone who is not against you is for you.'

This is the Gospel of the Lord.

Tuesday

FIRST READING

A reading from the book of Job   3:1-3. 11-17. 20-23

Why give light to a man of grief?

Job broke the silence and cursed the day of his birth. This is what he said:

> May the day perish when I was born,
> and the night that told of a boy conceived.
> Why did I not die new-born,
> not perish as I left the womb?
> Why were there two knees to receive me,
> two breasts for me to suck?

735

Had there not been, I should now be lying in peace,
wrapped in a restful slumber,
with the kings and high viziers of earth
who build themselves vast vaults,
or with princes who have gold and to spare
and houses crammed with silver.

Or put away like a still-born child that never came to be,
like unborn babes that never see the light.
Down there, bad men bustle no more,
there the weary rest.
Why give light to a man of grief?
Why give life to those bitter of heart,
who long for a death that never comes,
and hunt for it more than for a buried treasure?
They would be glad to see the grave-mound
and shout with joy if they reached the tomb.
Why make this gift of light to a man who does not see his way,
whom God baulks on every side?

This is the word of the Lord.

Responsial Psalm   Ps 87:2-8. ℟ v.3

℟   Let my prayer come before you, Lord.

1   I call to you, Lord, all the day long;
    to you I stretch out my hands.
    Will you work your wonders for the dead?
    Will the shades stand and praise you?   ℟

2   Will your love be told in the grave
    or your faithfulness among the dead?
    Will your wonders be known in the dark
    or your justice in the land of oblivion?   ℟

3   As for me, Lord, I call to you for help:
    in the morning my prayer comes before you.
    Lord, why do you reject me?
    Why do you hide your face?   ℟

Gospel Acclamation   Mk 10:45

> Alleluia, alleluia!
> The Son of Man came to serve
> and to give his life as a ransom for all.
> Alleluia!

GOSPEL

A reading from the holy Gospel according to Luke   9:51-56

He resolutely took the road to Jerusalem.

As the time drew near for him to be taken up to heaven, Jesus resolutely took the road for Jerusalem and sent messengers ahead of him. These set out, and they went into a Samaritan village to make preparations for him, but the people would not receive him because he was making for Jerusalem. Seeing this, the disciples James and John said, 'Lord, do you want us to call down fire from heaven to burn them up?' But he turned and rebuked them, and they went off to another village.

This is the Gospel of the Lord.

Wednesday

FIRST READING

A reading from the book of Job   9:1-13. 14-16

Human justice cannot be compared to God's.

Job spoke to his friends.

> Indeed, I know it is as you say:
> how can man be in the right against God?
> If any were so rash as to challenge him for reasons,
> one in a thousand would be more than they could answer.
> His heart is wise, and his strength is great:
> who then can successfully defy him?
> He moves the mountains, though they do not know it;
> he throws them down when he is angry.
> He shakes the earth, and moves it from its place,
> making all its pillars tremble.
> The sun, at his command, forbears to rise,

and on the stars he sets a seal.
He and no other stretched out the skies,
and trampled the Sea's tall waves.
The Bear, Orion too, are of his making,
the Pleiades and the Mansions of the South.
His works are great, beyond all reckoning,
his marvels, past all counting.
Were he to pass me, I should not see him,
nor detect his stealthy movement.
Were he to snatch a prize, who could prevent him,
or dare to say, 'What are you doing?'
How dare I plead my cause, then,
or choose arguments against him?
Suppose I am in the right, what use is my defence?
For he whom I must sue is judge as well.
If he deigned to answer my citation,
could I be sure that he would listen to my voice?

This is the word of the Lord.

Responsorial Psalm   Ps 87:10-15. ℟ v.3

℟   Let my prayer come before you, Lord.

1   I call to you, Lord, all the day long;
     to you I stretch out my hands.
     Will you work your wonders for the dead?
     Will the shades stand and praise you? ℟

2   Will your love be told in the grave
     or your faithfulness among the dead?
     Will your wonders be known in the dark
     or your justice in the land of oblivion? ℟

3   As for me, Lord, I call to you for help:
     in the morning my prayer comes before you.
     Lord, why do you reject me?
     Why do you hide your face? ℟

Gospel Acclamation   Ps 118:105

> Alleluia, alleluia!
> I count all things worthless but this:
> to gain Jesus Christ and to be found in him.
> Alleluia!

GOSPEL

A reading from the holy Gospel according to Luke   9:57-62

I will follow you wherever you go.

As Jesus and his disciples travelled along they met a man on the road who said to him, 'I will follow you wherever you go.' Jesus answered, 'Foxes have holes and the birds of the air have nests, but the Son of Man has nowhere to lay his head.'

Another to whom he said, 'Follow me' replied, 'Let me go and bury my father first.' But he answered, 'Leave the dead to bury their dead; your duty is to go and spread the news of the kingdom of God.'

Another said, 'I will follow you, sir, but first let me go and say good-bye to my people at home.' Jesus said to him, 'Once the hand is laid on the plough, no one who looks back is fit for the kingdom of God.'

This is the Gospel of the Lord.

Thursday

FIRST READING

A reading from the book of Job   19:21-27

I know that my Redeemer lives.

Job said:

> Pity me, pity me, you, my friends,
> for the hand of God has struck me.
> Why do you hound me down like God,
> will you never have enough of my flesh?
> Ah, would that these words of mine were written down,
> inscribed on some monument
> with iron chisel and engraving tool,
> cut into the rock for ever.

This I know: that my Avenger lives,
and he, the Last, will take his stand on earth.
After my awaking, he will set me close to him,
and from my flesh I shall look on God.
He whom I shall see will take my part:
these eyes will gaze on him and find him not aloof.

This is the word of the Lord.

Responsial Psalm   Ps 26:7-9. 13-14. ℟ v.13

℟   I believe that I shall see the good things of the Lord
     in the land of the living.

1   O Lord, hear my voice when I call;
     have mercy and answer.
     Of you my heart has spoken:
     'Seek his face.'   ℟

2   It is your face, O Lord, that I seek;
     hide not your face.
     Dismiss not your servant in anger;
     you have been my help.   ℟

3   I am sure I shall see the Lord's goodness
     in the land of the living.
     Hope in him, hold firm and take heart.
     Hope in the Lord!   ℟

Gospel Acclamation   Mk 1:15

Alleluia, alleluia!
The kingdom of God is near:
repent and believe the Good News!
Alleluia!

GOSPEL

A reading from the holy Gospel according to Luke   10:1-12

Your peace will rest on them.

The Lord appointed seventy-two others and sent them out ahead of
him, in pairs, to all the towns and places he himself was to visit. He
said to them, 'The harvest is rich but the labourers are few, so ask the

Lord of the harvest to send labourers to his harvest. Start off now, but remember, I am sending you out like lambs among wolves. Carry no purse, no haversack, no sandals. Salute no one on the road. Whatever house you go into, let your first words be, "Peace to this house!" And if a man of peace lives there, your peace will go and rest on him; if not, it will come back to you. Stay in the same house, taking what food and drink they have to offer, for the labourer deserves his wages; do not move from house to house. Whenever you go into a town where they make you welcome, eat what is set before you. Cure those in it who are sick, and say, "The kingdom of God is very near to you." But whenever you enter a town and they do not make you welcome, go out into its streets and say, "We wipe off the very dust of your town that clings to our feet, and leave it with you. Yet be sure of this: the kingdom of God is very near." I tell you, on that day it will not go as hard with Sodom as with that town.'

This is the Gospel of the Lord.

Friday

FIRST READING

A reading from the book of Job
38:1. 12-21; 40:3-5

Have you ever given orders to the morning, or journeyed to the depths of the sea?

From the heart of the tempest the Lord gave Job his answer. He said:

Have you ever in your life given orders to the morning
or sent the dawn to its post,
telling it to grasp the earth by its edges
and shake the wicked out of it,
when it changes the earth to sealing clay
and dyes it as a man dyes clothes;
stealing the light from wicked men
and breaking the arm raised to strike?
Have you journeyed all the way to the sources of the sea,
or walked where the Abyss is deepest?
Have you been shown the gates of Death
or met the janitors of Shadowland?
Have you an inkling of the extent of the earth?

Tell me all about it if you have!
Which is the way to the home of the light,
and where does darkness live?
You could then show them the way to their proper places,
or put them on the path to where they live!
If you know all this, you must have been born with them,
you must be very old by now!

Job replied to the Lord:

My words have been frivolous: what can I reply?
I had better lay my finger on my lips.
I have spoken once ... I will not speak again;
more than once ... I will add nothing.

This is the word of the Lord.

Responsorial Psalm   Ps 138:1-3. 7-10. 13-14. ℟ v.24

℟   Guide me, Lord, along the everlasting way.

1   O Lord, you search me and you know me,
    you know my resting and my rising,
    you discern my purpose from afar.
    You mark when I walk or lie down,
    all my ways lie open to you.   ℟

2   O where can I go from your spirit,
    or where can I flee from your face?
    If I climb the heavens, you are there.
    If I lie in the grave, you are there.   ℟

3   If I take the wings of the dawn
    and dwell at the sea's furthest end,
    even there your hand would lead me,
    your right hand would hold me fast.   ℟

4   For it was you who created my being,
    knit me together in my mother's womb.
    I thank you for the wonders of my being,
    for the wonders of all your creation.   ℟

Gospel Acclamation   cf. Ps 94:8

Alleluia, alleluia!
If today you hear his voice,
harden not your hearts.
Alleluia!

GOSPEL

A reading from the holy Gospel according to Luke   10:13-16

Whoever rejects me, rejects him who sent me.

Jesus said to his disciples: 'Alas for you, Chorazin! Alas for you, Bethsaida! For if the miracles done in you had been done in Tyre and Sidon, they would have repented long ago, sitting in sackcloth and ashes. And still, it will not go as hard with Tyre and Sidon at the Judgement as with you. And as for you, Capernaum, did you want to be exalted high as heaven? You shall be thrown down to hell.

'Anyone who listens to you listens to me; anyone who rejects you rejects me, and those who reject me reject the one who sent me.'

This is the Gospel of the Lord.

Saturday

FIRST READING

A reading from the book of Job   42:1-3. 5-6. 12-17

I have seen you with my own eyes, and I repent all I have said.

This was the answer Job gave to the Lord:

I know that you are all-powerful:
what you conceive, you can perform.
I am the man who obscured your designs
with my empty-headed words.
I have been holding forth on matters I cannot understand,
on marvels beyond me and my knowledge.
I knew you then only by hearsay;
but now, having seen you with my own eyes,
I retract all I have said,
and in dust and ashes I repent.

The Lord blessed Job's new fortune even more than his first one. He came to own fourteen thousand sheep, six thousand camels, a thousand yoke of oxen and a thousand she-donkeys. He had seven sons and three daughters; his first daughter he called 'Turtledove', the second 'Cassia' and the third 'Mascara'. Throughout the land there were no women as beautiful as the daughters of Job. And their father gave them inheritance rights like their brothers.

After his trials, Job lived on until he was a hundred and forty years old, and saw his children and his children's children up to the fourth generation. Then Job died, an old man and full of days.

This is the word of the Lord.

Responsorial Psalm   Ps 118:66. 71. 75. 91. 125. 130. ℟ v.135

℟   Lord, let your face shine on me.

1   Teach me discernment and knowledge
    for I trust in your commands.
    It was good for me to be afflicted,
    to learn your statutes.   ℟

2   Lord, I know that your decrees are right,
    that you afflicted me justly.
    By your decree the earth endures to this day;
    for all things serve you. ℟

3   I am your servant, make me understand;
    then I shall know your will.
    The unfolding of your word gives light
    and teaches the simple. ℟

Gospel Acclamation   cf. Mt 11:25

Alleluia, alleluia!
Blessed are you, Father, Lord of heaven and earth;
you have revealed to little ones the mysteries of the kingdom.
Alleluia!

GOSPEL

A reading from the holy Gospel according to Luke   10:17-24

Rejoice because your names are written in heaven.

The seventy-two came back rejoicing. 'Lord,' they said 'even the devils submit to us when we use your name.' Jesus said to them, 'I watched Satan fall like lighting from heaven. Yes, I have given you power to tread underfoot serpents and scorpions and the whole strength of the enemy; nothing shall ever hurt you. Yet do not rejoice that the spirits submit to you; rejoice rather that your names are written in heaven.'

It was then that, filled with joy by the Holy Spirit, he said, 'I bless you, Father, Lord of heaven and of earth, for hiding these things from the learned and the clever and revealing them to mere children. Yes, Father, for that is what it pleased you to do. Everything has been entrusted to me by my Father; and no one knows who the Son is except the Father, and who the Father is except the Son and those to whom the Son chooses to reveal him.'

Then turning to his disciples he spoke to them in private. 'Happy the eyes that see what you see, for I tell you that many prophets and kings wanted to see what you see, and never saw it; to hear what you hear, and never heard it.'

This is the Gospel of the Lord.

TWENTY-SEVENTH WEEK IN ORDINARY TIME
Year II

Monday

FIRST READING

A reading from the letter of St Paul to the Galatians   1:6-12

*The Good News I preached is not according to a human being ... it
is through a revelation of Jesus Christ.*

I am astonished at the promptness with which you have turned
away from the one who called you and have decided to follow a
different version of the Good News. Not that there can be more
than one Good News; it is merely that some troublemakers among
you want to change the Good News of Christ; and let me warn you
that if anyone preaches a version of the Good News different from
the one we have already preached to you, whether it be ourselves or
an angel from heaven, he is to be condemned. I am only repeating
what we told you before: if anyone preaches a version of the Good
News different from the one you have already heard, he is to be
condemned. So now whom am I trying to please – man, or God?
Would you say it is men's approval I am looking for? If I still
wanted that, I should not be what I am – a servant of Christ.

The fact is, brothers, and I want you to realise this, the Good
News I preached is not a human message that I was given by men,
it is something I learnt only through a revelation of Jesus Christ.

This is the word of the Lord.

Responsorial Psalm   Ps 110:1-2. 7-10. ℟ v.5

℟   The Lord will remember his covenant for ever.

or

℟   Alleluia!

1   I will thank the Lord with all my heart
    in the meeting of the just and their assembly.
    Great are the works of the Lord;
    to be pondered by all who love them.   ℟

746

℟ His works are justice and truth:
his precepts are all of them sure,
standing firm for ever and ever:
they are made in uprightness and truth.   ℟

℟ He has sent deliverance to his people
and established his covenant for ever.
Holy his name, to be feared;
his praise shall last for ever!   ℟

Gospel Acclamation   Jn 13:34

Alleluia, alleluia!
I give you a new commandment:
love one another as I have loved you.
Alleluia!

GOSPEL

A reading from the holy Gospel according to Luke   10:25-37

Who is my neighbour?

There was a lawyer who, to disconcert Jesus, stood up and said to him
'Master, what must I do to inherit eternal life?' He said to him, 'What
is written in the Law? What do you read there?' He replied, 'You must
love the Lord your God with all your heart, with all your soul, with all
your strength, and with all your mind, and your neighbour as
yourself.' 'You have answered right,' said Jesus 'do this and life is
yours.'

But the man was anxious to justify himself and said to Jesus, 'And
who is my neighbour?' Jesus replied, 'A man was once on his way
down from Jerusalem to Jericho and fell into the hands of brigands;
they took all he had, beat him and then made off, leaving him half
dead. Now a priest happened to be travelling down the same road, but
when he saw the man, he passed by on the other side. In the same way
a Levite who came to the place saw him, and passed by on the other
side. But a Samaritan traveller who came upon him was moved with
compassion when he saw him. He went up and bandaged his wounds,
pouring oil and wine on them. He then lifted him on to his own mount,
carried him to the inn and looked after him. Next day, he took out two
denarii and handed them to the innkeeper. "Look after him," he

said "and on my way back I will make good any extra expense you have." Which of these three, do you think, proved himself a neighbour to the man who fell into the brigands' hands?' 'The one who took pity on him' he replied. Jesus said to him, 'Go, and do the same yourself.'

This is the Gospel of the Lord.

Tuesday

FIRST READING

A reading from the letter of St Paul to the Galatians   1:13-24

He revealed his Son in me, that I might preach the Good News about him to the gentiles.

You must have heard of my career as a practising Jew, how merciless I was in persecuting the Church of God, how much damage I did to it, how I stood out among other Jews of my generation, and how enthusiastic I was for the traditions of my ancestors.

Then God, who had specially chosen me while I was still in my mother's womb, called me through his grace and chose to reveal his Son in me, so that I might preach the Good News about him to the pagans. I did not stop to discuss this with any human being, nor did I go up to Jerusalem to see those who were already apostles before me, but I went off to Arabia at once and later went straight back from there to Damascus. Even when after three years I went up to Jerusalem to visit Cephas and stayed with him for fifteen days, I did not see any of the other apostles; I only saw James, the brother of the Lord, and I swear before God that what I have just written is the literal truth. After that I went to Syria and Cilicia, and was still not known by sight to the churches of Christ in Judaea, who had heard nothing except that their one-time persecutor was now preaching the faith he had previously tried to destroy; and they gave glory to God for me.

This is the word of the Lord.

Responsorial Psalm   Ps 138:1-3. 13-15. ℟ v.24

℟   Guide me, Lord, along the everlasting way.

1   O Lord, you search me and you know me,
     you know my resting and my rising,
     you discern my purpose from afar.
     You mark when I walk or lie down,
     all my ways lie open to you.   ℟

2   For it was you who created my being,
     knit me together in my mother's womb.
     I thank you for the wonder of my being,
     for the wonders of all your creation.   ℟

3   Already you knew my soul,
     my body held no secret from you,
     when I was being fashioned in secret
     and moulded in the depths of the earth.   ℟

Gospel Acclamation   Lk 11:28

     Alleluia, alleluia!
     Blessed are they who hear the word of God
     and keep it.
     Alleluia!

GOSPEL

A reading from the holy Gospel according to Luke   10:38-42

Martha took up the duties in the house. Mary chose the better part.

Jesus came to a village, and a woman named Martha welcomed him
into her house. She had a sister called Mary, who sat down at the
Lord's feet and listened to him speaking. Now Martha who was
distracted with all the serving said, 'Lord, do you not care that my
sister is leaving me to do the serving all by myself? Please tell her to
help me.' But the Lord answered: 'Martha, Martha,' he said 'you worry
and fret about so many things, and yet few are needed, indeed only
one. It is Mary who has chosen the better part; it is not to be taken
from her.'

This is the Gospel of the Lord.

749

Wednesday

FIRST READING

A reading from the letter of St Paul to the Galatians   2:1-2. 7-14

They recognised the grace that had been given to me

It was not till fourteen years had passed that I went up to Jerusalem again. I went with Barnabas and took Titus with me. I went there as the result of a revelation, and privately I laid before the leading men the Good News as I proclaim it among the pagans; I did so for fear the course I was adopting or had already adopted would not be allowed. On the contrary, they recognised that I had been commissioned to preach the Good News to the uncircumcised just as Peter had been commissioned to preach it to the circumcised. The same person whose action had made Peter the apostle of the circumcised had given me a similar mission to the pagans. So, James, Cephas and John, these leaders, these pillars, shook hands with Barnabas and me as a sign of partnership: we were to go to the pagans and they to the circumcised. The only thing they insisted on was that we should remember to help the poor, as indeed I was anxious to do.

When Cephas came to Antioch, however, I opposed him to his face, since he was manifestly in the wrong. His custom had been to eat with the pagans, but after certain friends of James arrived he stopped doing this and kept away from them altogether for fear of the group that insisted on circumcision. The other Jews joined him in this pretence, and even Barnabas felt himself obliged to copy their behaviour.

When I saw they were not respecting the true meaning of the Good News, I said to Cephas in front of everyone, 'In spite of being a Jew, you live like the pagans and not like the Jews, so you have no right to make the pagans copy Jewish ways.'

This is the word of the Lord.

Responsorial Psalm   Ps 116. ℟ Mk 16:15

℟   Go out to all the world,
      and tell the Good News.

or

℟   Alleluia!

1 O praise the Lord, all you nations,
    acclaim him all you peoples!   ℟

2 Strong is his love for us;
    he is faithful for ever.   ℟

Gospel Acclamation   Rom 8:15

Alleluia, alleluia!
You have received the Spirit which makes us God's children,
and in that Spirit we call God our Father.
Alleluia!

GOSPEL

A reading from the holy Gospel according to Luke   11:1-4

Lord, teach us to pray.

Once Jesus was in a certain place praying, and when he had finished, one of his disciples said, 'Lord, teach us to pray, just as John taught his disciples.' He said to them, 'Say this when you pray:

"Father, may your name be held holy,
your kingdom come;
give us each day our daily bread,
and forgive us our sins,
for we ourselves forgive each one who is in debt to us.
And do not put us to the test." '

This is the Gospel of the Lord.

Thursday

FIRST READING

A reading from the letter of St Paul to the Galatians 3:1-5

Was it because you practised the law that you received the Spirit or because you believed what you heard?

Are you people in Galatia mad? Has someone put a spell on you, in spite of the plain explanation you have had of the crucifixion of Jesus Christ? Let me ask you one question: was it because you practised the Law that you received the Spirit, or because you believed what was preached to you? Are you foolish enough to end in outward observances what you began in the Spirit? Have all the favours you received been wasted? And if this were so, they would most certainly have been wasted. Does God give you the Spirit so freely and work miracles among you because you practise the Law, or because you believed what was preached to you?

This is the word of the Lord.

Responsorial Psalm Lk 1:69-75. ℟ cf. v.68

℟ Blessed is the Lord God of Israel;
  for he has come to his people.

1 God has raised up for us a mighty saviour
  in the house of David his servant,
  as he promised by the lips of holy men,
  those who were his prophets from of old. ℟

2 A saviour who would free us from our foes,
  from the hands of all who hate us.
  So his love for our fathers is fulfilled
  and his holy covenant remembered. ℟

3 He swore to Abraham our father
  to grant us, that free from fear,
  and saved from the hands of our foes,
  we might serve him in holiness and justice
  all the days of our life in his presence. ℟

Gospel Acclamation   cf. Acts 16:14

Alleluia, alleluia!
Open our hearts, O Lord,
to listen to the words of your Son.
Alleluia!

GOSPEL

A reading from the holy Gospel according to Luke   11:5-13

Seek and it will be given to you.

Jesus said to his disciples: 'Suppose one of you has a friend and goes to him in the middle of the night to say, "My friend, lend me three loaves, because a friend of mine on his travels has just arrived at my house and I have nothing to offer him"; and the man answers from inside the house, "Do not bother me. The door is bolted now, and my children and I are in bed; I cannot get up to give it you." I tell you, if the man does not get up and give it him for friendship's sake, persistence will be enough to make him get up and give his friend all he wants.

'So I say to you: Ask, and it will be given to you; search, and you will find; knock, and the door will be opened to you. For the one who asks always receives; the one who searches always finds; the one who knocks will always have the door opened to him. What father among you would hand his son a stone when he asked for bread? Or hand him a snake instead of a fish? Or hand him a scorpion if he asked for an egg? If you then, who are evil, know how to give your children what is good, how much more will the heavenly Father give the Holy Spirit to those who ask him!'

This is the Gospel of the Lord.

Friday

FIRST READING

A reading from the letter of St Paul to the Galatians 3:7-14

Those who rely on faith are blessed with the faith of Abraham.

Don't you see that it is those who rely on faith who are the sons of Abraham? Scripture foresaw that God was going to use faith to justify the pagans, and proclaimed the Good News long ago when Abraham was told: In you all the pagans will be blessed. Those therefore who rely on faith receive the same blessing as Abraham, the man of faith.

On the other hand, those who rely on the keeping of the Law are under a curse, since scripture says: Cursed be everyone who does not persevere in observing everything prescribed in the book of the Law. The Law will not justify anyone in the sight of God, because we are told: the righteous man finds life through faith. The Law is not even based on faith, since we are told: The man who practises these precepts finds life through practising them. Christ redeemed us from the curse of the Law by being cursed for our sake, since scripture says: Cursed be everyone who is hanged on a tree. This was done so that in Christ Jesus the blessing of Abraham might include the pagans, and so that through faith we might receive the promised Spirit.

This is the word of the Lord.

Responsorial Psalm   Ps 110:1-6. ℟ v.5

℟   The Lord will remember his covenant for ever.

or

℟   Alleluia!

1   I will thank the Lord with all my heart
    in the meeting of the just and their assembly.
    Great are the works of the Lord;
    to be pondered by all who love them.   ℟

2   Majestic and glorious his work,
    his justice stands firm for ever.
    He makes us remember his wonders.
    The Lord is compassion and love.   ℟

3 He gives food to those who fear him;
   keeps his covenant ever in mind.
   He has shown his might to his people
   by giving them the lands of the nations.   ℟

Alleluia, alleluia!
The prince of this world will now be cast out,
and when I am lifted up from the earth
I will draw all to myself, says the Lord.
Alleluia!

GOSPEL

A reading from the Gospel according to Luke   11:15-26

*If by the finger of God I cast out devils, the kingdom of God has
overtaken you.*

When Jesus had cast out a devil, some of the people said, 'It is through
Beelzebul, the prince of devils, that he casts out devils.' Others asked
Jesus, as a test, for a sign from heaven; but knowing what they were
thinking, he said to them, 'Every kingdom divided against itself is
heading for ruin, and a household divided against itself collapses. So
too with Satan: if he is divided against himself, how can his kingdom
stand? – since you assert that it is through Beelzebul that I cast out
devils. Now if it is through Beelzebul that I cast out devils through
whom do your own experts cast them out? Let them be your judges,
then. But if it is through the finger of God that I cast out devils, then
know that the kingdom of God has overtaken you. So long as a strong
man fully armed guards his own palace, his goods are undisturbed;
but when someone stronger than he is attacks and defeats him, the
stronger man takes away all the weapons he relied on and shares out
his spoil.

   'He who is not with me is against me; and he who does not gather
with me scatters.

   'When an unclean spirit goes out of a man it wanders through
waterless country looking for a place to rest, and not finding one it
says, "I will go back to the home I came from." But on arrival, finding
it swept and tidied, it then goes off and brings seven other spirits more

wicked than itself, and they go in and set up house there, so that the man ends up by being worse than he was before.'

This is the Gospel of the Lord

Saturday

FIRST READING

A reading from the letter of St Paul to the Galatians   3:22-29

All of you are children of God through faith.

Scripture makes no exceptions when it says that sin is master everywhere. In this way the promise can only be given through faith in Jesus Christ and can only be given to those who have this faith.

Before faith came, we were allowed no freedom by the Law; we were being looked after till faith was revealed. The Law was to be our guardian until the Christ came and we could be justified by faith. Now that that time has come we are no longer under that guardian, and you are, all of you, sons of God through faith in Christ Jesus. All baptised in Christ, you have all clothed yourselves in Christ, and there are no more distinctions between Jew and Greek, slave and free, male and female, but all of you are one in Christ Jesus. Merely by belonging to Christ you are the posterity of Abraham, the heirs he was promised.

This is the word of the Lord.

Responsorial Psalm   Ps 104:2-7. ℟ v.8

℟   The Lord will remember his covenant for ever.

or

℟   Alleluia!

1   O sing to the Lord, sing his praise;
      tell all his wonderful works!
      Be proud of his holy name,
      let the hearts that seek the Lord rejoice. ℟

2   Consider the Lord and his strength;
      constantly seek his face.
      Remember the wonders he has done,
      his miracles, the judgements he spoke. ℟

3   O children of Abraham, his servant,
     O sons of the Jacob he chose.
     He, the Lord, is our God:
     his judgements prevail in all the earth. ℟

Gospel Acclamation   Lk 11:28

    Alleluia, alleluia!
    Blessed are they who hear the word of God
    and keep it.
    Alleluia!

GOSPEL

A reading from the holy Gospel according to Luke   11:27-28

Happy the womb that bore you!
Happier still are those who hear the word of God.

As Jesus was speaking, a woman in the crowd raised her voice and said, 'Happy the womb that bore you and the breasts you sucked!' But he replied, 'Still happier those who hear the word of God and keep it!'

    This is the Gospel of the Lord.

TWENTY-EIGHTH WEEK IN ORDINARY TIME
Year II

Monday

FIRST READING

A reading from the letter of St Paul   4:22-24. 26-27. 31–5:1
to the Galatians

We are the children, not of the slave-girl, but of the free-born wife.

The Law says, if you remember, that Abraham had two sons, one by the slave-girl, and one by his free-born wife. The child of the slave-girl was born in the ordinary way; the child of the free woman was born as the result of a promise. This can be regarded as an allegory: the women stand for the two covenants. The first who comes from Sinai, and whose children are slaves, is Hagar. The Jerusalem above, however, is free and is our mother, since scripture says: Shout for joy, you barren women who bore no children! Break into shouts of joy and gladness, you who were never in labour. For there are more sons of the foresaken one than sons of the wedded wife. So, my brothers, we are the children, not of the slave-girl, but of the free-born wife.

When Christ freed us, he meant us to remain free. Stand firm, therefore, and do not submit again to the yoke of slavery.

This is the word of the Lord.

Responsorial Psalm

Ps 112:1-7. ℟ v.2

℟ Blessed be the name of the Lord for ever.

or

℟ Alleluia!

1 Praise, O servants of the Lord,
 praise the name of the Lord!
 May the name of the Lord be blessed
 both now and for evermore! ℟

2 From the rising of the sun to its setting
 praised be the name of the Lord!
 High above all nations is the Lord,
 above the heavens his glory. ℟

3 Who is like the Lord, our God,
 who stoops from the heights to look down,
 to look down upon heaven and earth?
 From the dust he lifts up the lowly,
 from the dungheap he raises the poor. ℟

Gospel Acclamation

cf. Ps 94:8

Alleluia, alleluia!
If today you hear his voice,
harden not your hearts.
Alleluia!

GOSPEL

A reading from the holy Gospel according to Luke   11:29-32

> *No sign will be given to this generation except the sign of Jonah*
> *the prophet.*

The crowds got even bigger and Jesus addressed them, 'This is a wicked generation; it is asking for a sign. The only sign it will be given is the sign of Jonah. For just as Jonah became a sign to the Ninevites, so will the Son of Man be to this generation. On Judgement day the Queen of the South will rise up with the men of this generation and condemn them, because she came from the ends of the earth to hear the wisdom of Solomon; and there is something greater than Solomon here. On Judgement day the men of Nineveh will stand up with this generation and condemn it, because when Jonah preached they repented; and there is something greater than Jonah here.'

This is the Gospel of the Lord.

Tuesday

FIRST READING

A reading from the letter of St Paul to the Galatians   5:1-6

> *Whether you are circumcised or not is not important, what does*
> *matter is faith which expresses itself through love.*

When Christ freed us, he meant us to remain free. Stand firm, therefore, and do not submit again to the yoke of slavery. It is I, Paul, who tell you this: if you allow yourselves to be circumcised, Christ will be of no benefit to you at all. With all solemnity I repeat my warning: Everyone who accepts circumcision is obliged to keep the whole Law. But if you do look to the Law to make you justified, then you have separated yourselves from Christ, and have fallen from grace. Christians are told by the Spirit to look to faith for those rewards that righteousness hopes for, since in Christ Jesus whether you are circumcised or not makes no difference – what matters is faith that makes its power felt through love.

This is the word of the Lord.

Responsorial Psalm   Ps 118:41. 43-45. 47-48. ℟ v.41

℟   Let your loving kindness come to me, O Lord.

1   Lord, let your love come upon me,
      the saving help of your promise.
      Do not take the word of truth from my mouth
      for I trust in your decrees.   ℟

2   I shall always keep your law
      for ever and ever.
      I shall walk in the path of freedom
      for I see your precepts.   ℟

3   Your commands have been my delight;
      these I have loved.
      I will worship your commands and love them
      and ponder your statutes.   ℟

Gospel Acclamation   Heb 4:12

Alleluia! alleluia!
The word of God is living and active;
it probes the thoughts and motives of our heart.
Alleluia!

GOSPEL

A reading from the holy Gospel according to Luke   11:37-41

Give alms and everything will be made clean for you.

Jesus had just finished speaking when a Pharisee invited him to dine
at his house. He went in and sat down at the table. The Pharisee saw
this and was surprised that he had not first washed before the meal.
But the Lord said to him, 'Oh, you Pharisees! You clean the outside of
cup and plate, while inside yourselves you are filled with extortion
and wickedness. Fools! Did not he who made the outside make the
inside too? Instead, give alms from what you have and then indeed
everything will be clean for you.'

This is the Gospel of the Lord.

Wednesday

FIRST READING

A reading from the letter of St Paul to the Galatians   5:18-25

You cannot belong to Christ unless you crucify the flesh with its passions.

If you are led by the Spirit, no law can touch you. When self-indulgence is at work the results are obvious: fornication, gross indecency and sexual irresponsibility; idolatry and sorcery; feuds and wrangling, jealousy, bad temper and quarrels; disagreements, factions, envy; drunkenness, orgies and similar things. I warn you now, as I warned you before: those who behave like this will not inherit the kingdom of God. What the Spirit brings is very different: love, joy, peace, patience, kindness, goodness, trustfulness, gentleness and self-control. There can be no law against things like that, of course. You cannot belong to Christ Jesus unless you crucify all self-indulgent passions and desires.

Since the Spirit is our life, let us be directed by the Spirit.

This is the word of the Lord.

Responsorial Psalm   Ps 1:1-4. 6. ℟ cf. Jn 8:12

℟   Those who follow you, Lord, will have the light of life.

1   Happy indeed is the man,
      who follows not the counsel of the wicked;
      nor lingers in the way of sinners
      nor sits in the company of scorners,
      but whose delight is the law of the Lord
      and who ponders his law day and night.   ℟

2   He is like a tree that is planted
      beside the flowing waters,
      that yields its fruit in due season
      and whose leaves shall never fade;
      and all that he does shall prosper.   ℟

3   Not so are the wicked, not so!
      For they like winnowed chaff
      shall be driven away by the wind.
      For the Lord guards the way of the just
      but the way of the wicked leads to doom.   ℟

Gospel Acclamation   Jn 10:27

Alleluia, alleluia!
My sheep listen to my voice, says the Lord;
I know them, and they follow me.
Alleluia!

GOSPEL

A reading from the holy Gospel according to Luke   11:42-46

Alas for you pharisees – and you lawyers, woe to you!

The Lord said to the Pharisees: 'Alas for you Pharisees! You who pay
your tithe of mint and rue and all sorts of garden herbs and overlook
justice and the love of God! These you should have practised, without
leaving the others undone. Alas for you Pharisees who like taking the
seats of honour in the synagogues and being greeted obsequiously in
the market squares! Alas for you, because you are like the unmarked
tombs that men walk on without knowing it!'

A lawyer then spoke up. 'Master,' he said 'when you speak like this
you insult us too.' 'Alas for you lawyers also,' he replied 'because you
load on men burdens that are unendurable, burdens that you
yourselves do not move a finger to lift.'

This is the Gospel of the Lord.

Thursday

FIRST READING

A reading from the letter of St Paul to the Ephesians   1:1-10

Before the world was made, he chose us.

From Paul, appointed by God to be an apostle of Christ Jesus, to the
saints who are faithful to Christ Jesus: Grace and peace to you from
God our Father and from the Lord Jesus Christ.

Blessed be God the Father of our Lord Jesus Christ,
who has blessed us with all the spiritual blessings of heaven in Christ.
Before the world was made, he chose us, chose us in Christ,
to be holy and spotless, and to live through love in his presence,

determining that we should become his adopted sons, through Jesus
    Christ

for his own kind purposes,

to make us praise the glory of his grace,

his free gift to us in the Beloved,

in whom, through his blood, we gain our freedom, the forgiveness of
    our sins.

Such is the richness of the grace

which he has showered on us

in all wisdom and insight.

He has let us know the mystery of his purpose,

the hidden plan he so kindly made in Christ from the beginning

to act upon when the times had run their course to the end:

that he would bring everything together under Christ, as head,

everything in the heavens and everything on earth.

    This is the word of the Lord.

Responsorial Psalm   Ps 97:1-6. ℟ v.2

    ℟   The Lord has made known his salvation.

1   Sing a new song to the Lord
     for he has worked wonders.
     His right hand and his holy arm
     have brought salvation.   ℟

2   The Lord has made known his salvation;
     has shown his justice to the nations.
     He has remembered his truth and love
     for the house of Israel.   ℟

3   All the ends of the earth have seen
     the salvation of our God.
     Shout to the Lord all the earth,
     ring out your joy.   ℟

4   Sing psalms to the Lord with the harp
     with the sound of music.
     With trumpets and the sound of the horn
     acclaim the King, the Lord.   ℟

Gospel Acclamation   Jn 14:6

> Alleluia, alleluia!
> I am the way, the truth, and the life, says the Lord;
> no one comes to the Father, except through me.
> Alleluia!

GOSPEL

A reading from the holy Gospel according to Luke   11:47-54

> *The blood of the prophets is required, from the blood of Abel to the*
> *blood of Zechariah.*

Jesus said: 'Alas for you who build the tombs of the prophets, the men your ancestors killed! In this way you both witness what your ancestors did and approve it; they did the killing, you do the building.

'And that is why the Wisdom of God said, "I will send them prophets and apostles; some they will slaughter and persecute, so that this generation will have to answer for every prophet's blood that has been shed since the foundation of the world, from the blood of Abel to the blood of Zechariah, who was murdered between the altar and the sanctuary." Yes, I tell you, this generation will have to answer for it all.

'Alas for you lawyers who have taken away the key of knowledge! You have not gone in yourselves, and have prevented others going in who wanted to.'

When he left the house, the scribes and the Pharisees began a furious attack on him and tried to force answers from him on innumerable questions, setting traps to catch him out in something he might say.

This is the Gospel of the Lord.

Friday

FIRST READING

A reading from the letter of St Paul to the Ephesians   1:11-14

> *We hoped in Christ before he came and we were sealed with the Holy Spirit.*

It is in Christ that we were claimed as God's own,
chosen from the beginning,

under the predetermined plan of the one who guides all things
as he decides by his own will;
chosen to be,
for his greater glory,
the people who would put their hopes in Christ before he came.
Now you too, in him,
have heard the message of the truth and the good news of your
    salvation,
and have believed it;
and you too have been stamped with the seal of the Holy Spirit of the
    Promise,
the pledge of our inheritance
which brings freedom for those whom God has taken for his own,
to make his glory praised.

This is the word of the Lord.

Responsorial Psalm   Ps 32:1-2. 4-5. 12-13. ℟ v.12

℟   Happy the people the Lord has chosen to be his own.

1   Ring out your joy to the Lord, O you just;
     for praise is fitting for loyal hearts.
     Give thanks to the Lord upon the harp,
     with a ten-stringed lute sing him songs.   ℟

2   For the word of the Lord is faithful
     and all his works to be trusted.
     The Lord loves justice and right
     and fills the earth with his love.   ℟

3   They are happy, whose God is the Lord,
     the people he has chosen as his own.
     From the heavens the Lord looks forth,
     he sees all the children of men.   ℟

Gospel Acclamation   Ps 32:22

    Alleluia, alleluia!
    Lord, let your mercy be on us,
    as we place our trust in you.
    Alleluia!

GOSPEL

A reading from the holy Gospel according to Luke 12:1-7

Every hair on your head has been numbered.

The people had gathered in their thousands so that they were treading on one another. And Jesus began to speak, first of all to his disciples. 'Be on your guard against the yeast of the Pharisees – that is, their hypocrisy. Everything that is now covered will be uncovered, and everything now hidden will be made clear. For this reason, whatever you have said in the dark will be heard in the daylight, and what you have whispered in hidden places will be proclaimed on the housetops.

'To you my friends I say: Do not be afraid of those who kill the body and after that can do no more. I will tell you whom to fear: fear him who, after he has killed, has the power to cast into hell. Yes, I tell you, fear him. Can you not buy five sparrows for two pennies? And yet not one is forgotten in God's sight. Why, every hair on your head has been counted. There is no need to be afraid: you are worth more than hundreds of sparrows.'

This is the Gospel of the Lord.

Saturday

FIRST READING

A reading from the letter of St Paul to the Ephesians 1:15-23

He made him the head of the Church, which is his body.

I, having once heard about your faith in the Lord Jesus, and the love that you show towards all the saints, have never failed to remember you in my prayers and to thank God for you. May the God of our Lord Jesus Christ, the Father of glory, give you a spirit of wisdom and perception of what is revealed, to bring you to full knowledge of him. May he enlighten the eyes of your mind so that you can see what hope his call holds for you, what rich glories he has promised the saints will inherit and how infinitely great is the power that he has exercised for us believers. This you can tell from the strength of his power at work in Christ, when he used it to raise him from the dead and to make him sit at his right hand, in heaven, far above every Sovereignty, Authority, Power or Domination, or any other name that can be named, not only in this age but also in the age to come. He has put all things under his feet, and made him, as the ruler of everything, the head of the Church; which is his body, the fullness of him who fills the whole creation.

This is the word of the Lord.

Responsorial Psalm   Ps 8:2-7. ℟ cf. v.7

℟   You gave your Son authority over all your creation.

1   How great is your name, O Lord our God,
    through all the earth!
    Your majesty is praised above the heavens;
    on the lips of children and of babes
    you have found praise to foil your enemy.   ℟

2   When I see the heavens, the works of your hands,
    the moon and the stars which you arranged,
    what is man that you should keep him in mind,
    mortal man that you care for him?   ℟

3   Yet you have made him little less than a god;
    with glory and honour you crowned him,
    gave him power over the works of your hand,
    put all things under his feet.   ℟

Gospel Acclamation   Jn 15:26. 27

Alleluia, alleluia!
The Spirit of Truth will bear witness to me, says the Lord,
and you also will be my witnesses.
Alleluia!

GOSPEL

A reading from the holy Gospel according to Luke   12:8-12

When the time comes, the Holy Spirit will teach you what you must say.

Jesus said to his disciples, 'I tell you, if anyone openly declares himself for me in the presence of men, the Son of Man will declare himself for him in the presence of God's angels. But the man who disowns me in the presence of men will be disowned in the presence of God's angels.

'Everyone who says a word against the Son of Man will be forgiven, but he who blasphemes against the Holy Spirit will not be forgiven.

'When they take you before synagogues and magistrates and authorities, do not worry about how to defend yourselves or what to say, because when the time comes, the Holy Spirit will teach you what you must say.'

This is the Gospel of the Lord.

TWENTY-NINTH WEEK IN ORDINARY TIME

Year II

Monday

FIRST READING

A reading from the letter of St Paul to the Ephesians   2:1-10

He has raised us up with Christ and has given us a place with him in heaven.

You were dead, through the crimes and the sins in which you used to live when you were following the way of this world, obeying the ruler who governs the air, the spirit who is at work in the rebellious. We all were among them too in the past, living sensual lives, ruled entirely by our own physical desires and our own ideas; so that by nature we were as much under God's anger as the rest of the world. But God loved us with so much love that he was generous with his mercy: when we were dead through our sins, he brought us to life with Christ – it is through grace that you have been saved – and raised us up with him and gave us a place with him in heaven, in Christ Jesus.

This was to show for all ages to come, through his goodness towards us in Christ Jesus, how infinitely rich he is in grace. Because it is by grace that you have been saved through faith; not by anything of your own, but by a gift from God; not by anything that you have done, so that nobody can claim the credit. We are God's work of art, created in Christ Jesus to live the good life as from the beginning he had meant us to live it.

This is the word of the Lord.

Responsorial Psalm   Ps 99. ℟ v.3

℟   The Lord made us, we belong to him.

1   Cry out with joy to the Lord, all the earth.
    Serve the Lord with gladness.
    Come before him, singing for joy.   ℟

2   Know that he, the Lord, is God.
    He made us, we belong to him,
    we are his people, the sheep of his flock.   ℟

3   Go within his gates, giving thanks.
    Enter his courts with songs of praise.
    Give thanks to him and bless his name.   ℟

4   Indeed, how good is the Lord,
    eternal his merciful love.
    He is faithful from age to age.   ℟

Gospel Acclamation   Mt 5:3

    Alleluia, alleluia!
    Happy the poor in spirit;
    the kingdom of heaven is theirs!
    Alleluia!

GOSPEL

A reading from the holy Gospel according to Luke   12:13-21

To whom will all this wealth of yours go?

A man in the crowd said to Jesus, 'Master, tell my brother to give me a
share of our inheritance.' 'My friend,' he replied 'who appointed me
your judge, or the arbitrator of your claims?' Then he said to them,
'Watch, and be on your guard against avarice of any kind, for a man's
life is not made secure by what he owns, even when he has more than
he needs.'

    Then he told them a parable: 'There was once a rich man who,
having had a good harvest from his land, thought to himself, "What
am I to do? I have not enough room to store my crops." Then he said,
"This is what I will do: I will pull down my barns and build bigger
ones, and store all my grain and my goods in them, and I will say to
my soul: My soul, you have plenty of good things laid by for many

years to come; take things easy, eat, drink, have a good time." But God said to him, "Fool! This very night the demand will be made for your soul; and this hoard of yours, whose will it be then?" So it is when a man stores up treasure for himself in place of making himself rich in the sight of God.'

This is the Gospel of the Lord.

Tuesday

FIRST READING

A reading from the letter of St Paul to the Ephesians   2:12-22

He is our peace; he has made the two into one.

Do not forget that you had no Christ and were excluded from membership of Israel, aliens with no part in the covenants with their Promise; you were immersed in this world, without hope and without God. But now in Christ Jesus, you that used to be so far apart from us have been brought very close, by the blood of Christ. For he is the peace between us, and has made the two into one and broken down the barrier which used to keep them apart, actually destroying in his own person the hostility caused by the rules and decrees of the Law. This was to create one single New Man in himself out of the two of them and by restoring peace through the cross, to unite them both in a single Body and reconcile them with God. In his own person he killed the hostility. Later he came to bring the good news of peace, peace to you who were far away and peace to those who were near at hand. Through him, both of us have in the one Spirit our way to come to the Father.

So you are no longer aliens or foreign visitors: you are citizens like all the saints, and part of God's household. You are part of a building that has the apostles and prophets for its main corner stone. As every structure is aligned on him, all grow into one holy temple in the Lord; and you too, in him, are being built into a house where God lives, in the Spirit.

This is the word of the Lord.

Responsorial Psalm   Ps 84:9-14. ℟ cf. v.9

℟   The Lord speaks of peace to his people.

1 I will hear what the Lord God has to say,
   a voice that speaks of peace.
   His help is near for those who fear him
   and his glory will dwell in our land.   ℟

2 Mercy and faithfulness have met;
   justice and peace have embraced.
   Faithfulness shall spring from the earth
   and justice look down from heaven.   ℟

3 The Lord will make us prosper
   and our earth shall yield its fruit.
   Justice shall march before him
   and peace shall follow his steps.   ℟

Gospel Acclamation   Lk 21:36

    Alleluia, alleluia!
    Be watchful, pray constantly,
    that you may be worthy to stand before the Son of Man.
    Alleluia!

GOSPEL

A reading from the holy Gospel according to Luke   12:35-38

Happy those servants whom the master finds awake when he comes.

Jesus said to his disciples: 'See that you are dressed for action and
have your lamps lit. Be like men waiting for their master to return
from the wedding feast, ready to open the door as soon as he comes and
knocks. Happy those servants whom the master finds awake when he
comes. I tell you solemnly, he will put on an apron, sit them down at
table and wait on them. It may be in the second watch he comes, or in
the third, but happy those servants if he finds them ready.'

    This is the Gospel of the Lord.

Wednesday

FIRST READING

A reading from the letter of St Paul to the Ephesians   3:2-12

The mystery of Christ now revealed to us was unknown to people in past generations.

You have probably heard how I have been entrusted by God with the grace he meant for you, and that it was by a revelation that I was given the knowledge of the mystery, as I have just described it very shortly. If you read my words, you will have some idea of the depths that I see in the mystery of Christ. This mystery that has now been revealed through the Spirit to his holy apostles and prophets was unknown to any men in past generations; it means that pagans now share the same inheritance, that they are parts of the same body, and that the same promise has been made to them, in Christ Jesus, through the gospel. I have been made the servant of that gospel by a gift of grace from God who gave it to me by his own power. I, who am less than the least of all the saints, have been entrusted with this special grace, not only of proclaiming to the pagans the infinite treasure of Christ but also of explaining how the mystery is to be dispensed. Through all the ages, this has been kept hidden in God, the creator of everything. Why? So that the Sovereignties and Powers should learn only now, through the Church, how comprehensive God's wisdom really is, exactly according to the plan which he had had from all eternity in Christ Jesus our Lord. This is why we are bold enough to approach God in complete confidence, through our faith in him.

This is the word of the Lord.

Responsorial Psalm   Is 12:2-6. ℟ cf. v.3

℟   You will draw water joyfully
     from the springs of salvation.

1   Truly, God is my salvation,
     I trust, I shall not fear.
     For the Lord is my strength, my song,
     he became my saviour.
     With joy you will draw water
     from the wells of salvation.   ℟

2　Give thanks to the Lord, give praise to his name!
　　make his mighty deeds known to the peoples!
　　Declare the greatness of his name,
　　sing a psalm to the Lord!　℟

3　For he has done glorious deeds,
　　made them known to all the earth!
　　People of Zion, sing and shout for joy
　　for great in your midst is the Holy One of Israel.　℟

Gospel Acclamation   Mt 24:42. 44

　　Alleluia, alleluia!
　　Be watchful and ready:
　　you know not when the Son of Man is coming.
　　Alleluia!

GOSPEL

A reading from the holy Gospel according to Luke   12:39-48

From the person who has received much, much will be demanded.

Jesus said to his disciples: 'You may be quite sure of this, that if the householder had known at what hour the burglar would come, he would not have let anyone break through the wall of his house. You too must stand ready, because the Son of Man is coming at an hour you do not expect.'

Peter said, 'Lord, do you mean this parable for us, or for everyone?' The Lord replied, 'What sort of steward, then, is faithful and wise enough for the master to place him over his household to give them their allowance of food at the proper time? Happy that servant if his master's arrival finds him at this employment. I tell you truly, he will place him over everything he owns. But as for the servant who says to himself, "My master is taking his time coming," and sets about beating the menservants and the maids, and eating and drinking and getting drunk, his master will come on a day he does not expect and at an hour he does not know. The master will cut him off and send him to the same fate as the unfaithful.

'The servant who knows what his master wants, but has not even started to carry out those wishes, will receive very many strokes of the lash. The one who did not know, but deserves to be beaten for what he has done, will receive fewer strokes. When a man has had a great

773

deal given him, a great deal will be demanded of him; when a man has had a great deal given him on trust, even more will be expected of him.'

This is the Gospel of the Lord.

Thursday

FIRST READING

A reading from the letter of St Paul to the Ephesians 3:14-21

Planted in love and built on love, you will grasp the fullness of God.

This is what I pray, kneeling before the Father, from whom every family, whether spiritual or natural, takes its name:

Out of his infinite glory, may he give you the power through his Spirit for your hidden self to grow strong, so that Christ may live in your hearts through faith, and then, planted in love and built on love, you will with all the saints have strength to grasp the breadth and the length, the height and the depth; until, knowing the love of Christ, which is beyond all knowledge, you are filled with the utter fullness of God.

Glory be to him whose power, working in us, can do infinitely more than we can ask or imagine; glory be to him from generation to generation in the Church and in Christ Jesus for ever and ever. Amen.

This is the word of the Lord.

Responsorial Psalm   Ps 32:1-2. 4-5. 11-12. 18-19. ℟ v.5

℟ The earth is full of the goodness of the Lord.

1 Ring out your joy to the Lord, O you just;
    for praise is fitting for loyal hearts.
    Give thanks to the Lord upon the harp,
    with a ten-stringed lute sing him songs. ℟

2 For the word of the Lord is faithful
    and all his works to be trusted.
    The Lord loves justice and right
    and fills the earth with his love. ℟

3   His own designs shall stand for ever,
    the plans of his heart from age to age.
    They are happy, whose God is the Lord,
    the people he has chosen as his own.   ℟

4   The Lord looks on those who revere him,
    on those who hope in his love,
    to rescue their souls from death,
    to keep them alive in famine.   ℟

Gospel Acclamation   Phil 3:8-9

    Alleluia, alleluia!
    I count all things worthless but this:
    to gain Jesus Christ and to be found in him.
    Alleluia!

                            GOSPEL

A reading from the holy Gospel according to Luke   12:49-53

                I have not come to bring peace, but separation.

Jesus said to his disciples: 'I have come to bring fire to the earth, and
how I wish it were blazing already! There is a baptism I must still
receive, and how great is my distress till it is over!

    'Do you suppose that I am here to bring peace on earth? No, I tell
you, but rather division. For from now on a household of five will be
divided: three against two and two against three; the father divided
against the son, son against father, mother against daughter, daughter against mother, mother-in-law against daughter-in-law, daughter-in-law against mother-in-law.'

    This is the Gospel of the Lord.

Friday

FIRST READING

A reading from the letter of St Paul to the Ephesians   4:1-6

There is one body, one Lord, one faith, one baptism.

I, the prisoner in the Lord, implore you to lead a life worthy of your vocation. Bear with one another charitably, in complete selflessness, gentleness and patience. Do all you can to preserve the unity of the Spirit by the peace that binds you together. There is one Body, one Spirit, just as you were all called into one and the same hope when you were called. There is one Lord, one faith, one baptism, and one God who is Father of all, over all, through all and within all.

This is the word of the Lord.

Responsorial Psalm   Ps 23:1-6. ℟ cf. v.6

℟   Lord, this is the people that longs to see your face.

1   The Lord's is the earth and its fullness,
     the world and all its people.
     It is he who set it on the seas;
     on the waters he made it firm.   ℟

2   Who shall climb the mountain of the Lord?
     Who shall stand in his holy place?
     The man with clean hands and pure heart,
     who desires not worthless things.   ℟

3   He shall receive blessings from the Lord
     and reward from the God who saves him.
     Such are the men who seek him,
     seek the face of the God of Jacob.   ℟

Gospel Acclamation   cf. Mt 11:25

Alleluia, alleluia!
Blessed are you, Father, Lord of heaven and earth;
you have revealed to little ones the mysteries of the kingdom.
Alleluia!

GOSPEL

A reading from the holy Gospel according to Luke   12:54-59

You know how to interpret the face of the earth and the sky. How is it you do not know how to interpret these times?

Jesus said to the crowds, 'When you see a cloud looming up in the west you say at once that rain is coming, and so it does. And when the wind is from the south you say it will be hot, and it is. Hypocrites! You know how to interpret the face of the earth and the sky. How is it you do not know how to interpret these times?

'Why not judge for yourselves what is right? For example: when you go to court with your opponent, try to settle with him on the way, or he may drag you before the judge and the judge hand you over to the bailiff and the bailiff have you thrown into prison. I tell you, you will not get out till you have paid the very last penny.'

This is the Gospel of the Lord.

Saturday

FIRST READING

A reading from the letter of St Paul to the Ephesians   4:7-16

Christ is the head by whom the whole body is fitted and joined together.

Each one of us has been given his own share of grace, given as Christ allotted it. It was said that he would:

When he ascended to the height, he captured prisoners,
he gave gifts to men.

When it says, 'he ascended', what can it mean if not that he descended right down to the lower regions of the earth? The one who rose higher than all the heavens to fill all things is none other than the one who descended. And to some, his gift was that they should be apostles; to some, prophets; to some, evangelists; to some, pastors and teachers; so that the saints together make a unity in the work of service, building up the body of Christ. In this way we are all to come to unity in our faith and in our knowledge of the Son of God, until we become the perfect Man, fully mature with the fullness of Christ himself.

Then we shall not be children any longer, or tossed one way and another and carried along by every wind of doctrine, at the mercy of all the tricks men play and their cleverness in practising deceit. If we live by the truth and in love, we shall grow in all ways into Christ, who is the head by whom the whole body is fitted and joined together, every joint adding its own strength, for each separate part to work according to its function. So the body grows until it has built itself up, in love.

This is the word of the Lord.

Responsorial Psalm   Ps 121:1-5. ℟ v.1

℟   Let us go rejoicing to the house of the Lord.

1   I rejoiced when I heard them say:
     'Let us go to God's house.'
     And now our feet are standing
     within your gates, O Jerusalem.   ℟

2   Jerusalem is built as a city
     strongly compact.
     It is there that the tribes go up,
     the tribes of the Lord.   ℟

3   For Israel's law it is,
     there to praise the Lord's name.
     There were set the thrones of judgement
     of the house of David.   ℟

Gospel Acclamation   Ez 33:1

Alleluia, alleluia!
I do not wish the sinner to die, says the Lord,
but to turn to me and live.
Alleluia!

GOSPEL

A reading from the holy Gospel according to Luke   13:1-9

Unless you repent you will all perish as they did.

Some people arrived and told Jesus about the Galileans whose blood Pilate had mingled with that of their sacrifices. At this he said to them, 'Do you suppose these Galileans who suffered like that were greater sinners than any other Galileans? They were not, I tell you. No; but unless you repent you will all perish as they did. Or those eighteen on whom the tower at Siloam fell and killed them? Do you suppose that they were more guilty than all the other people living in Jerusalem? They were not, I tell you. No; but unless you repent you will all perish as they did.'

He told this parable: 'A man had a fig tree planted in his vineyard, and he came looking for fruit on it but found none. He said to the man who looked after the vineyard. "Look here, for three years now I have been coming to look for fruit on this fig tree and finding none. Cut it down: why should it be taking up the ground?" "Sir," the man replied "leave it one more year and give me time to dig round it and manure it: it may bear fruit next year; if not, then you can cut it down." '

This is the Gospel of the Lord.

THIRTIETH WEEK IN ORDINARY TIME
Year II

Monday

FIRST READING

A reading from the letter of St Paul to the Ephesians   4:32–5:8

Walk in love as Christ loved us.

Be friends with one another, and kind, forgiving each other as readily as God forgave you in Christ.

Try, then, to imitate God, as children of his that he loves, and follow Christ by loving as he loved you, giving himself up in our place as a fragrant offering and a sacrifice to God. Among you there must be not even a mention of fornication or impurity in any of its forms, or promiscuity: this would hardly become the saints! There must be no coarseness, or salacious talk and jokes – all this is wrong for you: raise your voices in thanksgiving instead. For you can be quite certain that nobody who actually indulges in fornication or impurity or promiscuity – which is worshipping a false god – can inherit anything of the kingdom of God. Do not let anyone deceive you with empty arguments: it is for this loose living that God's anger comes down on those who rebel against him. Make sure that you are not included with them. You were darkness once, but now you are light in the Lord; be like children of light.

This is the word of the Lord.

Responsorial Psalm   Ps 1:1-4. 6. ℟ cf. Eph 5:1

℟   Behave like God as his very dear children.

1   Happy indeed is the man
who follows not the counsel of the wicked;
nor lingers in the way of sinners
nor sits in the company of scorners,
but whose delight is the law of the Lord
and who ponders his law day and night.   ℟

2   He is like a tree that is planted
beside the flowing waters,
that yields its fruit in due season
and whose leaves shall never fade;
and all that he does shall prosper.   ℟

3   Not so are the wicked, not so!
For they like winnowed chaff
shall be driven away by the wind.
For the Lord guards the way of the just
but the way of the wicked leads to doom.   ℟

Gospel Acclamation   cf. Jn 17:17

Alleluia, alleluia!
Your word, O Lord, is truth:
make us holy in the truth.
Alleluia!

GOSPEL

A reading from the holy Gospel according to Luke   13:10-17

*This daughter of Abraham, was it was not right t free her from
the bondage on the sabbath day?*

One sabbath day Jesus was teaching in one of the synagogues, and a woman was there who for eighteen years had been possessed by a spirit that left her enfeebled; she was bent double and quite unable to stand upright. When Jesus saw her he called her over and said, 'Woman, you are rid of your infirmity' and he laid his hands on her. And at once she straightened up, and she glorified God.

But the synagogue official was indignant because Jesus had healed on the sabbath, and he addressed the people present. 'There are six days' he said 'when work is to be done. Come and be healed on one of those days and not on the sabbath.' But the Lord answered him. 'Hypocrites!' he said 'Is there one of you who does not untie his ox or his donkey from the manger on the sabbath and take it out for watering? And this woman, a daughter of Abraham whom Satan has held bound these eighteen years – was it not right to untie her bonds on the sabbath day?' When he said this, all his adversaries were covered with confusion, and all the people were overjoyed at all the wonders he worked.

This is the Gospel of the Lord.

Tuesday

FIRST READING

A reading from the letter of St Paul to the Ephesians   5:21-33

This is a great mystery and it refers to Christ and the Church.

Give way to one another in obedience to Christ. Wives should regard their husbands as they regard the Lord, since as Christ is head of the Church and saves the whole body, so is a husband the head of his wife; and as the Church submits to Christ, so should wives to their husbands, in everything. Husbands should love their wives just as Christ loved the Church and sacrificed himself for her to make her holy. He made her clean by washing her in water with a form of words, so that when he took her to himself she would be glorious, with no speck or wrinkle or anything like that, but holy and faultless. In the same way, husbands must love their wives as they love their own bodies; for a man to love his wife is for him to love himself. A man never hates his own body, but he feeds it and looks after it; and that is the way Christ treats the Church, because it is the body – and we are its living parts. For this reason, a man must leave his father and mother and be joined to his wife, and the two will become one body. This mystery has many implications; but I am saying it applies to

Christ and the Church. To sum up; you too, each one of you, must love his wife as he loves himself; and let every wife respect her husband.

This is the word of the Lord.

Responsorial Psalm   Ps 127:1-5. ℟ cf. v.1

℟   Happy are those who fear the Lord.

1   O blessed are those who fear the Lord
    and walk in his ways!
    By the labour of your hands you shall eat.
    You will be happy and prosper.   ℟

2   Your wife like a fruitful vine
    in the heart of your house;
    your children like shoots of the olive
    around your table.   ℟

3   Indeed thus shall be blessed
    the man who fears the Lord.
    May the Lord bless you from Zion
    all the days of your life!   ℟

Gospel Acclamation   cf. Mt 11:25

Alleluia, alleluia!
Blessed are you, Father, Lord of heaven and earth;
you have revealed to little ones the mysteries of the kingdom.
Alleluia!

GOSPEL

A reading from the holy Gospel according to Luke   13:18-21

The seed grew and became a mighty tree.

Jesus said, 'What is the kingdom of God like? What shall I compare it with? It is like a mustard seed which a man took and threw into his garden: it grew and became a tree, and the birds of the air sheltered in its branches.'

Another thing he said, 'What shall I compare the kingdom of God with? It is like the yeast a woman took and mixed in with three measures of flour till it was leavened all through.'

This is the Gospel of the Lord.

Wednesday

FIRST READING

A reading from the letter of St Paul to the Ephesians 6:1-9

Be obedient, not as human servants but as servants of Christ.

Children, be obedient to your parents in the Lord – that is your duty. The first commandment that has a promise attached to it is: Honour your father and mother; and the promise is: and you will prosper and have a long life in the land. And parents, never drive your children to resentment but in bringing them up correct them and guide them as the Lord does.

Slaves, be obedient to the men who are called your masters in this world, with deep respect and sincere loyalty, as you are obedient to Christ: not only when you are under their eye, as if you had only to please men, but because you are slaves of Christ and wholeheartedly do the will of God. Work hard and willingly, but do it for the sake of the Lord and not for the sake of men. You can be sure that everyone, whether a slave or a free man, will be properly rewarded by the Lord for whatever work he has done well. And those of you who are employers, treat your slaves in the same spirit; do without threats, remembering that they and you have the same Master in heaven and he is not impressed by one person more than by another.

This is the word of the Lord.

Responsorial Psalm   Ps 144:10-14. ℟ v. 13

℟   The Lord is faithful in all his words.

1   All your creatures shall thank you, O Lord,
    and your friends shall repeat their blessing.
    They shall speak of the glory of your reign
    and declare your might, O God,
    to make known to men your mighty deeds
    and the glorious splendour of your reign.   ℟

2   Yours is an everlasting kingdom;
    your rule lasts from age to age.   ℟

3   The Lord is faithful in all his words
    and loving in all his deeds.
    The Lord supports all who fall
    and raises all who are bowed down.   ℟

Gospel Acclamation   cf. 2 Thess 2:14

Alleluia, alleluia!
God has called us with the gospel,
to share in the glory of our Lord Jesus Christ.
Alleluia!

GOSPEL

A reading from the holy Gospel according to Luke   cf. 13:22-30

*They will come from East and West to take their places at the feast in the
kingdom of God.*

Through towns and villages Jesus went teaching, making his way to
Jerusalem. Someone said to him, 'Sir, will there be only a few saved?'
He said to them, 'Try your best to enter by the narrow door, because, I
tell you, many will try to enter and will not succeed.

'Once the master of the house has got up and locked the door, you
may find yourself knocking on the door, saying, 'Lord, open to us' but
he will answer, 'I do not know where you come from.' Then you will
find yourself saying, 'We once ate and drank in your company; you
taught in our streets' but he will reply, 'I do not know where you come
from. Away from me, all you wicked men!'

'Then there will be weeping and grinding of teeth, when you see
Abraham and Isaac and Jacob and all the prophets in the kingdom of
God, and yourselves turned outside. And men from east and west,
from north and south, will come to take their places at the feast in the
kingdom of God.

'Yes, there are those now last who will be first, and those now first
who will be last.'

This is the Gospel of the Lord.

Thursday

FIRST READING

A reading from the letter of St Paul to the Ephesians 6:10-20

Put God's armour on so that you will be able to stand firm.

Grow strong in the Lord, with the strength of his power. Put God's armour on so as to be able to resist the devil's tactics. For it is not against human enemies that we have to struggle, but against the Sovereignties and the Powers who originate the darkness of this world, the spiritual army of evil in the heavens. That is why you must rely on God's armour, or you will not be able to put up any resistance when the worst happens, or have enough resources to hold your ground.

So stand your ground, with truth buckled round your waist, and integrity for a breastplate, wearing for shoes on your feet the eagerness to spread the gospel of peace and always carrying the shield of faith so that you can use it to put out the burning arrows of the evil one. And then you must accept salvation from God to be your helmet and receive the word of God from the Spirit to use as a sword.

Pray all the time, asking for what you need, praying in the Spirit on every possible occasion. Never get tired of staying awake to pray for all the saints; and pray for me to be given an opportunity to open my mouth and speak without fear and give out the mystery of the gospel of which I am an ambassador in chains; pray that in proclaiming it I may speak as boldly as I ought to.

This is the word of the Lord.

Responsorial Psalm Ps 143:1-2. 9-10. ℟ v.1

℟ Blessed be the Lord, my Rock!

1 Blessed be the Lord, my rock
who trains my arms for battle,
who prepares my hands for war. ℟

2 He is my love, my fortress;
he is my stronghold, my saviour,
my shield, my place of refuge.
He brings peoples under my rule. ℟

(continued)

3 To you, O God, will I sing a new song;
   I will play on the ten-stringed lute
   to you who give kings their victory,
   who set David your servant free.

   ℟ Blessed be the Lord, my Rock!

Gospel Acclamation   cf. Lk 19:38; 2:14

Alleluia, alleluia!
Blessed is the king who comes in the name of the Lord:
glory to God in the highest and peace to his people on earth.
Alleluia!

GOSPEL

A reading from the holy Gospel according to Luke   13:31-35

It is not right for the prophet to die outside Jerusalem.

Some Pharisees came up to Jesus. 'Go away' they said 'Leave this place, because Herod means to kill you.' He replied, 'You may go and give that fox this message: Learn that today and tomorrow I cast out devils and on the third day attain my end. But for today and tomorrow and the next day I must go out, since it would not be right for a prophet to die outside Jerusalem.

'Jerusalem, Jerusalem, you that kill the prophets and stone those who are sent to you! How often have I longed to gather your children, as a hen gathers her brood under her wings, and you refused! So be it! Your house will be left to you. Yes, I promise you, you shall not see me till the time comes when you say:

Blessings on him who comes in the name of the Lord!'

This is the Gospel of the Lord.

Friday

FIRST READING

A reading from the letter of St Paul to the Philippians   1:1-11

He who began this good work in you will see that it is perfected
when the day of Christ comes.

From Paul and Timothy, servants of Christ Jesus, to all the saints in
Christ Jesus, together with their presiding elders and deacons. We
wish you the grace and peace of God our Father and of the Lord Jesus
Christ.

I thank my God whenever I think of you; and every time I pray for
all of you, I pray with joy, remembering how you have helped to
spread the Good News from the day you first heard it right up to the
present. I am quite certain that the One who began this good work in
you will see that it is finished when the Day of Christ Jesus comes. It
is only natural that I should feel like this towards you all, since you
have shared the privileges which have been mine: both my chains and
my work defending and establishing the gospel. You have a perma-
nent place in my heart, and God knows how much I miss you all,
loving you as Christ Jesus loves you. My prayer is that your love for
each other may increase more and more and never stop improving
your knowledge and deepening your perception so that you can
always recognise what is best. This will help you to become pure and
blameless, and prepare you for the Day of Christ, when you will reach
the perfect goodness which Christ Jesus produces in us for the glory
and praise of God.

This is the word of the Lord.

Responsorial Psalm   Ps 110:1-6. ℟ v.2

    ℟ How great are the works of the Lord!

or

    ℟ Alleluia!

1 I will thank the Lord with all my heart
   in the meeting of the just and their assembly.
   Great are the works of the Lord;
   to be pondered by all who love them.   ℟

2 Majestic and glorious his work,
   his justice stands firm for ever.
   He makes us remember his wonders.
   The Lord is compassion and love.

   ℟   How great are the works of the Lord!
or
   ℟   Alleluia!

3 He gives food to those who fear him;
   keeps his covenant ever in mind.
   He has shown his might to his people
   by giving them the lands of the nations.   ℟

Gospel Acclamation   Jn 10:27

   Alleluia, alleluia!
   My sheep listen to my voice, says the Lord;
   I know them, and they follow me.
   Alleluia!

GOSPEL

A reading from the holy Gospel according to Luke   14:1-6

Which of you here, if his ass or ox falls into a well, will not pull him out on the
sabbath day?

On a sabbath day Jesus had gone for a meal to the house of one of the
leading Pharisees; and they watched him closely. There in front of
him was a man with dropsy, and Jesus addressed the lawyers and
Pharisees, 'Is it against the law' he asked 'to cure a man on the
sabbath, or not?' But they remained silent, so he took the man and
cured him and sent him away. Then he said to them, 'Which of you
here, if his son falls into a well, or his ox, will not pull him out on a
sabbath day without hesitation?' And to this they could find no
answer.

   This is the Gospel of the Lord.

Saturday

FIRST READING

A reading from the letter of St Paul to the Philippians 1:18-26

For me to live is Christ, and to die is gain.

Christ is proclaimed; and that makes me happy; and I shall continue being happy, because I know this will help to save me, thanks to your prayers and to the help which will be given to me by the Spirit of Jesus. My one hope and trust is that I shall never have to admit defeat, but that now as always I shall have the courage for Christ to be glorified in my body, whether by my life or by my death. Life to me, of course, is Christ, but then death would bring me something more; but then again, if living in this body means doing work which is having good results – I do not know what I should choose. I am caught in this dilemma: I want to be gone and be with Christ, which would be very much the better, but for me to stay alive in this body is a more urgent need for your sake. This weighs with me so much that I feel sure I shall survive and stay with you all, and help you to progress in the faith and even increase your joy in it; and so you will have another reason to give praise to Christ Jesus on my account when I am with you again.

This is the word of the Lord.

Responsorial Psalm Ps 42:2-3. 5. ℟ v.3

℟ My soul is thirsting for the living God.

1 Like the deer that yearns
  for running streams,
  so my soul is yearning
  for you, my God. ℟

2 My soul is thirsting for God,
  the God of my life;
  when can I enter and see
  the face of God? ℟

3 I would lead the rejoicing crowd
  into the house of God,
  amid cries of gladness and thanksgiving. ℟

Gospel Acclamation   Mt 11:29

Alleluia, alleluia!
Take my yoke upon you;
learn from me, for I am gentle and lowly in heart.
Alleluia!

GOSPEL

A reading from the holy Gospel according to Luke   14:1. 7-11

All who exalt themselves shall be humbled, and all who
humble themselves shall be exalted.

Now on a sabbath day Jesus had gone for a meal to the house of one of
the leading Pharisees; and they watched him closely.

He then told the guests a parable, because he had noticed how they
picked the places of honour. He said this, 'When someone invites you
to a wedding feast, do not take your seat in the place of honour. A
more distinguished person than you may have been invited, and the
person who invited you both may come and say, "Give up your place to
this man." And then, to your embarrassment, you would have to go
and take the lowest place. No; when you are a guest, make your way
to the lowest place and sit there, so that, when your host comes, he
may say, "My friend, move up higher." In that way, everyone with you
at the table will see you honoured. For everyone who exalts himself
will be humbled, and the man who humbles himself will be exalted.'

This is the Gospel of the Lord.

THIRTY-FIRST WEEK IN ORDINARY TIME

Year II

Monday

FIRST READING

A reading from the letter of St Paul to the Philippians   2:1-4

Be of one mind and make me happy.

If our life in Christ means anything to you, if love can persuade at all, or the Spirit that we have in common, or any tenderness and sympathy, then be united in your convictions and united in your love, with a common purpose and a common mind. That is the one thing which would make me completely happy. There must be no competition among you, no conceit; but everybody is to be self-effacing. Always consider the other person to be better than yourself, so that nobody thinks of his own interests first but everybody thinks of other people's interests instead.

This is the word of the Lord.

Responsorial Psalm   Ps 130

     ℟   In you, Lord, I have found my peace.

1   O Lord, my heart is not proud
     nor haughty my eyes.
     I have not gone after things too great
     nor marvels beyond me.   ℟

2   Truly I have set my soul
     in silence and peace.
     A weaned child on its mother's breast,
     even so is my soul.   ℟

3   O Israel, hope in the Lord,
     both now and for ever.   ℟

Gospel Acclamation   Jn 8:31-32

> Alleluia, alleluia!
> If you stay in my word, you will indeed be my disciples,
> and you will know the truth, says the Lord.
> Alleluia!

GOSPEL

A reading from the holy Gospel according to Luke   14:12-14

Do not invite just your friends, but the poor and the crippled.

Jesus said to his host, one of the leading Pharisees, 'When you give a
lunch or a dinner, do not ask your friends, brothers, relations or rich
neighbours, for fear they repay your courtesy by inviting you in
return. No; when you have a party, invite the poor, the crippled, the
lame, the blind; that they cannot pay you back means that you are
fortunate, because repayment will be made to you when the virtuous
rise again.'

This is the Gospel of the Lord.

Tuesday

FIRST READING

A reading from the letter of St Paul to the Philippians   2:5-11

Because of his humility, God raised him on high.

In your minds you must be the same as Christ Jesus:

> His state was divine,
> yet he did not cling
> to his equality with God
> but emptied himself
> to assume the condition of a slave,
> and became as men are;
> and being as all men are,
> he was humbler yet,
> even to accepting death,
> death on a cross.
> But God raised him high
> and gave him the name

which is above all other names
so that all beings
in the heavens, on earth and in the underworld,
should bend the knee at the name of Jesus
and that every tongue should acclaim
Jesus Christ as Lord,
to the glory of God the Father.

This is the word of the Lord.

Responsorial Psalm   Ps 21:26-32. ℟ v. 26

℟   I will praise you, Lord, in the assembly of your people.

My vows I will pay before those who fear the Lord.
The poor shall eat and shall have their fill.
They shall praise the Lord, those who seek him.
May their hearts live for ever and ever!   ℟

All the earth shall remember and return to the Lord,
all families of the nations worship before him
for the kingdom is the Lord's; he is ruler of the nations.
They shall worship him, all the mighty of the earth.   ℟

And my soul shall live for him, my children serve him.
They shall tell of the Lord to generations yet to come,
declare his faithfulness to peoples yet unborn:
'These things the Lord has done.'   ℟

Gospel Acclamation   Mt 11:28

Alleluia, alleluia!
Come to me, all you that labour and are burdened,
and I will give you rest, says the Lord.
Alleluia!

GOSPEL

A reading from the holy Gospel according to Luke   14:15-24

Go to the highway and force people to come that my house will be filled.

One of those gathered round the table said to Jesus, 'Happy the man
who will be at the feast in the kingdom of God!' But he said to him,

'There was a man who gave a great banquet, and he invited a larg
number of people. When the time for the banquet came, he sent hi
servant to say to those who had been invited, "Come along: everythin
is ready now." But all alike started to make excuses. The first said, '
have bought a piece of land and must go and see it. Please accept m
apologies." Another said, "I have bought five yoke of oxen and am o
my way to try them out. Please accept my apologies." Yet anothe
said, "I have just got married and so am unable to come."

'The servant returned and reported this to his master. Then th
householder, in a rage, said to his servant, "Go out quickly into th
streets and alleys of the town and bring in here the poor, the crippled
the blind and the lame." "Sir," said the servant "your orders hav
been carried out and there is still room." Then the master said to hi
servant, "Go to the open roads and the hedgerows and force people t
come in to make sure my house is full; because, I tell you, not one o
those who were invited shall have a taste of my banquet."'

This is the Gospel of the Lord.

Wednesday

FIRST READING

A reading from the letter of St Paul to the Philippians   2:12-1

Work out your salvation; God will put both the will and the action into you

My dear friends, continue to do as I tell you, as you always have; no
only as you did when I was there with you, but even more now that
am no longer there; and work for your salvation 'in fear an
trembling.' It is God, for his own loving purpose, who puts both th
will and the action into you. Do all that has to be done withou
complaining or arguing and then you will be innocent and genuine
perfect children of God among a deceitful and underhand brood, an
you will shine in the world like bright stars because you are offering i
the word of life. This would give me something to be proud of for th
Day of Christ, and would mean that I had not run in the race an
exhausted myself for nothing. And then, if my blood has to be shed a
part of your own sacrifice and offering – which is your faith – I sha
still be happy and rejoice with all of you, and you must be just a
happy and rejoice with me.

This is the word of the Lord.

Responsorial Psalm Ps 26:1. 4. 13-14. ℟ v.1

℟ The Lord is my light and my salvation.

1 The Lord is my light and my help;
   whom shall I fear?
   The Lord is the stronghold of my life;
   before whom shall I shrink? ℟

2 There is one thing I ask of the Lord,
   for this I long,
   to live in the house of the Lord,
   all the days of my life,
   to savour the sweetness of the Lord,
   to behold his temple. ℟

3 I am sure I shall see the Lord's goodness
   in the land of the living.
   Hope in him, hold firm and take heart.
   Hope in the Lord! ℟

Gospel Acclamation 1 Peter 4:14

Alleluia, alleluia!
If you are insulted for the name of Christ, blessed are you,
for the Spirit of God rests upon you.
Alleluia!

GOSPEL

A reading from the holy Gospel according to Luke 14:25-33

All who do not give up all their possessions cannot be my disciples.

Great crowds accompanied Jesus on his way and he turned and spoke to them. 'If any man comes to me without hating his father, mother, wife, children, brothers, sisters, yes and his own life too, he cannot be my disciple. Anyone who does not carry his cross and come after me cannot be my disciple.

'And indeed, which of you here, intending to build a tower, would not first sit down and work out the cost to see if he had enough to complete it? Otherwise, if he laid the foundation and then found himself unable to finish the work, the onlookers would all start making fun of him and saying, "Here is a man who started to build and was unable to finish." Or again, what king marching to war against another king would not first sit down and consider whether with ten thousand men he could stand up to the other who advanced against him with twenty thousand? If not, then while the other king was still a long way off, he would send envoys to sue for peace. So in the same way, none of you can be my disciple unless he gives up all his possessions.'

This is the Gospel of the Lord.

Thursday

FIRST READING

A reading from the letter of St Paul to the Philippians 3:3-8

I count everything else as loss, if only I can gain Christ.

We are the real people of the circumcision, we who worship in accordance with the Spirit of God; we have our own glory from Christ Jesus without having to rely on a physical operation. If it came to relying on physical evidence, I should be fully qualified myself. Take any man who thinks he can rely on what is physical: I am even better qualified. I was born of the race of Israel and of the tribe of Benjamin, a Hebrew born of Hebrew parents, and I was circumcised when I was eight days old. As for the Law, I was a Pharisee; as for working for religion, I was a persecutor of the Church; as far as the Law can make you perfect, I was faultless. But because of Christ, I have come to consider all the advantages that I had as disadvantages. Not only that, but I believe nothing can happen that will outweigh the supreme advantage of knowing Christ Jesus my Lord.

This is the word of the Lord.

Responsorial Psalm   Ps 104:2-7. ℟ v.3

℟   Let hearts rejoice who search for the Lord.

or

℟   Alleluia!

1   O sing to the Lord, sing his praise;
     tell all his wonderful works!
     Be proud of his holy name,
     let the hearts that seek the Lord rejoice.   ℟

2   Consider the Lord and his strength;
    constantly seek his face.
    Remember the wonders he has done,
    his miracles, the judgements he spoke. ℟

3   O children of Abraham, his servant,
    O sons of the Jacob he chose.
    He, the Lord, is our God:
    his judgements prevail in all the earth. ℟

Gospel Acclamation   Mt 11:28

Alleluia, alleluia!
Come to me, all you that labour and are burdened,
and I will give you rest, says the Lord.
Alleluia!

GOSPEL

A reading from the holy Gospel according to Luke   15:1-10

There will be great rejoicing in heaven over one repentant sinner.

The tax collectors and the sinners were all seeking the company of Jesus to hear what he had to say, and the Pharisees and the scribes complained. 'This man' they said 'welcomes sinners and eats with them.' So he spoke this parable to them:

'What man among you with a hundred sheep, losing one, would not leave the ninety-nine in the wilderness and go after the missing one till he found it? And when he found it, would he not joyfully take it on his shoulders and then, when he got home, call together his friends and neighbours? "Rejoice with me," he would say "I have found my sheep that was lost." In the same way, I tell you, there will be more rejoicing in heaven over one repentant sinner than over ninety-nine virtuous men who have no need of repentance.

'Or again, what woman with ten drachmas would not, if she lost one, light a lamp and sweep out the house and search thoroughly till she found it? And then, when she had found it, call together her friends and neighbours? "Rejoice with me," she would say "I have found the drachma I lost." In the same way, I tell you, there is rejoicing among the angels of God over one repentant sinner.'

This is the Gospel of the Lord.

Friday

FIRST READING

A reading from the letter of St Paul to the Philippians 3:17–4:

The Saviour we await will transfigure these wretched bodies to be like his own.

My brothers, be united in following my rule of life. Take as your models everybody who is already doing this and study them as you used to study us. I have told you often, and I repeat it today with tears, there are many who are behaving as the enemies of the cross of Christ. They are destined to be lost. They make foods into their god and they are proudest of something they ought to think shameful; the things they think important are earthly things. For us, our homeland is in heaven, and from heaven comes the saviour we are waiting for, the Lord Jesus Christ, and he will transfigure these wretched bodies of ours into copies of his glorious body. He will do that by the same power with which he can subdue the whole universe.

So then, my brothers and dear friends, do not give way but remain faithful in the Lord. I miss you very much, dear friends; you are my joy and my crown.

This is the word of the Lord.

Responsorial Psalm

Ps 121:1-5. ℟ v.1

℟ Let us go rejoicing to the house of the Lord.

1 I rejoiced when I heard them say:
  'Let us go to God's house.'
  And now our feet are standing
  within your gates, O Jerusalem. ℟

2 Jerusalem is built as a city
  strongly compact.
  It is there that the tribes go up,
  the tribes of the Lord. ℟

3 For Israel's law it is,
  there to praise the Lord's name.
  There were set the thrones of judgement
  of the house of David. ℟

Gospel Acclamation   1 Jn 2:5

Alleluia, alleluia!
Whoever keeps the word of Christ,
grows perfect in the love of God.
Alleluia!

GOSPEL

A reading from the holy Gospel according to Luke   16:1-8

*The children of this world are wiser in dealing with their own kind
than are the children of light.*

Jesus said to his disciples, 'There was a rich man and he had a steward
who was denounced to him for being wasteful with his property. He
called for the man and said, "What is this I hear about you? Draw me
up an account of your stewardship because you are not to be my
steward any longer." Then the steward said to himself, "Now that my
master is taking the stewardship from me, what am I to do? Dig? I am
not strong enough. Go begging? I should be too ashamed. Ah, I know
what I will do to make sure that when I am dismissed from office there
will be some to welcome me into their homes."

'Then he called his master's debtors one by one. To the first he
said, "How much do you owe my master?" "One hundred measures of
oil" was the reply. The steward said, 'Here, take your bond; sit down
straight away and write fifty." To another he said, "And you, sir, how
much do you owe?" "One hundred measures of wheat" was the reply.
The steward said, "Here, take your bond and write eighty."

'The master praised the dishonest steward for his astuteness. For
the children of this world are more astute in dealing with their own
kind than are the children of light.'

This is the Gospel of the Lord.

Saturday

FIRST READING

A reading from the letter of St Paul to the Philippians   4:10-19

In him who gives me strength, I have strength for everything.

It is a great joy to me, in the Lord, that at last you have shown some concern for me again; though of course you were concerned before, and only lacked an opportunity. I am not talking about shortage of money: I have learnt to manage on whatever I have, I know how to be poor and I know how to be rich too. I have been through my initiation and now I am ready for anything anywhere: full stomach or empty stomach, poverty or plenty. There is nothing I cannot master with the help of the One who gives me strength. All the same, it was good of you to share with me in my hardships. In the early days of the Good News, as you people of Philippi well know, when I left Macedonia, no other church helped me with gifts of money. You were the only ones; and twice since my stay in Thessalonika you have sent me what I needed. It is not your gift that I value; what is valuable to me is the interest that is mounting up in your account. Now for the time being I have everything that I need and more: I am fully provided now that I have received from Epaphroditus the offering that you sent, a sweet fragrance – the sacrifice that God accepts and finds pleasing. In return my God will fulfil all your needs, in Christ Jesus, as lavishly as only God can.

This is the word of the Lord.

Responsorial Psalm   Ps 111:1-2. 5-6. 8. 9. ℟ v.1

℟   Happy are those who fear the Lord.

or

℟   Alleluia!

1   Happy the man who fears the Lord,
     who takes delight in all his commands.
     His sons will be powerful on earth;
     the children of the upright are blessed.   ℟

2   The good man takes pity and lends,
he conducts his affairs with honour.
The just man will never waver:
he will be remembered for ever. ℟

3   With a steadfast heart he will not fear.
Open-handed, he gives to the poor;
his justice stands firm for ever.
His head will be raised in glory. ℟

Gospel Acclamation   2 Cor 8:9

Alleluia, alleluia!
Jesus Christ was rich but he became poor,
to make you rich out of his poverty.
Alleluia!

GOSPEL

A reading from the holy Gospel according to Luke   16:9-15

*If you cannot be trusted with money, who will trust you
with the true riches?*

Jesus said to his disciples, 'I tell you this: use money, tainted as it is, to win you friends, and thus make sure that when it fails you, they will welcome you into the tents of eternity. The man who can be trusted in little things can be trusted in great; the man who is dishonest in little things will be dishonest in great. If then you cannot be trusted with money, that tainted thing, who will trust you with genuine riches? And if you cannot be trusted with what is not yours, who will give you what is your very own?

'No servant can be the slave of two masters: he will either hate the first and love the second, or treat the first with respect and the second with scorn. You cannot be the slave both of God and of money.'

The Pharisees, who loved money, heard all this and laughed at him. He said to them, 'You are the very ones who pass yourselves off as virtuous in people's sight, but God knows your hearts. For what is thought highly of by men is loathsome in the sight of God.'

This is the Gospel of the Lord.

THIRTY-SECOND WEEK IN ORDINARY TIME
Year II

Monday

FIRST READING

A reading from the letter of St Paul to Titus   1:1-9

Appoint elders as I directed you.

From Paul, servant of God, an apostle of Jesus Christ to bring those whom God has chosen to faith and to the knowledge of the truth that leads to true religion; and to give them the hope of the eternal life that was promised so long ago by God. He does not lie and so, at the appointed time, he revealed his decision, and, by the command of God our saviour, I have been commissioned to proclaim it. To Titus, true child of mine in the faith that we share, wishing you grace and peace from God the Father and from Christ Jesus our saviour.

The reason I left you behind in Crete was for you to get everything organised there and appoint elders in every town, in the way that I told you: that is, each of them must be a man of irreproachable character: he must not have been married more than once, and his children must be believers and not uncontrollable or liable to be charged with disorderly conduct. Since, as president, he will be God's representative, he must be irreproachable: never an arrogant or hot-tempered man, nor a heavy drinker or violent, nor out to make money; but a man who is hospitable and a friend of all that is good; sensible, moral, devout and self-controlled; and he must have a firm grasp of the unchanging message of the tradition, so that he can be counted on for both expounding the sound doctrine and refuting those who argue against it.

This is the word of the Lord.

Responsorial Psalm
       Ps 23:1-6. ℟ cf. v.6

℟   Lord, this is the people that longs to see your face.

1   The Lord's is the earth and its fullness,
     the world and all its peoples.
     It is he who set it on the seas;
     on the waters he made it firm. ℟

2 Who shall climb the mountain of the Lord?
Who shall stand in his holy place?
The man with clean hands and pure heart,
who desires not worthless things. ℟

3 He shall receive blessings from the Lord
and reward from the God who saves him.
Such are the men who seek him,
seek the face of the God of Jacob. ℟

Gospel Acclamation   Phil 2:15-16

Alleluia, alleluia!
Shine on the world like bright stars;
you are offering it the word of life.
Alleluia!

GOSPEL

A reading from the holy Gospel according to Luke   17:1-6

*If your neighbour returns to you seven times a day and says I am
sorry, you must forgive that person.*

Jesus said to his disciples, 'Obstacles are sure to come, but alas for the
one who provides them! It would be better for him to be thrown into
the sea with a millstone put round his neck than that he should lead
astray a single one of these little ones. Watch yourselves!

'If your brother does something wrong, reprove him and, if he is
sorry, forgive him. And if he wrongs you seven times a day and seven
times comes back to you and says, "I am sorry," you must forgive him.'

The apostles said to the Lord, 'Increase our faith.' The Lord
replied, 'Were your faith the size of a mustard seed you could say to
this mulberry tree, "Be uprooted and planted in the sea," and it would
obey you.'

This is the Gospel of the Lord.

Tuesday

FIRST READING

A reading from the letter of St Paul to Titus   2:1-8. 11-14

We must live good lives while we wait in hope for the appearance
of our Lord and God, Jesus Christ.

It is for you to preach the behaviour which goes with healthy doctrine. The older men should be reserved, dignified, moderate, sound in faith and love and constancy. Similarly, the older women should behave as though they were religious, with no scandalmongering and no habitual wine-drinking – they are to be the teachers of the right behaviour and show the younger women how they should love their husbands and love their children, how they are to be sensible and chaste, and how to work in their homes, and be gentle, and do as their husbands tell them, so that the message of God is never disgraced. In the same way, you have got to persuade the younger men to be moderate and in everything you do make yourself an example to them of working for good: when you are teaching, be an example to them in your sincerity and earnestness and in keeping all that you say so wholesome that nobody can make objections to it; and then any opponent will be at a loss, with no accusation to make against us.

You see, God's grace has been revealed, and it has made salvation possible for the whole human race and taught us that what we have to do is to give up everything that does not lead to God, and all our worldly ambitions; we must be self-restrained and live good and religious lives here in this present world, while we are waiting in hope for the blessing which will come with the Appearing of the glory of our great God and saviour Christ Jesus. He sacrificed himself for us in order to set us free from all wickedness and to purify a people so that it could be his very own and would have no ambition except to do good.

This is the word of the Lord.

Responsorial Psalm   Ps 36:3-4. 18. 23. 27. 29. ℟ v.39

℟ The salvation of the just comes from the Lord.

1 If you trust in the Lord and do good,
   then you will live in the land and be secure.
   If you find your delight in the Lord,
   he will grant your heart's desire. ℟

2 He protects the lives of the upright,
   their heritage will last for ever.
   The Lord guides the steps of a man
   and makes safe the path of one he loves. ℟

3 Then turn away from evil and do good
   and you shall have a home for ever.
   The just shall inherit the land;
   there they shall live for ever. ℟

Gospel Acclamation   Jn 14:23

   Alleluia, alleluia!
   All who love me will keep my words,
   and my Father will love them, and we will come to them.
   Alleluia!

GOSPEL

A reading from the holy Gospel according to Luke   17:7-10

We are only servants: we have done our duty.

Jesus said to his disciples: 'Which of you, with a servant ploughing or
minding sheep, would say to him when he returned from the fields,
"Come and have your meal immediately?" Would he not be more
likely to say, "Get my supper laid; make yourself tidy and wait on me
while I eat and drink. You can eat and drink yourself afterwards?"
Must he be grateful to the servant for doing what he was told? So with
you: when you have done all you have been told to do, say, "We are
merely servants: we have done no more than our duty." '

   This is the Gospel of the Lord.

Wednesday

FIRST READING

A reading from the letter of St Paul to Titus   3:1-

There was a time when we were ignorant, but his compassion
saved us

Remind your people that it is their duty to be obedient to the officials
and representatives of the government; to be ready to do good at every
opportunity; not to go slandering other people or picking quarrels, but
to be courteous and always polite to all kinds of people. Remember
there was a time when we too were ignorant, disobedient and misled
and enslaved by different passions and luxuries; we lived then in
wickedness and ill-will, hating each other and hateful ourselves.

But when the kindness and love of God our saviour for mankind
were revealed, it was not because he was concerned with any
righteous actions we might have done ourselves; it was for no reason
except his own compassion that he saved us, by means of the cleansing
water of rebirth and by renewing us with the Holy Spirit which he so
generously poured over us through Jesus Christ our saviour. He did
this so that we should be justified by his grace, to become heirs
looking forward to inheriting eternal life.

This is the word of the Lord.

Responsorial Psalm   Ps 22. ℟ v.1

℟   The Lord is my shepherd;
      there is nothing I shall want.

1   The Lord is my shepherd;
    there is nothing I shall want.
    Fresh and green are the pastures
    where he gives me repose.
    Near restful waters he leads me,
    to revive my drooping spirit.   ℟

2   He guides me along the right path;
    he is true to his name.
    If I should walk in the valley of darkness
    no evil would I fear.
    You are there with your crook and your staff;
    with these you give me comfort.   ℟

℟ You have prepared a banquet for me
in the sight of my foes.
My head you have anointed with oil;
my cup is overflowing.   ℟

℟ Surely goodness and kindness shall follow me
all the days of my life.
In the Lord's own house shall I dwell
for ever and ever.   ℟

Gospel Acclamation   1 Thess 5:18

Alleluia, alleluia!
For all things give thanks to God,
because this is what he expects of you in Christ Jesus.
Alleluia!

GOSPEL

A reading from the holy Gospel according to Luke   17:11-19

*It seems that no one has returned to give thanks to God except this
foreigner.*

On the way to Jerusalem Jesus travelled along the border between
Samaria and Galilee. As he entered one of the villages, ten lepers
came to meet him. They stood some way off and called to him, 'Jesus!
Master! Take pity on us.' When he saw them he said, 'Go and show
yourselves to the priests.' Now as they were going away they were
cleansed. Finding himself cured, one of them turned back praising
God at the top of his voice and threw himself at the feet of Jesus and
thanked him. The man was a Samaritan. This made Jesus say, 'Were
not all ten made clean? The other nine, where are they? It seems that
no one has come back to give praise to God, except this foreigner.' And
he said to the man, 'Stand up and go on your way. Your faith has
saved you.'

This is the Gospel of the Lord.

Thursday

FIRST READING

A reading from the letter of St Paul to Philemon   7-2

Receive him, not as a slave any more, but a dear brother

I am so delighted, and comforted, to know of your love; they tell me brother, how you have put new heart into the saints.

Now, although in Christ I can have no diffidence about telling you to do whatever is your duty, I am appealing to your love instead reminding you that this is Paul writing, an old man now and, what i more, still a prisoner of Christ Jesus. I am appealing to you for a child of mine, whose father I became while wearing these chains: I mean Onesimus. He was of no use to you before, but he will be useful to you now, as he has been to me. I am sending him back to you, and with him – I could say – a part of my own self. I should have liked to keep him with me; he could have been a substitute for you, to help me while I am in the chains that the Good News has brought me. However, I did not want to do anything without your consent; it would have been forcing your act of kindness, which should be spontaneous. I know you have been deprived of Onesimus for a time, but it was only so that you could have him back for ever, not as a slave any more, but something better than a slave, a dear brother; especially dear to me, but how much more to you, as a blood-brother as well as a brother in the Lord So if all that we have in common means anything to you, welcome him as you would me; but if he has wronged you in any way or owes you anything, then let me pay for it. I am writing this in my own handwriting: I, Paul, shall pay it back – I will not add any mention o. your debt to me, which is yourself. Well then, brother, I am counting on you, in the Lord; put new heart into me, in Christ.

This is the word of the Lord.

Responsorial Psalm   Ps 145:7-10. ℟ v.5

℟   Blest are they whose help is the God of Jacob.

or

℟   Alleluia!

1   It is the Lord who keeps faith for ever,
     who is just to those who are oppressed.

It is he who gives bread to the hungry,
the Lord, who sets prisoners free.   ℟

2   It is the Lord who gives sight to the blind,
who raises up those who are bowed down.
It is the Lord who loves the just,
the Lord, who protects the stranger.   ℟

3   The Lord upholds the widow and orphan,
but thwarts the path of the wicked.
The Lord will reign for ever,
Zion's God from age to age.   ℟

Gospel Acclamation   Jn 15:5

Alleluia, alleluia!
I am the vine and you are the branches, says the Lord;
those who live in me, and I in them, will bear much fruit.
Alleluia!

GOSPEL

A reading from the holy Gospel according to Luke   17:20-25

The kingdom of God is among you.

Asked by the Pharisees when the kingdom of God was to come, Jesus gave them this answer, 'The coming of the kingdom of God does not admit of observation and there will be no one to say, "Look here! Look there!" For, you must know, the kingdom of God is among you.'

He said to the disciples, 'A time will come when you will long to see one of the days of the Son of Man and will not see it. They will say to you, "Look there!" or, "Look here!" Make no move; do not set off in pursuit; for as the lightning flashing from one part of heaven lights up the other, so will be the Son of Man when his day comes. But first he must suffer grievously and be rejected by this generation.'

This is the Gospel of the Lord.

Friday

FIRST READING

A reading from the second letter of St John   4-9

Whoever stands by that doctrine has the Father and the Son.

It has given me great joy to find that your children have been living the life of truth as we were commanded by the Father. I am writing now, dear lady, not to give you any new commandment, but the one which we were given at the beginning, and to plead: let us love one another.

To love is to live according to his commandments: this is the commandment which you have heard since the beginning, to live a life of love.

There are many deceivers about in the world, refusing to admit that Jesus Christ has come in the flesh. They are the Deceiver; they are the Antichrist. Watch yourselves, or all our work will be lost and not get the reward it deserves. If anybody does not keep within the teaching of Christ but goes beyond it, he cannot have God with him: only those who keep to what he taught can have the Father and the Son with them.

This is the word of the Lord.

Responsorial Psalm   Ps 118:1-2. 10-11. 17-18. ℟ v.1

℟   Happy are they who follow the law of the Lord!

1   They are happy whose life is blameless,
     who follow God's law!
     They are happy who do his will,
     seeking him with all their hearts.   ℟

2   I have sought you with all my heart:
     let me not stray from your commands.
     I treasure your promise in my heart
     lest I sin against you.   ℟

3   Bless your servant and I shall live
     and obey your word.
     Open my eyes that I may see
     the wonders of your law.   ℟

Gospel Acclamation   Lk 21:28

Alleluia, alleluia!
Lift up your heads and see;
your redemption is near at hand.
Alleluia!

GOSPEL

A reading from the holy Gospel according to Luke   17:26-37

It will be the same when the day comes the Son of Man is revealed.

Jesus said to the disciples: 'As it was in Noah's day, so will it also be in the days of the Son of Man. People were eating and drinking, marrying wives and husbands, right up to the day Noah went into the ark, and the Flood came and destroyed them all. It will be the same as it was in Lot's day: people were eating and drinking, buying and selling, planting and building, but the day Lot left Sodom, God rained fire and brimstone from heaven and it destroyed them all. It will be the same when the day comes for the Son of Man to be revealed.

'When that day comes, anyone on the housetop, with his possessions in the house, must not come down to collect them, nor must anyone in the fields turn back either. Remember Lot's wife. Anyone who tries to preserve his life will lose it; and anyone who loses it will keep it safe. I tell you, on that night two will be in one bed: one will be taken, the other left; two women will be grinding corn together: one will be taken, the other left.' The disciples interrupted. 'Where Lord?' they asked. He said, 'Where the body is, there too will the vultures gather.'

This is the Gospel of the Lord.

Saturday

FIRST READING

A reading from the third letter of St John   5-8

We must welcome our brothers and sisters and cooperate in their work of truth.

My friend, you have done faithful work in looking after these brothers, even though they were complete strangers to you. They are a proof to the whole Church of your charity and it would be a very good thing if you could help them on their journey in a way that God would approve. It was entirely for the sake of the name that they set out, without depending on the pagans for anything; it is our duty to welcome men of this sort and contribute our share to their work for the truth.

This is the word of the Lord.

Responsorial Psalm   Ps 111:1-6. ℞ v.1

℞   Happy are those who fear the Lord.

or

℞   Alleluia!

1   Happy the man who fears the Lord,
    who takes delight in all his commands.
    His sons will be powerful on earth;
    the children of the upright are blessed.   ℞

2   Riches and wealth are in his house;
    his justice stands firm for ever.
    He is a light in the darkness for the upright:
    he is generous, merciful and just.   ℞

3   The good man takes pity and lends,
    he conducts his affairs with honour.
    The just man will never waver:
    he will be remembered for ever.   ℞

Gospel Acclamation   cf. 2 Thess 2:14

Alleluia, alleluia!
God has called us with the gospel
to share in the glory of our Lord Jesus Christ.
Alleluia!

GOSPEL

A reading from the holy Gospel according to Luke   18:1-8

God will see justice done to his chosen who cry to him.

Jesus told his disciples a parable about the need to pray continually and never lose heart. 'There was a judge in a certain town' he said who had neither fear of God nor respect for men. In the same town there was a widow who kept on coming to him and saying, "I want justice from you against my enemy!" For a long time he refused, but at last he said to himself, "Maybe I have neither fear of God nor respect for man, but since she keeps pestering me I must give this widow her just rights, or she will persist in coming and worry me to death." '

And the Lord said, 'You notice what the unjust judge has to say? Now will not God see justice done to his chosen who cry to him day and night even when he delays to help them? I promise you, he will see justice done to them, and done speedily. But when the Son of Man comes, will he find any faith on earth?'

This is the Gospel of the Lord.

THIRTY-THIRD WEEK IN ORDINARY TIME

Year II

Monday

FIRST READING

A reading from the book of the Apocalypse   1:1-4; 2:1-5

Remember how far you have fallen, and repent

This is the revelation given by God to Jesus Christ so that he could tell his servants about the things which are now to take place very soon; he sent his angel to make it known to his servant John, and John has written down everything he saw and swears it is the word of God guaranteed by Jesus Christ. Happy the man who reads this prophecy, and happy those who listen to him, if they treasure all that it says, because the Time is close.

From John, to the seven churches of Asia: grace and peace to you from him who is, who was, and who is to come, from the seven spirits in his presence before his throne.

I heard the Lord saying to me: 'Write to the angel of the church in Ephesus and say, "Here is the message of the one who holds the seven stars in his right hand and who lives surrounded by the seven golden lampstands: I know all about you: how hard you work and how much you put up with. I know you cannot stand wicked men, and how you tested the impostors who called themselves apostles and proved they were liars. I know, too, that you have patience, and have suffered for my name without growing tired. Nevertheless, I have this complaint to make; you have less love now than you used to. Think where you were before you fell; repent, and do as you used to at first." '

This is the word of the Lord.

Responsorial Psalm   Ps 1:1-4. 6. ℟ Apoc 2:7

℟   Those who are victorious I will feed from the tree of life.

1   Happy indeed is the man
     who follows not the counsel of the wicked;
     nor lingers in the way of sinners

nor sits in the company of scorners,
but whose delight is the law of the Lord
and who ponders his law day and night.   ℟

2   He is like a tree that is planted
beside the flowing waters,
that yields its fruit in due season
and whose leaves shall never fade;
and all that he does shall prosper.   ℟

3   Not so are the wicked, not so!
For they like winnowed chaff
shall be driven away by the wind.
For the Lord guards the way of the just
but the way of the wicked leads to doom.   ℟

Gospel Acclamation   Jn 8:12

Alleluia, alleluia!
I am the light of the world, says the Lord:
whoever follows me will have the light of life.
Alleluia!

GOSPEL

A reading from the holy Gospel according to Luke   18:35-43

What do you want me to do? Lord, that I may see.

As Jesus drew near to Jericho there was a blind man sitting at the
side of the road begging. When he heard the crowd going past he
asked what it was all about, and they told him that Jesus the
Nazarene was passing by. So he called out, 'Jesus, Son of David, have
pity on me.' The people in front scolded him and told him to keep
quiet, but he shouted all the louder, 'Son of David, have pity on me.'
Jesus stopped and ordered them to bring the man to him, and when he
came up, asked him, 'What do you want me to do for you?' 'Sir,' he
replied 'let me see again.' Jesus said to him, 'Receive your sight. Your
faith has saved you.' And instantly his sight returned and he followed
him praising God, and all the people who saw it gave praise to God for
what had happened.

This is the Gospel of the Lord.

Tuesday

FIRST READING

A reading from the book of the Apocalypse 3:1-6. 14-2:

*If one of you hears me calling and opens the door, I will come and
share supper with you*

I, John, heard the Lord saying to me: 'Write to the angel of the church
in Sardis and say, "Here is the message of the one who holds the seven
spirits of God and the seven stars: I know all about you: how you are
reputed to be alive and yet are dead. Wake up; revive what little you
have left: it is dying fast. So far I have failed to notice anything in the
way you live that my God could possibly call perfect, and yet do you
remember how eager you were when you first heard the message?
Hold on to that. Repent. If you do not wake up, I shall come to you like
a thief, without telling you at what hour to expect me. There are a few
in Sardis, it is true, who have kept their robes from being dirtied, and
they are fit to come with me, dressed in white. Those who prove
victorious will be dressed, like these, in white robes; I shall not blot
their names out of the book of life, but acknowledge their names in the
presence of my Father and his angels. If anyone has ears to hear, let
him listen to what the Spirit is saying to the churches."

'Write to the angel of the church in Laodicea and say, "Here is the
message of the Amen, the faithful, the true witness, the ultimate
source of God's creation: I know all about you: how you are neither
cold nor hot. I wish you were one or the other, but since you are
neither, but only lukewarm, I will spit you out of my mouth. You say
to yourself, "I am rich, I have made a fortune, and have everything
want," never realising that you are wretchedly and pitiably poor, and
blind and naked too. I warn you, buy from me the gold that has been
tested in the fire to make you really rich, and white robes to clothe you
and cover your shameful nakedness, and eye ointment to put on your
eyes so that you are able to see. I am the one who reproves and
disciplines all those he loves: so repent in real earnest. Look, I am
standing at the door, knocking. If one of you hears me calling and
opens the door, I will come in to share his meal, side by side with him.
Those who prove victorious I will allow to share my throne, just as I
was victorious myself and took my place with my Father on his
throne. If anyone has ears to hear, let him listen to what the Spirit is
saying to the churches." '

This is the word of the Lord.

Responsorial Psalm   Ps 14:2-5. ℟ Apoc 3:21

℟   The one who is victorious I will sit beside me on my throne.

1   Lord, who shall be admitted to your tent?
     He who walks without fault;
     he who acts with justice
     and speaks the truth from his heart;
     he who does not slander with his tongue.   ℟

2   He who does no wrong to his brother,
     who casts no slur on his neighbour,
     who holds the godless in disdain,
     but honours those who fear the Lord.   ℟

3   He who takes no interest on a loan
     and accepts no bribes against the innocent.
     Such a man will stand firm for ever.   ℟

Gospel Acclamation   1 Jn 4:10

Alleluia, alleluia!
God first loved us
and sent his Son to take away our sins.
Alleluia!

GOSPEL

A reading from the holy Gospel according to Luke   19:1-10

The Son of Man has come to seek out and save what was lost.

Jesus entered Jericho and was going through the town when a man
whose name was Zacchaeus made his appearance; he was one of the
senior tax collectors and a wealthy man. He was anxious to see what
kind of man Jesus was, but he was too short and could not see him for
the crowd; so he ran ahead and climbed a sycamore tree to catch a
glimpse of Jesus who was to pass that way. When Jesus reached the
spot he looked up and spoke to him: 'Zacchaeus, come down. Hurry,
because I must stay at your house today.' And he hurried down and
welcomed him joyfully. They all complained when they saw what was
happening. 'He has gone to stay at a sinner's house' they said. But
Zacchaeus stood his ground and said to the Lord, 'Look, sir, I am

817

going to give half my property to the poor, and if I have cheated anybody I will pay him back four times the amount.' And Jesus said to him, 'Today salvation has come to this house, because this man too is a son of Abraham; for the Son of Man has come to seek out and save what was lost.'

This is the Gospel of the Lord.

Wednesday

FIRST READING

A reading from the book of the Apocalypse   4:1-11

Holy Lord God, the Almighty, who was and is and is to come.

In my vision, I, John, saw a door open in heaven and heard the same voice speaking to me, the voice like a trumpet, saying, 'Come up here: I will show you what is to come in the future.' With that, the Spirit possessed me and I saw a throne standing in heaven, and the One who was sitting on the throne, and the Person sitting there looked like a diamond and a ruby. There was a rainbow encircling the throne, and this looked like an emerald. Round the throne in a circle were twenty-four thrones, and on them I saw twenty-four elders sitting, dressed in white robes with golden crowns on their heads. Flashes of lightning were coming from the throne, and the sound of peals of thunder, and in front of the throne there were seven flaming lamps burning, the seven Spirits of God. Between the throne and myself was a sea that seemed to be made of glass, like crystal. In the centre, grouped round the throne itself, were four animals with many eyes, in front and behind. The first animal was like a lion, the second like a bull, the third animal had a human face, and the fourth animal was like a flying eagle. Each of the four animals had six wings and had eyes all the way round as well as inside; and day and night they never stopped singing:

'Holy, Holy, Holy
is the Lord God, the Almighty;
he was, he is and he is to come.'

Every time the animals glorified and honoured and gave thanks to the One sitting on the throne, who lives forever and ever, the twenty-four elders prostrated themelves before him to worship the One who lives for ever and ever, and threw down their crowns in front of the throne, saying, 'You are our Lord and our God, you are worthy of glory and honour and power, because you made all the universe and it was only by your will that everything was made and exists.'

This is the word of the Lord.

Responsorial Psalm   Ps 150. ℟ Apoc 4:8

℟   Holy, holy, holy Lord, mighty God!

or

℟   Alleluia!

1   Praise God in his holy place,
    praise him in his mighty heavens.
    Praise him for his powerful deeds,
    praise his surpassing greatness.   ℟

2   O praise him with sound of trumpet,
    praise him with lute and harp.
    Praise him with timbrel and dance,
    praise him with strings and pipes.   ℟

3   O praise him with resounding cymbals,
    praise him with clashing of cymbals.
    Let everything that lives and that breathes
    give praise to the Lord.   ℟

Gospel Acclamation   cf. Jn 15:16

Alleluia, alleluia!
I have chosen you from the world, says the Lord,
to go and bear fruit that will last.
Alleluia!

GOSPEL

A reading from the holy Gospel according to Luke   19:11-28

Why did you lend my money out?

While the people were listening, Jesus went on to tell a parable, because he was near Jerusalem and they imagined that the kingdom of God was going to show itself then and there. Accordingly he said, 'A man of noble birth went to a distant country to be appointed king and afterwards return. He summoned ten of his servants and gave them ten pounds. "Do business with these" he told them "until I get back." But his compatriots detested him and sent a delegation to follow him with this message, "We do not want this man to be our king."

'Now on his return, having received his appointment as king, he sent for those servants to whom he had given the money, to find out what profit each had made. The first came in and said, "Sir, your one pound has brought in ten." "Well done, my good servant!" he replied. "Since you have proved yourself faithful in a very small thing, you shall have the government of ten cities." Then came the second and said, "Sir, your one pound has made five." To this one also he said, "And you shall be in charge of five cities." Next came the other and said, "Sir, here is your pound. I put it away safely in a piece of linen because I was afraid of you; for you are an exacting man: you pick up what you have not put down and reap what you have not sown." "You wicked servant!" he said "Out of your own mouth I condemn you. So you knew I was an exacting man, picking up what I have not put down and reaping what I have not sown? Then why did you not put my money in the bank? On my return I could have drawn it out with interest." And he said to those standing by, "Take the pound from him and give it to the man who has ten pounds." And they said to him, "But, sir, he has ten pounds ..." "I tell you, to everyone who has will be given more; but from the man who has not, even what he has will be taken away.

"But as for my enemies who did not want me for their king, bring them here and execute them in my presence." '

When he had said this he went on ahead, going up to Jerusalem.

This is the Gospel of the Lord.

Thursday

FIRST READING

A reading from the book of the Apocalypse   5:1-10

The lamb that was slain redeemed us from every nation by his blood.

I, John, saw that in the right hand of the One sitting on the throne there was a scroll that had writing on back and front and was sealed with seven seals. Then I saw a powerful angel who called with a loud voice, 'Is there anyone worthy to open the scroll and break the seals of it?' But there was no one, in heaven or on the earth or under the earth, who was able to open the scroll and read it. I wept bitterly because there was nobody fit to open the scroll and read it, but one of the elders said to me, 'There is no need to cry: the Lion of the tribe of Judah, the Root of David, has triumphed, and he will open the scroll and the seven seals of it.'

Then I saw, standing between the throne with its four animals and the circle of the elders, a Lamb that seemed to have been sacrificed; it had seven horns, and it had seven eyes, which are the seven Spirits God has sent out all over the world. The Lamb came forward to take the scroll from the right hand of the One sitting on the throne, and when he took it, the four animals prostrated themselves before him and with them the twenty-four elders; each one of them was holding a harp and had a golden bowl full of incense made of the prayers of the saints. They sang a new hymn:

'You are worthy to take the scroll
and break the seals of it,
because you were sacrificed, and with your blood
you bought men for God
of every race, language, people and nation
and made them a line of kings and priests.
to serve our God and to rule the world.'

This is the word of the Lord.

Responsorial Psalm   Ps 149: 1-6. 9. ℟ Apoc 5:10

℟   The lamb has made us a kingdom of priests to serve our God.

or

℟   Alleluia!

1   Sing a new song to the Lord,
     his praise in the assembly of the faithful.
     Let Israel rejoice in its Maker,
     let Zion's sons exult in their king. ℟

2   Let them praise his name with dancing
     and make music with timbrel and harp.
     For the Lord takes delight in his people.
     He crowns the poor with salvation. ℟

3   Let the faithful rejoice in their glory,
     shout for joy and take their rest.
     Let the praise of God be on their lips:
     this honour is for all his faithful. ℟

Gospel Acclamation   cf. Ps 94:8

Alleluia, alleluia!
If today you hear his voice,
harden not your hearts.
Alleluia!

GOSPEL

A reading from the holy Gospel according to Luke   19:41-44

If only you knew on what your peace depends.

As Jesus drew near Jerusalem and came in sight of the city he shed
tears over it and said, 'If you in your turn had only understood on this
day the message of peace! But, alas, it is hidden from your eyes! Yes, a
time is coming when your enemies will raise fortifications all round
you, when they will encircle you and hem you in on every side; they
will dash you and the children inside your walls to the ground; they
will leave not one stone standing on another within you – and all
because you did not recognise your opportunity when God offered it!'

This is the Gospel of the Lord.

Friday

FIRST READING

A reading from the book of the Apocalypse   10:8-11

I took the book and swallowed it.

I, John, heard the voice I had heard from heaven speaking to me
again. 'Go', it said 'and take that open scroll out of the hand of the
angel standing on sea and land.' I went to the angel and asked him to
give me the small scroll, and he said, 'Take it and eat it; it will turn
your stomach sour, but in your mouth it will taste as sweet as honey.'
So I took it out of the angel's hand, and swallowed it; it was as sweet
as honey in my mouth, but when I had eaten it my stomach turned
sour. Then I was told, 'You are to prophesy again, this time about
many different nations and countries and languages and emperors.'

This is the word of the Lord.

Responsorial Psalm   Ps 118:14. 24. 72. 103. 111. 131. ℟ v.103

℟   How sweet to my taste is your promise!

1   I rejoiced to do your will
    as though all riches were mine.
    Your will is my delight;
    your statutes are my counsellors.   ℟

2   The law from your mouth means more to me
    than silver and gold.
    Your promise is sweeter to my taste
    than honey in the mouth.   ℟

3   Your will is my heritage for ever,
    the joy of my heart.
    I open my mouth and I sigh
    as I yearn for your commands.   ℟

Gospel Acclamation   Jn 10:27

    Alleluia, alleluia!
    My sheep listen to my voice, says the Lord;
    I know them, and they follow me.
    Alleluia!

GOSPEL

A reading from the holy Gospel according to Luke   19:45-48

You have turned the house of the Lord into a robber's den.

Jesus went into the Temple and began driving out those who were selling. 'According to scripture,' he said 'my house will be a house of prayer. But you have turned it into a robbers' den.'

He taught in the Temple every day. The chief priests and the scribes, with the support of the leading citizens, tried to do away with him, but they did not see how they could carry this out because the people as a whole hung on his words.

This is the Gospel of the Lord.

Saturday

FIRST READING

A reading from the book of the Apocalypse   11:4-12

These two prophets have been a plague to the earth.

I, John, heard a voice saying: 'These, my two witnesses, are the two olive trees and the two lamps that stand before the Lord of the world. Fire can come from their mouths and consume their enemies if anyone tries to harm them; and if anybody does try to harm them he will certainly be killed in this way. They are able to lock up the sky so that it does not rain as long as they are prophesying; they are able to turn water into blood and strike the whole world with any plague as often as they like. When they have completed their witnessing, the beast that comes out of the Abyss is going to make war on them and overcome them and kill them. Their corpses will lie in the main street of the Great City known by the symbolic names Sodom and Egypt, in which their Lord was crucified. Men out of every people, race, language and nation will stare at their corpses, for three-and-a-half days, not letting them be buried, and the people of the world will be glad about it and celebrate the event by giving presents to each other, because these two prophets have been a plague to the people of the world.'

After the three-and-a-half days, God breathed life into their corpses and they stood up, and everybody who saw it happen was terrified; then they heard a loud voice from heaven say to them, 'Come up here', and while their enemies were watching, they went up to heaven in a cloud.

This is the word of the Lord.

Responsorial Psalm   Ps 143:1-2. 9-10. ℟ v.1

℟   Blessed be the Lord, my Rock!

1   Blessed be the Lord, my rock
    who trains my arms for battle,
    who prepares my hands for war.   ℟

2   He is my love, my fortress;
    he is my stronghold, my saviour,
    my shield, my place of refuge.
    He brings peoples under my rule.   ℟

3   To you, O God, will I sing a new song;
    I will play on the ten-stringed lute
    to you who give kings their victory,
    who set David your servant free.   ℟

Gospel Acclamation   cf. 2 Tim 1:10

    Alleluia, alleluia!
    Our Saviour Jesus Christ has done away with death
    and brought us life through his gospel.
    Alleluia!

GOSPEL

A reading from the holy Gospel according to Luke   20:27-40

He is God, not of the dead, but of the living.

Some Sadducees – those who say that there is no resurrection – approached Jesus and they put this question to him, 'Master, we have it from Moses in writing, that if a man's married brother dies childless, the man must marry the widow to raise up children for his brother. Well then, there were seven brothers. The first, having married a wife, died childless. The second and then the third married the widow. And the same with all seven, they died leaving no

825

children. Finally the woman herself died. Now, at the resurrection, to which of them will she be wife since she had been married to all seven?'

Jesus replied, 'The children of this world take wives and husbands, but those who are judged worthy of a place in the other world and in the resurrection from the dead do not marry because they can no longer die, for they are the same as the angels, and being children of the resurrection they are sons of God. And Moses himself implies that the dead rise again, in the passage about the bush where he calls the Lord the God of Abraham, the God of Isaac and the God of Jacob. Now he is God, not of the dead, but of the living; for to him all men are in fact alive.'

Some scribes then spoke up. 'Well put, Master' they said – because they would not dare to ask him any more questions.

This is the Gospel of the Lord.

LAST WEEK IN ORDINARY TIME

Year II

Monday

FIRST READING

A reading from the book of the Apocalypse   14:1-5

They had names of Christ and his Father written on their foreheads.

In my vision I, John, saw Mount Zion, and standing on it a Lamb who had with him a hundred and forty-four thousand people, all with his name and his Father's name written on their foreheads. I heard a sound coming out of the sky like the sound of the ocean or the roar of thunder; it seemed to be the sound of harpists playing their harps. There in front of the throne they were singing a new hymn in the presence of the four animals and the elders, a hymn that could only be learnt by the hundred and forty-four thousand who had been redeemed from the world; they follow the Lamb wherever he goes; they have been redeemed from amongst men to be the first-fruits for God and for the Lamb. They never allowed a lie to pass their lips and no fault can be found in them.

This is the word of the Lord.

Responsorial Psalm   Ps 23:1-6. ℟ cf. v.6

℟   Lord, this is the people that longs to see your face.

1   The Lord's is the earth and its fullness,
    the world and all its peoples.
    It is he who set it on the seas;
    on the waters he made it firm.   ℟

2   Who shall climb the mountain of the Lord?
    Who shall stand in his holy place?
    The man with clean hands and pure heart,
    who desires not worthless things.   ℟

3   He shall receive blessings from the Lord
    and reward from the God who saves him.
    Such are the men who seek him,
    seek the face of the God of Jacob.   ℟

Gospel Acclamation   Mt 24:42. 44

Alleluia, alleluia!
Be watchful and ready:
you know not when the Son of Man is coming.
Alleluia!

GOSPEL

A reading from the holy Gospel according to Luke   21:1-4

He saw the poor widow give two small coins.

As Jesus looked up he saw rich people putting their offerings into the treasury; then he happened to notice a poverty-stricken widow putting in two small coins, and he said, 'I tell you truly, this poor widow has put in more than any of them; for these have all contributed money they had over, but she from the little she had has put in all she had to live on.'

This is the Gospel of the Lord.

Tuesday

FIRST READING

A reading from the book of the Apocalypse   14:14-19

Harvest time has come, and the harvest of the earth is ripe.

In my vision I, John, saw a white cloud and, sitting on it, one like a son of man with a gold crown on his head and a sharp sickle in his hand. Then another angel came out of the sanctuary, and shouted aloud to the one sitting on the cloud, 'Put your sickle in and reap: harvest time has and the harvest of the earth is ripe.' Then the one sitting on the cloud set his sickle to work on the earth, and the earth's harvest was reaped.

Another angel, who also carried a sharp sickle, came out of the temple in heaven, and the angel in charge of the fire left the altar and shouted aloud to the one with the sharp sickle, 'Put your sickle in and cut all the bunches off the vine of the earth; all its grapes are ripe. So the angel set his sickle to work on the earth and harvested the whole vintage of the earth and put it into a huge winepress, the winepress of God's anger.

This is the word of the Lord.

Responsorial Psalm   Ps 95:10-13. ℟ v.13

℟ The Lord comes to judge the earth.

1   Proclaim to the nations: 'God is king.'
    The world he made firm in its place;
    he will judge the peoples in fairness.
    Let the heavens rejoice and earth be glad,
    let the sea and all within it thunder praise.   ℟

2   Let the land and all it bears rejoice,
    all the trees of the wood shout for joy
    at the presence of the Lord for he comes,
    he comes to rule the earth.
    With justice he will rule the world,
    he will judge the peoples with his truth.   ℟

Gospel Acclamation   Apoc 2:10

Alleluia, alleluia!
Be faithful until death, says the Lord,
and I will give you the crown of life.
Alleluia!

GOSPEL

A reading from the holy Gospel according to Luke   21:5-11

Not a single stone will be left on the other.

When some were talking about the Temple, remarking how it was adorned with fine stonework and votive offerings, Jesus said, 'All these things you are staring at now – the time will come when not a single stone will be left on another: everything will be destroyed.' And they put to him this question: 'Master,' they said 'when will this happen, then, and what sign will there be that this is about to take place?'

'Take care not to be deceived,' he said 'because many will come using my name and saying, "I am he" and, "The time is near at hand." Refuse to join them. And when you hear of wars and revolutions, do not be frightened, for this is something that must happen but the end is not so soon.' Then he said to them, 'Nation will fight against nation, and kingdom against kingdom. There will be great earthquakes and plagues and famines here and there; there will be fearful sights and great signs from heaven.'

This is the Gospel of the Lord.

Wednesday

FIRST READING

A reading from the book of the Apocalypse   15:1-4

They sang the canticle of Moses and the canticle of the lamb.

What I, John, saw in heaven was a great and wonderful sign: seven angels were bringing the seven plagues that are the last of all, because they exhaust the anger of God. I seemed to see a glass lake suffused with fire, and standing by the lake of glass, those who had fought against the beast and won, and against his statue and the number which is his name. They all had harps from God, and they were singing the hymn of Moses, the servant of God, and of the Lamb:

'How great and wonderful are all your works,
Lord God Almighty;
just and true are all your ways,
King of nations.
Who would not revere and praise your name, O Lord?
You alone are holy,
and all the pagans will come and adore you
for the many acts of justice you have shown.'

This is the word of the Lord.

Responsorial Psalm   Ps 97:1-3. 7-9. ℟ Apoc 15:3

℟   Great and wonderful are all your works.
     Lord, mighty God.

1   Sing a new song to the Lord
    for he has worked wonders.

His right hand and his holy arm
have brought salvation. ℟

2 The Lord has made known his salvation;
   has shown his justice to the nations.
   He has remembered his truth and love
   for the house of Israel. ℟

3 Let the sea and all within it, thunder;
   the world, and all its peoples.
   Let the rivers clap their hands.
   and the hills ring out their joy
   at the presence of the Lord. ℟

4 For the Lord comes,
   he comes to rule the earth.
   He will rule the world with justice
   and the peoples with fairness. ℟

Gospel Acclamation   Apoc 2:10

   Alleluia, alleluia!
   Be faithful until death, says the Lord,
   and I will give you the crown of life.
   Alleluia!

GOSPEL

A reading from the holy Gospel according to Luke   21:12-19

You will be hated by all because of my name, but not a hair of your
head will be lost.

Jesus said to his disciples: 'Men will seize you and persecute you; they
will hand you over to the synagogues and to imprisonment, and bring
you before kings and governors because of my name – and that will be
your opportunity to bear witness. Keep this carefully in mind: you are
not to prepare your defence, because I myself shall give you an
eloquence and a wisdom that none of your opponents will be able to
resist or contradict. You will be betrayed even by parents and
brothers, relations and friends; and some of you will be put to death.
You will be hated by all men on account of my name, but not a hair of
your head will be lost. Your endurance will win you your lives.'

   This is the Gospel of the Lord.

Thursday

FIRST READING

A reading from the book of   18:1-2. 21-23; 19:1-3. 9
the Apocalypse

Babylon the Great has fallen.

I, John, saw an angel come down from heaven, with great authority given to him; the earth was lit up with his glory. At the top of his voice he shouted, 'Babylon has fallen, Babylon the Great has fallen, and has become the haunt of devils and a lodging for every foul spirit and dirty, loathsome bird.'

Then a powerful angel picked up a boulder like a great millstone, and as he hurled it into the sea, he said, 'That is how the great city of Babylon is going to be hurled down, never to be seen again.

'Never again in you, Babylon,
will be heard the song of harpists and minstrels,
the music of flute and trumpet;
never again will craftsmen of every skill be found
or the sound of the mill be heard;
never again will shine the light of the lamp,
never again will be heard
the voices of bridegroom and bride.
Your traders were the princes of the earth,
all the nations were under your spell.'

After this I seemed to hear the great sound of a huge crowd in heaven, singing, 'Alleluia! Victory and glory and power to our God! He judges fairly, he punishes justly, and he has condemned the famous prostitute who corrupted the earth with her fornication; he has avenged his servants that she killed.' They sang again, 'Alleluia! The smoke of her will go up for ever and ever.'

The angel said, 'Write this: Happy are those who are invited to the wedding feast of the Lamb.'

This is the word of the Lord.

Responsorial Psalm   Ps 99:2-5. ℟ Apoc 19:9

℟   Blessed are they who are called to the wedding feast of the
       Lamb.

1   Cry out with joy to the Lord, all the earth.
    Serve the Lord with gladness.
    Come before him, singing for joy.   ℟

2   Know that he, the Lord, is God.
    He made us, we belong to him,
    we are his people, the sheep of his flock.   ℟

3   Go within his gates, giving thanks.
    Enter his courts with songs of praise.
    Give thanks to him and bless his name.   ℟

4   Indeed, how good is the Lord,
    eternal his merciful love.
    He is faithful from age to age.   ℟

Gospel Acclamation   Lk 21:28

    Alleluia, alleluia!
    Lift up your heads and see;
    your redemption is near at hand.
    Alleluia!

GOSPEL

A reading from the holy Gospel according   21:20-28
to Luke

Jerusalem will be trampled by the Gentiles until the time of the
Gentiles is fulfilled.

Jesus said to his disciples: 'When you see Jerusalem surrounded by
armies, you must realise that she will soon be laid desolate. Then
those in Judaea must escape to the mountains, those inside the city
must leave it, and those in country districts must not take refuge in it.
For this is the time of vengeance when all that scripture says must be
fulfilled. Alas for those with child, or with babies at the breast, when
those days come!

    'For great misery will descend on the land and wrath on this
people. They will fall by the edge of the sword and be led captive to

every pagan country; and Jerusalem will be trampled down by the pagans until the age of the pagans is completely over.

'There will be signs in the sun and moon and stars; on earth nations in agony, bewildered by the clamour of the ocean and its waves; men dying of fear as they await what menaces the world, for the powers of heaven will be shaken. And then they will see the Son of Man coming in a cloud with power and great glory. When these things begin to take place, stand erect, hold your heads high, because your liberation is near at hand.'

This is the Gospel of the Lord.

Friday

FIRST READING

A reading from the book of the Apocalypse   20:1-4. 11 – 21:2

The dead were judged according to what they had done in their lives.
I saw the new Jerusalem coming down from heaven.

I, John, saw an angel come down from heaven with the key of the Abyss in his hand and an enormous chain. He overpowered the dragon, the primeval serpent which is the devil and Satan, and chained him up for a thousand years. He threw him into the Abyss, and shut the entrance and sealed it over him, to make sure he would not deceive the nations again until the thousand years had passed. At the end of that time he must be released, but only for a short while.

Then I saw thrones, and I saw those who are given the power to be judges take their seats on them. I saw the souls of all who had been beheaded for having witnessed for Jesus and for having preached God's word, and those who refused to worship the beast or his statue and would not have the brand-mark on their foreheads or hands; they came to life, and reigned with Christ for a thousand years.

Then I saw a great white throne and the One who was sitting on it. In his presence, earth and sky vanished, leaving no trace. I saw the dead, both great and small, standing in front of his throne, while the book of life was opened, and other books opened which were the record of what they had done in their lives, by which the dead were judged.

The sea gave up all the dead who were in it; Death and Hades were emptied of the dead that were in them; and every one was judged according to the way in which he had lived. Then Death and Hades were thrown into the burning lake. This burning lake is the second death; and anybody whose name could not be found written in the book of life was thrown into the burning lake.

Then I saw a new heaven and a new earth; the first heaven and the first earth had disappeared now, and there was no longer any sea. I saw the holy city, and the new Jerusalem, coming down from God out of heaven, as beautiful as a bride all dressed for her husband.

This is the word of the Lord.

Responsorial Psalm   Ps 83:3-6. 8. ℟ Apoc 21:3

℟   Here God lives among his people.

1   My soul is longing and yearning,
    is yearning for the courts of the Lord.
    My heart and my soul ring out their joy
    to God, the living God.   ℟

2   The sparrow herself finds a home
    and the swallow a nest for her brood;
    she lays her young by your altars,
    Lord of hosts, my king and my God.   ℟

3   They are happy, who dwell in your house,
    for ever singing your praise.
    They are happy, whose strength is in you.
    They walk with ever growing strength.   ℟

Gospel Acclamation   Lk 21:28

Alleluia, alleluia!
Lift up your heads and see;
your redemption is near at hand.
Alleluia!

GOSPEL

A reading from the holy Gospel according to Luke   21:29-33

When you see these things happen, know that the kingdom of God is near.

Jesus told his disciples a parable, 'Think of the fig tree and indeed every tree. As soon as you see them bud, you know that summer is now near. So with you when you see these things happening: know that the kingdom of God is near. I tell you solemnly, before this generation has passed away all will have taken place. Heaven and earth will pass away, but my words will never pass away.'

This is the Gospel of the Lord.

Saturday

FIRST READING

A reading from the book of the Apocalypse   22:1-7

It will never be night again, because the Lord God will shine on them.

The angel showed me, John, the river of life, rising from the throne of God and of the Lamb and flowing crystal-clear down the middle of the city street. On either side of the river were the trees of life, which bear twelve crops of fruit in a year, one in each month, and the leaves of which are the cure for the pagans.

The ban will be lifted. The throne of God and of the Lamb will be in its place in the city; his servants will worship him, they will see him face to face, and his name will be written on their foreheads. It will never be night again and they will not need lamplight or sunlight, because the Lord God will be shining on them. They will reign for ever and ever.

The angel said to me, 'All that you have written is sure and will come true: the Lord God who gives the spirit to the prophets has sent his angel to reveal to his servants what is soon to take place. Very soon now, I shall be with you again.' Happy are those who treasure the prophetic message of this book.

This is the word of the Lord.

Responsorial Psalm   Ps 94:1-7. ℟ 1 Cor 16:22; Apoc 22:20

℟   Marantha! Come, Lord Jesus!

1   Come, ring out our joy to the Lord;
     hail the rock who saves us.
     Let us come before him, giving thanks,
     with songs let us hail the Lord.   ℟

2   A mighty God is the Lord,
    a great king above all gods.
    In his hand are the depths of the earth;
    the heights of the mountains are his.
    To him belongs the sea, for he made it
    and the dry land shaped by his hands.   ℟

3   Come in; let us bow and bend low;
    let us kneel before the God who made us
    for he is our God and we
    the people who belong to his pasture,
    the flock that is led by his hand.   ℟

Gospel Acclamation   Lk 21:36

    Alleluia, alleluia!
    Be watchful, pray constantly,
    that you may be worthy to stand before the Son of Man.
    Alleluia!

GOSPEL

A reading from the holy Gospel according to Luke   21:34-36

Stay awake, that you might have the strength to survive all that is
going to happen.

Jesus said to his disciples: 'Watch yourselves, or your hearts will be
coarsened with debauchery and drunkenness and the cares of life, and
that day will be sprung on you suddenly, like a trap. For it will come
down on every living man on the face of the earth. Stay awake,
praying at all times for the strength to survive all that is going to
happen, and to stand with confidence before the Son of Man.'

    This is the Gospel of the Lord.

GOSPEL ACCLAMATIONS

For use *ad libitum* on the Weekdays in Ordinary Time

1

1 Sam 3:9; Jn 6:68

Alleluia, alleluia!
Speak, O Lord, your servant is listening;
you have the words of everlasting life.
Alleluia!

2

cf. Ps 18:9

Alleluia, alleluia!
Your words, O Lord, give joy to my heart,
your teaching is light to my eyes.
Alleluia!

3

Ps 24:4. 5

Alleluia, alleluia!
Teach me your paths, my God,
and lead me in your truth.
Alleluia!

4

cf. Ps 26:11

Alleluia, alleluia!
Teach me your way, O Lord,
and lead me on a straight road.
Alleluia!

5

cf. Ps 94:8

Alleluia, alleluia!
If today you hear his voice,
harden not your hearts.
Alleluia!

6

Ps 110:7. 8

Alleluia, alleluia!
Your laws are all made firm, O Lord,
established for ever more.
Alleluia!

7   Ps 118:18

Alleluia, alleluia!
Unveil my eyes, O Lord,
and I will see the marvels of your law.
Alleluia!

8   Ps 118:27

Alleluia, alleluia!
Instruct me in the way of your rules,
and I will reflect on all your wonders.
Alleluia!

9   Ps 118:34

Alleluia, alleluia!
Teach me the meaning of your law, O Lord,
and I will guard it with all my heart.
Alleluia!

10   Ps 118:36. 29

Alleluia, alleluia!
Turn my heart to do your will;
teach me your law, O God.
Alleluia!

11   Ps 118:88

Alleluia, alleluia!
Give me life, O Lord,
and I will do your commands.
Alleluia!

12   Ps 118:105

Alleluia, alleluia!
Your word is a lamp for my feet,
and a light on my path.
Alleluia!

13

Ps 118:135

Alleluia, alleluia!
Let your face shine on your servant,
and teach me your laws.
Alleluia!

14

Ps 129:5

Alleluia, alleluia!
I hope in the Lord,
I trust in his word.
Alleluia!

15

Ps 144:13

Alleluia, alleluia!
The Lord is faithful in all his words
and holy in his deeds.
Alleluia!

16

Ps 147:12. 15

Alleluia, alleluia!
O praise the Lord, Jerusalem;
he sends out his word to the earth.
Alleluia!

17

Mt 4:4

Alleluia, alleluia!
No one lives on bread alone,
but on every word that comes from the mouth of God.
Alleluia!

18

cf. Mt 11:25

Alleluia, alleluia!
Blessed are you, Father, Lord of heaven and earth;
you have revealed to little ones the mysteries of the kingdom.
Alleluia!

19   cf. Lk 8:15

Alleluia, alleluia!
Happy are they who have kept the word with a generous heart
and yield a harvest through perseverance.
Alleluia!

20   cf. Jn 6:63. 68

Alleluia, alleluia!
Your words, Lord, are spirit and life,
you have the words of everlasting life.
Alleluia!

21   Jn 8:12

Alleluia, alleluia!
I am the light of the world, says the Lord;
whoever follows me will have the light of life.
Alleluia!

22   Jn 10:27

Alleluia, alleluia!
My sheep listen to my voice, says the Lord;
I know them, and they follow me.
Alleluia!

23   Jn 14:6

Alleluia, alleluia!
I am the way, the truth, and the life, says the Lord;
no one comes to the Father, except through me.
Alleluia!

24   Jn 14:23

Alleluia, alleluia!
All who love me will keep my words,
and my Father will love them, and we will come to them.
Alleluia!

25   Jn 15:1

Alleluia, alleluia!
I call you my friends, says the Lord,
for I have made known to you all that the Father has told me.
Alleluia!

26   cf. Jn 17:1

Alleluia, alleluia!
Your word, O Lord, is truth;
make us holy in the truth.
Alleluia!

27   cf. Acts 16:1

Alleluia, alleluia!
Open our hearts, O Lord,
to listen to the words of your Son.
Alleluia!

28   2 Cor 5:1

Alleluia, alleluia!
God was in Christ, to reconcile the world to himself;
and the Good News of reconciliation he has entrusted to us.
Alleluia!

29   cf. Eph 1:17. 1

Alleluia, alleluia!
May the Father of our Lord Jesus Christ
enlighten the eyes of our heart
that we might see how great is the hope
to which we are called.
Alleluia!

30   Phil 2:15-1

Alleluia, alleluia!
Shine on the world like bright stars;
you are offering it the word of life.
Alleluia!

31   Col 3:16. 17

Alleluia, alleluia!
Give thanks to God our Father through Jesus Christ our Lord,
and may the fullness of his message live within you.
Alleluia!

32   cf. 1 Thess 2:13

Alleluia, alleluia!
Receive this message not as human words,
but as truly the word of God.
Alleluia!

33   cf. 2 Thess 2:14

Alleluia, alleluia!
God has called us with the gospel
to share in the glory of our Lord Jesus Christ.
Alleluia!

34   cf. 2 Tim 1:10

Alleluia, alleluia!
Our Saviour Jesus Christ has done away with death,
and brought us life through his gospel.
Alleluia!

35   Heb 4:12

Alleluia, alleluia!
The word of God is living and active;
it probes the thoughts and motives of our heart.
Alleluia!

36   James 1:18

Alleluia, alleluia!
The Father gave us birth by his message of truth,
that we might be as the first fruits of his creation.
Alleluia!

37   James 1:21

Alleluia, alleluia!
Receive and submit to the word planted in you;
it can save your souls.
Alleluia!

38   1 Peter 1:25

Alleluia, alleluia!
The word of the Lord stands for ever;
it is the word given to you, the Good News.
Alleluia!

39   1 Jn 2:5

Alleluia, alleluia!
Whoever keeps the word of Christ,
grows perfect in the love of God.
Alleluia!

For the last Week

1   Mt 24:42. 44

Alleluia, alleluia!
Be watchful and ready:
you know not when the Son of Man is coming.
Alleluia!

2   Lk 21:28

Alleluia, alleluia!
Lift up your heads and see;
your redemption is near at hand.
Alleluia!

3   Lk 21:36

Alleluia, alleluia!
Be watchful, pray constantly,
that you may be worthy to stand before the Son of Man.
Alleluia!

4   Apoc 2:10

Alleluia, alleluia!
Be faithful until death, says the Lord,
and I will give you the crown of life.
Alleluia!

Proper of Saints

JANUARY

1 January: Octave of Christmas
SOLEMNITY OF MARY, MOTHER OF GOD

See Proper of Seasons, Volume I, pp.138ff.

2 January

Ss Basil the Great and Gregory Nazianzen, bishops and doctors of the Church   Memorial

Common of pastors or Common of doctors of the Church.

FIRST READING

A reading from the letter of St Paul
to the Ephesians   4:1-7. 11-13

In the work of service we help in building up the body of Christ.

I, the prisoner in the Lord, implore you to lead a life worthy of your
vocation. Bear with one another charitably, in complete selflessness, gentleness and patience. Do all you can to preserve the
unity of the Spirit by the peace that binds you together. There is
one Body, one Spirit, just as you were all called into one and the
same hope when you were called. There is one Lord, one faith, one
baptism, and one God who is Father of all, over all, through all and
within all.

Each one of us, however, has been given his own share of grace,
given as Christ allotted it. To some his gift was that they should be
apostles; to some, prophets; to some, evangelists; to some, pastors
and teachers; so that the saints together make a unity in the work
of service, building up the body of Christ. In this way we are all to
come to unity in our faith and in our knowledge of the Son of God,
until we become the perfect man, fully mature with the fullness of
Christ himself.

This is the word of the Lord.

Responsorial Psalm

Ps 22. ℟ v.1

℟   The Lord is my shepherd; there is nothing I shall want.

1   The Lord is my shepherd;
      there is nothing I shall want.
      Fresh and green are the pastures
      where he gives me repose.
      Near restful waters he leads me,
      to revive my drooping spirit. ℟

2   He guides me along the right path;
      he is true to his name.
      If I should walk in the valley of darkness
      no evil would I fear.
      You are there with your crook and your staff;
      with these you give me comfort. ℟

3   You have prepared a banquet for me
      in the sight of my foes.
      My head you have anointed with oil;
      my cup is overflowing.   ℟

4   Surely goodness and kindness shall follow me
      all the days of my life.
      In the Lord's own house shall I dwell
      for ever and ever.   ℟

Gospel Acclamation

Mt 23:9-10

      Alleluia, alleluia!
      You have one Father, your Father in heaven;
      you have one teacher: the Lord Jesus Christ!
      Alleluia!

GOSPEL

A reading from the holy Gospel 23:8-12
according to Matthew

The greatest among you must be your servant.

Jesus said to his disciples: 'You must not allow yourselves to be called Rabbi, since you have only one master, and you are all brothers. You must call no one on earth your father, since you have only one Father, and he is in heaven. Nor must you allow yourselves to be called teachers, for you have only one Teacher, the Christ. The greatest among you must be your servant. Anyone who exalts himself will be humbled, and anyone who humbles himself will be exalted.'

This is the Gospel of the Lord.

7 January

St Raymond of Penyafort, priest

Optional memorial

Common of pastors.

FIRST READING

A reading from the second letter of St Paul to the Corinthians 5:14-20

God gave us the work of reconciliation.

The love of Christ overwhelms us when we reflect that if one man has died for all, then all men should be dead; and the reason he died for all was so that living men should live no longer for themselves, but for him who died and was raised to life for them.

From now onwards, therefore, we do not judge anyone by the standards of the flesh. Even if we did once know Christ in the flesh, that is not how we know him now. And for anyone who is in Christ, there is a new creation; the old creation has gone, and now the new one is here. It is all God's work. It was God who reconciled us to himself through Christ and gave us the work of handing on this reconciliation. In other words, God in Christ was reconciling the world to himself, not holding men's faults against them, and he has entrusted to us the news that they are reconciled. So we are ambassadors for Christ; it is as though God were appealing through us, and the appeal that we make in Christ's name is: be reconciled to God.

This is the word of the Lord.

Responsorial Psalm Ps 102: 1-4. 8-9. 13-14. 17-18. ℟ v.1

℟ O bless the Lord, my soul.

1 My soul, give thanks to the Lord,
   all my being, bless his holy name.
   My soul, give thanks to the Lord
   and never forget all his blessings. ℟

2 It is he who forgives all your guilt,
   who heals every one of your ills,
   who redeems your life from the grave,
   who crowns you with love and compassion. ℟

3 The Lord is compassion and love,
   slow to anger and rich in mercy.
   His wrath will come to an end;
   he will not be angry for ever. ℟

4 As a father has compassion on his sons,
   the Lord has pity on those who fear him;
   for he knows of what we are made,
   he remembers that we are dust. ℟

5 But the love of the Lord is everlasting
   upon those who hold him in fear;
   his justice reaches out to children's children
   when they keep his covenant in truth. ℟

Gospel Acclamation Lk 21:36

Alleluia, alleluia!
Be watchful, pray constantly,
that you may be worthy to stand before the Son of Man.
Alleluia!

GOSPEL

A reading from the holy Gospel according to Luke 12:35-40

Be prepared.

Jesus said to his disciples: 'See that you are dressed for action and
have your lamps lit. Be like men waiting for their master to return
from the wedding feast, ready to open the door as soon as he comes and

knocks. Happy those servants whom the master finds awake when he comes. I tell you solemnly, he will put on an apron, sit them down at table and wait on them. It may be in the second watch he comes, or in the third, but happy those servants if he finds them ready. You may be quite sure of this, that if the householder had known at what hour the burglar would come, he would not have let anyone break through the wall of his house. You too must stand ready, because the Son of Man is coming at an hour you do not expect.'

This is the Gospel of the Lord.

13 January

St Hilary, bishop and doctor of the Church

Optional memorial

Common of pastors or Common of doctors of the Church.

FIRST READING

A reading from the first letter of St John   2:18-25

Whoever acknowledges the Son possesses the Father also.

Children, these are the last days;
you were told that an Antichrist must come,
and now several antichrists have already appeared;
we know from this that these are the last days.
Those rivals of Christ came out of your own number,
but they had never really belonged;
if they had belonged, they would have stayed with us;
but they left us, to prove that not one of them
ever belonged to us.
But you have been anointed by the Holy One,
and have all received the knowledge.
It is not because you do not know the truth that I am writing to you
but rather because you know it already
and know that no lie can come from the truth.
The man who denies that Jesus is the Christ –
he is the liar,
he is Antichrist;
and he is denying the Father as well as the Son,
because no one who has the Father can deny the Son,

and to acknowledge the Son is to have the Father as well.
Keep alive in yourselves what you were taught in the beginning:
as long as what you were taught in the beginning is alive in you,
you will live in the Son
and in the Father;
and what is promised to you by his own promise
is eternal life.

This is the word of the Lord.

Responsorial Psalm   Ps 109: 1-4. ℞ v.4

℞ You are a priest for ever, in the line of Melchizedek.

1 The Lord's revelation to my Master:
  'Sit on my right:
  I will put your foes beneath your feet.'   ℞

2 The Lord will send from Zion
  your sceptre of power:
  rule in the midst of all your foes.   ℞

3 A prince from the day of your birth
  on the holy mountains;
  from the womb before the daybreak I begot you.   ℞

4 The Lord has sworn an oath he will not change.
  'You are a priest for ever,
  a priest like Melchizedek of old.'   ℞

Gospel Acclamation   Mt 5:16

Alleluia, alleluia!
Let your light shine before all
that they may see your good works and glorify your Father.
Alleluia!

GOSPEL

A reading from the holy Gospel according to Matthew   5:13-19

You are the light of the world.

Jesus said to his disciples: 'You are the salt of the earth. But if salt becomes tasteless, what can make it salty again? It is good for nothing, and can only be thrown out to be trampled underfoot by men.

'You are the light of the world. A city built on a hill-top cannot be hidden. No one lights a lamp to put it under a tub; they put it on the lamp-stand where it shines for everyone in the house. In the same way your light must shine in the sight of men, so that, seeing your good works, they may give the praise to your Father in heaven.

'Do not imagine that I have come to abolish the Law or the Prophets. I have come not to abolish but to complete them. I tell you solemnly, till heaven and earth disappear, not one dot, not one little stroke, shall disappear from the Law until its purpose is achieved. Therefore, the man who infringes even one of the least of these commandments and teaches others to do the same will be considered the least in the kingdom of heaven; but the man who keeps them and teaches them will be considered great in the kingdom of heaven.'

This is the Gospel of the Lord.

17 January

St Anthony, abbot   Memorial

Common of holy men and women: for religious.

FIRST READING

A reading from the letter of St Paul to the Ephesians   6:10-13. 18

Put on God's armour.

Grow strong in the Lord, with the strength of his power. Put God's armour on so as to be able to resist the devil's tactics. For it is not against human enemies that we have to struggle, but against the Sovereignties and the Powers who originate the darkness in this world, the spiritual army of evil in the heavens. That is why you must rely on God's armour, or you will not be able to put up any resistance when the worst happens, or have enough resources to hold your ground.

Pray all the time, asking for what you need, praying in the Spirit on every possible occasion. Never get tired of staying awake to pray for all the saints.

This is the word of the Lord.

Responsorial Psalm   Ps 15: 1-2. 5. 7-8. 11. ℟ cf. v.5

℟   You are my inheritance, O Lord.

1   Preserve me, God, I take refuge in you.
    I say to the Lord: 'You are my God.'
    O Lord, it is you who are my portion and cup;
    it is you yourself who are my prize.   ℟

2   I will bless the Lord who gives me counsel,
    who even at night directs my heart.
    I keep the Lord ever in my sight:
    since he is at my right hand, I shall stand firm.   ℟

3   You will show me the path of life,
    the fullness of joy in your presence,
    at your right hand happiness for ever.   ℟

Gospel Acclamation   Jn 8:31-32

    Alleluia, alleluia!
    If you stay in my word, you will indeed be my disciples,
    and you will know the truth, says the Lord.
    Alleluia!

GOSPEL

A reading from the holy Gospel according to Matthew   19:16-26

If you wish to be perfect, go and sell what you have.

There was a man who came to Jesus and asked, 'Master, what good
deed must I do to possess eternal life?' Jesus said to him, 'Why do you
ask me about what is good? There is one alone who is good. But if you
wish to enter into life, keep the commandments.' He said, 'Which?'
'These:' Jesus replied. 'You must not kill. You must not commit
adultery. You must not bring false witness. Honour your father and
mother, and: You must love your neighbour as yourself.' The young
man said to him, 'I have kept all these. What more do I need to do?'
Jesus said, 'If you wish to be perfect, go and sell what you own and
give the money to the poor, and you will have treasure in heaven; then
come, follow me'.

But when the young man heard these words he went away sad, for
he was a man of great wealth.

Then Jesus said to his disciples, 'I tell you solemnly, it will be hard for a rich man to enter the kingdom of heaven. Yes, I tell you again, it is easier for a camel to pass through the eye of a needle than for a rich man to enter the kingdom of heaven.' When the disciples heard this they were astonished. 'Who can be saved, then?' they said. Jesus gazed at them. 'For men' he told them 'this is impossible; for God everything is possible.'

This is the Gospel of the Lord.

20 January

St Fabian, pope and martyr   Optional Memorial

Common of martyrs or Common of pastors: for popes.

FIRST READING

A reading from the first letter of St Peter   5:1-4

Be the shepherds of the flock of God that is entrusted to you.

I have something to tell your elders: I am an elder myself, and a witness to the sufferings of Christ and with you I have a share in the glory that is to be revealed. Be the shepherds of the flock of God that is entrusted to you; watch over it, not simply as a duty but gladly, because God wants it; not for sordid money, but because you are eager to do it. Never be a dictator over any group that is put in your charge, but be an example that the whole flock can follow. When the chief shepherd appears, you will be given the crown of unfading glory.

This is the word of the Lord.

Responsorial Psalm   Ps 39:2. 4. 7-10. ℟ cf. vv. 8-9

℟   Here am I, Lord; I come to do your will.

1   I waited, I waited for the Lord
    and he stooped down to me;
    he heard my cry.
    He put a new song into my mouth,
    praise of our God.   ℟

2 You do not ask for sacrifice and offerings,
   but an open ear.
   You do not ask for holocaust and victim.
   Instead, here am I.

   ℟ Here am I, Lord; I come to do your will.

3 In the scroll of the book it stands written
   that I should do your will.
   My God, I delight in your law
   in the depth of my heart. ℟

4 Your justice I have proclaimed
   in the great assembly.
   My lips I have not sealed;
   you know it, O Lord. ℟

Gospel Acclamation   Jn 10:14

   Alleluia, alleluia!
   I am the good shepherd, says the Lord;
   I know my sheep, and mine know me.
   Alleluia!

GOSPEL

A reading from the holy Gospel according to John   21:15-17

Take care of my lambs and my sheep.

Jesus showed himself to his disciples, and after they had eaten he said
to Simon Peter, 'Simon son of John, do you love me more than these
others do?' He answered, 'Yes Lord, you know I love you.' Jesus said to
him, 'Feed my lambs.' A second time he said to him, 'Simon son of
John, do you love me?' He replied, 'Yes, Lord, you know I love you.'
Jesus said to him, 'Look after my sheep.' Then he said to him a third
time, 'Simon son of John, do you love me?' Peter was upset that he
asked him the third time, 'Do you love me?' and said, 'Lord, you know
everything; you know I love you.' Jesus said to him, 'Feed my sheep.'

   This is the Gospel of the Lord.

also 20 January

St Sebastian, martyr

Optional Memorial

Common of martyrs.

FIRST READING

A reading from the first letter of St Peter   3:14-17

There is no need to be afraid or to worry about them.

If you have to suffer for being good, you will count it a blessing. There is no need to be afraid or to worry about persecutors. Simply reverence the Lord Christ in your hearts, and always have your answer ready for people who ask you the reason for the hope that you all have. But give it with courtesy and respect and with a clear conscience, so that those who slander you when you are living a good life in Christ may be proved wrong in the accusations that they bring. And if it is the will of God that you should suffer, it is better to suffer for doing right than for doing wrong.

This is the word of the Lord.

Responsorial Psalm   Ps 33:2-9. ℟ v.5

℟   The Lord set me free from all my fears.

1   I will bless the Lord at all times,
     his praise always on my lips;
     in the Lord my soul shall make its boast.
     The humble shall hear and be glad.   ℟

2   Glorify the Lord with me.
     Together let us praise his name.
     I sought the Lord and he answered me;
     from all my terrors he set me free.   ℟

3   Look towards him and be radiant;
     let your faces not be abashed.
     This poor man called; the Lord heard him
     and rescued him from all his distress.   ℟

4   The angel of the Lord is encamped
     around those who revere him, to rescue them.
     Taste and see that the Lord is good.
     He is happy who seeks refuge in him.   ℟

Gospel Acclamation   James 1:12

> Alleluia, alleluia!
> Blessed are they who stand firm when trials come;
> when they have stood the test, they will win the crown of life.
> Alleluia!

GOSPEL

A reading from the holy Gospel according to Matthew   10:28-33

Do not fear those who kill the body.

Jesus said to his apostles: 'Do not be afraid of those who kill the body but cannot kill the soul; fear him rather who can destroy both body and soul in hell. Can you not buy two sparrows for a penny? And yet not one falls to the ground without your Father knowing. Why, every hair on your head has been counted. So there is no need to be afraid; you are worth more than hundreds of sparrows.

'So if anyone declares himself for me in the presence of men, I will declare myself for him in the presence of my Father in heaven. But the one who disowns me in the presence of men, I will disown in the presence of my Father in heaven.'

This is the Gospel of the Lord.

21 January

St Agnes, virgin and martyr   Memorial

Common of martyrs or Common of virgins.

FIRST READING

A reading from the first letter of St Paul   1:26-31
to the Corinthians

God has chosen those who are nothing at all.

Take yourselves, brothers, at the time when you were called: how many of you were wise in the ordinary sense of the word, how many were influential people, or came from noble families? No, it was to shame the wise that God chose what is foolish by human reckoning, and to shame what is strong that he chose what is weak by human reckoning; those whom the world think common and contemptible are the ones that God has chosen – those who are nothing at all to show up those who are everything. The human race has nothing to boast about to God, but you, God has made members of Christ Jesus and by God's doing he has become our wisdom, and our virtue, and our holiness, and our freedom. As scripture says: if anyone wants to boast, let him boast about the Lord.

This is the word of the Lord.

Responsorial Psalm   Ps 22. ℟ v.1

℟   The Lord is my shepherd; there is nothing I shall want.

1   The Lord is my shepherd;
    there is nothing I shall want.
    Fresh and green are the pastures
    where he gives me repose.
    Near restful waters he leads me,
    to revive my drooping spirit.   ℟

2   He guides me along the right path;
    he is true to his name.
    If I should walk in the valley of darkness
    no evil would I fear.
    You are there with your crook and your staff;
    with these you give me comfort.   ℟

3   You have prepared a banquet for me
    in the sight of my foes.
    My head you have anointed with oil;
    my cup is overflowing.   ℟

4   Surely goodness and kindness shall follow me
    all the days of my life.
    In the Lord's own house shall I dwell
    for ever and ever.   ℟

Gospel Acclamation   Jn 15:9.5

Alleluia, alleluia!
Remain in my love, says the Lord;
all who live in me and I in them will bear much fruit.
Alleluia!

GOSPEL

A reading from the holy Gospel according to Matthew   13:44-46

He sold all that he had and bought the field.

Jesus said to the crowds: 'The kingdom of heaven is like treasure hidden in a field which someone has found; he hides it again, goes off happy, sells everything he owns and buys the field.

'Again, the kingdom of heaven is like a merchant looking for fine pearls; when he finds one of great value he goes and sells everything he owns and buys it.'

This is the Gospel of the Lord.

22 January

St Vincent, deacon and martyr

Optional Memorial

Common of martyrs.

FIRST READING

A reading from the second letter of St Paul   4:7-15
to the Corinthians

We carry in our bodies the death and life of Jesus.

We are only the earthenware jars that hold this treasure, to make it clear that such an overwhelming power comes from God and not from us. We are in difficulties on all sides, but never cornered; we see no answer to our problems, but never despair; we have been persecuted, but never deserted; knocked down, but never killed; always, wherever we may be, we carry with us in our body the death of Jesus, so that the life of Jesus, too, may always be seen in our body. Indeed, while we are still alive, we are consigned to our death every day, for the sake of Jesus, so that in our mortal flesh the life of Jesus, too, may be openly shown. So death is at work in us, but life in you.

But as we have the same spirit of faith that is mentioned in scripture – I believed, and therefore I spoke – we too believe and therefore we too speak, knowing that he who raised the Lord Jesus to life will raise us with Jesus in our turn, and put us by his side and you with us. You see, all this is for your benefit, so that the more grace is multiplied among people, the more thanksgiving there will be, to the glory of God.

This is the word of the Lord.

Responsorial Psalm   Ps 33:2-9. ℟ v.5

> ℟   The Lord set me free from all my fears.

1   I will bless the Lord at all times,
    his praise always on my lips;
    in the Lord my soul shall make its boast.
    The humble shall hear and be glad.   ℟

2   Glorify the Lord with me.
    Together let us praise his name.
    I sought the Lord and he answered me;
    from all my terrors he set me free.   ℟

3   Look towards him and be radiant;
    let your faces not be abashed.
    This poor man called; the Lord heard him
    and rescued him from all his distress.   ℟

4   The angel of the Lord is encamped
    around those who revere him, to rescue them.
    Taste and see that the Lord is good.
    He is happy who seeks refuge in him.   ℟

Gospel Acclamation   Mt 5:10

> Alleluia, alleluia!
> Happy are they who suffer persecution for justice' sake;
> the kingdom of heaven is theirs.
> Alleluia!

GOSPEL

A reading from the holy Gospel according to Matthew   10:17-22

You will be dragged before governors and kings on account of me, to bear witness before them and all the people.

Jesus said to his apostles: 'Beware of men: they will hand you over to sanhedrins and scourge you in their synagogues. You will be dragged before governors and kings for my sake, to bear witness before them and the pagans. But when they hand you over, do not worry about how to speak or what to say; what you are to say will be given to you when the time comes; because it is not you who will be speaking; the Spirit of your Father will be speaking in you.

'Brother will betray brother to death, and the father his child; children will rise against their parents and have them put to death. You will be hated by all men on account of my name; but the man who stands firm to the end will be saved.'

This is the Gospel of the Lord.

24 January

St Francis de Sales, bishop and doctor of the Church   Memorial

Common of pastors or Common of doctors of the Church.

FIRST READING

A reading from the letter of St Paul to the Ephesians   3:8-12

The mission is to proclaim to all peoples the infinite treasure of Christ.

I, who am less than the least of all the saints, have been entrusted with this special grace, not only of proclaiming to the pagans the infinite treasure of Christ but also of explaining how the mystery is to be dispersed. Through all the ages, this has been kept hidden in God, the creator of everything. Why? So that the Sovereignties and Powers should learn only now, through the Church, how comprehensive God's wisdom really is, exactly according to the plan which he had from all eternity in Christ Jesus our Lord. This is why we are bold enough to approach God in complete confidence, through our faith in him.

This is the word of the Lord.

Responsorial Psalm   Ps 36:3-6. 30-31. ℟ v.30

℟   The mouths of the just murmur wisdom.

1   If you trust in the Lord and do good,
      then you will live in the land and be secure.
      If you find your delight in the Lord,
      he will grant your heart's desire.   ℟

2   Commit your life to the Lord,
      trust in him and he will act,
      so that your justice breaks forth like the light,
      your cause like the noon-day sun.   ℟

3   The just man's mouth utters wisdom
    and his lips speak what is right;
    the law of his God is in his heart,
    his steps shall be saved from stumbling.   ℟

Gospel Acclamation   Jn 13:34

    Alleluia, alleluia!
    I give you a new commandment:
    love one another as I have loved you.
    Alleluia!

GOSPEL

A reading from the holy Gospel according to John   15:9-17

You are my friends if you do what I command you.

Jesus said to his disciples:

    'As the Father has loved me,
    so I have loved you.
    Remain in my love.
    If you keep my commandments
    you will remain in my love,
    just as I have kept my Father's commandments
    and remain in his love.
    I have told you this
    so that my own joy may be in you
    and your joy be complete.
    This is my commandment:
    love one another,
    as I have loved you.
    A man can have no greater love
    than to lay down his life for his friends.
    You are my friends,
    if you do what I command you.
    I shall not call you servants any more,
    because a servant does not know
    his master's business;
    I call you friends,
    because I have made known to you

everything I have learnt from my Father.
You did not choose me,
no, I chose you;
and I commissioned you
to go out and to bear fruit,
fruit that will last;
and then the Father will give you
anything you ask him in my name.
What I command you
is to love one another.'

This is the Gospel of the Lord.

25 January

THE CONVERSION OF ST PAUL, APOSTLE Feast

FIRST READING

A reading from the Acts of the Apostles   22:3-16

Rise and be baptised and wash away your sins, calling on the name of Jesus.

Paul said to the people, 'I am a Jew and was born at Tarsus in Cilicia. I was brought up here in this city. I studied under Gamaliel and was taught the exact observance of the Law of our ancestors. In fact, I was as full of duty towards God as you are today. I even persecuted this Way to the death, and sent women as well as men to prison in chains as the high priest and the whole council of elders can testify, since they even sent me with letters to their brothers in Damascus. When I set off it was with the intention of bringing prisoners back from there to Jerusalem for punishment.

'I was on that journey and nearly at Damascus when about midday a bright light from heaven suddenly shone round me. I fell to the ground and heard a voice saying, "Saul, Saul, why are you persecuting me?" I answered: Who are you, Lord? and he said to me, "I am Jesus the Nazarene, and you are persecuting me." The people with me saw the light but did not hear his voice as he spoke to me. I said: What am I to do, Lord? The Lord answered, "Stand up and go into Damascus, and there you will be told what you have been appointed to do." The light had been so dazzling that I was blind and my companions had to take me by the hand; and so I came to Damascus.

'Someone called Ananias, a devout follower of the Law and highly thought of by all the Jews living there, came to see me; he stood beside me and said, "Brother Saul, receive your sight." Instantly my sight came back and I was able to see him. Then he said, "The God of our ancestors has chosen you to know his will, to see the Just One and hear his own voice speaking, because you are to be his witness before all mankind, testifying to what you have seen and heard. And now why delay? It is time you were baptised and had your sins washed away while invoking his name." '

This is the word of the Lord.

Alternative First Reading

A reading from the Acts of the Apostles   9:1-22

Lord, what do you want me to do?

Saul was still breathing threats to slaughter the Lord's disciples. He had gone to the high priest and asked for letters addressed to the synagogues in Damascus, that would authorise him to arrest and take to Jerusalem any followers of the Way, men or women, that he could find.

Suddenly, while he was travelling to Damascus and just before he reached the city, there came a light from heaven all round him. He fell to the ground, and then he heard a voice saying, 'Saul, Saul, why are you persecuting me?' 'Who are you, Lord?' he asked, and the voice answered, 'I am Jesus, and you are persecuting me. Get up now and go into the city, and you will be told what you have to do.' The men travelling with Saul stood there speechless, for though they heard the voice they could see no one. Saul got up from the ground, but even with his eyes wide open he could see nothing at all, and they had to lead him into Damascus by the hand. For three days he was without his sight, and took neither food nor drink.

A disciple called Ananias who lived in Damascus had a vision in which he heard the Lord say to him, 'Ananias!' When he replied, 'Here I am, Lord,' the Lord said, 'You must go to Straight Street and ask at the house of Judas for someone called Saul, who comes from Tarsus. At this moment he is praying, having had a vision of man called Ananias coming in and laying hands on him to give him back his sight.'

When he heard that, Ananias said, 'Lord, several people have told me about this man and all the harm he has been doing to your saints in Jerusalem. He has only come here because he holds a warrant from

865

the chief priests to arrest everybody who invokes your name.' The Lord replied, 'You must go all the same, because this man is my chosen instrument to bring my name before pagans and pagan kings and before the people of Israel; I myself will show him how much he himself must suffer for my name.' Then Ananias went. He entered the house, and at once laid his hands on Saul and said, 'Brother Saul, I have been sent by the Lord Jesus who appeared to you on your way here so that you may recover your sight and be filled with the Holy Spirit.' Immediately it was as though scales fell away from Saul's eyes and he could see again. So he was baptised there and then, and after taking some food he regained his strength.

After he had spent only a few days with the disciples in Damascus, he began preaching in the synagogues, 'Jesus is the Son of God.' All his hearers were amazed. 'Surely' they said 'this is the man who organised the attack in Jerusalem against the people who invoke this name, and who came here for the sole purpose of arresting them to have them tried by the chief priests?' Saul's power increased steadily, and he was able to throw the Jewish colony at Damascus into complete confusion by the way he demonstrated that Jesus was the Christ.

This is the word of the Lord.

Responsorial Psalm　　　　　　　　　　Ps 116:1-2. ℟ Mk 16:15

℟ Go out to all the world, and tell the Good News.

or

℟ Alleluia!

1 Praise the Lord, all you nations,
   acclaim him all you people. ℟

2 Strong is his love for us;
   he is faithful for ever. ℟

Gospel Acclamation　　　　　　　　　　　cf. Jn 15:16

Alleluia, alleluia!
I have chosen you from the world, says the Lord,
to go and bear fruit that will last.
Alleluia!

GOSPEL

A reading from the holy Gospel according to Mark   16:15-18

Go out to the whole world and make known the Good News.

Jesus showed himself to the Eleven and said to them, 'Go out to the whole world; proclaim the Good News to all creation. He who believes and is baptised will be saved; he who does not believe will be condemned. These are the signs that will be associated with believers: in my name they will cast out devils; they will have the gift of tongues; they will pick up snakes in their hands, and be unharmed should they drink deadly poison; they will lay their hands on the sick, who will recover.'

This is the Gospel of the Lord.

These readings are used in a Votive Mass of St Paul.

26 January

Ss Timothy and Titus, bishops   Memorial

Common of pastors.
The first reading is proper to this Memorial.

FIRST READING

A reading from the second letter of St Paul to Timothy   1:1-8

I have in mind your faith which is openly sincere.

From Paul, appointed by God to be an apostle of Christ Jesus in his design to promise life in Christ Jesus; to Timothy, dear child of mine, wishing you grace, mercy and peace from God the Father and from Christ Jesus our Lord.

Night and day I thank God, keeping my conscience clear and remembering my duty to him as my ancestors did, and always I remember you in my prayers; I remember your tears and long to see you again to complete my happiness. Then I am reminded of the sincere faith which you have; it came first to live in your grandmother Lois, and your mother Eunice, and I have no doubt that it is the same faith in you as well.

That is why I am reminding you now to fan into a flame the gift that God gave you when I laid my hands on you. God's gift was not a spirit of timidity, but the Spirit of power, and love, and self-control. So you are never to be ashamed of witnessing to the Lord, or ashamed of me for being his prisoner; but with me, bear the hardships for the sake of the Good News, relying on the power of God who has saved us and called us to be holy.

This is the word of the Lord.

Alternative First Reading

A reading from the letter of St Paul to Titus   1:1-5

> *To Titus, my beloved son in a common faith.*

From Paul, servant of God, an apostle of Jesus Christ to bring those whom God has chosen to faith and to the knowledge of the truth that leads to true religion; and to give them the hope of the eternal life that was promised so long ago by God. He does not lie and so, at the appointed time, he revealed his decision, and, by the command of God our saviour, I have been commissioned to proclaim it. To Titus, true child of mine in the faith that we share, wishing you grace and peace from God the Father and from Christ Jesus our saviour.

The reason I left you behind in Crete was for you to get everything organised there and appoint elders in every town, in the way that I told you.

This is the word of the Lord.

Responsorial Psalm   Ps 95: 1-3. 7-8. 10. ℟ v. 3

℟ Proclaim his marvellous deeds to all the nations.

1 O sing a new song to the Lord,
    sing to the Lord all the earth.
    O sing to the Lord, bless his name. ℟

2 Proclaim his help day by day,
    tell among the nations his glory
    and his wonders among all the people. ℟

3 Give the Lord, you families of peoples,
    give the Lord glory and power,
    give the Lord the glory of his name. ℟

4   Proclaim to the nations: 'God is king.'
    The world he made firm in its place;
    he will judge the peoples in fairness. ℟

Gospel Acclamation   Lk 4:18-19

    Alleluia, alleluia!
    The Lord sent me to bring Good News to the poor,
    and freedom to prisoners.
    Alleluia!

GOSPEL

A reading from the holy Gospel according to Luke   10:1-9

The harvest is rich but the labourers are few.

The Lord appointed seventy-two others and sent them out ahead of him, in pairs, to all the towns and places he himself was to visit. He said to them, 'The harvest is rich but the labourers are few, so ask the Lord of the harvest to send labourers to his harvest. Start off now, but remember, I am sending you out like lambs among wolves. Carry no purse, no haversack, no sandals. Salute no one on the road. Whatever house you go into, let your first words be, 'Peace to this house!' And if a man of peace lives there, your peace will go and rest on him; if not, it will come back to you. Stay in the same house, taking what food and drink they have to offer, for the labourer deserves his wages; do not move from house to house. Whenever you go into a town where they make you welcome, eat what is set before you. Cure those in it who are sick, and say, "The kingdom of God is very near to you" '.

    This is the Gospel of the Lord.

27 January

St Angela Merici, virgin   Optional Memorial

Common of virgins or Common of holy men and women: for teachers.

FIRST READING

A reading from the first letter of St Peter   4:7-11

Each one of you has received a special gift; put yourselves at the service of others.

Keep a calm and sober mind. Above all, never let your love for each other grow insincere, since love covers over many a sin. Welcome each other into your houses without grumbling. Each one of you has received a special grace, so, like good stewards responsible for all these different graces of God, put yourselves at the service of others. If you are a speaker, speak in words which seem to come from God; if you are a helper, help as though every action was done at God's orders; so that in everything God may receive the glory, through Jesus Christ, since to him belong all glory and power for ever and ever. Amen.

This is the word of the Lord.

Responsorial Psalm   Ps 148:1-2. 11-14. ℟ cf. vv.12.13

℟   Young men and women, praise the name of the Lord.

or

℟   Alleluia!

1   Praise the Lord from the heavens,
     praise him in the heights.
     Praise him, all his angels,
     praise him, all his host.   ℟

2   All earth's kings and peoples,
     earth's princes and rulers;
     young men and maidens,
     old men together with children.   ℟

3   Let them praise the name of the Lord
    for he alone is exalted.
    The splendour of his name
    reaches beyond heaven and earth.   ℟

4   He exalts the strength of his people.
    He is the praise of all his saints,
    of the sons of Israel,
    of the people to whom he comes close.   ℟

Gospel Acclamation   cf. Mt 11:25

    Alleluia, alleluia!
    Blessed are you, Father, Lord of heaven and earth,
    you have revealed to little ones the mysteries of the kingdom.
    Alleluia!

GOSPEL

A reading from the holy Gospel according to Mark   9:34-37

Whenever you have accepted graciously a small child, you
have accepted me.

On the road the disciples had been arguing which of them was the greatest. So Jesus sat down, called the Twelve to him and said, 'If anyone wants to be first, he must make himself last of all and servant of all.' He then took a little child, set him in front of them, put his arms round him, and said to them. 'Anyone who welcomes one of these little children in my name, welcomes me; and anyone who welcomes me welcomes not me but the one who sent me.'

    This is the Gospel of the Lord.

28 January

St Thomas Aquinas,
priest and doctor of the Church Memorial

Common of doctors of the Church or Common of pastors.

FIRST READING

A reading from the book of Wisdom 7:7-10. 15-16

I have loved wisdom more than health and beauty.

I prayed, and understanding was given me;
I entreated, and the spirit of Wisdom came to me.
I esteemed her more than sceptres and thrones;
compared with her, I held riches as nothing.
I reckoned no priceless stone to be her peer,
for compared with her, all gold is a pinch of sand,
and beside her silver ranks as mud.
I love her more than health or beauty,
preferred her to the light,
since her radiance never sleeps.
May God grant me to speak as he would wish
and express thoughts worthy of his gifts,
since he himself is the guide of Wisdom,
since he directs the sages.
We are indeed in his hand, we ourselves and our words,
with all our understanding, too, and technical knowledge.

This is the word of the Lord.

Responsorial Psalm Ps 118:9-14. ℟ v.12

℟ Lord, teach me your decrees.

1 How shall the young remain sinless?
 By obeying your word.
 I have sought you with all my heart:
 let me not stray from your commands. ℟

2 I treasure your promise in my heart
   lest I sin against you.
   Blessed are you, O Lord;
   teach me your statutes. ℟

3 With my tongue I have recounted
   the decrees of your lips.
   I rejoice to do your will
   as though all riches were mine. ℟

Gospel Acclamation   Mt 23:9-10

   Alleluia, alleluia!
   You have one Father, your Father in heaven;
   you have one teacher, the Lord Jesus Christ.
   Alleluia!

GOSPEL

A reading from the holy Gospel according to Matthew   23:8-12

You must not allow yourselves to be called teachers, for you have only one teacher, the Christ.

Jesus said to his disciples: 'You must not allow yourselves to be called Rabbi, since you have only one Master, and you are all brothers. You must call no one on earth your father, since you have only one Father, and he is in heaven. Nor must you allow yourselves to be called teachers, for you have only one Teacher, the Christ. The greatest among you must be your servant. Anyone who exalts himself will be humbled, and anyone who humbles himself will be exalted.'

   This is the Gospel of the Lord.

31 January

St John Bosco, priest

Memorial

Common of pastors or Common of holy men and women: for teachers.

FIRST READING

A reading from the letter of St Paul to the Philippians   4:4-9

Fill your minds with everything that is holy.

I want you to be happy, always happy in the Lord; I repeat, what I
want is your happiness. Let your tolerance be evident to everyone: the
Lord is very near. There is no need to worry; but if there is anything
you need, pray for it, asking God for it with prayer and thanksgiving,
and that peace of God, which is so much greater than we can
understand, will guard your hearts and your thoughts, in Christ
Jesus. Finally, brothers, fill your minds with everything that is true,
everything that is noble, everything that is good and pure, everything
that we love and honour, and everything that can be thought virtuous
or worthy of praise. Keep doing all the things that you learnt from me
and have been taught by me and have heard or seen that I do. Then
the God of peace will be with you.

This is the word of the Lord.

Responsorial Psalm   Ps 102:1-4. 8-9. 13-14. 17-18. ℟ v.1

℟ O bless the Lord, my soul.

1   My soul, give thanks to the Lord,
    all my being, bless his holy name.
    My soul, give thanks to the Lord.
    and never forget all his blessings.   ℟

2   It is he who forgives all your guilt,
    who heals every one of your ills,
    who redeems your life from the grave,
    who crowns you with love and compassion.   ℟

3   The Lord is compassion and love,
    slow to anger and rich in mercy.
    His wrath will come to an end;
    he will not be angry for ever.   ℟

4   As a father has compassion on his sons,
     the Lord has pity on those who fear him;
     for he knows of what we are made,
     he remembers that we are dust.   ℟

5   But the love of the Lord is everlasting
     upon those who hold him in fear;
     his justice reaches out to children's children
     when they keep his covenant in truth.   ℟

Gospel Acclamation   Mt 23:11. 12

     Alleluia, alleluia!
     Whoever is greatest among you will serve the rest.
     All who humble themselves shall be exalted.
     Alleluia!

GOSPEL

A reading from the holy Gospel according to Matthew   18:1-5

Whoever welcomes such a child for my sake, welcomes me.

The disciples came to Jesus and said, 'Who is the greatest in the
kingdom of heaven?' So he called a little child to him and set the child
in front of them. Then he said, 'I tell you solemnly, unless you change
and become like little children you will never enter the kingdom of
heaven. And so, the one who makes himself as little as this little child
is the greatest in the kingdom of heaven.

     'Anyone who welcomes a little child like this in my name wel-
comes me.'

     This is the Gospel of the Lord.

FEBRUARY

PRESENTATION OF THE LORD

Feast

FIRST READING

A reading from the prophet Malachi

3:1-4

The Lord whom you seek will come to his temple.

The Lord God says this: Look, I am going to send my messenger to prepare a way before me. And the Lord you are seeking will suddenly enter his Temple; and the angel of the covenant whom you are longing for, yes, he is coming, says the Lord of hosts. Who will be able to resist the day of his coming? Who will remain standing when he appears? For he is like the refiner's fire and the fullers' alkali. He will take his seat as refiner and purifier; he will purify the sons of Levi and refine them like gold and silver, and then they will make the offering to the Lord as it should be made. The offering of Judah and Jerusalem will then be welcomed by the Lord as in former days, as in the years of old.

This is the word of the Lord.

Responsorial Psalm   Ps 23:7-10. ℟ v.10

℟   Who is this king of glory? It is the Lord!

1   O gates, lift up your heads;
    grow higher, ancient doors.
    Let him enter, the king of glory!   ℟

2   Who is the king of glory?
    The Lord, the mighty, the valiant,
    the Lord, the valiant in war.   ℟

3   O gates, lift high your heads;
    grow higher, ancient doors.
    Let him enter, the king of glory!   ℟

4   Who is he, the king of glory?
    He, the Lord of armies,
    he is the king of glory.   ℟

SECOND READING

A reading from the letter to the Hebrews   2:14-18

He had to be made like us in all things.

Since all the children share the same blood and flesh, Jesus too shared equally in it, so that by his death he could take away all the power of the devil, who had power over death, and set free all those who had been held in slavery all their lives by the fear of death. For it was not the angels that he took to himself; he took to himself descent from Abraham. It was essential that he should in this way become completely like his brothers so that he could be a compassionate and trustworthy high priest of God's religion, able to atone for human sins. That is, because he has himself been through temptation he is able to help others who are tempted.

This is the word of the Lord.

Gospel Acclamation   Lk 2:32

Alleluia, alleluia!
This is the light of revelation to the nations,
and the glory of your people, Israel.
Alleluia!

GOSPEL

A reading from the holy Gospel according to Luke   2:22-40

My eyes have seen your saving power.

When the day came for them to be purified as laid down by the Law of Moses, the parents of Jesus took him up to Jerusalem to present him to the Lord – observing what stands written in the Law of the Lord: Every first-born male must be consecrated to the Lord – and also to offer in sacrifice, in accordance with what is said in the Law of the Lord, a pair of turtle-doves or two young pigeons. Now in Jerusalem there was a man named Simeon. He was an upright and devout man; he looked forward to Israel's comforting and the Holy Spirit rested on him. It had been revealed to him by the Holy Spirit that he would not see death until he had set eyes on the Christ of the Lord. Prompted by the Spirit he came to the Temple; and when the parents brought in the child Jesus to do for him what the Law required, he took him into his arms and blessed God, and he said:

'Now, Master, you can let your servant go in peace,
just as you promised;
because my eyes have seen the salvation
which you have prepared for all the nations to see,
a light to enlighten the pagans
and the glory of your people Israel.'

As the child's father and mother stood there wondering at the things that were being said about him, Simeon blessed them and said to Mary his mother, 'You see this child: he is destined for the fall and for the rising of many in Israel, destined to be a sign that is rejected – and a sword will pierce your own soul too – so that the secret thoughts of many may be laid bare.'

There was a prophetess also, Anna the daughter of Phanuel, of the tribe of Asher. She was well on in years. Her days of girlhood over, she had been married for seven years before becoming a widow. She was now eighty-four years old and never left the Temple, serving God night and day with fasting and prayer. She came by just at that moment and began to praise God; and she spoke of the child to all who looked forward to the deliverance of Jerusalem.

When they had done everything the Law of the Lord required, they went back to Galilee, to their own town of Nazareth. Meanwhile the child grew to maturity, and he was filled with wisdom; and God's favour was with him.

This is the Gospel of the Lord.

Shorter form

A reading from the holy Gospel according to Luke   2:22-32

My eyes have seen your saving power.

When the day came for them to be purified as laid down by the Law of Moses, the parents of Jesus took him up to Jerusalem to present him to the Lord – observing what stands written in the Law of the Lord: Every first-born male must be consecrated to the Lord – and also to offer in sacrifice, in accordance with what is said in the Law of the Lord, a pair of turtledoves or two young pigeons. Now in Jerusalem there was a man called Simeon. He was an upright and devout man; he looked forward to Israel's comforting and the Holy Spirit rested on him. It had been revealed to him by the Holy Spirit that he would not see death until he had set eyes on the Christ of the Lord. Prompted by the Spirit he came to the Temple: and when the parents brought in the child Jesus to do for him what the Law required, he took him into his arms and blessed God; and he said:

'Now, Master, you can let your servant go in peace,
just as you promised;
because my eyes have seen the salvation
which you have prepared for all the nations to see,
a light to enlighten the pagans
and the glory of your people Israel.'

This is the Gospel of the Lord.

---

3 February

St Blaise, bishop and martyr   Optional Memorial

Common of martyrs or Common of pastors.

FIRST READING

A reading from the letter of St Paul to the Romans   5:1-5

We boast about our sufferings.

Through our Lord Jesus Christ, by faith we are judged righteous and at peace with God, since it is by faith and through Jesus that we have entered this state of grace in which we can boast about looking forward to God's glory. But that is not all we can boast about; we can boast about our sufferings. These sufferings bring patience, as we know, and patience brings perseverance, and perseverance brings hope, and this hope is not deceptive, because the love of God has been poured into our hearts by the Holy Spirit which has been given us.

This is the word of the Lord.

Responsorial Psalm   Ps 116. ℟ Mk 16:15

   ℟   Go out to all the world, and tell the Good News.

or

   ℟   Alleluia!

1   O praise the Lord, all you nations,
    acclaim him all you peoples! ℟

2   Strong is his love for us;
    he is faithful for ever. ℟

Gospel Acclamation   Mt 28:19-20

   Alleluia, alleluia!
   Go and teach all people my gospel.
   I am with you always, until the end of the world.
   Alleluia!

GOSPEL

A reading from the holy Gospel according to Mark   16:15-20

Go out to the whole world; proclaim the Good News to all creation.

Jesus showed himself to the Eleven, and he said to them, 'Go out to the whole world; proclaim the Good News to all creation. He who believes and is baptised will be saved; he who does not believe will be condemned. These are the signs that will be associated with believers: in my name they will cast out devils; they will have the gift of tongues; they will pick up snakes in their hands, and be unharmed should they drink deadly poison; they will lay their hands on the sick, who will recover.'

And so the Lord Jesus, after he had spoken to them, was taken up into heaven: there at the right hand of God he took his place, while they, going out, preached everywhere, the Lord working with them and confirming the word by the signs that accompanied it.

This is the Gospel of the Lord.

also 3 February

St Ansgar, bishop   Optional Memorial

Common of pastors: for missionaries.

FIRST READING

A reading from the prophet Isaiah   52:7-10

All the ends of the earth shall see the salvation of our God.

How beautiful on the mountains,
are the feet of one who brings good news,
who heralds peace, brings happiness,
proclaims salvation,
and tells Zion
'Your God is king!'

Listen! Your watchmen raise their voices,
they shout for joy together,
for they see the Lord face to face,
as he returns to Zion.

Break into shouts of joy together,
you ruins of Jerusalem;
for the Lord is consoling his people,
redeeming Jerusalem.

The Lord bares his holy arm
in the sight of all the nations,
and all the ends of the earth shall see
the salvation of our God.

This is the word of the Lord.

Responsorial Psalm   Ps 95:1-3. 7-8. 10. ℟ v. 3

℟   Proclaim his marvellous deeds to all the nations.

1   O sing a new song to the Lord,
     sing to the Lord all the earth.
     O sing to the Lord, bless his name.   ℟

2   Proclaim his help day by day,
     tell among the nations his glory
     and his wonders among all the peoples.   ℟   (continued)

881

3   Give the Lord, you families of peoples,
     give the Lord glory and power,
     give the Lord the glory of his name.

     ℟   Proclaim his marvellous deeds to all the nations.

4   Proclaim to the nations: 'God is king.'
     The world he made firm in its place;
     he will judge the peoples in fairness.   ℟

Gospel Acclamation   Mk 1:17

          Alleluia, alleluia!
          Come, follow me, says the Lord,
          and I will make you fishers of my people.
          Alleluia!

GOSPEL

A reading from the holy Gospel according to Mark   1:14-20

I will make you fishers of my people.

After John had been arrested, Jesus went into Galilee. There he
proclaimed the Good News from God. 'The time has come,' he said,
'and the kingdom of God is close at hand. Repent, and believe the Good
News.'

     As he was walking along by the Sea of Galilee he saw Simon and
his brother Andrew casting a net in the lake – for they were
fishermen. And Jesus said to them, 'Follow me and I will make you
into fishers of men.' And at once they left their nets and followed him.

     Going on a little farther, he saw James son of Zebedee and his
brother John; they too were in their boat, mending their nets. He
called them at once and, leaving their father Zebedee in the boat with
the men he employed, they went after him.

     This is the Gospel of the Lord.

5 February

St Agatha, virgin and martyr   Memorial

Common of martyrs or Common of virgins.

FIRST READING

A reading from the first letter of St Paul to the Corinthians   1:26-31

God has chosen those who are nothing at all.

Take yourselves, brothers, at the time when you were called: how many of you were wise in the ordinary sense of the word, how many were influential people, or came from noble families? No, it was to shame the wise that God chose what is foolish by human reckoning, and to shame what is strong that he chose what is weak by human reckoning; those whom the world thinks common and contemptible are the ones that God has chosen – those who are nothing at all to show up those who are everything. The human race has nothing to boast about to God, but you, God has made members of Christ Jesus and by God's doing he has become our wisdom, and our virtue, and our holiness, and our freedom. As scripture says: if anyone wants to boast, let him boast about the Lord.

This is the word of the Lord.

Responsorial Psalm   Ps 30:3-4. 6. 8. 16. 17. ℟ v. 6

℟   Into your hands, O Lord, I entrust my spirit.

1   Be a rock of refuge for me,
   a mighty stronghold to save me,
   for you are my rock, my stronghold.
   For your name's sake, lead me and guide me.   ℟

2   Into your hands I commend my spirit.
   It is you who will redeem me, Lord.
   As for me, I trust in the Lord:
   let me be glad and rejoice in your love.   ℟

3   My life is in your hands, deliver me
   from the hands of those who hate me.
   Let your face shine on your servant.
   Save me in your love.   ℟

Gospel Acclamation   1 Peter 4:14

Alleluia, alleluia!
If you are insulted for the name of Christ, blessed are you,
for the Spirit of God rests upon you.
Alleluia!

GOSPEL

A reading from the holy Gospel according to Luke   9:23-26

Those who lose their lives for my sake will save them.

To all Jesus said, 'If anyone wants to be a follower of mine, let him
renounce himself and take up his cross every day and follow me. For
anyone who wants to save his life will lose it; but anyone who loses his
life for my sake, that man will save it. What gain, then, is it for a man
to have won the whole world and to have lost or ruined his very self?
For if anyone is ashamed of me and of my words, of him the Son of
Man will be ashamed when he comes in his own glory and in the glory
of the Father and the holy angels.'

This is the Gospel of the Lord.

6 February

Ss Paul Miki, priest
and companions, martyrs   Memorial

Common of martyrs.

FIRST READING

A reading from the letter of St Paul to the Galatians   2:19-20

I live now, not I but Christ lives in me.

Through the Law I am dead to the Law, so that now I can live for God.
I have been crucified with Christ, and I live now not with my own life
but with the life of Christ who lives in me. The life I now live in this
body I live in faith: faith in the Son of God who loved me and who
sacrificed himself for my sake.

This is the word of the Lord.

Responsorial Psalm   Ps 125. ℞ v.5

℞   Those who sow in tears, shall reap with shouts of joy.

1   When the Lord delivered Zion from bondage,
    it seemed like a dream.
    Then was our mouth filled with laughter,
    on our lips there were songs.   ℞

2   The heathens themselves said: 'What marvels
    the Lord worked for them!'
    What marvels the Lord worked for us!
    Indeed we were glad.   ℞

3   Deliver us, O Lord, from our bondage
    as streams in dry land.
    Those who are sowing in tears
    will sing when they reap.   ℞

4   They go out, they go out, full of tears,
    carrying seed for the sowing:
    they come back, they come back, full of song,
    carrying their sheaves.   ℞

Gospel Acclamation   Mt 28:19-20

Alleluia, alleluia!
Go and teach all people my gospel.
I am with you always, until the end of the world.
Alleluia!

GOSPEL

A reading from the holy Gospel according to Matthew   28:16-20

Go and make disciples of all the nations.

The eleven disciples set out for Galilee, to the mountain where Jesus
had arranged to meet them. When they saw him they fell down before
him, though some hesitated. Jesus came up and spoke to them. He
said, 'All authority in heaven and on earth has been given to me. Go,
therefore, make disciples of all the nations; baptise them in the name
of the Father and of the Son and of the Holy Spirit, and teach them to

observe all the commands I gave you. And know that I am with you always; yes, to the end of time.'

This is the Gospel of the Lord.

In celebrations between 8 February and 28 February, if the day falls within Lent, the acclamation used before the Gospel should be one of the Lenten phrases, and 'Alleluia' should be omitted.

---

8 February

St Jerome Emiliani   Optional Memorial

Common of holy men and women: for teachers.

FIRST READING

A reading from the book of Tobit   12:6-13

It is good to pray while fasting and giving alms.

Raphael took Tobit and his son Tobias aside and said, 'Bless God, utter his praise before all the living for all the favours he has given you. Bless and extol his name. Proclaim before all men the deeds of God as they deserve, and never tire of giving him thanks. It is right to keep the secret of a king, yet right to reveal and publish the works of God. Thank him worthily. Do what is good, and no evil can befall you.

'Prayer with fasting and alms with right conduct are better than riches with inquity. Better to practise almsgiving than to hoard up gold. Almsgiving saves from death and purges every kind of sin. Those who give alms have their fill of days; those who commit sin and do evil, bring harm on themselves.

'I am going to tell you the whole truth, hiding nothing from you. I have already told you that it is right to keep the secret of a king, yet right too to reveal in worthy fashion the works of God. So you must know that when you and Sarah were at prayer, it was I who offered your supplications before the glory of the Lord and who read them; so too when you were burying the dead. When you did not hesitate to get up and leave the table to go and bury a dead man, I was sent to test your faith.'

This is the word of the Lord.

886

Responsorial Psalm   Ps 33:2-11. ℟ v.2 Alt. ℟ v.9

℟   I will bless the Lord at all times.

or

℟   Taste and see the goodness of the Lord.

1   I will bless the Lord at all times,
    his praise always on my lips;
    in the Lord my soul shall make its boast.
    The humble shall hear and be glad.   ℟

2   Glorify the Lord with me.
    Together let us praise his name.
    I sought the Lord and he answered me;
    from all my terrors he set me free.   ℟

3   Look towards him and be radiant;
    let your faces not be abashed.
    This poor man called; the Lord heard him
    and rescued him from all his distress.   ℟

4   The angel of the Lord is encamped
    around those who revere him, to rescue them.
    Taste and see that the Lord is good.
    He is happy who seeks refuge in him.   ℟

5   Revere the Lord, you his saints.
    They lack nothing, those who revere him.
    Strong lions suffer want and go hungry
    but those who seek the Lord lack no blessing.   ℟

Gospel Acclamation   Mt 5:3

    Alleluia, alleluia!
    Happy the poor in spirit;
    the kingdom of heaven is theirs!
    Alleluia!

GOSPEL

A reading from the holy Gospel according to Mark   10:17-30

Sell whatever you have, and come follow me.

Jesus was setting out on a journey when a man ran up, knelt before him and put this question to him, 'Good master, what must I do to inherit eternal life?' Jesus said to him, 'Why do you call me good? No one is good but God alone. You know the commandments: You must not kill; You must not commit adultery; You must not steal; You must not bring false witness; You must not defraud; Honour your father and mother.' And he said to him, 'Master, I have kept all these from my earliest days.' Jesus looked steadily at him and loved him, and he said, 'There is one thing you lack. Go and sell everything you own and give the money to the poor, and you will have treasure in heaven; then come, follow me.' But his face fell at these words and he went away sad, for he was a man of great wealth.

Jesus looked round and said to his disciples, 'How hard it is for those who have riches to enter the kingdom of God!' The disciples were astounded by these words, but Jesus insisted. 'My children,' he said to them, 'how hard it is to enter the kingdom of God! It is easier for a camel to pass through the eye of a needle than for a rich man to enter the kingdom of God.' They were more astonished than ever. 'In that case,' they said to one another, 'who can be saved?' Jesus gazed at them. 'For men,' he said, 'it is impossible, but not for God: because everything is possible for God.'

Peter took this up. 'What about us?' he asked him. 'We have left everything and followed you.' Jesus said, 'I tell you solemnly, there is no one who has left house, brothers, sisters, father, children or land for my sake and for the sake of the gospel who will not be repaid a hundred times over, houses, brothers, sisters, mothers, children and land – not without persecutions – now in this present time and, in the world to come, eternal life.'

This is the Gospel of the Lord.

Shorter form

A reading from the holy Gospel according to Mark   10:17-27

Sell whatever you have, and come follow me.

Jesus was setting out on a journey when a man ran up, knelt before him and put this question to him, 'Good master, what must I do to inherit eternal life?' Jesus said to him, 'Why do you call me good? No one is good but God alone. You know the commandments: You must not kill; You must not commit adultery; You must not steal; You must not bring false witness; You must not defraud; Honour your father and mother.' And he said to him, 'Master, I have kept all these from my earliest days.' Jesus looked steadily at him and loved him, and he said, 'There is one thing you lack. Go and sell everything you own and give the money to the poor, and you will have treasure in heaven; then come, follow me.' But his face fell at these words and he went away sad, for he was a man of great wealth.

Jesus looked round and said to his disciples, 'How hard it is for those who have riches to enter the kingdom of God!' The disciples were astounded by these words, but Jesus insisted, 'My children,' he said to them, 'how hard it is to enter the kingdom of God! It is easier for a camel to pass through the eye of a needle than for a rich man to enter the kingdom of God.' They were more astonished than ever. 'In that case,' they said to one another, 'who can be saved?' Jesus gazed at them. 'For men,' he said, 'it is impossible, but not for God: because everything is possible for God.'

This is the Gospel of the Lord.

---

10 February
St Scholastica, virgin   Memorial

Common of virgins or Common of holy men and women.

FIRST READING

A reading from the Song of Songs   8:6-7

Love is as strong as Death.

Set me like a seal on your heart,
like a seal on your arm.
For love is strong as Death,
jealousy relentless as Sheol.
The flash of it is a flash of fire,
a flame of the Lord himself.
Love no flood can quench,
no torrents drown.

Were a man to offer all the wealth of his house to buy love, contempt is all he would purchase.

This is the word of the Lord.

Responsorial Psalm   Ps 148:1-2. 11-14. ℟ cf. vv.12. 13

℟   Young men and women, praise the name of the Lord.

or

℟   Alleluia!

1   Praise the Lord from the heavens,
    praise him in the heights.
    Praise him, all his angels,
    praise him, all his host.   ℟

2   All earth's kings and peoples,
    earth's princes and rulers;
    young men and maidens,
    old men together with children.   ℟

3   Let them praise the name of the Lord
    for he alone is exalted.
    The splendour of his name
    reaches beyond heaven and earth.   ℟

4   He exalts the strength of his people.
    He is the praise of all his saints,
    of the sons of Israel,
    of the people to whom he comes close.   ℟

Gospel Acclamation   Jn 14:23

    Alleluia, alleluia!
    All who love me will keep my words,
    and my Father will love them, and we will come to them.
    Alleluia!

GOSPEL

A reading from the holy Gospel according to Luke   10:38-42

Martha took up the duties in the house. Mary chose the better part.

In the course of their journey Jesus came to a village, and a woman
named Martha welcomed him into her house. She had a sister called
Mary, who sat down at the Lord's feet and listened to him speaking.

Now Martha who was distracted with all the serving said, 'Lord, do you not care that my sister is leaving me to do the serving all by myself? Please tell her to help me.' But the Lord answered: 'Martha, Martha,' he said, 'you worry and fret about so many things, and yet few are needed, indeed only one. It is Mary who has chosen the better part; it is not to be taken from her.'

This is the Gospel of the Lord.

11 February

Our Lady of Lourdes   Optional Memorial

Common of the Blessed Virgin Mary.

FIRST READING

A reading from the prophet Isaiah   66:10-14

I will send toward Jerusalem peace like a river.

Rejoice, Jerusalem,
be glad for her, all you who love her!
Rejoice, rejoice for her,
all you who mourned her!
That you may be suckled, filled,
from her consoling breast,
that you may savour with delight
her glorious breasts.
For thus says the Lord:
Now towards her I send flowing
peace, like a river,
and like a stream in spate
the glory of the nations.
At her breast will her nurslings be carried
and fondled in her lap.
Like a son comforted by his mother
will I comfort you.
(And by Jerusalem you will be comforted.)
At the sight your heart will rejoice,
and your bones flourish like the grass.
To his servants the Lord will reveal his hand.

This is the word of the Lord.

Responsorial Psalm   Jud 13:18-19. ℟ 15:9

℟   You are the highest honour of our race!

1   May you be blessed, my daughter, by God Most High,
    beyond all women on earth;
    and may the Lord God be blessed,
    the Creator of heaven and earth.   ℟

2   The trust you have shown
    shall not pass from the memories of men,
    but shall ever remind them
    of the power of God.   ℟

Gospel Acclamation   cf. Lk 1:45

    Alleluia, alleluia!
    Blessed are you, O Virgin Mary, for your firm believing,
    that the promises of the Lord would be fulfilled.
    Alleluia!

GOSPEL

A reading from the holy Gospel according to John   2:1-11

The mother of Jesus was at the wedding feast with him

There was a wedding at Cana in Galilee. The mother of Jesus was there, and Jesus and his disciples had also been invited. When they ran out of wine, since the wine provided for the wedding was all finished, the mother of Jesus said to him, 'They have no wine.' Jesus said, 'Woman, why turn to me? My hour has not come yet.' His mother said to the servants, 'Do whatever he tells you.' There were six stone water jars standing there, meant for the ablutions that are customary among the Jews: each could hold twenty or thirty gallons. Jesus said to the servants, 'Fill the jars with water,' and they filled them to the brim. 'Draw some out now,' he told them, 'and take it to the steward.' They did this; the steward tasted the water, and it had turned into wine. Having no idea where it came from – only the servants who had drawn the water knew – the steward called the bridegroom and said 'People generally serve the best wine first, and keep the cheaper sort till the guests have had plenty to drink; but you have kept the best wine till now.

This was the first of the signs given by Jesus: it was given at Cana in Galilee. He let his glory be seen, and his disciples believed in him.

This is the Gospel of the Lord.

14 February

Ss Cyril, monk, and Methodius, bishop   Memorial

Common of pastors: for missionaries or Common of holy men and women.

FIRST READING

A reading from the Acts of the Apostles   13:46-49

We must turn to the gentiles.

Paul and Barnabas spoke out boldly to the Jews, 'We had to proclaim the word of God to you first, but since you have rejected it, since you do not think yourselves worthy of eternal life, we must turn to the pagans. For this is what the Lord commanded us to do when he said:

'I have made you a light for the nations,
so that my salvation may reach the ends of the earth.'

It made the pagans very happy to hear this and they thanked the Lord for his message; all who were destined for eternal life became believers. Thus the word of the Lord spread through the whole countryside.

This is the word of the Lord.

Responsorial Psalm   Ps 116. ℞ Mk 16:15

℞   Go out to all the world, and tell the Good News.

or

℞   Alleluia!

1   O praise the Lord, all you nations,
acclaim him all you peoples! ℞

2   Strong is his love for us;
he is faithful for ever. ℞

893

Gospel Acclamation   Lk 4:18

Alleluia, alleluia!
The Lord sent me to bring Good News to the poor,
and freedom to prisoners.
Alleluia!

GOSPEL

A reading from the holy Gospel according to Luke   10:1-9

The harvest is rich but the labourers are few.

The Lord appointed seventy-two others and sent them out ahead of
him, in pairs, to all the towns and places he himself was to visit. He
said to them, 'The harvest is rich but the labourers are few, so ask the
Lord of the harvest to send labourers to his harvest. Start off now, but
remember, I am sending you out like lambs among wolves. Carry no
purse, no haversack, no sandals. Salute no one on the road. Whatever
house you go into, let your first words be, "Peace to this house!" And if
a man of peace lives there, your peace will go and rest on him; if not, it
will come back to you. Stay in the same house, taking what food and
drink they have to offer, for the labourer deserves his wages; do not
move from house to house. Whenever you go into a town where they
make you welcome, eat what is set before you. Cure those in it who are
sick and say, "The kingdom of God is very near to you." '

This is the Gospel of the Lord.

17 February

The Seven Founders of the Order of Servites

Optional Memorial

Common of holy men and women: for religious.

FIRST READING

A reading from the letter of St Paul to the Romans   8:26-30

With those he justified, he shared his glory.

The Spirit comes to help us in our weakness. For when we cannot
choose words in order to pray properly, the Spirit himself expresses

894

our plea in a way that could never be put into words, and God who knows everything in our hearts knows perfectly well what he means, and that the pleas of the saints expressed by the Spirit are according to the mind of God.

We know that by turning everything to their good God co-operates with all those who love him, with all those that he has called according to his purpose. They are the ones he chose specially long ago and intended to become true images of his Son, so that his Son might be the eldest of many brothers. He called those he intended for this; those he called he justified, and with those he justified he shared his glory.

This is the word of the Lord.

Responsorial Psalm   Ps 33:2-11. ℟ v.2. Alt. ℟ v.9

℟   I will bless the Lord at all times.

or

℟   Taste and see the goodness of the Lord.

1   I will bless the Lord at all times,
    his praise always on my lips;
    in the Lord my soul shall make its boast.
    The humble shall hear and be glad.   ℟

2   Glorify the Lord with me.
    Together let us praise his name.
    I sought the Lord and he answered me;
    from all my terrors he set me free.   ℟

3   Look towards him and be radiant;
    let your faces not be abashed.
    This poor man called; the Lord heard him
    and rescued him from all his distress.   ℟

4   The angel of the Lord is encamped
    around those who revere him, to rescue them.
    Taste and see that the Lord is good.
    He is happy who seeks refuge in him.   ℟

5   Revere the Lord, you his saints.
    They lack nothing, those who revere him.
    Strong lions suffer want and go hungry
    but those who seek the Lord lack no blessing.   ℟

Gospel Acclamation   Mt 5:3

> Alleluia, alleluia!
> Happy the poor in spirit;
> the kingdom of heaven is theirs!
> Alleluia!

GOSPEL

A reading from the holy Gospel according to Matthew   19:27-29

You who have left everything and followed me, will be rewarded a hundred-fold.

Peter said to Jesus: 'What about us? We have left everything and followed you. What are we to have, then?' Jesus said to him, 'I tell you solemnly, when all is made new and the Son of Man sits on his throne of glory, you will yourselves sit on twelve thrones to judge the twelve tribes of Israel. And everyone who has left houses, brothers, sisters, father, mother, children or land for the sake of my name will be repaid a hundred times over, and also inherit eternal life.'

This is the Gospel of the Lord.

21 February

St Peter Damian
bishop and doctor of the Church

Optional Memorial

Common of doctors of the Church or Common of pastors or Common of holy men and women: for religious.

FIRST READING

A reading from the second letter of St Paul to Timothy   4:1-5

Preach the Good News; fulfill your ministry.

Before God and before Christ Jesus who is to be judge of the living and the dead, I put this duty to you, in the name of his Appearing and of his kingdom: proclaim the message and, welcome or unwelcome, insist on it. Refute falsehood, correct error, call to obedience – but do all with patience and with the intention of teaching. The time is sure to come when, far from being content with sound teaching, people will be avid for the latest novelty and collect themselves a whole series of teachers according to their own tastes; and then, instead of listening to the truth, they will turn to myths. Be careful always to choose the right course; be brave under trials; make the preaching of the Good News your life's work, in thoroughgoing service.

This is the word of the Lord.

Responsorial Psalm   Ps 15:1-2. 5. 7-8. 11. ℟ cf. v.5

℟   You are my inheritance, O Lord.

1   Preserve me, God, I take refuge in you.
    I say to the Lord: 'You are my God.'
    O Lord, it is you who are my portion and cup;
    it is you yourself who are my prize.   ℟

2   I will bless the Lord who gives me counsel,
    who even at night directs my heart.
    I keep the Lord ever in my sight:
    since he is at my right hand, I shall stand firm.   ℟

3   You will show me the path of life,
    the fullness of joy in your presence,
    at your right hand happiness for ever.   ℟

Gospel Acclamation   Jn 15:9.5

    Alleluia, alleluia!
    Remain in my love, says the Lord;
    all who live in me, and I in them, will bear much fruit.
    Alleluia!

GOSPEL

A reading from the holy Gospel according to John   15:1-8

All who live in me, and I in them, bear fruit.

Jesus said to his disciples:

    'I am the true vine,
    and my Father is the vinedresser.
    Every branch in me that bears no fruit

he cuts away,
and every branch that does bear fruit he prunes
to make it bear even more.
You are pruned already,
by means of the word that I have spoken to you.
Make your home in me, as I make mine in you.
As a branch cannot bear fruit all by itself,
but must remain part of the vine,
neither can you unless you remain in me.
I am the vine,
you are the branches.
Whoever remains in me, with me in him,
bears fruit in plenty;
for cut off from me you can do nothing.
Anyone who does not remain in me
is like a branch that has been thrown away
– he withers;
these branches are collected and thrown on the fire,
and they are burnt.
If you remain in me
and my words remain in you,
you may ask what you will
and you shall get it.
It is to the glory of my Father that you should bear much fruit,
and then you will be my disciples.

This is the Gospel of the Lord.

22 February

THE CHAIR OF ST PETER, APOSTLE   Feast

FIRST READING

A reading from the first letter of St Peter   5:1-4

I myself am one of your leaders and a witness to the sufferings of Christ.

I have something to tell your elders: I am an elder myself, and a witness to the sufferings of Christ, and with you I have a share in the glory that is to be revealed. Be the shepherds of the flock of God that is entrusted to you: watch over it, not simply as a duty but gladly, because God wants it; not for sordid money, but because you are eager to do it. Never be a dictator over any group that is put in your charge, but be an example that the whole flock can follow. When the chief shepherd appears, you will be given the crown of unfading glory.

This is the word of the Lord.

Responsorial Psalm   Ps 22. ℟ v.1

℟   The Lord is my shepherd; there is nothing I shall want.

1   The Lord is my shepherd;
     there is nothing I shall want.
     Fresh and green are the pastures
     where he gives me repose.
     Near restful waters he leads me,
     to revive my drooping spirit.   ℟

2   He guides me along the right path;
     he is true to his name.
     If I should walk in the valley of darkness
     no evil would I fear.
     You are there with your crook and your staff;
     with these you give me comfort.   ℟

3   You have prepared a banquet for me
     in the sight of my foes.
     My head you have anointed with oil;
     my cup is overflowing.   ℟

4   Surely goodness and kindness shall follow me
     all the days of my life.
     In the Lord's own house shall I dwell
     for ever and ever.   ℟

Gospel Acclamation   Mt 16:18

Alleluia, alleluia!
You are Peter, the rock on which I will build my Church;
the gates of hell will not hold out against it.
Alleluia!

GOSPEL

A reading from the holy Gospel according to Matthew   16:13-19

You are Peter; and to you I will give the keys of the kingdom of heaven.

When Jesus came to the region of Caesarea Philippi he put this question to his disciples, 'Who do people say the Son of Man is?' And they said, 'Some say he is John the Baptist, some Elijah, and others Jeremiah or one of the prophets.' 'But you,' he said, 'who do you say I am?' Then Simon Peter spoke up, 'You are the Christ,' he said, 'the Son of the living God.' Jesus replied, 'Simon son of Jonah, you are a happy man! Because it was not flesh and blood that revealed this to you but my Father in heaven. So I now say to you: You are Peter and on this rock I will build my Church. And the gates of the underworld can never hold out against it. I will give you the keys of the kingdom of heaven: whatever you bind on earth shall be considered bound in heaven; whatever you loose on earth shall be considered loosed in heaven.'

These readings are used in a Votive Mass of St Peter.

23 February

St Polycarp, bishop and martyr   Memorial

Common of martyrs or Common of pastors.

FIRST READING

A reading from the book of the Apocalypse   2:8-11

I know your affliction and your poverty.

I, John, heard the Lord say to me: 'Write to the angel of the Church in Smyrna and say, "Here is the message of the First and the Last, who was dead and has come to life again: I know the trials you have had, and how poor you are – though you are rich – and the slanderous accusations that have been made by the people who profess to be Jews but are really members of the synagogue of Satan. Do not be afraid of the sufferings that are coming to you: I tell you, the devil is going to send some of you to prison to test you, and you must face an ordeal for ten days. Even if you have to die, keep faithful, and I will give you the crown of life for your prize. If anyone has ears to hear, let him listen to what the Spirit is saying to the Churches: for those who prove victorious there is nothing to be afraid of in the second death." '

This is the word of the Lord.

Responsorial Psalm   Ps 30:3-4. 6. 8. 16-17. ℟ v.6

℟   Into your hands, O Lord, I entrust my spirit.

1   Be a rock of refuge for me,
    a mighty stronghold to save me,
    for you are my rock, my stronghold.
    For your name's sake, lead me and guide me.   ℟

2   Into your hands I commend my spirit.
    It is you who will redeem me, Lord.
    As for me, I trust in the Lord:
    let me be glad and rejoice in your love.   ℟

3   My life is in your hands, deliver me
    from the hands of those who hate me.
    Let your face shine on your servant.
    Save me in your love.   ℟

Gospel Acclamation

    Alleluia, alleluia!
    You are God: we praise you; you are the Lord: we acclaim you;
    the white-robed army of martyrs praise you.
    Alleluia!

GOSPEL

A reading from the holy Gospel according to John   15:18-21

If they persecuted me, they will persecute you too.

Jesus said to his disciples:

    'If the world hates you,
    remember that it hated me before you.
    If you belonged to the world,
    the world would love you as its own;
    but because you do not belong to the world,

901

because my choice withdrew you from the world,
therefore the world hates you.
Remember the words I said to you:
A servant is not greater than his master.
If they persecuted me,
they will persecute you too;
if they kept my word,
they will keep yours as well.
But it will be on my account that they will do all this,
because they do not know the one who sent me.'

This is the Gospel of the Lord.

MARCH

4 March

St Casimir   Optional Memorial

Common of holy men and women.

FIRST READING

A reading from the letter of St Paul   3:8-14
to the Philippians

> *I am racing for the finish, for the prize to which God calls us*
> *upwards to receive in Christ Jesus.*

I believe nothing can happen that will outweigh the supreme
advantage of knowing Christ Jesus my Lord. For him I have
accepted the loss of everything, and I look on everything as so
much rubbish if only I can have Christ and be given a place in him.
I am no longer trying for perfection by my own efforts, the perfection that comes from the Law, but I want only the perfection that
comes through faith in Christ, and is from God and based on faith.
All I want to know is Christ and the power of his resurrection and
to share his sufferings by reproducing the pattern of his death.
That is the way I can hope to take my place in the resurrection of
the dead. Not that I have become perfect yet: I have not won, but I
am still running, trying to capture the prize for which Christ Jesus
captured me. I can assure you my brothers, I am far from thinking
that I have already won. All I can say is that I forget the past and I
strain ahead for what is still to come; I am racing for the finish, for
the prize to which God calls us upwards to receive in Christ Jesus.

This is the word of the Lord.

Responsorial Psalm   Ps 14:2-5. ℟ v.1

℟   The just shall live on your holy mountain, O Lord.

1   Lord, who shall dwell on your holy mountain?
    He who walks without fault;
    he who acts with justice
    and speaks the truth from his heart;
    he who does not slander with his tongue.   ℟

2   He who does no wrong to his brother,
who casts no slur on his neighbour,
who holds the godless in disdain,
but honours those who fear the Lord.

℟   The just shall live on your holy mountain, O Lord.

3   He who takes no interest on a loan
and accepts no bribes against the innocent,
such a man will stand firm for ever.   ℟

Gospel Acclamation   Jn 13:34

Praise to you, Lord Jesus Christ, king of endless glory!
I give you a new commandment:
love one another as I have loved you.
Praise to you, Lord Jesus Christ, king of endless glory!

GOSPEL

A reading from the holy Gospel according to John   15:9-17

You are my friends if you do what I command you.

Jesus said to his disciples:

'As the Father has loved me,
so I have loved you.
Remain in my love.
If you keep my commandments
you will remain in my love,
just as I have kept my Father's commandments
and remain in his love.
I have told you this
so that my own joy may be in you
and your joy be complete.
This is my commandment:
love one another,
as I have loved you.
A man can have no greater love
than to lay down his life for his friends.
You are my friends,
if you do what I command you.

I shall not call you servants any more,
because a servant does not know
his master's business;
I call you friends,
because I have made known to you
everything I have learnt from my Father.
You did not choose me,
no, I chose you;
and I commissioned you
to go out and to bear fruit,
fruit that will last;
and then the Father will give you
anything you ask him in my name.
What I command you
is to love one another.'

This is the Gospel of the Lord.

7 March

Ss Perpetua and Felicity, martyrs   Memorial

Common of martyrs.

FIRST READING

A reading from the letter of St Paul to the Romans   8:31-39

Neither death nor life can ever come between us and the love of God.

With God on our side who can be against us? Since God did not spare
his own Son, but gave him up to benefit us all, we may be certain,
after such a gift, that he will not refuse anything he can give. Could
anyone accuse those that God has chosen? When God acquits, could
anyone condemn? Could Christ Jesus? No! He not only died for us – he
rose from the dead, and there at God's right hand he stands and pleads
for us.

Nothing therefore can come between us and the love of Christ,
even if we are troubled or worried, or being persecuted, or lacking food
or clothes or being threatened or even attacked. As scripture promised: For your sake we are being massacred daily, and reckoned as
sheep for the slaughter. These are the trials through which we
triumph, by the power of him who loved us.

For I am certain of this: neither death nor life, no angel, no prince, nothing that exists, nothing still to come, not any power, or height or depth, nor any created thing, can ever come between us and the love of God made visible in Christ Jesus our Lord.

This is the word of the Lord.

Responsorial Psalm   Ps 123:2-5. 7-8. ℟ v.7

℟   Our soul has escaped like a bird from the hunter's net.

1   If the Lord had not been on our side
    when men rose against us,
    then would they have swallowed us alive
    when their anger was kindled.   ℟

2   Then would the waters have engulfed us,
    the torrent gone over us;
    over our head would have swept
    the raging waters.   ℟

3   Indeed the snare has been broken
    and we have escaped.
    Our help is in the name of the Lord,
    who made heaven and earth.   ℟

Gospel Acclamation   Mt 5:10

Praise and honour to you, Lord Jesus Christ!
Happy are they who suffer persecution for justice' sake;
the kingdom of heaven is theirs.
Praise and honour to you, Lord Jesus Christ!

GOSPEL

A reading from the holy Gospel according to Matthew   10:34-39

It is not peace I have come to bring, but a sword.

Jesus said to his apostles: 'Do not suppose that I have come to bring peace to the earth: it is not peace I have come to bring, but a sword. For I have come to set a man against his father, a daughter against her mother, a daughter-in-law against her mother-in-law. A man's enemies will be those of his own household.

'Anyone who prefers father or mother to me is not worthy of me. Anyone who prefers son or daughter to me is not worthy of me. Anyone who does not take his cross and follow in my footsteps is not worthy of me. Anyone who finds his life will lose it; anyone who loses his life for my sake will find it.'

This is the Gospel of the Lord.

8 March

St John of God, religious   Optional Memorial

Common of holy men and women: for religious or: for those who work for the underprivileged.

FIRST READING

A reading from the first letter of St John   3:14-18

We should lay down our lives for our brothers and sisters.

We have passed out of death and into life,
and of this we can be sure
because we love our brothers.
If you refuse to love, you must remain dead;
to hate your brother is to be a murderer,
and murderers, as you know, do not have eternal life in them.
This has taught us love –
that he gave up his life for us;
and we, too, ought to give up our lives for our brothers.
If a man who was rich enough in this world's goods
saw that one of his brothers was in need,
but closed his heart to him,
how could the love of God be living in him?
My children,
our love is not to be just words or mere talk,
but something real and active.

This is the word of the Lord.

Responsorial Psalm   Ps 111:1-9. ℟ v.1

    ℟   Happy are those who fear the Lord.

or

    ℟   Alleluia!

1   Happy the man who fears the Lord,
    who takes delight in his commands.
    His sons will be powerful on earth;
    the children of the upright are blessed. ℟

2   Riches and wealth are in his house;
    his justice stands firm for ever.
    He is a light in the darkness for the upright:
    he is generous, merciful and just. ℟

3   The good man takes pity and lends,
    he conducts his affairs with honour.
    The just man will never waver:
    he will be remembered for ever. ℟

4   He has no fear of evil news;
    with a firm heart he trusts in the Lord.
    With a steadfast heart he will not fear;
    he will see the downfall of his foes. ℟

5   Open-handed, he gives to the poor;
    his justice stands firm for ever.
    His head will be raised in glory. ℟

Gospel Acclamation   Jn 13:34

    Glory and praise to you, Lord Jesus Christ!
    I give you a new commandment:
    love one another as I have loved you.
    Glory and praise to you, Lord Jesus Christ!

GOSPEL

A reading from the holy Gospel according to Matthew   25:31-40

Whatever you have done to the very least of my brothers and sisters you have done to me.

Jesus said to his disciples: 'When the Son of Man comes in his glory, escorted by all the angels, then he will take his seat on his throne of glory. All the nations will be assembled before him and he will separate men one from another as the shepherd separates sheep from goats. He will place the sheep on his right hand and the goats on his left. Then the King will say to those on his right hand, "Come, you whom my Father has blessed, take for your heritage the kingdom prepared for you since the foundation of the world. For I was hungry and you gave me food; I was thirsty and you gave me drink; I was a stranger and you made me welcome; naked and you clothed me, sick and you visited me, in prison and you came to see me." Then the virtuous will say to him in reply, "Lord, when did we see you hungry and feed you; or thirsty and give you a drink? When did we see you a stranger and make you welcome; naked and clothe you; sick or in prison and go to see you?" And the King will answer, "I tell you solemnly, in so far as you did this to one of the least of these brothers of mine, you did it to me." '

This is the Gospel of the Lord.

9 March

St Frances of Rome, religious   Optional Memorial

Common of holy men and women.

FIRST READING

A reading from the book of Proverbs   31:10-13. 19-20. 30-31

It is the wise woman whom the Lord will praise.

A perfect wife – who can find her?
She is far beyond the price of pearls.
Her husband's heart has confidence in her,
from her he will derive no little profit.
Advantage and not hurt she brings him
all the days of her life.

She is always busy with wool and with flax,
she does her work with eager hands.
She sets her hands to the distaff,
her fingers grasp the spindle.
She holds out her hand to the poor,
she opens her arms to the needy.
Charm is deceitful, and beauty empty;
the woman who is wise is the one to praise.
Give her a share in what her hands have worked for,
and let her works tell her praises at the city gates.

This is the word of the Lord.

Responsorial Psalm   Ps 33:2-11. ℟ v.2. Alt. ℟ v.9

℟   I will bless the Lord at all times.

or

℟   Taste and see the goodness of the Lord.

1   I will bless the Lord at all times,
    his praise always on my lips;
    in the Lord my soul shall make its boast.
    The humble shall hear and be glad.   ℟

2   Glorify the Lord with me.
    Together let us praise his name.
    I sought the Lord and he answered me;
    from all my terrors he set me free.   ℟

3   Look towards him and be radiant;
    let your faces not be abashed.
    This poor man called; the Lord heard him
    and rescued him from all his distress.   ℟

4   The angel of the Lord is encamped
    around those who revere him, to rescue them.
    Taste and see that the Lord is good.
    He is happy who seeks refuge in him.   ℟

5   Revere the Lord, you his saints.
    They lack nothing, those who revere him.
    Strong lions suffer want and go hungry
    but those who seek the Lord lack no blessing. ℞

Gospel Acclamation   Jn 13:34

    Glory to you, Word of God, Lord Jesus Christ!
    I give you a new commandment:
    love one another as I have loved you.
    Glory to you, Word of God, Lord Jesus Christ!

GOSPEL

A reading from the holy Gospel according to Matthew   22:35-40

Love the Lord your God, and your neighbour as yourself.

To disconcert Jesus, one of the Pharisees, a lawyer, put a question, 'Master, which is the greatest commandment of the Law?' Jesus said, 'You must love the Lord your God with all your heart, with all your soul, and with all your mind. This is the greatest and the first commandment. The second resembles it: You must love your neighbour as yourself. On these two commandments hang the whole Law, and the Prophets also.'

    This is the Gospel of the Lord.

17 March

St Patrick, bishop   Optional Memoria

Common of pastors: for missionaries.
Proper readings for use in countries where this celebration is a solemnity or feas
will be found below, in the National Calendars, pp.1262ff.

FIRST READING

A reading from the first letter of St Peter   4:7-1

Each one of you has received a special gift; put yourselves at the
service of others

Keep a calm and sober mind. Above all, never let your love for each
other grow insincere, since love covers over many a sin. Welcome each
other into your houses without grumbling. Each one of you has
received a special grace, so, like good stewards responsible for all
these different graces of God, put yourselves at the service of others. If
you are a speaker, speak in words which seem to come from God; if you
are a helper, help as though every action was done at God's orders; so
that in everything God may receive the glory, through Jesus Christ,
since to him alone belong all glory and power for ever and ever. Amen.

This is the word of the Lord.

Responsorial Psalm   Ps 95:1-3. 7-8. 10. ℟ v.3

℟   Proclaim his marvellous deeds to all the nations.

1   O sing a new song to the Lord,
    sing to the Lord all the earth.
    O sing to the Lord, bless his name.   ℟

2   Proclaim his help day by day,
    tell among the nations his glory
    and his wonders among all the peoples.   ℟

3   Give the Lord, you families of peoples,
    give the Lord glory and power,
    give the Lord the glory of his name.   ℟

4   Proclaim to the nations: 'God is king.'
    The world he made firm in its place;
    he will judge the peoples in fairness.   ℟

Gospel Acclamation   Mk 1:17

Praise to you, Lord Jesus Christ, king of endless glory!
Come, follow me, says the Lord,
and I will make you fishers of my people.
Praise to you, Lord Jesus Christ, king of endless glory!

GOSPEL

A reading from the holy Gospel according to Luke   5:1-11

I will place my trust in your words.

Jesus was standing one day by the Lake of Gennesaret, with the crowd pressing round him listening to the word of God, when he caught sight of two boats close to the bank. The fishermen had gone out of them and were washing their nets. He got into one of the boats – it was Simon's – and asked him to put out a little from the shore. Then he sat down and taught the crowds from the boat.

When he had finished speaking he said to Simon, 'Put out into deep water and pay out your nets for a catch.' 'Master,' Simon replied, 'we worked hard all night long and caught nothing, but if you say so, I will pay out the nets.' And when they had done this they netted such a huge number of fish that their nets began to tear, so they signalled to their companions in the other boat to come and help them; when these came, they filled the two boats to sinking point.

When Simon Peter saw this he fell at the knees of Jesus saying, 'Leave me, Lord; I am a sinful man.' For he and all his companions were completely overcome by the catch they had made; so also were James and John, sons of Zebedee, who were Simon's partners. But Jesus said to Simon, 'Do not be afraid; from now on it is men you will catch.' Then, bringing their boats back to land, they left everything and followed him.

This is the Gospel of the Lord.

18 March

St Cyril of Jerusalem, bishop and doctor of the Church

Optional Memorial

Common of pastors or Common of doctors of the Church.

FIRST READING

A reading from the first letter of St John   5:1-5

This is the victory over the world – our faith

Whoever believes that Jesus is the Christ
has been begotten by God;
and whoever loves the Father that begot him
loves the child whom he begets.
We can be sure that we love God's children
if we love God himself and do what he has commanded us;
this is what loving God is –
keeping his commandments;
and his commandments are not difficult,
because anyone who has been begotten by God
has already overcome the world;
this is the victory over the world –
our faith.
Who can overcome the world?
Only the man who believes that Jesus is the Son of God.

This is the word of the Lord.

Responsorial Psalm   Ps 18:8-11. ℟ v.10. Alt. ℟ Jn 6:63

℟   The judgements of the Lord are true, and all of them are just.

or

℟   Your words, Lord, are spirit and life.

1   The law of the Lord is perfect,
     it revives the soul.
     The rule of the Lord is to be trusted,
     it gives wisdom to the simple.   ℟

2 The precepts of the Lord are right,
   they gladden the heart.
   The command of the Lord is clear,
   it gives light to the eyes.   ℟

3 The fear of the Lord is holy,
   abiding for ever.
   The decrees of the Lord are truth
   and all of them just.   ℟

4 They are more to be desired than gold,
   than the purest of gold
   and sweeter are they than honey,
   than honey from the comb.   ℟

Gospel Acclamation   Jn 15:9. 5

   Praise and honour to you, Lord Jesus Christ!
   Remain in my love, says the Lord;
   whoever lives in me and I in him will bear much fruit.
   Praise and honour to you, Lord Jesus Christ!

GOSPEL

A reading from the holy Gospel according to John   15:1-8

All who live in me, and I in them, bear fruit.

Jesus said to his disciples:

   'I am the true vine,
   and my Father is the vinedresser.
   Every branch in me that bears no fruit
   he cuts away,
   and every branch that does bear fruit he prunes
   to make it bear even more.
   You are pruned already,
   by means of the word that I have spoken to you.
   Make your home in me, as I make mine in you.
   As a branch cannot bear fruit all by itself,
   but must remain part of the vine,
   neither can you unless you remain in me.
   I am the vine,

915

you are the branches.
Whoever remains in me, with me in him,
bears fruit in plenty;
for cut off from me you can do nothing.
Anyone who does not remain in me
is like a branch that has been thrown away
– he withers;
these branches are collected and thrown on the fire,
and they are burnt.
If you remain in me
and my words remain in you,
you may ask what you will
and you shall get it.
It is to the glory of my Father that you should bear much fruit,
and then you will be my disciples.'

This is the Gospel of the Lord.

19 March

ST JOSEPH,
HUSBAND OF THE BLESSED VIRGIN MARY

Solemnity

FIRST READING

A reading from the second book of Samuel   7:4-5. 12-14. 16

The Lord God will give to him the throne of his Father, David.

The word of the Lord came to Nathan:

'Go and tell my servant David, "Thus the Lord speaks: When your days are ended and you are laid to rest with your ancestors, I will preserve the offspring of your body after you and make his sovereignty secure. (It is he who shall build a house for my name, and I will make his royal throne secure for ever.) I will be a father to him and he a son to me. Your House and your sovereignty will always stand secure before me and your throne be established for ever." '

This is the word of the Lord.

Responsorial Psalm   Ps 88:2-5. 27. 29. ℟ v.37

℟   The son of David will live for ever.

1   I will sing for ever of your love, O Lord;
     through all ages my mouth will proclaim your truth.
     Of this I am sure, that your love lasts for ever,
     that your truth is firmly established as the heavens.   ℟

2   'I have made a covenant with my chosen one;
     I have sworn to David my servant:
     I will establish your dynasty for ever
     and set up your throne through all ages.'   ℟

3   He will say to me: 'You are my father,
     my God, the rock who saves me.'
     I will keep my love for him always;
     for him my covenant shall endure.   ℟

SECOND READING

A reading from the letter of St Paul to the Romans   4:13. 16-18. 22

Against all hope he believed in hope.

The promise of inheriting the world was not made to Abraham and his
descendants on account of any law but on account of the righteousness
which consists in faith. That is why what fulfills the promise depends
on faith, so that it may be a free gift and be available to all of
Abraham's descendants, not only those who belong to the Law but
also to those who belong to the faith of Abraham who is the father of
all of us. As scripture says: I have made you the ancestor of many
nations – Abraham is our father in the eyes of God, in whom he put
his faith, and who brings the dead to life and calls into being what
does not exist.

   Though it seemed Abraham's hope could not be fulfilled, he hoped
and he believed, and through doing so he did become the father of
many nations exactly as he had been promised: Your descendants will
be as many as the stars. This is the faith that was 'considered as
justifying him'.

   This is the word of the Lord.

Gospel Acclamation   Ps 83:5

> Glory and praise to you, Lord Jesus Christ!
> How happy they who dwell in your house, O Lord;
> continually they sing your praise!
> Glory and praise to you, Lord Jesus Christ!

GOSPEL

A reading from the holy Gospel according to Matthew   1:16. 18-21. 24

Joseph did as the angel of the Lord commanded him.

Jacob was the father of Joseph the husband of Mary; of her was born Jesus who is called Christ.

This is how Jesus Christ came to be born. His mother Mary was betrothed to Joseph; but before they came to live together she was found to be with child through the Holy Spirit. Her husband Joseph, being a man of honour and wanting to spare her publicity, decided to divorce her informally. He had made up his mind to do this when the angel of the Lord appeared to him in a dream and said, 'Joseph son of David, do not be afraid to take Mary home as your wife, because she has conceived what is in her by the Holy Spirit. She will give birth to a son and you must name him Jesus, because he is the one who is to save his people from their sins.' When Joseph woke up he did what the angel of the Lord had told him to do.

This is the Gospel of the Lord.

Alternative Gospel

A reading from the holy Gospel according to Luke   2:41-51

See how your father and I have been in sorrow seeking you.

Every year the parents of Jesus used to go to Jerusalem for the feast of the Passover. When he was twelve years old, they went up for the feast as usual. When they were on their way home after the feast, the boy Jesus stayed behind in Jerusalem without his parents knowing it. They assumed he was with the caravan, and it was only after a day's journey that they went to look for him among their relations and acquaintances. When they failed to find him they went back to Jerusalem looking for him everywhere.

Three days later, they found him in the Temple, sitting among the doctors, listening to them, and asking them questions; and all those who heard him were astounded at his intelligence and his replies. They were overcome when they saw him, and his mother said to him, 'My child, why have you done this to us? See how worried your father and I have been, looking for you.' 'Why were you looking for me?' he replied 'Did you not know that I must be busy with my Father's affairs?' But they did not understand what he meant.

He then went down with them and came to Nazareth and lived under their authority.

This is the Gospel of the Lord.

---

23 March

St Turibius of Mongrovejo, bishop

Optional Memorial

Common of pastors.

FIRST READING

A reading from the second letter of St Paul to Timothy   1:13-14; 2:1-3

You have been entrusted to look after something precious; guard it with the help of the Holy Spirit who lives in us.

Keep as your pattern the sound teaching you have heard from me, in the faith and love that are in Christ Jesus. You have been trusted to look after something precious; guard it with the help of the Holy Spirit who lives in us. Accept the strength, my dear son, that comes from the grace of Christ Jesus. You have heard everything that I teach in public; hand it on to reliable people so that they in turn will be able to teach others.

Put up with your share of difficulties, like a good soldier of Christ Jesus.

This is the word of the Lord.

Responsorial Psalm   Ps 95: 1-3. 7-8. 10. ℟ v.3

℟   Proclaim his marvellous deeds to all the nations.

1   O sing a new song to the Lord,
    sing to the Lord all the earth.
    O sing to the Lord, bless his name.   ℟

2   Proclaim his help day by day,
    tell among the nations his glory
    and his wonders among all the peoples.   ℟

3   Give the Lord, you families of peoples,
    give the Lord glory and power,
    give the Lord the glory of his name.   ℟

4   Proclaim to the nations: 'God is king.'
    The world he made firm in its place;
    he will judge the peoples in fairness.   ℟

Gospel Acclamation   Jn 10:14

    Glory to you, Word of God, Lord Jesus Christ!
    I am the good shepherd, says the Lord;
    I know my sheep, and mine know me.
    Glory to you, Word of God, Lord Jesus Christ!

GOSPEL

A reading from the holy Gospel according to Matthew   9:35-37

The harvest is rich but the labourers are few.

Jesus made a tour through all the towns and villages, teaching in
their synagogues, proclaiming the Good News of the kingdom and
curing all kinds of diseases and sickness.

And when he saw the crowds he felt sorry for them because they
were harassed and dejected, like sheep without a shepherd. Then he
said to his disciples, 'The harvest is rich but the labourers are few, so
ask the Lord of the harvest to send labourers to his harvest.'

This is the Gospel of the Lord.

25 March

THE ANNUNCIATION OF THE LORD

Solemnity

FIRST READING

A reading from the prophet Isaiah   7:10-14. 8:10

Behold, the virgin shall conceive.

The Lord spoke to Ahaz and said, 'Ask the Lord your God for a sign for
yourself coming either from the depths of Sheol or from the heights
above.' 'No,' Ahaz answered, 'I will not put the Lord to the test.'
Then Isaiah said:

Listen now, House of David:
are you not satisfied with trying the patience of men
without trying the patience of my God, too?
The Lord himself, therefore,
will give you a sign.
It is this: the maiden is with child
and will soon give birth to a son
whom she will call Emmanuel,
a name which means, 'God-is-with-us'.

This is the word of the Lord.

Responsorial Psalm   Ps 39:7-11. ℟ vv.8. 9.

℟   Here am I, Lord; I come to do your will.

1   You do not ask for sacrifice and offerings,
    but an open ear.
    You do not ask for holocaust and victim.
    Instead, here am I.   ℟

2   In the scroll of the book it stands written
    that I should do your will.
    My God, I delight in your law
    in the depth of my heart.   ℟

3   Your justice I have proclaimed
    in the great assembly.
    My lips I have not sealed;
    you know it, O Lord.   ℟   (continued)

921

4   I have not hidden your justice in my heart
but declared your faithful help.
I have not hidden your love and your truth
from the great assembly.

℞   Here am I Lord; I come to do your will.

SECOND READING

A reading from the letter to the Hebrews   10:4-10

In the scroll of the book it was written of me that I should obey your
will, O God.

Bulls' blood and goats' blood are useless for taking away sins, and this
is what Christ said, on coming into the world:

You who wanted no sacrifice or oblation,
prepared a body for me.
You took no pleasure in holocausts or sacrifices for sin;
then I said,
just as I was commanded in the scroll of the book,
'God, here I am! I am coming to obey your will.'

Notice that he says first: You did not want what the Law lays down as
the things to be offered, that is: the sacrifices, the oblations, the
holocausts and the sacrifices for sin, and you took no pleasure in them;
and then he says: Here I am! I am coming to obey your will. He is
abolishing the first sort to replace it with the second. And this will
was for us to be made holy by the offering of his body made once and
for all by Jesus Christ.

This is the word of the Lord.

Gospel Acclamation   Jn 1:14

Praise to you, Lord Jesus Christ, king of endless glory!
The Word of God became flesh and dwelt among us;
and we saw his glory.
Praise to you, Lord Jesus Christ, king of endless glory!

GOSPEL

A reading from the holy Gospel according to Luke   1:26-38

You are to conceive and bear a son.

The angel Gabriel was sent by God to a town in Galilee called Nazareth, to a virgin betrothed to a man named Joseph, of the House of David; and the virgin's name was Mary. He went in and said to her, 'Rejoice, so highly favoured! The Lord is with you.' She was deeply disturbed by these words and asked herself what this greeting could mean, but the angel said to her, 'Mary, do not be afraid; you have won God's favour. Listen! You are to conceive and bear a son, and you must name him Jesus. He will be great and will be called Son of the Most High. The Lord God will give him the throne of his ancestor David; he will rule over the House of Jacob for ever and his reign will have no end.' Mary said to the angel, 'But how can this come about, since I am a virgin?' 'The Holy Spirit will come upon you,' the angel answered, 'and the power of the Most High will cover you with its shadow. And so the child will be holy and will be called Son of God. Know this too: your kinswoman Elizabeth has, in her old age, herself conceived a son, and she whom people called barren is now in her sixth month, for nothing is impossible to God.' 'I am the handmaid of the Lord,' said Mary, 'let what you have said be done to me.' And the angel left her.

This is the Gospel of the Lord.

In celebrations between 27 March and 22 April, if the day falls within Lent, the acclamation used before the Gospel should be one of the Lenten phrases, and 'Alleluia' should be omitted.

APRIL

2 April

St Francis of Paola, hermit   Optional Memorial

Common of holy men and women: for religious.

FIRST READING

A reading from the letter of St Paul to the Philippians   3:8-14

I am racing for the finish, for the prize to which God calls us
upwards to receive in Christ Jesus.

I believe nothing can happen that will outweigh the supreme advantage of knowing Christ Jesus my Lord. For him I have accepted the loss of everything, and I look on everything as so much rubbish if only I can have Christ and be given a place in him. I am no longer trying for perfection by my own efforts, the perfection that comes from the Law, but I want only the perfection that comes through faith in Christ, and is from God based on faith. All I want is to know Christ and the power of his resurrection and to share his sufferings by reproducing the pattern of his death. That is the way I can hope to take my place in the resurrection of the dead. Not that I have become perfect yet: I have not yet won, but I am still running, trying to capture the prize for which Christ Jesus captured me. I can assure you my brothers, I am far from thinking that I have already won. All I can say is that I forget the past and I strain ahead for what is still to come; I am racing for the finish, for the prize to which God calls us upwards to receive in Christ Jesus.

This is the word of the Lord.

Responsorial Psalm   Ps 15:1-2. 5. 7-8. 11. ℟ cf. v.5

℟   You are my inheritance, O Lord.

1   Preserve me, God, I take refuge in you.
    I say to the Lord: 'You are my God.'
    O Lord, it is you who are my portion and cup;
    it is you yourself who are my prize.   ℟

924

2   I will bless the Lord who gives me counsel,
    who even at night directs my heart.
    I keep the Lord ever in my sight:
    since he is at my right hand, I shall stand firm.   ℟

3   You will show me the path of life,
    the fullness of joy in your presence,
    at your right hand happiness for ever.   ℟

Gospel Acclamation   Mt 5:3

    Alleluia, alleluia!
    Happy the poor in spirit;
    the kingdom of heaven is theirs!
    Alleluia!

GOSPEL

A reading from the holy Gospel according to Luke   12:32-34

It has pleased the Father to give you the kingdom.

Jesus said to his disciples: 'There is no need to be afraid, little flock,
for it has pleased your Father to give you the kingdom.

'Sell your possessions and give alms. Get yourselves purses that do
not wear out, treasure that will not fail you, in heaven where no thief
can reach it and no moth destroy it. For where your treasure is, there
will your heart be also.'

This is the Gospel of the Lord.

4 April

St Isidore,
bishop and doctor of the Church

Optional Memorial

Common of pastors or Common of doctors.

FIRST READING

A reading from the second letter of St Paul   4:1-2. 5-7
to the Corinthians

We preach Christ Jesus and ourselves as your servants for Jesus' sake.

Since we have by an act of mercy been entrusted with this work of administration, there is no weakening on our part. On the contrary, we will have none of the reticence of those who are ashamed, no deceitfulness or watering down the word of God; but the way we commend ourselves to every human being with a conscience is by stating the truth openly in the sight of God. For it is not ourselves that we are preaching, but Christ Jesus as the Lord, and ourselves as your servants for Jesus' sake. It is the same God that said, 'Let there be light shining out of darkness', who has shone in our minds to radiate the light of the knowledge of God's glory, the glory on the face of Christ.

We are only the earthenware jars that hold this treasure, to make it clear that such an overwhelming power comes from God and not from us.

This is the word of the Lord.

Responsorial Psalm   Ps 36:3-6. 30-31. ℟ v.30

℟   The mouths of the just murmur wisdom.

1   If you trust in the Lord and do good,
    then you will live in the land and be secure.
    If you find your delight in the Lord,
    he will grant your heart's desire. ℟

2   Commit your life to the Lord,
    trust in him and he will act,
    so that your justice breaks forth like the light,
    your cause like the noon-day sun. ℟

3   The just man's mouth utters wisdom
    and his lips speak what is right;
    the law of his God is in his heart,
    his steps shall be saved from stumbling.   ℟

Gospel Acclamation   Jn 15:5

Alleluia, alleluia!
I am the vine and you are the branches, says the Lord:
those who live in me, and I in them, will bear much fruit.
Alleluia!

GOSPEL

A reading from the holy Gospel according to Luke   6:43-45

What a person says, comes from what is in the heart.

Jesus said to his disciples: 'There is no sound tree that produces rotten fruit, nor again a rotten tree that produces sound fruit. For every tree can be told by its own fruit: people do not pick figs from thorns, nor gather grapes from brambles. A good man draws what is good from the store of goodness in his heart; a bad man draws what is bad from the store of badness. For a man's words flow out of what fills his heart.'

    This is the Gospel of the Lord.

5 April

St Vincent Ferrer, priest

Optional Memorial

Common of pastors: for missionaries or Common of holy men and women: for religious.

FIRST READING

A reading from the second letter of St Paul to Timothy   4:1-5

Preach the Good News; fulfill your ministry.

Before God and before Christ Jesus who is to be judge of the living and the dead, I put this duty to you, in the name of his Appearing and of his kingdom: proclaim the message and, welcome or unwelcome, insist on it. Refute falsehood, correct error, call to obedience – but do all with patience and with the intention of teaching. The time is sure to come when, far from being content with sound teaching, people will be avid for the latest novelty and collect themselves a whole series of teachers according to their own tastes; and then, instead of listening to the truth, they will turn to myths. Be careful always to choose the right course; be brave under trials; make the preaching of the Good News your life's work, in thoroughgoing service.

This is the word of the Lord.

Responsorial Psalm   Ps 39:2. 4. 7-10. ℟ cf. vv.8-9

℟   Here am I, Lord; I come to do your will.

1   I waited, I waited for the Lord
    and he stooped down to me;
    he heard my cry.
    He put a new song into my mouth,
    praise of our God. ℟

2   You do not ask for sacrifice and offerings,
    but an open ear.
    You do not ask for holocaust and victim.
    Instead, here am I. ℟

3   In the scroll of the book it stands written
    that I should do your will.
    My God, I delight in your law
    in the depth of my heart. ℟

4   Your justice I have proclaimed
    in the great assembly.
    My lips I have not sealed;
    you know it, O Lord. ℟

Gospel Acclamation   Lk 21:36

Alleluia, alleluia!
Be watchful, pray constantly,
that you may be worthy to stand before the Son of Man.
Alleluia!

GOSPEL

A reading from the holy Gospel according to Luke   12:35-40

Be prepared.

Jesus said to his disciples:

'See that you are dressed for action and have your lamps lit. Be like men waiting for their master to return from the wedding feast, ready to open the door as soon as he comes and knocks. Happy those servants whom the master finds awake when he comes. I tell you solemnly, he will put on an apron, sit them down at table and wait on them. It may be in the second watch he comes, or in the third, but happy those servants if he finds them ready. You may be quite sure of this, that if the householder had known at what hour the burglar would come, he would not have let anyone break through the wall of his house. You too must stand ready, because the Son of Man is coming at an hour you do not expect.'

This is the Gospel of the Lord.

7 April

St John Baptist de la Salle, priest   Memorial

Common of pastors or Common of holy men and women: for teachers.

FIRST READING

A reading from the second letter of St Paul to Timothy   1:13-14; 2:1-3

You have been entrusted to look after something precious; guard it
with the help of the Holy Spirit who lives in us.

Keep as your pattern the sound teaching you have heard from me, in the faith and love that are in Christ Jesus. You have been trusted to look after something precious; guard it with the help of the Holy Spirit who lives in us. Accept the strength, my dear son, that comes from the grace of Christ Jesus. You have heard everything that I teach in public; hand it on to reliable people so that they in turn will be able to teach others.

Put up with your share of difficulties, like a good soldier of Christ Jesus.

This is the word of the Lord.

Responsorial Psalm   Ps 1:1-4. 6. ℟ v.2. Alt. ℟ Ps 39:5. Alt. ℟ Ps 91:13-14

℟ Happy are they who delight in the law of the Lord.

or

℟ Happy are they who hope in the Lord.

or

℟ The just will flourish like the palm-tree in the garden of the
Lord.

1   Happy indeed is the man
who follows not the counsel of the wicked;
nor lingers in the way of sinners
nor sits in the company of scorners,
but whose delight is the law of the Lord
and who ponders his law day and night.   ℟

2   He is like a tree that is planted
beside the flowing waters,
that yields its fruit in due season
and whose leaves shall never fade;
and all that he does shall prosper.   ℟

3   Not so are the wicked, not so!
For they like winnowed chaff
shall be driven away by the wind;
for the Lord guards the way of the just
but the way of the wicked leads to doom.   ℟

Gospel Acclamation   Mt 23:11. 12

Alleluia, alleluia!
Whoever is greatest among you will serve the rest.
All who humble themselves shall be exalted.
Alleluia!

GOSPEL

A reading from the holy Gospel according to Matthew   18:1-5

Whoever welcomes such a child for my sake, welcomes me.

The disciples came to Jesus and said, 'Who is the greatest in the kingdom of heaven?' So he called a little child to him and set the child in front of them. Then he said, 'I tell you solemnly, unless you change and become like little children you will never enter the kingdom of heaven. And so, the one who makes himself as little as this little child is the greatest in the kingdom of heaven. Anyone who welcomes a little child like this in my name welcomes me.'

This is the Gospel of the Lord.

11 April

St Stanislaus, bishop and martyr   Memorial

Common of martyrs or Common of pastors.

FIRST READING

A reading from the book of the Apocalypse   12:10-12

Even in the face of death these martyrs would not cling to life.

I, John, heard a voice shout from heaven, 'Victory and power and empire for ever have been won by our God, and all authority for his Christ, now that the persecutor, who accused our brothers day and night before our God, has been brought down. They have triumphed over him by the blood of the Lamb and by the witness of their martyrdom, because even in the face of death they would not cling to life. Let the heavens rejoice and all who live there.'

This is the word of the Lord.

Responsorial Psalm   Ps 33:2-9. ℟ v.5

℟ The Lord set me free from all my fears.

1 I will bless the Lord at all times,
   his praise always on my lips;
   in the Lord my soul shall make its boast.
   The humble shall hear and be glad.   ℟

2   Glorify the Lord with me.
Together let us praise his name.
I sought the Lord and he answered me;
from all my terrors he set me free.

℟   The Lord set me free from all my fears.

3   Look towards him and be radiant;
let your faces not be abashed.
This poor man called; the Lord heard him
and rescued him from all his distress.   ℟

4   The angel of the Lord is encamped
around those who revere him, to rescue them.
Taste and see that the Lord is good.
He is happy who seeks refuge in him.   ℟

Gospel Acclamation   2 Cor 1:3-4

Alleluia, alleluia!
Blessed be the Father of mercies and the God of all comfort,
who consoles us in all our afflictions.
Alleluia!

GOSPEL

A reading from the holy Gospel according to John   17:11-19

The world hates them.

Jesus raised his eyes to heaven and said,

'Holy Father,
keep those you have given me true to your name,
so that they may be one like us.
While I was with them,
I kept those you had given me true to your name.
I have watched over them and not one is lost
except the one who chose to be lost,
and this was to fulfil the scriptures.
But now I am coming to you
and while still in the world I say these things
to share my joy with them to the full.
I passed your word on to them,

and the world hated them,
because they belong to the world
no more than I belong to the world.
I am not asking you to remove them from the world,
but to protect them from the evil one.
They do not belong to the world
any more than I belong to the world.
Consecrate them in the truth;
your word is truth.
As you sent me into the world,
I have sent them into the world,
and for their sake I consecrate myself
so that they too may be consecrated in truth.'

This is the Gospel of the Lord.

13 April

St Martin I, pope and martyr   Optional Memorial

Common of martyrs or Common of pastors: for popes.

FIRST READING

A reading from the second letter of St Paul to Timothy   2:8-13; 3:10-12

*You must be aware that anybody who tries to live in devotion
to Christ is certain to suffer persecution.*

Remember the Good News that I carry, 'Jesus Christ risen from the dead, sprung from the race of David'; it is on account of this that I have my own hardships to bear, even to being chained like a criminal – but they cannot chain up God's news. So I bear it all for the sake of those who are chosen, so that in the end they may have the salvation that is in Christ Jesus and the eternal glory that comes with it.

Here is a saying that you can rely on:

If we have died with him, then we shall live with him.
If we hold firm, then we shall reign with him.
If we disown him, then he will disown us.
We may be unfaithful, but he is always faithful,
for he cannot disown his own self.

You know what I have taught, how I have lived, what I have aimed at; you know my faith, my patience and my love; my constancy and the persecutions and hardships that came to me in places like Antioch, Iconium and Lystra – all the persecutions I have endured; and the Lord has rescued me from every one of them. You are well aware, then, that anybody who tries to live in devotion to Christ is certain to be attacked.

This is the word of the Lord.

Responsial Psalm   Ps 125. ℟ v.5

℟ Those who sow in tears, shall reap with shouts of joy.

1   When the Lord delivered Zion from bondage,
     it seemed like a dream.
     Then was our mouth filled with laughter,
     on our lips there were songs.   ℟

2   The heathens themselves said: 'What marvels
     the Lord worked for them!'
     What marvels the Lord worked for us!
     Indeed we were glad.   ℟

3   Deliver us, O Lord, from our bondage
     as streams in dry land.
     Those who are sowing in tears
     will sing when they reap.   ℟

4   They go out, they go out, full of tears,
     carrying seed for the sowing:
     they come back, they come back, full of song,
     carrying their sheaves.   ℟

Gospel Acclamation

Alleluia, alleluia!
You are God: we praise you; you are the Lord: we acclaim you;
the white-robed army of martyrs praise you.
Alleluia!

GOSPEL

A reading from the holy Gospel according to John 15:18-21

If they persecuted me, they will persecute you too.

Jesus said to his disciples:

'If the world hates you,
remember that it hated me before you.
If you belonged to the world,
the world would love you as its own;
but because you do not belong to the world,
because my choice withdrew you from the world,
therefore the world hates you.
Remember the words I said to you:
A servant is not greater than his master.
If they persecuted me,
they will persecute you too;
if they kept my word,
they will keep yours as well.
But it will be on my account that they will do all this,
because they do not know the one who sent me.'

This is the Gospel of the Lord.

21 April

St Anselm, bishop and doctor of the Church

Optional Memorial

Common of pastors or Common of doctors of the Church.

FIRST READING

A reading from the letter of St Paul to the Ephesians 3:14-19

To know the love of Christ, which is beyond all knowledge.

This is what I pray, kneeling before the Father, from whom every family, whether spiritual or natural, takes its name:

Out of his infinite glory, may he give you the power through his Spirit for your hidden self to grow strong, so that Christ may live in your hearts through faith, and then, planted in love and built on love, you will with all the saints have strength to grasp the breadth and the length, the height and the depth; until, knowing the love of Christ,

which is beyond all knowlege, you are filled with the utter fullness of
God.

This is the word of the Lord.

Responsorial Psalm   Ps 33:2-11. ℟ v.2. Alt. ℟ v.9

℟   I will bless the Lord at all times.

or

℟   Taste and see the goodness of the Lord.

1   I will bless the Lord at all times,
    his praise always on my lips;
    in the Lord my soul shall make its boast.
    The humble shall hear and be glad.   ℟

2   Glorify the Lord with me.
    Together let us praise his name.
    I sought the Lord and he answered me;
    from all my terrors he set me free.   ℟

3   Look towards him and be radiant;
    let your faces not be abashed.
    This poor man called; the Lord heard him
    and rescued him from all his distress.   ℟

4   The angel of the Lord is encamped
    around those who revere him, to rescue them.
    Taste and see that the Lord is good.
    He is happy who seeks refuge in him.   ℟

5   Revere the Lord, you his saints.
    They lack nothing, those who revere him.
    Strong lions suffer want and go hungry
    but those who seek the Lord lack no blessing.   ℟

Gospel Acclamation   cf. Jn 6:63. 68

Alleluia, alleluia!
Your words, Lord, are spirit and life;
you have the words of everlasting life.
Alleluia!

GOSPEL

A reading from the holy Gospel according to Matthew 7:21-29

Jesus taught them with authority.

Jesus said to his disciples: 'It is not those who say to me, "Lord, Lord," who will enter the kingdom of heaven, but the person who does the will of my Father in heaven. When the day comes many will say to me, "Lord, Lord, did we not prophesy in your name, cast out demons in your name, work many miracles in your name?" Then I shall tell them to their faces: I have never known you; away from me, you evil men!

'Therefore, everyone who listens to these words of mine and acts on them will be like a sensible man who built his house on rock. Rain came down, floods rose, gales blew and hurled themselves against that house, and it did not fall; it was founded on rock. But everyone who listens to these words of mine and does not act on them will be like a stupid man who built his house on sand. Rain came down, floods rose, gales blew and struck that house, and it fell, and what a fall it had!'

Jesus had now finished what he wanted to say, and his teaching made a deep impression on the people because he taught them with authority, and not like their own scribes.

This is the Gospel of the Lord.

23 April

St George, martyr   Optional Memorial

Common of martyrs.

FIRST READING

A reading from the book of the Apocalypse 21:5-7

Whoever conquers shall have this heritage.

The One sitting on the throne spoke: 'Now I am making the whole of creation new', he said. 'Write this: that what I am saying is sure and will come true.' And then he said, 'It is already done. I am the Alpha and the Omega, the Beginning and the End. I will give water from the well of life free to anybody who is thirsty; it is the rightful inheritance of the one who proves victorious; and I will be his God and he a son to me.'

This is the word of the Lord.

Responsorial Psalm   Ps 125. ℞ v.5

℞   Those who sow in tears, shall reap with shouts of joy.

1   When the Lord delivered Zion from bondage,
    it seemed like a dream.
    Then was our mouth filled with laughter,
    on our lips there were songs. ℞

2   The heathens themselves said: 'What marvels
    the Lord worked for them!'
    What marvels the Lord worked for us!
    Indeed we are glad. ℞

3   Deliver us, O Lord, from our bondage
    as streams in dry land.
    Those who are sowing in tears
    will sing when they reap. ℞

4   They go out, they go out, full of tears,
    carrying seed for the sowing:
    they come back, they come back, full of song,
    carrying their sheaves. ℞

Gospel Acclamation   1 Peter 4:14

    Alleluia, alleluia!
    If you are insulted for the name of Christ, blessed are you,
    for the Spirit of God rests upon you.
    Alleluia!

GOSPEL

A reading from the holy Gospel according to Luke   9:23-26

Those who lose their lives for my sake will save them

To all Jesus said, 'If anyone wants to be a follower of mine, let him
renounce himself and take up his cross every day and follow me. For
anyone who wants to save his life will lose it, but anyone who loses his
life for my sake, that man will save it. What gain, then, is it for a man
to have won the whole world and to have lost or ruined his very self?
For if anyone is ashamed of me and of my words, of him the Son of
Man will be ashamed when he comes in his own glory and in the glory
of the Father and the holy angels.'

    This is the Gospel of the Lord.

24 April

St Fidelis of Sigmaringen, priest and martyr

Optional Memorial

Common of martyrs or Common of pastors.

FIRST READING

A reading from the letter of St Paul to the Colossians 1:24-29

I became the servant of the Church when God made me responsible for delivering his message to you.

It makes me happy to suffer for you, as I am suffering now, and in my own body to do what I can to make up all that has still to be undergone by Christ for the sake of his body, the Church. I became the servant of the Church when God made me responsible for delivering God's message to you, the message which was a mystery hidden for generations and centuries and has now been revealed to his saints. It was God's purpose to reveal it to them and to show all the rich glory of this mystery to pagans. The mystery is Christ among you, your hope of glory: this is the Christ we proclaim, this is the wisdom in which we thoroughly train everyone and instruct everyone, to make them all perfect in Christ. It is for this I struggle wearily on, helped only by his power driving me irresistibly.

This is the word of the Lord.

Responsorial Psalm   Ps 33:2-9. ℟ v. 5

℟   The Lord set me free from all my fears.

1   I will bless the Lord at all times,
      his praise always on my lips;
      in the Lord my soul shall make its boast.
      The humble shall hear and be glad. ℟

2   Glorify the Lord with me.
      Together let us praise his name.
      I sought the Lord and he answered me;
      from all my terrors he set me free. ℟

(continued)

939

3   Look towards him and be radiant;
let your faces not be abashed.
This poor man called; the Lord heard him
and rescued him from all his distress.

℟   The Lord set me free from all my fears.

4   The angel of the Lord is encamped
around those who revere him, to rescue them.
Taste and see that the Lord is good.
He is happy who seeks refuge in him.   ℟

Gospel Acclamation   Jn 13:34

Alleluia, alleluia!
I give you a new commandment:
love one another as I have loved you.
Alleluia!

GOSPEL

A reading from the holy Gospel according to John   17:20-26

I want those you have given me to be with me where I am.

Jesus raised his eyes to heaven and said:

'Holy Father,
I pray not only for these,
but for those also
who through their words will believe in me.
May they all be one.
Father, may they be one in us,
as you are in me and I am in you,
so that the world may believe it was you who sent me.
I have given them the glory you gave to me,
that they may be one as we are one.
With me in them and you in me,
may they be so completely one
that the world will realise that it was you who sent me
and that I have loved them as much as you loved me.
Father,
I want those you have given me

to be with me where I am,
so that they may always see the glory
you have given me
because you loved me
before the foundation of the world.
Father, Righteous One,
the world has not known you,
but I have known you,
and these have known
that you have sent me.
I have made your name known to them
and will continue to make it known,
so that the love with which you loved me may be in them,
and so that I may be in them.'

This is the Gospel of the Lord.

25 April

ST MARK, EVANGELIST

Feast

FIRST READING

A reading from the first letter of St Peter

5:5-14

My son, Mark, sends you greetings.

All wrap yourselves in humility to be servants of each other, because God refuses the proud and will always favour the humble. Bow down, then, before the power of God now, and he will raise you up on the appointed day; unload all your worries on to him, since he is looking after you. Be calm but vigilant, because your enemy the devil is prowling round like a roaring lion, looking for something to eat. Stand up to him, strong in faith and in the knowledge that your brothers all over the world are suffering the same things. You will have to suffer only for a little while: the God of all grace who called you to eternal glory in Christ will see that all is well again: he will confirm, strengthen and support you. His power lasts for ever and ever. Amen.

I write these few words to you through Silvanus, who is a brother I know I can trust, to encourage you never to let go this true grace of God to which I bear witness.

Your sister in Babylon, who is with you among the chosen, sends you greetings; so does my son, Mark.

Greet one another with a kiss of love.
Peace to you all who are in Christ.

This is the word of the Lord.

Responsorial Psalm   Ps 88:2-3. 6-7. 16-17. ℟ cf. v.2

℟   For ever I will sing the goodness of the Lord.

or

℟   Alleluia!

1   I will sing for ever of your love, O Lord;
    through all ages my mouth will proclaim your truth.
    Of this I am sure, that your love lasts for ever,
    that your truth is firmly established as the heavens.   ℟

2   The heavens proclaim your wonders, O Lord;
    the assembly of your holy ones proclaims your truth.
    For who in the skies can compare with the Lord
    or who is like the Lord among the sons of God?   ℟

3   Happy the people who acclaim such a king,
    who walk, O Lord, in the light of your face,
    who find their joy every day in your name,
    who make your justice the source of their bliss.   ℟

Gospel Acclamation   1 Cor 1:23-24

Alleluia, alleluia!
We preach a Christ who was crucified;
he is the power and the wisdom of God.
Alleluia!

GOSPEL

A reading from the holy Gospel according to Mark   16:15-20

Make known the Good News to every creature.

Jesus said to the Eleven, 'Go out to the whole world; proclaim the
Good News to all creation. He who believes and is baptised will be
saved; he who does not believe will be condemned. These are the signs
that will be associated with believers: in my name they will cast out

devils; they will have the gift of tongues; they will pick up snakes in their hands, and be unharmed should they drink deadly poison; they will lay their hands on the sick, who will recover.'

And so the Lord Jesus, after he had spoken to them, was taken up into heaven: there at the right hand of God he took his place, while they, going out, preached everywhere, the Lord working with them and confirming the word by the signs that accompanied it.

This is the Gospel of the Lord.

28 April

St Peter Chanel, priest and martyr

Optional Memorial

Common of martyrs or Common of pastors: for missionaries.

FIRST READING

A reading from the first letter of St Paul to the Corinthians   1:18-25

It was because God wanted to save those who have faith through the foolishness of the message that we preach.

The language of the cross may be illogical to those who are not on the way to salvation, but those of us who are on the way see it as God's power to save. As scripture says: I shall destroy the wisdom of the wise and bring to nothing all the learning of the learned. Where are the philosophers now? Where are the scribes? Where are any of our thinkers today? Do you see now how God has shown up the foolishness of human wisdom? If it was God's wisdom that human wisdom should not know God, it was because God wanted to save those who have faith through the foolishness of the message that we preach. And so, while the Jews demand miracles and the Greeks look for wisdom, here are we preaching a crucified Christ; to the Jews an obstacle that they cannot get over, to the pagans madness, but to those who have been called, whether they are Jews or Greeks, a Christ who is the power and the wisdom of God. For God's foolishness is wiser than human wisdom, and God's weakness is stronger than human strength.

This is the word of the Lord.

Responsorial Psalm Ps 116. ℟ Mk 16:15

℟ Go out to all the world, and tell the Good News.

or

℟ Alleluia!

1 O praise the Lord, all you nations,
   acclaim him all you peoples! ℟

2 Strong is his love for us;
   he is faithful for ever. ℟

Gospel Acclamation Mk 1:17

Alleluia, alleluia!
Come, follow me, says the Lord,
and I will make you fishers of my people.
Alleluia!

GOSPEL

A reading from the holy Gospel according to Mark 1:14-20

I will make you fishers of my people.

After John had been arrested, Jesus went into Galilee. There he proclaimed the Good News from God. 'The time has come,' he said, 'and the kingdom of God is close at hand. Repent, and believe the Good News.'

As he was walking along by the Sea of Galilee he saw Simon and his brother Andrew casting a net in the lake – for they were fishermen. And Jesus said to them, 'Follow me and I will make you into fishers of men.' And at once they left their nets and followed him.

Going on a little farther, he saw James son of Zebedee and his brother John; they too were in their boat, mending their nets. He called them at once and, leaving their father Zebedee in the boat with the men he employed, they went after him.

This is the Gospel of the Lord.

29 April

St Catherine of Siena,
virgin and doctor of the Church
Memorial

Common of virgins.

FIRST READING

A reading from the first letter of St John   1:5–2:2

The blood of Christ cleanses us of all sin.

This is what we have heard from Jesus Christ,
and the message that we are announcing to you:
God is light; there is no darkness in him at all.
If we say that we are in union with God
while we are living in darkness,
we are lying because we are not living the truth.
But if we live our lives in the light, as he is in the light,
we are in union with one another,
and the blood of Jesus, his Son,
purifies us from all sin.
If we say we have no sin in us,
we are deceiving ourselves
and refusing to admit the truth;
but if we acknowledge our sins,
then God who is faithful and just
will forgive our sins and purify us
from everything that is wrong.
To say that we have never sinned is to call God a liar
and to show that his word is not in us.
I am writing this, my children, to stop you sinning;
but if anyone should sin,
we have our advocate with the Father,
Jesus Christ, who is just;
he is the sacrifice that takes our sins away,
and not only ours, but the whole world's.

This is the word of the Lord.

945

Responsorial Psalm   Ps 102:1-4. 8-9. 13-14. 17-18. ℞ v.1

℞ O bless the Lord, my soul.

1 My soul, give thanks to the Lord,
   all my being, bless his holy name.
   My soul, give thanks to the Lord
   and never forget all his blessings. ℞

2 It is he who forgives all your guilt,
   who heals every one of your ills,
   who redeems your life from the grave,
   who crowns you with love and compassion. ℞

3 The Lord is compassion and love,
   slow to anger and rich in mercy.
   His wrath will come to an end;
   he will not be angry for ever. ℞

4 As a father has compassion on his sons,
   the Lord has pity on those who fear him;
   for he knows of what we are made,
   he remembers that we are dust. ℞

5 But the love of the Lord is everlasting
   upon those who hold him in fear;
   his justice reaches out to children's children
   when they keep his covenant in truth. ℞

Gospel Acclamation   cf. Mt 11:25

Alleluia, alleluia!
Blessed are you, Father, Lord of heaven and earth;
you have revealed to little ones the mysteries of the kingdom.
Alleluia!

GOSPEL

A reading from the holy Gospel according to Matthew   11:25-30

You have hidden these things from the learned and the clever and
revealed them to children.

Jesus exclaimed, 'I bless you, Father, Lord of heaven and of earth, for hiding these things from the learned and the clever and revealing them to mere children. Yes, Father, for that is what it pleased you to do. Everything has been entrusted to me by my Father; and no one knows the Son except the Father, just as no one knows the Father except the Son and those to whom the Son chooses to reveal him.

'Come to me, all you who labour and are overburdened, and I will give you rest. Shoulder my yoke and learn from me, for I am gentle and humble in heart, and you will find rest for your souls. Yes, my yoke is easy and my burden light.'

This is the Gospel of the Lord.

30 April

St Pius V, pope　　　　　Optional Memorial

Common of pastors: for popes.

FIRST READING

A reading from the first letter of St Paul　　　　4:1-5
to the Corinthians

We are to be as Christ's servants, stewards entrusted with the
mysteries of God.

People must think of us as Christ's servants, stewards entrusted with the mysteries of God. What is expected of stewards is that each one should be found worthy of his trust. Not that it makes the slightest difference to me whether you, or indeed any human tribunal, find me worthy or not. I will not even pass judgement on myself. True, my conscience does not reproach me at all, but that does not prove that I am acquitted: the Lord alone is my judge. There must be no passing of premature judgement. Leave that until the Lord comes: he will light up all that is hidden in the dark and reveal the secret intentions of men's hearts. Then will be the time for each one to have whatever praise he deserves, from God.

This is the word of the Lord.

Responsorial Psalm   Ps 109:1-4. ℟ v.4

℟   You are a priest for ever, in the line of Melchizedek.

1   The Lord's revelation to my Master:
    'Sit on my right:
    I will put your foes beneath your feet.'   ℟

2   The Lord will send from Zion
    your sceptre of power:
    rule in the midst of all your foes.   ℟

3   A prince from the day of your birth
    on the holy mountains;
    from the womb before the daybreak I begot you.   ℟

4   The Lord has sworn an oath he will not change.
    'You are a priest for ever,
    a priest like Melchizedek of old.'   ℟

Gospel Acclamation   Jn 10:14

Alleluia, alleluia!
I am the good shepherd, says the Lord;
I know my sheep, and mine know me.
Alleluia!

GOSPEL

A reading from the holy Gospel according to John   21:15-17

Take care of my lambs and my sheep.

Jesus showed himself to his disciples, and after they had eaten he said
to Simon Peter, 'Simon son of John, do you love me more than these
others do?' He answered, 'Yes Lord, you know I love you.' Jesus said to
him, 'Feed my lambs.' A second time he said to him, 'Simon son of
John, do you love me?' He replied, 'Yes, Lord, you know I love you.'
Jesus said to him, 'Look after my sheep'. Then he said to him a third
time, 'Simon son of John, do you love me?' Peter was upset that he
asked him the third time, 'Do you love me?' and said, 'Lord, you know
everything; you know I love you.' Jesus said to him, 'Feed my sheep.'

This is the Gospel of the Lord.

MAY

1 May

St Joseph the worker

Memorial

The Gospel is proper to this memorial.

FIRST READING

A reading from the book of Genesis   1:26–2:3

Fill the earth and subdue it.

God said, 'Let us make man in our own image, in the likeness of ourselves, and let them be masters of the fish of the sea, the birds of heaven, the cattle, all the wild beasts and all the reptiles that crawl upon the earth.'

God created man in the image of himself,
in the image of God he created him,
male and female he created them.

God blessed them, saying to them, 'Be fruitful, multiply, fill the earth and conquer it. Be masters of the fish of the sea, the birds of heaven and all living animals on the earth.' God said, 'See, I give you all the seed-bearing plants that are upon the whole earth, and all the trees with seed-bearing fruit; this shall be your food. To all wild beasts, all birds of heaven and all living reptiles on the earth I give all the foliage of plants for food.' And so it was. God saw all he had made, and indeed it was very good. Evening came and morning came: the sixth day.

Thus heaven and earth were completed with all their array. On the seventh day God completed the work he had been doing. He rested on the seventh day after all the work he had been doing. God blessed the seventh day and made it holy, because on that day he had rested after all his work of creating.

This is the word of the Lord.

Alternative First Reading

A reading from the letter of St Paul   3:14-15. 17. 23-24
to the Colossians

*Whatever the task, do it with all your heart, as serving the Lord
and not any human master.*

Over all these clothes, to keep them together and complete them,

949

put on love. And may the peace of Christ reign in your hearts, because it is for this that you were called together as parts of one body. Always be thankful. Never say or do anything except in the name of the Lord Jesus, giving thanks to God the Father through him. Whatever your work is, put your heart into it as if it were for the Lord and not for men, knowing that the Lord will repay you by making you his heirs. It is Christ the Lord that you are serving.

This is the word of the Lord.

Responsorial Psalm Ps 89:2-4. 12-14. 16. ℞ v.17

℞ Lord, give success to the work of our hands.

or

℞ Alleluia!

1 Before the mountains were born
or the earth or the world brought forth,
you are God, without beginning or end. ℞

2 You turn men back into dust
and say: 'Go back, sons of men.'
To your eyes a thousand years
are like yesterday, come and gone,
no more than a watch in the night. ℞

3 Make us know the shortness of our life
that we may gain wisdom of heart.
Lord, relent! Is your anger for ever?
Show pity to your servants. ℞

4 In the morning, fill us with your love;
we shall exult and rejoice all our days.
Show forth your work to your servants;
let your glory shine on their children. ℞

Gospel Acclamation Ps 67:20

Alleluia, alleluia!
Blessed be the Lord day after day,
the God who saves us and bears our burdens.
Alleluia!

GOSPEL

A reading from the holy Gospel according to Matthew   13:54-58

Is not this the carpenter's son?

Jesus came to his home town and taught the people in their synagogue in such a way that they were astonished and said, 'Where did the
man get this wisdom and these miraculous powers? This is the
carpenter's son, surely? Is not his mother the woman called Mary, and
his brothers James and Joseph and Simon and Jude? His sisters, too,
are they not all here with us? So where did the man get it all?' And
they would not accept him. But Jesus said to them, 'A prophet is only
despised in his own country and in his own house,' and he did not work
many miracles there because of their lack of faith.

This is the Gospel of the Lord.

2 May

St Athanasius,
bishop and doctor of the Church   Memorial

Common of pastors or Common of doctors of the Church.

FIRST READING

A reading from the first letter of St John   5:1-5

Our faith, this is the victory which overcomes the evils in the world.

Whoever believes that Jesus is the Christ
has been begotten by God;
and whoever loves the Father that begot him
loves the child whom he begets.
We can be sure that we love God's children
if we love God himself and do what he has commanded us;
this is what loving God is –
keeping his commandments;
and his commandments are not difficult,
because anyone who has been begotten by God
has already overcome the world;
this is the victory over the world –
our faith.

Who can overcome the world?
Only the man who believes that Jesus is the Son of God.

This is the word of the Lord.

Responsorial Psalm   Ps 36:3-6. 30-31. ℟ v.30

℟ The mouths of the just murmur wisdom.

1 If you trust in the Lord and do good,
   then you will live in the land and be secure.
   If you find your delight in the Lord,
   he will grant your heart's desire. ℟

2 Commit your life to the Lord,
   trust in him and he will act,
   so that your justice breaks forth like the light,
   your cause like the noon-day sun. ℟

3 The just man's mouth utters wisdom
   and his lips speak what is right;
   the law of his God is in his heart,
   his steps shall be saved from stumbling. ℟

Gospel Acclamation   Mt 5:10

   Alleluia, alleluia!
   Happy are they who suffer persecution for justice' sake;
   the kingdom of heaven is theirs.
   Alleluia!

GOSPEL

A reading from the holy Gospel according to Matthew   10:22-25

If they persecute you in one city, take refuge in the next.

Jesus said to his disciples: 'You will be hated by all men on account of
my name; but the man who stands firm to the end will be saved. If
they persecute you in one town, take refuge in the next; and if they
persecute you in that, take refuge in another. I tell you solemnly, you
will not have gone the round of the towns of Israel before the Son of
Man comes.

   'The disciple is not superior to his teacher, nor the slave to his master. It is enough for the disciple that he should grow to be like his teacher.'

This is the Gospel of the Lord.

3 May

SS PHILIP AND JAMES, APOSTLES   Feast

FIRST READING

A reading from the first letter of St Paul   15:1-8
to the Corinthians

The Lord appeared to James, and then to all the Apostles.

Brothers, I want to remind you of the gospel I preached to you, the gospel that you received and in which you are firmly established; because the gospel will save you only if you keep believing exactly what I preached to you – believing anything else will not lead to anything.

Well then, in the first place, I taught you what I had been taught myself, namely that Christ died for our sins, in accordance with the scriptures; that he was buried; and that he was raised to life on the third day, in accordance with the scriptures; that he appeared first to Cephas and secondly to the Twelve. Next he appeared to more than five hundred of the brothers at the same time, most of whom are still alive, though some have died; then he appeared to James, and then to all the apostles; and last of all he appeared to me too; it was as though I was born when no one expected it.

This is the word of the Lord.

Responsorial Psalm   Ps 18:2-5. ℟ v.5

℟   Their message goes out through all the earth.

or

℟   Alleluia!

1   The heavens proclaim the glory of God
and the firmament shows forth the work of his hands.
Day unto day takes up the story
and night unto night makes known the message.   ℟

2   No speech, no word, no voice is heard
    yet their span extends through all the earth,
    their words to the utmost bounds of the world.

℟   Their message goes out through all the earth.

Gospel Acclamation   Jn 14:6.9

Alleluia, alleluia!
I am the way, the truth, and the life, says the Lord;
Philip, whoever sees me sees the Father.
Alleluia!

GOSPEL

A reading from the holy Gospel according to John   14:6-14

Have I been with you so long and yet you do not know me?

Jesus said to Thomas:

'I am the Way, the Truth and the Life.
No one can come to the Father except through me.
If you know me, you know my Father too.
From this moment you know him and have seen him.'

Philip said, 'Lord, let us see the Father and then we shall be
satisfied.' 'Have I been with you all this time, Philip,' said Jesus to
him 'and you still do not know me?

'To have seen me is to have seen the Father,
so how can you say, "Let us see the Father?"
Do you not believe
that I am in the Father and the Father is in me?
The words I say to you I do not speak as from myself:
it is the Father, living in me, who is doing this work.
You must believe me when I say
that I am in the Father and the Father is in me;
believe it on the evidence of this work, if for no other reason.
I tell you most solemnly, whoever believes in me
will perform the same works as I do myself,
he will perform even greater works,
because I am going to the Father.
Whatever you ask for in my name I will do,

so that the Father may be glorified in the Son.
If you ask for anything in my name, I will do it.'

This is the Gospel of the Lord.

12 May

Ss Nereus and Achilleus, martyrs

Optional Memorial

Common of martyrs.

FIRST READING

A reading from the book of the Apocalypse   7:9-17

These are the people who have been through the great persecution.

I, John, saw a huge number, impossible to count, of people from every
nation, race, tribe and language; they were standing in front of the
throne and in front of the Lamb, dressed in white robes and holding
palms in their hands. They shouted aloud, 'Victory to our God, who
sits on the throne, and to the Lamb!' And all the angels who were
standing in a circle round the throne, surrounding the elders and the
four animals, prostrated themselves before the throne, and touched
the ground with their foreheads, worshipping God with these words,
'Amen. Praise and glory and wisdom and thanksgiving and honour
and power and strength to our God for ever and ever. Amen.'

One of the elders then spoke, and asked me, 'Do you know who
these people are, dressed in white robes, and where they have come
from?' I answered him, 'You can tell me, my Lord.' Then he said,
'These are the people who have been through the great persecution,
and because they have washed their robes white again in the blood of
the Lamb, they now stand in front of God's throne and serve him day
and night in his sanctuary; and the One who sits on the throne will
spread his tent over them. They will never hunger or thirst again;
neither the sun nor scorching wind will ever plague them, because the
Lamb who is at the throne will be their shepherd and will lead them to
springs of living water; and God will wipe away all tears from their
eyes.'

This is the word of the Lord.

Responsorial Psalm   Ps 123:2-5. 7-8. ℟ v.7

    ℟   Our soul has escaped like a bird from the hunter's net.

1   If the Lord had not been on our side
    when men rose against us,
    then would they have swallowed us alive
    when their anger was kindled. ℟

2   Then would the waters have engulfed us,
    the torrent gone over us;
    over our heads would have swept
    the raging waters. ℟

3   Indeed the snare has been broken
    and we have escaped.
    Our help is in the name of the Lord,
    who made heaven and earth. ℟

Gospel Acclamation   Mt 5:10

    Alleluia, alleluia!
    Happy are they who suffer persecution for justice' sake;
    the kingdom of heaven is theirs.
    Alleluia!

GOSPEL

A reading from the holy Gospel according to Matthew   10:17-22

You will be dragged before governors and kings on account of me, to bear
witness before them and all the people.

Jesus said to his apostles: 'Beware of men: they will hand you over to
sanhedrins and scourge you in their synagogues. You will be dragged
before governors and kings for my sake, to bear witness before them
and the pagans. But when they hand you over, do not worry about how
to speak or what to say; what you are to say will be given to you when
the time comes; because it is not you who will be speaking; the Spirit
of your Father will be speaking in you.

    'Brother will betray brother to death, and the father his child;
children will rise against their parents and have them put to death.

You will be hated by all men on account of my name; but the man who stands firm to the end will be saved.'

This is the Gospel of the Lord.

Also 12 May

St Pancras, martyr Optional Memorial

Common of martyrs.

FIRST READING

A reading from the book of the Apocalypse 19:1. 5-9

Happy are those who are invited to the wedding feast of the Lamb.

I, John, seemed to hear the great sound of a huge crowd in heaven, singing, 'Alleluia! Victory and glory and power to our God!'

Then a voice came from the throne; it said, 'Praise our God, you servants of his and all who, great or small, revere him.' And I seemed to hear the voices of a huge crowd, like the sound of the ocean or the great roar of thunder, answering, 'Alleluia! The reign of the Lord our God Almighty has begun; let us be glad and joyful and give praise to God, because this is the time for the marriage of the Lamb. His bride is ready, and she has been able to dress herself in dazzling white linen, because her linen is made of the good deeds of the saints.' The angel said, 'Write this: Happy are those who are invited to the wedding feast of the Lamb.'

This is the word of the Lord.

Responsorial Psalm Ps 102:1-4. 8-9. 13-14. 17-18. ℟ v.1

℟ O bless the Lord, my soul.

1 My soul, give thanks to the Lord.
all my being, bless his holy name.
My soul, give thanks to the Lord
and never forget all his blessings. ℟

2 It is he who forgives all your guilt,
who heals every one of your ills,
who redeems your life from the grave,
who crowns you with love and compassion. ℟ (continued)

3 The Lord is compassion and love,
   slow to anger and rich in mercy.
   His wrath will come to an end;
   he will not be angry for ever.

   ℟   O bless the Lord, my soul.

4 As a father has compassion on his sons,
   the Lord has pity on those who fear him;
   for he knows of what we are made,
   he remembers that we are dust.   ℟

5 But the love of the Lord is everlasting
   upon those who hold him in fear;
   his justice reaches out to children's children
   when they keep his covenant in truth.   ℟

Gospel Acclamation   Mt 11:25

Alleluia, alleluia!
Blessed are you, Father, Lord of heaven and earth;
you have revealed to little ones the mysteries of the kingdom.
Alleluia!

GOSPEL

A reading from the holy Gospel according to Matthew   11:25-30

You have hidden these things from the learned and the clever.

Jesus exclaimed, 'I bless you, Father, Lord of heaven and of earth, for hiding these things from the learned and the clever and revealing them to mere children. Yes, Father, for that is what it pleased you to do. Everything has been entrusted to me by my Father; and no one knows the Son except the Father, just as no one knows the Father except the Son and those to whom the Son chooses to reveal him.

'Come to me, all you who labour and are overburdened, and I will give you rest. Shoulder my yoke and learn from me, for I am gentle and humble in heart, and you will find rest for your souls. Yes, my yoke is easy and my burden light.'

This is the Gospel of the Lord.

14 May

ST MATTHIAS, APOSTLE   Feast

FIRST READING

A reading from the Acts of the Apostles   1:15-17. 20-26

The lot fell to Matthias, and he was numbered with the eleven Apostles.

One day Peter stood up to speak to the brothers – there were about a hundred and twenty persons in the congregation: 'Brothers, the passage of scripture has to be fulfilled in which the Holy Spirit, speaking through David, foretells the fate of Judas, who offered himself as a guide to the men who arrested Jesus – after having been one of our number and actually sharing this ministry of ours. Now in the Book of Psalms it says:

Let his camp be reduced to ruin,
let there be no one to live in it.

And again:

Let someone else take his office.

'We must therefore choose someone who has been with us the whole time that the Lord Jesus was travelling round with us, someone who was with us right from the time when Jesus was baptising until the day when he was taken up from us – and he can act with us as a witness to his resurrection.'

Having nominated two candidates, Joseph known as Barsabbas, whose surname was Justus, and Matthias, they prayed, 'Lord, you can read everyone's heart; show us therefore which of these two you have chosen to take over this ministry and apostolate, which Judas abandoned to go to his proper place.' They then drew lots for them, and as the lot fell to Matthias, he was listed as one of the twelve apostles.

This is the word of the Lord.

Responsorial Psalm   Ps 112:1-8. ℟ cf. v.8

℟ The Lord will give him a seat with the leaders of his people.

or

℟ Alleluia!

1 Praise, O servants of the Lord,
   praise the name of the Lord!
   May the name of the Lord be blessed
   both now and for evermore!   ℟

2 From the rising of the sun to its setting
   praised be the name of the Lord!
   High above all nations is the Lord,
   above the heavens his glory.   ℟

3 Who is like the Lord, our God,
   who has risen on high to his throne
   yet stoops from the heights to look down,
   to look down upon heaven and earth?   ℟

4 From the dust he lifts up the lowly,
   from the dungheap he raises the poor
   to set him in the company of princes,
   yes, with the princes of his people.   ℟

Gospel Acclamation   Jn 15:16

Alleluia, alleluia!
I have chosen you from the world, says the Lord,
to go out and bear fruit that will last.
Alleluia!

GOSPEL

A reading from the holy Gospel according to John   15:9-17

It was not you who chose me, but I chose you.

Jesus said to his disciples:

'As the Father has loved me.
so I have loved you.
Remain in my love.
If you keep my commandments
you will remain in my love,
just as I have kept my Father's commandments
and remain in his love.
I have told you this
so that my own joy may be in you
and your joy be complete.
This is my commandment:
love one another,
as I have loved you.
A man can have no greater love
than to lay down his life for his friends.
You are my friends,
if you do what I command you.
I shall not call you servants any more,
because a servant does not know
his master's business;
I call you friends,
because I have made known to you
everything I have learnt from my Father.
You did not choose me,
no, I chose you;
and I commissioned you
to go out and to bear fruit,
fruit that will last;
and then the Father will give you
anything you ask him in my name.
What I command you
is to love another.'

This is the Gospel of the Lord.

18 May

St John I, pope and martyr   Optional Memorial

Common of martyrs or Common of pastors: for popes.

FIRST READING

A reading from the book of the Apocalypse   3:14. 20-22

I will come in to share his meal, side by side with him.

Here is the message of the Amen, the faithful, the true witness, the ultimate source of God's creation:

'Look, I am standing at the door, knocking. If one of you hears me calling and opens the door, I will come in to share his meal, side by side with him. Those who prove victorious I will allow to share my throne, just as I was victorious myself and took my place with my Father on his throne. If anyone has ears to hear, let him listen to what the Spirit is saying to the churches.'

This is the word of the Lord.

Responsorial Psalm   Ps 22. ℟ v. 1

℟   The Lord is my shepherd; there is nothing I shall want.

1   The Lord is my shepherd;
     there is nothing I shall want.
     Fresh and green are the pastures
     where he gives me repose.
     Near restful waters he leads me,
     to revive my drooping spirit. ℟

2   He guides me along the right path;
     he is true to his name.
     If I should walk in the valley of darkness
     no evil would I fear.
     You are there with your crook and your staff;
     with these you give me comfort. ℟

3   You have prepared a banquet for me
     in the sight of my foes.
     My head you have anointed with oil;
     my cup is overflowing. ℟

4   Surely goodness and kindness shall follow me
    all the days of my life.
    In the Lord's own house shall I dwell
    for ever and ever.   ℟

Gospel Acclamation   Jn 15:15

    Alleluia, alleluia!
    I call you my friends, says the Lord,
    for I have made known to you all that the Father has told me.
    Alleluia!

GOSPEL

A reading from the holy Gospel according to Luke   22:24-30

I confer a kingdom on you, just as my Father conferred one on me.

A dispute arose between the apostles about which should be reckoned the greatest, but Jesus said to them, 'Among pagans it is the kings who lord it over them, and those who have authority over them are given the title Benefactor. This must not happen with you. No; the greatest among you must behave as if he were the youngest, the leader as if he were the one who serves. For who is the greater: the one at table or the one who serves? The one at table, surely? Yet here am I among you as one who serves!

    'You are the men who have stood by me faithfully in my trials; and now I confer a kingdom on you, just as my Father conferred one on me; you will eat and drink at my table in my kingdom, and you will sit on thrones to judge the twelve tribes of Israel.'

    This is the Gospel of the Lord.

20 May

St Bernardine of Siena, priest   Optional Memorial

Common of pastors: for missionaries.

FIRST READING

A reading from the Acts of the Apostles   4:8-12

There is no salvation in any other.

Peter, filled with the Holy Spirit, said, 'Rulers of the people, and elders! If you are questioning us today about an act of kindness to a cripple, and asking us how he was healed, then I am glad to tell you all, and would indeed be glad to tell the whole people of Israel, that it was by the name of Jesus Christ the Nazarene, the one you crucified, whom God raised from the dead, by this name and by no other that this man is able to stand up perfectly healthy, here in your presence, today. This is the stone rejected by you the builders, but which has proved to be the keystone. For of all the names in the world given to men, this is the only one by which we can be saved.'

This is the word of the Lord.

Responsorial Psalm   Ps 39:2. 4. 7-10. ℟ cf. vv. 8. 9

℟   Here am I, Lord; I come to do your will.

1   I waited, I waited for the Lord
    and he stooped down to me;
    he heard my cry.
    He put a new song into my mouth,
    praise of our God.   ℟

2   You do not ask for sacrifice and offerings,
    but an open ear.
    You do not ask for holocaust and victim.
    Instead, here am I.   ℟

3   In the scroll of the book it stands written
    that I should do your will.
    My God, I delight in your law
    in the depth of my heart.   ℟

964

4   Your justice I have proclaimed
    in the great assembly.
    My lips I have not sealed;
    you know it, O Lord.   ℟

Gospel Acclamation   Jn 8:12

    Alleluia, alleluia!
    I am the light of the world, says the Lord;
    whoever follows me will have the light of life.
    Alleluia!

GOSPEL

A reading from the holy Gospel according to Luke   9:57-62

I will follow you, wherever you go.

As Jesus and his disciples travelled along they met a man on the road
who said to him, 'I will follow you wherever you go'. Jesus answered,
'Foxes have holes and the birds of the air have nests, but the Son of
Man has nowhere to lay his head.'

    Another to whom he said, 'Follow me,' replied, 'Let me go and bury
my father first.' But he answered, 'Leave the dead to bury their dead;
your duty is to go and spread the news of the kingdom of God.'

    Another said, 'I will follow you, sir, but first let me go and say
good-bye to my people at home'. Jesus said to him, 'Once the hand is
laid on the plough, no one who looks back is fit for the kingdom of
God.'

    This is the Gospel of the Lord.

25 May

St Bede the Venerable, priest and doctor of the Church

Optional Memorial

Common of doctors or Common of pastors.

FIRST READING

A reading from the first letter of St Paul to the Corinthians   2:10-16

We are those who have the mind of Christ.

The Spirit reaches the depths of everything, even the depths of God. After all, the depths of a man can only be known by his own spirit, not by any other man, and in the same way the depths of God can only be known by the Spirit of God. Now instead of the spirit of the world, we have received the Spirit that comes from God, to teach us to understand the gifts that he has given us. Therefore we teach, not in the way in which philosophy is taught, but in the way that the Spirit teaches us: we teach spiritual things spiritually. An unspiritual person is one who does not accept anything of the Spirit of God: he sees it all as nonsense; it is beyond his understanding because it can only be understood by means of the Spirit. A spiritual man, on the other hand, is able to judge the value of everything, and his own value is not to be judged by other men. As scripture says: Who can know the mind of the Lord, so who can teach him? But we are those who have the mind of Christ.

This is the word of the Lord.

Responsorial Psalm   Ps 118:9-14. ℟ v. 12

℟   Lord, teach me your decrees.

1   How shall the young remain sinless?
     By obeying your word.
     I have sought you with all my heart:
     let me not stray from your commands.   ℟

2   I treasure your promise in my heart
     lest I sin against you.
     Blessed are you, O Lord;
     teach me your statutes.   ℟

3   With my tongue I have recounted
    the decrees of your lips.
    I rejoiced to do your will
    as though all riches were mine.   ℟

Gospel Acclamation   cf. Jn 6:63. 68

Alleluia, alleluia!
Your words, Lord, are spirit and life;
you have the words of everlasting life.
Alleluia!

GOSPEL

A reading from the holy Gospel according to Matthew   7:21-29

Jesus taught them with authority.

Jesus said to his disciples: 'It is not those who say to me, "Lord, Lord,"
who will enter the kingdom of heaven, but the person who does the
will of my Father in heaven. When the day comes many will say to
me, "Lord, Lord, did we not prophesy in your name, cast out demons in
your name, work many miracles in your name?" Then I shall tell them
to their faces: I have never known you; away from me, you evil men!

'Therefore, everyone who listens to these words of mine and acts on
them will be like a sensible man who built his house on rock. Rain
came down, floods rose, gales blew and hurled themselves against
that house, and it did not fall: it was founded on rock. But everyone
who listens to these words of mine and does not act on them will be
like a stupid man who built his house on sand. Rain came down, floods
rose, gales blew and struck that house, and it fell; and what a fall it
had!'

Jesus had now finished what he wanted to say, and his teaching
made a deep impression on the people because he taught them with
authority, and not like their own scribes.

This is the Gospel of the Lord.

Also 25 May

St Gregory VII, pope   Optional Memorial

Common of pastors: for popes.

FIRST READING

A reading from the Acts of the Apostles   20:17-18. 28-32. 36

*Be on guard for yourselves and for all whom the Holy Spirit has
made you the overseers.*

From Miletus Paul sent for the elders of the church of Ephesus. When
they arrived he addressed these words to them:

'Be on your guard for yourselves and for all the flock of which the
Holy Spirit has made you the overseers, to feed the Church of God
which he bought with his own blood. I know quite well that when I
have gone fierce wolves will invade you and will have no mercy on the
flock. Even from your own ranks there will be men coming forward
with a travesty of the truth on their lips to induce the disciples to
follow them. So be on your guard, remembering how night and day for
three years I never failed to keep you right, shedding tears over each
one of you. And now I commend you to God, and to the word of his
grace that has power to build you up and to give you your inheritance
among all the sanctified.'

When he had finished speaking he knelt down with them all and
prayed.

This is the word of the Lord.

Responsorial Psalm   Ps 109:1-4. ℟ v.4

℟   You are a priest for ever, in the line of Melchizedek.

1   The Lord's revelation to my Master:
     'Sit on my right:
     I will put your foes beneath your feet.'   ℟

2   The Lord will send from Zion
     your sceptre of power:
     rule in the midst of all your foes.   ℟

3   A prince from the day of your birth
     on the holy mountains;
     from the womb before the daybreak I begot you.   ℟

4   The Lord has sworn an oath he will not change.
    'You are a priest for ever,
    a priest like Melchizedek of old.' ℞

Gospel Acclamation   Mk 1:17

    Alleluia, alleluia!
    Come, follow me, says the Lord,
    and I will make your fishers of my people.
    Alleluia!

GOSPEL

A reading from the holy Gospel according to Matthew   16:13-19

You are Peter and on this rock I will build my Church.

When Jesus came to the region of Caesarea Philippi he put this question to his disciples, 'Who do people say the Son of Man is?' And they said, 'Some say he is John the Baptist, some Elijah, and others Jeremiah or one of the prophets.' 'But you,' he said, 'who do you say I am?' Then Simon Peter spoke up, 'You are the Christ,' he said, 'the Son of the living God.' Jesus replied, 'Simon son of Jonah, you are a happy man! Because it was not flesh and blood that revealed this to you but my Father in heaven. So I now say to you: You are Peter and on this rock I will build my Church. And the gates of the underworld can never hold out against it. I will give you the keys of the kingdom of heaven; whatever you bind on earth shall be considered bound in heaven; whatever you loose on earth shall be considered loosed in heaven.'

    This is the Gospel of the Lord.

Also 25 May

St Mary Magdalene de Pazzi, virgin

Optional Memorial

Common of virgins or Common of holy men and women: for religious.

FIRST READING

A reading from the first letter of St Paul to the Corinthians   7:25-35

A virgin can devote herself to the work of the Lord.

About remaining celibate, I have no directions from the Lord but give my own opinion as one who, by the Lord's mercy, has stayed faithful. Well then, I believe that in these present times of stress this is right: that it is good for a man to stay as he is. If you are tied to a wife, do not look for freedom; if you are free of a wife, then do not look for one. But if you marry, it is no sin, and it is not a sin for a young girl to get married. They will have their troubles, though, in their married life, and I should like to spare you that.

Brothers, this is what I mean: our time is growing short. Those who have wives should live as though they had none, and those who mourn should live as though they had nothing to mourn for; those who are enjoying life should live as though there were nothing to laugh about; those whose life is buying things should live as though they had nothing of their own; and those who have to deal with the world should not become engrossed in it. I say this because the world as we know it is passing away.

I would like to see you free from all worry. An unmarried man can devote himself to the Lord's affairs, all he need worry about is pleasing the Lord; but a married man has to bother about the world's affairs and devote himself to pleasing his wife: he is torn two ways. In the same way an unmarried woman, like a young girl, can devote herself to the Lord's affairs; all she need worry about is being holy in body and spirit. The married woman, on the other hand, has to worry about the world's affairs and devote herself to pleasing her husband. I say this only to help you, not to put a halter round your necks, but simply to make sure that everything is as it should be, and that you give your undivided attention to the Lord.

This is the word of the Lord.

Responsorial Psalm   Ps 148: 1-2. 11-14. ℟ vv. 12. 13

> ℟ Young men and women, praise the name of the Lord.

or

> ℟ Alleluia!

1 Praise the Lord from the heavens,
   praise him in the heights.
   Praise him, all his angels,
   praise him, all his host. ℟

2 All earth's kings and peoples,
   earth's princes and rulers;
   young men and maidens,
   old men together with children. ℟

3 Let them praise the name of the Lord
   for he alone is exalted.
   The splendour of his name
   reaches beyond heaven and earth. ℟

4 He exalts the strength of his people.
   He is the praise of all his saints,
   of the sons of Israel,
   of the people to whom he comes close. ℟

Gospel Acclamation   Jn 8:31-32

> Alleluia, alleluia!
> If you stay in my word, you will indeed be my disciples,
> and you will know the truth, says the Lord.
> Alleluia!

GOSPEL

A reading from the holy Gospel according to Mark   3:31-35

Whoever has done the will of God is my brother, my sister, and my mother.

The mother and brothers of Jesus arrived and, standing outside, sent in a message asking for him. A crowd was sitting round him at the time the message was passed to him, 'Your mother and brothers and sisters are outside asking for you'. He replied, 'Who are my mother and my brothers?' And looking round at those sitting in a circle about him, he said, 'Here are my mother and my brothers. Anyone who does the will of God, that person is my brother and sister and mother.'

This is the Gospel of the Lord.

26 May

St Philip Neri, priest

Memorial

Common of pastors or Common of holy men and women: for religious.

FIRST READING

A reading from the letter of St Paul to the Philippians   4:4-9

Fill your minds with everything that is holy.

I want you to be happy, always happy in the Lord, I repeat, what I want is your happiness. Let your tolerance be evident to everyone: the Lord is very near. There is no need to worry; but if there is anything you need, pray for it, asking God for it with prayer and thanksgiving, and that peace of God, which is so much greater than we can understand, will guard your hearts and your thoughts, in Christ Jesus. Finally, brothers, fill your minds with everything that is true, everything that is noble, everything that is good and pure, everything that we love and honour, and everything that can be thought virtuous or worthy of praise. Keep doing all the things that you learnt from me and have been taught by me and have heard or seen that I do. Then the God of peace will be with you.

This is the word of the Lord.

Responsorial Psalm   Ps 33:2-11. ℟ v.2. Alt. ℟. v.9

℟   I will bless the Lord at all times.

or

℟   Taste and see the goodness of the Lord.

1   I will bless the Lord at all times,
       his praise always on my lips;
       in the Lord my soul shall make its boast.
       The humble shall hear and be glad.   ℟

2 Glorify the Lord with me.
   Together let us praise his name.
   I sought the Lord and he answered me;
   from all my terrors he set me free. ℟

3 Look towards him and be radiant;
   let your faces not be abashed.
   This poor man called; the Lord heard him
   and rescued him from all his distress. ℟

4 The angel of the Lord is encamped
   around those who revere him, to rescue them.
   Taste and see that the Lord is good.
   He is happy who seeks refuge in him. ℟

5 Revere the Lord, you his saints.
   They lack nothing, those who revere him.
   Strong lions suffer want and go hungry
   but those who seek the Lord lack no blessing. ℟

Gospel Acclamation   Jn 15:9. 5

   Alleluia, alleluia!
   Remain in my love, says the Lord;
   all who live in me, and I in them, will bear much fruit.
   Alleluia!

GOSPEL

A reading from the holy Gospel according to John   17:20-26

I want those you have given me to be with me where I am.

Jesus raised his eyes to heaven and said:

   'Holy Father,
   I pray not only for these,
   but for those also
   who through their words will believe in me.
   May they all be one.
   Father, may they be one in us,
   as you are in me and I am in you,
   so that the world may believe it was you who sent me.
   I have given them the glory you gave to me,

973

that they may be one as we are one.
With me in them and you in me,
may they be so completely one
that the world will realise that it was you who sent me
and that I have loved them as much as you loved me.
Father,
I want those you have given me
to be with me where I am,
so that they may always see the glory
you have given me
because you loved me
before the foundation of the world.
Father, Righteous One,
the world has not known you,
but I have known you,
and these have known
that you have sent me.
I have made your name known to them
and will continue to make it known,
so that the love with which you loved me may be in them,
and so that I may be in them.'

This is the Gospel of the Lord.

27 May

St Augustine of Canterbury, bishop

Optional Memorial

Common or pastors: for missionaries.

FIRST READING

A reading from the first letter of St Paul to the Thessalonians 2:2-8

We were eager to hand over to you not only the Good News but our whole lives as well.

It was our God who gave us the courage to proclaim his Good News to you in the face of great opposition. We have not taken to preaching because we are deluded, or immoral, or trying to deceive anyone; it was God who decided that we were fit to be entrusted with the Good

News, and when we are speaking, we are not trying to please men but God, who can read our inmost thoughts. You know very well, and we can swear it before God, that never at any time have our speeches been simply flattery, or a cover for trying to get money; nor have we ever looked for any special honour from men, either from you or anybody else, when we could have imposed ourselves on you with full weight, as apostles of Christ.

Instead, we were unassuming. Like a mother feeding and looking after her own children, we felt so devoted and protective towards you, and had come to love you so much, that we were eager to hand over to you not only the Good News but our whole lives as well.

This is the word of the Lord.

Responsorial Psalm   Ps 95: 1-3. 7-8. 10. ℟ v.3

℟ Proclaim his marvellous deeds to all the nations.

1   O sing a new song to the Lord,
    sing to the Lord all the earth.
    O sing to the Lord, bless his name.   ℟

2   Proclaim his help day by day,
    tell among the nations his glory
    and his wonders among all the peoples.   ℟

3   Give the Lord, you families of peoples,
    give the Lord glory and power,
    give the Lord the glory of his name.   ℟

4   Proclaim to the nations: 'God is king.'
    The world he made firm in its place;
    he will judge the peoples in fairness.   ℟

Gospel Acclamation   Jn 10:14

Alleluia, alleluia!
I am the good shepherd, says the Lord;
I know my sheep, and mine know me.
Alleluia!

GOSPEL

A reading from the holy Gospel according to Matthew   9:35-37

The harvest is rich, but the labourers are few.

Jesus made a tour through all the towns and villages, teaching in their synagogues, proclaiming the Good News of the kingdom and curing all kinds of diseases and sickness.

And when he saw the crowds he felt sorry for them because they were harassed and dejected, like sheep without a shepherd. Then he said to his disciples, 'The harvest is rich but the labourers are few, so ask the Lord of the harvest to send labourers to his harvest.'

This is the Gospel of the Lord.

31 May

THE VISITATION OF THE BLESSED VIRGIN MARY

Feast

FIRST READING

A reading from the prophet Zephaniah   3:14-18

The king of Israel, the Lord, is in your midst.

Shout for joy, daughter of Zion,
Israel, shout aloud!
Rejoice, exult with all your heart,
daughter of Jerusalem!
The Lord has repealed your sentence;
he has driven your enemies away.
The Lord, the king of Israel, is in your midst;
you have no more evil to fear.
When that day comes, word will come to Jerusalem;
Zion, have no fear,
do not let your hands fall limp.
The Lord your God is in your midst,
a victorious warrior.
He will exult with joy over you,
he will renew you by his love;
he will dance with shouts of joy for you
as on a day of festival.

This is the word of the Lord.

Alternative First Reading

A reading from the letter of St Paul to the Romans   12:9-16

Contribute to the needs of God's people, and practise hospitality.

Do not let your love be a pretence, but sincerely prefer good to evil. Love each other as much as brothers should, and have a profound respect for each other. Work for the Lord with untiring effort and with great earnestness of spirit. If you have hope, this will make you cheerful. Do not give up if trials come; and keep on praying. If any of the saints are in need you must share with them; and you should make hospitality your special care.

Bless those who persecute you: never curse them, bless them. Rejoice with those who rejoice and be sad with those in sorrow. Treat everyone with equal kindness; never be condescending but make real friends with the poor.

This is the word of the Lord.

Responsorial Psalm   Is 12:2-6. ℟ v.6

℟   Among you is the great and Holy One of Israel.

1   Truly, God is my salvation,
    I trust, I shall not fear.
    For the Lord is my strength, my song,
    he became my saviour.
    With joy you will draw water
    from the wells of salvation.   ℟

2   Give thanks to the Lord, give praise to his name!
    Make his mighty deeds known to the peoples!
    Declare the greatness of his name.   ℟

3   Sing a psalm to the Lord!
    For he has done glorious deeds.
    make them known to all the earth!
    People of Zion, sing and shout for joy
    for great in your midst is the Holy One of Israel.   ℟

Gospel Acclamation

cf. Lk 1:45

Alleluia, alleluia!
Blessed are you, O Virgin Mary, for your firm believing,
that the promises of the Lord would be fulfilled.
Alleluia!

GOSPEL

A reading from the holy Gospel according to Luke

1:39-56

Why should I be honoured with a visit from the mother of my Lord?

Mary set out and went as quickly as she could to a town in the hill country of Judah. She went into Zechariah's house and greeted Elizabeth. Now as soon as Elizabeth heard Mary's greeting, the child leapt in her womb and Elizabeth was filled with the Holy Spirit. She gave a loud cry and said, 'Of all women you are the most blessed, and blessed is the fruit of your womb. Why should I be honoured with a visit from the mother of my Lord? For the moment your greeting reached my ears, the child in my womb leapt for joy. Yes, blessed is she who believed that the promise made her by the Lord would be fulfilled.'

And Mary said:

'My soul proclaims the greatness of the Lord
and my spirit exults in God my saviour;
because he has looked upon his lowly handmaid.
Yes, from this day forward all generations will call me blessed,
for the Almighty has done great things to me.
Holy is his name,
and his mercy reaches from age to age for those who fear him.
He has shown the power of his arm,
he has routed the proud of heart.
He has pulled down princes from their thrones and exalted the
    lowly.
The hungry he has filled with good things, the rich sent empty
    away.
He has come to the help of Israel his servant, mindful of his mercy
– according to the promise he made to our ancestors –
of his mercy to Abraham and to his descendants for ever.'

This is the Gospel of the Lord.

Saturday following the Second Sunday after Pentecost

The Immaculate Heart of Mary

Optional Memorial

The Gospel is proper to this memorial.
Common of the Blessed Virgin Mary.

FIRST READING

A reading from the prophet Isaiah   61:9-11

I will rejoice in my God.

Their race will be famous throughout the nations,
their descendants throughout the peoples.
All who see them will admit
that they are a race whom the Lord has blessed.
I exult for joy in the Lord,
my soul rejoices in my God,
for he has clothed me in the garments of salvation,
he has wrapped me in the cloak of integrity,
like a bridegroom wearing his wreath,
like a bride adorned in her jewels.
For as the earth makes fresh things grow,
as a garden makes seeds spring up,
so will the Lord make both integrity and praise
spring up in the sight of the nations.

This is the word of the Lord.

Responsorial Psalm   1 Sam 2:1. 4-8. ℟ cf. v.1

℟   My heart rejoices in the Lord my saviour.

1   My heart exults in the Lord,
     I find my strength in my God;
     my mouth laughs at my enemies
     as I rejoice in your saving help.   ℟

2   The bows of the mighty are broken,
     but the weak are clothed with strength.
     Those with plenty must labour for bread,
     but the hungry need work no more.
     The childless wife has children now
     but the fruitful wife bears no more.   ℟

(continued)

3   It is the Lord who gives life and death,
he brings men to the grave and back;
it is the Lord who gives poverty and riches.
He brings men low and raises them on high.

℟   My heart rejoices in the Lord my saviour.

4   He lifts up the lowly from the dust,
from the dungheap he raises the poor
to set them in the company of princes,
to give them a glorious throne. ℟

Gospel Acclamation   cf. Lk 2:19

Alleluia, alleluia!
Blessed is the Virgin Mary, who kept the word of God,
and pondered it in her heart.
Alleluia!

GOSPEL

A reading from the holy Gospel according to Luke   2:41-51
She stored up all these things in her heart.

Every year the parents of Jesus used to go to Jerusalem for the feast of
the Passover. When he was twelve years old, they went up for the
feast as usual. When they were on their way home after the feast, the
boy Jesus stayed behind in Jerusalem without his parents knowing it.
They assumed he was with the caravan, and it was only after a day's
journey that they went to look for him among their relations and
acquaintances. When they failed to find him they went back to
Jerusalem looking for him everywhere.

Three days later, they found him in the Temple, sitting among the
doctors, listening to them, and asking them questions; and all those
who heard him were astounded at his intelligence and his replies.
They were overcome when they saw him, and his mother said to him,
'My child, why have you done this to us? See how worried your father
and I have been, looking for you.' 'Why were you looking for me?' he
replied 'Did you not know that I must be busy with my Father's
affairs?' But they did not understand what he meant.

980

He then went down with them and came to Nazareth and lived under their authority. His mother stored up all these things in her heart.

This is the Gospel of the Lord.

JUNE

1 June

St Justin, martyr   Memorial

Common of martyrs.

FIRST READING

A reading from the first letter of St Paul   1:18-25
to the Corinthians

*It was because God wanted to save those who have faith through
the foolishness of the message that we preach.*

The language of the cross may be illogical to those who are not on the
way to salvation, but those of us who are on the way see it as God's
power to save. As scripture says: I shall destroy the wisdom of the wise
and bring to nothing all the learning of the learned. Where are the
philosophers now? Where are the scribes? Where are any of our
thinkers today? Do you see now how God has shown up the foolishness
of human wisdom? If it was God's wisdom that human wisdom should
not know God, it was because God wanted to save those who have
faith through the foolishness of the message that we preach. And so,
while the Jews demand miracles and the Greeks look for wisdom, here
are we preaching a crucified Christ; to the Jews an obstacle that they
cannot get over, to the pagans madness, but to those who have been
called, whether they are Jews or Greeks, a Christ who is the power
and the wisdom of God. For God's foolishness is wiser than human
wisdom, and God's weakness is stronger than human strength.

This is the word of the Lord.

Responsorial Psalm   Ps 33:2-9. ℟ v.5

℟   The Lord set me free from all my fears.

1   I will bless the Lord at all times,
     his praise always on my lips;
     in the Lord my soul shall make its boast.
     The humble shall hear and be glad.   ℟

2   Glorify the Lord with me.
     together let us praise his name.

I sought the Lord and he answered me;
from all my terrors he set me free. ℟

3   Look towards him and be radiant;
let your faces not be abashed.
This poor man called; the Lord heard him
and rescued him from all his distress. ℟

4   The angel of the Lord is encamped
around those who revere him, to rescue them.
Taste and see that the Lord is good.
He is happy who seeks refuge in him. ℟

Gospel Acclamation   Mt 5:16

Alleluia, alleluia!
Let your light shine before all
that they may see your good works and glorify your Father.
Alleluia!

GOSPEL

A reading from the holy Gospel according to Matthew   5:13-19

You are the light of the world.

Jesus said to his disciples: 'You are the salt of the earth. But if salt becomes tasteless, what can make it salty again? It is good for nothing, and can only be thrown out to be trampled underfoot by men.

'You are the light of the world. A city built on a hill-top cannot be hidden. No one lights a lamp to put it under a tub; they put it on the lamp-stand where it shines for everyone in the house. In the same way your light must shine in the sight of men, so that, seeing your good works, they may give the praise to your Father in heaven.

'Do not imagine that I have come to abolish the Law or the Prophets. I have come not to abolish but to complete them. I tell you solemnly, till heaven and earth disappear, not one dot, not one little stroke, shall disappear from the Law until its purpose is achieved. Therefore, the man who infringes even one of the least of these commandments and teaches others to do the same will be considered the least in the kingdom of heaven; but the man who keeps them and teaches them will be considered great in the kingdom of heaven.'

This is the Gospel of the Lord.

2 June

Ss Marcellinus and Peter, martyrs

Optional Memorial

Common of martyrs.

FIRST READING

A reading from the second letter of St Paul
to the Corinthians

6:4-10

We are said to be dying and yet here we are alive.

We prove we are servants of God by great fortitude in times of
suffering: in times of hardship and distress; when we are flogged, or
sent to prison, or mobbed; labouring, sleepless, starving. We prove we
are God's servants by our purity, knowledge, patience and kindness;
by a spirit of holiness, by a love free from affectation; by the word of
truth and by the power of God; by being armed with the weapons of
righteousness in the right hand and in the left, prepared for honour or
disgrace, for blame or praise; taken for impostors while we are
genuine; obscure yet famous; said to be dying and here we are alive;
rumoured to be executed before we are sentenced; thought most
miserable and yet we are always rejoicing; taken for paupers though
we make others rich, for people having nothing though we have
everything.

This is the word of the Lord.

Responsorial Psalm

Ps 123:2-5. 7-8. ℟ v.7

℟ Our soul has escaped like a bird from the hunter's net.

1 If the Lord had not been on our side
   when men rose against us,
   then would they have swallowed us alive
   when their anger was kindled. ℟

2 Then would the waters have engulfed us,
   the torrent gone over us;
   over our heads would have swept
   the raging waters. ℟

Indeed the snare has been broken
and we have escaped.
Our help is in the name of the Lord,
who made heaven and earth.   ℟

2 Cor 1:3-4

Alleluia, alleluia!
Blessed be the Father of mercies and the God of all comfort,
who consoles us in all our afflictions.
Alleluia!

GOSPEL

A reading from the holy Gospel according to John   17:11-19

The world hates them.

Jesus raised his eyes to heaven and said,

'Holy Father,
keep those you have given me true to your name,
so that they may be one like us.
While I was with them,
I kept those you had given me true to your name.
I have watched over them and not one is lost
except the one who chose to be lost,
and this was to fulfil the scriptures.
But now I am coming to you
and while still in the world I say these things
to share my joy with them to the full.
I passed your word on to them,
and the world hated them,
because they belong to the world
no more than I belong to the world.
I am not asking you to remove them from the world,
but to protect them from the evil one.
They do not belong to the world
any more than I belong to the world.
Consecrate them in the truth;
your word is truth.
As you sent me into the world,

I have sent them into the world,
and for their sake I consecrate myself
so that they too may be consecrated in truth.'

This is the Gospel of the Lord.

3 June

Ss Charles Lwanga and companions, martyrs

Memorial

Common of martyrs.

FIRST READING

A reading from the second book of Maccabees   7:1-2. 9-14

We are prepared to die rather than break the laws of our ancestors

There were seven brothers who were arrested with their mother. The
king tried to force them to taste pig's flesh, which the Law forbids, by
torturing them with whips and scourges. One of them, acting as
spokesman for the others, said, 'What are you trying to find out from
us? We are prepared to die rather than break the laws of our
ancestors.' With his last breath the second exclaimed, 'Inhuman fiend,
you may discharge us from this present life, but the King of the world
will raise us up, since it is for his laws that we die, to live again for
ever.'

After him, they amused themselves with the third, who on being
asked for his tongue promptly thrust it out and boldly held out his
hands, with these honourable words, 'It was heaven that gave me
these limbs; for the sake of his laws I disdain them; from him I hope to
receive them again.' The king and his attendants were astounded at
the young man's courage and his utter indifference to suffering.

When this one was dead they subjected the fourth to the same
savage torture. When he neared his end he cried, 'Ours is the better
choice, to meet death at men's hands, yet relying on God's promise
that we shall be raised up by him; whereas for you there can be no
resurection, no new life.'

This is the word of the Lord.

Responsorial Psalm　　　　　　　　　　Ps 123:2-5. 7-8. ℟ v.7

℟　Our soul has escaped like a bird from the hunter's net.

1　If the Lord had not been on our side `
　when men rose against us,
　then would they have swallowed us alive
　when their anger was kindled.　℟

2　Then would the waters have engulfed us,
　the torrent gone over us;
　over our head would have swept
　the raging waters.　℟

3　Indeed the snare has been broken
　and we have escaped.
　Our help is the name of the Lord,
　who made heaven and earth.　℟

Gospel Acclamation　　　　　　　　　　　　　Mt 5:3

　Alleluia, alleluia!
　Happy the poor in spirit;
　the kingdom of heaven is theirs!
　Alleluia!

GOSPEL

A reading from the holy Gospel according to Matthew　　5:1-12

Rejoice and be glad, for your reward will be great in heaven.

Seeing the crowds, Jesus went up the hill. There he sat down and was joined by his disciples. Then he began to speak. This is what he taught them:

　'How happy are the poor in spirit;
　theirs is the kingdom of heaven.
　Happy the gentle:
　they shall have the earth for their heritage.
　Happy those who mourn:
　they shall be comforted.
　Happy those who hunger and thirst for what is right:

987

they shall be satisfied.
Happy the merciful:
they shall have mercy shown them.
Happy the pure in heart:
they shall see God.
Happy the peacemakers:
they shall be called sons of God.
Happy those who are persecuted in the cause of right:
theirs is the kingdom of heaven.

'Happy are you when people abuse you and persecute you and speak all kinds of calumny against you on my account. Rejoice and be glad, for your reward will be great in heaven.'

This is the Gospel of the Lord.

5 June

St Boniface, bishop and martyr Memorial

Common of martyrs or Common of pastors: for missionaries.

FIRST READING

A reading from the Acts of the Apostles 26:19-23

Christ will proclaim light to the people and to the whole world.

Paul said, 'King Agrippa, I could not disobey the heavenly vision. On the contrary I started preaching, first to the people of Damascus, then to those of Jerusalem and all the countryside of Judaea, and also to the pagans, urging them to repent and turn to God, proving their change of heart by their deeds. This was why the Jews laid hands on me in the Temple and tried to do away with me. But I was blessed with God's help, and so I have stood firm to this day, testifying to great and small alike, saying nothing more than what the prophets and Moses himself said would happen: that the Christ was to suffer and that, as the first to rise from the dead, he was to proclaim that light now shone for our people and for the pagans too.'

This is the word of the Lord.

esponsorial Psalm   Ps 116. ℟ Mk 16:15

℟   Go out to all the world, and tell the Good News.

℟   Alleluia!

O praise the Lord, all you nations,
acclaim him all you peoples!   ℟

Strong is his love for us;
he is faithful for ever.   ℟

ospel Acclamation   Jn 10:14

Alleluia, alleluia!
I am the good shepherd, says the Lord,
I know my sheep and mine know me.
Alleluia!

GOSPEL

A reading from the holy Gospel according to John   10:11-16

The good shepherd is one who lays down his life for his sheep.

esus said:

'I am the good shepherd:
the good shepherd is one who lays down his life for his sheep.
The hired man, since he is not the shepherd
and the sheep do not belong to him,
abandons the sheep and runs away
as soon as he sees a wolf coming,
and then the wolf attacks and scatters the sheep;
this is because he is only a hired man
and has no concern for the sheep.
I am the good shepherd;
I know my own
and my own know me,
just as the Father knows me
and I know the Father;
and I lay down my life for my sheep.
And there are other sheep I have

that are not of this fold,
and these I have to lead as well.
They too will listen to my voice,
and there will be only one flock,
and one shepherd.'

This is the Gospel of the Lord.

6 June

St Norbert, bishop   Optional Memoria

Common of pastors or Common of holy men and women: for religious.

FIRST READING

A reading from the prophet Ezekiel   34:11-1

As a shepherd keeps all his flock in view, so shall I keep my sheep in view

The Lord says this: I am going to look after my flock myself and keep
all of it in view. As a shepherd keeps all his flock in view when he
stands up in the middle of his scattered sheep, so shall I keep my
sheep in view. I shall rescue them from wherever they have been
scattered during the mist and darkness. I shall bring them out of the
countries where they are; I shall gather them together from foreign
countries and bring them back to their own land. I shall pasture them
on the mountains of Israel, in the ravines and in every inhabited place
in the land. I shall feed them in good pasturage; the high mountains of
Israel will be their grazing ground. There they will rest in good
grazing ground; they will browse in rich pastures on the mountains of
Israel. I myself will pasture my sheep, I myself will show them where
to rest – it is the Lord who speaks. I shall look for the lost one, bring
back the stray, bandage the wounded and make the weak strong.
shall watch over the fat and healthy. I shall be a true shepherd to
them.

This is the word of the Lord.

Responsorial Psalm   Ps 22. ℟ v.1

℟   The Lord is my shepherd; there is nothing I shall want.

1   The Lord is my shepherd;
    there is nothing I shall want.
    Fresh and green are the pastures
    where he gives me respose.
    Near restful waters he leads me,
    to revive my drooping spirit.   ℟

2   He guides me along the right path;
    he is true to his name.
    If I should walk in the valley of darkness
    no evil would I fear.
    You are there with your crook and your staff;
    with these you give me comfort.   ℟

3   You have prepared a banquet for me
    in the sight of my foes.
    My head you have anointed with oil;
    my cup is overflowing.   ℟

4   Surely goodness and kindness shall follow me
    all the days of my life.
    In the Lord's own house shall I dwell
    for ever and ever.   ℟

Gospel Acclamation   Mt 5:3

    Alleluia, alleluia!
    Happy the poor in spirit;
    the kingdom of heaven is theirs!
    Alleluia!

GOSPEL

A reading from the holy Gospel according to Luke   14:25-33

Unless you are ready to give up all that you possess, you cannot be my disciple.

Great crowds accompanied Jesus on his way and he turned and spoke
to them. 'If any man comes to me without hating his father, mother,
wife, children, brothers, sisters, yes and his own life too, he cannot be
my disciple. Anyone who does not carry his cross and come after me
cannot be my disciple.

'And indeed, which of you here, intending to build a tower, would not first sit down and work out the cost to see if he had enough to complete it? Otherwise, if he laid the foundation and then found himself unable to finish the work, the onlookers would all star making fun of him and saying, 'Here is a man who started to build and was unable to finish.' Or again, what king marching to war against another king would not first sit down and consider whether with ten thousand men he could stand up to the other who advanced against him with twenty thousand? If not, then while the other king was still a long way off, he would send envoys to sue for peace. So in the same way, none of you can be my disciple unless he gives up all his possessions.'

This is the Gospel of the Lord.

9 June

St Ephrem, deacon and doctor of the Church

Optional Memorial

Common of doctors of the Church.

FIRST READING

A reading from the letter of St Paul to the Colossians   3:12-17

Above all have love, which is the bond of perfection

You are God's chosen race, his saints; he loves you, and you should be clothed in sincere compassion, in kindness and humility, gentleness and patience. Bear with one another; forgive each other as soon as a quarrel begins. The Lord has forgiven you; now you must do the same. Over all these clothes, to keep them together and complete them, put on love. And may the peace of Christ reign in your hearts, because it is for this that you were called together as parts of one body. Always be thankful.

Let the message of Christ, in all its richness, find a home with you. Teach each other, and advise each other, in all wisdom. With gratitude in your hearts sing psalms and hymns and inspired songs to God; and never say or do anything except in the name of the Lord Jesus, giving thanks to God the Father through him.

This is the word of the Lord.

Responsorial Psalm Ps 36: 3-6. 30-31. ℟ v.30

℟ The mouths of the just murmur wisdom.

1 If you trust in the Lord and do good,
   then you will live in the land and be secure.
   If you find your delight in the Lord,
   he will grant your heart's desire. ℟

2 Commit your life to the Lord,
   trust in him and he will act,
   so that your justice breaks forth like the light,
   your cause like the noon-day sun. ℟

3 The just man's mouth utters wisdom
   and his lips speak what is right;
   the law of his God is in his heart,
   his steps shall be saved from stumbling. ℟

Gospel Acclamation Jn 15:5

Alleluia, alleluia!
I am the vine and you are the branches, says the Lord:
those who live in me, and I in them, will bear much fruit.
Alleluia!

GOSPEL

A reading from the holy Gospel according to Luke 6:43-45

What a person says, comes from what is in the heart.

Jesus said to his disciples:
'There is no sound tree that produces rotten fruit, nor again a
rotten tree that produces sound fruit. For every tree can be told by its
own fruit: people do not pick figs from thorns, nor gather grapes from
brambles. A good man draws what is good from the store of goodness
in his heart; a bad man draws what is bad from the store of badness.
For a man's words flow out of what fills his heart.'

This is the Gospel of the Lord.

11 June

St Barnabas, apostle

Memoria

The First Reading is proper to this Memorial.

FIRST READING

A reading from the Acts of the Apostles

11:21-26; 13:1-

He was a good man, filled with the Holy Spirit and with faith

A great number believed and were converted to the Lord.

The church in Jerusalem heard about this and they sent Barnabas to Antioch. There he could see for himself that God had given grace and this pleased him, and he urged them all to remain faithful to the Lord with heartfelt devotion; for he was a good man, filled with the Holy Spirit and with faith. And a large number of people were won over to the Lord.

Barnabas then left for Tarsus to look for Saul, and when he found him he brought him to Antioch. As things turned out they were to live together in that church a whole year, instructing a large number of people. It was at Antioch that the disciples were first called 'Christ-ians'.

In the church at Antioch the following were prophets and teachers Barnabas, Simeon called Niger, and Lucius of Cyrene, Manaen, who had been brought up with Herod the tetrarch, and Saul. One day while they were offering worship to the Lord and keeping a fast, the Holy Spirit said, 'I want Barnabas and Saul set apart for the work to which I have called them.' So it was that after fasting and prayer they laid their hands on them and sent them off.

This is the word of the Lord.

Responsorial Psalm

Ps 97:1-6. ℟ v.2

℟   The Lord has revealed to the nations his saving power.

1   Sing a new song to the Lord
     for he has worked wonders.
     His right hand and his holy arm
     have brought salvation.   ℟

2 The Lord has made known his salvation;
has shown his justice to the nations.
He has remembered his truth and love
for the house of Israel. ℟

3 All the ends of the earth have seen
the salvation of our God.
Shout to the Lord all the earth,
ring out your joy. ℟

4 Sing psalms to the Lord with the harp,
with the sound of music.
With trumpets and the sound of the horn
acclaim the King, the Lord. ℟

Gospel Acclamation   Mt 28:18.20

Alleluia, alleluia!
Go and teach all people my gospel.
I am with you always until the end of the world.
Alleluia!

GOSPEL

A reading from the holy Gospel according to Matthew   10:7-13

You received without charge, give without charge.

Jesus said to his apostles, 'As you go, proclaim that the kingdom of heaven is close at hand. Cure the sick, raise the dead, cleanse the lepers, cast out devils. You received without charge, give without charge. Provide yourselves with no gold or silver, not even with a few coppers for your purse, with no haversack for the journey or spare tunic or footwear or a staff, for the workman deserves his keep.

'Whatever town or village you go into, ask for someone trustworthy and stay with him until you leave. As you enter his house, salute it, and if the house deserves it, let your peace descend upon it; if it does not, let your peace come back to you.'

This is the Gospel of the Lord.

13 June

St Anthony of Padua, priest and doctor of the Church

Memorial

Common of pastors or Common of doctors of the Church or Common of holy men and women: for religious.

FIRST READING

A reading from the prophet Isaiah

61:1-3

The Lord God anointed me and sent me to bring Good News to the poor.

The spirit of the Lord has been given to me,
for the Lord has anointed me.
He has sent me to bring good news to the poor,
to bind up hearts that are broken;
to proclaim liberty to captives,
freedom to those in prison;
to proclaim a year of favour from the Lord,
a day of vengeance for our God,
to comfort all those who mourn and to give them
for ashes a garland;
for mourning robe the oil of gladness,
for despondency, praise.

This is the word of the Lord.

Responsorial Psalm

Ps 88:2-5. 21-22. 25. 27. ℟ v.2

℟ For ever I will sing the goodness of the Lord.

1 I will sing for ever of your love, O Lord;
through all ages my mouth will proclaim your truth.
Of this I am sure, that your love lasts for ever,
that your truth is firmly established as the heavens. ℟

2 'I have made a covenant with my chosen one;
I have sworn to David my servant:
I will establish your dynasty for ever
and set up your throne through all ages. ℟

'I have found David my servant
and with my holy oil anointed him.
My hand shall always be with him
and my arm shall make him strong.   ℟

'My truth and my love shall be with him;
by my name his might shall be exalted.
He will say to me: "You are my father,
my God, the rock who saves me." '   ℟

Gospel Acclamation   Lk 4:18

Alleluia, alleluia!
The Lord sent me to bring Good News to the poor,
and freedom to prisoners.
Alleluia!

GOSPEL

A reading from the holy Gospel according to Luke   10:1-9

The harvest is rich but the labourers are few.

The Lord appointed seventy-two others and sent them out ahead of
him, in pairs, to all the towns and places he himself was to visit. He
said to them, 'The harvest is rich but the labourers are few, so ask the
Lord of the harvest to send labourers to his harvest. Start off now, but
remember, I am sending you out like lambs among wolves. Carry no
purse, no haversack, no sandals. Salute no one on the road. Whatever
house you go into, let your first words be, "Peace to this house!" And if
a man of peace lives there, your peace will go and rest on him; if not, it
will come back to you. Stay in the same house, taking what food and
drink they have to offer, for the labourer deserves his wages; do not
move from house to house. Whenever you go into a town where they
make you welcome, eat what is set before you. Cure those in it who are
sick, and say, "The kingdom of God is very near to you." '

This is the Gospel of the Lord.

19 June

St Romuald, abbot   Optional Memorial

Common of holy men and women: for religious.

FIRST READING

A reading from the letter of St Paul to the Philippians   3:8-14

*I am racing for the finish, for the prize to which God calls us upwards
to receive in Christ Jesus.*

I believe nothing can happen that will outweigh the supreme advantage of knowing Christ Jesus my Lord. For him I have accepted the loss of everything, and I look on everything as so much rubbish if only I can have Christ and be given a place in him. I am no longer trying for perfection by my own efforts, the perfection that comes from the Law, but I want only the perfection that comes through faith in Christ, and is from God and based on faith. All I want is to know Christ and the power of his resurrection and to share his sufferings by reproducing the pattern of his death. That is the way I can hope to take my place in the resurrection of the dead. Not that I have become perfect yet: I have not yet won, but I am still running, trying to capture the prize for which Christ Jesus captured me. I can assure you my brothers, I am far from thinking that I have already won. All I can say is that I forget the past and I strain ahead for what is still to come; I am racing for the finish, for the prize to which God calls us upwards to receive in Christ Jesus.

This is the word of the Lord.

Responsorial Psalm   Ps 130

℟   In you, Lord, I have found my peace.

1   O Lord, my heart is not proud
      nor haughty my eyes.
      I have not gone after things too great
      nor marvels beyond me. ℟

2   Truly I have set my soul
      in silence and peace.
      A weaned child on its mother's breast,
      even so is my soul. ℟

3   O Israel, hope in the Lord
    both now and for ever.   ℞

Gospel Acclamation   Mt 5:3

    Alleluia, alleluia!
    Happy the poor in spirit;
    the kingdom of heaven is theirs!
    Alleluia!

GOSPEL

A reading from the holy Gospel according to Luke   14:25-33

Unless you are ready to give up all that you possess, you cannot be my disciple.

Great crowds accompanied Jesus on his way and he turned and spoke to them. 'If any man comes to me without hating his father, mother, wife, children, brothers, sisters, yes and his own life too, he cannot be my disciple. Anyone who does not carry his cross and come after me cannot be my disciple.

'And indeed, which of you here, intending to build a tower, would not first sit down and work out the cost to see if he had enough to complete it? Otherwise, if he laid the foundation and then found himself unable to finish the work, the onlookers would all start making fun of him and saying, "Here is a man who started to build and was unable to finish." Or again, what king marching to war against another king would not first sit down and consider whether with ten thousand men he could stand up to the other who advanced against him with twenty thousand? If not, then while the other king was still a long way off, he would send envoys to sue for peace. So in the same way, none of you can be my disciple unless he gives up all his possessions.'

    This is the Gospel of the Lord.

21 June

St Aloysius Gonzaga, religious

Memorial

Common of holy men and women: for religious.

FIRST READING

A reading from the first letter of St John   5:1-5

This is the victory over the world – our faith.

Whoever believes that Jesus is the Christ
has been begotten by God;
and whoever loves the Father that begot him
loves the child whom he begets.
We can be sure that we love God's children
if we love God himself and do what he has commanded us;
this is what loving God is –
keeping his commandments;
and his commandments are not difficult,
because anyone who has been begotten by God
has already overcome the world;
this is the victory over the world –
our faith.
Who can overcome the world?
Only the man who believes that Jesus is the Son of God.

This is the word of the Lord.

Responsorial Psalm   Ps 15:1-2. 5. 7-8. ℟ cf. v.5

℟   You are my inheritance, O Lord..

1   Preserve me, God, I take refuge in you.
    I say to the Lord: 'You are my God.'
    O Lord, it is you who are my portion and cup;
    it is you yourself who are my prize.   ℟

2   I will bless the Lord who gives me counsel,
    who even at night directs my heart.
    I keep the Lord ever in my sight:
    since he is at my right hand, I shall stand firm.   ℟

1000

3   You will show me the path of life,
    the fullness of joy in your presence,
    at your right hand happiness for ever.   ℟

Gospel Acclamation   Jn 13:34

    Alleluia, alleluia!
    I give you a new commandment:
    love one another as I have loved you.
    Alleluia!

GOSPEL

A reading from the holy Gospel according to Matthew   22:34-40

Love the Lord your God, and your neighbour as yourself.

A lawyer, to disconcert Jesus, put a question, 'Master which is the
greatest commandment of the Law?' Jesus said, 'You must love the
Lord your God with all your heart, with all your soul, and with all
your mind. This is the greatest and the first commandment. The
second resembles it: You must love your neighbour as yourself. On
these two commandments hang the whole Law, and the Prophets
also.'

    This is the Gospel of the Lord.

22 June

St Paulinus of Nola, bishop   Optional Memorial

Common of pastors.

FIRST READING

A reading from the second letter of St Paul   8:9-15
to the Corinthians

He was rich, but he became poor for your sake: to make you rich out
of his poverty.

Remember how generous the Lord Jesus was: he was rich, but he
became poor for your sake, to make you rich out of his poverty. As I
say, I am only making a suggestion; it is only fair to you, since you
were the first, a year ago, not only in taking action but even in
deciding to. So now finish the work and let the results be worthy, as
far as you can afford it, of the decision you made so promptly. As long
as the readiness is there, a man is acceptable with whatever he can
afford; never mind what is beyond his means. This does not mean that
to give relief to others you ought to make things difficult for
yourselves: it is a question of balancing what happens to be your
surplus now against their present need, and one day they may have
something to spare that will supply your own need. That is how we
strike a balance: as scripture says: The man who gathered much had
none too much, the man who gathered little did not go short.

This is the word of the Lord.

Responsorial Psalm   Ps 39:2. 4. 7-10. ℟ vv.8-9

℟   Here am I, Lord; I come to do your will.

1   I waited, I waited for the Lord
    and he stooped down to me;
    he heard my cry.
    He put a new song into my mouth,
    praise of our God.   ℟

2   You do not ask for sacrifice and offerings,
    but an open ear.
    You do not ask for holocaust and victim.
    Instead, here am I.   ℟

3   In the scroll of the book it stands written
    that I should do your will.
    My God, I delight in your law
    in the depth of my heart.   ℟

4   Your justice I have proclaimed
    in the great assembly.
    My lips I have not sealed;
    you know it, O Lord.   ℟

Gospel Acclamation   Mt 5:3

    Alleluia, alleluia!
    Happy the poor in spirit;
    the kingdom of heaven is theirs!
    Alleluia!

GOSPEL

A reading from the holy Gospel according to Luke   12:32-34

It has pleased the Father to give you the kingdom.

Jesus said to his disciples: 'There is no need to be afraid, little flock,
for it has pleased your Father to give you the kingdom.

   'Sell your possessions and give alms. Get yourselves purses that do
not wear out, treasure that will not fail you, in heaven where no thief
can reach it and no moth destroy it. For where your treasure is, there
will your heart be also.'

   This is the Gospel of the Lord.

Also 22 June

Ss John Fisher, bishop,
and Thomas More, martyrs   Optional Memorial

Common of martyrs.

FIRST READING

A reading from the first letter of St Peter   4:12-19

Be glad when you are sharing in the suffering of Christ.

My dear people, you must not think it unaccountable that you should
be tested by fire. There is nothing extraordinary in what has happened to you. If you can have some share in the sufferings of Christ, be
glad, because you will enjoy a much greater gladness when his glory is
revealed. It is a blessing for you when they insult you for bearing the
name of Christ, because it means that you have the Spirit of glory, the
Spirit of God resting on you. None of you should ever deserve to suffer
for being a murderer, a thief, a criminal or an informer; but if anyone
of you should suffer for being a Christian, then he is not to be ashamed
of it; he should thank God that he has been called one. The time has
come for the judgement to begin at the household of God; and if what
we know now is only the beginning, what will it be when it comes
down to those who refuse to believe God's Good News? If it is hard for
a good man to be saved, what will happen to the wicked and to
sinners? So even those whom God allows to suffer must trust themselves to the constancy of the creator and go on doing good.

This is the word of the Lord.

Responsorial Psalm   Ps 125. ℟ v.5

℟   Those who sow in tears, shall reap with shouts of joy.

1   When the Lord delivered Zion from bondage,
    it seemed like a dream.
    Then was our mouth filled with laughter,
    on our lips there were songs.   ℟

2   The heathens themselves said : 'What marvels
    the Lord worked for them!'
    What marvels the Lord worked for us!
    Indeed we were glad.   ℟

3   Deliver us, O Lord, from our bondage
    as streams in dry land.
    Those who are sowing in tears
    will sing when they reap.   ℟

4   They go out, they go out, full of tears,
    carrying seed for the sowing:
    they come back, they come back, full of song.
    carrying their sheaves.   ℟

Gospel Acclamation   Mt 5:10

    Alleluia, alleluia!
    Happy are they who suffer persecution for justice' sake;
    the kingdom of heaven is theirs.
    Alleluia!

GOSPEL

A reading from the holy Gospel according to Matthew   10:34-39

It is not peace I have come to bring, but a sword.

Jesus said to his apostles: 'Do not suppose that I have come to bring
peace to the earth: it is not peace I have come to bring, but a sword.
For I have come to set a man against his father, a daughter against
her mother, a daughter-in-law against her mother-in-law. A man's
enemies will be those of his own household.

   'Anyone who prefers father or mother to me is not worthy of me.
Anyone who prefers son or daughter to me is not worthy of me.
Anyone who does not take his cross and follow in my footsteps is not
worthy of me. Anyone who finds his life will lose it; anyone who loses
his life for my sake will find it.'

   This is the Gospel of the Lord.

24 June

THE BIRTH OF ST JOHN THE BAPTIST

Solemnity

Vigil Mass

FIRST READING

A reading from the prophet Jeremiah   1:4-10

Before I formed you in the womb, I knew you.

In the days of Josiah, the word of the Lord was addressed to me, saying,

'Before I formed you in the womb I knew you;
before you came to birth I consecrated you;
I have appointed you as prophet to the nations.'

I said, 'Ah, Lord; look, I do not know how to speak: I am a child!' But the Lord replied,

'Do not say, "I am a child,"
Go now to those to whom I send you
and say whatever I command you.
Do not be afraid of them,
for I am with you to protect you –
it is the Lord who speaks!'

Then the Lord put out his hand and touched my mouth and said to me:

'There! I am putting my words into your mouth.
Look, today I am setting you
over nations and over kingdoms,
to tear up and to knock down,
to destroy and to overthrow,
to build and to plant.'

This is the word of the Lord.

Responsorial Psalm   Ps 70:1-6. 15. 17. ℟ v.6

℟   Since my mother's womb, you have been my strength.

1   In you, O Lord, I take refuge;
     let me never be put to shame.
     In your justice rescue me, free me:
     pay heed to me and save me. ℟

2   Be a rock where I can take refuge,
     a mighty stronghold to save me;
     for you are my rock, my stronghold.
     Free me from the hand of the wicked. ℟

3   It is you, O Lord, who are my hope,
     my trust, O Lord, since my youth.
     On you I have leaned from my birth,
     from my mother's womb you have been my help. ℟

4   My lips will tell of your justice
     and day by day of your help.
     O God, you have taught me from my youth
     and I proclaim your wonders still. ℟

SECOND READING

A reading from the first letter of St Peter   1:8-12

The prophets searched and inquired for this salvation.

You did not see Jesus Christ, yet you love him; and still without
seeing him, you are already filled with joy so glorious that it cannot be
described, because you believe; and you are sure of the end to which
your faith looks forward, that is, the salvation of your souls.

It was this salvation that the prophets were looking and searching
so hard for; their prophecies were about the grace which was to come
to you. The Spirit of Christ which was in them foretold the sufferings
of Christ and the glories that would come after them, and they tried to
find out at what time and in what circumstances all this was to be
expected. It was revealed to them that the news they brought of all the
things which have now been announced to you, by those who preached
to you the Good News through the Holy Spirit sent from heaven, was
for you and not for themselves. Even the angels long to catch a
glimpse of these things.

This is the word of the Lord.

Gospel Acclamation   cf. Jn 1:7; Lk 1:17

> Alleluia, alleluia!
> He came to bear witness to the light,
> to prepare an upright people for the Lord.
> Alleluia!

GOSPEL

A reading from the holy Gospel according to Luke   1:5-17

A son is born to you and you will name him John.

In the days of King Herod of Judaea there lived a priest called Zechariah who belonged to the Abijah section of the priesthood, and he had a wife, Elizabeth by name, who was a descendant of Aaron. Both were worthy in the sight of God, and scrupulously observed all the commandments and observances of the Lord. But they were childless: Elizabeth was barren and they were both getting on in years.

Now it was the turn of Zechariah's section to serve, and he was exercising his priestly office before God when it fell to him by lot, as the ritual custom was, to enter the Lord's sanctuary and burn incense there. And at the hour of incense the whole congregation was outside, praying.

Then there appeared to him the angel of the Lord, standing on the right of the altar of incense. The sight disturbed Zechariah and he was overcome with fear. But the angel said to him, 'Zechariah, do not be afraid, your prayer has been heard. Your wife Elizabeth is to bear you a son and you must name him John. He will be your joy and delight and many will rejoice at his birth, for he will be great in the sight of the Lord; he must drink no wine, no strong drink. Even from his mother's womb he will be filled with the Holy Spirit, and he will bring back many of the sons of Israel to the Lord their God. With the spirit and power of Elijah, he will go before him to turn the hearts of fathers towards their children and the disobedient back to the wisdom that the virtuous have, preparing for the Lord a people fit for him.'

This is the Gospel of the Lord.

Mass During the Day

FIRST READING

A reading from the prophet Isaiah   49:1-6

Behold I will make you a light to the nations.

Islands, listen to me,
pay attention, remotest peoples.
The Lord called me before I was born,
from my mother's womb he pronounced my name.

He made my mouth a sharp sword,
and hid me in the shadow of his hand.
He made me into a sharpened arrow,
and concealed me in his quiver.

He said to me, 'You are my servant, Israel,
in whom I shall be glorified';
while I was thinking, 'I have toiled in vain,
I have exhausted myself for nothing';

and all the while my cause was with the Lord,
my reward with my God.
I was honoured in the eyes of the Lord,
my God was my strength.

And now the Lord has spoken,
he who formed me in the womb to be his servant,
to bring Jacob back to him,
to gather Israel to him:

'It is not enough for you to be my servant,
to restore the tribes of Jacob and bring back the survivors of Israel;
I will make you the light of the nations
so that my salvation may reach to the ends of the earth.'

This is the word of the Lord.

Responsorial Psalm   Ps 138:1-3. 13-15. ℟ v.14

℟   I praise you for I am wonderfully made.

1   O Lord, you search me and you know me,
     you know my resting and my rising,
     you discern my purpose from afar.   (continued)

You mark when I walk or lie down,
all my ways lie open to you.

℟   I praise you for I am wonderfully made.

2   For it was you who created my being,
     knit me together in my mother's womb.
     I thank you for the wonder of my being,
     for the wonders of all your creation.   ℟

3   Already you knew my soul,
     my body held no secret from you
     when I was being fashioned in secret
     and moulded in the depths of the earth.   ℟

SECOND READING

A reading from the Acts of the Apostles   13:22-26

Christ's coming was announced beforehand by
the preaching of John.

Paul said: 'God made David the king of our ancestors, of whom he
approved in these words, "I have elected David son of Jesse, a man
after my own heart, who will carry out my whole purpose." To keep
his promise, God has raised up for Israel one of David's descendants,
Jesus, as Saviour, whose coming was heralded by John when he
proclaimed a baptism of repentance for the whole people of Israel.
Before John ended his career he said, "I am not the one you imagine
me to be; that one is coming after me and I am not fit to undo his
sandal."

'My brothers, sons of Abraham's race, and all you who fear God,
this message of salvation is meant for you.'

This is the word of the Lord.

Gospel Acclamation   cf. Lk 1:76

Alleluia, alleluia!
You, child, will be called the prophet of the Most High;
you will go before the Lord to prepare his ways.
Alleluia!

GOSPEL

A reading from the holy Gospel according to Luke   1:57-66. 80

John is his name.

The time came for Elizabeth to have her child, and she gave birth to a son; and when her neighbours and relations heard that the Lord had shown her so great a kindness, they shared her joy.

Now on the eighth day they came to circumcise the child; they were going to call him Zechariah after his father, but his mother spoke up. 'No,' she said 'he is to be called John.' They said to her, 'But no one in your family has that name', and made signs to his father to find out what he wanted him called. The father asked for a writing tablet and wrote, 'His name is John.' And they were all astonished. At that instant his power of speech returned and he spoke and praised God. All their neighbours were filled with awe and the whole affair was talked about throughout the hill country of Judaea. All those who heard of it treasured it in their hearts. 'What will this child turn out to be?' they wondered. And indeed the hand of the Lord was with him. The child grew up and his spirit matured. And he lived out in the wilderness until the day he appeared openly to Israel.

This is the Gospel of the Lord.

27 June

St Cyril of Alexandria,
bishop and doctor of the Church

Optional Memorial

Common of pastors or Common of doctors of the Church.

FIRST READING

A reading from the second letter of St Paul to Timothy   4:1-5

Preach the Good News; fulfill your ministry.

Before God and before Christ Jesus who is to be judge of the living and the dead, I put this duty to you, in the name of his Appearing and of his kingdom: proclaim the message and, welcome or unwelcome, insist on it. Refute falsehood, correct error, call to obedience – but do all with patience and with the intention of teaching. The time is sure to come when, far from being content with sound teaching, people will be avid for the latest novelty and collect themselves a whole series of teachers according to their own tastes; and then, instead of listening to the truth, they will turn to myths. Be careful always to choose the right course; be brave under trials; make the preaching of the Good News your life's work, in thoroughgoing service.

This is the word of the Lord.

Responsorial Psalm   Ps 88:2-5. 21-22. 25. 27. ℟ cf. v.2

℟   For ever I will sing the goodness of the Lord.

1   I will sing for ever of your love, O Lord;
     through all ages my mouth will proclaim your truth.
     Of this I am sure, that your love lasts for ever,
     that your truth is firmly established as the heavens.   ℟

2   'I have made a covenant with my chosen one;
     I have sworn to David my servant:
     I will establish your dynasty for ever
     and set up your throne through all ages.   ℟

3   'I have found David my servant
     and with my holy oil anointed him.
     My hand shall always be with him
     and my arm shall make him strong.   ℟

4   'My truth and my love shall be with him;
     by my name his might shall be exalted.
     He will say to me: "You are my father,
     my God, the rock who saves me."'   ℟

Gospel Acclamation   Mt 5:16

    Alleluia, alleluia!
    Let your light shine before all
    that they may see your good works and glorify your Father.
    Alleluia!

GOSPEL

A reading from the holy Gospel according to Matthew   5:13-19

You are the light of the world.

Jesus said to his disciples: 'You are the salt of the earth. But if salt becomes tasteless, what can make it salty again. It is good for nothing, and can only be thrown out to be trampled underfoot by men.

'You are the light of the world. A city built on a hill-top cannot be hidden. No one lights a lamp to put it under a tub; they put it on the lamp-stand where it shines for everyone in the house. In the same way your light must shine in the sight of men, so that, seeing your good works, they may give the praise to your Father in heaven.'

'Do not imagine that I have come to abolish the Law or the Prophets. I have come not to abolish but to complete them. I tell you solemnly, till heaven and earth disappear, not one dot, not one little stroke, shall disappear from the Law until its purpose is achieved. Therefore, the man who infringes even one of the least of these commandments and teaches others to do the same will be considered the least in the kingdom of heaven; but the man who keeps them and teaches them will be considered great in the kingdom of heaven.'

This is the Gospel of the Lord.

28 June

St Irenaeus, bishop and martyr   Memorial

Common of martyrs or Common of doctors of the Church.

FIRST READING

A reading from the second letter of St Paul to Timothy   2:22-26

The Lord's servant must be kind to everyone, correcting with gentleness.

Fasten your attention on holiness, faith, love and peace, in union with all those who call on the Lord with pure minds. Avoid these futile and silly speculations, understanding that they only give rise to quarrels; and a servant of the Lord is not to engage in quarrels, but has to be kind to everyone, a good teacher, and patient. He has to be gentle when he corrects people who dispute what he says, never forgetting that God may give them a change of mind so that they recognise the truth and come to their senses, once out of the trap where the devil caught them and kept them enslaved.

This is the word of the Lord.

Responsorial Psalm

Ps 36:3-6. 30-31. ℟ v.30

℟   The mouths of the just murmur wisdom.

1   If you trust in the Lord and do good,
    then you will live in the land and be secure.
    If you find your delight in the Lord,
    he will grant your heart's desire.   ℟

2   Commit your life to the Lord,
    trust in him and he will act,
    so that your justice breaks forth like the light,
    your cause like the noon-day sun.   ℟

3   The just man's mouth utters wisdom
    and his lips speak what is right;
    the law of his God is in his heart,
    his steps shall be saved from stumbling.   ℟

Gospel Acclamation

Jn 15:9. 5

Alleluia, alleluia!
Remain in my love, says the Lord;
all who live in me, and I in them, will bear much fruit.
Alleluia!

GOSPEL

A reading from the holy Gospel according to John   17:20-26

I want those you have given me to be with me where I am.

Jesus raised his eyes to heaven and said:

'Holy Father,
I pray not only for these,
but for those also
who through their words will believe in me.
May they all be one.

Father, may they be one in us,
as you are in me and I am in you,
so that the world may believe it was you who sent me.
I have given them the glory you gave to me,
that they may be one as we are one.
With me in them and you in me,
may they be so completely one
that the world will realise that it was you who sent me
and that I have loved them as much as you loved me.
Father,
I want those you have given me
to be with me where I am,
so that they may always see the glory
you have given me
because you loved me
before the foundation of the world.
Father, Righteous One,
the world has not known you,
but I have known you,
and these have known
that you have sent me.
I have made your name known to them
and will continue to make it known,
so that the love with which you loved me may be in them,
and so that I may be in them.'

This is the Gospel of the Lord.

SS PETER AND PAUL, APOSTLES   Solemnity

Vigil Mass

FIRST READING

A reading from the Acts of the Apostles   3:1-10

What I have, I give to you: in the name of Jesus stand up and walk.

Once, when Peter and John were going up to the Temple for the prayers at the ninth hour, it happened that there was a man being carried past. He was a cripple from birth; and they used to put him down every day near the Temple entrance called the Beautiful Gate so that he could beg from the people going in. When this man saw Peter and John on their way into the Temple he begged from them. Both Peter and John looked straight at him and said, 'Look at us.' He turned to them expectantly, hoping to get something from them, but Peter said, 'I have neither silver nor gold, but I will give you what I have: in the name of Jesus Christ the Nazarene, walk!' Peter then took him by the hand and helped him to stand up. Instantly his feet and ankles became firm, he jumped up, stood, and began to walk, and he went with them into the Temple, walking and jumping and praising God. Everyone could see him walking and praising God, and they recognised him as the man who used to sit begging at the Beautiful Gate of the Temple. They were all astonished and unable to explain what had happened to him.

This is the word of the Lord.

Responsorial Psalm   Ps 18:2-5. ℟ v.5

℟   Their message goes out through all the earth.

1   The heavens proclaim the glory of God
    and the firmament shows forth the work of his hands.
    Day unto day takes up the story
    and night unto night makes known the message.   ℟

2   No speech, no word, no voice is heard
    yet their span extends through all the earth,
    their words to the utmost bounds of the world.   ℟

SECOND READING

A reading from the letter of St Paul to the Galatians   1:11-20

God chose me while I was still in my mother's womb.

The Good News I preached is not a human message that I was given by men, it is something I learnt only through a revelation of Jesus Christ. You must have heard of my career as a practising Jew, how merciless I was in persecuting the Church of God, how much damage I did to it, how I stood out among other Jews of my generation, and how enthusiastic I was for the traditions of my ancestors.

Then God, who had specially chosen me while I was still in my mother's womb, called me through his grace and chose to reveal his Son to me, so that I might preach the Good News about him to the pagans. I did not stop to discuss this with any human being, nor did I go up to Jerusalem to see those who were already apostles before me, but I went off to Arabia at once and later went straight back from there to Damascus. Even when after three years I went up to Jerusalem to visit Cephas and stayed with him for fifteen days, I did not see any of the other apostles; I only saw James, the brother of the Lord, and I swear before God that what I have just written is the literal truth.

This is the word of the Lord.

Gospel Acclamation   Jn 21:17

Alleluia, alleluia!
Lord, you know all things;
you know that I love you.
Alleluia!

GOSPEL

A reading from the holy Gospel according to John   21:15-19

Feed my lambs, feed my sheep.

Jesus showed himself to his disciples, and after they had eaten he said to Simon Peter, 'Simon son of John, do you love me more than these others do?' He answered, 'Yes Lord, you know I love you.' Jesus said to him, 'Feed my lambs.' A second time he said to him, 'Simon son of John, do you love me?' He replied, 'Yes, Lord, you know I love you.' Jesus said to him, 'Look after my sheep.' Then he said to him a third time, 'Simon son of John, do you love me?' Peter was upset that he asked him the third time, "Do you love me?" and said, 'Lord, you know everything; you know I love you.' Jesus said to him, 'Feed my sheep.

'I tell you most solemnly,
when you were young
you put on your own belt
and walked where you liked;
but when you grow old
you will stretch out your hands,
and somebody else will put a belt round you
and take you where you would rather not go.'

In these words he indicated the kind of death by which Peter would give glory to God. After this he said, 'Follow me.'

This is the Gospel of the Lord.

Mass During the Day

FIRST READING

A reading from the Acts of the Apostles

12:1-11

Now I know it is indeed true: the Lord has saved me from the power of Herod.

King Herod started persecuting certain members of the Church. He beheaded James the brother of John, and when he saw that this pleased the Jews he decided to arrest Peter as well. This was during the days of Unleavened Bread, and he put Peter in prison, assigning four squads of four soldiers each to guard him in turns. Herod meant to try Peter in public after the end of Passover week. All the time Peter was under guard the Church prayed to God for him unremittingly.

On the night before Herod was to try him, Peter was sleeping between two soldiers, fastened with double chains, while guards kept watch at the main entrance to the prison. Then suddenly the angel of the Lord stood there, and the cell was filled with light. He tapped Peter on the side and woke him. 'Get up!' he said 'Hurry!' – and the chains fell from his hands. The angel then said, 'Put on your belt and sandals.' After he had done this, the angel next said, 'Wrap your cloak round you and follow me.' Peter followed him, but had no idea that what the angel did was all happening in reality; he thought he was seeing a vision. They passed through two guard posts one after the other, and reached the iron gate leading to the city. This opened of its own accord; they went through it and had walked the whole length of one street when suddenly the angel left him. It was only then that Peter came to himself. 'Now I know it is all true,' he said. 'The Lord really did send his angel and has saved me from Herod and from all that the Jewish people were so certain would happen to me.'

This is the word of the Lord.

Responsorial Psalm   Ps 33:2-9. ℟ v.5

℟   The Lord set me free from all my fears.

1   I will bless the Lord at all times.
    his praise always on my lips;
    in the Lord my soul shall make its boast.
    The humble shall hear and be glad.   ℟

2   Glorify the Lord with me.
    Together let us praise his name.
    I sought the Lord and he answered me;
    from all my terrors he set me free.   ℟

3   Look towards him and be radiant;
    let your faces not be abashed.
    This poor man called; the Lord heard him
    and rescued him from all his distress.   ℟

4   The angel of the Lord is encamped
    around those who revere him, to rescue them.
    Taste and see that the Lord is good.
    He is happy who seeks refuge in him.   ℟

SECOND READING

A reading from the second letter of St Paul to Timothy   4:6-8. 17-18

All that remains now is the crown of righteousness.

My life is already being poured away as a libation, and the time has come for me to be gone. I have fought the good fight to the end; I have run the race to the finish; I have kept the faith; all there is to come now is the crown of righteousness reserved for me, which the Lord, the righteous judge, will give to me on that Day; and not only to me but to all those who have longed for his Appearing.

The Lord stood by me and gave me power, so that through me the whole message might be proclaimed for all the pagans to hear; and so I was rescued from the lion's mouth. The Lord will rescue me from all evil attempts on me, and bring me safely to his heavenly kingdom. To him be glory for ever and ever. Amen.

This is the word of the Lord.

Gospel Acclamation   Mt 16:18

> Alleluia, alleluia!
> You are Peter, the rock on which I will build my Church;
> the gates of hell will not hold out against it.
> Alleluia!

GOSPEL

A reading from the holy Gospel according to Matthew   16:13-19

You are Peter; and I will give to you the keys of the kingdom of heaven.

When Jesus came to the region of Caesarea Philippi he put this question to his disciples, 'Who do people say the Son of Man is?' And they said, 'Some say he is John the Baptist, some Elijah, and others Jeremiah or one of the prophets.' 'But you,' he said 'who do you say I am?' Then Simon Peter spoke up, 'You are the Christ,' he said 'the Son of the living God.' Jesus replied, 'Simon son of Jonah, you are a happy man! Because it was not flesh and blood that revealed this to you but my Father in heaven. So I now say to you: You are Peter and on this rock I will build my Church. And the gates of the underworld can never hold out against it. I will give you the keys of the kingdom of heaven: whatever you bind on earth shall be considered bound in heaven; whatever you loose on earth shall be considered loosed in heaven.'

This is the Gospel of the Lord.

For a Votive Mass of St Peter, the readings are taken from the feast of the Chair of St Peter, apostle, see above, pp.898ff. For a Votive Mass of St Paul, the readings are taken from the feast of the Conversion of St Paul, apostle, see above pp.864ff.

30 June

The First Martyrs of the Church of Rome

Optional Memorial

Common of martyrs.

FIRST READING

A reading from the letter of St Paul to the Romans   8:31-39

Neither death nor life can ever come between us and the love of God.

With God on our side who can be against us? Since God did not spare his own Son, but gave him up to benefit us all, we may be certain, after such a gift, that he will not refuse anything he can give. Could anyone accuse those that God has chosen? When God acquits, could anyone condemn? Could Christ Jesus? No! He not only died for us – he rose from the dead, and there at God's right hand he stands and pleads for us.

Nothing therefore can come between us and the love of Christ, even if we are troubled or worried, or being persecuted, or lacking food or clothes or being threatened or even attacked. As scripture promised: For your sake we are being massacred daily, and reckoned as sheep for the slaughter. These are the trials through which we triumph, by the power of him who loved us.

For I am certain of this: neither death nor life, no angel, no prince, nothing that exists, nothing still to come, not any power, or height or depth, nor any created thing, can ever come between us and the love of God made visible in Christ Jesus our Lord.

This is the word of the Lord.

Responsorial Psalm   Ps 123:2-5. 7-8. ℟ v.7

℟   Our soul has escaped like a bird from the hunter's net.

1   If the Lord had not been on our side
    when men rose against us,
    then would they have swallowed us alive
    when their anger was kindled.   ℟

2   Then would the waters have engulfed us,
    the torrent gone over us;
    over our heads would have swept
    the raging waters.   ℟

(continued)

3   Indeed the snare has been broken
    and we have escaped.
    Our help is in the name of the Lord,
    who made heaven and earth.

℟   Our soul has escaped like a bird from the hunter's net.

Gospel Acclamation   Mt 5:10

    Alleluia, alleluia!
    Happy are they who suffer persecution for justice' sake;
    the kingdom of heaven is theirs.
    Alleluia!

GOSPEL

A reading from the holy Gospel according to Matthew   24:4-13

You will be hated by all nations for my name's sake.

Jesus said to his disciples, 'Take care that no one deceives you;
because many will come using my name and saying, "I am the
Christ", and they will deceive many. You will hear of wars and
rumours of wars; do not be alarmed, for this is something that must
happen, but the end will not be yet. For nation will fight against
nation, and kingdom against kingdom. There will be famines and
eathquakes here and there. All this is only the beginning of the
birthpangs.

    'Then they will hand you over to be tortured and put to death; and
you will be hated by all the nations on account of my name. And then
many will fall away; men will betray one another and hate one
another. Many false prophets will arise; they will deceive many, and
with the increase of lawlessness, love in most men will grow cold; but
the man who stands firm to the end will be saved.'

    This is the Gospel of the Lord.

JULY

3 July
ST THOMAS, APOSTLE Feast

FIRST READING

A reading from the letter of St Paul to the Ephesians 2:19-22

You are part of the building built on the foundation of the apostles.

You are no longer aliens or foreign visitors; you are citizens like all the saints, and part of God's household. You are part of a building that has the apostles and prophets for its foundations, and Christ Jesus himself for its main cornerstone. As every structure is aligned on him, all grow into one holy temple in the Lord; and you too, in him, are being built into a house where God lives, in the Spirit.

This is the word of the Lord.

Responsorial Psalm Ps 116. ℟ Mk 16:15

℟ Go out to all the world, and tell the Good News.

1 O praise the Lord, all you nations,
   acclaim him all you peoples! ℟

2 Strong is his love for us;
   he is faithful for ever. ℟

Gospel Acclamation Jn 20:29

Alleluia, alleluia!
You believe in me, Thomas, because you have seen me;
happy those who have not seen me, but still believe!
Alleluia!

GOSPEL

A reading from the holy Gospel according to John 20:24-29

My Lord and my God.

Thomas, called the Twin, who was one of the Twelve, was not with the disciples when Jesus came. When they said, 'We have seen the Lord', he answered, 'Unless I see the holes that the nails made in his hands and can put my finger into the holes they made, and unless I can put my hand into his side, I refuse to believe.' Eight days later the disciples were in the house again and Thomas was with them. The doors were closed, but Jesus came in and stood among them. 'Peace be with you,' he said. Then he spoke to Thomas, 'Put your finger here; look, here are my hands. Give me your hand; put it into my side. Doubt no longer but believe.' Thomas replied, 'My Lord and my God!' Jesus said to them:

'You believe because you can see me.
Happy are those who have not seen and yet believe.'

This is the Gospel of the Lord.

4 July

St Elizabeth of Portugal   Optional Memorial

Common of holy men and women: for those who work for the underprivileged.

FIRST READING

A reading from the first letter of St John   3:14-18

We should lay down our lives for our brothers and sisters.

We have passed out of death and into life,
and of this we can be sure
because we love our brothers.
If you refuse to love, you must remain dead;
to hate your brother is to be a murderer,
and murderers, as you know, do not have eternal life in them.
This has taught us love –
that he gave up his life for us;
and we, too, ought to give up our lives for our brothers.
If a man who was rich enough in this world's goods
saw that one of his brothers was in need,
but closed his heart to him,
how could the love of God be living in him?
My children,
our love is not to be just words or mere talk,
but something real and active.

This is the word of the Lord.

Responsorial Psalm   Ps 111:1-9. ℟ v.1

℟   Happy are those who fear the Lord.

1   Happy the man who fears the Lord,
    who takes delight in his commands.
    His sons will be powerful on earth;
    the children of the upright are blessed.   ℟

2   Riches and wealth are in his house;
    his justice stands firm for ever.
    He is a light in the darkness for the upright:
    he is generous, merciful and just.   ℟

3   The good man takes pity and lends,
    he conducts his affairs with honour.
    The just man will never waver:
    he will be remembered for ever.   ℟

4   He has no fear of evil news;
    with a firm heart he trusts in the Lord.
    With a steadfast heart he will not fear;
    he will see the downfall of his foes.   ℟

5   Open-handed, he gives to the poor;
    his justice stands firm for ever.
    His head will be raised in glory.   ℟

Gospel Acclamation   Jn 13:34

    Alleluia, alleluia!
    I give you a new commandment:
    love one another as I have loved you.
    Alleluia!

GOSPEL

A reading from the holy Gospel according to Matthew   25:31-46

Whatever you have done to the very least of my brothers and sisters
you have done to me.

Jesus said to his disciples: 'When the Son of Man comes in his glory,
escorted by all the angels, then he will take his seat on his

throne of glory. All the nations will be assembled before him and he will separate men one from another as the shepherd separates sheep from goats. He will place the sheep on his right hand and the goats on his left. Then the King will say to those on his right hand, "Come, you whom my Father has blessed, take for your heritage the kingdom prepared for you since the foundation of the world. For I was hungry and you gave me food; I was thirsty and you gave me drink; I was a stranger and you made me welcome; naked and you clothed me, sick and you visited me, in prison and you came to see me." Then the virtuous will say to him in reply, "Lord, when did we see you hungry and feed you; or thirsty and give you drink? When did we see you a stranger and make you welcome; naked and clothe you; sick or in prison and go to see you?" And the King will answer, "I tell you solemnly, in so far as you did this to one of the least of these brothers of mine, you did it to me."

'Next he will say to those on his left hand, "Go away from me, with your curse upon you, to the eternal fire prepared for the devil and his angels. For I was hungry and you never gave me food; I was thirsty and you never gave me anything to drink; I was a stranger and you never made me welcome, naked and you never clothed me, sick and in prison and you never visited me." Then it will be their turn to ask, "Lord, when did we see you hungry or thirsty, a stranger or naked, sick, or in prison, and did not come to your help?" Then he will answer, "I tell you solemnly, in so far as you neglected to do this to one of the least of these, you neglected to do it to me." And they will go away to eternal punishment, and the virtuous to eternal life.'

This is the Gospel of the Lord.

Shorter form

A reading from the holy Gospel according to Matthew   25:31-40

> *Whatever you have done to the very least of my brothers and sisters you have done to me.*

Jesus said to his disciples: 'When the Son of Man comes in his glory, escorted by all the angels, then he will take his seat on his throne of glory. All the nations will be assembled before him and he will separate men one from another as the shepherd separates sheep from goats. He will place the sheep on his right hand and the goats on his left. Then the King will say to those on his right hand,

"Come, you whom my Father has blessed, take for your heritage the kingdom prepared for you since the foundation of the world. For I was hungry and you gave me food; I was thirsty and you gave me drink; I was a stranger and you made me welcome; naked and you clothed me, sick and you visited me, in prison and you came to see me." Then the virtuous will say to him in reply, "Lord, when did we see you hungry and feed you; or thirsty and give you drink? When did we see you a stranger and make you welcome; naked and clothe you; sick or in prison and go to see you?" And the King will answer, "I tell you solemnly, in so far as you did this to one of the least of these brothers of mine, you did it to me".'

This is the Gospel of the Lord.

---

5 July

St Anthony Zaccaria, priest   Optional Memorial

Common of pastors or Common of holy men and women: for teachers or: for religious.

FIRST READING

A reading from the second letter of St Paul to Timothy   1:13-14; 2:1-3

You have been entrusted to look after something precious; guard it with the help of the Holy Spirit who lives in us.

Keep as your pattern the sound teaching you have heard from me, in the faith and love that are in Christ Jesus. You have been trusted to look after something precious; guard it with the help of the Holy Spirit who lives in us. Accept the strength, my dear son, that comes from the grace of Christ Jesus. You have heard everything that I teach in public; hand it on to reliable people so that they in turn will be able to teach others.

Put up with your share of difficulties, like a good soldier of Christ Jesus.

This is the word of the Lord.

Responsorial Psalm   Ps 1:1-4. 6. ℟ v.2. Alt. ℟ Ps 39:5. Alt. ℟ Ps 91:13-14

℟   Happy are those who fear the Lord.

or

℟   Happy are they who hope in the Lord.

or

℟   The just will flourish like the palm tree in the garden of the
     Lord.

1   Happy indeed is the man
    who follows not the counsel of the wicked;
    nor lingers in the way of sinners
    nor sits in the company of scorners,
    but whose delight is the law of the Lord
    and who ponders his law day and night.   ℟

2   He is like a tree that is planted
    beside the flowing waters,
    that yields its fruit in due season
    and whose leaves shall never fade;
    and all that he does shall prosper.   ℟

3   Not so are the wicked, not so!
    For they like winnowed chaff
    shall be driven away by the wind.
    For the Lord guards the way of the just
    but the way of the wicked leads to doom.   ℟

Gospel Acclamation   cf. Mt 11:25

    Alleluia, alleluia!
    Blessed are you, Father, Lord of heaven and earth;
    you have revealed to little ones the mysteries of the kingdom.
    Alleluia!

GOSPEL

A reading from the holy Gospel according to Mark   10:13-16

Do not keep the children from me.

People were bringing little children to Jesus, for him to touch them.

The disciples turned them away, but when Jesus saw this he was indignant and said to them, 'Let the little children come to me; do not stop them; for it is to such as these that the kingdom of God belongs. I tell you solemnly, anyone who does not welcome the kingdom of God like a little child will never enter it.' Then he put his arms round them, laid his hands on them and gave them his blessing.

This is the Gospel of the Lord.

6 July

St Maria Goretti, virgin and martyr

Optional Memorial

Common of martyrs or Common of virgins.

FIRST READING

A reading from the first letter of St Paul to the Corinthians   6:13-15. 17-20

Your bodies are members of Christ.

The body is not meant for fornication; it is for the Lord, and the Lord for the body. God, who raised the Lord from the dead, will by his power raise us up too.

You know, surely, that your bodies are members making up the body of Christ; anyone who is joined to the Lord is one spirit with him.

Keep away from fornication. All the other sins are committed ouside the body; but to fornicate is to sin against your own body. Your body, you know, is the temple of the Holy Spirit, which is in you since you have received him from God. You are not your own property; you have been bought and paid for. That is why you should use your body for the glory of God.

This is the word of the Lord.

Responsorial Psalm   Ps 30:3-4. 6-8. 16-17. ℟ v.6

℟   Into your hands, O Lord, I entrust my spirit.

1   Be a rock of refuge for me,
     a mighty stronghold to save me,
     for you are my rock, my stronghold.
     For your name's sake, lead me and guide me.   ℟

2   Into your hands I commend my spirit.
    It is you who will redeem me, Lord.
    As for me, I trust in the Lord:
    let me be glad and rejoice in your love.

    ℟   Into your hands, O Lord, I entrust my spirit.

3   My life is in your hands, deliver me
    from the hands of those who hate me.
    Let your face shine on your servant.
    Save me in your love.   ℟

Gospel Acclamation   James 1:12

    Alleluia, alleluia!
    Blessed are they who stand firm when trials come;
    when they have stood the test, they will win the crown of life.
    Alleluia!

GOSPEL

A reading from the holy Gospel according to John   12:24-26

If the grain of wheat in the ground dies, it yields a rich harvest.

Jesus said to his disciples:

    'I tell you, most solemnly,
    unless a wheat grain falls on the ground and dies,
    it remains only a single grain;
    but if it dies,
    it yields a rich harvest.
    Anyone who loves his life loses it;
    anyone who hates his life in this world
    will keep it for the eternal life.
    If a man serves me, he must follow me,
    wherever I am, my servant will be there too.
    If anyone serves me, my Father will honour him.'

This is the Gospel of the Lord.

11 July

St Benedict, abbot   Memorial

Common of holy men and women: for religious.

FIRST READING

A reading from the book of Proverbs   2:1-9

Apply your heart to learn wisdom.

My son, if you take my words to heart,
if you set store by my commandments,
tuning your ear to wisdom,
and applying your heart to truth:
yes, if your plea is for clear perception,
if you cry out for discernment,
if you look for it as if it were silver,
and search for it as for buried treasure,
you will then understand what the fear of the Lord is,
and discover the knowledge of God.
For the Lord himself is giver of wisdom,
from his mouth issue knowledge and discernment.
He keeps his help for honest men,
he is the shield of those whose ways are honourable;
he stands guard over the paths of justice,
he keeps watch on the way of his devoted ones.
Then you will understand what virtue is, justice, and fair dealing,
all paths that lead to happiness.

    This is the word of the Lord.

Responsorial Psalm   Ps 33:2-11. ℟ v.2

   ℟   I will bless the Lord at all times.

or

   ℟   Taste and see the goodness of the Lord.

1   I will bless the Lord at all times,
    his praise always on my lips;
    in the Lord my soul shall make its boast.
    The humble shall hear and be glad. ℟

2 Glorify the Lord with me.
   Together let us praise his name.
   I sought the Lord and he answered me;
   from all my terrors he set me free.

   ℟ I will bless the Lord at all time.

or

   ℟ Taste and see the goodness of the Lord.

3 Look towards him and be radiant;
   let your faces not be abashed.
   This poor man called; the Lord heard him
   and rescued him from all his distress. ℟

4 The angel of the Lord is encamped
   around those who revere him, to rescue them.
   Taste and see that the Lord is good.
   He is happy who seeks refuge in him. ℟

5 Revere the Lord, you his saints.
   They lack nothing, those who revere him.
   Strong lions suffer want and go hungry
   but those who seek the Lord lack no blessing. ℟

Gospel Acclamation

Mt 5:3

Alleluia, alleluia!
Happy the poor in spirit;
the kingdom of heaven is theirs!
Alleluia!

GOSPEL

A reading from the holy Gospel according to Matthew   19:27-29

You who have left everything and followed me, will be rewarded a hundred-fold.

Peter spoke to Jesus. 'What about us?' he said. 'We have left everything and followed you. What are we to have, then?' Jesus said to him, 'I tell you solemnly, when all is made new and the Son of Man sits on his throne of glory, you will yourselves sit on twelve thrones to judge the twelve tribes of Israel. And everyone who has left houses, brothers, sisters, father, mother, children or land for the sake of my name will be repaid a hundred times over, and also inherit eternal life.'

This is the Gospel of the Lord.

13 July

St Henry
Optional Memorial

Common of holy men and women.

FIRST READING

A reading from the prophet Micah
6:6-8

People, what is good has been explained to you; this is what the Lord
God asks of you.

'With what gift shall I come into the Lord's presence
and bow down before God on high?
Shall I come with holocausts,
with calves one year old?
Will he be pleased with rams by the thousand,
with libations of oil in torrents?
Must I give my first-born for what I have done wrong,
the fruit of my body for my own sin.'
– 'What is good has been explained to you, man;
this is what the Lord asks of you:
only this, to act justly,
to love tenderly
and to walk humbly with your God.'

This is the word of the Lord.

Responsial Psalm   Ps 1:1-4. 6. ℟ v.2. Alt. ℟ Ps 39:5. Alt. ℟ Ps 91:13-14

℟   Happy are they who delight in the law of the Lord.

or

℟   Happy are they who hope in the Lord.

or

℟   The just will flourish like the palm tree in the garden of the
Lord.

1   Happy indeed is the man
who follows not the counsel of the wicked;
nor lingers in the way of sinners
nor sits in the company of scorners,
but whose delight is the law of the Lord
and who ponders his law day and night.   ℟

2 He is like a tree that is planted
   beside the flowing waters,
   that yields its fruit in due season
   and whose leaves shall never fade;
   and all that he does shall prosper.

   ℟ Happy are they who delight in the law of the Lord.

or

   ℟ Happy are they who hope in the Lord.

or

   ℟ The just will flourish like the palm tree in the garden of the
      Lord.

3 Not so are the wicked, not so!
   for they like winnowed chaff
   shall be driven away by the wind.
   For the Lord guards the way of the just
   but the way of the wicked leads to doom. ℟

Gospel Acclamation   Jn 14:23

   Alleluia, alleluia!
   All who love me will keep my words,
   and my Father will love them and we will come to them.
   Alleluia!

GOSPEL

A reading from the holy Gospel according to Matthew   7:21-27

A wise man builds his house on rock, not on sand.

Jesus said to his disciples: 'It is not those who say to me, "Lord, Lord",
who will enter the kingdom of heaven, but the person who does the
will of my Father in heaven. When the day comes many will say to
me, "Lord, Lord, did we not prophesy in your name, cast out demons in
your name, work many miracles in your name?" Then I shall tell them
to their faces: I have never known you; away from me, you evil men!

'Therefore, everyone who listens to these words of mine and acts on
them will be like a sensible man who built his house on rock. Rain
came down, floods rose, gales blew and hurled themselves against

that house, and it did not fall: it was founded on rock. But everyone who listens to these words of mine and does not act on them will be like a stupid man who built his house on sand. Rain came down, floods rose, gales blew and struck that house, and it fell; and what a fall it had!'

This is the Gospel of the Lord.

14 July

St Camillus de Lellis, priest   Optional Memorial

Common of holy men and women: for those who work for the underprivileged.

FIRST READING

A reading from the first letter of St John   3:14-18

We should lay down our lives for our brothers and sisters.

We have passed out of death and into life,
and of this we can be sure
because we love our brothers.
If you refuse to love, you must remain dead;
to hate your brother is to be a murderer,
and murderers, as you know, do not have eternal life in them.
This has taught us love –
that he gave up his life for us;
and we, too, ought to give up our lives for our brothers.
If a man who was rich enough in this world's goods
saw that one of his brothers was in need,
but closed his heart to him,
how could the love of God be living in him?
My children,
our love is not to be just words or mere talk,
but something real and active.

This is the word of the Lord.

1035

Responsorial Psalm   Ps 111:1-9. ℟ v.1

    ℟   Happy are those who fear the Lord.

or

    ℟   Alleluia!

1   Happy the man who fears the Lord,
    who takes delight in his commands.
    His sons will be powerful on earth;
    the children of the upright are blessed.   ℟

2   Riches and wealth are in his house;
    his justice stands firm for ever.
    He is a light in the darkness for the upright:
    he is generous, merciful and just.   ℟

3   The good man takes pity and lends,
    he conducts his affairs with honour.
    The just man will never waver:
    he will be remembered for ever.   ℟

4   He has no fear of evil news:
    with a firm heart he trusts in the Lord.
    With a steadfast heart he will not fear;
    he will see the downfall of his foes.   ℟

5   Open-handed, he gives to the poor;
    his justice stands firm for ever.
    His head will be raised in glory.   ℟

Gospel Acclamation   Jn 13:34

    Alleluia, alleluia!
    I give you a new commandment:
    love one another as I have loved you.
    Alleluia!

GOSPEL

A reading from the holy Gospel according to John   15:9-17

You are my friends if you do what I command you.

Jesus said to his disciples:

'As the Father has loved me,
so I have loved you.
Remain in my love.
If you keep my commandments
you will remain in my love,
just as I have kept my Father's commandments
and remain in his love.
I have told you this
so that my own joy may be in you
and your joy be complete.
This is my commandment:
love one another,
as I have loved you.
A man can have no greater love
than to lay down his life for his friends.
You are my friends,
if you do what I command you.
I shall not call you servants any more,
because a servant does not know
his master's business;
I call you friends,
because I have made known to you
everything I have learnt from my Father.
You did not choose me,
no, I chose you;
and I commissioned you
to go out and to bear fruit,
fruit that will last;
and then the Father will give you
anything you ask him in my name.
What I command you
is to love one another.'

This is the Gospel of the Lord.

15 July

St Bonaventure,
bishop and doctor of the Church   Memorial

Common of pastors: for bishops or Common of doctors of the Church.

FIRST READING

A reading from the letter of St Paul to the Ephesians   3:14-19

To know the love of Christ, which is beyond all knowledge.

This is what I pray, kneeling before the Father, from whom every family, whether spiritual or natural, takes its name:

Out of his infinite glory, may he give you the power through his Spirit for your hidden self to grow strong so that Christ may live in your hearts though faith, and then, planted in love and built on love, you will with all the saints have strength to grasp the breadth and the length, the height and the depth; until, knowing the love of Christ, which is beyond all knowledge, you are filled with the utter fullness of God.

This is the word of the Lord.

Responsorial Psalm   Ps 118:9-14. ℟ v.12

℟ Lord, teach me your decrees.

1 How shall the young remain sinless?
   By obeying your word.
   I have sought you with all my heart:
   let me not stray from your commands. ℟

2 I treasure your promise in my heart
   lest I sin against you.
   Blessed are you, O Lord;
   teach me your statutes. ℟

3 With my tongue I have recounted
   the decrees of your lips.
   I rejoiced to do your will
   as though all riches were mine. ℟

Gospel Acclamation   Mt 23:9-10

> Alleluia! Alleluia!
> You have one Father, your Father in heaven;
> you have one teacher: the Lord Jesus Christ!
> Alleluia!

GOSPEL

A reading from the holy Gospel according to Matthew   23:8-12

The greatest among you must be your servant.

Jesus said to his disciples: 'You must not allow yourselves to be called Rabbi, since you have only one Master, and you are all brothers. You must call no one on earth your father, since you have only one Father, and he is in heaven. Nor must you allow yourselves to be called teachers, for you have only one Teacher, the Christ. The greatest among you must be your servant. Anyone who exalts himself will be humbled, and anyone who humbles himself will be exalted.'

This is the Gospel of the Lord.

16 July

Our Lady of Mount Carmel   Optional Memorial

Common of the Blessed Virgin Mary.

FIRST READING

A reading from the prophet Zechariah   2:14-17

Rejoice, daughter of Zion, for I am coming.

Sing, rejoice,
daughter of Zion;
for I am coming
to dwell in the middle of you
– it is the Lord who speaks.
Many nations will join the Lord,
on that day;
they will become his people.
But he will remain among you,
and you will know that the Lord of hosts has sent me to you.

But the Lord will hold Judah
as his portion in the Holy Land,
and again make Jerusalem his very own.
Let all mankind be silent before the Lord!
For he is awaking and is coming from his holy dwelling.

This is the word of the Lord.

Responsorial Psalm   Lk 1:46-55. ℟ v.49

℟   The Almighty has done great things for me, and holy is his
       Name.

or

℟   O blessed Virgin Mary, you carried the Son of the eternal
       Father.

1   My soul glorifies the Lord,
       my spirit rejoices in God, my saviour.   ℟

2   He looks on his servant in her nothingness;
       henceforth all ages will call me blessed.
       The Almighty works marvels for me.
       Holy his name!   ℟

3   His mercy is from age to age,
       on those who fear him.
       He puts forth his arm in strength
       and scatters the proud-hearted.   ℟

4   He casts the mighty from their thrones
       and raises the lowly.
       He fills the starving with good things,
       sends the rich away empty.   ℟

5   He protects Israel, his servant,
       remembering his mercy,
       the mercy promised to our fathers,
       to Abraham and his sons for ever.   ℟

Gospel Acclamation   Lk 11:28

Alleluia, alleluia!
Blessed are they who hear the word of God
and keep it.
Alleluia!

GOSPEL

A reading from the holy Gospel according to Matthew   12:46-50

*Extending his hands toward the disciples, he said: Here are my
mother and my brothers.*

Jesus was speaking to the crowds when his mother and his brothers
appeared; they were standing outside and were anxious to have a
word with him. But to the man who told him this Jesus replied, 'Who
is my mother? Who are my brothers?' And stretching out his hand
towards his disciples he said, 'Here are my mother and my brothers.
Anyone who does the will of my Father in heaven, he is my brother
and sister and mother.'

This is the Gospel of the Lord.

21 July

St Lawrence of Brindisi,
priest and doctor of the Church

Optional Memorial

Common of pastors or Common of doctors of the Church.

FIRST READING

A reading from the second letter of St Paul
to the Corinthians

4:1-2. 5-7

We preach Jesus Christ as Lord, with ourselves as your servants for Jesus' sake.

Since we have by an act of mercy been entrusted with this work of administration, there is no weakening on our part. On the contrary, we will have none of the reticence of those who are ashamed, no deceitfulness or watering down the word of God; but the way we commend ourselves to every human being with a conscience is by stating the truth openly in the sight of God. For it is not ourselves that we are preaching, but Christ Jesus as the Lord, and ourselves as your servants for Jesus' sake. It is the same God that said, 'Let there be light shining out of darkness,' who has shone in our minds to radiate the light of the knowledge of God's glory, the glory on the face of Christ.

We are only the earthenware jars that hold this treasure, to make it clear that such an overwhelming power comes from God and not from us.

This is the word of the Lord.

Responsorial Psalm

Ps 39:2. 4. 7-10. ℟ cf. vv. 8. 9

℟   Here am I, Lord; I come to do your will.

1   I waited, I waited for the Lord
    and he stooped down to me;
    he heard my cry.
    He put a new song into my mouth,
    praise of our God.   ℟

2   You do not ask for sacrifice and offerings,
    but an open ear.
    You do not ask for holocaust and victim.
    Instead, here am I.   ℟

3 In the scroll of the book it stands written
   that I should do your will.
   My God, I delight in your law
   in the depth of my heart. ℟

4 Your justice I have proclaimed
   in the great assembly.
   My lips I have not sealed;
   you know it, O Lord. ℟

Gospel Acclamation

   Alleluia, alleluia!
   The seed is the word of God, Christ is the sower;
   all who come to him will live for ever.
   Alleluia!

GOSPEL

A reading from the holy Gospel according to Mark   4:1-10. 13-20

The sower went out to sow seed.

Jesus began to teach by the lakeside, but such a huge crowd gathered round him that he got into a boat on the lake and sat there. The people were all along the shore, at the water's edge. He taught them many things in parables, and in the course of his teaching he said to them, 'Listen! Imagine a sower going out to sow. Now it happened that, as he sowed, some of the seed fell on the edge of the path, and the birds came and ate it up. Some seed fell on rocky ground where it found little soil and sprang up straightaway because there was no depth of earth; and when the sun came up it was scorched and, not having any roots, it withered away. Some seed fell into thorns, and the thorns grew up and choked it, and it produced no crop. And some seeds fell into rich soil and, growing tall and strong, produced crop; and yielded thirty, sixty, even a hundredfold.' And he said, 'Listen, anyone who has ears to hear!'

When he was alone, the Twelve, together with the others who formed his company, asked what the parables meant.

He said to them, 'Do you not understand this parable? Then how will you understand any of the parables? What the sower is sowing is the word. Those on the edge of the path where the word is sown are people who have no sooner heard it than Satan comes and carries away the word that was sown in them. Similarly, those who receive the seed on patches of rock are people who, when first they hear the word, welcome it at once with joy. But they have no root in them, they do not last; should some trial come, or some persecution on account of the word, they fall away at once. Then there are others who receive the seed in thorns. These have heard the word, but the worries of this world, the lure of riches and all the other passions come in to choke the word, and so it produces nothing. And there are those who have received the seed in rich soil: they hear the word and accept it and yield a harvest, thirty and sixty and a hundredfold.'

This is the Gospel of the Lord.

22 July
St Mary Magdalen
Memorial

The Gospel is proper to this memorial.

FIRST READING

A reading from the Song of Songs
3:1-4

I have found him whom my heart loves.

The bride says this:

> On my bed, at night, I sought him
> whom my heart loves.
> I sought but did not find him.
> So I will rise and go through the City;
> in the streets and the squares
> I will seek him whom my heart loves.
> I sought but did not find him.
> The watchmen came upon me
> on their rounds in the City:
> 'Have you seen him whom my heart loves?'
> Scarcely had I passed them
> than I found him whom my heart loves.

This is the word of the Lord.

Alternative First Reading

A reading from the second letter of St Paul
to the Corinthians   5:14-17

> *Even if we did once know Christ in the flesh, that is not how we know him now.*

The love of Christ overwhelms us when we reflect that if one man has
died for all, then all men should be dead; and the reason he died for all
was so that living men should live no longer for themselves, but for
him who died and was raised to life for them.

From now onwards, therefore, we do not judge anyone by the
standards of the flesh. Even if we did once know Christ in the flesh,
that is not how we know him now. And for anyone who is in Christ,
there is a new creation; the old creation has gone, and now the new
one is here.

This is the word of the Lord.

Responsorial Psalm   Ps 62:2-6. 8-9. ℟ v.2

   ℟   My soul is thirsting for you, O Lord, my God.

1   O God, you are my God, for you I long;
     for you my soul is thirsting.
     My body pines for you
     like a dry, weary land without water.   ℟

2   So I gaze on you in the sanctuary
     to see your strength and your glory.
     For your love is better than life,
     my lips will speak your praise.   ℟

3   So I will bless you all my life,
     in your name I will lift up my hands.
     My soul shall be filled as with a banquet,
     my mouth shall praise you with joy.   ℟

4   For you have been my help;
     in the shadow of your wings I rejoice.
     My soul clings to you;
     your right hand holds me fast.   ℟

Gospel Acclamation

> Alleluia, alleluia!
> Tell us Mary, what did you see on the way?
> I saw the glory of the risen Christ, I saw his empty tomb.
> Alleluia!

GOSPEL

A reading from the holy Gospel according to John   20:1-2. 11-18

Woman, why are you weeping? Whom are you seeking?

It was very early on the first day of the week and still dark, when Mary of Magdala came to the tomb. She saw that the stone had been moved away from the tomb and came running to Simon Peter and the other disciple, the one Jesus loved. 'They have taken the Lord out of the tomb' she said 'and we don't know where they have put him.'

Mary stayed outside near the tomb, weeping. Then, still weeping, she stooped to look inside, and saw two angels in white sitting where the body of Jesus had been, one at the head, the other at the feet. They said, 'Woman, why are you weeping?' 'They have taken my Lord away' she replied 'and I don't know where they have put him.' As she said this she turned round and saw Jesus standing there, though she did not recognise him. Jesus said, 'Woman why are you weeping? Who are you looking for?' Supposing him to be the gardener, she said, 'Sir, if you have taken him away, tell me where you have put him, and I will go and remove him.' Jesus said, 'Mary!' She knew him then and said to him in Hebrew, 'Rabbuni!' – which means Master. Jesus said to her, 'Do not cling to me, because I have not yet ascended to my Father. But go and find the brothers, and tell them: I am ascending to my Father and your Father, to my God and your God.' So Mary of Madgala went and told the disciples that she had seen the Lord and that he had said these things to her.

This is the Gospel of the Lord.

23 July

St Bridget, religious   Optional Memorial

Common of holy men and women: for religious.

FIRST READING

A reading from the letter of St Paul to the Galatians   2:19-20

I live now, not I but Christ lives in me.

Through the Law I am dead to the Law, so that now I can live for God. I have been crucified with Christ, and I live now not with my own life but with the life of Christ who lives in me. The life I now live in this body I live in faith: faith in the Son of God who loved me and who sacrificed himself for my sake.

This is the word of the Lord.

Responsorial Psalm   Ps 33:2-11. ℟ v.2. Alt. ℟ v.9

℟   I will bless the Lord at all times.

or

℟   Taste and see the goodness of the Lord.

1   I will bless the Lord at all times,
    his praise always on my lips;
    in the Lord my soul shall make its boast.
    The humble shall hear and be glad.   ℟

2   Glorify the Lord with me.
    Together let us praise his name.
    I sought the Lord and he answered me;
    from all my terrors he set me free.   ℟

3   Look towards him and be radiant;
    let your faces not be abashed.
    This poor man called; the Lord heard him
    and rescued him from all his distress.   ℟

4   The angel of the Lord is encamped
    around those who revere him, to rescue them.
    Taste and see that the Lord is good.
    He is happy who seeks refuge in him.   ℟

(continued)

5   Revere the Lord, you his saints.
They lack nothing, those who revere him.
Strong lions suffer want and go hungry
but those who seek the Lord lack no blessing.

℟   I will bless the Lord at all times.

or

℟   Taste and see the goodness of the Lord.

Gospel Acclamation   Jn 15:9. 5

Alleluia, alleluia!
Remain in my love, says the Lord;
all who live in me, and I in them, will bear much fruit.
Alleluia!

GOSPEL

A reading from the holy Gospel according to John   15:1-8

All who live in me, and I in them, bear fruit.

Jesus said to his disciples;

'I am the true vine,
and my Father is the vinedresser.
Every branch in me that bears no fruit
he cuts away,
and every branch that does bear fruit he prunes
to make it bear even more.
You are pruned already,
by means of the word that I have spoken to you.
Make your home in me, as I make mine in you.
As a branch cannot bear fruit all by itself,
but must remain part of the vine,
neither can you unless you remain in me.
I am the vine,
you are the branches.
Whoever remains in me, with me in him,
bears fruit in plenty;
for cut off from me you can do nothing.

Anyone who does not remain in me
is like a branch that has been thrown away
– he withers;
these branches are collected and thrown on the fire,
and they are burnt.
If you remain in me
and my words remain in you,
you may ask what you will
and you shall get it.
It is to the glory of my Father that you should bear much fruit,
and then you will be my disciples.

This is the Gospel of the Lord.

25 July

ST JAMES, APOSTLE Feast

FIRST READING

A reading from the second letter of St Paul to the Corinthians 4:7-15

We carry always in our bodies the death of Jesus.

We are only the earthenware jars that hold this treasure, to make it clear that such an overwhelming power comes from God and not from us. We are in difficulties on all sides, but never cornered; we see no answer to our problems, but never despair; we have been persecuted, but never deserted; knocked down, but never killed; always wherever we may be, we carry with us in our body the death of Jesus, so that the life of Jesus, too, may always be seen in our body. Indeed, while we are still alive, we are consigned to our death every day, for the sake of Jesus, so that in our mortal flesh the life of Jesus, too, may be openly shown. So death is at work in us, but life in you.

But as we have the same spirit of faith that is mentioned in scripture – I believed, and therefore I spoke – we too believe and therefore we too speak, knowing that he who raised the Lord Jesus to life will raise us with Jesus in our turn, and put us by his side and you with us. You see, all this is for your benefit, so that the more grace is multiplied among people, the more thanksgiving there will be, to the glory of God.

This is the word of the Lord.

Responsorial Psalm   Ps 125. ℟ v.5

℟   Those who sow in tears, shall reap with shouts of joy.

1   When the Lord delivered Zion from bondage,
    it seemed like a dream.
    Then was our mouth filled with laughter,
    on our lips there were songs.   ℟

2   The heathens themselves said: 'What marvels
    the Lord worked for them!'
    What marvels the Lord worked for us!
    Indeed we were glad.   ℟

3   Deliver us, O Lord, from our bondage
    as streams in dry land.
    Those who are sowing in tears
    will sing when they reap.   ℟

4   They go out, they go out, full of tears,
    carrying seed for the sowing:
    they come back, they come back, full of song,
    carrying their sheaves.   ℟

Gospel Acclamation   cf. Jn 15:16

    Alleluia, alleluia!
    I have chosen you from the world, says the Lord,
    to go and bear fruit that will last.
    Alleluia!

GOSPEL

A reading from the holy Gospel according to Matthew   20:20-28

You shall indeed drink my cup.

The mother of the sons of Zebedee came with them to make a request
of him, and bowed low; and he said to her, 'What is it you want?' She
said to him, 'Promise that these two sons of mine may sit one at your
right hand and the other at your left in your kingdom.' 'You do not

know what you are asking' Jesus answered. 'Can you drink the cup that I am going to drink?' They replied, 'We can.' 'Very well,' he said 'you shall drink my cup, but as for seats at my right hand and my left, these are not mine to grant; they belong to those to whom they have been allotted by my Father.'

When the other ten heard this they were indignant with the two brothers. But Jesus called them to him and said, 'You know that among the pagans the rulers lord it over them, and their great men make their authority felt. This is not to happen among you. No; anyone who wants to be great among you must be your servant, and anyone who wants to be first among you must be your slave, just as the Son of Man came not to be served but to serve, and to give his life as a ransom for many.'

This is the Gospel of the Lord.

26 July

Ss Joachim and Anne
parents of the Blessed Virgin Mary   Memorial

FIRST READING

A reading from the book of Ecclesiasticus   44:1. 10-15

Their name lives on for all generations.

Let us praise illustrious men,
our ancestors in their successive generations.
Here is a list of generous men
whose good works have not been forgotten.
In their descendants there remains
a rich inheritance born of them.
Their descendants stand by the covenants
and, thanks to them, so do their children's children.
Their offspring will last for ever,
their glory will not fade.
Their bodies have been buried in peace,
and their name lives on for all generations.
The peoples will proclaim their wisdom,
the assembly will celebrate their praises.

This is the word of the Lord.

Responsorial Psalm   Ps 131:11.13-14. 17-18. ℟ Lk 1:32

  ℟   God will give him the throne of David, his father.

1   The Lord swore an oath to David;
     he will not go back on his word:
     'A son, the fruit of your body,
     will I set upon your throne.'   ℟

2   For the Lord has chosen Zion;
     he has desired it for his dwelling:
     'This is my resting-place for ever,
     here have I chosen to live.   ℟

3   'There David's stock will flower:
     I will prepare a lamp for my anointed.
     I will cover his enemies with shame
     but on him my crown shall shine.'   ℟

Gospel Acclamation   cf. Lk 2:25

   Alleluia, alleluia!
   They yearned for the comforting of Israel,
   and the Holy Spirit dwelt in them.
   Alleluia!

GOSPEL

A reading from the holy Gospel according to Matthew   13:16-17

Many prophets and just people have longed to see what you see.

Jesus said to his disciples: 'Happy are your eyes because they see, your ears because they hear! I tell you solemnly, many prophets and holy men longed to see what you see, and never saw it; to hear what you hear, and never heard it.'

     This is the Gospel of the Lord.

29 July

St Martha

The Gospel is proper to this memorial. Common of holy men and women.

FIRST READING

A reading from the first letter of St John 4:7–16

If we love one another, God will live in us.

My dear people,
let us love one another
since love comes from God
and everyone who loves is begotten by God and knows God.
Anyone who fails to love can never have known God,
because God is love.
God's love for us was revealed
when God sent into the world his only Son
so that we could have life through him:
this is the love I mean:
not our love for God,
but God's love for us when he sent his Son
to be the sacrifice that takes our sins away.
My dear people,
since God has loved us so much,
we too should love one another.
No one has ever seen God;
but as long as we love one another
God will live in us
and his love will be complete in us.
We can know that we are living in him
and he is living in us
because he lets us share his Spirit.
We ourselves saw and we testify
that the Father sent his Son
as saviour of the world.
If anyone acknowledges that Jesus is the Son of God,
God lives in him, and he in God.
We ourselves have known and put our faith in
God's love towards ourselves.

God is love
and anyone who lives in love lives in God,
and God lives in him.

This is the word of the Lord.

Responsial Psalm   Ps 33:2-11. ℟ v.2. Alt. ℟ v.9

℟   I will bless the Lord at all times.

or

℟   Taste and see the goodness of the Lord.

1   I will bless the Lord at all times,
     his praise always on my lips;
     in the Lord my soul shall make its boast.
     The humble shall hear and be glad.   ℟

2   Glorify the Lord with me.
     Together let us praise his name.
     I sought the Lord and he answered me;
     from all my terrors he set me free.   ℟

3   Look towards him and be radiant;
     let your faces not be abashed.
     This poor man called; the Lord heard him
     and rescued him from all his distress.   ℟

4   The angel of the Lord is encamped
     around those who revere him, to rescue them.
     Taste and see that the Lord is good.
     He is happy who seeks refuge in him.   ℟

5   Revere the Lord, you his saints.
     They lack nothing, those who revere him.
     Strong lions suffer want and go hungry
     but those who seek the Lord lack no blessing.   ℟

Gospel Acclamation   Jn 8:12

     Alleluia, alleluia!
     I am the light of the world, says the Lord;
     whoever follows me will have the light of life.
     Alleluia!

GOSPEL

A reading from the holy Gospel according to John   11:19-27

I have believed that you are the Christ, the Son of the living God.

Many Jews had come to Martha and Mary to sympathise with them over their brother. When Martha heard that Jesus had come she went to meet him. Mary remained sitting in the house. Martha said to Jesus, 'If you had been here, my brother would not have died, but I know that, even now, whatever you ask of God, he will grant you.' 'Your brother' said Jesus to her 'will rise again.' Martha said, 'I know he will rise again at the resurrection on the last day.' Jesus said:

'I am the resurrection and the life.
If anyone believes in me, even though he dies he will live,
and whoever lives and believes in me
will never die.
Do you believe this?'

'Yes, Lord,' she said 'I believe that you are the Christ, the Son of God, the one who has to come into this world.'

This is the Gospel of the Lord.

Alternative Gospel

A reading from the holy Gospel according to Luke   10:38-42

Martha, Martha, you worry and fret about so many things.

Jesus came to a village, and a woman named Martha welcomed him into her house. She had a sister called Mary, who sat down at the Lord's feet and listened to him speaking. Now Martha who was distracted with all the serving said, 'Lord, do you not care that my sister is leaving me to do the serving all by myself? Please tell her to help me.' But the Lord answered: 'Martha, Martha' he said 'you worry and fret about so many things, and yet few are needed, indeed only one. It is Mary who has chosen the better part; it is not to be taken from her.'

This is the Gospel of the Lord.

---

30 July

St Peter Chrysologus,
bishop and doctor of the Church

Optional Memorial

Common of pastors or Common of doctors of the Church.

FIRST READING

A reading from the letter of St Paul to the Ephesians   3:8-12

The mission is to proclaim to all peoples the infinite treasure of Christ.

I, who am less than the least of all the saints, have been entrusted with this special grace, not only of proclaiming to the pagans the infinite treasure of Christ but also of explaining how the mystery is to be dispensed. Through all the ages, this has been kept hidden in God, the creator of everything. Why? So that the Sovereignties and Powers should learn only now, through the Church, how comprehensive God's wisdom really is, exactly according to the plan which he had had from all eternity in Christ Jesus our Lord. This is why we are bold enough to approach God in complete confidence, through our faith in him.

This is the word of the Lord.

Responsorial Psalm   Ps 118:9-14. ℟ v.12

℟   Lord, teach me your decrees.

1   How shall the young remain sinless?
     By obeying your word.
     I have sought you with all my heart:
     let me not stray from your commands.   ℟

2   I treasure your promise in my heart
     lest I sin against you.
     Blessed are you, O Lord;
     teach me your statutes.   ℟

3   With my tongue I have recounted
     the decrees of your lips.
     I rejoiced to do your will
     as though all riches were mine.   ℟

Gospel Acclamation

Jn 15:5

Alleluia, alleluia!
I am the vine and you are the branches, says the Lord:
he who lives in me, and I in him, will bear much fruit.
Alleluia!

GOSPEL

A reading from the holy Gospel according to Luke

6:43-45

What a person says, comes from what is in the heart.

Jesus said to his disciples: 'There is no sound tree that produces rotten fruit, nor again a rotten tree that produces sound fruit. For every tree can be told by its own fruit: people do not pick figs from thorns, nor gather grapes from brambles. A good man draws what is good from the store of goodness in his heart; a bad man draws what is bad from the store of badness. For a man's words flow out of what fills his heart.

This is the Gospel of the Lord.

31 July

St Ignatius of Loyola, priest

Memorial

Common of pastors or Common of holy men and women: for religious.

FIRST READING

A reading from the first letter of St Paul
to the Corinthians

10:31–11:1

Do all things for the glory of God.

Whatever you eat, whatever you drink, whatever you do at all, do it for the glory of God. Never do anything offensive to anyone – to Jews or Greeks or to the Church of God; just as I try to be helpful to everyone at all times, not anxious for my own advantage but for the advantage of everybody else, so that they may be saved.

Take me for your model, as I take Christ.

This is the word of the Lord.

Responsorial Psalm   Ps 33:2-11. ℟ v.2. Alt. ℟ v.9

> ℟   I will bless the Lord at all times.

or

> ℟   Taste and see the goodness of the Lord.

1   I will bless the Lord at all times,
    his praise always on my lips;
    in the Lord my soul shall make its boast.
    the humble shall hear and be glad.   ℟

2   Glorify the Lord with me.
    Together let us praise his name.
    I sought the Lord and he answered me;
    from all my terrors he set me free.   ℟

3   Look towards him and be radiant;
    let your faces not be abashed.
    This poor man called; the Lord heard him
    and rescued him from all his distress.   ℟

4   The angel of the Lord is encamped
    around those who revere him, to rescue them.
    Taste and see that the Lord is good.
    He is happy who seeks refuge in him.   ℟

5   Revere the Lord, you his saints.
    They lack nothing, those who revere him.
    Strong lions suffer want and go hungry
    but those who seek the Lord lack no blessing.   ℟

Gospel Acclamation   Mt 5:3

> Alleluia, alleluia!
> Happy the poor in spirit;
> the kingdom of heaven is theirs!
> Alleluia!

GOSPEL

A reading from the holy Gospel according to Luke   14:25-33

Unless you are ready to give up all that you possess, you cannot be my disciples.

Great crowds accompanied Jesus on his way and he turned and spoke to them. 'If any man comes to me without hating his father, mother, wife, children, brothers, sisters, yes and his own life too, he cannot be my disciple. Anyone who does not carry his cross and come after me cannot be my disciple.

'And indeed, which of you here, intending to build a tower, would not first sit down and work out the cost to see if he had enough to complete it? Otherwise, if he laid the foundation and then found himself unable to finish the work, the onlookers would all start making fun of him and saying, "Here is a man who started to build and was unable to finish." Or again, what king marching to war against another king would not first sit down and consider whether with ten thousand men he could stand up to the other who advanced against him with twenty thousand? If not, then while the other king was still a long way off, he would send envoys to sue for peace. So in the same way, none of you can be my disciple unless he gives up all his possessions.'

This is the Gospel of the Lord.

AUGUST

1 August

St Alphonsus Liguori,
bishop and doctor of the Church   Memorial

Common of pastors or Common of doctors of the Church.

FIRST READING

A reading from the letter of St Paul to the Romans   8:1-4

*The law of the spirit of life in Christ Jesus has set me free from the
law of sin and death.*

The reason why those who are in Christ Jesus are not condemned,
is that the law of the spirit of life in Christ Jesus has set you free
from the law of sin and death. God has done what the law, because
of our unspiritual nature, was unable to do. God dealt with sin by
sending his own Son in a body as physical as any sinful body, and in
that body God condemned sin. He did this in order that the Law's
just demands might be satisfied in us, who behave not as our
unspiritual nature but as the spirit dictates.

This is the word of the Lord.

Responsorial Psalm   Ps 118:9-14. ℟ v.12

℟   Lord, teach me your decrees.

1   How shall the young remain sinless?
     By obeying your word.
     I have sought you with all my heart:
     let me not stray from your commands.   ℟

2   I treasure your promise in my heart
     lest I sin against you.
     Blessed are you, O Lord;
     teach me your statutes.   ℟

3   With my tongue I have recounted
     the decreees of your lips.
     I rejoiced to do your will
     as though all riches were mine.   ℟

Gospel Acclamation   Mt 5:16

Alleluia, alleluia!
Let your light shine before all
that they may see your good works and glorify your Father.
Alleluia!

GOSPEL

A reading from the holy Gospel according to Matthew   5:13-19

You are the light of the world.

Jesus said to his disciples: 'You are the salt of the earth. But if salt becomes tasteless, what can make it salty again? It is good for nothing, and can only be thrown out to be trampled underfoot by men.

'You are the light of the world. A city built on a hill-top cannot be hidden. No one lights a lamp to put it under a tub; they put it on the lamp-stand where it shines for everyone in the house. In the same way your light must shine in the sight of men, so that, seeing your good works, they may give the praise to your Father in heaven.

'Do not imagine that I have come to abolish the Law or the Prophets. I have come not to abolish but to complete them. I tell you solemnly, till heaven and earth disappear, not one dot, not one little stroke, shall disappear from the Law until its purpose is achieved. Therefore, the man who infringes even one of the least of these commandments and teaches others to do the same will be considered the least in the kingdom of heaven; but the man who keeps them and teaches them will be considered great in the kingdom of heaven.'

This is the Gospel of the Lord.

2 August

St Eusebius of Vercelli, bishop

Optional Memorial

Common of pastors.

FIRST READING

A reading from the first letter of St John   5:1-5

This is the victory over the world – our faith.

Whoever believes that Jesus is the Christ
has been begotten by God;
and whoever loves the Father that begot him
loves the child whom he begets.
We can be sure that we love God's children
if we love God himself and do what he has commanded us;
this is what loving God is –
keeping his commandments;
and his commandments are not difficult,
because anyone who has been begotten by God
has already overcome the world;
this is the victory over the world –
our faith.
Who can overcome the world?
Only the man who believes that Jesus is the Son of God.

This is the word of the Lord.

Responsorial Psalm   Ps 88:2-5. 21-22. 25. 27. ℟ cf. v.2

℟   For ever I will sing the goodness of the Lord.

1   I will sing for ever of your love, O Lord;
     through all ages my mouth will proclaim your truth.
     Of this I am sure, that your love lasts for ever,
     that your truth is firmly established as the heavens.   ℟

2   'I have made a covenant with my chosen one;
     I have sworn to David my servant:
     I will establish your dynasty for ever
     and set up your throne through all ages.   ℟

3   'I have found David my servant
     and with my holy oil anointed him.

My hand shall always be with him
and my arm shall make him strong. ℟

4 'My truth and my love shall be with him;
by my name his might shall be exalted.
He will say to me: "You are my father,
my God, the rock who saves me." ' ℟

Gospel Acclamation   Mt 5:3

Alleluia, alleluia!
Happy the poor in spirit;
the kingdom of heaven is theirs!
Alleluia!

GOSPEL

A reading from the holy Gospel according to Matthew   5:1-12

Rejoice and be glad, for your reward will be great in heaven.

Seeing the crowds, Jesus went up the hill. There he sat down and was
joined by his disciples. Then he began to speak. This is what he taught
them:

'How happy are the poor in spirit;
theirs is the kingdom of heaven.
Happy the gentle:
they shall have the earth for their heritage.
Happy those who mourn:
they shall be comforted.
Happy those who hunger and thirst for what is right:
they shall be satisfied.
Happy the merciful:
they shall have mercy shown them.
Happy the pure in heart:
they shall see God.
Happy the peacemakers:
they shall be called sons of God.
Happy those who are persecuted in the cause of right:
theirs is the kingdom of heaven.

'Happy are you when people abuse you and persecute you and

speak all kinds of calumny against you on my account. Rejoice and be glad, for your reward will be great in heaven.'

This is the Gospel of the Lord.

4 August

St John Vianney, priest   Memorial

Common of pastors.

FIRST READING

A reading from the prophet Ezekiel   3:16-21

I have appointed you as sentry to the house of Israel.

The word of the Lord was addressed to me as follows, 'Son of man, I have appointed you as sentry to the House of Israel. Whenever you hear a word from me, warn them in my Name. If I say to a wicked man: You are to die, and you do not warn him; if you do not speak and warn him to renounce his evil ways and so live, then he shall die for his sin, but I will hold you responsible for his death. If, however, you do warn a wicked man and he does not renounce his wickedness and his evil ways, then he shall die for his sin, but you yourself will have saved your life. When the upright man renounces his integrity to do evil and I set a trap for him, he too shall die; since you failed to warn him, he shall die for his sin and the integrity he practised will no longer be remembered; but I will hold you responsible for his death. If, however, you warn the upright man not to sin and he abstains from sinning, he shall live, thanks to your warning, and you too will have saved your life.'

This is the word of the Lord.

Responsorial Psalm   Ps 116. ℟ Mk 16:15

℟   Go out to all the world, and tell the Good News.

or

℟   Alleluia!

1   O praise the Lord, all you nations,
        acclaim him all you peoples!   ℟

2   Strong his love for us;
    he is faithful for ever. ℟

Gospel Acclamation   Lk 4:18

Alleluia, alleluia!
The Lord sent me to bring Good News to the poor,
and freedom to prisoners.
Alleluia!

GOSPEL

A reading from the holy Gospel according to Matthew   9:35–10:1

When he saw the crowds, he had compassion for them.

Jesus made a tour through all the towns and villages, teaching in their synagogues, proclaiming the Good News of the kingdom and curing all kinds of diseases and sickness.

And when he saw the crowds he felt sorry for them because they were harassed and dejected, like sheep without a shepherd. Then he said to his disciples, 'The harvest is rich but the labourers are few, so ask the Lord of the harvest to send labourers to his harvest.'

He summoned his twelve disciples, and gave them authority over unclean spirits with power to cast them out and to cure all kinds of diseases and sickness.

This is the Gospel of the Lord.

5 August

The Dedication of the Basilica of St Mary Major

Optional Memorial

Common of the Blessed Virgin Mary.

FIRST READING

A reading from the book of the Apocalypse   21:1-5

I saw the new Jerusalem, as beautiful as a bride all dressed for her husband.

I, John, saw a new heaven and a new earth; the first heaven and the first earth had disappeared now, and there was no longer any sea. I saw the holy city, and the new Jerusalem, coming down from

God out of heaven, as beautiful as a bride all dressed for her husband. Then I heard a loud voice call from the throne, 'You see this city? Here God lives among men. He will make his home among them; they shall be his people, and he will be their God; his name is God-with-them. He will wipe away all tears from their eyes; there will be no more death, and no more mourning or sadness. The world of the past has gone.'

Then the One sitting on the throne spoke: 'Now I am making the whole of creation new.'

This is the word of the Lord.

Responsorial Psalm   Jud 13:18-19. ℟ 15:9

℟   You are the highest honour of our race!

1   May you be blessed, my daughter, by God Most High,
    beyond all women on earth;
    and may the Lord God be blessed,
    the Creator of heaven and earth.   ℟

2   The trust you have shown
    shall not pass from the memories of men,
    but shall ever remind them
    of the power of God.   ℟

Gospel Acclamation   Lk 11:28

    Alleluia, alleluia!
    Blessed are they who hear the word of God
    and keep it.
    Alleluia!

GOSPEL

A reading from the holy Gospel according to Luke   11:27-28

Happy the womb that bore you!

As Jesus was speaking, a woman in the crowd raised her voice and said, 'Happy the womb that bore you and the breasts you sucked!' But he replied, 'Still happier those who hear the word of God and keep it!'

This is the Gospel of the Lord.

6 August
THE TRANSFIGURATION OF THE LORD   Feast

FIRST READING

A reading from the book of Daniel   7:9-10. 13-14

His raiment was as white as snow.

As I watched:
Thrones were set in place
and one of great age took his seat.
His robe was white as snow,
the hair of his head as pure as wool.
His throne was a blaze of flames,
its wheels were a burning fire.
A stream of fire poured out,
issuing from his presence.
A thousand thousand waited on him,
ten thousand times ten thousand stood before him.
A court was held and the books were opened.
I gazed into the visions of the night.
And I saw, coming on the clouds of heaven,
one like a son of man.
He came to the one of great age
and was led into his presence.
On him was conferred sovereignty,
glory and kingship,
and men of all peoples, nations and languages became his servants.
His sovereignty is an eternal sovereignty
which shall never pass away,
nor will his empire ever be destroyed.

This is the word of the Lord.

Responsorial Psalm   Ps 96:1-2. 5-6. 9. ℟ vv.1. 9

℟   The Lord is king, the most high over all the earth.

1   The Lord is king, let earth rejoice,
      let all the coastlands be glad.
      Cloud and darkness are his raiment;
      his throne, justice and right.   ℟

2 The mountains melt like wax
   before the Lord of all the earth.
   the skies proclaim his justice;
   all peoples see his glory.

   ℟ The Lord is king, the most high over all the earth.

3 For you indeed are the Lord
   most high above all the earth
   exalted far above all spirits. ℟

SECOND READING

A reading from the second letter of St Peter   1:16-19

We heard this voice from out of heaven.

It was not any cleverly invented myths that we were repeating when
we brought you the knowledge of the power and the coming of our
Lord Jesus Christ; we had seen his majesty for ourselves. He was
honoured and glorified by God the Father, when the Sublime Glory
itself spoke to him and said, 'This is my Son, the Beloved; he enjoys
my favour.' We heard this ourselves, spoken from heaven, when we
were with him on the holy mountain.

So we have confirmation of what was said in prophecies; and you
will be right to depend on prophecy and take it as a lamp for lighting a
way through the dark until the dawn comes and the morning star
rises in your minds.

This is the word of the Lord.

Gospel Acclamation   Mt 17:5

Alleluia, alleluia!
This is my Son, my beloved, in whom is all my delight:
listen to him.
Alleluia!

Year A

GOSPEL

A reading from the holy Gospel according to Matthew   17:1-9

His face was shining like the sun.

Jesus took with him Peter and James and his brother John and led them up a high mountain where they could be alone. There in their presence he was transfigured: his face shone like the sun and his clothes became as white as the light. Suddenly Moses and Elijah appeared to them; they were talking with him. Then Peter spoke to Jesus. 'Lord,' he said 'it is wonderful for us to be here; if you wish, I will make three tents here, one for you, one for Moses and one for Elijah.' He was still speaking when suddenly a bright cloud covered them with shadow, and from the cloud there came a voice which said, 'This is my Son, the Beloved; he enjoys my favour. Listen to him.' When they heard this, the disciples fell on their faces, overcome with fear. But Jesus came up and touched them. 'Stand up,' he said 'do not be afraid.' And when they raised their eyes they saw no one but only Jesus.

As they came down from the mountain Jesus gave them this order. 'Tell no one about the vision until the Son of Man has risen from the dead.'

This is the Gospel of the Lord.

Year B

GOSPEL

A reading from the holy Gospel according to Mark   9:2-10

This is my Son, the Beloved.

Jesus took with him Peter and James and John and led them up a high mountain where they could be alone by themselves. There in their presence he was transfigured; his clothes became dazzlingly white, whiter than any earthly bleacher could make them. Elijah appeared to them with Moses; and they were talking with Jesus. Then Peter spoke to Jesus: 'Rabbi,' he said 'it is wonderful for us to be here; so let us make three tents, one for you, one for Moses and one for Elijah.' He did not know what to say; they were so frightened. And a cloud came, covering them in shadow; and there came a voice from the cloud, 'This is my Son, the Beloved. Listen to him.' Then suddenly, when they looked round, they saw no one with them any more but only Jesus.

As they came down from the mountain he warned them to tell no one what they had seen, until after the Son of Man had risen from the dead. They observed the warning faithfully, though among them-selves they discussed what 'rising from the dead' could mean.

This is the Gospel of the Lord.

Year C

GOSPEL

A reading from the holy Gospel according to Luke   9:28-36

As he prayed the aspect of his face was changed.

Jesus took with him Peter and John and James and went up the mountain to pray. As he prayed, the aspect of his face was changed and his clothing became brilliant as lightning. Suddenly there were two men there talking to him; they were Moses and Elijah appearing in glory, and they were speaking of his passing which he was to accomplish in Jerusalem. Peter and his companions were heavy with sleep, but they kept awake and saw his glory and the two men standing with him. As these were leaving him, Peter said to Jesus, 'Master, it is wonderful for us to be here; so let us make three tents, one for you, one for Moses and one for Elijah.' – He did not know what he was saying. As he spoke, a cloud came and covered them with shadow; and when they went into the cloud the disciples were afraid. And a voice came from the cloud, saying, 'This is my Son, the Chosen One. Listen to him.' And after the voice had spoken, Jesus was found alone. The disciples kept silence and, at that time, told no one what they had seen.

This is the Gospel of the Lord.

7 August

Ss Sixtus II, pope and martyr, and companions, martyrs   Optional Memorial

Common of martyrs.

FIRST READING

A reading from the book of Wisdom   3:1-9

He accepted them as a holocaust.

The souls of the virtuous are in the hands of God,
no torment shall ever touch them.
In the eyes of the unwise, they did appear to die,
their going looked like a disaster,
their leaving us, like annihilation;
but they are in peace.
If they experienced punishment as men see it,
their hope was rich with immortality;
slight was their affliction, great will their blessings be.
God has put them to the test
and proved them worthy to be with him;
he has tested them like gold in a furnace,
and accepted them as a holocaust.
When the time comes for his visitation they will shine out;
as sparks run through the stubble, so will they.
They shall judge nations, rule over peoples,
and the Lord will be their king for ever.
They who trust in him will understand the truth,
those who are faithful will live with him in love;
for grace and mercy await those he has chosen.

This is the word of the Lord.

Responsorial Psalm   Ps 125. ℟ v.5

℟   Those who sow in tears, shall reap with shouts of joy.

1   When the Lord delivered Zion from bondage,
      it seemed like a dream.
      Then was our mouth filled with laughter,
      on our lips there were songs.   ℟

2 The heathens themselves said: 'What marvels
the Lord worked for them!'
What marvels the Lord worked for us!
Indeed we were glad.

℟ Those who sow in tears, shall reap with shouts of joy.

3 Deliver us, O Lord, from our bondage
as streams in dry land.
Those who are sowing in tears
will sing when they reap. ℟

4 They go out, they go out, full of tears,
carrying seed for the sowing:
they come back, they come back, full of song,
carrying their sheaves. ℟

Gospel Acclamation   James 1:12

Alleluia, alleluia!
Blessed are they who stand firm when trials come;
when they have stood the test, they will win the crown of life.
Alleluia!

GOSPEL

A reading from the holy Gospel according to Matthew   10:28-33

Do not fear those who kill the body.

Jesus said to his apostles: 'Do not be afraid of those who kill the body
but cannot kill the soul; fear him rather who can destroy both body
and soul in hell. Can you not buy two sparrows for a penny? And yet
not one falls to the ground without your Father knowing. Why, every
hair on your head has been counted. So there is no need to be afraid;
you are worth more than hundreds of sparrows.

'So if anyone declares himself for me in the presence of men, I will
declare myself for him in the presence of my Father in heaven. But
the one who disowns me in the presence of men, I will disown in the
presence of my Father in heaven.'

This is the Gospel of the Lord.

Also 7 August

St Cajetan, priest   Optional Memorial

Common of pastors or Common of holy men and women: for religious.

FIRST READING

A reading from the book of Ecclesiasticus   2:7-13

You who fear the Lord, believe him, hope in him, love him.

You who fear the Lord, wait for his mercy;
do not turn aside in case you fall.
You who fear the Lord, trust him,
and you will not be baulked of your reward.
You who fear the Lord hope for good things,
for everlasting happiness and mercy.
Look at the generations of old and see:
who ever trusted in the Lord and was put to shame?

Or who ever feared him steadfastly and was left forsaken?
Or who ever called out to him, and was ignored?
For the Lord is compassionate and merciful,
he forgives sins, and saves in days of distress.

This is the word of the Lord.

Responsorial Psalm   Ps 111:1-9. ℟ v.1

℟   Happy are they who fear the Lord.

or

℟   Alleluia!

1   Happy the man who fears the Lord,
     who takes delight in his commands.
     His sons will be powerful on earth;
     the children of the upright are blessed.   ℟

2   Riches and wealth are in his house;
     his justice stands firm for ever.
     He is a light in the darkness for the upright:
     he is generous, merciful and just.   ℟

3   The good man takes pity and lends,
     he conducts his affairs with honour.

The just man will never waver:
he will be remembered for ever.

℟   Happy are they who fear the Lord.

or

℟   Alleluia!

4   He has no fear of evil news;
with a firm heart he trusts in the Lord.
With a steadfast heart he will not fear;
he will see the downfall of his foes.   ℟

5   Open-handed, he gives to the poor;
his justice stands firm for ever.
His head will be raised in glory.   ℟

Gospel Acclamation   Mt 5:3

Alleluia, alleluia!
Happy the poor in spirit;
the kingdom of heaven is theirs!
Alleluia!

GOSPEL

A reading from the holy Gospel according to Luke   12:32-34

It has pleased the Father to give you the kingdom.

Jesus said to his disciples: 'There is no need to be afraid, little flock,
for it has pleased your Father to give you the kingdom.

'Sell your possessions and give alms. Get yourselves purses that do
not wear out, treasure that will not fail you, in heaven where no thief
can reach it and no moth destroy it. For where your treasure is, there
will your heart be also.'

This is the Gospel of the Lord.

8 August

St Dominic, priest Memorial

Common of pastors: for missionaries or Common of holy men and women: for religious.

FIRST READING

A reading from the first letter of St Paul to the Corinthians   2:1-10

We teach the wisdom of God in mystery.

When I came to you, brothers, it was not with any show of oratory or philosophy, but simply to tell you what God had guaranteed. During my stay with you, the only knowledge I claimed to have was about Jesus and only about him as the crucified Christ. Far from relying on any power of my own, I came among you in great 'fear and trembling' and in my speeches and the sermons that I gave, there were none of the arguments that belong to philosophy; only a demonstration of the power of the Spirit. And I did this so that your faith should not depend on human philosophy but on the power of God.

But still we have a wisdom to offer those who have reached maturity, not a philosophy of our age, it is true, still less of the masters of our age, which are coming to their end. The hidden wisdom of God which we teach in our mysteries is the wisdom that God predestined to be for our glory before the ages began. It is a wisdom that none of the masters of this age have ever known, or they would not have crucified the Lord of Glory; we teach what scripture calls; the things that no eye has seen and no ear has heard, things beyond the mind of man, all that God has prepared for those who love him.

These are the very things that God has revealed to us through the Spirit.

This is the word of the Lord.

Responsorial Psalm   Ps 95:1-3. 7-8. 10. ℟ v.3

℟ Proclaim his marvellous deeds to all the nations.

1 O sing a new song to the Lord,
    sing to the Lord all the earth.
    O sing to the Lord, bless his name.   ℟

2   Proclaim his help day by day,
    tell among the nations his glory
    and his wonders among all the peoples.

    ℞   Proclaim his marvellous deeds to all the nations.

3   Give the Lord, you families of peoples,
    give the Lord glory and power,
    give the Lord the glory of his name.   ℞

4   Proclaim to the nations: 'God is king.'
    The world he made firm in its place;
    he will judge the peoples in fairness.   ℞

Gospel Acclamation   Jn 8:12

    Alleluia, alleluia!
    I am the light of the world, says the Lord;
    whoever follows me will have the light of life.
    Alleluia!

GOSPEL

A reading from the holy Gospel according to Luke   9:57-62

I will follow you wherever you go.

As Jesus and his disciples travelled along they met a man on the road
who said to him, 'I will follow you wherever you go.' Jesus answered,
'Foxes have holes and the birds of the air have nests, but the Son of
Man has nowhere to lay his head.'

    Another to whom he said, 'Follow me,' replied, 'Let me go and bury
my father first.' But he answered, 'Leave the dead to bury their dead;
your duty is to go and spread the news of the kingdom of God.'

    Another said, 'I will follow you, sir, but first let me go and say
good-bye to my people at home.' Jesus said to him, 'Once the hand is
laid on the plough, no one who looks back is fit for the kingdom of
God.'

    This is the Gospel of the Lord.

10 August
ST LAWRENCE, DEACON AND MARTYR   Feast

FIRST READING

A reading from the second letter of St Paul   9:6-10
to the Corinthians

God loves a cheerful giver.

Thin sowing means thin reaping; the more you sow, the more you reap.
Each one should give what he has decided in his own mind, not
grudgingly or because he is made to, for God loves a cheerful giver.
And there is no limit to the blessings which God can send you – he will
make sure that you will always have all you need for yourselves in
every possible circumstance, and still have something to spare for all
sorts of good works. As scripture says: He was free in almsgiving, and
gave to the poor: his good deeds will never be forgotten.

The one who provides seed for the sower and bread for food will
provide you with all the seed you want and make the harvest of your
good deeds a larger one.

This is the word of the Lord.

Responsorial Psalm   Ps 111:1-2. 5-9. ℟ v.5

℟   Happy the merciful who give to those in need.

1   Happy the man who fears the Lord,
    who takes delight in his commands.
    His sons will be powerful on earth;
    the children of the upright are blessed.   ℟

2   The good man takes pity and lends,
    he conducts his affairs with honour.
    The just man will never waver:
    he will be remembered for ever.   ℟

3   He has no fear of evil news;
    with a firm heart he trusts in the Lord.
    With a steadfast heart he will not fear;
    he will see the downfall of his foes.   ℟

4 Open-handed, he gives to the poor;
   his justice stands firm for ever.
   His head will be raised in glory.

   ℟ Happy the merciful who give to those in need.

Gospel Acclamation   Jn 8:12

   Alleluia, alleluia!
   I am the light of the world, says the Lord:
   whoever follows me will have the light of life.
   Alleluia!

GOSPEL

A reading from the holy Gospel according to John   12:24-26

The Father will honour all who serve me.

Jesus said to his disciples:

   'I tell you, most solemnly,
   unless a wheat grain falls on the ground and dies,
   it remains only a single grain;
   but if it dies,
   it yields a rich harvest.
   Anyone who loves his life loses it;
   anyone who hates his life in this world
   will keep it for the eternal life.
   If a man serves me, he must follow me,
   wherever I am, my servant will be there too.
   If anyone serves me, my Father will honour him.'

   This is the Gospel of the Lord.

11 August

St Clare, virgin
Memorial

Common of virgins or Common of holy men and women: for religious.

FIRST READING

A reading from the letter of St Paul to the Philippians 3:8-14

I am racing for the finish, for the prize to which God calls us upwards to receive in Christ Jesus.

I believe nothing can happen that will outweigh the supreme advantage of knowing Christ Jesus my Lord. For him I have accepted the loss of everything, and I look on everything as so much rubbish if only I can have Christ and be given a place in him. I am no longer trying for perfection by my own efforts, the perfection that comes from the Law, but I want only the perfection that comes through faith in Christ, and is from God and based on faith. All I want is to know Christ and the power of his resurrection and to share his sufferings by reproducing the pattern of his death. That is the way I can hope to take my place in the resurrection of the dead. Not that I have become perfect yet: I have not yet won, but I am still running, trying to capture the prize for which Christ Jesus captured me. I can assure you, my brothers, I am far from thinking that I have already won. All I can say is that I forget the past and I strain ahead for what is still to come; I am racing for the finish, for the prize to which God calls us upwards to receive in Christ Jesus.

This is the word of the Lord.

Responsorial Psalm
Ps 15:1-2. 5. 7-8. 11. ℟ cf. v.5

℟ You are my inheritance, O Lord.

1 Preserve me, God, I take refuge in you.
   I say to the Lord: 'You are my God.'
   O Lord, it is you who are my portion and cup;
   it is you yourself who are my prize. ℟

2 I will bless the Lord who gives me counsel,
   who even at night directs my heart.
   I keep the Lord ever in my sight:
   since he is at my right hand, I shall stand firm. ℟ (continued)

3   You will show me the path of life,
     the fullness of joy in your presence,
     at your right hand happiness for ever.

℞   You are my inheritance, O Lord.

Gospel Acclamation   Mt 5:3

     Alleluia, alleluia!
     Happy the poor in spirit;
     the kingdom of heaven is theirs!
     Alleluia!

GOSPEL

A reading from the holy Gospel according to Matthew   19:27-29

You who have left everything and followed me, will be rewarded a
hundred-fold.

Peter spoke to Jesus. 'What about us?' he said, 'We have left
everything and followed you. What are we to have, then?' Jesus said
to him, 'I tell you solemnly, when all is made new and the Son of Man
sits on his throne of glory, you will yourselves sit on twelve thrones to
judge the twelve tribes of Israel. And everyone who has left houses,
sisters, father, mother, children or land for the sake of my name will
be repaid a hundred times over, and also inherit eternal life.'

     This is the Gospel of the Lord.

13 August

Ss Pontian, pope
and Hippolytus, priest, martyrs   Optional Memorial

Common of martyrs or Common of pastors.

FIRST READING

A reading from the first letter of St Peter   4:12-19

Be glad when you are sharing in the suffering of Christ.

My dear people, you must not think it unaccountable that you should
be tested by fire. There is nothing extraordinary in what has happened to you. If you can have some share in the sufferings of Christ, be

glad, because you will enjoy a much greater gladness when his glory is revealed. It is a blessing for you when they insult you for bearing the name of Christ, because it means that you have the Spirit of glory, the Spirit of God resting on you. None of you should ever deserve to suffer for being a murderer, a thief, a criminal or an informer; but if anyone of you should suffer for being a Christian, then he is not to be ashamed of it; he should thank God that he has been called one. The time has come for the judgement to begin at the household of God; and if what we know now is only the beginning, what will it be when it comes down to those who refuse to believe God's Good News? If it is hard for a good man to be saved, what will happen to the wicked and to sinners? So even those whom God allows to suffer must trust themselves to the constancy of the creator and go on doing good.

This is the word of the Lord.

Responsorial Psalm   Ps 123:2-5. 7-8. ℟ v.7

℟   Our soul has escaped like a bird from the hunter's net.

1   If the Lord had not been on our side
    when men rose against us,
    then would they have swallowed us alive
    when their anger was kindled.   ℟

2   Then would the waters have engulfed us,
    the torrent gone over us;
    over our head would have swept
    the raging waters.   ℟

3   Indeed the snare has been broken
    and we have escaped.
    Our help is in the name of the Lord,
    who made heaven and earth.   ℟

Gospel Acclamation

    Alleluia, alleluia!
    You are God: we praise you; you are the Lord: we acclaim you;
    the white-robed army of martyrs praise you.
    Alleluia.

GOSPEL

A reading from the holy Gospel according to John 15:18-21

If they have persecuted me, they will persecute you too.

Jesus said to his disciples:

'If the world hates you,
remember that it hated me before you.
If you belonged to the world,
the world would love you as its own;
but because you do not belong to the world,
because my choice withdrew you from the world,
therefore the world hates you.
Remember the words I said to you:
A servant is not greater than his master.
If they persecuted me,
they will persecute you too;
if they kept my word
they will keep yours as well.
But it will be on my account that they will do all this,
because they do not know the one who sent me.'

This is the Gospel of the Lord.

15 August

THE ASSUMPTION OF THE BLESSED VIRGIN MARY

Solemnity

Vigil Mass

FIRST READING

A reading from the first book of Chronicles 15:3-4. 15-16; 16:1-2

*They brought in the ark of God and set it inside the tent which
David had pitched for it.*

David gathered all Israel together in Jerusalem to bring the ark of
God up to the place he had prepared for it. David called together the
sons of Aaron and the sons of Levi, and the Levites carried the ark of
God with the shafts on their shoulders, as Moses had ordered in
accordance with the word of the Lord.

David then told the heads of the Levites to assign duties for their kinsmen as cantors, with their various instruments of music, harps and lyres and cymbals, to play joyful tunes.

They brought the ark of God in and put it inside the tent that David had pitched for it; and they offered holocausts before God, and communion sacrifices. And when David had finished offering holocausts and communion sacrifices, he blessed the people in the name of the Lord.

This is the word of the Lord.

Responsorial Psalm   Ps 131:6-7. 9-10. 13-14. ℟ v.8

℟ Lord, go up to the place of your rest, you and the ark of your
    holiness.

1 At Ephrata we heard of the ark;
   we found it in the plains of Yearim.
   'Let us go to the place of his dwelling;
   let us go to kneel at his footstool.'   ℟

2 Your priests shall be clothed with holiness:
   your faithful shall ring out their joy.
   For the sake of David your servant
   do not reject your anointed.   ℟

3 For the Lord has chosen Zion;
   he has desired it for his dwelling:
   'This is my resting-place for ever,
   here have I chosen to live.'   ℟

SECOND READING

A reading from the first letter of St Paul   15:54-57
to the Corinthians

He gives us victory through Jesus Christ.

When this perishable nature has put on imperishability, and when this mortal nature has put on immortality, then the words of scripture will come true: Death is swallowed up in victory. Death, where is your victory? Death, where is your sting? Now the sting of death is sin, and sin gets its power from the Law. So let us thank God for giving us the victory through our Lord Jesus Christ.

This is the word of the Lord.

Gospel Acclamation   Lk 11:28

Alleluia, alleluia!
Blessed are they who hear the word of God
and keep it.
Alleluia!

GOSPEL

A reading from the holy Gospel according to Luke   11:27-28

Blessed is the womb that bore you.

As Jesus was speaking, a woman in the crowd raised her voice and said, 'Happy the womb that bore you and the breasts you sucked!' But he replied, 'Still happier those who hear the word of God and keep it!'

This is the Gospel of the Lord.

Mass During the Day

FIRST READING

A reading from the book of the Apocalypse   11:19; 12:1-6. 10

I saw a woman clothed with the sun and with the moon beneath her feet.

The sanctuary of God in heaven opened, and the ark of the covenant could be seen inside it. Now a great sign appeared in heaven: a woman, adorned with the sun, standing on the moon, and with the twelve stars on her head for a crown. She was pregnant, and in labour, crying aloud in the pangs of childbirth. Then a second sign appeared in the sky, a huge red dragon which had seven heads and ten horns, and each of the seven heads crowned with a coronet. Its tail dragged a third of the stars from the sky and dropped them to the earth, and the dragon stopped in front of the woman as she was having the child, so that he could eat it as soon as it was born from its mother. The woman brought a male child into the world, the son who was to rule all the nations with an iron sceptre, and the child was taken straight up to God and to his throne, while the woman escaped into the desert, where God had made a place of safety ready. Then I heard a voice shout from heaven, 'Victory and power and empire for ever have been won by our God, and all authority for his Christ.'

This is the word of the Lord.

Responsorial Psalm   Ps 44:10-12. 16. ℟ v.10

> ℟   The queen stands at your right hand, arrayed in gold.

1   The daughters of kings are among your loved ones.
     On your right stands the queen in gold of Ophir.
     Listen, O daughter, give ear to my words:
     forget your own people and your father's house.   ℟

2   So will the king desire your beauty:
     He is your lord, pay homage to him.
     They are escorted amid gladness and joy;
     they pass within the palace of the king.   ℟

SECOND READING

A reading from the first letter of St Paul   15:20-26
to the Corinthians

> *As members of Christ all people will be raised, Christ first, and*
> *after him all who belong to him.*

Christ has been raised from the dead, the first-fruits of all who have
fallen asleep. Death came through one man and in the same way the
resurrection of the dead has come through one man. Just as all men
die in Adam, so all men will be brought to life in Christ; but all of
them in their proper order; Christ as the first-fruits and then, after
the coming of Christ, those who belong to him. After that will come
the end, when he hands over the kingdom to God the Father, having
done away with every sovereignty, authority and power. For he must
be king until he has put all his enemies under his feet and the last of
the enemies to be destroyed is death, for everything is to be put under
his feet.

     This is the word of the Lord.

Gospel Acclamation

     Alleluia, alleluia!
     Mary is taken up to heaven,
     and the angels of God shout for joy.
     Alleluia!

GOSPEL

A reading from the holy Gospel according to Luke   1:39-56

The Almighty has done great things for me; he has lifted up the lowly.

Mary set out and went as quickly as she could to a town in the hill country of Judah. She went into Zechariah's house and greeted Elizabeth. Now as soon as Elizabeth heard Mary's greeting, the child leapt in her womb and Elizabeth was filled with the Holy Spirit. She gave a loud cry and said, 'Of all women you are the most blessed, and blessed is the fruit of your womb. Why should I be honoured with a visit from the mother of my Lord? For the moment your greeting reached my ears, the child in my womb leapt for joy. Yes, blessed is she who believed that the promise made her by the Lord would be fulfilled.'

And Mary said:

'My soul proclaims the greatness of the Lord
and my spirit exults in God my saviour;
because he has looked upon his lowly handmaid.
Yes, from this day forward all generations will call me blessed,
for the Almighty has done great things for me.
Holy is his name,
and his mercy reaches from age to age for those who fear him.
He has shown the power of his arm,
he has routed the proud of heart.
He has pulled down princes from their thrones and exalted the lowly.
The hungry he has filled with good things, the rich sent empty away.
He has come to the help of Israel his servant, mindful of his mercy
– according to the promise he made to our ancestors –
of his mercy to Abraham and to his descendants for ever.'

Mary stayed with Elizabeth about three months and then went back home.

This is the Gospel of the Lord.

16 August

St Stephen of Hungary   Optional Memorial

Common of holy men and women.

FIRST READING

A reading from the book of Deuteronomy   6:3-9

Love the Lord your God with your whole heart.

Moses said to the people:

'Listen Israel, keep and observe what will make you prosper and give you great increase, as the Lord, the God of your fathers has promised you, giving you a land where milk and honey flow.

'Listen, Israel: the Lord our God is the one Lord. You shall love the Lord your God with all your heart, with all your soul, with all your strength. Let these words I urge on you today be written on your heart. You shall repeat them to your children and say them over to them whether at rest in your house or walking abroad, at your lying down or at your rising; you shall fasten them on your hand as a sign and on your forehead as a circlet; you shall write them on the doorposts of your house and on your gates.'

This is the word of the Lord.

Responsorial Psalm   Ps 111:1-9. ℟ v.1

℟   Happy are those who fear the Lord.

or

℟   Alleluia!

1   Happy the man who fears the Lord,
       who takes delight in his commands.
       His sons will be powerful on earth;
       the children of the upright are blessed.   ℟

2   Riches and wealth are in his house;
       his justice stands firm for ever.
       He is a light in the darkness for the upright:
       he is generous, merciful and just.   ℟   (continued)

3   The good man takes pity and lends,
    he conducts his affairs with honour.
    The just man will never waver:
    he will be remembered for ever.

    ℟   Happy are those who fear the Lord.

or

    ℟   Alleluia!

4   He has no fear of evil news;
    with a firm heart he trusts in the Lord.
    With a steadfast heart he will not fear;
    he will see the downfall of his foes.   ℟

5   Open-handed he gives to the poor;
    his justice stands firm for ever.
    His head will be raised in glory.   ℟

Gospel Acclamation   Jn 14:23

    Alleluia, alleluia!
    All who love me will keep my words
    and my Father will love them, and we will come to them.
    Alleluia!

GOSPEL

A reading from the holy Gospel according to Matthew   25:14-30

Because you have been faithful in a few things, enter into the joy of your Lord.

Jesus spoke this parable to his disciples: 'A man on his way abroad
summoned his servants and entrusted his property to them. To one he
gave five talents, to another two, to a third, one; each in proportion to
his ability. Then he set out. The man who had received the five talents
promptly went and traded with them and made five more. The man
who had received two made two more in the same way. But the man
who had received one went off and dug a hole in the ground and hid
his master's money. Now a long time after, the master of those
servants came back and went through his accounts with them. The
man who had received the five talents came forward bringing five
more. "Sir," he said, "you entrusted me with five talents; here are five

more that I have made." His master said to him, "Well done, good and faithful servant; you have shown you can be faithful in small things, I will trust you with greater; come and join in your master's happiness." Next the man with the two talents came forward. "Sir," he said, "you entrusted me with two talents; here are two more that I have made." His master said to him, "Well done, good and faithful servant; you have shown you can be faithful in small things, I will trust you with greater; come and join in your master's happiness."

Last came forward the man who had the one talent. "Sir," said he, "I had heard you were a hard man, reaping where you have not sown and gathering where you have not scattered; so I was afraid, and I went off and hid your talent in the ground. Here it is; it was yours, you have it back." But his master answered him, "You wicked and lazy servant! So you knew that I reap where I have not sown and gather where I have not scattered? Well then, you should have deposited my money with the bankers, and on my return I would have recovered my capital with interest. So now, take the talent from him and give it to the man who has the five talents. For to everyone who has will be given more, and he will have more than enough; but from the man who has not, even what he has will be taken away. As for this good-for-nothing servant, throw him out into the dark, where there will be weeping and grinding of teeth." '

This is the Gospel of the Lord.

Shorter form

A reading from the holy Gospel according to Matthew   25:14-23

Because you have been faithful in a few things, enter into the joy of your Lord.

Jesus spoke this parable to his disciples: 'A man on his way abroad summoned his servants and entrusted his property to them. To one he gave five talents, to another two, to a third, one; each in proportion to his ability. Then he set out. The man who had received the five talents promptly went and traded with them and made five more. The man who had received two made two more in the same way. But the man who had received one went off and dug a hole in the ground and hid his master's money. Now a long time after, the master of those servants came back and went through his accounts with them. The man who had received the five talents came forward bringing five more. "Sir," he said, "you entrusted me with five talents; here are five more that I have made." His master said to him, "Well done, good and faithful servant; you have shown you can be faithful in small things, I will trust you with greater; come and join in your master's happiness.' Next the man with the two talents came forward. "Sir," he said, "you entrusted me with two talents; here are two more that I have made." His master said to him, "Well done, good and faithful servant; you have shown you can be faithful in small things, I will trust you with greater; come and join in your master's happiness." '

This is the Gospel of the Lord.

---

19 August

St John Eudes, priest   Optional Memorial

Common of pastors or Common of holy men and women.

FIRST READING

A reading from the letter of St Paul to the Ephesians   3:14-19

To know the love of Christ, which is beyond all knowledge.

This is what I pray, kneeling before the Father, from whom every family, whether spiritual or natural, takes its name:

Out of his infinite glory, may he give you the power through his Spirit for your hidden self to grow strong, so that Christ may live in your hearts through faith, and then, planted in love and built on love, you will with all the saints have strength to grasp the breadth and the length, the height and the depth; until, knowing the love of Christ, which is beyond all knowledge, you are filled with the utter fullness of God.

This is the word of the Lord.

Responsorial Psalm   Ps 130

℟   In you, Lord, I have found my peace.

1   O Lord, my heart is not proud
      nor haughty my eyes.
      I have not gone after things too great
      nor marvels beyond me.   ℟

2   Truly I have set my soul
    in silence and peace.
    A weaned child on its mother's breast,
    even so is my soul.   ℟

3   O Israel, hope in the Lord
    both now and for ever.   ℟

Gospel Acclamation   cf. Mt 11:25

Alleluia, alleluia!
Blessed are you, Father, Lord of heaven and earth;
you have revealed to little ones the mysteries of the kingdom.
Alleluia!

GOSPEL

A reading from the holy Gospel according to Matthew   11:25-30

You have hidden these things from the learned and the clever and
revealed them to children.

Jesus exclaimed, 'I bless you, Father, Lord of heaven and of earth, for
hiding these things from the learned and the clever and revealing
them to mere children. Yes, Father, for that is what it pleased you to
do. Everything has been entrusted to me by my Father; and no one
knows the Son except the Father, just as no one knows the Father
except the Son and those to whom the Son chooses to reveal him.

'Come to me, all you who labour and are overburdened, and I will
give you rest. Shoulder my yoke and learn from me, for I am gentle
and humble in heart, and you will find rest for your souls. Yes, my
yoke is easy and my burden light.'

This is the Gospel of the Lord.

20 August

St Bernard,
abbot and doctor of the Church
Memorial

Common of doctors of the Church or Common of holy men and women: for religious.

FIRST READING

A reading from the book of Ecclesiasticus
15:1-6

He filled them with the spirit of wisdom and understanding.

Whoever fears the Lord will act like this,
and whoever grasps the Law will obtain wisdom.
She will come to meet him like a mother,
and receive him like a virgin bride.
She will give him the bread of understanding to eat,
and the water of wisdom to drink.
He will lean on her and will not fall,
he will rely on her and not be put to shame.
She will raise him high above his neighbours,
and in full assembly she will open his mouth.
He will find happiness and a crown of joy,
he will inherit an everlasting name.

This is the word of the Lord.

Responsorial Psalm
Ps 118:9-14. ℟ v.12

℟   Lord, teach me your decrees.

1   How shall the young remain sinless?
    By obeying your word.
    I have sought you with all my heart:
    let me not stray from your commands.   ℟

2   I treasure your promise in my heart
    lest I sin against you.
    Blessed are you, O Lord;
    teach me your statutes.   ℟

3   With my tongue I have recounted
    the decrees of your lips.
    I rejoiced to do your will
    as though all riches were mine.   ℟

Gospel Acclamation Jn 15:9. 5

Alleluia, alleluia!
Remain in my love, says the Lord;
all who live in me, and I in them, will bear much fruit.
Alleluia!

GOSPEL

A reading from the holy Gospel according to John 17:20-26

I want those you have given me to be with me where I am.

Jesus raised his eyes to heaven and said:

'Holy Father,
I pray not only for these,
but for those also
who through their words will believe in me.
May they all be one.
Father, may they be one in us,
as you are in me and I am in you,
so that the world may believe it was you who sent me.
I have given them the glory you gave to me,
that they may be one as we are one.
With me in them and you in me,
may they be so completely one
that the world will realise that it was you who sent me
and that I have loved them as much as you loved me.
Father,
I want those you have given me
to be with me where I am,
so that they may always see the glory
you have given me
because you loved me
before the foundation of the world.
Father, Righteous One,
the world has not known you,
but I have known you,
and these have known
that you have sent me.
I have made your name known to them
and will continue to make it known,

so that the love with which you loved me may be in them,
and so that I may be in them.'

This is the Gospel of the Lord.

21 August

St Pius X, pope   Memorial

Common of pastors: for popes.

FIRST READING

A reading from the first letter of St Paul   2:2-8
to the Thessalonians

> *We were eager to hand over to you not only the Good News but our*
> *whole lives as well.*

It was our God who gave us the courage to proclaim his Good News to
you in the face of great opposition. We have not taken to preaching
because we are deluded, or immoral, or trying to deceive anyone; it
was God who decided that we were fit to be entrusted with the Good
News, and when we are speaking, we are not trying to please men but
God, who can read our inmost thoughts. You know very well, and we
can swear it before God, that never at any time have our speeches
been simply flattery, or a cover for trying to get money; nor have we
ever looked for any special honour from men, either from you or
anybody else, when we could have imposed ourselves on you with full
weight, as apostles of Christ.

Instead, we were unassuming. Like a mother feeding and looking
after her own children, we felt so devoted and protective towards you,
and had come to love you so much, that we were eager to hand over to
you not only the Good News but our whole lives as well.

This is the word of the Lord.

Responsorial Psalm   Ps 88:2-5. 21-22. 25. 27. ℟ cf. v.2

℟ For ever I will sing the goodness of the Lord.

1   I will sing for ever of your love, O Lord;
    through all ages my mouth will proclaim your truth.
    Of this I am sure, that your love lasts for ever,
    that your truth is firmly established as the heavens.   ℟

2 'I have made a covenant with my chosen one;
   I have sworn to David my servant:
   I will establish your dynasty for ever
   and set up your throne through all ages. ℟

3 'I have found David my servant
   and with my holy oil anointed him.
   My hand shall always be with him
   and my arm shall make him strong. ℟

4 'My truth and my love shall be with him;
   by my name his might shall be exalted.
   He will say to me: "You are my father,
   my God, the rock who saves me." ' ℟

Gospel Acclamation   Jn 10:14

   Alleluia, alleluia!
   I am the good shepherd, says the Lord;
   I know my sheep, and mine know me.
   Alleluia!

GOSPEL

A reading from the holy Gospel according to John   21:15-17

Take care of my lambs and my sheep.

Jesus showed himself to his disciples, and after they had eaten he said to Simon Peter, 'Simon son of John, do you love me more than these others do?' He answered, 'Yes Lord, you know I love you.' Jesus said to him, 'Feed my lambs.' A second time he said to him, 'Simon son of John, do you love me?' He replied, 'Yes, Lord, you know I love you.' Jesus said to him, 'Look after my sheep.' Then he said to him a third time, 'Simon son of John, do you love me?' Peter was upset that he asked him the third time, 'Do you love me?' and said, 'Lord, you know everything; you know I love you.' Jesus said to him, 'Feed my sheep.'

   This is the Gospel of the Lord.

22 August

The Queenship of Mary   Memorial

Common of the Blessed Virgin Mary.

FIRST READING

A reading from the prophet Isaiah   9:1-6

A Son is born to us.

The people that walked in darkness
has seen a great light;
on those who live in a land of deep shadow
a light has shone.
You have made their gladness greater,
you have made their joy increase;
they rejoice in your presence
as men rejoice at harvest time,
as men are happy when they are dividing the spoils.

For the yoke that was weighing on him,
the bar across his shoulders,
the rod of his oppressor,
these you break as on the day of Midian.

For all the footgear of battle,
every cloak rolled in blood,
is burnt
and consumed by fire.
For there is a child born for us,
a son given to us
and dominion is laid on his shoulders;
and this is the name they give him:
Wonder-Counsellor, Mighty-God,
Eternal-Father, Prince-of-Peace.
Wide is his dominion
in a peace that has no end,
for the throne of David
and for his royal power,
which he establishes and makes secure
in justice and integrity.
From this time onwards and for ever,
the jealous love of the Lord of hosts will do this.

This is the word of the Lord.

Responsorial Psalm   Ps 112:1-8. ℟ v.2

℟   Blessed be the name of the Lord for ever.

or

℟   Alleluia!

1   Praise, O servants of the Lord,
    praise the name of the Lord!
    May the name of the Lord be blessed
    both now and for evermore!   ℟

2   From the rising of the sun to its setting
    praised be the name of the Lord!
    High above all nations is the Lord,
    above the heavens his glory.   ℟

3   Who is like the Lord, our God,
    who has risen on high to his throne
    yet stoops from the heights to look down,
    to look down upon heaven and earth?   ℟

4   From the dust he lifts up the lowly,
    from the dungheap he raises the poor
    to set him in the company of princes,
    yes, with the princes of his people.   ℟

Gospel Acclamation   cf. Lk 1:28

    Alleluia, alleluia!
    Hail, Mary, full of grace, the Lord is with you;
    blessed are you among women.
    Alleluia!

GOSPEL

A reading from the holy Gospel according to Luke   1:26-38

You will conceive and bear a son.

The angel Gabriel was sent by God to a town in Galilee called
Nazareth, to a virgin betrothed to a man named Joseph, of the
House of David; and the virgin's name was Mary. He went in and
said to her, 'Rejoice, so highly favoured! The Lord is with you.' She
was deeply disturbed by these words and asked herself what

1097

this greeting could mean, but the angel said to her, 'Mary, do not be afraid; you have won God's favour. Listen! You are to conceive and bear a son, and you must name him Jesus. He will be great and will be called Son of the Most High. The Lord God will give him the throne of his ancestor David; he will rule over the House of Jacob for ever and his reign will have no end.' Mary said to the angel, 'But how can this come about, since I am a virgin?' 'The Holy Spirit will come upon you,' the angel answered, 'and the power of the Most High will cover you with its shadow. And so the child will be holy and will be called Son of God. Know this too: your kinswoman Elizabeth has, in her old age, herself conceived a son, and she whom people called barren is now in her sixth month, for nothing is impossible to God.' 'I am the handmaid of the Lord,' said Mary, 'let what you have said be done to me.' And the angel left her.

This is the Gospel of the Lord.

23 August

St Rose of Lima, virgin   Optional Memorial

Common of virgins or Common of holy men and women: for religious.

FIRST READING

A reading from the second letter of St Paul   10:17–11:2
to the Corinthians

I have betrothed you to one man, as a chaste virgin for Christ.

If anyone wants to boast, let him boast of the Lord. It is not the man who commends himself that can be accepted, but the man who is commended by the Lord.

I only wish you were able to tolerate a little foolishness from me. But of course: you are tolerant towards me. You see, the jealousy that I feel for you is God's own jealousy: I arranged for you to marry Christ so that I might give you away as a chaste virgin to this one husband.

This is the word of the Lord.

Gospel Acclamation   Ps 148:1-2. 11-14. ℟ vv.12. 13

    ℟   Young men and women, praise the name of the Lord.

or

    ℟   Alleluia!

1   Praise the Lord from the heavens,
    praise him in the heights.
    Praise him, all his angels,
    praise him, all his host. ℟

2   All earth's kings and peoples,
    earth's princes and rulers;
    young men and maidens,
    old men together with children. ℟

3   Let them praise the name of the Lord
    for he alone is exalted.
    The splendour of his name
    reaches beyond heaven and earth. ℟

4   He exalts the strength of his people.
    He is the praise of all his saints,
    of the sons of Israel,
    of the people to whom he comes close. ℟

Gospel Acclamation   Jn 15:9.5

    Alleluia, alleluia!
    Remain in my love, says the Lord;
    whoever lives in me and I in him will bear much fruit.
    Alleluia!

GOSPEL

A reading from the holy Gospel according to Matthew   13:44-46

He sold all that he had and bought the field.

Jesus said to the crowds: 'The kingdom of heaven is like treasure hidden in a field which someone has found; he hides it again, goes off happy, sells everything he owns and buys the field.

   'Again, the kingdom of heaven is like a merchant looking for fine pearls; when he finds one of great value he goes and sells everything he owns and buys it.'

This is the Gospel of the Lord.

24 August

ST BARTHOLOMEW, APOSTLE Feast

FIRST READING

A reading from the book of the Apocalypse 21:9-14

On the foundations are the names of the twelve Apostles of the Lamb.

The angel came to speak to me, and said, 'Come here and I will show you the bride that the Lamb has married.' In the spirit he took me to the top of an enormous high mountain and showed me Jerusalem, the holy city, coming down from God out of heaven. It had all the radiant glory of God and glittered like some precious jewel of crystal-clear diamond. The walls of it were of a great height, and had twelve gates; at each of the twelve gates there was an angel, and over the gates were written the names of the twelve tribes of Israel; on the east there were three gates, on the north three gates, on the south three gates, and on the west three gates. The city walls stood on twelve foundation stones, each one of which bore the name of the one of the twelve apostles of the Lamb.

This is the word of the Lord.

Responsorial Psalm Ps 144:10-13. 17-18. ℟ cf. v.12

℟ Your friends tell the glory of your kingship, Lord.

1 All your creatures shall thank you, O Lord,
and your friends shall repeat their blessing.
They shall speak of the glory of your reign
and declare your might, O God. ℟

2 They make known to me your mighty deeds
and the glorious splendour of your reign.
Yours is an everlasting kingdom;
your rule lasts from age to age. ℟

3   The Lord is just in all his ways
    and loving in all his deeds.
    He is close to all who call him,
    who call on him from their hearts.   ℟

Gospel Acclamation   Jn 1:49

   Alleluia, alleluia!
   Master, you are the Son of God,
   you are the king of Israel.
   Alleluia!

GOSPEL

A reading from the holy Gospel according to John   1:45-51

There is a true Israelite, in whom there is no deceit.

Philip found Nathanael and said to him, 'We have found the one
Moses wrote about in the Law, the one about whom the prophets
wrote: he is Jesus son of Joseph, from Nazareth.' 'From Nazareth?'
said Nathanael. 'Can anything good come from that place?' 'Come and
see' replied Philip. When Jesus saw Nathanael coming he said of him,
'There is an Israelite who deserves the name, incapable of deceit.'
'How do you know me?' said Nathanael. 'Before Philip came to call
you,' said Jesus 'I saw you under the fig tree.' Nathanael answered,
'Rabbi, you are the Son of God, you are the King of Israel.' Jesus
replied, 'You believe that just because I said: I saw you under the fig
tree. You will see greater things than that.' And then he added, 'I tell
you most solemnly, you will see heaven laid open and, above the Son
of Man, the angels of God ascending and descending.'

   This is the Gospel of the Lord.

25 August

St Louis   Optional Memorial

Common of holy men and women.

FIRST READING

A reading from the prophet Isaiah   58:6-11

Share your bread with the hungry.

Is not this the sort of fast that pleases me
– it is the Lord who speaks –
to break unjust fetters
and undo the thongs of the yoke,

to let the oppressed go free,
and break every yoke,
to share your bread with the hungry,
and shelter the homeless poor,

to clothe the man you see to be naked
and not turn from your own kin?
Then will your light shine like the dawn
and your wound be quickly healed over.

Your integrity will go before you
and the glory of the Lord behind you.
Cry, and the Lord will answer;
call, and he will say, 'I am here.'
If you do away with the yoke,
the clenched fist, the wicked word,
if you give your bread to the hungry,
and relief to the oppressed,

your light will rise in the darkness,
and your shadows become like noon,
The Lord will always guide you,
giving you relief in desert places.

He will give strength to your bones
and shall be like a watered garden,
like a spring of water
whose waters never run dry.

This is the word of the Lord.

Responsorial Psalm   Ps 111:1-9. ℟ v.1

℟ Happy are those who fear the Lord.

or

℟ Alleluia!

1 Happy the man who fears the Lord,
   who takes delight in his commands.
   His sons will be powerful on earth;
   the children of the upright are blessed.   ℟

2 Riches and wealth are in his house;
   his justice stands firm for ever.
   He is a light in the darkness for the upright:
   he is generous, merciful and just.   ℟

3 The good man takes pity and lends,
   he conducts his affairs with honour.
   The just man will never waver:
   he will be remembered for ever.   ℟

4 He has no fear of evil news;
   with a firm heart he trusts in the Lord.
   With a steadfast heart he will not fear;
   he will see the downfall of his foes.   ℟

5 Open-handed, he gives to the poor;
   his justice stands firm for ever.
   His head will be raised in glory.   ℟

Gospel Acclamation   Jn 13:34

   Alleluia, alleluia!
   I give you a new commandment:
   love one another as I have loved you.
   Alleluia!

GOSPEL

A reading from the holy Gospel according to Matthew   22:35-40

Love the Lord your God, and your neighbour as yourself.

To disconcert Jesus, one of the Pharisees, a lawyer, put a question,
'Master, which is the greatest commandment of the Law?' Jesus said,

'You must love the Lord your God with all your heart, with all your soul, and with all your mind. This is the greatest and the first commandment. The second resembles it: You must love your neighbour as yourself. On these two commandments hang the whole Law, and the Prophets also.'

This is the Gospel of the Lord.

Also 25 August

St Joseph Calasanz, priest   Optional Memorial

Common of pastors or Common of holy men and women: for teachers.

FIRST READING

A reading from the first letter of St Paul   12:31–13:13
to the Corinthians

Love never ends.

Be ambitious for the higher gifts. And I am going to show you a way that is better than any of them.

If I have all the eloquence of men or of angels, but speak without love, I am simply a gong booming or a cymbal clashing. If I have the gift of prophecy, understanding all the mysteries there are, and knowing everything, and if I have faith in all its fullness, to move mountains, but without love, then I am nothing at all. If I give away all that I possess, piece by piece, and if I even let them take my body to burn it, but am without love, it will do me no good whatever.

Love is always patient and kind; it is never jealous; love is never boastful or conceited; it is never rude or selfish; it does not take offence, and is not resentful. Love takes no pleasure in other people's sins but delights in the truth; it is always ready to excuse, to trust, to hope, and to endure whatever comes.

Love does not come to an end. But if there are gifts of prophecy, the time will come when they must fail; or the gift of languages, it will not continue for ever; and knowledge – for this, too, the time will come when it must fail. For our knowledge is imperfect and our prophesying is imperfect; but once perfection comes, all imperfect things will disappear. When I was a child, I used to talk like a child, and think like a child, and argue like a child, but now I am a man, all childish ways are put behind me. Now we are seeing a dim reflection in a mirror; but then we shall be seeing face to face. The knowledge that I have now is imperfect; but then I shall know as fully as I am known.

In short, there are three things that last: faith, hope and love; and the greatest of these is love.

This is the word of the Lord.

Shorter form

A reading from the first letter of St Paul
to the Corinthians

13:4-13

Love never ends.

Love is always patient and kind; it is never jealous; love is never boastful or conceited; it is never rude or selfish; it does not take offence, and is not resentful. Love takes no pleasure in other people's sins but delights in the truth; it is always ready to excuse, to trust, to hope, and to endure whatever comes.

Love does not come to an end. But if there are gifts of prophecy, the time will come when they must fail; or the gift of languages, it will not continue for ever; and knowledge – for this, too, the time will come when it must fail. For our knowledge is imperfect and our prophesying is imperfect; but once perfection comes, all imperfect things will disappear. When I was a child, I used to talk like a child, and think like a child, and argue like a child, but now I am a man, all childish ways are put behind me. Now we are seeing a dim reflection in a mirror; but then we shall be seeing face to face. The knowledge that I have now is imperfect; but then I shall know as fully as I am known.

In short, there are three things that last: faith, hope and love; and the greatest of these is love.

This is the word of the Lord.

Responsorial Psalm   Ps 33:2-11. ℟ v.2. Alt ℟ v.9

℟   I will bless the Lord at all times.

or

℟   Taste and see the goodness of the Lord.

1   I will bless the Lord at all times,
     his praise always on my lips;
     in the Lord my soul shall make its boast.
     The humble shall hear and be glad.   ℟

2   Glorify the Lord with me.
    Together let us praise his name.
    I sought the Lord and he answered me;
    from all my terrors he set me free.

    ℟   I will bless the Lord at all times.

or

    ℟   Taste and see the goodness of the Lord.

3   Look towards him and be radiant;
    let your faces not be abashed.
    This poor man called; the Lord heard him
    and rescued him from all his distress.   ℟

4   The angel of the Lord is encamped
    around those who revere him, to rescue them.
    Taste and see that the Lord is good.
    He is happy who seeks refuge in him.   ℟

5   Revere the Lord, you his saints.
    They lack nothing, those who revere him.
    Strong lions suffer want and go hungry
    but those who seek the Lord lack no blessing.   ℟

Gospel Acclamation   Jn 15:9. 5

    Alleluia, alleluia!
    Remain in my love, says the Lord;
    all who live in me and I in them will bear much fruit.
    Alleluia!

GOSPEL

A reading from the Gospel according to Matthew   18:1-5

Unless you become like little children you will never enter the kingdom of heaven.

The disciples came to Jesus and said, 'Who is the greatest in the kingdom of heaven?' So he called a little child to him and set the child in front of them. Then he said, 'I tell you solemnly, unless you change and become like little children you will never enter the kingdom of heaven. And so, the one who makes himself as little as this little child is the greatest in the kingdom of heaven. Anyone who welcomes a little child like this in my name welcomes me.'

    This is the Gospel of the Lord.

27 August

St Monica Memorial

Common of holy men and women.

FIRST READING

A reading from the book of Ecclesiasticus 26:1-4. 13-16

The beauty of a good wife in a well-kept house is like the beauty of the rising sun.

Happy the husband of a really good wife;
the number of his days will be doubled.
A perfect wife is the joy of her husband,
he will live out the years of his life in peace.
A good wife is the best of portions,
reserved for those who fear the Lord;
rich or poor, they will be glad of heart,
cheerful of face, whatever the season.
The grace of a wife will charm her husband,
her accomplishment will make him the stronger.
A silent wife is a gift from the Lord,
no price can be put on a well-trained character.
A modest wife is a boon twice over,
a chaste character cannot be weighed on scales.
Like the sun rising over the mountains of the Lord
is the beauty of a good wife in a well-kept house.

This is the word of the Lord.

Responsorial Psalm Ps 130

℟ In you, Lord, I have found my peace.

1 O Lord, my heart is not proud
nor haughty my eyes.
I have not gone after things too great
nor marvels beyond me. ℟

2 Truly I have set my soul
in silence and peace.
A weaned child on its mother's breast,
even so is my soul. ℟

3 O Israel, hope in the Lord
both now and for ever. ℟

Gospel Acclamation   Jn 8:12

> Alleluia, alleluia!
> I am the light of the world, says the Lord;
> whoever follows me will have the light of life.
> Alleluia!

GOSPEL

A reading from the holy Gospel according to Luke   7:11-17

> *She bore me in the arms of her prayer that you might say to the son of*
> *the widow: Young man, I command you – rise up.*

Jesus went to a town called Nain, accompanied by his disciples and a great number of people. When he was near the gate of the town it happened that a dead man was being carried out for burial, the only son of his mother, and she was a widow. And a considerable number of the townspeople were with her. When the Lord saw her he felt sorry for her. 'Do not cry' he said. Then he went up and put his hand on the bier and the bearers stood still, and he said, 'Young man, I tell you to get up.' And the dead man sat up and began to talk, and Jesus gave him to his mother. Everyone was filled with awe and praised God saying, 'A great prophet has appeared among us; God has visited his people.' And this opinion of him spread throughout Judaea and all over the countryside.

This is the Gospel of the Lord.

28 August

St Augustine,
bishop and doctor of the Church   Memorial

Common of pastors or Common of doctors of the Church.

FIRST READING

A reading from the first letter of St John   4:7-16

> *If we love one another, God will live in us.*

My dear people,
let us love one another

since love comes from God
and everyone who loves is begotten by God and knows God.
Anyone who fails to love can never have known God,
because God is love.
God's love for us was revealed
when God sent into the world his only Son
so that we could have life through him;
this is the love I mean:
not our love for God,
but God's love for us when he sent his Son
to be the sacrifice that takes our sins away.
My dear people,
since God has loved us so much,
we too should love one another.
No one has ever seen God;
but as long as we love one another
God will live in us
and his love will be complete in us.
We can know that we are living in him
and he is living in us
because he lets us share his Spirit.
We ourselves saw and we testify
that the Father sent his Son
as saviour of the world.
If anyone acknowledges that Jesus is the Son of God,
God lives in him, and he in God.
We ourselves have known and put our faith in
God's love towards ourselves.
God is love
and anyone who lives in love lives in God,
and God lives in him.

This is the word of the Lord.

Responsial Psalm   Ps 118:9-14. ℞ v.12

℞   Lord, teach me your decrees.

1   How shall the young remain sinless?
     By obeying your word.
     I have sought you with all my heart:
     let me not stray from your commands.   ℞

2   I treasure your promise in my heart
    lest I sin against you.
    Blessed are you, O Lord;
    teach me your statutes.

   ℟   Lord, teach me your decrees.

3   With my tongue I have recounted
    the decrees of your lips.
    I rejoiced to do your will
    as though all riches were mine.   ℟

Gospel Acclamation   Mt 23:9-10

   Alleluia, alleluia!
   You have one Father, your Father in heaven;
   you have one teacher: the Lord Jesus Christ!
   Alleluia!

GOSPEL

A reading from the holy Gospel according to Matthew   23:8-12

The greatest among you must be your servant.

Jesus said to his disciples: 'You must not allow yourselves to be called
Rabbi, since you have only one Master, and you are all brothers. You
must call no one on earth your father, since you have only one Father,
and he is in heaven. Nor must you allow yourselves to be called
teachers, for you have only one Teacher, the Christ. The greatest
among you must be your servant. Anyone who exalts himself will be
humbled, and anyone who humbles himself will be exalted.'

   This is the Gospel of the Lord.

29 August

The Beheading of John the Baptist

Memorial

The Gospel is proper to this memorial.

FIRST READING

A reading from the prophet Jeremiah   1:17-19

Say to them everything that I tell you; do not be afraid of their presence.

The word of the Lord was addressed to me, saying:

'Brace yourself for action.
Stand up and tell them
all I command you.
Do not be dismayed at their presence,
or in their presence I will make you dismayed.
I, for my part, today will make you
into a fortified city,
a pillar of iron,
and a wall of bronze
to confront all this land:
the kings of Judah, its princes,
its priests and the country people.
They will fight against you
but shall not overcome you,
for I am with you to deliver you –
it is the Lord who speaks.'

This is the word of the Lord.

Responsorial Psalm   Ps 70:1-6. 15. 17. ℟ v.15

℟   I will sing your salvation.

1   In you, O Lord, I take refuge;
let me never be put to shame.
In your justice rescue me, free me:
pay heed to me and save me.   ℟

2 Be a rock where I can take refuge,
    a mighty stronghold to save me;
    for you are my rock, my stronghold.
    Free me from the hand of the wicked.

    ℟ I will sing your salvation.

3 It is you, O Lord, who are my hope,
    my trust, O Lord, since my youth.
    On you I have leaned from my birth,
    from my mother's womb you have been my help. ℟

4 My lips will tell of your justice
    and day by day of your help.
    O God, you have taught me from my youth
    and I proclaim your wonders still. ℟

Gospel Acclamation   Mt 5:10

    Alleluia, alleluia!
    Happy are they who suffer persecution for justice' sake;
    the kingdom of heaven is theirs.
    Alleluia!

GOSPEL

A reading from the holy Gospel according to Mark   6:17-29

I want you to give me the head of John the Baptist on a dish.

Herod had sent to have John arrested, and had him chained up in
prison because of Herodias, his brother Philip's wife whom he had
married. For John had told Herod, 'It is against the law for you to
have your brother's wife.' As for Herodias, she was furious with him
and wanted to kill him; but she was not able to, because Herod was
afraid of John, knowing him to be a good and holy man, and gave him
his protection. When he had heard him speak he was greatly perplexed, and yet he liked to listen to him.

    An opportunity came on Herod's birthday when he gave a banquet
for the nobles of his court, for his army officers and for the leading
figures in Galilee. When the daughter of this same Herodias came in
and danced, she delighted Herod and his guests; so the king said to the
girl, 'Ask me anything you like and I will give it you.' And he swore

1112

her an oath, 'I will give you anything you ask, even half my kingdom.' She went out and said to her mother, 'What shall I ask for?' She replied, 'The head of John the Baptist.' The girl hurried straight back to the king and made her request, 'I want you to give me John the Baptist's head, here and now, on a dish.' The king was deeply distressed, but thinking of the oaths he had sworn and of his guests, he was reluctant to break his word to her. So the king at once sent one of the bodyguard with orders to bring John's head. The man went off and beheaded him in prison; then he brought the head on a dish and gave it to the girl, and the girl gave it to her mother. When John's disciples heard about this, they came and took his body and laid it in a tomb.

This is the Gospel of the Lord.

SEPTEMBER

3 September

St Gregory the Great,
pope and doctor of the Church

Common of pastors or Common of doctors of the Church.

FIRST READING

A reading from the second letter of St Paul
to the Corinthians   4:1-2. 5-7

*We preach Jesus Christ as Lord, with ourselves as your servants
for Jesus' sake.*

Since we have by an act of mercy been entrusted with this work of
administration, there is no weakening on our part. On the contrary,
we will have none of the reticence of those who are ashamed, no
deceitfulness or watering down the word of God; but the way we
commend ourselves to every human being with a conscience is by
stating the truth openly in the sight of God. For it is not ourselves that
we are preaching, but Christ Jesus as the Lord, and ourselves as your
servants for Jesus' sake. It is the same God that said, 'Let there be
light shining out of darkness', who has shone in our minds to radiate
the light of the knowledge of God's glory, the glory on the face of
Christ.

We are only the earthenware jars that hold this treasure, to make
it clear that such an overwhelming power comes from God and not
from us.

This is the word of the Lord.

Responsorial Psalm   Ps 95:1-3. 7-8. 10. ℟ v.3

℟ Proclaim his marvellous deeds to all the nations.

1   O sing a new song to the Lord,
    sing to the Lord all the earth.
    O sing to the Lord, bless his name.   ℟

2   Proclaim his help day by day,
    tell among the nations his glory
    and his wonders among all the peoples.   ℟

3   Give the Lord, you families of peoples,
    give the Lord glory and power,
    give the Lord the glory of his name.   ℟

4   Proclaim to the nations: 'God is king.'
    The world he made firm in its place;
    he will judge the peoples in fairness.   ℟

Gospel Acclamation   Jn 15:15

   Alleluia, alleluia!
   I call you my friends, says the Lord,
   for I have made known to you all that the Father has told me.
   Alleluia!

GOSPEL

A reading from the holy Gospel according to Luke   22:24-30

I confer a kingdom on you, just as my Father conferred one on me.

A dispute arose between the apostles about which should be reckoned the greatest, but Jesus said to them, 'Among pagans it is the kings who lord it over them, and those who have authority over them are given the title Benefactor. This must not happen with you. No; the greatest among you must behave as if he were the youngest, the leader as if he were the one who serves. For who is the greater: the one at table or the one who serves? The one at table, surely? Yet here am I among you as one who serves!

'You are the men who have stood by me faithfully in my trials; and now I confer a kingdom on you, just as my Father conferred one on me: you will eat and drink at my table in my kingdom, and you will sit on thrones to judge the twelve tribes of Israel.'

   This is the Gospel of the Lord.

8 September

THE BIRTHDAY OF THE BLESSED VIRGIN MARY

Feast

FIRST READING

A reading from the prophet Micah   5:1-4

This is the time when she who is in labour is to give birth.

The Lord says this:

'You Bethlehem Ephrathah, the least of the clans of Judah,
out of you will be born for me
the one who is to rule over Israel;
his origin goes back to the distant past,
to the days of old.
The Lord is therefore going to abandon them
till the time when she who is to give birth gives birth.
Then the remnant of his brothers will come back
to the sons of Israel.
He will stand and feed his flock
with the power of the Lord,
with the majesty of the name of his God.
They will live secure, for from then on he will extend his power
to the ends of the land.
He himself will be peace.'

This is the word of the Lord.

Alternative First Reading

A reading from the letter of St Paul to the Romans   8:28-30

Those whom God knew beforehand and predestined.

We know that by turning everything to their good God co-operates
with all those who love him, with all those that he has called
according to his purpose. They are the ones he chose specially long ago
and intended to become true images of his Son, so that his Son might
be the eldest of many brothers. He called those he intended for this;
those he called he justified, and with those he justified he shared his
glory.

This is the word of the Lord.

Responsorial Psalm   Ps 12:6-7. ℟ Is 61:10

℟   With delight I rejoice in the Lord.

1   Lord, I trust in your merciful love.
    Let my heart rejoice in your saving help.   ℟

2   Let me sing to the Lord for his goodness to me,
    singing psalms to the name of the Lord, the Most High.   ℟

Gospel Acclamation

Alleluia, alleluia!
Happy are you, holy Virgin Mary, deserving of all praise;
from you rose the sun of justice, Christ the Lord.
Alleluia!

GOSPEL

A reading from the holy Gospel according to Matthew   1:1-16. 18-23

She has conceived what is in her by the Holy Spirit.

A genealogy of Jesus Christ, son of David, son of Abraham:

Abraham was the father of Isaac,
Isaac the father of Jacob,
Jacob the father of Judah and his brothers,
Judah was the father of Perez and Zerah, Tamar being their
    mother,
Perez was the father of Hezron,
Hezron the father of Ram,
Ram was the father of Amminadab,
Amminadab the father of Nahshon,
Nahshon the father of Salmon,
Salmon was the father of Boaz, Rahab being his mother,
Boaz was the father of Obed, Ruth being his mother,
Obed was the father of Jesse;
and Jesse was the father of King David.

David was the father of Solomon, whose mother had been Uriah's
    wife,
Solomon was the father of Rehoboam,
Rehoboam the father of Abijah,
Abijah the father of Asa,

Asa was the father of Jehoshaphat,
Jehoshaphat the father of Joram,
Joram the father of Azariah,
Azariah was the father of Jotham,
Jotham the father of Ahaz,
Ahaz the father of Hezekiah,
Hezekiah was the father of Manasseh,
Manasseh the father of Amon,
Amon the father of Josiah;
and Josiah was the father of Jechoniah and his brothers.
Then the deportation to Babylon took place.

After the deportation to Babylon:
Jechoniah was the father of Shealtiel,
Shealtiel the father of Zerubbabel,
Zerubbabel was the father of Abiud,
Abiud the father of Eliakim,
Eliakim the father of Azor,
Azor was the father of Zadok,
Zadok the father of Achim,
Achim the father of Eliud,
Eliud was the father of Eleazar,
Eleazar the father of Matthan,
Matthan the father of Jacob;

and Jacob was the father of Joseph the husband of Mary; of her was born Jesus who is called Christ.

This is how Jesus Christ came to be born. His mother Mary was betrothed to Joseph; but before they came to live together she was found to be with child through the Holy Spirit. Her husband Joseph, being a man of honour and wanting to spare her publicity, decided to divorce her informally. He had made up his mind to do this when the angel of the Lord appeared to him in a dream and said, 'Joseph son of David, do not be afraid to take Mary home as your wife, because she has conceived what is in her by the Holy Spirit. She will give birth to a son and you must name him Jesus, because he is the one who is to save his people from their sins.' Now all this took place to fufil the words spoken by the Lord through the prophet:

The virgin will conceive and give birth to a son
and they will call him Emmanuel,

a name which means 'God-is-with-us.'

This is the Gospel of the Lord.

Shorter form

A reading from the holy Gospel according to Matthew   1:18-23

She has conceived what is in her by the Holy Spirit.

This is how Jesus Christ came to be born. His mother Mary was betrothed to Joseph; but before they came to live together she was found to be with child through the Holy Spirit. Her husband Joseph, being a man of honour and wanting to spare her publicity, decided to divorce her informally. He had made up his mind to do this when the angel of the Lord appeared to him in a dream and said, 'Joseph son of David, do not be afraid to take Mary home as your wife, because she has conceived what is in her by the Holy Spirit. She will give birth to a son and you must name him Jesus, because he is the one who is to save his people from their sins.' Now all this took place to fulfil the words spoken by the Lord through the prophet:

The virgin will conceive and give birth to a son
and they will call him Emmanuel,

a name which means 'God-is-with-us'.

This is the Gospel of the Lord.

---

13 September

St John Chrysostom,
bishop and doctor of the Church   Memorial

Common of pastors or Common of doctors of the Church.

FIRST READING

A reading from the letter of St Paul   4:1-7. 11-13
to the Ephesians

In the work of service we help in building up the body of Christ.

I, the prisoner in the Lord, implore you to lead a life worthy of your vocation. Bear with one another charitably, in complete selflessness, gentleness and patience. Do all you can to preserve the unity of the Spirit by the peace that binds you together. There is one Body, one Spirit, just as you were all called into one and the same hope when you were called. There is one Lord, one faith, one baptism, and one God who is Father of all, over all, through all and within all.

1119

Each one of us, however, has been given his own share of grace, given as Christ allotted it. To some his gift was that they should be apostles; to some, prophets; to some, evangelists; to some, pastors and teachers; so that the saints together make a unity in the work of service, building up the body of Christ. In this way we are all to come to unity in our faith and in our knowledge of the Son of God, until we become the perfect Man, fully mature with the fullness of Christ himself.

This is the word of the Lord.

Responsorial Psalm   Ps 39:2. 4. 7-10. ℟ cf. vv.8. 9.

℟   Here am I, Lord; I come to do your will.

1   I waited, I waited for the Lord
    and he stooped down to me;
    he heard my cry.
    He put a new song into my mouth,
    praise of our God.   ℟

2   You do not ask for sacrifice and offerings,
    but an open ear.
    You do not ask for holocaust and victim.
    Instead, here am I.   ℟

3   In the scroll of the book it stands written
    that I should do your will.
    My God, I delight in your law
    in the depth of my heart.   ℟

4   Your justice I have proclaimed
    in the great assembly.
    My lips I have not sealed;
    you know it, O Lord.   ℟

Gospel Acclamation

Alleluia, alleluia!
The seed is the word of God, Christ is the sower;
all who come to him will live for ever.
Alleluia!

GOSPEL

A reading from the holy Gospel according to Mark   4:1-10. 13-20

The sower went out to sow seed.

Jesus began to teach by the lakeside, but such a huge crowd gathered round him that he got into a boat on the lake and sat there. The people were all along the shore, at the water's edge. He taught them many things in parables, and in the course of his teaching he said to them, 'Listen! Imagine a sower going out to sow. Now it happened that, as he sowed, some of the seed fell on the edge of the path, and the birds came and ate it up. Some seed fell on rocky ground where it found little soil and sprang up straightaway, because there was no depth of earth; and when the sun came up it was scorched and, not having any roots, it withered away. Some seed fell into thorns, and the thorns grew up and choked it, and it produced no crop. And some seeds fell into rich soil, and growing tall and strong, produced crop; and yielded thirty, sixty, even a hundredfold.' And he said, 'Listen, anyone who has ears to hear!'

When he was alone, the Twelve, together with the others who formed his company, asked what the parables meant.

He said to them, 'Do you not understand this parable? Then how will you understand any of the parables? What the sower is sowing is the word. Those on the edge of the path where the word is sown are people who have no sooner heard it than Satan comes and carries away the word that was sown in them. Similarly, those who receive the seed on patches of rock are people who, when first they hear the word, welcome it at once with joy. But they have no root in them, they do not last; should some trial come, or some persecution on account of the word, they fall away at once. Then there are others who receive the seed in thorns. These have heard the word, but the worries of this world, the lure of riches and all the other passions come in to choke the word, and so it produces nothing. And there are those who have received the seed in rich soil: they hear the word and accept it and yield a harvest, thirty and sixty and a hundredfold.'

This is the Gospel of the Lord.

Shorter form

A reading from the holy Gospel according to Mark   4:1-9

The sower went out to sow seed.

Jesus began to teach by the lakeside, but such a huge crowd gathered round him that he got into a boat on the lake and sat there. The people were all along the shore, at the water's edge. He taught them many things in parables, and in the course of his teaching he said to them, 'Listen! Imagine a sower going out to sow. Now it happened that, as he sowed, some of the seed fell on the edge of the path, and the birds came and ate it up. Some seed fell on rocky ground where it found little soil and sprang up straightaway, because there was no depth of earth; and when the sun came up it was scorched and, not having any roots, it withered away. Some seed fell into thorns, and the thorns grew up and choked it, and it produced no crop. And some seeds fell into rich soil and, growing tall and strong, produced crop; and yielded thirty, sixty, even a hundredfold.'

This is the Gospel of the Lord.

14 September

THE TRIUMPH OF THE CROSS   Feast

FIRST READING

A reading from the book of Numbers   21:4-9

When those that were afflicted looked upon it, they were healed.

On the way through the wilderness the people lost patience. They spoke against God and against Moses, 'Why did you bring us out of Egypt to die in this wilderness? For there is neither bread nor water here: we are sick of this unsatisfying food.'

At this God sent fiery serpents among the people; their bite brought death to many in Israel. The people came and said to Moses, 'We have sinned by speaking against the Lord and against you. Intercede for us with the Lord to save us from these serpents.' Moses interceded for the people, and the Lord answered him, 'Make a fiery serpent and put it on a standard. If anyone is bitten and looks at it, he shall live.' So Moses fashioned a bronze serpent which he put on a standard, and if anyone was bitten by a serpent, he looked at the bronze serpent and lived.

This is the word of the Lord.

Responsorial Psalm   Ps 77:1-2. 34-38. ℟ v.7

℟   Do not forget the works of the Lord!

1   Give heed, my people, to my teaching;
      turn your ear to the words of my mouth.
      I will open my mouth in a parable
      and reveal hidden lessons of the past. ℟

2   When he slew them then they would seek him,
      return and seek him in earnest.
      They would remember that God was their rock,
      God the Most High their redeemer. ℟

3   But the words they spoke were mere flattery;
      they lied to him with their lips.
      For their hearts were not truly with him;
      they were not faithful to his covenant.   ℟

4   Yet he who is full of compassion
      forgave their sin and spared them.
      So often he held back his anger
      when he might have stirred up his rage. ℟

SECOND READING

A reading from the letter of St Paul to the Philippians   2:6-11

He humbled himself, therefore God had exalted him.

The state of Jesus Christ was divine,
yet he did not cling
to his equality with God
but emptied himself
to assume the condition of a slave,
and became as men are:
and being as all men are,
he was humbler yet,
even to accepting death,
death on a cross.

1123

But God raised him high
and gave him the name
which is above all other names
so that all beings
in the heavens, on earth and in the underworld,
should bend the knee at the name of Jesus
and that every tongue should acclaim
Jesus Christ as Lord,
to the glory of God the Father.

This is the word of the Lord.

Gospel Acclamation

Alleluia, alleluia!
We adore you, O Christ, and we praise you,
because by your cross you have redeemed the world.
Alleluia!

GOSPEL

A reading from the holy Gospel according to John   3:13-17

The Son of Man must be lifted up.

Jesus said to Nicodemus:

'No one has gone up to heaven
except the one who came down from heaven,
the Son of Man who is in heaven;
and the Son of Man must be lifted up
as Moses lifted up the serpent in the desert,
so that everyone who believes may have eternal life in him.
Yes, God loved the world so much
that he gave his only Son,
so that everyone who believes in him may not be lost
but may have eternal life.
For God sent his Son into the world
not to condemn the world
but so that through him the world might be saved.'

This is the Gospel of the Lord.

15 September

Our Lady of Sorrows
Memorial

The Gospel is proper to this memorial.

FIRST READING

A reading from the letter to the Hebrews
5:7-9

He learned obedience and became the source of eternal salvation.

During his life on earth, Christ offered up prayer and entreaty, aloud and in silent tears, to the one who had the power to save him out of death, and he submitted so humbly that his prayer was heard. Although he was Son, he learnt to obey through suffering; but having been made perfect, he became for all who obey him the source of eternal salvation.

This is the word of the Lord.

Responsorial Psalm
Ps 30:2-6. 15-16. 20. ℟ v.17

℟   Save me, O Lord, in your steadfast love.

1   In you, O Lord, I take refuge.
Let me never be put to shame.
In your justice, set me free,
hear me and speedily rescue me.   ℟

2   Be a rock of refuge for me,
a mighty stronghold to save me,
for you are my rock, my stronghold,
For your name's sake, lead me and guide me.   ℟

3   Release me from the snares they have hidden
for you are my refuge, Lord.
Into your hands I commend my spirit.
It is you who will redeem me, Lord.   ℟

4   As for me, I trust in you, Lord,
I say: 'You are my God.
My life is in your hands, deliver me
from the hands of those who hate me.'   ℟
(continued)

5 How great is the goodness, Lord,
   that you keep for those who fear you,
   that you show to those who trust you
   in the sight of men.

℟ Save me, O Lord, in your steadfast love.

Sequence

The sequence may be said or sung.

At the cross her station keeping
stood the mournful Mother weeping,
close to Jesus to the last;

through her heart, his sorrow sharing,
all his bitter anguish bearing,
now at length the sword had passed.

Oh, how sad and sore distressed
was that Mother highly blessed
of the sole-begotten One.

Christ above in torments hangs;
she beneath beholds the pangs
of her dying glorious Son.

Is there one who would not weep,
whelmed in miseries so deep,
Christ's dear Mother to behold?

Can the human heart refrain
from partaking in her pain,
in that Mother's pain untold?

Bruised, derided, cursed, defiled
she beheld her tender child
all with bloody scourges rent;

for the sins of his own nation
saw him hang in desolation,
till his spirit forth he sent.

O you Mother, fount of love!
Touch my spirit from above,
make my heart with yours accord:

make me feel as you have felt;
make my soul to glow and melt
with the love of Christ our Lord.

Holy Mother, pierce me through;
in my heart each wound renew
of my Saviour crucified:

let me share with you his pain
who for all my sins was slain,
who for me in torments died.

Let me mingle tears with you,
mourning him who mourned for me
all the days that I may live:

by the cross with you to stay,
there with you to weep and pray,
is all I ask of you to give.

Virgin of all virgins best,
listen to my fond request:
let me share your grief divine;

let me, to my latest breath,
in my body bear the death
of that dying Son of yours.

Wounded with his every wound,
steep my soul till it has swooned
in his very blood away;

be to me, O Virgin, nigh,
lest in flames I burn and die
in his awful judgement day.

Christ, when you shall call me hence,
be your Mother my defence,
be your cross my victory.

While my body here decays,
may my soul your goodness praise,
safe in paradise with you.

1126

Gospel Acclamation

> Alleluia, alleluia!
> Happy are you, O blessed Virgin Mary;
> without dying you won the martyr's crown beside the cross of the
>   Lord.
> Alleluia!

GOSPEL

A reading from the holy Gospel according to John   19:25-27

> *How that loving mother was pierced with grief and anguish when she*
> *saw the sufferings of her son.*

Near the cross of Jesus stood his mother and his mother's sister, Mary the wife of Clopas, and Mary of Magdala. Seeing his mother and the disciple he loved standing near her, Jesus said to his mother, 'Woman, this is your son.' Then to the disciple he said, 'This is your mother.' And from that moment the disciple made a place for her in his home.

> This is the Gospel of the Lord.

Alternative Gospel

A reading from the holy Gospel according to Luke   2:33-35

> *A sword will pierce your very soul.*

As the father and mother of Jesus stood wondering at the things that were being said about him, Simeon blessed them and said to Mary his mother, 'You see this child: he is destined for the fall and for the rising of many in Israel, destined to be a sign that is rejected – and a sword will pierce your own soul too – so that the secret thoughts of many may be laid bare.'

> This is the Gospel of the Lord.

---

16 September

Ss Cornelius, pope, and Cyprian, bishop, martyrs

Memorial

Common of martyrs or Common of pastors.

FIRST READING

A reading from the second letter of St Paul to the Corinthians

4:7-15

We carry in our bodies the death and life of Jesus.

We are only the earthenware jars that hold this treasure, to make it clear that such an overwhelming power comes from God and not from us. We are in difficulties on all sides, but never cornered; we see no answer to our problems, but never despair; we have been persecuted, but never deserted; knocked down, but never killed; always, wherever we may be, we carry with us in our body the death of Jesus, so that the life of Jesus, too, may always be seen in our body. Indeed, while we are still alive, we are consigned to our death every day, for the sake of Jesus, so that in our mortal flesh the life of Jesus, too, may be openly shown. So death is at work in us, but life in you.

But as we have the same spirit of faith that is mentioned in scripture – I believed, and therefore I spoke – we too believe and therefore we too speak, knowing that he who raised the Lord Jesus to life will raise us with Jesus in our turn, and put us by his side and you with us. You see, all this is for your benefit, so that the more grace is multiplied among people, the more thanksgiving there will be, to the glory of God.

This is the word of the Lord.

Responsorial Psalm

Ps 125. ℟ v.5

℟ Those who sow in tears, shall reap with shouts of joy.

1 When the Lord delivered Zion from bondage,
   it seemed like a dream.
   Then was our mouth filled with laughter,
   on our lips there were songs. ℟

2 The heathens themselves said: 'What marvels
   the Lord worked for them!'

What marvels the Lord worked for us!
Indeed we were glad.   ℞

3 Deliver us, O Lord, from our bondage
as streams in dry land.
Those who are sowing in tears
will sing when they reap.   ℞

4 They go out, they go out, full of tears,
carrying seed for the sowing:
they come back, they come back, full of song,
carrying their sheaves.   ℞

Gospel Acclamation   2 Cor 1:3-4

Alleluia, alleluia!
Blessed be the Father of mercies and the God of all comfort,
who consoles us in all our afflictions.
Alleluia!

GOSPEL

A reading from the holy Gospel according to John   17:11-19

The world hates them.

Jesus raised his eyes to heaven and said,

'Holy Father,
keep those you have given me true to your name,
so that they may be one like us.
While I was with them,
I kept those you had given me true to your name.
I have watched over them and not one is lost
except the one who chose to be lost,
and this was to fulfil the scriptures.
But now I am coming to you
and while still in the world I say these things
to share my joy with them to the full.
I passed your word on to them,
and the world hated them,
because they belong to the world
no more than I belong to the world.

I am not asking you to remove them from the world,
but to protect them from the evil one.
They do not belong to the world
any more than I belong to the world.
Consecrate them in the truth;
your word is truth.
As you sent me into the world,
I have sent them into the world,
and for their sake I consecrate myself
so that they too may be consecrated in truth.'

This is the Gospel of the Lord.

17 September

St Robert Bellarmine,
bishop and doctor of the Church

Optional Memorial

Common of pastors or Common of doctors of the Church.

FIRST READING

A reading from the book of Wisdom   7:7-10. 15-16

I have loved wisdom more than health and beauty.

I prayed, and understanding was given me;
I entreated, and the spirit of Wisdom came to me.
I esteemed her more than sceptres and thrones;
compared with her, I held riches as nothing.
I reckoned no priceless stone to be her peer,
for compared with her, all gold is a pinch of sand,
and beside her silver ranks as mud.
I loved her more than health or beauty,
preferred her to the light,
since her radiance never sleeps.
May God grant me to speak as he would wish
and express thoughts worthy of his gifts,
since he himself is the guide of Wisdom,
since he directs the sages.
We are indeed in his hand, we ourselves and our words,
with all our understanding, too, and technical knowledge.

This is the word of the Lord.

Responsorial Psalm   Ps 18:8-11. ℟ v.10. Alt. ℟ Jn 6:63

℟   The judgements of the Lord are true, and all of them are just.

or

℟   Your words, Lord, are spirit and life.

1   The law of the Lord is perfect,
    it revives the soul.
    The rule of the Lord is to be trusted,
    it gives wisdom to the simple.   ℟

2   The precepts of the Lord are right,
    they gladden the heart.
    The command of the Lord is clear,
    it gives light to the eyes.   ℟

3   The fear of the Lord is holy,
    abiding for ever.
    The decrees of the Lord are truth
    and all of them just.   ℟

4   They are more to be desired than gold,
    than the purest of gold,
    and sweeter are they than honey,
    than honey from the comb.   ℟

Gospel Acclamation   cf. Jn 6:63. 68

    Alleluia, alleluia!
    Your words, Lord, are spirit and life;
    you have the words of everlasting life.
    Alleluia!

GOSPEL

A reading from the holy Gospel according to Matthew   7:21-29

Jesus taught them with authority.

Jesus said to his disciples: 'It is not those who say to me, "Lord, Lord,"
who will enter the kingdom of heaven, but the person who does the
will of my Father in heaven. When the day comes many will say to
me, "Lord, Lord, did we not prophesy in your name, cast out demons in

your name, work many miracles in your name?" Then I shall tell them to their faces: I have never known you; away from me, you evil men!

'Therefore, everyone who listens to these words of mine and acts on them will be like a sensible man who built his house on rock. Rain came down, floods rose, gales blew and hurled themselves against that house, and it did not fall: it was founded on rock. But everyone who listens to these words of mine and does not act on them will be like a stupid man who built his house on sand. Rain came down, floods rose, gales blew and struck that house, and it fell; and what a fall it had!'

Jesus had now finished what he wanted to say, and his teaching made a deep impression on the people because he taught them with authority, and not like their own scribes.

This is the Gospel of the Lord.

19 September

St Januarius, bishop and martyr

Optional Memorial

Common of martyrs or Common of pastors.

FIRST READING

A reading from the letter to the Hebrews   10:32-36

You have suffered greatly.

Remember all the sufferings that you had to meet after you received the light, in earlier days; sometimes by being yourselves publicly exposed to insults and violence, and sometimes as associates of others who were treated in the same way. For you not only shared in the sufferings of those who were in prison, but you happily accepted being stripped of your belongings, knowing that you owned something that was better and lasting. Be as confident now, then, since the reward is so great. You will need endurance to do God's will and gain what he has promised.

This is the word of the Lord.

Responsorial Psalm   Ps 125. ℟ v.5

℟ Those who sow in tears, shall reap with shouts of joy.

1 When the Lord delivered Zion from bondage,
   it seemed like a dream.
   Then was our mouth filled with laughter,
   on our lips there were songs. ℟

2 The heathens themselves said: 'What marvels
   the Lord worked for them!'
   What marvels the Lord worked for us!
   Indeed we were glad. ℟

3 Deliver us, O Lord, from our bondage
   as streams in dry land.
   Those who are sowing in tears
   will sing when they reap. ℟

4 They go out, they go out, full of tears,
   carrying seed for the sowing:
   they come back, they come back, full of song,
   carrying their sheaves. ℟

Gospel Acclamation   James 1:12

   Alleluia, alleluia!
   Blessed are they who stand firm when trials come;
   when they have stood the test, they will win the crown of life.
   Alleluia!

GOSPEL

A reading from the holy Gospel according to John   12:24-26

If the grain of wheat in the ground dies, it yields a rich harvest.

Jesus said to his disciples:

   'I tell you, most solemnly,
   unless a wheat grain falls on the ground and dies,
   it remains only a single grain;
   but if it dies,
   it yields a rich harvest.
   Anyone who loves his life loses it;

anyone who hates his life in this world
will keep it for the eternal life.
If a man serves me, he must follow me,
wherever I am, my servant will be there too.
If anyone serves me, my Father will honour him.'

This is the Gospel of the Lord.

21 September

ST MATTHEW, APOSTLE AND EVANGELIST

Feast

FIRST READING

A reading from the letter of St Paul   4:1-7. 11-13
to the Ephesians

It was his gift that some should be apostles, others evangelists.

I, the prisoner in the Lord, implore you to lead a life worthy of your vocation. Bear with one another charitably, in complete selflessness, gentleness and patience. Do all you can to preserve the unity of the Spirit by the peace that binds you together. There is one Body, one Spirit, just as you were all called into one and the same hope when you were called. There is one Lord, one faith, one baptism, and one God who is Father of all, over all, through all and within all.

Each one of us, however, has been given his own share of grace, given as Christ allotted it. And to some, his gift was that they should be apostles; to some, prophets; to some, evangelists; to some, pastors and teachers; so that the saints together make a unity in the work of service, building up the body of Christ. In this way we are all to come to unity in our faith and in our knowledge of the Son of God, until we become the perfect Man, fully mature with the fullness of Christ himself.

This is the word of the Lord.

Responsorial Psalm   Ps 18:2-5. ℟ v.5

℟   Their message goes out through all the earth.

1   The heavens proclaim the glory of God
     and the firmament shows forth the work of his hands.
     Day unto day takes up the story
     and night unto night makes known the message.   ℟

2   No speech, no word, no voice is heard
     yet their span extends through all the earth,
     their words to the utmost bounds of the world.   ℟

Gospel Acclamation

     Alleluia, alleluia!
     You are God: we praise you; you are the Lord: we acclaim you;
     the glorious company of apostles praise you.
     Alleluia!

GOSPEL

A reading from the holy Gospel according to Matthew   9:9-13

Follow me. And standing up, he followed him.

As Jesus was walking on he saw a man named Matthew sitting by the
customs house, and he said to him, 'Follow me.' And he got up and
followed him.

While he was at dinner in the house it happened that a number of
tax collectors and sinners came to sit at the table with Jesus and his
disciples. When the Pharisees saw this, they said to his disciples,
'Why does your master eat with tax collectors and sinners?' When he
heard this he replied, 'It is not the healthy who need the doctor, but
the sick. Go and learn the meaning of the words: What I want is
mercy, not sacrifice. And indeed I did not come to call the virtuous,
but sinners.'

This is the Gospel of the Lord.

26 September

Ss Cosmas and Damian, martyrs

Optional Memorial

Common of martyrs.

FIRST READING

A reading from the book of Wisdom   3:1-9

He accepted them as a holocaust.

The souls of the virtuous are in the hands of God,
no torment shall ever touch them.
In the eyes of the unwise, they did appear to die,
their going looked like a disaster,
their leaving us, like annihilation;
but they are in peace.
If they experienced punishment as men see it,
their hope was rich with immortality;
slight was their affliction, great will their blessings be.
God has put them to the test
and proved them worthy to be with him;
he has tested them like gold in a furnace,
and accepted them as a holocaust.
When the time comes for his visitation they will shine out;
as sparks run through the stubble, so will they.
They shall judge nations, rule over peoples,
and the Lord will be their king for ever.
They who trust in him will understand the truth,
those who are faithful will live with him in love;
for grace and mercy await those he has chosen.

This is the word of the Lord.

Responsorial Psalm   Ps 125. ℟ v.5

℟   Those who sow in tears, shall reap with shouts of joy.

1   When the Lord delivered Zion from bondage,
    it seemed like a dream.
    Then was our mouth filled with laughter,
    on our lips there were songs.   ℟

2   The heathens themselves said: 'What marvels
    the Lord worked for them!
    What marvels the Lord worked for us!
    Indeed we were glad. ℟

3   Deliver us, O Lord, from our bondage
    as streams in dry land.
    Those who are sowing in tears
    will sing when they reap. ℟

4   They go out, they go out, full of tears,
    carrying seed for the sowing:
    they come back, they come back, full of song,
    carrying their sheaves. ℟

Gospel Acclamation   James 1:12

    Alleluia, alleluia!
    Blessed are they who stand firm when trials come;
    when they have stood the test, they will win the crown of life.
    Alleluia!

GOSPEL

A reading from the holy Gospel according to Matthew   10:28-33

Do not fear those who kill the body.

Jesus said to his apostles: 'Do not be afraid of those who kill the body
but cannot kill the soul; fear him rather who can destroy both body
and soul in hell. Can you not buy two sparrows for a penny? And yet
not one falls to the ground without your Father knowing. Why, every
hair on your head has been counted. So there is no need to be afraid;
you are worth more than hundreds of sparrows.

'So if anyone declares himself for me in the presence of men, I will
declare myself for him in the presence of my Father in heaven. But
the one who disowns me in the presence of men, I will disown in the
presence of my Father in heaven.'

    This is the Gospel of the Lord.

27 September

St Vincent de Paul, priest
Memorial

Common of pastors: for missionaries or Common of holy men and women: for those engaged in works of mercy.

FIRST READING

A reading from the first letter of St Paul to the Corinthians 1:26-31

God has chosen those who are nothing at all.

Take yourselves, brothers, at the time when you were called: how many of you were wise in the ordinary sense of the word, how many were influential people, or came from noble families? No, it was to shame the wise that God chose what is foolish by human reckoning, and to shame what is strong that he chose what is weak by human reckoning; those whom the world thinks common and contemptible are the ones that God has chosen – those who are nothing at all to show up those who are everything. The human race has nothing to boast about to God, but you, God has made members of Christ Jesus and by God's doing he has become our wisdom, and our virtue, and our holiness, and our freedom. As scripture says: if anyone wants to boast let him boast about the Lord.

This is the word of the Lord.

Responsorial Psalm Ps 111:1-9. ℟ v.1

℟ Happy are those who fear the Lord.

or

℟ Alleluia!

1 Happy the man who fears the Lord,
   who takes delight in his commands.
   His sons will be powerful on earth;
   the children of the upright are blessed. ℟

2 Riches and wealth are in his house;
   his justice stands firm for ever.
   He is a light in the darkness for the upright:
   he is generous, merciful and just. ℟

3   The good man takes pity and lends,
    he conducts his affairs with honour.
    The just man will never waver:
    he will be remembered for ever.   ℟

4   He has no fear of evil news;
    with a firm heart he trusts in the Lord.
    With a steadfast heart he will not fear;
    he will see the downfall of his foes.   ℟

5   Open-handed, he gives to the poor;
    his justice stands firm for ever.
    His head will be raised in glory.   ℟

Gospel Acclamation   Jn 10:14

    Alleluia, alleluia!
    I am the good shepherd, says the Lord;
    I know my sheep, and mine know me.
    Alleluia!

GOSPEL

A reading from the holy Gospel according to Matthew   9:35-37

The harvest is rich but the labourers are few.

Jesus made a tour through all the towns and villages, teaching in their synagogues, proclaiming the Good News of the kingdom and curing all kinds of diseases and sickness.

And when he saw the crowds he felt sorry for them because they were harassed and dejected, like sheep without a shepherd. Then he said to his disciples, 'The harvest is rich but the labourers are few, so ask the Lord of the harvest to send labourers to his harvest'.

This is the Gospel of the Lord.

28 September

St Wenceslaus, martyr   Optional Memorial

Common of martyrs.

FIRST READING

A reading from the first letter of St Peter   3:14-17

There is no need to be afraid or to worry about them.

If you have to suffer for being good, you will count it a blessing. There is no need to be afraid or to worry about persecutors. Simply reverence the Lord Christ in your hearts, and always have your answer ready for people who ask you the reson for the hope that you all have. But give it with courtesy and respect and with a clear conscience, so that those who slander you when you are living a good life in Christ may be proved wrong in the accusations that they bring. And if it is the will of God that you should suffer, it is better to suffer for doing right than for doing wrong.

This is the word of the Lord.

Responsorial Psalm   Ps 125. ℟ v.5

℟   Those who sow in tears, shall reap with shouts of joy.

1   When the Lord delivered Zion from bondage,
    it seemed like a dream.
    Then was our mouth filled with laughter,
    on our lips there were songs.   ℟

2   The heathens themselves said: 'What marvels
    the Lord worked for them!'
    What marvels the Lord worked for us!
    Indeed we were glad.   ℟

3   Deliver us, O Lord, from our bondage
    as streams in dry land.
    Those who are sowing in tears
    will sing when they reap.   ℟

4   They go out, they go out, full of tears,
    carrying seed for the sowing:
    they come back, they come back, full of song,
    carrying their sheaves.   ℟

Gospel Acclamation   Mt 5:10

> Alleluia, alleluia!
> Happy are they who suffer persecution for justice' sake;
> the kingdom of heaven is theirs.
> Alleluia!

GOSPEL

A reading from the holy Gospel according to Matthew   10:34-39

It is not peace I have come to bring, but a sword.

Jesus said to his apostles: 'Do not suppose that I have come to bring peace to the earth: it is not peace I have come to bring, but a sword. For I have come to set a man against his father, a daughter against her mother, a daughter-in-law against her mother-in-law. A man's enemies will be those of his own household.

'Anyone who prefers father or mother to me is not worthy of me. Anyone who prefers son or daughter to me is not worthy of me. Anyone who does not take his cross and follow in my footsteps is not worthy of me. Anyone who finds his life will lose it; anyone who loses his life for my sake will find it.'

This is the Gospel of the Lord.

29 September

SS MICHAEL, GABRIEL AND RAPHAEL, ARCHANGELS   Feast

FIRST READING

A reading from the prophet Daniel   7:9-10. 13-14

Countless thousands ministered to him.

As I watched:
'Thrones were set in place
and one of great age took his seat.
His robe was white as snow,
the hair of his head as pure as wool.
His throne was a blaze of flames,
its wheels were a burning fire.
A stream of fire poured out,

issuing from his presence.
A thousand thousand waited on him,
ten thousand times ten thousand stood before him.
A court was held
and the books were opened.
I gazed into the visions of the night.
And I saw, coming on the clouds of heaven,
one like a son of man.
He came to the one of great age
and was led into his presence.
On him was conferred sovereignty,
glory and kingship,
and men of all peoples, nations and languages became his servants.
His sovereignty is an eternal sovereignty
which shall never pass away,
nor will his empire ever be destroyed.'

This is the word of the Lord.

Alternative First Reading

A reading from the book of the Apocalypse   12:7-12

Michael and his angels battled with the dragon.

Now war broke out in heaven, when Michael with his angels attacked the dragon. The dragon fought back with his angels, but they were defeated and driven out of heaven. The great dragon, the primeval serpent, known as the devil of Satan, who had deceived all the world, was hurled down to the earth and his angels were hurled down with him. Then I heard a voice shout from heaven, 'Victory and power and empire for ever have been won by our God, and all authority for his Christ, now that the persecutor, who accused our brothers day and night before our God, has been brought down. They have triumphed over him by the blood of the Lamb and by the witness of their martyrdom, because even in the face of death they would not cling to life. Let the heavens rejoice and all who live there.'

This is the word of the Lord.

Responsorial Psalm   Ps 137:1-5. ℟ v.1

℟   In the sight of the angels I will sing your praises Lord.

1   I thank you, Lord, with all my heart,
    you have heard the words of my mouth,
    in the presence of the angels I will bless you.
    I will adore before your holy temple.   ℟

2   I thank you for your faithfulness and love
    which excel all we ever knew of you.
    On the day I called, you answered;
    you increased the strength of my soul.   ℟

3   All the earth's kings shall thank you
    when they hear the words of your mouth.
    They shall sing of the Lord's ways:
    'How great is the glory of the Lord!'   ℟

Gospel Acclamation   Ps 102:21

    Alleluia, alleluia!
    Bless the Lord, all you his angels,
    his ministers who do his will.
    Alleluia!

GOSPEL

A reading from the holy Gospel according to John   1:47-51

Above the Son of Man you will see the angels of God ascending and descending.

When Jesus saw Nathanael coming he said of him, 'There is an
Israelite who deserves the name, incapable of deceit.' 'How do you
know me?' said Nathanael. 'Before Philip came to call you,' said Jesus
'I saw you under the fig tree.' Nathanael answered, 'Rabbi, you are the
Son of God, you are the King of Israel.' Jesus replied, 'You believe that
just because I said: I saw you under the fig tree. You will see greater
things than that.' And then he added, 'I tell you most solemnly, you
will see heaven laid open and, above the Son of Man, the angels of God
ascending and descending.'

    This is the Gospel of the Lord.

30 September

St Jerome, priest and doctor of the Church

Memorial

Common of doctors of the Church or Common of pastors.

FIRST READING

A reading from the second letter of St Paul to Timothy   3:14-17

All scripture is inspired by God and can profitably be used for teaching.

You must keep to what you have been taught and know to be true; remember who your teachers were, and how, ever since you were a child, you have known the holy scriptures – from these you can learn the wisdom that leads to salvation through faith in Christ Jesus. All scripture is inspired by God and can profitably be used for teaching, for refuting error, for guiding people's lives and teaching them to be holy. This is how the man who is dedicated to God becomes fully equipped and ready for any good work.

This is the word of the Lord.

Responsorial Psalm   Ps 118:9-14. ℟ v.12

℟   Lord, teach me your decrees.

1   How shall the young remain sinless?
    By obeying your word.
    I have sought you with all my heart:
    let me not stray from your commands.   ℟

2   I treasure your promise in my heart
    lest I sin against you.
    Blessed are you, O Lord;
    teach me your statutes.   ℟

3   With my tongue I have recounted
    the decrees of your lips.
    I rejoiced to do your will
    as though all riches were mine.   ℟

Gospel Acclamation   cf. Acts 16:14

Alleluia, alleluia!
Open our hearts, O Lord,
to listen to the words of your Son.
Alleluia!

GOSPEL

A reading from the holy Gospel according to Matthew   13:47-52

The new and the old.

Jesus said to the crowds: 'The kingdom of heaven is like a dragnet cast into the sea that brings in a haul of all kinds. When it is full, the fishermen haul it ashore; then, sitting down, they collect the good ones in a basket and throw away those that are no use. This is how it will be at the end of time; the angels will appear and separate the wicked from the just to throw them into the blazing furnace where there will be weeping and grinding of teeth.

'Have you understood all this?' They said, 'Yes.' And he said to them, 'Well then, every scribe who becomes a disciple of the kingdom of heaven is like a householder who brings out from his storeroom things both new and old.'

This is the Gospel of the Lord.

OCTOBER

1 October

St Teresa of the child Jesus, virgin Memorial

Common of virgins or Common of holy men and women: for religious.

FIRST READING

A reading from the prophet Isaiah 66:10-14

Now towards her I send flowing peace, like a river.

Rejoice, Jerusalem,
be glad for her, all you who love her!
Rejoice, rejoice for her,
all you who mourned her!
That you may be suckled, filled,
from her consoling breast,
that you may savour with delight
her glorious breasts.
For thus says the Lord:
Now towards her I send flowing
peace, like a river,
and like a stream in spate
the glory of the nations.
At her breast will her nurslings be carried
and fondled in her lap.
Like a son comforted by his mother
will I comfort you.
(And by Jerusalem you will be comforted.)
At the sight your heart will rejoice,
and your bones flourish like the grass.
To his servants the Lord will reveal his hand.

This is the word of the Lord.

Responsorial Psalm   Ps 130

℟   In you, Lord, I have found my peace.

1   O Lord, my heart is not proud
    nor haughty my eyes.
    I have not gone after things too great
    nor marvels beyond me.   ℟

2   Truly I have set my soul
    in silence and peace.
    A weaned child on its mother's breast,
    even so is my soul.   ℟

3   O Israel, hope in the Lord
    both now and for ever.   ℟

Gospel Acclamation   cf. Mt 11:25

    Alleluia, alleluia!
    Blessed are you, Father, Lord of heaven and earth;
    you have revealed to little ones the mysteries of the kingdom.
    Alleluia!

GOSPEL

A reading from the holy Gospel according to Matthew   18:1-5

Unless you have the genuineness of little children, you will not enter
the kingdom of God.

The disciples came to Jesus and said, 'Who is the greatest in the
kingdom of heaven?' So he called a little child to him and set the child
in front of them. Then he said, 'I tell you solemnly, unless you change
and become like little children you will never enter the kingdom of
heaven. And so, the one who makes himself as little as this little child
is the greatest in the kingdom of heaven. Anyone who welcomes a
little child like this in my name welcomes me.'

    This is the Gospel of the Lord.

2 October

The Guardian Angels Memorial

The Gospel is proper to this memorial.

FIRST READING

A reading from the book of Exodus 23:20-23

My angel will go before you.

The Lord says this: 'I myself will send an angel before you to guard you as you go and to bring you to the place that I have prepared. Give him reverence and listen to all that he says. Offer him no defiance; he would not pardon such a fault, for my name is in him. If you listen carefully to his voice and do all that I say, I shall be enemy to your enemies, foe to your foes. My angel will go before you.'

This is the word of the Lord.

Responsorial Psalm Ps 90:1-6. 10-11. ℟ v.11

℟ He has put his angels in charge of you, to guard you in all your
　 ways.

1 He who dwells in the shelter of the Most High
　 and abides in the shade of the Almighty
　 says to the Lord: 'My refuge,
　 my stronghold, my God in whom I trust!' ℟

2 It is he who will free you from the snare
　 of the fowler who seeks to destroy you;
　 he will conceal you with his pinions
　 and under his wings you will find refuge. ℟

3 You will not fear the terror of the night
　 nor the arrow that flies by day,
　 nor the plague that prowls in the darkness
　 nor the scourge that lays waste at noon. ℟

4 Upon you no evil shall fall,
　 no plague approach where you dwell.
　 For you has he commanded his angels,
　 to keep you in all your ways. ℟

Gospel Acclamation   Ps 102:21

> Alleluia, alleluia!
> Bless the Lord, all you his angels,
> his ministers who do his will.
> Alleluia!

GOSPEL

A reading from the holy Gospel according to Matthew   18:1-5. 10

> *Their angels in heaven are always in the presence of my Father,*
> *who is in heaven.*

The disciples came to Jesus and said, 'Who is the greatest in the kingdom of heaven?' So he called a little child to him and set the child in front of them. Then he said, 'I tell you solemnly, unless you change and become like little children you will never enter the kingdom of heaven. And so, the one who makes himself as little as this little child is the greatest in the kingdom of heaven.

'Anyone who welcomes a little child like this in my name welcomes me.

'See that you never despise any of these little ones, for I tell you that their angels in heaven are continually in the presence of my Father in heaven.'

This is the Gospel of the Lord.

4 October

St Francis of Assisi   Memorial

Common of holy men and women: for religious.

FIRST READING

A reading from the letter of St Paul to the Galatians   6:14-18

> *Through him the world is crucified to me, and I to the world.*

As for me, the only thing I can boast about is the cross of our Lord Jesus Christ, through whom the world is crucified to me, and I to the world. It does not matter if a person is circumcised or not; what matters is for him to become an altogether new creature. Peace and mercy to all who follow this rule, who form the Israel of God.

I want no more trouble from anybody after this; the marks on my body are those of Jesus. The grace of our Lord Jesus Christ be with your spirit, my brothers. Amen.

This is the word of the Lord.

Responsorial Psalm   Ps 15:1-2. 5. 7-8. 11. ℟ cf. v.5

℟   You are my inheritance, O Lord.

1   Preserve me, God, I take refuge in you.
    I say to the Lord, 'You are my God.'
    O Lord, it is you who are my portion and cup;
    it is you yourself who are my prize.   ℟

2   I will bless the Lord who gives me counsel,
    who even at night directs my heart.
    I keep the Lord ever in my sight:
    since he is at my right hand, I shall stand firm.   ℟

3   You will show me the path of life,
    the fullness of joy in your presence,
    at your right hand happiness for ever.   ℟

Gospel Acclamation   cf. Mt 11:25

Alleluia, alleluia!
Blessed are you, Father, Lord of heaven and earth;
you have revealed to little ones the mysteries of the kingdom.
Alleluia!

GOSPEL

A reading from the holy Gospel according to Matthew   11:25-30

*You have hidden these things from the learned and the clever, and
revealed them to children.*

Jesus exclaimed, 'I bless you, Father, Lord of heaven and of earth, for hiding these things from the learned and the clever and revealing them to mere children. Yes, Father, for that is what it pleased you to do. Everything has been entrusted to me by my Father; and no one knows the Son except the Father, just as no one knows the Father except the Son and those to whom the Son chooses to reveal him.

'Come to me, all you who labour and are overburdened, and I will give you rest. Shoulder my yoke and learn from me, for I am gentle and humble in heart, and you will find rest for your souls. Yes, my yoke is easy and my burden light.'

This is the Gospel of the Lord.

6 October

St Bruno, priest   Optional Memorial

Common of holy men and women: for religious.

FIRST READING

A reading from the letter of St Paul to the Philippians   3:8-14

I am racing for the finish, for the prize to which God calls us upwards to receive in Christ Jesus.

I believe nothing can happen that will outweigh the supreme advantage of knowing Christ Jesus my Lord. For him I have accepted the loss of everything, and I look on everything as so much rubbish if only I can have Christ and be given a place in him. I am no longer trying for perfection by my own efforts, the perfection that comes from the Law, but I want only the perfection that comes through faith in Christ, and is from God and based on faith. All I want is to know Christ and the power of his resurrection and to share his sufferings by reproducing the pattern of his death. That is the way I can hope to take my place in the resurrection of the dead. Not that I have become perfect yet: I have not yet won, but I am still running, trying to capture the prize for which Christ Jesus captured me. I can assure you, my brothers, I am far from thinking that I have already won. All I can say is that I forget the past and I strain ahead for what is still to come; I am racing for the finish, for the prize to which God calls us upwards to receive in Christ Jesus.

This is the word of the Lord.

Responsorial Psalm   Ps 1:1-4. 6. ℟ v.2. Alt. ℟ Ps 39:5. Alt. ℟ Ps 91:13-14

    ℟ Happy are they who delight in the law of the Lord.

or

    ℟ Happy are they who hope in the Lord.

or

    ℟ The just will flourish like the palm-tree in the garden of the
        Lord.

1 Happy indeed is the man
    who follows not the counsel of the wicked;
    nor lingers in the way of sinners
    nor sits in the company of scorners,
    but whose delight is the law of the Lord
    and who ponders his law day and night.   ℟

2 He is like a tree that is planted
    beside the flowing waters,
    that yields its fruit in due season
    and whose leaves shall never fade;
    and all that he does shall prosper.   ℟

3 Not so are the wicked, not so!
    For they like winnowed chaff
    shall be driven away by the wind.
    For the Lord guards the way of the just
    but the way of the wicked leads to doom.   ℟

Gospel Acclamation   Jn 8:12

Alleluia, alleluia!
I am the light of the world, says the Lord,
  whoever follows me will have the light of life.
Alleluia!

GOSPEL

A reading from the holy Gospel according to Luke   9:57-62

I will follow you wherever you go.

As Jesus and his disciples travelled along they met a man on the road
who said to him, 'I will follow you wherever you go.' Jesus answered,

'Foxes have holes and the birds of the air have nests, but the Son of Man has nowhere to lay his head.'

Another to whom he said, 'Follow me,' replied, 'Let me go and bury my father first.' But he answered, 'Leave the dead to bury their dead; your duty is to go and spread the news of the kingdom of God.'

Another said, 'I will follow you, sir, but first let me go and say good-bye to my people at home.' Jesus said to him, 'Once the hand is laid on the plough, no one who looks back is fit for the kingdom of God.'

This is the Gospel of the Lord.

7 October

Our Lady of the Rosary   Memorial

Common of the Blessed Virgin Mary.

FIRST READING

A reading from the Acts of the Apostles   1:12-14

They all joined in continuous prayer together with Jesus' mother Mary.

After Jesus had ascended into heaven, the apostles went back to Jerusalem, a short distance away, no more than a sabbath walk; and when they reached the city they went to the upper room where they were staying; there were Peter and John, James and Andrew, Philip and Thomas, Bartholomew and Matthew, James son of Alphaeus and Simon the Zealot, and Jude son of James. All these joined in continuous prayer, together with several women, including Mary the mother of Jesus, and with his brothers.

This is the word of the Lord.

Responsorial Psalm   Lk 1:46-55. ℟ v.49

> ℟ The Almighty has done great things for me, and holy is his Name.

or

> ℟ O Blessed Virgin Mary, you carried the Son of the Eternal Father.

1   My soul glorifies the Lord,
    my spirit rejoices in God, my saviour.   ℟

2 He looks on his servant in her nothingness;
   henceforth all ages will call me blessed.
   The Almighty works marvels for me.
   Holy his name!

   ℟ The Almighty has done great things for me, and holy is his
      Name.

   ℟ O Blessed Virgin Mary, you carried the Son of the Eternal
      Father.

3 His mercy is from age to age,
   on those who fear him.
   He puts forth his arm in strength
   and scatters the proud-hearted. ℟

4 He casts the mighty from their thrones
   and raises the lowly.
   He fills the starving with good things,
   sends the rich away empty. ℟

5 He protects Israel, his servant,
   remembering his mercy,
   the mercy promised to our fathers,
   to Abraham and his sons for ever. ℟

Gospel Acclamation   cf. Lk 1:28

   Alleluia, alleluia!
   Hail Mary, full of grace; the Lord is with you.
   Blessed are you among women.
   Alleluia!

GOSPEL

A reading from the holy Gospel according to Luke   1:26-38

You will conceive and bear a son.

The angel Gabriel was sent by God to a town in Galilee called
Nazareth, to a virgin betrothed to a man named Joseph, of the House
of David; and the virgin's name was Mary. He went in and said to her,
'Rejoice, so highly favoured! The Lord is with you.' She was deeply
disturbed by these words and asked herself what this greeting could
mean, but the angel said to her, 'Mary, do not be afraid;

you have won God's favour. Listen! You are to conceive and bear a son, and you must name him Jesus. He will be great and will be called Son of the Most High. The Lord God will give him the throne of his ancestor David; he will rule over the House of Jacob for ever and his reign will have no end.' Mary said to the angel, 'But how can this come about, since I am a virgin?' 'The Holy Spirit will come upon you,' the angel answered, 'and the power of the Most High will cover you with its shadow. And so the child will be holy and will be called Son of God. Know this too: your kinswoman Elizabeth has, in her old age, herself conceived a son, and she whom people called barren is now in her sixth month, for nothing is impossible to God.' 'I am the handmaid of the Lord,' said Mary, 'Let what you have said be done to me.' And the angel left her.

This is the Gospel of the Lord.

9 October

St Denis, bishop and martyr, and companions, martyrs   Optional Memorial

Common of martyrs.

FIRST READING

A reading from the second letter of St Paul   6:4-10
to the Corinthians

We are said to be dying and yet here we are alive.

We prove we are servants of God by great fortitude in times of suffering: in times of hardship and distress; when we are flogged, or sent to prison, or mobbed; labouring, sleepless, starving. We prove we are God's servants by our purity, knowledge, patience and kindness; by a spirit of holiness, by a love free from affectation; by the word of truth and by the power of God; by being armed with the weapons of righteousness in the right hand and in the left, prepared for honour or disgrace, for blame or praise; taken for impostors while we are genuine; obscure yet famous; said to be dying and here we are alive; rumoured to be executed before we are sentenced; thought most miserable and yet we are always rejoicing; taken for paupers though we make others rich, for people having nothing though we have everything.

This is the word of the Lord.

Responsorial Psalm   Ps 125. ℟v.5

℟   Those who sow in tears, shall reap with shouts of joy.

1   When the Lord delivered Zion from bondage,
    it seemed like a dream.
    Then was our mouth filled with laughter,
    on our lips there were songs. ℟

2   The heathens themselves said: 'What marvels
    the Lord worked for them!'
    What marvels the Lord worked for us!
    Indeed we were glad. ℟

3   Deliver us, O Lord, from our bondage
    as streams in dry land.
    Those who are sowing in tears
    will sing when they reap. ℟

4   They go out, they go out, full of tears,
    carrying seed for the sowing:
    they come back, they come back, full of song,
    carrying their sheaves. ℟

Gospel Acclamation   Jn 8:12

Alleluia alleluia!
I am the light of the world, says the Lord,
whoever follows me will have the light of life.
Alleluia!

GOSPEL

A reading from the holy Gospel according to Matthew   5:13-16

You are the light of the world.

Jesus said to his disciples: 'You are the salt of the earth. But if salt
becomes tasteless, what can make it salty again? It is good for
nothing, and can only be thrown out to be trampled underfoot by men.

'You are the light of the world. A city built on a hill-top cannot be
hidden. No one lights a lamp to put it under a tub; they put it on the
lamp-stand where it shines for everyone in the house. In the same way

your light must shine in the sight of men, so that, seeing your good works, they may give the praise to your Father in heaven.'

This is the Gospel of the Lord.

Also 9 October

St John Leonardi, priest

Optional Memorial

Common of pastors or Common of holy men and women: for those engaged in works of mercy.

FIRST READING

A reading from the second letter of St Paul to the Corinthians

4:1-2. 5-7

We preach Jesus Christ as Lord, with ourselves as your servants for Jesus' sake.

Since we have by an act of mercy been entrusted with this work of administration, there is no weakening on our part. On the contrary, we will have none of the reticence of those who are ashamed, no deceitfulness or watering down the word of God; but the way we commend ourselves to every human being with a conscience is by stating the truth openly in the sight of God. For it is not ourselves that we are preaching, but Christ Jesus as the Lord, and ourselves as your servants for Jesus' sake. It is the same God that said, 'Let there be light shining out of darkness,' who has shone in our minds to radiate the light of the knowledge of God's glory, the glory on the face of Christ.

We are only the earthenware jars that hold this treasure, to make it clear that such an overwhelming power comes from God and not from us.

This is the word of the Lord.

Responsorial Psalm   Ps 95:1-3. 7-8. 10. ℟ v.3

℟   Proclaim his marvellous deeds to all the nations.

1   O sing a new song to the Lord,
    sing to the Lord all the earth.
    O sing to the Lord, bless his name.   ℟

2 Proclaim his help day by day,
   tell among the nations his glory
   and his wonders among all the peoples.

   ℞ Proclaim his marvellous deeds to all the nations.

3 Give the Lord, you families of peoples,
   give the Lord glory and power,
   give the Lord the glory of his name. ℞

4 Proclaim to the nations: 'God is king,'
   The world he made firm in its place;
   he will judge the peoples in fairness. ℞

Gospel Acclamation   Mk 1:17

   Alleluia, alleluia!
   Come, follow me, says the Lord,
   and I will make you fishers of my people.
   Alleluia!

GOSPEL

A reading from the holy Gospel according to Luke   5:1-11

I will place my trust in your words.

Jesus was standing one day by the Lake of Gennesaret, with the
crowd pressing round him listening to the word of God, when he
caught sight of two boats close to the bank. The fishermen had gone
out of them and were washing their nets. He got into one of the boats –
it was Simon's – and asked him to put out a little from the shore. Then
he sat down and taught the crowds from the boat.

When he had finished speaking he said to Simon, 'Put out into
deep water and pay out your nets for a catch.' 'Master,' Simon replied,
'we worked hard all night long and caught nothing, but if you say so, I
will pay out the nets.' And when they had done this they netted such a
huge number of fish that their nets began to tear, so they signalled to
their companions in the other boat to come and help them; when these
came, they filled the two boats to sinking point.

When Simon Peter saw this he fell at the knees of Jesus saying,
'Leave me, Lord; I am a sinful man.' For he and all his companions
were completely overcome by the catch they had made; so also were

James and John, sons of Zebedee, who were Simon's partners. But Jesus said to Simon, 'Do not be afraid; from now on it is men you will catch.' Then, bringing their boats back to land, they left everything and followed him.

This is the Gospel of the Lord.

14 October

St Callistus I, pope and martyr

Optional Memorial

Common of martyrs or Common of pastors: for popes.

FIRST READING

A reading from the first letter of St Peter   5:1-4

Be the shepherds of the flock of God that is entrusted to you.

I have something to tell your elders: I am an elder myself, and a witness to the sufferings of Christ, and with you I have a share in the glory that is to be revealed. Be the shepherds of the flock of God that is entrusted to you: watch over it, not simply as a duty but gladly, because God wants it; not for sordid money, but because you are eager to do it. Never be a dictator over any group that is put in your charge, but be an example that the whole flock can follow. When the chief shepherd appears, you will be given the crown of unfading glory.

This is the word of the Lord.

Responsorial Psalm   Ps 39:2. 4. 7-10. ℞ cf. vv.8. 9

℞   Here am I, Lord; I come to do your will.

1   I waited, I waited for the Lord
    and he stooped down to me;
    he heard my cry.
    He put a new song into my mouth,
    praise of our God.   ℞

2   You do not ask for sacrifice and offerings,
    but an open ear.

(continued)

You do not ask for holocaust and victim.
Instead, here am I. ℟

℟   Here am I, Lord; I come to do your will.

3 In the scroll of the book it stands written
   that I should do your will.
   My God, I delight in your law
   in the depth of my heart. ℟

4 Your justice I have proclaimed
   in the great assembly.
   My lips I have not sealed;
   you know it, O Lord. ℟

Gospel Acclamation   Jn 15:15

   Alleluia, alleluia!
   I call you my friends, says the Lord,
   for I have made known to you all that the Father has told me.
   Alleluia!

GOSPEL

A reading from the holy Gospel according to Luke   22:24-30

I confer a kingdom on you, just as my Father conferred one on me.

A dispute arose between the apostles about which should be reckoned
the greatest, but Jesus said to them, 'Among pagans it is the kings
who lord it over them, and those who have authority over them are
given the title Benefactor. This must not happen with you. No; the
greatest among you must behave as if he were the youngest, the
leader as if he were the one who serves. For who is the greater: the one
at table or the one who serves? The one at table, surely? Yet here am I
among you as one who serves!

   'You are the men who have stood by me faithfully in my trials;
and now I confer a kingdom on you, just as my Father conferred one on
me; you will eat and drink at my table in my kingdom, and you will sit
on thrones to judge the twelve tribes of Israel.'

   This is the Gospel of the Lord.

15 October

St Teresa of Avila,
virgin and doctor of the Church   Memorial

Common of virgins or Common of holy men and women: for religious.

FIRST READING

A reading from the letter of St Paul to the Romans   8:22-27

The Spirit himself intercedes for us with longings too deep for words.

From the beginning till now the entire creation, as we know, has been groaning in one great act of giving birth; and not only creation, but all of us who possess the first-fruits of the Spirit, we too groan inwardly as we wait for our bodies to be set free. For we must be content to hope that we shall be saved – our salvation is not in sight, we should not have to be hoping for it if it were – but, as I say, we must hope to be saved since we are not saved yet – it is something we must wait for with patience.

The Spirit too comes to help us in our weakness. For when we cannot choose words in order to pray properly, the Spirit himself expresses our plea in a way that could never be put into words, and God who knows everything in our hearts knows perfectly well what he means, and that the pleas of the saints expressed by the Spirit are according to the mind of God.

This is the word of the Lord.

Responsorial Psalm   Ps 18:8-11. ℟ v.10. Alt. ℟ Jn 6:63

℟   The judgements of the Lord are true, and all of them are just.

or

℟   Your words, Lord, are spirit and life.

1   The law of the Lord is perfect,
       it revives the soul.
       The rule of the Lord is to be trusted,
       it gives wisdom to the simple.   ℟

2　The precepts of the Lord are right,
　　they gladden the heart.
　　The command of the Lord is clear,
　　it gives light to the eyes.

　　℟　The judgements of the Lord are true, and all of them are just.

or

　　℟　Your words, Lord are spirit and life.

3　The fear of the Lord is holy,
　　abiding for ever.
　　The decrees of the Lord are truth
　　and all of them just.　℟

4　They are more to be desired than gold,
　　than the purest of gold
　　and sweeter are they than honey,
　　than honey from the comb.　℟

Gospel Acclamation　　　　　　　　　　　　　　　　　　Jn 15:9. 5

　　Alleluia, alleluia!
　　Remain in my love, says the Lord;
　　all who live in me, and I in them, will bear much fruit.
　　Alleluia!

GOSPEL

A reading from the holy Gospel according to John　　　　15:1-8

All who live in me, and I in them, bear fruit.

Jesus said to his disciples:

　　'I am the true vine,
　　and my Father is the vinedresser.
　　Every branch in me that bears no fruit
　　he cuts away,
　　and every branch that does bear fruit he prunes
　　to make it bear even more.
　　You are pruned already,
　　by means of the word that I have spoken to you.
　　Make your home in me, as I make mine in you.

As a branch cannot bear fruit all by itself,
but must remain part of the vine,
neither can you unless you remain in me.
I am the vine,
you are the branches.
Whoever remains in me, with me in him,
bears fruit in plenty;
for cut off from me you can do nothing.
Anyone who does not remain in me
is like a branch that has been thrown away
– he withers;
these branches are collected and thrown on the fire,
and they are burnt.
If you remain in me
and my words remain in you,
you may ask what you will
and you shall get it.
It is to the glory of my Father that you should bear much fruit,
and then you will be my disciples.'

This is the Gospel of the Lord.

16 October

St Hedwig, religious   Optional Memorial

Common of holy men and women: for religious.

FIRST READING

A reading from the book of Ecclesiasticus   26:1-4. 13-16

*The beauty of a good wife in a well-kept house is like the beauty of the
rising sun.*

Happy the husband of a really good wife;
the number of his days will be doubled.
A perfect wife is the joy of her husband,
he will live out the years of his life in peace.
A good wife is the best of portions,
reserved for those who fear the Lord;
rich or poor, they will be glad of heart,
cheerful of face, whatever the reason.
The grace of a wife will charm her husband,

her accomplishments will make him the stronger.
A silent wife is a gift from the Lord,
no price can be put on a well-trained character.
A modest wife is a boon twice over,
a chaste character cannot be weighed on scales.
Like the sun rising over the mountains of the Lord
is the beauty of a good wife in a well-kept house.

This is the word of the Lord.

Responsial Psalm   Ps 127:1-5. ℟ v.1

℟   Happy are those who fear the Lord.

1   O blessed are those who fear the Lord
    and walk in his ways!
    By the labour of your hands you shall eat.
    you will be happy and prosper.   ℟

2   Your wife will be like a fruitful vine
    in the heart of your house;
    your children like shoots of the olive,
    around your table.   ℟

3   Indeed thus shall be blessed
    the man who fears the Lord.
    May the Lord bless you from Zion
    all the days of your life!   ℟

Gospel Acclamation   Jn 8:31-32

Alleluia, alleluia!
If you stay in my word, you will indeed be my disciples,
and you will know the truth, says the Lord.
Alleluia!

GOSPEL

A reading from the holy Gospel according to Mark   3:31-35

Whoever has done the will of God is my brother, my sister,
and my mother.

The mother and brothers of Jesus arrived and, standing outside, sent
in a message asking for him. A crowd was sitting round him at the
time the message was passed to him, 'Your mother and brothers and
sisters are outside asking for you.' He replied, 'Who are my mother
and my brothers?' And looking round at those sitting in a circle about
him, he said, 'Here are my mother and my brothers. Anyone who does
the will of God, that person is my brother and sister and mother.'

This is the Gospel of the Lord.

Also 16 October

St Margaret Mary Alacoque, virgin

Optional Memorial

Common of virgins or Common of holy men and women: for religious.

FIRST READING

A reading from the letter of St Paul to the Ephesians   3:14-19

To know the love of Christ, which is beyond all knowledge.

This is what I pray, kneeling before the Father, from whom every
family, whether spiritual or natural, takes its name:

Out of his infinite glory, may he give you the power through his
Spirit for your hidden self to grow strong, so that Christ may live in
your hearts through faith, and then, planted in love and built on love,
you will with all the saints have strength to grasp the breadth and the
length, the height and the depth; until, knowing the love of Christ,
which is beyond all knowledge, you are filled with the utter fullness of
God.

This is the word of the Lord.

Responsorial Psalm   Ps 22. ℟ v.1

℟   The Lord is my shepherd; there is nothing I shall want.

1   The Lord is my shepherd;
     there is nothing I shall want.
     Fresh and green are the pastures
     where he gives me repose.
     Near restful waters he leads me,
     to revive my drooping spirit.   ℟

2   He guides me along the right path;
     he is true to his name.
     If I should walk in the valley of darkness
     no evil would I fear.
     You are there with your crook and your staff;
     with these you give me comfort.   ℟

3   You have prepared a banquet for me
     in the sight of my foes.
     My head you have anointed with oil;
     my cup is overflowing.   ℟

4   Surely goodness and kindness shall follow me
     all the days of my life.
     In the Lord's own house shall I dwell
     for ever and ever.   ℟

Gospel Acclamation   cf. Mt 11:25

     Alleluia, alleluia!
     Blessed are you, Father, Lord of heaven and earth;
     you have revealed to little ones the mysteries of the kingdom.
     Alleluia!

GOSPEL

A reading from the holy Gospel according to Matthew   11:25-30

*You have hidden these things from the learned and the clever and
revealed them to children.*

Jesus exclaimed, 'I bless you, Father, Lord of heaven and of earth, for hiding these things from the learned and the clever and revealing them to mere children. Yes, Father, for that is what it pleased you to do. Everything has been entrusted to me by my Father; and no one knows the Son except the Father, just as no one knows the Father except the Son and those to whom the Son chooses to reveal him.

'Come to me, all you who labour and are overburdened, and I will give you rest. Shoulder my yoke and learn from me, for I am gentle and humble in heart, and you will find rest for your souls. Yes, my yoke is easy and my burden light.'

This is the Gospel of the Lord.

17 October

St Ignatius of Antioch, bishop and martyr   Memorial

Common of martyrs or Common of pastors.

FIRST READING

A reading from the letter of St Paul to the Philippians   3:17–4:1

Our homeland is in heaven.

My brothers, be united in following my rule of life. Take as your models everybody who is already doing this and study them as you used to study us. I have told you often, and I repeat it today with tears, there are many who are behaving as the enemies of the cross of Christ. They are destined to be lost. They make foods into their god and they are proudest of something they ought to think shameful; the things they think important are earthly things. For us, our homeland is in heaven, and from heaven comes the saviour we are waiting for, the Lord Jesus Christ, and he will transfigure these wretched bodies of ours into copies of his glorious body. He will do that by the same power with which he can subdue the whole universe.

So then, my brothers and dear friends, do not give way but remain faithful to the Lord. I miss you very much, dear friends; you are my joy and my crown.

This is the word of the Lord.

Responsorial Psalm   Ps 33:2-9. ℟ v.5

℟   The Lord set me free from all my fears.

1   I will bless the Lord at all times,
     his praise always on my lips;
     in the Lord my soul shall make its boast.
     the humble shall hear and be glad.   ℟

2   Glorify the Lord with me.
     Together let us praise his name.
     I sought the Lord and he answered me;
     from all my terrors he set me free.   ℟

3   Look towards him and be radiant;
     let your faces not be abashed.
     This poor man called; the Lord heard him
     and rescued him from all his distress.   ℟

4   The angel of the Lord is encamped
     around those who revere him, to rescue them.
     Taste and see that the Lord is good.
     He is happy who seeks refuge in him.   ℟

Gospel Acclamation   James 1:12

Alleluia, alleluia!
Blessed are they who stand firm when trials come;
when they have stood the test, they will win the crown of life.
Alleluia!

GOSPEL

A reading from the holy Gospel according to John   12:24-26

If the grain of wheat in the ground dies, it yields a rich harvest.

Jesus said to his disciples:

'I tell you, most solemnly,
unless a wheat grain falls on the ground and dies,
it remains only a single grain;
but if it dies,
it yields a rich harvest.

Anyone who loves his life loses it;
anyone who hates his life in this world
will keep it for the eternal life.
If a man serves me, he must follow me,
wherever I am, my servant will be there too.
If anyone serves me, my Father will honour him.'

This is the Gospel of the Lord.

18 October

ST LUKE, EVANGELIST

Feast

FIRST READING

A reading from the second letter of St Paul to Timothy   4:10-17

Luke alone is with me.

Demas has deserted me for love of this life and gone to Thessalonika, Crescens has gone to Galatia and Titus to Dalmatia; only Luke is with me. Get Mark to come and bring him with you; I find him a useful helper in my work. I have sent Tychicus to Ephesus. When you come, bring the cloak I left with Carpus in Troas, and the scrolls, especially the parchment ones. Alexander the coppersmith has done me a lot of harm; the Lord will repay him for what he has done. Be on your guard against him yourself, because he has been bitterly contesting everything that we say.

The first time I had to present my defence, there was not a single witness to support me. Everyone of them deserted me – may they not be held accountable for it. But the Lord stood by me and gave me power, so that through me the whole message might be proclaimed for all the pagans to hear.

This is the word of the Lord.

Responsorial Psalm   Ps 144:10-13. 17-18. ℟ v.12

℟   Your friends tell the glory of your kingship, Lord.

1   All your creatures shall thank you, O Lord,
     and your friends shall repeat their blessing.
     They shall speak of the glory of your reign
     and declare your might, O God.   ℟

2   They make known to men your mighty deeds
    and the glorious splendour of your reign.
    Yours is an everlasting kingdom;
    your rule lasts from age to age.

    ℟   Your friends tell the glory of your kingship, Lord.

3   The Lord is just in all his ways
    and loving in all his deeds.
    He is close to all who call him,
    who call on him from their hearts.   ℟

Gospel Acclamation   cf. Jn 15:16

    Alleluia, alleluia!
    I have chosen you from the world, says the Lord.
    to go and bear fruit that will last.
    Alleluia!

GOSPEL

A reading from the holy Gospel according to Luke   10:1-9

The harvest is plentiful but the labourers are few.

The Lord appointed seventy-two others and sent them out ahead of him, in pairs, to all the towns and places he himself was to visit. He said to them, 'The harvest is rich but the labourers are few, so ask the Lord of the harvest to send labourers to his harvest. Start off now, but remember, I am sending you out like lambs among wolves. Carry no purse, no haversack, no sandals. Salute no one on the road. Whatever house you go into, let your first words be, "Peace to this house!" And if a man of peace lives there, your peace will go and rest on him; if not, it will come back to you. Stay in the same house, taking what food and drink they have to offer, for the labourer deserves his wages; do not move from house to house. Whenever you go into a town where they make you welcome, eat what is set before you. Cure those in it who are sick, and say, "The kingdom of God is very near to you." '

This is the Gospel of the Lord.

19 October

Ss John de Brébeuf and Isaac Jogues, priests and martyrs, and companions, martyrs

Optional Memorial

Common of martyrs or Common of pastors: for missionaries.

FIRST READING

A reading from the second letter of St Paul to the Corinthians   4:7-15

We carry in our bodies the death and life of Christ.

We are only the earthenware jars that hold this treasure, to make it clear that such an overwhelming power comes from God and not from us. We are in difficulties on all sides, but never cornered; we see no answer to our problems, but never despair; we have been persecuted, but never deserted; knocked down, but never killed; always, wherever we may be, we carry with us in our body the death of Jesus, so that the life of Jesus, too, may always be seen in our body. Indeed, while we are still alive, we are consigned to our death every day, for the sake of Jesus, so that in our mortal flesh the life of Jesus, too, may be openly shown. So death is at work in us, but life in you.

But as we have the same spirit of faith that is mentioned in scripture – I believed, and therefore I spoke – we too believe and therefore we too speak, knowing that he who raised the Lord Jesus to life will raise us with Jesus in our turn, and put us by his side and you with us. You see, all this is for your benefit, so that the more grace is multiplied among people, the more thanksgiving there will be, to the glory of God.

This is the word of the Lord.

Responsorial Psalm   Ps 125.℞ v.5

℞   Those who sow in tears, shall reap with shouts of joy.

1   When the Lord delivered Zion from bondage,
     it seemed like a dream.
     Then was our mouth filled with laughter,
     on our lips there were songs.   ℞

2　The heathens themselves said : 'What marvels
　　the Lord worked for them!'
　　What marvels the Lord worked for us!
　　Indeed we were glad.

　　　℟　Those who sow in tears, shall reap with shouts of joy.

3　Deliver us, O Lord, from our bondage
　　as streams in dry land.
　　Those who are sowing in tears
　　will sing when they reap.　℟

4　They go out, they go out, full of tears,
　　carrying seed for the sowing:
　　they come back, they come back, full of song,
　　carrying their sheaves.　℟

Gospel Acclamation　　　　　　　　　　　　　　　Mt 28:19-20

　　Alleluia, alleluia!
　　Go and teach all people my gospel.
　　I am with you always, until the end of the world.
　　Alleluia!

GOSPEL

A reading from the holy Gospel according to Matthew　　28:16-20

Go and make disciples of all the nations.

The eleven disciples set out for Galilee, to the mountain where Jesus
had arranged to meet them. When they saw him they fell down before
him, though some hesitated. Jesus came up and spoke to them. He
said, 'All authority in heaven and on earth has been given to me. Go,
therefore, make disciples of all the nations; baptise them in the name
of the Father and of the Son and of the Holy Spirit, and teach them to
observe all the commands I gave you. And know that I am with you
always; yes, to the end of time.'

　　This is the Gospel of the Lord.

1172

Also 19 October

St Paul of the Cross, priest Optional Memorial

Common of pastors or Common of holy men and women: for religious.

FIRST READING

A reading from the first letter of St Paul to the Corinthians 1:18-25

It was because God wanted to save those who have faith through the foolishness of the message that we preach.

The language of the cross may be illogical to those who are not on the way to salvation, but those of us who are on the way see it as God's power to save. As scripture says: I shall destroy the wisdom of the wise and bring to nothing all the learning of the learned. Where are the philosophers now? Where are the scribes? Where are any of our thinkers today? Do you see now how God has shown up the foolishness of human wisdom? If it was God's wisdom that human wisdom should not know God, it was because God wanted to save those who have faith through the foolishness of the message that we preach. And so, while the Jews demand miracles and the Greeks look for wisdom, here are we preaching a crucified Christ; to the Jews an obstacle that they cannot get over, to the pagans madness, but to those who have been called, whether they are Jews or Greeks, a Christ who is the power and the wisdom of God. For God's foolishness is wiser than human wisdom, and God's weakness is stronger than human strength.

This is the word of the Lord.

Responsorial Psalm Ps 116. ℟ Mk 16:15

℟ Go out to all the world, and tell the Good News.

or

℟ Alleluia!

1 O praise the Lord, all you nations,
    acclaim him all you peoples! ℟

2 Strong is his love for us;
    he is faithful for ever. ℟

1173

Gospel Acclamation   Mt 5:6

> Alleluia, alleluia!
> Happy are those who hunger and thirst for what is right;
> they shall be satisfied.
> Alleluia!

GOSPEL

A reading from the holy Gospel according to Matthew   16:24-27

> *All who lose their lives on account of me will really save their lives.*

Jesus said to his disciples, 'If anyone wants to be a follower of mine, let him renounce himself and take up his cross and follow me. For anyone who wants to save his life will lose it; but anyone who loses his life for my sake will find it. What, then, will a man gain if he wins the whole world and ruins his life? Or what has a man to offer in exchange for his life?

'For the Son of Man is going to come in the glory of his Father with his angels, and, when he does, he will reward each one according to his behaviour.'

This is the Gospel of the Lord.

23 October

St John of Capistrano, priest   Optional Memorial

Common of pastors: for missionaries.

FIRST READING

A reading from the second letter of St Paul   5:14-20
to the Corinthians

> *God gave us the work of reconciliation.*

The love of Christ overwhelms us when we reflect that if one man has died for all, then all men should be dead; and the reason he died for all was so that living men should live no longer for themselves, but for him who died and was raised to life for them.

From now onwards, therefore, we do not judge anyone by the standards of the flesh. Even if we did once know Christ in the flesh, that is not how we know him now. And for anyone who is in Christ, there is a new creation; the old creation has gone, and now the new one is here. It is all God's work. It was God who reconciled us to himself through Christ and gave us the work of handing on this reconciliation. In other words, God in Christ was reconciling the world to himself, not holding men's faults against them, and he has entrusted to us the news that they are reconciled. So we are ambassadors for Christ; it is as though God were appealing through us, and the appeal that we make in Christ's name is: be reconciled to God.

This is the word of the Lord.

Responsorial Psalm   Ps 15:1-2. 5. 7-8. 11. ℟ v.5

℟   You are my inheritance, O Lord.

1   Preserve me, God, I take refuge in you.
     I say to the Lord: 'You are my God.'
     O Lord it is you who are my portion and cup;
     it is you yourself who are my prize.   ℟

2   I will bless the Lord who gives me counsel,
     who even at night directs my heart.
     I keep the Lord ever in my sight:
     since he is at my right hand, I shall stand firm.   ℟

3   You will show me the path of life,
     the fullness of joy in your presence,
     at your right hand happiness for ever.   ℟

Gospel Acclamation   Jn 8:12

     Alleluia, alleluia!
     I am the light of the world, says the Lord;
     whoever follows me will have the light of life.
     Alleluia!

GOSPEL

A reading from the holy Gospel according to Luke   9:57-62

I will follow you wherever you go.

As Jesus and his disciples travelled along they met a man on the road who said to him, 'I will follow you wherever you go'. Jesus answered, 'Foxes have holes and the birds of the air have nests, but the Son of

Man has nowhere to lay his head'.

Another to whom he said, 'Follow me', replied, 'Let me go and bury my father first'. But he answered. 'Leave the dead to bury their dead; your duty is to go and spread the news of the kingdom of God'.

Another said, 'I will follow you, sir, but first let me go and say good-bye to my people at home'. Jesus said to him, 'Once the hand is laid on the plough, no one who looks back is fit for the kingdom of God.'

This is the Gospel of the Lord.

24 October

St Anthony Claret, bishop

Optional Memorial

Common of pastors: for missionaries.

FIRST READING

A reading from the prophet Isaiah 52:7-10

All the ends of the earth shall see the salvation of our God.

How beautiful on the mountains,
are the feet of one who brings good news,
who heralds peace, brings happiness,
proclaims salvation,
and tells Zion,
'Your God is king!'

Listen! Your watchmen raise their voices,
they shout for joy together,
for they see the Lord face to face,
as he returns to Zion.
Break into shouts of joy together,
you ruins of Jerusalem;
for the Lord is consoling his people,
redeeming Jerusalem.

The Lord bares his holy arm
in the sight of all the nations,
and all the ends of the earth shall see
the salvation of our God.

This is the word of the Lord.

Responsorial Psalm   Ps 95:1-3. 7-8. 10. ℟ v.3

℟   Proclaim his marvellous deeds to all the nations.

1   O sing a new song to the Lord,
     sing to the Lord all the earth.
     O sing to the Lord, bless his name. ℟

2   Proclaim his help day by day,
     tell among the nations his glory
     and his wonders among all the peoples. ℟

3   Give the Lord, you families of peoples,
     give the Lord glory and power,
     give the Lord the glory of his name. ℟

4   Proclaim to the nations: 'God is king.'
     The world he made firm in its place;
     he will judge the peoples in fairness. ℟

Gospel Acclamation   Mk 1:17

     Alleluia, alleluia!
     Come, follow me, says the Lord,
     and I will make you fishers of my people.
     Alleluia!

GOSPEL

A reading from the holy Gospel according to Mark   1:14-20

I will make you fishers of my people.

After John had been arrested, Jesus went into Galilee. There he
proclaimed the Good News from God. 'The time has come,' he said,
'and the kingdom of God is close at hand. Repent, and believe the Good
News.'

As he was walking along by the Sea of Galilee he saw Simon and
his brother Andrew casting a net in the lake – for they were
fishermen. And Jesus said to them, 'Follow me and I will make you
into fishers of men.' And at once they left their nets and followed him.

Going on a little farther, he saw James son of Zebedee and his
brother John; they too were in their boat, mending their nets. He

called them at once and, leaving their father Zebedee in the boat with the men he employed, they went after him.

This is the Gospel of the Lord.

28 October

SS SIMON AND JUDE, APOSTLES   Feast

FIRST READING

A reading from the letter of St Paul to the Ephesians   2:19-22

You are part of the building built on the foundation of the apostles.

You are no longer aliens or foreign visitors: you are citizens like all the saints, and part of God's household. You are part of a building that has the apostles and prophets for its foundations, and Christ Jesus himself for its main cornerstone. As every structure is aligned on him, all grow into one holy temple in the Lord; and you too, in him, are being built into a house where God lives, in the spirit.

This is the word of the Lord.

Responsorial Psalm   Ps 18:2-5. ℟ v.5

℟   Their message goes out through all the earth.

1   The heavens proclaim the glory of God
    and the firmament shows forth the work of his hands.
    Day unto day takes up the story
    and night unto night makes known the message.   ℟

2   No speech, no word, no voice is heard
    yet their span goes forth through all the earth,
    their words to the utmost bounds of the world.   ℟

Gospel Acclamation

    Alleluia, alleluia!
    You are God: we praise you; you are the Lord: we acclaim you;
    the glorious company of apostles praise you.
    Alleluia!

GOSPEL

A reading from the holy Gospel according to Luke   6:12-19

He chose twelve from among them, whom he named Apostles.

Jesus went out into the hills to pray; and he spent the whole night in prayer to God. When day came he summoned his disciples and picked out twelve of them; he called them 'apostles': Simon whom he called Peter, and his brother Andrew; James, John, Philip, Bartholomew, Matthew, Thomas, James son of Alphaeus, Simon called the Zealot, Judas son of James, and Judas Iscariot who became a traitor.

He then came down with them and stopped at a piece of level ground where there was a large gathering of his disciples with a great crowd of people from all parts of Judaea and from Jerusalem and from the coastal region of Tyre and Sidon who had come to hear him and to be cured of their diseases. People tormented by unclean spirits were also cured, and everyone in the crowd was trying to touch him because power came out of him that cured them all.

This is the Gospel of the Lord.

These readings are used in Votive Masses of the apostles, or of one apostle.

NOVEMBER

1 November
ALL SAINTS Solemnity

FIRST READING

A reading from the book of the Apocalypse 7:2-4. 9-14

*I saw an immense crowd, beyond hope of counting, of people from
every nation, race, tribe and language.*

I, John, saw another angel rising where the sun rises, carrying the
seal of the living God; he called in a powerful voice to the four
angels whose duty was to devastate land and sea, 'Wait before you
do any damage on land or at sea or to the trees, until we have put
the seal on the foreheads of the servants of our God.' Then I heard
how many were sealed: a hundred and forty-four thousand, out of
all the tribes of Israel.

After that I saw a huge number, impossible to count, of people
from every nation, race, tribe and language; they were standing in
front of the throne and in front of the Lamb, dressed in white robes
and holding palms in their hands. They shouted aloud, 'Victory to
our God, who sits on the throne, and to the Lamb!' And all the
angels who were standing in a circle round the throne, surrounding
the elders and the four animals, prostrated themselves before the
throne, and touched the ground with their foreheads, worshipping
God with these words, 'Amen. Praise and glory and wisdom and
thanksgiving and honour and power and strength to our God for
ever and ever. Amen.'

One of the elders then spoke, and asked me, 'Do you know who
these people are, dressed in white robes, and where they have come
from?' I answered him, 'You can tell me, my lord.' Then he said,
'These are the people who have been through the great persecution,
and they have washed their robes white again in the blood of the
Lamb.'

This is the word of the Lord.

Responsorial Psalm   Ps 23:1-6. ℟ cf. v.6

℟   Lord, this is the people that longs to see your face.

1   The Lord's is the earth and its fullness,
      the world and all its peoples.
      It is he who set it on the seas;
      on the waters he made it firm.   ℟

2   Who shall climb the mountain of the Lord?
      Who shall stand in his holy place?
      The man with clean hands and pure heart,
      who desires not worthless things.   ℟

3   He shall receive blessings from the Lord
      and reward from the God who saves him.
      Such are the men who seek him,
      seek the face of the God of Jacob.   ℟

SECOND READING

A reading from the first letter of St John   3:1-3

We shall see God as he really is.

Think of the love that the Father has lavished on us,
by letting us be called God's children;
and that is what we are.
Because the world refused to acknowledge him,
therefore it does not acknowledge us.
My dear people, we are already the children of God
but what we are to be in the future has not yet been revealed;
all we know is, that when it is revealed
we shall be like him
because we shall see him as he really is.
Surely everyone who entertains this hope
must purify himself, must try to be as pure as Christ.

   This is the word of the Lord.

Gospel Acclamation   Mt 11:28

   Alleluia, alleluia!
   Come to me, all you that labour and are burdened,
   and I will give you rest, says the Lord.
   Alleluia!

GOSPEL

A reading from the holy Gospel according to Matthew   5:1-12

Rejoice and be glad for your reward will be great in heaven.

Seeing the crowds, Jesus went up the hill. There he sat down and was joined by his disciples. Then he began to speak. This is what he taught them:

'How happy are the poor in spirit;
theirs is the kingdom of heaven.
Happy the gentle:
they shall have the earth for their heritage.
Happy those who mourn:
they shall be comforted.
Happy those who hunger and thirst for what is right:
they shall be satisfied.
Happy the merciful:
they shall have mercy shown them.
Happy the pure in heart:
they shall see God.
Happy the peacemakers:
they shall be called sons of God.
Happy those who are persecuted in the cause of right:
theirs is the kingdom of heaven.

'Happy are you when people abuse you and persecute you and speak all kinds of calumny against you on my account. Rejoice and be glad, for your reward will be great in heaven.'

This is the Gospel of the Lord.

2 November

THE COMMEMORATION
OF ALL THE FAITHFUL DEPARTED

Readings are taken from those given in Masses for the Dead, vol.III, pp.849ff. A selection of readings is also given in volume I.

3 November

St Martin de Porres, religious

Optional Memorial

Common of holy men and women: for religious.

FIRST READING

A reading from the letter of St Paul to the Philippians   4:4-9

Fill your minds with everything that is holy.

I want you to be happy, always happy in the Lord; I repeat, what I want is your happiness. Let your tolerance be evident to everyone: the Lord is very near. There is no need to worry; but if there is anything you need, pray for it, asking God for it with prayer and thanksgiving, and that peace of God, which is so much greater than we can understand, will guard your hearts and your thoughts, in Christ Jesus. Finally, brothers, fill your minds with everything that is true, everything that is noble, everything that is good and pure, everything that we love and honour, and everything that can be thought virtuous or worthy of praise. Keep doing all the things that you learnt from me and have been taught by me and have heard or seen that I do. Then the God of peace will be with you.

This is the word of the Lord.

Responsorial Psalm   Ps 130

℟   In you, Lord, I have found my peace.

1   O Lord, my heart is not proud
    nor haughty my eyes.
    I have not gone after things too great
    nor marvels beyond me.   ℟

2   Truly I have set my soul
    in silence and peace.
    A weaned child on its mother's breast,
    even so is my soul.   ℟

3   O Israel, hope in the Lord
    both now and for ever.   ℟

Gospel Acclamation   Jn 13:34

Alleluia, alleluia!
I give you a new commandment:
love one another as I have loved you.
Alleluia!

GOSPEL

A reading from the holy Gospel according to Matthew   22:34-40

Love the Lord your God, and your neighbour as yourself.

When the Pharisees heard that Jesus had silenced the Sadducees they got together and, to disconcert him, one of them put a question, 'Master, which is the greatest commandment of the Law?' Jesus said, 'You must love the Lord your God with all your heart, with all your soul, and with all your mind. This is the greatest and the first commandment. The second resembles it: You must love your neighbour as yourself. On these two commandments hang the whole Law, and the Prophets also.'

This is the Gospel of the Lord.

4 November

St Charles Borromeo, bishop   Memorial

Common of pastors.

FIRST READING

A reading from the letter of St Paul to the Romans   12:3-13

Our gifts differ according to the grace given to us.

In the light of the grace I have received I want to urge each one among you not to exaggerate his real importance. Each of you must judge himself soberly by the standards of the faith God has given him. Just as each of our bodies has several parts and each part has a separate function, so all of us, in union with Christ, form one body, and as parts of it we belong to each other. Our gifts differ according to the grace given us. If your gift is prophecy, then use it as your faith suggests; if administration, then use it for administration; if teaching, then use it for teaching. Let the preachers deliver sermons, the almsgivers give freely, the officials be diligent and those who do works of mercy do them cheerfully.

Do not let your love be a pretence, but sincerely prefer good to evil. Love each other as much as brothers should, and have a profound respect for each other. Work for the Lord with untiring effort and with great earnestness of spirit. If you have hope, this will make you cheerful. Do not give up if trials come; and keep on praying. If any of the saints are in need you must share with them; and you should make hospitality your special care.

This is the word of the Lord.

Responsival Psalm   Ps 88:2-5. 21-22. 25. 27. ℟ cf. v.2

℟   For ever I will sing the goodness of the Lord.

1   I will sing for ever of your love, O Lord;
    through all ages my mouth will proclaim your truth.
    Of this I am sure, that your love lasts for ever,
    that your truth is firmly established as the heavens.   ℟

2   'I have made a covenant with my chosen one;
    I have sworn to David my servant:
    I will establish your dynasty for ever
    and set up your throne through all ages.   ℟

3   'I have found David my servant
    and with my holy oil anointed him.
    My hand shall always be with him
    and my arm shall make him strong.   ℟

4   'My truth and my love shall be with him;
    by my name his might shall be exalted.
    He will say to me: "You are my father,
    my God, the rock who saves me." '   ℟

Gospel Acclamation   Jn 10:14

    Alleluia, alleluia!
    I am the good shepherd, says the Lord;
    I know my sheep, and mine know me.
    Alleluia!

GOSPEL

A reading from the holy Gospel according to John   10:11-16

The good shepherd is one who lays down his life for his sheep.

Jesus said:

'I am the good shepherd:
the good shepherd is one who lays down his life for his sheep.
The hired man, since he is not the shepherd
and the sheep do not belong to him,
abandons the sheep and runs away
as soon as he sees a wolf coming,
and then the wolf attacks and scatters the sheep;
this is because he is only a hired man
and has no concern for the sheep.
I am the good shepherd;
I know my own
and my own know me
just as the Father knows me
and I know the Father;
and I lay down my life for my sheep.
And there are other sheep I have
that are not of this fold,
and these I have to lead as well.
They too will listen to my voice,
and there will be only one flock,
and one shepherd.'

This is the Gospel of the Lord.

9 November

THE DEDICATION OF THE LATERAN BASILICA
Feast

FIRST READING

A reading from the prophet Ezekiel   47:1-2. 8-9. 12

*I see water flowing from the temple and all who were touched by it
were saved.*

The angel brought me to the entrance of the Temple, where a
stream came out from under the Temple threshold and flowed
eastwards, since the Temple faced east. The water flowed from

under the right side of the Temple, south of the altar. He took me out by the north gate and led me right round outside as far as the outer east gate where the water flowed out on the right-hand side. He said, 'This water flows east down to the Arabah and to the sea; and flowing into the sea it makes its waters wholesome. Wherever the river flows, all living creatures teeming in it will live. Fish will be very plentiful, for wherever the water goes it brings health, and life teems wherever the river flows. Along the river, on either bank, will grow every kind of fruit tree with leaves that never wither and fruit that never fails; they will bear new fruit every month, because this water comes from the sanctuary. And their fruit will be good to eat and the leaves medicinal.'

This is the word of the Lord.

Responsorial Psalm   Ps 45:2-3. 5-6. 8-9. ℟ v.5

℟   The waters of the river gladden the city of God.

1   God is for us a refuge and strength,
    a helper close at hand, in time of distress:
    so we shall not fear though the earth should rock,
    though the mountains fall into the depths of the sea.   ℟

2   The waters of a river give joy to God's city,
    the holy place where the Most High dwells.
    God is within, it cannot be shaken;
    God will help it at the dawning of the day.   ℟

3   The Lord of hosts is with us:
    the God of Jacob is our stronghold.
    Come, consider the works of the Lord,
    the redoubtable deeds he has done on the earth.   ℟

SECOND READING

A reading from the first letter of St Paul   3:9-11. 16-17
to the Corinthians

You are the temple of God.

You are God's building. By the grace God gave me, I succeeded as an architect and laid the foundations, on which someone else is doing the building. Everyone doing the building must work carefully. For the foundation, nobody can lay any other than the one which has already been laid, that is Jesus Christ.

Didn't you realise that you were God's temple and that the Spirit of God was living among you? If anybody should destroy the temple of God, God will destroy him, because the temple of God is sacred; and you are that temple.

This is the word of the Lord.

Gospel Acclamation   2 Chron 7:16

Alleluia, alleluia!
I have chosen and sanctified this house, says the Lord,
that my name may remain in it for all time.
Alleluia!

GOSPEL

A reading from the holy Gospel according to John   2:13-22

He spoke about the temple of his own body.

Just before the Jewish Passover Jesus went up to Jerusalem, and in the Temple he found people selling cattle and sheep and pigeons, and the money changers sitting at their counters there. Making a whip out of some cord, he drove them all out of the Temple, cattle and sheep as well, scattered the money changers' coins, knocked their tables over and said to the pigeon-sellers, 'Take all this out of here and stop turning my Father's house into a market'. Then his disciples remembered the words of scripture: Zeal for your house will devour me. The Jews intervened and said, 'What sign can you show us to justify what you have done?' Jesus answered, 'Destroy this sanctuary, and in three days I will raise it up'. The Jews replied, 'It has taken forty-six years to build this sanctuary: are you going to raise it up in three days?' But he was speaking of the sanctuary that was his body, and when Jesus rose from the dead, his disciples remembered that he had said this, and they believed the scripture and the words he had said.

This is the Gospel of the Lord.

10 November

St Leo the Great,
pope and doctor of the Church Memorial

Common of pastors: for popes or Common of doctors of the Church.

FIRST READING

A reading from the book of Ecclesiasticus 39:6-10

Understanding will fill him up.

If it is the will of the great Lord,
the scholar will be filled with the spirit of understanding,
he will shower forth words of wisdom,
and in prayer give thanks to the Lord.
He will grow upright in purpose and learning,
he will ponder the Lord's hidden mysteries.
He will display the instruction he has received,
taking his pride in the Law of the Lord's covenant.
Many will praise his understanding,
and it will never be forgotten.
His memory will not disappear,
generation after generation his name will live.
Nations will proclaim his wisdom,
the assembly will celebrate his praises.

This is the word of the Lord.

Responsorial Psalm Ps 36:3-6. 30-31. ℟ v.30

℟ The mouths of the just murmur wisdom.

1 If you trust in the Lord and do good,
   then you will live in the land and be secure.
   If you find your delight in the Lord,
   he will grant your heart's desire. ℟

2 Commit your life to the Lord,
   trust in him and he will act,
   so that your justice breaks forth like the light,
   your cause like the noon-day sun. ℟

3 The just man's mouth utters wisdom
   and his lips speak what is right;
   the law of his God is in his heart,
   his steps shall be saved from stumbling. ℟

Gospel Acclamation   Mk 1:17

> Alleluia, alleluia!
> Come, follow me, says the Lord,
> and I will make you fishers of my people.
> Alleluia!

GOSPEL

A reading from the holy Gospel according to Matthew   16:13-19

You are Peter and on this rock I will build my Church.

When Jesus came to the region of Caesarea Philippi he put this question to his disciples, 'Who do people say the Son of Man is?' And they said, 'Some say he is John the Baptist, some Elijah, and others Jeremiah or one of the prophets'. 'But you,' he said,' who do you say I am?' Then Simon Peter spoke up, 'You are the Christ,' he said, 'the Son of the living God'. Jesus replied, 'Simon son of Jonah, you are a happy man! Because it was not flesh and blood that revealed this to you but my Father in heaven. So I now say to you: You are Peter and on this rock I will build my Church. And the gates of the underworld can never hold out against it. I will give you the keys of the kingdom of heaven: whatever you bind on earth shall be considered bound in heaven; whatever you loose on earth shall be considered loosed in heaven.'

This is the Gospel of the Lord.

11 November

St Martin of Tours, bishop   Memorial

Common of pastors or Common of holy men and women: for religious.

FIRST READING

A reading from the prophet Isaiah   61:1-3

The Lord God has anointed me and sent me to bring Good News to the poor.

The spirit of the Lord has been given to me,
for the Lord has anointed me.
He has sent me to bring good news to the poor,

to bind up hearts that are broken;

to proclaim liberty to captives,
freedom to those in prison;
to proclaim a year of favour from the Lord,
a day of vengeance for our God,
to comfort all those who mourn and to give them
for ashes a garland;
for mourning robe the oil of gladness,
for despondency, praise.

This is the word of the Lord.

Responsorial Psalm   Ps 88: 2-5. 21-22. 25. 27. ℟ cf. v.2

℟   For ever I will sing the goodness of the Lord.

1   I will sing for ever of your love, O Lord;
    through all ages my mouth will proclaim your truth.
    Of this I am sure, that your love lasts for ever,
    that your truth is firmly established as the heavens.   ℟

2   'I have made a covenant with my chosen one;
    I have sworn to David my servant:
    I will establish your dynasty for ever
    and set up your throne through all ages.   ℟

3   'I have found David my servant
    and with my holy oil anointed him.
    My hand shall always be with him
    and my arm shall make him strong.   ℟

4   'My truth and my love shall be with him;
    by my name his might shall be exalted.
    He will say to me: "You are my father,
    my God, the rock who saves me." '   ℟

Gospel Acclamation   Jn 13:34

Alleluia, alleluia!
I give you a new commandment:
love one another, as I have loved you.
Alleluia!

GOSPEL

A reading from the holy Gospel according to Matthew   25:31-40

Whatever you have done to the very least of my brothers and sisters
you have done to me.

Jesus said to his disciples: 'When the Son of Man comes in his glory, escorted by all the angels, then he will take his seat on his throne of glory. All the nations will be assembled before him and he will separate men one from another as the shepherd separates sheep from goats. He will place the sheep on his right hand and the goats on his left. Then the King will say to those on his right hand, "Come, you whom my Father has blessed, take for your heritage the kingdom prepared for you since the foundation of the world. For I was hungry and you gave me food; I was thirsty and you gave me drink; I was a stranger and you made me welcome; naked and you clothed me, sick and you visited me, in prison and you came to see me." Then the virtuous will say to him in reply, "Lord, when did we see you hungry and feed you; or thirsty and give you drink? When did we see you a stranger and make you welcome; naked and clothe you; sick or in prison and go to see you?" And the King will answer, "I tell you solemnly, in so far as you did this to one of the least of these brothers of mine, you did it to me." '

This is the Gospel of the Lord.

12 November

St Josaphat, bishop and martyr   Memorial

Common of martyrs or Common of pastors.

FIRST READING

A reading from the letter of St Paul to the Ephesians   4:1-7. 11-13

In the work of service we help in building up the body of Christ.

I, the prisoner in the Lord, implore you to lead a life worthy of your vocation. Bear with one another charitably, in complete selflessness, gentleness and patience. Do all you can to preserve the unity of the Spirit by the peace that binds you together. There is one Body, one Spirit, just as you were all called into one and the same hope when you were called. There is one Lord, one faith, one baptism, and one God who is Father of all, over all, through all and within all.

Each one of us, however, has been given his own share of grace, given as Christ allotted it. And to some, his gift was that they should be apostles, to some, prophets; to some, evangelists; to some, pastors and teachers so that the saints together make a unity in the work of service, building up the body of Christ. In this way we are all to come to unity in our faith and in our knowledge of the Son of God, until we become the perfect Man, fully mature with the fullness of Christ himself.

This is the word of the Lord.

Responsorial Psalm   Ps 1:1-4. 6. ℟ v.2. Alt ℟ Ps 39:5. Alt. ℟ Ps 91:13-14

℟   Happy are they who delight in the law of the Lord.

or

℟   Happy are they who hope in the Lord.

or

℟   The just will flourish like the palm-tree in the garden of the
     Lord.

1   Happy indeed is the man
     who follows not the counsel of the wicked;
     nor lingers in the way of sinners
     nor sits in the company of scorners,
     but whose delight is the law of the Lord
     and who ponders his law day and night.   ℟

2   He is like a tree that is planted
     beside the flowing waters,
     that yields its fruit in due season
     and whose leaves shall never fade;
     and all that he does shall prosper.   ℟

3   Not so are the wicked, not so!
     For they like winnowed chaff
     shall be driven away by the wind;
     for the Lord guards the way of the just
     but the way of the wicked leads to doom.   ℟

Gospel Acclamation   Jn 15:9. 5

> Alleluia, alleluia!
> Remain in my love, says the Lord;
> all who live in me, and I in them, will bear much fruit.
> Alleluia!

GOSPEL

A reading from the holy Gospel according to John   17:20-26

I want those you have given me to be with me where I am.

Jesus raised his eyes to heaven and said:

> 'Holy Father,
> I pray not only for these,
> but for those also
> who through their words will believe in me.
> May they all be one.
> Father, may they be one in us,
> as you are in me and I am in you,
> so that the world may believe it was you who sent me.
> I have given them the glory you gave to me,
> that they may be one as we are one.
> With me in them and you in me,
> may they be so completely one
> that the world will realise that it was you who sent me
> and that I have loved them as much as you loved me.
> Father,
> I want those you have given me
> to be with me where I am,
> so that they may always see the glory
> you have given me
> because you loved me
> before the foundation of the world.
> Father, Righteous One,
> the world has not known you,
> but I have known you,
> and these have known
> that you have sent me.
> I have made your name known to them
> and will continue to make it known,

so that the love with which you loved me may be in them,
and so that I may be in them.'

This is the Gospel of the Lord.

15 November

St Albert the Great,
bishop and doctor of the Church

Optional Memorial

Common of pastors or Common of doctors of the Church.

FIRST READING

A reading from the book of Ecclesiasticus   15:1-6

He filled them with the spirit of wisdom and understanding.

Whoever fears the Lord will act like this,
and whoever grasps the Law will obtain wisdom.
She will come to meet him like a mother,
and receive him like a virgin bride.
She will give him the bread of understanding to eat,
and the water of wisdom to drink.
He will lean on her and will not fall,
he will rely on her and not be put to shame.
She will raise him high above his neighbours,
and in full assembly she will open his mouth.
He will find happiness and a crown of joy,
he will inherit an everlasting name.

This is the word of the Lord.

Responsorial Psalm   Ps 118:9-14. ℟ v.12

℟   Lord, teach me your decrees.

1   How shall the young remain sinless?
    By obeying your word.
    I have sought you with all my heart:
    let me not stray from your commands.   ℟

2   I treasure your promise in my heart
    lest I sin against you.
    Blessed are you, O Lord;
    teach me your statutes.

    ℞   Lord, teach me your decrees.

3   With my tongue I have recounted
    the decrees of your lips.
    I rejoiced to do your will
    as though all riches were mine.   ℞

Gospel Acclamation   cf. Acts 16:14

    Alleluia, alleluia!
    Open our hearts, O Lord,
    to listen to the words of your Son.
    Alleluia!

GOSPEL

A reading from the holy Gospel according to Matthew   13:47-52

The new and the old.

Jesus said to the crowds: 'The kingdom of heaven is like a dragnet cast
out into the sea that brings in a haul of all kinds. When it is full, the
fishermen haul it ashore; then, sitting down, they collect the good
ones in a basket and throw away those that are no use. This is how it
will be at the end of time; the angels will appear and separate the
wicked from the just to throw them into the blazing furnace where
there will be weeping and grinding of teeth.

    'Have you understood all this?' They said, 'Yes.' And he said to
them 'Well then, every scribe who becomes a disciple of the kingdom
of heaven is like a householder who brings out from his storeroom
things both new and old.'

    This is the Gospel of the Lord.

16 November

St Margaret of Scotland Optional Memorial

Common of holy men and women: for those who work for the underprivileged.

FIRST READING

A reading from the prophet Isaiah   58:6-11

Share your bread with the hungry.

Is not this the sort of fast that pleases me
– it is the Lord who speaks –
to break unjust fetters
and undo the thongs of the yoke,

to let the oppressed go free,
and break every yoke,
to share your bread with the hungry,
and shelter the homeless poor,

to clothe the man you see to be naked
and not turn from your own kin?
Then will your light shine like the dawn
and your wound be quickly healed over.

Your integrity will go before you
and the glory of the Lord behind you.
Cry, and the Lord will answer;
call, and he will say, 'I am here.'

If you do away with the yoke,
the clenched fist, the wicked word,
if you give your bread to the hungry,
and relief to the oppressed,

your light will rise in the darkness,
and your shadows become like noon.
The Lord will always guide you,
giving you relief in desert places.

He will give strength to your bones
and you shall be like a watered garden,
like a spring of water
whose waters never run dry.

This is the word of the Lord.

Responsorial Psalm

Ps 111:1-9. ℟ v.1

℟ Happy are those who fear the Lord.

or

℟ Alleluia!

1 Happy the man who fears the Lord,
   who takes delight in his commands.
   His sons will be powerful on earth;
   the children of the upright are blessed. ℟

2 Riches and wealth are in his house;
   his justice stands firm for ever.
   He is a light in the darkness for the upright:
   he is generous, merciful and just. ℟

3 The good man takes pity and lends,
   he conducts his affairs with honour.
   The just man will never waver:
   he will be remembered for ever. ℟

4 He has no fear of evil news;
   with a firm heart he trusts in the Lord.
   With a steadfast heart he will not fear;
   he will see the downfall of his foes. ℟

5 Open-handed, he gives to the poor;
   his justice stands firm for ever.
   His head will be raised in glory. ℟

Gospel Acclamation

Jn 13:34

Alleluia, alleluia!
I give you a new commandment:
love one another as I have loved you.
Alleluia!

GOSPEL

A reading from the holy Gospel according to John   15:9-17

You are my friends if you do what I command you.

Jesus said to his disciples,

'As the Father has loved me,
so I have loved you.
Remain in my love.
If you keep my commandments
you will remain in my love,
just as I have kept my Father's commandments
and remain in his love.
I have told you this
so that my own joy may be in you
and your joy be complete.
This is my commandment:
love one another,
as I have loved you.
A man can have no greater love
than to lay down his life for his friends.
You are my friends,
if you do what I command you.
I shall not call you servants any more,
because a servant does not know
his master's business;
I call you friends,
because I have made known to you
everything I have learnt from my Father.
You did not choose me,
no, I chose you;
and I commissioned you
to go out and to bear fruit,
fruit that will last;
and then the Father will give you
anything you ask him in my name.
What I command you
is to love one another.'

This is the Gospel of the Lord.

Also 16 November

St Gertrude, virgin   Optional Memorial

Common of virgins or Common of holy men and women: for religious.

FIRST READING

A reading from the letter of St Paul to the Ephesians   3:14-19

To know the love of Christ, which is beyond all knowledge.

This is what I pray, kneeling before the Father, from whom every family, whether spiritual or natural, takes its name:

Out of his infinite glory, may he give you the power through his Spirit for your hidden self to grow strong, so that Christ may live in your hearts through faith, and then, planted in love and built on love, you will with all the saints have strength to grasp the breadth and the length, the height and the depth, until, knowing the love of Christ which is beyond all knowledge, you are filled with the utter fullness of God.

This is the word of the Lord.

Responsorial Psalm   Ps 22. ℟ v.1

℟   The Lord is my shepherd; there is nothing I shall want.

1   The Lord is my shepherd;
    there is nothing I shall want.
    Fresh and green are the pastures
    where he gives me repose.
    Near restful waters he leads me,
    to revive my drooping spirit.   ℟

2   He guides me along the right path;
    he is true to his name.
    If I should walk in the valley of darkness
    no evil would I fear.
    You are there with your crook and your staff;
    with these you give me comfort.   ℟

3   You have prepared a banquet for me
    in the sight of my foes.
    My head you have anointed with oil;
    my cup is overflowing.   ℟

4 Surely goodness and kindness shall follow me
   all the days of my life.
   In the Lord's own house shall I dwell
   for ever and ever. ℟

Gospel Acclamation   Jn 15:9. 5

   Alleluia, alleluia!
   Remain in my love, says the Lord;
   all who live in me, and I in them, will bear much fruit.
   Alleluia!

GOSPEL

A reading from the holy Gospel according to John   15:1-8

All who live in me, and I in them, bear fruit.

Jesus said to his disciples:

   'I am the true vine,
   and my Father is the vinedresser.
   Every branch in me that bears no fruit
   he cuts away,
   and every branch that does bear fruit he prunes
   to make it bear even more.
   You are pruned already,
   by means of the word that I have spoken to you.
   Make your home in me, as I make mine in you.
   As a branch cannot bear fruit all by itself,
   but must remain part of the vine,
   neither can you unless you remain in me.
   I am the vine,
   you are the branches.
   Whoever remains in me, with me in him,
   bears fruit in plenty;
   for cut off from me you can do nothing.
   Anyone who does not remain in me
   is like a branch that has been thrown away
   – he withers;
   these branches are collected and thrown on the fire,
   and they are burnt.
   If you remain in me

1201

and my words remain in you,
you may ask what you will
and you shall get it.
It is the glory of my Father that you should bear much fruit,
and then you will be my disciples.'

This is the Gospel of the Lord.

17 November

St Elizabeth of Hungary, religious   Memorial

Common of holy men and women: for those who work for the underprivileged.

FIRST READING

A reading from the first letter of St John   3:14-18

We should lay down our lives for our brothers and sisters.

We have passed out of death and into life,
and of this we can be sure
because we love our brothers.
If you refuse to love, you must remain dead;
to hate your brother is to be a murderer,
and murderers, as you know, do not have eternal life in them.
This has taught us love –
that he gave up his life for us;
and we, too, ought to give up our lives for our brothers.
If a man who was rich enough in this world's goods
saw that one of his brothers was in need,
but closed his heart to him,
how could the love of God be living in him?
My children,
our love is not to be just words or mere talk,
but something real and active.

This is the word of the Lord.

Responsorial Psalm   Ps 33:2-11. ℟ v.2

℟   I will bless the Lord at all times.

or

℟   Taste and see the goodness of the Lord.

1   I will bless the Lord at all times,
     his praise always on my lips;
     in the Lord my soul shall make its boast.
     The humble shall hear and be glad.   ℟

2   Glorify the Lord with me.
     Together let us praise his name.
     I sought the Lord and he answered me;
     from all my terrors he set me free.   ℟

3   Look towards him and be radiant;
     let your faces not be abashed.
     This poor man called; the Lord heard him
     and rescued him from all his distress.   ℟

4   The angel of the Lord is encamped
     around those who revere him, to rescue them.
     Taste and see that the Lord is good.
     He is happy who seeks refuge in him.   ℟

5   Revere the Lord, you his saints.
     They lack nothing, those who revere him.
     Strong lions suffer want and go hungry
     but those who seek the Lord lack no blessing.   ℟

Gospel Acclamation   Jn 13:34

     Alleluia, alleluia!
     I give you a new commandment:
     love one another as I have loved you.
     Alleluia!

GOSPEL

A reading from the holy Gospel according to Luke 6:27-38

Be merciful, as your Father is merciful.

Jesus said to his disciples: 'I say this to you who are listening: Love your enemies, do good to those who hate you, bless those who curse you, pray for those who treat you badly. To the man who slaps you on one cheek, present the other cheek too; to the man who takes your cloak from you, do not refuse your tunic. Give to everyone who asks you, and do not ask for your property back from the man who robs you. Treat others as you would like them to treat you. If you love those who love you, what thanks can you expect? Even sinners love those who love them. And if you do good to those who do good to you, what thanks can you expect? For even sinners do that much. And if you lend to those from whom you hope to receive, what thanks can you expect? Even sinners lend to sinners to get back the same amount. Instead, love your enemies and do good, and lend without any hope of return. You will have a great reward, and you will be sons of the Most High, for he himself is kind to the ungrateful and the wicked.

'Be compassionate as your Father is compassionate. Do not judge, and you will not be judged yourselves; do not condemn, and you will not be condemned yourselves; grant pardon, and you will be pardoned. Give, and there will be gifts for you: a full measure, pressed down, shaken together, and running over, will be poured into your lap; because the amount you measure out is the amount you will be given back.'

This is the Gospel of the Lord.

18 November

The Dedication of the Basilicas of Ss Peter and Paul, Apostles

Optional Memorial

The readings are proper to this memorial.

FIRST READING

A reading from the Acts of the Apostles   28:11-16. 30-31

So we came to Rome.

At the end of three months we set sail in a ship that had wintered in the island; she came from Alexandria and her figurehead was the Twins. We put in at Syracuse and spent three days there; from there we followed the coast up to Rhegium. After one day there a south wind sprang up and on the second day we made Puteoli, where we found some brothers and were much rewarded by staying a week with them. And so we came to Rome.

When the brothers there heard of our arrival they came to meet us, as far as the Forum of Appius and the Three Taverns. When Paul saw them he thanked God and took courage. On our arrival in Rome Paul was allowed to stay in lodgings of his own with the soldier who guarded him.

Paul spent the whole of the two years in his own rented lodging. He welcomed all who came to visit him, proclaiming the kingdom of God and teaching the truth about the Lord Jesus Christ with complete freedom and without hindrance from anyone.

This is the word of the Lord.

Responsorial Psalm   Ps 97:1-6. ℟ v.2

℟   The Lord has revealed to the nations his saving power.

1   Sing a new song to the Lord
     for he has worked wonders.
     His right hand and his holy arm
     have brought salvation.   ℟

2   The Lord has made known his salvation;
    has shown his justice to the nations.
    He has remembered his truth and love
    for the house of Israel.

    ℟   The Lord has revealed to the nations his saving power.

3   All the ends of the earth have seen
    the salvation of our God.
    Shout to the Lord all the earth,
    ring out your joy.   ℟

4   Sing psalms to the Lord with the harp
    with the sound of music.
    With trumpets and the sound of the horn
    acclaim the King, the Lord.   ℟

Gospel Acclamation

Alleluia, alleluia!
You are God; we praise you; you are the Lord; we acclaim you;
the glorious company of apostles praise you.
Alleluia!

GOSPEL

A reading from the holy Gospel according to Matthew   14:22-33

Tell me to come to you over the water.

After the crowds had eaten as much as they wanted, Jesus made the
disciples get into the boat and go on ahead to the other side while he
would send the crowds away. After sending the crowds away he went
up into the hills by himself to pray. When evening came, he was there
alone, while the boat, by now far out on the lake, was battling with a
heavy sea for there was a head-wind. In the fourth watch of the night
he went towards them, walking on the lake, and when the disciples
saw him walking on the lake they were terrified. 'It is a ghost' they
said, and cried out in fear. But at once Jesus called out to them saying,
'Courage! It is I! Do not be afraid.' It was Peter who answered. 'Lord,'
he said 'if it is you, tell me to come to you across the water.' 'Come'
said Jesus. Then Peter got out of the boat and started walking towards
Jesus across the water, but as soon as he felt the force of the wind, he

took fright and began to sink. 'Lord! Save me!' he cried. Jesus put out his hand at once and held him. 'Man of little faith,' he said, 'why did you doubt?' And as they got into the boat the wind dropped. The men in the boat bowed down before him and said, 'Truly, you are the Son of God.'

This is the Gospel of the Lord.

21 November

The Presentation of the Blessed Virgin Mary

Memorial

Common of the Blessed Virgin Mary.

FIRST READING

A reading from the prophet Zechariah   2:14-17

Rejoice, daughter of Zion, for I am coming.

Sing, rejoice,
daughter of Zion;
for I am coming
to dwell in the middle of you
– it is the Lord who speaks.
Many nations will join the Lord,
on that day;
they will become his people.
But he will remain among you,
and you will know that the Lord of hosts has sent me to you.
But the Lord will hold Judah
as his portion in the Holy Land,
and again make Jerusalem his very own.
Let all mankind be silent before the Lord!
For he is awakening and is coming from his holy dwelling.

This is the word of the Lord.

Responsorial Psalm

Lk 1:46-55. ℟ v.49

℟ The Almighty has done great things for me, and holy is his
   Name.

or

℟ O blessed Virgin Mary, you carried the Son of the eternal
   Father.

1 My soul glorifies the Lord,
   my spirit rejoices in God, my saviour. ℟

2 He looks on his servant in her nothingness;
   henceforth all ages will call me blessed.
   The Almighty works marvels for me.
   Holy his name! ℟

3 His mercy is from age to age,
   on those who fear him.
   He puts forth his arm in strength
   and scatters the proud-hearted. ℟

4 He casts the mighty from their thrones
   and raises the lowly.
   He fills the starving with good things,
   sends the rich away empty. ℟

5 He protects Israel, his servant,
   remembering his mercy,
   the mercy promised to our fathers,
   to Abraham and his sons for ever. ℟

Gospel Acclamation

Lk 11:28

Alleluia, alleluia!
Blessed are they who hear the word of God
and keep it.
Alleluia!

GOSPEL

A reading from the holy Gospel according to Matthew   12:46-50

*Extending his hands towards the disciples, he said: Here are my
mother and my brothers.*

Jesus was speaking to the crowds when his mother and his brothers
appeared; they were standing outside and were anxious to have a
word with him. But to the man who told him this Jesus replied, 'Who
is my mother? Who are my brothers?' And stretching out his hand
towards his disciples he said, 'Here are my mother and my brothers.
Anyone who does the will of my Father in heaven, he is my brother
and sister and mother.'

This is the Gospel of the Lord.

22 November

St Cecilia virgin and martyr   Memorial

Common of martyrs or Common of Virgins.

FIRST READING

A reading from the prophet Hosea   2:16-17. 21-22

I will betroth you to myself for ever.

The Lord says this:

I am going to lead her out into the wilderness
and speak to her heart.
There she will respond to me as she did when she was young,
as she did when she came out of the land of Egypt.
I will betroth you to myself for ever,
betroth you with integrity and justice,
with tenderness and love;
I will betroth you to myself with faithfulness,
and you will come to know the Lord.

This is the word of the Lord.

Responsorial Psalm   Ps 44:11-12. 14-17. ℟ v.11. Alt. ℟ Mt 25:6

℟   Listen to me, daughter; see and bend your ear.

or

℟   The bridegroom is here; let us go out to meet Christ the Lord.

1   Listen, O daughter, give ear to my words:
     forget your own people and your father's house.
     So will the king desire your beauty:
     He is your lord, pay homage to him.   ℟

2   The daughter of the king is clothed with splendour,
     her robes embroidered with pearls set in gold.
     She is led to the king with her maiden companions.   ℟

3   They are escorted amid gladness and joy;
     they pass within the palace of the king.
     Sons shall be yours in place of your fathers:
     you will make them princes over all the earth.   ℟

Gospel Acclamation

Alleluia, alleluia!
This is a wise bridesmaid, whom the Lord found waiting;
at his coming, she went in with him to the wedding feast.
Alleluia!

GOSPEL

A reading from the holy Gospel according to Matthew   25:1-13

The bridegroom is here, go out and meet him.

Jesus spoke this parable to his disciples:
     'The kingdom of heaven will be like this: Ten bridesmaids took their lamps and went to meet the bridegroom. Five of them were foolish and five were sensible: the foolish ones did take their lamps, but they brought no oil, whereas the sensible ones took flasks of oil as well as their lamps. The bridegroom was late, and they all grew drowsy and fell asleep. But at midnight there was a cry, "The bridegroom is here! Go out and meet him." At this, all those bridesmaids woke up and trimmed their lamps, and the foolish ones

said to the sensible ones, "Give us some of your oil: our lamps are going out". But they replied, "There may not be enough for us and for you; you had better go to those who sell it and buy some for yourselves". They had gone off to buy it when the bridegroom arrived. Those who were ready went in with him to the wedding hall and the door was closed. The other bridesmaids arrived later, "Lord, Lord," they said, "open the door for us." But he replied, "I tell you solemnly, I do not know you". So stay awake, because you do not know either the day or the hour.'

This is the Gospel of the Lord.

23 November

St Clement I, pope and martyr

Optional Memorial

Common of martyrs or Common of pastors: for popes.

FIRST READING

A reading from the first letter of St Peter   5:1-4

Be the shepherds of the flock of God that is entrusted to you.

I have something to tell your elders: I am an elder myself, and a witness to the sufferings of Christ, and with you I have a share in the glory that is to be revealed. Be the shepherds of the flock of God that is entrusted to you: watch over it, not simply as a duty but gladly, because God wants it; not for sordid money, but because you are eager to do it. Never be a dictator over any group that is put in your charge, but be an example that the whole flock can follow. When the chief shepherd appears, you will be given the crown of unfading glory.

This is the word of the Lord.

Responsorial Psalm   Ps 88:2-5. 21-22. 25. 27. ℟ cf. v.2

℟ For ever I will sing the goodness of the Lord.

1 I will sing for ever of your love, O Lord;
    through all ages my mouth will proclaim your truth.
    Of this I am sure, that your love lasts for ever,
    that your truth is firmly established as the heavens. ℟

2 'I have made a covenant with my chosen one;
    I have sworn to David my servant:
    I will establish your dynasty for ever
    and set up your throne through all ages.

    ℟   For ever I will sing the goodness of the Lord.

3 'I have found David my servant
    and with my holy oil anointed him.
    My hand shall always be with him
    and my arm shall make him strong.   ℟

4 'My truth and my love shall be with him;
    by my name his might shall be exalted.
    He will say to me: "You are my father,
    my God, the rock who saves me." '   ℟

Gospel Acclamation   Mk 1:17

        Alleluia, alleluia!
        Come follow me, says the Lord,
        and I will make you fishers of my people.
        Alleluia!

                            GOSPEL

A reading from the holy Gospel according to Matthew   16:13-19

                   You are Peter and on this rock I will build my Church.

When Jesus came to the region of Caesarea Philippi he put this
question to his disciples, 'Who do people say the Son of Man is?' And
they said, 'Some say he is John the Baptist, some Elijah, and others
Jeremiah or one of the prophets'. 'But you,' he said, 'who do you say I
am?' Then Simon Peter spoke up, 'You are the Christ,' he said, 'the
Son of the living God'. Jesus replied, 'Simon son of Jonah, you are a
happy man! Because it was not flesh and blood that revealed this to
you but my Father in heaven. So I now say to you: You are Peter and
on this rock I will build my Church. And the gates of the underworld
can never hold out against it. I will give you the keys of the kingdom
of heaven: whatever you bind on earth shall be considered bound in
heaven; whatever you loose on earth shall be considered loosed in
heaven.'

    This is the Gospel of the Lord.

Also 23 November

St Columban, abbot   Optional Memorial

Common of pastors: for missionaries or Common of holy men and women: for
religious.

FIRST READING

A reading from the prophet Isaiah   52:7-10

All the ends of the earth shall see the salvation of our God.

How beautiful on the mountains,
are the feet of one who brings good news,
who heralds peace, brings happiness,
proclaims salvation,
and tells Zion,
'Your God is king!'

Listen! Your watchmen raise their voices,
they shout for joy together,
for they see the Lord face to face,
as he returns to Zion.
Break into shouts of joy together,
you ruins of Jerusalem;
for the Lord is consoling his people,
redeeming Jerusalem.

The Lord bares his holy arm
in the sight of all the nations,
and all the ends of the earth shall see
the salvation of our God.

This is the word of the Lord.

Responsorial Psalm   Ps 95:1-3. 7-8. 10. ℟ v.3

℟   Proclaim his marvellous deeds to all the nations.

1   O sing a new song to the Lord,
    sing to the Lord all the earth.
    O sing to the Lord, bless his name.   ℟

2   Proclaim his help day by day,
    tell among the nations his glory
    and his wonders among all the peoples.   ℟

3   Give the Lord, you families of peoples,
    give the Lord glory and power,
    give the Lord the glory of his name.   ℟

4   Proclaim to the nations: 'God is king.'
    The world he made firm in its place;
    he will judge the peoples in fairness.   ℟

Gospel Acclamation   Jn 8:12

Alleluia, alleluia!
I am the light of the world, says the Lord;
whoever follows me will have the light of life.
Alleluia!

GOSPEL

A reading from the holy Gospel according to Luke   9:57-62

I will follow you, wherever you go.

As Jesus and his disciples travelled along they met a man on the road
who said to him, 'I will follow you wherever you go'. Jesus answered,
'Foxes have holes and the birds of the air have nests, but the Son of
Man has nowhere to lay his head'.

Another to whom he said, 'Follow me', replied, 'Let me go and bury
my father first'. But he answered, 'Leave the dead to bury their dead;
your duty is to go and spread the news of the kingdom of God'.

Another said, 'I will follow you, sir, but first let me go and say
good-bye to my people at home'. Jesus said to him, 'Once the hand is
laid on the plough, no one who looks back is fit for the kingdom of
God'.

This is the Gospel of the Lord.

30 November

ST ANDREW, APOSTLE

Feast

FIRST READING

A reading from the letter of St Paul to the Romans   10:9-18

*Faith comes from what is heard and what is heard comes from
the preaching of Christ.*

If your lips confess that Jesus is Lord and if you believe in your heart
that God raised him from the dead, then you will be saved. By
believing from the heart you are made righteous; by confessing with
your lips you are saved. When scripture says: those who believe in
him will have no cause for shame, it makes no distinction between
Jew and Greek: all belong to the same Lord who is rich enough
however many ask his help, for everyone who calls on the name of the
Lord will be saved.

But they will not ask his help unless they believe in him, and they
will not believe in him unless they have heard of him, and they will
not hear of him unless they get a preacher, and they will never have a
preacher unless one is sent, but as scripture says: The footsteps of
those who bring good news are a welcome sound. Not everyone, of
course, listens to the Good News. As Isaiah says: Lord, how many
believed what we proclaimed? So faith comes from what is preached,
and what is preached comes from the word of Christ.

Let me put the question: is it possible that they did not hear?
Indeed they did; in the words of the psalm, their voice has gone out
through all the earth, and their message to the ends of the world.

This is the word of the Lord.

Responsorial Psalm   Ps 18:2-5. ℟ v.5

℟   Their message goes out through all the earth.

1   The heavens proclaim the glory of God
     and the firmament shows forth the work of his hands.
     Day unto day takes up the story
     and night unto night makes known the message.   ℟

2   No speech, no word, no voice is heard
     yet their span goes forth through all the earth,
     their words to the utmost bounds of the world.   ℟

Gospel Acclamation

Mt 4:19

> Alleluia, alleluia!
> Come, follow me, says the Lord,
> and I will make you fishers of my people.
> Alleluia!

GOSPEL

A reading from the holy Gospel according to Matthew 4:18-22

Immediately they left their nets and followed him.

As Jesus was walking by the Sea of Galilee he saw two brothers, Simon, who was called Peter, and his brother Andrew; they were making a cast in the lake with their net, for they were fishermen. And he said to them, 'Follow me and I will make you fishers of men.' And they left their nets at once and followed him.

Going on from there he saw another pair of brothers, James son of Zebedee and his brother John; they were in their boat with their father Zebedee, mending their nets, and he called them. At once, leaving the boat and their father, they followed him.

This is the Gospel of the Lord.

DECEMBER

3 December

St Francis Xavier, priest Memorial

Common of pastors: for missionaries.

FIRST READING

A reading from the first letter of St Paul 9:16-19. 22-23
to the Corinthians

Unless I preach the gospel, I shall be punished.

I do not boast of preaching the gospel, since it is a duty which has been laid on me; I should be punished if I did not preach it! If I had chosen this work myself, I might have been paid for it, but as I have not, it is a responsibility which has been put into my hands. Do you know what my reward is? It is this: in my preaching, to be able to offer the Good News free, and not insist on the rights which the Gospel gives me.

So though I am not a slave of any man I have made myself the slave of everyone so as to win as many as I could. For the weak I made myself weak. I made myself all things to all men in order to save some at any cost; and I still do this, for the sake of the Gospel, to have a share in its blessings.

This is the word of the Lord.

Responsorial Psalm Ps 116:1.2. ℟ Mk 16:15

℟ Go out to all the world, and tell the Good News.

or

℟ Alleluia!

1 O praise the Lord, all you nations,
   acclaim him all you peoples! ℟

2 Strong is his love for us;
   he is faithful for ever. ℟

Gospel Acclamation   Mt 28:19. 20

Alleluia, alleluia!
Go and teach all people my gospel.
I am with you always, until the end of the world.
Alleluia!

GOSPEL

A reading from the holy Gospel according to Mark   16:15-20

Go out to the whole world; proclaim the Good News to all creation.

Jesus showed himself to the Eleven, and he said to them, 'Go out to the whole world; proclaim the Good News to all creation. He who believes and is baptised will be saved; he who does not believe will be condemned. These are the signs that will be associated with believers: in my name they will cast out devils; they will have the gift of tongues; they will pick up snakes in their hands, and be unharmed should they drink deadly poison; they will lay their hands on the sick, who will recover.'

And so the Lord Jesus, after he had spoken to them, was taken up into heaven: there at the right hand of God he took his place, while they, going out, preached everywhere, the Lord working with them and confirming the word by the signs that accompanied it.

This is the Gospel of the Lord.

4 December

St John Damascene,
priest and doctor of the Church

Optional Memorial

Common of pastors or Common of doctors of the Church.

FIRST READING

A reading from the second letter of St Paul   1:13-14; 2:1-3
to Timothy

You have been entrusted to look after something precious; guard it
with the help of the Holy Spirit who lives in us.

Keep as your pattern the sound teaching you have heard from me, in the faith and love that are in Christ Jesus. You have been trusted to look after something precious; guard it with the help of the Holy Spirit who lives in us. Accept the strength, my dear son, that comes from the grace of Christ Jesus. You have heard everything that I teach in public; hand it on to reliable people so that they in turn will be able to teach others.

Put up with your share of difficulties, like a good soldier of Christ Jesus.

This is the word of the Lord.

Responsorial Psalm   Ps 18:8-11. ℟ v.10. Alt. ℟ Jn 6:63

℟   The judgements of the Lord are true, and all of them are just.

or

℟   Your words, Lord, are spirit and life.

1   The law of the Lord is perfect,
    it revives the soul.
    The rule of the Lord is to be trusted,
    it gives wisdom to the simple.   ℟

2   The precepts of the Lord are right,
    they gladden the heart.
    The command of the Lord is clear,
    it gives light to the eyes.   ℟

3   The fear of the Lord is holy,
    abiding for ever.
    The decrees of the Lord are truth
    and all of them just.   ℟

4   They are more to be desired than gold,
    than the purest of gold
    and sweeter are they than honey,
    than honey from the comb.   ℟

Gospel Acclamation   Jn 14:23

Alleluia, alleluia!
All who love me will keep my words
and my Father will love them, and we will come to them.
Alleluia!

GOSPEL

A reading from the holy Gospel according to Matthew   25:14-30

Because you have been faithful in a few things, enter into the joy of
your Lord.

Jesus spoke this parable to his disciples: 'A man on his way abroad
summoned his servants and entrusted his property to them. To one he
gave five talents, to another two, to a third, one; each in proportion to
his ability. Then he set out. The man who had received the five talents
promptly went and traded with them and made five more. The man
who had received two made two more in the same way. But the man
who had received one went off and dug a hole in the ground and hid
his master's money. Now a long time after, the master of those
servants came back and went through his accounts with them. The
man who had received the five talents came forward bringing five
more. 'Sir,' he said, 'you entrusted me with five talents; here are five
more that I have made.' His master said to him, 'Well done, good and
faithful servant; you have shown you can be faithful in small things, I
will trust you with greater; come and join in your master's happiness.'
Next the man with the two talents came forward. 'Sir,' he said, 'you
entrusted me with two talents; here are two more that I have made.'
His master said to him, 'Well done, good and faithful servant; you
have shown you can be faithful in small things, I will trust you with
greater; come and join in your master's happiness.'

'Last came forward the man who had the one talent. "Sir," said he,
"I had heard you were a hard man, reaping where you have not sown
and gathering where you have not scattered; so I was afraid, and I
went off and hid your talent in the ground. Here it is; it was yours, you
have it back." But his master answered him, "You wicked and lazy
servant! So you knew I reap where I have not sown and gather where I
have not scattered? Well then, you should have deposited my money
with the bankers, and on my return I would have recovered my capital
with interest. So now, take the talent from him and give it to the man
who has the five talents. For to everyone who has will be given more,

and he will have more than enough; but from the man who has not, even what he has will be taken away. As for this good-for-nothing servant, throw him out into the dark, where there will be weeping and grinding of teeth." '

This is the Gospel of the Lord.

6 December

St Nicholas, bishop   Optional Memorial

Common of pastors.

FIRST READING

A reading from the prophet Isaiah   6:1-8

Whom shall I send? Who will be our messenger?

In the year of King Uzziah's death I saw the Lord seated on a high throne; his train filled the sanctuary; above him stood seraphs, each one with six wings:two to cover its face, two to cover its feet and two for flying.

And they cried out one to another in this way,

'Holy, holy, holy is the Lord of hosts.
His glory fills the whole earth.'

The foundations of the threshold shook with the voice of the one who cried out, and the Temple was filled with smoke. I said:

'What a wretched state I am in! I am lost,
for I am a man of unclean lips
and I live among a people of unclean lips.
and my eyes have looked at the King, the Lord of hosts.'

Then one of the seraphs flew to me, holding in his hand a live coal which he had taken from the altar with a pair of tongs. With this he touched my mouth and said:

'See now, this has touched your lips,
your sin is taken away,
your iniquity is purged.'

Then I heard the voice of the Lord saying: 'Whom shall I send? Who will be our messenger?' I answered, 'Here I am, send me.'

This is the word of the Lord.

Responsorial Psalm   Ps 39:2. 4. 7-10. ℟ cf. vv. 8.9

℟   Here am I, Lord; I come to do your will.

1   I waited, I waited for the Lord
     and he stooped down to me;
     he heard my cry.
     He put a new song into my mouth,
     praise of our God.   ℟

2   You do not ask for sacrifice and offerings,
     but an open ear.
     You do not ask for holocaust and victim.
     Instead, here am I.   ℟

3   In the scroll of the book it stands written
     that I should do your will.
     My God, I delight in your law
     in the depth of my heart.   ℟

4   Your justice I have proclaimed
     in the great assembly.
     My lips I have not sealed;
     you know it, O Lord.   ℟

Gospel Acclamation   Lk 4:18

     Alleluia, alleluia!
     The Lord sent me to bring Good News to the poor,
     and freedom to prisoners.
     Alleluia!

GOSPEL

A reading from the holy Gospel according to Luke   10:1-9

The harvest is rich but the labourers are few.

The Lord appointed seventy-two others and sent them out ahead of him, in pairs, to all the towns and places he himself was to visit. He said to them, 'The harvest is rich but the labourers are few, so ask the Lord of the harvest to send labourers to his harvest. Start off now, but remember, I am sending you out like lambs among wolves. Carry no purse, no haversack, no sandals. Salute no one on the road. Whatever house you go into, let your first words be, "Peace to this house!" And if a man of peace lives there, your peace will go and rest on him; if not, it will come back to you. Stay in the same house, taking what food and drink they have to offer, for the labourer deserves his wages; do not move from house to house. Whenever you go into a town where they make you welcome, eat what is set before you. Cure those in it who are sick, and say, "The kingdom of God is very near to you." '

This is the Gospel of the Lord.

7 December

St Ambrose,
bishop and doctor of the Church   Memorial

Common of pastors or Common of doctors of the Church.

FIRST READING

A reading from the letter of St Paul to the Ephesians   3:8-12

The mission is to proclaim to all peoples the infinite treasure of Christ.

I, who am less than the least of all the saints, have been entrusted with this special grace, not only of proclaiming to the pagans the infinite treasure of Christ but also of explaining how the mystery is to be dispensed. Through all the ages, this has been kept hidden in God, the creator of everything. Why? So that the Sovereignties and Powers should learn only now, through the Church, how comprehensive God's wisdom really is, exactly according to the plan which he had had from all eternity in Christ Jesus our Lord. This is why we are bold enough to approach God in complete confidence, through our faith in him.

This is the word of the Lord.

Responsorial Psalm   Ps 88:2-5. 21-22. 25. 27. ℟ cf. v.2

℟   For ever I will sing the goodness of the Lord.

1   I will sing for ever of your love, O Lord;
     through all ages my mouth will proclaim your truth.
     Of this I am sure, that your love lasts for ever,
     that your truth is firmly established as the heavens.   ℟

2 'I have made a covenant with my chosen one;
   I have sworn to David my servant:
   I will establish your dynasty for ever
   and set up your throne through all ages.

   ℟ For ever I will sing the goodness of the Lord.

3 'I have found David my servant
   and with my holy oil anointed him.
   My hand shall always be with him
   and my arm shall make him strong. ℟

4 'My truth and my love shall be with him;
   by my name his might shall be exalted.
   He will say to me: "You are my father,
   my God, the rock who saves me." ' ℟

Gospel Acclamation   Jn 10:14

   Alleluia, alleluia!
   I am the good shepherd, says the Lord;
   I know my sheep, and mine know me.
   Alleluia!

GOSPEL

A reading from the holy Gospel according to John   10:11-16
The good shepherd is one who lays down his life for his sheep.
Jesus said:

   'I am the good shepherd:
   the good shepherd is one who lays down his life for his sheep.
   The hired man, since he is not the shepherd
   and the sheep do not belong to him,
   abandons the sheep and runs away
   as soon as he sees a wolf coming,
   and then the wolf attacks and scatters the sheep;
   this is because he is only a hired man
   and has no concern for the sheep.
   I am the good shepherd;
   I know my own
   and my own know me,

just as the Father knows me
and I know the Father;
and I lay down my life for my sheep.
And there are other sheep I have
that are not of this fold,
and these I have to lead as well.
They too will listen to my voice,
and there will be only one flock,
and one shepherd.'

This is the Gospel of the Lord.

8 December

THE IMMACULATE CONCEPTION OF
THE BLESSED VIRGIN MARY   Solemnity

FIRST READING

A reading from the book of Genesis   3:9-15. 20

I will put enmity between your offspring and her offspring.

After Adam had eaten of the tree the Lord God called to him, 'Where
are you?' he asked. 'I heard the sound of you in the garden,' he replied.
'I was afraid because I was naked, so I hid.' 'Who told you that you
were naked?' he asked. 'Have you been eating of the tree I forbade you
to eat?' The man replied, 'It was the woman you put with me; she gave
me the fruit, and I ate it.' Then the Lord God asked the woman, 'What
is this you have done?' The woman replied, 'The serpent tempted me
and I ate.'

Then the Lord God said to the serpent, 'Because you have done
this,

'Be accursed beyond all cattle,
all wild beasts.
You shall crawl on your belly and eat dust
every day of your life.
I will make you enemies of each other:
you and the woman,
your offspring and her offspring.
It will crush your head
and you will strike its heel.'

The man named his wife 'Eve' because she was the mother of all those who live.

This is the word of the Lord.

Responsorial Psalm   Ps 97:1-4. ℟ v.1

℟   Sing to the Lord a new song, for he has done marvellous deeds.

1   Sing a new song to the Lord
    for he has worked wonders.
    His right hand and his holy arm
    have brought salvation.   ℟

2   The Lord has made known his salvation;
    has shown his justice to the nations.
    He has remembered his truth and love
    for the house of Israel.   ℟

3   All the ends of the earth have seen
    the salvation of our God.
    Shout to the Lord all the earth,
    ring out your joy.   ℟

SECOND READING

A reading from the letter of St Paul to the Ephesians   1:3-6. 11-12

God chose us in Christ before the foundation of the world.

Blessed be God the Father of our Lord Jesus Christ,
who has blessed us with all the spiritual blessings of heaven in Christ.
Before the world was made, he chose us, chose us in Christ,
to be holy and spotless, and to live through love in his presence,
determining that we should become his adopted sons, through Jesus
    Christ
for his own kind purposes,
to make us praise the glory of his grace,
his free gift to us in the Beloved.
And it is in him that we were claimed as God's own,
chosen from the beginning,

under the predetermined plan of the one who guides all things
as he decides by his own will;
chosen to be,
for his greater glory,
the people who would put their hopes in Christ before he came.

This is the word of the Lord.

Gospel Acclamation   cf. Lk 1:28

Alleluia, alleluia!
Hail, Mary, full of grace, the Lord is with you;
blessed are you among women.
Alleluia!

GOSPEL

A reading from the holy Gospel according to Luke   1:26-38

Rejoice, favoured one, the Lord is with you.

The angel Gabriel was sent by God to a town in Galilee called
Nazareth, to a virgin betrothed to a man named Joseph, of the House
of David; and the virgin's name was Mary. He went in and said to her,
'Rejoice, so highly favoured! The Lord is with you.' She was deeply
disturbed by these words and asked herself what this greeting could
mean, but the angel said to her, 'Mary, do not be afraid; you have won
God's favour. Listen! You are to conceive and bear a son, and you must
name him Jesus. He will be great and will be called Son of the Most
High. The Lord God will give him the throne of his ancestor David; he
will rule over the House of Jacob for ever and his reign will have no
end.' Mary said to the angel, 'But how can this come about, since I am
a virgin?' 'The Holy Spirit will come upon you' the angel answered
'and the power of the Most High will cover you with its shadow. And
so the child will be holy and will be called Son of God. Know this too:
your kinswoman Elizabeth has, in her old age, herself conceived a son,
and she whom people called barren is now in her sixth month, for
nothing is impossible to God.' 'I am the handmaid of the Lord,' said
Mary 'let what you have said be done to me.' And the angel left her.

This is the Gospel of the Lord.

11 December

St Damasus I, pope
Optional Memorial

Common of pastors: for popes.

FIRST READING

A reading from the Acts of the Apostles
20:17-18. 28-32. 36

Be on guard for yourselves and for all of whom the Holy Spirit has made you the overseers.

From Miletus Paul sent for the elders of the church of Ephesus. When they arrived he addressed these words to them:

'Be on your guard for yourselves and for all the flock of which the Holy Spirit has made you the overseers, to feed the Church of God which he bought with his own blood. I know quite well that when I have gone fierce wolves will invade you and will have no mercy on the flock. Even from your own ranks there will be men coming forward with a travesty of the truth on their lips to induce the disciples to follow them. So be on your guard, remembering how night and day for three years I never failed to keep you right, shedding tears over each one of you. And now I commend you to God, and to the word of his grace that has power to build you up and to give you your inheritance among all the sanctified.'

When he had finished speaking he knelt down with them all and prayed.

This is the word of the Lord.

Responsorial Psalm
Ps 109:1-4. ℟ v.4

℟ You are a priest for ever, in the line of Melchizedek.

1 The Lord's revelation to my Master:
  'Sit on my right:
  I will put your foes beneath your feet.' ℟

2 The Lord will send from Zion
  your sceptre of power:
  rule in the midst of all your foes. ℟

3   A prince from the day of your birth
     on the holy mountains;
     from the womb before the daybreak I begot you. ℟

4   The Lord has sworn an oath he will not change.
     'You are a priest for ever,
     a priest like Melchizedek of old.' ℟

Gospel Acclamation   Jn 15:15

     Alleluia, alleluia!
     I call you my friends, says the Lord,
     for I have made known to you all that the Father has told me.
     Alleluia!

GOSPEL

A reading from the holy Gospel according to John   15:9-17

You are my friends if you do what I command you.

Jesus said to his disciples:

     'As the Father has loved me,
     so I have loved you.
     Remain in my love.
     If you keep my commandments
     you will remain in my love,
     just as I have kept my Father's commandments
     and remain in his love.
     I have told you this
     so that my own joy may be in you
     and your joy be complete.
     This is my commandment:
     love one another
     as I have loved you.
     A man can have no greater love
     than to lay down his life for his friends.
     You are my friends,
     if you do what I command you.
     I shall not call you servants any more,
     because a servant does not know

his master's business;
I call you friends,
because I have made known to you
everything I have learnt from my Father.
You did not choose me,
no, I chose you;
and I commissioned you
to go out and to bear fruit,
fruit that will last;
and then the Father will give you
anything you ask him in my name.
What I command you
is to love one another.'

This is the Gospel of the Lord.

12 December

St Jane Frances de Chantal, religious

Optional Memorial

Common of holy men and women: for religious.

FIRST READING

A reading from the book of Proverbs 31:10-13. 19-20. 30-31

It is the wise woman whom the Lord will praise.

A perfect wife – who can find her?
She is far beyond the price of pearls.

Her husband's heart has confidence in her,
from her he will derive no little profit.

Advantage and not hurt she brings him
all the days of her life.

She is always busy with wool and with flax,
she does her work with eager hands.

She sets her hands to the distaff,
her fingers grasp the spindle.

She holds out her hand to the poor,
she opens her arms to the needy.

Charm is deceitful, and beauty empty;
the woman who is wise is the one to praise.

Give her a share in what her hands have worked for,
and let her works tell her praises at the city gates.

This is the word of the Lord.

Responsorial Psalm   Ps 130

R̸ In you, Lord, I have found my peace.

1   O Lord my heart is not proud
    nor haughty my eyes.
    I have not gone after things too great
    nor marvels beyond me.   R̸

2   Truly I have set my soul
    in silence and peace.
    A weaned child on its mother's breast,
    even so is my soul.   R̸

3   O Israel, hope in the Lord
    both now and for ever.   R̸

Gospel Acclamation   Jn 8:31-32

Alleluia, alleluia!
If you stay in my word, you will indeed by my disciples,
and you will know the truth, says the Lord.
Alleluia!

GOSPEL

A reading from the holy Gospel according to Mark   3:31-35

Whoever has done the will of God is my brother, my sister, and my
mother.

The mother and brothers of Jesus arrived and, standing outside, sent
in a message asking for him. A crowd was sitting round him at the
time the message was passed to him, 'Your mother and brothers and
sisters are outside asking for you.' He replied, 'Who are my mother
and my brothers?' And looking round at those sitting in a

circle about him, he said, 'Here are my mother and my brothers. Anyone who does the will of God, that person is my brother and sister and mother.'

This is the Gospel of the Lord.

13 December

St Lucy, virgin and martyr
Memorial

Common of martyrs or Common of virgins.

FIRST READING

A reading from the second letter of St Paul to the Corinthians
10:17–11:2

I have betrothed you to one man, as a chaste virgin for Christ.

If anyone wants to boast, let him boast of the Lord. It is not the man who commends himself that can be accepted, but the man who is commended by the Lord.

I only wish you were able to tolerate a little foolishness from me. But of course: you are tolerant towards me. You see, the jealousy that I feel for you is God's own jealousy: I arranged for you to marry Christ so that I might give you away as a chaste virgin to this one husband.

This is the word of the Lord.

Responsorial Psalm
Ps 30:3-4. 6-8. 16-17. ℟ v.6

℟   Into your hands, O Lord, I entrust my spirit.

1   Be a rock of refuge for me,
    a mighty stronghold to save me,
    for you are my rock, my stronghold.
    For your name's sake, lead me and guide me.   ℟

2   Into your hands I commend my spirit.
    It is you who will redeem me, Lord.
    As for me, I trust in the Lord:
    let me be glad and rejoice in your love.   ℟

3 My life is in your hands, deliver me
from the hands of those who hate me.
Let your face shine on your servant.
Save me in your love.

℟ Into your hands, O Lord, I entrust my spirit.

Gospel Acclamation

Alleluia, alleluia!
This is the wise bridesmaid, whom the Lord found waiting;
at his coming she went in with him to the wedding feast.
Alleluia!

GOSPEL

A reading from the holy Gospel according to Matthew   25:1-13

The bridegroom is here, go out and meet him.

Jesus spoke this parable to his disciples:

'The kingdom of heaven will be like this: Ten bridesmaids took their lamps and went to meet the bridegroom. Five of them were foolish and five were sensible: the foolish ones did take their lamps, but they brought no oil, whereas the sensible ones took flasks of oil as well as their lamps. The bridegroom was late, and they all grew drowsy and fell asleep. But at midnight there was a cry, "The bridegroom is here! Go out and meet him." At this, all those bridesmaids woke up and trimmed their lamps, and the foolish ones said to the sensible ones, "Give us some of your oil: our lamps are going out". But they replied, "There may not be enough for us and for you; you had better go to those who sell it and buy some for yourselves". They had gone off to buy it when the bridegroom arrived. Those who were ready went in with him to the wedding hall and the door was closed. The other bridesmaids arrived later. "Lord, Lord," they said, "open the door for us." But he replied, "I tell you solemnly, I do not know you". So stay awake, because you do not know either the day or the hour.'

This is the Gospel of the Lord.

14 December

St John of the Cross,
priest and doctor of the Church   Memorial

Common of doctors of the Church or Common of holy men and women: for religious.

FIRST READING

A reading from the first letter of St Paul   2:1-10
to the Corinthians

We teach the wisdom of God in mystery.

When I came to you, brothers, it was not with any show of oratory or philosophy, but simply to tell you what God had guaranteed. During my stay with you, the only knowledge I claimed to have was about Jesus, and only about him as the crucified Christ. Far from relying on any power of my own, I came among you in great 'fear and trembling' and in my speeches and the sermons that I gave, there were none of the arguments that belong to philosophy; only a demonstration of the power of the Spirit. And I did this so that your faith should not depend on human philosophy but on the power of God.

But still we have a wisdom to offer those who have reached maturity: not a philosophy of our age, it is true, still less of the masters of our age, which are coming to their end. The hidden wisdom of God which we teach in our mysteries is the wisdom that God predestined to be for our glory before the ages began. It is a wisdom that none of the masters of this age have ever known, or they would not have crucified the Lord of Glory; we teach what scripture calls: the things that no eye has seen and no ear has heard, things beyond the mind of man, all that God has prepared for those who love him.

These are the very things that God has revealed to us through the Spirit.

This is the word of the Lord.

Responsorial Psalm   Ps 36:3-6. 30-31. ℟ v.30

℟   The mouths of the just murmur wisdom.

1   If you trust in the Lord and do good,
    then you will live in the land and be secure.
    If you find your delight in the Lord,
    he will grant your heart's desire.   ℟

2   Commit your life to the Lord,
trust in him and he will act,
so that your justice breaks forth like the light,
your cause like the noon-day sun. ℞

3   The just man's mouth utters wisdom
and his lips speak what is right;
the law of his God is in his heart,
his steps shall be saved from stumbling. ℞

Gospel Acclamation   Mt 5:3

Alleluia, alleluia!
Happy the poor in spirit;
the kingdom of heaven is theirs!
Alleluia!

GOSPEL

A reading from the holy Gospel according to Luke   14:25-33

Unless you are ready to give up all that you possess, you cannot be my disciples.

Great crowds accompanied Jesus on his way and he turned and spoke to them. 'If any man comes to me without hating his father, mother, wife, children, brothers, sisters, yes and his own life too, he cannot be my disciple. Anyone who does not carry his cross and come after me cannot be my disciple.

'And indeed, which of you here, intending to build a tower, would not first sit down and work out the cost to see if he had enough to complete it? Otherwise, if he laid the foundation and then found himself unable to finish the work, the onlookers would all start making fun of him and saying, "Here is a man who started to build and was unable to finish." Or again, what king marching to war against another king would not first sit down and consider whether with ten thousand men he could stand up to the other who advanced against him with twenty thousand? If not, then while the other king was still a long way off, he would send envoys to sue for peace. So in the same way, none of you can be my disciple unless he gives up all his possessions.'

This is the Gospel of the Lord.

1235

21 December

St Peter Canisius,
priest and doctor of the Church

Optional Memorial

Common of pastors or Common of doctors of the Church.

FIRST READING

A reading from the second letter of St Paul to Timothy   4:1-5

Preach the Good News; fulfill your ministry.

Before God and before Christ Jesus who is to be judge of the living and the dead, I put this duty to you, in the name of his Appearing and of his kingdom: proclaim the message and, welcome or unwelcome, insist on it. Refute falsehood, correct error, call to obedience – but do all with patience and with the intention of teaching. The time is sure to come when, far from being content with sound teaching, people will be avid for the latest novelty and collect themselves a whole series of teachers according to their own tastes; and then, instead of listening to the truth, they will turn to myths. Be careful always to choose the right course; be brave under trials; make the preaching of the Good News your life's work, in thoroughgoing service.

This is the word of the Lord.

Responsorial Psalm   Ps 39:2. 4. 7-10. ℟ vv.8. 9

℟   Here am I , Lord; I come to do your will.

1   I waited, I waited for the Lord
     and he stooped down to me;
     he heard my cry.
     He put a new song into my mouth,
     praise of our God.   ℟

2   You do not ask for sacrifice and offerings,
     but an open ear.
     You do not ask for holocaust and victim.
     Instead, here am I.   ℟

3 In the scroll of the book it stands written
   that I should do your will.
   My God, I delight in your law
   in the depth of my heart.

   ℟ Here am I, Lord; I come to do your will.

4 Your justice I have proclaimed
   in the great assembly.
   My lips I have not sealed;
   you know it, O Lord. ℟

Gospel Acclamation   Mt 5:16

   Alleluia, alleluia!
   Let your light shine before all
   that they may see your good works and glorify your Father.
   Alleluia!

GOSPEL

A reading from the holy Gospel according to Matthew   5:13-19

                                        You are the light of the world.

Jesus said to his disciples: 'You are the salt of the earth. But if salt
becomes tasteless, what can make it salty again? It is good for
nothing, and can only be thrown out to be trampled underfoot by men.

   'You are the light of the world. A city built on a hill-top cannot be
hidden. No one lights a lamp to put it under a tub; they put it on the
lamp-stand where it shines for everyone in the house. In the same way
your light must shine in the sight of men, so that, seeing your good
works, they may give the praise to your Father in heaven.

   'Do not imagine that I have come to abolish the Law or the
Prophets. I have come not to abolish but to complete them. I tell you
solemnly, till heaven and earth disappear, not one dot, not one little
stroke, shall disappear from the Law until its purpose is achieved.
Therefore, the man who infringes even one of the least of these
commandments and teaches others to do the same will be considered
the least in the kingdom of heaven; but the man who keeps them and
teaches them will be considered great in the kingdom of heaven.'

   This is the Gospel of the Lord.

23 December

St John of Kanty, priest

Optional Memorial

Common of pastors or Common of holy men and women: for those who work for the underprivileged.

FIRST READING

A reading from the letter of St James

2:14-17

If good works do not go with faith then it is quite dead.

Take the case, my brothers, of someone who has never done a single good act but claims that he has faith. Will that faith save him? If one of the brothers or one of the sisters is in need of clothes and has not enough food to live on, and one of you says to them, 'I wish you well; keep yourself warm and eat plenty', without giving them these bare necessities of life, then what good is that? Faith is like that: if good works do not go with it, it is quite dead.

This is the word of the Lord.

Responsorial Psalm

Ps 111:1-9. ℟ v.1

℟   Happy are those who fear the Lord.

or

℟   Alleluia!

1   Happy the man who fears the Lord,
    who takes delight in his commands.
    His sons will be powerful on earth;
    the children of the upright are blessed.   ℟

2   Riches and wealth are in his house;
    his justice stands firm for ever.
    He is a light in the darkness for the upright:
    he is generous, merciful and just.   ℟

3   The good man takes pity and lends,
    he conducts his affairs with honour.
    The just man will never waver:
    he will be remembered for ever.   ℟

4   He has no fear of evil news;
    with a firm heart he trusts in the Lord.
    With a steadfast heart he will not fear;
    he will see the downfall of his foes.   ℟

5   Open-handed, he gives to the poor;
    his justice stands firm for ever.
    His head will be raised in glory.   ℟

Gospel Acclamation   Jn 13:34

    Alleluia, alleluia!
    I give you a new commandment:
    love one another as I have loved you.
    Alleluia!

GOSPEL

A reading from the holy Gospel according to Luke   6:27-38

Be merciful, as your Father is merciful.

Jesus said to his disciples: 'I say this to you who are listening: Love
your enemies, do good to those who hate you, bless those who curse
you, pray for those who treat you badly. To the man who slaps you on
one cheek, present the other cheek too; to the man who takes your
cloak from you, do not refuse your tunic. Give to everyone who asks
you, and do not ask for your property back from the man who robs you.
Treat others as you would like them to treat you. If you love those who
love you, what thanks can you expect? Even sinners love those who
love them. And if you do good to those who do good to you, what
thanks can you expect? For even sinners do that much. And if you
lend to those from whom you hope to receive, what thanks can you
expect? Even sinners lend to get back the same amount. Instead, love
your enemies and do good, and lend without any hope of return. You
will have a great reward, and you will be sons of the Most High, for he
himself is kind to the ungrateful and the wicked.

    'Be compassionate as your Father is compassionate. Do not judge,
and you will not be judged yourselves; do not condemn, and you will
not be condemned yourselves; grant pardon, and you will be pardoned.
Give, and there will be gifts for you: a full measure, pressed down,
shaken together, and running over, will be poured into your lap;

because the amount you measure out is the amount you will be given back.'

This is the Gospel of the Lord.

26 December
ST STEPHEN, FIRST MARTYR   Feast

FIRST READING

A reading from the Acts of the Apostles   6:8-10; 7:54-59

I can see heaven thrown open.

Stephen was filled with grace and power and began to work miracles and great signs among the people. But then certain people came forward to debate with Stephen, some from Cyrene and Alexandria who were members of the synagogue called the Synagogue of Freedmen, and others from Cilicia and Asia. They found they could not get the better of him because of his wisdom, and because it was the Spirit that prompted what he said. They were infuriated when they heard what he said, and ground their teeth at him.

But Stephen, filled with the Holy Spirit, gazed into heaven and saw the glory of God, and Jesus standing at God's right hand. 'I can see heaven thrown open' he said 'and the Son of Man standing at the right hand of God.' At this all the members of the council shouted out and stopped their ears with their hands; then they all rushed at him, sent him out of the city and stoned him. The witnesses put down their clothes at the feet of a young man called Saul. As they were stoning him, Stephen said in invocation, 'Lord Jesus, receive my spirit.' Then he knelt down and said aloud, 'Lord, do not hold this sin against them'; and with these words he fell asleep. Saul entirely approved of the killing.

This is the word of the Lord.

Responsorial Psalm   Ps 30:3-4. 6. 8. 16-17. ℟ v.6

℟   Into your hands, O Lord, I entrust my spirit.

1   Be a rock of refuge for me,
    a mighty stronghold to save me,
    for you are my rock, my stronghold.
    For your name's sake, lead me and guide me.   ℟

2   Into your hands I commend my spirit.
    It is you who will redeem me, Lord.
    As for me, I trust in the Lord:
    let me be glad and rejoice in your love.   ℟

3   My life is in your hands, deliver me
    from the hands of those who hate me.
    Let your face shine on your servant.
    Save me in your love.   ℟

Gospel Acclamation   Ps 117:26. 27

    Alleluia, alleluia!
    Blessed is he who comes in the name of the Lord;
    the Lord God shines upon us.
    Alleluia!

GOSPEL

A reading from the holy Gospel according to Matthew   10:17-22

It is not you who will be speaking but the Spirit of your Father.

Jesus said to his apostles: 'Beware of men: they will hand you over to
sanhedrins and scourge you in their synagogues. You will be dragged
before governors and kings for my sake, to bear witness before them
and the pagans. But when they hand you over, do not worry about how
to speak or what to say; what you are to say will be given to you when
the time comes; because it is not you who will be speaking; the Spirit
of your Father will be speaking in you.

    'Brother will betray brother to death, and the father his child;
children will rise against their parents and have them put to death.
You will be hated by all men on account of my name; but the man who
stands firm to the end will be saved.'

    This is the Gospel of the Lord.

27 December

ST JOHN, APOSTLE AND EVANGELIST   Feast

FIRST READING

A reading from the first letter of St John   1:1-4

What we have seen and heard we are making known to you.

Something which has existed since the beginning,
that we have heard,
and we have seen with our own eyes;
that we have watched
and touched with our hands:
the Word, who is life –
this is our subject.
That life was made visible:
we saw it and we are giving our testimony,
telling you of the eternal life
which was with the Father and has been made visible to us.
What we have seen and heard
we are telling you
so that you too may be in union with us,
as we are in union
with the Father
and with his Son Jesus Christ.
We are writing this to you to make our own joy complete.

> This is the word of the Lord.

Responsorial Psalm   Ps 96:1-2. 5-6. 11-12. ℟ v.12

℟   Let the just rejoice in the Lord.

1   The Lord is king, let earth rejoice,
      the many coastlands be glad.
      Cloud and darkness are his raiment;
      his throne, justice and right.   ℟

2   The mountains melt like wax
      before the Lord of all the earth.
      The skies proclaim his justice;
      all peoples see his glory.   ℟

3   Light shines forth for the just
    and joy for the upright of heart.
    Rejoice, you just, in the Lord;
    give glory to his holy name. ℟

Gospel Acclamation

    Alleluia, alleluia!
    You are God: we praise you; you are the Lord: we acclaim you;
    the glorious company of apostles praise you.
    Alleluia!

GOSPEL

A reading from the holy Gospel according to John   20:2-8

The other disciple outran Peter and came first to the tomb.

On the first day of the week Mary of Magdala came running to Simon Peter and the other disciple, the one Jesus loved. 'They have taken the Lord out of the tomb' she said 'and we don't know where they have put him.'

So Peter set out with the other disciple to go to the tomb. They ran together, but the other disciple, running faster than Peter, reached the tomb first; he bent down and saw the linen cloths lying on the ground, but did not go in. Simon Peter who was following now came up, went right into the tomb, saw the linen cloths on the ground, and also the cloth that had been over his head; this was not with the linen cloths but rolled up in a place by itself. Then the other disciple who had reached the tomb first also went in; he saw and he believed.

This is the Gospel of the Lord.

28 December

THE HOLY INNOCENTS, MARTYRS   Feast

FIRST READING

A reading from the first letter of St John   1:5 – 2:2

The blood of Jesus Christ cleanses us of all sin.

This is what we have heard from Jesus Christ,
and the message that we are announcing to you:
God is light; there is no darkness in him at all.
If we say that we are in union with God
while we are living in darkness,
we are lying because we are not living the truth.
But if we live our lives in the light,
as he is in the light,
we are in union with one another,
and the blood of Jesus, his Son,
purifies us from all sin.
If we say we have no sin in us,
we are deceiving ourselves
and refusing to admit the truth;
but if we acknowledge our sins,
then God who is faithful and just
will forgive our sins and purify us
from everything that is wrong.
To say that we have never sinned
is to call God a liar
and to show that his word is not in us.
I am writing this, my children,
to stop you sinning;
but if anyone should sin,
we have our advocate with the Father,
Jesus Christ, who is just;
he is the sacrifice that takes our sins away,
and not only ours,
but the whole world's.

This is the word of the Lord.

Responsorial Psalm   Ps 123:2-5. 7-8. ℟ v.7

℟   Our soul has escaped like a bird from the hunter's net.

1   If the Lord had not been on our side
    when men rose against us,
    then would they have swallowed us alive
    when their anger was kindled.   ℟

2   Then would the waters have engulfed us,
    the torrent gone over us;
    over our head would have swept
    the raging waters.   ℟

3   Indeed the snare has been broken
    and we have escaped.
    Our help is in the name of the Lord,
    who made heaven and earth.   ℟

Gospel Acclamation

    Alleluia, alleluia!
    You are God: we praise you; you are the Lord: we acclaim you;
    the white-robed army of martyrs praise you.
    Alleluia!

GOSPEL

A reading from the holy Gospel according to Matthew   2:13-18

Herod killed all the male children who were in Bethlehem.

After the wise men had left, the angel of the Lord appeared to Joseph
in a dream and said, 'Get up, take the child and his mother with you,
and escape into Egypt, and stay there until I tell you, because Herod
intends to search for the child and do away with him.' So Joseph got
up and, taking the child and his mother with him, left that night for
Egypt, where he stayed until Herod was dead. This was to fulfil what
the Lord had spoken through the prophet:

    I called my son out of Egypt.

    Herod was furious when he realised that he had been outwitted by
the wise men and in Bethlehem and its surrounding district he had all

the male children killed who were two years old or under, reckoning by the date he had been careful to ask the wise men. It was then that the words spoken through the prophet Jeremiah were fulfilled:

A voice was heard in Ramah,
sobbing and loudly lamenting:
it was Rachel weeping for her children,
refusing to be comforted
because they were no more.

This is the Gospel of the Lord.

29 December

St Thomas à Becket, bishop and martyr

Optional Memorial

Common of martyrs or Common of pastors.

FIRST READING

A reading from the second letter of St Paul to Timothy   2:8-13; 3:10-12

*You must be aware that anybody who tries to live in devotion to
Christ is certain to suffer persecution.*

Remember the Good News that I carry, 'Jesus Christ risen from the dead, sprung from the race of David'; it is on account of this that I have my own hardships to bear, even to being chained like a criminal – but they cannot chain up God's news. So I bear it all for the sake of those who are chosen, so that in the end they may have the salvation that is in Christ Jesus and the eternal glory that comes with it.
    Here is a saying that you can rely on:

If we have died with him, then we shall live with him.
If we hold firm, then we shall reign with him.
If we disown him, then he will disown us.
We may be unfaithful, but he is always faithful,
for he cannot disown his own self.

You know what I have taught, how I have lived, what I have aimed at; you know my faith, my patience and my love; my constancy and the persecutions and hardships that came to me in places like Antioch, Iconium and Lystra – all the persecutions I have endured; and the Lord has rescued me from every one of them. You are well aware, then, that anybody who tries to live in devotion to Christ is certain to be attacked.

This is the word of the Lord.

Responsorial Psalm   Ps 33:2-9. ℟ v.5

℟   The Lord set me free from all my fears.

1   I will bless the Lord at all times,
    his praise always on my lips;
    in the Lord my soul shall make its boast.
    The humble shall hear and be glad.   ℟

2   Glorify the Lord with me.
    Together let us praise his name.
    I sought the Lord and he answered me;
    from all my terrors he set me free.   ℟

3   Look towards him and be radiant;
    let your faces not be abashed.
    This poor man called; the Lord heard him
    and rescued him from all his distress.   ℟

4   The angel of the Lord is encamped
    around those who revere him, to rescue them.
    Taste and see that the Lord is good.
    He is happy who seeks refuge in him.   ℟

Gospel Acclamation   Mt 5:6

Alleluia, alleluia!
Happy are those who hunger and thirst for what is right;
they shall be satisfied.
Alleluia!

GOSPEL

A reading from the holy Gospel according to Matthew   16:24-27

All who lose their lives on account of me will really save their lives.

Jesus said to his disciples, 'If anyone wants to be a follower of mine, let him renounce himself and take up his cross and follow me. For anyone who wants to save his life will lose it; but anyone who loses his life for my sake will find it. What, then, will a man gain if he wins the whole world and ruins his life? Or what has a man to offer in exchange for his life?

'For the Son of Man is going to come in the glory of his Father with his angels, and, when he does, he will reward each one according to his behaviour.'

This is the Gospel of the Lord.

31 December

St Sylvester I, pope
Optional Memorial

Common of pastors: for popes.

FIRST READING

A reading from the prophet Ezekiel
34:11-16

As a shepherd keeps all his flock in view, so shall I keep my sheep in view.

The Lord says this: I am going to look after my flock myself and keep all of it in view. As a shepherd keeps all his flock in view when he stands up in the middle of his scattered sheep, so shall I keep my sheep in view. I shall rescue them from wherever they have been scattered during the mist and darkness. I shall bring them out of the countries where they are; I shall gather them together from foreign countries and bring them back to their own land. I shall pasture them on the mountains of Israel, in the ravines and in every inhabited place in the land. I shall feed them in good pasturage; the high mountains of Israel will be their grazing ground. There they will rest in good grazing ground; they will browse in rich pastures on the mountains of Israel. I myself will pasture my sheep, I myself will show them where to rest – it is the Lord who speaks. I shall look for the lost one, bring back the stray, bandage the wounded and make the weak strong. I shall watch over the fat and healthy. I shall be a true shepherd to them.

This is the word of the Lord.

Responsorial Psalm   Ps 22. ℟ v.1

℟   The Lord is my shepherd; there is nothing I shall want.

1   The Lord is my shepherd;
    there is nothing I shall want.
    Fresh and green are the pastures
    where he gives me repose.
    Near restful waters he leads me,
    to revive my drooping spirit.   ℟

2   He guides me along the right path;
    he is true to his name.
    If I should walk in the valley of darkness
    no evil would I fear.
    You are there with your crook and your staff;
    with these you give me comfort.   ℟

3   You have prepared a banquet for me
    in the sight of my foes.
    My head you have anointed with oil;
    my cup is overflowing.   ℟

4   Surely goodness and kindness shall follow me
    all the days of my life.
    In the Lord's own house shall I dwell
    for ever and ever.   ℟

Gospel Acclamation   Mk 1:17

    Alleluia, alleluia!
    Come, follow me, says the Lord,
    and I will make you fishers of my people.
    Alleluia!

GOSPEL

A reading from the holy Gospel according to Matthew   16:13-19

You are Peter and on this rock I will build my Church.

When Jesus came to the region of Caesarea Philippi he put this question to his disciples, 'Who do people say the Son of Man is?' And they said, 'Some say he is John the Baptist, some Elijah, and others Jeremiah or one of the prophets'. 'But you,' he said, 'who do you say I am?' Then Simon Peter spoke up, 'You are the Christ,' he said, 'the Son of the living God'. Jesus replied, 'Simon son of Jonah, you are a happy man! Because it was not flesh and blood that revealed this to you but my Father in heaven. So I now say to you: You are Peter and on this rock I will build my Church. And the gates of the underworld can never hold out against it. I will give you the keys of the kingdom of heaven: whatever you bind on earth shall be considered bound in heaven; whatever you loose on earth shall be considered loosed in heaven.'

This is the Gospel of the Lord.

National Calendars

for England, Wales, Australia, Ireland, Scotland

In the supplement of national propers following the universal calendar (January-December) is observed, and the area and degree of each celebration is defined under the heading of the date.

NATIONAL CALENDAR FOR ENGLAND

Approved by the Sacred Congregation for Divine Worship
on 21 November 1971 (Prot. Num: 25/71)

March	1	ST DAVID, BISHOP, PATRON OF WALES	Feas
	17	ST PATRICK, BISHOP, PATRON OF IRELAND	Feas
April	21	St Anselm, bishop and doctor of the Church	Memoria
	23	ST GEORGE, MARTYR, PATRON OF ENGLAND	Feas
May	4	THE BEATIFIED MARTYRS OF ENGLAND AND WALES	Feas
	25	St Bede the Venerable, priest and doctor of the Church	Memoria
	27	ST AUGUSTINE OF CANTERBURY, BISHOP, APOSTLE OF ENGLAND	Feas
June	20	St Alban, protomartyr of England	Memoria
	22	SS JOHN FISHER, BISHOP, AND THOMAS MORE, MARTYRS	Feas
August	26	*Bl Dominic of the Mother of God, priest**	
September	3	ST GREGORY THE GREAT, POPE AND DOCTOR OF THE CHURCH, APOSTLE OF THE ENGLISH	Feast
	24	Our Lady of Ransom	Memorial
October	13	St Edward the Confessor, king	Memorial
	25	THE FORTY MARTYRS OF ENGLAND AND WALES	Feast
December	29	ST THOMAS À BECKET, BISHOP AND MARTYR, PATRON OF THE PASTORAL CLERGY OF ENGLAND	Feast

*When no rank is given, it is an optional memorial.

NATIONAL CALENDAR FOR WALES

February	9	*St Teilo, bishop*	
March	1	ST DAVID, BISHOP, PATRON OF WALES	Solemnity
	17	ST PATRICK, BISHOP, PATRON OF IRELAND	Feast
April	20	*St Beuno, abbot*	
	23	ST GEORGE, MARTYR, PATRON OF ENGLAND	Feast
May	4	*The Beatified Martyrs of England and Wales*	
	5	*St Asaph, bishop*	
June	20	Ss Alban, Julius and Aaron, protomartyrs of Britain	Memorial
	22	Ss John Fisher, bishop, and Thomas More, martyrs	Memorial
July	12	*St John Jones, priest and martyr*	
	23	*Ss Philip Evans and John Lloyd, priests and martyrs*	
August	3	*St Germanus of Auxerre, bishop*	
	26	*St David Lewis, priest and martyr*	
September	11	*St Deiniol, bishop*	
October	16	*St Richard Gwyn, schoolmaster, martyr*	
	25	THE SIX WELSH MARTYRS AND COMPANIONS, MARTYRS	Feast
November	3	*St Winefride, virgin*	
	6	*St Illtud, abbot*	
	8	ALL SAINTS OF WALES	Feast
	14	*St Dyfrig, bishop*	
December	10	*St John Roberts, priest and martyr*	

NATIONAL CALENDAR FOR AUSTRALIA

Approved by the Sacred Congregation for Divine Worship
on 4 February 1974 (Prot. Num: 1892/73)

March	17	ST PATRICK, BISHOP, PATRON OF IRELAND	Solemnity
April	28	St Peter Chanel, priest and martyr	Memorial
May	24*	OUR LADY HELP OF CHRISTIANS	Solemnity
October	1	St Teresa of the Child Jesus, Virgin	Memorial
December	3	St Francis Xavier, Priest	Memorial

In Australia and New Zealand the Epiphany is assigned to the Sunday from 2 January to 8 January; Corpus Christi is assigned to the Sunday after Trinity Sunday.

*Or, if this day is a Sunday, May 23.

NATIONAL CALENDAR FOR IRELAND

Approved by the Sacred Congregation for Divine Worship
on 6 November 1972 (Prot. Num. 203/72)

February	1	ST BRIGID, VIRGIN	Feast
March	17	ST PATRICK, BISHOP, PATRON OF IRELAND	Solemnity
June	9	ST COLUMBA (COLUM CILLE), ABBOT	Feast
July	1	ST OLIVER PLUNKETT BISHOP AND MARTYR	Feast
November	6	ALL SAINTS OF IRELAND	Feast
	23	ST COLUMBAN, ABBOT	Feast

NATIONAL CALENDAR FOR SCOTLAND

Approved by the Sacred Congregation for Divine Worship
on 14 March 1972 (Prot. Num: 2222/70)

January	13	St Kentigern, bishop	Memorial
March	8	ST JOHN OGILVIE, PRIEST AND MARTYR	Feast
	17	ST PATRICK, BISHOP	Feast
June	9	St Columba, abbot	Memorial
August	26	St Ninian, bishop	Memorial
November	16	ST MARGARET, SECONDARY PATRON OF SCOTLAND	Feast
	30	ST ANDREW, APOSTLE, PRINCIPAL PATRON OF SCOTLAND	Solemnity

JANUARY

13 January
St Kentigern, bishop In Scotland: Memorial

Common of pastors: for bishops.

FEBRUARY

1 February
ST BRIGID, VIRGIN In Ireland: Feast

Common of virgins or Common of holy men and women.

FIRST READING

A reading from the letter of St Paul to the Romans 12:3-13

Our gifts differ according to the grace given us.

In the light of the grace I have received I want to urge each one among you not to exaggerate his real importance. Each of you must judge himself soberly by the standard of the faith God has given him. Just as each of our bodies has several parts and each part has a separate function, so all of us, in union with Christ, form one body, and as parts of it we belong to each other. Our gifts differ according to the grace given us. If your gift is prophecy, then use it as your faith suggests; if administration, then use it for administration; if teaching, then use it for teaching. Let the preachers deliver sermons, the almsgivers give freely, the officials be diligent, and those who do works of mercy do them cheerfully.

Do not let your love be a pretence, but sincerely prefer good to evil. Love each other as much as brothers should, and have a profound respect for each other. Work for the Lord with untiring effort and with great earnestness of spirit. If you have hope, this will make you cheerful. Do not give up if trials come; and keep on praying. If any of the saints are in need you must share with them; and you should make hospitality your special care.

This is the word of the Lord.

Responsorial Psalm   Ps 148:1-2. 11-14

℟   Praise the name of the Lord.

1   Praise the Lord from the heavens,
    praise him in the heights.
    praise him, all his angels,
    praise him, all his host.   ℟

2   All earth's kings and peoples,
    earth's princes and rulers;
    young men and maidens,
    old men together with children.   ℟

3   Let them praise the name of the Lord
    for he alone is exalted.
    The splendour of his name
    reaches beyond heaven and earth.   ℟

4   He exalts the strength of his people.
    He is the praise of all his saints,
    of the sons of Israel,
    of the people to whom he comes close.   ℟

Gospel Acclamation   Mt 5:8

Alleluia, alleluia!
Happy are the pure of heart:
for they shall see God.
Alleluia!

GOSPEL

A reading from the holy Gospel according to Mark   3:31-35

Whoever has done the will of God is my brother, my sister, and my mother.

The mother and brothers of Jesus arrived and, standing outside, sent
in a message asking for him. A crowd was sitting round him at the
time the message was passed to him, 'Your mother and brothers and
sisters are outside asking for you'. He replied, 'Who are my mother
and my brothers?' And looking round at those sitting in a circle about
him, he said, 'Here are my mother and my brothers. Anyone who does
the will of God, that person is my brother and sister and mother.'

This is the Gospel of the Lord.

Alternative Gospel

A reading from the holy Gospel according to Luke   11:27-28

Happy the womb that bore you!

As Jesus was speaking, a woman in the crowd raised her voice and said, 'Happy the womb that bore you and the breasts you sucked!' But he replied, 'Still happier those who hear the word of God and keep it!'

This is the Gospel of the Lord.

MARCH

1 March
ST DAVID, BISHOP
Patron of Wales   In Wales: Solemnity
In England: Feast

Common of pastors: for bishops or Common of holy men and women, for example:

FIRST READING

A reading from the letter of St Paul to the Philippians   3:8-14

I am racing for the finish, for the prize to which God calls us upwards to receive in Christ Jesus.

I believe nothing can happen that will outweigh the supreme advantage of knowing Christ Jesus my Lord. For him I have accepted the loss of everything, and I look on everything as so much rubbish if only I can have Christ and be given a place in him. I am no longer trying for perfection by my own efforts, the perfection that comes from the Law, but I want only the perfection that comes through faith in Christ, and is from God and based on faith. All I want is to know Christ and the power of his resurrection and to share his sufferings by reproducing the pattern of his death. That is the way I can hope to take my place in the resurrection of the dead. Not that I have become perfect yet: I have not yet won, but I am still running, trying to capture the prize for which Christ Jesus captured me. I can assure you my brothers, I am far from thinking that I have already won. All I can say is that I forget the past and I strain ahead for what is still to come; I am racing for the finish, for the prize to which God calls us upwards to receive in Christ Jesus.

This is the word of the Lord.

Responsorial Psalm   Ps 1. ℟ Ps 39:5

℟ Happy are they who hope in the Lord.

1   Happy indeed is the man
    who follows not the counsel of the wicked;
    nor lingers in the way of sinners
    nor sits in the company of scorners,
    but whose delight is the law of the Lord
    and who ponders his law day and night.   ℟

2   He is like a tree that is planted
    beside the flowing waters,
    that yields its fruit in due season
    and whose leaves shall never fade;
    and all that he does shall prosper.   ℟

3   Not so are the wicked, not so!
    For they like winnowed chaff
    shall be driven away by the wind;
    for the Lord guards the way of the just
    but the way of the wicked leads to doom.   ℟

Gospel Acclamation   Jn 8:31-32

Alleluia, alleluia!
If you stay in my word, you will indeed be my disciples,
and you will know the truth, says the Lord.
Alleluia!

GOSPEL

A reading from the holy Gospel according to Matthew   5:13-16

You are the light of the world.

Jesus said to his disciples: 'You are the salt of the earth. But if salt becomes tasteless, what can make it salty again? It is good for nothing, and can only be thrown out to be trampled underfoot by men.

'You are the light of the world. A city built on a hill-top cannot be hidden. No one lights a lamp to put it under a tub; they put it on the lamp-stand where it shines for everyone in the house. In the same way your light must shine in the sight of men, so that, seeing your good works, they may give the praise to your Father in heaven.'

This is the Gospel of the Lord.

10 March

ST JOHN OGILVIE, PRIEST AND MARTYR

In Scotland: Feast

Common of martyrs or Common of pastors: for missionaries, for example:

FIRST READING

A reading from the prophet Isaiah   50:5-9

I offered my back to those who struck me.

The Lord has opened my ear.
For my part, I made no resistance,
neither did I turn away.
I offered my back to those who struck me,
my cheeks to those who tore at my beard;
I did not cover my face
against insult and spittle.

The Lord comes to my help,
so that I am untouched by the insults.
So, too, I set my face like flint;
I know I shall not be shamed.
My vindicator is here at hand. Does anyone start proceedings against
     me?
Then let us go to court together.
Who thinks he has a case against me?

Let him approach me.

The Lord is coming to my help,
who dare condemn me?

This is the word of the Lord.

Responsorial Psalm   Ps 76:12-16. 21. ℟ v.12

℟   I remember the deeds of the Lord.

1   I remember the deeds of the Lord,
    I remember your wonders of old,
    I muse on all your works
    and ponder your mighty deeds.   ℟

2   Your ways, O God, are holy.
    What god is great as our God?
    You are the God who works wonders.
    You showed your power among the peoples.   ℟

3   Your strong arm redeemed your people,
    the sons of Jacob and Joseph.
    You guided your people like a flock
    by the hand of Moses and Aaron.   ℟

SECOND READING

A reading from the second letter of St Paul to the Corinthians   1:3-7

God comforts us that we might comfort others in their sorrows.

Blessed be the God and Father of our Lord Jesus Christ, a gentle
Father and the God of all consolation, who comforts us in all our
sorrows, so that we can offer others, in their sorrows, the consolation
that we have received from God ourselves. Indeed, as the sufferings of
Christ overflow to us, so, through Christ, does our consolation
overflow. When we are made to suffer, it is for your consolation and
salvation. When, instead, we are comforted, this should be a consolation to you, supporting you in patiently bearing the same sufferings as
we bear. And our hope for you is confident, since we know that,
sharing our sufferings, you will also share our consolations.

This is the word of the Lord.

Gospel Acclamation   Jn 12:26

> Alleluia, alleluia!
> If you serve me, follow me, says the Lord;
> and where I am, my servant will also be.
> Alleluia!

GOSPEL

A reading from the holy Gospel according to John   12:24-26

If the grain of wheat in the ground dies, it yields a rich harvest.

Jesus said to his disciples:

> 'I tell you, most solemnly,
> unless a wheat grain falls on the ground and dies,
> it remains only a single grain;
> but if it dies,
> it yields a rich harvest.
> Anyone who loves his life loses it;
> anyone who hates his life in this world
> will keep it for the eternal life.
> If a man serves me, he must follow me,
> wherever I am, my servant will be there too.
> If anyone serves me, my Father will honour him.'

This is the Gospel of the Lord.

ST PATRICK, BISHOP

Patron of Ireland

In Ireland and Australia: Solemnity
In England, Wales and Scotland: Feast

Common of pastors: for missionaries or: for bishops.

FIRST READING

A reading from the prophet Jeremiah   1:4-9

Go now to those to whom I send you.

The word of the Lord was addressed to me, saying,

'Before I formed you in the womb I knew you;
before you came to birth I consecrated you;
I have appointed you as prophet to the nations.'

I said, 'Ah, Lord; look, I do not know how to speak: I am a child!'
But the Lord replied,

'Do not say, "I am a child."
Go now to those to whom I send you
and say whatever I command you.
Do not be afraid of them,
for I am with you to protect you –
it is the Lord who speaks!'

Then the Lord put out his hand and touched my mouth and said to me:

'There! I am putting my words into your mouth.'

This is the word of the Lord.

Responsorial Psalm   Ps 116. ℞ Mk 16:15

℞   Go out to all the world,
      and tell the Good News.

or (outside Lent only)

℞   Alleluia!

1   O praise the Lord, all you nations,
    acclaim him all you peoples! ℞

2   Strong is his love for us;
    he is faithful for ever. ℞

SECOND READING

A reading from the Acts of the Apostles   13:46-49

We must turn to the pagans.

Paul and Barnabas spoke out boldly to the Jews, 'We had to proclaim
the word of God to you first, but since you have rejected it, since you do
not think yourselves worthy of eternal life, we must turn to the
pagans. For this is what the Lord commanded us to do when he said:

'I have made you a light for the nations,
so that my salvation may reach the ends of the earth.'

It made the pagans very happy to hear this and they thanked the
Lord for his message; all who were destined for eternal life became
believers. Thus the word of the Lord spread through the whole
countryside.

This is the word of the Lord.

Gospel Acclamation   Lk 4:18-19

Outside Lent

Alleluia, alleluia!
The Lord sent me to bring Good News to the poor,
and freedom to prisoners.
Alleluia!

In Lent

Praise and honour to you, Lord Jesus Christ!
The Lord sent me to bring Good News to the poor,
and freedom to prisoners.
Praise and honour to you, Lord Jesus Christ!

GOSPEL

A reading from the holy Gospel according to Luke   10:1-12. 17-20

Your peace will rest on that man.

The Lord appointed seventy-two others and sent them out ahead of him, in pairs, to all the towns and places he himself was to visit. He said to them, 'The harvest is rich but the labourers are few, so ask the Lord of the harvest to send labourers to his harvest. Start off now, but remember, I am sending you out like lambs among wolves. Carry no purse, no haversack, no sandals. Salute no one on the road. Whatever house you go into, let your first words be, "Peace to this house!" And if a man of peace lives there, your peace will go and rest on him; if not, it will come back to you. Stay in the same house, taking what food and drink they have to offer, for the labourer deserves his wages; do not move from house to house. Whenever you go into a town where they make you welcome, eat what is set before you. Cure those in it who are sick, and say, "The kingdom of God is very near to you." But whenever you enter a town and they do not make you welcome, go out into its streets and say, "We wipe off the very dust of your town that clings to our feet, and leave it with you. Yet be sure of this: the kingdom of God is very near." I tell you, on that day it will not go as hard with Sodom as with that town.'

The seventy-two came back rejoicing. 'Lord,' they said 'even the devils submit to us when we use your name.' He said to them, 'I watched Satan fall like lightning from heaven. Yes, I have given you power to tread underfoot serpents and scorpions and the whole strength of the enemy; nothing shall ever hurt you. Yet do not rejoice that the spirits submit to you; rejoice rather that your names are written in heaven.'

This is the Gospel of the Lord.

APRIL

St Anselm, bishop and doctor of the Church

In England: Memorial

Common of pastors: for bishops or Common of doctors of the Church.

23 April

ST GEORGE, MARTYR

Patron of England

In England and Wales: Feast

FIRST READING

A reading from the book of the Apocalypse   12:10-12

Even in the face of death these martyrs would not cling to life.

I, John, heard a voice shout from heaven, 'Victory and power and empire for ever have been won by our God, and all authority for his Christ, now that the persecutor, who accused our brothers day and night before our God, has been brought down. They have triumphed over him by the blood of the Lamb and by the witness of their martyrdom, because even in the face of death they would not cling to life. Let the heavens rejoice and all who live there.'

This is the word of the Lord.

Responsorial Psalm   Ps 125. ℟ v.5

℟   Those who sow in tears, shall reap with shouts of joy.

1   When the Lord delivered Zion from bondage,
    it seemed like a dream.
    Then was our mouth filled with laughter,
    on our lips there were songs.   ℟

2   The heathens themselves said: 'What marvels
    the Lord worked for them!'
    What marvels the Lord worked for us!
    Indeed we were glad.   ℟

(continued)

3   Deliver us, O Lord, from our bondage
    as streams in dry land.
    Those who are sowing in tears
    will sing when they reap.

    ℟   Those who sow in tears shall reap with shouts of joy.

4   They go out, they go out, full of tears,
    carrying seed for the sowing;
    they come back, they come back, full of song,
    carrying their sheaves.   ℟

Gospel Acclamation   James 1:12

    Alleluia, alleluia!
    Blessed are they who stand firm when trials come;
    when they have stood the test, they will win the crown of life.
    Alleluia!

GOSPEL

A reading from the holy Gospel according to John   15:18-21

If they persecuted me, they will persecute you too.

Jesus said to his disciples:

    'If the world hates you,
    remember that it hated me before you.
    If you belonged to the world,
    the world would love you as its own;
    but because you do not belong to the world,
    because my choice withdrew you from the world,
    therefore the world hates you.
    Remember the words I said to you:
    A servant is not greater than his master.
    If they persecuted me,
    they will persecute you too;
    if they kept my word,
    they will keep yours as well.
    But it will be on my account that they will do this,
    because they do not know the one who sent me.'

    This is the Gospel of the Lord.

Alternative Gospel

A reading from the holy Gospel according to John   15:1-8

All who live in me, and I in them, bear fruit.

Jesus said to his disciples:

'I am the true vine,
and my Father is the vinedresser.
Every branch in me that bears no fruit
he cuts away,
and every branch that does bear fruit he prunes
to make it bear even more.
You are pruned already,
by means of the word that I have spoken to you.
Make your home in me, as I make mine in you.
As a branch cannot bear fruit all by itself,
but must remain part of the vine,
neither can you unless you remain in me.
I am the vine,
you are the branches.
Whoever remains in me, with me in him,
bears fruit in plenty;
for cut off from me you can do nothing.
Anyone who does not remain in me
is like a branch that has been thrown away
– he withers;
these branches are collected and thrown on the fire,
and they are burnt.
If you remain in me
and my words remain in you,
you may ask what you will
and you shall get it.
It is to the glory of my Father that you should bear much fruit,
and then you will be my disciples.'

This is the Gospel of the Lord.

28 April

St Peter Chanel, priest and martyr

Australia: Memoria

Common of martyrs or Common of pastors: for missionaries.

MAY

4 May

THE BEATIFIED MARTYRS OF ENGLAND AND WALES

In England: Feast

In Wales: Memorial

Common of martyrs.

FIRST READING

A reading from the Acts of the Apostles   7:55-60

Lord Jesus, receive my spirit

Stephen, filled with the Holy Spirit, gazed into heaven and saw the glory of God, and Jesus standing at God's right hand. 'I can see heaven thrown open', he said, 'and the Son of Man standing at the right hand of God.' At this all the members of the council shouted out and stopped their ears with their hands; then they all rushed at him, sent him out of the city and stoned him. The witnesses put down their clothes at the feet of a young man called Saul. As they were stoning him, Stephen said in invocation, 'Lord Jesus, receive my spirit'. Then he knelt down and said aloud, 'Lord, do not hold this sin against them'; and with these words he fell asleep.

This is the word of the Lord.

Responsorial Psalm   Ps 30:3-4. 6. 8. 17. 21. ℟ v.6

℟   Into your hands, O Lord, I entrust my spirit.

1   Be a rock of refuge for me,
     a mighty stronghold to save me,
     for you are my rock, my stronghold.
     For your name's sake, lead me and guide me.   ℟

2   Into your hands I commend my spirit.
    It is you who will redeem me, Lord.
    As for me, I trust in the Lord:
    let me be glad and rejoice in your love.   ℟

3   Let your face shine on your servant.
    Save me in your love.
    You hide them in the shelter of your presence
    from the plotting of men.   ℟

Gospel Acclamation

   Alleluia, alleluia!
   You are God: we praise you; you are Lord: we acclaim you;
   the white-robed army of martyrs praise you.
   Alleluia!

GOSPEL

A reading from the holy Gospel according to Matthew   10:17-20

You will be dragged before governors and kings on account of me,
to bear witness before them and all the people.

Jesus said to his apostles: 'Beware of men: they will hand you over to
sanhedrins and scourge you in their synagogues. You will be dragged
before governors and kings for my sake, to bear witness before them
and the pagans. But when they hand you over, do not worry about how
to speak or what to say; what you are to say will be given to you when
the time comes; because it is not you who will be speaking; the Spirit
of your Father will be speaking in you.

   'Brother will betray brother to death, and the father his child;
children will rise against their parents and have them put to death.
You will be hated by all men on account of my name; but the man who
stands firm to the end will be saved.'

   This is the Gospel of the Lord.

OUR LADY HELP OF CHRISTIANS

In Australia: Solemnity

Common of the Blessed Virgin Mary.

Year A

FIRST READING

A reading from the book of Ecclesiasticus 4:11-18

God loves those who love wisdom.

Wisdom brings up her own sons,
and cares for those who seek her.
Whoever loves her loves life,
those who wait on her early will be filled with happiness.
Whoever holds her close will inherit honour,
and wherever he walks the Lord will bless him.
Those who serve her minister to the Holy One,
and the Lord loves those who love her.
Whoever obeys her judges aright,
and whoever pays attention to her dwells secure.
If he trusts himself to her he will inherit her,
and his descendants will remain in possession of her;
for though she takes him at first through winding ways,
bringing fear and faintness on him,
plaguing him with her discipline until she can trust him,
and testing him with her ordeals,
in the end she will lead him back to the straight road,
and reveal her secrets to him.

This is the word of the Lord.

Responsorial Psalm Ps 112:1-8. ℟ v.2

℟ Blessed be the name of the Lord for ever.

or

℟ Alleluia!

1 Praise, O servants of the Lord,
praise the name of the Lord!

May the name of the Lord be blessed
both now and for evermore! ℟

2   From the rising of the sun to its setting
    praised be the name of the Lord!
    High above all nations is the Lord,
    above the heavens his glory. ℟

3   Who is like the Lord, our God,
    who has risen on high to his throne
    yet stoops from the heights to look down,
    to look down upon heaven and earth! ℟

4   From the dust he lifts up the lowly,
    from the dungheap he raises the poor
    to set him in the company of princes,
    yes, with the princes of his people. ℟

SECOND READING

A reading from the first letter of St Paul   1:18-25
to the Corinthians

*It was because God wanted to save those who have faith through
the foolishness of the message that we preach.*

The language of the cross may be illogical to those who are not on the
way to salvation, but those of us who are on the way see it as God's
power to save. As scripture says: I shall destroy the wisdom of the wise
and bring to nothing all the learning of the learned. Where are the
philosophers now? Where are the scribes? Where are any of our
thinkers today? Do you see now how God has shown up the foolishness
of human wisdom? If it was God's wisdom that human wisdom should
not know God, it was because God wanted to save those who have
faith through the foolishness of the message that we preach. And so,
while the Jews demand miracles and the Greeks look for wisdom, here
are we preaching a crucified Christ; to the Jews an obstacle that they
cannot get over, to the pagans madness, but to those who have been
called, whether they are Jews or Greeks, a Christ who is the power
and the wisdom of God. For God's foolishness is wiser than human
wisdom, and God's weakness is stronger than human strength.

This is the word of the Lord.

Gospel Acclamation

Alleluia, alleluia!
Happy are you, O Blessed Virgin Mary;
without dying you won the martyr's crown beside the cross of the
    Lord.
Alleluia!

GOSPEL

A reading from the holy Gospel according to John   19:25-27

This is your mother.

Near the cross of Jesus stood his mother and his mother's sister, Mary
the wife of Clopas, and Mary of Magdala. Seeing his mother and the
disciple he loved standing near her, Jesus said to his mother, 'Woman,
this is your son'. Then to the disciple he said, 'This is your mother'.
And from that moment the disciple made a place for her in his home.

This is the Gospel of the Lord.

Year B

FIRST READING

A reading from the Book of Proverbs   31:10-13. 19-20. 30-31

It is the wise woman whom the Lord will praise.

A perfect wife – who can find her?
She is far beyond the price of pearls.

Her husband's heart has confidence in her,
from her he will derive no little profit.

Advantage and not hurt she brings him
all the days of her life.

She is always busy with wool and with flax,
she does her work with eager hands.

She sets her hands to the distaff,
her fingers grasp the spindle.

She holds out her hand to the poor,
she opens her arms to the needy.

Charm is deceitful, and beauty empty;
the woman who is wise is the one to praise.

Give her a share in what her hands have worked for,
and let her works tell her praises at the city gates.

This is the word of the Lord.

Responsorial Psalm   Judith 13:18-20

℟   You are the highest honour of our race.

1   May you be blessed, my daughter, by God Most High,
    beyond all women on earth;
    and may the Lord God be blessed,
    the Creator of heaven and earth.   ℟

2   The trust you have shown
    shall not pass from the memories of men,
    but shall ever remind them
    of the power of God.   ℟

3   God grant you be always held in honour,
    and rewarded with blessings,
    since you did not consider your own life
    when our nation was brought to its knees.   ℟

SECOND READING

A reading from the letter of St James   3:13-18

The harvest of justice is sown in peace by those who make peace.

If there are any wise or learned men among you, let them show it by
their good lives, with humility and wisdom in their actions. But if at
heart you have the bitterness of jealousy, or a self-seeking ambition,
never make any claims for yourself or cover up the truth with lies –
principles of this kind are not the wisdom that comes down from
above: they are only earthly, animal and devilish. Wherever you find
jealousy and ambition, you find disharmony, and wicked things of
every kind being done; whereas the wisdom that comes down from
above is essentially something pure; it also makes for peace, and is

kindly and considerate; it is full of compassion and shows itself by doing good; nor is there any trace of partiality or hypocrisy in it. Peacemakers, when they work for peace, sow the seeds which will bear fruit in holiness.

This is the word of the Lord.

Gospel Acclamation   Lk 1:45

Alleluia, alleluia!
Blessed are you, O Virgin Mary, for your firm believing,
that the promises of the Lord would be fulfilled.
Alleluia!

GOSPEL

A reading from the holy Gospel according to Luke   1:39-56

Why should I be honoured with a visit from the mother of my Lord?

Mary set out and went as quickly as she could to a town in the hill country of Juda. She went into Zechariah's house and greeted Elizabeth. Now as soon as Elizabeth heard Mary's greeting, the child leapt in her womb and Elizabeth was filled with the Holy Spirit. She gave a loud cry and said, 'Of all women you are the most blessed, and blessed is the fruit of your womb. Why should I be honoured with a visit from the mother of my Lord? For the moment your greeting reached my ears, the child in my womb leapt for joy. Yes, blessed is she who believed that the promise made her by the Lord would be fulfilled.'

And Mary said:

'My soul proclaims the greatness of the Lord
and my spirit exults in God my saviour;
because he has looked upon his lowly handmaid.
Yes, from this day forward all generations will call me blessed,
for the Almighty has done great things for me.
Holy is his name,
and his mercy reaches from age to age for those who fear him.
He has shown the power of his arm,
he has routed the proud of heart.
He has pulled down princes from their thrones and exalted the
    lowly.

The hungry he has filled with good things, the rich sent empty
away.
He has come to the help of Israel his servant, mindful of his mercy
– according to the promise he made to our ancestors –
of his mercy to Abraham and to his descendants for ever.'

Mary stayed with Elizabeth about three months and then went
back home.

This is the Gospel of the Lord.

Year C

FIRST READING

A reading from the book of Genesis   3:1-15. 20

I will put enmity between your offspring and her offspring.

After Adam had eaten of the tree the Lord God called to him. 'Where
are you?' he asked. 'I heard the sound of you in the garden,' he replied.
'I was afraid because I was naked, so I hid.' 'Who told you that you
were naked?' he asked. 'Have you been eating of the tree I forbade you
to eat?' The man replied, 'It was the woman you put with me; she gave
me the fruit, and I ate it'. Then the Lord God asked the woman, 'What
is this you have done?' The woman replied, 'The serpent tempted me
and I ate'.
    Then the Lord God said to the serpent, 'Because you have done
this,

'Be accursed beyond all cattle,
all wild beasts.
You shall crawl on your belly and eat dust
every day of your life.
I will make you enemies of each other:
you and the woman,
your offspring and her offspring.
It will crush your head
and you will crush its heel,'

The man named his wife 'Eve' because she was the mother of all
those who live.

This is the word of the Lord.

Responsorial Psalm Ps 102:1-4. 8-9. 11-12. ℟ v.10. Alt. ℟ v.8

℟ Lord, do not deal with us as our sins deserve,
   nor punish us for our faults.

or

℟ The Lord is kind and merciful.

1 My soul, give thanks to the Lord,
  all my being, bless his holy name.
  My soul, give thanks to the Lord
  and never forget all his blessings. ℟

2 It is he who forgives all your guilt,
  who heals every one of your ills,
  who redeems your life from the grave,
  who crowns you with love and compassion. ℟

3 The Lord is compassion and love,
  slow to anger and rich in mercy.
  His wrath will come to an end;
  he will not be angry for ever. ℟

4 For as the heavens are high above the earth
  so strong is his love for those who fear him.
  As far as the east is from the west
  so far does he remove our sins. ℟

SECOND READING

A reading from the letter of St Paul 3:14-19
to the Ephesians

To know the love of Christ, which is beyond all knowledge.

This is what I pray, kneeling before the Father, from whom every family, whether spiritual or natural, takes its name:

Out of his infinite glory, may he give you the power through his Spirit for your hidden self to grow strong, so that Christ may live in your hearts through faith, and then, planted in love and built on love, you will with all the saints have strength to grasp the breadth and the length, the height and the depth; until, knowing the love of Christ, which is beyond all knowledge, you are filled with the utter fullness of God.

This is the word of the Lord.

Gospel Acclamation   Lk 2:19

> Alleluia, alleluia!
> Blessed is the Virgin Mary who kept the word of God,
> and pondered it in her heart.
> Alleluia!

GOSPEL

A reading from the holy Gospel according to Luke   8:19-21

My mother and my brothers are those who hear the word of God and put it into practice.

His mother and his brothers came looking for him, but they could not get to him because of the crowd. He was told, 'Your mother and brothers are standing outside and want to see you'. But he said in answer, 'My mother and my brothers are those who hear the word of God and put it into practice'.

This is the Gospel of the Lord.

25 May

St Bede the Venerable, priest and doctor of the Church
In England: Memorial

Common of doctors of the Church or Common of holy men and women.

FIRST READING

A reading from the book of Ecclesiasticus   39:6-10

He filled him with the spirit of wisdom and understanding.

If it is the will of the great Lord,
the scholar will be filled with the spirit of understanding,
he will shower forth words of wisdom,
and in prayer give thanks to the Lord.
He will grow upright in purpose and learning,
he will ponder the Lord's hidden mysteries.
He will display the instruction he has received,
taking his pride in the Law of the Lord's covenant.
Many will praise his understanding,
and it will never be forgotten.
His memory will not disappear,
generation after generation his name will live.
Nations will proclaim his wisdom,

the assembly will celebrate his praises.

This is the word of the Lord.

Responsorial Psalm   Ps 36:3-6. 20-21. ℟ v.30

℟   The mouths of the just murmur wisdom.

1   If you trust in the Lord and do good,
    then you will live in the land and be secure.
    If you find your delight in the Lord,
    he will grant your heart's desire.   ℟

2   Commit your life to the Lord,
    trust in him and he will act,
    so that your justice breaks forth like the light,
    your cause like the noon-day sun.   ℟

3   The just man's mouth utters wisdom
    and his lips speak what is right;
    the law of his God is in his heart,
    his steps shall be saved from stumbling.   ℟

Gospel Acclamation   Mt 5:16

Alleluia, alleluia!
Let your light shine before all,
that they may see your good works and glorify your Father.
Alleluia!

GOSPEL

A reading from the holy Gospel according to Matthew   5:13-16

You are the light of the world.

Jesus said to his disciples: 'You are the salt of the earth. But if salt
becomes tasteless, what can make it salty again? It is good for
nothing, and can only be thrown out to be trampled underfoot by men.

'You are the light of the world. A city built on a hill-top cannot be
hidden. No one lights a lamp to put it under a tub, they put it on the
lamp-stand where it shines for everyone in the house. In the same way
your light must shine in the sight of men, so that, seeing your good
works, they may give the praise to your Father in heaven.'

This is the Gospel of the Lord.

27 May

ST AUGUSTINE OF CANTERBURY, BISHOP

In England : Feast

Common of pastors.

FIRST READING

A reading from the first letter of St Paul to the Thessalonians 2:2-8

We were eager to hand over to you not only the Good News but our whole lives as well.

It was our God who gave us the courage to proclaim his Good News to you in the face of great opposition. We have not taken to preaching because we are deluded, or immoral, or trying to deceive anyone; it was God who decided that we were fit to be entrusted with the Good News, and when we are speaking, we are not trying to please men but God, who can read our inmost thoughts. You know very well, and we can swear it before God, that never at any time have our speeches been simply flattery, or a cover for trying to get money; nor have we ever looked for any special honour from men, either from you or anybody else, when we could have imposed ourselves on you with full weight, as apostles of Christ.

Instead, we were unassuming. Like a mother feeding and looking after her own children we felt so devoted and protective towards you, and had come to love you so much, that we were eager to hand over to you not only the Good News but our whole lives as well.

This is the word of the Lord.

Responsorial Psalm   Ps 116. ℟ Mk 6:15

℟   Go out to all the world, and tell the Good News.

or

℟   Alleluia!

1   O praise the Lord, all you nations,
      acclaim him all you peoples!   ℟

2   Strong is his love for us;
      he is faithful for ever.   ℟

Gospel Acclamation   Lk 4:18-19

> Alleluia, alleluia!
> The Lord sent me to bring Good News to the poor,
> and freedom to prisoners.
> Alleluia!

GOSPEL

A reading from the holy Gospel according to Luke   10:1-9

The harvest is rich but the labourers are few.

The Lord appointed seventy-two others and sent them out ahead of him, in pairs, to all the towns and places he himself was to visit. He said to them, 'The harvest is rich but the labourers are few, so ask the Lord of the harvest to send labourers to his harvest. Start off now, but remember, I am sending you out like lambs among wolves. Carry no purse, no haversack, no sandals. Salute no one on the road. Whatever house you go into, let your first words be, "Peace to this house!" And if a man of peace lives there, your peace will go and rest on him; if not, it will come back to you. Stay in the same house, taking what food and drink they have to offer, for the labourer deserves his wages; do not move from house to house. Whenever you go into a town where they make you welcome, eat what is set before you. Cure those in it who are sick, and say, "The kingdom of God is very near to you".'

This is the Gospel of the Lord.

JUNE

9 June

ST COLUMBA (COLUM CILLE), ABBOT

In Ireland: Feast
In Scotland: Memorial

Common of pastors: for missionaries or Common of holy men and women: for religious.

FIRST READING

A reading from the letter of St Paul to the Colossians 1:24-29

I became the servant of the Church when God made me responsible for delivering his message to you.

It makes me happy to suffer for you, as I am suffering now, and in my own body to do what I can to make up all that has still to be undergone by Christ for the sake of his body, the Church. I became the servant of the Church when God made me responsible for delivering God's message to you, the message which was a mystery hidden for generations and centuries and has now been revealed to his saints. It was God's purpose to reveal it to them and to show all the rich glory of this mystery to pagans. The mystery is Christ among you, your hope of glory: this is the Christ we proclaim, this is the wisdom in which we thoroughly train everyone and instruct everyone, to make them all perfect in Christ. It is for this I struggle wearily on, helped only by his power driving me irresistibly.

This is the word of the Lord.

Responsorial Psalm   Ps 15:1-2. 5. 7-8. 11. ℟ cf. v.5

℟   You are my inheritance, O Lord.

1   Preserve me, God, I take refuge in you.
    I say to the Lord: 'You are my God.'
    O Lord, it is you who are my portion and cup;
    it is you yourself who are my prize.   ℟

2   I will bless the Lord who gives me counsel,
    who even at night directs my heart.   (continued)

1281

I keep the Lord ever in my sight:
since he is at my right hand, I shall stand firm.   ℟

℟   You are my inheritance, O Lord.

3   You will show me the path of life,
the fullness of joy in your presence,
at your right hand happiness for ever.   ℟

Gospel Acclamation   Mt 28:19-20

Alleluia, alleluia!
Go and teach all my people my gospel.
I am with you always, until the end of the world.
Alleluia!

GOSPEL

A reading from the holy Gospel according to Mark   10:17-30

Sell whatever you have, and come follow me.

Jesus was setting out on a journey when a man ran up, knelt before
him and put this question to him, 'Good master, what must I do to
inherit eternal life?' Jesus said to him, 'Why do you call me good? No
one is good but God alone. You know the commandments: You must
not kill; You must not commit adultery; You must not steal; You must
not bring false witness; You must not defraud; Honour your father
and mother.' And he said to him, 'Master, I have kept all these from
my earliest days'. Jesus looked steadily at him and loved him, and he
said, 'There is one thing you lack. Go and sell everything you own and
give the money to the poor, and you will have treasure in heaven; then
come, follow me.' But his face fell at these words and he went away
sad, for he was a man of great wealth.

Jesus looked round and said to his disciples, 'How hard it is for
those who have riches to enter the kingdom of God!' The disciples were
astounded by these words, but Jesus insisted, 'My children,' he said to
them, 'how hard it is to enter the kingdom of God! It is easier for a
camel to pass through the eye of a needle than for a rich man to enter
the kingdom of God.' They were more astonished than ever. 'In that
case,' they said to one another, 'who can be saved?' Jesus gazed at
them. 'For men,' he said, 'it is impossible, but not for God: because
everything is possible for God.'

Peter took this up. 'What about us?' he asked him. 'We have left
everything and followed you.' Jesus said, 'I tell you solemnly, there is

no one who has left house, brothers, sisters, father, children or land for my sake and for the sake of the gospel who will not be repaid a hundred times over, houses, brothers, sisters, mothers, children and land – not without persecutions – now in this present time and, in the world to come, eternal life.'

This is the Gospel of the Lord.

In the Easter Season

Alternative Gospel

A reading from the holy Gospel according to John   15:9-17

You are my friends if you do what I command you.

Jesus said to his disciples:

'As the Father has loved me,
so I have loved you.
Remain in my love.
If you keep my commandments
you will remain in my love,
just as I have kept my Father's commandments
and remain in his love.
I have told you this
so that my own joy may be in you
and your joy be complete.
This is my commandment:
love one another,
as I have loved you.
A man can have no greater love
than to lay down his life for his friends.
You are my friends,
if you do what I command you.
I shall not call you servants any more,
because a servant does not know
his master's business:
I call you friends,
because I have made known to you
everything I have learnt from my Father.
You did not choose me,
no, I chose you;
and I commissioned you
to go out and to bear fruit,
fruit that will last;

and then the Father will give you
anything you ask him in my name.
What I command you
is to love one another.'

This is the Gospel of the Lord.

---

20 June

St Alban,
protomartyr of Britain

In England: Memorial

Ss Alban, Julius
and Aaron, protomartyrs

In Wales: Memorial

FIRST READING

A reading from the second letter of St Paul
to Timothy

2:8-13; 3:10-12

*You must be aware that anybody who tries to live in devotion to
Christ is certain to suffer persecution.*

Remember the Good News that I carry, 'Jesus Christ risen from the
dead, sprung from the race of David'; it is on account of this that I
have my own hardships to bear, even to being chained like a criminal
– but they cannot chain up God's news. So I bear it all for the sake of
those who are chosen, so that in the end they may have the salvation
that is in Christ Jesus and the eternal glory that comes with it.
  Here is a saying that you can rely on:

If we have died with him, then we shall live with him.
If we hold firm, then we shall reign with him.
If we disown him, then he will disown us.
We may be unfaithful, but he is always faithful,
for he cannot disown his own self.

  You know, though, what I have taught, how I have lived, what I
have aimed at; you know my faith, my patience and my love; my
constancy and the persecutions and hardships that came to me in
places like Antioch, Iconium and Lystra – all the persecutions I have
endured; and the Lord has rescued me from every one of them. You
are all aware, then, that anybody who tries to live in devotion to
Christ is certain to be attacked.

  This is the word of the Lord.

Responsorial Psalm   Ps 123:2-5. 7-8. ℟ v.7

  ℟ Our soul has escaped like a bird from the hunter's net.

1 If the Lord had not been on our side
   when men rose against us
   then would they have swallowed us alive
   when their anger was kindled.   ℟

2 Then would the waters have engulfed us,
   the torrent gone over us;
   over our head would have swept
   the raging waters.   ℟

3 Indeed the snare has been broken
   and we have escaped.
   Our help is in the name of the Lord,
   who made heaven and earth.   ℟

Gospel Acclamation   2 Cor 1:3-4

   Alleluia, alleluia!
   Blessed be the Father of mercies and the God of all comfort,
   who consoles us in all our afflictions.
   Alleluia!

GOSPEL

A reading from the holy Gospel according to John   12:24-26

          If the grain of wheat in the ground dies, it yields a rich harvest.
Jesus said to his disciples:

   'I tell you, most solemnly,
   unless a wheat grain falls on the ground and dies,
   it remains only a single grain;
   but if it dies,
   it yields a rich harvest.
   Anyone who loves his life loses it;
   anyone who hates his life in this world
   will keep it for the eternal life.
   If a man serves me, he must follow me,

wherever I am, my servant will be there too.
If anyone serves me, my Father will honour him.'

This is the Gospel of the Lord.

22 June

SS JOHN FISHER, BISHOP
AND ST THOMAS MORE, MARTYRS

In England: Feast
In Wales: Memorial

FIRST READING

A reading from the second book of Maccabees   6:18. 21. 24-31

Because of the awe the Lord inspires in me, I will suffer gladly.

Eleazar, one of the foremost teachers of the Law, a man already advanced in years and of most noble appearance, was being forced to open his mouth wide to swallow pig's flesh. Those in charge of the impious banquet, because of their long-standing friendship with him, took him aside and privately urged him to have meat brought of a kind he could properly use, prepared by himself, and only pretend to eat the portions of sacrificial meat as prescribed by the king. 'Such pretence', he said, 'does not square with our time of life; many young people would suppose that Eleazar at the age of ninety had conformed to the foreigners' way of life, and because I had played this part for the sake of a paltry brief spell of life might themselves be led astray on my account; I should only bring defilement and disgrace on my old age. Even though for the moment I avoid execution by man, I can never, living or dead, elude the grasp of the Almighty. Therefore if I am man enough to quit this life here and now I shall prove myself worthy of my old age, and I shall have left the young a noble example of how to make a good death eagerly and generously, for the venerable and holy laws.'

With these words he went straight to the block. His escorts, so recently well disposed towards him, turned against him after this declaration, which they regarded as sheer madness. Just before he died under the blows, he groaned aloud and said, 'The Lord whose knowledge is holy sees clearly that, though I might have escaped death, whatever agonies of body I now endure under this bludgeoning, in my soul I am glad to suffer, because of the awe which he inspires in me'.

This was how he died, leaving his death as an example of nobility and a record of virtue not only for the young but for the great majority of the nation.

This is the word of the Lord.

Responsorial Psalm   Ps 30:2. 6. 8-9. 15-17. 25. ℟ Lk 23:46

℟   Into your hands, O Lord, I entrust my spirit.

1   In you, O Lord, I take refuge,
     Let me never be put to shame.
     In your justice, set me free.
     Into your hands I commend my spirit.
     It is you who will redeem me, Lord. ℟

2   You who have seen my affliction
     and taken heed of my soul's distress,
     have not handed me over to the enemy,
     but set my feet at large. ℟

3   But as for me, I trust in you, Lord,
     I say: 'You are my God.
     My life is in your hands, deliver me
     from the hands of those who hate me. ℟

4   'Let your face shine on your servant.
     Save me in your love.'
     Be strong, let your heart take courage,
     all who hope in the Lord. ℟

Gospel Acclamation   James 1:12

     Alleluia, alleluia!
     Blessed are they who stand firm when trials come;
     when they have stood the test, they will win the crown of life.
     Alleluia!

                                   GOSPEL

A reading from the holy Gospel according to Matthew   24:4-13

                   You will be hated by all nations for my name's sake,

Jesus said to his disciples, 'Take care that no one deceives you;

because many will come using my name and saying, "I am the Christ", and they will deceive many. You will hear of wars and rumours of wars; do not be alarmed, for this is something that must happen, but the end will not be yet. For nation will fight against nation, and kingdom against kingdom. There will be famines and earthquakes here and there. All this is only the beginning of the birthpangs.

'Then they will hand you over to be tortured and put to death; and you will be hated by all the nations on account of my name. And then many will fall away; men will betray one another and hate one another. Many false prophets will arise; they will deceive many, and with the increase of lawlessness, love in most men will grow cold; but the man who stands firm to the end will be saved.'

This is the Gospel of the Lord

JULY

1 July
ST OLIVER PLUNKETT, BISHOP AND MARTYR

In Ireland: Feast

FIRST READING

A reading from the prophet Ezekiel   34:11-16

As a shepherd keeps all his flock in view, so shall I keep my sheep in view.

The Lord says this: I am going to look after my flock myself and keep all of it in view. As a shepherd keeps all his flock in view when he stands up in the middle of his scattered sheep, so shall I keep my sheep in view. I shall rescue them from wherever they have been scattered during the mist and darkness. I shall bring them out of the countries where they are; I shall gather them together from foreign countries and bring them back to their own land. I shall pasture them on the mountains of Israel, in the ravines and in every inhabited place in the land. I shall feed them in good pasturage; the high mountains of Israel will be their grazing ground. There they will rest in good grazing ground; they will browse in rich pastures on the mountains of Israel. I myself will pasture my sheep, I myself will show them where to rest – it is the Lord who speaks. I shall look for the lost one, bring back the stray, bandage the wounded and make the weak strong. I shall watch over the fat and healthy. I shall be a true shepherd to them.

This is the word of the Lord.

Alternative First Reading

A reading from the first letter of St Peter 3:8-18

> *He must never yield to evil but must practise good; he must seek peace and pursue it.*

You should all agree among yourselves and be sympathetic; love the brothers, have compassion and be self-effacing. Never pay back one wrong with another, or an angry word with another one; instead, pay back with a blessing. That is what you are called to do, so that you inherit a blessing yourself. Remember: Anyone who wants to have a happy life and to enjoy prosperity must banish malice from his tongue, deceitful conversation from his lips; he must never yield to evil but must practise good; he must seek peace and pursue it. Because the face of the Lord frowns on evil men, but the eyes of the Lord are turned towards the virtuous.

No one can hurt you if you are determined to do only what is right; if you do have to suffer for being good, you will count it a blessing. There is no need to be afraid or to worry about them. Simply reverence the Lord Christ in your hearts, and always have your answer ready for people who ask you the reason for the hope that you all have. But give it with courtesy and respect and with a clear conscience, so that those who slander you when you are living a good life in Christ may be proved wrong in the accusations that they bring. And if it is the will of God that you should suffer, it is better to suffer for doing right than for doing wrong.

Why, Christ himself, innocent though he was, had died once for sins, died for the guilty, to lead us to God. In the body he was put to death, in the spirit he was raised to life.

This is the word of the Lord.

Responsorial Psalm Ps 30:3-4. 6. 8. 17. 21. ℟ v.6

℟ Into your hands, O Lord, I entrust my spirit.

1 Be a rock of refuge for me,
a mighty stronghold to save me,
for you are my rock, my stronghold.
For your name's sake, lead me and guide me. ℟

2 Into your hands I commend my spirit.
It is you who will redeem me, Lord.
As for me, I trust in the Lord:
let me be glad and rejoice in your love. ℟

3 Let your face shine on your servant.
Save me in your love.
You hide them in the shelter of your presence
from the plotting of men. ℟

Gospel Acclamation James 1:12

Alleluia, alleluia!
Blessed are they who stand firm when trials come;
when they have stood the test, they will win the crown of life.
Alleluia!

GOSPEL

A reading from the holy Gospel according to John 10:11-16

The good shepherd is one who lays down his life for his sheep.

Jesus said:

'I am the good shepherd:
the good shepherd is one who lays down his life for his sheep.
The hired man, since he is not the shepherd
and the sheep do not belong to him,
abandons the sheep and runs away
as soon as he sees a wolf coming,
and then the wolf attacks and scatters the sheep;
this is because he is only a hired man
and has no concern for the sheep.
I am the good shepherd;

I know my own
and my own know me,
just as the Father knows me
and I know the Father;
and I lay down my life for my sheep.
And there are other sheep I have
that are not of this fold,
and these I have to lead as well.
They too will listen to my voice,
and there will be only one flock,
and one shepherd.'

This is the Gospel of the Lord.

AUGUST

26 August

St Ninian, Bishop   In Scotland: Memorial

Common of pastors: for bishops.

Also 26 August

Blessed Dominic of the Mother of God, priest

In England: Optional Memorial

Common of pastors.

FIRST READING

A reading from the first letter of St Paul   1:18-25
to the Corinthians

It was because God wanted to save those who have faith through
the foolishness of the message that we preach.

The language of the cross may be illogical to those who are not on
the way to salvation, but those of us who are on the way see it as
God's power to save. As scripture says: I shall destroy the wisdom
of the wise and bring to nothing all the learning of the learned.
Where are the philosophers now? Where are the scribes? Where are
any of our thinkers today? Do you see how God has shown up

the foolishness of human wisdom? If it was God's wisdom that human wisdom should not know God, it was because God wanted to save those who have faith through the foolishness of the message that we preach. And so, while the Jews demand miracles and the Greeks look for wisdom, here are we preaching a crucified Christ; to the Jews an obstacle that they cannot get over, to the pagans madness, but to those who have been called, whether they are Jews or Greeks, a Christ who is the power and the wisdom of God. For God's foolishness is wiser than human wisdom, and God's weakness is stronger than human strength.

This is the word of the Lord.

Responsorial Psalm   Ps 116. ℟ Mk 6:15

℟   Go out to the whole world, and tell the Good News.

or

℟   Alleluia!

1   O praise the Lord, all you nations,
     acclaim him all you peoples!   ℟

2   Strong is his love for us;
     he is faithful for ever.   ℟

Gospel Acclamation   2 Cor 5:19

Alleluia, alleluia!
God was in Christ, to reconcile the world to himself;
and the Good News of reconciliation he has entrusted to us.
Alleluia!

GOSPEL

A reading from the holy Gospel according to Mark   1:14-20

I will make you fishers of my people.

After John had been arrested, Jesus went into Galilee. There he proclaimed the Good News from God. 'The time has come,' he said, 'and the kingdom of God is close at hand. Repent, and believe the Good News.'

As he was walking along by the Sea of Galilee he saw Simon and his brother Andrew casting a net in the lake – for they were fishermen. And Jesus said to them, 'Follow me and I will make you into fishers of men.' And at once they left their nets and followed him.

Going on a little farther, he saw James son of Zebedee and his brother John; they too were in their boat, mending their nets. He called them at once and, leaving their father Zebedee in the boat with the men he employed, they went after him.

This is the Gospel of the Lord.

SEPTEMBER

3 September
ST GREGORY THE GREAT, POPE AND DOCTOR OF THE CHURCH
Apostle of the English

In England: Feast

Common of pastors of Common of doctors of the Church.

FIRST READING

A reading from the first letter of St Paul to the Thessalonians 2:2-8

We were eager to hand over to you not only the Good News but our whole lives as well.

It was our God who gave us the courage to proclaim his Good News to you in the face of great opposition. We have not taken to preaching because we are deluded, or immoral, or trying to deceive anyone; it was God who decided that we were fit to be entrusted with the Good News, and when we are speaking, we are not trying to please men but God, who can read our inmost thoughts. You know very well, and we can swear it before God, that never at any time have our speeches been simply flattery, or a cover for trying to get money; nor have we ever looked for any special honour from men, either from you or anybody else, when we could have imposed ourselves on you with full weight, as apostles of Christ.

Instead, we were unassuming. Like a mother feeding and looking after her own children, we felt so devoted and protective towards you, and had come to love you so much, that we were eager to hand over to you not only the Good News but our whole lives as well.

This is the word of the Lord.

Responsorial Psalm   Ps 95:1-3. 7-8. 10. ℟ v.3

℟   Proclaim his marvellous deeds to all the nations.

1   O sing a new song to the Lord,
    sing to the Lord all the earth.
    O sing to the Lord, bless his name.   ℟

2   Proclaim his help day by day,
    tell among the nations his glory
    and his wonders among all the peoples.   ℟

3   Give the Lord, you families of peoples,
    give the Lord glory and power,
    give the Lord the glory of his name.   ℟

4   Proclaim to the nations: 'God is king.'
    The world he made firm in its place;
    he will judge the peoples in fairness.   ℟

Gospel Acclamation   Lk 4:18-19

    Alleluia, alleluia!
    The Lord sent me to bring Good News to the poor,
    and freedom to prisoners.
    Alleluia!

GOSPEL

A reading from the holy Gospel according to Matthew   16:13-19

You are Peter and on this rock I will build my Church.

When Jesus came to the region of Caesarea Philippi he put this question to his disciples, 'Who do people say the Son of Man is?' And they said, 'Some say he is John the Baptist, some Elijah, and others Jeremiah or one of the prophets'. 'But you,' he said, 'who do you say I am?' Then Simon Peter spoke up, 'You are the Christ,' he said, 'the Son of the living God'. Jesus replied, 'Simon son of Jonah, you are a happy man! Because it was not flesh and blood that revealed this to you but my Father in heaven. So I now say to you: You are Peter and on this rock I will build my Church. And the gates of the underworld can never hold out against it. I will give you the keys of the kingdom of heaven; whatever you bind on earth shall be considered bound in heaven; whatever you loose on earth shall be considered loosed in heaven.'

This is the Gospel of the Lord.

24 September

Our Lady of Ransom   In England: Memorial

Common of the Blessed Virgin Mary.

FIRST READING

A reading from the letter of St Paul to the Galatians   4:4-7

God sent his Son, born of a woman.

When the appointed time came, God sent his Son, born of a woman, born a subject of the Law, to redeem the subjects of the Law and to enable us to be adopted as sons. The proof that you are sons is that God has sent the Spirit of his Son into our hearts: the Spirit that cries, 'Abba, Father', and it is this that makes you a son, you are not a slave any more; and if God has made you son, then he has made you heir.

This is the word of the Lord.

Responsional Psalm   Lk 1:46-55. ℟ v.49

℟ The Almighty has done great things for me, and holy is his
    Name.

or

℟ O Blessed Virgin Mary, you carried the Son of the eternal
    Father.

1 My soul glorifies the Lord,
    my spirit rejoices in God, my saviour. ℟

2 He looks on his servant in her nothingness;
henceforth all ages will call me blessed.
The Almighty works marvels for me.
Holy his name!

℟ The Almighty has done great things for me, and holy is his
Name.

or

℟ O Blessed Virgin Mary, you carried the Son of the eternal
Father.

3 His mercy is from age to age,
on those who fear him.
He puts forth his arm in strength
and scatters the proud-hearted. ℟

4 He casts the mighty from their thrones
and raises the lowly.
He fills the starving with good things,
sends the rich away empty. ℟

5 He protects Israel, his servant,
remembering his mercy,
the mercy promised to our fathers,
to Abraham and his sons for ever. ℟

Gospel Acclamation   Lk 2:19

Alleluia, alleluia!
Blessed is the Virgin Mary who kept the word of God,
and pondered it in her heart.
Alleluia!

GOSPEL

A reading from the holy Gospel according to John   19:25-27

Woman, this is your son. This is your mother.

Near the cross of Jesus stood his mother and his mother's sister, Mary
the wife of Clopas, and Mary of Magdala. Seeing his mother and the
disciple he loved standing near her, Jesus said to his mother,

'Woman, this is your son'. Then to the disciple he said, 'This is your mother'. And from that moment the disciple made a place for her in his home.

This is the Gospel of the Lord.

OCTOBER

1 October

St Teresa of the child Jesus, Virgin
In Australia: Memorial

As in the Proper of Saints, General Calendar pp.1146ff.

13 October

St Edward the Confessor, king
In England: Memorial

Common of holy men and women.

FIRST READING

A reading from the letter of St Paul to the Romans   8:26-30

With those he justified, he shared his glory.

The Spirit comes to help us in our weakness. For when we cannot choose words in order to pray properly, the Spirit himself expresses our plea in a way that could never be put into words, and God who knows everything in our hearts knows perfectly well what he means, and that the pleas of the saints expressed by the Spirit are according to the mind of God.

We know that by turning everything to their good God co-operates with all those who love him, with all those that he has called according to his purpose. They are the ones he chose specially long ago and intended to become true images of his Son, so that his Son might be the eldest of many brothers. He called those he intended for this; those he called he justified, and with those he justified he shared his glory.

This is the word of the Lord.

Responsorial Psalm   Ps 130

℟   In you, Lord, I have found my peace.

1   O Lord, my heart is not proud
    nor haughty my eyes.
    I have not gone after things too great
    nor marvels beyond me.   ℟

2   Truly I have set my soul
    in silence and peace.
    A weaned child on its mother's breast,
    even so is my soul.   ℟

3   O Israel, hope in the Lord
    both now and for ever.   ℟

Gospel Acclamation   Mt 5:3

    Alleluia, alleluia!
    Happy the poor in spirit;
    the kingdom of heaven is theirs!
    Alleluia!

GOSPEL

A reading from the holy Gospel according to Matthew   5:1-12

Rejoice and be glad, for your reward will be great in heaven.

Seeing the crowds, Jesus went up the hill. There he sat down and was
joined by his disciples. Then he began to speak. This is what he taught
them:

    'How happy are the poor in spirit;
    theirs is the kingdom of heaven.
    Happy the gentle:
    they shall have the earth for their heritage.
    Happy those who mourn:
    they shall be comforted.
    Happy those who hunger and thirst for what is right:
    they shall be satisfied.
    Happy the merciful:
    they shall have mercy shown them.

Happy the pure in heart:
they shall see God.
Happy the peacemakers:
they shall be called sons of God.
Happy those who are persecuted in the cause of right:
theirs is the kingdom of heaven.

'Happy are you when people abuse you and persecute you and speak all kinds of calumny against you on my account. Rejoice and be glad, for your reward will be great in heaven.'

This is the Gospel of the Lord.

25 October

THE FORTY MARTYRS OF
ENGLAND AND WALES   In England: Feast

THE SIX WELSH MARTYRS AND
COMPANIONS, MARTYRS   In Wales: Feast

FIRST READING

A reading from the letter to the Hebrews   11:33-40

Through faith they conquered kingdoms. God will provide for us
something better.

Gideon, Barak, Samson, Jephthah, David, Samuel and the prophets – these were men who through faith conquered kingdoms, did what is right and earned the promises. They could keep a lion's mouth shut, put out blazing fires and emerge unscathed from battle. They were weak people who were given strength, to be brave in war and drive back foreign invaders. Some came back to their wives from the dead, by resurrection; and others submitted to torture, refusing release so that they would rise again to a better life. Some had to bear being pilloried and flogged, or even chained up in prison. They were stoned or sawn in half, or beheaded; they were homeless, and dressed in the skins of sheep and goats; they were penniless and were given nothing but ill-treatment. They were too good for the world and they went out to live in deserts and mountains and in caves and ravines. These are all heroes of faith, but they did not receive what was promised, since God had made provision for us to have something better, and they were not to reach perfection except with us.

This is the word of the Lord.

Responsorial Psalm   Ps 15:1-2. 5. 7. 8-11 ℟ v.5

℟   You are my inheritance, O Lord.

1   Preserve me, God, I take refuge in you.
    I say to the Lord: 'You are my God.'
    O Lord, it is you who are my portion and cup;
    it is you yourself who are my prize.   ℟

2   I will bless the Lord who gives me counsel,
    who even at night directs my heart.
    I keep the Lord ever in my sight:
    since he is at my right hand, I shall stand firm.   ℟

3   You will show me the path of life,
    the fullness of joy in your presence,
    at your right hand happiness for ever.   ℟

Gospel Acclamation

    Alleluia, alleluia!
    You are God: we praise you; you are Lord: we acclaim you;
    the white-robed army of martyrs praise you.
    Alleluia!

GOSPEL

A reading from the holy Gospel according to John   12:24-26

If the grain of wheat in the ground dies, it yields a rich harvest.

Jesus said to his disciples:

    'I tell you, most solemnly,
    unless a wheat grain falls on the ground and dies,
    it remains only a single grain;
    but if it dies,
    it yields a rich harvest.

Anyone who loves his life loses it;
anyone who hates his life in this world
will keep it for the eternal life.
If a man serves me, he must follow me,
wherever I am, my servant will be there too.
If anyone serves me, my Father will honour him.'

This is the Gospel of the Lord.

Alternative Gospel 1

A reading from the holy Gospel according to John   15:18-21

If they have persecuted me, they will persecute you too.

Jesus said to his disciples:

'If the world hates you,
remember that it hated me before you.
If you belonged to the world,
the world would love you as its own;
but because you do not belong to the world,
because my choice withdrew you from the world,
therefore the world hates you.
Remember the words I said to you:
A servant is not greater than his master.
If they persecuted me,
they will persecute you too;
if they kept my word,
they will keep yours as well.
But it will be on my account that they will do all this,
because they do not know the one who sent me.'

This is the Gospel of the Lord.

Alternative Gospel 2

A reading from the holy Gospel according to John   17:11-19

The world hates them.

Jesus raised his eyes to heaven and said,

'Holy Father,
keep those you have given me true to your name,
so that they may be one like us.

While I was with them,
I kept those you had given me true to your name.
I have watched over them and not one is lost
except the one who chose to be lost,
and this was to fulfil the scriptures.
But now I am coming to you
and while still in the world I say these things
to share my joy with them to the full.
I passed your word on to them,
and the world hated them,
because they belong to the world
no more than I belong to the world.
I am not asking you to remove them from the world,
but to protect them from the evil one.
They do not belong to the world
any more than I belong to the world.
Consecrate them in the truth;
your word is truth.
As you sent me into the world,
I have sent them into the world,
and for their sake I consecrate myself
so that they too may be consecrated in truth.'

This is the Gospel of the Lord.

NOVEMBER

6 November

ALL SAINTS OF IRELAND   In Ireland: Feast

FIRST READING

A reading from the book of Ecclesiasticus   44:1-15

Their name lives on for all generations.

Let us praise illustrious men,
our ancestors in their successive generations.
The Lord has created an abundance of glory,
and displayed his greatness from earliest times.
Some wielded authority as kings
and were renowned for their strength;
others were intelligent advisers
and uttered prophetic oracles.
Others directed the people by their advice,
by their understanding of the popular mind,
and by the wise words of their teaching;
others composed musical melodies,
and set down ballads;
others were rich and powerful,
living peacefully in their homes.
All these were honoured by their contemporaries,
and were the glory of their day.
Some of them left a name behind them,
so that their praises are still sung.
While others have left no memory,
and disappeared as though they had not existed,
they are now as though they had never been,
and so too, their children after them.

Here is a list of generous men
whose good works have not been forgotten.
In their descendants there remains
a rich inheritance born of them.
Their descendants stand by the covenants
and, thanks to them, so do their children's children.

Their offspring will last for ever,
their glory will not fade.
Their bodies have been buried in peace,
and their name lives on for all generations.
The peoples will proclaim their wisdom,
the assembly will celebrate their praises.

This is the word of the Lord.

Responsorial Psalm   Ps 14:2-5. ℟ Ps 39:5

℟   Happy are they who hope in the Lord.

1   Lord, who shall dwell on your holy mountain?
    He who walks without fault;
    he who acts with justice
    and speaks the truth from his heart;
    he who does not slander with his tongue.   ℟

2   He who does no wrong to his brother,
    who casts no slur on his neighbour,
    who holds the godless in disdain,
    but honours those who fear the Lord.   ℟

3   He who takes no interest on a loan
    and accepts no bribes against the innocent.
    Such a man will stand firm for ever.   ℟

Gospel Acclamation   Mt 11:28

Alleluia, alleluia!
Come to me all you that labour and are burdened,
and I will give you rest, says the Lord.
Alleluia!

GOSPEL

A reading from the holy Gospel according to Luke   6:17-23

Happy are the poor. Their reward will be great.

Jesus came down with the Twelve and stopped at a piece of level
ground where there was a large gathering of his disciples with a great
crowd of people from all parts of Judaea and from Jerusalem

and from the coastal region of Tyre and Sidon who had come to hear him and to be cured of their diseases. People tormented by unclean spirits were also cured, and everyone in the crowd was trying to touch him because power came out of him that cured them all.

Then fixing his eyes on his disciples he said:

'How happy are you who are poor: yours is the kingdom of God.
Happy you who are hungry now: you shall be satisfied.
Happy you who weep now: you shall laugh.

'Happy are you when people hate you, drive you out, abuse you, denounce your name as criminal, on account of the Son of Man. Rejoice when that day comes and dance for joy, for then your reward will be great in heaven.'

This is the Gospel of the Lord.

16 November

ST MARGARET
Secondary patron of Scotland

In Scotland: Feast

FIRST READING

A reading from the book of Proverbs   31:10-13. 19-20. 30-31

It is the wise woman whom the Lord will praise.

A perfect wife – who can find her?
She is far beyond the price of pearls.

Her husband's heart has confidence in her,
from her he will derive no little profit.

Advantage and not hurt she brings him
all the days of her life.

She is always busy with wool and with flax,
she does her work with eager hands.

She sets her hands to the distaff,
her fingers grasp the spindle.

She holds out her hand to the poor,
she opens her arms to the needy.

Charm is deceitful, and beauty empty;
the woman who is wise is the one to praise.

Give her a share in what her hands have worked for,
and let her works tell her praises at the city gates.

This is the word of the Lord.

Responsorial Psalm   Ps 127:1-5. ℟ v.1

℟   O blessed are those who fear the Lord.

1   O blessed are those who fear the Lord
    and walk in his ways!
    By the labour of your hands you shall eat.
    You will be happy and prosper.   ℟

2   Your wife like a fruitful vine
    in the heart of your house;
    your children like shoots of the olive,
    around your table.   ℟

3   Indeed thus shall be blessed
    the man who fears the Lord.
    May the Lord bless you from Zion
    in a happy Jerusalem
    all the days of your life.   ℟

SECOND READING

A reading from the first letter of St Paul   12:31–13:13
to the Corinthians

Love never ends.

Be ambitious for the higher gifts. And I am going to show you a way
that is better than any of them.

If I have all the eloquence of men or of angels, but speak without
love, I am simply a gong booming or a cymbal clashing. If I have the
gift of prophecy, understanding all the mysteries there are, and
knowing everything, and if I have faith in all its fullness, to move
mountains, but without love, then I am nothing at all. If I give away
all that I possess, piece by piece, and if I even let them take my body to
burn it, but am without love, it will do me no good whatever.

Love is always patient and kind; it is never jealous; love is never boastful or conceited; it is never rude or selfish; it does not take offence, and is not resentful. Love takes no pleasure in other people's sins but delights in the truth; it is always ready to excuse, to trust, to hope, and to endure whatever comes.

Love does not come to an end. But if there are gifts of prophecy, the time will come when they must fail; or the gift of languages, it will not continue for ever; and knowledge – for this, too, the time will come when it must fail. For our knowledge is imperfect and our prophesying is imperfect; but once perfection comes, all imperfect things will disappear. When I was a child, I used to talk like a child, and think like a child, and argued like a child, but now I am a man, all childish ways are put behind me. Now we are seeing a dim reflection in a mirror; but then we shall be seeing face to face. The knowledge that I have now is imperfect; but then I shall know as fully as I am known.

In short, there are three things that last: faith, hope and love; and the greatest of these is love.

This is the word of the Lord.

Gospel Acclamation   Mt 25:34

Alleluia, alleluia!
Come, you whom my Father has blessed, says the Lord;
inherit the kingdom prepared for you since the foundation of the
    world.
Alleluia!

GOSPEL

A reading from the holy Gospel according to Matthew   25:31-46

*Whatever you have done to the very least of my brothers and sisters
you have done to me.*

Jesus said to his disciples: 'When the Son of Man comes in his glory, escorted by all the angels, then he will take his seat on his throne of glory. All the nations will be assembled before him and he will separate men one from another as the shepherd separates sheep from goats. He will place the sheep on his right hand and the goats on his left. Then the King will say to those on his right hand, 'Come, you whom my Father has blessed, take for your heritage the kingdom prepared for you since the foundation of the world. For I was hungry and you gave me food; I was thirsty and you gave me drink; I was a stranger and you made me welcome; naked and you clothed me sick and you visited me, in prison and you came to see me.' Then the virtuous will say to him in reply, 'Lord, when did we see you hungry and feed you; or thirsty and give you drink? When did we see you a stranger and make you welcome; naked and clothe you; sick or in prison and go to see you?' And the King will answer, 'I tell you solemnly, in so far as you did this to one of the least of these brothers of mine, you did it to me'. Next he will say to those on his left hand, 'Go away from me, with your curse upon you, to the eternal fire prepared for the devil and his angels. For I was hungry and you never gave me food; I was thirsty and you never gave me anything to drink; I was a stranger and you never made me welcome, naked and you never clothed me, sick and in prison and you never visited me.' Then it will be their turn to ask, 'Lord, when did we see you hungry or thirsty, a stranger or naked, sick or in prison, and did not come to your help?' Then he will answer, 'I tell you solemnly, in so far as you neglected to do this to one of the least of these, you neglected to do it to me'. And they will go away to eternal punishment, and the virtuous to eternal life.'

This is the Gospel of the Lord.

23 November

ST COLUMBAN, ABBOT   In Ireland: Feast

As in the Proper of Saints, General Calendar, pp.1213ff..

ST ANDREW, APOSTLE

Principal patron of Scotland

In Scotland: Solemnity

FIRST READING

A reading from the book of Wisdom   3:1-9

He accepted them as a holocaust.

The souls of the virtuous are in the hands of God,
no torment shall ever touch them.
In the eyes of the unwise, they did appear to die,
their going looked like a disaster,
their leaving us, like annihilation;
but they are in peace.
If they experienced punishment as men see it,
their hope was rich with immortality;
slight was their affliction, great will their blessings be.
God has put them to the test
and proved them worthy to be with him;
he has tested them like gold in a furnace,
and accepted them as a holocaust.
When the time comes for his visitation they will shine out;
as sparks run through the stubble, so will they.
They shall judge nations, rule over peoples,
and the Lord will be their king for ever.
They who trust in him will understand the truth,
those who are faithful will live with him in love;
for grace and mercy await those he has chosen.

This is the word of the Lord.

Responsorial Psalm   Ps 30:3-4. 6. 8. 17. 21. ℟ v.6

℟   Into your hands, O Lord, I entrust my spirit.

1   Be a rock of refuge for me,
    a mighty stronghold to save me,
    for you are my rock, my stronghold.
    For your name's sake, lead me and guide me.   ℟

2 Into your hands I commend my spirit.
It is you who will redeem me, Lord.
As for me, I trust in the Lord:
let me be glad and rejoice in your love.

℟ Into your hands, O Lord, I entrust my spirit.

3 Let your face shine on your servant.
Save me in your love.
You hide them in the shelter of your presence
from the plotting of men. ℟

SECOND READING

A reading from the letter of St Paul to the Romans   10:9-18

*Faith comes from what is heard and what is heard comes from the
preaching of Christ.*

If your lips confess that Jesus is Lord and if you believe in your heart
that God raised him from the dead, then you will be saved. By
believing from the heart you are made righteous; by confessing with
your lips you are saved. When scripture says: those who believe in
him will have no cause for shame, it makes no distinction between
Jew and Greek: all belong to the same Lord who is rich enough,
however many ask his help, for everyone who calls on the name of the
Lord will be saved.

But they will not ask his help unless they believe in him, and they
will not believe in him unless they have heard of him, and they will
not hear of him unless they get a preacher, and they will never have a
preacher unless one is sent, but as scripture says: The footsteps of
those who bring good news are a welcome sound. Not everyone, of
course, listens to the Good News. As Isaiah says: Lord, how many
believed what we proclaimed? So faith comes from what is preached,
and what is preached comes from the word of Christ.

Let me put the question: is it possible that they did not hear?
Indeed they did; in the words of the psalm, their voice has gone out
through all the earth, and their message to the ends of the world.

This is the word of the Lord.

Gospel Acclamation   Mt 4:19

Alleluia, alleluia!
Come follow me, says the Lord,
and I will make you fishers of my people.
Alleluia!

GOSPEL

A reading from the holy Gospel according to Matthew   4:18-22

Immediately they left their nets and followed him.

As Jesus was walking by the Sea of Galilee he saw two brothers, Simon, who was called Peter, and his brother Andrew; they were making a cast in the lake with their net, for they were fishermen. And he said to them, 'Follow me and I will make you fishers of men.' And they left their nets at once and followed him.

Going on from there he saw another pair of brothers, James son of Zebedee and his brother John; they were in their boat with their father Zebedee, mending their nets, and he called them. At once, leaving the boat and their father, they followed him.

This is the Gospel of the Lord.

DECEMBER

3 December

St Francis Xavier, Priest

In Australia: Memorial

As in Proper of Saints, General Calendar, pp.1217ff.

29 December

ST THOMAS OF CANTERBURY, BISHOP AND MARTYR

In England: Feast

Common of martyrs or Common of pastors.

FIRST READING

A reading from the letter of St Paul to the Colossians   1:24-29

I became the servant of the Church when God made me responsible for delivering his message to you.

It makes me happy to suffer for you, as I am suffering now, and in my own body to do what I can to make up all that has still to be undergone by Christ for the sake of his body, the Church. I became the servant of the Church when God made me responsible for delivering God's message to you, the message which was a mystery hidden for generations and centuries and has now been revealed to his saints. It was God's purpose to reveal it to them and to show all the rich glory of this mystery to pagans. The mystery is Christ among you, your hope of glory: this is the Christ we proclaim, this is the wisdom in which we thoroughly train everyone and instruct everyone, to make them all perfect in Christ. It is for this I struggle wearily on, helped only by his power driving me irresistibly.

This is the word of the Lord.

Responsorial Psalm   Ps 22. ℟ v.1

℟   The Lord is my shepherd; there is nothing I shall want.

1   The Lord is my shepherd;
    there is nothing I shall want.

Fresh and green are the pastures
where he gives me repose.
Near restful waters he leads me,
to revive my drooping spirit. ℟

2 He guides me along the right path;
he is true to his name.
If I should walk in the valley of darkness
no evil would I fear.
You are there with your crook and your staff;
with these you give me comfort. ℟

3 You have prepared a banquet for me
in the sight of my foes.
My head you have anointed with oil;
my cup is overflowing. ℟

4 Surely goodness and kindness shall follow me
all the days of my life.
In the Lord's own house shall I dwell
for ever and ever. ℟

Gospel Acclamation   Jn 10:14

Alleluia, alleluia!
I am the good shepherd, says the Lord;
I know my sheep, and mine know me.
Alleluia!

or   Mt 5:10

Alleluia, alleluia!
Happy are those who suffer persecution for justice' sake;
the kingdom of heaven is theirs.
Alleluia!

GOSPEL

A reading from the holy Gospel according to Luke   22:24-30

I confer a kingdom on you, just as my Father conferred one on me.

A dispute arose between the apostles about which should be reckoned
the greatest, but Jesus said to them, 'Among the pagans it is the kings
who lord it over them, and those who have authority over them

are given the title Benefactor. This must not happen with you. No; the greatest among you must behave as if he were the youngest, the leader as if he were the one who serves. For who is the greater: the one at table or the one who serves? The one at table, surely? Yet here am I among you as one who serves!

'You are the men who have stood by me faithfully in my trials; and now I confer a kingdom on you, just as my Father conferred one on me: you will eat and drink at my table in my kingdom, and you will sit on thrones to judge the twelve tribes of Israel.'

This is the Gospel of the Lord.

Alternative Gospel

A reading from the holy Gospel according to Matthew   10:28-33

Do not fear those who kill the body.

Jesus said to his apostles: 'Do not be afraid of those who kill the body but cannot kill the soul; fear him rather who can destroy both body and soul in hell. Can you not buy two sparrows for a penny? And yet not one falls to the ground without your Father knowing. Why, every hair on your head has been counted. So there is no need to be afraid; you are worth more than hundreds of sparrows.

'So if anyone declares himself for me in the presence of men, I will declare myself for him in the presence of my Father in heaven. But the one who disowns me in the presence of men, I will disown in the presence of my Father in heaven.'

This is the Gospel of the Lord.

Commons

In the Commons, readings are presented in pairs: a first reading with a responsorial psalm; a Gospel acclamation with a Gospel reading. These pairings are suggestions only. Any other suitable pairing may be used, having regard to the pastoral needs of the occasion.

Some readings are marked for use 'Outside the Easter Season'. This does not preclude their use at other times.

COMMON OF THE DEDICATION OF A CHURCH

I On the Day of Dedication

FIRST READING

A reading from the book of Nehemiah   8:2-4. 5-6. 8-10

They read from the book of Law and they understood what was read.

Ezra the priest brought the Law before the assembly, consisting of men, women, and children old enough to understand. This was the first day of the seventh month. On the square before the Water Gate, in the presence of the men and women, and children old enough to understand, he read from the book from early morning till noon; all the people listened attentively to the Book of the Law.

Ezra the scribe stood on a wooden dais erected for the purpose. In full view of all the people – since he stood higher than all the people – Ezra opened the book; and when he opened it all the people stood up. Then Ezra blessed the Lord, the great God, and all the people raised their hands and answered, 'Amen! Amen!'; then they bowed down and, face to the ground, prostrated themselves before the Lord. And Ezra read from the Law of God, translating and giving the sense, so that the people understood what was read.

Then Nehemiah – His Excellency – and Ezra, priest and scribe (and the Levites who were instructing the people) said to all the people, 'This day is sacred to the Lord your God. Do not be mournful, do not weep.' For the people were all in tears as they listened to the words of the Law.

He then said, 'Go, eat the fat, drink the sweet wine, and send a portion to the man who has nothing prepared ready. For this day is sacred to our Lord. Do not be sad: the joy of the Lord is your stronghold.'

This is the word of the Lord.

Responsorial Psalm   Ps 18:8-10. 15. ℟ cf. Jn 6:63

℟   Your words, Lord, are spirit and life.

1   The law of the Lord is perfect,
    it revives the soul.
    The rule of the Lord is to be trusted,
    it gives wisdom to the simple.   ℟

2   The precepts of the Lord are right,
    they gladden the heart.
    The command of the Lord is clear,
    it gives light to the eyes.   ℟

3   The fear of the Lord is holy,
    abiding for ever.
    The decrees of the Lord are truth
    and all of them just.   ℟

4   May the spoken words of my mouth,
    the thoughts of my heart,
    win favour in your sight, O Lord,
    my rescuer, my rock!   ℟

SECOND READING

Readings are chosen from the Anniversary of Dedication. pp.1337ff. below.

During the Easter Season, Apoc 21:1-5 (p.1335) or Apoc 21:9-14 (p.1336) may be chosen, or the reading may be taken from the Anniversary of Dedication, first readings for use during the Easter Season, pp.1333.

GOSPEL

Readings are chosen from the Anniversary of Dedication, pp.1338ff. below.

II Dedication of an Altar

FIRST READING FROM THE OLD TESTAMENT

Outside the Easter Season

1

A reading from the book of Genesis   28:11-18

*Jacob arose and took the stone that he put under his head, set it up
as a memorial stone, and poured oil on top of it.*

When Jacob had reached a certain place he passed the night there,
since the sun had set. Taking one of the stones to be found at that
place, he made it his pillow and lay down where he was. He had a
dream: a ladder was there, standing on the ground with its top
reaching to heaven; and there were angels of God going up it and
coming down. And the Lord was there, standing over him, saying, 'I
am the Lord, the God of Abraham your father, and the God of Isaac. I
will give to you and your descendants the land on which you are lying.
Your descendants shall be like the specks of dust on the ground; you
shall spread to the west and the east, to the north and the south, and
all tribes of the earth shall bless themselves by you and your
descendants. Be sure that I am with you; I will keep you safe wherever
you go, and bring you back to this land, for I will not desert you before
I have done all that I have promised you.' Then Jacob awoke from his
sleep and said, 'Truly, the Lord is in this place and I never knew it!' He
was afraid and said, 'How awe-inspiring this place is! This is nothing
less than a house of God; this is the gate of heaven!' Rising early in the
morning, Jacob took the stone he had used for his pillow, and set it up
as a monument, pouring oil over the top of it.

This is the word of the Lord.

Responsorial Psalm   Ps 94:1-7. ℟ cf. v.2

℟   Let us come before the Lord and praise him.

1   Come, ring out our joy to the Lord;
    hail the rock who saves us.
    Let us come before him, giving thanks,
    with songs let us hail the Lord.   ℟

2 A mighty God is the Lord,
   a great king above all gods.
   In his hand are the depths of the earth;
   the heights of the mountains are his.
   To him belongs the sea, for he made it
   and the dry land shaped by his hands.

   ℟ Let us come before the Lord and praise him.

3 Come in; let us bow and bend low;
   let us kneel before the God who made us
   for he is our God and we
   the people who belong to his pasture,
   the flock that is led by his hand. ℟

2

A reading from the book of Joshua   8:30-35

Joshua built an altar to the Lord.

Joshua built an altar to the Lord the God of Israel on Mount Ebal, as
Moses, the Lord's servant, had ordered the sons of Israel, as is written
in the Book of the Law of Moses, 'an altar of undressed stones that no
iron tool has ever worked'. On this they offered holocausts to the Lord
and offered communion sacrifices as well.

There Joshua wrote on the stones a copy of the Law which Moses
had written for the Israelites. Then, on both sides of the ark, and
facing the levitical priests who carried the ark of the covenant of the
Lord, all Israel with their elders and scribes and judges – strangers as
well as Israelites born – all took their places, half of them in front of
Mount Gerizim and half in front of Mount Ebal, as Moses the servant
of the Lord had ordered originally for the blessing of the people of
Israel. After this, Joshua read all the words of the Law – the blessing
and the cursing – exactly as it stands written in the Book of the Law.
Of every word laid down by Moses there was not one left unread by
Joshua in the presence of the full assembly of Israel, with the women
and children there, and the strangers living among the people.

   This is the word of the Lord.

Responsorial Psalm   Ps 83:3-5. 10-11. ℟ v.2. Alt. ℟ Apoc 21:3

   ℟   How lovely is your dwelling place, Lord, mighty God!

or

   ℟   Here God lives among his people.

or

   ℟   God who is with them will be their God.

1   My soul is longing and yearning,
    is yearning for the courts of the Lord.
    My heart and my soul ring out their joy
    to God, the living God. ℟

2   The sparrow herself finds a home
    and the swallow a nest for her brood;
    she lays her young by your altars,
    Lord of hosts, my king and my God.   ℟

3   They are happy, who dwell in your house,
    for ever singing your praise.
    Turn your eyes, O God, our shield,
    look on the face of your anointed.   ℟

4   One day within your courts
    is better than a thousand elsewhere.
    The threshold of the house of God
    I prefer to the dwelling of the wicked.   ℟

3

A reading from the first book of Maccabees   4:52-59

They dedicated the altar, and the people celebrated with great joy.

On the twenty-fifth of the ninth month, Chislev, in the year one hundred and forty-eight, the priests rose at dawn and offered a lawful sacrifice on the new altar of holocausts which they had made. The altar was dedicated, to the sound of zithers, harps and cymbals, at the same time of year and on the same day on which the pagans had originally profaned it. The whole people fell prostrate in adoration, praising to the skies him who had made them so successful. For eight days they celebrated the dedication of the altar, joyfully offering holocausts, communion sacrifices and thanksgivings. They ornamented the front of the Temple with crowns and bosses of gold, repaired the gates and the storerooms and fitted them with doors. There was no end to the rejoicing among the people, and the reproach of the pagans was lifted from them. Judas, with his brothers and the whole assembly of Israel, made it a law that the days of the dedication of the altar should be celebrated yearly at the proper season, for eight days beginning on the twenty-fifth of the month Chislev, with rejoicing and gladness.

This is the word of the Lord.

Responsorial Psalm   Ps 121:1-4. 8-9. ℟ v.1

℟   Let us go rejoicing to the house of the Lord.

1   I rejoiced when I heard them say:
    'Let us go to God's house.'
    And now our feet are standing
    within your gates, O Jerusalem.   ℟

2   Jerusalem is built as a city
    strongly compact.
    It is there that the tribes go up,
    the tribes of the Lord.
    For Israel's law it is,
    there to praise the Lord's name.   ℟

3   For love of my brethren and friends
    I say: 'Peace upon you!'
    For love of the house of the Lord
    I will ask for your good.   ℟

FIRST READING FROM THE NEW TESTAMENT

In the Easter Season

1

A reading from the Acts of the Apostles   2:42-47

They continued in fellowship with the apostles and in the breaking of bread.

The whole community remained faithful to the teaching of the apostles, to the brotherhood, to the breaking of bread and to the prayers.

The many miracles and signs worked through the apostles made a deep impression on everyone.

The faithful all lived together and owned everything in common; they sold their goods and possessions and shared out the proceeds among themselves according to what each one needed.

They went as a body to the Temple every day but met in their houses for the breaking of bread; they shared their food gladly and generously; they praised God and were looked up to by everyone. Day by day the Lord added to their community those destined to be saved.

This is the word of the Lord.

Responsorial Psalm   Ps 117:15-16. 19-20. 22-23. 27. ℟ v.1

℟   Give thanks to the Lord, for he is good, his love is everlasting.

1   There are shouts of joy and victory
     in the tents of the just.
     The Lord's right hand has triumphed;
     his right hand raised me up.
     The Lord's right hand has triumphed.   ℟

2   Open to me the gates of holiness;
     I will enter and give thanks.
     This is the Lord's own gate
     where the just may enter.   ℟

3   The stone which the builders rejected
     has become the corner stone.
     This is the work of the Lord,
     a marvel in our eyes.   ℟   (continued)

1323

4   The Lord God is our light.
     Go forward in procession with branches
     even to the altar.

    ℟   Give thanks to the Lord, for he is good, his love is everlasting.

2

A reading from the book of the Apocalypse   8:3-4

The angel stood before the altar.

I, John, saw in my vision another angel, who had a golden censer, and who came and stood at the altar. A large quantity of incense was given to him to offer with the prayers of all the saints on the golden altar that stood in front of the throne; and so from the angel's hand the smoke of the incense went up in the presence of God and with it the prayers of the saints.

    This is the word of the Lord.

Responsorial Psalm   Ps 121:1-4. 8-9. ℟ cf. v.1

    ℟   Let us go rejoicing to the house of the Lord.

1   I rejoiced when I heard them say:
     'Let us go to God's house.'
     And now our feet are standing
     within your gates, O Jerusalem.   ℟

2   Jerusalem is built as a city
     strongly compact.
     It is there that the tribes go up,
     the tribes of the Lord.
     For Israel's law it is,
     there to praise the Lord's name.   ℟

3   For love of my brethren and friends
     I say: 'Peace upon you!'
     For love of the house of the Lord
     I will ask for your good.   ℟

SECOND READING FROM THE NEW TESTAMENT

1

A reading from the first letter of St Paul
to the Corinthians

10:16-21

You cannot partake of the table of the Lord and that of demons also.

The blessing-cup that we bless is a communion with the blood of Christ, and the bread that we break is a communion with the body of Christ. The fact that there is only one loaf means that, though there are many of us, we form a single body because we all have a share in this one loaf.

Look at the other Israel, the race, where those who eat the sacrifices are in communion with the altar. Does this mean that the food sacrificed to idols has a real value, or that the idol itself is real? Not at all. It simply means that the sacrifices that they offer they sacrifice to demons who are not God. I have no desire to see you in communion with demons. You cannot drink the cup of the Lord and the cup of demons. You cannot take your share at the table of the Lord and at the table of demons.

This is the word of the Lord.

2

A reading from the letter to the Hebrews

13:8-15

We have an altar from which those who serve the tabernacle have no right to eat.

Jesus Christ is the same today as he was yesterday and as he will be for ever. Do not let yourselves be led astray by all sorts of strange doctrines: it is better to rely on grace for inner strength than on dietary laws which have done no good to those who kept them. We have our own altar from which those who serve the tabernacle have no right to eat. The bodies of the animals whose blood is brought into the sanctuary by the high priest for the atonement of sin are burnt outside the camp, and so Jesus too suffered outside the gate to sanctify the people with his own blood. Let us go to him then, outside the camp, and share his degradation. For there is no eternal city for us in this life but we look for one in the life to come. Through him, let us offer God an unending sacrifice of praise, a verbal sacrifice that is offered every time we acknowledge his name.

This is the word of the Lord.

GOSPEL

1

Gospel Acclamation   Ez 37:27

> Alleluia, alleluia!
> My dwelling-place shall be with them, says the Lord,
> and I will be their God and they will be my people.
> Alleluia!

A reading from the holy Gospel according to Matthew   5:23-24

Go and make peace with your neighbour first, then come and offer your gift.

Jesus said to his disciples: 'If you are bringing your offering to the altar and there remember that your brother has something against you, leave your offering there before the altar, go and be reconciled with your brother first, and then come back and present your offering.'

This is the Gospel of the Lord.

2

Gospel Acclamation   cf. Jn 4:23.24

> Alleluia, alleluia!
> The Father seeks worshippers
> who will worship him in spirit and in truth.
> Alleluia!

A reading from the holy Gospel according to John   4:19-24

The Father seeks worshippers who will worship him in spirit and in truth.

The Samaritan woman said to Jesus, 'I see you are a prophet, sir. Our fathers worshipped on this mountain, while you say that Jerusalem is the place where one ought to worship.' Jesus said:

> 'Believe me, woman, the hour is coming
> when you will worship the Father
> neither on this mountain nor in Jerusalem.

You worship what you do not know;
we worship what we do know;
for salvation comes from the Jews.
But the hour will come – in fact it is here already –
when true worshippers will worship the Father in spirit and truth;
that is the kind of worshipper
the Father wants.
God is spirit,
and those who worship
must worship in spirit and truth.'

This is the Gospel of the Lord.

3

Gospel Acclamation   Heb 13:8

Alleluia, alleluia!
Jesus Christ is the same yesterday, today, and for ever.
Alleluia!

A reading from the holy Gospel according to John   12:31-36

When I am lifted up from the earth I will draw all people to myself.

Jesus said to the crowd:

'Now sentence is being passed on this world:
now the prince of this world is to be overthrown.
And when I am lifted up from the earth,
I shall draw all men to myself.'

By these words he indicated the kind of death he would die. The crowd
answered. 'The Law has taught us that the Christ will remain for
ever. How can you say, "The Son of Man must be lifted up"? Who is
this Son of Man?' Jesus then said:

'The light will be with you only a little longer now.
Walk while you have the light,
or the dark will overtake you;
he who walks in the dark does not know where he is going.
While you still have the light,
believe in the light
and you will become sons of light.'

This is the Gospel of the Lord.

III Anniversary of Dedication of a Church

FIRST READING FROM THE OLD TESTAMENT

Outside the Easter Season

1

A reading from the first book of the Kings   8:22-23. 27-30

Let your eyes watch over this house.

In the presence of the whole assembly of Israel, Solomon stood before the altar of the Lord and, stretching out his hands towards heaven, said, 'Lord, God of Israel, not in heaven above nor on earth beneath is there such a God as you, true to your covenant and your kindness towards your servants when they walk wholeheartedly in your way. Yet will God really live with men on the earth? Why, the heavens and their own heavens cannot contain you. How much less this house that I have built! Listen to the prayer and entreaty of your servant, Lord my God; listen to the cry and to the prayer your servant makes to you today. Day and night let your eyes watch over this house, over this place of which you have said, "My name shall be there". Listen to the prayer that your servant will offer in this place.

'Hear the entreaty of your servant and of Israel your people as they pray in this place. From heaven where your dwelling is, hear; and, as you hear, forgive.'

This is the word of the Lord.

Responsorial Psalm   Ps 83:3-5. 10-11. ℟ v.2. Alt. ℟ Apoc 21:3

℟   How lovely is your dwelling place, Lord, mighty God!

or

℟   Here God lives among his people.

1   My soul is longing and yearning,
    is yearning for the courts of the Lord.
    My heart and my soul ring out their joy
    to God, the living God.   ℟

2   The sparrow herself finds a home
     and the swallow a nest for her brood;
     she lays her young by your altars,
     Lord of hosts, my king and my God.   ℟

3   They are happy, who dwell in your house,
     for ever singing your praise.
     Turn your eyes, O God, our shield,
     look on the face of your anointed.   ℟

4   One day within your courts
     is better than a thousand elsewhere.
     The threshold of the house of God
     I prefer to the dwelling of the wicked.   ℟

2

A reading from the second book of Chronicles   5:6-11. 13–6:2

I have built a dwelling-place for you to live in for ever.

King Solomon, and all the community of Israel gathering with him in front of the ark, sacrificed sheep and oxen, countless, innumerable. The priests brought the ark of the covenant of the Lord to its place, in the Debir of the Temple, that is, in the Holy of Holies, under the cherubs' wings. For there where the ark was placed the cherubs spread out their wings and sheltered the ark and its shafts. These were long enough for their ends to be seen from the Holy Place in front of the Debir, but not from outside. There was nothing in the ark except the two tablets that Moses had placed in it at Horeb, where the Lord had made a covenant with the Israelites when they came out of Egypt.

Now when the priests came out of the sanctuary, a cloud filled the sanctuary, the Temple of the Lord.

All those who played the trumpet, or who sang, united in giving praise and glory to the Lord. Lifting their voices to the sound of the trumpet and cymbal and instruments of music, they gave praise to the Lord, 'for he is good, for his love is everlasting'.

Because of the cloud the priests could no longer perform their duties; the glory of the Lord filled the Temple of God.

Then Solomon said:

'The Lord has chosen to dwell in the thick cloud.
Yes, I have built you a dwelling,
a place for you to live in for ever.'

This is the word of the Lord.

Responsorial Psalm   1 Chron 29:10-12. ℞ v.13

℞   We praise your glorious name, O mighty God.

1   Blessed are you, O Lord,
    the God of Israel our father,
    for ever, for ages unending.   ℞

2   Yours, Lord, are greatness and power,
    and splendour, triumph and glory.
    All is yours, in heaven and on earth.   ℞

3   Yours, O Lord, is the kingdom,
    you are supreme over all.
    Both honour and riches come from you.   ℞

4   You are the ruler of all,
    from your hand come strength and power,
    from your hand come greatness and might.   ℞

3

A reading from the prophet Isaiah   56:1. 6-7

My house will be called a house of prayer for all the peoples.

Thus says the Lord: Have a care for justice, act with integrity, for soon
my salvation will come and my integrity be manifest.

Foreigners who have attached themselves to the Lord to serve him
and to love his name and be his servants – all who observe the
sabbath, not profaning it, and cling to my covenant – these I will bring
to my holy mountain. I will make them joyful in my house of prayer.
Their holocausts and their sacrifices will be accepted on my altar, for
my house will be called a house of prayer for all the peoples.

This is the word of the Lord.

Responsorial Psalm   Ps 83:3-5. 10-11. ℟ v.2. Alt. ℟ Apoc 21:3

℟   How lovely is your dwelling place, Lord, mighty God.

or

℟   Here God lives among his people.

1   My soul is longing and yearning,
    is yearning for the courts of the Lord.
    My heart and my soul ring out their joy
    to God, the living God.   ℟

2   The sparrow herself finds a home
    and the swallow a nest for her brood;
    she lays her young by your altars,
    Lord of hosts, my king and my God.   ℟

3   They are happy, who dwell in your house
    for ever singing your praise.
    Turn your eyes, O God, our shield,
    look on the face of your anointed.   ℟

4   One day within your courts
    is better than a thousand elsewhere.
    The threshold of the house of God
    I prefer to the dwelling of the wicked.   ℟

4

A reading from the prophet Ezekiel   43:1-2. 4-7

The glory of the Lord God filled the temple.

The angel took me to the gate, the one facing east. I saw the glory of
the God of Israel approaching from the east. A sound came with it,
like the sound of the ocean, and the earth shone with his glory.
    The glory of the Lord arrived at the Temple by the east gate. The
spirit lifted me up and brought me into the inner court; I saw the glory
of the Lord fill the Temple. And I heard someone speaking to me from
the Temple while the man stood beside me. The voice said, 'Son of
man, this is the dais of my throne, the step on which I rest my feet. I
shall live here among the sons of Israel for ever.'

    This is the word of the Lord.

Responsorial Psalm   1 Chron 29:10-12. ℟ v.13

℟   We praise your glorious name, O mighty God.

1   Blessed are you, O Lord,
    the God of Israel our father,
    for ever, for ages unending. ℟

2   Yours, Lord, are greatness and power,
    and splendour, triumph and glory.
    All is yours, in heaven and on earth. ℟

3   Yours, O Lord, is the kingdom,
    you are supreme over all.
    Both honour and riches come from you. ℟

4   You are the ruler of all,
    from your hand come strength and power,
    from your hand come greatness and might. ℟

5

A reading from the prophet Ezekiel   47:1-2. 8-9. 12

I see water flowing from the temple and all who were touched by it
were saved.

The angel brought me to the entrance of the Temple, where a stream
came out from under the Temple threshold and flowed eastwards,
since the Temple faced east. The water flowed from under the right
side of the Temple, south of the altar. He took me out by the north
gate and led me right round outside as far as the outer east gate where
the water flowed out on the right-hand side. He said, 'This water flows
east down to the Arabah and to the sea; and flowing into the sea it
makes its waters wholesome. Wherever the river flows, all living
creatures teeming in it will live. Fish will be very plentiful, for
wherever the water goes it brings health, and life teems wherever the
river flows. Along the river, on either bank, will grow every kind of
fruit tree with leaves that never wither and fruit that never fails; they
will bear new fruit every month, because this water comes from
the sanctuary. And their fruit will be good to eat and the leaves
medicinal.

This is the word of the Lord.

Responsorial Psalm   Ps 45:2-3. 5-6. 8-9. ℟ v.5

℟   The waters of the river gladden the city of God.

1   God is for us a refuge and strength,
     a helper close at hand, in time of distress:
     so we shall not fear though the earth should rock,
     though the mountains fall into the depths of the sea.   ℟

2   The waters of a river give joy to God's city,
     the holy place where the Most High dwells.
     God is within, it cannot be shaken;
     God will help it at the dawning of the day.   ℟

3   The Lord of hosts is with us:
     the God of Jacob is our stronghold.
     Come, consider the works of the Lord
     the redoubtable deeds he has done on the earth.   ℟

FIRST READING FROM THE NEW TESTAMENT

In the Easter Season

1

A reading from the Acts of the Apostles   7:44-50

God does not live in houses made by human hands.

Stephen said to the people, the elders and scribes, 'While they were in the desert our ancestors possessed the Tent of Testimony that had been constructed according to the instructions God gave Moses, telling him to make an exact copy of the pattern he had been shown. It was handed down from one ancestor of ours to another until Joshua brought it into the country we had conquered from the nations which were driven out by God as we advanced. Here it stayed until the time of David. He won God's favour and asked pemission to have a temple built for the House of Jacob, though it was Solomon who actually built God's house for him. Even so the Most High does not live in a house that human hands have built: for as the prophet says:

"With heaven my throne
and earth my footstool,
what house could you build me,

what place could you make for my rest?
Was not all this made by my hand?" '

This is the word of the Lord.

Responsorial Psalm   Ps 94:1-7. ℟ v.2

℟   Let us come before the Lord and praise him.

1   Come, ring out our joy to the Lord;
     hail the rock who saves us.
     Let us come before him, giving thanks,
     with songs let us hail the Lord.   ℟

2   A mighty God is the Lord,
     a great king above all gods.
     In his hand are the depths of the earth;
     the heights of the mountains are his.
     To him belongs the sea, for he made it
     and the dry land shaped by his hands.   ℟

3   Come in; let us bow and bend low;
     let us kneel before the God who made us
     for he is our God and we
     the people who belong to his pasture,
     the flock that is led by his hand.   ℟

2

A reading from the book of the Apocalypse   21:1-5

Behold, the home of God is among his people.

I, John, saw a new heaven and a new earth; the first heaven and the first earth had disappeared now, and there was no longer any sea. I saw the holy city, and the new Jerusalem, coming down from God out of heaven, as beautiful as a bride all dressed for her husband. Then I heard a loud voice call from the throne, 'You see this city? Here God lives among men. He will make his home among them; they shall be his people, and he will be their God; his name is God-with-them. He will wipe away all tears from their eyes; there will be no more death, and no more mourning or sadness. The world of the past has gone.'

Then the One sitting on the throne spoke: 'Now I am making the whole of creation new.'

This is the word of the Lord.

Responsorial Psalm   Ps 83:3-5. 10-11. ℟ v.2. Alt ℟ Apoc 21:3

℟   How lovely is your dwelling place, Lord, mighty God!

or

℟   Here God lives among his people.

1   My soul is longing and yearning,
    is yearning for the courts of the Lord.
    My heart and my soul ring out their joy
    to God, the living God.   ℟

2   The sparrow herself finds a home
    and the swallow a nest for her brood;
    she lays her young by your altars,
    Lord of hosts, my king and my God.   ℟

3   They are happy, who dwell in your house,
    for ever singing your praise.
    Turn your eyes, O God, our shield,
    look on the face of your anointed.   ℟

4   One day within your courts
    is better than a thousand elsewhere.
    The threshold of the house of God
    I prefer to the dwelling of the wicked.   ℟

3

A reading from the book of the Apocalypse   21:9-14

I will show you the bride the Lamb has married.

The angel said to me, 'Come here and I will show you the bride that the Lamb has married.' In the spirit, he took me to the top of an enormous high mountain and showed me Jerusalem, the holy city, coming down from God out of heaven. It had all the radiant glory of God and glittered like some precious jewel of crystal-clear diamond. The walls of it were of a great height, and had twelve gates; at each of the twelve gates there was an angel, and over the gates were written the names of the twelve tribes of Israel; on the east there were three gates, on the north three gates, on the south three gates, and on the west three gates. The city walls stood on twelve foundation stones, each one of which bore the name of one of the twelve apostles of the Lamb.

This is the word of the Lord.

Responsorial Psalm   Ps 121:1-4. 8-9. ℟ v.1

℟   Let us go rejoicing to the house of the Lord.

1   I rejoiced when I heard them say:
     'Let us go to God's house.'
     And now our feet are standing
     within your gates, O Jerusalem.   ℟

2   Jerusalem is built as a city
     strongly compact.
     It is there that the tribes go up,
     the tribes of the Lord.
     For Israel's law it is,
     there to praise the Lord's name.   ℟

3   For love of my brethren and friends
     I say: 'Peace upon you!'
     For love of the house of the Lord
     I will ask for your good.   ℟

SECOND READING FROM THE NEW TESTAMENT

1

A reading from the first letter of St Paul to the Corinthians 3:9-11. 16-17

You are the temple of God.

You are God's building. By the grace God gave me, I succeeded as an architect and laid the foundations, on which someone else is doing the building. Everyone doing the building must work carefully. For the foundation, nobody can lay other than the one which has already been laid, that is Jesus Christ.

Didn't you realise that you were God's temple and that the Spirit of God was living among you? If anybody should destroy the temple of God, God will destroy him, because the temple of God is sacred; and you are that temple.

This is the word of the Lord.

2

A reading from the letter of St Paul to the Ephesians 2:19-22

All grow into one holy temple in the Lord.

You are no longer aliens or foreign visitors: you are citizens like all the saints, and part of God's household. You are part of a building that has the apostles and prophets for its foundations, and Christ Jesus himself for its main cornerstone. As every structure is aligned on him, all grow into one holy temple in the Lord; and you too, in him, are being built into a house where God lives, in the Spirit.

This is the word of the Lord.

3

A reading from the letter to the Hebrews 12:18-19. 22-24

As living stones, you will be built into a spiritual temple.

What you have come to is nothing known to the senses: not a blazing fire, or a gloom turning to total darkness, or a storm; or trumpeting thunder or the great voice speaking which made everyone that heard it beg that no more should be said to them. But what you have come to is Mount Zion and the city of the living God, the heavenly Jerusalem

1337

where the millions of angels have gathered for the festival, with the whole church in which everyone is a 'first-born son' and a citizen of heaven. You have come to God himself, the supreme Judge, and been placed with spirits of the saints who have been made perfect; and to Jesus, the mediator who brings a new covenant and a blood for purification which pleads more insistently than Abel's.

This is the word of the Lord.

4

A reading from the first letter of St Peter   2:4-9

So that you too may be living stones making a spiritual house.

Jesus Christ is the living stone, rejected by men but chosen by God and precious to him; set yourselves close to him so that you too, the holy priesthood that offers the spiritual sacrifices which Jesus Christ has made acceptable to God, may be living stones making a spiritual house. As scripture says: See how I lay in Zion a precious cornerstone that I have chosen and the man who rests his trust on it will not be disappointed. That means that for you who are believers, it is precious; but for unbelievers, the stone rejected by the builders has proved to be the keystone, a stone to stumble over, a rock to bring men down. They stumble over it because they do not believe in the word; it was the fate in store for them.

But you are a chosen race, a royal priesthood, a consecrated nation, a people set apart to sing the praises of God who called you out of the darkness into his wonderful light.

This is the word of the Lord.

GOSPEL

1

Gospel Acclamation   Mt 16:18

Alleluia, alleluia!
You are Peter, the rock on which I will build my Church;
the gates of hell will not hold out against it.
Alleluia!

A reading from the holy Gospel according to Matthew   16:13-19

You are Peter; and to you I will give the keys of the kingdom of heaven.

When Jesus came to the region of Caesarea Philippi he put this question to his disciples, 'Who do people say the Son of Man is?' And they said, 'Some say he is John the Baptist, some Elijah, and others Jeremiah or one of the prophets.' 'But you,' he said, 'who do you say I am?' Then Simon Peter spoke up, 'You are the Christ,' he said, 'the Son of the living God.' Jesus replied, 'Simon son of Jonah, you are a happy man! Because it was not flesh and blood that revealed this to you but my Father in heaven. So I now say to you: You are Peter and on this rock I will build my Church. And the gates of the underworld can never hold out against it. I will give you the keys of the kingdom of heaven: whatever you bind on earth shall be considered bound in heaven; whatever you loose on earth shall be considered loosed in heaven.'

This is the Gospel of the Lord.

2

Gospel Acclamation   cf. Mt 7:8

Alleluia, alleluia!
In my house, says the Lord, everyone who asks will receive;
whoever seeks shall find; and to those who knock it shall be
    opened.
Alleluia!

A reading from the holy Gospel according to Luke   19:1-10

Today salvation has come to this house.

Jesus entered Jericho and was going through the town when a man whose name was Zacchaeus made his appearance; he was one of the senior tax collectors and a wealthy man. He was anxious to see what kind of man Jesus was, but he was too short and could not see him for the crowd; so he ran ahead and climbed a sycamore tree to catch a glimpse of Jesus who was to pass that way. When Jesus reached the spot he looked up and spoke to him: 'Zacchaeus, come down. Hurry, because I must stay at your house today.' And he hurried down and welcomed him joyfully. They all complained when they saw what was happening. 'He has gone to stay at a sinner's house,' they said. But Zacchaeus stood his ground and said to the Lord, 'Look, sir, I am going to give half my property to the poor, and if I have cheated anybody I will pay him back four times the amount.' And Jesus said to him, 'Today salvation has come to this house, because this man too is a son of Abraham; for the Son of Man has come to seek out and save what was lost.'

This is the Gospel of the Lord.

3

Gospel Acclamation   2 Chron 7:16

Alleluia, alleluia!
I have chosen and sanctified this house, says the Lord,
that my name may remain in it for all time.
Alleluia!

A reading from the holy Gospel according to John   2:13-22

He spoke about the temple of his own body.

Just before the Jewish Passover Jesus went up to Jerusalem, and in the Temple he found people selling cattle and sheep and pigeons, and the money changers sitting at their counters there. Making a whip out of some cord, he drove them all out of the Temple, cattle and sheep as well, scattered the money changers' coins, knocked their tables over and said to the pigeon-sellers, 'Take all this out of here and stop turning my Father's house into a market.' Then his disciples remembered the words of scripture: Zeal for your house will devour me. The Jews intervened and said, 'What sign can you show us to justify what you have done?' Jesus answered, 'Destroy this sanctuary, and in three days I will raise it up.' The Jews replied, 'It has taken forty-six years to build this sanctuary: are you going to raise it up in three days?' But he was speaking of the sanctuary that was his body, and when Jesus rose from the dead, his disciples remembered that he had said this, and they believed the scripture and the words he had said.

This is the Gospel of the Lord.

4

Gospel Acclamation   Is 66:1

Alleluia, alleluia!
Heaven is my throne and earth is my footstool, says the Lord;
what is the house that you would build for me?
Alleluia!

or   Ez 37:27

Alleluia, alleluia!
My dwelling-place shall be with them, says the Lord,
and I will be their God and they will be my people.
Alleluia!

A reading from the holy Gospel according to John   4:19-24

True worshippers will worship the Father in spirit and truth.

The Samaritan woman said to Jesus, 'I see you are a prophet, sir. Our
fathers worshipped on this mountain, while you say that Jerusalem is
the place where one ought to worship.' Jesus said:

'Believe me, woman, the hour is coming
when you will worship the Father
neither on this mountain nor in Jerusalem.
You worship what you do not know;
we worship what we do know;
for salvation comes from the Jews.
But the hour will come – in fact it is here already –
when true worshippers will worship the Father in spirit and truth:
that is the kind of worshipper
the Father wants.
God is spirit,
and those who worship
must worship in spirit and truth.'

This is the Gospel of the Lord.

RITES OF DEDICATION
CHURCH AND ALTAR

The readings for these Rites are given here, as an appendix to the Common of the Dedication of a Church, to facilitate cross references.

I Laying of a Foundation Stone

The readings may be taken from the Common, pp.1317ff., or, especially if a foundation stone is used in the rite, it is appropriate to choose one of the following readings.

FIRST READING

1

A reading from the first book of the Kings   5:2-18

At the King's orders they quarried huge stones, special stones, for the laying of the temple foundations.

Solomon sent this message to Hiram, 'You are aware that David my father was unable to build a temple for the name of the Lord his God, because his enemies waged war on him from all sides, until the Lord should put them under his control. But now the Lord my God has given me rest on every side: not one enemy, no calamities. I therefore plan to build a temple for the name of the Lord my God, just as the Lord said to David my father, "Your son whom I will place on your throne to succeed you shall be the man to build a temple for my name". So now have cedars of Lebanon cut down for me; my servants will work with your servants, and I will pay for the hire of your servants at whatever rate you fix. As you know, we have no one as skilled in felling trees as the Sidonians.' When Hiram heard what Solomon had said, he was delighted. 'Now blessed be the Lord' he said 'who has given David a wise son to rule over this great people!' And Hiram sent word to Solomon, 'I have received your message. For my part, I will supply all you want in the way of cedar wood and juniper. Your servants will bring these down from Lebanon to the sea, and I shall have them towed by sea to any place you name; I shall discharge them there, and you will take them over. For your part, you will see to the provisioning of

1342

my household as I direct.' So Hiram provided Solomon with all the cedar wood and juniper he wanted, while Solomon gave Hiram twenty thousand kors of wheat to feed his household, and twenty thousand kors of pure oil. Solomon gave Hiram this every year. The Lord gave Solomon wisdom as he had promised him; good relations persisted between Solomon and Hiram, and the two of them concluded a treaty.

King Solomon raised a levy throughout Israel for forced labour: the levy numbered thirty thousand men. He sent these to Lebanon in relays, ten thousand a month; they spent one month in Lebanon and two months at home. Adoram was in charge of the forced labour. Solomon also had seventy thousand porters and eighty thousand quarrymen in the mountains, as well as the administrators' officials who supervised the work, three thousand three hundred of them in charge of the men employed in the work. At the king's orders they quarried stones, special stones, for the laying of the temple foundations, dressed stones. Solomon's workmen and Hiram's workmen and the Giblites cut and assembled the wood and stone for the building of the Temple.

This is the word of the Lord.

2

A reading from the prophet Isaiah   28:16-17

See how I lay in Zion a stone of witness, a precious cornerstone, a foundation stone.

The Lord says this:

See how I lay in Zion
a stone of witness,
a precious cornerstone, a foundation stone:
The believer shall not stumble.
And I will make justice the measure,
integrity the plumb-line.

This is the word of the Lord.

3

A reading from the Acts of the Apostles   4:8-12

Jesus Christ, the one you crucified, has proved to be the keystone.

Peter, filled with the Holy Spirit, said, 'Rulers of the people, and elders! If you are questioning us today about an act of kindness to a cripple, and asking us how he was healed, then I am glad to tell you all, and would indeed be glad to tell the whole people of Israel, that it was by the name of Jesus Christ the Nazarene, the one you crucified, whom God raised from the dead, by this name and by no other that this man is able to stand up perfectly healthy, here in your presence, today. This is the stone rejected by you the builders, but which has proved to be the keystone. For of all the names in the world given to men, this is the only one by which we can be saved.'

This is the word of the Lord.

4

A reading from the first letter of St Paul to the Corinthians

10:1-6

And that rock was Christ.

I want to remind you, brothers, how our fathers were all guided by a cloud above them and how they all passed through the sea. They were all baptised into Moses in this cloud and in this sea; all ate the same spiritual food and all drank the same spiritual drink, since they all drank from the spiritual rock that followed them as they went, and that rock was Christ. In spite of this, most of them failed to please God and their corpses littered the desert.

These things all happened as warnings for us, not to have the wicked lusts for forbidden things that they had.

This is the word of the Lord.

RESPONSORIAL PSALM

1

Ps 23:1-6. ℟ 2 Chron 7:16

℟ I have chosen and sanctified this place.

1 The Lord's is the earth and its fullness,
   the world and all its peoples.
   It is he who set it on the seas;
   on the waters he made it firm. ℟

2   Who shall climb the mountain of the Lord?
     Who shall stand in his holy place?
     The man with clean hands and pure heart,
     who desires not worthless things. ℟

3   He shall receive blessings from the Lord
     and reward from the God who saves him.
     Such are the men who seek him,
     seek the face of the God of Jacob. ℟

2

Ps 41:3. 5; Ps 42:3. 4. ℟ 42:3

℟   Lord, may your truth lead me to your holy mountain.

1   My soul is thirsting for God,
     the God of my life;
     when can I enter and see
     the face of God? ℟

2   These things will I remember
     as I pour out my soul:
     how I would lead the rejoicing crowd
     into the house of God,
     amid cries of gladness and thanksgiving,
     the throng wild with joy. ℟

3   O send forth your light and your truth;
     let these be my guide.
     Let them bring me to your holy mountain
     to the place where you dwell. ℟

4   And I will come to the altar of God,
     the God of my joy.
     My redeemer, I will thank you on the harp,
     O God, my God. ℟

3

Ps 86. ℟ v.1

℟ The city of God is founded on the holy mountains.

1 On the holy mountain is his city
  cherished by the Lord.
  The Lord prefers the gates of Zion
  to all Jacob's dwellings.
  Of you are told glorious things,
  O city of God! ℟

2 'Babylon and Egypt I will count
  among those who know me;
  Philistia, Tyre, Ethiopia,
  these will be her children
  and Zion shall be called "Mother"
  for all shall be her children.' ℟

3 It is he, the Lord Most High,
  who gives each his place.
  In his register of peoples he writes:
  'These are her children'
  and while they dance they will sing:
  'In you all find their home.' ℟

4

Ps 99:1-3. 5. ℟ cf. Ez 37:27

℟ I will make my dwelling place among the people.

1 Cry out with joy to the Lord, all the earth.
  Serve the Lord with gladness.
  Come before him, singing for joy. ℟

2 Know that he, the Lord, is God.
  He made us, we belong to him,
  we are his people, the sheep of his flock. ℟

3 Indeed, how good is the Lord,
  eternal his merciful love.
  He is faithful from age to age. ℟

5

Ps 117:1-2. 16-17. 22-23. ℟ cf. 1 Cor 3:11

℟　There is no other foundation than Christ Jesus.

1　Give thanks to the Lord for he is good,
　　for his love has no end.
　　Let the sons of Israel say:
　　'His love has no end.'　℟

2　The Lord's right hand has triumphed;
　　his right hand raised me up.
　　I shall not die, I shall live
　　and recount his deeds.　℟

3　The stone which the builders rejected
　　has become the corner stone.
　　This is the work of the Lord,
　　a marvel in our eyes.　℟

GOSPEL

1

A reading from the holy Gospel according to Matthew　　7:21-29

A house built on rock and a house built on sand.

Jesus said to his disciples: 'It is not those who say to me, "Lord, Lord," who will enter the kingdom of heaven, but the person who does the will of my Father in heaven. When the day comes many will say to me, "Lord, Lord, did we not prophesy in your name, cast out demons in your name, work many miracles in your name?" Then I shall tell them to their faces: I have never known you ; away from me, you evil men!

'Therefore, everyone who listens to these words of mine and acts on them will be like a sensible man who built his house on rock. Rain came down, floods rose, gales blew and hurled themselves against that house, and it did not fall: it was founded on rock. But everyone who listens to these words of mine and does not act on them will be like a stupid man who built his house on sand. Rain came down, floods rose, gales blew and struck that house, and it fell; and what a fall it had!'

Jesus had now finished what he wanted to say, and his teaching made a deep impression on the people because he taught them with authority, and not like their own scribes.

This is the Gospel of the Lord.

2

A reading from the holy Gospel according to Matthew   16:13-18

On this rock I will build my church.

When Jesus came to the region of Caesarea Philippi he put this question to his disciples, 'Who do people say the Son of Man is?' And they said, 'Some say he is John the Baptist, some Elijah, and others Jeremiah or one of the prophets'. 'But you,' he said 'who do you say I am?' Then Simon Peter spoke up, 'You are the Christ,' he said 'the Son of the living God'. Jesus replied, 'Simon son of Jonah, you are a happy man! Because it was not flesh and blood that revealed this to you but my Father in heaven. So I now say to you: You are Peter and on this rock I will build my church. And the gates of the underworld can never hold out against it.'

This is the Gospel of the Lord.

3

A reading from the holy Gospel according to Mark   12:1-12

It was the stone rejected by the builders that became the keystone.

Jesus spoke to the chief priests and the scribes and the elders in parables: 'A man planted a vineyard; he fenced it round, dug out a trough for the winepress and built a tower; then he leased it to tenants and went abroad. When the time came, he sent a servant to the tenants to collect from them his share of the produce from the vineyard. But they seized the man, thrashed him and sent him away empty-handed. Next he sent another servant to them; him they beat about the head and treated shamefully. And he sent another and him they killed; then a number of others, and they thrashed some and killed the rest. He had still someone left: his beloved son. He sent him to them last of all. "They will respect my son" he said. But those tenants said to each other, "This is the heir. Come on, let us kill him, and the inheritance will be ours." So they seized him and killed him and threw him out of the vineyard. Now what will the owner of the vineyard do? He will come and make an end of the tenants and give the vineyard to others. Have you not read this text of scripture:

It was the stone rejected by the builders
that became the keystone.
This was the Lord's doing
and it is wonderful to see?'

And they would have liked to arrest him, because they realised
that the parable was aimed at them, but they were afraid of the
crowds. So they left him alone and went away.

This is the Gospel of the Lord.

4

A reading from the holy Gospel according to Luke   6:46-49

He laid the foundations on rock.

Jesus said to his disciples: 'Why do you call me, "Lord, Lord" and not
do what I say?

'Everyone who comes to me and listens to my words and acts on
them – I will show you what he is like. He is like the man who when
he built his house dug, and dug deep, and laid the foundations on rock;
when the river was in flood it bore down on that house but could not
shake it, it was so well built. But the one who listens and does nothing
is like the man who built his house on soil, with no foundations: as
soon as the river bore down on it, it collapsed; and what a ruin that
house became!'

This is the Gospel of the Lord.

II Dedication of a Church

The first reading and responsorial psalm given below are always used for the Rite of Dedication of a Church. The second reading and Gospel are taken from the Common of the Dedication of a Church, pp.1337ff.

FIRST READING

A reading from the book of Nehemiah 8:2-6. 8-10

They read from the book of Law and they understood what was read.

Ezra the priest brought the Law before the assembly, consisting of men, women, and children old enough to understand. This was the first day of the seventh month. On the square before the Water Gate, in the presence of the men and women, and children old enough to understand, he read from the book from early morning till noon; all the people listened attentively to the book of the Law.

Ezra the scribe stood on a wooden dais erected for the purpose. In full view of all the people – since he stood higher than all the people – Ezra opened the book; and when he opened it all the people stood up. Then Ezra blessed the Lord, the great God, and all the people raised their hands and answered, 'Amen! Amen!'; then they bowed down and, face to the ground, prostrated themselves before the Lord. And Ezra read from the Law of God, translating and giving the sense, so that the people understood what was read.

Then (Nehemiah – His Excellency – and) Ezra priest and scribe (and the Levites who were instructing the people) said to all the people, 'This day is sacred to the Lord your God. Do not be mournful, do not weep.' For the people were all in tears as they listened to the words of the Law.

He then said, 'Go, eat the fat, drink the sweet wine, and send a portion to the man who has nothing prepared ready. For this day is sacred to our Lord. Do not be sad: the joy of the Lord is your stronghold.'

This is the word of the Lord.

Responsorial Psalm   Ps 18:8-10. 15. ℟ Jn 6:63

> ℟   Your words, Lord, are spirit and life.

1   The law of the Lord is perfect,
it revives the soul.
The rule of the Lord is to be trusted,
it gives wisdom to the simple. ℟

2   The precepts of the Lord are right,
they gladden the heart,
The command of the Lord is clear,
it gives light to the eyes. ℟

3   The fear of the Lord is holy,
abiding for ever.
The decrees of the Lord are truth
and all of them just. ℟

4   May the spoken words of my mouth,
the thoughts of my heart,
win favour in your sight, O Lord,
my rescuer, my rock! ℟

III Dedication of a Church already in General Use for Sacred Celebrations

Readings are chosen from the Common of the Dedication of a Church, pp.1317ff.

IV Dedication of an Altar

Readings are chosen either from the Mass of the day, or from the Common of the Dedication of a Church: for the Dedication of an Altar, pp.1319ff.

V Blessing of a Church

Readings are chosen either from the Common of the Dedication of a Church, pp.1317ff., or from the Mass of the day.

VI Blessing of an Altar

For the blessing of a fixed altar, readings are chosen from the Common of the Dedication of a Church: for the Dedication of an Altar, pp.1319ff. For the blessing of a moveable altar, readings are chosen from the Mass of the day.

VII Blessing of a Chalice and Paten

When this takes place during Mass, apart from the days listed on the Table of Liturgical Days, nos. 1-9, one or two readings may be chosen from those given below. These may also be used when the Blessing takes place outside Mass, or other suitable readings may be chosen.

NEW TESTAMENT READING

1

A reading from the first letter of St Paul to the Corinthians

10:14-22

Our blessing-cup is a communion with the blood of Christ.

My dear brothers, you must keep clear of idolatry. I say to you as sensible people: judge for yourselves what I am saying. The blessing-cup that we bless is a communion with the blood of Christ, and the bread that we break is a communion with the body of Christ. The fact that there is only one loaf means that, though there are many of us, we form a single body because we all have a share in this one loaf. Look at the other Israel, the race, where those who eat the sacrifices are in communion with the altar. Does this mean that the food sacrificed to idols has a real value, or that the idol itself is real? Not at all. It simply means that the sacrifices that they offer they sacrifice to demons who are not God. I have no desire to see you in communion with demons. You cannot drink the cup of the Lord and the cup of demons. You cannot take your share at the table of the Lord and at the table of demons. Do we want to make the Lord angry; are we stronger than he is?

This is the word of the Lord.

2

A reading from the first letter of St Paul   11:23-26
to the Corinthians

This cup is the new covenant in my blood.

For this is what I received from the Lord, and in turn passed on to you: that on the same night that he was betrayed, the Lord Jesus took some bread, and thanked God for it and broke it, and he said, 'This is my body, which is for you; do this as a memorial of me.' In the same way he took the cup after supper and said. 'This cup is the new covenant in my blood. Whenever you drink it, do this as a memorial of me.' Until the Lord comes, therefore, every time you eat this bread and drink this cup, you are proclaiming his death.

This is the word of the Lord.

RESPONSORIAL PSALM

1

Ps 15:5. 8-11. ℟ v.5

℟   The Lord is my inheritance and my cup.

1   O Lord it is you who are my portion and cup;
    it is you yourself who are my prize.
    I keep the Lord ever in my sight:
    since he is at my right hand, I shall stand firm. ℟

2   And so my heart rejoices, my soul is glad;
    even my body shall rest in safety.
    For you will not leave my soul among the dead,
    nor let your beloved know decay. ℟

3   You will show me the path of life,
    the fullness of joy in your presence,
    at your right hand happiness for ever. ℟

2

Responsorial Psalm
Ps 22. ℟ v.5

℟ You prepared a banquet before me; my cup overflows.

1 The Lord is my shepherd;
there is nothing I shall want.
Fresh and green are the pastures
where he gives me repose.
Near restful waters he leads me,
to revive my drooping spirit. ℟

2 He guides me along the right path;
he is true to his name.
If I should walk in the valley of darkness
no evil would I fear.
You are there with your crook and your staff;
with these you give me comfort. ℟

3 You have prepared a banquet for me
in the sight of my foes.
My head you have anointed with oil;
my cup is overflowing. ℟

4 Surely goodness and kindness shall follow me
all the days of my life.
In the Lord's own house shall I dwell
for ever and ever. ℟

GOSPEL ACCLAMATION

1

Jn 6:56

Alleluia, alleluia!
All who eat my flesh and drink my blood
live in me and I in them, says the Lord.
Alleluia!

2

Jn 6:57

Alleluia, alleluia!
As the living Father sent me, and I live because of the Father,
so whoever feeds on me will live because of me.
Alleluia!

GOSPEL

1

A reading from the holy Gospel according to Matthew   20:20-28

You shall indeed drink my cup.

The mother of Zebedee's sons came to Jesus with her sons to make a request of him, and bowed low; and he said to her, 'What is it you want?' She said to him, 'Promise that these two sons of mine may sit one at your right hand and the other at your left in your kingdom.' 'You do not know what you are asking' Jesus answered. 'Can you drink the cup that I am going to drink?' They replied, 'We can.' 'Very well,' he said 'you shall drink my cup, but as for seats at my right hand and my left, these are not mine to grant; they belong to those to whom they have been allotted by my Father.'

When the other ten heard this they were indignant with the two brothers. But Jesus called them to him and said, 'You know that among the pagans the rulers lord it over them, and their great men make their authority felt. This is not to happen among you. No; anyone who wants to be great among you must be your servant, and anyone who wants to be first among you must be your slave, just as the Son of Man came not to be served but to serve, and to give his life as a ransom for many.'

This is the Gospel of the Lord.

2

A reading from the holy Gospel according to Mark   14:12-16. 22-26

He took a cup, gave thanks, and passed it to them, and they all drank from it.

On the first day of Unleavened Bread, when the Passover lamb was sacrificed, the disciples of Jesus said to him, 'Where do you want us to go and make the preparations for you to eat the passover?' So he sent two of his disciples, saying to them, 'Go into the city and you will meet a man carrying a pitcher of water. Follow him, and say to the owner of the house which he enters, "The Master says: Where is my dining room in which I can eat the passover with my disciples?" He will show you a large upper room furnished with couches, all prepared. Make the preparations for us there.' The disciples set out and went to the city and found everything as he had told them, and prepared the Passover.

And as they were eating he took some bread, and when he had said the blessing he broke it and gave it to them. 'Take it,' he said 'this is my body.' Then he took a cup, and when he had returned thanks he gave it to them, and all drank from it, and he said to them, 'This is my blood, the blood of the covenant, which is to be poured out for many. I tell you solemnly, I shall not drink any more wine until the day I drink the new wine in the kingdom of God.'

After psalms had been sung they left for the Mount of Olives.

This is the Gospel of the Lord.

COMMON OF THE BLESSED VIRGIN MARY

FIRST READING FROM THE OLD TESTAMENT

Outside the Easter Season

1

A reading from the book of Genesis   3:9-15. 20

I will put enmity between your offspring and her offspring.

After Adam had eaten of the tree the Lord God called to him. 'Where are you?' he asked. 'I heard the sound of you in the garden,' he replied. 'I was afraid because I was naked, so I hid.' 'Who told you that you were naked?' he asked. 'Have you been eating of the tree I forbade you to eat?' The man replied, 'It was the woman you put with me; she gave me the fruit, and I ate it'. Then the Lord God asked the woman, 'What is this you have done?' The woman replied, 'The serpent tempted me and I ate.'

Then the Lord God said to the serpent, 'Because you have done this,

'Be accursed beyond all cattle,
all wild beasts.
You shall crawl on your belly and eat dust
every day of your life.
I will make you enemies of each other:
you and the woman,
your offspring and her offspring.
It will crush your head
and you will strike its heel.'

The man named his wife 'Eve' because she was the mother of all those who live.

This is the word of the Lord.

Responsorial Psalm   Jud 13:18-19. ℟ 15:9

℟ You are the highest honour of our race!

1 May you be blessed, my daughter, by God Most High,
   beyond all women on earth;
   and may the Lord God be blessed,
   the Creator of heaven and earth. ℟

2 The trust you have shown
   shall not pass from the memories of men,
   but shall ever remind them
   of the power of God. ℟

2

A reading from the book of Genesis   12:1-7

He spoke to our ancestors, to Abraham and his seed for ever.

The Lord said to Abram, 'Leave your country, your family and your
father's house, for the land I will show you. I will make you a great
nation; I will bless you and make your name so famous that it will be
used as a blessing.

   'I will bless those who bless you:
   I will curse those who slight you.
   All the tribes of the earth
   shall bless themselves by you.'

So Abram went as the Lord told him, and Lot went with him.
Abram was seventy-five years old when he left Haran. Abram took his
wife Sarai, his nephew Lot, all the possessions they had amassed and
the people they had acquired in Haran. They set off for the land of
Canaan, and arrived there.

Abram passed through the land as far as Shechem's holy place, the
Oak of Moreh. At that time the Canaanites were in the land. The Lord
appeared to Abram and said, 'It is to your descendants that I will give
this land.' So Abram built there an altar for the Lord who had
appeared to him.

This is the word of the Lord.

Responsorial Psalm   Lk 1:46-55. ℟ v.49

℟   The Almighty has done great things for me, and holy is his
Name.

1 My soul glorifies the Lord,
my spirit rejoices in God, my saviour. ℟

2 He looks on his servant in her nothingness;
henceforth all ages will call me blessed.
The Almighty works marvels for me.
Holy his name! ℟

3 His mercy is from age to age,
on those who fear him.
He puts forth his arm in strength
and scatters the proud-hearted. ℟

4 He casts the mighty from their thrones
and raises the lowly.
He fills the starving with good things,
sends the rich away empty. ℟

5 He protects Israel, his servant,
remembering his mercy,
the mercy promised to our fathers,
to Abraham and his sons for ever. ℟

3

A reading from the second book of Samuel   7:1-5. 8-11. 16

God will give him the seat of David, his father.

Once David had settled into his house and the Lord had given him rest
from all the enemies surrounding him, the king said to the prophet
Nathan, 'Look, I am living in a house of cedar while the ark of God
dwells in a tent. Nathan said to the king, 'Go and do all that is in your
mind, for the Lord is with you.'

But that very night the word of the Lord came to Nathan:

'Go and tell my servant David, "Thus the Lord speaks: Are you the
man to build me a house to dwell in? I took you from the pasture, from
following the sheep, to be leader of my people Israel; I have been with
you on all your expeditions; I have cut off all your enemies before you.
I will give you fame as great as the fame of the greatest on earth. I will
provide a place for my people Israel; I will plant them there and

they shall dwell in that place and never be disturbed again; nor shall the wicked continue to oppress them as they did, in the days when I appointed judges over my people Israel; I will give them rest from all their enemies. The Lord will make you great; the Lord will make you a House. Your House and your sovereignty will always stand secure before me and your throne be established for ever." '

This is the word of the Lord.

Responsorial Psalm   1 Sam 2:1. 4-8. ℟ cf. v.1

℟ My heart rejoices in the Lord, my Saviour.

1 My heart exults in the Lord,
   I find my strength in my God;
   my mouth laughs at my enemies
   as I rejoice in your saving help. ℟

2 The bows of the mighty are broken,
   but the weak are clothed with strength.
   Those with plenty must labour for bread,
   but the hungry need work no more.
   The childless wife has children now
   but the fruitful wife bears no more. ℟

3 It is the Lord who gives life and death,
   he brings men to the grave and back;
   it is the Lord who gives poverty and riches.
   He brings men low and raises them on high. ℟

4 He lifts up the lowly from the dust,
   from the dungheap he raises the poor
   to set them in the company of princes,
   to give them a glorious throne. ℟

4

A reading from the first book of Chronicles   15:3-4. 15-16; 16:1-2

They brought in the ark of God and set it inside the tent that David had pitched for it.

David gathered all Israel together in Jerusalem to bring the ark of God up to the place he had prepared for it. David called together the sons of Aaron and the sons of Levi, and the Levites carried the ark of God with the shafts on their shoulders, as Moses had ordered in accordance with the word of the Lord.

David then told the heads of the Levites to assign duties for their kinsmen as cantors, with their various instruments of music, harps and lyres and cymbals, to play joyful tunes.

They brought the ark of God in and put it inside the tent that David had pitched for it; and they offered holocausts before God, and communion sacrifices. And when David had finished offering holocausts and communion sacrifices, he blessed the people in the name of the Lord.

This is the word of the Lord.

Responsorial Psalm   Ps 112:1-8. ℟ v.2

℟ Blessed be the name of the Lord for ever.

1 Praise, O servants of the Lord,
   praise the name of the Lord!
   May the name of the Lord be blessed
   both now and for evermore!   ℟

2 From the rising of the sun to its setting
   praised be the name of the Lord!
   High above all nations is the Lord,
   above the heavens his glory.   ℟

3 Who is like the Lord, our God,
   who has risen on high to his throne
   yet stoops from the heights to look down,
   to look down upon heaven and earth?   ℟

4 From the dust he lifts up the lowly,
   from the dungheap he raises the poor
   to set him in the company of princes,
   yes, with the princes of his people.   ℟

5

A reading from the book of Proverbs   8:22-31

Mary, seat of Wisdom.

Thus speaks the Wisdom of God:

> The Lord created me when his purpose first unfolded,
> before the oldest of his works.
> From everlasting I was firmly set,
> from the beginning, before earth came into being.
> The deep was not, when I was born,
> there were no springs to gush with water.
> Before the mountains were settled,
> before the hills, I came to birth;
> before he made the earth, the countryside,
> or the first grains of the world's dust.
> When he fixed the heavens firm, I was there,
> when he drew a ring on the surface of the deep,
> when he thickened the clouds above,
> when he fixed fast the springs of the deep,
> when he assigned the sea its boundaries
> – and the waters will not invade the shore –
> when he laid down the foundations of the earth,
> I was by his side, a master craftsman,
> delighting him day after day,
> ever at play in his presence,
> at play everywhere in his world,
> delighting to be with the sons of men.

This is the word of the Lord.

Responsorial Psalm   Ps 44:11-12. 14-17. ℟ v.11

℟   Listen to me, daughter; see and bend your ear.

1   Listen, O daughter, give ear to my words:
    forget your own people and your father's house.
    So will the king desire your beauty:
    He is your lord, pay homage to him.   ℟

2   The daughter of the king is clothed with splendour,
    her robes embroidered with pearls set in gold.
    She is led to the king with her maiden companions.   ℟

3   They are escorted amid gladness and joy;
       they pass within the palace of the king.
       Sons shall be yours in place of your fathers:
       you will make them princes over all the earth. ℞

6

A reading from the book of Ecclesiasticus   24:1. 3-4. 8-12. 19-22

Mary, seat of Wisdom.

Wisdom speaks her own praises,
in the midst of her people she glories in herself.

  'I came forth from the mouth of the Most High,
    and I covered the earth like mist.
  I had my tent in the heights,
    and my throne in a pillar of cloud.
  Then the creator of all things instructed me.
    and he who created me fixed a place for my tent.
  He said, "Pitch your tent in Jacob,
    make Israel your inheritance".
  From eternity, in the beginning, he created me,
    and for eternity I shall remain.
  I ministered before him in the holy tabernacle,
    and thus was I established on Zion.
  In the beloved city he has given me rest,
    and in Jerusalem I wield my authority.
  I have taken root in a privileged people,
    in the Lord's property, in his inheritance.
  Approach me, you who desire me,
    and take your fill of my fruits,
  for memories of me are sweeter than honey,
    inheriting me is sweeter than the honeycomb.
  They who eat me will hunger for more,
    they who drink me will thirst for more.
  Whoever listens to me will never have to blush,
    whoever acts as I dictate will never sin.'

This is the word of the Lord.

Responsorial Psalm Ps 44:11-12. 14-17. ℟ v.11

℟ Listen to me, daughter; see and bend your ear.

1 Listen, O daughter, give ear to my words:
   forget your own people and your father's house.
   So will the king desire your beauty:
   He is your lord, pay homage to him. ℟

2 The daughter of the king is clothed with splendour,
   her robes embroidered with pearls set in gold.
   She is led to the king with her maiden companions. ℟

3 They are escorted amid gladness and joy;
   they pass within the palace of the king.
   Sons shall be yours in place of your fathers:
   you will make them princes over all the earth. ℟

7

A reading from the prophet Isaiah 7:10-14

Behold, the virgin shall conceive.

The Lord spoke to Ahaz and said, 'Ask the Lord your God for a sign for yourself coming either from the depths of Sheol or from the heights above.' 'No,' Ahaz answered, 'I will not put the Lord to the test.'
   Then Isaiah said:

Listen now, House of David:
are you not satisfied with trying the patience of men
without trying the patience of my God, too?
The Lord himself, therefore,
will give you a sign.
It is this: the maiden is with child
and will soon give birth to a son
whom she will call Emmanuel,
a name which means 'God-is-with-us'.

This is the word of the Lord.

Responsorial Psalm 1 Sam 2:1. 4-8. ℟ cf. v.1

℟ My heart rejoices in the Lord, my Saviour.

1 My heart exults in the Lord,
   I find my strength in my God;

my mouth laughs at my enemies
as I rejoice in your saving help. ℟

2 The bows of the mighty are broken,
   but the weak are clothed with strength.
   Those with plenty must labour for bread,
   but the hungry need work no more.
   The childless wife has children now
   but the fruitful wife bears no more. ℟

3 It is the Lord who gives life and death,
   he brings men to the grave and back;
   it is the Lord who gives poverty and riches.
   He brings men low and raises them on high. ℟

4 He lifts up the lowly from the dust,
   from the dungheap he raises the poor
   to set them in the company of princes,
   to give them a glorious throne. ℟

8

A reading from the prophet Isaiah   9:1-6

A Son is born to us.

The people that walked in darkness
has seen a great light;
on those who live in a land of deep shadow
a light has shone.
You have made their gladness greater,
you have made their joy increase;
they rejoice in your presence
as men rejoice at harvest time,
as men are happy when they are dividing the spoils.
For the yoke that was weighing on him,
the bar across his shoulders,
the rod of his oppressor,
these you break as on the day of Midian.
For all the footgear of battle,
every cloak rolled in blood,
is burnt,
and consumed by fire.
For there is a child born for us,

a son given to us
and dominion is laid on his shoulders;
and this is the name they give him:
Wonder-Counsellor, Mighty-God,
Eternal-Father, Prince-of-Peace.
Wide is his dominion
in a peace that has no end,
for the throne of David
and for his royal power,
which he establishes and makes secure
in justice and integrity.
From this time onwards and for ever,
the jealous love of the Lord of Hosts will do this.

This is the word of the Lord.

Responsorial Psalm   Ps 112:1-8. ℟ v.2

℟   Blessed be the name of the Lord for ever.

or

℟   Alleluia!

1   Praise, O servants, of the Lord,
    praise the name of the Lord!
    May the name of the Lord be blessed
    both now and for evermore!   ℟

2   From the rising of the sun to its setting
    praised be the name of the Lord!
    High above all nations is the Lord,
    above the heavens his glory.   ℟

3   Who is like the Lord, our God,
    who has risen on high to his throne
    yet stoops from the heights to look down,
    to look down upon heaven and earth?   ℟

4   From the dust he lifts up the lowly,
    from the dungheap he raises the poor
    to set him in the company of princes,
    yes, with the princes of his people.   ℟

9

A reading from the prophet Isaiah   61:9-11

I will rejoice in my God.

My people will be famous throughout the nations,
their descendants throughout the peoples.
All who see them will admit
that they are a race whom the Lord has blessed.
I exult for joy in the Lord,
my soul rejoices in my God,
for he has clothed me in the garments of salvation,
he has wrapped me in the cloak of integrity,
like a bridegroom wearing his wreath,
like a bride adorned in her jewels.
For as the earth makes fresh things grow,
as a garden makes seeds spring up,
so will the Lord make both integrity and praise
spring up in the sight of the nations.

This is the word of the Lord.

Responsorial Psalm   1 Sam 2:1. 4-8. ℟ v.1

℟ My heart rejoices in the Lord, my Saviour.

1 My heart exults in the Lord,
   I find my strength in my God;
   my mouth laughs at my enemies
   as I rejoice in your saving help. ℟

2 The bows of the mighty are broken
   but the weak are clothed with strength.
   Those with plenty must labour for bread,
   but the hungry need work no more.
   The childless wife has children now
   but the fruitful wife bears no more. ℟

3 It is the Lord who gives life and death,
   he brings men to the grave and back;
   it is the Lord who gives poverty and riches.
   He brings men low and raises them on high. ℟

4 He lifts up the lowly from the dust,
   from the dungheap he raises the poor
   to set them in the company of princes,
   to give them a glorious throne.

℟ My heart rejoices in the Lord, my Saviour.

10

A reading from the prophet Micah   5:1-4

The remnant will return when she who is pregnant gives birth.

The Lord says this:

You, Bethlehem, Ephrathah,
the least of the clans of Judah,
out of you will be born for me
the one who is to rule over Israel;
his origin goes back to the distant past,
to the days of old.
The Lord is therefore going to abandon them
till the time when she who is to give birth gives birth.
Then the remnant of his brothers will come back
to the sons of Israel.
He will stand and feed his flock
with the power of the Lord,
with the majesty of the name of his God.
They will live secure, for from then on he will extend his power
to the ends of the land.
He himself will be peace.

This is the word of the Lord.

Responsorial Psalm   Ps 112:1-8. ℟ v.2

℟ Blessed be the name of the Lord for ever.

or

℟ Alleluia!

1 Praise, O servants of the Lord,
   praise the name of the Lord!

May the name of the Lord be blessed
both now and for evermore! ℟

From the rising of the sun to its setting
praised be the name of the Lord!
High above all nations is the Lord,
above the heavens his glory. ℟

Who is like the Lord, our God,
who has risen on high to his throne
yet stoops from the heights to look down,
to look down upon heaven and earth? ℟

From the dust he lifts up the lowly,
from the dungheap he raises the poor
to set him in the company of princes,
yes, with the princes of his people. ℟

11

A reading from the prophet Zechariah   2:14-17

Rejoice, daughter of Zion, for I am coming.

Sing, rejoice,
daughter of Zion;
for I am coming
to dwell in the middle of you
- it is the Lord who speaks.
Many nations will join the Lord,
on that day;
they will become his people.
But he will remain among you,
and you will know that the Lord of hosts has sent me to you.
But the Lord will hold Judah
as his portion in the Holy Land,
and again make Jerusalem his very own.
Let all mankind be silent before the Lord!
For he is awaking and is coming from his holy dwelling.

This is the word of the Lord.

Responsorial Psalm   Lk 1:46-55

℟ O Blessed Virgin Mary, you carried the Son of the eternal
     Father.

1 My soul glorifies the Lord,
   my spirit rejoices in God, my saviour.   ℟

2 He looks on his servant in her nothingness;
   henceforth all ages will call me blessed.
   The Almighty works marvels for me.
   Holy his name!   ℟

3 His mercy is from age to age,
   on those who fear him.
   He puts forth his arm in strength
   and scatters the proud-hearted.   ℟

4 He casts the mighty from their thrones
   and raises the lowly.
   He fills the starving with good things,
   sends the rich away empty.   ℟

5 He protects Israel, his servant,
   remembering his mercy,
   the mercy promised to our fathers,
   to Abraham and his sons for ever.   ℟

FIRST READING FROM THE NEW TESTAMENT

In the Easter Season

1

A reading from the Acts of the Apostles   1:12-14

They all joined in continuous prayer together with Jesus' mother, Mary.

After Jesus had ascended into heaven, the apostles went back to
Jerusalem, a short distance away, no more that a sabbath walk; and
when they reached the city they went to the upper room where they
were staying; there were Peter and John, James and Andrew, Philip
and Thomas, Bartholomew and Matthew, James son of Alphaeus and
Simon the Zealot, and Jude son of James. All these joined in
continuous prayer, together with several women, including Mary the
mother of Jesus, and with his brothers.

This is the word of the Lord.

Responsorial Psalm   Lk 1:46-55

℟ O Blessed Virgin Mary, you carried the Son of the eternal
    Father.

1 My soul glorifies the Lord,
    my spirit rejoices in God, my saviour. ℟

2 He looks on his servant in her nothingness;
    henceforth all ages will call me blessed.
    The Almighty works marvels for me.
    Holy his name! ℟

3 His mercy is from age to age,
    on those who fear him.
    He puts forth his arm in strength
    and scatters the proud-hearted. ℟

4 He casts the mighty from their thrones
    and raises the lowly.
    He fills the starving with good things,
    sends the rich away empty. ℟

5 He protects Israel, his servant,
    remembering his mercy,
    the mercy promised to our fathers,
    to Abraham and his sons for ever. ℟

2

A reading from the book of the Apocalypse   11:19; 12:1-6. 10

A great sign appeared in the heavens.

The sanctuary of God in heaven opened, and the ark of the covenant
could be seen inside it.

Now a great sign appeared in heaven: a woman, adorned with the
sun, standing on the moon, and with the twelve stars on her head for a
crown. She was pregnant, and in labour, crying aloud in the pangs of
childbirth. Then a second sign appeared in the sky, a huge red dragon
which had seven heads and ten horns, and each of the seven heads
crowned with a coronet. Its tail dragged a third of the stars from the
sky and dropped them to the earth, and the dragon stopped in front of
the woman as she was having the child, so that he could eat it as soon
as it was born from its mother. The woman brought a male child into

the world, the son who was to rule all the nations with an iron sceptre, and the child was taken straight up to God and to his throne, while the woman escaped into the desert, where God had made a place of safety ready. Then I heard a voice shout from heaven, 'Victory and power and empire for ever have been won by our God, and all authority for his Christ.'

This is the word of the Lord.

Responsorial Psalm   Ps 44:11-12. 14-17. ℟ v.11

℟   Listen to me, daughter; see and bend your ear.

1   Listen, O daughter, give ear to my words:
    forget your own people and your father's house.
    So will the king desire your beauty:
    He is your lord, pay homage to him.   ℟

2   The daughter of the king is clothed with splendour,
    her robes embroidered with pearls set in gold.
    She is led to the king with her maiden companions.   ℟

3   They are escorted amid gladness and joy;
    they pass within the palace of the king.
    Sons shall be yours in place of your fathers:
    you will make them princes over all the earth.   ℟

3

A reading from the book of the Apocalypse   21:1-5

I saw the new Jerusalem as beautiful as a bride all dressed for her husband.

I, John, saw a new heaven and a new earth; the first heaven and the first earth had disappeared now, and there was no longer any sea. I saw the holy city, and the new Jerusalem, coming down from God out of heaven, as beautiful as a bride all dressed for her husband. Then I heard a loud voice call from the throne, 'You see this city? Here God lives among men. He will make his home among them; they shall be his people, and he will be their God; his name is God-with-them. He will wipe away all tears from their eyes; there will be no more death, and no more mourning or sadness. The world of the past has gone.'

Then the One sitting on the throne spoke: 'Now I am making the whole of creation new.'

This is the word of the Lord.

Responsorial Psalm   Judith 13:18-19. ℞ 15:9

℞   You are the highest honour of our race!

1   May you be blessed, my daughter, by God Most High,
     beyond all women on earth;
     and may the Lord God be blessed,
     the Creator of heaven and earth.   ℞

2   The trust you have shown
     shall not pass from the memories of men,
     but shall ever remind them
     of the power of God.   ℞

SECOND READING FROM THE NEW TESTAMENT

1

A reading from the letter of St Paul to the Romans   5:12. 17-19

However great the number of sins committed, grace was even greater.

Sin entered the world through one man, and through sin death, and
thus death has spread through the whole human race because
everyone has sinned. If it is certain that death reigned over everyone
as the consequence of one man's fall, it is even more certain that one
man, Jesus Christ, will cause everyone to reign in life who receives
the free gift that he does not deserve, of being made righteous. Again,
as one man's fall brought condemnation on everyone, so the good act
of one man brings everyone life and makes them justified. As by one
man's disobedience many were made sinners, so by one man's obedience many will be made righteous.

This is the word of the Lord.

2

A reading from the letter of St Paul to the Romans   8:28-30

God knew them and called them to justification.

We know that by turning everything to their good God co-operates with all those who love him, with all those that he has called according to his purpose. They are the ones he chose specially long ago and intended to become true images of his Son, so that his Son might be the eldest of many brothers. He called those he intended for this; those he called he justified, and with those he justified he shared his glory.

This is the word of the Lord.

3

A reading from the letter of St Paul to the Galatians   4:4-7

God sent his Son, born of a woman.

When the appointed time came, God sent his Son, born of a woman, born a subject of the Law, to redeem the subjects of the Law and to enable us to be adopted as sons. The proof that you are sons is that God has sent the Spirit of his Son into our hearts: the Spirit that cries, 'Abba, Father', and it is this that makes you a son, you are not a slave any more; and if God has made you son, then he has made you heir.

This is the word of the Lord.

4

A reading from the letter of St Paul to the Ephesians   1:3-6. 11-12

Before the world was made, God chose us in Christ.

Blessed be God the Father of our Lord Jesus Christ,
 who has blessed us with all the spiritual blessings of heaven in
   Christ.
Before the world was made, he chose us, chose us in Christ,
to be holy and spotless, and to live through love in his presence,
determining that we should become his adopted sons, through Jesus
   Christ
for his own kind purposes,
to make us praise the glory of his grace,

his free gift to us in the Beloved.
And it is in him that we were claimed as God's own,
chosen from the beginning,
under the predetermined plan of the one who guides all things
as he decides by his own will;
chosen to be,
for his greater glory,
the people who would put their hopes in Christ before he came.

This is the word of the Lord.

GOSPEL

1

Gospel Acclamation

Alleluia, alleluia!
Happy are you, holy Virgin Mary, deserving of all praise;
from you rose the sun of justice, Christ the Lord.
Alleluia!

A reading from the holy Gospel according   1:1-16. 18-23
to Matthew

She has conceived what is in her by the Holy Spirit.

A genealogy of Jesus Christ, son of David, son of Abraham:

Abraham was the father of Isaac,
Isaac the father of Jacob,
Jacob the father of Judah and his brothers,
Judah was the father of Perez and Zerah, Tamar being their
    mother,
Perez was the father of Hezron,
Hezron the father of Ram,
Ram was the father of Amminadab,
Amminadab the father of Nahshon,
Nahshon the father of Salmon,
Salmon was the father of Boaz, Rahab being his mother,
Boaz was the father of Obed, Ruth being his mother,

Obed was the father of Jesse;
and Jesse was the father of King David.

David was the father of Solomon, whose mother had been Uriah's
   wife,
Solomon was the father of Rehoboam,
Rehoboam the father of Abijah,
Abijah the father of Asa,
Asa was the father of Jehoshaphat,
Jehoshaphat the father of Joram,
Joram the father of Azariah,
Azariah was the father of Jotham,
Jotham the father of Ahaz,
Ahaz the father of Hezekiah,
Hezekiah was the father of Manasseh,
Manasseh the father of Amon,
Amon the father of Josiah;
and Josiah was the father of Jechoniah and his brothers.
Then the deportation to Babylon took place.

After the deportation to Babylon:
Jechoniah was the father of Shealtiel,
Shealtiel the father of Zerubbabel,
Zerubbabel was the father of Abiud,
Abiud the father of Eliakim,
Eliakim the father of Azor,
Azor was the father of Zadok,
Zadok the father of Achim,
Achim the father of Eliud,
Eliud was the father of Eleazar,
Eleazar the father of Matthan,
Matthan the father of Jacob;
and Jacob was the father of Joseph the husband of Mary;
of her was born Jesus who is called Christ.

This is how Jesus Christ came to be born. His mother Mary was
betrothed to Joseph; but before they came to live together she was
found to be with child through the Holy Spirit. Her husband Joseph,
being a man of honour and wanting to spare her publicity, decided to
divorce her informally. He had made up his mind to do this when the
angel of the Lord appeared to him in a dream and said, 'Joseph son of
David, do not be afraid to take Mary home as your wife, because she

has conceived what is in her by the Holy Spirit. She will give birth to a son and you must name him Jesus, because he is the one who is to save his people from their sins.' Now all this took place to fulfil the words spoken by the Lord through the prophet:

The virgin will conceive and give birth to a son
and they will call him Emmanuel,

a name which means 'God-is-with-us'.

This is the Gospel of the Lord.

Shorter form

A reading from the holy Gospel according to Matthew   1:18-23

She has conceived what is in her by the Holy Spirit.

This is how Jesus Christ came to be born. His mother Mary was betrothed to Joseph; but before they came to live together she was found to be with child through the Holy Spirit. Her husband Joseph, being a man of honour and wanting to spare her publicity, decided to divorce her informally. He had made up his mind to do this when the angel of the Lord apeared to him in a dream and said, 'Joseph son of David, do not be afraid to take Mary home as your wife, because she has conceived what is in her by the Holy Spirit. She will give birth to a son and you must name him Jesus, because he is the one who is to save his people from their sins.' Now all this took place to fulfil the words spoken by the Lord through the prophet:

The virgin will conceive and give birth to a son
and they will call him Emmanuel,

a name which means 'God-is-with-us'.

This is the Gospel of the Lord.

2

Gospel Acclamation   cf. Lk 1:45

> Alleluia, alleluia!
> Blessed are you, O Virgin Mary, for your firm believing
> that the promises of the Lord would be fulfilled.
> Alleluia!

A reading from the holy Gospel according to Matthew   2:13-15. 19-23

Take the child and his mother and flee into Egypt.

After the wise men had left, the angel of the Lord appeared to Joseph in a dream and said, 'Get up, take the child and his mother with you, and escape into Egypt, and stay there until I tell you, because Herod intends to search for the child and do away with him.' So Joseph got up and, taking the child and his mother with him, left that night for Egypt, where he stayed until Herod was dead. This was to fulfil what the Lord had spoken through the prophet:

> I called my son out of Egypt.

After Herod's death, the angel of the Lord appeared in a dream to Joseph in Egypt and said, 'Get up, take the child and his mother with you and go back to the land of Israel, for those who wanted to kill the child are dead.' So Joseph got up and, taking the child and his mother with him, went back to the land of Israel. But when he learnt that Archelaus had succeeded his father Herod as ruler of Judaea he was afraid to go there, and being warned in a dream he left for the region of Galilee. There he settled in a town called Nazareth. In this way the words spoken through the prophets were to be fulfilled:

> He will be called a Nazarene.

This is the Gospel of the Lord.

3

Gospel Acclamation   Lk 11:28

Alleluia, alleluia!
Blessed are they who hear the word of God
and keep it.
Alleluia!

A reading from the holy Gospel according to Matthew   12:46-50

Extending his hands towards the disciples, he said: Here are my
mother and my brothers.

Jesus was speaking to the crowds when his mother and his brothers
appeared; they were standing outside and were anxious to have a
word with him. But to the man who told him this Jesus replied, 'Who
is my mother? Who are my brothers?' And stretching out his hand
towards his disciples he said, 'Here are my mother and my brothers.
Anyone who does the will of my Father in heaven, he is my brother
and sister and mother.'

This is the Gospel of the Lord.

4

Gospel Acclamation   cf. Lk 1:28

Alleluia, alleluia!
Hail, Mary, full of grace, the Lord is with you;
blessed are you among women.
Alleluia!

A reading from the holy Gospel according to Luke   1:26-38

You will conceive and bear a son.

The angel Gabriel was sent by God to a town in Galilee called
Nazareth, to a virgin betrothed to a man named Joseph, of the House
of David; and the virgin's name was Mary. He went in and said to her,
'Rejoice, so highly favoured! The Lord is with you.' She was deeply
disturbed by these words and asked herself what this greeting could
mean, but the angel said to her, 'Mary, do not be afraid; you have won
God's favour. Listen! You are to conceive and bear a son,

and you must name him Jesus. He will be great and will be called Son of the Most High. The Lord God will give him the throne of his ancestor David; he will rule over the House of Jacob for ever and his reign will have no end. 'Mary said to the angel, 'But how can this come about, since I am a virgin?' 'The Holy Spirit will come upon you,' the angel answered, 'and the power of the Most High will come over you with its shadow. And so the child will be holy and will be called Son of God. Know this too: your kinswoman Elizabeth has, in her old age, herself conceived a son, and she whom people called barren is now in her sixth month, for nothing is impossible to God.' 'I am the handmaid of the Lord,' said Mary, 'let what you have said to be done to me.' And the angel left her.

This is the Gospel of the Lord.

5

Gospel Acclamation   cf. Lk 1:45

Alleluia, alleluia!
Blessed are you, O Virgin Mary, for your firm believing,
that the promises of the Lord would be fulfilled.
Alleluia!

A reading from the holy Gospel according to Luke   1:39-47

Blessed is she who believed.

Mary set out and went as quickly as she could to a town in the hill country of Judah. She went into Zechariah's house and greeted Elizabeth. Now as soon as Elizabeth heard Mary's greeting, the child leapt in her womb and Elizabeth was filled with the Holy Spirit. She gave a loud cry and said, 'Of all women you are the most blessed, and blessed is the fruit of your womb. Why should I be honoured with a visit from the mother of my Lord? For the moment your greeting reached my ears, the child in my womb leapt for joy. Yes, blessed is she who believed that the promise made her by the Lord would be fulfilled.'

And Mary said:

'My soul proclaims the greatness of the Lord
and my spirit exults in God my saviour.'

This is the Gospel of the Lord.

6

Gospel Acclamation

Alleluia, alleluia!
Happy are you, holy Virgin Mary, deserving of all praise;
from you rose the sun of justice, Christ the Lord.
Alleluia!

A reading from the holy Gospel according to Luke   2:1-14

She gave birth to a son, her first born.

Caesar Augustus issued a decree for a census of the whole world to be taken. This census – the first – took place while Quirinius was governor of Syria, and everyone went to his own town to be registered. So Joseph set out from the town of Nazareth in Galilee and travelled up to Judaea, to the town of David called Bethlehem, since he was of David's House and line, in order to be registered together with Mary, his betrothed, who was with child. While they were there the time came for her to have her child, and she gave birth to a son, her first-born. She wrapped him in swaddling clothes, and laid him in a manger because there was no room for them at the inn. In the countryside close by there were shepherds who lived in the fields and took it in turns to watch their flocks during the night. The angel of the Lord appeared to them and the glory of the Lord shone round them. They were terrified, but the angel said, 'Do not be afraid. Listen, I bring you news of great joy, a joy to be shared by the whole people. Today in the town of David a saviour has been born to you; he is Christ the Lord. And here is a sign for you: you will find a baby wrapped in swaddling clothes and lying in a manger.' And suddenly with the angel there was a great throng of the heavenly host, praising God and singing:

'Glory to God in the highest heaven,
and peace to men who enjoy his favour.'

This is the Gospel of the Lord.

7

Gospel Acclamation

cf. Lk 2:19

> Alleluia, alleluia!
> Blessed is the Virgin Mary who kept the word of God,
> and pondered it in her heart.
> Alleluia!

A reading from the holy Gospel according to Luke

2:15-19

Mary treasured all these things and pondered them in her heart.

The shepherds said to one another, 'Let us go to Bethlehem and see this thing that has happened which the Lord has made known to us'. So they hurried away and found Mary and Joseph, and the baby lying in the manger. When they saw the child they repeated what they had been told about him, and everyone who heard it was astonished at what the shepherds had to say. As for Mary, she treasured all these things and pondered them in her heart.

> This is the Gospel of the Lord.

8

Gospel Acclamation

> Alleluia, alleluia!
> Happy are you, holy Virgin Mary, deserving of all praise;
> from you rose the sun of justice, Christ the Lord.
> Alleluia!

A reading from the holy Gospel according to Luke

2:27-35

A sword will pierce your own soul.

Prompted by the Spirit Simeon came to the Temple; and when the parents brought in the child Jesus to do for him what the Law required, he took him into his arms and blessed God; and he said:

> 'Now, Master, you can let your servant go in peace,
> just as you promised;
> because my eyes have seen the salvation
> which you have prepared for all the nations to see,
> a light to enlighten the pagans
> and the glory of your people Israel.'

As the child's father and mother stood there wondering at the things that were being said about him, Simeon blessed them and said to Mary his mother, 'You see this child: he is destined for the fall and for the rising of many in Israel, destined to be a sign that is rejected – and a sword will pierce your own soul too – so that the secret thoughts of many may be laid bare.'

This is the Gospel of the Lord.

9

Gospel Acclamation   cf. Lk 2:19

Alleluia, alleluia!
Blessed is the Virgin Mary who kept the word of God,
and pondered it in her heart.
Alleluia!

A reading from the holy Gospel according to Luke   2:41-52

Your father and I have been looking for you.

Every year the parents of Jesus used to go to Jerusalem for the feast of the Passover. When he was twelve years old, they went up for the feast as usual. When they were on their way home after the feast, the boy Jesus stayed behind in Jerusalem without his parents knowing it. They assumed he was with the caravan, and it was only after a day's journey that they went to look for him among their relations and acquaintances. When they failed to find him they went back to Jerusalem looking for him everywhere.

Three days later, they found him in the Temple, sitting among the doctors, listening to them, and asking them questions; and all those who heard him were astounded at his intelligence and his replies. They were overcome when they saw him, and his mother said to him, 'My child, why have you done this to us? See how worried your father and I have been, looking for you.' 'Why were you looking for me?' he replied. 'Did you not know that I must be busy with my Father's affairs?' But they did not understand what he meant.

He then went down with them and came to Nazareth and lived under their authority. His mother stored up all these things in her heart. And Jesus increased in wisdom, in stature, and in favour with God and men.

This is the Gospel of the Lord.

10

Gospel Acclamation   cf. Lk 11:28

Alleluia, alleluia!
Blessed are they who hear the word of God
and keep it.
Alleluia!

A reading from the holy Gospel according to Luke   11:27-28

Happy the womb that bore you!

As Jesus was speaking, a woman in the crowd raised her voice and
said, 'Happy the womb that bore you and the breasts you sucked!' But
he replied, 'Still happier those who hear the word of God and keep it!'

This is the Gospel of the Lord.

11

Gospel Acclamation   cf. Lk 1:45

Alleluia, alleluia!
Blessed are you, O Virgin Mary, for your firm believing,
that the promises of the Lord would be fulfilled.
Alleluia!

A reading from the holy Gospel according to John   2:1-11

The mother of Jesus was at the wedding feast with him.

There was a wedding at Cana in Galilee. The mother of Jesus was
there, and Jesus and his disciples had also been invited. When they
ran out of wine, since the wine provided for the wedding was all
finished, the mother of Jesus said to him, 'They have no wine.' Jesus
said, 'Woman, why turn to me? My hour has not come yet.' His mother
said to the servants, 'Do whatever he tells you.' There were six stone
water jars standing there, meant for the ablutions that are customary
among the Jews: each could hold twenty or thirty gallons. Jesus said
to the servants, 'Fill the jars with water,' and they filled them to the
brim. 'Draw some out now,' he told them, 'and take it to the steward.'
They did this; the steward tasted the water, and it had turned into

wine. Having no idea where it came from – only the servants who had drawn the water knew – the steward called the bridegroom and said, 'People generally serve the best wine first, and keep the cheaper sort till the guests have had plenty to drink; but you have kept the best wine till now.'

This was the first of the signs given by Jesus: it was given at Cana in Galilee. He let his glory be seen, and his disciples believed in him.

This is the Gospel of the Lord.

12

Gospel Acclamation

Alleluia, alleluia!
Happy are you, O Blessed Virgin Mary;
without dying you won the martyr's crown beside the cross of the
    Lord.
Alleluia!

A reading from the holy Gospel according to John   19:25-27

Woman, this is your son. This is your mother.

Near the cross of Jesus stood his mother and his mother's sister, Mary the wife of Clopas, and Mary of Magdala. Seeing his mother and the disciple he loved standing near her, Jesus said to his mother, 'Woman, this is your son.' Then to the disciple he said, 'This is your mother.' And from that moment the disciple made a place for her in his home.

This is the Gospel of the Lord.

COMMON OF MARTYRS

Outside the Easter Season

1

A reading from the second book of Chronicles   24:18-22

Zechariah, whom you murdered between the sanctuary and the altar.

The Judaeans abandoned the Temple of the Lord, the God of their ancestors, for the worship of sacred poles and idols. Because of their guilt, God's anger fell on Judah and Jerusalem. He sent them prophets to bring them back to the Lord, but when these gave their message, they would not listen. The spirit of God took possession of Zechariah son of Jehoiada the priest. He stood up before the people and said, 'God says this, "Why do you transgress the commandments of the Lord, to no good purpose? You have deserted the Lord, now he deserts you." ' They then plotted against him and by order of the king stoned him in the court of the Temple of the Lord. King Joash, forgetful of the kindness that Jehoiada, the father of Zechariah, had shown him, killed Jehoiada's son who cried out as he died, 'The Lord sees and he will avenge!'

This is the word of the Lord.

Responsorial Psalm   Ps 30:3-4. 6. 8. 16. 17. ℟ v.6

℟   Into your hands, O Lord, I entrust my spirit.

1   Be a rock of refuge for me,
    a mighty stronghold to save me,
    for you are my rock, my stronghold.
    For your name's sake, lead me and guide me.   ℟

2   Into your hands I commend my spirit.
    It is you who will redeem me, Lord.
    As for me, I trust in the Lord:
    let me be glad and rejoice in your love.   ℟

3   My life is in your hands, deliver me
    from the hands of those who hate me.
    Let your face shine on your servant.
    Save me in your love.   ℟

2

A reading from the second book of Maccabees   6:18. 21. 24-31

Because of the awe the Lord inspires in me, I will suffer gladly.

Eleazar, one of the foremost teachers of the Law, a man already
advanced in years and of most noble appearance, was being forced to
open his mouth wide to swallow pig's flesh. Those in charge of the
impious banquet, because of their long-standing friendship with him
took him aside and privately urged him to have meat brought of a
kind he could properly use, prepared by himself, and only pretend to
eat the portions of sacrificial meat as prescribed by the king. 'Such
pretence', he said, 'does not square with our time of life; many young
people would suppose that Eleazar at the age of ninety had conformed
to the foreigners' way of life, and because I had played this part for the
sake of a paltry brief spell of life might themselves be led astray on my
account; I should only bring defilement and disgrace on my old age.
Even though for the moment I avoid execution by man, I can never,
living or dead, elude the grasp of the Almighty. Therefore if I am man
enough to quit this life here and now I shall prove myself worthy of
my old age, and I shall have left the young a noble example of how to
make a good death, eagerly and generously, for the venerable and
holy laws.'

With these words he went straight to the block. His escorts, so
recently well disposed towards him, turned against him after this
declaration, which they regarded as sheer madness. Just before he
died under the blows, he groaned aloud and said, 'The Lord whose
knowledge is holy sees clearly that, though I might have escaped
death, whatever agonies of body I now endure under this bludgeoning,
in my soul I am glad to suffer, because of the awe which he inspires in
me'.

This was how he died, leaving his death as an example of nobility
and a record of virtue not only for the young but for the great majority
of the nation.

This is the word of the Lord.

Responsorial Psalm   Ps 33:2-9. ℟ v.5

℟   The Lord set me free from all my fears.

1   I will bless the Lord at all times,
    his praise always on my lips;
    in the Lord my soul shall make its boast.
    The humble shall hear and be glad.   ℟

2   Glorify the Lord with me.
    Together let us praise his name.
    I sought the Lord and he answered me;
    from all my terrors he set me free.   ℟

3   Look towards him and be radiant;
    let your faces not be abashed.
    This poor man called; the Lord heard him
    and rescued him from all his distress.   ℟

4   The angel of the Lord is encamped
    around those who revere him, to rescue them.
    Taste and see that the Lord is good.
    He is happy who seeks refuge in him.   ℟

3

A reading from the second book of Maccabees   7:1-2. 9-14

We are prepared to die rather than break the laws of our ancestors.

There were seven brothers who were arrested with their mother. The
king tried to force them to taste pig's flesh, which the Law forbids, by
torturing them with whips and scourges. One of them, acting as
spokesman for the others, said, 'What are you trying to find out from
us? We are prepared to die rather than break the laws of our
ancestors.' With his last breath the second exclaimed, 'Inhuman fiend,
you may discharge us from this present life, but the King of the world
will raise us up, since it is for his laws that we die, to live again for
ever.'

    After him, they amused themselves with the third, who on being
asked for his tongue promptly thrust it out and boldly held out his
hands, with these honourable words, 'It was heaven that gave me
these limbs; for the sake of his laws I disdain them; from him I hope to
receive them again.' The king and his attendants were astounded at
the young man's courage and his utter indifference to suffering.

When this one was dead they subjected the fourth to the same savage torture. When he neared his end he cried, 'Ours is the better choice, to meet death at men's hands, yet relying on God's promise that we shall be raised up by him; whereas for you there can be no resurrection, no new life.'

This is the word of the Lord.

Responsorial Psalm   Ps 123:2-5. 7-8. ℟ v.7

℟   Our soul has escaped like a bird from the hunter's net.

1   If the Lord had not been on our side
    when men rose against us,
    then would they have swallowed us alive
    when their anger was kindled.   ℟

2   Then would the waters have engulfed us,
    the torrent gone over us;
    over our heads would have swept
    the raging waters.   ℟

3   Indeed the snare has been broken
    and we have escaped.
    Our help is in the name of the Lord,
    who made heaven and earth.   ℟

4

A reading from the second book of Maccabees   7:1. 20-23. 27-29

Because of her hopes in the Lord, this admirable mother bore their deaths with
honour.

There were seven brothers who were arrested with their mother. The king tried to force them to taste pig's flesh, which the Law forbids, by torturing them with whips and scourges.

The mother was especially admirable and worthy of honourable remembrance, for she watched the death of seven sons in the course of a single day, and endured it resolutely because of her hopes in the Lord. Indeed she encouraged each of them in the language of their ancestors; filled with noble conviction, she reinforced her womanly argument with manly courage, saying to them, 'I do not know how you appeared in my womb; it was not I who endowed you with breath and life, I had not the shaping of your every part. It is the creator of the world, ordaining the process of man's birth and presiding over the origin of all things, who in his mercy will most surely give you back both breath and life, seeing that you now despise your own existence for the sake of his laws.' To her youngest son she said: 'My son, have pity on me; I carried you nine months in my womb and suckled you three years, fed you and reared you to the age you are now and cherished you, I implore you, my child, observe heaven and earth, consider all that is in them, and acknowledge that God made them out of what did not exist, and that mankind comes into being in the same way. Do not fear this executioner, but prove yourself worthy of your brothers, and make death welcome, so that in the day of mercy I may receive you back in your brothers' company.'

This is the word of the Lord.

Responsial Psalm — Ps 30:3-4. 6-8. 16. 17. ℟ v.6

℟   Into your hands, O Lord, I entrust my spirit.

1   Be a rock of refuge for me,
    a mighty stronghold to save me,
    for you are my rock, my stronghold.
    For your name's sake, lead me and guide me.   ℟

2   Into your hands I commend my spirit.
    It is you who will redeem me, Lord.
    As for me, I trust in the Lord:
    let me be glad and rejoice in your love.   ℟

3   My life is in your hands, deliver me
    from the hands of those who hate me.
    Let your face shine on your servant.
    Save me in your love.   ℟

5

A reading from the book of Wisdom — 3:1-9

He accepted them as a holocaust.

The souls of the virtuous are in the hands of God,
no torment shall ever touch them.
In the eyes of the unwise, they did appear to die,

their going looked like a disaster,
their leaving us like annihilation;
but they are in peace.
If they experienced punishment as men see it,
their hope was rich with immortality;
slight was their affliction, great will their blessings be.
God has put them to the test
and proved them worthy to be with him;
he has tested them like gold in a furnace,
and accepted them as a holocaust.
When the time comes for his visitation they will shine out;
as sparks run through the stubble, so will they.
They shall judge nations, rule over peoples,
and the Lord will be their king for ever.
They who trust in him will understand the truth,
those who are faithful will live with him in love;
for grace and mercy await those he has chosen.

This is the word of the Lord.

Responsorial Psalm   Ps 125. ℟ v.5

℟ Those who sow in tears, shall reap with shouts of joy.

1   When the Lord delivered Zion from bondage,
    it seemed like a dream.
    Then was our mouth filled with laughter,
    on our lips there were songs.   ℟

2   The heathens themselves said: 'What marvels
    the Lord worked for them!'
    What marvels the Lord worked for us!
    Indeed we were glad.   ℟

3   Deliver us, O Lord, from our bondage
    as streams in dry land.
    Those who are sowing in tears
    will sing when they reap.   ℟

4   They go out, they go out, full of tears,
    carrying seed for the sowing:
    they come back, they come back, full of song,
    carrying their sheaves.   ℟

6

A reading from the book of Ecclesiasticus 51:1-8

You have redeemed me, true to the greatness of your mercy and of your name.

I will give praise to you, Lord and King,
and praise you, God my saviour,
I give thanks to your name;
for you have been protector and support to me,
and redeemed my body from destruction,
from the snare of the lying tongue,
from lips that fabricate falsehood;
and in the presence of those around me
you have been my support, you have redeemed me,
true to the greatness of your mercy and of your name,
from the fangs of those who would devour me,
from the hands of those seeking my life,
from the many ordeals which I have endured,
from the stifling heat which hemmed me in,
from the heart of a fire which I had not kindled,
from deep in the belly of Sheol,
from the unclean tongue and the lying word –
the perjured tongue slandering me to the king.
My soul has been close to death,
my life had gone down to the brink of Sheol.
They were surrounding me on every side, there was no one to support
    me;
I looked for someone to help – in vain.
Then I remembered your mercy, Lord,
and your deeds from earliest times,
how you deliver those who wait for you patiently,
and save them from the clutches of their enemies.

This is the word of the Lord.

Responsorial Psalm   Ps 123:2-5. 7-8. ℟ v.7

℟   Our soul has escaped like a bird from the hunter's net.

1   If the Lord had not been on our side
    when men rose against us,
    then would they have swallowed us alive
    when their anger was kindled.   ℟

2   Then would the waters have engulfed us,
    the torrent gone over us;
    over our heads would have swept
    the raging waters.   ℟

3   Indeed the snare has been broken
    and we have escaped.
    Our help is in the name of the Lord,
    who made heaven and earth.   ℟

FIRST READING FROM THE NEW TESTAMENT

In the Easter Season

1

A reading from the Acts of the Apostles   7:55-60

Lord Jesus, receive my spirit.

Stephen, filled with the Holy Spirit, gazed into heaven and saw the glory of God, and Jesus standing at God's right hand. 'I can see heaven thrown open,' he said, 'and the Son of Man standing at the right hand of God.' At this all the members of the council shouted out and stopped their ears with their hands; then they all rushed at him, sent him out of the city and stoned him. The witnesses put down their clothes at the feet of a young man called Saul. As they were stoning him, Stephen said in invocation, 'Lord Jesus, receive my spirit.' Then he knelt down and said aloud, 'Lord, do not hold this sin against them'; and with these words he fell asleep.

This is the word of the Lord.

Responsorial Psalm   Ps 30:3-4. 6-8. 16-17. ℟ v.6

℟   Into your hands, O Lord, I entrust my spirit.

1   Be a rock of refuge for me,
    a mighty stronghold to save me,
    for you are my rock, my stronghold.
    For your name's sake, lead me and guide me.   ℟

2   Into your hands I commend my spirit.
    It is you who will redeem me, Lord.
    As for me, I trust in the Lord:
    let me be glad and rejoice in your love.   ℟

3   My life is in your hands, deliver me
    from the hands of those who hate me.
    Let your face shine on your servant.
    Save me in your love.   ℟

2

A reading from the book of the Apocalypse   7:9-17

These are the people who have been through the great persecution.

I, John, saw a huge number, impossible to count, of people from every
nation, race, tribe and language; they were standing in front of the
throne and in front of the Lamb, dressed in white robes and holding
palms in their hands. They shouted aloud, 'Victory to our God, who
sits on the throne, and to the Lamb!' And all the angels who were
standing in a circle round the throne, surrounding the elders and the
four animals, prostrated themselves before the throne, and touched
the ground with their foreheads, worshipping God with these words,
'Amen. Praise and glory and wisdom and thanksgiving and honour
and power and strength to our God for ever and ever. Amen.'

   One of the elders then spoke, and asked me. 'Do you know who
these people are, dressed in white robes, and where they have come
from?' I answered him, 'You can tell me, my lord.' Then he said, 'These
are the people who have been through the great persecution, and
because they have washed their robes white again in the blood of the
Lamb, they now stand in front of God's throne and serve him day and
night in his sanctuary; and the One who sits on the throne will spread
his tent over them. They will never hunger or thirst again; neither the

sun nor scorching wind will ever plague them, because the Lamb who is at the throne will be their shepherd and will lead them to springs of living water; and God will wipe away all tears from their eyes.'

This is the word of the Lord.

Responsorial Psalm   Ps 123:2-5. 7-8. ℟ v.7

℟   Our soul has escaped like a bird from the hunter's net.

1   If the Lord had not been on our side
     when men rose against us,
     then would they have swallowed us alive
     when their anger was kindled. ℟

2   Then would the waters have engulfed us,
     the torrent gone over us;
     over our heads would have swept
     the raging waters. ℟

3   Indeed the snare has been broken
     and we have escaped.
     Our help is in the name of the Lord,
     who made heaven and earth. ℟

3

A reading from the book of the Apocalypse   12:10-12

Even in the face of death these martyrs would not cling to life.

I, John, heard a voice shout from heaven, 'Victory and power and empire for ever have been won by our God, and all authority for his Christ, now that the persecutor, who accused our brothers day and night before our God, has been brought down. They have triumphed over him by the blood of the Lamb and by the witness of their martyrdom, because even in the face of death they would not cling to life. Let the heavens rejoice and all who live there.'

This is the word of the Lord.

Responsorial Psalm   Ps 33:2-9. ℞ v.5

℞   The Lord set me free from all my fears.

1   I will bless the Lord at all times,
    his praise always on my lips;
    in the Lord my soul shall make its boast.
    The humble shall hear and be glad.   ℞

2   Glorify the Lord with me.
    Together let us praise his name.
    I sought the Lord and he answered me;
    from all my terrors he set me free.   ℞

3   Look towards him and be radiant;
    let your faces not be abashed.
    This poor man called; the Lord heard him
    and rescued him from all his distress.   ℞

4   The angel of the Lord is encamped
    around those who revere him, to rescue them.
    Taste and see that the Lord is good.
    He is happy who seeks refuge in him.   ℞

4

A reading from the book of the Apocalypse   21:5-7

Whoever conquers shall have this heritage.

The One sitting on the throne spoke: 'Now I am making the whole of
creation new,' he said. 'Write this: that what I am saying is sure and
will come true.' And then he said, 'It is already done. I am the Alpha
and the Omega, the Beginning and the End. I will give water from the
well of life free to anybody who is thirsty; it is the rightful inheritance
of the one who proves victorious; and I will be his God and he a son to
me.'

This is the word of the Lord.

Responsorial Psalm   Ps 125. ℞ v.5

℞   Those who sow in tears, shall reap with shouts of joy.

1   When the Lord delivered Zion from bondage,
    it seemed like a dream.

Then was our mouth filled with laughter,
on our lips there were songs. ℟

2   The heathens themselves said: 'What marvels
the Lord worked for them!'
What marvels the Lord worked for us!
Indeed we were glad. ℟

3   Deliver us, O Lord, from our bondage
as streams in dry land.
Those who are sowing in tears
will sing when they reap. ℟

4   They go out, they go out, full of tears,
carrying seed for the sowing:
they come back, they come back, full of song,
carrying their sheaves. ℟

SECOND READING FROM THE NEW TESTAMENT

1

A reading from the letter of St Paul to the Romans   5:1-5

We boast about our sufferings.

Through our Lord Jesus Christ, by faith we are judged righteous and at peace with God, since it is by faith and through Jesus that we have entered this state of grace in which we can boast about looking forward to God's glory. But that is not all we can boast about; we can boast about our sufferings. These sufferings bring patience, as we know, and patience brings perseverance, and perseverance brings hope, and this hope is not deceptive because the love of God has been poured into our hearts by the Holy Spirit which has been given us.

This is the word of the Lord.

2

A reading from the letter of St Paul to the Romans   8:31-39

Neither death nor life can ever come between us and the love of God.

With God on our side who can be against us? Since God did not spare his own Son, but gave him up to benefit us all, we may be certain, after such a gift, that he will not refuse anything he can give. Could anyone accuse those that God has chosen? When God acquits, could anyone condemn? Could Christ Jesus? No! He not only died for us – he rose from the dead, and there at God's right hand he stands and pleads for us.

Nothing therefore can come between us and the love of Christ, even if we are troubled or worried, or being persecuted, or lacking food or clothes, or being threatened or even attacked. As scripture promised: For your sake we are being massacred daily, and reckoned as sheep for the slaughter. These are the trials through which we triumph, by the power of him who loved us.

For I am certain of this: neither death nor life, no angel, no prince, nothing that exists, nothing still to come, not any power, or height or depth, nor any created thing, can ever come between us and the love of God made visible in Christ Jesus our Lord.

This is the word of the Lord.

3

A reading from the second letter of St Paul
to the Corinthians   4:7-15

We carry in our bodies the death and life of Jesus.

We are only the earthenware jars that hold this treasure, to make it clear that such an overwhelming power comes from God and not from us. We are in difficulties on all sides, but never cornered; we see no answer to our problems, but never despair; we have been persecuted, but never deserted; knocked down, but never killed; always, wherever we may be, we carry with us in our body the death of Jesus, so that the life of Jesus, too, may always be seen in our body. Indeed, while we are still alive, we are consigned to our death every day, for the sake of Jesus, so that in our mortal flesh the life of Jesus, too, may be openly shown. So death is at work in us, but life in you.

But as we have the same spirit of faith that is mentioned in scripture – I believed, and therefore I spoke – we too believe and therefore we too speak, knowing that he who raised the Lord Jesus to life will raise us with Jesus in our turn, and put us by his side and you with us. You see, all this is for your benefit, so that the more grace is mutiplied among people, the more thanksgiving there will be, to the glory of God.

This is the word of the Lord.

4

A reading from the second letter of St Paul to the Corinthians   6:4-10

We are said to be dying and yet here we are alive.

We prove we are servants of God by great fortitude in times of suffering: in times of hardship and distress; when we are flogged, or sent to prison, or mobbed; labouring, sleepless, starving. We prove we are God's servants by our purity, knowledge, patience and kindness; by a spirit of holiness, by a love free from affectation; by the word of truth and by the power of God; by being armed with the weapons of righteousness in the right hand and in the left, prepared for honour or disgrace, for blame or praise; taken for impostors while we are genuine; obscure yet famous; said to be dying and here are we alive; rumoured to be executed before we are sentenced; thought most miserable and yet we are always rejoicing; taken for paupers though we make others rich, for people having nothing though we have everything.

This is the word of the Lord.

5

A reading from the second letter of St Paul to Timothy   2:8-13; 3:10-12

You must be aware that anybody who tries to live in devotion to Christ is certain to suffer persecution.

Remember the Good News that I carry, 'Jesus Christ risen from the dead, sprung from the race of David'; it is on account of this that I have my own hardships to bear, even to being chained like a criminal – but they cannot chain up God's news. So I bear it all for the sake of those who are chosen, so that in the end they may have the salvation that is in Christ Jesus and the eternal glory that comes with it.

Here is a saying that you can rely on:
If we have died with him, then we shall live with him.
If we hold firm, then we shall reign with him.
If we disown him, then he will disown us.
We may be unfaithful, but he is always faithful,
for he cannot disown his own self.

You know what I have taught, how I have lived, what I have

aimed at; you know my faith, my patience and my love; my constancy and the persecutions and hardships that came to me in places like Antioch, Iconium and Lystra – all the persecutions I have endured; and the Lord has rescued me from every one of them. You are well aware, then, that anybody who tries to live in devotion to Christ is certain to be attacked.

This is the word of the Lord.

6

A reading from the letter to the Hebrews   10:32-36

You have suffered greatly.

Remember all the sufferings that you had to meet after you received the light, in earlier days; sometimes by being yourselves publicly exposed to insults and violence, and sometimes as associates of others who were treated in the same way. For you not only shared in the sufferings of those who were in prison, but you happily accepted being stripped of your belongings, knowing that you owned something that was better and lasting. Be as confident now, then, since the reward is so great. You will need endurance to do God's will and gain what he has promised.

This is the word of the Lord.

7

A reading from the letter of St James   1:2-4. 12

Happy are they who stand firm when trials come.

My brothers, you will always have your trials but, when they come, try to treat them as a happy privilege; you understand that your faith is only put to the test to make you patient, but patience too is to have its practical results so that you will become fully-developed, complete, with nothing missing.

Happy the man who stands firm when trials come. He has proved himself, and will win the prize of life, the crown that the Lord has promised to those who love him.

This is the word of the Lord.

8

A reading from the first letter of St Peter   3:14-17

There is no need to be afraid or to worry about them.

If you have to suffer for being good, you will count it a blessing. There is no need to be afraid or to worry about persecutors. Simply reverence the Lord Christ in your hearts, and always have your answer ready for people who ask you the reason for the hope that you all have. But give it with courtesy and respect and with a clear conscience, so that those who slander you when you are living a good life in Christ may be proved wrong in the accusations that they bring. And if it is the will of God that you should suffer, it is better to suffer for doing right than for doing wrong.

This is the word of the Lord.

9

A reading from the first letter of St Peter   4:12-19

Be glad when you are sharing in the suffering of Christ.

My dear people, you must not think it unaccountable that you should be tested by fire. There is nothing extraordinary in what has happened to you. If you can have some share in the sufferings of Christ, be glad, because you will enjoy a much greater gladness when his glory is revealed. It is a blessing for you when they insult you for bearing the name of Christ, because it means that you have the Spirit of glory, the Spirit of God resting on you. None of you should ever deserve to suffer for being a murderer, a thief, a criminal or an informer; but if anyone of you should suffer for being a Christian, then he is not to be ashamed of it; he should thank God that he has been called one. The time has come for the judgement to begin at the household of God; and if what we know now is only the beginning, what will it be when it comes down to those who refuse to believe God's Good News? If it is hard for a good man to be saved, what will happen to the wicked and to sinners? So even those whom God allows to suffer must trust themselves to the constancy of the creator and go on doing good.

This is the word of the Lord.

10

A reading from the first letter of St John   5:1-5

Our faith, this is the victory which overcomes the evils in the world.

Whoever believes that Jesus is the Christ
has been begotten by God;
and whoever loves the Father that begot him
loves the child whom he begets.
We can be sure that we love God's children
if we love God himself and do what he has commanded us;
this is what loving God is –
keeping his commandments;
and his commandments are not difficult,
because anyone who has been begotten by God
has already overcome the world;
this is the victory over the world –
our faith.
Who can overcome the world?
Only the man who believes that Jesus is the Son of God.

This is the word of the Lord.

GOSPEL

1

Gospel Acclamation   Mt 5:10

Alleluia, alleluia!
Happy are they who suffer persecution for justice' sake;
the kingdom of heaven is theirs.
Alleluia!

A reading from the holy Gospel according to Matthew   10:17-22

You will be dragged before governors and kings on account of me, to
bear witness before them and all the people.

Jesus said to his apostles: 'Beware of men: they will hand you over to
sanhedrins and scourge you in their synagogues. You will be dragged
before governors and kings for my sake, to bear witness before

them and the pagans. But when they hand you over, do not worry about how to speak or what to say; what you are to say will be given to you when the time comes; because it is not you who will be speaking; the Spirit of your Father will be speaking in you.

'Brother will betray brother to death, and the father his child; children will rise against their parents and have them put to death. You will be hated by all men on account of my name; but the man who stands firm to the end will be saved.'

This is the Gospel of the Lord.

2

Gospel Acclamation   James 1:12

Alleluia, alleluia!
Blessed are they who stand firm when trials come;
when they have stood the test, they will win the crown of life.
Alleluia!

A reading from the holy Gospel according to Matthew   10:28-33

Do not fear those who kill the body.

Jesus said to his apostles: 'Do not be afraid of those who kill the body but cannot kill the soul; fear him rather who can destroy both body and soul in hell. Can you not buy two sparrows for a penny? And yet not one falls to the ground without your Father knowing. Why, every hair on your head has been counted. So there is no need to be afraid; you are worth more than hundreds of sparrows.

'So if anyone declares himself for me in the presence of men, I will declare myself for him in the presence of my Father in heaven. But the one who disowns me in the presence of men, I will disown in the presence of my Father in heaven.'

This is the Gospel of the Lord.

3

Gospel Acclamation   Mt 5:10

> Alleluia, alleluia!
> Happy are they who suffer persecution for justice' sake;
> the kingdom of heaven is theirs.
> Alleluia!

A reading from the holy Gospel according to Matthew   10:34-39

It is not peace I have come to bring, but a sword.

Jesus said to his apostles: 'Do not suppose that I have come to bring peace to the earth: it is not peace I have come to bring, but a sword. For I have come to set a man against his father, a daughter against her mother, a daughter-in-law against her mother-in-law. A man's enemies will be those of his own household.

'Anyone who prefers father or mother to me is not worthy of me. Anyone who prefers son or daughter to me is not worthy of me. Anyone who does not take his cross and follow in my footsteps is not worthy of me. Anyone who finds his life will lose it; anyone who loses his life for my sake will find it.'

This is the Gospel of the Lord.

4

Gospel Acclamation   1 Peter 4:14

> Alleluia, alleluia!
> If you are insulted for the name of Christ, blessed are you,
> for the Spirit of God rests upon you.
> Alleluia!

A reading from the holy Gospel according to Luke   9:23-26

Those who lose their lives for my sake will save them.

To all Jesus said, 'If anyone wants to be a follower of mine, let him renounce himself and take up his cross every day and follow me. For anyone who wants to save his life will lose it; but anyone who loses his life for my sake, that man will save it. What gain, then, is it for a

man to have won the whole world and to have lost or ruined his very
self? For if anyone is ashamed of me and of my words, of him the Son
of Man will be ashamed when he comes in his own glory and in the
glory of the Father and the holy angels.'

This is the Gospel of the Lord.

5

Gospel Acclamation   2 Cor 1:3-4

Alleluia, alleluia!
Blessed be the Father of mercies and the God of all comfort,
who consoles us in all our afflictions.
Alleluia!

A reading from the holy Gospel according to John   12:24-26

If the grain of wheat in the ground dies, it yields a rich harvest.

Jesus said to his disciples:

'I tell you, most solemnly,
unless a wheat grain falls on the ground and dies,
it remains only a single grain;
but if it dies,
it yields a rich harvest.
Anyone who loves his life loses it;
anyone who hates his life in this world
will keep it for the eternal life.
If a man serves me, he must follow me,
wherever I am, my servant will be there too.
If anyone serves me, my Father will honour him.'

This is the Gospel of the Lord.

6

Gospel Acclamation

Alleluia, alleluia!
You are God: we praise you; you are Lord: we acclaim you;
the white-robed army of martyrs praise you.
Alleluia!

A reading from the holy Gospel according to John   15:18-21

If they have persecuted me, they will persecute you too.

Jesus said to his disciples:

'If the world hates you,
remember that it hated me before you.
If you belonged to the world,
the world would love you as its own;
but because you do not belong to the world,
because my choice withdrew you from the world,
therefore the world hates you.
Remember the words I said to you:
A servant is not greater than his master.
If they persecuted me,
they will persecute you too;
if they kept my word
they will keep yours as well.
But it will be on my account that they will do all this,
because they do not know the one who sent me.'

This is the Gospel of the Lord.

7

Gospel Acclamation   Jn 17:19

Alleluia alleluia!
For their sake I consecrate myself, says the Lord,
so that they too may be consecrated in the truth.
Alleluia!

A reading from the holy Gospel according to John   17:11-19

The world hates them.

Jesus raised his eyes to heaven and said,

'Holy Father,
keep those you have given me true to your name,
so that they may be one like us.
While I was with them,
I kept those you had given me true to your name.
I have watched over them and not one is lost

except the one who chose to be lost,
and this was to fulfil the scriptures.
But now I am coming to you
and while still in the world I say these things
to share my joy with them to the full.
I passed your word on to them,
and the world hated them,
because they belong to the world
no more than I belong to the world.
I am not asking you to remove them from the world,
but to protect them from the evil one.
They do not belong to the world
any more than I belong to the world.
Consecrate them in the truth;
your word is truth.
As you sent me into the world,
I have sent them into the world,
and for their sake I consecrate myself
so that they too may be consecrated in truth.'

This is the Gospel of the Lord.

COMMON OF PASTORS

1

A reading from the book of Exodus 32:7-14

He thought of destroying them but Moses, his chosen one, interceded in the hopes of turning away his anger.

The Lord spoke to Moses, 'Go down now, because your people whom you brought out of Egypt have apostasised. They have been quick to leave the way I marked out for them; they have made themselves a calf of molten metal and have worshipped it and offered it sacrifice. "Here is your God, Israel," they have cried, "who brought you up from the land of Egypt!" I can see how headstrong these people are! Leave me now, my wrath shall blaze out against them and devour them; of you, however, I will make a great nation.'

But Moses pleaded with the Lord his God. 'Lord,' he said, 'why should your wrath blaze out against this people of yours whom you brought out of the land of Egypt with arm outstretched and mighty hand? Why let the Egyptians say, "Ah, it was in treachery that he brought them out, to do them to death in the mountains and wipe them off the face of the earth?" Leave your burning wrath; relent and do not bring this disaster on your people. Remember Abraham, Isaac and Jacob, your servants to whom by your own self you swore and made this promise: I will make your offspring as many as the stars of heaven, and all this land which I promised I will give to your descendants, and it shall be their heritage for ever.' So the Lord relented and did not bring on his people the disaster he had threatened.

This is the word of the Lord.

Responsorial Psalm   Ps 105:19-23. ℟ v.4

℟   Lord, remember us, for the love you bear your people.

1   They fashioned a calf at Horeb
     and worshipped an image of metal,
     exchanging the God who was their glory
     for the image of a bull that eats grass. ℟

2   They forgot the God who was their saviour,
     who had done such great things in Egypt,
     such portents in the land of Ham,
     such marvels at the Red Sea.   ℟

3   For this he said he would destroy them,
     but Moses, the man he had chosen,
     stood in the breach before him,
     to turn back his anger from destruction.   ℟

2

A reading from the book of Deuteronomy   10:8-9

The Lord God is the inheritance of those who serve him.

Moses said to the people: 'The Lord set apart the tribe of Levi to carry
the ark of the Lord's covenant, to stand in the presence of the Lord, to
do him service and in his name to pronounce blessing as they still do
today. Levi therefore had no share or inheritance with his brothers:
the Lord is his inheritance, as the Lord your God told him.'

This is the word of the Lord.

Responsorial Psalm   Ps 15:1-2. 5. 7-8. 11. ℟ cf v.5

℟   You are my inheritance, O Lord.

1   Preserve me, God, I take refuge in you.
     I say to the Lord: 'You are my God.'
     O Lord, it is you who are my portion and cup;
     it is you yourself who are my prize.   ℟

2   I will bless the Lord who gives me counsel,
     who even at night directs my heart.
     I keep the Lord ever in my sight:
     since he is at my right hand, I shall stand firm.   ℟   (continued)

3 You will show me the path of life,
   the fullness of joy in your presence,
   at your right hand happiness for ever.

℟   You are my inheritance, O Lord.

3

A reading from the first book of Samuel   16:1. 6-13

Come, anoint the young shepherd; he is the one who will be king.

The Lord said to Samuel, 'Fill your horn with oil and go. I am sending you to Jesse of Bethlehem, for I have chosen myself a king among his sons.'

When he arrived, he caught sight of Eliab and thought, 'Surely the Lord's anointed one stands there before him,' but the Lord said to Samuel, 'Take no notice of his appearance or his height for I have rejected him; God does not see as man sees; man looks at appearances but the Lord looks at the heart.' Jesse then called Abinadab and presented him to Samuel, who said, 'The Lord has not chosen this one either.' Jesse then presented Shammah, but Samuel said, 'The Lord has not chosen this one either.' Jesse presented his seven sons to Samuel, but Samuel said to Jesse, 'The Lord has not chosen these.' He then asked Jesse, 'Are these all the sons you have?' He answered, 'There is still one left, the youngest; he is out looking after the sheep.' Then Samuel said to Jesse, 'Send for him; we will not sit down to eat until he comes.' Jesse had him sent for, a boy of fresh complexion, with fine eyes and pleasant bearing. The Lord said, 'Come, anoint him, for this is the one.' At this, Samuel took the horn of oil and anointed him where he stood with his brothers; and the spirit of the Lord seized on David and stayed with him from that day on.

This is the word of the Lord.

Responsorial Psalm   Ps 88:2-5. 21-22. 25. 27. ℟ cf. v.2

℟   For ever I will sing the goodness of the Lord.

1 I will sing for ever of your love, O Lord;
   through all ages my mouth will proclaim your truth.
   Of this I am sure, that your love lasts for ever,
   that your truth is firmly established as the heavens. ℟

2 'I have made a covenant with my chosen one;
  I have sworn to David my servant:
  I will establish your dynasty for ever
  and set up your throne through all ages. ℟

3 'I have found David my servant
  and with my holy oil anointed him.
  My hand shall always be with him
  and my arm shall make him strong. ℟

4 'My truth and my love shall be with him;
  by my name his might shall be exalted.
  He will say to me: "You are my father,
  my God, the rock who saves me." ' ℟

4

A reading from the prophet Isaiah   6:1-8

Whom shall I send? Who will be our messenger?

In the year of King Uzziah's death I saw the Lord seated on a high throne; his train filled the sanctuary; above him stood seraphs, each one with six wings: two to cover its face, two to cover its feet and two for flying.
  And they cried out one to another in this way,

'Holy, holy, holy is the Lord of hosts.
His glory fills the whole earth.'

The foundations of the threshold shook with the voice of the one who cried out, and the Temple was filled with smoke. I said:

'What a wretched state I am in! I am lost,
for I am a man of unclean lips
and I live among a people of unclean lips,
and my eyes have looked at the King, the Lord of hosts.'

Then one of the seraphs flew to me, holding in his hand a live coal which he had taken from the altar with a pair of tongs. With this he touched my mouth and said:

'See now, this has touched your lips,
your sin is taken away,
your iniquity is purged.'

Then I heard the voice of the Lord saying:

'Whom shall I send? Who will be our messenger?'

I answered, 'Here I am, send me.'

This is the word of the Lord.

Responsorial Psalm   Ps 39:2. 4. 7-10. ℟ cf. v.8. 9

> ℟ Here am I, Lord; I come to do your will.

1 I waited, I waited for the Lord
   and he stooped down to me;
   he heard my cry.
   He put a new song into my mouth,
   praise of our God.   ℟

2 You do not ask for sacrifice and offerings,
   but an open ear.
   You do not ask for holocaust and victim.
   Instead, here am I.   ℟

3 In the scroll of the book it stands written
   that I should do your will.
   My God, I delight in your law
   in the depth of my heart.   ℟

4 Your justice I have proclaimed
   in the great assembly.
   My lips I have not sealed;
   you know it, O Lord.   ℟

5

For missionaries

A reading from the prophet Isaiah   52:7-10

All the ends of the earth shall see the salvation of our God.

How beautiful on the mountains,
are the feet of one who brings good news,
who heralds peace, brings happiness,
proclaims salvation,
and tells Zion,
'Your God is king!'

Listen! Your watchmen raise their voices,
they shout for joy together,
for they see the Lord face to face,
as he returns to Zion.
Break into shouts of joy together,
you ruins of Jerusalem;
for the Lord is consoling his people,
redeeming Jerusalem.

The Lord bares his holy arm
in the sight of all the nations,
and all the ends of the earth shall see
the salvation of our God.

This is the word of the Lord.

Responsorial Psalm   Ps 95:1-3. 7-8. 10. ℟ v.3

℟   Proclaim his marvellous deeds to all the nations.

1   O sing a new song to the Lord,
     sing to the Lord all the earth.
     O sing to the Lord, bless his name.   ℟

2   Proclaim his help day by day,
     tell among the nations his glory
     and his wonders among all the peoples.   ℟

3   Give the Lord, you families of peoples,
     give the Lord glory and power,
     give the Lord the glory of his name.   ℟

4   Proclaim to the nations: 'God is king.'
     The world he made firm in its place;
     he will judge the peoples in fairness.   ℟

6

A reading from the prophet Isaiah   61:1-3

The Lord God anointed me and sent me to bring Good News to the poor.

The spirit of the Lord has been given to me,
for the Lord has anointed me.
He has sent me to bring good news to the poor,
to bind up hearts that are broken;

to proclaim liberty to captives,
freedom to those in prison;
to proclaim a year of favour from the Lord,
a day of vengeance for our God,

to comfort all those who mourn and to give them
for ashes a garland;
for mourning robe the oil of gladness,
for despondency, praise.

This is the word of the Lord.

Responsorial Psalm   Ps 88:2-5. 21-22. 25. 27. ℟ v.2

℟   For ever I will sing the goodness of the Lord.

1   I will sing for ever of your love, O Lord;
    through all ages my mouth will proclaim your truth.
    Of this I am sure, that your love lasts for ever,
    that your truth is firmly established as the heavens.   ℟

2   'I have made a covenant with my chosen one;
    I have sworn to David my servant:
    I will establish your dynasty for ever
    and set up your throne through all ages.   ℟

3   'I have found David my servant
    and with my holy oil anointed him.
    My hand shall always be with him
    and my arm shall make him strong.   ℟

4   'My truth and my love shall be with him;
    by my name his might shall be exalted.
    He will say to me: "You are my father,
    my God, the rock who saves me." '   ℟

7

A reading from the prophet Jeremiah   1:4-9

Go to those to whom I send you.

The word of the Lord was addressed to me, saying,

'Before I formed you in the womb I knew you;
before you came to birth I consecrated you;
I have appointed you as prophet to the nations'.

I said, 'Ah, Lord; look, I do not know how to speak: I am a child!'

> But the Lord replied,
> 'Do not say, "I am a child".
> Go now to those to whom I send you
> and say whatever I command you.
> Do not be afraid of them,
> for I am with you to protect you –
> it is the Lord who speaks!'

Then the Lord put out his hand and touched my mouth and said to me:

> 'There! I am putting my words into your mouth.'

This is the word of the Lord.

Responsorial Psalm   Ps 95:1-3. 7-8. 10. ℟ v.3

℟   Proclaim his marvellous deeds to all the nations.

1   O sing a new song to the Lord,
    sing to the Lord all the earth.
    O sing to the Lord, bless his name.   ℟

2   Proclaim his help day by day,
    tell among the nations his glory
    and his wonders among all the peoples.   ℟

3   Give the Lord, you families of peoples,
    give the Lord glory and power,
    give the Lord the glory of his name.   ℟

4   Proclaim to the nations: 'God is king.'
    The world he made firm in its place;
    he will judge the peoples in fairness.   ℟

8

A reading from the prophet Ezekiel   3:16-21

I have appointed you as sentry to the house of Israel.

The word of the Lord was addressed to me as follows, 'Son of man, I have appointed you as sentry to the House of Israel. Whenever you hear a word from me, warn them in my name. If I say to a wicked man:

You are to die, and you do not warn him; if you do not speak and warn him to renounce his evil ways and so live, then he shall die for his sin, but I will hold you responsible for his death. If, however, you do warn a wicked man and he does not renounce his wickedness and his evil ways, then he shall die for his sin, but you yourself will have saved your life. When the upright man renounces his integrity to do evil and I set a trap for him, he too shall die; since you failed to warn him, he shall die for his sin and the integrity he practised will no longer be remembered; but I will hold you responsible for his death. If, however, you warn the upright man not to sin and he abstains from sinning, he shall live, thanks to your warning, and you too will have saved your life.'

This is the word of the Lord.

Responsorial Psalm   Ps 116. ℟ Mk 16:15

℟   Go out to all the world, and tell the Good News.

or

℟   Alleluia!

1   O praise the Lord, all you nations,
    acclaim him all you peoples!   ℟

2   Strong is his love for us;
    he is faithful for ever.   ℟

9

A reading from the prophet Ezekiel   34:11-16

As a shepherd keeps all his flock in view, so shall I keep my sheep in view.

The Lord says this: 'I am going to look after my flock myself and keep all of it in view. As a shepherd keeps all his flock in view when he stands up in the middle of his scattered sheep, so shall I keep my sheep in view. I shall rescue them from wherever they have been scattered during the mist and darkness. I shall bring them out of the countries where they are; I shall gather them together from foreign countries and bring them back to their own land. I shall pasture them on the mountains of Israel, in the ravines and in every inhabited place in the land. I shall feed then in good pasturage; the high mountains of

Israel will be their grazing ground. There they will rest in good grazing ground; they will browse in rich pastures on the mountains of Israel. I myself will pasture my sheep, I myself will show them where to rest – it is the Lord who speaks. I shall look for the lost one, bring back the stray, bandage the wounded and make the weak strong. I shall watch over the fat and healthy. I shall be a true shepherd to them.

This is the word of the Lord.

Responsorial Psalm   Ps 22. ℟ v.1

℟   The Lord is my shepherd; there is nothing I shall want.

1   The Lord is my shepherd;
    there is nothing I shall want.
    Fresh and green are the pastures
    where he gives me repose.
    Near restful waters he leads me,
    to revive my drooping spirit.   ℟

2   He guides me along the right path;
    he is true to his name.
    If I should walk in the valley of darkness
    no evil would I fear.
    You are there with your crook and your staff;
    with these you give me comfort.   ℟

3   You have prepared a banquet for me
    in the sight of my foes.
    My head you have anointed with oil;
    my cup is overflowing.   ℟

4   Surely goodness and kindness shall follow me
    all the days of my life.
    In the Lord's own house shall I dwell
    for ever and ever.   ℟

FIRST READING FROM THE NEW TESTAMENT

In the Easter Season

1

For missionaries

A reading from the Acts of the Apostles   13:46-49

We must turn to the gentiles.

Paul and Barnabas spoke out boldly to the Jews, 'We had to proclaim the word of God to you first, but since you have rejected it, since you do not think yourselves worthy of eternal life, we must turn to the pagans. For this is what the Lord commanded us to do when he said:

'I have made you a light for the nations,
so that my salvation may reach the ends of the earth.'

It made the pagans very happy to hear this and they thanked the Lord for his message; all who were destined for eternal life became believers. Thus the word of the Lord spread through the whole countryside.

This is the word of the Lord.

Responsorial Psalm   Ps 116. ℟ Mk 16:15

℟   Go out to all the world, and tell the Good News.

or

℟   Alleluia!

1   O praise the Lord, all you nations,
     acclaim him all you peoples!   ℟

2   Strong is his love for us;
     he is faithful for ever.   ℟

2

A reading from the Acts of the Apostles   20:17-18. 28-32. 36

Be on guard for yourselves and for all of whom the Holy Spirit has made you the
overseers.

From Miletus Paul sent for the elders of the church of Ephesus. When
they arrived he addressed these words to them:

'Be on your guard for yourselves and for all the flock of which the
Holy Spirit has made you the overseers, to feed the Church of God
which he bought with his own blood. I know quite well that when I
have gone fierce wolves will invade you and will have no mercy on the
flock. Even from your own ranks there will be men coming forward
with a travesty of the truth on their lips to induce the disciples to
follow them. So be on your guard, remembering how night and day for
three years I never failed to keep you right, shedding tears over each
one of you. And now I commend you to God, and to the word of his
grace that has power to build you up and to give you your inheritance
among all the sanctified.'

When he had finished speaking he knelt down with them all and
prayed.

This is the word of the Lord.

Responsorial Psalm   Ps 109:1-4. ℟ v.4

℟ You are a priest for ever, in the line of Melchizedek.

1 The Lord's revelation to my Master:
  'Sit on my right:
  I will put your foes beneath your feet.' ℟

2 The Lord will send from Zion
  your sceptre of power:
  rule in the midst of all your foes. ℟

3 A prince from the day of your birth
  on the holy mountains;
  from the womb before the daybreak I begot you. ℟

4 The Lord has sworn an oath he will not change.
  'You are a priest for ever,
  a priest like Melchizedek of old.' ℟

3

A reading from the Acts of the Apostles   26:19-23

Christ will proclaim light to the people and to the whole world.

Paul said, 'King Agrippa, I could not disobey the heavenly vision. On the contrary I started preaching, first to the people of Damascus, then to those of Jerusalem and all the countryside of Judaea, and also to the pagans, urging them to repent and turn to God, proving their change of heart by their deeds. This was why the Jews laid hands on me in the Temple and tried to do away with me. But I was blessed with God's help, and so I have stood firm to this day, testifying to great and small alike, saying nothing more than what the prophets and Moses himself said would happen: that the Christ was to suffer and that, as the first to rise from the dead, he was to proclaim that light now shone for our people and for the pagans too.'

This is the word of the Lord.

Responsorial Psalm   Ps 116. ℟ Mk 16:15

℟   Go out to all the world, and tell the Good News.

or

℟   Alleluia!

1   O praise the Lord, all you nations,
     acclaim him all you peoples!   ℟

2   Strong is his love for us;
     he is faithful for ever.   ℟

SECOND READING FROM THE NEW TESTAMENT

1

A reading from the letter of St Paul to the Romans   12:3-13

Our gifts differ according to the grace given us.

In the light of the grace I have received I want to urge each one among
you not to exaggerate his real importance. Each of you must judge
himself soberly by the standard of the faith God has given him. Just
as each of our bodies has several parts and each part has a separate
function, so all of us, in union with Christ, form one body, and as parts
of it we belong to each other. Our gifts differ according to the grace
given us. If your gift is prophecy, then use it as your faith suggests; if
administration, then use it for administration; if teaching, then use it
for teaching. Let the preachers deliver sermons, the almsgivers give
freely, the officials be diligent, and those who do works of mercy do
them cheerfully.

Do not let your love be a pretence, but sincerely prefer good to evil.
Love each other as much as brothers should, and have a profound
respect for each other. Work for the Lord with untiring effort and with
great earnestness of spirit. If you have hope, this will make you
cheerful. Do not give up if trials come; and keep on praying. If any of
the saints are in need you must share with them; and you should
make hospitality your special care.

This is the word of the Lord.

2

For missionaries

A reading from the first letter of St Paul   1:18-25
to the Corinthians

It was because God wanted to save those who have faith through the
foolishness of the message that we preach.

The language of the cross may be illogical to those who are not on the
way to salvation, but those of us who are on the way see it as God's
power to save. As scripture says: I shall destroy the wisdom of the wise
and bring to nothing all the learning of the learned. Where are the
philosophers now? Where are the scribes? Where are any of our
thinkers today? Do you see now how God has shown up the foolishness

of human wisdom? If it was God's wisdom that human wisdom should not know God, it was because God wanted to save those who have faith through the foolishness of the message that we preach. And so, while the Jews demand miracles and the Greeks look for wisdom, here are we preaching a crucified Christ; to the Jews an obstacle that they cannot get over, to the pagans madness, but to those who have been called, whether they are Jews or Greeks, a Christ who is the power and the wisdom of God. For God's foolishness is wiser than human wisdom, and God's weakness is stronger than human strength.

This is the word of the Lord.

3

A reading from the first letter of St Paul
to the Corinthians

4:1-5

We are to be as Christ's servants, stewards entrusted with the mysteries of God.

People must think of us as Christ's servants, stewards entrusted with the mysteries of God. What is expected of stewards is that each one should be found worthy of his trust. Not that it makes the slightest difference to me whether you, or indeed any human tribunal, find me worthy, or not. I will not even pass judgement on myself. True, my conscience does not reproach me at all, but that does not prove that I am acquitted: the Lord alone is my judge. There must be no passing of premature judgement. Leave that until the Lord comes: he will light up all that is hidden in the dark and reveal the secret intentions of men's hearts. Then will be the time for each one to have whatever praise he deserves, from God.

This is the word of the Lord.

4

A reading from the first letter of St Paul
to the Corinthians

9:16-19. 22-23

Unless I preach the gospel, I shall be punished.

I do not boast of preaching the gospel, since it is a duty which has been laid on me; I should be punished if I did not preach it! If I had chosen this work myself, I might have been paid for it, but as I have not, it is a responsibility which has been put into my hands. Do you know what my reward is? It is this: in my preaching, to be able to offer the Good

News free, and not insist on the rights which the Gospel gives me.

So though I am not a slave of any man I have made myself the slave of everyone so as to win as many as I could. For the weak I made myself weak. I made myself all things to all men in order to save some at any cost; and I still do this, for the sake of the Gospel, to have a share in its blessings.

This is the word of the Lord.

5

A reading from the second letter of St Paul   3:1-6
to the Corinthians

God has given us the qualifications to be ministers of the new covenant.

Does this sound like a new attempt to commend ourselves to you? Unlike other people, we need no letters of recommendation either to you or from you, because you are yourselves our letter, written in our hearts, that anybody can see and read, and it is plain that you are a letter from Christ, drawn up by us, and written not with ink but with the Spirit of the living God, not on stone tablets but on the tablets of your living hearts.

Before God, we are confident of this through Christ: not that we are qualified in ourselves to claim anything as our own work: all our qualifications come from God. He is the one who has given us the qualifications to be the administrators of this new covenant, which is not a covenant of written letters but of the Spirit.

This is the word of the Lord.

6

A reading from the second letter of St Paul   4:1-2. 5-7
to the Corinthians

We preach Jesus Christ as Lord, with ourselves as your servants for Jesus' sake.

Since we have by an act of mercy been entrusted with this work of administration, there is no weakening on our part. On the contrary, we will have none of the reticence of those who are ashamed, no deceitfulness or watering down the word of God; but the way we commend ourselves to every human being with a conscience is by stating the truth openly in the sight of God. For it is not ourselves that we are preaching, but Christ Jesus as the Lord, and ourselves as your servants for Jesus' sake. It is the same God that said, 'Let there be light shining out of darkness,' who has shone in our minds to radiate the light of the knowledge of God's glory, the glory on the face of Christ.

We are only the earthenware jars that hold this treasure, to make it clear that such an overwhelming power comes from God and not from us.

This is the word of the Lord.

7

A reading from the second letter of St Paul to the Corinthians   5:14-20

God gave us the work of reconciliation.

The love of Christ overwhelms us when we reflect that if one man has died for all, then all men should be dead; and the reason he died for all was so that living men should live no longer for themselves, but for him who died and was raised to life for them.

From now onwards, therefore, we do not judge anyone by the standards of the flesh. Even if we did once know Christ in the flesh, that is not how we know him now. And for anyone who is in Christ, there is a new creation; the old creation has gone, and now the new one is here. It is all God's work. It was God who reconciled us to himself through Christ and gave us the work of handing on this reconciliation. In other words, God in Christ was reconciling the world to himself, not holding men's faults against them, and he has entrusted to us the news that they are reconciled. So we are ambassadors for Christ; it is as though God were appealing through us, and the appeal that we make in Christ's name is: be reconciled to God.

This is the word of the Lord.

8

A reading from the letter of St Paul to the Ephesians   4:1-7. 11-13

In the work of service we help in building up the body of Christ.

I, the prisoner in the Lord, implore you to lead a life worthy of your vocation. Bear with one another charitably, in complete selflessness, gentleness and patience. Do all you can to preserve the unity of the Spirit by the peace that binds you together. There is one Body, one Spirit, just as you were all called into one and the same hope when you were called. There is one Lord, one faith, one baptism, and one God who is Father of all, over all, through all and within all.

Each one of us, however, has been given his own share of grace, given as Christ allotted it. To some his gift was that they should be apostles; to some, prophets; to some, evangelists; to some, pastors and teachers; so that the saints together make a unity in the work of service, building up the body of Christ. In this way we are all to come to unity in our faith and in our knowledge of the Son of God, until we become the perfect Man, fully mature with the fullness of Christ himself.

This is the word of the Lord.

9

A reading from the letter of St Paul   1:24-29
to the Colossians

I became the servant of the Church when God made me responsible for delivering his message to you.

It makes me happy to suffer for you, as I am suffering now, and in my own body to do what I can to make up all that has still to be undergone by Christ for the sake of his body, the Church. I became the servant of the Church when God made me responsible for delivering God's message to you, the message which was a mystery hidden for generations and centuries and has now been revealed to his saints. It was God's purpose to reveal it to them and to show all the rich glory of this mystery to pagans. The mystery is Christ among you, your hope of glory: this is the Christ we proclaim, this is the wisdom in which we thoroughly train everyone and instruct everyone, to make them all perfect in Christ. It is for this I struggle wearily on, helped only by his power driving me irresistibly.

This is the word of the Lord.

10

A reading from the first letter of St Paul
to the Thessalonians

2:2-8

*We were eager to hand over to you not only the Good News
but our whole lives as well.*

It was our God who gave us the courage to proclaim his Good News to
you in the face of great opposition. We have not taken to preaching
because we are deluded, or immoral, or trying to deceive anyone; it
was God who decided that we were fit to be entrusted with the Good
News, and when we are speaking, we are not trying to please men but
God, who can read our inmost thoughts. You know very well, and we
can swear it before God, that never at any time have our speeches
been simply flattery, or a cover for trying to get money; nor have we
ever looked for any special honour from men, either from you or
anybody else, when we could have imposed ourselves on you with full
weight, as apostles of Christ.

Instead, we were unassuming. Like a mother feeding and looking
after her own children, we felt so devoted and protective towards you,
and had come to love you so much, that we were eager to hand over to
you not only the Good News but our whole lives as well.

This is the word of the Lord.

11

A reading from the second letter of St Paul
to Timothy

1:13-14; 2:1-3

*You have been entrusted to look after something precious; guard it
with the help of the Holy Spirit who lives in us.*

Keep as your pattern the sound teaching you have heard from me, in
the faith and love that are in Christ Jesus. You have been trusted to
look after something precious; guard it with the help of the Holy
Spirit who lives in us. Accept the strength, my dear son, that comes
from the grace of Christ Jesus. You have heard everything that I
teach in public; hand it on to reliable people so that they in turn will
be able to teach others.

Put up with your share of difficulties, like a good soldier of Christ
Jesus.

This is the word of the Lord.

12

A reading from the second letter of St Paul to Timothy   4:1-5

Preach the Good News; fulfill your ministry.

Before God and before Christ Jesus who is to be judge of the living and the dead, I put this duty to you, in the name of his Appearing and of his kingdom: proclaim the message and, welcome or unwelcome, insist on it. Refute falsehood, correct error, call to obedience – but do all with patience and with the intention of teaching. The time is sure to come when, far from being content with sound teaching, people will be avid for the latest novelty and collect themselves a whole series of teachers according to their own tastes; and then instead of listening to the truth, they will turn to myths. Be careful always to choose the right course; be brave under trials; make the preaching of the Good News your life's work, in thoroughgoing service.

This is the word of the Lord.

13

A reading from the first letter of St Peter   5:1-4

Be the shepherds of the flock of God that is entrusted to you.

I have something to tell your elders: I am an elder myself, and a witness to the sufferings of Christ, and with you I have a share in the glory that is to be revealed. Be the shepherds of the flock of God that is entrusted to you: watch over it, not simply as a duty but gladly, because God wants it; not for sordid money, but because you are eager to do it. Never be a dictator over any group that is put in our charge, but be an example that the whole flock can follow. When the chief shepherd appears, you will be given the crown of unfading glory.

This is the word of the Lord.

GOSPEL

1

Gospel Acclamation   2 Cor 5:19

Alleluia, alleluia!
God was in Christ, to reconcile the world to himself;
and the Good News of reconciliation he has entrusted to us.
Alleluia!

A reading from the holy Gospel according to Matthew   9:35-37

The harvest is rich, but the labourers are few.

Jesus made a tour through all the towns and villages, teaching in
their synagogues, proclaiming the Good News of the kingdom and
curing all kinds of diseases and sickness.

And when he saw the crowds he felt sorry for them because they
were harassed and dejected, like sheep without a shepherd. Then he
said to his disciples, 'The harvest is rich but the labourers are few, so
ask the Lord of the harvest to send labourers to his harvest.'

This is the Gospel of the Lord.

2

For a pope

Gospel Acclamation   Mk 1:17

Alleluia, alleluia!
Come, follow me, says the Lord,
and I will make you fishers of my people.
Alleluia!

A reading from the holy Gospel according to Matthew   16:13-19

You are Peter and on this rock I will build my Church.

When Jesus came to the region of Caesarea Philippi he put this
question to his disciples, 'Who do people say the Son of Man is?' And
they said, 'Some say he is John the Baptist, some Elijah, and others

Jeremiah or one of the prophets.' 'But you,' he said, 'who do you say I am?' Then Simon Peter spoke up, 'You are the Christ,' he said, 'the Son of the living God.' Jesus replied, 'Simon son of Jonah, you are a happy man! Because it was not flesh and blood that revealed this to you but my Father in heaven. So I now say to you: You are Peter and on this rock I will build my Church. And the gates of the underworld can never hold out against it. I will give you the keys of the kingdom of heaven: whatever you bind on earth shall be considered bound in heaven; whatever you loose on earth shall be considered loosed in heaven.'

This is the gospel of the Lord.

3

Gospel Acclamation   Mt 23:9-10

Alleluia, alleluia!
You have one Father, your Father in heaven;
you have one teacher: the Lord Jesus Christ!
Alleluia!

A reading from the holy Gospel according to Matthew   23:8-12

The greatest among you must be your servant.

Jesus said to his disciples: 'You must not allow yourselves to be called Rabbi, since you have only one Master, and you are all brothers. You must call no one on earth your father, since you have only one Father, and he is in heaven. Nor must you allow yourselves to be called teachers, for you have only one Teacher, the Christ. The greatest among you must be your servant. Anyone who exalts himself will be humbled, and anyone who humbles himself will be exalted.'

This is the Gospel of the Lord.

4

For missionaries

Gospel Acclamation   Mt 28:19-20

Alleluia, alleluia!
Go and teach all people my gospel.
I am with you always, until the end of the world.
Alleluia!

A reading from the holy Gospel according to Matthew   28:16-20

Go and make disciples of all the nations.

The eleven disciples set out for Galilee, to the mountain where Jesus had arranged to meet them. When they saw him they fell down before him, though some hesitated. Jesus came up and spoke to them. He said, 'All authority in heaven and on earth has been given to me. Go, therefore, make disciples of all the nations; baptise them in the name of the Father and of the Son and of the Holy Spirit, and teach them to observe all the commands I gave you. And know that I am with you always; yes, to the end of time.'

This is the Gospel of the Lord.

5

Gospel Acclamation   Mk 1:17

Alleluia, alleluia!
Come, follow me, says the Lord,
and I will make you fishers of my people.
Alleluia!

A reading from the holy Gospel according to Mark   1:14-20

I will make you fishers of my people.

After John had been arrested, Jesus went into Galilee. There he proclaimed the Good News from God. 'The time has come,' he said, 'and the kingdom of God is close at hand. Repent, and believe the Good News.'

As he was walking along by the Sea of Galilee he saw Simon and his brother Andrew casting a net in the lake – for they were fishermen. And Jesus said to them, 'Follow me and I will make you into fishers of men.' And at once they left their nets and followed him.

Going on a little farther, he saw James son of Zebedee and his brother John; they too were in their boat, mending their nets. He called them at once and, leaving their father Zebedee in the boat with the men he employed, they went after him.

This is the Gospel of the Lord.

6

For missionaries

Gospel Acclamation   Mt 28:19-20

Alleluia, alleluia!
Go, and teach all people my gospel.
I am with you always, until the end of the world.
Alleluia!

A reading from the holy Gospel according to Mark   16:15-20

Go out to the whole world; proclaim the Good News to all creation.

Jesus showed himself to the Eleven, and he said to them, 'Go out to the whole world; proclaim the Good News to all creation. He who believes and is baptised will be saved; he who does not believe will be condemned. These are the signs that will be associated with believers: in my name they will cast out devils; they will have the gift of tongues; they will pick up snakes in their hands, and be unharmed should they drink deadly poison; they will lay their hands on the sick, who will recover.'

And so the Lord Jesus, after he had spoken to them, was taken up into heaven: there at the right hand of God he took his place, while they, going out, preached everywhere, the Lord working with them and confirming the word by the signs that accompanied it.

This is the Gospel of the Lord.

7

For missionaries

Gospel Acclamation   Mk 1:17

> Alleluia, alleluia!
> Come, follow me, says the Lord,
> and I will make you fishers of my people.
> Alleluia!

A reading from the holy Gospel according to Luke   5:1-11

I will place my trust in your words.

Jesus was standing one day by the Lake of Gennesaret, with the crowd pressing round him listening to the word of God, when he caught sight of two boats close to the bank. The fishermen had gone out of them and were washing their nets. He got into one of the boats – it was Simon's – and asked him to put out a little from the shore. Then he sat down and taught the crowds from the boat.

When he had finished speaking he said to Simon, 'Put out into deep water and pay out your nets for a catch.' 'Master,' Simon replied, 'we worked hard all night long and caught nothing, but if you say so, I will pay out the nets.' And when they had done this they netted such a huge number of fish that their nets began to tear, so they signalled to their companions in the other boat to come and help them; when these came, they filled the two boats to sinking point.

When Simon Peter saw this he fell at the knees of Jesus saying, 'Leave me, Lord; I am a sinful man.' For he and all his companions were completely overcome by the catch they had made; so also were James and John, sons of Zebedee, who were Simon's partners. But Jesus said to Simon, 'Do not be afraid; from now on it is men you will catch.' Then, bringing their boats back to land, they left everything and followed him.

This is the Gospel of the Lord.

8

Gospel Acclamation   Lk 4:18

Alleluia, alleluia!
The Lord sent me to bring Good News to the poor,
and freedom to prisoners.
Alleluia!

A reading from the holy Gospel according to Luke   10:1-9

The harvest is rich but the labourers are few.

The Lord appointed seventy-two others and sent them out ahead of
him, in pairs, to all the towns and places he himself was to visit. He
said to them, 'The harvest is rich but the labourers are few, so ask the
Lord of the harvest to send labourers to his harvest. Start off now, but
remember, I am sending you out like lambs among wolves. Carry no
purse, no haversack, no sandals. Salute no one on the road. Whatever
house you go into, let your first words be, "Peace to this house!" And if
a man of peace lives there, your peace will go and rest on him; if not, it
will come back to you. Stay in the same house, taking what food and
drink they have to offer, for the labourer deserves his wages; do not
move from house to house. Whenever you go into a town where they
make you welcome, eat what is set before you. Cure those in it who are
sick, and say, "The kingdom of God is very near to you." '

This is the Gospel of the Lord.

9

Gospel Acclamation   Jn 15:15

Alleluia, alleluia!
I call you my friends, says the Lord,
for I have made known to you all that the Father has told me.
Alleluia!

A reading from the holy Gospel according to Luke   22:24-30

I confer a kingdom on you, just as my Father conferred one on me.

A dispute arose between the apostles about which should be reckoned
the greatest, but Jesus said to them, 'Among pagans it is the kings

who lord it over them, and those who have authority over them are given the title Benefactor. This must not happen with you. No; the greatest among you must behave as if he were the youngest, the leader as if he were the one who serves. For who is the greater: the one at table or the one who serves? The one at table, surely? Yet here am I among you as one who serves!

'You are the men who have stood by me faithfully in my trials; and now I confer a kingdom on you, just as my Father conferred one on me: you will eat and drink at my table in my kingdom, and you will sit on thrones to judge the twelve tribes of Israel.'

This is the Gospel of the Lord.

10

Gospel Acclamation   Jn 10:14

Alleluia, alleluia!
I am the good shepherd, says the Lord,
I know my sheep and mine know me.
Alleluia!

A reading from the holy Gospel according to John   10:11-16

The good shepherd is one who lays down his life for his sheep.

Jesus said:

'I am the good shepherd:
the good shepherd is one who lays down his life for his sheep.
The hired man, since he is not the shepherd
and the sheep do not belong to him,
abandons the sheep and runs away
as soon as he sees a wolf coming,
and then the wolf attacks and scatters the sheep;
this is because he is only a hired man
and has no concern for the sheep.
I am the good shepherd;
I know my own
and my own know me,
just as the Father knows me
and I know the Father;
and I lay down my life for my sheep.

1434

And there are other sheep I have
that are not of this fold,
and these I have to lead as well.
They too will listen to my voice,
and there will be only one flock,
and one shepherd.'

This is the Gospel of the Lord.

11

Gospel Acclamation   Jn 15:5

Alleluia, alleluia!
I am the vine and you are the branches, says the Lord:
he who lives in me, and I in him, will bear much fruit.
Alleluia!

A reading from the holy Gospel according to John   15:9-17

I shall not call you servants any more, I call you friends.

Jesus said to his disciples:

'As the Father has loved me,
so I have loved you.
Remain in my love.
If you keep my commandments
you will remain in my love,
just as I have kept my Father's commandments
and remain in his love.
I have told you this
so that my own joy may be in you
and your joy be complete.
This is my commandment:
love one another,
as I have loved you.
A man can have no greater love
than to lay down his life for his friends.
You are my friends,
if you do what I command you.
I shall not call you servants any more,
because a servant does not know

1435

his master's business;
I call you friends,
because I have made known to you
everything I have learnt from my Father.
You did not choose me,
no, I chose you;
and I commissioned you
to go out and to bear fruit,
fruit that will last;
and then the Father will give you
anything you ask him in my name.
What I command you
is to love one another.'

This is the Gospel of the Lord.

12

For a pope

Gospel Acclamation   Jn 10:14

Alleluia, alleluia!
I am the good shepherd, says the Lord;
I know my own sheep and my own know me.
Alleluia!

A reading from the holy Gospel according to John   21:15-17

Take care of my lambs and my sheep.

Jesus showed himself to his disciples, and after they had eaten he said
to Simon Peter, 'Simon son of John, do you love me more than these
others do?' He answered, 'Yes Lord, you know I love you.' Jesus said to
him, 'Feed my lambs.' A second time he said to him, 'Simon son of
John, do you love me?' He replied, 'Yes, Lord, you know I love you.'
Jesus said to him, 'Look after my sheep.' Then he said to him a third
time, 'Simon son of John, do you love me?' and he said, 'Lord, you
know everything; you know I love you.' Jesus said to him, 'Feed my
sheep.'

This is the Gospel of the Lord.

COMMON OF DOCTORS OF THE CHURCH

FIRST READING FROM THE OLD TESTAMENT

Outside the Easter Season

1

A reading from the first book of the Kings   3:11-14

I give you a heart wise and shrewd.

The Lord said to Solomon, 'Since you have not asked for long life for yourself or riches or the lives of your enemies, but have asked for a discerning judgement for yourself, here and now I do what you ask. I give you a heart wise and shrewd as none before you has had and none will have after you. What you have not asked I shall give you too: such riches and glory as no other king ever had. And I will give you a long life, if you follow my ways, keeping my laws and commandments, as your father David followed them.'

This is the word of the Lord.

Responsorial Psalm   Ps 36:3-6. 30-31. ℟ v.30

℟   The mouth of the just man murmurs wisdom.

1 If you trust in the Lord and do good,
   then you will live in the land and be secure.
   If you find your delight in the Lord,
   he will grant your heart's desire. ℟

2 Commit your life to the Lord,
   trust in him and he will act,
   so that your justice breaks forth like the light,
   your cause like the noon-day sun. ℟

3 The just man's mouth utters wisdom
   and his lips speak what is right;
   the law of his God is in his heart,
   his steps shall be saved from stumbling. ℟

2

A reading from the book of Wisdom 7:7-10. 15-16

I loved wisdom more than health and beauty.

I prayed, and understanding was given me;
I entreated, and the spirit of Wisdom came to me.
I esteemed her more than sceptres and thrones;
compared with her, I held riches as nothing.
I reckoned no priceless stone to be her peer,
for compared with her, all gold is a pinch of sand,
and beside her silver ranks as mud.
I loved her more than health or beauty,
preferred her to the light,
since her radiance never sleeps.
May God grant me to speak as he would wish
and express thoughts worthy of his gifts,
since he himself is the guide of Wisdom,
since he directs the sages.
We are indeed in his hand, we ourselves and our words,
with all our understanding, too, and technical knowledge.

This is the word of the Lord.

Responsorial Psalm Ps 18:8-11. ℞ v.10

℞ The judgements of the Lord are true, and all of them are just.

1 The law of the Lord is perfect,
  it revives the soul.
  The rule of the Lord is to be trusted,
  it gives wisdom to the simple. ℞

2 The precepts of the Lord are right,
  they gladden the heart.
  The command of the Lord is clear,
  it gives light to the eyes. ℞

3 The fear of the Lord is holy,
  abiding for ever.
  The decrees of the Lord are truth
  and all of them just. ℞

4   They are more to be desired than gold,
      than the purest of gold
      and sweeter are they than honey,
      than honey from the comb. ℟

3

A reading from the book of Ecclesiasticus   15:1-6

He filled him with the spirit of wisdom and understanding.

Whoever fears the Lord will act like this,
and whoever grasps the Law will obtain wisdom.
She will come to meet him like a mother,
and receive him like a virgin bride.
She will give him the bread of understanding to eat
and the water of wisdom to drink.
He will lean on her and will not fall,
he will rely on her and not be put to shame.
She will raise him high above his neighbours,
and in full assembly she will open his mouth.
He will find happiness and a crown of joy,
he will inherit an everlasting name.

    This is the word of the Lord.

Responsorial Psalm   Ps 118:9-14. ℟ v.12

   ℟ Lord, teach me your decrees.

1   How shall the young remain sinless?
     By obeying your word.
     I have sought you with all my heart:
     let me not stray from your commands. ℟

2   I treasure your promise in my heart
     lest I sin against you.
     Blessed are you, O Lord;
     teach me your statutes. ℟

3   With my tongue I have recounted
     the decrees of your lips.
     I rejoiced to do your will
     as though all riches were mine. ℟

4

A reading from the book of Ecclesiasticus   39:6-10

Understanding will fill him up.

If it is the will of the great Lord,
he will be filled with the spirit of understanding,
he will shower forth words of wisdom,
and in prayer give thanks to the Lord.
He will grow upright in purpose and learning,
he will ponder the Lord's hidden mysteries.
He will display the instruction he has received,
taking his pride in the Law of the Lord's covenant.
Many will praise his understanding,
and it will never be forgotten.
His memory will not disappear,
generation after generation his name will live.
Nations will proclaim his wisdom,
the assembly will celebrate his praises.

This is the word of the Lord.

Responsorial Psalm   Ps 36:3-6. 30-31. ℟ v.30

℟ The mouth of the just man murmurs wisdom.

1 If you trust in the Lord and do good,
      then you will live in the land and be secure.
      If you find your delight in the Lord,
      he will grant your heart's desire.   ℟

2 Commit your life to the Lord,
      trust in him and he will act,
      so that your justice breaks forth like the light,
      your cause like the noon-day sun.   ℟

3 The just man's mouth utters wisdom
      and his lips speak what is right;
      the law of his God is in his heart,
      his steps shall be saved from stumbling.   ℟

FIRST READING FROM THE NEW TESTAMENT

In the Easter Season

1

A reading from the Acts of the Apostles   2:14. 22-24. 32-36

God has made him both Lord and Christ.

On Pentecost day Peter stood up with the Eleven and said in a loud voice:

'Men of Israel, listen to what I am going to say: Jesus the Nazarene was a man commended to you by God by the miracles and portents and signs that God worked through him when he was among you, as you all know. This man, who was put into your power by the deliberate intention and foreknowledge of God, you took and had crucified by men outside the Law. You killed him, but God raised him to life, freeing him from the pangs of Hades; for it was impossible for him to be held in its power.

'God raised this man Jesus to life, and all of us are witnesses to that. Now raised to the heights by God's right hand, he has received from the Father the Holy Spirit, who was promised, and what you see and hear is the outpouring of that Spirit. For David himself never went up to heaven; and yet these words are his:

"The Lord said to my Lord:
Sit at my right hand
until I make your enemies
a footstool for you."

'For this reason the whole house of Israel can be certain that God has made this Jesus whom you crucified both Lord and Christ.'

This is the word of the Lord.

Responsorial Psalm   Ps 18:8-11. ℟ Jn 6:63

   ℟   Your words, Lord, are spirit and life.

1   The law of the Lord is perfect,
    it revives the soul.
    The rule of the Lord is to be trusted,
    it gives wisdom to the simple.   ℟

2   The precepts of the Lord are right,
    they gladden the heart.
    The command of the Lord is clear,
    it gives light to the eyes.

    ℟   Your words, Lord, are spirit and life.

3   The fear of the Lord is holy,
    abiding for ever.
    The decrees of the Lord are truth
    and all of them just.   ℟

4   They are more to be desired than gold,
    than the purest of gold
    and sweeter are they than honey,
    than honey from the comb.   ℟

2

A reading from the Acts of the Apostles   13:26-33

God fulfilled the promise by raising Jesus from the dead.

When Paul reached Antioch in Pisidia, he spoke in the synagogue:

'My brothers, sons of Abraham's race, and all you who fear God, this message of salvation is meant for you. What the people of Jerusalem and their rulers did, though they did not realise it, was in fact to fulfil the prophecies read on every sabbath. Though they found nothing to justify his death, they condemned him and asked Pilate to have him executed. When they had carried out everything that scripture foretells about him they took him down from the tree and buried him in a tomb. But God raised him from the dead, and for many days he appeared to those who had accompanied him from Galilee to Jerusalem: and it is these same companions of his who are now his witnesses before our people.

'We have come here to tell you the Good News. It was to our ancestors that God made the promise but it is to us, their children, that he has fulfilled it, by raising Jesus from the dead. As scripture says in the first psalm: You are my son: today I have become your father.'

This is the word of the Lord.

Responsorial Psalm   Ps 36:3-6. 30-31. ℟ v.30

  ℟ The mouth of the just man murmurs wisdom.

1 If you trust in the Lord and do good,
    then you will live in the land and be secure.
    If you find your delight in the Lord,
    he will grant your heart's desire. ℟

2 Commit your life to the Lord,
    trust in him and he will act,
    so that your justice breaks forth like the light,
    your cause like the noon-day sun. ℟

3 The just man's mouth utters wisdom
    and his lips speak what is right;
    the law of his God is in his heart,
    his steps shall be saved from stumbling. ℟

SECOND READING FROM THE NEW TESTAMENT

1

A reading from the first letter of St Paul   1:18-25
to the Corinthians

It has pleased God to save those who have faith through the
foolishness of the message that we preach.

Tha language of the cross may be illogical to those who are not on the
way to salvation, but those of us who are on the way see it as God's
power to save. As scripture says: I shall destroy the wisdom of the wise
and bring to nothing all the learning of the learned. Where are the
philosophers now? Where are the scribes? Where are any of our
thinkers today? Do you see now how God has shown up the foolishness
of human wisdom? If it was God's wisdom that human wisdom should
not know God, it was because God wanted to save those who have
faith through the foolishness of the message that we preach. And so,
while the Jews demand miracles and the Greeks look for wisdom, here
are we preaching a crucified Christ; to the Jews an obstacle that they
cannot get over, to the pagans madness, but to those who have been
called, whether they are Jews or Greeks, a Christ who is the power

and the wisdom of God. For God's foolishness is wiser than human wisdom, and God's weakness is stronger than human strength.

This is the word of the Lord.

2

A reading from the first letter of St Paul 2:1-10
to the Corinthians

We teach the wisdom of God in mystery.

When I came to you, brothers, it was not with any show of oratory or philosophy, but simply to tell you what God had guaranteed. During my stay with you, the only knowledge I claimed to have was about Jesus, and only about him as the crucified Christ. Far from relying on any power of my own, I came among you in great 'fear and trembling' and in my speeches and the sermons that I gave, there were none of the arguments that belong to philosophy; only a demonstration of the power of the Spirit. And I did this so that your faith should not depend on human philosophy but on the power of God.

But still we have a wisdom to offer those who have reached maturity: not a philosophy of our age, it is true, still less of the masters of our age, which are coming to their end. The hidden wisdom of God which we teach in our mysteries is the wisdom that God predestined to be for our glory before the ages began. It is a wisdom that none of the masters of this age have ever known, or they would not have crucified the Lord of Glory; we teach what scripture calls: the things that no eye has seen and no ear has heard, things beyond the mind of man, all that God has prepared for those who love him.

These are the very things that God has revealed to us through the Spirit.

This is the word of the Lord.

3

A reading from the first letter of St Paul 2:10-16
to the Corinthians

We are those who have the mind of Christ.

The Spirit reaches the depths of everything, even of God. After all, the depths of a man can only be known by his own spirit, not by any other man, and in the same way the depths of God can only be known by the

Spirit of God. Now instead of the spirit of the world, we have received the Spirit that comes from God, to teach us to understand the gifts that he has given us. Therefore we teach, not in the way in which philosophy is taught, but in the way that the Spirit teaches us: we teach spiritual things spiritually. An unspiritual person is one who does not accept anything of the Spirit of God: he sees it all as nonsense; it is beyond his understanding because it can only be understood by means of the Spirit. A spiritual man, on the other hand, is able to judge the value of everything, and his own value is not to be judged by other men. As scripture says: Who can know the mind of the Lord, so who can teach him? But we are those who have the mind of Christ.

This is the word of the Lord.

4

A reading from the letter of St Paul 3:8-12
to the Ephesians

The mission is to proclaim to all peoples the infinite treasure of Christ.

I, who am less than the least of all the saints, have been entrusted with this special grace, not only of proclaiming to the pagans the infinite treasure of Christ but also of explaining how the mystery is to be dispensed. Through all the ages, this has been kept hidden in God, the creator of everything. Why? So that the Sovereignties and Powers should learn only now, through the Church, how comprehensive God's wisdom really is, exactly according to the plan which he had had from all eternity in Christ Jesus our Lord. This is why we are bold enough to approach God in complete confidence, through our faith in him.

This is the word of the Lord.

5

A reading from the letter of St Paul 4:1-7. 11-13
to the Ephesians

Our mission is to build up the body of Christ.

I, the prisoner in the Lord, implore you to lead a life worthy of your vocation. Bear with one another charitably, in complete selflessness, gentleness and patience. Do all you can to preserve the unity of the Spirit by the peace that binds you together. There is one Body, one Spirit, just as you were all called into one and the same hope when you were called. There is one Lord, one faith, one baptism, and one God who is Father of all, over all, through all and within all.

Each one of us, however, has been given his own share of grace, given as Christ allotted it. And to some, his gift was that they should be apostles; to some, prophets; to some, evangelists; to some, pastors and teachers; so that the saints together make a unity in the work of service, building up the body of Christ. In this way we are all to come to unity in our faith and in our knowledge of the Son of God, until we become the perfect Man, fully mature with the fullness of Christ himself.

This is the word of the Lord.

6

A reading from the second letter of St Timothy   1:13-14; 2:1-3

You have been trusted to look after something precious; guard it with the help of the Holy Spirit who lives in us.

Keep as your pattern the sound teaching you have heard from me, in the faith and love that are in Christ Jesus. You have been trusted to look after something precious; guard it with the help of the Holy Spirit who lives in us. Accept the strength, my dear son, that comes from the grace of Christ Jesus. You have heard everything that I teach in public; hand it on to reliable people so that they in turn will be able to teach others.

Put up with your share of difficulties, like a good soldier of Christ Jesus.

This is the word of the Lord.

7

A reading from the second letter of St Timothy   4:1-5

Preach the Good News; fulfill your ministry.

Before God and before Christ Jesus who is to be judge of the living and the dead, I put this duty to you, in the name of his Appearing and of his kingdom: proclaim the message and, welcome or unwelcome, insist on it. Refute falsehood, correct error, call to obedience – but do all with patience and with the intention of teaching. The time is sure to come when, far from being content with sound teaching, people will be avid for the latest novelty and collect themselves a whole series of teachers according to their own tastes; and then, instead of listening to the truth, they will turn to myths. Be careful always to choose the right course; be brave under trials; make the preaching of the Good News your life's work, in thoroughgoing service.

This is the word of the Lord.

GOSPEL

1

Gospel Acclamation   Mt 5:16

Alleluia, alleluia!
Let your light shine before all,
that they may see your good works and glorify your Father.
Alleluia!

A reading from the holy Gospel according to Matthew   5:13-16

You are the light of the world.

Jesus said to his disciples: 'You are the salt of the earth. But if salt becomes tasteless, what can make it salty again? It is good for nothing, and can only be thrown out to be trampled underfoot by men.

'You are the light of the world. A city built on a hill-top cannot be hidden. No one lights a lamp to put it under a tub; they put it on the lamp-stand where it shines for everyone in the house. In the same way your light must shine in the sight of men, so that, seeing your good works, they may give the praise to your Father in heaven.'

This is the Gospel of the Lord.

2

Gospel Acclamation   cf. Jn 6:63. 68

Alleluia, alleluia!
Your words, Lord, are spirit and life;
you have the message of eternal life.
Alleluia!

A reading from the holy Gospel according to Matthew   7:21-29

Jesus taught them with authority.

Jesus said to his disciples: 'It is not those who say to me, "Lord, Lord," who will enter the kingdom of heaven, but the person who does the will of my Father in heaven. When the day comes many will say to me, "Lord, Lord, did we not prophesy in your name, cast out demons in your name, work many miracles in your name?" Then I shall tell them to their faces: I have never known you; away from me, you evil men!

'Therefore, everyone who listens to these words of mine and acts on them will be like a sensible man who built his house on rock. Rain came down, floods rose, gales blew and hurled themselves against that house, and it did not fall: it was founded on rock. But everyone who listens to these words of mine and does not act on them will be like a stupid man who built his house on sand. Rain came down, floods rose, gales blew and struck that house, and it fell; and what a fall it had!'

Jesus had now finished what he wanted to say, and his teaching made a deep impression on the people because he taught them with authority, and not like their own scribes.

This is the Gospel of the Lord.

3

Gospel Acclamation   cf. Acts 16:14

Alleluia, alleluia!
Open our hearts, O Lord,
to listen to the words of your Son.
Alleluia!

or   1 Cor 1:18

Alleluia, alleluia!
The message of the cross is folly to those who turn away,
but to those who are saved it is the power of God.
Alleluia!

A reading from the holy Gospel according to Matthew   13:47-52

The new and the old.

Jesus said to the crowds: 'The kingdom of heaven is like a dragnet cast into the sea that brings a haul of all kinds. When it is full, the fishermen haul it ashore; then, sitting down, they collect the good ones in a basket and throw away those that are no use. This is how it will be at the end of time; the angels will appear and separate the wicked from the just to throw them into the blazing furnace where there will be weeping and grinding of teeth.

'Have you understood all this?' They said, 'Yes.' And he said to them, 'Well then, every scribe who becomes a disciple of the kingdom of heaven is like a householder who brings out from his storeroom things both new and old.'

When Jesus had finished these parables he left the district.

This is the Gospel of the Lord.

4

Gospel Acclamation   Mt 23:9-10

Alleluia, alleluia!
You have one Father, your Father in heaven;
you have one teacher: the Lord Jesus Christ!
Alleluia!

A reading from the holy Gospel according to Matthew   23:8-12

You must not allow yourselves to be called teachers, for you have only one teacher, the Christ.

Jesus said to his disciples: 'You must not allow yourselves to be called Rabbi, since you have only one Master, and you are all brothers. You must call no one on earth your father, since you have only one Father, and he is in heaven. Nor must you allow yourselves to be called teachers, for you have only one Teacher, the Christ. The greatest among you must be your servant. Anyone who exalts himself will be humbled, and anyone who humbles himself will be exalted.'

This is the Gospel of the Lord.

5

Gospel Acclamation

> Alleluia, alleluia!
> The seed is the word of God, Christ is the sower;
> all who come to him will live for ever.
> Alleluia!

or   1 Cor 2:7

> Alleluia, alleluia!
> We teach a secret and hidden wisdom of God,
> which he decreed for our glory before time began.
> Alleluia!

A reading from the holy Gospel according to Mark   4:1-10. 13-20

The sower went out to sow seed.

Jesus began to teach by the lakeside, but such a huge crowd gathered round him that he got into a boat on the lake and sat there. The people were all along the shore, at the water's edge. He taught them many things in parables, and in the course of his teaching he said to them, 'Listen! Imagine a sower going out to sow. Now it happened that, as he sowed, some of the seed fell on the edge of the path, and the birds came and ate it up. Some seed fell on rocky ground where it found little soil and sprang up straightaway, because there was no depth of earth; and when the sun came up it was scorched and, not having any roots, it withered away. Some seed fell into thorns, and the thorns grew up and choked it, and it produced no crop. And some seeds fell into rich soil and, growing tall and strong, produced crop; and yielded thirty, sixty, even a hundredfold.' And he said, 'Listen, anyone who has ears to hear!'

When he was alone, the Twelve, together with the others who formed his company, asked what the parables meant.

He said to them, 'Do you not understand this parable? Then how will you understand any of the parables? What the sower is sowing is the word. Those on the edge of the path where the word is sown are people who have no sooner heard it than Satan comes and carries away the word that was sown in them. Similarly, those who receive the seed on patches of rock are people who, when first they hear the word, welcome it at once with joy. But they have no root in them, they do not last; should some trial come, or some persecution on account of the word, they fall away at once. Then there are others who receive the seed in thorns. These have heard the word, but the worries of this world, the lure of riches and all the other passions come in to choke the word, and so it produces nothing. And there are those who have received the seed in rich soil: they hear the word and accept it and yield a harvest, thirty and sixty and a hundredfold.'

This is the Gospel of the Lord.

Shorter form

A reading from the holy Gospel according to Mark   4:1-9

The sower went out to sow seed.

Jesus began to teach by the lakeside, but such a huge crowd gathered round him that he got into a boat on the lake and sat there. The people were all along the shore, at the water's edge. He taught them many things in parables, and in the course of his teaching he said to them, 'Listen! Imagine a sower going out to sow. Now it happened that, as he sowed, some of the seed fell on the edge of the path, and the birds came and ate it up. Some seed fell on rocky ground where it found little soil and sprang up straightaway, because there was no depth of earth; and when the sun came up it was scorched and, not having any roots, it withered away. Some seed fell into thorns, and the thorns grew up and choked it, and it produced no crop. And some seeds fell into rich soil and, growing tall and strong, produced crop; and yielded thirty, sixty, even a hundredfold.'

This is the Gospel of the Lord.

6

Gospel Acclamation   Jn 15:5

Alleluia, alleluia!
I am the vine and you are the branches, says the Lord:
he who lives in me, and I in him, will bear much fruit.
Alleluia!

A reading from the holy Gospel according to Luke   6:43-45

What a person says, comes from what is in the heart.

Jesus said to his disciples: 'There is no sound tree that produces rotten fruit, nor again a rotten tree that produces sound fruit. For every tree can be told by its own fruit: people do not pick figs from thorns, nor gather grapes from brambles. A good man draws what is good from the store of goodness in his heart; a bad man draws what is bad from the store of badness. For a man's words flow out of what fills his heart.'

This is the Gospel of the Lord.

COMMON OF VIRGINS

FIRST READING FROM THE OLD TESTAMENT

Outside the Easter Season

1

A reading from the Song of Songs   8:6-7

Love is as strong as death.

Set me like a seal on your heart,
like a seal on your arm.
For love is strong as Death,
jealousy relentless as Sheol.
The flash of it is a flash of fire,
a flame of the Lord himself.
Love no flood can quench,
no torrents drown.

Were a man to offer all the wealth of his house to buy love,
contempt is all he would purchase.

This is the word of the Lord.

Responsorial Psalm   Ps 148:1-2. 11-14. ℟ cf. vv.12. 13

℟   Alleluia!

or

℟   Young men and women, praise the name of the Lord.

1   Praise the Lord from the heavens,
    praise him in the heights.
    Praise him, all his angels,
    praise him, all his host.   ℟

2   All earth's kings and peoples,
    earth's princes and rulers;
    young men and maidens,
    old men together with children.   ℟

3   Let them praise the name of the Lord
    for he alone is exalted.   (continued)

The splendour of his name
reaches beyond heaven and earth.

℟   Alleluia!

or

℟   Young men and women, praise the name of the Lord.

4   He exalts the strength of his people.
He is the praise of all his saints,
of the sons of Israel,
of the people to whom he comes close.   ℟

2

A reading from the prophet Hosea   2:16-17. 21-22

I will betroth you to myself for ever.

The Lord says this:

I am going to lead her out into the wilderness
and speak to her heart.
There she will respond to me as she did when she was young,
as she did when she came out of the land of Egypt.
I will betroth you to myself for ever,
betroth you with integrity and justice,
with tenderness and love;
I will betroth you to myself with faithfulness,
and you will come to know the Lord.

This is the word of the Lord.

Responsorial Psalm   Ps 44:11-12. 14-17. ℟ v.11. Alt. ℟ Mt 25:6

℟   Listen to me, daughter; see and bend your ear.

or

℟   The bridegroom is here; let us go out to meet Christ the Lord.

1   Listen, O daughter, give ear to my words:
forget your own people and your father's house.
So will the king desire your beauty:
He is your lord, pay homage to him.   ℟

2 The daughter of the king is clothed with splendour,
 her robes embroidered with pearls set in gold.
 She is led to the king with her maiden companions. ℟

3 They are escorted amid gladness and joy;
 they pass within the palace of the king.
 Sons shall be yours in place of your fathers:
 you will make them princes over all the earth. ℟

FIRST READING FROM THE NEW TESTAMENT

In the Easter Season

1

A reading from the book of the Apocalypse   19:1. 5-9

Happy are those who are invited to the wedding feast of the Lamb.

I, John, seemed to hear the great sound of a huge crowd in heaven, singing, 'Alleluia! Victory and glory and power to our God!'

Then a voice came from the throne; it said, 'Praise our God, you servants of his and all who, great or small, revere him.' And I seemed to hear the voices of a huge crowd, like the sound of the ocean or the great roar of thunder, answering, 'Alleluia! The reign of the Lord our God Almighty has begun; let us be glad and joyful and give praise to God, because this is the time for the marriage of the Lamb. His bride is ready, and she has been able to dress herself in dazzling white linen, because her linen is made of the good deeds of the saints.' The angel said, 'Write this: Happy are those who are invited to the wedding feast of the Lamb.'

This is the word of the Lord.

Responsorial Psalm   Ps 148:1-2. 11-14. ℟ cf. vv.12. 13

   ℟   Alleluia!

or

   ℟   Young men and women, praise the name of the Lord.

1 Praise the Lord from the heavens,
 praise him in the heights.
 Praise him, all his angels,
 praise him, all his host. ℟

2   All earth's kings and peoples,
    earth's princes and rulers;
    young men and maidens,
    old men together with children.

    ℟   Alleluia!

or

    ℟   Young men and women, praise the name of the Lord.

3   Let them praise the name of the Lord
    for he alone is exalted.
    The splendour of his name
    reaches beyond heaven and earth.   ℟

4   He exalts the strength of his people.
    He is the praise of all his saints,
    of the sons of Israel,
    of the people to whom he comes close.   ℟

2

A reading from the book of the Apocalypse   21:1-5

I saw the new Jerusalem, as beautiful as a bride all dressed for her husband.

I, John, saw a new heaven and a new earth; the first heaven and the first earth had disappeared now, and there was no longer any sea. I saw the holy city, and the new Jerusalem, coming down from God out of heaven, as beautiful as a bride all dressed for her husband. Then I heard a loud voice call from the throne, 'You see this city? Here God lives among men. He will make his home among them; they shall be his people, and he will be their God; his name is God-with-them. He will wipe away all tears from their eyes; there will be no more death, and no more mourning or sadness. The world of the past has gone.'

Then the One sitting on the throne spoke: 'Now I am making the whole of creation new.'

This is the word of the Lord.

Responsorial Psalm   Ps 44:11-12. 14-17. ℞ v.11. Alt. ℞ Mt 25:6

℞   Listen to me, daughter; see and bend your ear.

or

℞   The bridegroom is here; let us go out to meet Christ the Lord.

1   Listen, O daughter, give ear to my words:
    forget your own people and your father's house.
    So will the king desire your beauty:
    He is your lord, pay homage to him. ℞

2   The daughter of the king is clothed with splendour,
    her robes embroidered with pearls set in gold.
    She is led to the king with her maiden companions. ℞

3   They are escorted amid gladness and joy;
    they pass within the palace of the king.
    Sons shall be yours in place of your fathers:
    you will make them princes over all the earth. ℞

SECOND READING FROM THE NEW TESTAMENT

1

A reading from the first letter of St Paul   7:25-35
to the Corinthians

A virgin can devote herself to the work of the Lord.

About remaining celibate, I have no directions from the Lord but give my own opinion as one who, by the Lord's mercy, has stayed faithful. Well then, I believe that in these present times of stress this is right: that it is good for a man to stay as he is. If you are tied to a wife, do not look for freedom; if you are free of a wife, then do not look for one. But if you marry, it is no sin, and it is not a sin for a young girl to get married. They will have their troubles, though, in their married life, and I should like to spare you that.

Brothers, this is what I mean: our time is growing short. Those who have wives should live as though they had none, and those who mourn should live as though they had nothing to mourn for; those who are enjoying life should live as though there were nothing to laugh about; those whose life is buying things should live as though they had nothing of their own; and those who have to deal with the world should not become engrossed in it. I say this because the world as we know it is passing away.

I would like to see you free from all worry. An unmarried man can devote himself to the Lord's affairs, all he need worry about is pleasing the Lord; but a married man has to bother about the world's affairs and devote himself to pleasing his wife: he is torn two ways. In the same way an unmarried woman, like a young girl, can devote herself to the Lord's affairs; all she need worry about is being holy in body and spirit. The married woman, on the other hand, has to worry about the world's affairs and devote herself to pleasing her husband. I say this only to help you, not to put a halter round your necks, but simply to make sure that everything is as it should be, and that you give your undivided attention to the Lord.

This is the word of the Lord.

2

A reading from the second letter of St Paul to the Corinthians   10:17–11:2

I have betrothed you to one man, as a chaste virgin for Christ.

If anyone wants to boast, let him boast of the Lord. It is not the man who commends himself that can be accepted, but the man who is commended by the Lord.

I only wish you were able to tolerate a little foolishness from me. But of course: you are tolerant towards me. You see, the jealousy that I feel for you is God's own jealousy: I arranged for you to marry Christ so that I might give you away as a chaste virgin to this one husband.

This is the word of the Lord.

GOSPEL

1

Gospel Acclamation

> Alleluia, alleluia!
> Come, bride of Christ, and receive the crown,
> which the Lord has prepared for you for ever.
> Alleluia!

A reading from the holy Gospel according to Matthew   19:3-12

*There are some who have chosen to remain single
for the sake of the kingdom of God.*

Some Pharisees approached Jesus, and to test him they said, 'Is it against the Law for a man to divorce his wife on any pretext whatever?' He answered, 'Have you not read that the creator from the beginning made them male and female and that he said: This is why a man must leave father and mother, and cling to his wife, and the two become one body. They are no longer two, therefore, but one body. So then, what God has united, man must not divide.'

They said to him, 'Then why did Moses command that a writ of dismissal should be given in cases of divorce?' 'It was because you were so unteachable,' he said, 'that Moses allowed you to divorce your wives, but it was not like this from the beginning. Now I say this to you: the man who divorces his wife – I am not speaking of fornication – and marries another, is guilty of adultery.'

The disciples said to him, 'If that is how things are between husband and wife, it is not advisable to marry.' But he replied, 'It is not everyone who can accept what I have said, but only those to whom it is granted. There are eunuchs born that way from their mother's womb, there are eunuchs made so by men and there are eunuchs who have made themselves that way for the sake of the kingdom of heaven. Let anyone accept this who can.'

This is the Gospel of the Lord.

2

Gospel Acclamation

A¹leluia, alleluia!
This is the wise bridesmaid, whom the Lord found waiting;
at his coming, she went in with him to the wedding feast.
Alleluia!

A reading from the holy Gospel according to Matthew   25:1-13

The bridegroom is here; go out and meet him.

Jesus spoke this parable to his disciples: 'The kingdom of heaven will be like this: Ten bridesmaids took their lamps and went to meet the bridegroom. Five of them were foolish and five were sensible: the foolish ones did take their lamps, but they brought no oil, whereas the sensible ones took flasks of oil as well as their lamps. The bridegroom was late, and they all grew drowsy and fell asleep. But at midnight there was a cry, "The bridegroom is here! Go out and meet him." At this, all those bridesmaids woke up and trimmed their lamps, and the foolish ones said to the sensible ones, "Give us some of your oil: our lamps are going out." But they replied, "There may not be enough for us and for you; you had better go to those who sell it and buy some for yourselves." They had gone off to buy it when the bridegroom arrived. Those who were ready went in with him to the wedding hall and the door was closed. The other bridesmaids arrived later. "Lord, Lord," they said, "open the door for us." But he replied, "I tell you solemnly, I do not know you." So stay awake, because you do not know either the day or the hour.'

This is the Gospel of the Lord.

3

Gospel Acclamation

Alleluia, alleluia!
All who love me will keep my words,
and my Father will love them, and we will come to him.
Alleluia!

A reading from the holy Gospel according to Luke   10:38-42

Martha took up the duties in the house. Mary chose the better part.

Jesus came to a village, and a woman named Martha welcomed him into her house. She had a sister called Mary, who sat down at the Lord's feet and listened to him speaking. Now Martha who was distracted with all the serving said, 'Lord, do you not care that my sister is leaving me to do the serving all by myself? Please tell her to help me.' But the Lord answered: 'Martha, Martha,' he said, 'you worry and fret about so many things, and yet few are needed, indeed only one. It is Mary who has chosen the better part; it is not to be taken from her.'

This is the Gospel of the Lord.

COMMON OF HOLY MEN AND WOMEN

FIRST READING FROM THE OLD TESTAMENT

Outside the Easter Season

1

A reading from the book of Genesis   12:1-4

Leave your country, your family, and come.

The Lord said to Abram, 'Leave your country, your family and your
father's house, for the land I will show you. I will make you a great
nation; I will bless you and make your name so famous that it will be
used as a blessing.

> 'I will bless those who bless you:
> I will curse those who slight you.
> All the tribes of the earth
> shall bless themselves by you.'

So Abram went as the Lord told him.

This is the word of the Lord.

Responsorial Psalm   Ps 15:1-2. 5. 7-8. 11. ℟ cf. v.5

℟   You are my inheritance, O Lord.

1   Preserve me, God, I take refuge in you.
    I say to the Lord: 'You are my God.'
    O Lord, it is you who are my portion and cup;
    it is you yourself who are my prize.   ℟

2   I will bless the Lord who gives me counsel,
    who even at night directs my heart.
    I keep the Lord ever in my sight:
    since he is at my right hand, I shall stand firm.   ℟

3   You will show me the path of life,
    the fullness of joy in your presence,
    at your right hand happiness for ever.   ℟

2

A reading from the book of Leviticus 19:1-2. 17-18

Love your neighbour as you love yourself.

The Lord spoke to Moses; he said:

'Speak to the whole community of the sons of Israel and say to them: "Be holy, for I, the Lord your God, am holy. You must not bear hatred for your brother in your heart. You must openly tell him, your neighbour, of his offence; this way you will not take a sin upon yourself. You must not exact vengeance, nor must you bear a grudge against the children of your people. You must love your neighbour as yourself. I am the Lord. You must keep my laws." '

This is the word of the Lord.

Responsorial Psalm Ps 14:2-5. ℟ v.1

℟ The just shall live on your holy mountain, O Lord.

1 Lord, who shall dwell on your holy mountain?
 He who walks without fault;
 he who acts with justice
 and speaks the truth from his heart;
 he who does not slander with his tongue. ℟

2 He who does no wrong to his brother,
 who casts no slur on his neighbour,
 who holds the godless in disdain,
 but honours those who fear the Lord. ℟

3 He who takes no interest on a loan
 and accepts no bribes against the innocent,
 such a man will stand firm for ever. ℟

3

A reading from the book of Deuteronomy 6:3-9

Love the Lord your God with your whole heart.

Moses said to the people: 'Listen, Israel, keep and observe what will make you prosper and give you great increase, as the Lord, the God of your fathers has promised you, giving you a land where milk and honey flow.

'Listen, Israel: the Lord our God is the one Lord. You shall love the

Lord your God with all your heart, with all your soul, with all your strength. Let these words I urge on you today be written on your heart. You shall repeat them to your children and say them over to them whether at rest in your house or walking abroad, at your lying down or at your rising; you shall fasten them on your hand as a sign and on your forehead as a circlet; you shall write them on the doorposts of your house and on your gates.'

This is the word of the Lord.

Responsorial Psalm   Ps 111:1-9. ℟ v.1

℟   Happy are those who fear the Lord.

or

℟   Alleluia!

1   Happy the man who fears the Lord;
    who takes delight in his commands.
    His sons will be powerful on earth;
    the children of the upright are blessed.   ℟

2   Riches and wealth are in his house;
    his justice stands firm for ever.
    He is a light in the darkness for the upright:
    he is generous, merciful and just.   ℟

3   The good man takes pity and lends,
    he conducts his affairs with honour.
    The just man will never waver:
    he will be remembered for ever.   ℟

4   He has no fear of evil news;
    with a firm heart he trusts in the Lord.
    With a steadfast heart he will not fear;
    he will see the downfall of his foes.   ℟

5   Open-handed, he gives to the poor;
    his justice stands firm for ever.
    His head will be raised in glory.   ℟

4

For religious

A reading from the book of Deuteronomy   10:8-9

The Lord is your inheritance.

Moses said to the people:

'The Lord set apart the tribe of Levi to carry the ark of the Lord's covenant, to stand in the presence of the Lord, to do him service and in his name to pronounce blessing as they still do today. Levi therefore had no share or inheritance with his brothers: the Lord is his inheritance, as the Lord your God told him.'

This is the word of the Lord.

Responsorial Psalm   Ps 15:1-2. 5. 7-8. 11. ℟ cf. v.5

℟ You are my inheritance, O Lord.

1 Preserve me, God, I take refuge in you.
I say to the Lord: 'You are my God.'
O Lord, it is you who are my portion and cup;
it is you yourself who are my prize.   ℟

2 I will bless the Lord who gives me counsel,
who even at night directs my heart.
I keep the Lord ever in my sight:
since he is at my right hand, I shall stand firm.   ℟

3 You will show me the path of life,
the fullness of joy in your presence,
at your right hand happiness for ever.   ℟

5

For religious

A reading from the first book of the Kings   19:4-9. 11-15

Go out and stand on the mountain-top in the presence of your God.

Elijah went on into the wilderness, a day's journey, and sitting under a furze bush wished he were dead. 'Lord' he said, 'I have had enough. Take my life; I am no better than my ancestors.' Then he lay down and went to sleep. But an angel touched him and said, 'Get up and eat.' He looked round, and there at his head was a scone baked on hot stones, and a jar of water. He ate and drank and then lay down again. But the angel of the Lord came back a second time and touched him and said, 'Get up and eat, or the journey will be too long for you.' So he got up and ate and drank, and strengthened by that food he walked for forty days and forty nights until he reached Horeb, the mountain of God. There he went into the cave and spent the night in it.

Then he was told, 'Go out and stand on the mountain before the Lord.' Then the Lord himself went by. There came a mighty wind, so strong it tore the mountains and shattered the rocks before the Lord. But the Lord was not in the wind. After the wind came an earthquake. But the Lord was not in the earthquake. After the earthquake came a fire. But the Lord was not in the fire. And after the fire came the sound of a gentle breeze. And when Elijah heard this, he covered his face with his cloak and went out and stood at the entrance of the cave. Then a voice came to him, which said, 'What are you doing here, Elijah?' He replied, 'I am filled with jealous zeal for the Lord of hosts, because the sons of Israel have deserted you, broken down your altars and put your prophets to the sword. I am the only one left and they want to kill me.'

'Go,' the Lord said, 'go back by the same way to the wilderness of Damascus.'

This is the word of the Lord.

Responsorial Psalm   Ps 14:2-5. ℟ v.1

℟ The just shall live on your holy mountain, O Lord.

1 Lord, who shall dwell on your holy mountain?
 He who walks without fault;
 he who acts with justice
 and speaks the truth from his heart;
 he who does not slander with his tongue. ℟

2 He who does no wrong to his brother,
 who casts no slur on his neighbour,
 who holds the godless in disdain,
 but honours those who fear the Lord.

3 He who takes no interest on a loan
 and accepts no bribes against the innocent,
 such a man will stand firm for ever. ℟

6

For religious

A reading from the first book of the Kings   19:16. 19-21

Elisha rose up and followed Elijah.

The Lord said to Elijah: 'You are to anoint Elisha son of Shaphat, of Abel Meholah, as prophet to succeed you.'

Leaving Horeb, he came on Elisha son of Shaphat as he was ploughing behind twelve yoke of oxen, he himelf being with the twelfth. Elijah passed near to him, and threw his cloak over him. Elisha left his oxen and ran after Elijah. 'Let me kiss my father and mother, then I will follow you,' he said. Elijah answered, 'Go, go back; for have I done anything to you?' Elisha turned away, took the pair of oxen and slaughtered them. He used the plough for cooking the oxen, then gave to his men, who ate. He then rose, and followed Elijah and became his servant.

This is the word of the Lord.

Responsorial Psalm   Ps 15:1-2. 7-8. 11. ℟ v.5

℟ You are my inheritance, O Lord.

1 Preserve me, God, I take refuge in you.
   I say to the Lord: 'You are my God.'
   O Lord, it is you who are my portion and cup;
   it is you yourself who are my prize. ℟

2 I will bless the Lord who gives me counsel,
   who even at night directs my heart.
   I keep the Lord ever in my sight:
   since he is at my right hand, I shall stand firm. ℟

3 You will show me the path of life,
   the fullness of joy in your presence,
   at your right hand happiness for ever. ℟

7

A reading from the book of Tobit   8:4-8

Bring us to old age together.

On the evening of their marriage, Tobias said to Sarah, 'Get up, my sister! You and I must pray and petition our Lord to win his grace and his protection.' She stood up and they began praying for protection, and this was how he began:

> 'You are blessed, O God of our fathers;
> blessed, too, is your name
> for ever and ever.
> Let the heavens bless you
> and all things you have made
> for evermore.
> It was you who created Adam,
> you who created Eve his wife
> to be his help and support;
> and from these two the human race was born.
> It was you who said,
> "It is not good that the man should be alone;
> let us make him a helpmate like himself."
> And so I do not take my sister
> for any lustful motive;
> I do it in singleness of heart.
> Be kind enough to have pity on her and on me
> and bring us to old age together.'

And together they said, 'Amen, Amen.'

This is the word of the Lord.

Responsorial Psalm   Ps 127:1-5. v.1

℟ Happy are those who fear the Lord.

1 O blessed are those who fear the Lord
   and walk in his ways!
   By the labour of your hands you shall eat.
   You will be happy and propser. ℟

2 Your wife will be like a fruitful vine
   in the heart of your house;

your children like shoots of the olive,
around your table. ℟

3 Indeed thus shall be blessed
the man who fears the Lord.
May the Lord bless you from Zion
all the days of your life! ℟

8

For those who work for the underprivileged

A reading from the book of Tobit   12:6-13

It is good to pray while fasting and giving alms.

Raphael took Tobit and his son Tobias aside and said, 'Bless God,
utter his praise before all the living for all the favours he has given
you. Bless and extol his name. Proclaim before all men the deeds of
God as they deserve, and never tire of giving him thanks. It is right to
keep the secret of a king, yet right to reveal and publish the works of
God. Thank him worthily. Do what is good, and no evil can befall you.

'Prayer with fasting and alms with right conduct are better than
riches with iniquity. Better to practise almsgiving than to hoard up
gold. Almsgiving saves from death and purges every kind of sin.
Those who give alms have their fill of days; those who commit sin and
do evil, bring harm on themselves.

'I am going to tell you the whole truth, hiding nothing from you. I
have already told you that it is right to keep the secret of a king, yet
right too to reveal in worthy fashion the works of God. So you must
know that when you and Sarah were at prayer, it was I who offered
your supplications before the glory of the Lord and who read them; so
too when you were burying the dead. When you did not hesitate to get
up and leave the table to go and bury a dead man, I was sent to test
your faith.'

This is the word of the Lord.

Responsorial Psalm   Ps 102:1-4. 8-9. 13-14. 17-18. ℟ v.1

℟ O bless the Lord, my soul.

1 My soul, give thanks to the Lord,
all my being, bless his holy name.
My soul, give thanks to the Lord
and never forget all his blessings. ℟

2 It is he who forgives all your guilt,
   who heals every one of your ills,
   who redeems your life from the grave,
   who crowns you with love and compassion.

   ℟ O bless the Lord, my soul.

3 The Lord is compassion and love,
   slow to anger and rich in mercy.
   His wrath will come to an end;
   he will not be angry for ever. ℟

4 As a father has compassion on his sons,
   the Lord has pity on those who fear him;
   for he knows of what we are made,
   he remembers that we are dust. ℟

5 But the love of the Lord is everlasting
   upon those who hold him in fear;
   his justice reaches out to children's children
   when they keep his covenant in truth. ℟

9

For widows

A reading from the book of Judith   8:2-8

She feared the Lord greatly.

Judith's husband Manasseh, of her own tribe and family, had died at the time of barley harvest. He was supervising the men as they bound up the sheaves in the field when he caught sunstroke and had to take to his bed. He died in Bethulia, his home town, and was buried with his ancestors in the field that lies between Dothan and Balamon. As a widow, Judith stayed inside her home for three years and four months. She had had an upper room built for herself on the roof. She wore sackcloth round her waist and dressed in widow's weeds. She fasted every day of her widowhood except for the sabbath eve, the sabbath itself, the eve of New Moon, the feast of New Moon and the festival of days of the House of Israel. Now, she was very beautiful, charming to see. Her husband Manasseh had left her gold and silver, manservants and maidservants, cattle and lands; and she lived among all her possessions without anyone finding a word to say against her, so devoutly did she fear God.

This is the word of the Lord.

Responsorial Psalm   Ps 130

℟   In you, Lord, I have found my peace.

1   O Lord, my heart is not proud
     nor haughty my eyes.
     I have not gone after things too great
     nor marvels beyond me. ℟

2   Truly I have set my soul
     in silence and peace.
     A weaned child on its mother's breast,
     even so is my soul. ℟

3   O Israel, hope in the Lord
     both now and for ever. ℟

10

A reading from the book of Esther   13:8-14. 17

Human glory is not above the glory of God.

Calling to mind all the wonderful works of the Lord, Mordecai offered
this prayer:

   'Lord, Lord, King and Master of all things,
   everything is subject to your power,
   and there is no one who can withstand you
   in your will to save Israel.

   'Yes, you have made heaven and earth,
   and all the marvels that are under heaven.
   You are the Lord of all,
   and there is none who can resist you, Lord.

   'You know all things;
   you know, Lord, you know,
   that no insolence, arrogance, vainglory
   prompted me to this,
   to this refusal to bow down
   before proud Haman.

   'I would readily have kissed his feet
   . for the safety of Israel.

'But what I did, I did
rather than place the glory of a man
above the glory of God;
and I will not bow down to any
but to you, Lord;
in so refusing I will not act in pride.
Hear my supplication,
have mercy on your heritage,
and turn our grief into rejoicing,
that we may live to hymn your name, Lord.
Do not suffer the mouths
of those who praise you to perish.'

This is the word of the Lord.

Responsorial Psalm   Ps 33:2-11. ℟ v.2

℟ I will bless the Lord at all times.

1 I will bless the Lord at all times,
   his praise always on my lips;
   in the Lord my soul shall make its boast.
   The humble shall hear and be glad. ℟

2 Glorify the Lord with me,
   together let us praise his name.
   I sought the Lord and he answered me;
   from all my terrors he set me free. ℟

3 Look towards him and be radiant;
   let your faces not be abashed.
   This poor man called; the Lord heard him
   and rescued him from all his distress. ℟

4 The angel of the Lord is encamped
   around those who revere him, to rescue them.
   Taste and see that the Lord is good.
   He is happy who seeks refuge in him. ℟

5 Revere the Lord, you his saints.
   They lack nothing, those who revere him.
   Strong lions suffer want and go hungry
   but those who seek the Lord lack no blessing. ℟

11

A reading from the book of Proverbs   31:10-13. 19-20. 30-31

It is the wise woman whom the Lord will praise.

A perfect wife – who can find her?
She is far beyond the price of pearls.

Her husband's heart has confidence in her,
from her he will derive no little profit.

Advantage and not hurt she brings him
all the days of her life.

She is always busy with wool and with flax,
she does her work with eager hands.

She sets her hands to the distaff,
her fingers grasp the spindle.

She holds out her hand to the poor,
she opens her arms to the needy.

Charm is deceitful, and beauty empty;
the woman who is wise is the one to praise.

Give her a share in what her hands have worked for,
and let her works tell her praises at the city gates.

This is the word of the Lord.

Responsorial Psalm   Ps 130

℟   In you, Lord, I have found my peace.

1   O Lord, my heart is not proud
     nor haughty my eyes.
     I have not gone after things too great
     nor marvels beyond me. ℟

2   Truly I have set my soul
     in silence and peace.
     A weaned child on its mother's breast,
     even so is my soul. ℟

3   O Israel, hope in the Lord
     both now and for ever. ℟

12

A reading from the book of Ecclesiasticus   2:7-13

You who fear the Lord, believe him, hope in him, love him.

You who fear the Lord, wait for his mercy;
do not turn aside in case you fall.
You who fear the Lord, trust him,
and you will not be baulked of your reward.
You who fear the Lord hope for good things,
for everlasting happiness and mercy.
Look at the generations of old and see:
who ever trusted in the Lord and was put to shame?

Or who ever feared him steadfastly and was left forsaken?
Or who ever called out to him, and was ignored?
For the Lord is compassionate and merciful,
he forgives sins, and saves in days of distress.

This is the word of the Lord.

Responsorial Psalm   Ps 111:1-9. ℟ v.1

℟   Happy are those who fear the Lord.

or

℟   Alleluia!

1   Happy the man who fears the Lord,
who takes delight in his commands.
His sons will be powerful on earth;
the children of the upright are blessed. ℟

2   Riches and wealth are in his house;
his justice stands firm for ever.
He is a light in the darkness for the upright:
he is generous, merciful and just. ℟

3   The good man takes pity and lends,
he conducts his affairs with honour.
The just man will never waver:
he will be remembered for ever. ℟

4   He has no fear of evil news;
with a firm heart he trusts in the Lord.

With a steadfast heart he will not fear;
he will see the downfall of his foes. ℟

5   Open-handed, he gives to the poor;
his justice stands firm for ever.
His head will be raised in glory. ℟

13

A reading from the book of Ecclesiasticus   3:17-24

Humble yourselves and you will find grace in the eyes of God.

My son, be gentle in carrying out your business,
and you will be better loved than a lavish giver.
The greater you are, the more you should behave humbly,
and then you will find favour with the Lord;
for great though the power of the Lord is,
he accepts the homage of the humble.
Do not try to understand things that are too difficult for you,
or try to discover what is beyond your powers.
Concentrate on what has been assigned you,
you have no need to worry over mysteries.
Do not meddle with matters that are beyond you;
what you have been taught already exceeds the scope of the human
    mind.
For many have been misled by their own presumption,
and wrong-headed opinions have warped their ideas.

This is the word of the Lord.

Responsorial Psalm   Ps 130

℟   In you, Lord, I have found my peace.

1   O Lord, my heart is not proud
nor haughty my eyes.
I have not gone after things too great
nor marvels beyond me. ℟

2   Truly I have set my soul
in silence and peace.
A weaned child on its mother's breast,
even so is my soul. ℟

(continued)

3   O Israel, hope in the Lord
    both now and for ever.

R̹   In you, Lord, I have found my peace.

14

A reading from the book of Ecclesiasticus   26:1-4. 13-16

The beauty of a good wife in a well-kept house is like the beauty of the rising sun.

Happy the husband of a really good wife;
the number of his days will be doubled.
A perfect wife is the joy of her husband,
he will live out the years of his life in peace.
A good wife is the best of portions,
reserved for those who fear the Lord;
rich or poor, they will be glad of heart,
cheerful of face, whatever the season.
The grace of a wife will charm her husband,
her accomplishments will make him the stronger.
A silent wife is a gift from the Lord,
no price can be put on a well-trained character.
A modest wife is a boon twice over,
a chaste character cannot be weighed on scales.
Like the sun rising over the mountains of the Lord
is the beauty of a good wife in a well-kept house.

    This is the word of the Lord.

Responsorial Psalm   Ps 127. R̹ v.1

    R̹   Happy are those who fear the Lord.

1   O blessed are those who fear the Lord
    and walk in his ways!
    By the labour of your hands you shall eat.
    You will be happy and prosper.   R̹

2   Your wife will be like a fruitful vine
    in the heart of your house;
    your children like shoots of the olive,
    around your table.   R̹

3 Indeed thus shall be blessed `
  the man who fears the Lord.
  May the Lord bless you from Zion
  all the days of your life! ℟

15

For those who work for the underprivileged

A reading from the prophet Isaiah   58:6-11

Share your bread with the hungry.

Is not this the sort of fast that pleases me
– it is the Lord who speaks –
to break unjust fetters
and undo the thongs of the yoke,

to let the oppressed go free,
and break every yoke,
to share your bread with the hungry,
and shelter the homeless poor,

to clothe the man you see to be naked
and not turn from your own kin?
Then will your light shine like the dawn
and your wound be quickly healed over.

Your integrity will go before you
and the glory of the Lord behind you.
Cry, and the Lord will answer;
call, and he will say, 'I am here.'

If you do away with the yoke,
the clenched fist, the wicked word,
if you give your bread to the hungry,
and relief to the oppressed,

your light will rise in the darkness,
and your shadows become like noon.
The Lord will always guide you,
giving you relief in desert places.

He will give strength to your bones
and you shall be like a watered garden,
like a spring of water
whose waters never run dry.

    This is the word of the Lord.

Responsorial Psalm   Ps 111:1-9. ℟ v.1

℟   Happy are those who fear the Lord.

or

℟   Alleluia!

1   Happy the man who fears the Lord,
     who takes delight in his commands.
     His sons will be powerful on earth;
     the children of the upright are blessed.   ℟

2   Riches and wealth are in his house;
     his justice stands firm for ever.
     He is a light in the darkness for the upright:
     he is generous, merciful and just.   ℟

3   The good man takes pity and lends,
     he conducts his affairs with honour.
     The just man will never waver:
     he will be remembered for ever.   ℟

4   He has no fear of evil news;
     with a firm heart he trusts in the Lord.
     With a steadfast heart he will not fear;
     he will see the downfall of his foes.   ℟

5   Open-handed, he gives to the poor;
     his justice stands firm for ever.
     His head will be raised in glory.   ℟

16

A reading from the prophet Jeremiah   20:7-9

*The desire to speak the word of the Lord seemed to be like a fire
burning in my heart.*

You have seduced me, Lord, and I have let myself be seduced;
you have overpowered me: you were the stronger.
I am a daily laughing-stock,
everybody's butt.
Each time I speak the word, I have to howl
and proclaim: 'Violence and ruin!'
The word of the Lord has meant for me

insult, derision, all day long.
I used to say, 'I will not think about him,
I will not speak in his name any more.'
Then there seemed to be a fire burning in my heart,
imprisoned in my bones.
The effort to restrain it wearied me,
I could not bear it.

This is the word of the Lord.

Responsorial Psalm   Ps 15:1-2. 5. 7-8. 11. ℟ v.5

℟   You are my inheritance, O Lord.

1   Preserve me, God, I take refuge in you.
I say to the Lord: 'You are my God.
O Lord, it is you who are my portion and cup;
it is you yourself who are my prize.'   ℟

2   I will bless the Lord who gives me counsel,
who even at night directs my heart.
I keep the Lord ever in my sight:
since he is at my right hand, I shall stand firm.   ℟

3   You will show me the path of life,
the fullness of joy in your presence,
at your right hand happiness for ever.   ℟

17

A reading from the prophet Micah   6:6-8

People, what is good has been explained to you; this is what the Lord
God asks of you.

– 'With what gift shall I come into the Lord's presence
and bow down before God on high?

Shall I come with holocausts,
with calves one year old?
Will he be pleased with rams by the thousand,
with libations of oil in torrents?
Must I give my first-born for what I have done wrong,
the fruit of my body for my own sin?'
– 'What is good has been explained to you, man;
this is what the Lord asks of you:

only this, to act justly,
to love tenderly
and to walk humbly with your God.'

This is the word of the Lord.

Responsorial Psalm   Ps 1:1-4. 6. ℟ v.2. Alt. ℟ Ps 39:5. Alt. ℟ Ps 91:13-14

     ℟   Happy are they who delight in the law of the Lord.

or

     ℟   Happy are they who hope in the Lord.

or

     ℟   The just will flourish like the palm tree in the garden of the
Lord.

1   Happy indeed is the man
who follows not the counsel of the wicked;
nor lingers in the way of sinners
nor sits in the company of scorners,
but whose delight is the law of the Lord
and who ponders his law day and night.   ℟

2   He is like a tree that is planted
beside the flowing waters,
that yields its fruit in due season
and whose leaves shall never fade;
and all that he does shall prosper.   ℟

3   Not so are the wicked, not so!
For they like winnowed chaff
shall be driven away by the wind;
for the Lord guards the way of the just
but the way of the wicked leads to doom.   ℟

18

A reading from the prophet Zephaniah   2:3; 3:12-13

I will leave in your midst a people humble and lowly.

Seek the Lord,
all you, the humble of the earth,
who obey his commands.

Seek integrity,
seek humility:
you may perhaps find shelter
on the day of the anger of the Lord.
In your midst I will leave
a humble and lowly people,
and those who are left in Israel will seek refuge in the name of the
    Lord.
They will do no wrong,
will tell no lies;
and the perjured tongue will no longer
be found in their mouths.
But they will be able to graze and rest
with no one to disturb them.

This is the word of the Lord.

Responsial Psalm   Ps 33:2-9. ℟ v.9

℟   Taste and see the goodness of the Lord.

1   I will bless the Lord at all times,
    his praise always on my lips;
    in the Lord my soul shall make its boast.
    The humble shall hear and be glad.   ℟

2   Glorify the Lord with me.
    Together let us praise his name.
    I sought the Lord and he answered me;
    from all my terrors he set me free.   ℟

3   Look towards him and be radiant;
    let your faces not be abashed.
    This poor man called; the Lord heard him
    and rescued him from all his distress.   ℟

4   The angel of the Lord is encamped
    around those who revere him, to rescue them.
    Taste and see that the Lord is good.
    He is happy who seeks refuge in him.   ℟

5   Revere the Lord, you his saints.
    They lack nothing, those who revere him.
    Strong lions suffer want and go hungry
    but those who seek the Lord lack no blessing.   ℟

FIRST READING FROM THE NEW TESTAMENT

In the Easter Season

1

For religious

A reading from the Acts of the Apostles   4:32-35

The whole group of believers was united, heart and soul.

The whole group of believers was united, heart and soul; no one claimed for his own use anything that he had, as everything they owned was held in common.

The apostles continued to testify to the resurrection of the Lord Jesus with great power, and they were all given great respect.

None of their members was ever in want, as all those who owned land or houses would sell them, and bring the money from them, to present it to the apostles; it was then distributed to any members who might be in need.

This is the word of the Lord.

Responsorial Psalm   Ps 15:1-2. 5. 7-8. 11. ℟ v.5

℟   You are my inheritance, O Lord.

1   Preserve me, God, I take refuge in you.
     I say to the Lord: 'You are my God.'
     O Lord, it is you who are my portion and cup;
     it is you yourself who are my prize. ℟

2   I will bless the Lord who gives me counsel,
     who even at night directs my heart.
     I keep the Lord ever in my sight:
     since he is at my right hand, I shall stand firm. ℟

3   You will show me the path of life,
     the fullness of joy in your presence,
     at your right hand happiness for ever. ℟

2

A reading from the book of the Apocalypse   3:14. 20-22

I will come in to share his meal, side by side with him.

Here is the message of the Amen, the faithful, the true witness, the ultimate source of God's creation:

'Look, I am standing at the door, knocking. If one of you hears me calling and opens the door, I will come in to share his meal, side by side with him. Those who prove victorious I will allow to share my throne, just as I was victorious myself and took my place with my Father on his throne. If anyone has ears to hear, let him listen to what the Spirit is saying to the churches.'

This is the word of the Lord.

Responsorial Psalm   Ps 22. ℟ v.1

℟   The Lord is my shepherd; there is nothing I shall want.

1   The Lord is my shepherd;
     there is nothing I shall want.
     Fresh and green are the pastures
     where he gives me repose.
     Near restful waters he leads me,
     to revive my drooping spirit. ℟

2   He guides me along the right path;
     he is true to his name.
     If I should walk in the valley of darkness
     no evil would I fear.
     You are there with your crook and your staff;
     with these you give me comfort. ℟

3   You have prepared a banquet for me
     in the sight of my foes.
     My head you have anointed with oil;
     my cup is overflowing. ℟

4   Surely goodness and kindness shall follow me
     all the days of my life.
     In the Lord's own house shall I dwell
     for ever and ever. ℟

3

A reading from the book of the Apocalypse   19:1. 5-9

Happy are those who are invited to the wedding feast of the Lamb.

I, John, seemed to hear the great sound of a huge crowd in heaven, singing, 'Alleluia! Victory and glory and power to our God!'

Then a voice came from the throne; it said, 'Praise our God, you servants of his and all who, great or small, revere him.' And I seemed to hear the voices of a huge crowd, like the sound of the ocean or the great roar of thunder, answering 'Alleluia! The reign of the Lord our God Almighty has begun; let us be glad and joyful and give praise to God, because this is the time for the marriage of the Lamb. His bride is ready, and she has been able to dress herself in dazzling white linen because her linen is made of the good deeds of the saints.' The angel said, 'Write this: Happy are those who are invited to the wedding feast of Lamb'.

This is the word of the Lord.

Responsorial Psalm   Ps 102:1-4. 8-9. 13-14. 17-18. ℟ v.1

℟   O bless the Lord, my soul.

1   My soul, give thanks to the Lord,
     all my being, bless his holy name.
     My soul, give thanks to the Lord
     and never forget all his blessings. ℟

2   It is he who forgives all your guilt
     who heals every one of your ills,
     who redeems your life from the grave,
     who crowns you with love and compassion. ℟

3   The Lord is compassion and love,
     slow to anger and rich in mercy.
     His wrath will come to an end;
     he will not be angry for ever. ℟

4   As a father has compassion on his sons,
     the Lord has pity on those who fear him;
     for he knows of what we are made,
     he remembers that we are dust. ℟

5   But the love of the Lord is everlasting
     upon those who hold him in fear;
     his justice reaches out to children's children
     when they keep his covenant in truth. ℟

4

A reading from the book of the Apocalypse   21:5-7

The Lord said: I will give water from the well of life to anybody who is thirsty.

The One sitting on the throne spoke: 'Now I am making the whole of creation new,' he said. 'Write this: that what I am saying is sure and will come true.' And then he said, 'It is already done. I am the Alpha and the Omega, the Beginning and the End. I will give water from the well of life free to anybody who is thirsty; it is the rightful inheritance of the one who proves victorious; and I will be his God and he a son to me.'

    This is the word of the Lord.

Responsorial Psalm   Ps 14:2-5. ℟ v.1

  ℟   The just shall live on your holy mountain, O Lord.

1   Lord, who shall dwell on your holy mountain?
     He who walks without fault;
     he who acts with justice
     and speaks the truth from his heart;
     he who does not slander with his tongue. ℟

2   He who does no wrong to his brother,
     who casts no slur on his neighbour,
     who holds the godless in disdain,
     but honours those who fear the Lord. ℟

3   He who takes no interest on a loan
     and accepts no bribes against the innocent,
     such a man will stand firm for ever. ℟

SECOND READING FROM THE NEW TESTAMENT

1

A reading from the letter of St Paul to the Romans   8:26-30

With those he justified, he shared his glory.

The Spirit comes to help us in our weakness. For when we cannot choose words in order to pray properly, the Spirit himself expresses our plea in a way that could never be put into words, and God who knows everything in our hearts knows perfectly well what he means, and that the pleas of the saints expressed by the Spirit are according to the mind of God.

We know that by turning everything to their good God co-operates with all those who love him, with all those that he has called according to his purpose. They are the ones he chose specially long ago and intended to become true images of his Son, so that his Son might be the eldest of many brothers. He called those he intended for this; those he called he justified, and with those he justified he shared his glory.

This is the word of the Lord.

2

A reading from the first letter of St Paul   1:26-31
to the Corinthians

God has chosen those who are nothing at all.

Take yourselves, brothers, at the time when you were called: how many of you were wise in the ordinary sense of the word, how many were influential people, or came from noble families? No, it was to shame the wise that God chose what is foolish by human reckoning, and to shame what is strong that he chose what is weak by human reckoning; those whom the world thinks common and contemptible are the ones that God has chosen – those who are nothing at all to show up those who are everything. The human race has nothing to boast about to God, but you, God has made members of Christ Jesus and by God's doing he has become our wisdom, and our virtue, and our holiness, and our freedom. As scripture says: if anyone wants to boast, let him boast about the Lord.

This is the word of the Lord.

3

A reading from the first letter of St Paul   12:31–13:13
to the Corinthians

Love never ends.

Be ambitious for the higher gifts. And I am going to show you a way
that is better than any of them.

If I have all the eloquence of men or of angels, but speak without
love, I am simply a gong booming or a cymbal clashing. If I have the
gift of prophecy, understanding all the mysteries there are, and
knowing everything, and if I have faith in all its fullness, to move
mountains, but without love, then I am nothing at all. If I give away
all that I possess, piece by piece, and if I even let them take my body to
burn it, but am without love, it will do me no good whatever.

Love is always patient and kind; it is never jealous; love is never
boastful or conceited; it is never rude or selfish; it does not take
offence, and is not resentful. Love takes no pleasure in other people's
sins but delights in the truth; it is always ready to excuse, to trust, to
hope, and to endure whatever comes.

Love does not come to an end. But if there are gifts of prophecy, the
time will come when they must fail; or the gift of languages, it will not
continue for ever; and knowledge – for this, too, the time will come
when it must fail. For our knowledge is imperfect and our prophesying is imperfect; but once perfection comes, all imperfect things will
disappear. When I was a child, I used to talk like a child, and think
like a child, and argue like a child, but now I am a man, all childish
ways are put behind me. Now we are seeing a dim reflection in a
mirror; but then we shall be seeing face to face. The knowledge that I
have now is imperfect; but then I shall know as fully as I am known.

In short, there are three things that last: faith, hope and love; and
the greatest of these is love.

This is the word of the Lord.

Shorter form

A reading from the first letter of St Paul   13:4-13
to the Corinthians

Love never ends.

Love is always patient and kind; it is never jealous; love is never
boastful or conceited; it is never rude or selfish; it does not take

offence, and is not resentful. Love takes no pleasure in other people's sins but delights in the truth; it is always ready to excuse, to trust, to hope, and to endure whatever comes.

Love does not come to an end. But if there are gifts of prophecy, the time will come when they must fail; or the gift of languages, it will not continue for ever; and knowledge – for this, too, the time will come when it must fail. For our knowledge is imperfect and our prophesying is imperfect; but once perfection comes, all imperfect things will disappear. When I was a child, I used to talk like a child, and think like a child, and argue like a child, but now I am a man, all childish ways are put behind me. Now we are seeing a dim reflection in a mirror; but then we shall be seeing face to face. The knowledge that I have now is imperfect; but then I shall know as fully as I am known.

In short, there are three things that last: faith, hope and love; and the greatest of these is love.

This is the word of the Lord

4

A reading from the second letter of St Paul
to the Corinthians   10:17–11:2

I arranged for you to marry Christ so that I might give you away as a chaste virgin to this one husband.

If anyone wants to boast, let him boast of the Lord. It is not the man who commends himself that can be accepted, but the man who is commended by the Lord.

I only wish you were able to tolerate a little foolishness from me. But of course: you are tolerant towards me. You see, the jealousy that I feel for you is God's own jealousy: I arranged for you to marry Christ so that I might give you away as a chaste virgin to this one husband.

This is the word of the Lord.

5

A reading from the letter of St Paul
to the Galatians   2:19-20

I live, now not I but Christ lives in me.

Through the law I am dead to the Law, so that now I can live for God. I have been crucified with Christ, and I live now not with my own life

life but with the life of Christ who lives in me. The life I now live in this body I live in faith: faith in the Son of God who loved me and who sacrificed himself for my sake.

This is the word of the Lord.

6

A reading from the letter of St Paul to the Galatians   6:14-16

Through which the world is crucified to me, and I to the world.

The only thing I can boast about is the cross of our Lord Jesus Christ, through whom the world is crucified to me, and I to the world. It does not matter if a person is circumcised or not; what matters is for him to become an altogether new creature. Peace and mercy to all who follow this rule, who form the Israel of God.

This is the word of the Lord.

7

A reading from the letter of St Paul to the Ephesians   3:14-19

To know the love of Christ, which is beyond all knowledge.

This is what I pray, kneeling before the Father, from whom every family, whether spiritual or natural, takes its name:

Out of his infinite glory, may he give you the power through his Spirit for your hidden self to grow strong, so that Christ may live in your hearts through faith, and then, planted in love and built on love, you will with all the saints have strength to grasp the breadth and the length, the height and the depth; until, knowing the love of Christ, which is beyond all knowledge, you are filled with the utter fullness of God.

This is the word of the Lord.

8

A reading from the letter of St Paul to the Ephesians   6:10-13. 18

Put on God's armour.

Grow strong in the Lord, with the strength of his power. Put God's armour on so as to be able to resist the devil's tactics. For it is not against human enemies that we have to struggle, but against the

Sovereignties and the Powers who originate the darkness in this world, the spiritual army of evil in the heavens. That is why you must rely on God's armour, or you will not be able to put up any resistance when the worst happens, or have enough resources to hold your ground.

Pray all the time, asking for what you need, praying in the Spirit on every possible occasion. Never get tired of staying awake to pray for all the saints.

This is the word of the Lord.

9

A reading from the letter of St Paul to the Philippians   3:8-14

I am racing for the finish, for the prize to which God calls us upwards to receive in Christ Jesus.

I believe nothing can happen that will outweigh the supreme advantage of knowing Christ Jesus my Lord. For him I have accepted the loss of everything, and I look on everything as so much rubbish if only I can have Christ and be given a place in him. I am no longer trying for perfection by my own efforts, the perfection that comes from the Law, but I want only the perfection that comes through faith in Christ, and is from God and based on faith. All I want is to know Christ and the power of his resurrection and to share his sufferings by reproducing the pattern of his death. That is the way I can hope to take my place in the resurrection of the dead. Not that I have become perfect yet: I have not yet won, but I am still running, trying to capture the prize for which Christ Jesus captured me. I can assure you my brothers, I am far from thinking that I have already won. All I can say is that I forget the past and I strain ahead for what is still to come; I am racing for the finish, for the prize to which God calls us upwards to receive in Christ Jesus.

This is the word of the Lord.

10

A reading from the letter of St Paul to the Philippians   4:4-9

Fill your minds with everything that is holy.

I want you to be happy, always happy in the Lord; I repeat, what I want is your happiness. Let your tolerance be evident to everyone: the Lord is very near. There is no need to worry; but if there is anything you need, pray for it, asking God for it with prayer and thanksgiving, and that peace of God, which is so much greater than we can understand, will guard your hearts and your thoughts, in Christ Jesus. Finally, brothers, fill your minds with everything that is true, everything that is noble, everything that is good and pure, everything that we love and honour, and everything that can be thought virtuous or worthy of praise. Keep doing all the things that you learnt from me and have been taught by me and have heard or seen that I do. Then the God of peace will be with you.

This is the word of the Lord.

11

A reading from the letter of St Paul to the Colossians   3:12-17

Above all have love, which is the bond of perfection.

You are God's chosen race, his saints; he loves you, and you should be clothed in sincere compassion, in kindness and humility, gentleness and patience. Bear with one another; forgive each other as soon as a quarrel begins. The Lord has forgiven you; now you must do the same. Over all these clothes, to keep them together and complete them, put on love. And may the peace of Christ reign in your hearts, because it is for this that you were called together as parts of one body. Always be thankful.

Let the message of Christ, in all its richness, find a home with you. Teach each other, and advise each other, in all wisdom. With gratitude in your hearts sing psalms and hymns and inspired songs to God; and never say or do anything except in the name of the Lord Jesus, giving thanks to God the Father through him.

This is the word of the Lord.

12

For widows

A reading from the first letter of St Paul to Timothy   5:3-10

A woman who is a widow and left without anybody can give herself up to God.

Be considerate to widows; I mean those who are truly widows. If a widow has children or grandchildren, they are to learn first of all to do their duty to their own families and repay their debt to their parents, because this is what pleases God. But a woman who is really widowed and left without anybody can give herself up to God and consecrate all her days and nights to petition and prayer. The one who thinks only of pleasure is already dead while she is still alive: remind them of all this, too, so that their lives may be blameless. Anyone who does not look after his own relations, especially if they are living with him, has rejected the faith and is worse than an unbeliever.

Enrolment as a widow is permissible only for a woman at least sixty years old who has had only one husband. She must be a woman known for her good works and for the way in which she has brought up her children, shown hospitality to strangers and washed the saints' feet, helped people who are in trouble and been active in all kinds of good work.

This is the word of the Lord.

13

A reading from the letter of St James   2:14-17

If good works do not go with faith then it is quite dead.

Take the case, my brothers, of someone who has never done a single good act but claims that he has faith. Will that faith save him? If one of the brothers or one of the sisters is in need of clothes and has not enough food to live on, and one of you says to them, 'I wish you well; keep yourself warm and eat plenty', without giving them these bare necessities of life, then what good is that? Faith is like that: if good works do not go with it, it is quite dead.

This is the word of the Lord.

14

A reading from the first letter of St Peter   3:1-9

Holy women hoped in God.

Wives should be obedient to their husbands. Then, if there are some husbands who have not yet obeyed the word, they may find themselves won over, without a word spoken, by the way their wives behave, when they see how faithful and conscientious they are. Do not dress up for show: doing up your hair, wearing gold bracelets and fine clothes; all this should be inside, in a person's heart, imperishable: the ornament of a sweet and gentle disposition – this is what is precious in the sight of God. That was how the holy women of the past dressed themselves attractively – they hoped in God and were tender and obedient to their husbands; like Sarah, who was obedient to Abraham, and called him her lord. You are now her children, as long as you live good lives and do not give way to fear or worry.

In the same way, husbands must always treat their wives with consideration in their life together, respecting a woman as one who, though she may be the weaker partner, is equally an heir to the life of grace. This will stop anything from coming in the way of your prayers.

Finally: you should all agree among yourselves and be sympathetic; love the brothers, have compassion and be self-effacing. Never pay back one wrong with another, or an angry word with another one; instead, pay back with a blessing. That is what you are called to do, so that you inherit a blessing yourself.

This is the word of the Lord.

15

A reading from the first letter of St Peter   4:7-11

Each one of you has received a special gift; put yourselves at the service of others.

Keep a calm and sober mind. Above all, never let your love for each other grow insincere, since love covers over many a sin. Welcome each other into your houses without grumbling. Each one of you has received a special grace, so, like good stewards responsible for all these different graces of God, put yourselves at the service of others. If you are a speaker, speak in words which seem to come from God; if you are a helper, help as though every action was done at God's orders; so that in everything God may receive the glory, through Jesus Christ, since to him alone belong all glory and power for ever and ever. Amen.

This is the word of the Lord.

16

For those who work for the underprivileged

A reading from the first letter of St John   3:14-18

We should lay down our lives for our brothers and sisters.

We have passed out of death and into life,
and of this we can be sure
because we love our brothers.

If you refuse to love, you must remain dead;
to hate your brother is to be a murderer,
and murderers, as you know, do not have eternal life in them.
This has taught us love –
that he gave up his life for us;
and we, too, ought to give up our lives for our brothers.
If a man who was rich enough in this world's goods
saw that one of his brothers was in need,
but closed his heart to him,
how could the love of God be living in him?
My children,
our love is not to be just words or mere talk,
but something real and active.

This is the word of the Lord.

17

A reading from the first letter of St John   4:7-16

If we love one another, God will live in us.

My dear people,
let us love one another
since love comes from God
and everyone who loves is begotten by God and knows God.
Anyone who fails to love can never have known God,
because God is love.
God's love for us was revealed
when God sent into the world his only Son
so that we could have life through him:
this is the love I mean:
not our love for God,
but God's love for us when he sent his Son
to be the sacrifice that takes our sins away.
My dear people,
since God has loved us so much,
we too should love one another.
No one has ever seen God;
but as long as we love one another
God will live in us
and his love will be complete in us.
We can know that we are living in him

and he is living in us
because he lets us share his Spirit.
We ourselves saw and we testify
that the Father sent his Son
as saviour of the world.
If anyone acknowledges that Jesus is the Son of God,
God lives in him, and he in God.
We ourselves have known and put our faith in
God's love towards ourselves.
God is love
and anyone who lives in love lives in God,
and God lives in him.

This is the word of the Lord.

18

A reading from the first letter of St John   5:1-5

This is the victory over the world – our faith.

Whoever believes that Jesus is the Christ
has been begotten by God;
and whoever loves the Father that begot him
loves the child whom he begets.
We can be sure that we love God's children
if we love God himself and do what he has commanded us;
this is what loving God is –
keeping his commandments;
and his commandments are not difficult,
because anyone who has been begotten by God
has already overcome the world;
this is the victory over the world –
our faith.
Who can overcome the world?
Only the man who believes that Jesus is the Son of God.

This is the word of the Lord.

GOSPEL

1

Gospel Acclamation   Mt 5:3

> Alleluia, alleluia!
> Happy the poor in spirit;
> the kingdom of heaven is theirs!
> Alleluia!

A reading from the holy Gospel according to Matthew   5:1-12

Rejoice and be glad, for your reward will be great in heaven.

Seeing the crowds, Jesus went up the hill. There he sat down and was joined by his disciples. Then he began to speak. This is what he taught them:

> 'How happy are the poor in spirit;
> theirs is the kingdom of heaven.
> Happy the gentle:
> they shall have the earth for their heritage.
> Happy those who mourn:
> they shall be comforted.
> Happy those who hunger and thirst for what is right:
> they shall be satisfied.
> Happy the merciful:
> they shall have mercy shown them.
> Happy the pure in heart:
> they shall see God.
> Happy the peacemakers:
> they shall be called sons of God.
> Happy those who are persecuted in the cause of right;
> theirs is the kingdom of heaven.

'Happy are you when people abuse you and persecute you and speak all kinds of calumny against you on my account. Rejoice and be glad, for your reward will be great in heaven.'

This is the Gospel of the Lord.

2

Gospel Acclamation   Jn 8:12

> Alleluia, alleluia!
> I am the light of the world, says the Lord;
> whoever follows me will have the light of life.
> Alleluia!

A reading from the holy Gospel according to Matthew   5:13-19

You are the light of the world.

Jesus said to his disciples: 'You are the salt of the earth. But if salt becomes tasteless, what can make it salty again? It is good for nothing, and can only be thrown out to be trampled underfoot by men.

'You are the light of the world. A city built on a hill-top cannot be hidden. No one lights a lamp to put it under a tub; they put it on the lamp-stand where it shines for everyone in the house. In the same way your light must shine in the sight of men, so that, seeing your good works, they may give the praise to your Father in heaven.

'Do not imagine that I have come to abolish the Law or the Prophets. I have come not to abolish but to complete them. I tell you solemnly, till heaven and earth disappear, not one dot, not one little stroke, shall disappear from the Law until its purpose is achieved. Therefore, the man who infringes even one of the least of these commandments and teaches others to do the same will be considered the least in the kingdom of heaven: but the man who keeps them and teaches them will be considered great in the kingdom of heaven.'

This is the Gospel of the Lord.

3

Gospel Acclamation   Jn 14:23

> Alleluia, alleluia!
> All who love me will keep my words,
> and my Father will love them and we will come to them.
> Alleluia!

A reading from the holy Gospel according to Matthew   7:21-27

Those who are wise build their house on rock, not on sand.

Jesus said to his disciples: 'It is not those who say to me, "Lord, Lord", who will enter the kingdom of heaven. When the day comes many will say to me, "Lord, Lord, did we not prophesy in your name, cast out demons in your name, work many miracles in your name?" Then I shall tell them to their faces: I have never known you; away from me, you evil men!'

'Therefore, everyone who listens to these words of mine and acts on them will be like a sensible man who built his house on rock. Rain came down, floods rose, gales blew and hurled themselves against that house, and it did not fall: it was founded on rock. But everyone who listens to these words of mine and does not act on them will be like a stupid man who built his house on sand. Rain came down, floods rose, gales blew and struck that house, and it fell; and what a fall it had!'

This is the Gospel of the Lord.

4

Gospel Acclamation   Mt 11:28

Alleluia, alleluia!
Come to me, all you that labour and are burdened,
and I will give you rest.
Alleluia!

A reading from the holy Gospel according to Matthew   11:25-30

*You have hidden these things from the learned and the clever and
revealed them to children.*

Jesus exclaimed, 'I bless you, Father, Lord of heaven and of earth, for hiding these things from the learned and the clever and revealing them to mere children. Yes, Father, for that is what it pleased you to do. Everything has been entrusted to me by my Father; and no one knows the Son except the Father, just as no one knows the Father except the Son and those to whom the Son chooses to reveal him.

'Come to me, all you who labour and are overburdened, and I will give you rest. Shoulder my yoke and learn from me, for I am gentle and humble in heart, and you will find rest for your souls. Yes, my yoke is easy and my burden light.'

This is the Gospel of the Lord.

5

Gospel Acclamation   Jn 15:4. 5

> Alleluia, alleluia!
> Live in me and let me live in you, says the Lord;
> my branches bear much fruit.
> Alleluia!

A reading from the holy Gospel according to Matthew   13:44-46

He sold all that he had and bought the field.

Jesus said to the crowds:

'The kingdom of heaven is like treasure hidden in a field which someone has found; he hides it again, goes off happy, sells everything he owns and buys the field.

'Again the kingdom of heaven is like a merchant looking for fine pearls; when he finds one of great value he goes and sells everything he owns and buys it.'

This is the Gospel of the Lord.

6

Gospel Acclamation   Mt 5:6

> Alleluia, alleluia!
> Happy are those who hunger and thirst for what is right;
> they shall be satisfied.
> Alleluia!

A reading from the holy Gospel according to Matthew   16:24-27

All who lose their lives on account of me will really save their lives.

Jesus said to his disciples, 'If anyone wants to be a follower of mine, let him renounce himself and take up his cross and follow me. For anyone who wants to save his life will lose it; but anyone who loses his life for my sake will find it. What, then, will a man gain if he wins the whole world and ruins his life? Or what has a man to offer in exchange for his life?

'For the Son of Man is going to come in the glory of his Father with his angels, and, when he does, he will reward each one according to his behaviour.'

This is the Gospel of the Lord.

7

Gospel Acclamation   Mt 23:11. 12

Alleluia, alleluia!
Whoever is greatest among you will serve the rest.
All who humble themselves shall be exalted.
Alleluia!

A reading from the holy Gospel according to Matthew   18:1-5

Unless you become like little children you will never enter the kingdom of heaven.

The disciples came to Jesus and said, 'Who is the greatest in the kingdom of heaven?' So he called a little child to him and set the child in front of them. Then he said, 'I tell you solemnly, unless you change and become like little children you will never enter the kingdom of heaven. And so, the one who makes himself as little as this little child is the greatest in the kingdom of heaven. Anyone who welcomes a little child like this in my name welcomes me.'

This is the Gospel of the Lord.

8

For religious

Gospel Acclamation   Jn 8:31-32

Alleluia, alleluia!
If you stay in my word, you will indeed be my disciples,
and you will know the truth, says the Lord.
Alleluia!

A reading from the holy Gospel according to Matthew 19:3-12

Some persons have chosen to remain single for the sake of the kingdom of heaven.

Some Pharisees approached Jesus, and to test him they said, 'Is it against the Law for a man to divorce his wife on any pretext whatever?' He answered, 'Have you not read that the creator from the beginning made them male and female and that he said: This is why a man must leave father and mother, and cling to his wife, and the two become one body. They are no longer two, therefore, but one body. So then, what God has united, man must not divide.'

They said to him, 'Then why did Moses command that a writ of dismissal should be given in cases of divorce?' 'It was because you were so unteachable,' he said, 'that Moses allowed you to divorce your wives, but it was not like this from the beginning. Now I say this to you: the man who divorces his wife – I am not speaking of fornication – and marries another, is guilty of adultery.'

The disciples said to him, 'If that is how things are between husband and wife, it is not advisable to marry.' But he replied, 'It is not everyone who can accept what I have said, but only those to whom it is granted. There are eunuchs born that way from their mother's womb, there are eunuchs made so by men and there are eunuchs who have made themselves that way for the sake of the kingdom of heaven. Let anyone accept this who can.'

This is the Gospel of the Lord.

9

Gospel Acclamation Mt 5:3

Alleluia, alleluia!
Happy the poor in spirit;
the kingdom of heaven is theirs!
Alleluia!

A reading from the holy Gospel according to Matthew 19:27-29

You who have left everything and followed me, will be rewarded a hundred-fold.

Peter spoke to Jesus. 'What about us?' he said 'We have left everything and followed you. What are we to have, then?' Jesus said to him, 'I tell you solemnly, when all is made new and the Son of Man sits on his throne of glory, you will yourselves sit on twelve thrones to judge the twelve tribes of Israel. And everyone who has left houses, brothers, sisters, father, mother, children or land for the sake of my name will be repaid a hundred times over, and also inherit eternal life.'

This is the Gospel of the Lord.

10

Gospel Acclamation   Jn 13:34

Alleluia, alleluia!
I give you a new commandment:
love one another as I have loved you.
Alleluia!

A reading from the holy Gospel according to Matthew   22:35-40

Love the Lord your God, and your neighbour as yourself.

A lawyer, to disconcert Jesus, put a question, 'Master, which is the greatest commandment of the Law?' Jesus said, 'You must love the Lord your God with all your heart, with all your soul, and with all your mind. This is the greatest and the first commandment. The second resembles it: You must love your neighbour as yourself. On these two commandments hang the whole Law, and the Prophets also.'

This is the Gospel of the Lord.

11

Gospel Acclamation   Mt 5:8

Alleluia, alleluia!
Happy are the pure of heart,
for they shall see God.
Alleluia!

A reading from the holy Gospel according to Matthew   25:1-13

The groom is coming; go and meet him.

Jesus spoke this parable to his disciples: 'The kingdom of heaven will be like this: Ten bridesmaids took their lamps and went to meet the bridegroom. Five of them were foolish and five were sensible: the foolish ones did take their lamps, but they brought no oil, whereas the sensible ones took flasks of oil as well as their lamps. The bridegroom was late, and they all grew drowsy and fell asleep. But at midnight there was a cry, "The bridegroom is here! Go out and meet him." At this, all those bridesmaids woke up and trimmed their lamps, and the foolish ones said to the sensible ones, "Give us some of your oil: our lamps are going out". But they replied, "There may not be enough for us and for you; you had better go to those who sell it and buy some for yourselves". They had gone off to buy it when the bridegroom arrived. Those who were ready went in with him to the wedding hall and the door was closed. The other bridesmaids arrived later. "Lord, Lord," they said, "open the door for us." But he replied, "I tell you solemnly, I do not know you". So stay awake, because you do not know either the day or the hour.'

This is the Gospel of the Lord.

12

Gospel Acclamation   Jn 14:23

Alleluia, alleluia!
All who love me will keep my words,
and my Father will love them and we will come to them.
Alleluia!

A reading from the holy Gospel according to Matthew   25:14-30

Because you have been faithful in a few things, enter into the joy of your Lord.

Jesus spoke this parable to his disciples: 'A man on his way abroad summoned his servants and entrusted his property to them. To one he gave five talents, to another two, to a third, one; each in proportion to his ability. Then he set out. The man who had received the five talents promptly went and traded with them and made five more. The man who had received two made two more in the same way. But the man who had received one went off and dug a hole in the ground and hid his master's money. Now a long time after, the master of those servants came back and went through his accounts with them. The man who had received the five talents came forward bringing five more. "Sir," he said, "You entrusted me with five talents; here are five more that I have made." His master said to him, "Well done, good and faithful servant; you have shown you can be faithful in small things, I will trust you with greater; come and join in your master's happiness." Next the man with the two talents came forward. "Sir," he said, "you entrusted me with two talents; here are two more that I have made.' His master said to him, "Well done, good and faithful servant; you have shown you can be faithful in small things, I will trust you with greater; come and join in your master's happiness."

'Last came forward the man who had the one talent. "Sir," said he, "I had heard you were a hard man, reaping where you have not sown and gathering where you have not scattered; so I was afraid, and I went off and hid your talent in the ground. Here it is; it was yours, you have it back." But his master answered him, "You wicked and lazy servant! So you knew that I reap where I have not sown and gather where I have not scattered? Well then, you should have deposited my money with the bankers, and on my return I would have recovered my capital with interest. So now, take the talent from him and give it to the man who has the five talents. For to everyone who has will be given more, and he will have more than enough; but from the man who has not, even what he has will be taken away. As for this good-for-nothing servant, throw him out into the dark, where there will be weeping and grinding of teeth." '

This is the Gospel of the Lord.

Shorter form

A reading from the holy Gospel according to Matthew   25:14-23

Because you have been faithful in a few things, enter into the joy of your Lord.

Jesus spoke this parable to his disciples: 'A man on his way abroad summoned his servants and entrusted his property to them. To one he gave five talents, to another two, to a third, one; each in proportion to his ability. Then he set out. The man who had received the five talents promptly went and traded with them and made five more. The man who had received two made two more in the same way . But the man who had received one went off and dug a hole in the ground and hid his master's money. Now a long time after, the master of those servants came back and went through his accounts with them. The man who had received the five talents came forward bringing five more. "Sir," he said, "you entrusted me with five talents; here are five more that I have made." His master said to him, "Well done, good and faithful servant; you have shown you can be faithful in small things, I will trust you with greater; come and join in your master's happiness." Next the man with the two talents came forward. "Sir," he said, "you entrusted me with two talents; here are two more that I have made." His master said to him, "Well done, good and faithful servant; you have shown you can be faithful in small things, I will trust you with greater; come and join in your master's happiness." '

This is the Gospel of the Lord.

13

For those who work for the underprivileged

Gospel Acclamation Jn 13:34

Alleluia, alleluia!
I give you a new commandment:
love one another as I have loved you.
Alleluia!

A reading from the holy Gospel according to Matthew 25:31-46

Whatever you have done to the very least of my brothers and sisters
you have done to me.

Jesus said to his disciples:
'When the Son of Man comes in his glory, escorted by all the angels, then he will take his seat on his throne of glory. All the nations will be assembled before him and he will separate men one from another as the shepherd separates sheep from goats. He will place the sheep on his right hand and the goats on his left. Then the King will say to those on his right hand "Come, you whom my Father has blessed, take for your heritage the kingdom prepared for you since the foundation of the world. For I was hungry and you gave me food; I

was thirsty and you gave me drink; I was a stranger and you made me welcome; naked and you clothed me, sick and you visited me, in prison and you came to see me." Then the virtuous will say to him in reply, "Lord, when did we see you hungry and feed you; or thirsty and give you drink? When did we see you a stranger and make you welcome; naked and clothe you; sick or in prison and go to see you?" And the King will answer, "I tell you solemnly, in so far as you did this to one of the least of these brothers of mine, you did it to me". Next he will say to those on his left hand, "Go away from me, with your curse upon you, to the eternal fire prepared for the devil and his angels. For I was hungry and you never gave me food; I was thirsty and you never gave me anything to drink; I was a stranger and you never made me welcome, naked and you never clothed me, sick and in prison and you never visited me." Then it will be their turn to ask, "Lord, when did we see you hungry or thirsty, a stranger or naked, sick or in prison, and did not come to your help?" Then he will answer, "I tell you solemnly, in so far as you neglected to do this to one of the least of these, you neglected to do it to me". And they will go away to eternal punishment, and the virtuous to eternal life. '

This is the Gospel of the Lord.

Shorter form

A reading from the holy Gospel according to Matthew   25:31-40

> *Whatever you have done to the very least of my brothers and sisters you have done to me.*

Jesus said to his disciples: 'When the Son of Man comes in his glory, escorted by all the angels, then he will take his seat on his throne of glory. All the nations will be assembled before him and he will separate men one from another as the shepherd separates sheep from goats. He will place the sheep on his right hand and the goats on his left. Then the King will say to those on his right hand, "Come, you whom my Father has blessed, take for your heritage the kingdom prepared for you since the foundation of the world. For I was hungry and you gave me food; I was thirsty and you gave me drink; I was a stranger and you made me welcome; naked and you clothed me, sick and you visited me, in prison and you came to see me." Then the virtuous will say to him in reply, "Lord, when did we see you hungry and feed you; or thirsty and give you a drink? When did we see you a stranger and make you welcome; naked and clothe you; sick or in prison and go to see you?" And the King will answer, "I tell you solemnly, in so far as you did this to one of the least of these brothers of mine, you did it to me." '

This is the Gospel of the Lord.

14

Gospel Acclamation   Jn 8:31-32

Alleluia, alleluia!
If you stay in my word, you will indeed be my disciples,
and you will know the truth, says the Lord.
Alleluia!

A reading from the holy Gospel according to Mark   3:31-35

Whoever has done the will of God is my brother, my sister, and my mother.

The mother and brothers of Jesus arrived and, standing outside, sent in a message asking for him. A crowd was sitting round him at the time the message was passed to him, 'Your mother and brothers and sisters are outside asking for you.' He replied, 'Who are my mother and my brothers?' And looking round at those sitting in a circle about him, he said, 'Here are my mother and my brothers. Anyone who does the will of God, that person is my brother and sister and mother.'

This is the Gospel of the Lord.

15

For teachers

Gospel Acclamation   cf. Mt 11:25

Alleluia, alleluia!
Blessed are you, Father, Lord of heaven and earth;
you have revealed to little ones the mysteries of the kingdom.
Alleluia!

A reading from the holy Gospel according to Mark   9:34-37

Whenever you have accepted graciously a small child, you have
accepted me.

On the road the disciples had been arguing which of them was the
greatest. So Jesus sat down, called the Twelve to him and said, 'If
anyone wants to be first, he must make himself last of all and servant
of all.' He then took a little child, set him in front of them, put his
arms round him, and said to them, 'Anyone who welcomes one of these
little children in my name, welcomes me; and anyone who welcomes
me welcomes not me but the one who sent me.'

This is the Gospel of the Lord.

16

For teachers

Gospel Acclamation   cf. Mt 11:25

Alleluia, alleluia!
Blessed are you, Father, Lord of heaven and earth;
you have revealed to little ones the mysteries of the kingdom.
Alleluia!

A reading from the holy Gospel according to Mark   10:13-16

Do not keep the children from me.

People were bringing little children to Jesus, for him to touch them.
The disciples turned them away, but when Jesus saw this he was
indignant and said to them, 'Let the little children come to me; do not
stop them; for it is to such as these that the kingdom of God belongs. I
tell you solemnly, anyone who does not welcome the kingdom of God
like a little child will never enter it.' Then he put his arms round
them, laid his hands on them and gave them his blessing.

This is the Gospel of the Lord.

17

For religious

Gospel Acclamation Mt 5:3

 Alleluia, alleluia!
 Happy the poor in spirit;
 the kingdom of heaven is theirs!
 Alleluia!

A reading from the holy Gospel according to Mark 10:17-30

Sell whatever you have, and come follow me.

Jesus was setting out on a journey when a man ran up, knelt before him and put this question to him, 'Good master, what must I do to inherit eternal life?' Jesus said to him, 'Why do you call me good? No one is good but God alone. You know the commandments: You must not kill; You must not commit adultery; You must not steal; You must not bring false witness; You must not defraud; Honour your father and mother.' And he said to him, 'Master, I have kept all these from my earliest days.' Jesus looked steadily at him and loved him, and he said, 'There is one thing you lack. Go and sell everything you own and give the money to the poor, and you will have treasure in heaven; then come, follow me,' But his face fell at these words and he went away sad, for he was a man of great wealth.

Jesus looked round and said to his disciples, 'How hard it is for those who have riches to enter the kingdom of God!' The disciples were astounded by these words, but Jesus insisted. 'My children,' he said to them, 'how hard it is to enter the kingdom of God!' It is easier for a camel to pass through the eye of a needle than for a rich man to enter the kingdom of God.' They were more astonished than ever. 'In that case,' they said to one another, 'who can be saved?' Jesus gazed at them. 'For men,' he said, 'it is impossible, but not for God: because everything is possible for God.'

Peter took this up. 'What about us?' he asked him. 'We have left everything and followed you.' Jesus said, 'I tell you solemnly, there is no one who has left house, brothers, sisters, father, children or land for my sake and for the sake of the gospel who will not be repaid a hundred times over, houses, brothers, sisters, mothers, children and land – not without persecutions – now in this present time and, in the world to come, eternal life.'

This is the Gospel of the Lord.

Shorter form

A reading from the holy Gospel acording to Mark   10:17-27

Sell whatever you have, and come follow me.

Jesus was setting out on a journey when a man ran up, knelt before him and put this question to him, 'Good master, what must I do to inherit eternal life?' Jesus said to him, 'Why do you call me good? No one is good but God alone. You know the commandments: You must not kill; You must not commit adultery; You must not steal; You must not bring false witness; You must not defraud; Honour your father and mother.' And he said to him, 'Master, I have kept all these from my earliest days.' Jesus looked steadily at him and loved him, and he said, 'There is one thing you lack. Go and sell everything you own and give the money to the poor, and you will have treasure in heaven; then come, follow me.' But his face fell at these words and he went away sad, for he was a man of great wealth.

Jesus looked round and said to his disciples, 'How hard it is for those who have riches to enter the kingdom of God!' The disciples were astounded by these words, but Jesus insisted. 'My children,' he said to them, 'it is easier for a camel to pass through the eye of a needle than for a rich man to enter the kingdom of God.' They were more astonished than ever. 'In that case,' they said to one another, 'who can be saved?' Jesus gazed at them. 'For men,' he said, 'it is impossible, but not for God: because everything is possible for God.'

This is the Gospel of the Lord.

18

Gospel Acclamation   Jn 13:34

Alleluia, alleluia!
I give you a new commandment:
love one another as I have loved you.
Alleluia!

A reading from the holy Gospel according to Luke 6:27-38

Be merciful, as your Father is merciful.

Jesus said to his disciples: 'I say this to you who are listening: Love your enemies, do good to those who hate you, bless those who curse you, pray for those who treat you badly. To the man who slaps you on one cheek, present the other cheek too; to the man who takes your cloak from you, do not refuse your tunic. Give to everyone who asks you, do not ask for your property back from the man who robs you. Treat others as you would like them to treat you. If you love those who love you, what thanks can you expect? Even sinners love those who love them. And if you do good to those who do good to you, what thanks can you expect? For even sinners do that much. And if you lend to those from whom you hope to receive, what thanks can you expect? Even sinners lend to get back the same amount. Instead, love your enemies and do good, and lend without any hope of return. You will have a great reward, and you will be sons of the Most High, for he himself is kind to the ungrateful and the wicked.

'Be compassionate as your Father is compassionate. Do not judge, and you will not be judged yourselves; do not condemn, and you will not be condemned yourselves; grant pardon, and you will be pardoned. Give, and there will be gifts for you: a full measure, pressed down, shaken together, and running over, will be poured into your lap; because the amount you measure out is the amount you will be given back.'

This is the Gospel of the Lord.

19

For religious

Gospel Acclamation Jn 8:12

Alleluia, alleluia!
I am the light of the world, says the Lord;
whoever follows me will have the light of life.
Alleluia!

A reading from the holy Gospel according to Luke 9:57-62

I will follow you wherever you go.

As Jesus and his disciples travelled along they met a man on the road who said to him, 'I will follow you wherever you go.' Jesus answered, 'Foxes have holes and the birds of the air have nests, but the Son of Man has nowhere to lay his head.'

Another to whom he said, 'Follow me,' replied, 'Let me go and bury my father first.' But he answered, 'Leave the dead to bury their dead; your duty is to go and spread the news of the kingdom of God.'

Another said, 'I will follow you, sir, but first let me go and say goodbye to my people at home.' Jesus said to him, 'Once the hand is laid on the plough, no one who looks back is fit for the kingdom of God.'

This is the Gospel of the Lord.

20

Gospel Acclamation Jn 14:23

Alleluia, alleluia!
All who love me will keep my words,
and my Father will love them and we will come to them.
Alleluia!

A reading from the holy Gospel according to Luke 10:38-42

Jesus accepts the hospitality of Martha and praises the attentiveness of Mary.

Jesus came to a village, and a woman name Martha welcomed him into her house. She had a sister called Mary, who sat down at the Lord's feet and listened to him speaking. Now Martha who was distracted with all the serving said, 'Lord, do you not care that my sister is leaving me to do the serving all by myself? Please tell her to help me.' But the Lord answered: 'Martha, Martha,' he said, 'you worry and fret about so many things, and yet few are needed, indeed only one. It is Mary who has chosen the better part; it is not to be taken from her.'

This is the Gospel of the Lord.

21

For religious

Gospel Acclamation   Mt 5:3

Alleluia, alleluia!
Happy the poor in spirit;
the kingdom of heaven is theirs!
Alleluia!

A reading from the holy Gospel according to Luke   12:32-34

It has pleased the Father to give you the kingdom.

Jesus said to his disciples: 'There is no need to be afraid, little flock, for it has pleased your Father to give you the kingdom.

'Sell your possessions and give alms. Get yourselves purses that do not wear out, treasure that will not fail you, in heaven where no thief can reach it and no moth destroy it. For where your treasure is, there will your heart be also.'

This is the Gospel of the Lord.

22

Gospel Acclamation   Lk 21:36

Alleluia, alleluia!
Be watchful, pray constantly,
that you may be worthy to stand before the Son of Man.
Alleluia!

A reading from the holy Gospel according to Luke   12:35-40

Be prepared.

Jesus said to his disciples: 'See that you are dressed for action and have your lamps lit. Be like men waiting for their master to return from the wedding feast, ready to open the door as soon as he comes and knocks. Happy those servants whom the master finds awake when he comes. I tell you solemnly, he will put on an apron, sit them down at table and wait on them. It may be in the second watch he comes, or in the third, but happy those servants if he finds them ready. You may be quite sure of this, that if the householder had known at what hour the burglar would come, he would not have let anyone break through the wall of his house. You too must stand ready, because the Son of Man is coming at an hour you do not expect.'

This is the Gospel of the Lord.

23

For religious

Gospel Acclamation   Mt 5:3

Alleluia, alleluia!
Happy the poor in spirit;
the kingdom of heaven is theirs!
Alleluia!

A reading from the holy Gospel according to Luke   14:25-33

Unless you are ready to give up all that you possess, you cannot be my disciple.

Great crowds accompanied Jesus on his way and he turned and spoke to them. 'If any man comes to me without hating his father, mother, wife, children, brothers, sisters, yes and his own life too, he cannot be my disciple. Anyone who does not carry his cross and come after me cannot be my disciple.

'And indeed, which of you here, intending to build a tower, would not first sit down and work out the cost to see if he had enough to complete it? Otherwise, if he laid the foundation and then found himself unable to finish the work, the onlookers would all start making fun of him and saying, 'Here is a man who started to build and was unable to finish.' Or again, what king marching to war against another king would not first sit down and consider whether with ten thousand men he could stand up to the other who advanced against him with twenty thousand? If not, then while the other king was still a long way off, he would send envoys to sue for peace. So in the same way, none of you can be my disciple unless he give up all his possessions.'

This is the Gospel of the Lord.

24

Gospel Acclamation   Jn 15:9.5

Alleluia, alleluia!
Remain in my love, says the Lord;
all who live in me, and I in them, will bear much fruit.
Alleluia!

A reading from the holy Gospel according to John   15:1-8

All who live in me, and I in them, bear fruit.

Jesus said to his disciples:

'I am the true vine,
and my Father is the vinedresser.
Every branch in me that bears no fruit
he cuts away,
and every branch that does bear fruit he prunes
to make it bear even more.
You are pruned already,
by means of the word that I have spoken to you.
Make your home in me, as I make mine in you.
As a branch cannot bear fruit all by itself,
but must remain part of the vine,
neither can you unless you remain in me.
I am the vine,
you are the branches.
Whoever remains in me, with me in him,
bears fruit in plenty;
for cut off from me you can do nothing.
Anyone who does not remain in me
is like a branch that has been thrown away
– he withers;
these branches are collected and thrown on the fire,
and they are burnt.
If you remain in me
and my words remain in you,
you may ask what you will
and you shall get it.

It is to the glory of my Father that you should bear much fruit,
and then you will be my disciples.'

This is the Gospel of the Lord.

25

Gospel Acclamation   Jn 13:34

Alleluia, alleluia!
I give you a new commandment:
love one another as I have loved you.
Alleluia!

A reading from the holy Gospel according to John   15:9-17

You are my friends if you do what I command you.

Jesus said to his disciples:

'As the Father has loved me,
so I have loved you.
Remain in my love.
If you keep my commandments
you will remain in my love,
just as I have kept my Father's commandments
and remain in his love.
I have told you this
so that my own joy may be in you
and your joy be complete.
This is my commandment:
love one another,
as I have loved you.
A man can have no greater love
than to lay down his life for his friends.
You are my friends,
if you do what I command you.
I shall not call you servants any more,
because a servant does not know
his master's business;
I call you friends,
because I have made known to you

everything I have learnt from my Father.
You did not choose me,
no, I chose you;
and I commissioned you
to go out and to bear fruit,
fruit that will last;
and then the Father will give you
anything you ask him in my name.
What I command you
is to love one another.'

This is the Gospel of the Lord.

26

Gospel Acclamation   Jn 15:9. 5

Alleluia, alleluia!
Remain in my love says the Lord;
all who live in me, and I in them, will bear much fruit.
Alleluia!

A reading from the holy Gospel according to John   17:20-26

I want those you have given me to be with me where I am.

Jesus raised his eyes to heaven and said:

'Holy Father,
I pray not only for these,
but for those also
who through their words will believe in me.
May they all be one.
Father, may they be one in us,
as you are in me and I am in you,
so that the world may believe it was you who sent me.
I have given them the glory you gave to me
that they may be one as we are one.
With me in them and you in me,
may they be so completely one
that the world will realise that it was you who sent me
and that I have loved them as much as you loved me.

Father,
I want those you have given me
to be with me where I am,
so that they may always see the glory
you have given me
because you loved me
before the foundation of the world.
Father, Righteous One,
the world has not known you,
but I have known you,
and these have known
that you have sent me.
I have made your name known to them
and will continue to make it known,
so that the love with which you loved me may be in them,
and so that I may be in them.'

This is the Gospel of the Lord.

INDEX OF READINGS

INDEX OF CANTICLES

INDEX OF GOSPEL ACCLAMATIONS

INDEX OF CELEBRATIONS
GENERAL ROMAN CALENDAR

INDEX OF CELEBRATIONS
NATIONAL CALENDARS

For England, Wales, Australia, Ireland, Scotland

The Blessed Virgin Mary
Our Lady Help of Christians (A)   1270
Our Lady of Ransom, (E) 24 September   1295
Aaron (W), 20 June   1284
Alban (E, W), 20 June   1284
All Saints of Ireland (I), 6 November   1303
Andrew (S), 30 November   1309
Anselm (E), 21 April   1265
Augustine of Canterbury (E), 27 May   1279

Beatified martyrs of England and Wales (E, W),
4 May   1268
Bede the Venerable (E), 25 May
Brigid (I), 1 February   1255

Columba (Colum Cille) (I, S), 9 June   1281
Columban (I), 23 November   1308

David (E, W), 1 March   1257
Dominic of the Mother of God (E),
13 October   1299

Edward the Confessor (E), 13 October   1297

Forty Martyrs of England and Wales (E),
25 October   1299

Francis Xavier (A), 3 December   1312

George (E), 23 April   1265
Gregory the Great (E), 3 September   1293

John Fisher (E & W), 22 June   1286
John Ogilvie (S), 10 March   1259
Julius (W), 20 June   1284

Kentigern (S), 13 January   1255

Margaret (S), 16 November   1305

Ninian (S), 16 November   1291

Oliver Plunkett (I), 1 July   1288

Patrick (A, E, I, S, W), 17 March   1262
Peter Chanel (A), 28 April   1268

Six Welsh Martyrs and companions,
25 October   1299

Teresa of the Child Jesus (A), 1 October   1297
Thomas of Canterbury (E, W)
29 December   1312
Thomas More (E, W), 22 June   1286

(A) Australia; (E) England; (I) Ireland; (S) Scotland; (W) Wales